European
Accounting
Guide

MILLER

European
Accounting
Guide

Second Edition

Edited by
David Alexander and Simon Archer

HARCOURT BRACE PROFESSIONAL PUBLISHING

A Division of
Harcourt Brace & Company
SAN DIEGO   NEW YORK   LONDON

Preface

For many years, we have been involved with accounting in a specifically European context, as teachers, researchers, writers, or as practitioners. Twenty years ago, while one could write about "accounting in Europe," one could hardly have produced a book about "European accounting" as such, for national rules and practices were too diverse for such an expression to be easily understood. Today, although European accounting is certainly characterized by significant national diversities, the term has acquired a meaning. How has this come about? The answer lies in the development of the European Union and its impact not merely on its own member states but on Europe as a whole.

During the past two decades, the goal of creating a single European "economic space" has been progressively realized. This process did not end at midnight on December 31, 1992, both because the task of harmonization is incomplete and because new members will subsequently join the existing community of twelve. Nevertheless, the official commencement of the Single European Market on January 1, 1993 was a significant milestone in European history.

Accounting rules, practices, and concepts form an important part of the infrastructure of this single economic space. There are many reasons why it may be necessary or desirable to make comparisons of profitability, solvency, and other financial attributes of firms and sectors in different countries, including the functioning of capital markets and the capital allocation process, mergers and acquisitions, industrial relations, antitrust and competition surveillance, and taxation policy, just to name the most obvious. Therefore, the European Union (EU) has itself placed great emphasis on accounting harmonization, while recognizing that this is a slow process, since national idiosyncrasies in accounting are deeply rooted and intertwined with ideas and practices outside the confines of accounting itself. Thus, it is important to appreciate both the achievements in accounting harmonization and its present limitations.

To observers in countries outside Europe, the harmonization process may well appear lumbering and its results meager. For a number of European countries, however, both within and outside the EU, its implications have been dramatic. In addition to the major changes that occurred in, say, German financial reporting in the late 1980s, developments of similar magnitude have taken place in, for example, Italy and Spain in the early 1990s. Even greater changes are in the process of taking place in the former communist countries of Central and Eastern Europe. European countries outside the EU and hoping to join it or to enjoy a number of the benefits of membership are already aligning changes in their accounting rules with EU requirements.

When we started preparing the first edition of the Guide in 1990, it seemed to us that the production of a European accounting guide was a timely as well as fascinating project. The continuing developments just mentioned have made it imperative to produce a new edition, with chapters on countries not previously included, as well as many extensively revised chapters.

We have sought to provide the reader with not just an authoritative description of accounting rules and practices in each country but also an informed understanding of the processes affecting them.

We are grateful to our authors, whose expertise and effort has given the Guide its authoritative character, and to our publishers for their backing. We hope you will find the Guide both useful and interesting.

David Alexander
University of Hull

Simon Archer
University of Surrey

CONTENTS

About the Editors

David Alexander teaches at the University of Hull, United Kingdom. He is the author or coauthor of major British and European textbooks on accounting. He is a chief examiner for the Chartered Association of Certified Accountants (ACCA) in London and has extensive experience in the development of distance-learning packages, including translations of this material for the expanding eastern European market.

Simon Archer, a former partner of Price Waterhouse, Paris, has had many years' experience working in Continental Europe. He is currently Professor of Accounting at the University of Surrey, Guildford, United Kingdom.

AN OVERVIEW OF EUROPEAN ACCOUNTING

1. Introduction

1.1 Introductory Remarks

The *European Accounting Guide* is a companion volume to the Miller *GAAP Guide* (guide to U.S. Generally Accepted Accounting Principles). It is, however, of necessity, a different kind of book. One reason for this is fairly obvious: not even the European Union of Twelve, let alone the whole of Europe, constitutes a unified entity as far as accounting is concerned. The harmonization within the European Union of those institutional characteristics that directly affect financial accounting and reporting, namely, company law and tax law, is only in its initial stages. Thus, European accounting consists of nationally based sets of rules and practices, subject to a limited degree of harmonization in the case of European Union member states.

There is, however, another reason for the differences between the two books, and this concerns the very concept of *generally accepted accounting principles* (GAAP). GAAP is a concept that has its origins in a national system (that of the United States), in which neither the law nor government agencies seek to lay down detailed accounting rules. Instead, they lay down a few general principles and leave the promulgation of detailed rules or standards to the private sector, that is, to a body created by the accounting profession and the business community. Because this body lacks legal authority, it must look elsewhere in order to find an authoritative basis for the standards that it sets.

It seeks this basis in the notion of general acceptance. Such a system for laying down national accounting rules owes much to the tradition of common law in the English-speaking countries. With one important exception (the Netherlands), this rule-based system is not found in countries that do not share the tradition of common law. In these latter countries, detailed commercial codes provide the legal infrastructure of business activity, and accounting rules are part of that codified legal infrastructure. To apply the concept of "generally accepted accounting principles" to such accounting rules is potentially misleading. For what matters in these countries is not whether such rules are generally accepted, but whether they are the law; and these are different issues.

Nevertheless, the European Union Directives dealing with financial accounting and reporting may be considered not merely to constitute a minimalist core of accounting principles for the twelve existing member states, but also to provide a focus for other European countries that wish to keep open the option to join the Union. There is no doubt that the principles adopted in the Directives are influential in such countries as Sweden, Turkey, Switzerland, and Poland.

Another influence on European accounting is provided by the standards issued by the International Accounting Standards Committee (IASC). These standards have acquired a status as indicators of internationally acceptable practice that gives them an influence complementary to that of the EU Directives. In some countries, such as Italy, it is the practice to apply these International Accounting Standards (IAS) to issues not covered by a national standard. The possibility of conflict between IAS and the EU Directives has created a certain tension, which, together with the difficulties experienced in agreeing and implementing the Directives, has led to a view that the European Union should issue no more Accounting Directives but should support the international standard-setting efforts of the IASC. It remains to be seen, however, whether this view will prevail. These matters, and the relevant institutions at both the European and international level, are discussed later in this chapter.

1.2 Accounting Harmonization and the Single European Market

As far as the twelve members of the EU are concerned, accounting harmonization is an integral part of the development of the Union into a single "economic space." In this connection, a distinction needs to be made between two objectives of accounting harmonization. One is the establishment of a "level playing field" for enterprises competing within the single market, and the other is the promotion of an efficient, integrated capital market for the Union.

According to the principle of the level playing field, enterprises within the EU should be able to compete throughout the Union on equal terms as far as the legal and regulatory environment is concerned, being neither favored nor disfavored by particular requirements in individual member states. The application of this principle to financial reporting implies a need for the harmonization of financial reporting requirements—but not necessarily for the standard of financial reporting within the Union to be "leveled upward."

By contrast, the promotion of an efficient, integrated capital market has implications for the quality and quantity of financial disclosure provided by firms seeking capital in that market, so that arguably a need for "leveling upward" *is* implied. Much research has been carried out, both in order to measure the extent to which actors in capital markets derive information from published financial reports and to evaluate the effects of differences in accounting and reporting practices on this process. The evidence suggests that, while in many cases information contained in published financial reports may already be known to the market from other sources (such as analysts' reports), in some circumstances published financial reports do convey new information about capital market participants. The crucial role of financial reporting lies in the reduction of information asymmetries that may inhibit the entry of new participants into the market. The better the information provided in published financial reports, the more effective it can be in removing these information asymmetries and promoting market efficiency.

The integration of capital markets within the European Union implies that market participants situated in member state X do not face significant barriers to entry if they wish to seek capital from, or to provide capital to, market participants in member states Y or Z. One form of barrier to entry is the lack of consistency in financial reporting practice, especially if it is accompanied by substantial differences in the quantity and quality of information provided. Such differences represent one form of information asymmetry facing potential providers of capital based in one member state in their dealings with potential seekers of capital in other member states. Hence, in seeking to promote capital market integration, the harmonization program is concerned not just with the reduction of heterogeneity but with "leveling up."

The orientation of financial accounting and reporting toward meeting the information needs of participants in capital markets is associated with the requirement, stated in the Fourth Directive, that financial statements should give "a true and fair view of the company's assets, liabilities, financial position, and profit and loss." This requirement was written into the draft of the Directive only after the entry of the United Kingdom and the Republic of Ireland into the EU, and its inclusion has been a crucial and, in some respects, controversial factor in European accounting harmonization.

The harmonization process within the EU has also been affected by influences from outside the Union and particularly from the United States and other English-speaking countries whose attachment to "fair presentation" and "substance over form" has reinforced the position of the United Kingdom and Ireland. In addition, the harmonization process has also had an influence on European countries not currently members of the Union, such as Sweden. The major institutional influences on the development of European accounting are reviewed in the next section.

2. Institutional Influences on European Accounting

It is useful to consider institutional influences on European Accounting under three headings: national, European, and international institutions.

2.1 National Institutions

Relevant details about national law-making bodies, about national professional bodies of accountants and auditors, and about the creation of accounting regulations by such professional bodies will be found in the individual chapters on each country. The point to emphasize here is that the existence and importance of the national organizations cannot be ignored. Even within the EU, such national organizations have a responsibility to their members, close interrelationships with the local business (and political) communities, and often long and sometimes esoteric traditions. Indeed, in some countries, a number of national accounting bodies exist, each with its own particular constituency and ax to grind.

We must remember, therefore, as we look through our optimistic European spectacles, that the wishes, hopes, and fears of national and subnational accounting organizations must be taken into account.

2.2 European Institutions

The coordinating organization for the accountancy profession in Europe is the Fédération des Experts Comptables Européens, known as FEE. FEE formally began on January 1, 1987 and was formed by the merger of two earlier organizations, the Union Européene des Experts Comptables, Economiques et Financiers (UEC), founded in 1951, and the Groupe d'Etudes des Experts Comptables de la CEE (Groupe d'Etudes), founded in 1961.

The main objectives of FEE have been stated as follows:

- To work generally toward the enhancement and harmonization of the practice of accountancy in the broadest sense
- To promote cooperation among the professional accountancy bodies in Europe in relation to issues of common interest in both the public and private sectors
- To represent the European accountancy profession at the international level
- To be the sole consultative organization of the European accountancy profession in relation to the EC authorities

The members of FEE are formally national professional bodies. Some thirty-four such bodies are members, representing twenty-two countries, including all twelve EU member states. FEE is gradually increasing its role and influence as the "spokesperson" for European professional accounting bodies, and therefore for European accountants. Thus, it represents a regional grouping within the International Federation of Accountants (IFAC), a similarly constituted body with an international membership (see below). FEE does not intend to act as a standard-setting body but proposes to promote accounting harmonization in line with the policies of IFAC. The speed with which FEE emerges as a heavyweight influence in its own right depends, of course, on the extent to which the member national accounting bodies are prepared to give up their own individual attempts at direct influence.

2.3 International Institutions

The International Federation of Accountants (IFAC) is the worldwide umbrella organization of accountancy bodies. It is independent of government or pseudogovernment control. Its stated purpose is "to develop and enhance a coordinated worldwide accountancy profession with harmonized standards." IFAC was created in 1973, and its constitution was formally approved in 1977. Perhaps the most important aspect of IFAC so far has been its relationship with the International Accounting Standards Committee (IASC). The IASC was also created in 1973, and all member bodies of IFAC are automatically members of IASC. IASC is independent and has total autonomy in the setting of international accounting standards. Its main objectives are:

- To formulate and publish in the public interest accounting standards to be observed in the presentation of financial statements and to promote their worldwide acceptance and observation
- To work generally for the improvement and harmonization of regulations, accounting standards, and procedures relating to the presentation of financial statements

3. Cultural Influences on European Accounting

To consider cultural influences, it is again useful to consider three categories—influences from within the existing EU members, from other European countries, and from the rest of the world. This division is merely one of convenience, however, and consistent with the structure of the Guide as a whole. Many attempts have been made in recent years to divide the world into accounting "zones." Such an analysis is in the end simplistic and approximate and not particularly helpful.

The Guide is divided into three major sections:

- The EU member states
- The EFTA (European Free Trade Association) countries and independents
- The countries of Central and Eastern Europe, which are in the process of adopting market economies and of developing accounting practices suited to such economies.

Each of these sections is prefaced by an overview and introduction, highlighting both the similarities and the differences of the countries within the section.

Four very general strands can be considered at this early stage, all of which influence (and explain) differences in specific practice and regulation.

3.1 The Relative Importance of Law

The question is the extent to which the "law of the land" determines the details of accounting and financial reporting. Tradition in the United Kingdom, for example, is that the law specifies general principle only, while in countries heavily influenced by the Roman Law tradition, the law tends to include more detail. Germany is often quoted as an example of the latter approach.

3.2 Prescriptiveness or Flexibility

If regulation is not specified in full detail in legislation, then two alternatives are still available. First, regulation might be created in detail by professional accounting bodies. Second, the broad regulation, whether created by legislation or by professional accounting body, may be explicitly designed on the assumption that the *individual* expert, in each unique situation, can and should choose the appropriate course of action, within the broad parameters laid down. The principle of a "true and fair view" exemplifies this approach.

The distinction between prescriptiveness and flexibility is in practice relative rather than absolute. This is well illustrated by the nuances of distinction between "fair presentation" as applied in the United States and "a true and fair view" as applied in the United Kingdom. It might appear that these two terms refer to quite similar concepts. However, the full expression used in U.S. auditors' reports is that the financial statements "present fairly . . . in accordance with generally accepted accounting principles" (GAAP), and especially with "promulgated GAAP" (i.e., the standards laid down by the Financial Accounting Standards Board and its predecessor bodies). Given the ever growing number of detailed and prescriptive Statements of Financial Accounting Standards, "fair presentation" in the United States can increasingly be considered as being a matter of formal compliance with a set of accounting rules. In other words, total compliance is both a necessary and a sufficient condition for providing "fair presentation."

By contrast, "a true and fair view" in the United Kingdom has historically implied not just compliance with a set of accounting rules but also respect for an overriding principle or meta-rule that the financial statements, in the judgment of the preparer and the auditor, fairly reflect the economic substance of the situation reported upon, to which end a departure from one or more of the accounting rules may be called for. Total compliance with the rules has thus been considered as neither a sufficient nor even a necessary condition for providing a true and fair view. Legal opinions regarding the implications of the 1989 U.K. Companies Act, however, suggest that the significance of accounting standards in delineating a true and fair view is tending to increase, so that total compliance might now be considered a necessary (and even, perhaps, a sufficient) condition for providing a true and fair view. This remains to be tested in the courts. All the same, the degree of prescriptiveness, as measured by the volume of detailed, technical accounting standards, is still markedly less in the United Kingdom than in the United States.

3.3 The Providers of Finance

The roots of most of the accounting practices discussed in this Guide predate the arguments of recent years that accounting statements must satisfy the needs of a wide variety of users. Generally, the suppliers of finance to business were the only users seriously considered until late in this century (sometimes quite late). Different countries have different financial institutional structures and finance-raising traditions. It follows that accounting practice has adapted to suit the local dominant sources of finance. In some countries, tradition tends to focus on the shareholder, and therefore on profit and on the matching of expenses and revenues. Other countries have more active banking sectors and less shareholder investors. Accounting there will tend to focus on creditors and, therefore, on the balance sheet and on the convention of prudence. Germany and Switzerland are often quoted as examples of this second approach.

A more obvious but less often quoted example of the influence of finance provision on financial reporting can be seen by considering the systems of Eastern Europe, as they begin to emerge from a half-century during which all finance was provided by the state.

3.4 The Influence of Taxation

The scope and extent of the influence of taxation law on financial statements varies considerably. Perceptions of this are often simplistic and extremist. In reality, no country can justly claim that tax considerations do not influence published results, and no country can be accused of blindly taking tax-based results and publishing them just as they are. Within these nonexistent extremes, however, lies a very real variety of tradition and practice. It is common in many countries, for instance, for some tax allowances to be claimable only if the identical figure from the tax computation is also used in the published financial statements.

3.5 Implications

The four strands of influence just described are, of course, to some extent interrelated. They are also—a crucial point too often forgotten—embedded in and emergent from the broad culture and "attitude to life" of each community to which they are applied. A number of important implications arise from this.

First, it helps us to understand the reasons why accounting philosophy and practice are where they are in each of the various states of Europe. Second, it carries an important message about the process of accounting harmonization or, more accurately, of movement toward harmonization within or beyond Europe. A true single European accounting way of thinking would imply a true single economic market and a common body of commercial law (which are both a long way away) embedded in a truly European culture. Third, we must remember that such interaction between accounting *per se* and its environment is a two-way process. Accounting needs to move as Europe moves. Accounting will be moved whether it likes it or not, as Europe moves.

At rock bottom, a fundamental question arises. We could conclude that the implication is that the ideal target of an accounting framework is theoretically attainable and that we must seek to move gradually and steadily toward it, though in full cognizance of the issues involved, which include the more general harmonization on company and commercial law with which accounting is intimately intertwined. Alternatively, we could conclude that such legal matters reflect different national histories with regard to business affairs and that a single European accounting frame-work would require a greater degree of homogeneity in approach than is likely in the near future or, arguably, even desirable. According to the latter way of thinking, harmonization would imply not ever-greater similarity but ever-greater recognition and mutual understanding across Europe of the different subcultures involved. This choice may appear semantic, but it is fundamental in its attitudinal and political implications.

4. The Non-European Influences

Before we explore the EU influences emerging, to use a convenient shorthand, "from Brussels," we should briefly consider the other international influences on financial reporting.

There is inevitably some direct influence from North America, as outlined above, if only because of its size and economic importance. More directly significant, however, is the existence and work of the International Accounting Standards Committee (IASC), already mentioned briefly. The IASC has issued an important series of standards (IASs), the major elements of which are included in the Appendix. The IASC has operated throughout its existence in the knowledge that when the crunch came, it and its standards had no formal authority. It therefore has had all along to rely on persuasion and the quality of its analysis and argument. As a general comment, this can be seen to have had two major effects. First, the quality of logic and discussion in its publications has generally been high, and its conclusions—if sometimes debatable—feasible and clearly articulated. Second, however, the conclusions and recommendations of many of the published IAS documents have often had to accommodate two or more alternative acceptable treatments, simply because both or all were already being practiced in countries that were members of IASC and were too significant to be ignored.

The disadvantages of this state of affairs are obvious and were well recognized by the IASC itself. Toward the end of the 1980s, the IASC decided it would attempt a more proactive approach, and early in 1989 it published an Exposure Draft (E32) on the comparability of financial statements. This proposed the elimination of certain treatments permitted by particular IASs and the expression of a clear preference for one particular treatment even where two alternatives were still to be regarded as acceptable. A summary of these proposals appears in Table 1.

There are also signs of closer cooperation between IASC and the International Organization of Securities Commissions (IOSCO). IOSCO has indicated its support for mutually acceptable accounting standards, and clearly any suggestion, however gently expressed, that quoted companies failing to follow standards would be investigated by Stock Exchange authorities can only strengthen the movement toward greater acceptance of such standards.

It is interesting to look, in summary form, at the detailed changes introduced by IASC to its IASs as part of the process of increasing comparability by reducing the range of acceptable alternatives. Readers already familiar with accounting standards or the equivalent in their own national accounting systems will find of considerable interest a comparison between those national details and the various treatments regarded as acceptable or unacceptable by the IASC. Readers not in that position should regard these proposals more as a table of reference against which to compare the various regional practices discussed later. IASC has designated three possible descriptions for any particular treatment. These are "required or benchmark treatment," the clear preference, "allowed alternative treatment," regarded as acceptable, and "treatment eliminated," re-

TABLE 1 International Accounting Standards Committee Summary of Proposals for the Comparability of Financial Statements

IAS	Paragraphs	Issues	Required or Preferred Treatment	Proposals Allowed Alternative Treatment	Treatment Eliminated
2	24, 25, & 26	Assignment of cost to inventories	• FIFO and weighted average cost formulas	• LIFO formula	• Base stock formula
8	19	Correction of fundamental errors and omissions and adjustments resulting from accounting policy changes	• Adjust opening retained earnings • Amend comparative information	• Include in income of the current period • Present amended pro forma comparative information	
9	16 & 17	Recognition of development costs	• Recognize immediately as expenses	• Recognize as assets when they meet specified criteria	
11	42 & 43	Recognition of revenue and net income on construction contracts	• Percentage of completion method • When the conditions for profit recognition are not met, recognize revenue to the extent of related costs		• Completed contract method
16	36	Measurement of property, plant, and equipment	• Measure at cost		• Measure at revalued amounts
16	39	Measurement of property, plant, and equipment acquired in exchange for another asset	• Fair value for dissimilar assets acquired • Net carrying amount of asset given up for similar assets acquired		• Net carrying amount of assets given up for dissimilar assets acquired • Fair value for similar assets acquired

			Benchmark treatment	Allowed alternative treatment
16	47	Recognition of a revaluation increase relating to a revaluation decrease previously charged to income	• Recognize in income of the current period	• Recognize in shareholders' interest
17	49	Recognition of finance income on finance leases by a lessor	• Net investment method for finance leases other than leveraged leases • Net cash investment methods for leveraged leases	• Net cash investment method for finance leases other than leveraged leases • Net investment method for leveraged leases
18	24	Recognition of revenue on transactions involving the rendering of services	• Percentage of completion method	• Completed contract method
19	45(a)	Determining the cost of retirement benefits	• Accrued benefit valuation methods	• Projects benefit valuation methods
19	5	Use of projected salaries in determining the cost of retirement benefits	• Incorporate an assumption about projected salaries	• Do not incorporate an assumption about projected salaries
19	45(c)	Recognition of past service costs, experience adjustments and the effects of changes in actuarial assumptions	• Recognize systematically over a period approximating the average of the expected remaining working lives of participating employees	• Recognize in income of the current period as they arise

(Table continues)

TABLE 1 (Continued)

IAS	Paragraphs	Issues	Required or Preferred Treatment	Proposals Allowed Alternative Treatment	Treatment Eliminated
21	28, 29, & 30	Recognition of foreign exchange gains and losses on long-term monetary items	• Recognize in income of the period unless hedged		• Defer and recognize in income of current and future periods
21	31	Recognition of foreign exchange losses on the acquisition of an asset that result from a severe devaluation against which there is no practical means of hedging	• Recognize in income of the current period	• Recognize as part of the cost of the asset	
21	32(c)	• Exchange rate for use in translating income statement items of foreign entities	• Exchange rates at the dates of the transactions (or average rate)		• Closing exchange rates
		• Treatment of differences on income statement items translated at other than the closing rate	• Recognize in share-holders' interests		• Recognize in income of the current period
21	33	Subsidiaries operating in hyperinflationary economies	• Restate financial statements in accordance with IAS, "Financial Reporting in Hyperinflationary Economies," before translation		• Translate financial statements without prior restatement

#	Para	Topic			
21	34(i) & (ii)	Treatment of exchange differences on foreign operations integral to those of the parent	• Recognize in income of the period unless hedged	• Recognize as part of the cost of an asset when they result from a severe devaluation against which there is no practical means of hedging	• Defer and recognize in income of current and future periods
22	36, 37, & 38	Accounting for business combinations	• Purchase method for acquisitions • Pooling of interests method for uniting of interests		• Purchase method for uniting of interests
22	40, 41, & 42	Treatment of positive goodwill	• Recognize as an asset and amortize to income on a systematic basis over its useful life. The amortization period should not exceed 5 years unless a longer period can be justified, which should not, in any case, exceed 20 years		• Adjust immediately to shareholders' interests
		Treatment of negative goodwill	• Allocate over individual nonmonetary assets. After such an allocation, if negative goodwill remains, treat as deferred income and recognize on a systematic basis as for positive goodwill	• Treat as deferred income and recognize in income on a systematic basis as for positive goodwill	• Adjust immediately to shareholders' interests

(Table continues)

TABLE 1 (Continued)

IAS	Paragraphs	Issues	Required or Preferred Treatment	Proposals Allowed Alternative Treatment	Treatment Eliminated
22	45	Measurement of minority interest arising on a business combination	• Measure at preacquisition carrying amounts	• Measure at postacquisition fair values	
23	21	Recognition of borrowing costs	• Recognize immediately as expenses	• Recognize as part of the cost of an asset if it takes a substantial period of time to get it ready for its intended use or sale	
25	47(a), (b), & (c)	Measurement of long-term investments	• Measure at cost	• Measure at revalued amounts	
		Measurement of marketable equity securities held as long-term investments	• Measure at cost recognizing declines in value that are other than temporary on an individual investment basis	• Measure at revalued amounts	• Measure at the lower of cost and market value on a portfolio basis
25	45(a) & (b)	Measurement of investment properties	• Measure at cost with depreciation	• Measure at revalued amounts	• Measure at cost without depreciation
25	46	Measure of current investments	• Measure at market value	• Measure at the lower of cost and market value on an individual investment basis	• Measure at the lower of cost and market value on a portfolio basis

| 25 | 48 & 49 | Recognition of increases and decreases in market values of current investments | • Recognize in income of the current period | • Recognize in revaluation surplus |
| 25 | 50 | Recognition of a realized gain previously recognized in revaluation surplus | • Transfer to retained earnings | • Recognize in income of the current period |

garded as unacceptable. Most of the proposed changes announced in E32 in 1989 have now been confirmed and incorporated in revised International Accounting Standards already published and operative for financial statements covering periods beginning on or after January 1, 1995. These changes, substantially in accordance with the E32 proposals, are summarized in Table 2.

Three issues proved rather more difficult. Table 3 sets out the proposals made by IASC on these issues in 1989. Table 4 gives the revised proposals made by IASC in 1991. Table 5 gives the actual requirements of the new International Accounting Standards operative from January 1, 1995.

Comparison of Tables 3, 4, and 5 will show that in two of the three cases, that is, assignment of costs to inventories and treatment of borrowing costs, the final proposals are the same as the original (1989) proposals, and in only one case, the treatment of development costs, does the revised 1991 proposal persist. It appears that minds have changed several times.

It is important to put these apparently considerable changes and inconsistencies of attitude into context. First, as Table 2 shows, the majority of changes were agreed on and maintained. Second, these are complicated issues from a theoretical perspective, and genuine alternative arguments exist. Third, and perhaps most importantly, we must not forget that the Board, that is, the IASC, is not as such a decision-making mechanism. It is the *members* of IASC who collectively make the decisions, if necessary by voting, when consensus cannot be reached. The members are a small number of individuals, representing particular countries. Table 6 shows the Board members of IASC in 1993.

5. The EU Directives

For many years the major method of engendering change across the EU has been by means of Directives. Once agreed (a process that can take more than 20 years), a Directive is a binding agreement by all the member states of the EU that they will introduce national legislation. It is important to clarify precisely what this means and what it does not mean. It does mean that all member states are required to implement the Directives. It does not mean that citizens or institutions within a member state are required to follow the Directive, unless and until the contents of the

Directive are enacted by legislation within the state. Another important point is that each Directive exists not just in one language version but in each of the nine European Union languages. It is the language version applicable to a particular member state that is to be enacted into the law of that country. There may not be perfect semantic equivalence among different language versions of the Directives. Furthermore, when the contents of the national legislation following from a Directive differ from that Directive (either by restricting allowed options or by going against the terms of the Directive itself), it is the national legislation only that must be followed within that state.

5.1 The Accounting Directives

The fundamental EU Directive relating to financial reporting is the Fourth Company Law Directive of July 25, 1978. This relates to the accounts of limited companies. It was followed by the Seventh Company Law Directive of June 13, 1983, which extends the principles of the Fourth Directive to the preparation of consolidated (group) accounts. The Fourth Directive seeks to provide a minimum of coordination of national provisions for the content and presentation of annual financial accounts and reports, of the valuation methods used within them, and of the rules for publication. It applies to "certain companies with limited liability"—broadly, all those above defined minimum size criteria—and aims to ensure that annual accounts disclose comparable and equivalent information.

The Fourth and Seventh Directives do not apply to the banking and insurance industries, but two industry-specific directives have been issued that are adaptations of the contents of the Fourth and Seventh directives to banking and insurance.

It is important to place the Fourth Directive into its historical context. It was drafted and debated over a period of some 10 years, beginning when the European Community had six members and ending when it had ten. The pre-Directive national characteristics of the accounting practices of the member states were significantly different, both in degree of sophistication and in direction. When appraising the success (or otherwise) of this Directive, we must measure its achievements against those at times startlingly diverse existing practices.

TABLE 2 *Some IASC Proposals in 1991*

Issues	Required or Benchmark Treatment	Allowed Alternative Treatment	Treatment Eliminated
Correction of fundamental errors and omissions, and adjustments resulting from accounting policy changes	• Adjust opening retained earnings (subject to certain exceptions) • Amend comparative information	• Include in income of the current period. • Present amended pro forma comparative information	
Recognition of revenue and net income on construction contracts	• Percentage of completion method • When the conditions for profit recognition are not met, recognize revenue to the extent of costs incurred that are recoverable		• Completed contract method
Measurement of property, plant, and equipment	• Measure at cost	• Measure at revalued amounts	
Measurement of property, plant, and equipment acquired in exchange for another asset	• Fair value for dissimilar assets acquired • Net carrying amount of asset given up for similar assets acquired		• Net carrying amount of asset given up for dissimilar assets acquired. • Fair value for similar assets acquired
Recognition of a revaluation increase relating to a revaluation decrease previously charged to income	• Recognize in income of the current period		• Recognize in shareholders' interests

Issue		
Recognition of revenue on transactions involving the rendering of services	• Percentage of completion method • When the outcome of the contract cannot be reliably estimated, recognize revenue to the extent of costs incurred that are recoverable	• Completed contract method
Determining the cost of retirement benefits	• Accrued benefit valuation methods	• Projected benefit valuation methods
Use of projected salaries in determining the cost of retirement benefits	• Incorporate an assumption about projected salaries	• Do not incorporate an assumption about projected salaries
Recognition of past service costs, experience adjustments and the effects of changes in actuarial assumption	• Recognize systematically over a period approximating the average of the expected remaining working lives of participating employees (subject to certain exceptions)	• Recognize in income of the current period as they arise
Recognition of foreign exchange gains and losses on long-term monetary items	• Recognize in income of the current period unless hedged	• Defer and recognize in income of current and future periods
Recognition of foreign exchange losses on the acquisition of an asset that result from a severe devluation against which there is no practical means of hedging	• Recognize in income of the current period	• Recognize as part of the cost of the asset

(Table continues)

TABLE 2 *(Continued)*

Issues	Required or Benchmark Treatment	Allowed Alternative Treatment	Treatment Eliminated
Exchange rate for use in translating income statement items of foreign entities	• Exchange rates at the dates of the transactions (or average rate)		• Closing exchange rates
Treatment of differences on income statement items translated at other than the closing rate	• Recognize in shareholders' interests		• Recognize in income of the current period
Subsidiaries operating in hyperinflation economies	• Restate financial statements in accordance with IAS 29, "Financial Reporting in Hyperinflationary Economies," before translation		• Translate financial statements without prior restatement
Exchange differences on foreign operations integral to those of the parent	• Recognize in income of the period unless hedged	• Recognize as part of the cost of an asset when they result from a severe devaluation against which there is no practical means of hedging	• Defer and recognize in income of current and future periods
Accounting for business combinations	• Purchase method for acquisitions • Pooling of interests method for uniting of interests		• Pooling of interests meethod for acquisitons • Purchase method for uniting of interests

	Benchmark treatment	Allowed alternative	
Positive goodwill	• Recognize as an asset and amortize to income on a systematic basis over its useful life. The amortization period should not exceed 5 years unless a longer period can be justified, which should not, in any case, exceed 20 years		• Adjust immediately to shareholders' interests
Negative goodwill	• Allocate over individual nonmonetary assets. After such an allocation, if negative goodwill remains, treat as deferred income and recognize in income on a systematic basis as for positive goodwill	• Treat as deferred income and recognize in income on a systematic basis as for positive goodwill	• Adjust immediately to shareholders' interests
Measurement of minority interest arising on a business combination	• Measure at preacquisition carrying amounts	• Measure at postacquisition fair values	
Measurement of investment properties	• Measure at cost with depreciation	• Measure at revalued amounts	• Measure at cost without depreciation
Recognition of a realized gain previously recognized in revaluation surplus	• Transfer to retained earnings		• Recognize in income of the current period

From IASC Statement of Intent, 1991.

TABLE 3   *Some IASC Proposals in 1989 (extracted from E32)*

Issues	Required or Benchmark Treatment	Allowed Alternative Treatment	Treatment Eliminated
Assignment of cost to inventories	• FIFO and weighted average cost formulas	• LIFO formula	• Base stock formula
Development costs	• Recognize immediately as expenses	• Recognize as assets when they meet specified criteria	
Borrowing costs	• Recognize immediately as expenses	• Recognize as part of the cost of an asset if it takes a substantial period of time to get it ready for its intended use or sale	

5.3 The True and Fair View

The key provision of the Fourth Directive is Article 2, reproduced in its entirety in Table 7. As some readers will recognize, the overriding requirement to show a true and fair view, over and above "the provisions of this Directive," is essentially taken from the philosophy and wording of the 1948 U.K. Companies Act. Also taken from the philosophy of the U.K. Companies Act is the fact that no attempt whatever is made to define "true and fair view." This article changed radically during the various drafts of the Directive. Its later interpretation, both in terms of the wording of resulting national legislation and, even more importantly, in terms of the philosophy of interpretation applied to it in practice in the various EU member states, has been highly varied. This, we suggest, is not surprising and reflects and illustrates the points made earlier about tradition and cultural influences being a vital consideration, both in understanding present practices and in predicting and influencing the future.

While the term *true and fair view* originated in U.K. company law, U.K.

TABLE 4 *Some Revised IASC Proposals, 1991 from IASC Statement of Intent 1991*

Issues	Required or Benchmark Treatment	Allowed Alternative Treatment	LIFO and Base Stock Formulas
Assignment of cost to inventories	• FIFO and weighted average cost formulas		• LIFO and base stock formulas
Development costs	• Recognize as assets when they meet specified criteria and as expenses when they do not meet criteria		• Recognize developments that meet the specified criteria as expenses
Borrowing costs	• Recognize as part of the cost of an asset if it takes a substantial period of time to get it ready for its intended use or sale; recognize as expense in other circumstances		• Recognize borrowing costs that meet criteria for capitalization as expenses

law does not spell out what the term means. The concept certainly does not mean, for example, that assets must be stated at their current values, and it is generally applied within the context of the historical cost convention (as is its counterpart, *fair presentation*, in the United States). But it is clearly understood to exclude the use of hidden reserves and also to entail a distinction between write-downs of assets that are made for tax purposes and those that are made for financial reporting purposes. The latter need to have an economic rationale in terms of the loss or expiry of value. The existence of tax allowances in respect of a write-off is not, of itself, such a rationale, for one form of tax concession to businesses is to allow write-offs for tax purposes in excess of what is economically justified. In addition, providing a true and fair view is understood to imply that

TABLE 5   *IASC Changes to the Proposed Changes to the E32 Changes*

Issues	Required or Benchmark Treatment	Allowed Alternative Treatment	Treatment Eliminated
Assignment of cost to inventories	• FIFO and weighted average cost formulas	• LIFO formula	• Base stock formula
Development costs	• Recognize as assets when they meet specified criteria and as expenses when they do not meet criteria		• Recognize developments that do meet the specified criteria as expenses
Borrowing costs	• Recognize immediately as expenses	• Recognize as part of the cost of an asset if it takes a substantial period of time to get it ready for its intended use or sale	

Exracted from revised IASs issued 1993, operative from Jan. 1, 1995.

economic substance should prevail over legal form (as in the requirement to capitalize finance leases).

This orientation toward a true and fair view differs considerably from the tradition in most countries in mainland Europe, where the emphasis has been on a conservative statement of profits and net assets in order to prevent excessive dividend distributions, coupled with the use of tax rules for asset valuation and setting up reserves. These tax rules are normally conservative (i.e., they represent a form of concession with respect to calculating taxable profits), but some of them may have an opposite effect. For example, the former rule in Germany (now modified by the 1985 Accounting Directives Law) that the costs of funding employee pension liabilities were not tax deductible led to such liabilities being materially understated in published accounts. Whether their effects are conservative or otherwise, such practices are in any event clearly inconsistent with giving a true and fair view, and their use in preparing published financial statements seems baffling to persons educated to believe that such state-

TABLE 6	*Board Members of IASC, 1993*
Australia	Japan
Canada	Jordan
France	Netherlands
Germany	Nordic Federation of
India	Public Accountants
Italy	South Africa
International Coordinating	United Kingdom
Committee of Financial	United States
Analysts Associations	

ments should provide a true and fair view. Conversely, people brought up to consider the use of financial statements in terms of constraints on dividends and of providing a basis for company taxation are equally baffled by the attachment of accountants from English-speaking countries to a concept of the true and fair view, which seems to elude satisfactory definition.

According to the thinking of the Germans, and to a certain extent of most other member states, the true and fair view is not an operational concept; accounting measurement rules are simply conventions that are agreed on by due democratic process, and if they allow hidden reserves, then such reserves are fair. From this standpoint, the idea that the results of such convention-laden calculations are "true" in the sense of being "representationally faithful" is bizarre. The conventions are considered to be part of a system of rules for governing the disposition of the wealth flows resulting from business activity and providing an equitable basis for dividends and taxation, while protecting creditors from overstatement of assets or overdistribution of dividends.

This is another example of the cultural divide mentioned at the start of this chapter, between the common law tradition and the tradition of codified law. In the former, definitions of such concepts are typically provided by courts in relation to specific situations, rather than by legislative texts intended to apply to many different situations. In the latter, the converse is true; the courts have a role of interpretation and clarification of legislative texts but not of providing situationally appropriate legal defini-

---

Table 7 *Article 2 of the Fourth Directive*

---

1. The annual accounts shall comprise the balance sheet, the profit and loss account and the notes on the accounts. These documents shall constitute a composite whole.

2. They shall be drawn up clearly and in accordance with the provisions of this Directive.

3. The annual accounts shall give a true and fair view of the company's assets, liabilities, financial position and profit or loss.

4. Where the application of the provisions of this Directive would not be sufficient to give a true and fair view within the meaning of paragraph 3, additional information must be given.

5. Where in exceptional cases the application of a provision of this Directive is incompatible with the obligation laid down in paragraph 3, that provision must be departed from in order to give a true and fair view within the meaning of paragraph 3. Any such departure must be disclosed in the notes on the accounts together with an explanation of the reasons for it and a statement of its effect on the assets, liabilities, financial position and profit or loss. The Member States may define the exceptional cases in question and lay down the relevant special rules.

6. The Member States may authorize or require the disclosure in the annual accounts of other information as well as that which must be disclosed in accordance with this Directive.

---

tions. Thus, the tradition of economic liberalism of the English-speaking countries, the faith in markets and the suspicion of technocracy, go hand-in-hand with an essentially pragmatic common law tradition and a belief that the accounting profession can largely lay down its own rules in the form of "generally accepted accounting principles." By contrast, the countries of Continental Europe have less historical attachment to economic liberalism, more faith in technocracy, and a preference for explicit legal texts, which extends to the framing of accounting rules. Harmonization of accounting within the EU has involved bringing these two traditions into some degree of harmony, and it is in this respect that the inclusion of the true and fair requirement in the Fourth Directive was both crucial and controversial.

One school of thought about the true and fair view prevalent in some European countries argues that it represents the totality of all the detailed regulations. The opposite school of thought argues that the true and fair view represents precisely that extra element resulting from the integration of the various separate regulatory strands into a coherent whole. In other words, professional judgment about whether financial statements fairly represent that which they purport to represent can transcend particular regulatory requirements about the applications of accounting principles; thus, substance prevails over form. The U.K. tradition, embodied in the wording of the final version of the Fourth Directive, is firmly in the latter camp: correct following of every detailed regulation cannot, of itself, be relied on to give the adequate (true and fair) overall picture. Such a concept is alien to centuries of culture and tradition in some other areas of Europe. Individual national attitudes to this issue should emerge from the relevant chapters. Some general implications for the next decade are discussed, or at least guessed at, later in this chapter.

5.4 Specific Provision of the Fourth Directive

The Fourth Directive defines and illustrates some detailed layouts and formats for published income statements and balance sheets. The content and sequence of presentation are precisely defined. However, following from the diversity of the existing practice, two different formats for balance sheets and four for income statements are allowed. The Directive continues to prescribe requirements for particular items in the balance sheet and income statement. The other major consideration in this Directive concerns the rules of valuation. The major methodology is based firmly on the historic cost principle, that is, on "purchase price or production cost." However, the Directive also "allows national governments to allow" alternative valuation methods, as specified in Article 33(1), see Table 8. Whichever valuation method is used, the general rules of Article 31 apply, see Table 9.

5.5 The Seventh Directive

The Seventh Directive applied and broadly extended the provisions of the Fourth Directive to the preparation and publication of consolidated accounts. Article 1(1) is reproduced in Table 10. The extent of the publication of consolidated accounts varied widely in the EU member states in pre-Seventh Directive days. This Directive required much development and change in some countries and very little in others.

TABLE 8 *Article 33(1) of the Fourth Directive*

---

1. The Member States may declare to the Commission that they reserve the power by way of derogation from Article 32 and pending subsequent coordination, to permit or require in respect of all companies or any classes of companies:

    (a) valuation by the replacement value method for tangible fixed assets with limited useful economic lives and for stocks;

    (b) valuation by methods other than that provided for in (a) which are designed to take account of inflation for the items shown in annual accounts, including capital and reserves;

    (c) revaluation of tangible fixed assets and financial fixed assets.Where national law provides for valuation methods as indicated in (a), (b) and (c), it must define their content and limits and the rules for their application. The application of any such method, the balance sheet and profit and loss account items concerned and the method by which the values shown are calculated shall be disclosed in the notes on the accounts.

---

6. Toward European Generally Accepted Accounting Principles?

It has been suggested that pre-EU accounting practices in the member states varied widely. The Fourth and Seventh Directives set out to harmonize these practices as far as possible, given the situation at the time. The extent to which practice had been harmonized by the early 1990s can be judged from the individual chapters later in this Guide. It has frequently been suggested in recent years that the Directives were always, and necessarily, seen very much as a first step. In retrospect, and given the divergences of practice and attitude discussed and illustrated throughout this volume, the point seems obvious.

Given that there is increasing recognition that the current EU accounting harmonization is obviously less than total in surface appearance, and where it does exist is often only skin-deep, what is the way forward? This is a complicated issue, and the following brief sketch attempts to outline the major elements in general terms in a way that will not date too quickly.

It is generally recognized that formal Directives are not an effective

---

TABLE 9 *Article 31 of the Fourth Directive*

---

1. The Member States shall ensure that the items shown in the annual accounts are valued in accordance with the following general principles:

    (a) the company must be presumed to be carrying on its business as a going concern;

    (b) the methods of valuation must be applied consistently from one financial year to another;

    (c) valuation must be made on a prudent basis, and in particular:

        (aa) only profits made at the balance sheet date may be included,

        (bb) account must be taken of all foreseeable liabilities and potential losses arising in the course of the financial year concerned or of a previous one, even if such liabilities or losses become apparent only between the date of the balance sheet and the date on which it is drawn up,

        (cc) account must be taken of all depreciation, whether the result of the financial year is a loss or a profit;

    (d) account must be taken of income and charges relating to the financial year, irrespective of the date of receipt or payment of such income or charges;

    (e) the components of asset and liability items must be valued separately;

    (f) the opening balance sheet for each financial year must correspond to the closing balance sheet for the preceding financial year.

2. Departures from these general principles shall be permitted in exceptional cases. Any such departures must be disclosed in the notes on the accounts and the reasons for them given together with an assessment of their effect on the assets, liabilities, financial position and profit or loss.

---

way of moving forward. They are too cumbersome in approach and too time-consuming in development. As an alternative mechanism, a European Accounting Forum has been set up under the auspices of the EC. This is intended as a gathering together of all major interested parties—the EC Commission, accounting standard-setting bodies, regulatory and government organizations, and business interest groups. The effectiveness of this forum seems to be highly uncertain, as perhaps was its original purpose.

One fundamental issue causing considerable uncertainty and aggrava-

---

TABLE 10   *Article 1 of the Seventh Directive*

---

1. A Member State shall require any undertaking governed by its national law to draw up consolidated accounts and a consolidated annual report if that undertaking (a parent undertaking):

   (a) has a majority of the shareholders' or members' voting rights in another undertaking (a subsidiary undertaking); or

   (b) has the right to appoint or remove a majority of the members of the administrative, management or supervisory body of another undertaking (a subsidiary undertaking) and is at the same time a shareholder in or member of that undertaking; or

   (c) has the right to exercise a dominant influence over an undertaking (a subsidiary undertaking) of which it is a shareholder or member, pursuant to a contract entered into with that undertaking or to a provision in its memorandum or articles of association, where the law governing that subsidiary undertaking permits its being subject to such contracts or provisions. A Member State need not prescribe that a parent undertaking must be a shareholder in or member of its subsidiary undertaking. Those Member States the laws of which do not provide for such contracts or clauses shall not be required to apply this provision; or

   (d) is a shareholder in or member of an undertaking, and:

      (aa) a majority of the members of the administrative, management or supervisory bodies of that undertaking (a subsidiary undertaking) who have held office during the financial year, during the preceding financial year and up to the time when the consolidated accounts are drawn up, have been appointed solely as a result of the exercise of its voting rights; or

      (bb) controls alone, pursuant to an agreement with other shareholders in or members of that undertaking (a subsidiary undertaking), a majority of shareholders' or members' voting rights in that undertaking. The Member States may introduce more detailed provisions concerning the form and contents of such agreements.

The Member States shall prescribe at least the arrangements referred to in (bb) above.

They may make the application of (aa) above dependent upon the holding's representing 20% or more of the shareholders' or members' voting rights.

However, (aa) above shall not apply where another undertaking has the rights referred to in subparagraphs (a), (b) or (c) above with regard to that subsidiary undertaking.

tion concerns the relationship between *European* accounting and harmonization, and *international* accounting and harmonization. One school of thought would argue that to attempt further harmonization at the European level is merely to introduce an unnecessary, artificial, and distracting middle layer into the wider movement toward greater international harmonization and comparability. The other school of thought, to which the European Commission appears attracted, takes the view that Europe, consistent with its emergence as a single economic market, needs a single accounting and reporting framework within that market. The reader will perceive the possible political undertones beneath this apparently economically based debate.

It should be remembered also, at the same time as the European Forum and the debate at EU level is slowly gathering pace, that the IASC, as discussed above, is becoming more active in the international sphere.

So where does this leave the prospects for European GAAP? We would summarize the position as follows.

- Practice among the twelve EU members started from a diverse base.
- The achievements of the Fourth and Seventh Directives within the EU have been real but more successful at the presentation level than at the content, valuation and attitudinal level. There is no European consensus on what a "true and fair view" means or implies.
- The organizational way forward—who or what will legislate or regulate: EU, Pan-European, or international dimension—is most unclear.
- The cultural dimension of accounting means that progress will of necessity be slow.
- The EU is about to acquire three or four new members (Austria, Finland, Sweden, and possibly Norway). Additionally, a number of Baltic, Central and Eastern European countries (starting with the Czech Republic, Hungary, and Poland) have announced their intention to seek membership. These countries will bring their own institutional and intellectual traditions into the Union and will influence, as well as be influenced by, European thinking on such matters as accounting.
- The way forward, the crucial way and the only effective way, is through ever increasing mutual understanding of differences and of the reasons for them.
- It is to this increase in mutual understanding that this Guide is dedicated.

BELGIUM

Ann Jorissen
UFSIA, University of Antwerp, Belgium

1. A Brief History of Belgian Accounting Legislation

1.1 Introduction

By the mid-1970s, the existing Belgian legislation on companies' accounting and financial reporting was outdated and obsolete. In response both to pressure from various users of accounting data (financial analysts, investors, employees, etc.) and to anticipated European legislation, on July 17, 1975 the Belgian legislature enacted the Law on Accounting and Companies' Annual Accounts. This basic law gave accounting a judicial status it had not had before, stating the fundamental principles by which annual accounts must abide, and also providing legal sanctions for the nonobservance of these principles.

After the 1975 law, two important royal decrees were passed:

- On October 8, 1976, on companies' annual accounts
- On March 7, 1978, on a minimum standard chart of accounts

These decrees revolutionized accounting and financial reporting in Belgium. Since then, the 1975 law and these decrees have been amended several times.

Other laws and royal decrees have been passed in recent years. At the present stage in the development of accounting, financial reporting, audit requirements, and company law, it clearly can be asserted that the relevant European Directives have been almost completely implemented. The requirement for larger companies to appoint an external auditor, introduced in 1985, was also part of that implementation.

1.2 Early Belgian Accounting Legislation

The first legislation concerning accounting and financial reporting in Belgium can be traced back to the Napoleonic Code of Commerce of 1807. This code contained provisions regarding bookkeeping and served as the foundation for the elaboration of the basic Company Law of 1873, in which were regulated the issuance of stock, the statutes of the limited company, the disclosure of annual accounts, and the statute of the directors and commissioners. Since then, Belgian company law has been amended on several occasions, and this process led, eventually, to the so-called Coordinated Law of Companies of 1935, which remained in effect until it was superseded by the Royal Decree of October 8, 1976 on Companies' Annual Accounts. The more recent developments in company law will be examined later.

Section 9 of the coordinated Law of Companies of 1935 spelled out the various requirements with which companies had to comply regarding their bookkeeping and financial reporting. These requirements concerned only balance sheets and income statements and were minimal. The type of balance sheets companies had to prepare were often referred to as "pocket-sized" balance sheets, for, in order to meet the official requirements, companies had to publish only six items in their balance sheet: two on the asset side (fixed assets and accounts receivable) and four on the liability side (shareholders' equity, bond loans, secured debts, and unsecured debts). On the other hand, the only requirement regarding the income statement that the law imposed was that depreciation be "true and fair." Although a number of large companies went beyond those minimum legal requirements and disclosed additional information on a voluntary basis, this additional information often fell short of meeting users' needs and was not standardized.

These surprisingly limited disclosure requirements can be explained partly by historical and institutional factors. One of these is the existence in Belgium of a handful of quite powerful holding companies (such as the Société Générale established in 1822), which played a major role in financing the country's industrial sector. These holding companies were reluctant to disclose information to outsiders. In addition, only a small number of shares were in the hands of third parties, which explains why the general public showed little interest in those financial statements.

The remaining part of trade and industry in Belgium was and still is in the hands of small family-run companies. When those family-run companies needed extra financial sources to finance their growth or other investments, they always turned to banks and other financial institutions. There was no tradition for these companies to go public once they had reached a certain size. For that reason, stock exchanges in Belgium (Brussels, Antwerp, Liège, and Gent) were quite small and had only a few listed companies.

As a result, Belgian companies were and are to a large extent financed by banks and other creditors. Therefore, financial reporting in Belgium was viewed for a long time as providing information to creditors. Consequently, the emphasis was put on the balance sheet at the expense of the income statement in the belief that a positive net worth was the best protection a company could give its creditors. Indeed, disclosure requirements were imposed mainly on companies to protect creditors and insiders rather than to inform outside investors. In this context, the financial position of a company as shown on a conservative balance sheet took precedence over the detailed determination of its earnings.

1.3 Toward a Comprehensive Accounting and Financial Reporting Legislation

1.3.1 Development up to 1975

From the late 1960s, financial analysts, accounting professionals, workers' councils, academics, and government agencies began to urge companies to disclose a broader range of information to the public. Among these pressure groups, workers' councils played a pivotal role in the process that led to the 1976 Royal Decree on accounting standards and financial reporting. The action of workers' councils can be traced back to the Economic and Social Conference of 1970, which called for a broadening of accounting disclosure requirements in Belgium and the provision of financial and economic information to workers' councils. The recommendations that emerged from that conference were embodied in the decree of November 27, 1973 (Royal Decree on Financial and Economic Information to Workers' Councils). The fundamental objective of this decree was to provide employees with a true and fair view of the economic and financial condition of their companies and to provide workers' councils with as much information as shareholders had.

After the Economic and Social Conference of 1970, several legislative committees were set up under the leadership of the Belgian government. These committees organized a series of hearings that allowed the accounting profession and different users of financial information (financial analysts, investors, academics) to present their views on the reform of the existing accounting legislation in Belgium. Various drafts of new accounting and financial reporting legislation were proposed by these committees.

Simultaneously, the European Commission was drafting its Fourth Directive, the purpose of which was to improve companies' accounting standards and to harmonize disclosure rules for annual accounts across member countries.

1.3.2 Crucial Legislation, 1975–1976

Drawing on the provisions of what later became the Fourth Directive, and on the various drafts proposed by the legislative committees set up in the early 1970s, the Belgian Parliament passed a law on July 17, 1975 calling for a major overhaul of accounting standards and financial reporting in Belgium. Detailed regulations concerning the reporting of corporate accounting data and the establishment of a minimum standard chart of accounts were later specified in the Royal Decrees of October 1976 and March 1978.

The Royal Decree of October 8, 1976 was a turning point in the history of accounting and financial reporting legislation in Belgium. As pointed out, the decree required corporations for the first time to divulge to the public a substantial amount of financial information: it defined the form and content of the annual accounts, the valuation rules, and the prescribed disclosure thereof. The disclosure of additional information in the income statement has had the greatest impact on accounting and reporting practice, because disclosure requirements before 1976 were quite limited in that respect.

Furthermore, it is interesting to note that the Belgian legislature attached great importance to the information to be disclosed in the notes to the balance sheet and the profit and loss account. The legislature even prescribed a format for these notes.

As Belgium has a tradition of a codified system of law, the accounting law of 1976 and the Royal Decrees have all the characteristics of this legal system. The Belgian accounting law consists of some general principles with an enormous amount of detailed regulation.

1.3.3 Subsequent Development

The 1976 Decree was later updated several times. The most recent accounting and financial reporting legislation (for nonconsolidated accounts) is as follows:

- The Royal Decree on Companies' Annual Accounts of September 12, 1983 (amended by the Royal Decrees of May 5, 1985; November 6, 1987; March 6, 1990; December 31, 1991; and December 3, 1993).
- The Royal Decree on the Minimum Standard Chart of Accounts of September 12, 1983 (amended by the Royal Decree of November 6, 1987).

1.3.4 Consolidated Accounts

As to the consolidated accounts, the law of July 17, 1975 stipulated that the government (formally, the King) could by royal decree oblige enterprises to establish and publish consolidated accounts. The first executive measure of this provision found its way into the Royal Decree of November 29, 1977. This decree imposes such requirements on holdings companies (*a*) which, on their own or through subsidiaries, have resorted to raising funds from the public; or (*b*) which have shareholdings worth either half their own equity or at least 500 million Belgian francs (BF).

This decree also deals with the nonconsolidated accounts of holding companies.

A second royal decree, that of September 1, 1986, related to the same companies. First, it adapted the decree of November 29, 1977 to recent changes in accounting legislation. Second, it incorporated into the first decree both the experience on consolidated accounts gained since 1977

and, to some extent, the European norm dealing with consolidation (the Seventh EC Directive of June 13, 1983). For holding companies, the Royal Decree of 1986 has been replaced by that of November 25, 1991.

Finally, the Royal Decree of March 6, 1990 sets up the rules that will regulate the drawing up of companies' consolidated accounts: hence, it affects a much wider range of companies than did the 1977 and 1986 decrees.

1.3.5 Chronology of Accounting and Financial Reporting Legislation in Belgium

Table 1 summarizes the history of accounting and financial reporting legislation in Belgium, from the Napoleonic Code of commerce of 1807 to the 1990 Royal Decree on Consolidated Accounts.

1.3.6 The Commission for Accounting Standards

The Commission for Accounting Standards was created by the law of 1975 (*Commission des Normes Comptables/Commissie voor Boekhoudkundige Normen*). According to Article 14 of the law, the task of the commission is to give opinions to the government and Parliament as required, or on its own initiative, and to develop an accounting doctrine and to formulate the principles of proper accounting by way of opinion or recommendation. Since its establishment, the Commission on Accounting Standards has issued 30 bulletins. These bulletins contain opinions on the application of various articles of the Law of 1975 and the Royal Decrees. The opinions of the Commission are authoritative pronouncements but have no binding character.

1.4 Company Law

1.4.1 Origins

Belgian company law stems from a distant past. The Code of Commerce of 1807 took in most of the provisions already contained in the Order of Colbert of 1673. The Code of 1807 was revised by the Law of May 18,

TABLE 1 *Chronology of Accounting and Financial Reporting Legislation in Belgium*

1807	Napoleonic Code of Commerce
May 18, 1873	Basic Company Law
July 22, 1913	Company Coordinated Law (Section 9, Article 75 spelled out the requirements with which companies had to comply regarding their bookkeeping and financial reporting)
July 9, 1935	Establishment of the Banking Commission: Royal Decree No. 18 on the legal status/control of banks and on the control of appeals to public saving (amended by the Laws of July 17, 1985 and of March 9, 1989)
November 30, 1935	Company Coordinated Law: new version (Section 9, article 77 spelled out the same requirements as those contained in Article 75 of the Law of July 22, 1913): this law has been amended several times
July 22, 1953	Establishment of the Public Auditors' Institute
November 27, 1973	Royal Decree on Financial and Economic Information to Workers' Councils (amended by the Royal Decrees of August 12, 1981 and of March 6, 1990)
July 17, 1975	Basic Law on Accounting and Companies' Annual Accounts (amended by the Laws of March 30, 1976 and of March 24, 1978; the Royal Decree of December 15, 1978; the Law of July 1, 1983; the Royal Decree of January 16, 1986; the Law of July 1989)
October 21, 1975	Establishment of the Accounting Standards Commission
October 8, 1976	Royal Decree on Companies' Annual Accounts (amended by the Royal Decrees of December 27, 1977; February 14 , 1979; September 12, 1983; March 5, 1985; November 6, 1987; March 6, 1990)
September 1986 November 29, 1971	Royal Decrees on Annual Accounts and Consolidated Accounts of Holding Companies
March 7, 1978	Royal Decree on a Minimum Standard Chart of Accounts (repealed by the Royal Decree of September 12, 1983)
November 12, 1979 October 19, 1981	Royal Decrees on Annual Accounts of Insurance companies

(Table continues)

(Table 1, continued)

June 9, 1981	Royal Decree on a Minimum Standard Chart of Accounts for the oil industry
September 12, 1983	Royal Decree on a Minimum Standard Chart of Accounts (amended by the Royal Decree of November 6, 1987)
December 5, 1984	Law modifying the Company Coordinated Law of November 30, 1935 (last amendment)
February 21, 1985	Law on Public Auditing Function (revision of the Law of July 22, 1953); establishment of the Institute of Chartered Accountants
March 6, 1990	Royal Decree on Companies' Consolidated Accounts

1873, which remains the fundamental root of present company law. At the end of the past century, there was further modification by Royal Decree in 1935: some of the texts that still govern today date back to this period. Since 1949 there have been numerous reforms.

1.4.2 Company Form

In earlier days, many trade and industry activities were carried out by individuals or groups of individuals. During the past 10 years we have witnessed an evolution. Unlimited liability companies are little by little being abandoned. The limited liability companies are taking over in number. The most popular legal forms of business are the private limited liability company (±103,000 in 1990), the public limited liability company (±69,000 in 1990), and the cooperative societies (±60,000 in 1990). Furthermore, there is a clear tendency for companies to create subsidiaries for various activities. This sometimes leads to the creation of holding companies.

The Belgian legislature has allowed the formation of "single person limited liability companies": this is an innovation introduced by the Law of July 14, 1985.

1.4.3 Reform of Company Law

A Reform Commission for company laws was set up in 1951 with a view to undertaking a reform of all outdated legislation. It was necessary to rethink old concepts. The same process was occurring in neighboring countries, which have all been proceeding, since the end of the Second World War, with a more or less complete overhaul of their legislation. The work of this commission continued up to 1968, although it was not until 10 years later that the government decided to deposit the project with the Chamber of Representatives (1979). As such, the project has had no follow-up on the parliamentary level.

It is important to note that the Belgian legislature is working on adapting the Company Law to European Directives as and when these become mandatory. But it is also taking initiatives that have been dictated by circumstances. Some texts stem from the works of the Reform Commission.

The Second EC Directive of December 13, 1976 provides for a harmonization of norms and procedures relative to the constitution, the minimum and the modifications of the capital of limited companies. One cannot say that Belgium was eager to assume its EC responsibilities regarding this matter. It took 8 years to adapt Belgian Company Law to the Second Directive (Law of December 5, 1984).

The 1984 law not only adapts Belgian Company Law to the Second Directive (see Section 3 for certain implications for the analyst), it also assures the transposition into Belgian law of the rules of the Fourth Directive that are directly linked with company law, especially

- The content and publication of the annual management report of directors accompanying the annual accounts
- The content and publication of the annual control report of statutory auditors (see below)
- The possibility of publishing abridged annual accounts
- The determination of distributable income (see Section 3)

1.5 Organization of the Auditing Profession

1.5.1 Introduction

In Belgium, the Institute of Recognized Auditors (*Institut des Réviseurs d'Entreprises* or *Institut van Bedvijfsrevisoren*) was created by the Law of

July 22, 1953. The reform of the auditing profession was realized by the Law of February 21, 1985. This law appears to be a codification of procedures in force, containing the necessary specifications for rendering the former system in accordance with the Eighth EC Directive of April 10, 1984 (relative to the qualifications and work of auditors). This law also adapted the Belgian legislation to the Fourth Directive.

When the certification of annual accounts or other information is required by law, only recognized auditors are entitled to issue such certification.

In principle, all limited companies, private limited companies, cooperative companies, and limited partnerships with shares must appoint an auditor to control their annual accounts (including consolidated accounts). Small and medium-sized companies are exempt from this requirement. However, if a shareholder of a small or medium-sized company wants an audit of the company, the shareholder has the right to ask for it. Such audits of small and medium-sized companies might also be carried out by a member of the Institute of Accountants.

There are workers' councils in all Belgian companies and institutions that employ an average of more than one hundred workers annually. Economic and financial information must be provided to the workers' councils in accordance with the Royal Decree of November 27, 1973. A recognized auditor must be appointed to make a report to the workers' council, especially on the annual accounts and on the economic and financial information. This legal requirement represents a considerable extension of the social role of auditors: this is a peculiarity of the Belgian system.

The auditor has a control function. The auditor does not have the power to interfere with the management of the company. The Company Law provides that auditors be appointed from among the members of the Institute of Recognized Auditors. In order to be recognized as an auditor, the candidate must

- Be Belgian or resident in Belgium
- Be at least 25 years old and no older than 65
- Never have been deprived of civil and political rights
- Hold a university diploma of at least 4 years of study or be registered for 2 years on the roll of chartered accountants

- Have successfully passed an admission examination
- Have completed a 3-year training period with a professional auditor
- Have passed an aptitude exam at the end of the training period
- Have made an oath before the President of the Commerce Tribunal

1.5.2 *Attestation and Report of the Recognized Auditor (for the Annual General Meeting of Shareholders)*

The outcome of the auditor's work is an annual report, the content of which is specified by Article 65 of the Company Law of December 5, 1984 (this law anticipates the auditing reform). The auditor draws up for the general meeting of shareholders a detailed written report that specifically indicates:

- How they carried out their control and if they obtained from the administrators and managers of the company the explanations and information they requested
- Whether the accounting records are maintained and the annual accounts prepared in conformity with the legal and statutory requirements applicable in Belgium
- Whether in their opinion, the annual accounts give, taking into account the legal and statutory requirements that govern them, a true and fair view of the assets and liabilities, of the financial position and of the results of the company, and if the supplementary information given in the notes is adequate
- Whether the management report of the directors includes all information required by law and is in accordance with the annual accounts
- Whether the allocation of the profits proposed to the general meeting is in conformity with legal and statutory requirements
- Whether they have any knowledge at all of transactions or decisions made in violation of the statutes or of the Company Law

In their report, the auditors indicate and justify with precision any qualifications or objections that they consider necessary. Otherwise, they expressly mention that they have none at all to formulate. Obviously, Belgian law did not opt for a report in a brief and standardized form. The auditor's report must accompany any complete publication of the annual accounts.

The auditor's attestation must appear at the conclusion of the auditor's report; it concerns only the annual accounts. The law specifies that if the auditor has attested the annual accounts without formulating any qualifications, the text of the report can be replaced by the auditor's "attestation."

1.5.3 Types of Attestations (Audit Opinions)

The Company Law distinguishes three types of attestation:

- Attestation without qualification (if the annual accounts correspond to the legal and statutory requirements, if the rules of evaluation were applied in a consistent manner, and if all of the necessary information is given with clarity)
- Attestation with qualification (if the auditor cannot indicate agreement with the content or the form of one or several items of the annual accounts)
- The refusal to attest (when the auditor disapproves of the accounts because of disagreement with the managers on one or several essential points: no true and fair view)

2. The Form and Content of Published Financial Statements and Notes

2.1 Introduction

As noted in Section 1.3, the present legal requirements regarding financial disclosure in Belgium originated in the Royal Decrees of October 1976 and November 1987. These decrees were modified by subsequent legislation, in particular by the Royal Decrees of September 1983, September 1986, November 1987, March 1990, December 1991, and November 1993. This legislation, together with the Law of December 5, 1984, served to implement the Fourth and Seventh EC Directives within Belgium.

The requirements lay down the format and content of the balance sheet and the income statement and the numbering and content of the notes.

There is no requirement for other statements, such as of sources and applications of funds or value added.

2.2 Disclosure

2.2.1 General Provisions

The annual accounts shall comprise the balance sheet, the income statement, and the notes to the accounts. These documents constitute a composite whole; they are stated in Belgian francs.

The annual accounts shall give a true and fair view of the enterprise's assets, liabilities, financial position, and result. They shall be prepared clearly and must set out systematically the nature and the amount of the enterprise's assets and rights, its debts and commitments, and its capital and reserves as of the balance sheet date, as well as the nature and the amount of its income and expense for the financial period then ended.

The opening balance sheet for each financial period shall correspond to the closing balance sheet for the preceding financial period. Any set-off between assets and liabilities, contingent assets and rights and contingent liabilities, or between income and expenses, shall not be permitted except as provided in the Accounting Decree (Royal Decree of October 1976, amended by Royal Decrees of September 1983 and November 1987).

2.2.2 Presentation of the Annual Accounts

The balance sheet and the income statement shall be drawn up in accordance with the layout provided in the Accounting Decree. The notes to the accounts shall contain the information and statements prescribed by the Accounting Decree.

Small and medium-sized enterprises (the accounting definition of these enterprises is given below) may, however, prepare their balance sheet and income statement in accordance with the abbreviated form provided for in the Accounting Decree, together with an abbreviated version of the notes.

Where assets or liabilities can be classified under more than one caption or subcaption of the balance sheet, and income or expenses under more than one caption or subcaption of the income statement, they shall be included under whichever item is most appropriate.

In order to provide more details, enterprises may further subdivide the prescribed captions and subcaptions in the notes. In order to comply with the true and fair view requirements, the nomenclature of captions preceded by a capital letter and subcaptions in the standard layout shall be adapted to the particular nature of the activity, the assets and liabilities, and the income and expenses of the enterprise.

2.2.3 Special Provisions Relating to the Annual Accounts

The balance sheet shall be prepared after appropriation, that is, after accounting for the results of appropriation, the result of the income statement, and the result brought forward. With respect to each caption and subcaption of the balance sheet and income statement, the amounts related to the corresponding item for the preceding financial period must be shown. Where the amounts of a financial period are not comparable with those of the preceding financial period, the figures of the preceding financial period may be adjusted in order to make them comparable: in that case the adjustments, where material, shall be disclosed and explained in the notes. Where the amounts of the preceding financial period are not adjusted, the notes must include the necessary details to allow comparison. Accumulated depreciation and amounts written off are deducted from the assets to which they relate.

The notes to the accounts shall state, by category, the contingent assets and liabilities not included in the balance sheet that may have a significant effect on the assets and liabilities or the financial position or result of the enterprise. Material contingent assets and liabilities that cannot be quantified shall be appropriately disclosed in the notes to the accounts.

2.3 Formats of Financial Statements

In the Appendix to this chapter, a real life example is given in the form of the financial statements of Petrofina, which include group accounts. The notes to the financial statements are also included.

Of the various options offered by the Fourth Directive, the formats adopted in Belgium are the horizontal form of balance sheet (liabilities being added to capital and reserves, not deducted from assets) and either the vertical form or the horizontal form of income statement, with operating expenses analyzed by nature, not by function. The latter analysis is, however, acceptable for the purpose of consolidated accounts (article 29, para. 2 of the Royal Decree of 6 March 1990). Each statement must include the comparative figures for the previous financial year.

Enterprises, irrespective of their legal form, that do not exceed more than one of the following criteria are allowed to present their annual accounts in abbreviated format:

- Personnel: 50
- Turnover: BF 170,000,000
- Balance sheet total: BF 85,000,000

If the number of employees exceeds 100, the enterprise must prepare its annual accounts using the full layout.

Individuals carrying on a commercial activity and general or limited partnerships with a turnover of less than BF 20 million may set up a simplified system of accounting, and they do not have to use the official formats, defined in the royal decrees, for the preparation of their annual accounts. (This turnover criterion is raised to BF 25 million for traders whose main activity is the retail sale of gaseous or liquid hydrocarbons for the propulsion of motor vehicles on public highways.)

With regard to the publication of the annual accounts, the following requirements exist:

1. Enterprises incorporated as companies or partnerships with varying degrees of limited liability (private limited liability companies, public limited liability companies, partnerships limited by shares, cooperative societies with limited liability) must publish their annual accounts by filing them with the National Bank of Belgium after approval by the general meeting (Article 80 of the Company Law)

2. For enterprises otherwise incorporated, one must make a distinction between those enterprises that are allowed to prepare their annual accounts using the abbreviated format and those enterprises that are obliged to use the full layout.

- The enterprises with an abbreviated format have no obligation to publish their annual accounts.
- The enterprises with a full layout must publish their annual accounts through filing with the National Bank of Belgium, except for individuals carrying on a commercial activity and general and limited partnerships of which all partners are individuals.

2.4 The Auditor's Report

The situation in Belgium with regard to auditing was described in Section 1.5. In the case of an unqualified audit report, only a short "attestation" need be published. Otherwise, the full text of the report should be published. An example of an unqualified attestation on the accounts of Petrofina is given in the Appendix.

3. Accounting Policies and Practices in Valuation and Income Measurement: Implications for the Analyst

3.1 Introduction

Since the enactment of the EC Fourth Directive into Belgian law, Belgian financial statements have been required to provide a "true and fair view." In Belgium's two main languages, French and Flemish, this phrase is translated as *une image fidele* and *een getrouw beeld*, respectively; that is to say, literally, "a faithful image" or "a true picture."

This concept was new to the Belgian world of preparers of financial statements and the profession. Until then, preparers, together with the profession, took a legal approach. If the annual accounts complied with the provisions of the law and the royal decrees and the prudence principle was respected, the annual accounts fulfilled all expectations. The notion of the predominance of the true and fair view over other dispositions of the Directive (Article 2, paragraph 5 of the Directive) is in Belgium, however, not interpreted to mean (as it is in the United Kingdom) that specific accounting rules should be overridden. Rather, the Belgian interpretation is similar to the French, namely that the notion of the true and fair view should be used to choose an accounting method when the specific rules leave a choice or are imprecise. This implies that when the balance sheet and the profit and loss account as such do not provide a true and fair view, it is sufficient to mention this in the notes in order to comply with the true and fair view. For this purpose, the notes to the accounts (*annexe*) must be considered an integral part of the financial statements. An example of this phenomenon can be found when, because of the influence of tax law, discussed below, the balance sheet and income statement by themselves may not give a true and fair view, and reference to the notes may be essential in order to be aware of the implications of this. A number of likely cases of divergence from a true and fair view are noted under the relevant headings in the rest of this section.

3.1.1 The Influence of Tax Law on Published Accounts

Somewhat like France and Germany, but unlike the United Kingdom, the United States, and the Netherlands, Belgium has a tax regime under which the published annual accounts serve as the basis for corporate taxation.

Companies are obliged to provide the tax authorities with a balance sheet and a detailed income statement and are bound by their contents. At the same time, the tax authorities may discuss the contents of the financial statements and make adjustments to them to establish the tax basis. Companies naturally tend to draw up their accounts in a manner that will not lead to adjustments for tax purposes.

3.1.2 Accounting Legislation and the Tax Law

Accounting legislation specifies that the rules regarding revaluation, depreciation, and so on, will be accepted by the fiscal administration, except insofar as they would be explicitly contravened by the fiscal legislation. The aim of accounting legislation is to render exceptional the cases in which fiscal rules can diverge from accounting rules. Therefore, it can be asserted that, on the fiscal level, the rule is the accounting law, apart from the exceptions provided for in fiscal legislation. The conditional preeminence of accounting legislation was translated into a circular of the fiscal administration dated March 31, 1978, placing in parallel the fiscal legislation and the accounting legislation of October 1976. At present, this preeminence is equally admitted by jurisprudence. Sometimes fiscal legislation requires a specific way of valuation and reporting for a certain item in order to be tax deductible. In those cases fiscal law dominates accounting law.

3.2 Group Accounts

3.2.1 Introduction

As noted in Section 1, the requirement for holding companies to publish consolidated accounts was introduced in Belgium by the law of September 1, 1986. The Royal Decree of March 1990 introduced the obligation to prepare consolidated accounts for commercial and industrial enterprises.

Significant changes were made by the Royal Decree of March 8, 1990, and at the same time the required treatment in company accounts of financial fixed assets (participations in related companies, see Section 3.8.6) was harmonized with the rules for consolidated accounts. The Royal Decree of March 1990 was, above all, intended to clarify the definitions of relationships between business entities that are crucial in establishing the existence and membership of a group for the purpose of consolidation and equity accounting.

The requirement to consolidate applies to any company that meets the relevant criteria, irrespective of its legal form (public corporation, private limited liability company, limited partnership, etc.).

3.2.2 Size Limits

A company is exempted from the requirement to publish consolidated accounts if it, together with its subsidiaries, does not exceed at least two of the following limits:

- Annual turnover, excluding value added tax: BF 680 million
- Balance sheet total: BF 340 million
- Average number of employees during the period: 250

For the financial periods commencing before January 1, 1999, the limits mentioned above shall be increased as follows:

- Annual turnover, excluding value added tax: BF 1700 million
- Balance sheet total: BF 850 million
- Average number of employees during the period: 500

3.2.3 Scope of Consolidation

Consolidated accounts are defined as comprising a consolidated balance sheet, a consolidated income statement, and consolidated notes (*annexe*), providing a financial presentation of a set of enterprises between which there exists a relationship of affiliation or subordination (parent–subsidiary), or which are placed under unified management within a relationship of coordination (consortium), such that they form an economic entity over and above the various legal forms involved.

The relationship of subordination includes *de facto* as well as *de jure* control. *De facto* control is presumed to exist when a shareholding entity has exercised a majority of the votes in the last two general meetings, unless proof to the contrary is provided. The notion behind the inclusion of *de facto* control is the so-called entity approach, which focuses on the group as such, as opposed to the proprietorial approach, which simply considers the parent company together with its subsidiaries. In certain cases, however, it is considered that use of the equity method may be more conducive to providing a true and fair view (see below).

The relationship of coordination (unified management) is presumed to exist when unified management results from contractual or statutory dispositions, or when the boards of directors are composed in the majority of the same persons. It is also presumed to exist, in the absence of proof to the contrary, when a majority of equity shares is held by the same persons or legal entities, except when they are held by state bodies.

The equity method (normally used for associated companies) is used for subsidiaries when:

- There are serious and lasting restrictions on the effective exercise of the power of control over the subsidiary or on the exercise by the subsidiary of power over its assets.

- The shareholding in the subsidiary is held exclusively with a view to ultimate disposal.
- In the case of a *de facto* subsidiary, but only in that case, the activities of the subsidiary are so different from those of the rest of the group that their inclusion would not be conducive to giving a true and fair view. The mere fact that the subsidiary belongs to a different sector of activity does not by itself constitute a reason for nonconsolidation.
- The subsidiary is in liquidation, has decided to discontinue its activities, or is in a condition such that the "going concern" principle cannot be applied.

It is also permissible to exclude smaller subsidiaries from consolidation if, collectively, their impact on the group's financial position or results would be immaterial. A subsidiary may also be excluded if the difficulties and costs of obtaining the necessary information outweigh the benefits of consolidating it. When a subsidiary is excluded from consolidation, the fact and the reasons for it must be mentioned in the *annexe*.

With respect to subconsolidations, Belgium has exercised the option given by the Seventh Directive not to require these in cases in which the overall consolidating entity is situated within the EC. However, in these cases the *Conseil d'Entreprise* (workers' council) may still require them, although they would not need to be published.

3.2.4 Proportional Consolidation

The proportional consolidation method is used in Belgium for participations in joint ventures, not only when the joint venture partners have equal shares, but even in the case of majority participations. In all other cases, full consolidation is used.

3.2.5 The Equity Method (Equitization)

As well as being used for certain categories of subsidiary (see Section 3.2.3), equitization is required for associated companies. These are defined as companies in which an enterprise included in the consolidation holds a participation and over which it exercises a significant influence on the orientation of its management. This significant influence is presumed to exist (in the absence of proof to the contrary) if the voting rights attached to the participation represent 20% or more of the total voting rights of the investee company's shareholders.

3.2.6 Harmonization of Accounting Rules

The accounting policies used in preparing the group accounts should be applied uniformly to the accounts of all the entities included by consolidation or by the equity method.

3.2.7 Capital Consolidation and Treatment of Goodwill

As envisaged in the Seventh Directive, the method of capital consolidation used in Belgium is the "acquisition" or the "purchase" method, according to which a consolidation difference is established at the time of the first consolidation after the acquisition of a participation (this also applies to increases in existing participations). This is the difference between the fair value of consideration given (recorded as the cost of the participation in the accounts of the consolidating company) and the fair value of the net assets attributable to the participation. It may be positive ("goodwill") or negative. In the latter case, it is treated as a nondistributable reserve. Positive goodwill must be capitalized as an intangible asset and amortized over an appropriate period, normally not to exceed 5 years; a longer period may be used if it can be justified, in which case such justification must be given in the *annexe*.

Goodwill does not appear in the accounts of the entity holding the participation (as it does in the Netherlands) but arises only on consolidation or equitization.

3.3 Foreign Currency Translation

3.3.1 Introduction

The rules for foreign currency translation in the accounts of single entities are set out in an opinion (or Statement of Recommended Practice) issued by the Accounting Standards Commission in December 1987. As such, they are not legally binding, but departure from them would not normally be considered consistent with giving a true and fair view. For consolidated accounts, the relevant rules are set out in Part II, Section 3 of the Royal Decree of March 6, 1990, which is legally binding.

3.3.2 Foreign Currency Translation in Consolidated Accounts

The provisions are similar to those of International Accounting Standard (IAS) 21, in that, depending on the circumstances of the subsidiary, either the closing rate–net investment method or a method involving a mixture of current and historical rates is to be used. The chosen method must be applied consistently over time to any one subsidiary (subject to its circumstances remaining the same), while subsidiaries whose circumstances differ may be treated according to different methods. Unlike IAS 21, however, the Royal Decree does not specify these circumstances; it is up to groups to specify their own criteria. In practice, the IAS 21 criteria are generally used.

The closing rate–net investment method involves translating all balance sheet amounts at the average buying and selling rates at the close of the balance sheet date, except where the exchange rate risk from a monetary item is explicitly hedged, when the rate for the hedging transaction may be used. Income statement items are translated at an approximation of "actual" rates of the transactions, normally an average calculated on a monthly, quarterly, or annual basis. This method gives rise to two kinds of translation difference. The difference arising on the subsidiary's beginning-of-year capital and reserves (net investment) translated at the previous year's closing rate and at the current year's closing rate is not considered a gain or loss and is transferred to the end-of-year consolidated reserves and, where appropriate, minority interests. The difference arising on the subsidiary's net income translated as described above and at the closing rate may be treated similarly, or transferred to the consolidated income statement, with the minority interest's share being appropriately classified as such.

The alternative method is not the "temporal method" described in IAS 21 but the older "monetary-nonmonetary method." All monetary assets, liabilities, monetary rights, and commitments are translated at the closing rate, except where the exchange rate risk from a monetary item is explicitly hedged, when the rate for the hedging transaction may be used. All other items (nonmonetary assets) are translated at historical rates applicable at the time on recording the assets in the accounts of the subsidiary. The translation differences arising on the items translated at closing rates are considered gains or losses and, as such, are included in the consolidated income statement.

3.3.3 *Foreign Currency Translation in Company Accounts*

The Commission for Accounting Standards has issued Bulletin No. 20 on the topic of foreign currency translation in company accounts. A brief summary is given here simply to indicate the general principles adopted.

All items that are expressed in a foreign currency should be translated into Belgian francs. A difference is made between monetary and nonmonetary items. Nonmonetary items should be translated into Belgian francs, when the transaction occurs, at the exchange rate of that date. The value of the nonmonetary items will not be influenced any more by changes in the exchange rate between the original currency and the Belgian franc.

Foreign currency monetary items are first recorded in the accounts at the relevant spot rate, unless they are specifically hedged, in which case the relevant forward rate should be used. In the case of an immediate and complete hedge, no exchange difference may arise.

At the balance sheet date, foreign currency monetary items must be valued at the spot rate of that moment. As a result, conversion differences will arise. Unrealized gains are not transferred to income (following the prudence principle) but are treated as a deferred income in the balance sheet. Following the same principle, unrealized losses are first offset against any balance of unrealized gains in the same currency, and any excess is transferred to income. Realized gains and losses from exchange differences are reported as such in the income statement.

In the same bulletin the Commission for Accounting Standards also issued advice with regard to the valuation of foreign currency forward contracts. For the valuation of those contracts a difference is made between forward contracts for hedging purposes and forward contracts for trading purposes.

3.4 Capital and Reserves

3.4.1 Introduction

Capital and reserves are divided into six main balance sheet headings:

- Capital
- Share premium
- Revaluation surpluses
- Reserves
- Profit and loss balance awaiting disposition
- Capital subsidies (government grants)

Capital may be subdivided into capital subscribed and uncalled capital. The amounts of called-up capital still unpaid shall be accounted for as a receivable.

In addition to the share capital of corporations (shown at nominal value), the term covers the capital of noncorporations such as cooperatives and various forms of partnership.

Share premium or paid-in surplus is the difference between the issue price and the nominal or par value of shares. Share premium is not distributable.

Revaluation surplus arises on the revaluation of physical and financial fixed assets; the surpluses must be "certain but not realized." Such surpluses are not distributable but may effectively enter distributable reserves through being credited to income in line with depreciation charges in respect of the related assets. Alternatively, they may be capitalized if they are certain and durable, but account needs to be taken of the tax impact in case the related assets are realized.

3.4.2 Reserves

Reserves are divided into four categories:

- Legal reserves
- Unavailable (nondistributable) reserves

- Untaxed reserves
- Available (distributable) reserves

The legal reserve is a nondistributable reserve established by transferring at least 5% of annual net income until the reserve amounts to 10% of the share capital. Article 77 of the Company Law obliges companies to build up this legal reserve in the books of the company.

Unavailable reserves consist of two categories: an amount equal to the total of share capital repurchased and held as treasury stock and reserves that the shareholders' meeting cannot freely dispose of by normal majority. With regard to the first category, own shares may only be repurchased subject to the constitution of such a reserve of the appropriate amount (as in Germany). The effect of this is that the repurchase of the shares does not impair the total of the company's capital plus nondistributable reserves.

The untaxed reserves are equal to the realized gains and profits, after deduction of related deferred taxes, of which the tax exemption or tax deferral depends on their being retained within the enterprise. This is an example in which tax regulation dominates accounting regulation.

Available reserves are those over which the shareholders in general meeting have power of disposal. They are generally constituted by the disposition of the net income (profit and loss balance) for the year, after transfers to dividends payable and to other reserve categories as required by law or decided by the shareholders in general meeting.

The reserves are followed by the caption profit (losses) brought forward. This caption is used when the General Assembly approves that losses will be carried forward. In case of a profit this caption will be used when the definite appropriation (dividends or transfer to the reserves) is postponed to future financial periods.

3.4.3 Capital Subsidies

Government grants may be of two kinds: capital grants and operating subsidies. Only capital grants appear in the balance sheet, where they are shown as part of the enterprise's own funds, not as a liability.

Capital grants are obtained in respect of investment in fixed assets. The amount of the investment grant will after deduction of deferred taxes be recorded under capital subsidies. The total amount of these grants will be released systematically to the profit and loss account at the same rate as the depreciation of the related fixed asset. The amounts recorded under capital subsidies will be reported then as other financial income. The amounts recorded under deferred taxes will be presented on the profit and loss account under caption IX.bis B. Transfer from deferred taxes. Any remaining balance will be released when the assets are disposed of or taken out of service.

3.5 Liabilities and Provisions

Caption VII on the liability side of the balance sheet consists of provisions for risks and charges and deferred taxes.

3.5.1 Provisions for Risks and Charges

Four main categories of such provisions are recognized:

- Pensions and similar obligations
- Taxation
- Provisions for major repairs and maintenance
- Other provisions for risks and charges

3.5.2 Pension Obligations

Since January 1, 1986 pension promises made to the whole workforce or a part of it must be funded externally through a pension fund or by taking out an insurance contract. If the minimum funding requirements (stipulated in the Royal Decree of May 14 and 15, 1985) are met, then no pension provision will appear on the balance sheet of the employer. If there is a shortfall in the minimum funding level, a provision will appear on the balance sheet for that particular amount, unless the company is exempted from compliance with that minimum funding level, because the company complies with the transitional provisions foreseen in the Royal Decree of 1985. Provisions for pensions on the balance sheet will usually be used in case of pension commitments made to individuals and in the case of prepensions.

3.5.3 *Provisions for Taxation*

Provisions for taxes include provisions made to cover tax charges resulting from adjustments of taxable income or from changes in the method of computing taxes.

3.5.4 *Major Repairs and Maintenance*

The subcaption major repairs and maintenance is not foreseen in the layout of the Fourth Directive. When the future expense is certain but subject to estimation, it is acceptable to spread it over a number of years, corresponding to the periodicity of the repairs or maintenance in question. When the expenditure takes place, the balance of the provision is released to income, offsetting the charge.

It should be noted that the amounts of the provisions are determined by the maximum allowed for tax purposes, rather than by what would be necessary to show a true and fair view.

3.5.5 *Other Provisions for Risks and Charges*

Other provisions for risks and charges include provisions for several types of situation, including the following:

- Risks under sales commitments
- Risks from futures markets in currencies or commodities
- Risks from orders placed or received for the supply of fixed assets
- Commitments relative to the acquisition or disposal of fixed assets
- Indemnities for redundancy to staff when closure of a company is certain but the amount of the indemnities is not yet established
- Warranties related to the supply of goods or services
- Items acquired in consideration for an annuity payment

The amounts of such provisions are likely to be tax-driven and may not necessarily represent what would be required to show a true and fair view.

3.5.6 Deferred Taxes

Only in the following circumstances will deferred taxes be presented on the balance sheet:

1. Taxes deferred to later financial periods on investment grants obtained from public authorities for investment in fixed assets
2. Taxes deferred to later financial periods on gains on disposal of tangible and intangible fixed assets and of securities issued by Belgian public authorities, when the taxes on these gains are deferred
3. Foreign taxes of the same nature as the taxes referred to in items 1 and 2 deferred to later financial periods.

3.5.7 Financial Debts Due in More Than One Year

It should be noted that financial debts due in more than one year include the capitalized value of finance lease obligations (*contracts de location-financement* and similar), under which the lessee has an option to acquire the asset at the end of the contract. In this respect, the Belgian rules differ from those in France, where capitalization of finance leases is allowed in consolidated accounts only. See also Section 3.8.5.

For all debts due in more than one year, the current portion is classified as a current liability.

Article 27bis stipulates that all liabilities, except for leasing liabilities, should be valued at nominal value.

3.6 Assets: General Points on Principles of Valuation

These general points concern the definition of acquisition value or original (historical) cost and also revaluations.

Belgian accounting legislation provides that all assets are assessed at acquisition value, after deduction of depreciation and related reductions in value (excepting some particular cases discussed below).

Acquisition value refers to the purchase price, the production cost, or the assigned value that corresponds to the agreed value of contributions in kind.

1. The purchase price includes not only the purchase price, but also additional costs such as registration fee, transport costs, and installation costs.

2. The production cost includes not only the acquisition price, but also raw material, consumption and supplies, and the costs of manufacturing directly chargeable to the product or range of products—just as the proportion of production costs (is) only indirectly chargeable to the same product or range of products, in that these costs can be ascribed to the usual period of manufacturing. It should be stressed that companies do not have to include all or part of the indirect costs of production in the cost price (in which case an explanation to that effect should be set out in the notes). Further, companies may include in the acquisition value of tangible and intangible fixed assets interest on capital borrowed to finance their acquisition or production, inasmuch as such interest relates to the period preceding the date on which such assets become ready for operation. Production cost of stocks and contracts in progress may include interest on capital borrowed to finance their production, inasmuch as such interest relates to stocks or contracts, the production or completion of which exceeds one year and relates to the normal production period for these stocks or the normal completion term for these contracts.

3. The share price corresponds to its agreed contractual/conventional value. This cannot exceed the market price of the assets at the moment of transfer of ownership.

3.6.1 Revaluation of Assets

A company can carry out revaluation of fixed assets, and of holdings and shares figuring under fixed assets, if the following conditions are fulfilled:

1. The value of the asset to be revalued must display a definite and durable surplus in relation to its accounting value.
2. The capital gain must be justified by the profitability of the company.
3. The capital gain must be justified in the explanatory notes in the annual accounts in the year of the evaluation.

4. The capital gain on fixed-term assets must be subject to depreciation.

5. The capital gains are credited to the "Revaluation surpluses" heading in the capital and reserves section, and held there as long as the assets to which they refer are not realized. These capital gains can nevertheless

   — Be taken to reserve to an amount not exceeding the depreciation on the capital gains

   — Be incorporated into the capital

   — Be withdrawn if they are discovered subsequently not to be funded, to an amount not exceeding the undepreciated figure.

Intangible assets and stocks can no longer be subject to revaluation. "Capital gains revaluation on intangible assets" accounts and "Capital gains revaluation in stock" accounts are, however, retained in the accounting plan in order to register capital gains accruing from before the financial year that began on December 31, 1983.

3.7 Intangible Assets

3.7.1 Formation Expenses

The Belgian legislature created a separate caption for formation expenses. Falling under this heading are those expenses connected with formation, further development, or restructuring of a company, such as those incurred by setting up a company, an increase in capital, loan issue expenses, and restructuring expenses, if not charged against income in the period incurred.

Restructuring expenses may be recorded as assets when they are incurred insofar as they concern expenses (*a*) precisely defined, (*b*) relating to a substantial modification in the structure of the organization of the company, and (*c*) intended to have a favorable and long-lasting effect on the company's profitability. The fulfillment of these conditions must be set out in the notes.

Formation expenses are valued on a historical cost basis and are subject to amortization by annual installments of at least 20%, except for loan issue expenses, whose amortization can be spread out through the period of the loan.

3.7.2 Intangible Fixed Assets

Belgian accounting legislation distinguishes among the following intangibles:

1. Research and development costs: these are the costs of research, production, and development of prototypes, products, discoveries, and know-how relevant to the development of the company's future activities.
2. Franchises, patents, licenses, know-how, trademarks, and similar/simulated rights
3. Goodwill: Goodwill is defined as the excess of the acquisition cost of a company or a division/sphere of activities over and above the value of the assets and liabilities acquired—like the difference in a merger or takeover, for example, between the agreed share value and the net value of the assets and liabilities of the company being taken over
4. Installments paid on intangible assets.

Principles of Valuation Intangible assets acquired by a third party or by the owners/second party are valued at their acquisition value. Those set up by the company itself are valued at their production cost. Intangible assets may not be subject to revaluation, dating from the financial year that started after December 31, 1983.

Interest expenses can be included under the acquisition value of intangible assets.

Tax-Permitted Methods of Amortization For intangible assets with finite life, see the section on fixed assets. Amortization can be imposed on intangible assets with indefinite life. In this case, reductions in value must be imposed in order to take account of lasting depreciations/tax allowance.

Research and development costs and goodwill are generally amortized over a maximum of 5 years. If the period of amortization exceeds this term, it must be justified in the supplementary notes.

Complementary or special one-off amortization must be imposed when the accounting value exceeds the use value/recoverable amount as a result of changing economic or technological circumstances.

Declining Balance Depreciation   Since the 1989 tax reform, intangible assets may no longer be subject to declining balance depreciation, from the beginning of the 1991 tax year. The minimum period allowed for straight-line depreciation is fixed at 5 years; for research and development costs the minimum period is 3 years.

3.8 Tangible Fixed Assets

3.8.1 Introduction

Belgian accounting legislation distinguishes among the following categories of tangible fixed assets:

1. Land and buildings
2. Plant, machinery, and equipment
3. Furniture and vehicles
4. Leasing and other similar rights
5. Other tangible assets
6. Assets under construction and advance payments

For the subcaption "other tangible fixed assets," the legislature has presented the following definition:

(a) Immovable property held in reserve for later use, dwellings, fixed assets which are idle or have been retired by the enterprise as well as any movable and immovable property, the use of which is granted to others by virtue of long term leases, building rights, rental or agricultural rental (except to the extent that the receivables arising from these contracts are to be included under caption V "Amounts receivable after

one year" and caption VII "Amounts receivable within one year").
Immovable property acquired or constructed for resale is not included
under this caption but recorded separately under stocks (caption VI);

(b) The expenses of improvements to immovable property rented by the
enterprise, if they have not been charged to income in the period
incurred.

3.8.2 Principles of Valuation

Fixed assets acquired or set up by the company itself are valued at their
acquisition price. Valuation at replacement cost is no longer permitted.
According to the Law of July 17, 1975, however, companies may apply the
replacement price (by ministerial authorization). The revaluation of fixed
assets is permitted.

3.8.3 Tax-Permitted Methods of Amortization

The depreciation plan must aim to spread the cost of fixed assets over their
probable period of use and must be systematic. Accelerated depreciation
can be applied in conformity with tax regulations.

Accounting legislation conforms with tax-permitted methods of amortization:

- Straight-line depreciation
- Declining balance depreciation
- Double straight-line depreciation (law of economic expansion)
- Accelerated depreciation on certain assets (e.g., energy-saving in-
vestments)

Additional or exceptional depreciation must be charged in respect of
tangible fixed assets with a finite economic life if their net book value
exceeds their value to the business, as a result of exceptional deterioration
or changes in economic or technological conditions.

In accordance with the relevant tax regulations, accelerated depreciation may be used. Should this lead to a more rapid rate of depreciation than
can be economically justified, however, the amount of the excess depre-

ciation must be disclosed in the notes. (This disclosure requirement does not apply to assets acquired during financial years before December 31, 1983.)

3.8.4 Oil, Gas, and Other Mineral Resources

The accounting treatment of the acquisition and subsequent depreciation of a natural resource is set out in opinion No. 158/1 of the *Commission des Normes Comptables* (Accounting Standards Commission), published in December 1988. The acquisition of land that includes a natural resource is considered an acquisition of a tangible fixed asset. Its acquisition cost includes the costs of preparing it for effective exploitation.

A natural resource of unlimited life does not require any depreciation. In the case of limited life, depreciation is calculated on the basis of the units of production method. According to this method, the depreciation chargeable in respect of each unit produced is calculated by dividing the cost of acquisition by the estimated number of units likely to be produced in normal operating conditions. If the value to the business is lower than the net book value, an exceptional depreciation charge must be made.

Revaluation of natural resource assets is permitted.

3.8.5 Assets Held under Financial Lease Contracts

As indicated in Section 3.5.6, financial lease contacts are capitalized in Belgium. The criteria for including leases under this heading are as follows:

1. Long-term rights to use developed immovable property that the enterprise has by virtue of long-term leases, building rights, leasing, and other similar noncancellable contracts, on condition that the installments foreseen in the contract cover the entire capital invested by the lessor in the property, including interest and ancillary costs

2. The rights to use movable property that the enterprise has by virtue of leasing or similar noncancellable contracts, on condition that the installments foreseen in the contract, increased by the amounts payable if the purchase option is exercised, cover the entire capital invested by the lessor for the acquisition of the property, including interest and ancillary costs

Until the Royal Decree of December 1993, the lease contract had to include a particular condition in order to be recognized as a financial lease contract for financial reporting purposes. The condition was that the title to the property must be transferred by right to the enterprise at the end of the contract, or that the contract had to include a purchase option for the enterprise.

Valuation Rules   For the lessee, the value of the fixed asset leased is the value of the right to use the asset during the term of the contract. This will normally be equal to the present value of the stream of lease payments, calculated by using the rate of interest implicit in the lease contract, and this amount will be debited to fixed assets and credited to the lease liability. The fixed asset is written off over its useful life or (if it is shorter) the life of the lease, subject to its residual value less the cost of exercising any option to acquire it at the end of the lease. Each lease payment is divided into an interest portion and a capital portion, and the latter reduces the amount of the lease liability. Interest is calculated at the rate of interest used to capitalize the lease, which is applied to the balance of the lease liability.

For the lessor, an amount corresponding to the lessee's lease liability (plus the present value of any amount receivable by the lessor at the end of the contract) is treated as a debtor, namely a trade-receivable due in more than one year (with the current portion being classified as a current trade receivable). The lessor's financial income from the lease transaction is equal to the rate of interest applied to the balance on capital outstanding. This balance receivable is calculated in a similar way to the lessee's balance payable, as described above.

Lease contracts that do not meet the criteria mentioned above are treated as operating leases and are not capitalized.

3.9 Financial Fixed Assets

3.9.1 Definitions

The caption "financial assets" includes participating interests and amounts receivable held in affiliated enterprises, enterprises linked by participating interests, and other enterprises.

For the application of the Royal Decree of March 1990, the following are considered affiliated enterprises of an enterprise:

1. The enterprises that it controls
2. The enterprises that control it
3. The enterprises with which the enterprise forms a consortium
4. The other enterprises that, to the knowledge of management, are controlled by the enterprises referred to in 1, 2, and 3, above.

"Control over an enterprise" is defined in the Royal Decree of 1990 as the power *de jure* or *de facto* to exercise a decisive influence on the appointment of the majority of the board of directors or general management or on the orientation of the management policy.

According to the provisions of the Royal Decree, control *de jure* exists and shall be presumed to be irrefutable in the following situations:

1. When it results from the holding of the majority of the voting rights attached to all of the shares of the enterprise concerned
2. When a shareholder or member has the right to appoint or remove the majority of the board of directors or general management
3. When a shareholder or member has the power of control by virtue of the memorandum and articles of association of the enterprise concerned or agreements entered into with that enterprise
4. When, pursuant to agreements entered into with other shareholders or members of the enterprise concerned, a shareholder or member has the majority of the voting rights attached to all of the shares of that enterprise
5. In the event of joint control

The control is *de facto* where it results from other factors than those referred to above. In the absence of evidence to the contrary, a shareholder or member of an enterprise shall be presumed to have *de facto* control over the enterprise if, at the two previous general meetings of the enterprise, the shareholder or member has exercised voting rights representing the majority of the votes attached to the shares represented at those general meetings.

In the second category of the financial fixed assets the enterprises linked by participating interests are found. Enterprises linked by participating interests are those enterprises in which the holding of the rights is intended through establishing a lasting and specific relationship with these enterprises, to permit the enterprise to increase influence on the orientation of the management policy of these enterprises.

The following enterprises, if they are not affiliated enterprises, fall into the category "other enterprises linked by participating interest":

1. Those in which the enterprise or its subsidiaries have a participating interest

2. Those that, to the knowledge of management, have a direct participating interest in the enterprise or participating interest through subsidiaries

3. Those that, to the knowledge of management, are subsidiaries of enterprises mentioned under item 2.

In the absence of evidence to the contrary given in the notes to the accounts, the following are considered participating interests:

1. Possession of rights representing one-tenth of the capital or of a particular category of shares of an enterprise

2. Possession of rights representing a lower proportion than 10%
   a. when by addition of the rights held by the enterprise and its subsidiaries (...), this participating interest represents one-tenth of the capital or of a particular category of shares of the enterprise
   b. when the disposal of the shares or the exercise of the related rights are subject to agreements or unilateral commitments which the enterprise has entered into

Shares are reported under the subcaption "other financial assets" when the rights held in these enterprises are not considered participating interests but the holding is intended for a lasting relationship.

3.9.2 *Valuation Rules for Financial Fixed Assets*

Participations are valued at cost but may be revalued in appropriate cases. Write-downs must be made in cases on a durable impairment of value because of the situation, level on profitability, or future prospects of the company in which they are held. Such write-downs are reported as "exceptional items" in the income statement. Loans and advances are stated at nominal value.

Transaction costs incurred in acquiring financial fixed assets may be taken directly to the income statement.

3.9.3 *Amounts Receivable in More than One Year*

Amounts receivable must be valued at nominal value (Article 27bis). The current portion of such amounts receivable is reclassified as a current asset. In case of doubtful or incomplete collectibility a write-down should be recorded.

3.10 Current Assets

3.10.1 *Inventories*

The sixth caption on the balance sheet includes stocks and contracts in progress. The following breakdown is presented on the balance sheet:

A. Stocks

1. Raw materials and consumables
2. Work in progress
3. Finished goods
4. Goods purchased for resale, which include goods purchased as such or after minor treatment
5. Immovable property acquired or constructed for resale
6. Advance payments

B. Contracts in progress

Contracts in progress include:

1. Work in progress, which is carried out for the account of third parties but has not yet been completed

2. Goods in progress, which are manufactured for the account of third parties and have not yet been delivered, except where these relate to standard production

3. Services that are performed for the account of third parties and have not yet been fulfilled, except where these relate to standard services

3.10.2 Valuation Rules

The following rules are accepted for tax purposes. The general rule is that of the lower of cost and market value. If a write-down from cost to market value has been made and the market value subsequently increases, this increase must be reflected but not so that the value exceeds cost. Work in process is valued at production cost.

Contracts-in-progress are treated consistently with IAS 11. They may be valued by using the percentage-of-completion method to recognize profit, when the profit may be estimated with reasonable certainty. On the other hand, the completed contract method, under which no profit is recognized until completion, may be used. Different methods may be used for different contracts, provided this is done consistently for each contract and also providing the reasons are disclosed in the notes.

Cost may be determined by identifying individually the price of each item, or according to various cost-flow assumptions: weighted average, first-in-first-out (FIFO) or last-in-first-out (LIFO). If cost on a LIFO basis is substantially lower than market value, this fact should be mentioned in the notes. Standard cost is not accepted as such, and companies that use standard costs must adjust such costs so that they approximate one of the other types of cost just mentioned.

Cost is normally understood to include production overheads (full cost), but some or all of the indirect production overheads may be omitted, in which case this must be mentioned in the notes.

As well as write-downs of inventories from cost to market value if lower, as mentioned above, contracts-in-progress and work-in-process may have to be written down if the estimated total costs to complete exceed the net selling price.

The use of replacement cost for inventories was permitted under the Royal Decree of October 8, 1976 but later excluded by the Royal Decree of September 12, 1983.

Raw materials and consumables that are regularly replenished, whose quantity, value, and composition do not vary significantly from one period to another, and whose total amount is immaterial, may be recorded in the same way as small tools, described below.

3.10.3 Advances Received on Contracts-in-Progress

Advances received on contracts-in-progress are not deducted from the balance of the inventory accounts but are shown as current liabilities.

3.10.4 Small Tools

If small tools are regularly replenished, and their quantity, value, and composition do not vary significantly from one period to another, and their total amount is immaterial, they may be recorded at a fixed amount, with the cost of replenishment being recorded as an expense.

3.10.5 Short-Term Investments

Short-term investments are financial assets acquired for short-term treasury purposes and not as long-term investments. Deposits are stated at nominal value, while securities are stated following the rule of lower of cost or market value as described above for inventories.

Own shares acquired and held as treasury stock are classified under the caption "investments."

If an enterprise has bought bonds, they should be valued at acquisition price. The difference between the acquisition price and the redemption value shall be released to the income statement as a component of interest and added to or deducted from the acquisition cost of the securities on the basis of the actuarial yield.

3.11 Exceptional Items in the Income Statement

Exceptional items in the income statement include the following:

Exceptional income

- Write-backs of depreciation and of amounts written off against intangible and physical fixed assets
- Write-backs of amounts written off against financial fixed assets
- Write-backs of provisions for exceptional risks and charges
- Realized surpluses on disposal of fixed assets
- Other income

Exceptional charges

- Exceptional depreciation and write-offs against organization cost and intangible and tangible fixed assets
- Write-offs against financial fixed assets
- Provisions for exceptional risks and charges
- Losses on disposal of fixed assets
- Other charges
- Exceptional costs of restructuring, treated as deferred charges

The criterion for inclusion is that the item is such that it is not part of the normal activity of the business.

There is no distinction between "exceptional items" and "extraordinary items and prior year adjustments," and the items reported as "exceptional" in Belgium should not be equated with "extraordinary" items in the sense used in some other countries, although some of them may have this character.

4. Expected Future Developments

With the Royal Decree of March 1990 on Consolidated Accounts, a period of 15 years of development of financial accounting and reporting in Belgium reached its conclusion. During the 1970s and 1980s, it is probably fair to say that development of Belgian financial accounting lagged behind that of its neighbors in the Netherlands and in France. The decision taken in the mid-1970s to modernize Belgian accounting took time to come to fruition; similar decisions were taken in France in the late 1960s.

Consequently, the expected future developments in Belgian financial accounting and reporting are essentially consolidation of recent improvements. From the standpoint of the informational quality of Belgian financial statements, one major problem remains: the decision that accounting rules for financial reporting should follow tax accounting rules with resultant departures from a "true and fair view" being indicated in the notes. The experience of using published financial statements suggests that this is not a satisfactory solution. It is possible to find a way around this essentially legalistic problem by emancipating group accounts, as opposed to legal entity accounts, from the domination of tax accounting. However, it is not yet clear whether Belgian accounting will adopt this solution.

Useful Addresses

Institut des Experts Comptables
Rue Blanche 25
1050 Bruxelles
Belgium
Tel: +(2) 537.67.35
Fax: +(2) 537.53.63

FEE
Rue de la Loi 83
B-1040 Brussels
Belgium
Tel: +(2) 2310555
Fax: +(2) 231 1112

Institut des Réviseurs d'Entreprises
Avenue Marnix 22
1050 Bruxelles
Belgium
Tel: +(2) 512 5136
Fax: +(2) 512 7886

Financial Statements

BILANS CONSOLIDES

AUX 31 DECEMBRE 1992 et 31 DECEMBRE 1993

(en millions BEF)

ACTIF		1992		1993
ACTIFS IMMOBILISES		216.069		231.558
II. IMMOBILISATIONS INCORPORELLES *(page 54)*		2.597		2,438
III. ECARTS DE CONSOLIDATION *(page 54)*		143		94
IV. IMMOBILISATIONS CORPORELLES *(page 55)*		203.280		222.284
A. Terrains et constructions	26.800		26.512	
B. Installations, machines, outillage, mobilier, matériel roulant	88.871		91.777	
C. Installations recherche-production	71.133		76.970	
D. Location-financement et droits similaires	1.708		1.726	
E. Autres immobilisations corporelles	1.883		1.821	
F. Immobilisations en cours	12.885		23.478	
V. IMMOBILISATIONS FINANCIERES *(page 56)*		10.049		6.742
A. Entreprises mises en équivalence				
1. Participations	3.252		3.195	
2. Créances	317		266	
	3.569		3.461	
B. Autres entreprises				
1. Participations, actions et parts	5.237		2.135	
2. Créances	1.243		1.146	
	6.480		3.281	
ACTIFS CIRCULANTS		138.333		127.095
VI. CREANCES A PLUS D'UN AN *(page 56)*		16.690		17.655
B. Autres créances	16.690		17.655	
VII. STOCKS *(page 57)*		47.181		41.209
VIII. CREANCES A UN AN AU PLUS *(page 57)*		65.803		61.096
A. Créances commerciales	53.924		52.164	
B. Autres créances	11.879		8.932	
IX. PLACEMENTS DE TRESORERIE		1.454		1.595
B. Autres placements	1.454		1.595	
X. VALEURS DISPONIBLES		1.285		1.217
XI. COMPTES DE REGULARISATION *(page 57)*		5.920		4.323
TOTAL DE L'ACTIF		**354.402**		**358.653**

(en millions BEF)

PASSIF	1992		1993	
CAPITAUX PROPRES *(page 58)*		121.280		127.064
I. CAPITAL		43.291		43.291
A. Capital souscrit	43.291		43.291	
II. PRIMES D'EMISSION		24.304		24.305
IV. RESERVES		78.192		78.606
V. ECARTS DE CONSOLIDATION		572		562
VI. ECARTS DE CONVERSION		– 25.676		– 20.239
VII. SUBSIDES EN CAPITAL		597		539
INTERETS DE TIERS *(page 59)*		4.315		4.956
VIII. INTERETS DE TIERS	4.315		4.956	
PROVISIONS, IMPOTS DIFFERES ET LATENCES FISCALES *(page 59)*		45.484		46.998
IX. A. PROVISIONS POUR RISQUES ET CHARGES		30.227		31.596
1. Pensions et obligations similaires	9.938		10.939	
3. Grosses réparations et entretiens	374		171	
4. Autres risques et charges	19.915		20.486	
B. IMPOTS DIFFERES ET LATENCES FISCALES		15.257		15.402
DETTES		183.323		179.635
X. DETTES A PLUS D'UN AN *(page 60)*		59.989		60.521
A. Dettes financières				
2. Emprunts obligataires non subordonnés	29.415		46.832	
3. Dettes de location - financement et assimilées	1.593		1.298	
4. Etablissements de crédit	18.579		12.036	
5. Autres emprunts	10.402		355	
XI. DETTES A UN AN AU PLUS *(page 61)*		116.471		110.413
A. Dettes à plus d'un an échéant dans l'année	8.992		9.615	
B. Dettes financières				
1. Etablissements de crédit	14.505		11.550	
2. Autres emprunts	16.020		9.812	
	30.525		21.362	
C. Dettes commerciales				
1. Fournisseurs	41.301		42.168	
2. Effets à payer	611		361	
	41.912		42.529	
E. Dettes fiscales, salariales et sociales				
1. Impôts	18.422		21.359	
2. Rémunérations et charges sociales	4.335		4.553	
	22.757		25.912	
F. Autres dettes	12.285		10.995	
XII. COMPTES DE REGULARISATION *(page 61)*		6.863		8.701
TOTAL DU PASSIF		**354.402**		**358.653**

47

GECONSOLIDEERDE BALANSEN

PER 31 DECEMBER 1992 en 31 DECEMBER 1993

(miljoen BEF)

ACTIVA	1992		1993	
VASTE ACTIVA		216.069		231.558
II. IMMATERIELE VASTE ACTIVA *(pag. 54)*		2.597		2.438
III. CONSOLIDATIEVERSCHILLEN *(pag. 54)*		143		94
IV. MATERIELE VASTE ACTIVA *(pag. 55)*		203.280		222.284
A. Terreinen en gebouwen	26.800		26.512	
B. Installaties, machines, uitrusting, meubilair en rollend materieel	88.871		91.777	
C. Exploratie- en winningsinstallaties	71.133		76.970	
D. Huurfinanciering en soortgelijke rechten	1.708		1.726	
E. Overige materiële vaste activa	1.883		1.821	
F. Vaste activa in aanbouw	12.885		23.478	
V. FINANCIELE VASTE ACTIVA *(pag. 56)*		10.049		6.742
A. Ondernemingen opgenomen volgens de netto-vermogenswaardemethode				
1. Deelnemingen	3.252		3.195	
2. Vorderingen	317		266	
	3.569		3.461	
B. Overige ondernemingen				
1. Deelnemingen	5.237		2.135	
2. Vorderingen	1.243		1.146	
	6.480		3.281	
VLOTTENDE ACTIVA		138.333		127.095
VI. VORDERINGEN MET EEN LOOPTIJD VAN LANGER DAN EEN JAAR *(pag. 56)*		16.690		17.655
B. Overige vorderingen	16.690		17.655	
VII. VOORRADEN *(pag. 57)*		47.181		41.209
VIII. VORDERINGEN MET EEN LOOPTIJD VAN TEN HOOGSTE EEN JAAR *(pag. 57)*		65.803		61.096
A. Handelsvorderingen	53.924		52.164	
B. Overige vorderingen	11.879		8.932	
IX. THESAURIEBELEGGINGEN		1.454		1.595
B. Overige beleggingen	1.454		1.595	
X. LIQUIDE MIDDELEN		1.285		1.217
XI. OVERLOPENDE REKENINGEN *(pag. 57)*		5.920		4.323
TOTAAL VAN DE ACTIVA		**354.402**		**358.653**

(miljoen BEF)

PASSIVA		1992		1993
EIGEN VERMOGEN *(pag. 58)*		121.280		127.064
I. KAPITAAL		43.291		43.291
A. Geplaatst kapitaal	43.291		43.291	
II. EMISSIEPREMIE		24.304		24.305
IV. RESERVES		78.192		78.606
V. CONSOLIDATIEVERSCHILLEN		572		562
VI. OMREKENINGSVERSCHILLEN		−25.676		−20.239
VII. KAPITAALSUBSIDIES		597		539
AANDEEL VAN DERDEN *(pag. 59)*		4.315		4.956
VIII. AANDEEL VAN DERDEN	4.315		4.956	
VOORZIENINGEN, UITGESTELDE BELASTING- **VERPLICHTINGEN EN FISCALE LATENTIES** *(pag. 59)*		45.484		46.998
IX. A. VOORZIENING VOOR RISICO'S EN LASTEN		30.227		31.596
1. Pensioenen en soortgelijke verplichtingen	9.938		10.939	
3. Belangrijke herstellings- en				
onderhoudswerkzaamheden	374		171	
4. Overige risico's en lasten	19.915		20.486	
B. UITGESTELDE BELASTINGVERPLICHTINGEN				
EN FISCALE LATENTIES		15.257		15.402
SCHULDEN		183.323		179.635
X. SCHULDEN MET EEN LOOPTIJD VAN LANGER				
DAN EEN JAAR *(pag. 60)*		59.989		60.521
A. Financiële schulden				
2. Niet-achtergestelde obligatieleningen	29.415		46.832	
3. Schulden van huurfinanciering en				
soortgelijke schulden	1.593		1.298	
4. Kredietinstellingen	18.579		12.036	
5. Overige leningen	10.402		355	
XI. SCHULDEN MET EEN LOOPTIJD VAN TEN				
HOOGSTE EEN JAAR *(pag. 61)*		116.471		110.413
A. Tijdens het boekjaar vervallende schulden				
met een looptijd van langer dan een jaar	8.992		9.615	
B. Financiële schulden				
1. Kredietinstellingen	14.505		11.550	
2. Overige schulden	16.020		9.812	
	30.525		21.362	
C. Handelsschulden				
1. Leveranciers	41.301		42.168	
2. Te betalen wissels	611		361	
	41.912		42.529	
E. Belastingen, salarissen en sociale lasten				
1. Belastingen	18.422		21.359	
2. Salarissen en sociale lasten	4.335		4.553	
	22.757		25.912	
F. Overige schulden	12.285		10.995	
XII. OVERLOPENDE REKENINGEN *(pag. 61)*		6.863		8.701
TOTAAL VAN DE PASSIVA		**354.402**		**358.653**

47

CONSOLIDATED BALANCE SHEET

AT 31 DECEMBER 1992 and 31 DECEMBER 1993

(million BEF)

ASSETS	1992		1993	
FIXED ASSETS		216,069		231,558
II. INTANGIBLE ASSETS *(page 54)*		2,597		2,438
III. ADJUSTMENTS ON CONSOLIDATION *(page 54)*		143		94
IV. TANGIBLE ASSETS *(page 55)*		203,280		222,284
A. Land and buildings	26,800		26,512	
B. Plant, machinery, equipment, furniture and vehicles	88,871		91,777	
C. Exploration and production equipment	71,133		76,970	
D. Leasing and similar rights	1,708		1,726	
E. Other tangible assets	1,883		1,821	
F. Assets under construction	12,885		23,478	
V. INVESTMENTS *(page 56)*		10,049		6,742
A. Companies accounted for by the equity method				
1. Shareholdings	3,252		3,195	
2. Receivables	317		266	
	3,569		3,461	
B. Other companies				
1. Shareholdings	5,237		2,135	
2. Receivables	1,243		1,146	
	6,480		3,281	
CURRENT ASSETS		138,333		127,095
VI. RECEIVABLES OF MORE THAN ONE YEAR *(page 56)*		16,690		17,655
B. Other receivables	16,690		17,655	
VII. INVENTORIES *(page 57)*		47,181		41,209
VIII. RECEIVABLES OF LESS THAN ONE YEAR *(page 57)*		65,803		61,096
A. Trade receivables	53,924		52,164	
B. Other receivables	11,879		8,932	
IX. MARKETABLE SECURITIES		1,454		1,595
B. Other securities	1,454		1,595	
X. CASH		1,285		1,217
XI. PREPAID EXPENSES AND ACCRUED INCOME *(page 57)*		5,920		4,323
TOTAL OF THE ASSETS		**354,402**		**358,653**

(million BEF)

LIABILITIES		1992		1993
SHAREHOLDERS' FUNDS *(page 58)*		121,280		127,064
I. SHARE CAPITAL		43,291		43,291
A. Issued capital subscribed	43,291		43,291	
II. SHARE PREMIUM		24,304		24,305
IV. RESERVES		78,192		78,606
V. ADJUSTMENTS ON CONSOLIDATION		572		562
VI. EXCHANGE ADJUSTMENTS		− 25,676		− 20,239
VII. CAPITAL GRANTS		597		539
MINORITY INTERESTS *(page 59)*		4,315		4,956
VIII. MINORITY INTERESTS	4,315		4,956	
PROVISIONS, DEFERRED TAXES AND FISCAL TIME DIFFERENCES *(page 59)*		45.484		46.998
IX. A. PROVISIONS FOR CLAIMS AND LOSSES		30,227		31,596
1. Pensions and similar liabilities	9,938		10,939	
3. Major repairs and maintenance	374		171	
4. Other claims and losses	19,915		20,486	
B. DEFERRED TAXES AND FISCAL TIME DIFFERENCES		15,257		15,402
DEBT		183,323		179,635
X. DEBT OF MORE THAN ONE YEAR *(page 60)*		59,989		60,521
A. Financial debt				
2. Unsubordinated bonds and notes	29,415		46,832	
3. Leasing and similar obligations	1,593		1,298	
4. Banks and financial institutions	18,579		12,036	
5. Others	10,402		355	
XI. DEBT OF LESS THAN ONE YEAR (CURRENT LIABILITIES) *(page 61)*		116,471		110,413
A. Debt of more than one year maturing within the year	8,992		9,615	
B. Financial debt				
1. Banks and financial institutions	14,505		11,550	
2. Others	16,020		9,812	
	30,525		21,362	
C. Trade debt				
1. Suppliers	41,301		42,168	
2. Bills of exchange payable	611		361	
	41,912		42,529	
E. Taxes, salaries and social security				
1. Taxes	18,422		21,359	
2. Salaries and social security	4,335		4,553	
	22,757		25,912	
F. Others	12,285		10,995	
XII. ACCRUED EXPENSES AND INCOME RECEIVED IN ADVANCE *(page 61)*		6,863		8,701
TOTAL OF THE LIABILITIES		**354,402**		**358,653**

47

RESULTATS CONSOLIDES

AUX 31 DECEMBRE 1992 et 31 DECEMBRE 1993

(en millions BEF)

	1992		1993	
I. VENTES ET PRESTATIONS *(page 62)*		555.758		558.982
A. Chiffre d'affaires	537.294		540.893	
C. Production immobilisée	758		946	
D. Autres produits d'exploitation	17.706		17.143	
II. COUTS DES VENTES ET PRESTATIONS		− 538.703		− 538.571
A. Approvisionnements et marchandises				
1. Achats	− 264.644		− 243.142	
2. Variations des stocks	− 221		− 4.358	
3. Droits et taxes sur produits	− 161.759		− 180.852	
	− 426.624		− 428.352	
B. Services et biens divers	− 43.866		− 43.426	
C. Rémunérations, charges sociales et pensions	− 30.543		− 29.869	
D. Amortissements et réductions de valeur sur immobilisations incorporelles et corporelles	− 26.320		− 23.342	
E. Réductions de valeur sur stocks et créances commerciales	− 707		− 3.800	
F. Provisions pour risques et charges	472		214	
G. Autres charges d'exploitation	− 11.115		− 9.996	
III. BENEFICE D'EXPLOITATION		17.055		20.411
IV. PRODUITS FINANCIERS *(page 63)*		6.053		5.317
A. Produits des immobilisations financières	2.199		2.047	
B. Produits des actifs circulants	1.962		1.642	
C. Autres produits financiers	1.892		1.628	
V. CHARGES FINANCIERES *(page 63)*		10.466		− 9.236
A. Charges des dettes	− 8.386		− 7.485	
B. Réductions de valeur sur actifs financiers	− 260		78	
C. Autres charges financières	− 1.820		− 1.829	
VI. BENEFICE COURANT AVANT IMPOTS		12.642		16.492

VII.	PRODUITS EXCEPTIONNELS *(page 64)*		3.229	2.358
	C. Reprises de provisions pour risques et charges exceptionnels	5		718
	D. Plus-values sur réalisation d'actifs immobilisés	806		1.421
	E. Autres produits exceptionnels	2.418		219
VIII.	CHARGES EXCEPTIONNELLES *(page 64)*		– 6.804	– 4.510
	A. Amortissements et réductions de valeur sur immobilisations incorporelles et corporelles	– 480		– 1.458
	C. Provisions pour risques et charges exceptionnels	– 2.620		– 1.038
	E. Autres charges exceptionnelles	– 3.704		– 2.014
IX.	BENEFICE DE L'EXERCICE AVANT IMPOTS		9.067	14.340
X.	IMPOTS DIFFERES *(page 64)*		1.959	1.274
	B. Prélèvements sur impôts différés	1.959		1.274
XI.	IMPOTS SUR LE RESULTAT *(page 64)*		– 7.447	– 8.577
	A. Impôts courants	– 7.447		– 8.577
XII.	BENEFICE DES ENTREPRISES CONSOLIDEES		3.579	7.037
XIII.	QUOTE-PART DANS LE RESULTAT DES ENTREPRISES MISES EN EQUIVALENCE		1.031	576
	A. Résultats en bénéfice	1.276		646
	B. Résultats en perte	– 245		– 70
XIV.	BENEFICE CONSOLIDE		4.610	7.613
XV.	PART DES TIERS DANS LE RESULTAT		– 21	469
XVI.	PART DU GROUPE DANS LE RESULTAT		4.631	7.144

GECONSOLIDEERDE RESULTATENREKENINGEN

PER 31 DECEMBER 1992 en 31 DECEMBER 1993

(miljoen BEF)

	1992		1993	
I. OMZET EN DIENSTEN *(pag. 62)*		555.758		558.982
A. Omzet	537.294		540.893	
C. Geproduceerde vaste activa	758		946	
D. Overige bedrijfsopbrengsten	17.706		17.143	
II. KOSTPRIJS VAN OMZET EN DIENSTEN		– 538.703		– 538.571
A. Aankopen en handelsvoorraden				
1. Aankopen	– 264.644		– 243.142	
2. Voorraadwijzigingen	– 221		– 4.358	
3. Rechten en belastingen op produkten	– 161.759		– 180.852	
	– 426.624		– 428.352	
B. Diensten en diverse goederen	– 43.866		– 43.426	
C. Salarissen, sociale lasten en pensioenen	– 30.543		– 29.869	
D. Afschrijvingen en waardeverminderingen op immateriële en materiële vaste activa	– 26.320		– 23.342	
E. Waardeverminderingen op voorraden en handelsvorderingen	– 707		– 3.800	
F. Voorzieningen voor risico's en lasten	472		214	
G. Overige bedrijfskosten	– 11.115		– 9.996	
III. BEDRIJFSWINST		17.055		20.411
IV. FINANCIELE OPBRENGSTEN *(pag. 63)*		6.053		5.317
A. Opbrengsten van financiële vaste activa	2.199		2.047	
B. Opbrengsten van vlottende activa	1.962		1.642	
C. Overige financiële opbrengsten	1.892		1.628	
V. FINANCIELE KOSTEN *(pag. 63)*		– 10.466		– 9.236
A. Kosten van schulden	– 8.386		– 7.485	
B. Waardeverminderingen op financiële activa	– 260		78	
C. Overige financiële kosten	– 1.820		– 1.829	
VI. WINST UIT DE GEWONE BEDRIJFSUITOEFENING VOOR BELASTINGEN		12.642		16.492

VII. BIJZONDERE OPBRENGSTEN *(pag. 64)*		3.229	2.358
C. Terugneming van voorzieningen voor bijzondere risico's en lasten	5		718
D. Meerwaarden op de verkoop van vaste activa	806		1.421
E. Overige bijzondere opbrengsten	2.418		219
VIII. BIJZONDERE KOSTEN *(pag. 64)*		– 6.804	– 4.510
A. Afschrijvingen en waardeverminderingen op immateriële en materiële vaste activa	– 480		– 1.458
C. Voorzieningen voor bijzondere risico's en lasten	– 2.620		– 1.038
E. Overige bijzondere kosten	– 3.704		– 2.014
IX. WINST VAN HET BOEKJAAR VOOR BELASTINGEN		9.067	14.340
X. UITGESTELDE BELASTINGVERPLICHTINGEN *(pag. 64)*		1.959	1.274
B. Aanwending van voorziening voor uitgestelde belastingverplichtingen	1.959		1.274
XI. BELASTINGEN OP DE WINST *(pag. 64)*		– 7.447	– 8.577
A. Belastingen	– 7.447		– 8.577
XII. WINST VAN DE GECONSOLIDEERDE ONDERNEMINGEN		3.579	7.037
XIII. AANDEEL IN HET RESULTAAT VAN ONDERNEMINGEN OPGENOMEN VOLGENS DE NETTO-VERMOGENSWAARDEMETHODE		1.031	576
A. Resultaten winst	1.276		646
B. Resultaten verlies	– 245		– 70
XIV. GECONSOLIDEERDE WINST		4.610	7.613
XV. AANDEEL VAN DERDEN IN DE WINST		– 21	469
XVI. AANDEEL VAN DE GROEP IN DE WINST		4.631	7.144

49

CONSOLIDATED STATEMENT OF INCOME

AT 31 DECEMBER 1992 and 31 DECEMBER 1993

(million BEF)

	1992		1993	
I. SALES AND OPERATING REVENUES *(page 62)*		555,758		558,982
A. Turnover	537,294		540,893	
C. Income from land and buildings	758		946	
D. Other operating income	17,706		17,143	
II. COST OF SALES AND SERVICES		– 538,703		– 538,571
A. Supplies and goods				
1. Purchases	– 264,644		– 243,142	
2. Movements in inventories	– 221		– 4,358	
3. Duties and taxes on products	– 161,759		– 180,852	
	– 426,624		– 428,352	
B. Other goods and services	– 43,866		– 43,426	
C. Salaries, social security and pensions	– 30,543		– 29,869	
D. Depreciation and reductions in value of intangible and tangible assets	– 26,320		– 23,342	
E. Reductions in value of trade receivables and inventories	– 707		– 3,800	
F. Provisions for claims and losses	472		214	
G. Other operating expenses	– 11,115		– 9,996	
III. OPERATING PROFIT		17,055		20,411
IV. FINANCIAL REVENUES *(page 63)*		6,053		5,317
A. Investment income	2,199		2,047	
B. Income from securities and cash	1,962		1,642	
C. Other financial income	1,892		1,628	
V. FINANCIAL CHARGES *(page 63)*		– 10,466		– 9,236
A. Interest on debt	– 8,386		– 7,485	
B. Reductions in value of investments	– 260		78	
C. Other financial charges	– 1,820		– 1,829	
VI. ORDINARY NET INCOME BEFORE TAXATION		12,642		16,492

VII. EXTRAORDINARY INCOME *(page 64)*		3,229		2,358
C. Write-back of provisions for extraordinary claims and losses	5		718	
D. Gain on disposal of fixed assets	806		1,421	
E. Other extraordinary income	2,418		219	
VIII. EXTRAORDINARY CHARGES *(page 64)*		− 6,804		− 4,510
A. Depreciation and reductions in value of intangible and tangible assets	− 480		− 1,458	
C. Provisions for extraordinary claims and losses	− 2,620		− 1,038	
E. Other extraordinary charges	− 3,704		− 2,014	
IX. NET INCOME BEFORE TAXATION		9,067		14,340
X. DEFERRED TAXES *(page 64)*		1,959		1,274
B. Transfer from deferred taxes	1,959		1,274	
XI. TAXATION *(page 64)*		− 7,447		− 8,577
A. Current taxation	− 7,447		− 8,577	
XII. NET INCOME OF CONSOLIDATED COMPANIES		3,579		7,037
XIII. SHARE OF RESULTS OF COMPANIES ACCOUNTED FOR BY THE EQUITY METHOD		1,031		576
A. Profits	1,276		646	
B. Losses	− 245		− 70	
XIV. CONSOLIDATED NET INCOME		4,610		7,613
XV. MINORITY INTERESTS' NET INCOME		− 21		469
XVI. PETROFINA SHAREHOLDERS' NET INCOME		4,631		7,144

AFFECTATIONS

(en millions BEF)

RESULTATS DE L'EXERCICE	
a) Part du Groupe	7.144
b) Part des tiers	469
Disponible pour affectations	7.613
Rémunération du capital	6.511
Intéressement du Conseil, de la Direction, des Cadres	
et Mécénat	222
Réserves	411
Intérêts de tiers	469
	7.613

TABLEAU DES FLUX DE TRESORERIE

(en millions BEF)

OPERATIONS D'EXPLOITATION		
Bénéfice d'exploitation	23.481	
Dotation aux amortissements	23.342	
Dotation aux provisions	– 183	
Marge brute d'autofinancement		46.640
Variation du fonds de roulement d'exploitation	13.259	
Charges et produits exceptionnels	– 2.152	
Dotations exceptionnelles aux amortissements et aux provisions	2.088	
Charges financières payées	– 8.883	
Impôts payés	– 8.455	
Flux nets des opérations d'exploitation		– 4.143
OPERATIONS D'INVESTISSEMENT		
Investissements de l'exercice	– 35.653	
Valeur comptable des actifs cédés	5.763	
Produits des immobilisations financières	3.024	
Autres produits financiers	2.979	
Flux nets des opérations d'investissement		– 23.887
OPERATIONS DE FINANCEMENT		
Augmentation de capital	48	
Variations des dettes financières à plus d'un an	– 2.517	
Variations des dettes financières à un an au plus	– 9.231	
Dividende payé	– 7.008	
Flux nets des opérations de financement		– 18.708
VARIATIONS DE LA TRESORERIE		– 98

Le tableau de financement est élaboré sur base des flux réels de l'exercice.

Les modifications intervenues dans le périmètre de consolidation ainsi que les variations résultant des fluctuations monétaires en sont exclues.

50

RESULTAATVERWERKING

(miljoen BEF)

RESULTAAT VAN HET BOEKJAAR	
a) Aandeel van de Groep	7.144
b) Aandeel van derden	469
Beschikbaar voor verdeling	7.613
Vergoeding van het kapitaal	6.511
Ter beschikking van de Raad van Bestuur, de Directie, het Stafpersoneel en het Mecenaat	222
Reserves	411
Aandeel van derden	469
	7.613

THESAURIESTROMEN

(miljoen BEF)

BEDRIJFSACTIVITEITEN		
Bedrijfswinst	23.481	
Dotatie aan afschrijvingen	23.342	
Dotatie aan voorzieningen	-183	
Bruto zelffinancieringsmarge		46.640
Wijziging van het werkkapitaal	13.259	
Bijzondere opbrengsten en kosten	-2.152	
Bijzondere dotatie aan afschrijvingen en voorzieningen	2.088	
Betaalde financiële kosten	-8.883	
Betaalde belastingen	-8.455	
Netto thesauriestroom uit bedrijfsactiviteiten		-4.143
INVESTERINGEN		
Investeringen van het boekjaar	-35.653	
Boekwaarde van de verkochte en afgeboekte vaste activa	5.763	
Opbrengsten van financiële vaste activa	3.024	
Overige financiële opbrengsten	2.979	
Netto thesauriestroom uit investeringsactiviteiten		-23.887
FINANCIERING		
Kapitaalverhoging	48	
Wijzigingen van de financiële schulden met een looptijd van langer dan een jaar	-2.517	
Wijzigingen van de financiële schulden met een looptijd van ten hoogste een jaar	-9.231	
Uitgekeerd dividend	-7.008	
Netto thesauriestroom uit financieringsactiviteiten		-18.708
WIJZIGINGEN IN DE THESAURIESITUATIE		-98

De financieringsstaat is opgesteld op basis van de reële thesauriestromen gedurende het boekjaar.
Wijzigingen in de grondslagen van de consolidatie en mutaties ten gevolge van monetaire schommelingen zijn hierin niet begrepen.

ALLOCATION OF NET INCOME

(million BEF)

NET INCOME FOR THE YEAR	
a) Group net income	7,144
b) Minority shareholders' net income	469
Available for allocation	7,613
Dividends	6,511
Bonuses to directors, officers and senior staff and donations to the Benevolent Fund	222
Allocation to reserves	411
Minority interests	469
	7,613

TREASURY FLOW

(million BEF)

OPERATING ACTIVITIES		
Operating profit	23,481	
Allocation to depreciation	23,342	
Allocation to provisions	− 183	
Internally generated funds from operations		46,640
Movement in working capital	13,259	
Extraordinary income and charges	− 2,152	
Extraordinary allocation to depreciation and provisions	2,088	
Financial charges paid	− 8,883	
Taxes paid	− 8,455	
Net treasury flow from operating activities		− 4,143
INVESTMENT ACTIVITIES		
Capital investment for the year	− 35,653	
Book value of sales and deletions	5,763	
Dividends received	3,024	
Other financial income	2,979	
Net treasury flow from investment activities		− 23,887
FINANCIAL ACTIVITIES		
Capital increase	48	
Movement in financial debt of more than one year	− 2,517	
Movement in financial debt of less than one year	− 9,231	
Dividend paid	− 7,008	
Net treasury flow from financial activities		− 18,708
MOVEMENT IN TREASURY POSITION		− 98

The financial statement is based on real treasury flows during the year.

It does not include the effect of changes in the scope of the consolidation and exchange adjustments.

NOTES TO THE CONSOLIDATED ACCOUNTS

In drawing up these consolidated accounts, the Group complied with the Royal Decree of November 25, 1991, concerning the annual accounts of industrial holding companies. However, for accounting practices specific to the petroleum industry or those not yet implemented under Belgian accounting law, the Group has followed FAS standards set by the Financial Accounting Standards Board.

Accordingly, since 1991 Petrofina has applied FAS 19 to account for its oil and gas exploration and production expenditure using the Successful Efforts method. Likewise, since 1992 the Group has applied FAS 109 to value the provision for deferred taxes.

I. CRITERIA FOR CONSOLIDATION

Companies which Petrofina effectively or legally controls have been fully consolidated. Under this method, the book value of the parent company's investment is replaced with the assets and liabilities of the relevant company. The balance-sheet heading "Adjustments on consolidation" represents the consolidation differences resulting from this substitution. "Minority interests" represents the share of minority shareholders in the shareholders' funds of the consolidated companies. In the income statement, the subsidiaries' income and charges are combined with those of the parent company, and the Group's net income and that of the minority interests is shown separately.

Companies which are jointly controlled with a limited number of shareholders are proportionally consolidated, when only the relevant Group interest in the assets, liabilities, income and charges are accounted for.

Certain subsidiaries are excluded from the scope of the consolidation. This applies when a company's total capital employed, total assets and turnover amount to less than 1‰ of the total corresponding items in the consolidated balance sheet of the previous financial year. Due to their negligible significance there is little interest in including these subsidiaries when valuing the Group's assets, financial position or consolidated profit.

A subsidiary is not consolidated when effective control is significantly affected due to serious and long-term restrictions. Companies which are planned to be sold are treated likewise.

The equity method applies to companies in which the group holds 20% to 50% of the capital and over which it exercises significant control. Under this method, the book value of the investment is replaced with the corresponding proportion of net assets of the consolidated company, and the fraction of profit due to the Group is recorded in the income statement. The equity method, however, does not apply to companies in which the Group owns less than 100 million BEF of the shareholders' funds: their significance is deemed negligible.

When the investments are not covered by the above criteria they are shown in the consolidated accounts at the book value in their parent company's accounts.

II. CONSOLIDATION SCOPE

A) On page 38 of this annual report the reader will find a list and summary of the main companies consolidated by the methods described above. A full list of consolidated companies and companies excluded from the scope is available from the Public Relations and Communication Department of Petrofina s.a., rue de l'Industrie 52, 1040 Brussels.

B) At December 31, 1993, the companies excluded from the consolidation because of restrictions affecting the exercise of control or due to their negligible significance represent less than 1% of all the consolidated companies' turnover, balance-sheet totals and capital employed. Therefore there is no benefit in including these companies in the consolidation and its valuation of the Group's assets, financial position or consolidated profit.

VI. VALUATION RULES

A) METHODS OF CONVERSION

The assets and liabilities on the balance sheet of the consolidated companies denominated in currencies other than their working currency are valued at the exchange rate on December 31. In the consolidation process, the balance sheets of foreign companies are converted into Belgian francs using the closing rate method. Under this method, all the assets and liabilities on the foreign companies' balance sheets are converted into Belgian francs at the year-end exchange rate, with the exception of shareholders' funds which are left at historical rates. The income and charges on the income statement of foreign companies are converted at the average exchange rate for the year. The differences arising from accounting with exchange rates other than the closing rate – i.e. yearly average and historical rates – are recorded under the heading "Exchange adjustments". The amount attributable to third parties is included under the heading "Minority interests".

B) DIFFERENCES ARISING FROM INITIAL CONSOLIDATION

When a company is consolidated for the first time, a comparison of its cost of acquisition and the proportion of its shareholders' funds relating to the Group's interest creates a difference, which as far as is possible, is allocated to the assets and liabilities of the subsidiary. The remainder is shown on the consolidated balance sheet under the heading "Adjustments on consolidation". The rate of depreciation of the assets allocation depends upon the specific nature of the asset.

C) METHODS OF VALUATION AND RESTATEMENT

The consolidated balance sheet is based on the accounts as at December 31. The valuation rules used in the consolidated accounts follow the valuation principles used by the parent company.

The use of these standard accounting rules and valuation methods throughout all subsidiaries means that the consolidated accounts can be drawn up with no major restatement of figures. Receivables, and inter-company payables are eliminated, as well as capital gains within the Group. Sales of raw materials and finished products between consolidated companies are subject to market conditions.

1. Oil and gas exploration and production costs

The Group uses the Successful Efforts method whereby only those costs which have led to the discovery and development of economically recoverable reserves are capitalized.

Under this method:

– the costs of purchasing drilling rights or property rights are capitalized;
– the costs of exploration and geological, geophysical and seismic studies are expensed as occurred;
– dryhole costs are also expensed as occurred;
– the costs of drilling wells that are considered economically viable and the cost of developing them are capitalized and treated as assets.

This method is applied field by field.

Financial charges are capitalized from the date of the decision to develop until the field begins production. All fixed assets related to production are depreciated by a unit of production method based on proven and developed reserves.

2. Intangible assets and incorporation expenses

Incorporation expenses are charged to the income statement of the year in which they occurred.
Intangible assets with a limited useful life are depreciated at 20% a year.

3. Tangible assets

Tangible assets are valued at their cost of acquisition or transfer value. Depreciation is calculated based on the economic useful life of the relevant asset. In certain circumstances, depreciation can be accelerated. Financial expenses for financing assets under construction are incorporated in the cost price of the capital expenditure.

4. Investments

Shareholdings under the heading "Other companies" are shown at their acquisition cost. Reductions in value are recorded when the year-end review indicates that there will be a permanent depreciation.

5. Inventories

Crude oil and petroleum and chemical finished products are valued at their market or cost price, whichever is the lower. Cost price is determined according to the last-in-first-out (LIFO) method. Other products are valued at the lower of the market price or the weighted average purchase price.

6. Receivables and payables

Receivables and payables are accounted for at their nominal value, and are reduced in value when their year-end valuation indicates that there will be a permanent reduction in value.

7. Marketable securities

Shares, shareholdings or fixed-income instruments are valued at the lower of market price or cost.

8. Provisions

Provisions for claims and losses account for clearly identifiable losses or expenses which are likely or certain by year-end but of which the actual amount can only be estimated.

a) The Group makes provisions for the future costs of cleaning up industrial sites. These provisions are entered under "Provisions for other claims and losses".
b) The Group accounts for the costs of pension and health schemes according to the regulations of each country where it operates. These costs are either covered by transfers to outside organizations or recorded under the heading "Pensions and similar liabilities". In the latter case, the actuarial value of the provisions is determined by independent experts.
c) In 1992, FINA, Inc. adopted FAS 106 to value and make a provision for supplementary post-retirement health-care benefits. Standard FAS 106 applies mainly

to the United States, where the social-security system is much less developed than in Europe.

d) The provision for deferred taxes was established on the basis of rules defined under FAS 109.

Under these rules, the company must value its provisions for deferred taxes on the basis of all temporary differences between its accounting net income and that calculated for fiscal purposes.

The provision for deferred taxes is reviewed each year to take account of the change in the tax base and any changes in legislation. Fiscal time differences are reflected in the consolidated accounts only if they are reasonably likely to materialize in the foreseeable future.

VII. FIXED ASSETS

(million BEF)

1° Fixed assets: geographical breakdown	1992	%	1993	%
Belgium	59,482	27.5	68,060	29.4
Other European countries	87,690	40.6	94,634	40.8
North America	65,591	30.4	66,370	28.7
Africa and others	3,306	1.5	2,494	1.1
TOTAL	216,069	100.0	231,558	100.0
2° Capital expenditure: geographical breakdown	1992	%	1993	%
Belgium	11,191	25.5	16,294	45.7
Other European countries	22,155	50.5	13,325	37.4
North America	8,714	19.8	5,189	14.5
Africa and others	1,854	4.2	845	2.4
TOTAL	43,914	100.0	35,653	100.0
3° Fixed assets: sector breakdown	1992	%	1993	%
Exploration, Production	76,457	35.4	82,229	35.5
Refining, Marketing, Transportation	89,337	41.3	102,918	44.5
Chemicals, Paints	40,605	18.8	39,841	17.2
Other activities	9,670	4.5	6,570	2.8
TOTAL	216,069	100.0	231,558	100.0

4° Capital expenditure: sector breakdown	1992	%	1993	%	Budget 1994	%
Exploration, Production	21,468 (*)	48.9	11,678 (**)	32.8	11,009	33.4
Refining, Marketing, Transportation	15,906	36.2	20,467	57.4	17,309	52.6
Chemicals, Paints	5,312	12.1	2,547	7.1	3,140	9.5
Other activities	1,228	2.8	961	2.7	1,469	4.5
TOTAL	43,914	100.0	35,653	100.0	32,927	100.0

5° Intercalary interests on assets under construction included in capital expenditure	1992	1993
	1,031	2,024

(*) includes depreciated exploration of 4,012 million BEF.

(**) includes depreciated exploration of 1,551 million BEF.

VIII. INTANGIBLE ASSETS

(million BEF)

	Research and development expenses	Patents and licences	Costumer goodwill	Other intangible assets	Total
A. COST PRICE					
At 31 December 1992	868	2,737	1,775	10,596	15,976
Changes in the year:					
– Acquisitions	152	2	285	193	632
– Variations in scope	0	0	– 2	0	– 2
– Sales and deletions	– 19	– 1	– 22	– 771	– 813
– Transfers	0	284	1	– 285	0
– Exchange adjustments	0	11	4	654	669
At 31 December 1993	1,001	3,033	2,041	10,387	16,462
C. DEPRECIATION AND REDUCTIONS IN VALUE					
At 31 December 1992	– 521	– 1,941	– 1,061	– 9,856	– 13,379
Changes in the year:					
– Allocation for the year	– 80	– 172	– 342	– 262	– 856
– Variations in scope	0	0	1	0	1
– Sales and deletions	19	0	7	770	796
– Transfers	0	– 2	0	2	0
– Exchange adjustments	0	– 1	– 4	– 581	– 586
At 31 December 1993	– 582	– 2,116	– 1,399	– 9,927	– 14,024
D. NET BOOK VALUE					
At 31 December 1993	419	917	642	460	2,438

VIII. ᴮᴵˢ ADJUSTMENTS ON CONSOLIDATION

(million BEF)

At 31 December 1992	143
Depreciation	– 45
Exchange adjustments	– 4
At 31 December 1993	94

IX. TANGIBLE ASSETS

(million BEF)

| | Land and buildings | Equipment | | Leasing | Other tangible assets | Assets under construction | Total |
		Machinery, furniture, vehicles	Exploration, production				
A. COST PRICE							
At 31 December 1992	39,612	169,013	165,514	7,049	3,336	12,885	397,409
Changes in the year:							
– Acquisitions	894	5,922	11,444	10	240	16,076	34,586
– Variations in scope	18	37	– 3		– 6		46
– Sales and deletions	– 1,242	– 3,934	– 9,869	– 136	– 115	– 70	– 15,366
– Transfers	– 121	5,837	306	– 338	– 96	– 5,588	0
– Exchange adjustments	1,236	5,379	14,134	328	179	175	21,431
At 31 December 1993	40,397	182,254	181,526	6,913	3,538	23,478	438,106
C. DEPRECIATION AND REDUCTIONS IN VALUE							
At 31 December 1992	– 12,812	– 80,142	– 94,381	– 5,341	– 1,453		– 194,129
Changes in the year:							
– Allocation for the year	– 1,681	– 11,637	– 9,645	– 199	– 368		– 23,530
– Variations in scope	– 7	– 17			– 2		– 26
– Sales and deletions	674	3,643	8,233	135	114		12,799
– Transfers	169	– 224	– 541	504	92		0
– Exchange adjustments	– 228	– 2,100	– 8,222	– 286	– 100		– 10,936
At 31 December 1993	– 13,885	– 90,477	– 104,556	– 5,187	– 1,717		– 215,822
D. NET BOOK VALUE							
At 31 December 1993	26,512	91,777	76,970	1,726	1,821	23,478	222,284

X. INVESTMENTS

(million BEF)

	Purchase price	Reductions in value	Receivables	Accounted for by the equity method	Total
A. COMPANIES ACCOUNTED FOR BY THE EQUITY METHOD					
At 31 December 1992	3,923	− 10	317	− 661	3,569
Changes in the year:					
– Acquisitions, capital increases	254				254
– Variations in scope	− 5			191	186
– Sales	− 285				− 285
– Profit accounted for by the equity method				576	576
– Dividends received				− 978	− 978
– Reductions in value		− 25			− 25
– Exchange adjustments	− 87	10	− 51	292	164
At 31 December 1993	3,800	− 25	266	− 580	3,461
B. OTHER COMPANIES					
At 31 December 1992	7,712	− 2,475	1,243		6,480
Changes in the year:					
– Acquisitions, capital increases	127		54		181
– Variations in scope	21				21
– Sales	− 2,959	270	− 205		− 2,894
– Reductions in value		− 342			− 342
– Exchange adjustments	− 219		54		− 165
At 31 December 1993	4,682	− 2,547	1,146		3,281

X. BIS CURRENT ASSETS

A. RECEIVABLES OF MORE THAN ONE YEAR

(million BEF)

	1992	1993
b) Placement of technical reserves relating to insurance operations	10,564	12,158
c) Other receivables	6,126	5,497
	16,690	17,655

56

B. INVENTORIES *(million BEF)*

	1992	1993
a) Petroleum products	26,339	21,983
b) Petrochemical products and paints	13,920	12,684
c) Other products	6,922	6,542
	47,181	41,209

At December 31, 1993, the Group has reduced the value of crude oil and petroleum products inventories by 3.1 billion BEF to bring them into line with their market value. In December 1992 the rise of the dollar rate allowed a write-back of 1 billion BEF of the reduction in value of inventories recorded in 1991.

C. RECEIVABLES OF LESS THAN ONE YEAR *(million BEF)*

1° Trade receivables	1992	1993
Trade receivables	56,586	54,882
Reduction in value of trade receivables	− 2,662	− 2,718
	53,924	52,164

During the 1993 financial year the title of 7.8 billion BEF in trade receivables was transferred to several banks.

(million BEF)

2° Other receivables	1992	1993
Recoverable rights and taxes	5,312	4,082
Claims relating to exploration and production activities	1,047	754
Short-term financial loans	568	570
Other receivables	4,952	3,526
	11,879	8,932

D. PREPAID EXPENSES AND ACCRUED INCOME *(million BEF)*

	1992	1993
− Pro rata of revenues accrued but not collected	2,810	1,979
− Charges relating to later years	2,038	2,295
− Evaluation differences on guarantees and commitments	1,072	49
	5,920	4,323

XI. LIABILITIES

A. EVOLUTION OF SHAREHOLDERS' FUNDS

(million BEF)

	Share capital	Share premium	Reserves	Adjustments on consolidation	Exchange adjustments	Capital grants	Total
At 31 December 1992	43,291	24,304	78,192	572	− 25,676	597	121,280
Changes in the year:							
− Increases in the year		1			5,437	33	5,471
− Variations in scope			3	− 10		1	− 6
− Transfers						− 92	− 92
− Profit for the year			7,144				7,144
− Proposed distribution			− 6,733				− 6,733
At 31 December 1993	43,291	24,305	78,606	562	− 20,239	539	127,064

B. SHARE CAPITAL

At December 31, 1993, the share capital of Petrofina s.a., totalled 43,291,318,836 BEF (represented by 23,251,817 shares), an increase of 212,268 BEF from December 31, 1992, as a result of the issue of 114 shares. The conversion price per share has been allocated in respect of 1,862 BEF as share capital and the balance as share premium.

C. SHARE PREMIUM

This amounted to 24,305,024,218 BEF, an increase of 956,688 BEF from December 31, 1992, as a result of the exercice of 114 warrants attached to the 1991 bond issue reserved for personnel.

D. RESERVES

The change in reserves arises from the movement in the allocation and deductions for the year, or a total of 7,144 million BEF and the transfer to the heading other debt (current liabilities) of the proposed allocation of dividends and directors' and staff bonuses (6,733 million BEF).

E. ADJUSTMENTS ON CONSOLIDATION

This reflects past adjustments on initial consolidations. The movement for the year of 10 million BEF corresponds to changes in the scope of the consolidation.

F. EXCHANGE ADJUSTMENTS

This heading shows exchange adjustments arising in the valuation of subsidiaries' shareholders' funds when converted into Belgian francs at either historical or closing rates. The variation of the year mainly resulted from the increase in the value of the dollar.

G. CAPITAL GRANTS

These are investment grants from public authorities. They are depreciated at the same rate as is applied to the relevant investments. Grants received in 1993 amounted to 33 million BEF, 92 million BEF were transferred to other financial income.

H. MINORITY INTERESTS

This reflects minority interests in the fully consolidated subsidiaries, mainly the minority interests in FINA, Inc.

(million BEF)

	1992	1993
At beginning of year	5,640	4,315
Deconsolidation of the Angolan subsidiary	− 1,290	—
Other changes in the scope of consolidation	− 8	47
Minority interests' profits for the year	− 21	469
Dividends paid to minority interests	− 270	− 241
Exchange adjustments	264	366
At end of year	4,315	4,956

The balance of exchange adjustments at 31 December 1993 totals − 199 million BEF.

I. PROVISIONS FOR CLAIMS AND LOSSES

1. Pensions and similar liabilities

This covers provisions established by the Group to cover personnel benefits in the form of pensions and health care.

3. Major repairs and maintenance

(million BEF)

	1992	1993
At beginning of year	709	374
Charge for the year	194	97
Utilization of previous provisions	− 492	− 336
Exchange adjustments	7	16
Other movements	− 44	20
At end of year	374	171

4. Provisions for other claims and losses

(million BEF)

	1992	1993
a) Technical provisions for insurance	12,415	12,366
b) Abandonment provisions (dismantling and environmental protection)	2,379	3,256
c) Other provisions for claims and losses	5,121	4,864
At end of year	19,915	20,486

XIII. DEBT OF MORE THAN ONE YEAR

(million BEF)

1° Analysis by category	1992		1993	
	Less than 5 years	More than 5 years	Less than 5 years	More than 5 years
− Bonds and notes	18,068	11,347	28,560	18,272
− Leasing	980	613	852	446
− Banks and financial institutions	13,031	5,548	9,051	2,985
− Other debts	9,956	446	147	208
TOTAL	42,035	17,954	38,610	21,911

2° Analysis by maturity	1992	1993
− 1994	11,515	—
− 1995	11,600	11,381
− 1996	11,234	13,902
− 1997	7,686	8,769
− 1998	2,885	4,558
− 1999	356	2,144
− 2000	11,445	13,283
− Later	3,268	6,484
	59,989	60,521

3° Analysis by currency	1992 (%)	1993 (%)
− Belgian francs	25	24
− US dollars	68	69
− Pounds sterling	5	1
− French francs	2	2
− Other currencies	0	4
This analysis takes swap transactions into account	100	100

4° Analysis by nature	1993 *(million BEF)*	1993 (%)
a. Bonds and notes	46,832	77
b. Leasing	1,298	2
c. Banks and financial institutions	12,036	20
− fixed rates	5,570	
− variable rates	6,466	
d. Other loans	355	1
	60,521	100

5° Changes in the year	1992 *(million BEF)*	1993 *(million BEF)*
At beginning of year	47,241	59,989
New loans	22,097	15,375
Transfers to short-term debt	− 8,992	− 9,611
Repayments on maturity	− 328	− 8,281
Exchange adjustments	96	3,045
Changes in scope of consolidation	− 125	4
At end of year	59,989	60,521

XIII. ᴮᴵˢ TOTAL FINANCIAL DEBT

(million BEF)

	1992	1993
Debt of more than one year	59,989	60,521
Debt of more than one year maturing within the year	8,992	9,615
Financial debt of less than one year	30,525	21,362
	99,506	91,498

XIII. ᵀᴱᴿ TAXES, SALARIES AND SOCIAL SECURITY CONTRIBUTIONS AND OTHER LIABILITIES

A. TAXES, SALARIES AND SOCIAL SECURITY CONTRIBUTIONS *(million BEF)*

	1992	1993
1° Taxes		
VAT payable	2,614	3,370
Corporate taxes payable	3,699	4,102
Excise duties on petroleum products	11,228	13,066
Miscellaneous taxes	881	821
	18,422	21,359
2° Salaries and social security contributions	4,335	4,553
	22,757	25,912

B. OTHER LIABILITIES *(million BEF)*

	1992	1993
Proposed dividend and bonuses	6,767	6,733
Liabilities resulting from exploration and production operations	2,984	2,377
Other miscellaneous liabilities	2,534	1,885
	12,285	10,995

XIII. ۹ᵁᴬᵀᴱᴿ ACCRUED EXPENSES AND INCOME RECEIVED IN ADVANCE

(million BEF)

	1992	1993
– Charged in the year but payable later		
• Interest payable	2,643	2,894
• Goods and services payable	1,944	2,333
– Income relating to subsequent years	2,276	3,474
	6,863	8,701

XIV. STATEMENT OF INCOME

(million BEF)

A. RESULTS BY SECTOR	Exploration, Production	Refining, Marketing, Transport	Chemicals, Paints	Other activities	Total
Sales and operating income	55,198	449,772	87,970	3,665	596,605
Internal sales					− 37,623
Net sales and operating income					558,982
Operating profit	14,652	7,508	3,282	− 1,961	23,481
Investment income	433	580	453	581	2,047
Income from companies accounted for by the equity method	232	145	25	174	576
Reductions in value of financial assets	− 2	− 31	− 8	119	78
Sector profit	15,315	8,202	3,752	− 1,087	26,182
Reductions in value of inventories					− 3,070
Net financial charges					− 6,044
Taxation					− 7,303
Extraordinary items (net)					− 2,152
Consolidated net income					7,613
Share of minority interests					469
Groups' share					7,144
Capital investment for the year	11,678	20,467	2,547	961	35,653
Net fixed assets	82,229	102,918	39,841	6,570	231,558

B. 1° TURNOVER	Petroleum products		Chemicals, paints		Other products		Total	
	1992	1993	1992	1993	1992	1993	1992	1993
Europe	357,769	355,294	58,227	54,130	5.990	6,856	421,986	416,280
North America	91,287	97,261	22,249	25,693	1,604	1,642	115,140	124,596
Africa and others	44	17	124	0			168	17
TOTAL	449,100	452,572	80,600	79,823	7,594	8,498	537,294	540,893

2° CAPITALIZED PRODUCTION	Total	
	1992	1993
Europe	758	797
North America		149
TOTAL	758	946

3° OTHER OPERATING INCOME	Total	
	1992	1993
Europe	14,932	11,435
North America	1,362	4,843
Africa and others	1,412	865
TOTAL	17,706	17,143

The heading "Other operating income" includes gains on disposal of exploration and production assets.

C. PAYROLL COSTS	Full consolidation		Proportional consolidation		Total	
	1992	1993	1992	1993	1992	1993
						(number of people)
1. Personnel						
Operational employees	4,727	4,537	705	675	5,432	5,212
Administrative employees	5,322	4,511	316	289	5,638	4,800
Management	4,064	4,325	356	359	4,420	4,684
TOTAL	14,113	13,373	1,377	1,323	15,490	14,696
2. Payroll costs						*(million BEF)*
Salaries and direct social security	20,516	20,061	2,234	2,194	22,750	22,255
Employer's social security contributions	4,459	4,352	665	657	5,124	5,009
Employer's contribution to private insurance schemes	739	696	62	57	801	753
Other payroll costs	965	965	104	95	1,069	1,060
Pensions	658	647	141	145	799	792
TOTAL	27,337	26,721	3,206	3,148	30,543	29,869

(million BEF)

D. FINANCIAL REVENUES	1992	1993
1. Investment income Investment income includes dividends from shareholdings which were neither consolidated nor accounted for by the equity method.	2,199	2,047
2. Income from securities and cash This heading shows income relating to securities and cash.	1,962	1,642
3. Other financial income This heading includes gains on disposal of current assets, capital and interest grants, exchange rate gains and other financial income.	1,892	1,628

(million BEF)

E. FINANCIAL CHARGES	1992	1993
1. Interests on debt Interests relating to short-term and long-term financial debt	– 9,417	– 9,509
Intercalary interests relating to assets under construction	1,031	2,024
	– 8,386	– 7,485
2. Reductions in value of current assets This heading shows reductions in value of marketable securities and of non-commercial receivables	– 260	78
3. Other financial charges This heading includes reductions in value of sales of marketable securities and non-commercial receivables, commissions and financial charges, exchange rate losses, discount charges and other financial charges	– 1,820	– 1,829

(million BEF)

F. EXTRAORDINARY ITEMS	1992	1993
1. Extraordinary charges		
a. Depreciation and reduction in value	− 480	− 1,458
c. Provisions for extraordinary claims and losses	− 2,620	− 1,038
e. Other extraordinary charges	− 3,704	− 2,014
TOTAL	− 6,804	− 4,510
Other extraordinary charges for 1993 mainly include 1.4 billion BEF for restructuring costs and 0.4 billion BEF for taxes.		
2. Extraordinary income		
c. Write-back of provisions for extraordinary claims and losses	5	718
d. Gains on the sale of assets	806	1,421
e. Other extraordinary income	2,418	219
TOTAL	3,229	2,358

(million BEF)

G. TAXATION	1992	1993
1. Current taxation		
At beginning of year	2,828	3,699
Charge entered on income statement	7,447	8,577
Taxes paid during the year	− 6,501	− 8,455
Variations in the scope of consolidation	− 199	4
Exchange adjustments	124	277
At end of year	3,699	4,102
2. Deferred taxes		
At beginning of year	15,521	15,257
Charge for the year	1,237	2,276
Extraordinary charge	2,425	370
Utilized in the year	− 3,196	− 3,550
Extraordinary utilization	− 2,158	− 60
Current timing differences	598	− 99
Exchange adjustments	861	1,189
Other movements	− 31	19
At end of year	15,257	15,402

The reduction in value of the Norwegian crown against the dollar allowed a write-back of the provision for deferred taxes and fiscal time differences of 1.5 billion BEF in 1992 and of 1.1 billion BEF in 1993.

XV. GUARANTEES AND COMMITMENTS NOT SHOWN ON THE BALANCE SHEET

(million BEF)

	1993
A. 1. Guarantees given by the Group as security for loans and commitments of third parties.	9,084
2. Garantees given by the Group in respect of its own assets.	334
3. Goods and values held by third parties, in their name, but at the risk or gain of companies included in the consolidation.	579
4. Purchase or sale commitments for fixed assets.	6,493

XVI. RELATIONS WITH COMPANIES NOT INCLUDED IN THE CONSOLIDATION

(million BEF)

	1993	
	Subsidiaries	Affiliates
1. INVESTMENTS		
• Shares	1,943	3,387
• Subordinated receivables	266	1,146
2. RECEIVABLES		
• of more than one year		11
• of less than one year	1,473	514
4. DEBT		
• of more than one year	2	
• of less than one year	490	231
7. FINANCIAL RESULTS		
• Revenues:		
– from investments	397	564
– from current assets	60	5

XVII. A. FINANCIAL RELATIONS WITH DIRECTORS AND MANAGERS

Salaries attributed to staff in charge of daily management (four executive directors with permanent functions and seven directeurs généraux) as well as the managers of the main subsidiaries (16 people) amounted to 201,485,511 BEF.
In the allocation of profit, the share of members of the Board of Directors and the four directeurs généraux totalled 69,010,000 BEF. That of the other members of management, senior staff and honorary directors totalled 65,930,000 BEF. An allocation of 47,400,000 was made to the Benevolent Fund.

COMPARATIVE STATISTICS

		1989	1990 (1)	1991 (2)	1992	1993
Turnover	*million BEF*	577,673	577,692	596,470	555,758	558,982
Cash flow	*million BEF*	53,264	49,626	47,675	32,464	34,578
Consolidated Group net income	*million BEF*	21,822	21,715	16,293	4,631	7,144
Gross dividend	*million BEF*	12,014	12,428	13,051	6,510	6,511
Gross dividend per share	*BEF*	555	561	561	280	280
Investments	*million BEF*	46,894	67,340	54,944	43,914	35,653
Average number of shares		21,220,632	21,684,477	22,838,704	23,251,239	23,251,784
Number of shares at 31 December		21,660,445	22,140,057	23,249,477	23,251,703	23,251,817
Crude oil production *(thousand metric tonnes)*		5,865	5,733	5,387	5,067	4,576
Natural gas sales *(million cubic metres)*		5,652	5,938	6,146	6,283	6,177
Crude oil processed in Group refineries						
(thousand metric tonnes)		27,635	27,566	28,018	27,125	27,027
Product sales *(thousand metric tonnes)*		36,293	35,777	36,318	37,029	36,582
Polymers and thermoplastic rubber manufactured						
(thousand metric tonnes)		1,165	1,220	1,300	1,425	1,565

(1) Calculated, from 1990, according to accounting standard FAS 52 concerning the conversion of the accounts of foreign subsidiaries into Belgian francs.

(2) Calculated, from 1991, according to accounting standard FAS 19 concerning the Successful Efforts method of accounting for oil and gas exploration and production.

ESTIMATED PROVEN OIL AND GAS RESERVES (*)

	Europe	North America	Africa & Middle East	Total	Europe	North America	Africa & Middle East	Total
CRUDE OIL (including condensate and LNG)	*(million tonnes)*				*(million barrels)*			
Proven developed and undeveloped reserves								
At 31 December 1991	52.5	6.6	5.4	64.5	410.2	49.9	39.9	500.0
Revisions and improved recovery	4.5	0.1	0.6	5.2	40.7	0.8	4.8	46.3
Discoveries and extensions	1.7	0.3	0.2	2.2	12.4	2.2	1.4	16.0
Purchases of minerals in place		0.4		0.4		3.1		3.1
Sales of minerals in place		− 0.5		− 0.5		− 3.8		− 3.8
Production (**)								
− consolidated companies	− 3.4	− 1.0	− 0.1	− 4.5	− 27.3	− 7.4	− 1.0	− 35.7
− other companies			− 0.5	− 0.5			− 3.9	− 3.9

	Europe	North America	Africa & Middle East	Total	Europe	North America	Africa & Middle East	Total
At 31 December 1992	55.3	5.9	5.6	66.8	436.0	44.8	41.2	522.0
Revisions and improved recovery	1.9	− 0.8		1.1	14.5	− 6.3	0.1	8.3
Discoveries and extensions	3.9	1.1		5.0	30.8	8.4		39.2
Purchases of minerals in place		0.1		0.1		0.4		0.4
Sales of minerals in place		− 0.4	− 0.2	− 0.6		− 3.0	− 1.2	− 4.2
Production (**)								
− consolidated companies	− 3.4	− 0.9	− 0.2	− 4.5	− 27.1	− 6.2	− 1.2	− 34.5
− other companies			− 0.1	− 0.1			− 1.0	− 1.0
At 31 December 1993	57.7	5.0	5.1	67.8	454.2	38.1	37.9	530.2
Proven developed reserves								
At 31 December 1991	36.3	5.1	5.4	46.8	283.2	39.2	39.9	362.3
At 31 December 1992	37.5	4.8	4.7	47.0	296.0	36.8	34.4	367.2
At 31 December 1993	44.9	3.3	4.9	53.1	350.4	25.5	36.3	412.2

	Europe	North America	Africa & Middle East	Total	Europe	North America	Africa & Middle East	Total
NATURAL GAS (***)	*(billion cubic metres)*				*(billion cubic feet)*			
Proven developed and undeveloped reserves								
At 31 December 1991	36.1	21.1		57.2	1,343.4	786.9		2,130.3
Revisions and improved recovery	2.9	− 0.2		2.7	109.0	− 8.9		100.1
Discoveries and extensions	2.4	0.9		3.3	87.9	35.3		123.2
Purchases of minerals in place	0.1	0.3		0.4	4.7	9.8		14.5
Sales of minerals in place		− 0.5		− 0.5	− 0.2	− 18.7		− 18.9
Production (**)	− 4.2	− 2.1		− 6.3	− 155.4	− 78.5		− 233.9
At 31 December 1992	37.3	19.5		56.8	1,389.4	725.9		2,115.3
Revisions and improved recovery	− 0.1	− 0.5		− 0.6	− 4.1	− 18.2		− 22.3
Discoveries and extensions	10.6	0.8		11.4	396.4	30.3		426.7
Purchases of minerals in place		0.1		0.1		2.7		2.7
Sales of minerals in place		− 4.3		− 4.3		− 158.7		− 158.7
Production (**)	− 4.1	− 2.0		− 6.1	− 152.6	− 75.9		− 228.5
At 31 December 1993	43.7	13.6		57.3	1,629.1	506.1		2,135.2
Proven developed reserves								
At 31 December 1991	32.2	13.9		46.1	1,198.4	518.3		1,716.7
At 31 December 1992	31.0	13.3		44.3	1,154.0	496.6		1,650.6
At 31 December 1993	31.0	9.6		40.6	1,154.1	363.7		1,517.8

(*) 1. Proven reserves are those that the Group estimates to be recoverable based on known technology and certain economic conditions.

    2. After deduction of royalties claimable in kind; in the US, net of all royalties.

    3. Proven reserves of natural gas include only quantities covered by sales contracts or which can be considered as such.

(**) Net of royalties taken in kind; in the US, net of all royalties.

(***) Gas produced and sold.

REPORT OF THE JOINT STATUTORY AUDITORS

TO THE ANNUAL GENERAL MEETING OF SHAREHOLDERS OF PETROFINA ON THE CONSOLIDATED ANNUAL ACCOUNTS
FOR THE YEAR ENDED DECEMBER 31, 1993

Ladies and Gentlemen,

On completion of the audit assignment you entrusted to us in accordance with legal requirements we have the honour to report to you on the consolidated accounts as of December 31, 1993.

Our examination was made in accordance with the general auditing standards issued by the "Institut des Reviseurs d'Entreprises". The administrative and accounting organization and its system of internal controls have been considered adequate for the fulfilment of our mission.

The company's management supplied all explanations and information we requested.

Our examination of the financial statements of the companies included in the consolidation was based on documents supplied by the various companies and checked by company auditors or qualified auditors in the relevant country.

The consolidated accounts have been prepared in accordance with legal and statutory requirements. Valuation rules have been applied correctly.

The Directors' report on the consolidated accounts contains the information required by law and is consistent with the consolidated annual accounts.

In conclusion, we certify without qualification, that the annual consolidated accounts as of December 31, 1993, with a balance sheet total of 358,653 million BEF and a statement of income showing consolidated net income for the year of 7,144 million BEF (Group's share), give a true and fair view of the assets and liabilities, the financial position and results of the Group, taking into account the applicable legal and statutory requirements, and that the supplementary information given in the notes is appropriate.

Brussels, April 15, 1994

The joint statutory auditors,

G.M. Timmerman
Partner of
Klynveld, Peat Marwick, Goerdeler,
Corporate auditors

M.C. Vaes
Partner of Tinnemans,
Pourbaix, Vaes & Co,
Member of Deloitte, Touche,
Tohmatsu International

DENMARK

Merete Christiansen
Copenhagen Business School

1. Background

1.1 History

The first known accounting regulation in Denmark was related to the kingdom and public administration in the sixteenth century, when the vassals and the nobility were obliged to render accounts concerning crown land. During the period of absolute monarchy and centralized administration, accounting requirements were extended. By 1840, all royal treasurers were required to keep books, and special royal cash controllers were appointed. Until the twentieth century, however, both the preparation and auditing of accounts were restricted to the state and municipal sectors.

The oldest limited companies in Denmark go back to the seventeenth century. The development of accounting at that time reflected the fact that Denmark relied mainly on agricultural production and fishing and that the capitalist society lacked momentum. No accounting regulation existed, and when the first limited companies voluntarily published their annual accounts, considerable flexibility in the choice of accounting principles was observed. Gradually, the number of limited companies grew as a result of continuing industrialization. Around the beginning of the twentieth century there were about 1,000 limited companies, and by 1909 the number had increased to about 2,500. The misuse of limited liability and financial scandals at that time led to demands for the adoption of a limited companies act.

In 1908 one of the largest financial scandals in Denmark's financial history took place, involving Minister of Justice P. A. Alberti, who gave himself up to the authorities, admitting to fraud and deception on an unprecedented scale as chairman of a Danish savings bank. In 1909 a State-Authorized Public Accountants Act (*Lov om Statsautoriserede revisorer*) was passed as a consequence of the Alberti case. In this law the

111

British/Dutch model based on an independent auditing profession was chosen in preference to the German model based on a close relationship between the auditing profession and the banks, the so-called *Treuhandsgesellschaften*. In Denmark, however, it was the state (Ministry of Trade and Shipping, later called the Ministry of Industry) that was to authorize auditors rather than professional bodies, as in the United Kingdom.

In 1912 a Bookkeeping Act (*Bogføringsloven*) was adopted. Under its provisions all kinds of businesses were required to keep books relating to their financial affairs, the only important exceptions being farmers and craftsmen.

The growth of limited companies and the problems of speculation and profiteering during the First World War increased pressure for a limited companies act, and in 1917 Denmark introduced its first Limited Companies Act (*Aktieselskabsloven*). It was one of the last countries in Europe to do so. This law was influenced particularly by the German *Handelsgesetzbuch* of 1897, as well as by the newly adopted companies acts in Norway and Sweden. The accounting sections of the law, however, were framed in accordance with the English legal tradition by quoting a general clause as the only guideline for accounting practice. The law included only two sections regarding financial reporting and two sections regarding the audit. The law stated that limited companies must prepare a profit and loss account and a balance sheet showing the true position of the company in accordance with the best estimate of management. This formulation embodied the concept of "orderly and prudent business practice." The law applied to all limited companies, and it required the financial statements to be audited. All limited companies had to submit a copy of their financial statements to the public registry (*Aktieselskabsregisteret*, later called the Danish Commerce and Companies Agency, *Erhvervs- og Selskabsstyrelsen*). The only exception regarding publication was for family owned companies, defined as companies that had ten or fewer shareholders and that were not open to inspection.

The Limited Companies Act of 1917 proved weak and ineffective, and during the 1920s attempts were made to introduce a new and stronger version. At that time, limited companies were primarily small and family-owned companies that were mainly debt financed; shareholders were relatively unimportant users of accounting information. The pressure for more accounting regulation, therefore, was rather weak, and a new Limited Companies Act was not adopted until 1930.

The Limited Companies Act of 1930 increased the amount of information that was to be presented in the financial statements. The requirements were embodied in a general clause, "orderly and prudent business practice," which became the leading principle of valuation. Prudence was emphasized to the extent that it allowed—perhaps even recommended—the creation of hidden reserves. The law also supported a prudent dividend policy in order to protect creditors by requiring that a legal reserve be set aside. Besides the general clause, the law included specific rules for revaluation, formation costs, and goodwill, but it went into no further detail about the items and formats of the accounts. The law was in force for more than 40 years, during which there were no major changes in accounting legislation.

Although the legal system of financial reporting remained unaltered from 1930 to 1973, accounting practice changed in several ways during these decades, with the accounting profession as one of the main driving forces.

One of the most significant changes began to make itself felt in the 1950s, when Danish companies moved from absorption costing to marginal costing. With marginal costing, inventory is valued at variable cost and the profit and loss account shows variable and fixed costs, the contribution margin being a subtotal if the vertical format is used. The driving force behind this development was Professor Palle Hansen (1911–1991), of the Copenhagen Business School, who was a strong advocate of the marginal costing principle for both management accounting and financial accounting purposes. During the 1960s marginal costing came to be used more and more and gradually established itself as a generally accepted accounting principle.

From 1917 to the Second World War, companies mainly used tax rules for the valuation of inventories, fixed assets, and so on, in the financial statements. In those days, tax law required only that the same inventory value be used in both statements, and the tax authorities would not accept higher depreciation charges (lower asset values) in the tax statement than in the financial statement. After the war there continued to be a close relationship between tax rules and accounting rules, creating considerable confusion in Danish accounting practice. The problems increased during the 1950s and later, when new tax rules were introduced that were oriented toward fiscal objectives rather than income measurement. The auditing profession recommended that companies ignore tax rules in the financial statements but was divided about how to reflect this in the statements. Generally, the separation between the taxation and accounting concepts of profit was not achieved until the implementation of the Fourth Directive in 1981.

After the Second World War, the German influence decreased and the accounting profession became more oriented toward the United Kingdom and the United States. During the 1960s the number of foreign groups establishing Danish subsidiaries, especially groups of U.S. origin, increased, and international audit firms like Arthur Andersen and Price Waterhouse set up affiliations in Denmark. U.S. and British accounting principles gradually penetrated Danish accounting practice (for example, the equity method and deferred taxation), and the international trends in financial accounting, especially the accounting developments taking place in the United Kingdom and the United States, became important driving forces for accounting changes.

In the late 1940s and afterwards, technological development stimulated discussions regarding the use of modern bookkeeping systems. The Bookkeeping Act and a relating order were revised in 1959, and in 1990, the Bookkeeping Order was revised once more to reflect developments in information technology.

During the 1960s demand grew for regulation of unauthorized auditors, and in 1970 a second-tier group of auditors was created by the adoption of the Registered Public Accountants Act (*Lov om Registrerede Revisorer*). After the implementation of the Eighth Directive, registered public accountants were allowed to audit only small and medium-sized companies and groups.

By 1934 the Nordic countries had already decided to harmonize company law in Denmark, Finland, Norway, and Sweden and published a proposal in 1942. This proposal for a new companies act was never implemented, however, because of the Second World War. In 1957 the Danish parliament appointed a commission to draft a new limited companies act. The commission published a draft in 1964, which was never implemented because about that time the Nordic countries decided to continue their efforts to harmonize their company law. On the basis of these efforts and the estimated future membership of the European Community (EC), a new proposal was put forward in 1969, and in 1973 the Limited Companies Act was replaced by two new acts relating to large and small limited companies, respectively: the Public Limited Companies Act and the Private Limited Companies Act. Its thirteen sections concerning financial reporting were primarily a codification of existing accounting practice and concentrated on broad-brush principles and requirements that did little to affect actual practice.

The most important changes were the following:

1. The directors' report became a mandatory part of financial reporting.
2. Specifications and notes regarding the accounts were introduced.
3. The notion of a group, which was for the first time defined in the legislation, was introduced. All Danish groups with a limited-liability parent company were now required to publish a consolidated balance sheet for the group as a whole or at least a so-called group statement, including information about intergroup outstandings and debt and the profit shown separately for the parent company and the subsidiaries. The auditor's report should cover both parent and group accounts.

The accounting regulation for public limited companies applied to private limited companies as well. The former privilege of nonpublication was withdrawn from family-owned companies, and all limited companies now had to prepare audited financial statements and to submit them to the Danish Commerce and Companies Agency, where they were open for inspection by anyone.

The former general clause "orderly and prudent business practice" was reformulated in modern terminology as "good accounting practice," the term used in all the Nordic Countries. "Prudence" was not mentioned in the general clause, but it remained an important concept.

In 1976 the auditing profession decided to join the International Federation of Accountants (IFAG). It thus became represented on the International Accounting Standards Committee (IASC) and in subsequent years published the International Accounting Standards in Danish, with Danish comments, as a substitute for national accounting standards. The International Accounting Standards have no legal enforcement and so far have not had the regulatory impact expected by the profession.

1.2 Recent History Leading to the Present Situation

Denmark became a member of the EC in 1973 and implemented the Fourth Directive in 1981,[1] being the first EC member state to do so. Accounting regulation was removed from the Limited Companies Acts, and a new Financial Statements Act, containing 68 sections, was promulgated.

Generally, the Financial Statements Act follows the Fourth Directive quite meticulously and takes advantage of the disclosure exemption rules in only a few cases. The directive is heavily represented, article by article. In cases in which it provides options (e.g., between the use of different valuation methods or formats), the Financial Statements Act generally includes the same options.

In 1990 the Seventh Directive was adopted in an amendment to the Financial Statements Act. At the same time the majority of disclosure rules and almost all the measurement rules relating to groups were removed from the act and incorporated in a special Financial Statements Order published by the Ministry of Industry (Commerce and Companies Agency).[2] A comparison between the accounting regulation of a single company (parent company) and that of groups exposes a shift of power involving the tactical level of accounting regulation. For single and parent companies, only rules regarding disclosure and sanctions are covered by the Financial Statements Order, whereas basic accounting principles and valuation principles are to be found in the Financial Statements Act. For groups, disclosure rules, basic accounting principles, and valuation principles are to be found in the Ministerial Order. Most regulation affecting groups is based on the Financial Statements Order. The separation was designed to avoid parliamentary involvement in highly technical matters concerning group accounting.

The most important innovations regarding group accounting were:

1. Small groups and subgroups do not need to prepare consolidated financial statements. It is estimated that the number of groups that need to present consolidated financial statements will be reduced

by 60%–75% because small groups no longer need to prepare and file consolidated financial statements. A small group must meet two of the following criteria:

- Net turnover less than 24 million Danish krone (DKr)
- Balance sheet less than 12 million DKr
- Average number of employees during the financial year less than 50 (100 DKr = 13 ECU).

2. Under certain circumstances a subsidiary may be excluded from consolidation.

3. The consolidated financial statement must include notes.

4. The past equity (purchase) method has become obligatory. The pooling of interests method is not acceptable.

5. The equity method must be used for associated undertakings in the consolidated financial statement and becomes an option in the financial statements of the parent company.

6. The treatment of the elimination difference (goodwill or negative goodwill) has changed (see Section 3.5).

The implementation of the Fourth and Seventh Directives brought significant changes in Danish accounting practice (for example, the number of notes, changes in formats, the introduction of "true and fair view") but did not have as radical an effect as many had expected. Only a few major changes in valuation principles were required, and accounting practice continued to be relatively diverse. Danish accounting regulation remained fairly flexible.

The Financial Statements Act was revised in 1988, incorporating a transfer of the audit regulations from the Limited Companies Acts.

Since the mid-1980s there has been a series of bankruptcies and financial scandals in which accounting legislation has been violated by companies and by auditors. The biggest scandal was the bankruptcy of Northern Feather in 1991. Such events have raised serious doubt about the concept of self-regulation.

The Institute of State-Authorized Public Accountants (*Foreningen af Statsautoriserede Revisorer*, FSR) has been obliged to publish Danish Accounting Standards since 1988. The approval or disapproval of Danish

Accounting Standards was the responsibility of the FSR, although a hearing procedure took place before final adoption. After the financial collapse of Northern Feather, the government and parliament demanded a reorganization of the standard-setting process. The Accounting Panel was established under the leadership of the auditing profession but including representatives from producers and users. The FSR is still responsible for the issue of the standards, however, the Accounting Panel being an advisory body.

So far, the Copenhagen Stock Exchange has been reluctant to participate in the standard-setting process and to exercise any kind of control.

As a result of the financial scandals, some revisions of the Financial Statements Act were made, tightening the disclosure requirements and introducing control as an obligation of the Danish Commerce and Companies Agency.

Figure 1 shows the development of accounting regulation over time, and Figure 2 presents an overview of existing accounting regulation. The scope of the Financial Statements Act has been widened and now includes partnerships and limited partnerships in which all partners and limited partners are public limited companies, limited partnership that have a public limited company as a general partner, private limited companies or companies with a similar legal form or in which all partners and limited partners respectively are covered by the previous formulation.

1.3 Driving Forces Behind the Development of Danish Accounting Regulation

Until the end of the 1950s Denmark was primarily an agricultural country; it is a relatively young industrial nation. Furthermore, most Danish companies are small, and most Danish industries are light industry. Danish companies require only limited amounts of capital, and the main sources of capital are banks and similar financial institutions, although trade and other creditors also play an important role. Little state capital is invested in companies. About 260 Danish companies are listed on the Copenhagen Stock Exchange, which is the only stock exchange in Denmark. Until now, the Copenhagen Stock Exchange has played a relatively minor role as a market for capital.

FIGURE 1 *The Development of Danish Accounting Regulation*

1912 The first Bookkeeping Act
1917 The first Limited Companies Act
1930 The Limited Companies Act is revised.
1959 The Bookkeeping Act is revised.
A Ministerial Order on the Accounting, Financial Statements and Preservation of Accounting Records of Commercial undertakings is issued.
1973 The Limited Companies Act is split into two acts, the Public Limited Companies Act and the Private Limited Companies Act.
1978 The Institute of State-Authorized Public Accountants publishes the International Accounting Standards in Danish.
1981 The sections dealing with the annual accounts of limited companies are separated from the two limited companies acts, and the Financial Statements Act is adopted (the implementation of the Fourth Directive).
1987 The Copenhagen Stock Exchange adopts the Information Obligations for Issuers of Listed Securities, in which it is stated that the financial statements of publicly listed companies must be in accordance with the highest level of accounting standard in the industry in which the company operates.
1988 The Financial Statements Act is revised: The chapter on auditing is transferred from the Limited Companies Acts to the Financial Statements Act.
1988 The first Danish Accounting Standard is published by the Institute of State-Authorized Public Accountants.
1989 The Information Obligations for Issuers of Listed Securities is revised
1990 The Ministerial Order on Accounting, Financial Statements and Preservation of Accounting Records of Commercial Undertakings is revised.
A Ministerial Guideline Concerning Bookkeeping is issued.
1991 The Financial Statements Act is revised (the implementation of the Seventh Directive).
A Ministerial Order relating to the Format of Annual Accounts and Group Accounts is adopted.
A Ministerial Guideline concerning Group Accounts is issued.
1991 The Public Limited Companies Act is revised: The limit for information obligations concerning important shareholders is decreased from shareholders owning 10% of the share capital to shareholders owning 5% of the share capital.
1991 The Financial Statements Act is revised:
— If a company changes its financial year, no financial period may exceed 12 months.
— If a company changes its accounting policy, the accumulated change must be transferred directly to the equity and the comparative figures must be adjusted accordingly.
— An outgoing auditor of a publicly listed company must immediately inform Copenhagen Stock Exchange and must inform the new elected auditor about the reason for no longer being the auditor.

(Figure 1 continues)

(Figure 1, continued)

— The auditor must attend the general meeting of publicly listed companies and answer questions relating to the annual accounts that are signed by him or her.

— The auditor must check that the board of directors follows the legislation laid down in the Limited Companies Acts and the Financial Statements Act.

— The financial report must be filed with the Danish Commerce and Companies Agency within 5 months after the end of the financial year.

1991   The Information Obligations for Issuers of Listed Securities is revised:

— A publicly listed company must follow the Danish Accounting Standards.

— Information must be given in the annual financial report if not all group companies are audited by at least one of the auditors of the parent company, their international affiliations, or a reputable international audit firm.

— The time limit for publishing the semiannual and annual reports is shortened.

1992   The Financial Statements Act is revised:

— Partnerships and limited partnerships must follow the act if all the partners or limited partners are companies covered by the law.

— The Danish Commerce and Companies Agency may request such information as is necessary in order to determine whether the act, provisions laid down pursuant to the act, and the company's articles of association have been complied with.

1992   The Public Limited Companies Act is revised:

— Information must be given on the annual general meeting and in the annual financial report concerning the position of the members of the board of directors in other public limited companies

1994   The Financial Statements Act is revised.

— The Danish Commerce and Companies Agency must carry out statistical tests to examine whether the companies follow the act and the provisions laid down pursuant to the act

— An Accounting Council is established as an advisory forum of the Ministry of Industry on accounting issues.

Future: Information concerning the audit fee in the financial report for large companies
Denmark enacted its first Act on State-Authorized Public Accountants in 1909 and the first Act on Public Registered Accountants in 1971. The Eighth Directive was implemented in 1988.

These are some of the factors that may help to explain why, until recently, accounting regulation has been liberal and almost without professional self-regulation to support the loose legal regulation.

Developments during the past decade, however, seem to indicate that a change is taking place toward a growing and broader interest concerning accounting regulation and toward a tighter accounting regulation, especially for publicly listed companies. The two driving forces behind this

---

FIGURE 2 *An Overview of Existing Accounting Regulation*

Laws and associated Ministerial Orders and Guidelines
- The Bookkeeping Act
- The Ministerial Order on Accounting, Financial Statements and Preservation of Accounting Records of Commercial Undertakings
- Ministerial Guideline Concerning Bookkeeping
- The Financial Statements Act
- The Ministerial Order relating to the Format of Annual Accounts and Group Accounts and the Preparation of Group Accounts
- Ministerial Guideline Concerning Group Accounts
- Special legislation exists concerning banks, insurance companies, mortgage credit institutions and other credit institutions

Accounting Standards and Recommendations
- Danish Accounting Standards:
  — No. 1: Objective and Contents of the Annual Accounts
  — No. 2: Disclosure of Accounting Policies
  — No. 3: Changes in Accounting Policies and Accounting Estimates
  — No. 4: Contingent Liabilities and Events Occurring after the Balance Sheet Date
  — No. 5: Extraordinary Items
  — No. 6: Long-term Contracts
  — No. 7: Research and Development
  — No. 8: Inventories
  — No. 9: Foreign Currency Translation

  These standards are mandatory for publicly listed companies.
- Information Obligations for Issuers of Listed Securities
  These obligations are mandatory for publicly listed companies.
- The International Accounting Standards
  Generally, these are recommended by the audit profession.
- Opinions issued by the Institute of State-Authorized Public Accountants (*Foreningen af Statsautoriserede Revisorer*, FSR)

Other Sources of Regulation
- *Revision & Regnskabsvæsen* (*Auditing & Accounting*, the professional journal of the FSR)
- *Revisorbladet* (*The Auditor's Journal*, the professional journal of the FRR (*Foreningen af Registrerede Revisorer*, FRR)
- Olaf Hasselager & Aksel Runge Johansen: *Årsregnskaber —Kommentarer til regnskabslovgivningen.* København: G.E.C. Gad 1992 (The standard commentary text concerning Danish accounting regulation)

---

change are growing internationalization and a series of bankruptcies and financial scandals.

2. The Form and Content of Published Financial Statements

2.1 Types of Financial Statement

In Denmark, both the parent company and the group as a whole must prepare and publish financial statements. Both sets of financial statements include a profit and loss account, balance sheet, and notes. The directors' report refers to the whole group, while the auditor's report covers both sets of financial statements.

The Financial Statements Act stresses that the directors' report should give a reliable statement concerning the development of the company, as well as supplementary information, should the financial statement be influenced by any exceptional circumstances or uncertainties. Twenty-two publicly listed trade, service, and industrial groups (18%) discussed exceptional circumstances in their financial statements for 1992.

Additionally, the directors' report must at a minimum include comments on:

1. Important events that have occurred subsequent to the end of the financial year
2. The company's expected future development
3. Research and development activities
4. The company's branches in foreign countries, if any

Normally, directors' reports of publicly listed companies go far beyond these minimum requirements. But the scope, the depth, and the precision vary considerably from company to company. A growing number of publicly listed trade, service, and industrial groups discuss topics related to environmental protection and standardization of quality. Twenty-four groups (20%) discussed state approval of their environmental policy and/ or investments related to environmental protection, and thirty-two groups discussed ISO-Certification in their financial statements for 1992.

According to the Financial Statements Act, no obligation exists to present any additional key figures or statements. The Copenhagen Stock Exchange has published Information Obligations for Issuers of Listed Securities, which was revised in 1991. In the revised guideline it is stressed that the financial statement of a publicly listed company must include comparative key figures for the previous 4 years and a cash flow statement. At the moment there is a move toward a cash flow statement based on the so-called direct method, used by 51% of publicly listed groups in 1992.

Furthermore, the Copenhagen Stock Exchange requires that the financial statements of publicly listed companies be in accordance with the highest level of accounting standards in the industry in which the company operates, and with generally accepted Danish accounting standards. At present the Danish Accounting Standards No. 1–8 are considered to be part of generally accepted Danish accounting practices. Foreign companies must fulfill the same obligations in relation to accounting standards in their home country. The financial statement must also include an introductory description of the accounting policies used by the company, and the company shall state whether the accounts are presented in compliance with generally accepted Danish accounting principles. Deviation from the foregoing obligations must be explained. An annual financial statement that is a summary of the financial report must be published when the directors' board has adopted the financial report. The Copenhagen Stock Exchange also requires that a semiannual financial statement be published.

All public and private limited companies must be audited by at least one state-authorized public accountant or one registered public accountant. After the implementation of the Eighth Directive, however, registered public accountants are allowed to audit only small and medium-sized companies and groups. The audit report must confirm that the financial statement has been audited and whether it is found to be in accordance with legal requirements and the articles of the company. An unqualified audit report signifies that:

1. The financial statement is correctly prepared in accordance with the books of the company in accordance with existing values, rights, and liabilities.

2. The directors' report includes the information required by law, including information about the development of the company, and the directors' report is not contradicted by the financial statements (profit and loss account, balance sheet and notes).

3. The financial statement gives a true and fair view of the company's assets, liabilities, financial position, and profit or loss.

4. The audit has not resulted in a qualified opinion.

Since 1978 the FSR has issued Danish Auditing Standards, with auditing recommendations. Standard No. 7 of 1988, for instance, concerning the audit report, includes recommendations reflected in the audit report presented by Lundbeck A/S (see page 151).

2.2 Scope of Consolidation

A parent company must be a public or a private limited company or a partnership or a limited partnership, and a subsidiary may likewise have different legal forms, limited as well as unlimited.

After the implementation of the Seventh Directive, full consolidation takes place if one of the following criteria is met:

1. The company has the majority of the shareholders' voting rights in the other undertaking.

2. The company owns shares in another undertaking and:
    (a) has the right to appoint a majority of the management or supervisory board of the other undertaking; or
    (b) has the right to exercise a dominant influence over an undertaking pursuant to a contract or to a provision in its memorandum or articles of association; or
    (c) exercises dominant influence as a result of agreements with other investors; or
    (d) exercises *de facto* dominant influence.

As can be seen, "dominant influence" is the key criterion to determine whether there is a parent/subsidiary relationship. In accordance with the

Seventh Directive, a subsidiary can be excluded from the consolidation under special circumstances. The subsidiary is then treated as "investment in a subsidiary" (a participating interest).

Before implementation of the Seventh Directive, all groups had to prepare and publish consolidated financial statements. Two general exceptions now exist:

1. Subgroups that are not publicly listed do not need to present consolidated financial statements. A reference must be made in the financial statement of the parent company in which the subsidiary is consolidated.
2. Small groups in which none of the companies is publicly listed in an EU country do not need to present consolidated financial statements, provided certain criteria are met.

It has been estimated that between 1,500 and 2,000 Danish companies will be required to present consolidated financial statements. Denmark has not implemented the provisions of the Seventh Directive concerning horizontal groups.

2.3 Form of the Published Financial Statements

Companies may choose freely among the four formats of the profit and loss account provided by the Fourth Directive. In practice, however, only the two vertical formats tend to be used by publicly listed trade, service, and industrial groups.

The mix of different formats makes it difficult for financial analysts to carry out cross-sectional analysis between companies. Comparability is obtainable only on a very aggregated level:

Net turnover	XXXXX
Staff costs[3]	XXXXX
Other costs except depreciation etc.	XXXXX
Depreciation and write-offs on tangible and intangible fixed assets	XXXXX

Financial analysts should also be aware of the lack of professional self-regulation in this area. Some companies provide more detailed information than required, and there is sometimes a lack of consensus about the placing of certain items. For instance, provision for bad debts may be found variously as a production cost, as a distribution cost, or as a general administrative charge. The extent to which this problem is a serious one is, as yet, unknown.

It is noteworthy too, that the EU formats of the profit and loss account did not correspond to Danish accounting traditions. Denmark had a long tradition of using the marginal costing principle for both management and financial accounting purposes. The use of marginal costing makes it possible to analyze the composition of variable and fixed costs. When the Fourth Directive was implemented, some people expected a shift toward absorption costing, but that has not taken place so far (see Table 1). The marginal costing era may have come to an end, however. The Danish Accounting Standard No. 8 on inventories recommends that, in addition to the direct production costs, the production cost should include overheads that have been incurred during the course of production and that are attributable to the goods in question. The Standard was adopted in 1993 after more than a year of discussion and is effective for financial statements covering financial years beginning on July 1, 1993 or later.

TABLE 1 *Methods of Inventory Costing Used by Publicly Quoted Trade, Service, and Industrial Groups*

Finished goods	1988 No. (%)	1989 No. (%)	1990 No. (%)	1991 No. (%)	1992 No. (%)
Marginal costing	48 (35)	48 (38)	48 (40)	57 (46)	52 (43)
Absorption costing	14 (10)	14 (11)	12 (9)	12 (10)	19 (15)
Mixed principles	4 (3)	3 (3)	5 (5)	4 (4)	6 (5)
Realization value	4 (3)	2 (2)	2 (2)	4 (4)	0 (0)
No information/ not relevant	44 (33)	37 (28)	29 (23)	24 (19)	18 (15)
Not relevant, no finished goods	22 (16)	24 (18)	25 (21)	20 (19)	26 (22)
Total	136 (100)	128 (100)	121 (100)	123 (100)	121 (100)

Source: *ACCOUNT DATA - DK*, Copenhagen Business School.

The formats make it difficult to show the distinction between variable and fixed costs. Here it should be remembered that most Danish companies are small or medium-sized, with relatively narrow bases of activity, which improves the usefulness of the contribution margin as a subtotal. In 1992, 28% of publicly listed trade, service, and industrial companies disclosed a contribution margin. Most of the industrial companies did so by distinguishing between direct and indirect production costs. This can lead to errors if distribution costs include important groups of variable costs.

The marginal costing approach also explains another Danish phenomenon, namely a tradition of showing subtotals in the profit and loss account. Since the EU harmonization, it has become far more difficult to present relevant subtotals, although Danish companies still try to do so, and a great variety of subtotals can be found. Therefore, financial analysts must reach their own conclusions concerning relevant subtotals.

A more detailed subdivision of the items in the financial statement is allowed, and new items may be added, provided that their contents are not included in any of the items prescribed by the formats. Items may be summarized if they are insignificant, or if a better overview is provided. This requires a note. More than two-thirds of publicly listed companies included subdivisions, aggregations, or additions in their profit and loss accounts in 1992.

In Danish accounting practice a great variety of transactions come under the heading "extraordinary items." There is no consensus about the proper definition of extraordinary items. In accordance with the Fourth Directive, the Financial Statements Act defines extraordinary items as items that are separate from ordinary activity. In accordance with IAS No. 8, Danish Accounting Standard No. 5 defines extraordinary items as gains and losses that derive from events or transactions that are distinct from the ordinary activities of the company and are therefore not expected to recur frequently or regularly. This Danish Accounting Standard has been mandatory for publicly listed companies for financial years beginning on July 1, 1990 or later. So far, accounting practice has been little aware of the time dimension in the definition of extraordinary items. It should be noted that many Danish companies have included gains and losses arising from the sale of tangible fixed assets as extraordinary items, in spite of their ordinary character (Table 2).

The financial analyst should be aware of the possible use of the distinction between ordinary and extraordinary activities for "creative accounting" purposes, where the matching principle is violated by categorizing income as ordinary and the corresponding charges as extraordinary over a span of financial years.

The format requirements concerning the balance sheet have not presented the same difficulties as the profit and loss account for accounting practice. Both the vertical and horizontal formats are allowed, but almost all companies use the horizontal format. It was new to Danish practice to disclose information concerning the maturity of debt. In practice, all companies divide debt into long-term debt and short-term debt. The short-term debt element of long-term debt, however, may be presented in at least two different ways: as an integral part of corresponding short-term debt items, or as a special item labeled "short-term part of long-term debt." It seems that Lundbeck A/S uses the first method.

The Financial Statements Order requires comparative figures for one year for the profit and loss account, the balance sheet, and some of the notes. The Information Obligations for Issuers of Listed Securities requires that the accounts shall contain comparative figures for the previous year. In case of break of consistency, the comparative figures must be changed accordingly.

The implementation of the Fourth Directive made notes compulsory only for the financial statements of the parent companies. The consoli-

TABLE 2   *Treatment of Gains or Losses Arising from the Sale of Tangible Assets by Publicly Listed Trade, Service, and Industrial Groups*

	1988 No. (%)	1989 No. (%)	1990 No. (%)	1991 No. (%)	1992 No. (%)
As ordinary item	10 (7)	13 (10)	25 (21)	31 (21)	41 34)
As extraordinary item	55 (41)	42 (33)	30 (25)	21 (17)	12 (10)
As both ordinary and extraordinary items	10 (7)	9 (7)	8 (7)	13 (11)	11 (9)
No information/ not relevant	61 (45)	64 (50)	58 (47)	58 (47)	57 (47)
Total	136 (100)	128 (100)	121 (100)	123 (100)	121 (100)

Source: *ACCOUNT DATA - DK*, Copenhagen Business School.

dated financial statement was required to include as a minimum only the profit and loss account and the balance sheet. The implementation of the Seventh Directive has introduced the requirement for notes in consolidated financial statement. This requirement came into force in 1992.

3. Accounting Policies and Practices in Valuation and Income Measurement: Implications for the Analyst

3.1 Fundamental Principles

In accordance with the Financial Statements Act, information must be given about valuation methods, methods of calculating depreciation, write-offs and revaluations, and the basis of foreign currency translation. Danish Accounting Standard No. 2 recommends that information be given about accounting practice in all areas that are important for a proper understanding of a financial statement. The information must be given in a separate section, before the profit and loss account, the balance sheet, and the notes. Almost all publicly listed companies give some such information, but precise and exhaustive information is sometimes still lacking. An examination of the information provided over the years, however, shows that the information provided in the 1992-accounts is far more precise and exhaustive than the information given in the 1988 accounts. The financial analyst should read both this section and the notes carefully.

3.2 The True and Fair View

There is an overriding principle that the financial statement shall present a "true and fair view" of the assets and liabilities of the group and the company, its financial position, and of the profit and loss. Moreover, it is a legal obligation to provide further information when the basic provisions of the law are not themselves sufficient to present a true and fair view. Finally, it is obligatory to deviate from the law in cases in which the application of other provisions of the law do not meet the requirements of this omnibus clause (the so-called true and fair override included in the EU

Fourth Directive). Such a deviation demands an explanation and information about its consequences for assets, liabilities, financial position, and profit. In practice, such deviations from statutory provisions, in order to give a true and fair view, seldom occur.

The true and fair view was at least conceptually somewhat different from the previous "good accounting practice," although both the Company Law Panel (*Det Selskabsretlige Panel*), which participated in the preparation for the Financial Statements Bill, and the auditing profession considered the two general clauses as practically identical. "Good accounting practice" was more an operational term than "a true and fair view." It was a process-oriented concept relating to the working methods normally used in the preparation of individual accounts. A true and fair view is a holistic concept relating to the desired attributes of the end-product as a whole, seen from the users' point of view. Until recently the true and fair view has never been debated in Denmark, but the latest edition of the standard Commentary Text on the Financial Statements published by two authors who have both been involved in the negotiations and implementation of the Fourth and Seventh Directives[4] includes a remarkable initiative by introducing and integrating the IASC Framework as an attempt to give substance to the notion of a true and fair view. To do so requires careful consideration, however. First, the information needs of financial statement users have never been a focal point in the Danish accounting debate, although a clarification on this level forms the basis for the following interpretation and implementation of the framework. Second, the forward-looking (decision-usefulness) theory on which the framework is based is contradictory to the backward-looking (stewardship) tradition of Danish accounting thinking during the past three decades. Third, different emphasis seems to be put on the prudence principle in the Directives and in the IASC Framework.

3.3 The Prudence Principle

Generally, the prudence principle is deeply rooted in Danish accounting regulation and practice. In spite of the inherent conflict in relation to the true and fair view, and the general prohibition of the creation of hidden reserves, the prudence principle is heavily supported in law, which stresses "the lower of cost and market value" as a basic principle, within the overall historical cost principle. Here the financial analyst should remember that both the typical financial structure of most Danish companies, which tends to stress the need for creditor protection, and the importance of the former connection between accounting and taxation income have inevitably supported prudent accounting practice. At the same time, the financial analyst should be aware of existing possibilities of revaluing assets, as described in more depth in subsequent sections.

The liberal accounting regulation therefore opens up a broad variety of "true and fair views," from quite prudent ones to rather optimistic ones. This sometimes makes time-series analysis and cross-sectional analysis rather complicated to carry out.

3.4 The Principle of Consistency

According to the Financial Statements Act, consistency is one of the basic accounting principles. In case of a break in consistency, the annual accounts for the year in which the change takes place must be prepared by applying the new method. The total effect on the company's assets and liabilities, its financial position, and profit or loss shall be disclosed in the notes. This also includes the effect on the tax on the profit or loss for the year and deferred taxation. The opening balance sheet for the year in which the change takes place must be adjusted accordingly.

Danish Accounting Standard No. 3 distinguishes between changes in accounting method (break in consistency) and changes in accounting estimates. According to the standard, a change in accounting method must take place only:

1. If the change is a consequence of a law
2. If the change is a consequence of a Danish National Standard
3. If the change serves the omnibus true and fair view clause in a better way than the old principle

Both concrete circumstances and international development may lead to changes in accounting methods. In the event of changes of accounting method, the following information must be given:

1. Confirmation that such a change has taken place
2. A description of the change
3. The reasoning behind the change
4. A description of the consequences of the change on assets, liabilities, financial position, and profit or loss
5. Confirmation that a corresponding change in the comparative figures of the last year or years has been made

The change must be mentioned in the directors' report, too. Changes to accounting estimates normally affect the ordinary profit and loss figure. Significant changes must be described in the notes.

Accounting Standard No. 3 was implemented on July 1, 1989. Depending on the year, between 20% and 35% of publicly listed companies (trade, service, and industrial) have adopted one or more changes in accounting method in recent years, and not all of these changes were easily apparent or understood. An acceptable reason for this large number of changes undoubtedly lies in the fact that, as a consequence of EU harmonization and growing internationalization, Denmark is going through a period of transition from old accounting rules and practice to a more internationally oriented practice. In a few cases, however, "creative accounting" combined with a lack of effective accounting control seems to be another possible factor, which the financial analyst must take into consideration.

3.5 Consolidated Financial Statements

In Denmark the most common method of business combination is for one company to become a subsidiary of another. In this situation the consolidation is based on the acquisition (purchase) method, and the subsidiary is consolidated at the time of acquisition (the past equity method). Before implementation of the Seventh Directive, most groups considered goodwill as merely a technical elimination difference between the cost of acquisition and the total capital employed in the subsidiary at the time of acquisition. Usually no revaluations of assets were considered, and the total difference was computed as goodwill. Implementation of the Seventh Directive requires revaluation of net assets at their fair value to the purchaser.

The elimination difference could and can be treated in different ways. It can be expensed in the profit and loss account, capitalized and depreciated as intangible assets, or eliminated directly against reserves. Even after the implementation of the Seventh Directive, only a few companies revalue net assets, and the most commonly used treatment is elimination against reserves. Lundbeck A/S revalues its net assets and offsets the remaining goodwill directly against reserves (see page 149).

Negative goodwill must appear separately as part of the total capital employed, offset against positive goodwill, or as a provision if it corresponds to a foreseeable loss or expense incurred in connection with the acquired subsidiary.

The pooling of interests method is not mentioned in the Financial Statements Act, but the Public Limited Companies Act presumes adoption of this method when a so-called legal merger takes place, which is a merger in which one of the companies continues the combined activities of all the merged undertakings by exchange of shares, and the other undertakings are legally dissolved. The number of legal mergers has increased in recent years, and so has the use of the pooling of interests method. One publicly listed company used the pooling of interests method when it bought another publicly listed company and paid by a new issue of shares.

One-line consolidation (the equity method, see Section 3.14 below) is used for nonconsolidated subsidiaries and associated undertakings. Joint ventures may be proportionally consolidated, but other methods may be used as well.

3.6 Foreign Currency Translation

The EU Directives do not deal with accounting problems relating to foreign currency translation, and Denmark has no legal rules for this.

So far, accounting practice among publicly listed companies is in favor of the closing rate method, and both realized and unrealized gains and losses are reported in the profit and loss account. It should be noted, however, that many companies do not disclose full information about their practice in this area, especially about where the differences are placed in the profit and loss account. Supplementary information about hedging or speculating policies and activities is often inadequate. The lack of such information makes it difficult for the financial analyst to evaluate the quality of earnings. In this area the financial analyst should carefully study the distinction between ordinary and extraordinary items and movements on the equity account.

Danish Accounting Standard No. 9 on foreign currency translation, which is effective for annual accounts covering financial years beginning on July 1, 1995 or later, recommends that transactions in foreign currency be translated to Danish krone by using the exchange rate at the date of the transaction and that the exchange rate at the end of the financial year is used for translation of transactions that are not yet completed. All translation differences must be disclosed in the profit and loss account.

The standard also deals with hedged transactions including hedging of future transactions.

For subsidiaries that qualify as foreign entities, the closing rate-net investment method is required, and for subsidiaries that do not qualify as foreign entities the temporal method is required (as recommended in IAS 21). In both cases the exchange rate at the time of the transaction is used when the profit and loss account is translated to Danish krone. This will be a new accounting practice in Denmark. Normally, the closing rate has been used for both the profit and loss account and the balance sheet. All exchange differences are recognized in capital employed according to the new standard.

3.7 Capital and Reserves

The equity account consists of the following categories:

1. Subscribed capital: The nominal value of the share capital. The directors' report must include a list of all equity investors in possession of more than 5% of the share capital or of voting rights. The parent company and its subsidiaries may hold the parent company's own shares, up to a total maximum limit of 10% of the share capital or of voting rights.

2. Share premium account

3. Revaluation reserve: A negative elimination difference of consolidation is placed separately under this heading. Negative goodwill may be included as a provision if it reflects foreseeable losses of, or expenses incurred in reorganizing, the subsidiary.

4. Reserves:

    a. Net revaluation reserve arising through use of the equity method: Net revaluations concerning both unconsolidated subsidiaries and associated undertakings are placed here—their accumulated net results, eventual revaluations, exchange rate differences, etc.

    b. Reserve for own shares: Danish law allows own shares to be valued either at zero or at another unspecified value. Valuation at a value other than zero requires the creation of a parallel reserve of the same value. However, the most common practice is to value own shares at zero.

    c. Legal reserves: The Companies Law requires companies to keep sufficient reserves according to their financial position. The exact requirements are no longer prescribed.

    d. Reserves provided by the articles of association.

    e. Other reserve funds: Different types of reserve fund can be observed in practice, their titles dating mainly from the time before implementation of the Fourth Directive:

        —Disposition reserve fund

        —Common reserve fund

        —Exchange and security reserve fund

        —Extra reserve fund

        —Special reserve fund

        —Investment reserve fund

    f. Profit or loss brought forward

    g. Profit or loss for the financial year: Profit or loss for the financial year less dividend.

The financial analyst must carefully examine movements of the total capital employed. Items related to foreign currency translation can be shown either in the profit and loss account or directly as total capital employed. Revaluations or write-offs of revalued assets may be found as movements in the total capital employed, and goodwill may be offset directly against reserves. Danish law does not require a note showing movements of the total capital employed concerning groups.

Minority interests can be shown as part of the total capital employed, or as a separate item between the total capital employed and provisions for liabilities and charges. Most groups show minority interests as a separate item.

3.8 Provisions for Liabilities and Charges

Provisions for liabilities and charges are intended to cover losses, debts, or charges, the nature of which is clearly defined and which at the date of the end of the financial year are either likely to be incurred or certain to be incurred but uncertain as to the amount or as to the date on which they will arise. Provisions for liabilities and charges must not be used to regulate the value of assets. Consequently, reserves for bad debts or write-downs of fixed assets do not qualify as provisions for liabilities and charges. Furthermore, provisions for liabilities and charges must not be used to create "hidden reserves." Important provisions for liabilities and charges must be explained in the notes.

In accounting practice, provision for deferred taxation is the most common item in provisions for liabilities and charges. In the construction industry, guarantees, for example, are treated as provisions for liabilities and charges. Negative goodwill, gains on sale and leaseback arrangements, and negative equity of subsidiaries may, in practice, also be treated as provisions for liabilities and charges. Sometimes the titles suggest a use in contravention of the legal requirements, and the financial analyst should carefully examine such provisions for liabilities and charges.

3.9 Property, Plant, and Equipment

By law, tangible fixed assets are valued at acquisition cost or production cost and amortized during their useful life. Production costs may include overheads and financial costs related to the production period, but few firms mention the inclusion of overheads and financial costs. Neither law nor the Danish Accounting Standards regulate the choice of depreciation method or the useful life of different categories of assets. Regarding estimation of useful life, considerable variation can be observed in practice. Tangible assets may be revalued if the value of an asset has increased as a result of factors that do not seem to be temporary. If a depreciable asset is revalued, the depreciation must be based on the revaluation. Revaluations must not be shown in the profit and loss account before realization (sale). A special revaluation reserve exists as part of the equity account. If the value of a revalued asset drops, the revaluation reserve must be adjusted accordingly. When a revalued asset is sold, the revaluation reserve must be transferred, but the company may decide whether the revaluation shall be shown in the profit and loss account as part of the realized gain or removed directly from the revaluation reserve to so-called free reserve funds. In the latter case, a part of the realized gain will never pass through the profit and loss account.

In practice, revaluation is often seen in relation to land and buildings. Approximately 20% of Danish listed groups make such revaluations in any one year, and more than 50% had revaluation reserves in their balance sheets in 1992. The reason for the revaluation of land and buildings may lie in the existence of a public valuation system affecting land and buildings, for tax purposes. Revaluations are carried out on all land and buildings each year for tax purposes on either a statistical basis or by official surveyors. The results of those revaluations are not automatically suitable for accounting purposes, but before implementation of the Fourth Directive, land and buildings were normally valued at those amounts, and they may also be used today as guidance in the valuation process. Furthermore, special statistics show the sales prices for different types of property in different parts of the country every 6 months.

Both the absolute and relative numbers of groups with yearly revaluations seem to be declining, which supports a hypothesis of such revaluations being a tradition carried on from the time before EU harmonization. The increase in the number of companies with accumulated revaluations may be caused simply by the fact that now more companies disclose information concerning their revaluations.

Write-downs must be made if the useful value of an asset has declined as a result of factors that do not seem to be temporary. The company decides whether such write-offs shall be included as part of depreciation in operating expenses or shown as extraordinary charges. In Denmark no provision exists for uncertain declining values or for tax purposes.

Profit, assets, and equity all change when companies carry out revaluation. Most significant of these is the change in equity. The financial analyst must be aware of such revaluations, because they may distort both time-series analysis of the single group and cross-sectional analyses between different groups.

3.10 Financial Assets

The measurement rules relating to financial fixed assets other than investments in subsidiaries and associated undertakings in most respects follow the measurement rules for tangible fixed assets, but write-downs can be made even if a drop in value is only temporary.

Financial current assets are measured at the lower of cost or market value. Financial current assets that are publicly traded may be valued at their quoted price. The Financial Statements Act provides that unrealized gains must be placed in a revaluation reserve. In practice, however, a growing number of companies redefine the realization principle in accordance with IAS No. 25, and unrealized gains are shown in the profit and loss account. Hereby a symmetric treatment of gains and losses is established, in accordance with the matching principle and at the expense of the prudence principle.

In practice, some companies stick strictly to the historical cost principle, while others use the possibility of revaluation. The financial analyst should be aware of those differences.

3.11 Leasing

The only legal requirement concerning leasing is an obligation to show leasing liabilities in the notes. In practice, few groups show leased assets and leasing liabilities in the balance sheet. It is impossible to know whether this indicates that the distinction between operating leases and financial leases in IAS No. 17 is not followed or that financial leases are not very common. When IAS No. 17 was introduced in Denmark it was followed by some debate concerning the treatment of financial leases. The FSR recommends both the legal requirements and the treatment according to IAS No. 17 and anticipates a gradual movement toward the approach of IAS No. 17.

3.12 Oil, Gas, and Other Mineral Resources

In Denmark no special accounting regulation exists in the area of oil, gas, and other mineral resources. DONG (Danish Oil and Natural Gas Company), one of the few Danish firms involved in oil and gas activities, uses the full cost method.

3.13 Intangible Assets

As mentioned earlier, the prudence principle is an important one in both Danish accounting regulation and Danish accounting practice. The Danish Financial Statements Act allows intangible assets bought from a third party to be capitalized. Research and development costs also may be capitalized. In practice, however, such a capitalization seldom occurs. Most companies expense intangible assets immediately. Capitalized intangible assets must be depreciated over a maximum of 5 years. A longer period of depreciation is permissible, but special arguments must be presented by the company. Intangible assets may not be revalued.

Write-downs must be made if the useful value of an asset has declined owing to factors that do not seem to be temporary. The company decides whether the write-offs shall be shown as part of "depreciation and write-offs" or as extraordinary charges. No provisions exist for uncertain declining values. Formation costs may not be capitalized. The financial analyst should be aware of companies changing policy from immediate expensing to capitalization and depreciation. In spite of relevant considerations related to the matching principle, it may be a sign of "creative accounting," aimed at restoration of equity.

The Danish Accounting Standard No. 7 concerning research and development is quite similar to IAS No. 9, but the Danish Standard does not recommend disclosure of total research and development costs.

3.14 Participating Interests

In the single company's financial statement, investments in subsidiaries and in associated undertakings may be treated in different ways, in accordance with the Financial Statements Act:

1. Historical cost
2. Intrinsic value in accordance with the general rules of valuation
3. The equity method

Before the implementation of the Seventh Directive, the equity method was allowed only for the treatment of investments in subsidiaries, and in practice both historical cost and intrinsic value were used also.

The equity method used in relation to associated undertakings is a new rule, resulting from the implementation of the Seventh Directive for group accounts. Before harmonization, accounting practice was divided equally among three methods: historical cost, intrinsic value, and the equity method. Now practice is moving toward the equity method, to avoid different treatment in the single company's financial statement and the consolidated financial statements.

Denmark permits combined taxation of the parent company and some or all of its wholly owned subsidiaries (joint taxation schemes). In the annual accounts the total tax amount may be divided among the different companies according to their pretax profit, or it may be charged to the parent company alone. When examining the financial statements of a parent company, the financial analyst should be aware of the treatment of profit from its subsidiaries.

Goodwill and negative goodwill are generally treated parallel to their treatment in the consolidated financial statements, so that profit or loss and the total capital employed will be similar in both the financial statements of the parent company and the consolidated financial statements.

No legal requirements are formulated in the case of a subsidiary that has negative equity. The negative equity may be offset against other positive equities or against loans to the subsidiary. Eventually the negative equity is shown as a provision for liabilities and charges.

In the consolidated financial statement, investments in both unconsolidated subsidiaries and associated undertakings must be treated according to the equity method.

Before the implementation of the Seventh Directive, no rules existed concerning joint ventures, and in accounting practice historical cost, one-line consolidation, and proportional consolidation could be observed. Since harmonization, joint ventures may be proportionally consolidated, so companies may still choose freely among the different methods.

The financial analyst must be aware of the lack of regulation in this area. He or she should also remember that Danish companies are often small companies with a relatively low capital strength in comparison with undertakings in some other countries.

3.15 Inventories

As mentioned earlier, both marginal and absorption costing are allowed in Denmark according to the Financial Statements Act, and marginal costing is still the most widely used principle. Lundbeck A/S uses marginal costing (see page 149 under Stocks and Table 1). However, the Danish Accounting Standard No. 8 recommends absorption costing and that standard is effective for annual accounts covering financial years beginning on July 1, 1993 or later.

The financial analyst should be aware of the definition used. If turnover and production differ, the method used will influence profit, balance sheet, and total capital employed. Danish accounting regulations do not specify the criteria by which costs are judged to be variable or fixed. Neither do the regulations define the content of absorption cost. The Financial Statements Law allows weighted average, FIFO, LIFO, and other similar methods to be used. Danish Accounting Standard No. 8 does not allow the LIFO method. No common practice in this area can be identified, because many companies omit information about the calculation principle. In defining the "lower of cost or market principle," the expression "today's price" (*dagsværdi*) is used. Before the adoption of the standard there seemed to be some confusion in Danish practice concerning the interpretation of that concept. Both "net realizable value" and "replacement cost" were used. According to the standard, "today's price" equals the "net realizable value." Inventories may be revalued to a limit of their replacement cost, but such a revaluation is seldom seen in practice. Nothing is said in the standard about interest during the production process. It is concluded that interest should not be included in the valuation of inventory.

3.16 Profit on Construction Contracts

Income from sales of goods and services is realized when the goods or services are delivered and the risk is transferred to the customer. According to the Financial Statements Act, production bases can be used only through reference to the true and fair view. A special rule allows companies to value long-term contracts at their sales price, but that rule is a measurement rule and does not affect the net turnover. Changes in contribution margin and gross profit must therefore be shown as part of production cost or as other ordinary income. This rule is not recommended in Danish Accounting Standard No. 6 concerning long-term contracts. The standard recommends that the percentage of completion method be used for long-term contracts. Billings on account under an individual long-term contract should be deducted from the asset "Work in progress on behalf of third parties" if they relate to stage payments for work already performed on the contract. Billings on account exceeding the value of work performed on the contract are recorded as advances from customers under current liabilities.

Today, most publicly listed firms that are involved in long-term contracts use the percentage of completion method, without any reference to the true and fair view.

3.17 Taxation

In Denmark the Fourth Directive established a separation between taxation and accounting, which was almost fully implemented by the end of 1985. Provision for deferred taxation is therefore necessary in Danish financial statements (Table 3). Accounting rules relating to taxation are summarized in Table 4.

Accounting practice is divided on the question whether deferred taxation due to timing differences should be shown fully or partly in the profit and loss account. One might say that Denmark is stuck in the middle of the international dispute, the two sides of which are represented by the United Kingdom and the United States. The Financial Statements Act does not include rules on how to compute deferred taxation. The liability method is the method most commonly used.

As mentioned earlier, taxable and accounting income differ considerably. Deferred taxation therefore often has a significant influence on the bottom line result in the profit and loss account, as well as on the division between equity and provisions. The financial analyst should pay attention to the principle used when time-series analysis and cross-sectional analysis are carried out.

TABLE 3 *Treatment of Deferred Taxation by Publicly Listed Trade, Service, and Industrial Groups*

	1988 No. (%)	1989 No. (%)	1990 No. (%)	1991 No. (%)	1992 No. (%)
Tax payable	8 (6)	7 (5)	9 (7)	5 (4)	6 (5)
Tax payable and partial deferred taxation	41(30)	40 (31)	40 (33)	40 (32)	39 (32)
Tax payable and fully deferred taxation	58 (43)	57 (45)	54 (45)	63 (51)	66 (55)
Tax payable, fully deferred taxation, and contingent taxation	5 (4)	2 (2)	1 (1)	1 (1)	1 (1)
Taxation not specified	1 (0)	0 (0)	2 (2)	2 (2)	1 (1)
No information/ not relevant	23 (17)	22 (17)	15 (12)	12 (10)	8 (6)
Total	136 (100)	128 (100)	121 (100)	123 (100)	121 (100)

Source: *ACCOUNT DATA - DK*, Copenhagen Business School.

Fully deferred taxation often includes the following timing differences between accounting and taxation:

1. Timing differences between accounting depreciation and tax-based depreciation. The tax rules are based on the declining balance sheet method, using price-indexed values.

2. Tax-based write-offs on inventories

TABLE 4 *Accounting Rules Relating to Taxation*

	Tax Payable	Deferred Taxation	Taxation Contingency[a]
Description	Tax to be paid	Owing to timing differences	Owing to possible realization at revalued book value
Information	In the accounts	In the accounts or in the notes	In the accounts or in the notes

[a] In a few areas Denmark taxes capital gains. If a taxable gain is made by selling an asset at its book value, a tax liability arises. A potential tax liability (a tax contingency) occurs when assets are revalued.

3. Timing differences between accounting write-offs on bad debts and the tax-based write-offs.

Information concerning tax relating to extraordinary items is of special interest when the financial analyst is analyzing the sources of income. According to the Financial Statements Act, the single company (the parent company) must give information concerning the impact of extraordinary items on tax expenses, but no information is required by groups. In 1992, 20 publicly listed trade, service, and industrial groups (16%) gave information about tax relating to extraordinary items, 46 did not give such information (38%), and for 19 groups it was impossible to know whether such information should have been given or was not relevant. Thirty-nine groups (32%) had no extraordinary items or they disclosed that the tax was not influenced by such items.

3.18 Pensions

Pension obligations are rarely seen in Danish Financial Statements. The Pension Act demands pension obligations to be transferred to insurance companies, and most pension arrangements therefore are classified as "defined contribution" plans. Only directors may have pension agreements directly with their company. Pension obligations may exist owing to pension obligations in foreign subsidiaries. A few companies have set up pension funds. These pension obligations are either capitalized in the balance sheet or mentioned in the notes. The method of capitalization is seldom explained.

3.19 Government Grants

Government grants are an unregulated area. Neither the Financial Statements Act nor any Danish Accounting Standard deals with the treatment of government grants, and few companies disclose any information about the methods used. Only three of the publicly listed trade, service, and industrial groups disclosed such information in their 1992 accounts. One group deducted the grant in arriving at the carrying amount of the asset, one offset the grant directly against equity, and the last group set up the grant as deferred income for later income recognition.

4. Expected Future Developments

Even after the implementation of the Fourth and Seventh Directives, Danish accounting regulation remained fairly flexible. Furthermore, self-regulation in the private sectors was fairly weak, and there was no control over the financial statements published by quoted companies on the Copenhagen Stock Exchange. The shortcomings of the accounting regulations were and to some extent still are reflected in accounting practice in several ways:

1. A variety of disclosure rules and measurement methods is used in accounting practice. Profit, assets, and liabilities can be measured differently, even for identical companies.
2. Several quoted companies do not comply with the law, and some even engage in creative accounting.

Financial scandals and bankruptcies, however, together with the growing awareness of internationalization, have been the driving forces that have pushed Danish accounting regulation further forward. The collapse of the Northern Feather Group in late 1990 is the largest economic scandal in the modern economic history of Denmark, and it has had serious economic consequences, both nationally and internationally. The critique in the wake of the scandal has focused on subjects like:

1. The need to establish a mechanism of accounting control and sanctions at the Copenhagen Stock Exchange
2. The need to place accounting users in a more central position in the regulation process
3. The need to reduce the existing scope of choice provided by the disclosure and measurement rules

It is now stated in the Financial Statements Act that the Danish Commerce and Companies Agency has both the right and the obligation to examine the financial statements of limited companies. Furthermore, an Accounting Council will be established in the near future with representatives from the parties concerned as an advisory forum of the Ministry of Industry. Finally, the standard-setting process has been speeded up and broadened by the adoption so far of nine Danish Accounting Standards.

Denmark still faces one of the fundamental contradictions that also delayed the adoption of the first Limited Companies Act in the beginning of the century: the conflict between a liberal antiregulatory ideology on the one hand, represented mainly by financial statement preparers from certain industries, and a social protectionist regulatory approach mainly represented by some of the financial statement user groups on the other hand.

Notes

1. Companies had to prepare financial statements in accordance with the law in respect of any financial year beginning on February 1, 1982 or later.

2. Groups must prepare financial statements in accordance with the amended law and the order in respect of any financial year beginning on April 1, 1991 or later.

3. With the format classified by function, information about staff costs is provided in the notes (for groups after April 1, 1991).

4. Hasselager, O., and Johansen, A.R. (1992): *Årsregnskaber—Kommentarer til regnskabslovgivningen*. København: G.E.C. Gads Forlag. The book, which includes commentary to all the sections in the Financial Statements Act and the Order on Financial Statements, has become a standard commentary textbook. Olaf Hasselager is head of the department of accounting of the Danish Commerce and Companies Agency, and Aksel Runge Johansen is state-authorized public accountant and partner in KPMG C. Jespersen.

Useful Addresses

Copenhagen Stock Exchange
Københavns Fondsbørs
Nikolaj Plads 6
DK-1067 Copenhagen K.
Denmark
Tel: +45 3393 3366
Fax: +45 3312 8613

The Danish Commerce and Companies Agency
Erhvervs- og Selskabsstyrelsen
Kampmannsgade 1
DK-1604 Copenhagen V.
Denmark
Tel: +45 3312 4280
Fax: +45 3332 4480

The Institute of Registered Public Accountants
Foreningen af Registrerede Revisorer (FRR)
Flintholm Alle 8
DK-2000 Frederiksberg
Denmark
Tel: +45 3186 4422
Fax: +45 3833 1318

The Institute of State-authorised Public Accountants
Foreningen af Statsautoriserede Revisorer (FSR)
Kronprinsessegade 8
DK-1306 Copenhagen K.
Denmark
Tel: +45 3393 9191
Fax: +45 3311 0913

H. Lundbeck A/S
Key figures for the Group, 1986-1993

Operating figures (DKK million)	1993	1992	1991	1990	1989	1988	1987	1986
Net turnover	933.9	768.4	745.5	609.0	588.1	584.0	524.1	498.8
Result before research costs	202.5	184.0	144.0	93.1	90.4	64.0	67.5	77.7
Research costs	181.4	133.4	92.5	86.9	78.1	70.3	66.4	63.1
Result of primary operations	30.0	54.4	53.9	11.0	14.7	(1.0)	0.4	15.0
Result before tax	53.4	55.9	223.2	28.6	26.7	26.8	8.9	36.8
Result after tax	37.6	40.3	212.6	19.6	44.6	29.9	2.2	21.0

Note: The result before tax in 1991 includes extraordinary income of DKK 172.6 million derived from the disposal of business activities.

Assets (DKK million)	1993	1992	1991	1990	1989	1988	1987	1986
Fixed assets	457.0	365.4	260.4	269.4	245.3	234.1	162.3	178.7
Stocks	102.7	88.6	82.6	74.8	78.7	83.3	94.6	89.0
Receivables	210.7	162.0	155.6	141.6	121.9	104.7	102.5	92.0
Cash and securities	404.0	445.4	448.8	196.8	221.0	217.4	242.8	233.7
Total assets	1174.4	1061.4	947.4	682.6	666.9	639.5	602.2	593.4

Liabilities (DKK million)	1993	1992	1991	1990	1989	1988	1987	1986
Equity capital	739.0	720.7	685.9	473.6	457.5	416.2	385.1	385.9
Provisions	48.4	31.5	44.9	60.3	60.4	86.9	94.7	93.7
Long-term debt	80.3	81.4	26.5	29.1	22.3	27.0	19.4	16.0
Short-term debt	306.7	227.8	190.1	119.6	126.7	109.4	103.0	97.8
Total liabilities	1174.4	1061.4	947.4	682.6	666.9	639.5	602.2	593.4

Key figures and ratios	1993	1992	1991	1990	1989	1988	1987	1986
Capital investment (DKK million)	141.1	145.0	53.8	57.0	58.8	67.4	37.5	38.0
Average number of employees	978	887	862	949	953	980	973	928
Net profit ratio								
before research costs (%)	21.7	23.9	19.3	15.3	15.4	11.0	12.9	15.6
Net profit ratio (%)	3.2	7.1	7.2	1.8	2.5	(0.2)	0.1	3.0
Return on assets (%)	2.6	5.1	5.7	1.6	2.2	(0.2)	0.1	2.5
Capital turnover rate (%)	79.5	72.4	78.7	89.2	88.2	91.3	87.0	84.1
Solidity (%)	62.9	67.9	72.4	69.4	68.6	65.1	63.9	65.0
Return on equity capital (%)	7.3	7.9	38.5	6.1	6.1	6.7	2.3	9.8

Net profit ratio before research and development costs:	Result before research and development costs as a percentage of net turnover.
Net profit ratio:	Result of primary operations as a percentage of net turnover.
Return on assets:	Result of primary operations as a percentage of total assets.
Capital turnover rate:	Net turnover as a percentage of total assets.
Solidity:	Equity capital as a percentage of total liabilities.
Return on equity capital:	Result before tax as a percentage of average equity capital.

Accounting principles

General
The annual accounts and consolidated accounts have been prepared in accordance with the Danish Company Accounts Act, good accounting practice and generally recognised Danish accounting guidelines.

As a departure from practice in former years, research and development costs are shown as a separate item, to increase the information value of the profit and loss account. Research costs are shown after administration costs and a new subtotal "Result before research and development costs" has been included in the profit and loss account. This change in practice has been made to show the year's earnings in direct relation to net sales, as research costs are solely related to earnings in future years.

The key figures and comparative figures have been adjusted accordingly.

Consolidation principles
The consolidated accounts comprise H. Lundbeck A/S (the parent company) and companies in which the parent company holds more than 50% of the votes or exercises a controlling influence in another way. A Group overview is given in note 7.

The consolidated accounts have been prepared as a synthesis of the audited accounts of the individual companies which, in all important respects, have been prepared in accordance with the accounting principles described below.

Intra-group income and costs, shareholdings, receivables, dividends and unrealised profits on stocks have been eliminated.

In the consolidated accounts, the book value of the parent company's shareholdings in subsidiaries has been set off against the parent company's share of subsidiaries' equity capital calculated at the point in time at which the Group relationship was established (past-equity method). Resulting differences have been allocated to the assets and liabilities which, at establishment of the Group relationship and in compliance with Group accounting principles, had a higher or lower value than the value at which they were entered in the subsidiaries' accounts.

Remaining balances (Group goodwill) are deducted from reserves which can be used to issue bonus shares.

Newly acquired or newly established subsidiaries are included in the profit and loss account from the date of acquisition. Subsidiaries which are sold or wound up are included until the date on which they are sold or wound up.

Currency conversion
Receivables and debts in foreign currencies are converted to DKK at the rate of exchange at the end of the financial year. Both realised and unrealised currency gains and losses are included in the profit and loss account.

Forward contracts at the balance sheet date are entered at the forward rate at the balance sheet date and unrealised capital gains and losses compared with the forward rates agreed upon are entered in the profit and loss account. However, unrealised capital gains relating to forward contracts entered into to cover exchange risks on future income are deferred until that sales income is realised.

The profit and loss accounts and balance sheets of foreign subsidiaries are converted to Danish kroner at the rate of exchange at the balance sheet date. Any difference from the net assets of these companies at the beginning of the financial year is entered under equity capital, cf. note 10.

Profit and loss account

Net turnover
Sales are booked as income when goods are despatched and net turnover comprises the year's invoiced sales less value-added tax, return goods and price reductions directly connected with sales.

Net turnover also includes fees and royalties, as well as non-refundable down payments received during the year. Large down-payments received counterbalanced by an obligation to meet future costs are accrued.

Research and development costs
Research and development costs comprise costs, including fees and depreciation, attributable to the company's research and development activities. As a general rule, the Group charges research and development costs over the profit and loss account as those costs are incurred.

Research and development costs linked to product-related development loans are activated.

Discontinued and acquired activities
The results of divested and acquired business areas are included under relevant primary operations items until the divestment date or after the acquisition date. The profit or loss on divestment or purchase is included under extraordinary items, after deduction of costs related to the divestment or acquisition.

Taxation
Tax on the result for the year includes both actual tax and deferred tax.

Provision for deferred tax is the calculated tax effect of accumulated timing differences between accounting and fiscal statements.

The effect of any changes in taxation rates is booked in the profit and loss account such that deferred tax is calculated in accordance with prevailing tax rates in the countries concerned.

Balance sheet

Intangible fixed assets
Intangible fixed assets are booked at purchase price less accumulated depreciation and write-downs.

Activated research and development costs are depreciated by the straight-line method in pace with earnings over a period which is equivalent to the remaining period of the relevant patents, with a maximum of 20 years.

Other intangible fixed assets are depreciated by the straight-line method over the following periods:

Patents and trademarks:
Contract period, with a maximum of 20 years.

Leasehold improvements:
Period of lease, with a maximum of 10 years.

Tangible fixed assets
Tangible fixed assets are booked at purchase price with the addition of any revaluation and with the deduction of accumulated depreciation and write-downs.

Tangible fixed assets are depreciated by the straight-line method over the expected useful life of the asset concerned, as follows:

Buildings	30 years
Installations	10 years
Technical equipment and machinery	3-10 years
Other operating equipment, fixtures and fittings	5-10 years

Improvements and purchases valued at less than DKK 30,000 are booked in full in the profit and loss account in the year in which they occur.

Financial fixed assets
Equity participation in subsidiaries is booked in the parent company's accounts in accordance with the equity method, i.e. at their book value with adjustment for divergences and deduction of unrealised intra-group profits, calculated in accordance with the same principles as in the consolidated accounts.

The parent company's share of subsidiaries' results is booked in the profit and loss account less changes in unrealised intra-group profits of the year and less depreciation on balances. Shares of net results booked as income are transferred to reserves for undistributed profits in subsidiaries to the extent that they exceed the dividends received from subsidiaries.

Other capital shares comprise investments in shares, which are valued at

purchase price. Other receivables comprise deposits related to property leases, which are valued at the amount paid in.

Stocks
Raw materials, packaging and goods bought for resale are valued at the last known purchase price at end-year, which very largely equates with purchase price calculated on the FIFO principle.

Work in progress and finished goods from own production are valued at cost price, which includes the cost of materials, energy used in production and direct production wages.

If the net realisation value is lower than purchase or cost price, the value of the products concerned is written down.

Receivables
Receivables are booked following individual evaluations of the risk of loss.

Securities
Securities include listed bonds, which are booked at the lower of purchase price and the official market value at the balance sheet date.

Other securities are booked at purchase price.

Write-downs to below purchase price are booked in the profit and loss account.

Other long-term debt
Other long-term debt comprises a loan from the Development Fund for the financing of research and development projects. As far as current research projects are concerned, the loan will be written off if the company does not market the product concerned.

The loan is offset by activated research and development projects, cf. note 6.

Sources and application of funds
The statement of sources and application of funds is a cash-flow analysis presented in accordance with the indirect method and based on the result for the year.

The statement shows the parent company's and the Group's cash-flow for the year and the liquidity position at the balance sheet date.

Cash and securities include instruments of debt related to sales of business activities, deposits with banks and cash in hand.

Currency adjustments occur in the conversion of foreign subsidiaries' liquid holdings at the beginning of the financial year to the balance-sheet exchange rates at the end of the financial year.

30

Bestyrelsens og direktionens underskrifter

København, den 17. marts 1994

Direktion:

Erik Sprunk-Jansen
adm.

Kurt Kruhöffer

Carl-Emil R. Sandberg

Eva Steiness

Bestyrelse:

Birgit Bundgaard
valgt af medarbejderne

Arne V. Jensen
formand

Jørgen Fakstorp

Jan Gottliebsen
valgt af medarbejderne

Torben Grandt

Henrik Hertz

Bent Jakobsen

Sven Dyrløv Madsen

Torben Skarsfeldt
valgt af medarbejderne

Revisionspåtegning

Vi har revideret årsregnskabet og koncern-
regnskabet for 1993 for H. Lundbeck A/S.
Revisionen er udført i overensstemmelse
med almindeligt anerkendte revisionsprin-
cipper og har omfattet de revisionshandlin-
ger, som vi har anset for nødvendige.

Regnskaberne for moderselskabet og koncernen er aflagt i overensstemmelse med
lovgivningens og vedtægternes krav til
regnskabsaflæggelse og giver efter vor
opfattelse et retvisende billede af aktiver og
passiver, den økonomiske stilling samt
resultat.

København, den 17. marts 1994

SCHØBEL & MARHOLT
Revisionsaktieselskab

Søren Bjerre-Nielsen
statsautoriseret revisor

Carsten Vaarby
statsautoriseret revisor

27

Signatures of the Supervisory Board and the Executive Management

Copenhagen, 17th March 1994

Executive Management:

Erik Sprunk-Jansen
President

Kurt Kruhöffer   Carl-Emil R. Sandberg   Eva Steiness

Supervisory Board:

Birgit Bundgaard   Arne V. Jensen   Jørgen Fakstorp
Elected by the employees   Chairman

Jan Gottliebsen   Torben Grandt   Henrik Hertz
Elected by the employees

Bent Jakobsen   Sven Dyrløv Madsen   Torben Skarsfeldt
                                                                           Elected by the employees

Auditors' report

We have audited the accounts and consolidated accounts for 1993 of H. Lundbeck A/S. The audit was carried out in accordance with generally accepted auditing principles as applied in Denmark and included the auditing actions we considered to be necessary.
The parent company's accounts and consolidated accounts have been prepared in compliance with the requirements of legislation and the articles of association in relation to the presentation of accounts and in our view give a true and fair view of the assets and liabilities, financial position and result.

SCHØBEL & MARHOLT
Revisionsaktieselskab

Søren Bjerre-Nielsen   Carsten Vaarby
State-authorised public accountant   State-authorised public accountant

Resultatopgørelse

Moderselskab					Koncernen	
1992 1000 DKK	1993 1000 DKK		Noter		1993 1000 DKK	1992 1000 DKK
525.169	612.165	Nettoomsætning	1		933.897	768.475
265.832	321.301	Produktionsomkostninger	2		335.559	274.365
35.646	71.338	Distributionsomkostninger	2		191.760	139.182
76.035	87.836	Administrationsomkostninger	2		204.121	170.961
147.656	131.690	**Resultat før forskningsomkostninger**			202.457	183.967
126.431	178.698	Forskningsomkostninger	2		181.384	133.360
5.396	15.597	Andre driftsindtægter			17.726	8.050
4.216	7.516	Andre driftsudgifter			8.823	4.216
22.405	(38.927)	**Resultat af primær drift**			29.976	54.441
11.715	69.946	Resultat før skat i datterselskaber	5,7			
38.266	47.908	Finansielle indtægter	9		48.045	38.598
19.763	14.283	Finansielle udgifter	9		13.377	15.560
52.623	64.644	**Resultat før ekstraordinære poster**			64.644	77.479
17.482	0	Ekstraordinære indtægter	3		0	47.800
14.215	11.219	Ekstraordinære udgifter	4		11.219	69.389
55.890	53.425	**Resultat før skat**			53.425	55.890
15.554	15.859	Skat af årets resultat	5		15.859	15.554
40.336	37.566	**Årets resultat**			37.566	40.336

Profit and loss account

Parent company					Group	
1992 DKK '000	1993 DKK '000		Notes		1993 DKK '000	1992 DKK '000
525,169	612,165	Net turnover	1		933,897	768,475
265,832	321,301	Production costs	2		335,559	274,365
35,646	71,338	Distribution costs	2		191,760	139,182
76,035	87,836	Administration costs	2		204,121	170,961
147,656	131,690	**Result before research costs**			202,457	183,967
126,431	178,698	Research costs	2		181,384	133,360
5,396	15,597	Other operating income			17,726	8,050
4,216	7,516	Other operating costs			8,823	4,216
22,405	(38,927)	**Result of primary operations**			29,976	54,441
11,715	69,946	Subsidiaries' result before tax	5,7			
38,266	47,908	Financial income	9		48,045	38,598
19,763	14,283	Financial costs	9		13,377	15,560
52,623	64,644	**Result before extraordinary items**			64,644	77,479
17,482	0	Extraordinary income	3		0	47,800
14,215	11,219	Extraordinary costs	4		11,219	69,389
55,890	53,425	**Result before tax**			53,425	55,890
15,554	15,859	Tax on result for the year	5		15,859	15,554
40,336	37,566	**Result for the year**			37,566	40,336

Balance pr. 31. december 1993
Aktiver

Moderselskab				Koncernen	
1992 1000 DKK	1993 1000 DKK		Noter	1993 1000 DKK	1992 1000 DKK
12.341	12.341	Forskning og udviklingsprojekter		12.341	12.341
8.797	9.790	Patenter og varemærker m.v.		9.790	8.797
1.479	3.646	Indretning af lejede lokaler		5.152	2.627
22.617	25.777	**Immaterielle anlægsaktiver**	6	27.283	23.765
130.969	201.104	Grunde og bygninger		208.534	132.410
45.446	68.699	Tekniske anlæg og maskiner		81.634	45.446
56.965	82.201	Andre driftsanlæg og inventar		105.616	74.958
84.280	23.271	Igangværende investeringer		28.702	84.280
317.660	375.275	**Materielle anlægsaktiver**	6	424.486	337.094
30.032	30.136	Kapitalinteresser i datterselskaber	7	0	0
760	760	Kapitalandele	8	760	760
2.707	2.804	Andre tilgodehavender	8	4.476	3.817
14.536	32.732	Lån til datterselskaber	8	0	0
48.035	66.432	**Finansielle anlægsaktiver**		5.236	4.577
388.312	467,484	**Anlægsaktiver i alt**		457.005	365.436
31.310	40.589	Råvarer og emballage		42.657	31.310
25.137	29.413	Varer under fremstilling		29.413	25.137
28.701	29.248	Færdigvarer		30.672	32.186
85.148	99.250	**Varebeholdninger**		102.742	88.633
13.587	6.803	Tilgodehavender fra salg		163.814	111.785
70.833	137.417	Tilgodehavender hos datterselskaber		0	0
58.359	41.857	Udbytte		0	0
0	13.038	Tilgodehavende selskabsskat	5	804	0
20.877	19.448	Andre tilgodehavender		37.470	40.738
3.550	3.724	Periodeafgrænsning		8.625	9.478
167.206	222.287	**Tilgodehavender**		210.713	162.001
375.315	275,107	**Værdipapirer**	9	275.107	375.315
23.772	61.223	**Likvide beholdninger**		128.914	70.067
651.441	657.867	**Omsætningsaktiver i alt**		717.476	696.016
1.039.753	1.125.351	**Aktiver i alt**		1.174.481	1.061.452

Balance sheet at 31st December 1993
Assets

Parent company				Group	
1992 DKK '000	1993 DKK '000		Notes	1993 DKK '000	1992 DKK '000
12,341	12,341	Research and development projects		12,341	12,341
8,797	9,790	Patents and trademarks etc.		9,790	8,797
1,479	3,646	Leasehold improvements		5,152	2,627
22,617	25,777	**Intangible fixed assets**	6	27,283	23,765
130,969	201,104	Land and buildings		208,534	132,410
45,446	68,699	Technical installations and machinery		81,634	45,446
56,965	82,201	Other fixtures and equipment		105,616	74,958
84,280	23,271	Construction in progress		28,702	84,280
317,660	375,275	**Tangible fixed assets**	6	424,486	337,094
30,032	30,136	Shares in subsidiaries	7	0	0
760	760	Other shareholdings	8	760	760
2,707	2,804	Deposits, etc.	8	4,476	3,817
14,536	32,732	Loans to subsidiaries	8	0	0
48,035	66,432	**Financial fixed assets**		5,236	4,577
388,312	467,484	**Total fixed assets**		457,005	365,436
31,310	40,589	Raw materials and packaging		42,657	31,310
25,137	29,413	Work in progress		29,413	25,137
28,701	29,248	Finished goods		30,672	32,186
85,148	99,250	**Stock**		102,742	88,633
13,587	6,803	Accounts receivable from sales		163,814	111,785
70,833	137,417	Accounts receivable from subsidiaries		0	0
58,359	41,857	Dividend		0	0
0	13,038	Corporate tax receivable	5	804	0
20,877	19,448	Other receivables		37,470	40,738
3,550	3,724	Accruals and deferred expenses		8,625	9,478
167,206	222,287	**Total receivables**		210,713	162,001
375,315	275,107	**Securities**	9	275,107	375,315
23,772	61,223	**Cash**		128,914	70,067
651,441	657,867	**Total current assets**		717,476	696,016
1,039,753	1,125,351	**Total assets**		1,174,481	1,061,452

32

Balance pr. 31. december 1993
Passiver

			Moderselskab			Koncernen	

1992 1000 DKK	1993 1000 DKK		Noter	1993 1000 DKK	1992 1000 DKK
110.000	110.000	Selskabskapital		110.000	110.000
14.663	14.663	Opskrivningshenlæggelser		14.663	14.663
21.408	16.458	Ikke udloddede overskud i datterselskaber			
150.000	150.000	Andre reserver		150.000	150.000
424.605	447.882	Overført overskud		464.340	446.013
720.676	739.003	**Egenkapital**	10	739.003	720.676
39.391	52.265	Hensættelser til eventualskat	11	48.416	31.589
39.391	52.265	**Hensættelser**		48.416	31.589
66.802	65.852	Prioritetsgæld, langfristet del	12	65.852	66.802
14.561	14.498	Anden gæld		14.498	14.561
81.363	80.350	**Langfristet gæld**		80.350	81.363
24.989	46.054	Bankgæld og udviklingslån		46.520	25.314
1.747	924	Prioritetsgæld, kortfristet del		924	1.747
44.720	25.928	Lån i datterselskaber		0	0
40.054	52.218	Leverandørgæld		66.713	55.380
1.378	0	Selskabsskat	5	0	22.764
35.464	47.422	Merværdiafgift, skatter og feriepengeforpligtelser		67.029	51.987
30.267	46.683	Anden gæld		91.022	50.928
19.704	12.504	Periodeafgrænsningsposter		12.504	19.704
	22.000	Udbytte for regnskabsåret		22.000	
198.323	253.733	**Kortfristet gæld**		306.712	227.824
279.686	334.083	**Gæld i alt**		387.062	309.187
1.039.753	1.125.351	**Passiver i alt**		1.174.481	1.061.452
		Forpligtelser	13		

Balance sheet at 31st December 1993
Liabilities

Parent company				Group	
1992 DKK '000	1993 DKK '000		Notes	1993 DKK '000	1992 DKK '000
110,000	110,000	Share capital		110,000	110,000
14,663	14,663	Appreciation reserve		14,663	14,663
21,408	16,458	Retained profit of subsidiaries			
150,000	150,000	Other reserves		150,000	150,000
424,605	447,882	Profit carried forward		464,340	446,013
720,676	739,003	**Equity capital**	10	739,003	720,676
39,391	52,265	Provision for deferred tax	11	48,416	31,589
39,391	52,265	**Total provisions**		48,416	31,589
66,802	65,852	Mortgage debt, long-term	12	65,852	66,802
14,561	14,498	Other debt		14,498	14,561
81,363	80,350	**Total long-term debt**		80,350	81,363
24,989	46,054	Bank debt and development loans		46,520	25,314
1,747	924	Mortgage debt, short-term		924	1,747
44,720	25,928	Loans in subsidiaries		0	0
40,054	52,218	Debt to suppliers		66,713	55,380
1,378	0	Corporate tax	5	0	22,764
35,464	47,422	VAT, employees' income tax and holiday pay		67,029	51,987
30,267	46,683	Other debt		91,022	50,928
19,704	12,504	Accruals and deferred income		12,504	19,704
	22,000	Dividend for the year		22,000	
198,323	253,733	**Short-term debt**		306,712	227,824
279,686	334,083	**Total debt**		387,062	309,187
1,039,753	1,125,351	**Total liabilities**		1,174,481	1,061,452
		Contractual commitments	13		

Finansieringsanalyse

Moderselskab				Koncernen	
1992 1000 DKK	1993 1000 DKK		Noter	1993 1000 DKK	1992 1000 DKK
40.336	37.566	Årets resultat		37.566	40.336
(3.809)	12.874	Hensættelser	11	16.034	(13.188)
27.586	32.262	Af- og nedskrivninger	2,6	40.951	34.588
0	(22.000)	Udbytte for regnskabsåret		(22.000)	0
64.113	60.702	**Selvfinansiering**		72.551	61.736
35.610	55.081	Tilgodehavender		48.415	15.234
4.303	14.102	Varebeholdninger		14.263	6.067
(18.168)	(53.960)	Rentefri kortfristet gæld		(55.855)	(33.068)
21.745	15.223	**Nettoinvestering i omsætningsaktiver**		6.823	(11.767)
42.368	45.479	**Driftens likviditetsbidrag**		65.728	73.503
131.148	95.107	Anlægsinvestering	6	141.122	144.983
(1.722)	(2.070)	Salgssummer for solgte anlæg	2,3,6	(9.611)	(4.116)
(18.823)	(2.657)	Kapitalinteresser i datterselskaber	7		
14.119	18.293	Anden finansinvestering		652	(319)
124.722	108.673	**Nettoinvestering i anlægskapital**		132.163	140.548
(82.354)	(63.194)	**Selvfinansiering netto**		(66.435)	(67.045)
90.871	21.066	Låntagning		25.767	76.110
(7.200)	(20.629)	Afdrag på lån		(1.783)	(8.484)
83.671	437	**Låntagning netto**		23.984	67.626
1.317	(62.757)	**Likvide midler**		(42.451)	581
397.770	399.087	Likvide beholdninger og værdipapirer primo		445.382	448.781
1.317	(62.757)	Årets bevægelse		(42.451)	581
		Valutakursomregning primo		1.090	(3.980)
399.087	336.330	**Likvide beholdninger og værdipapirer ultimo**		404.021	445.382

Statement of sources and application of funds

Parent company				Group	
1992 DKK '000	1993 DKK '000		Notes	1993 DKK '000	1992 DKK '000
40,336	37,566	Result for the year		37,566	40,336
(3,809)	12,874	Provisions	11	16,034	(13,188)
27,586	32,262	Depreciation	2,6	40,951	34,588
0	(22,000)	Dividend for the year		(22,000)	0
64,113	60,702	**Self-finance**		72,551	61,736
35,610	55,081	Receivables		48,415	15,234
4,303	14,102	Stock		14,263	6,067
(18,168)	(53,960)	Interest-free short-term debt		(55,855)	(33,068)
21,745	15,223	**Net investment in current assets**		6,823	(11,767)
42,368	45,479	**Cash contribution from operations**		65,728	73,503
131,148	95,107	Capital investment	6	141,122	144,983
(1,722)	(2,070)	Proceeds from sales of assets	2,3,6	(9,611)	(4,116)
(18,823)	(2,657)	Shares in subsidiaries	7	0	0
14,119	18,293	Other financial investment		652	(319)
124,722	108,673	**Net investment in fixed capital**		132,163	140,548
(82,354)	(63,194)	**Self-finance, net**		(66,435)	(67,045)
90,871	21,066	Borrowings		25,767	76,110
(7,200)	(20,629)	Instalments on loans		(1,783)	(8,484)
83,671	437	**Borrowings, net**		23,984	67,626
1,317	(62,757)	**Liquid funds**		(42,451)	581
397,770	399,087	Cash and securities at 1st January		445,382	448,781
1,317	(62,757)	Movements during the year		(42,451)	581
		Conversion of foreign currency at 1st January		1,090	(3,980)
399,087	336,330	**Cash and securities at 31st December**		404,021	445,382

Notes to the 1993 annual accounts
Unless otherwise stated, amounts are expressed in DKK '000

1 Net turnover

Parent company			Group	
1992	1993		1993	1992
136,606	211,325	Denmark	189,389	164,435
388,563	400,840	Exports	744,508	604,040
525,169	612,165	Total	933,897	768,475

2 Production, distribution, administration and research costs

Production, distribution, administration and research costs include salaries and wages etc. distributed as follows:

Supervisory Board and Executive Management:

Parent company		
1992	1993	
644	1,031	Fees to Board members
2,455	5,109	Executive Management's remuneration
3,099	6,140	Total

At 1st January 1993, the Group's Executive Management was expanded to include, besides Erik Sprunk-Jansen, President, Carl-Emil R. Sandberg, Executive Vice-President, Production and Engineering, Kurt Kruhöffer, Executive Vice-President, Corporate Sales and Marketing, and Eva Steiness, Executive Vice-President, Research and Development.

Other employees:

Parent company			Group	
1992	1993		1993	1992
165,213	187,231	Staff salaries and wages	290,658	243,876
10,204	12,868	Contribution to pension schemes	17,989	15,945
929	1,077	Other social security costs	11,504	8,735
176,346	201,176	Total	320,151	268,556

Number of employees:

Parent company			Group	
1992	1993		1993	1992
631	674	Average number of employees during the year	978	887

Production, distribution, administration and research costs include depreciation etc., distributed as follows:

Parent company			Group	
1992	1993		1993	1992
879	1,131	Intangible fixed assets	1,233	1,060
5,617	6,470	Land and buildings	6,586	5,647
8,527	9,853	Machinery and installations	11,024	8,527
11,992	14,873	Fixtures and equipment	22,984	18,921
27,015	32,327		41,827	34,155
571	(65)	Losses and gains on disposal	(876)	433
27,586	32,262	Total	40,951	34,588

Depreciation is allocated as follows:

Parent company			Group	
1992	1993		1993	1992
17,068	19,478	Production	20,766	17,068
642	402	Distribution	2,854	2,662
4,001	5,329	Administration	10,278	8,983
5,875	7,053	Research	7,053	5,875
27,586	32,262	Total	40,951	34,588

3 Extraordinary income

Parent company			Group	
1992	1993		1993	1992
17,482	0	Disposal of business activity	0	47,531
0	0	Miscellaneous	0	269
17,482	0	Total	0	47,800

4 Extraordinary costs

Parent company			Group	
1992	1993		1993	1992
11,451	0	Purchase of previously licensed sales rights	0	18,381
		Acquisition of product portfolio	0	45,682
0	11,219	Discontinuance of partnership agreement	11,219	0
2,764	0	Miscellaneous	0	5,326
14,215	11,219	Total	11,219	69,389

5 Tax on the year's result

Parent company			Group	
1992	1993		1993	1992
17,813	(1,348)	Tax due on the year's income	1,953	31,757
(3,341)	(3,517)	Adjustment re previous years	(2,921)	(2,959)
(4,547)	0	Adjustment of deferred tax at 1st January due to changed corporate tax rate	0	(4,677)
(10,535)	(15,580)	Corporate taxes paid between jointly taxed subsidiaries and parent company		
15,426	25,199	Subsidiaries' tax	0	0
	(1,769)	Deferred tax of jointly taxed subsidiary carried forward		
738	12,874	Provision for deferred tax	16,827	(8,567)
15,554	15,859	Total	15,859	15,554

In 1993, tax instalments totalling DKK 6.548 million have been paid by the parent company and DKK 9.388 million by the Group. In 1992, tax of DKK 14.772 million was paid by the parent company and DKK 28.652 million by the group. Tax on extraordinary items for 1993 amounts to DKK 3.366 million for the parent company and the Group.

6 Intangible and tangible fixed assets

Group	Research and development projects	Patents and trade-marks etc.	Leasehold improve-ments	Total intangible fixed assets	Land and buildings	Technical installations and machinery	Other fixtures and equipment	Construction in progress	Total tangible fixed assets	Total
Purchase price:										
Balance at 1.1.1993	12,341	11,415	8,042	31,798	186,902	92,154	152,471	84,280	515,807	547,605
Conversion of foreign currency	0	0	72	72	108	0	507	0	615	687
Additions	0	2,468	780	3,248	88,105	47,212	58,135	(55,578)	137,874	141,122
Disposals	0	969	675	1,644	3,872	42	18,082	0	21,996	23,640
Purchase price	12,341	12,914	8,219	33,474	271,243	139,324	193,031	28,702	632,300	665,774
Appreciations	0	0	0	0	14,663	0	0	0	14,663	14,663
Balance at 31.12.1993	12,341	12,914	8,219	33,474	285,906	139,324	193,031	28,702	646,963	680,437
Depreciation:										
Balance at 1.1.1993	0	2,618	3,271	5,889	71,299	46,708	77,513	0	195,520	201,409
Conversion of foreign currency	0	0	34	34	26	0	277	0	303	337
Additions	0	796	437	1,233	6,586	11,024	22,984	0	40,594	41,827
Disposals	0	290	675	965	539	42	13,359	0	13,940	14,905
Balance at 31.12.1993	0	3,124	3,067	6,191	77,372	57,690	87,415	0	222,477	228,668
Book value at 31.12.1993	12,341	9,790	5,152	27,283	208,534	81,634	105,616	28,702	424,486	451,769

Parent company:	Research and development projects	Patents and trade-marks etc.	Leasehold improve-ments	Total intangible fixed assets	Land and buildings	Technical installations and machinery	Other fixtures and equipment	Construction in progress	Total tangible fixed assets	Total
Purchase price:										
Balance at 1.1.1993	12,341	11,415	5,390	29,146	184,981	92,154	114,958	84,280	476,373	505,519
Additions	0	2,468	358	2,826	78,749	33,106	41,435	(61,009)	92,281	95,107
Disposals	0	969	0	969	0	42	7,006	0	7,048	8,017
Purchase price	12,341	12,914	5,748	31,003	263,730	125,218	149,387	23,271	561,606	592,609
Appreciations	0	0	0	0	14,663	0	0	0	14,663	14,663
Balance at 31.12.1993	12,341	12,914	5,748	31,003	278,393	125,218	149,387	23,271	576,269	607,272
Depreciation:										
Balance at 1.1.1993	0	2,618	1,767	4,385	70,819	46,708	57,993	0	175,520	179,905
Additions	0	796	335	1,131	6,470	9,853	14,873	0	31,196	32,327
Disposals	0	290	0	290	0	42	5,680	0	5,722	6,012
Balance at 31.12.1993	0	3,124	2,102	5,226	77,289	56,519	67,186	0	200,994	206,220
Book value at 31.12.1993	12,341	9,790	3,646	25,777	201,104	68,699	82,201	23,271	375,275	401,052

The cash value of property at 1.1.1993 or later amounts to DKK 190.948 million.
The book value of mortgaged fixed assets in the parent company and the Group amounts to DKK 183.388 million.

7   Shares in subsidiaries

	Total	Purchase price	Acc. appreciation	Acc. depreciation
Book value at 1.1.1993	(12,841)	55.393	21,408	(89,642)
	0			0
Conversion of foreign currency, 1.1.1993	2.761		3,472	(711)
Capital infusion	16,969	16,969		
Realised revaluations on payment of dividends by subsidiaries	(41,857)		(31,066)	(10,791)
Profits of subsidiaries	54.843		31,735	23,108
Losses of subsidiaries	(10,097)		(9,092)	(1,005)
Total	9,778	72,362	16,457	(79,041)
Of which transferred to offset loans to and claims on subsidiaries	20.358			
Total	30.136			

Specified as follows:

	Book value at 31.12.1993 DKK '000	Result for the year DKK '000	Ownership
H. Lundbeck A/S, Sandvika, Norway	444	14	100%
H. Lundbeck AB, Helsingborg, Sweden	9,370	9,009	100%
OY H. Lundbeck AB, Åbo, Finland	1,092	3,542	100%
Lundbeck AS, Tartu, Estonia	7	0	100%
Lundbeck Pharma A/S, Copenhagen, Denmark	1,658	21,883	100%
Lundbeck Medimerc A/S, Copenhagen, Denmark	622	1,322	100%
A/S Lundbeck Export Division Ltd., Copenhagen, Denmark	5,095	6,788	100%
Lundbeck Limited, Milton Keynes, UK	10,144	(8,836)	100%
Lundbeck B.V., Amsterdam, The Netherlands	3,011	2,425	100%
Lundbeck N.V., Vilvoorde, Belgium	581	(499)	100%
Lundbeck S.A., Paris, France	(628)	1,012	100%
Lundbeck (Schweiz) AG, Zürich, Switzerland	3,153	2,425	100%
Lundbeck Italia S.p.A., Milan, Italy	284	(507)	100%
Lundbeck Arzneimittel G.m.b.H., Vienna, Austria	1,556	(256)	100%
Lundbeck South Africa (PTY) Limited, Ferndale, Randburg, South Africa	247	(44)	100%
Total	36,636	38,278	
Total group eliminations	(26,858)	6,468	
Book value at 31.12.1993 / result for the year	9,778	44,746	

Group eliminations primarily constitute eliminations
for activated rights and unrealised internal profits on stocks.

8   Shareholdings and other receivables

Parent company				Group	
Other share-holdings	Loans to subsidiaries	Receivables		Other share-holdings	Receivables
760	14,536	2,707	Book value at 1.1.1993	760	3,817
0	18,196	97	Additions/disposals during the year	0	659
760	32,732	2,804	Book value at 31.12.1993	760	4,476
760	32,732	2,804	Market value 31.12.1993	760	4,476

9   Securities

The item Securities includes an instrument of debt relating to the winding-up of a business area. The instrument has one year to maturity.

In 1993, financial income totalled DKK 48.045 million for the Group and DKK 47.908 million for the parent company, including DKK 3.869 million from Group-affiliated companies.

The financial income of the parent company includes realised capital gains of DKK 21.138 million.

In 1993, financial costs amounted to DKK 13.377 million for the Group and DKK 14.283 million for the parent company, including DKK 1.939 million attributable to Group-affiliated companies. Financial costs include the year's depreciation of unrealised capital losses at 31.12.1993 of DKK 0.614 million and realised capital losses of DKK 1.108 million.

10 Parent company's equity capital

	Share capital	Appreciation reserve	Non-distributed profit in subsidiaries	Extra reserve fund	Profit carried forward	Total
Equity capital at 1.1.1993	110,000	14,663	21,408	150,000	424,605	720,676
Conversion of foreign currencies			3,472		(711)	2,761
Dividends from subsidiaries			(31,066)		31,066	0
Profit for the year			22,644		14,922	37,566
Dividend for the year					(22,000)	(22,000)
Equity capital at 31.12.1993	110,000	14,663	16,458	150,000	447,882	739,003

11 Provision for deferred tax

Group	Balance at 1.1.1993	Conversion of foreign currencies	Movement in the year	Balance at 31.12.1993
Timing differences between accounting and tax statements				
Intangible and tangible fixed assets	92,719	2,833	43,803	139,355
Stocks	22,139		(1,816)	20,323
Other non-taxed reserves	27,468)	60	6,593	(20,815)
Total timing differences	87,390	2,893	48,580	138,863
Provision for deferred tax	31,589	793	16,034	48,416

The item Movement in the year includes provision for deferred tax relating to the calculated tax effect of the difference between the year's accounting and taxation statements. The timing differences are assessed as a net difference, as deferred tax is activated for foreign subsidiaries.

Parent company	Balance at 1.1.1993	Movements in the year	Balance at 31.12.1993
Timing differences between accounting and tax statements			
Intangible and tangible fixed assets	131,293	35,613	166,906
Stocks	22,139	(1,816)	20,323
Other non-taxed reserves	37,577)	4,068	(33,509)
Total timing differences	115,855	37,865	153,720
Provision for deferred tax	39,391	12,874	52,265

The item Movement in the year includes provision for deferred tax relating to the calculated tax effect of the difference between the year's accounting and tax statements.

12 Long-term mortgage debt

Of the Group's total long-term mortgage debt of DKK 65.852 million, DKK 54.902 million falls due after 5 years. The cash value of the mortgage debt amounts to DKK 67.477 million.

13 Contractual commitments

The parent company has assumed commitments amounting to DKK 36.6 million in the form of leasing contracts with special termination provisions, guarantee commitments and security commitments on behalf of subsidiaries. The subsidiaries have assumed commitments amounting to DKK 30.6 million, including pension commitments of DKK 0.2 million.

The Group has no further guarantee commitments apart from normal commercial delivery commitments.

Comments on the accounts

Growth in the period 1988-1993
The Lundbeck Group has undergone substantial change as a result of the expansion and focusing strategy defined in 1988. The comments below describe the trend in the Group's turnover and the "result of primary operations" in the period 1988-1993.

Net turnover
Since 1991, business interests etc. accounting for a total turnover of just

Net turnover
1988-1993 (DKK m)

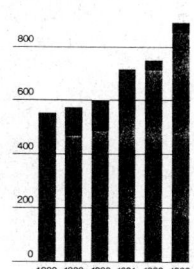

■ Present business activities

■ Business activities disposed of

▓ New markets

Currency conversion

The increase in turnover in the remainder of the company's product portfolio includes new markets in Europe, Asia and South America, which between them accounted for turnover of just under DKK 50 million in 1993.

Result before research costs and result of primary operations in the period 1988-1993
The trend in the Group's primary operating result from break-even in 1988 to DKK 30 million in 1993 is based on the following background:

Result of primary operations
1988-1993 (DKK m)

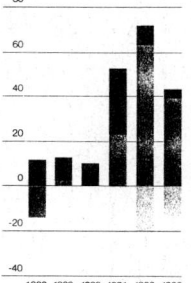

■ Present business activities

■ Business activities disposed of

▓ New markets

Currency conversion

The trend in the result of primary operations has also been strongly influenced by the increase in research costs from DKK 70 million in 1988 to almost three times that figure in 1993. Total research and development costs amounted to DKK 181 million in 1993, or 19% of turnover.

Thus, the continued modest level of profit has to be seen in the light of the significant expansion of the Group's market coverage, research

Result before research costs
1988-1993 (DKK m)

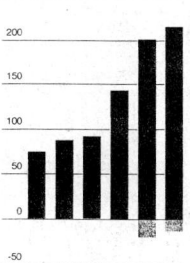

■ Present business activities

■ Business activities disposed of

▓ New markets

Currency conversion

under DKK 150 million have been sold. In addition, the annual turnover in low-return distribution products has been reduced during this period from just over DKK 50 million to less than DKK 20 million. In spite of this adjustment of the product range, overall growth of more than 60% has been achieved, from turnover of DKK 584 million in 1988 to DKK 934 million in 1993.

The increase in turnover of DKK 166 million between 1992 and 1993 is very largely attributable to the new antidepressant Cipramil® which, with sales of DKK 237 million, enjoyed growth of more than 100% in 1993. As in earlier years, the remaining products in the company's portfolio also achieved satisfactory growth, at 10%.

- Substantial operational investment in the establishment of new markets and the further development of existing markets. Expenditure on the establishment of new markets and the acquisition of a synthesis factory in the United Kingdom in 1993 had a DKK 20 million influence on the result in 1992 and DKK 13 million in 1993. In addition, product rights were purchased. These have been booked under other operating costs.

- There has also been significant investment in production capacity and new office and laboratory accommodation in recent years, with a consequential increase in annual depreciation. Depreciation was just under DKK 20 million higher in 1993 than in 1988.

and development, and production capacity.

Cancellation of distribution agreement/Extraordinary cost
With the aim of achieving improved control and monitoring of Lundbeck's distribution in the United Kingdom, a long-term cooperation with an external distributor was wound up in 1993.

The winding up of this distribution agreement had a DKK 13 million impact on the Group's primary operation result in 1993. In addition, in the preparation of the 1993 accounts, a provision of DKK 11 million has been made in relation to an obligation to buy back remaining inventory on 1st February 1994. This provision has been booked under extraordinary costs.

Provision for research project and movement relating to down-payments in 1993
In 1991, in connection with the signing of licence agreements for Sertindole in the USA and Japan, an amount was accrued to cover future obligations under two contracts. In 1993, DKK 7 million was applied. Thereafter, there remained a provision of DKK 12 million at 31st December 1993.

A major research project was initiated at the end of 1993. The project will be completed at the beginning of 1995. As the Group committed itself to the entire project in 1993, the entire contract sum was booked in that year. The total provision, which covers expected costs in 1994 and 1995, has had an impact of DKK 27 million on the operating result.

The sum of DKK 17 million was applied to a second project in 1993. The amount had been booked in the 1992 accounts. This project will be completed at the beginning of 1994.

Hereafter, at end-1993, the total accrued to cover future research costs was just over DKK 40 million.

The Danish Fund for Industrial Growth
In 1993, Lundbeck raised a loan from the Danish Fund for Industrial Growth for a promising project. However, the project had to be wound up at end-1993. In this connection, the Fund has written down the amount due to it under the project by DKK 2 million. The amount has been booked as income under primary operations.

Currency trends
The 1993 result was not influenced by the currency unrest during the year as the overwhelming proportion of the company's sales in foreign currencies had been hedged by end-1992.

No significant hedging of the company's sales of currency in 1994 had occurred by the end of 1993. This is because of the great uncertainty in relation to future exchange rates following the breakdown of the EMS in 1993. Hedging will be resumed when currency fluctuations have steadied to a normal situation.

Financial items
The financial result amounts to a net DKK 35 million, against DKK 23 million in 1992. The background to this

includes a reduction in interest-bearing funds as a result of a high level of investment. Interest income fell by DKK 4 million in 1993. Capital gains of DKK 21 million were realised on securities in 1993, compared with DKK 5 million in 1992, cf. note 9.

The year's taxation and result
After tax, the result for the year was DKK 38 million, which was on a par with 1992.

The just under DKK 16 million tax paid during the year resulted from deferred tax of DKK 17 million and a net repayment of approx. DKK 1 million. This is due partly to the favourable tax reversal rules in the United Kingdom, resulting in repayment of tax paid in previous years and partly to favourable Danish tax rules permitting the immediate write-off of certain capital investment in connection with research and development.

Statement of sources and application of funds

Fixed investment
There was again significant investment in fixed assets in 1993. In both 1992 and 1993 investment amounted to more than DKK 140 million. One of the biggest investments in fixed assets in 1993 was the purchase of the synthesis factory at Seal Sands in the United Kingdom, which accounted for a total of DKK 30 million in 1993. In addition, a research laboratory and a new tablet factory were established during the year. The total investment in these two projects in 1992 and 1993 combined was DKK 75 million.

Net self-finance
As a result of the high level of investment in fixed assets and the investment in new markets, research and development etc. charged as oper-

ating costs in both 1992 and 1993, there was a financing requirement - i.e. the liquidity contribution from operations less net investment in fixed assets - of approx. DKK 67 million in both years.

The financing requirement in 1993 was met by the raising of loans to a net value of DKK 24 million and the use of cash and securities totalling DKK 43 million.

Equity capital
At end-1993, equity capital amounted to DKK 739 million, equivalent to a solidity ratio of 63%.

A dividend of DKK 22 million will be paid to the company's shareholder, the Lundbeck Foundation.

Holdings of cash and securities
At 31st December 1993, in spite of the increase in operational and capital investment in recent years, Lundbeck continued to have cash and securities amounting to more than DKK 400 million, or 34% of total assets. If short and long-term interest-bearing debt is set against this sum, net liquidity is DKK 276 million, or 26% of the adjusted balance.

Because of its relatively modest borrowings, the Group has substantial potential to raise loans.

As expansion will continue in the years to come, controlled development of current and fixed assets is the means to secure the necessary financial resources.

Shareholders
In compliance with s.28A of the Danish Companies Act, it is stated that the Lundbeck Foundation, Ottilia-vej 9, DK-2500 Copenhagen-Valby, owns 100% of the share capital.

Proposed distribution of the parent company's profit of DKK 37,566,000:

	DKK '000
Result for the year	37,566
Dividend	22,000
Transfer to the company's reserves	15,566

Allocated as follows:

Transfer to "Account for undistributed profits of subsidiaries" in accordance with the book-value method	22,644
Transfer to "Account for transferred profit" (cf. note 10)	-7,078

·FRANCE

Jean-Claude Scheid
*Institut National des Techniques Economiques et Commerciales
(INTEC), Conservatoire Nationale des Arts et Métiers, France*

Peter Walton
Geneva University, Switzerland

1. Background

1.1 Introduction

The pace of change in French accounting was extremely fast in the 1980s, with the result that Anglo-Saxon perceptions of French accounting are frequently out of step with the reality. This is further compounded by a failure to recognize that the existence of a detailed set of regulations does not necessarily mean that (*a*) all those regulations are complied with in the normal course of business or (*b*) accountants do not think to go beyond these official requirements.

A modern capital market with an active supervisory body, a thriving and competitive multinational business, and a benevolent involvement by the state in supporting business provide an environment in which accounting has progressed rapidly, and standards of reporting and disclosure are high. The days of profit-smoothing, inconsistency of accounting policies and minimal disclosures are fading into the past, even if France did pass through that stage of development historically later than did Great Britain or the United States.

Inevitably the development of reporting in a jurisdiction is one of evolution, sometimes slow, sometimes taking sudden leaps. Accounting meets new challenges and finds new solutions, but usually the process involves grafting onto or modifying what has already been established, rather than scrapping the existing rules and starting again. A consequence is that an outsider taking an overview at any given moment will see a set of rules and regulations that may well be inconsistent and may appear convoluted and even illogical. A further complication is that accepted practice and existing regulations do not necessarily match exactly.

This chapter provides a guide through the French version of the regulatory labyrinth, and it seems useful to approach the subject with a brief analysis of the historical development of both accounting and business, in order to illustrate the evolution of reporting.

1.2 Accountants and Auditors

Whereas accounting as an essential feature of business activity first made its appearance in many Western countries in the nineteenth century, alongside the spread of the industrial revolution, in France accounting was introduced as a compulsory feature of business in 1673 by a law (known as the Savary law) that required traders to maintain daybooks of their business transactions and prepare an annual list of assets, as well as to keep copies of all letters.

In 1807 the Savary Law was incorporated into a Commercial Code, as French law was reorganized into Napoleonic codes. The next major reform of company law was in 1867, when the *Société Anonyme* (share-issuing company) was introduced and with it the profession of auditor (*Commissaire aux Comptes*).

It is a particular feature of the French professional accounting scene that the profession of auditor historically has been separate from that of accountant. Indeed, it is an apposite example of the complexity of France that there are today two quite distinct professional organizations, one for accountants and one for auditors, giving the impression of two separate professions. Nearly all auditors are also members of the accounting body, however.

In fact, diversity of organization has been a feature of the development of the profession. The first professional body, the *Société de Comptabilité de France* (SCF) was formed in 1881 and embraced everyone involved in accounting activity, classifying members as *teneurs de livres*, *comptables*, and *expert-comptables*, titles that have no exact English equivalent. The term *expert-comptable* has since become established as meaning the top tier of accounting professionals, excluding statutory auditors.

The SCF offered its own professional examinations at the three levels, but it was followed over the years by a large number of other accounting bodies that aimed to promote the interests of particular segments (geographic or technical or both) of the profession. The appearance of income tax on corporate profits in 1917 provided an extra stimulus to demand for accounting services. Most of these bodies offered their own examinations and the state even offered a State Accounting Diploma from 1927.

It was clear that some rationalization was necessary, and plans under consideration before the outbreak of the Second World War progressed during the Vichy government and gave rise to a 1945 government order that created the *Ordre des Experts Comptables et des Comptables Agréés* (OECCA) as it now exists.

The OECCA is a two-tier body, as a compromise gesture toward acknowledging the diversity of the bodies that it superseded. The *expert comptable* was distinguished by the right to draw up annual statements, while the *comptable agréé* ran the bookkeeping system. In practice, the distinctions were not so clear, and over the years since 1945 the profession of *comptable agréé* has declined; it was closed to new entrants in 1972.

Only members of the OECCA are allowed to call themselves *expert comptable* and provide specialist accounting services (OECCA pursues a policy of actively protecting this, bringing about a hundred cases a year before the courts against people who are offering the same services). Furthermore, only partners in an accounting practice or employees of a practice are eligible to be members. This means that someone leaving a firm to work in industry automatically loses his or her membership in the professional body. There is a body, the *Association des Directeurs de Comptabilité* (APDC), that brings together senior accounting executives from industry, but this organization has more the characteristics of a pressure group than a professional body. The bulk of accountants in commerce and industry have no formal professional representation.

Several different training routes exist, reflecting the diversity of qualifications offered by the public and private educational institutions in France. A student must, however, spend 3 years with a professional firm (a *cabinet*) and take the OECCA professional examinations. The final part of the process consists of writing a dissertation on which the candidate is also given an oral examination. Currently more than one thousand students a year gain their *diplôme d'expertise comptable*, and approximately four thousand students are on training contracts with firms.

Accounting firms have seen a rapid expansion in the past 30 years, with some concentration of activity in the hands of large firms (although not on a scale comparable with the United States or the United Kingdom) and (discreet) linkages by some of the firms with the international networks of the Anglo-American firms.

The development of auditing has taken a rather different line, as may be symbolized by the fact that accounting comes under the jurisdiction of the Ministry of the Economy, while auditing is under the Ministry of Justice.

The statutory auditor, as envisaged by French company law in 1867, was required to make a report to the annual general meeting on the company's situation and on the balance sheet presented by the company's directors. The function, though, could be carried out by anyone.

The position changed in 1935, when a major reform took place. The task of the auditor was extended to one of verifying the books and assets of the company and the information given by the directors, as well as making a report to the shareholders. An auditor was always to be appointed for a 3-year period. At the same time, the equivalent of the county courts were given the duty of establishing a list of official auditors, consisting of those who had passed a state examination. From this point on, auditors had a strongly regional base, and although they formed professional associations, these associations tended to parallel the regional basis of the courts.

The next major reform in auditing occurred in the late 1960s. In 1966, auditors' role was widened and their fees fixed in relation to the size of clients, and a new professional organization, the *Compagnie Nationale des Commissaires aux Comptes* (CNCC) was formed in 1969. In particular, auditors were required from 1966 to make a report giving their opinion on the individual accounts of SAs (*Société Anonyme*) and SARLs (*Société à Responsibilité Limitée*). They were required to certify (or not) the *regularité* of the accounts (conforming with legal requirements) and their *sincerité* (application of accepted valuation methods in good faith). At that time, many auditors feared that their role would become quasi-judicial, being required to assess other people's accounts, but as events turned out, the CNCC progressively has developed the audit function down the lines of Anglo-American practice and issues regular auditing guidelines on much the same basis.

Nonetheless, the role of the auditor and, in particular, what is understood by "sincerity" and "regularity" in the accounts has been open to question. In the 1970s there were a number of fairly spectacular audit failures, such as Creusot-Loire, where companies went into liquidation after several years of showing either small profits or a zero result. Increasing losses had been masked by transfers from reserves and changes in accounting policy, all of which were certified as "sincere and regular." It was felt that the auditor was obliged to give a positive certificate if individually all the transactions were sanctioned by the law or conformed with established practice, even if taken altogether the effect was to give a misleading picture of the company as a whole.

Since 1984, when the EC Fourth Directive was implemented in France, French companies also have been obliged to give a true and fair view of the state of affairs of the company, and this is believed to have led to auditors approaching matters differently. One should, however, be wary of assuming that the French auditor now automatically has the same reaction as an Anglo-Saxon auditor. For example, where a company normally charges accelerated depreciation for tax purposes in its individual accounts (see Section 2.2) and in a poor year decides only to charge economic depreciation, this would not be regarded as worthy of mention.

1.3 Accounting, Business, and the State

There is a popular misconception that French accounting is heavily controlled by the state (this is often paralleled by another misconception, that the state does not intervene in accounting in the Anglo-American world). This idea probably derives from misunderstanding a long tradition of centralization in France and one of seeking state endorsement to lend authority. This is compounded by the idea that French enterprise accounting is designed to create inputs for a national accounting system through which the government controls the economy. In fact, the enterprise accounting arrangements predate the national accounting arrangements, and attempts to reconcile the two have largely failed. Having said that, however, it should be made clear that INSEE, the state statistical office, does collect and aggregate the financial statements of enterprises, thereby producing useful statistics about industry sectors, margins, and so on, even if they do not fit neatly into the national accounting system used for economic measurement. The major state impact on accounting rather has been through the impact of taxation and the requirement that all expenses claimed for tax purposes should appear in the shareholder accounts.

Insofar as it is acceptable to generalize, the French state, since the Second World War, has taken an interventionist stance with industry, but this has usually been with a view to promoting or protecting industry, providing, for example, grants for research and development and accelerated tax allowances for investment.

In the period between the World Wars, successive French governments took a *laissez-faire* attitude to industry, and the economy was stagnant during that period. Industry was polarized between a small number of quite large concerns and a multitude of small, family businesses. After the collapse of France in the Second World War, a reaction blamed military failure on economic weakness, and economic weakness on the lack of initiative of French industry. It was resolved that after the war the economy would be revitalized, but through the leadership of the state.

France, influenced by Jean Monnet, a prominent political figure who was also influential in the creation of the European Community, started on a succession of 5-year economic plans designed to rebuild the economy in partnership with the private sector, to create an *économie concertée*, where public and private investment worked together. At the same time, the state nationalized a large slice of the economy. It was decided that a uniform accounting system should be installed in the nationalized industries to make management control easier, and such a system would also be compulsory for all bodies receiving grant aid from the state (a draft system had been prepared during the War under the Vichy government but had been abandoned). A commission was established (*Commission de Normalisation de la Comptabilité*, 1946) to prepare the new system. The Commission consisted of civil servants, senior accountants, auditors, business people, lawyers, academics, and others, a grouping typical of the many committees set up under Monnet's influence to deal with particular issues of rebuilding the economy.

This Commission produced in 1947 its Plan Comptable Général (PCG), a chart of accounts that provided a system of ledger codes and annual statements that should emerge from the records kept in this way. What then happened was that, over a period of many years, private industry gradually adopted the PCG voluntarily, until the tax authorities (the *Fisc*) adopted it as the basis for tax returns in 1965, after which it was used by practically all enterprises.

There have been many further developments. The Commission changed its name to the *Conseil National de la Comptabilité* (CNC, National Accounting Council). The PCG was revised in 1957, largely to go some way toward meeting the needs of the national accounting system, which had been introduced progressively since 1952. From 1959 the CNC was given the task of preparing industry-specific variants of the basic 1957 plan, and from that time it can be judged as spreading eventually to all French industry.

In fact, a key period of change for French industry occurred in the late 1960s. Company law underwent a major revision in 1966, including the revision of the audit function and the introduction into the law of definitions of the form and content of the balance sheet and profit and loss account (albeit without any direct reference to the PCG1957) and more precise details of what other information should be included in annual reports to shareholders.

This was accompanied by reform in the capital markets, including in 1967 the creation of a stock exchange regulatory authority, the *Commission des Opérations de Bourse* (COB), which has since been quite influential in pressing for better accounting and disclosure. At the same time, management attitudes were also changing: the first contested takeover bid. was made, and there were the strikes of 1968. The old attitudes of secrecy started to change, and managers began to perceive that it was necessary to inform both workers and shareholders about what was going on.

Since 1945 companies having more than 50 workers had been obliged to have a *Comité d'Entreprise*, a workers' council, whose rights were extended at this time to include receiving management reports. From 1965 the CNC started to issue guidance on numerous points of interpretation and amplification of the PCG1957, by way of notes or recommendations. At the same time, the OECCA also started to issue technical guidance, thus creating to some extent competition between the two organizations.

Starting in 1968, the COB asked quoted companies to give more information either in prospectuses issued when raising funds or in the annual reports sent to shareholders. Such information concerned primarily further detail of elements of the balance sheet and profit and loss account and was asked for in the form of notes to the accounts.

It was also in the late 1960s and early 1970s that companies themselves began to prepare and publish consolidated accounts on a voluntary basis and using a wide range of accounting policies. An important development from a user perspective was the appearance of "secondary" reports, voluntary disclosures often framed in English and giving consolidated figures that were intended as public relations documents both for the international capital markets and for international business generally.

The COB made it a requirement in 1971 to produce consolidated accounts as part of the prospectus when raising funds, and from 1973 it was required that such accounts be audited.

1.4 European Harmonization

The 1980s were a period of substantial change for French accounting, seeing the introduction of both the Fourth and Seventh Directives. Plans to revise the PCG had been held back by a desire to introduce a new version in line with European Union harmonization initiatives, and the new plan was first exposed in 1979, after final approval of the Fourth Directive by the Council of Ministers. The new plan (PCG1982) was published in its final form in 1982, to be followed by the Accounting Act of April 1983 (Act 83 353 of April 30, 1983) and the Decree of November 29, 1983, providing for implementation of the Fourth European Directive for the accounting year 1984.

Part of the particularity of the system is that the Accounting Act and implementing decree make barely any mention of the PCG1982, although much of the detailed accounting implementation, standard ledger codes, and their relationship with the annual statements, and so on, are contained in the PCG1982. The accounting law and decree introduced into the legal framework the requirements of the Fourth Directive: standard formats for the profit and loss account and balance sheet, explanatory notes to the accounts (*annexe*), and an overall obligation to give a true and fair view (*image fidèle*). An Act of March 1, 1984 extended the audit requirement to all enterprises classified as medium or large and introduced a requirement that the auditor be presented with forecasts, which were not submitted to shareholders but were shown to the Comité d'*Entreprise*. Company law required that managers provide accounts that give a true and fair view— and provided penal sanctions in the event that they failed to do this.

The Seventh Directive was implemented through an Act of January 3, 1985 and a Decree of February 17, 1986, requiring listed companies to produce consolidated accounts from 1986 and unlisted companies to do so from the accounting year 1990. The PCG82 was modified (December 9, 1986) to include rules for consolidated statements.

A number of particularities about the way in which the Directives were implemented in France will be considered in detail below. However, two main points need to be borne in mind. First, the requirements to show all deductions to be claimed for tax purposes remained in force for individual company accounts, but consolidated accounts do not have to be in line with tax regulations, and companies are free to restate the individual figures for inclusion in group accounts.

Second, group accounts do not necessarily have to comply with French generally accepted accounting principles (GAAP). Companies that operate in other markets are free to produce group accounts using the GAAP of the appropriate market (Act of January 3, 1985). In effect this means that where, for example, a French multinational was already producing two sets of accounts, one set of individual accounts complying with tax regulations and submitted formally to shareholders for approval and the other based on U.S. GAAP for international business purposes, the U.S. GAAP accounts could become the official group accounts: no French GAAP group accounts need be prepared. Consequently, a number of French companies (e.g., Peugeot) publish group accounts based on U.S. GAAP, and a number of companies use International Accounting Standards (e.g., Thomson).

1.5 Business Finance

France has a tradition of family businesses, and although this image is changing, notably with the enormous growth of old family businesses such as Peugeot, Bouygues, and Bic, companies often seek to finance themselves through debt rather than equity funding. It is not, therefore, unusual to see companies that have only bonds quoted on the Bourse. This tendency is further reinforced by nationalized industries that make major borrowings on the public market. The State does not wish to subscribe new share capital, and such companies as Electricité de France, Renault, and the SNCF (French railways) are frequent and major issuers of bonds.

Further, the State itself is a regular borrower on the capital markets for its own financing needs. It holds a weekly auction of Treasury bonds with the banks, as well as making large public issues from time to time with varying conditions attached, and such government securities are quite actively traded. All of this goes to explain why turnover in bonds on the stock exchanges is 10 times that of shares.

Since the beginning of the 1980s, however, the French financial markets have undergone a number of important changes. First, the nationalized industries (whose number increased significantly in 1982 with the nationalizations carried out after the election of President Mitterand in 1981) wished to increase their equity without issuing any new shares, leading to the creation of new equity instruments:

- The *titre participatif* (certificate of participation), which gives a dividend payout that varies with the success of the company, albeit with a minimum dividend, is not repaid except if the issuer wishes to redeem it and carries no voting rights.
- The *certificat d'investissement* (investment certificate) is a straightforward ordinary share except that it does not carry any voting rights

These are bound up in voting certificates (*certificat de droit de vote*), which are themselves separately quoted on the Bourse.

There are also new financial instruments, such as floating rate bonds, redeemable bonds, renewable bonds, and convertible bonds with various types of warrant attached. A considerable variety of instruments now exist, situated on a spectrum between debt and equity.

A second development is the creation of new markets to deal in new types of financial instruments:

- Share options (*marché d'options négociables de Paris*, or MONEP)
- Financial futures: interest rates, fixed term contracts, options, future rate agreements (*marché à terme des instruments financiers*, or MATIF)
- Index funds: options on the CAC40 index of the 40 top listed shares (part of MONEP)

France has seven provincial stock exchanges (Nantes, Nancy, Lille, Bordeaux, Toulouse, Lyon, and Marseilles), as well as the Paris Bourse, but the last is by far the most active and has both a senior market and a junior market *(Second Marché)*. The French financial markets have become the most active in Europe after London.

A particular phenomenon of the late 1980s was the arrival of medium-sized family businesses on the market, looking either for a quotation on the *Second Marché* or to be taken over because of the absence of a management successor within the family. There is an active market in such businesses, which, although not obvious, has as much economic significance as the few large public takeover bids that receive substantial press coverage in France and abroad.

The banking sector has undergone a number of changes during the 1980s, with nationalization in 1982, followed by some privatization in 1987, as well as large scale changes in banking regulation in 1984 and 1986. The commercial banking scene is a mixture of retail banks and smaller specialist banks. The retail banks include some that started as mutual banks (e.g., Crédit Agricole, Banque Populaire) and some that have always been commercial (Société Générale, Banque Nationale de Paris, Crédit Lyonnais), though some have been under state control for many years. The private banks, which may, like Indosuez, have substantial international connections, often specialize in loans to industry without offering any clearing or similar retail services. The banks are an important source of financing, particularly to small and medium-sized companies, and some have strong regional and industry bases (particularly the mutual organizations). Large companies typically maintain banking ties with a number of different banks at the same time.

A right-wing government came to power in 1993 and has set about reducing the state's holdings in commercial businesses. In a major privatization program it has sold stakes in Banque Nationale de Paris, Elf Aquitaine, Rhône Poulenc and insurance group UAP. It plans to sell its shares in more problematic holdings such as Crédit Lyonnais and Bull Computers. The privatization program has generated a great deal of interest from private buyers.

1.6 State of Play in the Mid-1990s

We have given an idea of the development of accounting in France and in this section will pull together a number of strands and present a sketch of the overall accounting environment as it exists today.

The first point to make is that the law is the paramount authority, and that different sources of law (act of parliament, decree, government order) have different priorities in relation to each other, so not all incorporated entities are necessarily subject to exactly the same legal requirements (for example, banks are theoretically subject to the Accounting Act and Decree but do not have to comply because there are specific laws concerning banks). Equally, there are statutes that apply to accounting, to company management, and to taxation, all of which may have an impact on reporting.

Looking first at legal types of business entity, five legal forms are considered to be "commercial" to which the Commercial Code applies: *Société Anonyme* (SA, a public, share-issuing company), *Société à Responsibilité Limitée* (SARL, normally described as a private company but by contrast with American or British private companies does not issue shares as such; modeled on the German *Gesellschaft mit beschrankter Haftung*, or GmbH), *Société en Commandite par actions* (SCA, a sort of limited partnership and not much used now, although this was the earliest form of incorporation to exist in France—Michelin is incorporated in this form), *Société en nom collectif*, and *Société en commandite simple*. There are also corporate forms outside the Commercial Code, the most important being the *Société Civile* (SC, which is in Anglo-Saxon terms a cross between a partnership and a limited company, members' liabilities for the company's obligations are limited only in proportion to the individual member's interest) and the *Etablissement Public à activité Industrielle et Commerciale* (EPIC, a business with profit-making objectives but 100% state control, e.g., Renault, SNCF, EDF).

Government statistics show that at the beginning of 1992 there were the following entities:

Form	Total (in thousands)
Unincorporated	1,674
SARL	631
SA	169
1901 Associations	192
Sociétés Civiles	297
Others	335
	3,298

It should be said that the system for compiling the above figures is thought to be accurate for recording new entities becoming active but suspect in identifying those that have ceased to exist: it probably overstates the number of entities, perhaps by as much as 10%.

Starting in 1983, the following legal instruments affecting accounting were passed:

- Act 83-353 of April 30, 1983 to harmonize the accounting requirements for "commercial" entities and some other corporate bodies with the Fourth Directive
- Decree 83-1020 of November 29, 1983, which set out the details of how the Accounting Act 83-353 should be applied
- Decree 84-184 of March 14, 1984, which recognized the previous instruments as providing accounting definitions that were to be applied in tax law
- Act 84-148 of March 1, 1984, on the prevention and regulation of business difficulties (which extended the accounting obligations to all legal bodies constituted under private law, as opposed to public law, which have a business activity but are not classified as "commercial")
- Decree 85-295 of March 1, 1985, which set out the method of application of Act 84-148
- Act 85-11 of January 3, 1985, to harmonize requirements for consolidated accounts for certain commercial companies and public enterprises with the Seventh Directive
- Decree 86-221 of February 17, 1986, which applied Act 85-11

It is likely that users will most frequently be concerned with the accounts of an SA or SARL, but it is possible that they will meet an SC (frequently used as a vehicle for professional firms and also for property companies) or even an EPIC. Generally, the Fourth Directive accounting requirements and the statutory audit requirement apply to all "commercial" entities (incorporated or not but subject to the different levels of disclosure provided in the Directive) and noncommercial entities that exceed two of three size criteria (balance sheet 4 million francs (Fr), Turnover Fr 8 million, employees 250). They also apply to banks and insurance companies, but these are subject to other specific legislation in addition, which may override some of the more general requirements.

In addition to statutory requirements of one sort or another, the main sources of accounting regulation are the CNC (PCG1982 and guidance notes and recommendations on particular issues), COB (regulations for listed companies), OECCA, and CNCC (professional guidance). The accounts preparer in fact has a maze of potential regulations to wade through and assess to determine whether or not the regulations apply to a particular business. This may help make more understandable the notion of a specialist accounting body. At the same time, there are a number of professional guides, notably *Memento Comptable Francis Lefebvre*, which publishes annual GAAP handbooks detailing the regulations and their sources on an issue-by-issue basis. These handbooks are a convenient and useful tool for anyone wanting to look at some point in detail.

In general, accounting harmonization has been taken seriously, and the attitudes behind harmonization of greater disclosure and more reliable information for the capital markets have coincided with changes in the French business environment. In some ways (for example, the extension of reporting requirements beyond the SA and SARL specified by the Fourth Directive) France has gone well beyond the minimum requirements. Nonetheless, the revised requirements have been part of a period of enormous change in the capital markets, and there is still a relatively wide diversity of attitude and, indeed, measurement technique, which may well disappear as accountants become accustomed to the new approaches and a new consensus emerges on various issues.

A particular feature of the French scene is that there is a complex web of legislation or quasi-legislation, but the existence of the regulation does not necessarily mean that companies comply with it. Sometimes there are no penalties for nonobservance, sometimes there is no machinery to police compliance, and sometimes there appears to be a tacit agreement that some regulations will simply be ignored.

For example, the 1983 Accounting Act and Decree specifies in considerable detail what information is to be given in the notes to the accounts. The CNC, however, under pressure from the auditing body, subsequently took the position that all this information needed to be disclosed only if it was material. This position was confirmed by an Order of December 9,

1986 (the main focus of which was consolidated accounts), even though there is no established concept of materiality in French accounting.

Similarly, the statutes require disclosure in the notes of the remuneration of the directors, but the CNCC took the position (Bulletin Trimestriel, December 1986, p. 446) that "information on remuneration is by nature not material" and left it to the individual auditor to decide if the information might be material to the reader in any particular case.

2. The Form and Content of Published Accounts

An analyst approaching a set of French financial statements will need to check thoroughly the basis on which the accounts have been prepared— the first port of call must be the accounting policies because of the choices that are open to preparers. Broadly, an analyst could expect to have available in the annual report of a French group (*a*) the parent company ("individual") accounts, framed according to the Fourth Directive and the 1983 Accounting Act and Decree, and (*b*) group accounts (only from 1990 onward if the company is not listed), which might have been prepared on one of three bases. These bases are (*a*) same measurement rules as the individual accounts, therefore including, for instance, tax depreciation; (*b*) options available within the French GAAP group rules to restate the figures disregarding tax rules; and (*c*) U.S. GAAP, or those of some other financial market.

Majority practice is that French groups use version (*b*), French GAAP without the tax distortion—a recent survey of published accounts,[1] which reviewed the published accounts of 100 listed companies (for fiscal 1992) found that 36 referred to non-French GAAP, of which 22 cited International Accounting Standards Committee (IASC) standards, 9 U.S .GAAP, and 5 "international" GAAP.

We will present below two sets of accounts, group accounts based on option (*b*) and individual accounts so that readers have the opportunity to review both. We will deal with the French GAAP measurement rules used in group accounts in the next section but point out where individual accounts diverge significantly from these. We do not believe that it would serve any purpose to review measurement rules based on U.S. GAAP, since users may well be familiar with U.S. GAAP, but in any event there is plenty of literature available on the subject.

2.1 Group Accounts

The accounts used are those of Pernod Ricard, the drinks group, ranked 164th in size in Europe by market capitalization (*The Financial Times* FT500 January 20, 1994) and easily within the top 50 in France. It has operations not only in Western Europe but also in the United States and Australia. Its major non-French companies are Austin Nichols in the United States, Orlando Wyndham in Australia, and Irish Distillers. Its major brands include, apart from Pernod and Ricard, Cinzano, Cognac Bisquit, Jameson Irish Whisky, Bushmills, Wild Turkey Bourbon, Jacob's Creek wine, and Orangina. Of its 1992 turnover 54% was from outside France.

Following our own advice, we will look first at the note on accounting policies, which is reproduced at the end of this chapter. The first statement confirms that the group accounts conform with the group accounting legislation, and although the note does not specify that the accounts are framed in accordance with French GAAP (as opposed to IASC or U.S. standards), this would be the normal assumption.

Looking at specific details, it seems that the company uses 50% ownership of voting shares of "effective control" as the criteria for inclusion of a company as a subsidiary. A joint venture (L'Igloo) is accounted for by using proportional consolidation, while the equity method is used where the group has a "sizable interest." Foreign currency translation has been done on the net investment basis (balance sheets translated at closing rate, exchange differences taken to reserves), with the average rate used for the income statements. Exchange differences arising on loans in foreign currency, where the loans were used to acquire a foreign subsidiary (Irish Distillers), have been taken to reserves.

Taking the intangible asset note with the goodwill note, goodwill arising on consolidation before 1987 has been written off against reserves, while goodwill arising on subsequent acquisitions is being amortized over a period "appropriate to the acquisition but not exceeding forty years." The amortization expense is disclosed as a separate item after tax in the consolidated income statement, which complies with a COB recommendation (October 1988) that goodwill expense be separately disclosed in this way. An extraordinary items note shows a further Fr 92m of goodwill depreciation). Goodwill is calculated after allocating the excess of acquisition cost over book value to acquired assets and, in particular, to brands. The intangibles in the balance sheet (excluding goodwill, which is disclosed separately on the balance sheet, and after tangible fixed assets) amount to Fr 2140 million in 1992. They consist mostly of brands and trademarks and are held at "original cost" and depreciated only if market value drops below cost.

The notes indicate that tangible fixed assets are carried at historical cost or valuation where that is in accordance with legal dispositions. The effect of the latter is likely to be minimal because the last "legal" revaluation in France was in 1976. The note points out that real estate assets held under finance leases have been capitalized. This is a possibility under French group accounting rules but not a requirement as such. The company does not, however, disclose in its notes whether other leased assets have been capitalized, and one must assume not, which seems rather inconsistent. There is no disclosure of what value of real estate is held under finance leases, nor what proportion of the company's debt is in the form of leasing. The only additional information given is the commitment to rental payments (note 13).

The note analyzing the tangible fixed assets (note 6) gives relatively little information, confining itself to a breakdown of gross cost and accumulated depreciation with the previous year's net figure for comparison. There is no reconciliation between opening and closing fixed assets, no detail of acquisitions and disposals, and no indication of the depreciation charge for the year. The income statement format was changed in 1992 to approximate to a disclosure of expenses by function, and there is therefore no disclosure of depreciation expense for the year.

The consolidated statements themselves comprise:

1. Income statement

2. Balance sheet

3. Changes in shareholders' equity (voluntary disclosure)

4. Changes in financial position (not required for shareholders; however, many French companies publish it voluntarily: the 1993 survey found that 88% of the sample included a funds flow statement)

The income statement is set out in vertical format, based loosely on the functional approach. This represents a change from previous years, when the presentation was more in line with that used in individual statements in France, showing the nature of expenditure (e.g., employment, raw materials, external services). The 1983 Accounting Act and Decree allows only a horizontal format and expenses disclosed by nature, but the full Fourth Directive range of vertical or horizontal formats and expenses either by function or by nature are available for group accounts. Note 4 gives some details of the change although does not restate the 1992 figures to reconcile with the previous presentation. Another particularity is that the interest expense is shown net, although the European Directives, and indeed French custom, do not allow offset of revenues and expenses. There is no note to amplify the interest expense figure. The group's share of the profits of associated companies should normally also be included in this section of the income statement, but instead it appears after deduction of taxes.

There is a legal requirement that any French company (this applies to individual companies, not the group as such) having more than 100 employees should have a profit-sharing scheme for employees, and the deduction for employees' share of profits is usually shown as an appropriation; however, Pernod Ricard has attributed this in the 1992 group accounts to employment costs.

In France, gains and losses on disposals of fixed assets are normally treated as being outside the ordinary operating result, regardless of the nature of the disposal. The notes show extraordinary items of gains of Fr 163m after tax on asset sales. The note does not make clear where this item appears in the income statement, but there is an "exceptional items" line that one must assume includes this figure. The confusion is compounded by the fact that the French word for extraordinary is *exceptionnel*.

The English language balance sheet and income statement include an extra column, which gives the 1992 figures converted to U.S. dollars. This is a "convenience translation," which simply converts all the French franc numbers to dollars at the average rate for 1992 (income statement) and closing rate (balance sheet) and is intended presumably for the use of those more accustomed to thinking in terms of dollars—it does not imply the use of U.S. GAAP, even though some other French companies do restate to U.S. GAAP.

The balance sheet follows broadly the standard PCG82/Fourth Directive format of a horizontal presentation, with assets on the left, set out in reverse order of liquidity. At the same time, goodwill is presented after tangible fixed assets and not with other intangibles, as noted above, and the final asset entries (accrued income and prepaid expense, currency translation adjustment) are specific to the French adaptation of the Fourth Directive. Pernod Ricard has included here all its *comptes de régularisation* (there is no direct English version, the nearest being perhaps "suspense account") into which it has put not only prepayments but also deferred charges that may be carried forward over more than one year. This is set out in more detail in the parent company accounts. There is a corresponding account in the liabilities and equity side of the balance sheet for deferred credits and accruals.

The right-hand side of the balance sheet shows equity before deduction of the final dividend *(avant répartition)*, which is the correct procedure in terms of legal requirements. Many companies also show the situation after attribution of dividend *(après répartition)*, but this is a voluntary disclosure.

Pernod Ricard has translated *provisions pour risques et charges* as "provisions for contingencies" and includes a breakdown between pensions and other contingencies in the notes—there is no other breakdown. The deferred tax provision is shown separately; it is calculated on the accrual method.

The information given on debt is minimal—note 11 breaks this down by repayment term, which is all the French requirements call for and gives no indication of the split among leasing, bank loans, market securities, and so on. There is no breakdown at all of short-term liabilities: the balance sheet gives trade and other accounts payable of Fr 2,908 million and other liabilities of Fr 687 million.

The company issued undated subordinated notes (TSDI, *titres subordinés à durée indeterminée*) during 1992, a form of hybrid capital instrument that is not clearly debt or equity (see note 12). These have been classified in the group balance sheet as debt.

There follows a statement of changes in equity, showing the progression over the 2 years. However, there is no information in the notes or on the face of the balance sheet to give details of how equity is made up—

shares in issue, share premium, etc. For more information, one is obliged
to look in the parent company accounts.

The statement of changes in financial position (*tableau de financement*)
follows broadly the U.S. cash flow statement. This provides an operating
cash flow derived by using the indirect method (reported profit with add
backs of noncash items), followed by details of investing activities, financing activities, and net change in cash. This is in line with the OECCA
recommendation.

Precise details are given of the name and location of all subsidiaries
(legal requirement), but segment information is limited in French regulations to turnover by major product and geographic area, in line with the
Fourth Directive. The 1993 survey found (p. 130) that 95% of its sample
published segment information but 35 companies disclosed more than just
turnover information. Pernod Ricard gives a breakdown that goes through
to net profit, split four ways between wines and spirits in France and sold
outside France, and nonalcoholic beverages in France and sold outside
France. In some ways, this is useful in that it allows a matrix analysis
(usually companies provide product breakdown and geographic breakdown separately so that it is not possible to identify sales of one product
line in one geographic area), but it is also limited in that it lumps every-
thing outside France into one segment, whereas it is likely that if one
applied IAS14 rules, there would be several more geographic segments,
including Ireland, the United States, and Australia, in each of which the
group has major subsidiaries. The company does, though, identify the
main manufacturing locations and trademarks used around the world. No
information is given on net assets used, so no computation of comparative
return on capital employed is possible.

2.2 Individual Accounts

Whereas there is little of interest in terms of evaluating the group to be
found in the individual accounts, in general these statements comply with
the Accounting Act and Decree of 1983 and the Fourth Directive and are
therefore an illustration of the different presentation used for single companies.

The balance sheet is more detailed than the version used for the consolidated accounts. It gives an analysis of fixed assets among land, buildings,

plant, and other items, although the analyst would have to do a little work to reintegrate the information given in note 2 (acquisitions and disposals) with that in note 3 (depreciation). The *comptes de régularisation* (after current assets) are spelled out in more detail, giving a split among prepayments, deferred expenses, and translation differences.

The equity section is given in much more detail than in the group accounts, although there is still no note to give details of shares in issue, etc. The detailed components are explained in Section 3.

2.3 Income Statement

The income statement is presented in vertical form (both vertical and horizontal are permitted) but gives expenses by nature (the French have not implemented the option of giving expenses by function for individual accounts, the majority British practice). This contrasts with the new presentation used for the group accounts. The income statement can be broken down, as the Fourth Directive requires, into (*a*) operating income and expense, (*b*) financial income and expense, (*c*) extraordinary items, and (*d*) taxation.

The extraordinary items section represents some difficulties for analysis. Depreciation that is in excess of economic depreciation but that is charged to reduce taxation is expensed here. In addition, French tax law permits the establishment of some special reserves (which are basically tax incentives); they too appear in this section, as do profits and losses on sales of nonfinancial assets, regardless of the nature of the underlying transaction.

A peculiarity of the Pernod Ricard accounts is that only one figure is given for extraordinary income and one for extraordinary expense, with no breakdown. This would make life quite difficult if the analyst were using these accounts rather than the group accounts.

In the balance sheet the company's undated subordinated notes are shown as a separate line item between equity and debt. In the French balance sheet this is *autres fonds propres*, a special category in the French balance sheet that is generally used for complex capital instruments (e.g., perpetual loans, nonvoting shares).

In general terms, the Pernod Ricard accounts are typical of what an analyst might expect to find—detailed disclosures in some areas (e.g., financial investments, subsidiary companies) and little in others (e.g., movements on fixed assets, borrowings). In fairness, however, it should be pointed out that there are a significant number of companies whose disclosures go well beyond this.

3. Measurement Policies: Implications for the Analyst

3.1 Group Accounts

The history of group accounting in France has been one of diversity, in the absence of any formal group accounting requirement. Companies preparing group accounts have largely done so on a voluntary basis and have therefore adopted accounting principles that seemed useful to them. The 1986 consolidation requirements specified rules for consolidation but at the same time gave companies the freedom to use rules acceptable in other financial markets. Research evidence so far suggests that the majority of companies that have published group accounts since 1986 are converging on the 1986 rules. Analysts should check the accounting policy notes for clarification.

The 1986 rules specify that all companies over which the parent company has exclusive control should be included as subsidiaries. Exclusive control may be determined by (*a*) direct or indirect majority voting power; (*b*) direct or indirect voting power of 40% of the votes if no other partner or shareholder holds a higher percentage; (*c*) controlling influence as a result of a management or other agreement (provided that the parent has a share of the capital). Subsidiaries whose activities are significantly different from those of the parent may be accounted for by the equity method.

Associates, where the parent has significant influence (normally deemed to occur with a holding of 20% or more) should be accounted for by the equity method. Joint ventures, however, are accounted for by using proportional consolidation. A joint venture is defined as a business run by a limited number of associates in such a way that decisions are taken in common.

Subsidiaries are accounted for on an acquisition basis, and any excess of purchase consideration over book value of the acquired subsidiary should be allocated in the first instance to the individual assets and liabilities acquired. Any unallocated balance is capitalized as goodwill and should be amortized on a regular basis.

Actual practice on the treatment of goodwill is becoming quite uniform. The 1993 survey of the published accounts of 100 listed companies gave the following figures:

Of the 97 companies that amortize, the useful life was:

No. of Companies	Life (years)
3	0–10
31	11–20
55	21–40
8	Not disclosed

In recent years there has emerged a tendency to write off goodwill over a longer period and also to allocate a larger amount to specific intangible assets such as trademarks, market share, and brands and treat these as nondepreciable.

3.2 Foreign Currency Translation

Translation of the statements of foreign subsidiaries, since it only arises from group accounting, has not been an issue in France, and many different variants are to be found. The 1986 rules do not specify any particular methodology. Some researchers suggest that majority practice is to use closing rate for translating the balance sheet, with differences taken into equity, and average rate for the income statement. Analysts should check the policy note carefully on this point.

There are, however, detailed rules for the treatment of individual transactions, and these rules give rise to some of the long-term deferred charges and credits seen in the Pernod Ricard balance sheet. Unsettled monetary assets and liabilities denominated in a foreign currency must be restated to their closing value at each balance sheet date. Where this results in an exchange gain, the gain is posted as a long-term deferred credit and released when the account is settled. Where translation results in an exchange loss, there are four entries to be made: the original account is adjusted and the equal and opposite entry is as a deferred charge in the balance sheet; at the same time a balance sheet provision is created, with a corresponding debit to the income statement (but there are five exceptions to creating a provision in that case). Analysts should adjust the balance sheet by offsetting the deferred charge against provisions.

There are no rules for the conversion of individual sale or purchase transactions and the *Memento Comptable Francis Lefebvre* takes the view that items may be translated at the rate used as the basis for negotiations, the rate ruling on the day the order was passed, the rate ruling at the time of invoice, or the rate ruling when the invoice was accounted for.

3.3 Capital and Reserves

The definition of equity (*capitaux propres*) includes some elements that would be classified differently in other jurisdictions, and within equity the PCG82 distinguishes a figure (*situation nette*), which excludes these items. The plan calls for disclosure of equity in the following way:

> Nominal share capital
> Share premium
> Revaluation reserve
> Other reserves:
>> Legal
>> Contractual
>> Regulated capital gains
>> Others
> Retained profits
> Profit and loss for the year
> Subtotal = Net position
> Investment grants
> Special tax allowances
> Total = Equity

French limited companies are obliged to have a minimum legal reserve of 10% of their share capital. The contractual reserves are those that may be called for by the company's articles of association or similar voluntary reserves. The revaluation reserve arises because revaluation of assets normally gives rise to a tax liability, but from time to time the government has allowed companies to revalue fixed assets free of tax liability. The last such occasion was in 1976, and so the incidence of this normally should be slight.

There is also the regulated capital gains reserve. This arises from a tax concession: where a company realizes a capital gain by disposing of an asset, it may claim a special tax rate of 18% on the gain, and this is given on the condition that the gain remains in reserves. If the company wishes to distribute the gain, then it becomes liable to full taxation.

A gain of 100 will have suffered tax at 18%, so appearing as a reserve of 82; if distributed the tax rate would move up to $33^1/_3$%, so giving rise to an additional tax charge of $15^2/_3$ and leaving $66^2/_3$ available for distribution. Analysts could allocate therefore $15^1/_3/82$ to deferred tax and $66^2/_3/82$ as permanent equity.

Government grants appear within equity and are subsequently released to the income statement in line with the depreciation of the asset for which the grant was given. Special tax allowances (*provisions réglementées*) consist largely of accelerated depreciation, but there are also other concessions that provide tax incentives for export activities and similar objectives and are included here. For analytical purposes, it would be reasonable to treat both these items as being part equity and part deferred taxation.

French companies may buy and sell their own shares but only in specific circumstances, such as to give to employees, to reduce the share capital overall, or to steady the market if the company is listed (in which case it may deal in no more than 10% of its shares). When a company owns its own shares they appear in the balance sheet as an asset, compared with the U.S. practice of netting them against equity.

After equity there is a special category in individual company accounts called *autres fonds propres*. This is a French adaptation of the Fourth Directive and was created to allow state-owned companies to raise near-equity funding from the markets without diluting the state's holdings. This is sometimes used for hybrid capital instruments by commercial companies.

3.4 Liabilities and Provisions

French accounting distinguishes among three major classes of provision: (*a*) provision for depreciation: a nondefinitive diminution of the value of an asset, where the balance sheet credit is offset against the asset; (*b*) special tax provision: a provision that, in effect, is a special tax allowance and not concerned with the economic valuation of the company (this appears within equity, as described above); (*c*) provision for contingencies and expenses (*provisions pour risques et charges*), which are disclosed in a separate component of the liabilities side of the balance sheet, usually split into the two types. The provision for contingencies might include amounts for pending litigation, foreign exchange risk, guarantees, and so on. The provision for expenses would include provisions for deferred expenses, pension obligations, and similar items. It may include items that would be considered as creditors in other jurisdictions, such as the provision for Corporation Tax.

The question of pension obligations is potentially a delicate one for the analyst. Whereas many companies rely first on participation in the state pension scheme and second on special industry schemes, there are often top-up or other arrangements that are not necessarily funded. Companies are permitted to recognize a pension liability in the balance sheet for these items and take an expense, but for the present only disclosure in the notes is required.

As far as liabilities are concerned, different categories of liability (convertible debt, bank overdraft, trade creditors, tax and social security creditors, etc.) are distinguished separately on the face of the accounts, with details in the notes dividing debt into that falling due within 1 year, from 2 to 5 years, and in more than 5 years. Contingent liabilities, such as debt guarantees, are disclosed in the notes.

3.5 Property, Plant, and Equipment

French law permits tangible fixed assets and investments to be held at valuation, but recognition of a gain in value normally involves a liability to capital gains tax (except in the special case of fiscal revaluation discussed above). Consequently, companies do not revalue assets in their individual accounts. Given that companies are freed from this constraint in their consolidated accounts, it may be that in due course revaluation of some assets may become the norm, but so far this is not the case. Where a revaluation takes place, it should give rise to a revaluation reserve as part of equity. Depreciable revalued assets would subsequently be depreciated on the new carrying value.

As previously discussed, the individual accounts show commercial depreciation within the ordinary result and extra tax-driven depreciation in the extraordinary result. For group accounts, only commercial depreciation normally should be charged. Commercial depreciation is usually allocated on a straight line basis over the useful life of the asset but generally without reference to a residual value.

Interest costs incurred during the construction of assets may be capitalized, but this is not widespread practice. The interest is available as an immediate tax deduction regardless of capitalization.

Property companies (*sociétés civiles de placements immobiliers*) are entitled to revalue their property folio, building by building, at each balance sheet date (decree of 27 February 1985). Gains arising are credited to a revaluation reserve as part of equity (and exceptionally do not give rise to a tax liability); losses are provided for with an expense to the income statement.

3.6 Leased Assets

The French consolidation regulations leave the question of capitalization of finance leases to the discretion of the preparer, and analysts should check the notes to the accounts to confirm whether or not such leases have been capitalized. Early evidence suggests that majority practice is to follow IAS17. For individual accounts, assets acquired under a finance lease may be capitalized only where the lease includes a purchase option and the lessee has exercised that option—so effectively finance leases are not capitalized in such accounts. Rental obligations are disclosed in the notes to the accounts, however, so analysts may make some adjustment to capitalize on the basis of an assumed interest rate.

3.7 Oil, Gas, and Other Mineral Resources

There is no special requirement for the disclosure of oil, gas, or other mineral reserves. The regulations for mining companies (which extend to oil companies) allow some concessions in terms of research and development. In general the regular research and development rules apply: pure research must be expensed, but applied research and development may be capitalized and amortized over a maximum of 5 years. However, the costs of successful exploration may be capitalized and amortization deferred until the asset is exploited commercially; the amortization period may be the whole economic life of the asset. Unsuccessful exploration costs must be taken directly to the income statement, however, and companies that have unamortized research and development costs may not pay a dividend unless they have reserves greater than the outstanding asset, or a parent company guarantees the absorption of unamortized research and development in a subsidiary.

Oil companies benefit from a particular tax concession in that they can create tax-free reserves to rebuild their mineral reserves as existing resources are consumed.

3.8 Intangible Assets

Purchased intangibles may be capitalized, and where one company acquires another, any excess of purchase price over book value of the acquired company should in the first instance be attributed to the assets, including intangibles, acquired. The CNC ruling on this specifically mentions allocating purchase cost to such intangibles as brands, trademarks, and even market share. Intangible assets should then be amortized over their useful life. It is not possible to revalue intangibles nor recognize internally developed intangibles.

3.9 Participations

A "participation" in a company, according to French law, starts when the investor holds 10% or more in the investee. Once the holding reaches 20%, the investor is deemed to have significant influence, and the investment should then be accounted for by using either proportional consolidation or the equity method. Proportional consolidation is required where the investment is in a joint venture, which is defined by the 1985 law as where there is joint control, that is, the company is managed jointly by a limited number of associates in such a way that decisions are made by common agreement.

Where a minority holding involves significant influence but is not a joint venture, however, this will be accounted for under the equity method. The notes to the accounts are required to specify whether any participations are accounted for under these methods.

3.10 Inventories

The basic rule for inventory is lower of cost or market value. For individual accounts only FIFO and average cost are allowed, with average cost as majority practice. LIFO can be used for consolidated accounts. Where market value is applied, a provision is expensed and the stock is carried at the written-down value.

For long-term contracts profit may be recognized either on the percentage of completion basis (majority practice) or on final completion of the contract. Analysts should check the disclosure in the accounting policies note.

3.11 Taxation

The basic rates of corporation tax in 1994 are $33^1/_3\%$ on undistributed profits, $33^1/_3\%$ on distributions, and 18% on long-term capital gains (assets held more than 2 years), subject to the gain being held in reserves. As far as individual accounts are concerned, taxable profit is the same as that reported to shareholders, and no deferred taxation provisions arise in the accounts. As indicated above, the *provisions réglementées* included in equity should be split between deferred taxation (say $33^1/_3\%$) and equity.

In consolidated accounts the special tax effects should in theory have been adjusted out and appropriate deferred tax provisions created. The 1993 survey notes that the majority of its sample (51%) provided for deferred taxation, while 33% gave deferred tax information as a note, rather than incorporating it into the balance sheet and 16% gave no information.

3.12 Pensions

As a general rule the main provision for pensions is made through the state pension scheme applying to that industry sector, with both employer and employee making a regular contribution. It is not uncommon, however, for large companies to have supplementary schemes, often with insurance companies. Where these are funded, they will probably be defined contribution schemes, but there is growing evidence that many companies have unfunded pension obligations. For the moment, the COB requires listed companies to disclose in a note to the accounts any unfunded liability, with a view to creating a balance sheet provision. Many companies already have some provision in the balance sheet. Self-invested schemes as such are not a feature of French pension accounting.

3.13 Other Matters

A general point that should be made is that analysts who have been trained in an Anglo-Saxon environment are probably accustomed to operating with relatively few regulations, but these are carefully followed. In a code law environment in which there is a proliferation of detailed regulation, noncompliance is quite common, and the relevant question is not so much "Is there a rule?" but "Does anyone observe the rule?"

In French accounting this has always been a relevant point, and it is even more so at the end of a decade of rapid change. Whereas the regulations have changed a great deal, the people responsible for preparing and auditing accounts are largely the same. While the spirit that is abroad is one of greater disclosure, it will take some years before that permeates all participants in corporate accounting, and analysts must expect in the short term to find the notes to the accounts occasionally silent on matters that patently should be there.

4. Expected Future Developments

The main expected development would be that the practices of accountants will catch up with the legislative developments and some consensus will emerge on the treatment of such items as pensions, goodwill, and deferred taxation in group accounts. Because companies that produced group accounts in the past did so on a voluntary basis, there is an inheritance of diversity of practice. There is bound to be some inertia, but the likelihood is that the more widespread use of consolidated accounts will cause many of the more anomalous practices to disappear. Given that France has always been a major participant in the IASC, it may well be that its standards will have a major influence on future regulation of such matters as foreign currency translation, leasing, and pension obligations.

An important feature of the new arrangements is that the group accounts are free from the stranglehold of tax legislation. This development paves the way for a freer development of reporting, and it is likely that while for the moment most people still associate annual accounts with taxation, perceptions will change gradually and the group accounts will come to take on a much higher profile.

On the legislative front, it is fairly unlikely that there will be any radical new legislation in the short to medium term that will affect accounting disclosures. The Fourth and Seventh Directives have been implemented, and the European Commission seems now to be of a mind to seek further harmonization through negotiation rather than new directives. On the other hand, the *Conseil National de la Comptabilité* is likely to be under pressure to issue more and more detailed guidance on individual accounting issues.

Notes

1. *L'Information financière: 100 groupes industriel et commerciaux* BDA, CCAS, GCC, Guérard Viala, HSD published by Interéditions, 1993.

Useful Addresses

Ordre des Experts Comptables
153 rue de Courcelles
75817 Paris Cedex
Tel 1.44.15.60.00

Compagnie Nationale des Commissaires aux Comptes
8 rue de l'Amiral de Coligny
75001 Paris
Tel: 1.44.77.82.82

Financial Statements

40

BILAN CONSOLIDÉ

(en millions de francs)

ACTIF	1992			1991
	Valeur brute	Amortissements et provisions	Valeur nette	Valeur nette
Actif immobilisé	**11 889**	**(3 399)**	**8 490**	**8 556**
Immobilisations incorporelles	2 413	(273)	2 140	2 131
Immobilisations corporelles	5 693	(2 717)	2 976	2 943
Survaleur	1 621	(314)	1 307	1 362
Immobilisations financières	2 162	(95)	2 067	2 120
Actif circulant	**9 167**	**(281)**	**8 886**	**9 507**
Stocks	4 161	(58)	4 103	4 356
Créances d'exploitation diverses	4 346	(200)	4 146	4 367
Valeurs mobilières de placement	211	(23)	188	192
Disponibilités	449		449	592
Comptes de régularisation Actif	**138**	**(7)**	**131**	**166**
Ecart de conversion Actif	**4**		**4**	**4**
TOTAL ACTIF	**21 198**	**(3 687)**	**17 511**	**18 233**

GROUP

40

CONSOLIDATED BALANCE SHEET

(As at December 31, in millions)

ASSETS	US$ 1992*	FF 1992	FF 1991
Fixed assets	**1,540**	**8,490**	**8,556**
Intangible assets	388	2,140	2,131
Property, plant and equipment	540	2,976	2,943
Goodwill	237	1,307	1,362
Investments	375	2,067	2,120
Current assets	**1,613**	**8,886**	**9,507**
Inventories	745	4,103	4,356
Trade and other accounts receivable	753	4,146	4,367
Marketable securities	34	188	192
Cash	81	449	592
Prepaid expenses	**24**	**131**	**166**
Currency translation adjustment	**1**	**4**	**4**
TOTAL ASSETS	**3,178**	**17,511**	**18,233**

*Exchange rate at December 31, 1992: US$1 = FF 5.51.

41

(en millions de francs)

PASSIF

	1992	1991
Capitaux propres du Groupe	7 663	7 046
Dont droits du Groupe dans le résultat	1 100	956
Droits des tiers dans les capitaux propres	320	295
Dont droits des tiers dans le résultat	30	27
Provisions pour risques et charges	270	198
Impôt différé Passif	85	51
Dettes	9 136	10 618
Dettes financières	5 432	6 571
Emballages consignés	109	179
Dettes d'exploitation	2 908	3 193
Dettes diverses	687	675
Comptes de régularisation Passif	37	25
Ecart de conversion Passif	–	–
TOTAL PASSIF	17 511	18 233

41

LIABILITIES AND SHAREHOLDERS' EQUITY	US$ 1992*	FF 1992	FF 1991
Shareholders' equity	**1,391**	**7,663**	**7,046**
Of which net income after minority interests	208	1,100	956
Minority interests in shareholders' equity	**58**	**320**	**295**
Of which minority interests in net income	6	30	27
Provisions for contingencies	**49**	**270**	**198**
Deferred income taxes	**15**	**85**	**51**
Liabilities	**1,658**	**9,136**	**10,618**
Long-term debt	986	5,432	6,571
Returnable containers	20	109	179
Trade and other accounts payable	528	2,908	3,193
Other liabilities	124	687	675
Deferred income	**7**	**37**	**25**
Currency translation adjustment	–	–	–
TOTAL LIABILITIES AND SHAREHOLDERS' EQUITY	**3,178**	**17,511**	**18,233**

*Exchange rate at December 31, 1992 : US$1 = FF 5.51.

42

COMPTE DE RÉSULTAT CONSOLIDÉ

(en millions de francs)	1992	1991	Variation en %
Chiffre d'affaires H.D.T.	14 497	15 221	− 4,8 %
Achats consommés	(6 099)	(6 768)	− 9,9 %
Marge brute	8 398	8 453	− 0,6 %
Frais de production et de distribution	(2 051)	(2 122)	− 3,3 %
Frais de commercialisation et d'administration	(4 367)	(4 279)	2,1 %
Résultat opérationnel	1 980	2 052	− 3,5 %
Frais financiers nets	(470)	(569)	− 17,4 %
Résultat courant	1 510	1 483	1,8 %
Charges et produits exceptionnels nets	264	16	NS
Impôts sur les bénéfices	(522)	(509)	2,6 %
Résultat des sociétés intégrées	1 252	990	26,5 %
Résultat des sociétés mises en équivalence	15	40	− 62,5 %
Résultat avant amortissement de survaleurs	1 267	1 030	23,0 %
Amortissement de survaleurs	(137)	(47)	NS
Bénéfice net	1 130	983	15,0 %
Droits des tiers dans le résultat	30	27	11,1 %
Droits du Groupe dans le résultat	1 100	956	15,1 %
Capacité d'autofinancement	1 447	1 387	4,3 %

GROUP

42

CONSOLIDATED STATEMENT OF INCOME

(For the years ended December 31, in millions)	US$ 1992*	FF 1992	FF 1991	% Change
Net sales excluding taxes and duties	**2,740**	**14,497**	**15,221**	**− 4.8%**
Cost of goods sold	(1,153)	(6,099)	(6,768)	− 9.9%
Gross margin	**1,587**	**8,398**	**8,453**	**− 0.6%**
Production and distribution expenses	(388)	(2,051)	(2,122)	− 3.3%
Marketing and administrative expenses	(825)	(4,367)	(4,279)	2.1%
Operating profit	**374**	**1,980**	**2,052**	**− 3.5%**
Net interest expense	(89)	(470)	(569)	− 17.4%
Pretax profit before exceptional items	**285**	**1,510**	**1,483**	**1.8%**
Exceptional items	50	264	16	N/A
Income taxes	(98)	(522)	(509)	2.6%
Net income of consolidated companies	**237**	**1,252**	**990**	**26.5%**
Interest in earnings of equity companies	3	15	40	− 62.5%
Net income before amortization of goodwill	**240**	**1,267**	**1,030**	**23.0%**
Amortization of goodwill	(26)	(137)	(47)	N/A
Net income	**214**	**1,130**	**983**	**15.0%**
Minority interests	6	30	27	11.1%
Net income after minority interests	**208**	**1,100**	**956**	**15.1%**
Cash flow	**274**	**1,447**	**1,387**	**4.3%**

* Average 1992 Exchange rate: US$1 = FF 5.29.

TABLEAU DE VARIATION DES CAPITAUX PROPRES DU GROUPE 43

(en millions de francs)

	Capitaux propres du Groupe
Au 31 décembre 1990	**6 331**
Dividendes payés aux actionnaires	(352)
Changement de périmètre de consolidation	(6)
Variation des réserves	129
Variation de l'écart de conversion	(12)
Résultat net consolidé 1991 - part du Groupe	956
Au 31 décembre 1991	**7 046**
Dividendes payés aux actionnaires	(372)
Changement de périmètre de consolidation	9
Variation des réserves	(17)
Variation de l'écart de conversion	(103)
Résultat net consolidé 1992 - part du Groupe	1 100
Au 31 décembre 1992	**7 663**

CONSOLIDATED STATEMENT OF CHANGES IN SHAREHOLDERS' EQUITY 43

(FF millions)

	Group shareholders' equity
Shareholders' equity at December 31, 1990	**6,331**
Dividends paid	(352)
Change in scope of consolidation	(6)
Net change in reserves	129
Change in currency translation adjustment	(12)
Consolidated net income after minority interests for 1991	956
Shareholders' equity at December 31, 1991	**7,046**
Dividends paid	(372)
Change in scope of consolidation	9
Net change in reserves	(17)
Change in currency translation adjustment	(103)
Consolidated net income after minority interests for 1992	1,100
Shareholders' equity at December 31, 1992	**7,663**

44   TABLEAU DE FINANCEMENT CONSOLIDÉ AU 31 DÉCEMBRE 1992

(en millions de francs)

	1992
Résultat net consolidé part du Groupe	1 100
Résultat net consolidé part des intérêts minoritaires	30
Résultat des sociétés mises en équivalence (net des dividendes)	(14)
Dotation aux amortissements sur immobilisations	443
Dotation aux amortissements des survaleurs	137
Variation des provisions et de l'impôt différé	169
Plus-values sur cessions d'immobilisations (nettes d'impôt)	(418)
Capacité d'autofinancement	**1 447**
Variation du besoin en fonds de roulement	(189)
Variation de la trésorerie issue des opérations d'exploitation	**1 258**
Acquisition d'immobilisations non financières (nette des cessions)	(589)
Acquisition d'immobilisations financières (nette des cessions)	46
Incidence des variations du périmètre de consolidation	618
Variation des créances et dettes sur immobilisations	(147)
Variation de la trésorerie issue des opérations d'investissement	**(72)**
Augmentation de capital	–
Emission d'emprunts et nouvelles dettes financières	327
Dividendes versés	(382)
Variation de la trésorerie issue des opérations de financement	**(55)**
Incidence des écarts de conversion	17
Variation nette de la trésorerie	**1 148**
Trésorerie à l'ouverture de l'exercice	(3 303)
Trésorerie à la clôture de l'exercice	(2 155)

44

CONSOLIDATED STATEMENT OF CHANGES IN FINANCIAL POSITION

(FF millions)

	1992
Consolidated net income after minority interests	1,100
Minority interests	30
Interest in earnings of equity companies (net of dividends)	(14)
Depreciation of fixed assets	443
Amortization of goodwill	137
Change in provisions and deferred taxes	169
Gains on disposals of fixed assets (net of taxes)	(418)
Cash flow	**1,447**
Change in working capital requirements	(189)
Cash provided by operating activities	**1,258**
Acquisition of property, plant and equipment (net of disposals)	(589)
Acquisition of investments (net of disposals)	46
Effect of change in scope of consolidation	618
Net change in long-term liabilities	(147)
Cash used in investment activities	**(72)**
Increase in capital	–
Issue of borrowings and increase in long-term debt	327
Dividends paid	(382)
Cash used in financing activities	**(55)**
Currency translation adjustment	17
Increase in cash	**1,148**
Cash position, beginning of year	(3,303)
Cash position, end of year	(2,155)

GROUP

NOTES TO THE CONSOLIDATED FINANCIAL STATEMENTS

45

NOTE 1 - ACCOUNTING PRINCIPLES

1.1. PRINCIPLES OF CONSOLIDATION

The Group's consolidated financial statements have been prepared in compliance with French legal requirements as set forth in Law No. 85-11 of January 3, 1985 and the related Application Decree No. 86-221 of February 17, 1986.

The financial statements of significant subsidiaries which are over 50%-owned or effectively controlled are included in the consolidated financial statements.

Companies over which the Group exercises joint control with another partner are consolidated using the proportional method.

Companies in which the Group exercises a sizeable influence are accounted for by the equity method.

All intercompany and intra-Group transactions have been eliminated.

A list of the consolidated companies is provided in Note 16. For purposes of simplification and to avoid any serious prejudice to the Group, only the names and addresses of the main companies included in the scope of consolidation are listed.

1.2. FOREIGN CURRENCY TRANSLATION

a) Financial statements prepared in foreign currencies have been translated according to the following principles:
- Balance sheets have been translated at official year-end rates.
- Statements of income have been translated using the average yearly rate for each currency.
- Differences in currency translation resulting from the effect of fluctuations in the year-end to year-end exchange rate on opening shareholders' equity and from the use of different rates in translating the balance sheet and the statement of income have been included in consolidated reserves.

b) Foreign currency transactions are translated at the exchange rate prevailing at the transaction date. Gains and losses resulting from foreign currency translation up until December 31, 1992 are recorded in the statement of income.

1.3. INTANGIBLE ASSETS

Intangible assets are valued at original cost; they are amortized when their market value falls below cost.

In compliance with the Law of January 3, 1985 concerning French companies' consolidated financial statements, goodwill arising from mergers prior to 1987 was fully amortized that year by a direct charge to shareholders' equity.

1.4. PROPERTY, PLANT AND EQUIPMENT

Property, plant and equipment are valued at cost or, when applicable, at a revalued cost in compliance with legal requirements.

Depreciation is calculated according to the straight-line method or, when applicable, according to the declining-balance method over the estimated useful life of the underlying asset.

Average periods of depreciation for these assets are as follows:

Buildings	15 to 50 years
Machinery and equipment	5 to 15 years
Other fixed assets	3 to 5 years

Real estate of significant value which is acquired through leasing contracts is capitalized and depreciated over the estimated useful life of the asset.

Buildings under sale and leaseback agreements are subject to a similar restatement. Any resulting capital gains are eliminated from the year's income.

Returnable containers are valued at cost. Based on statistics provided by each company, this item is restated to adjust the asset value of the containers to reflect losses from breakages and to recognize unrealized income from non-returns. In the case of changes in deposit rates, the debt corresponding to non-returned containers is valued at the new rates, with possible losses charged to expenses. Obsolescence is reflected in the depreciation calculations.

1.5. INVESTMENTS

Equity investments in non-consolidated companies are valued at acquisition cost. A provision for depreciation is made if the market value falls below cost.

1.6. GOODWILL

Since January 1, 1986, goodwill on acquisition is reflected in assets and assigned by brand name if appropriate.

Goodwill is amortized on a straight-line basis over a period appropriate to the acquisition but not exceeding 40 years.

1.7. INVENTORIES

Inventories are valued at the lower of cost or market value, mainly using average weighted costs.

The cost of long-term inventories is uniformly determined to include distilling and aging costs but excludes interest expense. These inventories are classified in current assets according to prevailing business practices, although a large part remains in inventory for over one year before being sold.

1.8. BORROWINGS DENOMINATED IN IRISH POUNDS

The effects of exchange rate fluctuations on repayments at maturity of all borrowings denominated in Irish pounds made to finance the acquisition of the Irish Distillers group have been eliminated in the consolidated statement of income and charged to currency translation adjustments in the balance sheet, since the borrowings are backed by assets denominated in Irish pounds.

1.9. PROVISIONS FOR CONTINGENCIES

This item records all provisions for contingencies made by Group companies, notably provisions for retirement benefits, excluding related social charges.

The Group's foreign companies provide for their retirement-related commitments in compliance with local practice and legislation. The Group's French companies record retirement benefits accrued at year-end for those employees 45 years of age and older.

1.10. INCOME TAXES

Since January 1, 1977, Groupe Pernod Ricard's tax liability had been determined according to the regulations governing tax consolidation of French companies more than 95% owned. As of January 1, 1988, the Group opted for the new tax system applicable to consolidated groups, and the tax liability was calculated accordingly.

Deferred tax credits or liabilities resulting from timing differences between taxable income and accounting income are accounted for by the accrual method. These concern primarily timing differences, cancellations of regulated provisions and restatements on consolidation. The resulting long-term and short-term tax liability is recorded as deferred income taxes.

1.11. INTEREST RATE HEDGING INSTRUMENTS

Groupe Pernod Ricard periodically subscribes for guaranteed interest rate contracts to hedge against major interest rate fluctuations.

Income and expense from these contractual guarantees are recorded in Groupe Pernod Ricard's statement of income on a prorated basis over the life of the operation:

• premiums paid are spread over the life of the contract;

• interest income or expense is recognized in the year it is earned or incurred;

• as these contracts hedge real positions only, no gain or loss is recognized at year-end.

NOTE 2 - EXTRAORDINARY ITEMS

Consolidated net income for the 1992 fiscal year includes extraordinary items which increased net income by FF 71 million.

(FF millions)	Amount after taxes
Gain on disposal of assets, less provisions for contingencies (1)	163
Additional amortization of goodwill (2)	(92)
Total	**71**

(1) This concerns the capital gain after income taxes realized in April 1992 on the disposal of Société des Vins de France, effective retroactively to January 1, 1992, after accounting for the costs of restructuring certain assets kept by the Group, less provisions for costs and depreciation of assets, which will probably be recognized by the Group in future years.

(2) In accordance with the accounting principles set forth in Note 1.6, the Group has accounted for additional amortization of goodwill of FF 92 million. This amortization results from the update as at December 31, 1992 of the assumptions retained upon acquisition of various companies, in accordance with the conservatism principle.

NOTE 3 - SCOPE OF CONSOLIDATION

In 1992, the scope of consolidation was expanded as follows:

• Cidreries Mignard, a producer and distributor of cider in France;

• Cidrerie et Vergers du Duché de Longueville, a producer and distributor of cider in France;

• Prasia, a distributor of wines, spirits and nonalcoholic beverages in Singapore;

• Vallade, a distributor of wines and spirits in Switzerland;

• Cusenier Saic and its subsidiary Etchart, producers and distributors of wines and spirits in Argentina.

SIAS Port, a company specializing in the production and marketing of fruit preparations in Mexico, has been fully consolidated since January 1, 1992.

Société des Vins de France, which the Group sold in May 1992, was withdrawn from the scope of consolidation as at January 1, 1992. However, the fine wine distribution companies, which have merged under the name Crus et Domaines de France, are still included in the consolidated financial statements.

NOTE 4 - PRESENTATION OF STATEMENT OF INCOME

In 1992, the Group adopted a new consolidated statement of income, which reclassified items as revenues or expenses. This new form of presentation provides a more streamlined picture of the Group's operations.

The 1991 statement of income has been restated for comparative purposes; the two presentations appear below.
(FF millions)

Former 1991 presentation		New 1991 presentation	
Sales net of sales and excise taxes	15,221	Net sales excluding taxes and duties	15,221
Gross margin	8,453	Gross margin	8,453
Outside services	(3,159)		
Taxes	(235)		
Payroll	(2,557)	Production and distribution expenses	(2,122)
Other income (expense)	45		
Provision for depreciation	(412)	Marketing and administrative expenses	(4,279)
Operating profit	**2,135**	**Operating profit**	**2,052**

The FF 83 million difference in operating profit derives almost fully from the inclusion of the provision for employee profit-sharing, which had until now been regarded as part of so-called "exceptional" items, in operating expenses in the new presentation.

NOTE 5 - INTANGIBLE ASSETS

The intangible assets recorded at year-end mainly consist of trademarks.
The value of acquired trademarks is determined according to the Company's sector of activity and the importance of their international distribution.

NOTE 6 - PROPERTY, PLANT AND EQUIPMENT

	1992			1991
(FF millions)	Gross value	Depreciation and provisions	Net value	Net value
Land	353	(9)	344	396
Buildings	1,827	(620)	1,207	1,162
Machinery and equipment	2,491	(1,528)	963	888
Other	918	(560)	358	393
Work in process	97	–	97	73
Advances	7	–	7	31
Total	**5,693**	**(2,717)**	**2,976**	**2,943**

NOTE 7 - INVESTMENTS

	1992			1991
(FF millions)	Gross value	Provisions	Net value	Net value
Shareholdings accounted for by the equity method	169	–	169	162
Other equity investments	1,896	(81)	1,815	1,894
Receivables on investments	52	(11)	41	17
Other	45	(3)	42	47
Total	**2,162**	**(95)**	**2,067**	**2,120**

Companies accounted for by the equity method include Heublein do Brazil, Heublein Japan, Edward Dillon, Dillon Bass and Mulligans and Malting Company of Ireland.
Other equity investments include Société Générale shares (2.06% of capital) and Compagnie de Suez shares (1.82% of capital).

NOTE 8 - INVENTORIES AND WORK IN PROCESS

Inventories and work in process at 1992 and 1991 year-end were as follows:

(FF millions)	1992	1991
Raw materials	857	819
Work in process	2,233	2,203
Goods in inventory	376	478
Finished products	637	856
Total	**4,103**	**4,356**

NOTE 9 - PROVISIONS FOR CONTINGENCIES

(FF millions)	1992	1991
Provisions for retirement benefits	106	91
Provisions for other risks	164	107
Total	**270**	**198**

NOTE 10 - INCOME TAXES

(FF millions)	1992	1991
Taxes payable	(488)	(481)
Deferred taxes	(34)	(28)
Total	**(522)**	**(509)**

48

Deferred taxes are calculated according to the accrual method. They are broken down as follows on the balance sheet:

(FF millions)	1992	1991
Deferred tax credit	149	164
Deferred tax liability	(234)	(215)
Net deferred tax	**85**	**51**

NOTE 11 - LONG-TERM DEBT

The breakdown of long-term debt by maturity date is as follows:

(FF millions)	1992	1991
Short term (less than one year) including bank loans	2,936 2,792	4,087 4,087
Medium term (from one to five years)	2,163	1,381
Long term (over five years)	333	1,103
Total	**5,432**	**6,571**

In December 1990 and January 1991, Groupe Pernod Ricard entered into a total of FF 1,600 million of confirmed lines of credit for a four and five year period. At December 31, 1992, none of these lines of credit had been used.

NOTE 12 - UNDATED SUBORDINATED NOTES ("TSDI")

On March 20, 1992, Pernod Ricard issued undated subordinated notes (TSDI), for a nominal amount of FF 400 million, outside of France.

The issue conditions include the following main conditions:
• The notes, for which no redemption period is provided, will only be redeemed at their par value in the event of liquidation, or voluntary early winding up of Pernod Ricard, except in the event of a merger or split.
• Redemption will be subordinated to prior complete paying off of all creditors of Pernod Ricard, with the exclusion of equity shares which may be issued by Pernod Ricard.
• Payment of interest may be suspended in the event that:
– the consolidated financial statements show losses for an amount greater than 25% of the consolidated shareholders' equity; and
– the decision has been made not to distribute any dividend for the most recent fiscal year.

The TSDI's are qualified as "repackaged" following the signing with a third party of an agreement concurrent with the issue.

Through this agreement, the third party which, by a separate agreement signed with the underwriters, undertakes to purchase the subordinated notes after a 15-year period, waives the right to collect interest as of the 16th year, in return for the initial payment by Pernod Ricard of an amount of FF 96 million.

In the event of early redemption or repayment prior to the end of the 15-year period, the third-party company would

partially assume the burden of paying off holders of the subordinate notes jointly with Pernod Ricard.

As a result of these provisions:
• at the issue date, the TSDI's have been recorded on the balance sheet at their net amount, that is FF 304 million;
• the consolidated income for each fiscal year backs the interest paid on the nominal amount of the issue, after deduction of the proceeds generated by the investment of the FF 96 million. These proceeds are charged against the balance at the closing date of the TSDI's.

The TSDI's have been issued in return for payment of the nominal amount at a fixed rate of 10.07%.

The issue tax system has been defined by the Service de la Législation Fiscale by a letter sent to the Company.

The net amount as at December 31, 1992 (FF 296 million) has been included in long-term debt.

NOTE 13 - FINANCIAL COMMITMENTS

(FF millions)

Commitments given:	1992	1991
Leasing	6	28
Bank guarantees	743	1,039
Purchasing commitments	88	248

The guarantee given to Société Générale by Pernod Ricard for the notes issued to finance part of the acquisition of Irish Distillers Group and secured for the principal by Société Générale was reduced from FF 966 million to FF 679 million between 1991 and 1992, in light of the repayments made.

NOTE 14 - GUARANTEED RATE CONTRACTS

As mentioned in Note 1.11, Pernod Ricard has subscribed for guaranteed rate contracts which as at December 31, 1992 were as follows:

	Collar 1	Collar 2	Collar 3
Amount (FF millions)	500	500	400
Guaranteed rate:			
• maximum	10%	9.75%	9.50%
• minimum	9 - 9.40%	8.25%	8.28%
Term	3 years	3 years	5 years
Beginning	11/01/1990	03/01/1991	11/29/1991
Maturity	10/31/1993	02/28/1994	11/28/1996

NOTE 15 - AVERAGE NUMBER OF EMPLOYEES AND PAYROLL EXPENSES

The average number of employees in 1992 was 9,381.

Payroll expenses totalled FF 2,495 million in 1992 compared with FF 2,690 million in 1991. These figures include employee profit-sharing and temporary personnel costs and are therefore not directly comparable with 1991 figures.

GROUP

NOTE 16 - PRINCIPAL CONSOLIDATED COMPANIES

49

Company	Head Office	% Interest	Consolidation Method	Register
Pernod Ricard	142, boulevard Haussmann, 75008 Paris	Parent Company		582041943
Ricard	4-6, rue Berthelot, 13014 Marseille	100	Full	303656375
• Renault Bisquit	Domaine de Lignères, 16170 Rouillac	100	Full	905420170
Pernod	120, avenue du Maréchal-Foch, 94105 Créteil	100	Full	302208301
SEGM	2, rue de Solférino, 75007 Paris	100	Full	302453592
• Prac SA (Spain)	Avenida Diagonal 477, Planta 14, Barcelona 36	100	Full	
• Perisem (Switzerland)	44, route de St-Julien, 1227 Carouge, Geneva	100	Full	
• Ramazzotti (Italy)	9, via San Petro All Orto, 20121 Milan	100	Full	
• IGM Deutschland (Germany)	Poststrasse N° 8, 5400 Koblenz	100	Full	
• Koninklijke Cooymans BV (Netherlands)	De Kroonstraat 1, 5048 AP Tilburg	100	Full	
• Lizas & Lizas (Greece)	L. Anthousas, 15344 Palini Attiki	90.0	Full	
• Pernod Ricard Japan KK (Japan)	Tamaya Building, 3rd Floor, 14-12 Shinjuku 1 - Chome Shinjuku-Ku, Tokyo 160	100	Full	
• Casella Far East Ltd. (Hong Kong)	1007-8 New Kowloon Plaza - 38 Tai Kok Tsui Road, Kowloon, Hong Kong	100	Full	
• Cusenier Saic (Argentina)	Lima 187 - 4° - 1073 Buenos Aires	100	Full	
Cusenier	142, boulevard Haussmann, 75008 Paris	100	Full	308198670
Austin Nichols (USA)	156 East, 46th Street, New York N.Y. 10017	100	Full	
• Orangina International (USA)	156 East, 46th Street New York N.Y. 10017	100	Full	
• Boulevard Distillers (USA)	156 East, 46th Street New York N.Y. 10017	70.0	Full	
• Yoo-Hoo Industries (USA)	156 East, 46th Street New York N.Y. 10017	100	Full	
• Heublein Japan	Roppongi Building, 3 Fl. 4-11-4 Roppongi Minceto Ku, Tokyo 106	30.0	Equity	
JFA Pampryl	12, rue François-Mignotte, 21700 Nuits-Saint-Georges	99.9	Full	035680016
CSR	2 bis, rue de Solférino - 75007 Paris	99.0	Full	552024275
• Cidrerie et Vergers du Duché de Longueville	Anneville-sur-Scie - 76590 Longueville-sur-Scie	100	Full	552750291
• Cidreries Mignard	BP 1 - 77510 Bellot	100	Full	745750448
Campbell Distillers (UK)	West Byrehill, Kilwinning, Ayrshire KA 136 LE	100	Full	
• White Heather Distillers (UK)	West Byrehill, Kilwinning, Ayrshire KA 136 LE	100	Full	
• Aberlour Glenlivet Distillery (UK)	West Byrehill, Kilwinning, Ayrshire KA 136 LE	100	Full	
• Campbell Whisky Holding (UK)	West Byrehill, Kilwinning, Ayrshire KA 136 LE	100	Full	
Santa Lina	Rue du Soleil-Levant, 20000 Ajaccio	100	Full	045920105
SIAS-MPA	142, boulevard Haussmann, 75008 Paris	100	Full	436380521
• SIAS-France	17, avenue du 8-Mai-1945, 77290 Mitry-Mory	100	Full	341826006
• Ramsey Laboratoires (USA)	2742, Grand Avenue, Cleveland, Ohio 44104 3191	100	Full	
• DSF (Germany)	Lilienthalstrasse 1, 7750 Konstanz	60.0	Full	
• SIAS Port (Mexico)	Labastida 912 B, 59650 Zamora, Michoacan	99.0	Full	
• SIAS Australia (Australia)	CNR George Downs Drive & Wisemans Ferry Road, Central Mangrove, NS W 2250	100	Full	
• SIAS Korea (Korea)	160-18 Sam Sung-Dong, Kang Nam Ku - Seoul	93.0	Full	
• SIAS UK (UK)	Oakley Hay Lodge, Great Fold Road, Corby NN 189 AS	100	Full	
• San Giorgio Flavors (Italy)	Via Fossata 114, 1047 Torino	100	Full	
Compagnie Financière des Produits Orangina	1, La Canebière, 13001 Marseille	100	Full	061801245
• Orangina France	7, Première Avenue, 13127 Vitrolles	95.1	Full	056807076
• L'igloo	7, Première Avenue, 13127 Vitrolles	50.0	Proportionate	085720217
• Centre d'Elaboration des Concentrés Orangina	Parc d'activités du plateau de Signes, 83870 Signes	100	Full	382255016
Crus et Domaines de France	109, rue Achard - 33000 Bordeaux	100	Full	384093290
Comrie Plc (Ireland)	61 Fitzwilliam Square, Dublin 2 (Registered Office)	100	Full	
Irish Distillers Group (Ireland)	Bow Street Distillery, Smithfield, Dublin 7	100	Full	
• Irish Distillers Ltd.	Bow Street Distillery, Smithfield, Dublin 7	100	Full	
• BWG Limited	Greenhills Road, Walkinstown, Dublin 12	100	Full	
Pernod Ricard Australia (Australia)	Grosvenor Place, 225 George Street, Sydney NSW 2000, Australia	100	Full	
• Orlando Wyndham Group Pty Limited	P.O. Box 2248, Adelaide, 100 South Australia 5001	80.7	Full	
Heublein do Brazil (Brazil)	655, rue Araporé, Sao Paulo	30.0	Equity	

GROUP

50   **NOTE 17 - BUSINESS SEGMENT INFORMATION**

WINES AND SPIRITS, FRANCE

Volumes sold (millions of liters)	129
Employees	2,975
21 production facilities in France	

Major trademarks:

- Ricard, Pastis 51, Pernod, Alaska.
- Suze.
- Ambassadeur, Dubonnet, Cinzano, Byrrh, Americano 505, Vabé, Bartissol.
- Whiskies Clan Campbell, White Heather, Aberlour, Cutty Sark(*).
- Whiskeys Jameson, Bushmills, Tullamore Dew, Power.
- Bourbon Wild Turkey.
- Vodkas Stolichnaya(*) and Karinskaya.
- Calvados Busnel and Lancelot.
- Cognac Bisquit, Armagnac Marquis de Montesquiou.
- Ports Cintra, Warre and Feist.
- Rums Vana and Naura.
- Liqueurs and White Brandies La Duchesse and Cusenier.
- Gins Gilbey's(*), Epsom, Black Jack.
- Carlton.
- Café de Paris, Blancs de fruits.
- Baroque, Soho.
- Alexis Lichine, Cruse, Victor Bérard, Pasquier Desvignes.
(*) Concessions

Companies operating in the segment:

- Ricard and its subsidiaries: Galibert & Varon, Tinville, Renault Bisquit.
- Pernod and its subsidiaries: SPA, Distillerie Laurent.
- Cusenier.
- Cidreries et Sopagly Réunies.
- Crus et Domaines de France.

Wines and Spirits, France

(FF millions)	1992	1991	% Change
Net sales excluding taxes and duties	3,824	5,332	−28.3
Cost of goods sold	(869)	(1,793)	−51.5
Gross margin	2,955	3,539	−16.5
Production and distribution expenses	(374)	(684)	−45.3
Marketing and administrative expenses	(1,602)	(1,829)	−12.4
Operating profit	979	1,026	− 4.6

WINES AND SPIRITS, INTERNATIONAL

Volumes sold (millions of liters)	215
Employees	2,883

31 production and bottling facilities:

- United States: Lawrenceburg.
- Great Britain: Aberlour, Edradour, Kilwinning, Glenalachie.
- Ireland: Bushmills, Fox and Geese, Waterford, Cork, Midleton.
- Australia: Rowland Flat, Griffith, Rutherglen, Dalwood, Pokolbin-Hunter Estate, Broke, Mudgee-Montrose, Pokolbin-Richmond Grove, Mudgee-Craigmoor, Eurunderee.
- Spain: Pamplona.
- Switzerland: Geneva.
- Argentina: Buenos Aires, Mendoza Etchart, Cafayatte Etchart.
- Italy: Milan, Canelli.
- Netherlands: Almelo, Tilburg, Bois-le-Duc.
- Greece: Palini.

Major trademarks:

- Pernod, Ricard, Pastis 51.
- Suze.
- Dubonnet.
- Carlton, Cruse, Alexis Lichine, Victor Bérard, Pasquier Desvignes, Canei, Orlando, Jacob's Creek, Wyndham.
- Bisquit, Renault.
- Clan Campbell, White Heather, Aberlour, Wild Turkey.
- Jameson, Bushmills, Tullamore Dew, Paddy, Power.
- King's Ransom, House of Lords, Glenforres.
- Amaro, Sambuca, Fior di Vite, Mariposa, Ocho Hermanos.
- Zoco.
- Advocaat de Korenaer, Surfers.
- Cork Dry Gin, vodka Huzzar.
- Eoliki.

Companies operating in the segment:

- SEGM and its subsidiaries: Perisem (Switzerland) and its subsidiary Vallade, Prac SA (Spain), Ramazzotti (Italy), IGM Deutschland (Germany), Cooymans & Kerstens (Netherlands), Lizas & Lizas (Greece), Casella Far East (Hong Kong), Cusenier Saic (Argentina), Prasia (Singapore), Pernod Ricard Japan (Japan).
- Irish Distillers.
- Campbell Distillers and its subsidiary Caxton Tower.
- Orlando Wyndham.
- Cusenier.
- Ricard and its subsidiaries: Renault Bisquit, Galibert & Varon.
- Pernod and its subsidiary SPA.
- Cidreries et Sopagly Réunies.
- Crus et Domaines de France.

Wines and Spirits, International

(FF millions)	1992	1991	% Change
Net sales excluding taxes and duties	4,123	4,094	0.7
Cost of goods sold	(1,518)	(1,675)	− 9.4
Gross margin	2,605	2,419	7.7
Production and distribution expenses	(563)	(495)	13.7
Marketing and administrative expenses	(1,424)	(1,302)	9.4
Operating profit	618	622	−0.6

GROUP

NONALCOHOLIC BEVERAGES AND PRODUCTS, FRANCE

Volumes sold (*) (millions of liters)	428
Employees	1,942

16 production facilities in France

Major trademarks:

- Banga.
- Pampryl, Pam Pam.
- Agruma, Janero.
- Sirups: Cusenier, Sironimo.
- Ciders: La Cidraie, Loïc Raison, Anée, Clos Normand, Jacques de Toy, Duché de Longueville.
- Pacific.
- Orangina, Matangi.
- Brut de Pomme.
- Champomy.

(*) Excluding flavors and fruit preparations.

NONALCOHOLIC BEVERAGES AND PRODUCTS, EXPORT AND INTERNATIONAL

Volumes sold (*) (millions of liters)	249
Employees	1,581

18 production facilities abroad:

- Germany: Constance, Nauen.
- Great Britain: Corby.
- Australia: Mangrove Mountain.
- United States: Cleveland (Ohio), Anna (Ohio), Winter Haven (Florida), Fort Worth (Texas), Carlstadt (New Jersey), Hialeah (Florida), Opelousas (Louisiana).
- Mexico: Zamora, Jacuna.
- Italy: Turin.
- Greece: Piraeus.
- Korea: Seoul.
- Fiji: Fiji.
- Austria: Kröllendorf.

(*) Excluding flavors and fruit preparations.

Major trademarks:

- Orangina.
- Yoo-Hoo.
- Pampryl.
- Minerva.

Companies operating in the segment:

- JFA Pampryl and its subsidiary Agruma.
- SIAS-MPA and its subsidiaries SIAS-France and Retext.
- Cusenier.
- Cidreries et Sopagly Réunies and its subsidiaries: Mignard, Duché de Longueville.
- Ricard.
- CFPO and its subsidiaries: Orangina France, L'Igloo.

Companies operating in the segment:

- SEGM and its subsidiaries.
- SIAS-MPA and its subsidiaries: DSF and Agrota (Germany), Ramsey (United States), SIAS Foods UK (Great Britain), San Giorgio Flavors (Italy), SIAS Australia (Australia), SPF Fiji (Fiji), SIAS Mexico and SIAS Port (Mexico), SIAS Korea (Korea), YB SIAS (Autria).
- JFA Pampryl.
- Cidreries et Sopagly Réunies and its subsidiaries: Mignard, Duché de Longueville.
- CFPO and its subsidiary Orangina France.
- Orangina International.
- Yoo-Hoo Industries.
- B.W.G.

Nonalcoholic Beverages and Products, France

(FF millions)	1992	1991	% Change
Net sales excluding taxes and duties	2,793	2,468	13.2
Cost of goods sold	(1,169)	(1,041)	12.3
Gross margin	1,624	1,427	13.8
Production and distribution expenses	(629)	(535)	17.6
Marketing and administrative expenses	(768)	(642)	19.6
Operating profit	227	250	− 9.2

Nonalcoholic Beverages and Products, Export and International

(FF millions)	1992	1991	% Change
Net sales excluding taxes and duties	3,757	3,327	12.9
Cost of goods sold	(2,543)	(2,259)	12.6
Gross margin	1,214	1,068	13.7
Production and distribution expenses	(485)	(409)	18.6
Marketing and administrative expenses	(573)	(505)	13.5
Operating profit	156	154	1.5

GROUPE

52   RAPPORT DES COMMISSAIRES AUX COMPTES
SUR LES COMPTES CONSOLIDÉS

Mesdames, Messieurs,

En exécution de la mission qui nous a été confiée par vos assemblées générales des 14 mai 1992 et 11 juin 1987, nous vous présentons notre rapport sur :

• le contrôle des comptes consolidés de la Société Pernod Ricard, tels qu'ils sont annexés au présent rapport,

• la vérification du rapport sur la gestion du Groupe, relatifs à l'exercice clos le 31 décembre 1992.

1 - OPINION SUR LES COMPTES CONSOLIDÉS

Nous avons procédé au contrôle des comptes consolidés en effectuant les diligences que nous avons estimées nécessaires selon les normes de la profession.

Nous certifions que les comptes consolidés sont réguliers et sincères et donnent une image fidèle du patrimoine, de la situation financière, ainsi que du résultat de l'ensemble constitué par les entreprises comprises dans la consolidation.

2 - VÉRIFICATIONS SPÉCIFIQUES

Nous avons également procédé, conformément aux normes de la profession, aux vérifications spécifiques prévues par la loi.

Nous n'avons pas d'observation à formuler sur la sincérité et la concordance avec les comptes consolidés des informations données dans le rapport sur la gestion du Groupe.

Fait à Paris, le 9 avril 1993

Les Commissaires aux Comptes

Jean Delquié

Société d'Expertise Comptable A. et L. Genot
Alain Genot
Louis Genot

Cabinet Robert Mazars
Frédéric Allilaire
Patrick de Cambourg

GROUP

52   REPORT OF THE AUDITORS
ON THE CONSOLIDATED FINANCIAL STATEMENTS FOR THE YEAR ENDED DECEMBER 31, 1992

In conformity with the mission ascribed to us by the General Meetings of May 14, 1992 and June 11, 1987, we hereby submit to you our report concerning:

• the audit of the consolidated financial statements of Pernod Ricard, as attached to this report,

• the examination of the Group's Management Report,

for the year ended December 31, 1992.

1 - OPINION ON THE CONSOLIDATED FINANCIAL STATEMENTS

We have examined the consolidated financial statements performing such tests as we deemed necessary in accordance with professional standards.

We certify that the consolidated financial statements are regular and present fairly the assets, the financial position and the results of the operations of Pernod Ricard and its subsidiaries.

2 - SPECIFIC EXAMINATIONS

We have also performed, in accordance with professional standards, the specific examinations required by French law.

We have no comment to make on the sincerity of the information given in the Management Report or on the consistency of this information with the consolidated financial statements.

Paris, April 9, 1993

The Statutory Auditors:

Jean Delquié

Société d'Expertise Comptable A. & L. Genot
Alain Genot
Louis Genot

Robert Mazars
Frédéric Allilaire
Patrick de Cambourg

54

BILAN PERNOD RICARD

(en milliers de francs)

ACTIF	31.12.1992 Brut	Amortissements et provisions	Net	31.12.1991 Net
Immobilisations incorporelles	222734	(7903)	214831	189557
Licences, marques	222734	(7903)	214831	189557
Immobilisations corporelles	34573	(18326)	16247	18779
Terrains	5410		5410	5527
Constructions	11529	(6862)	4667	4840
Matériel et outillage	988	(967)	21	38
Autres	16646	(10497)	6149	8374
Immobilisations financières	6964624	(157879)	6806745	6896370
Participations	4581479	(149200)	4432279	4590359
Créances rattachées à des participations	2382262	(8679)	2373583	2303034
Prêts	686		686	672
Autres	197		197	2305
TOTAL ACTIF IMMOBILISÉ	7221931	(184108)	7037823	7104706
Avances et acomptes versés sur commandes	1402		1402	726
Créances d'exploitation	78125		78125	79768
• Créances clients et comptes rattachés	72117		72117	74476
• Autres	6008		6008	5292
Créances diverses	955729		955729	261045
Valeurs mobilières de placement	120318	(22792)	97526	109099
Disponibilités	8793		8793	11535
TOTAL ACTIF CIRCULANT	1164367	(22792)	1141575	462173
Charges constatées d'avance	7406		7406	11548
Charges à répartir sur plusieurs exercices	8213		8213	3013
Écart de conversion - Actif	374		374	477
TOTAL COMPTES DE RÉGULARISATION	15993		15993	15038
TOTAL GÉNÉRAL	8402291	(206900)	8195391	7581917

54

PARENT COMPANY BALANCE SHEET

(As at December 31, in FF thousands)

ASSETS	Gross value	1992 Depreciation, amortization and provisions	Net value	1991 Net value
Intangible assets	222,734	(7,903)	214,831	189,557
Licenses, trademarks	222,734	(7,903)	214,831	189,557
Property, plant and equipment	34,573	(18,326)	16,247	18,779
Land	5,410		5,410	5,527
Buildings	11,529	(6,862)	4,667	4,840
Machinery and equipment	988	(967)	21	38
Other	16,646	(10,497)	6,149	8,374
Investments	6,964,624	(157,879)	6,806,745	6,896,370
Equity investments	4,581,479	(149,200)	4,432,279	4,590,359
Receivables related to equity investments	2,382,262	(8,679)	2,373,583	2,303,034
Loans	686		686	672
Other	197		197	2,305
TOTAL FIXED ASSETS	7,221,931	(184,108)	7,037,823	7,104,706
Advances and down payments to suppliers	1,402		1,402	726
Operating receivables	78,125		78,125	79,768
• Trade and other accounts receivable	72,117		72,117	74,476
• Other	6,008		6,008	5,292
Sundry receivables	955,729		955,729	261,045
Marketable securities	120,318	(22,792)	97,526	109,099
Cash	8,793		8,793	11,535
TOTAL CURRENT ASSETS	1,164,367	(22,792)	1,141,575	462,173
Prepaid expenses	7,406		7,406	11,548
Deferred expenses	8,213		8,213	3,013
Currency translation adjustment	374		374	477
TOTAL ACCRUALS	15,993		15,993	15,038
TOTAL ASSETS	8,402,291	(206,900)	8,195,391	7,581,917

SOCIÉTÉ

55

(en milliers de francs)

PASSIF	31.12.1992	31.12.1991
Capital	**939 777**	**939 777**
Primes d'émission, de fusion, d'apport	**248 967**	**248 967**
Écarts de réévaluation	**–**	**–**
Réserves	**1 871 936**	**1 856 835**
• Réserve légale	93 978	93 978
• Réserves réglementées	1 777 958	1 762 857
Report à nouveau	**472 402**	**368 546**
Résultat de l'exercice	**1 175 716**	**490 560**
Provisions réglementées	**8 565**	**8 634**
TOTAL DES CAPITAUX PROPRES	**4 717 363**	**3 913 319**
AUTRES FONDS PROPRES (TSDI)	**296 426**	**–**
PROVISIONS POUR RISQUES ET CHARGES	**12 124**	**11 642**
Dettes financières	**2 377 135**	**2 816 237**
• Emprunts obligataires non convertibles	900 000	900 000
• Emprunts et dettes auprès des établissements de crédit	1 374 952	1 817 706
• Emprunts et dettes financières diverses	102 183	98 531
Dettes d'exploitation	**42 133**	**40 291**
• Dettes fournisseurs et comptes rattachés	20 962	16 955
• Dettes fiscales et sociales	21 171	23 336
Dettes diverses	**750 144**	**800 428**
• Dettes fiscales (impôts sur les bénéfices)		35 366
• Autres	750 144	765 062
TOTAL DES DETTES	**3 169 412**	**3 656 956**
Écart de conversion - Passif	**66**	**–**
TOTAL COMPTES DE RÉGULARISATION	**66**	**–**
TOTAL GÉNÉRAL	**8 195 391**	**7 581 917**

COMPANY

55

(As at December 31, in FF thousands)

LIABILITIES AND SHAREHOLDERS' EQUITY

	1992	1991
Capital stock	939,777	939,777
Additional paid-in capital	248,967	248,967
Appraisal increase credit	–	–
Reserves	1,871,936	1,856,835
• Legal reserve	93,978	93,978
• Regulated reserves	1,777,958	1,762,857
Retained earnings	472,402	368,546
Net income	1,175,716	490,560
Regulated provisions	8,565	8,634
TOTAL SHAREHOLDERS' EQUITY	4,717,363	3,913,319
UNDATED SUBORDINATED NOTES	296,426	–
PROVISIONS FOR CONTINGENCIES	12,124	11,642
Long-term debt	2,377,135	2,816,237
• Non-convertible bond loans	900,000	900,000
• Borrowings and loans from lending institutions	1,374,952	1,817,706
• Other long-term debt	102,183	98,531
Current liabilities	42,133	40,291
• Trade and other accounts payable	20,962	16,955
• Taxes and social security	21,171	23,336
Sundry liabilities	750,144	800,428
• Income taxes	–	35,366
• Other	750,144	765,062
TOTAL LIABILITIES	3,169,412	3,656,956
Currency translation adjustment	66	–
TOTAL ACCRUALS	66	–
TOTAL LIABILITIES AND SHAREHOLDERS' EQUITY	8,195,391	7,581,917

56 COMPTE DE RÉSULTAT PERNOD RICARD

(en milliers de francs)

	31.12.1992	31.12.1991
Redevances	230 361	222 003
Autres produits	29 938	25 665
Reprises sur provisions		328
Total des produits d'exploitation	**260 299**	**247 996**
Services extérieurs	(160 086)	(159 696)
Impôts, taxes et versements assimilés	(5 108)	(4 238)
Charges de personnel	(33 117)	(33 140)
Dotations aux amortissements et aux provisions	(4 773)	(3 577)
Autres charges	(1 856)	(1 768)
Total des charges d'exploitation	**(204 940)**	**(202 419)**
RÉSULTAT D'EXPLOITATION AVANT OPÉRATIONS FINANCIÈRES	**55 359**	**45 577**
Produits de participations	996 076	655 788
Produits d'autres valeurs mobilières	2	48
Autres intérêts et produits assimilés	141 629	83 937
Reprises sur provisions	1 442	566
Différences positives de change	5 306	1 817
Produits nets sur cessions de valeurs mobilières de placement	228	4 232
Total des produits financiers	**1 144 683**	**746 388**
Dotations aux provisions	(1 775)	(7 828)
Intérêts et charges assimilées	(320 987)	(326 726)
Différences négatives de change	(6 167)	(4 161)
Total des charges financières	**(328 929)**	**(338 715)**
RÉSULTAT FINANCIER	**815 754**	**407 673**
RÉSULTAT COURANT	**871 113**	**453 250**
Produits exceptionnels	672 099	53 166
Charges exceptionnelles	(359 187)	(53 510)
RÉSULTAT EXCEPTIONNEL	**312 912**	**(344)**
RÉSULTAT AVANT IMPÔT	**1 184 025**	**452 906**
Impôt sur les bénéfices	(8 309)	37 654
BÉNÉFICE DE L'EXERCICE	**1 175 716**	**490 560**

56

PARENT COMPANY STATEMENTS OF INCOME

(For the years ended December 31, in FF thousands)

	1992	1991
Royalties	230,361	222,003
Other income	29,938	25665
Reversals of provisions	–	328
Total operating income	**260,299**	**247,996**
Outside services	(160,086)	(159,696)
Taxes and duties	(5,108)	(4,238)
Payroll expenses	(33,117)	(33,140)
Depreciation, amortization and provisions	(4,773)	(3,577)
Other expenses	(1,856)	(1,768)
Total operating expenses	**(204,940)**	**(202,419)**
OPERATING PROFIT	**55,359**	**45,577**
Income from equity investments	996,076	655,788
Income from other securities	2	48
Other interest and related income	141,629	83,937
Reversals of provisions	1,442	566
Currency translation gains	5,306	1,817
Gains on disposals of marketable securities	228	4,232
Total financial income	**1,144,683**	**746,388**
Provisions	(1,775)	(7,828)
Interest and related expenses	(320,987)	(326,726)
Currency translation losses	(6,167)	(4,161)
Total financial expense	**(328,929)**	**(338,715)**
NET FINANCIAL INCOME (EXPENSE)	**815,754**	**407,673**
PRETAX PROFIT BEFORE EXCEPTIONAL ITEMS	**871,113**	**453,250**
Exceptional income	672,099	53,166
Exceptional expense	(359,187)	(53,510)
NET EXCEPTIONAL INCOME (EXPENSE)	**312,912**	**(344)**
INCOME BEFORE INCOME TAXES	**1,184,025**	**452,906**
Income taxes	(8,309)	37,654
NET INCOME	**1,175,716**	**490,560**

GERMANY

Günter Seckler
Wirtschaftsprüfer
Steuerberater
Partner of Arthur Andersen & Co. GmbH
Wirtschaftsprüfungsgesellschaft, Steuerberatungsgesellschaft
Friedrich-Ebert-Anlage 2 - 14
60036 Frankfurt am Main

1. Background

1.1 History of German Accounting Regulations

German accounting regulations and, especially, German accounting law have only a relatively brief history compared with those of other European countries. In 1937 general accounting standards and principles were codified for the first time in the Stock Corporation Law. This came about as a reaction to the large number of companies going bankrupt during the worldwide economic crisis of the late 1920s and early 1930s. Existing accounting practice failed to protect adequateley the creditors of German companies in cases of bankruptcy. Consequently, the dominating principle incorporated in the Stock Corporation Law of 1937 was that of prudence in order best to protect the interests of creditors.

A significant modification of the Stock Corporation Law of 1937 took place in 1965. Under the revised law the interests of the shareholders were given more consideration than under the previous law. Particularly, the opportunities for asset underevaluations were limited. The principle of prudence and the idea of creditor protection remained important, however, if no longer dominant.

Until 1985 the Stock Corporation Law of 1965 was more or less the sole source of accounting law in Germany, codifying accounting principles and standards. No other specific regulations existed, either for other corporations like limited liability companies or for noncorporations such as partnerships. There was, however, a broad understanding that the standards incorporated in the Stock Corporation Law represented to a large extent generally accepted accounting principles. This applied especially to the rules regarding the format and content of the balance sheet and the income statement. Furthermore, certain evaluation rules were broadly accepted also for companies of other legal forms. Nevertheless, there were no really binding rules for nonstock corporations, and therefore, those companies could be highly flexible in their accounting approaches.

In 1985, however, the Fourth, Seventh, and Eighth EC Directives were embodied in German law, thereby completely changing the existing regulatory systems with regard to preparation, publication, and auditing of single and group accounts.

Technically, the modification of German law was achieved by incorporating the three EC Directives into the Accounting Directives Law, which is a pure modification law covering in total 39 separate laws. Of supreme importance was the revision of the Commercial Code and, especially, the insertion of a third book (last amended on July 25, 1994) with accounting and auditing rules applicable to all businesses.

Second, supplementary rules were retained or codified in separate laws for specific legal forms (e.g., in Stock Corporation Law and Limited Liability Company Law) as well as for specific industries (e.g., in Banking Law and the Insurance Supervisory Law). Third, specific provisions for large noncorporations included in the Publicity Law of 1969 were modified.

With the adoption of the three EC Directives, the most important Anglo-Saxon accounting principles were implemented into German accounting law. The reader of German financial statements should always remember, however, that to a large extent, new and old accounting standards still can be applied in parallel.

The Accounting Directives Law itself became effective on January 1, 1986. For single company financial statements it had to be applied not later than for fiscal years commencing after December 31, 1986. The latest application for group financial statements were fiscal years beginning after December 31, 1989. The law could be applied as of an earlier date but generally only *in toto*. Many exceptions and generous transitional rules were provided for in the law, however.

1.2 The German Auditing Profession

As with German accounting law, the German auditing profession has a rather short tradition compared with those of some other European countries. The first auditing firms were formed at the turn of the twentieth century. Their main purpose was to audit and to provide consultancy services for large businesses on a voluntary basis. The first official professional organization was not established until 1931, when the consequences of the worldwide economic crisis demonstrated the need for audited financial statements.

A decree of the *Reichspräsident* dated September 19, 1931, announcing statutory audits by independent auditors, can be regarded as the birth of the German auditing profession. Further milestones in its development are represented by the statutory audit requirements established for stock corporations in 1937, for large nonstock corporations in 1969, and for (at least medium-sized) limited liability companies in 1985.

The growing demands of stockholders, banks, and other creditors for audited financial statements, as well as a dramatic expansion of the range of services provided by audit firms, has led to considerable growth of the profession during the past 30–40 years. Today the German auditing profession is headed by the Chamber of Auditors (*Wirtschaftsprüferkammer*), an independent professional organization supervised by the Federal Minister of Economics. The tasks of the Chamber of Auditors range from the supervision of its members to the representation of the profession to other parties.

Members of the Wirtschaftsprüferkammer are both certified auditors (*Wirtschaftsprüfer*, or WP) as well as certified accountants (*vereidigte Buchprüfer*, or vBP). The difference between the two types of professional is that certified accountants benefit from simplified admission and examination procedures, while on the other hand, they are allowed to perform only voluntary audits, as well as statutory audits of medium-sized limited liability companies, or *Gesellschaften mit beschränkter Haftung* (GmbHs). All other statutory audits must be performed by certified auditors.

Before one may be appointed as a certified auditor, one must surmount many hurdles. In general, this requires study in business administration, law, and general economics or a similar subject. Furthermore, candidates must usually have 5 years of practical experience, including at least 4 years as an auditor. In addition, certain personal criteria need to be met before one may be admitted for the professional examination, which includes accounting, auditing, business administration, law, taxation, and general economics.

Because of stringent admission, examination, and supervisory regulations, the German Professional Law (*Wirtschaftsprüferordnung*) is widely regarded as one of the strictest worldwide.

Besides the Chamber of Auditors, the Institute of Certified Auditors (*Institut der Wirtschaftsprüfer*, IdW) is the other important organization of the profession. Its main task is to publish statements on principal accounting and auditing questions that then usually serve as generally accepted standards and principles within the profession. Unlike the Chamber of Auditors, the membership of the Institute of Certified Auditors is voluntary.

Auditing financial statements and rendering opinions thereon are the exclusive right of certified auditors and certified accountants. The requirements concerning financial statements are set out in Section 2.3.

1.3 General Accounting Rules in Germany

As a general rule, applicable for all businesses, financial statements are to be drawn up in accordance with generally accepted accounting principles (§243 (1) HGB).

For corporations only, the general rule has been expanded. Their financial statements must, in compliance with generally accepted accounting principles, present a true and fair view of the net worth, the financial position, and the results of the company (§264 (2) HGB).

Both general rules require that the financial statements comply with GAAP, which mostly were incorporated into the German Commercial Code in connection with the adoption of the Fourth Directive. They can be briefly summarized as follows:

- The financial statements must be clear and understandable.
- They must be complete.
- Offsetting of assets against liabilities and income against expenses is prohibited.

- The amounts included in the opening balance sheet must agree with the closing balance sheet of the preceding year.
- To the extent not disproved by facts or action of law, a going concern must be assumed.
- Valuation must be made on an item-by-item basis.
- Accounting must be done prudently; that is, all anticipated risks and losses that arise up to the balance sheet date are to be recognized, even if they become known only after the balance sheet date but before the date of preparation of the financial statements; profits may be recognized only if they are realized (realization and imparity principle).
- Accounting must be made on an accrual basis and with due consideration of the matching principle.
- Valuation principles must be applied consistently over the years.
- Valuation is based on historical cost.

Deviations from the above principles are allowed only to the extent that exceptional circumstances exist. It should also be noted that in accordance with the prudence principle, provisions and allowances can be set up if it is possible, but not necessarily probable, that an asset has been impaired or a liability has been incurred.

As mentioned earlier, the general rule for corporations requires not only that their financial statements comply with GAAP, but also that they provide a true and fair view. This principle has been taken over from Anglo-Saxon countries. In Germany, however, its interpretation may be different. It still seems to be the dominant opinion in Germany that compliance with legal requirements ensures a true and fair presentation, even if the law allows exceptions from GAAP, for instance, the creation of hidden reserves. It is broadly understood that the form and content of financial statements are derived first from the specific rules of laws and ordinances. The general rule needs to be referred to only if doubts arise in the interpretation and application of individual rules or if uncertainties in the legal provisions need to be resolved.

With regard to the transformation of significant option rights established by the Fourth and Seventh EC Directive into the German Commercial Code and the comparison of material differences between German

GAAP and U.S. GAAP as well as International Accounting Standards (IAS), reference is made to Exhibits I through IV at the end of the chapter.

1.4 The Relationship Between Commercial and Tax Accounting

It is of supreme practical importance to recognize that commercial accounts in Germany are linked directly with tax accounts. According to the so-called authoritative principle (*Maßgeblichkeitsprinzip*), which is incorporated in §5 EStG (German Income Tax Law) and which is almost unknown in the accounting rules of other countries, commercial financial statements form an authoritative basis for tax accounts. Tax accounts do not represent an independent set of accounts but are derived from the commercial accounts.

As a consequence, the accounting treatment in the commercial financial statements in general directly affects the tax position of a company. In addition, most of the tax incentives can be claimed only if the same treatment is applied to the items in question in the commercial financial statements. This, in practice, leads to a reversal of the authoritative nature of commercial financial statements for tax accounts.

As a result, German companies are compelled to evaluate their assets at the lowest amount possible and their liabilities at their highest amount possible under GAAP in their commercial financial statements in order to minimize their tax liability. Furthermore, in order to benefit from tax incentives, they may be led to record in their commercial accounts special tax-allowed depreciations and reserves, or to not reverse write-downs even though the reasons for them no longer exist, even if this leads to a departure from the true and fair view.

1.5 Financing of German Industry

Financing of German industry is characterized by a relatively low number of companies traded on the stock exchange, a relatively low equity ratio, and typically high financing via pension accruals. Another important source of financing, if not the most important, is banks.

Of about 440,000 corporations, only around 550 were listed on the stock exchange at the end of 1990. Traditionally, these were very large stock corporations (*Aktiengesellschaft*, AG). This picture has changed to a certain extent, since, especially in the second half of the 1980s, a considerable number of medium-sized corporations decided to go public. The main reasons for this development were considered to be:

- The inability or unwillingness of the old shareholders to provide additional equity funds
- The relative reduction of disadvantages (e.g., publication requirements) attributed to AGs, compared with other legal forms

For a number of years the average equity ratio of German companies has been only 20%, or even lower. This rather low ratio is often attributed to the fact that from a tax point of view, loan capital financing is preferable compared with equity financing, since unlike equity financing, debt financing reduces the tax basis for net worth tax and for trade tax on capital and—via interest expense—also for income taxes. This also explains the tendency for shareholders to try to classify a high portion of their investments in firms as loans and not as equity capital.

The high degree of funding via pension accruals is mainly due to the fact that from a tax, administrative, and financial point of view, this form of funding is often preferable to external funding.

2. The Form and Content of Published Financial Statements

2.1 Introductiory Notes

As described in Section 1.1 above, the German accounting and disclosure rules are codified in various laws, although the majority of the regulations are now incorporated in the third book of the Commercial Code (last revised on July 25, 1994). Nevertheless, within the framework of this accounting guide, it would be impossible to cover every particular rule. Accordingly, all rules and regulations specifically relating to registered cooperatives, as well as to companies of particular industries like banks and insurance companies, are not further commented on. This limits the range of entities taken into account to the following:

- Corporations, for example, stock corporations (AGs), partnerships limited by shares (*Kommanditgesellschaft auf Aktien*, KGaAs) and limited liability companies (GmbHs).
- Small noncorporations, for example, sole proprietorships, partnerships (*Offene Handelsgesellschaft*, OHG; and *Kommanditgesellschaft*, KG) and partnerships with at least one limited liability company as general partner (e.g., GmbH & Co.'s).
- Large noncorporations, with the same legal form as above but exceeding certain size criteria (see Section 2.3)

Whereas the first two types of company are governed by the Commercial Code, the accounting, auditing, and disclosure rules for noncorporations are included in the Publicity Law.

As a particular point, it should be mentioned that GmbH & Co.'s and AG & Co.'s are partnerships that, until December 31, 1994, must follow only the less stringent requirements for noncorporations (e.g., the absence of net worth taxes on company level, comparatively low accounting, audit, and publication requirements), although they contain strong corporation elements from an economic point of view. This regulation has been greatly discussed in the EC in past years. As a result, beginning on January 1, 1995, such partnerships will have to meet the requirements set up for corporations as well.

2.2 Components of Single and Group Financial Statements

The financial statements must include at least the following components:

	Corporations	Noncorporations Small	Large
Balance sheet	X	X	X
Income statement	X	X	X
Notes	X		X
Management report	X*a*		X

a Except for small corporations (since 8/94)

In the terminology of German law, financial statements consist of the first three components; the management report is a separate element of year-end reporting. For the purpose of this guide, however, this stringent interpretation is not followed, and the management report is regarded as an integral part of the financial statements. It should be noted, however, that the auditors' opinion must state whether the management report is consistent with the financial statements.

2.3 Differentiation of Financial Statements According to Legal Form and Size

In order to establish different levels of requirements for the preparation, audit, and disclosure of single entity and group financial statements, certain size criteria were incorporated into the Commercial Code and the Publicity Law, in addition to the differentiation according to legal form. These are shown in Table 1.

The figures in parentheses represent the increased limits for corporations that were incorporated into the German Commercial Code on July 25, 1994. It is permissible to apply the increased limits retroactively for fiscal years commencing after December 31, 1990.

The requirements set out in the following paragraphs and sections apply only if at least two of the three size criteria are met by corporations in two consecutive years and by noncorporations in three consecutive years. It should be noted that quoted stock corporations, or those that are traded over the counter, are always deemed to be "large" corporations.

2.4 Overview of Preparation, Audit, and Disclosure Requirements

Table 2 provides an overview of the minimum legal requirements concerning financial statements. Companies are free to establish stricter requirements in their statutes.

In addition to the requirements shown in Table 2, corporations must publish the proposal for the appropriation of the result and the report of the supervisory board, if applicable. The latter also applies to noncorporations. Furthermore, the auditor's opinion or disclaimer, but not the full auditor's report, which usually is a long-form report, must be disclosed in the case of statutory audits.

TABLE 1 *Size Criteria for Disclosure of Single Entity and Group Financial Statements*

	Balance Sheet Total (thousands DM)	Sales (thousands DM)	Number of Employees
A. Corporations			
I. Single entity financial statements (§267 HGB)			
1. Small	< 3,900	< 8,000	< 50
	(< 5,310)	(< 10,620)	No change
2. Medium-sized	> 3,900 < 15,500	> 8,000 < 32,000	> 50 < 250
	(> 5,310 < 21,240)	(> 10,620 < 42,480)	No change
3. Large	> 15,500	> 32,000	> 250
	(> 21,240)	(> 42,480)	No change
II. Consolidated financial statements (§293 HGB)			
1. Consolidated	> 39,000	> 80,000	> 500
	(> 53,100)	(> 106,200)	No change
2. Combined	> 46,800	> 96,000	> 500
	(> 63,720)	(> 127,440)	No change
B. Noncorporations			
I. Single entity financial statements (§1 PublG)			
1. Small	< 125,000	< 250,000	< 5,000
2. Large	> 125,000	> 250,000	> 5,000
II. Consolidated financial statements (§11 PublG)			
Consolidated	> 125,000	> 250,000	> 5,000

DM, Deutsche marks.

The company's management must forward a full auditor's report to the members of the supervisory board only. On a voluntary basis, this is usually also made available to selected other addressees (e.g., banks and other important creditors).

It should be recognized that despite the legal requirements, the quota of firms that publish financial statements is currently estimated to be far below 20%. Small and medium-sized companies in particular still prefer to make their financial statements available only to selected outside addressees (e.g., banks), in order not to disclose any information that might be of interest to competitors. The Commercial Code does not adequately prevent such practice, since no serious penalties are incorporated for nonpublication.

TABLE 2 *Minimum Legal Requirements for Financial Statements*

	Single Entity Financial Statements					Group Financial Statements	
	Corporations			Noncorporations		Corpor- ations	Noncor- porations
	Small	Medium-sized	Large	Small	Large		
Balance sheet							
Preparation	yes	yes	yes	yes	yes	yes	yes
Disclosure	CR	CR	FG	≅	FG	FG	FG
Income statement							
Preparation	yes	yes	yes	yes	yes	yes	yes
Disclosure	≅	CR	FG	≅	(FG)	FG	FG
Notes							
Preparation	yes	yes	yes	≅	yes	yes	yes
Disclosure	CR	CR	FG	≅	FG	FG	FG
Management report							
Preparation	yes	yes	yes	≅	yes	yes	yes
Disclosure	≅	CR	FG	≅	FG	FG	FG
Statutory audit	≅	yes	yes	≅	yes	yes	yes
Maximum preparation period (months)	6	3	3	"Adequate period"	3	5	5
Maximum disclosure period (months)	12	9	9	≅	9	9	9

Abbreviations: CR, Commercial Register; FG, Federal Gazette

Notes: Except for small corporations (since August 1994) and small noncorporations (since January 1987), all other companies must prepare a full set of financial statements.

Except for small noncorporations and small corporations, statutory audits are required.

Except for small noncorporations, all other companies must publish a full set or at least part of their financial statements.

Large companies must publish their single entity and group financial statements in the Federal Gazette before filing them with the Commercial Register; the disclosure requirement for small and medium-sized corporations is limited to the Commercial Register; however, small and medium-sized corporations must announce in the Federal Gazette that the financial statements have been filed with the Commercial Register.

Large noncorporations do not have to publish their income statement, provided they disclose limited information (sales, investment income, payroll expenses, number of employees, depreciation/evaluation methods) in an annex to the balance sheet (§9 (2) PublG).

2.5 Published Financial Statements and the Management Report

2.5.1 General Remarks

Detailed legal regulations concerning the form and content of financial statements exist for corporations only. Large noncorporations must also follow them. No such detailed rules exist for small noncorporations. It is common practice, however, for these companies to prepare their financial statements similarly to those of corporations but mostly to a less detailed extent. Because of the lack of regulations and the absence of disclosure requirements for these companies, the following paragraphs deal only with corporations and large noncorporations.

2.5.2 Balance Sheet

The basic format of the balance sheet to be applied by corporations and large noncorporations in their single and group financial statements is presented in §266 HGB. The main captions within the prescribed accounts format are:

Assets	*Equity and Liabilities*
A. Fixed assets	A. Equity
I. Intangible assets	I. Subscribed capital
II. Tangible assets	II. Capital reserves
III. Financial assets	III. Revenue reserves
	IV. Retained profits/accumulated losses brought forward
	V. Result for the year
B. Current assets	B. Accruals
I. Inventories	
II. Receivables and other current assets	
III. Securities	
IV. Liquid funds	
C. Prepaid expenses	C. Liabilities
D. Deferred income	

Whereas small corporations are allowed to present and disclose their balance sheet in the above format, all other companies must break down the subheadings into various prescribed items.

In addition to the general principles, which require a clear, understandable, and complete presentation and forbid the netting of items, the following presentation and disclosure rules are incorporated in §265 HGB:

- Continuity of disclosure and classification
- Presentation of comparative figures
- Notes, where items belong to more than one heading
- Extension of the basic classification, if different industries require
- Differing disclosures are combined in one legal entity
- Change of classification/description, if appropriate
- Option to add new items, if appropriate
- Option to eliminate items with no amount
- Combination of headings in case of immaterial amounts or to improve the clarity of presentation

Other important rules are the options to present in the notes to financial statements, instead of on the face of the balance sheet:

- The fixed assets movements analysis
- The remaining terms of liabilities (less than 1 year, over 5 years) and of receivables (over 1 year)
- The type and amounts of contingent liabilities

In order to avoid overloading the balance sheet and to improve the clarity of presentation, there is a strong tendency to put as many disclosures as possible into the notes, where optional, and also to use the legal opportunities to combine headings in the balance sheet with supplementary analyses in the notes.

2.5.3 Income Statement

The basic formats of the income statement for corporations and noncorporations are incorporated in §275 HGB. They apply to the single entity as well as to the group financial statements.

The income statement must be presented in a vertical form following either the "type-of-expenditure" or the "functional" format. The general presentation principles as described earlier also apply to the profit and loss account.

The traditional format in Germany, the type-of-expenditure format is a production-oriented presentation. According to the underlying philosophy, the measurement for the performance of a company is not only sales but also inventories produced on or taken from stock, as well as the value of internal resources used to create or improve fixed assets.

Accordingly, the change in work-in-progress and finished goods as well as own work capitalized are disclosed separately. Together with sales, they make up the "gross performance" for the year. As a further typical characteristic, income and expense items are disclosed according to their type, disregarding where they were incurred.

The type-of-expenditure format as defined in §275 (2) HGB shows the following structure:

	Item no.
Sales	1
± Change in work in progress/finished goods	2
+ Own work capitalized	3
Gross performance	1 – 3
+ Other operating income	4
– Cost of materials	5
– Personnel expenses	6
– Depreciation	7
– Other operating expenses	8
Operating result	1 – 8
± Financial result	9 – 13
Result from ordinary operations	14
± Extraordinary result	15 – 17
– Taxation	18 – 19
Result for the year	20

The traditional format for the income statement in Anglo-Saxon countries is the "functional" format. Although that format was allowed to

German non-AGs before 1987, it achieved some importance only after incorporation into the Commercial Code.

According to its underlying philosophy, the measurement for the performance of a company is primarily sales. Consequently, the change in inventories and own cost capitalized are not disclosed separately. Instead, expenses are mainly structured according to the "cost centers" or functions where they are incurred.

The "functional" format as prescribed in §275 (3) HGB shows the following structure:

	Item no.
Sales	1
– Cost of sales	2
Gross profit	3
– Selling expenses	4
– Administrtive expenses	5
+ Other operating income	6
– Other operating expense	7
Operating result	1 – 7
+ Financial result	8 – 12
Result from ordinary operations	13
+ Extraordinary result	14 – 16
– Taxation	17 – 18
Result for the year	19

It should be noted that the subheadings used above for the most part are not official line descriptions according to §275 HGB and, therefore, are mostly not disclosed separately. However, they are frequently used by financial analysts in order to structure the income statement.

It should further be noted that the contents of subheadings and single lines are not identical in both formats, even if the same descriptions are used. This makes the comparison of companies more difficult and is mainly a result of the following:

- Companies applying the functional format partly allocate nonincome taxes and interest expenses to cost of sales, selling, or general and administrative (G&A) expenses. Accordingly, there may be differences with regard to taxation, financial, and operating results, since under the type-of-expenditure approach such allocations are not known.

- "Other operating expenses" in the cost-of-sales format are usually lower, since only those amounts not allocable to cost of sales, selling, or G&A are classified under this line.
- On the other hand, "other operating expenses" in the cost-of-sales format may also show a higher amount. As a German peculiarity, and deviating from international practice, it is regarded as acceptable to classify the difference between direct and full cost valuation of inventories as other operating expense, if the company has decided to price its inventories at direct cost only (reference is also made to this in Section 3.2.4).
- Small and medium-sized corporations are allowed to combine lines 1–5 (type-of-expenditure format), or lines 1–3 and 6 (functional format) into a heading described "gross results" (§276 HGB) and need not split up this heading for disclosure purposes; it should be borne in mind that the contents of this heading may be completely different, depending on the format used.

Apart from these particulars, the contents of the single lines in the German cost-of-sales income statement comply with international standards and do not need further comment. On the other hand, the internationally less well-known type-of-expenditure format requires some additional explanations:

- The "change in work in progress and finished goods" line represents the difference in values compared with the previous year. Thus, the amount disclosed includes changes in units, in prices, and in allowances.
- With respect to the background of this line as well as of "own cost capitalized," reference is made to the previous explanations.
- Material costs must be broken down into cost of raw material, consumables, supplies, and purchased merchandise, as well as cost of purchased services. It is broadly accepted that the latter should include only costs of the same character as for material, for instance, expenses for having goods manufactured by other parties.

- Personnel expenses must be split into wages and salaries, social security, and old-age pensions.

- Depreciation must be split into usual and unusual portions, if any. The latter refers only to depreciation on current assets to the extent that it exceeds a level, for example, a percentage or absolute amount, that is deemed to be usual for the company. Because it remains doubtful what exactly is to be understood by the term usual, particular attention should be given to the explanations in the notes.

- Separate disclosure of income from participations, particularly from those in affiliated companies, is required within the financial results caption. Although not required by law, it is common practice to disclose income or losses resulting from income and loss pooling contracts separately.

  Such contracts are mostly concluded in order to arrive at taxation on a group basis. A second, usually less important, reason for such contracts is that funds for dividend payments are available at the parent company level in the same year in which they are incurred in the group companies.

- The amounts to be classified as extraordinary income or expense are defined as those incurring outside the regular activities of a company (§277 (4) HGB).

  Although a common interpretation and practice of what exactly is to be understood by "extraordinary" has not yet been achieved, there seems to be a strong trend toward the Anglo-American understanding. More and more, *extraordinary* is characterized by nonrecurring events resulting in significant amounts. On the other hand, typical results of a recurring nature, such as gains/losses from the disposal of fixed assets or from the release of excess accruals, are regarded as contributing to the results of ordinary activities, unless of very high amounts.

- Taxation must be split into income taxes and other taxes. Deferred tax expenses need not be disclosed separately.

  Although a netting of income and expenses is not allowed in general, some important commentaries consider it to be acceptable or even preferable to net income from reversal of tax accruals or tax refunds with the tax expense of the year, since it is regarded as misleading to classify that income as "other operating income," as is still common practice.

It is to be noted that common practice for many classification issues, particularly with regard to the cost-of-sales format income statement and "unusual" or "exceptional" items, has not yet been finally developed. Therefore, particular attention should be given to the corresponding explanations in the notes to financial statements.

2.5.4 Notes to Financial Statements

The notes form an integral part of financial statements. Before 1987, notes had to be prepared and disclosed only by stock corporations and large companies falling within the scope of the Publicity Law (but with less quantity of information); they are frequently regarded as representing the most important change brought about by the Accounting Directives Law.

As with Anglo-Saxon disclosure practice, notes provide additional information for the interpretation of the balance sheet and income statement. Furthermore, they fulfill a replacement function, since they contain information that otherwise would need to be incorporated in the balance sheet or income statement.

The form and structure of the notes are not prescribed by law. Accordingly, various presentation formats can be found in practice. The most common basic structure used is:

- I. General information to financial statements
  - 1. Significant accounting principles
  - 2. Other
- II. Specific information to financial statements
  - 1. Disclosures to balance sheet
  - 2. Disclosures to income statement
- III. Sundry disclosures

The provisions concerning individual disclosures to be included in the single and group notes are spread over a large number of paragraphs in the Commercial Code and other specific laws. Therefore, completeness of disclosure usually can be achieved only by using checklists, although §§284–288 (single entity financial statements) and §§313–314 HGB (group financial statements) can be regarded as key provisions. Using the above basic format, the most important disclosures are:

General information:

- Accounting principles applied to single entity balance sheet and income statement items
- Method of foreign currency translation
- Departures from consistency
- Note, if contents or amounts of items are not comparable
- Disclosure of hidden reserves in inventories, if values are significantly below market
- Disclosure of the extent to which the results were affected by claiming tax benefits
- Method of goodwill amortization

Specific information, balance sheet:

- Fixed assets movement analysis, if not on the face of the balance sheet
- Amounts due to or due from shareholders (GmbHs only)
- Receivables with a term of more than 1 year; payables with a term of less than 1 year or more than 5 years, if not disclosed in the balance sheet
- Amount and type of collaterals on payables
- Disclosures to capitalized start-up/expansion costs and to deferred taxes
- Pension obligations not accrued for
- Details to sundry accruals, if significant
- Details of equity investment of at least a 20% interest (information can also be given in a separate listing, not to be published in the Federal Gazette but only in the Commercial Register)

Specific information, income statement:

- Details of extraordinary and prior period items, if material
- If a functional format is adopted, disclosure of materials and personnel costs as in the type-of-expenditure format
- Analysis of depreciation by balance sheet item
- Breakdown of sales by areas of activity and geographically defined markets
- Breakdown of tax expense relating to ordinary and extraordinary activities

Sundry disclosures:

- Type and amounts of contingent liabilities, if not set out in the balance sheet
- Total amount of other financial commitments
- Average number of employees
- The names of and financial relations with current and previous members the management and supervisory boards
- Total remuneration of the current and previous management and supervisory boards (separately for each group), unless the remuneration for single board members can be determined by such a disclosure

It should be noted that small and medium-sized corporations are granted certain simplifications for preparation and/or publication. For instance, small corporations neither have to provide details on extraordinary items and a fixed assets movement analysis, nor do they have to publish any disclosures relating to the income statement. Medium-sized corporations do not have to disclose the breakdown of sales by product lines and geographic markets. It is to be noted that apart from the analysis of sales (to be disclosed only by large corporations), no segment reporting is required by German law.

To a large extent, the above-described disclosures are also to be made in the notes to group financial statements. Important further disclosures in the group notes are:

- Uniform accounting and valuation principles applied
- Consolidation principles applied
- Details of consolidated and nonconsolidated group companies
- Translation of foreign currency financial statements

2.5.5 *Management Report*

The provisions (§§285 and 315 HGB) relating to the contents of the single entity and group management report are quite limited.

At a minimum, the management report must include a true and fair description of the company's/group's position and the business development during the fiscal year. In addition, the management report should include:

- Past balance sheet date events of great importance
- Anticipated future developments
- Disclosures regarding research and development

It should be noted that the management reports of smaller companies or groups mostly reflect only the minimum requirements and are quite brief. Usually they do not contribute further important information.

On the other hand, large and, especially, public companies use their management report as a promotional tool by adding analyses of accounts, by commenting on variations from previous years, by giving details of new products and markets, as well as by including a social report or a funds statement. Unlike Anglo-Saxon countries, the funds statement is not a compulsory component of financial statements, and if it is included, several different formats may be used, including those based on "net working capital" or "cash and equivalents" or variations thereof.

2.6 Auditor's Opinion

As previously mentioned, certified auditors/audit firms have the exclusive right to perform statutory audits and to issue opinions thereon. As an exception, certified accountants are allowed to perform statutory audits of medium-sized corporations.

The auditor must report on the audit. In particular, the auditor must confirm that the financial statements comply with the law. In addition, mention must be made of all material negative changes in net worth, financial position, and results, as well as of material losses that could jeopardize the going-concern assumption.

Unlike some other European countries, it is professional practice to prepare long-form audit reports only. The auditor's opinion included in the report (but not the rest of the report) must be published by the companies along with their financial statements. The standard audit opinion provided in §322 HGB reads as follows:

> Based on my/our audit performed in accordance with my/our professional duties, the accounting records and the (consolidated) financial statements comply with the legal regulations. The (consolidated) financial statements present, in compliance with generally accepted accounting principles, a true and fair view of the net worth, financial position and results of the company (group). The (group) management report is in agreement with the (consolidated) financial statements.

The audit opinion must be modified, if additional comments appear necessary in order to avoid creating an incorrect impression concerning the scope of the audit and the scope of the opinion, or if single entity and consolidated financial statements are combined in one set (see Section 2.7 below). Reference to the company's statutes is to be made, if they contain accounting-related regulations.

If there are objections, the auditor must qualify or disclaim his opinion. The objections must be explained in the opinion. Additions to the opinion like those described above do not represent qualifications.

According to statistics provided by the professional organizations, additions, qualifications, or disclaimers usually occur in less than 5% of cases.

It should be noted that the audit opinion refers to the financial statements as prepared. The auditor is not responsible for the correct publication of these financial statements.

2.7 Combination of Single Entity and Group Financial Statements

According to §298 and §315 HGB, parent companies are allowed to combine their single and consolidated financial statements and management reports. It is to be expected that in future an increasing number of companies will make use of this provision.

2.8 Sample Set of Financial Statements

As a sample, excerpts of the 1993 annual report of Friedrich Grohe AG are presented at the end of this chapter. Friedrich Grohe AG has recently been cited for its exemplary 1992 annual report by one of the most reputable business magazines in Germany.

We regard the statements of Friedrich Grohe AG as typical insofar as:

- They combine single entity and consolidated accounts.
- The balance sheet and income statements are presented in a simplified manner with supplementary analyses included in the notes.
- The content of the notes is limited mostly to the pure legal requirements.

On the other hand, we believe that the content of the management report might be typical only for very large companies; the majority of German companies tend to publish less information.

3. Accounting Policies and Practices: Implications for the Analyst

3.1 Consolidated Financial Statements

3.1.1 Overview

Consolidated financial statements are not the basis for either taxation or profit distributions but are of growing importance because of increasing national and international economic integration.

Regulations and principles for consolidated financial statements are largely the same for corporations and noncorporations. Important differences are described at the end of this section.

The basic consolidation provisions are incorporated in §§290–315 HGB. These are:

- Parent companies with a domestic head office are obliged to prepare and to publish consolidated financial statements, either:
  - —if they exercise *de facto* control over one or more companies in which they own a participation of usually more than 20% (traditional German concept); or
  - —if in principle they are able to exercise control by having the majority of voting rights, by being able to appoint or dismiss the members of the subsidiary boards, or because of a contract of domination or a domination clause incorporated in the bylaws of the subsidiary (Anglo-Saxon control concept).

There are exemptions for groups not exceeding certain size criteria (see Section 2.3 above), or if an ultimate parent having its head office in the EC reports on the group including the German subgroup on a statutory or voluntary basis.

- The group financial statements must include the parent and all domestic and foreign subsidiaries. Enterprises must be excluded from full consolidation if their inclusion would conflict with the requirement of a true and fair view (e.g., as a result of extremely divergent activities). Subsidiaries can be excluded, for instance, if they are immaterial or if the shares are held solely for the purpose of resale. Furthermore, exclusion of subsidiaries is allowed if the parent company's rights with regard to the subsidiary's assets are limited significantly or if the required information cannot be obtained from the subsidiary within a reasonable period of time or only at excessive costs.
- According to the one entity theory, the fiscal year-end and the accounting and valuation principles of all group companies must be identical. (As an important exception, however, German law allows consolidation of single entity financial statements if their closing date is earlier than the group's closing date but by not more than 3 months).

- Three forms of consolidation are permitted by law:
  - —Full consolidation for subsidiaries under control (e.g., over 50% of the voting rights)
  - —Proportional consolidation for joint ventures with uniform management by equal partners
  - —Equity accounting for associated enterprises on which a significant influence is exerted (e.g., 20%–50% of the voting rights).

Instead of proportional consolidation, joint ventures also may be included by using the equity method.

The new consolidation rules must be applied for fiscal years commencing in 1990. Generous transitional provisions were granted to companies adopting the new regulations earlier, mainly the option to exclude foreign subsidiaries, not to apply identical accounting and valuation principles, and most importantly, simplifications regarding capital consolidation (see Section 3.1.2 below).

As mentioned previously, only a few important deviations are allowed to noncorporations. These are:

- Group financial statements must be prepared only if control over subsidiaries actually is exercised (traditional German concept); the ability alone to exercise such control is not sufficient.
- The less stringent valuation principles for noncorporations (§253 HGB) can be applied (mainly retention of written-down values, even if the reasons for them no longer exist; write-downs of fixed and intangible assets also in case of a nonpermanent impairment in value; opportunity to create hidden reserves via "excess" depreciation within the framework of sound business judgment).

3.1.2 Capital Consolidation

Full Consolidation   The primary method of capital consolidation is the Anglo-Saxon purchase or acquisition method (§301 HGB). Under exceptional circumstances (e.g., exchange of shares), the pooling of interests or merger method may be applied, although this method is quite rare and not expected to become important. Therefore, the following comments focus on the purchase method, two sub-forms of which are permitted by law for the first consolidation:

- According to the book value method, the book values in the individual balance sheets (as adjusted because of the application of identical valuation principles) are compared with the cost of the investment. If a debit balance arises (e.g., because hidden reserves have been paid for in the purchase price), this must be allocated to the relevant balance sheet headings in the proportion of shares held. Any amount remaining is to be recorded as goodwill. Any credit balance arising must be recorded as a consolidation difference on the liability side of the balance sheet (negative goodwill, or "badwill").
- According to the current value method, the subsidiaries' book values are replaced by market values so that hidden reserves are fully reflected. After the revaluation, however, the proportional net equity of the subsidiary is not allowed to exceed the cost of the investment. Thus, no badwill can arise from applying this method.

Any debit or credit balances between proportional net equity and acquisition cost of the shares are classified as goodwill or badwill. Disclosed hidden reserves relating to other shareholders are dealt with by inclusion in the minority interest.

Because there is no specific regulation as to how upward revaluations ust be assigned to various categories of item, future income can be manipulated to a certain and often not insignificant extent. This is because revaluations reverse quickly, slowly, or not at all, depending on whether inventories, fixed assets, or other items are revalued upwards.

Goodwill arising at the time of the first consolidation either can be offset against equity reserves or can be amortized systematically over the years that are likely to benefit (§309 (1) HGB). Although a 4-year period is mentioned by law as the regular amortization period, a range of 0–40 years is widely regarded as acceptable.

Badwill must be shown as a consolidation difference on the liability side of the balance sheet and in principle should remain unchanged in future consolidations. Depending on its character, a reclassification to capital reserves or to accrued liabilities may be acceptable, if not even preferred. A release to income is allowed only if it becomes clear that it corresponds to a realized profit (a "lucky buy") or if the unfavorable developments anticipated in a reduced purchase price actually occur (§309 (2) HGB).

It is broadly understood that there are only classification differences between the book value and the current value method.

Determination of goodwill or badwill can be made on the basis of the values at the time of the acquisition of shares, at the time of the first consolidation, at the time the new consolidation regulations are first applied, or, in the case of a successive purchase of shares, at the time the enterprise becomes a subsidiary.

Furthermore, parent companies that adopted the new regulations for fiscal years before 1990 as a transitional simplification are allowed:

- To treat the full consolidation differences obtained by applying the former German method as goodwill/badwill; or
- To revalue the subsidiaries' assets and to interpret the remaining amounts as goodwill/badwill.

The characteristics of the former German method were:

- The annual determination of the consolidation difference (not named goodwill or badwill) by simply comparing the book values of the investments with the proportional subscribed capital and reserves of the subsidiaries at each balance sheet date;
- The absence of restatements to current value; and
- As a result of both, no impacts on subsequent years' consolidated income statements, since the consolidation differences were not amortized and there was no additional depreciation as a result of revaluations.

As described in the preceeding paragraphs, there are several options with regard to capital consolidation. Common practice has not yet been developed. However, surveys performed by German Institute of Certified Public Accountants (IdW) revealed the following indications:

- The clearly preferred capital consolidation method is the book value method.

- A clear majority of groups offsets goodwill arising at the time of the first consolidation against equity reserves; this partly is spread over 2 or more years.
- Of the remainder, most groups use an amortization period of more than 4 years. There is a tendency toward a 15-year period, which corresponds to the regular amortization period prescribed by the German Income Tax Law for goodwill arising in the single equity financial statements (see the section "Fixed Asset Movement Analysis below).

Proportional and Equity Consolidation   As far as it can be foreseen currently, proportional consolidation will not become important in Germany. If exceptionally it is applied, the same principles as for full consolidations (see preceeding section) are to be followed (§310 (2) HGB).

The time and method of goodwill determination as described above are basically also applicable to equity consolidation (§311 HGB). Classification can follow two methods: Either the full equity value of the investment can be shown on the balance sheet, with separate disclosure of the goodwill portion in the notes, or the equity value can be split between a participation value and goodwill already on the balance sheet.

3.1.3 Debt and Income Consolidation

Elimination of intercompany debt, of intercompany income and expnses, as well as of intercompany profits and losses in principle follow international standards. It should be noted, however, that in the first year of including subsidiaries in a consolidation, consolidation impacts may be directly offset against reserves, instead of affecting profit and loss (Article 27 EGHGB).

3.1.4 Deferred Taxation

According to §306 HGB, timing differences incurred in connection with consolidation measures (e.g., intercompany profit elimination) must be addressed by accounting for deferred taxes. This applies to deferred tax liabilities as well as to deferred tax assets.

At the same time, the deferred taxation provision for single entity financial statements (§274 HGB) applies, and this requires accounting for deferred tax liabilities but offers the option to account for a deferred tax asset.

Thus, timing differences resulting from the (revaluated) single entity financial statements and from consolidation entries may be handled differently. Furthermore, there is no general understanding with regard to the tax rules and/or tax rates to be applied. Consequently, there is a broad range of choice for deferred tax accounting policy.

3.1.5 Foreign Currency Translation

Neither the Commercial Code nor the Seventh Directive defines a method of translating foreign currency financial statements. Furthermore, common practice has not yet been established in Germany in that regard, so that the IdW has not yet issued a statement on this subject, although a draft version has been available since 1986. Consequently, a broad variety of methods like the current/noncurrent, the monetary/nonmonetary, the temporal, the closing, and the current rate method (FAS-52/IAS 21) and variants thereof are used.

Translation differences are dealt with in very different ways. Whereas some companies neutralize the differences in the balance sheet via cumulative translation adjustments, others let them affect profit and loss. A third group charges profit and loss in cases of translation losses and neutralizes translation gains via corresponding accruals.

Special attention must be given to the explanations in the notes to group financial statements, since the translation of foreign currency statements often materially affects the financial position and results of a group.

3.1.6 Summary

In Germany there is great scope for affecting consolidated financial statements by the choice of accounting policies. When analyzing financial statements, particular attention should be given to notes regarding capital consolidation, foreign currency translation, and deferred taxation.

3.2 Single Entity Financial Statements

3.2.1 *Capital and Reserves*

The minimum subscribed capital is DM 100,000 for AGs and DM 50,000 for GmbHs. The subscribed capital represents the maximum liability of the shareholders for liabilities of the company and is divided into single shares. Whereas GmbHs are allowed to acquire their own shares without restriction, if certain provisions, as described in §33 GmbHG, are met, the purchase of own shares by stock corporations is limited to 10% and to specific purposes (§71 Aktiengesetz, AktG, Stock Corporation Law).

Sole proprietorships and partnerships cannot have a subscribed capital by nature. Nevertheless, the so-called fixed capital accounts are sometimes described as subscribed capital, since those accounts have a similar function.

Regulations concerning reserves exist only for corporations. Reserves can be split into capital and revenue reserves. Capital reserves need not be broken down on the balance sheet and can include funds provided from outside. Revenue reserves must be split on the balance sheet by type and are created by transfers from retained earnings.

Capital reserves mainly consist of:

1. The premiums paid in connection with the issuance of new shares
2. Amounts received on the issuance of debentures with convertible rights and share options
3. Contributions from shareholders as consideration for preferential rights of their shares
4. Other shareholders' contributions to the capital

Revenue reserves are composed of:

5. Legal revenue reserves
6. Statutory reserves
7. Reserves for own shares
8. Other reserves

Provisions for reserves 1–7 are prescribed by law. Provisions for "other reserves" out of retained earnings are usually subject to the management board's decision. The reserve for own shares must be set up in an amount corresponding to the value of own shares capitalized. It must be established by transfer from free reserves or retained earnings. A legal revenue reserve is compulsory for AGs and KGaAs only. According to §150 AktG, the annual provision is 5% of the annual net income until the reserves 1–3 and 5 reach 10% (or a higher amount if required by the bylaws) of the corporation's subscribed capital. No such regulations exist for GmbHs.

Whereas the reversal of reserves for GmbHs is only restricted to types 6 and 7, AGs and KGaAs are also restricted regarding types 1–3 and 5. These reserves may be reversed only in order to compensate accumulated losses or to serve as funds for the increase of the subscribed capital. Special reference is made to §150 AktG.

3.2.2 Liabilities, Accruals, and Special Tax Items

Definitions

- Liabilities are obligations that are certain regarding existence, value, and maturity.
- *Accruals* are provisons for uncertain obligations, anticipated losses, and certain expenses incurred before the balance sheet date.
- *Special tax items* represent one element of the influence of the German tax law on commercial financial statements. They can include items with an equity portion, as well as items having a contra asset character.

The following comments focus on accruals and special tax items, which are of special importance to the analyst of German financial statements.

Special Tax Items Special tax items are usually classified under a heading placed between equity and accruals on the face of the balance sheet. Such items can contain items with an equity portion or differences between commercially required and tax-allowed depreciation.

The first type represents untaxed reserves and includes a liability portion (for deferred taxation) as well as an equity portion (for retained net income).

The item may be accounted for only if the item would otherwise not be tax deductible, as is usually the case for corporations.

Mainly capital gains from the disposal of fixed and financial assets (§6b EStG reserve) are "parked" here. Taxes on such capital gains are postponed if and to the extent that the capital gains are reinvested in qualifying assets.

The second type is a contra asset by nature. It includes the accumulated difference between depreciation allowed for tax purposes and that which is commercially justified. Special tax depreciation in particular is allowed in the area of the former German Democratic Republic as well as for research and development (R&D) assets. Alternatively, the special tax depreciation can also be accounted for as a reduction of assets (see Section 3.4 below).

The Commercial Code requires that the rules for setting up special tax items be disclosed. Since analysis by types and single items is not required, future income implications, in particular the timing of the reversal of these items, cannot be adequately determined by external analysts. This is partly addressed by the requirement to disclose in the notes the amounts by which the current year's income as well as subsequent years' income will be affected by setting up items with an equity portion or by applying special tax depreciation.

Accruals   German accounting legislation differs in the treatment of pension, tax, and other accruals to be separately shown on the balance sheet. Whereas pension and tax accruals represent provisions for uncertain liabilities, other accruals also include amounts to reflect loss contingencies and expense equalization accruals.

Accrued Pensions. German pension plans are mostly of a defined benefit type and generally are funded via:

- Pension accruals (internal funding) (the most common instrument)
- Companies' welfare funds (a common instrument)
- Independent pension funds (preferred by very large companies)
- Direct insurance policies (preferred by small companies)

Accrued pensions are one of the most critical issues in analyzing German financial statements, since there are significant exceptions from the need to accrue for pensions, and the accruals may be understated because of the calculation method usually applied.

The exceptions from setting up pension accruals are defined in Article 27 EGHGB. They refer to:

1. Pensions based on direct promises granted before 1987 (this also applies to claims increased thereafter but obtained before 1987)

2. Pensions based on indirect promises (mostly via companies' welfare funds)

Exception 1 must be interpreted as a transitional compromise (a so-called biological solution) with respect to companies that before the implementation of the Accounting Directives Law did not or did not fully account for pensions.

No such explanation is available for exception 2, which is important for companies financing their pensions via welfare funds. Because of certain labor court decisions, companies remain liable for the pension claims although the promises (formally) were granted by the welfare fund. In case of underfunding, therefore, from an economic point of view (but not by law), additional accruals for those indirect obligations are required. (It should be noted that such obligations do not occur if indirect promises are funded via pension funds or direct insurance policies.)

In order to compensate for the lack of accounting duties for certain direct and indirect claims, the amounts not accrued for must be disclosed in the notes. Overfunding of welfare funds, however, need not be disclosed.

As previously mentioned, the second significant problem in connection with pension accounting in Germany is the actuarial method normally used to determine the present value of the pension liabilities. This is a method prescribed in §6a of the German Income Tax Law, which works with a fixed discount rate of 6% but disregards future payroll increases and forbids the establishment of accruals for employees less than 30 years old. The latter may be regarded as an indirect consideration of the staff turnover factor, which is also not taken directly into account.

Because of the above weaknesses, the present values determined according to the tax method are mostly below the amounts determined according to more reasonable methods, for instance, below the projected benefit obligation as calculated according to the provisions of FAS-106. Although German companies may choose other methods to determine their pension obligations, the majority apply the tax method. This must be seen in connection with the close relationship between commercial and tax accounting (see Section 1.4 above) in Germany.

Other Accruals. Other accruals contain provisions for uncertain liabilities, anticipated losses, and for expense equalizations.

The legal requirements and common practice for the first two categories mostly comply with international standards. As an exception, it may be recognized that provisions for anniversary grants (cash payments or other benefits offered to employees if they stay, for instance, 5, 10, 15 years with the firm) often are not accounted for, since they will become tax deductible only to the extent that claims occur after 1992.

Expense equalization accruals mainly include repair and maintenance measures as well as other specific expenses to be allocated to past periods, if probable but uncertain with regard to amount or time.

Repairs and maintenance must be accrued for if carried out within 3 months of the balance sheet date. They may be provided for if carried out within 12 months.

Provisions for other specific expenses are optional, too. These provisions can include amounts for major repairs, for advertising campaigns and R&D projects not yet executed, or similar items. However, because of the lack of precision of the rule, adequate discretion is left to the preparers.

In this connection it should be noted that the external reader may be unable to determine to what extent various accounting options have been used, since this is not subject to a separate disclosure. Furthermore, it is becoming increasingly common practice not to break down other accruals by amounts but to comply with the disclosure requirements in the notes by mentioning only the type of significant other accruals.

In addition, it should be noted that optional accruals are not tax deductible and that, according to the prudence principle, the amounts accrued for need not be probable (except for expense equalization accruals) but only possible. This leaves considerable scope for conservative accounting.

3.2.3 *Fixed Assets*

Property, Plant, and Equipment: Overview As a part of fixed assets, property, plant, and equipment (PPE) include only items that are supposed to remain in the business for a long period of time. Corporations must disclose separately land, land rights, and buildings, machinery, factory and office equipment, and advanced payments and construction in progress.

As a general rule, PPE should be evaluated at acquisition or manufacturing cost, less regular depreciation. Acquisition cost includes the purchase price (after price reductions) plus incidental cost and expenses incurred to render the asset ready for use. Details of the definition of manufacturing cost are given in Section 3.2.4 below.

No specific methods are prescribed by law as to how to determine regular depreciation. The most common methods are the straight-line and the declining balance methods. Estimated useful lives are taken mostly from the tax tables available for various industries. The assumptions used in these tables are in general conservative.

Provisions for extraordinary depreciation are required if a permanent impairment of value is anticipated. It should be noted, however, that noncorporations are also allowed to write down PPE, if the impairment is only of a temporary nature. For corporations this option is applicable for financial assets only.

Furthermore, noncorporations are permitted to write down PPE within the framework of "sound business judgment." This rule has been incorporated explicitly into the Commercial Code in order to further allow noncorporations to create hidden reserves. Because small noncorporations are not obliged to prepare notes, and large noncorporations do not have to include a specific disclosure regarding the use of "sound business judgment," external analysts are hardly able to determine to what extent net worth and results are affected by extremely conservative accounting.

Another important simplification for noncorporations is that a written-down value may be retained, even if the reasons for the write-down no longer apply. Principally, corporations are obliged to reverse write-downs accounted for in the past if the reasons that had caused an extraordinary depreciation have become void. This ruling becomes optional if the retention of the lower carrying value is accepted for tax purposes and necessary for being accepted taxwise (i.e., the "authoritative principle," see also Section 1.4).

As a result, there are only two situations for corporations that make a reversal of a previously performed write-down mandatory:

- The write-down was recognized in the commercial books only but disregarded for tax purposes.
- Reasons for a write-down permissible only for tax purposes have become void.

It should be noted that the retention option for corporations has been implemented in the Commercial Code in order not to force such companies to create taxable income by making the write-ups.

Special Tax Depreciation   Valuation of PPE is highly influenced by tax regulations. This applies not only to the use of tax tables or the retention option as described earlier but also to special tax depreciation, which is accepted as a tax-deductible item only if accounted for in the commercial financial statements, too. In this case, however, the effect of special tax depreciation on the current and future years' results (but not the cumulative effect from previous years) needs to be disclosed in the notes.

The limit for capitilization (DM 800) commonly used for low value items, as well as the common practice of depreciating moveable fixed assets acquired in the first half of the year with the full annual rate and those acquired in the second half with half of the annual rate, are taken from German Income Tax Law.

Treatment of Government Grants   There is still no generally accepted practice in Germany with respect to accounting for government grants. Whereas some German companies immediately take those grants into income when received, others prefer to amortize the grants over the period that benefits therefrom. The latter method is becoming dominant, and it complies with a corresponding statement of the main technical committee of the IdW issued in 1984. The main provisions of that statement are as follows:

- Government grants must be accounted for at the time the claim is made, not just at the time cash payments are received.

- Investment grants are to be amortized according to the useful lives of the assets for which they are received.
- Grants to compensate expenses must be taken into profit and loss in the periods when the respective expenses are incurred.
- Unamortized portions of government grants preferably should be shown as a special item on the liability side of the balance sheet.
- Alternatively, investment grants may also reduce the "at cost" values of the corresponding assets.

Although it is broadly accepted that corporations and large noncorporations should disclose the accounting method applied for government grants in their notes, the relating impact on the income statement is in general hardly recognizable to external analysts. In addition, misinterpretations of the fixed asset movement analysis may occur if companies directly reduce the "at cost" values instead of presenting the unamortized portion of the grants in a separate item.

Intangible Assets   Intangible fixed assets are to be capitalized, if purchased. They may not be capitalized if created by the use of internal resources. Intangible current assets, however, are to be capitalized if not purchased from third parties.

The Commercial Code differs with regard to concessions, industrial rights, patents, licences, and similar rights on the one hand and goodwill and advances on intangibles on the other.

Accounting for Leases   As for many other issues, accounting for leases is in practice dominated by tax regulations, which are incorporated in various statements of the fiscal authorities.

The basic principles applicable to real estate as well as to other fixed assets leases are as follows:

- The leased asset must be accounted for by the lessor unless the lease is a financial lease.
- Financial leases are assumed to exist if the basic lease term is less than 40% or more than 90% of the useful life of the lease asset, and/or if bargain purchase or lease prolongation options have been agreed on.

- Special leased assets only usable by the lessee always must be accounted for by the lessee.

It should be noted that standard lease contracts are mostly structured in such a manner that the leased assets are to be capitalized by the lessor.

The IdW recommends that lessors show the leased assets separately on the balance sheet, but this cannot yet be regarded as a general accounting practice.

Lessees do not need to disclose details about the amounts of their financial or operating leases. Although corporations and large noncorporations must disclose future financial commitments in their notes, they need not distinguish between lease and other commitments, and they also do not have to give an analysis of the obligations by year.

Participations   Participations are defined as holdings in other enterprises that are designed to serve a business through a long-term relationship with the other business (§271 HGB).

According to the Commercial Code, two types of participation, namely, shares in affiliated companies and investments, must be differentiated. Whereas investments need comply only with the general definition provided above, shares in affiliated companies are only shown if the other company should in principle be included in the consolidated statements of the ultimate parent, according to the provisions for full consolidation.

For the application of this rule, it is irrelevant whether or not group financial statements are actually prepared or if the other company must be or can be excluded from consolidation in agreement with the legal provisions.

Bearing in mind the above, participations usually qualify as investments if 20%–50% of the other entity's nominal share capital is held. They normally qualify as shares in affiliated companies if the interest exceeds 50%.

It should be noted that there is a second definition of affiliated companies included in the Stock Corporation Law, which is not applicable to accounting questions but to other issues like the duty of AGs to prepare a dependency report. Such a dependency report is required in case of a dominating influence of a parent without a domination agreement. Another important definition in the Stock Corporation Law is the question of how many members of the supervisory board must be representatives of employees.

Like other financial assets, participations are to be carried at cost, unless exceptional depreciation is required. Participations in partnerships are an exception from historical cost accounting, being partly accounted for on an equity basis, as is usual for tax purposes.

Provisions for exceptional depreciation must be made in cases of a permanent impairment of capitalized value. They can be also made in cases of a temporary impairment. Unlike for property, plant, and equipment, the latter is applicable to corporations, too.

As a further special point, it should be mentioned that exceptional write-downs of participations can be retained, if once accepted by the tax authorities, even if their *raison d'être* no longer applies.

Fixed Asset Movement Analysis   Corporations and large noncorporations must provide a fixed asset movement analysis, either on the balance sheet or in the notes, which must include tangible, intangible, and financial assets as well as capitalized start-up/business expansion costs. Small noncorporations usually provide such an analysis on a voluntary basis in the balance sheet.

The format used by Friedrich Grohe AG in its 1993 notes to financial statements is the most commonly used format in Germany. As a particular point, it should be noted that German accounting legislation does not require the development of accumulated depreciation from the opening to the closing balance but only the disclosure of the closing balance and the depreciation expense of the year on an item-by-item basis.

The amounts classified as acquisition or manufacturing cost may include a mixture of historical cost and net book values as presented in the last financial statements prepared according to the old accounting legislation (mostly fiscal year 1986). This is because of a transitional simplification permitted by the Accounting Directives Law, making it difficult for external analysts to analyze the real aging of the fixed assets. Special attention therefore should be given to any reference to Article 24 (6) EGHGB in the notes.

It should be added that as an accounting convenience, start-up and business expansion costs may be capitalized. If so, annual amortization must be at least 25%. Furthermore, the amounts capitalized are unavailable for profit distribution. This rule also applies to deferred tax assets, if capitalized (see Section 3.2.6 below).

The valuation principles to be applied are the same as for PPE. Specific provisions exist for the depreciation of goodwill. Such provisions define a regular annual amortization rate of at least 25% but also allow a longer or faster amortization, if justifiable.

In this connection the 15-year depreciation period, as defined in the German Income Tax Law, plays a special role. Because of the common practice of differentiating between the commercial and tax accounts only where unavoidable, this 15-year period is often applied in commercial financial statements, too. The maximum period recognized by most commentators is 40 years.

It should be noted that goodwill in the single entity financial statements must be differentiated from that incurred through consolidation. It arises, for example, if a business is bought at a price exceeding the fair market value of the acquired assets. It can also occur when a partnership is merged at a net asset value that is below the book value of the participation. It cannot occur when shares are acquired, since all costs incurred in this connection are to be reflected as acquisition cost of the investment. With respect to the goodwill arising from consolidation, reference is made to Section 3.1.2 above.

3.2.4 Inventories

Inventories are usually divided into raw materials, work-in-progress, and finished goods and merchandise. Advance payments received on orders of material may be openly deducted from inventories or, alternatively, shown as liabilities.

Inventories must be stated at the lower of historical cost or market value. Historical cost can be derived by applying simplifying assumptions with regard to the usage of inventories like FIFO, LIFO, or average cost. It is to be expected that the LIFO method will become more important in the future, since starting in 1990 it has been accepted for tax purposes. Currently, average cost followed by FIFO are the most common methods.

Acquisition cost, which represents the basic values for raw material and merchandise, has been defined under Section 3.2.3 above.

Manufacturing cost, which is the basic value for work-in-progress and finished goods, comprises expenditures that are incurred through the consumption of goods and services in order to manufacture, enlarge, or improve an asset significantly beyond its original state. Table 3 identifies those cost components that need to or may be capitalized.

As Table 3 shows, German companies have a wide range of options by which to value their inventories. In practice, most companies comply with the tax regulations that require the capitalization of components 1–6. Only a minority of companies capitalize fewer or more components in their commercial accounts.

Interest expenses may be included in manufacturing cost only under exceptional conditions. They may be capitalized if incurred for the production of an asset but only to the extent that they are incurred during the production period. Idle capacity costs must be excluded from manufacturing costs.

Write-downs of inventories must be made if market values fall below historical cost (lower of cost or market principle). The applicable market for raw materials and supplies is usually the purchase market (replacement value). The market for finished goods is the sales market (net realizable value). For work-in-progress and merchandise, either market may apply. In any case, the lowest amount reasonably applicable must be used. This also means, for instance, that unlike the rule in some other countries, the replacement value is to be used if lower than historical cost, even if the net realizable value is above historical cost.

As a second peculiarity, the net realizable value in Germany is often determined by considering a mark-down to the sales price for an adequate entrepreneur's profit, since this is allowed for tax purposes.

A third point is the opportunity to anticipate expected future price reductions ("future" often being defined as up to 2 years) via inventory reserves, and the option for noncorporations to set up reserves within the framework of "sound business judgment."

Fourth, §80 of the Income Tax Execution Regulation (EStDV) allows the setting up of special allowances on imported goods like tobacco, coffee, and tea of up to 10% of the replacement cost at the balance sheet date, if also reflected in the commercial accounts.

Whereas the latter may be of importance for specific industries only, the definition of manufacturing cost and the option to set up allowances for

TABLE 3

	Commercial Accounts		Tax Accounts	
	Compulsory	*Optional*	*Compulsory*	*Optional*
1. Direct material cost	x		x	
2. Direct labor cost	x		x	
3. Special production costs	x		x	
4. Material overhead costs		x	x	
5. Labor overhead cost		x	x	
6. Depreciation of fixed assets		x	x	
7. General administration costs		x		x
8. Pensions and other social benefits		x		x
9. Interest expense		(x)		(x)
10. Selling expenses		—		—

future price reductions in particular provide great latitude for valuation. In addition, there remain judgmental areas with respect to the definition and evaluation of obsolete and excess items.

External analysts may find it difficult to estimate to what extent these options have been used, because the explanations in the notes are mostly limited to general remarks concerning accounting policy.

Deferred Income and Expenses   As a special feature of German accounting regulations, certain qualifying cash receipts and expenditures, respectively, must be recognized as deferral items shown seperately on the balance sheet. These captions are not to be qualified as assets or liabilities but only as mere deferral positions set up for proper allocation of income and expenses.

This ruling mainly applies to

- Expenditures made before the balance sheet date insofar as they must be reflected as expense within a distinct and identifiable period after year-end; as a result, these expenditures must be capitalized as deferred expense.
- Cash collected before the balance sheet date insofar as this must be reflected as income within a distinct and identifiable period after

year-end; these cash receipts must be set up separately on the liability side as deferred income.

In practice, the main components of these captions are cash receipts or expenditures, respectively, with regard to services that will be rendered or claimed after year-end only (e.g., prepaid leases and insurance premiums).

Long-term Production Projects   As a general rule, income may be recognized only if the agreed-upon product or service has been (almost) completely rendered. Exceptions to this basic principle are accepted for long-term production projects in order to avoid high fluctuations of income. Thus, besides the still dominant completed-contract-method, the percentage-of-completion method optionally can be applied.

Because of the absence of specific provisions, the income recognition principles as outlined in IAS 11 are widely accepted by German accounting practice. In either case, the income recognition method must be described in the notes, if material amounts are concerned.

3.2.5 Receivables

Accounting for receivables and other current assets in Germany is quite similar to practice in other European countries and, therefore, will not be commented on in detail. It should be noted, however, that other current assets mostly also include items of a long-term nature, such as cash surrender values of pension reinsurances. This may lead to misinterpretations. Additionally, and differing from practice in other countries, receivables denominated in foreign currencies are mostly not translated at the closing date rate but at the lower of the closing date or historical rates. For payables, the opposite rule is applied, which leads to the result that translation losses are always considered but translation gains never.

Whereas this practice might comply with the so-called imparity principle, departures from a true and fair presentation may well occur, particularly if there are corresponding foreign currency receivables and payables. Therefore, exceptions to the stringent imparity principle are widely accepted, at least in the case of corresponding assets and liabilities denominated in foreign currencies, as well as in the case of forward contracts.

The translation method applied must be disclosed in the notes.

3.2.6 *Taxation*

The following comments are confined to income taxes, two types of which are levied in Germany.

The trade tax on income (TTI) is a municipal tax set at between 10% and 20% of the taxable income, depending on the rates fixed locally. Except for timing differences, the main deviation between taxable and commercial income is usually that 50% of interest expenses on long-term loans must be added back to the commercial income. Corporations and noncorporations are subject to TTI.

Only corporations are subject to the corporation income tax (CIT), which is a federal tax. There is a split tax rate, amounting to 30% (36% up to 1993 inclusive) if profits are fully distributed, and to 45% (50% up to 1993 inclusive), if profits are fully retained. Because of the imputation system, from a German shareholder's point of view, the CIT qualifies as a prepayment of personal income taxes. For foreign investors the CIT typically results in a definite tax charge. Except for timing differences, the taxable income for CIT purposes can be determined roughly as equal to commercial income after deducting TTI and adding back property taxes and 50% of the supervisory board's compensation.

Depending on the local TTI rate and the decision whether to retain or distribute profits, the total income tax burden for corporations may range between approximately 37% and 56% of pretax income for fiscal year 1994 and between 39% and 59% of pretax income for fiscal years from 1995 on because of a 7.5% surtax that will be imposed on CIT resulting from the additional fiscal needs due to the still ongoing reunification process in Germany.

Although the majority of German companies tend to prepare only one set of financial statements, there can be many differences between commercial and taxable income, due to technical reasons. In addition, those differences may occur because of accounting measures that are not acceptable for tax purposes. For instance:

- If start-up or business expansion cost is capitalized
- If gross inventories are priced below the minimum amounts accepted for tax purposes

- If inventory reserves are established at amounts exceeding the amounts allowed for tax purposes (e.g., anticipation of future price reductions, reserves based on "sound business judgment")
- If accruals are not accepted for tax purposes (e.g., expense equalization accruals, repair and maintenance accruals for accruals not spent within 3 months of the balance sheet date, retrieval of pension reserves not accrued for in the past).

Although the above deviations are in principle subject to deferred taxation, accounting for deferred taxation does not play an important role in Germany, since in most cases a deferred tax asset arises that does not need to be capitalized according to §274 HGB and usually is not capitalized by German companies. Thus, analysts may still find discrepancies between the tax expense and the pretax income reported in the commercial financial statements.

It should be added that the Commercial Code mainly follows the liability method of deferred tax accounting as presented in IAS 12.

As a side point, the substantially higher CIT rate on retained profits has been established in order to persuade German companies to distribute their profits rather than retain them. The shareholders in this case must decide whether to reinvest the dividends in the company or in an alternative investment. It is commonly understood that this decision process contributes to a better allocation of funds within the whole economy.

4. Expected Future Developments

As mentioned in the introductory part of this chapter, the implementation of the Fourth and Seventh EC Directives into German law represented an important step in German accounting history. At present there are no further indications that its significance will change in the short to medium term.

The most important change to be faced in the near future is the extension of the stringent accounting, auditing, and disclosure requirements for corporations to GmbH & Co.'s, which formally represent partnerships but contain strong elements of corporations. The exclusion of GmbH & Co.'s from the regulations applicable to corporations never was accepted by the majority of the other European countries and the above extension decision recently passed by the Cabinet Council of the EC will be applicable commencing January 1, 1995 for all partnerships whose only general partner is a corporation.

Further, less important, changes might be Pan-European upward adjustments to the size criteria for corporations, in order to reflect inflation or to focus more directly on larger companies. The latest upward adjustments were incorporated into the Commercial Code on July 25, 1994. They can be applied retroactively for fiscal years beginning after January 1, 1990. In addition, the German government is aiming to restructure the disclosure requirements for small and medium-sized companies, which are regarded as excessive and too complex.

Because of the increasing internationalization and the extension of the legal requirement to prepare group accounts to GmbHs, which are below the size criteria of the Publicity Law, consolidated financial statements have become more and more important. Since the transition of the Seventh EC Directive into the German Commercial Code, which had to be applied by German companies in 1990 at the latest, significant progress has been made in establishing widely accepted and standardized group accounting practices.

At present it seems that the number of companies publishing their single entity and group financial statements is decreasing rather than increasing. Considering the low incidence of publication in past years, it seems doubtful that an improvement can be achieved without increasing the legal penalties for nonpublication.

Companies in the former German Democratic Republic had to adopt West German accounting legislation beginning in mid-1990. So far, no major deviations are expected in the long term. In the short term, however, a considerable number of discrepancies and particularities must be taken into account. For instance, it should be noted that the Deutsche mark values of the opening balance sheet as of July 1, 1990 need to be adjusted retroactively until fiscal year 1994, if material discrepancies are identified subsequently. This will further complicate the analysis of the net worth and financial position of East German companies for external analysts during the next few years.

Useful Addresses

Institut der Wirtschaftsprufer
Tersteegenstrasse 14
4000 Dusseldorf 30
Germany
Tel: +(211) 45610
Fax: +(211) 454 1097

Wirtschaftspruferkammer
Tersteegenstrasse 14
4000 Dusseldorf 30
Germany
Tel: +(211) 45610
Fax: +(211) 4561 193

Friedrich Grohe AG, Hemer
Konzernbilanz zum 31. Dezember 1993

AKTIVA	Anhang IV	1993 DM	1993 DM	*1992 TDM*
A. Anlagevermögen	(1)			
I. Immaterielle Vermögensgegenstände				
Software			1.359.731	*1.251*
II. Sachanlagen				
1. Grundstücke und Bauten		100.381.538		*75.274*
2. Technische Anlagen und Maschinen ...		40.725.931		*31.149*
3. Andere Anlagen, Betriebs- und Geschäftsausstattung		59.282.063		*47.816*
4. Geleistete Anzahlungen und Anlagen im Bau		22.770.289		*27.791*
			223.159.821	*182.030*
III. Finanzanlagen				
1. Anteile an verbundenen Unternehmen		–		*9.000*
2. Beteiligungen an assoziierten Unternehmen		821.600		*–*
3. Beteiligungen		44.197		*–*
4. Wertpapiere des Anlagevermögens		313.957		*304*
5. Sonstige Ausleihungen		300.000		*571*
			1.479.754	*9.875*
			225.999.306	*193.156*
B. Umlaufvermögen				
I. Vorräte	(2)			
1. Roh-, Hilfs- und Betriebsstoffe		30.072.485		*36.195*
2. Unfertige Erzeugnisse		56.329.041		*59.272*
3. Fertige Erzeugnisse und Waren		84.936.350		*89.239*
			171.337.876	*184.706*
II. Forderungen und sonstige Vermögensgegenstände				
1. Forderungen aus Lieferungen und Leistungen	(3)	140.840.331		*131.497*
2. Forderungen gegen verbundene Unternehmen	(3)	–		*27.676*
3. Sonstige Vermögensgegenstände	(4)	19.947.744		*19.303*
			160.788.075	*178.476*
III. Kassenbestand, Postgiroguthaben, Guthaben bei Kreditinstituten			120.241.816	*89.094*
			452.367.767	*452.276*
C. Rechnungsabgrenzungsposten	(5)		491.653	*435*
D. Abgrenzungsposten für latente Steuern ..	(6)		9.370.042	*10.645*
			688.228.768	*656.512*

34

Friedrich Grohe AG, Hemer
Consolidated Balance Sheet as of December 31, 1993

ASSETS	Note IV	1993 DM	1993 DM	1992 KDM
A. Fixed assets	(1)			
I. Intangible assets				
Software			1,359,731	1,251
II. Tangible assets				
1. Land and buildings		100,381,538		75,274
2. Technical equipment and machinery		40,725,931		31,149
3. Other equipment, factory and office equipment		59,282,063		47,816
4. Advance payments and construction in progress		22,770,289		27,791
			223,159,821	182,030
III. Financial assets				
1. Shares in affiliated companies		–		9,000
2. Investments in associated companies		821,600		–
3. Participating interests		44,197		–
4. Other long-term investments		313,957		304
5. Other loans		300,000		571
			1,479,754	9,875
			225,999,306	193,156
B. Current assets				
I. Inventories	(2)			
1. Raw materials and supplies		30,072,485		36,195
2. Work in progress		56,329,041		59,272
3. Finished goods and goods purchased for resale		84,936,350		89,239
			171,337,876	184,706
II. Receivables and other assets				
1. Trade receivables	(3)	140,840,331		131,497
2. Receivables from affiliated companies	(3)	–		27,676
3. Other assets	(4)	19,947,744		19,303
			160,788,075	178,476
III. Cash in hand, in postal giro accounts and at banks			120,241,816	89,094
			452,367,767	452,276
C. Prepaid expenses and deferred charges	(5)		491,653	435
D. Deferred taxes	(6)		9,370,042	10,645
			688,228,768	656,512

34

PASSIVA	Anhang IV	1993 DM	1993 DM	1992 TDM
A. Eigenkapital				
I. Gezeichnetes Kapital	(7)			
Stammaktien		65.000.000		*65.000*
Vorzugsaktien ohne Stimmrecht		51.000.000		*51.000*
Bedingtes Kapital: DM 58.000.000			116.000.000	*116.000*
II. Kapitalrücklage	(8)		183.000.000	*183.000*
III. Andere Gewinnrücklagen	(9)		27.865.297	*18.759*
IV. Bilanzgewinn			49.243.847	*47.326*
V. Ausgleichsposten für Anteile anderer Gesellschafter am Eigenkapital	(10)		439.462	*439*
			376.548.606	*365.524*
B. Sonderposten mit Rücklageanteil			–	*215*
C. Sonderposten für Investitionszuschüsse und -zulagen zum Anlagevermögen	(11)		6.066.335	*–*
D. Rückstellungen				
1. Rückstellungen für Pensionen		114.450.048		*105.549*
2. Steuerrückstellungen	(12)	11.363.054		*18.468*
3. Sonstige Rückstellungen	(13)	83.302.366		*69.408*
			209.115.468	*193.425*
E. Verbindlichkeiten	(14)			
1. Verbindlichkeiten gegenüber Kreditinstituten		37.558.295		*45.530*
2. Verbindlichkeiten aus Lieferungen und Leistungen		31.327.280		*28.659*
3. Verbindlichkeiten gegenüber assoziierten Unternehmen		487.589		*–*
4. Sonstige Verbindlichkeiten		27.125.195		*23.159*
– davon aus Steuern: DM 4.187.078 (1992: TDM 3.366)				
– davon im Rahmen der sozialen Sicherheit: DM 8.236.431 (1992: TDM 6.995)				
			96.498.359	*97.348*
			688.228.768	*656.512*

35

SHAREHOLDERS' EQUITY AND LIABILITIES	Note IV	1993 DM	1993 DM	1992 KDM
A. Shareholders' equity				
I. Subscribed capital	(7)			
Ordinary share capital		65,000,000		65,000
Non-voting preference share capital		51,000,000		51,000
Conditional capital: DM 58,000,000			116,000,000	116,000
II. Capital reserve	(8)		183,000,000	183,000
III. Other revenue reserves	(9)		27,865,297	18,759
IV. Retained earnings			49,243,847	47,326
V. Minority interests	(10)		439,462	439
			376,548,606	365,524
B. Special items with an equity portion			–	215
C. Special items for investment grants and premiums to fixed assets	(11)		6,066,335	–
D. Accruals				
1. Accruals for pensions		114,450,048		105,549
2. Accrued taxes	(12)	11,363,054		18,468
3. Other accruals	(13)	83,302,366		69,408
			209,115,468	193,425
E. Accounts payable	(14)			
1. Amounts owed to banks		37,558,295		45,530
2. Trade payables		31,327,280		28,659
3. Amounts owed to associated companies		487,589		–
4. Other payables		27,125,195		23,159
– thereof for taxes: DM 4,187,078 (1992: KDM 3,366)				
– thereof for social security: DM 8,236,431 (1992: KDM 6,995)				
			96,498,359	97,348
			688,228,768	656,512

35

Friedrich Grohe AG, Hemer
Bilanz zum 31. Dezember 1993

AKTIVA

	Anhang IV	1993 DM	1993 DM	1992 TDM
A. Anlagevermögen	(1)			
I. Immaterielle Vermögensgegenstände				
Software			1.225.488,—	1.218
II. Sachanlagen				
1. Grundstücke und Bauten		13.708.124,50		13.630
2. Technische Anlagen und Maschinen		10.918.927,—		12.660
3. Andere Anlagen, Betriebs- und Geschäftsausstattung		29.294.538,—		24.930
4. Geleistete Anzahlungen und Anlagen im Bau		14.797.267,45		9.529
			68.718.856,95	60.749
III. Finanzanlagen				
1. Anteile an verbundenen Unternehmen		44.940.600,—		38.878
2. Ausleihungen an verbundene Unternehmen		4.431.250,—		4.468
3. Beteiligungen		4.700.000,—		–
4. Sonstige Ausleihungen		300.000,—		571
			54.371.850,—	43.917
			124.316.194,95	105.884
B. Umlaufvermögen				
I. Vorräte	(2)			
1. Roh-, Hilfs- und Betriebsstoffe		9.676.491,—		12.483
2. Unfertige Erzeugnisse		21.666.816,—		24.060
3. Fertige Erzeugnisse und Waren		26.084.384,—		26.490
			57.427.691,—	63.033
II. Forderungen und sonstige Vermögensgegenstände				
1. Forderungen aus Lieferungen und Leistungen	(3)	66.547.913,65		61.528
2. Forderungen gegen verbundene Unternehmen	(3)	167.878.849,86		199.069
3. Sonstige Vermögensgegenstände	(4)	7.545.397,83		6.963
			241.972.161,34	267.560
III. Kassenbestand, Postgiroguthaben, Guthaben bei Kreditinstituten			99.342.159,44	72.017
			398.742.011,78	402.610
C. Rechnungsabgrenzungsposten	(5)		250.841,—	128
			523.309.047,73	508.622

36

Friedrich Grohe AG, Hemer
Balance Sheet as of December 31, 1993

ASSETS

	Note IV	1993 DM	1993 DM	1992 KDM
A. Fixed assets	(1)			
I. Intangible assets				
Software			1,225,488.—	1,218
II. Tangible assets				
1. Land and buildings		13,708,124.50		13,630
2. Technical equipment and machinery		10,918,927.—		12,660
3. Other equipment, factory and office equipment		29,294,538.—		24,930
4. Advance payments and construction in progress		14,797,267.45		9,529
			68,718,856.95	60,749
III. Financial assets				
1. Shares in affiliated companies ..		44,940,600.—		38,878
2. Loans to affiliated companies ...		4,431,250.—		4,468
3. Participating interests		4,700,000.—		–
4. Other loans		300,000.—		571
			54,371,850.—	43,917
			124,316,194.95	105,884
B. Current assets				
I. Inventories	(2)			
1. Raw materials and supplies		9,676,491.—		12,483
2. Work in progress		21,666,816.—		24,060
3. Finished goods and goods purchased for resale		26,084,384.—		26,490
			57,427,691.—	63,033
II. Receivables and other assets				
1. Trade receivables	(3)	66,547,913.65		61,528
2. Receivables from affiliated companies..................	(3)	167,878,849.86		199,069
3. Other assets	(4)	7,545,397.83		6,963
			241,972,161.34	267,560
III. Cash in hand, in postal giro accounts and at banks			99,342,159.44	72,017
			398,742,011.78	402,610
C. Prepaid expenses and deferred charges	(5)		250,841.—	128
			523,309,047.73	508,622

PASSIVA

	Anhang IV	1993 DM	1993 DM	1992 TDM
A. Eigenkapital				
I. Gezeichnetes Kapital	(7)			
Stammaktien		65.000.000,—		65.000
Vorzugsaktien ohne Stimmrecht . . .		51.000.000,—		51.000
Bedingtes Kapital: DM 58.000.000,—			116.000.000,—	116.000
II. Kapitalrücklage	(8)		183.000.000,—	183.000
III. Andere Gewinnrücklagen	(9)		20.000.000,—	–
IV. Bilanzgewinn			40.135.221,15	40.600
			359.135.221,15	339.600
B. Sonderposten mit Rücklageanteil . .			–	141
C. Rückstellungen				
1. Rückstellungen für Pensionen		71.879.574,—		65.825
2. Steuerrückstellungen	(12)	4.038.819,—		13.693
3. Sonstige Rückstellungen	(13)	49.364.034,13		42.118
			125.282.427,13	121.636
D. Verbindlichkeiten	(14)			
1. Verbindlichkeiten gegenüber				
Kreditinstituten		2.872.181,08		12.947
2. Verbindlichkeiten aus Lieferungen				
und Leistungen		21.584.431,14		19.617
3. Verbindlichkeiten gegenüber				
verbundenen Unternehmen		757.297,22		2.847
4. Verbindlichkeiten gegenüber				
Unternehmen, mit denen ein				
Beteiligungsverhältnis besteht		487.589,—		–
5. Sonstige Verbindlichkeiten		13.189.901,01		11.834
– davon aus Steuern: DM 2.439.325,92				
(1992: TDM 1.995)				
– davon im Rahmen der sozialen				
Sicherheit: DM 2.878.400,85				
(1992: TDM 2.586)				
			38.891.399,45	47.245
			523.309.047,73	508.622

37

SHAREHOLDERS' EQUITY AND LIABILITIES

	Note IV	1993 DM	1993 DM	1992 KDM
A. Shareholders' equity				
I. Subscribed capital	(7)			
Ordinary share capital		65,000,000.—		65,000
Non-voting preference share capital		51,000,000.—		51,000
Conditional capital: DM 58,000,000.–			116,000,000.—	116,000
II. Capital reserve	(8)		183,000,000.—	183,000
III. Other revenue reserves	(9)		20,000,000.—	–
IV. Retained earnings			40,135,221.15	40,600
			359,135,221.15	339,600
B. Special items with an equity portion			–	141
C. Accruals				
1. Accruals for pensions		71,879,574.—		65,825
2. Accrued taxes	(12)	4,038,819.—		13,693
3. Other accruals	(13)	49,364,034.13		42,118
			125,282,427.13	121,636
D. Accounts payable	(14)			
1. Amounts owed to banks		2,872,181.08		12,947
2. Trade payables		21,584,431.14		19,617
3. Amounts owed to affiliated companies		757,297.22		2,847
4. Amounts owed to other group companies		487,589.—		–
5. Other payables		13,189,901.01		11,834
– thereof for taxes: DM 2,439,325.92 (1992: KDM 1,995)				
– thereof for social security: DM 2,878,400.85 (1992: KDM 2,586)				
			38,891,399.45	47,245
			523,309,047.73	508,622

37

Friedrich Grohe AG, Hemer
Konzerngewinn- und -verlustrechnung für das Geschäftsjahr 1993

	Anhang V	1993 DM	1992 TDM
1. Umsatzerlöse	(1)	881.482.441	836.038
2. Herstellungskosten der zur Erzielung der Umsatzerlöse erbrachten Leistungen		589.151.118	569.574
3. Bruttoergebnis vom Umsatz		292.331.323	266.464
4. Vertriebskosten		189.504.971	169.286
5. Allgemeine Verwaltungskosten		23.559.932	23.242
6. Sonstige betriebliche Erträge	(4)	13.367.501	7.654
7. Sonstige betriebliche Aufwendungen	(5)	11.781.073	8.173
8. Erträge aus assoziierten Unternehmen		444.600	–
9. Erträge aus anderen Wertpapieren und Ausleihungen des Finanzanlagevermögens		25.934	35
10. Sonstige Zinsen und ähnliche Erträge		6.274.314	8.818
– davon aus verbundenen Unternehmen: DM – (1992: TDM 2.481)			
11. Zinsen und ähnliche Aufwendungen		3.401.304	4.531
12. Ergebnis der gewöhnlichen Geschäftstätigkeit		84.196.392	77.739
13. Steuern vom Einkommen und vom Ertrag	(6)	35.658.971	35.976
14. Jahresüberschuß		48.537.421	41.763
15. Anderen Gesellschaftern zustehender Gewinn		80.000	80
16. Gewinnvortrag aus dem Vorjahr		20.786.426	5.643
17. Einstellung in andere Gewinnrücklagen		20.000.000	–
18. Bilanzgewinn		49.243.847	47.326

38

Friedrich Grohe AG, Hemer
Consolidated Statement of Income for the Financial Year 1993

	Note V	1993 DM	1992 KDM
1. Sales	(1)	881,482,441	836,038
2. Cost of sales		589,151,118	569,574
3. Gross profit		292,331,323	266,464
4. Sales-related expenses		189,504,971	169,286
5. General administrative expenses		23,559,932	23,242
6. Other operating income	(4)	13,367,501	7,654
7. Other operating expenses	(5)	11,781,073	8,173
8. Income from associated companies		444,600	–
9. Income from other long-term investments and loans		25,934	35
10. Other interest and similar income		6,274,314	8,818
– thereof from affiliated companies: DM – (1992: KDM 2,481)			
11. Interest and similar expenses		3,401,304	4,531
12. Profit on ordinary activities		84,196,392	77,739
13. Taxes on income	(6)	35,658,971	35,976
14. Net income		48,537,421	41,763
15. Profit attributable to minority interests		80,000	80
16. Unappropriated surplus carried forward from previous year		20,786,426	5,643
17. Transfer to other revenue reserves		20,000,000	–
18. Retained earnings		49,243,847	47,326

Friedrich Grohe AG, Hemer
Gewinn- und Verlustrechnung für das Geschäftsjahr 1993

	Anhang V	1993 DM	1993 DM	1992 TDM
1. Umsatzerlöse	(1)		771.928.147,24	706.222
2. Herstellungskosten der zur Erzielung der Umsatzerlöse erbrachten Leistungen			603.702.553,61	541.428
3. Bruttoergebnis vom Umsatz			168.225.593,63	164.794
4. Vertriebskosten			109.424.016,38	92.435
5. Allgemeine Verwaltungskosten			10.912.125,—	9.336
6. Sonstige betriebliche Erträge	(4)		24.022.512,49	23.842
7. Sonstige betriebliche Aufwendungen . . .	(5)		24.106.758,66	25.300
8. Erträge aus Beteiligungen			6.170.023,47	2.753
– davon aus verbundenen Unternehmen: DM 6.170.023,47 (1992: TDM 2.753)				
9. Erträge aus Gewinnabführungsverträgen			18.615.023,71	11.302
10. Erträge aus Ausleihungen des Finanzanlagevermögens			2.515,—	10
11. Sonstige Zinsen und ähnliche Erträge . . .			4.983.649,83	10.628
– davon aus verbundenen Unternehmen: DM 461.180,— (1992: TDM 5.471)				
12. Abschreibungen auf Finanzanlagen			–	505
13. Aufwendungen aus Verlustübernahme . .			3.458.769,92	10.378
14. Zinsen und ähnliche Aufwendungen			962.111,17	2.058
– davon an verbundene Unternehmen: DM 162.790,20 (1992: TDM 379)				
15. Ergebnis der gewöhnlichen Geschäftstätigkeit			73.155.537,—	73.317
16. Steuern vom Einkommen und vom Ertrag	(6)	30.011.722,—		30.981
Umlagen Konzerngesellschaften		(2.931.500,—)	27.080.222,—	1.736
17. Jahresüberschuß			46.075.315,—	40.600
18. Gewinnvortrag			14.059.906,15	
19. Einstellung in andere Gewinnrücklagen			20.000.000,—	–
20. Bilanzgewinn			40.135.221,15	40.600

39

Friedrich Grohe AG, Hemer
Statement of Income for the Financial Year 1993

	Note V	1993 DM	1993 DM	1992 KDM
1. Sales	(1)		771,928,147.24	706,222
2. Cost of sales			603,702,553.61	541,428
3. Gross profit			168,225,593.63	164,794
4. Sales-related expenses			109,424,016.38	92,435
5. General administrative expenses			10,912,125.—	9,336
6. Other operating income	(4)		24,022,512.49	23,842
7. Other operating expenses	(5)		24,106,758.66	25,300
8. Income from participating interests			6,170,023.47	2,753
– thereof from affiliated companies: DM 6,170,023.47 (1992: KDM 2,753)				
9. Income from profit and loss absorption agreements			18,615,023.71	11,302
10. Income from long-term loans			2,515.—	10
11. Other interest and similar income			4,983,649.83	10,628
– thereof from affiliated companies: DM 461,180.— (1992: KDM 5,471)				
12. Depreciation on financial assets			–	505
13. Expenses from profit and loss absorption agreements			3,458,769.92	10,378
14. Interest and similar expenses			962,111.17	2,058
– thereof to affiliated companies: DM 162,790.20 (1992: KDM 379)				
15. Profit on ordinary activities			73,155,537.—	73,317
16. Taxes on income	(6)	30,011,722.—		30,981
Allocations to group companies		(2,931,500.—)	27,080,222.—	1,736
17. Net income			46,075,315.—	40,600
18. Unappropriated surplus carried forward ..			14,059,906.15	–
19. Transfer to other revenue reserves			20,000,000.—	–
20. Retained earnings			40,135,221.15	40,600

39

Friedrich Grohe AG, Hemer
Konzernanlagespiegel für das Geschäftsjahr 1993

	Anschaffungs-/ Herstellungskosten 1. Januar 1993 DM	Zugänge DM
I. Immaterielle Vermögensgegenstände		
Software	1.899.011	826.608
II. Sachanlagen		
1. Grundstücke und Bauten	133.952.793	23.780.273
2. Technische Anlagen und Maschinen	150.429.915	19.504.952
3. Andere Anlagen, Betriebs- und Geschäftsausstattung	134.140.615	23.906.437
4. Geleistete Anzahlungen und Anlagen im Bau	27.790.781	17.278.907
	446.314.104	84.470.569
III. Finanzanlagen		
1. Anteile an verbundenen Unternehmen	9.000.000	–
2. Beteiligungen an assoziierten Unternehmen	–	821.600
3. Beteiligungen	–	44.197
4. Wertpapiere des Anlagevermögens	304.315	9.642
5. Sonstige Ausleihungen	570.700	–
	9.875.015	875.439
	458.088.130	86.172.616

40

Abgänge DM	Umbuchungen DM	Kumulierte Abschreibungen DM	Buchwert 31. Dezember 1993 DM	Abschreibungen des Geschäfts- jahres DM
193.472	–	1.172.416	1.359.731	673.085
372.907	6.509.372	63.487.993	100.381.538	4.125.979
8.382.126	8.061.439	128.888.249	40.725.931	14.851.554
7.540.672	6.669.090	97.893.407	59.282.063	17.253.176
1.059.498	(21.239.901)	–	22.770.289	–
17.355.203	–	290.269.649	223.159.821	36.230.709
9.000.000	–	–	–	–
–	–	–	821.600	–
–	–	–	44.197	–
–	–	–	313.957	–
270.700	–	–	300.000	–
9.270.700	–	–	1.479.754	–
26.819.375	–	291.442.065	225.999.306	36.903.794

41

Friedrich Grohe AG, Hemer
Consolidated Statement of Movements in Fixed Assets and
Related Depreciation for the Financial Year 1993

	At cost, January 1, 1993 DM	Additions DM
I. Intangible assets		
Software	1,899,011	826,608
II. Tangible assets		
1. Land and buildings	133,952,793	23,780,273
2. Technical equipment and machinery	150,429,915	19,504,952
3. Other equipment, factory and office equipment	134,140,615	23,906,437
4. Advance payments and construction in progress	27,790,781	17,278,907
	446,314,104	84,470,569
III. Financial assets		
1. Shares in affiliated companies	9,000,000	–
2. Investments in associated companies	–	821,600
3. Participating interests	–	44,197
4. Other long-term investments	304,315	9,642
5. Other loans	570,700	–
	9,875,015	875,439
	458,088,130	86,172,616

Disposals DM	Re- classifications DM	Accumulated depreciation DM	Net book value, December 31, 1993 DM	Depreciation during financial year DM
193,472	–	1,172,416	1,359,731	673,085
372,907	6,509,372	63,487,993	100,381,538	4,125,979
8,382,126	8,061,439	128,888,249	40,725,931	14,851,554
7,540,672	6,669,090	97,893,407	59,282,063	17,253,176
1,059,498	(21,239,901)	–	22,770,289	–
17,355,203	–	290,269,649	223,159,821	36,230,709
9,000,000	–	–	–	–
–	–	–	821,600	–
–	–	–	44,197	–
–	–	–	313,957	–
270,700	–	–	300,000	–
9,270,700	–	–	1,479,754	–
26,819,375	–	291,442,065	225,999,306	36,903,794

Friedrich Grohe AG, Hemer
Anlagespiegel für das Geschäftsjahr 1993

	Anschaffungs-/ Herstellungskosten 1. Januar 1993 DM	Zugänge DM
I. Immaterielle Vermögensgegenstände		
Software	1.671.658,24	608.152,88
II. Sachanlagen		
1. Grundstücke und Bauten	44.913.858,21	12.310,94
2. Technische Anlagen und Maschinen	60.309.321,37	1.996.927,33
3. Andere Anlagen, Betriebs- und Geschäftsausstattung	65.526.174,94	8.371.640,47
4. Geleistete Anzahlungen und Anlagen im Bau	9.529.111,93	10.796.356,82
	180.278.466,45	21.177.235,56
III. Finanzanlagen		
1. Anteile an verbundenen Unternehmen	39.383.334,—	6.062.266,—
2. Ausleihungen an verbundene Unternehmen	4.467.863,—	–
3. Beteiligungen	–	4.700.000,—
4. Sonstige Ausleihungen	570.700,—	–
	44.421.897,—	10.762.266,—
	226.372.021,69	32.547.654,44

Abgänge DM	Umbuchungen DM	Kumulierte Abschreibungen DM	Buchwert 31. Dezember 1993 DM	Abschreibungen des Geschäfts- jahres DM
6.293,35	–	1.048.029,77	1.225.488,—	600.992,52
9.980,07	701.200,74	31.909.265,32	13.708.124,50	635.294,08
1.963.884,96	272.277,31	49.695.714,05	10.918.927,—	3.996.959,64
4.389.218,86	4.494.390,55	44.708.449,10	29.294.538,—	8.330.347,12
60.332,70	(5.467.868,60)	–	14.797.267,45	–
6.423.416,59	–	126.313.428,47	68.718.856,95	12.962.600,84
–	–	505.000,—	44.940.600,—	–
36.613,—	–	–	4.431.250,—	–
–	–	–	4.700.000,—	–
270.700,—	–	–	300.000,—	–
307.313,—	–	505.000,—	54.371.850,—	–
6.737.022,94	–	127.866.458,24	124.316.194,95	13.563.593,36

43

Friedrich Grohe AG, Hemer
Statement of Movements in Fixed Assets and Related Depreciation for the Financial Year 1993

	At cost, January 1, 1993 DM	Additions DM
I. Intangible assets		
Software	1,671,658.24	608,152.88
II. Tangible assets		
1. Land and buildings	44,913,858.21	12,310.94
2. Technical equipment and machinery	60,309,321.37	1,996,927.33
3. Other equipment, factory and office equipment	65,526,174.94	8,371,640.47
4. Advance payments and construction in progress	9,529,111.93	10,796,356.82
	180,278,466.45	21,177,235.56
III. Financial assets		
1. Shares in affiliated companies	39,383,334.—	6,062,266.—
2. Loans to affiliated companies	4,467,863.—	–
3. Participating interests	–	4,700,000.—
4. Other loans	570,700.—	–
	44,421,897.—	10,762,266.—
	226,372,021.69	32,547,654.44

Disposals DM	Re-classifications DM	Accumulated depreciation DM	Net book value, December 31, 1993 DM	Depreciation during financial year DM
6,293.35	–	1,048,029.77	1,225,488.—	600,992.52
9,980.07	701,200.74	31,909,265.32	13,708,124.50	635,294.08
1,963,884.96	272,277.31	49,695,714.05	10,918,927.—	3,996,959.64
4,389,218.86	4,494,390.55	44,708,449.10	29,294,538.—	8,330,347.12
60,332.70	(5,467,868.60)	–	14,797,267.45	–
6,423,416.59	–	126,313,428.47	68,718,856.95	12,962,600.84
–	–	505,000.—	44,940,600.—	–
36,613.—	–	–	4,431,250.—	–
–	–	–	4,700,000.—	–
270,700.—	–	–	300,000.—	–
307,313.—	–	505,000.—	54,371,850.—	–
6,737,022.94	–	127,866,458.24	124,316,194.95	13,563,593.36

Friedrich Grohe AG, Hemer
Combined Notes to the Consolidated Financial Statements and the Financial Statements of Friedrich Grohe AG for the Financial Year 1993

The financial statements and consolidated financial statements of Friedrich Grohe AG (in the following referred to as the "Company") are prepared in line with the regulations of the German Commercial Code *(Handelsgesetzbuch)* applicable to corporations, and the regulations of the German Stock Corporation Law *(Aktiengesetz)*. For the purpose of these notes, the Company and the consolidated financial statements are considered together, and unless otherwise stated, the comments contained herein apply to both.

I. Companies included in the consolidation

Friedrich Grohe AG holds shares, directly or indirectly, in the following companies, all of which are included in the consolidation:

Name and location of the company	Percentage of share capital held
Grohe Thermostat GmbH, Lahr	98
Schmöle GmbH & Co., Menden	100
Grohe Wohnungsbau GmbH, Hemer	100
Grohe Verwaltungs-GmbH, Hemer	100
H. D. Eichelberg & Co. GmbH, Iserlohn	100
Herzberger Armaturen GmbH, Herzberg	100
Grohe Gesellschaft mbH, Vienna	100
Grohe S.A.R.L., Issy-les-Moulineaux	100
Grohe S.p.A., Milan	100
Grohe N.V., Winksele	100
Grohe Japan K.K., Tokyo	100
Grohe A/S, Vaerløse	100
Grohe Nederland B.V., Zoetermeer	98 *
Barking-Grohe Ltd., Barking	98 *
Grohe Ltd., Barking	98 *
Grohe España S.A., Barcelona	98 *
Grohe America Inc., Bloomingdale	98 *
Grohe Canada Inc., Stoney Creek	98 *

* The shares are held indirectly through Grohe Thermostat GmbH.

Herzberger Armaturen GmbH, Herzberg, which was not consolidated in the financial year 1992, was included in the consolidated financial statements of the year effective January 1, 1993 (date of initial consolidation). Furthermore, Grohe A/S, Vaerløse, which was acquired a 100% by Friedrich Grohe AG effective January 1, 1993, was consolidated accordingly.

44

The 50% share in Grome Marketing (Cyprus) Ltd., Nicosia, which was purchased by Friedrich Grohe AG effective June 30, 1993, was accounted for as investment in associated companies in the consolidated financial statements in accordance with section 311 of the Commercial Code.

The information required by sections 285 (11) and 313 (2) of the Commercial Code is disclosed separately, in a list of shareholdings filed under sections 287 and 313 (4) of the Commercial Code with the Commercial Register maintained by the Municipal Court of Iserlohn.

II. Consolidation policies

The Friedrich Grohe Group (in the following referred to as the "Group") is consolidated on the basis of the financial statements of the individual Group companies. The financial statements of foreign subsidiaries are prepared in conformity with the accounting principles generally accepted in the respective countries. The financial statements of all consolidated companies are then adjusted, where necessary, as required by sections 300 and 308 of the Commercial Code, to conform to the uniform accounting and valuation policies applied in preparing the consolidated financial statements. Formats and account classifications used in the balance sheet and statement of income are in conformity with sections 266 and 275 (3), respectively, of the Commercial Code. The financial year of all consolidated companies is the calendar year.

Capital is consolidated by the book value method under section 301 of the Commercial Code, whereby the carrying value of shares in a consolidated subsidiary is offset against the amount of corresponding equity in that subsidiary as arrived at on the basis of the book values of the assets, liabilities and other defined items. Differences arising in this process are added to the value of the fixed assets to the extent they represent hidden reserves. Any remaining debit balances are treated as goodwill and written off against reserves under section 309 of the Commercial Code.

In the consolidated financial statements the interest in Grome Marketing (Cyprus) Ltd. was accounted for by the equity method according to section 312 of the Commercial Code. The capitalisation difference at the time of acquisition of the interest was offset against reserves according to section 312 (2) in connection with section 309 (1) of the Commercial Code.

Intercompany profits in inventories have been eliminated. Resulting deferred taxes are shown as a deferred tax asset.

Items in the balance sheets of foreign subsidiaries are translated into D-marks at the rate of exchange ruling at the balance sheet date. Items in the statements of income are translated at average rates. Foreign currency differences arising from translation and from consolidation are dealt with generally in the statement of income.

45

All other intercompany receivables and payables and intercompany income and expenses have been eliminated.

Minority shareholders' equity in consolidated subsidiaries is shown separately ("Minority interests") in the shareholders' equity section of the balance sheet, in compliance with section 307 (1) of the Commercial Code.

III. Accounting policies

As in previous years, the consolidated financial statements have been prepared in accordance with accounting policies applied uniformly throughout the Group.

1. **Tangible and intangible fixed assets** are stated at purchase or production cost less depreciation mainly on a straight-line basis over the estimated useful lives of the individual assets. Estimated useful lives are in accordance with those allowed by tax regulations. Low-value items costing not more than DM 800 each are fully depreciated in the year of acquisition under section 6 (2) of the German Income Tax Law *(Einkommensteuergesetz)*.

2. In the Company's balance sheet **shares in affiliated companies** are stated at cost or at such lower values as were attributable to them at the balance sheet date.

   Loans to affiliated companies are stated at nominal value at balance sheet date.

   In the financial statements of Friedrich Grohe AG, the interest in Grome Marketing (Cyprus) Ltd. is accounted for at cost under **participating interests**. Concerning the disclosure in the consolidated balance sheet reference is made to II.

   The other **participating interests** reported in the consolidated balance sheet are stated at cost.

   The **remaining financial assets** are stated at cost.

3. **Raw materials and supplies and goods purchased for resale** are stated at average cost or lower market price.

Work in progress and finished goods are stated at production cost consisting of direct labour and material costs as well as production and material overheads. Production and material overheads include only those costs as must be capitalised under German tax regulations.

Reasonable valuation allowances are provided to reflect inventory risks.

4. **Receivables and other assets** are stated at nominal value less adequate valuation allowances to reflect specific risks of loss and general valuation allowances to cover general credit risks. Receivables denominated in foreign currencies are translated at the rate of exchange ruling at the balance sheet date. Losses arising from exchange rate movements up to the balance sheet date have been recognised.

5. **Special items for investment grants and premiums to fixed assets** shown in the consolidated balance sheet refer to accrued subsidies and premiums granted to Herzberger Armaturen GmbH. The special items are amortised systematically according to the average useful lives of the respective fixed assets.

6. **Pension accruals** are stated at actuarial valuations arrived at by the "Teilwert" method described in section 6a of the German Income Tax Law (roughly equivalent to the "entry-age normal" method), applying an interest rate of 6% p.a.

7. **Other accruals** represent reasonable provision for all identifiable risks of loss and uncertain liabilities.

8. **Accounts payable** are stated at the amounts (re)payable.

IV. Notes to the balance sheets

1. Details of the Group's and the Company's **fixed assets** for the financial year 1993 are presented in the Statement of Movements in Fixed Assets and Related Depreciation appended to these notes.

In the Group, additions include KDM 34,481 and KDM 858, respectively, due to initial consolidations of Herzberger Armaturen GmbH and Grohe A/S.

Higher depreciations made in line with tax provisions in previous years led to higher results of KDM 33 in the Company and KDM 606 in the Group, respectively, in the year under review.

2. For certain imported **inventories** valuation allowances have been set up under section 80 of the German Income Tax Implementation Ordinance *(Einkommensteuer-Durchführungsverordnung)* for the Company KDM 49; for the Group KDM 132.

3. As in the previous years, Group's and Company's **trade receivables** remain due within one year. The same applies to **receivables from affiliated companies** included in the balance sheet of the Company.

4. **Other assets** include KDM 1,719 (previous year: KDM 1,619) for the Group and KDM 80 (previous year: KDM 502) for the Company due after more than one year.

5. **Prepaid expenses and deferred charges** include debt discounts of KDM 238 (previous year: KDM 343) for the Group and KDM 33 (previous year: KDM 49) for the Company.

6. **Deferred tax assets** relate mainly to deferred taxes on intercompany profit eliminations.

7. As in the previous year, **subscribed capital** is divided into

	Number	KDM
Ordinary shares	1,300,000	65,000
Preference shares	1,020,000	51,000
	2,320,000	116,000

All shares are bearer shares with a nominal value of DM 50.

Since the formation of the Company all ordinary shares have been held by Grohe Handelsgesellschaft mbH.

Subject to Supervisory Board approval, the Board of Management
is authorised to increase the Company's share capital by not more
than DM 58 million by October 31, 1996 at the latest by issuing on
one or several occasions bearer shares for cash deposits or contributions in kind (authorised capital).

8. The **capital reserve** consists entirely of premiums in compliance
   with section 272 (2) paragraph 1 of the Commercial Code.

9. The **other revenue reserves** in the consolidated balance sheet
   result from initial consolidations as well as from the transfer of net
   income of the financial year 1993 of the Company, in the balance
   sheet of which a respective reserve is reported. In financial year
   1993, debit balances totalling KDM 10,893 arising on initial consolidations were written off against these reserves in compliance
   with sections 309 and 312 of the Commercial Code.

10. **Minority interests** in the consolidated balance sheet consist of the
    2% interest in Grohe Thermostat GmbH held by Grohe Industrie-
    beteiligungen GmbH & Co. KG.

11. **Special items for investment grants and premiums to fixed assets**
    shown in the consolidated balance sheet will be amortised during
    a period of 7 to 10 years.

12. **Accrued taxes** include KDM 983 of deferred taxes for the Group
    and KDM 622 for the Company.

13. **Other accruals** (the Group and the Company) principally reflect
    sales deductions and warranty obligations, personnel-related
    liabilities including accruals for long-service awards, and other
    uncertain liabilities and unbilled costs.

14. The **structure of accounts payable** by maturity is set out below:

	1993				1992
	not more than 1 year KDM	between 1 and 5 years KDM	more than 5 years KDM	Total KDM	not more than 1 year KDM
The Group					
Amounts owed to banks ..	16,218	16,310	5,030	37,558	19,814
Trade payables	31,327	–	–	31,327	28,659
Amounts owed to associated companies ..	488	–	–	488	–
Other payables	26,353	772	–	27,125	22,377
The Company					
Amounts owed to banks ..	1,122	1,750	–	2,872	10,697
Trade payables	21,584	–	–	21,584	19,617
Amounts owed to affiliated companies	757	–	–	757	2,847
Amounts owed to other group companies	488	–	–	488	–
Other payables	12,418	772	–	13,190	11,052

As of December 31, 1993, security of amounts owed to banks of KDM 11,853 for the Group and KDM 2,250 for the Company had been provided by pledging assets financed by loans. KDM 13,862 of amounts owed to banks (the Group) was secured by mortgages.

V. Notes to the statements of income

1. **Sales** by geographical markets can be subdivided as follows:

	The Group KDM	The Company KDM
Germany	292,278	294,476
Rest of Europe	405,933	319,856
Rest of world	183,272	157,596
	881,483	771,928

2. **Personnel expenses and employees**

	The Group KDM	The Company KDM
Personnel expenses:		
Wages and salaries	251,203	110,785
Social security, pension and other benefits	57,899	26,899
	309,102	137,684
Thereof for pensions	13,309	8,553
Employees (annual average):		
Wage earners	2,664	916
Salaried staff	1,321	623
	3,985	1,539
Trainees and apprentices	88	39
	4,073	1,578

3. **Material costs** consist of:

	The Group KDM	The Company KDM
Raw materials and supplies; goods purchased for resale	281,648	489,805
Purchased services	15,076	6,593
	296,724	496,398

4. **Other operating income** includes income from the reversal of special items with an equity portion of KDM 218 for the Group and KDM 141 for the Company. Furthermore, income due to the reversal of special items for investment grants and premiums to fixed assets in the amount of KDM 750 is included in other operating income for the Group. Remaining other operating income refers mainly to currency exchange profits.

   This heading includes income of the Company of KDM 22,453 resulting from charging expenses to other Group companies shown in the same amount under other operating expenses.

5. Remaining **other operating expenses** for the Group include restructuring expenses and basically currency exchange losses.

6. **Taxes on income** for the Group include, in addition to the Company's corporate income tax and trade tax on income, own income taxes and, as far as there is an interlocking relationship, allocations to Group companies for trade tax on income of the companies in Germany except for Herzberger Armaturen GmbH, for which no income taxes are payable due to settlement with tax losses carried forward. Moreover, local-law income taxes of the consolidated foreign subsidiaries and the effect of setting up deferred tax accruals and assets based on consolidation adjustments are taken into account. The calculation of the corporate income tax for the Company assumes a dividend payment in line with the proposed distribution of retained earnings. The income tax charge both for the Group and the Company has been reduced by depreciation from taxable surplus in the tax balance of the Company.

   Other taxes are included under operating expenses.

VI. Other particulars

1. **Contingent liabilities**

	The Group KDM	The Company KDM
Notes discounted	12,118	6,835
Guarantees	73	73

The Group's and the Company's commitments from purchase orders are normal for the industry.

2. **Other financial commitments**

At the balance sheet date, the Group's financial commitments from lease agreements of various kinds aggregated KDM 24,082, including the Company's commitments of KDM 10,019. The Company had further commitments totalling KDM 40,160 from a lease agreement with an affiliated company.

Furthermore, the Company and Grohe Thermostat GmbH have submitted letters of comfort for some subsidiaries.

3. **Board of Management and Supervisory Board**

Members of the **Board of Management** in the financial year 1993 were:

Dipl.-Volkswirt Klaus Weisshaar, Frankfurt/ Main, (Spokesman, since November 5, 1993 Chairman)
Dipl.-Ing. Manfred Baab, Langenselbold
Dipl.-Betriebswirt Peter Körfer-Schün, Dortmund
Dr.-Ing. Dietrich Steude, Menden (until March 31, 1993)

Emoluments of members of the Board of Management for the financial year 1993 aggregated KDM 2,359.

A loan of KDM 200 which was granted to one member of the Board of Management at an interest rate of 5.5% p.a. was totally redeemed by payment of the outstanding amount of KDM 183 in the financial year 1993.

Members of the **Supervisory Board** in the financial year 1993 were:

Charles R. Grohe, Pully/Switzerland, Chairman
Gustel Stockmayer*, Neuried
  (Vice Chairman since April 20, 1993)
Dipl.-Finanzwirt Wilhelm Braune, Hagen
  (Vice Chairman until April 20, 1993)
Bernd Grohe, Clarens/Switzerland
Jost Kingler*, Cologne
Hans-Joachim Manthey*, Menden
Prof. Georg Neumann, Freudenberg
Peter Paulokat*, Hemer
Jürgen Steinmetz*, Iserlohn
Dipl.-Ing. Karl-Ernst Vaillant, Remscheid-Reinshagen
Dipl.-Ing. Hans Hermann Voss, Wipperfürth
Dieter Woop*, Lahr

---

* Staff representative since March 3, 1993

Subject to approval by the Annual Meeting of the proposed distribution of dividends, total emoluments of members of the Supervisory Board amount to KDM 295 for the financial year 1993.

Hemer, February 16, 1994

The Board of Management

Proposed allocation of distributable profit of Friedrich Grohe AG

The Board of Management proposes that the distributable profit of Friedrich Grohe AG as of December 31, 1993 should be allocated as follows:

	DM
Distribution to shareholders	
– payment of dividend of DM 12.50 per ordinary share	16,250,000.00
– payment of dividend of DM 13.50 per preference share	13,770,000.00
	30,020,000.00
Amount carried forward	10,115,221.15
Retained earnings	40,135,221.15

Including the tax credit, the dividend for shareholders entitled for tax credit amounts to approx. DM 17.86 per ordinary share and DM 19.29 per preference share.

Hemer, February 1993

The Board of Management

Payment on coupon no. 2 at the following banks and their branches:

Commerzbank AG
CS First Boston Effectenbank AG
Banque Paribas Capital Markets GmbH
Berliner Handels- und Frankfurter Bank
Westdeutsche Landesbank Girozentrale
Westfalenbank AG

Bestätigungsvermerk

Zu dem vorstehenden Jahresabschluß und Konzernabschluß der Friedrich Grohe AG zum 31. Dezember 1993 und dem beigefügten zusammengefaßten Lagebericht und Konzernlagebericht für das Geschäftsjahr 1993 erteilen wir den folgenden Bestätigungsvermerk:

„Die Buchführung, der Jahresabschluß und der Konzernabschluß entsprechen nach unserer pflichtgemäßen Prüfung den gesetzlichen Vorschriften. Der Jahresabschluß und der Konzernabschluß vermitteln unter Beachtung der Grundsätze ordnungsmäßiger Buchführung ein den tatsächlichen Verhältnissen entsprechendes Bild der Vermögens-, Finanz- und Ertragslage der Kapitalgesellschaft und des Konzerns. Der zu einem Bericht zusammengefaßte Lagebericht und Konzernlagebericht steht im Einklang mit dem Jahresabschluß und dem Konzernabschluß."

ARTHUR ANDERSEN & CO. G.M.B.H.
Wirtschaftsprüfungsgesellschaft
Steuerberatungsgesellschaft

Borchert Voß
Wirtschaftsprüfer Wirtschaftsprüfer

Frankfurt am Main,
den 16. Februar 1994

Auditor's Opinion

On the financial statements and consolidated financial statements of Friedrich Grohe AG as of December 31, 1993 and the combined management report for the Company and the Group for the financial year 1993 we hereby express the following opinion:

"The accounting, the financial statements and the consolidated financial statements, which we have audited in accordance with professional standards, comply with the German legal provisions. With due regard to the generally accepted accounting principles the financial statements and the consolidated financial statements give a true and fair view of the assets, liabilities, financial position and profit or loss of the Company and of the Group. The combined management report for the Company and the Group is consistent with the annual financial statements and the consolidated financial statements."

ARTHUR ANDERSEN & CO. G.M.B.H.
Wirtschaftsprüfungsgesellschaft
Steuerberatungsgesellschaft

Borchert
Wirtschaftsprüfer

Voss
Wirtschaftsprüfer

Frankfurt/ Main
February 16, 1994

Exhibit I Survey of Transfer of Significant Option Rights Established by the 4th EC Directive into German Commercial Code (GCC)

Article 4th Dir.	Description of Option	Codif- ication §§ GCC	Remarks
2 VI	Optional codification of the statements, i.e., in particular to attach a cash-flow statement as an integral part of the annual statements	n/a	No transfer of this option into GCC
6	Optional disclosure of disposition of earnings as part of the income statement	268 I	Option has been fully transferred to the reporting entity
17,2	Qualification of investments as participations optional up to a capital share of 20% (from a share > 20% disclosure as participation is compulsory)	271 I	Application of the 20% (=max.) limit
20 II	Option for setting up certain identified accruals for future expenses	249 II	Option has been fully transferred to the reporting entity
30	Optional aggregation of tax expense due from both ordinary and extraordinary results within income statement	275	Option has been exerted by GCC
33	Option for deviating from the purchase cost method with regard to the presentation of certain balance sheet items, i.e., inflation accounting, valuation at replacement value and face value, respectively	253	No transfer of this option into GCC
35 I, 39 I	Option for extraordinary depreciation of PP&E, financial assets, and current assets under certain identified conditions	253, 255	Option has been fully transferred to the reporting entity

Article 4th Dir.	Description of Option	Codification §§ GCC	Remarks
37 I	Optional capitalization of R&D expenses	n/a	No transfer of this option into GCC; handling of R&D related expenses is covered by general GAAP not codified by German commercial law
37 II	Option with respect to the extension of the amortization period applicable to goodwill beyond the standard period of 5 years	255 IV	Option has been fully transferred to the reporting entity, i.e., the amortization period can be extended to the estimated period of benefit from the goodwill
38, 40 I	Optional valuation of movable PP&E and Inventories by application of the weighted average method, LIFO- and FIFO-method, or minimum-balance method	240, 256	Option has been fully transferred to the reporting entity
45 I	Application of a protection clause optional re disclosure of participation details such as name of the respective entity, investor's capital share, and entity's results for the year ended; previous authorization can be demanded by each member country	286 III, 287	Option has been transferred to the reporting entity with the exception that no previous authorization is required
47	Optional facilities with regard to identified footnote disclosure requirements dependent upon size of the respective company	288	Option has been fully transferred to the reporting entity
51	Optional exemption from audit requirements dependent on company's size	316 I	Option has been exerted by GCC

(Exhibit continues)

Exhibit I (continued)

Article 4th Dir.	Description of Option	Codif- ication §§ GCC	Remarks
59	Optional accounting for investments in affiliated subsidiaries under the equity method	253 II, 271 II	No transfer of this option into GCC; interests in affiliated entities must be recorded at cost

Exhibit II Survey of Transfer of Significant Option Rights Established by the 7th EC Directive into German Commercial Code (GCC)

Article 7th Dir.	Description of Option	Codif- ication §§ GCC	Remarks
1. Composition of companies to be included into consolidation:			
1 c)	Compulsory inclusion of an entity into consolidation can be combined with the requirement of a 20% interest in the subsidiary in the case that the parent company has direct control over the formation of the entity's management and/or supervisory board	290 II Nr.2	No transfer of this option into GCC
1 d) aa)	Compulsory inclusion of an entity into consolidation can be combined with the requirement of a minimum 20% interest in the subsidiary in the case that the parent company has direct control over the formation of the entity's management and/or supervisory board	290 II Nr.3	No transfer of this option into GCC
2. Exemption rules:			
6	Optional exemption from consolidation requirements dependent on entity's size	293	Option has been exerted by GCC
7 III	Option for nonapplication of Article 7 (general exemption rules) for companies quoted at an EC stock exchange	291 I, II	No transfer of this option into GCC
8	Option for application of Article 7 only under the condition that shareholders of the parent company owning a determined minimum share have not claimed for the presentation of consolidated financial statements within a period of 6 months prior to year-end	291 III	Option has been exerted by GCC

(Exhibit continues)

Exhibit I (continued)

Article 7th Dir.	Description of Option	Codification §§ GCC	Remarks
9	Option for application of Articles 7 and 8 only under the condition that additional disclosure requirements determinable by each member country have been considered by the reporting entity	n/a	No transfer of this option into GCC
11	Option for exemption of an EC parent company from presenting consolidated financial statements in the case that this company and all its subsidiaries are included in the con-solidated statements of a non-EC parent company that meets the requirements of consolidated statements set up under the 7th EC Directive	292	Option has been exerted by GCC
15	Option to exempt a parent company from consolidation in the case that this company —is not active in the commercial or trade area and —is shareholder of a subsidiary owing to an agreement with one or more companies not included in the consolidated financial statements	n/a	No transfer of this option into GCC

3. Techniques of capital consolidation:

19	Option to offset the investment in the subsidiary against its proportional equity at the time of purchase of shares or, in the case that shares have been acquired subsequently, at the moment when the entity has become a subsidiary company (i e., the parent's investment equals or exceeds 20% of the subsidiary's share capital)	301 II	Option has been exerted by GCC

Article 7th Dir.	Description of Option	Codif-ication §§ GCC	Remarks
20	Option for application of Article 19 only in the case that a minimum capital share of 90% is owned by the parent company	n/a	No transfer of this option into GCC
30	Option to offset goodwill from consolidation within the equity section against earned or capital surplus; the offsetting entry has to be shown separately	309 I	Option has been fully transferred to the reporting entity

4. Other consolidation items:

27	Option for deviation of balance sheet dates between parent company's single financial statements and consolidated statements, i.e., presentation of consolidated financial statements as of a cut-off date applied by the most significant entities or the majority of entities included in consolidation, respectively	299 I	Option has been exerted by GCC
28	Option for adjustment of a subsequent year's opening balance sheet in case of significant changes with respect to the composition of the consolidated companies	n/a	No transfer of this option into GCC
29	Optional adoption of allowances from single financial statements that had been set up for tax purposes only under the condition that appropriate disclosure concerning these impacts is made in the footnotes	308 I	Option has been exerted by GCC

(Exhibit continues)

Exhibit II (continued)

Article 7th Dir.	Description of Option	Codif-ication §§ GCC	Remarks
	5. Other consolidation methods:		
32	Optional application of the proportional consolidation method in the case of an investment in an entity together with nonconsolidated companies	310	Option has been fully transferred to the reporting entity
33 II	Option for applying the equity method either by presenting the carrying amount of the respective investment or by disclosing the investment at an amount equal to the proportional share in the subsidiary's equity	312 I	No transfer of this option into GCC; by application of the equity method both alternatives are available
33 III	Under the equity method application of valuation methods used for consolidation purposes can be prescribed in the case that the investment shall be recorded at an amount equal to the pro-rata portion of the subsidiary's equity	312 V	No transfer of this option into GCC, application of valuation method used for consolidation purposes is optional
	6. Specific disclosure requirements		
34 Nr. 12	Option to demand disclosure of compensation received by management or supervisory board members regarding activities at companies consolidated under the proportional method or the equity method	314 I Nr. 6	No transfer of this option into GCC
35 I a)	Option for separate presentation of specific details with regard to the parent company's investments in subsidiaries in order to avoid public	313 IV	Option has been fully transferred to the reporting entity

Article 7th Dir.	Description of Option	Codif- ication §§ GCC	Remarks
	disclosure (i.e., name and place of registration of the respective subsidiary as well as capital share of the parent company or the subsidiary's equity and its net income, if available)		
35 I b)	Option to omit disclosure of details mentioned under Article 35 I a) in the case that disclosure would prove a significant handicap to the respective subsidiaries; omittance can be made dependent on prior approval by administration authorities or court decision	313	No transfer of this option into GCC

312

Exhibit III Comparison of Significant Differences between German GAAP and U.S. GAAP

Caption	German GAAP	Source HGB	U.S. GAAP	Source FAS, APB, ARB
ASSETS				
Current Assets				
Deferred charges/ prepaid expenses	Optional capitalization of start-up costs as an accounting convenience, disclosed under a separate caption and amortized over a period up to 5 years	§269	Current and noncurrent portion of prepaid expenses are disclosed separately as prepaid expenses or other assets, respectively	ARB 43
Deferred tax asset	Optional for individual financial statements; compulsory for tax assets resulting from consolidation entries; no recognition of a future tax benefit resulting from a loss carryforward in the year the loss has been incurred; only the reversal of deferred tax liabilities is possible to an extent that future tax expenses are compensation for by the loss carryforward	§§274 II, 306	Compulsory both for individual and consolidated financial statements; future tax benefits due to loss carryforwards have to be recognized if future realization is "more likely than not" (i.e., likelihood >50%), the tax asset is subject to a valuation allowance in case the asset becomes impaired	FAS-109
Marketable securities	Basically separate valuation of each single item, group valuation possible for homogeneous kinds of securities	§§252 I, 240 IV	Portfolio approach for securities representing ownership rights, i.e., allowances are calculated on the basis of the portfolio balance as of balance sheet date	FAS-12
Accounts receivable, trade	Simultaneous recognition of bad debt allowances and lump sum allowance for general risk of collection permissible	§253 III	Recognition of lump sum allowances not approved	APB 12

Item	Description	§	Description	Standard
Inventories	Wide range of options for capitalization of manufacturing costs between direct and full costs; capitalization of interest only in case of direct relation of interest expense incurred by identified projects, in addition to determination of net realizable value as of balance sheet date allowance due to anticipation of expected future price reductions are optional; for noncorporations additional volume of write-downs is available within the range of "sound business judgment"	§255	Capitalization of full costs	ARB 43
			Capitalization of interest for qualifying assets	FAS-34
		§253 III	Application of the lower of cost or market principle; no devaluation down to lower replacement costs in the case that net realizable value less mark-down still exceeds replacement costs: then inventory write-down is limited to NRV less an allowance for a normal profit margin	ARB 43
Noncurrent assets				
Investments	Application of the cost method; if decrease of value is —nontemporary: write-down is compulsory —temporary: write-down is optional For investments in noncorporations additional volume of write-downs is optional within the range of "sound business judgment"	§255	In general application of	APB 18
		§§253 II, 279 §253 IV	—the equity method for investments of 20% or more of the voting stock —the cost method for investments of less than 20% of the voting stock Nontemporary losses in value of the investment:	
	Reversal of previous extraordinary write-downs when reasons for write-down have become void: • for corporations only compulsory when —write-down was performed in trade books only but disregarded for tax purposes —reasons for write-down permissible for tax purposes only have become void • for noncorporations generally optional	§280	—reversal of previous extraordinary write-downs is generally mandatory in case reasons for extraordinary write-downs have become void	
		§253V	For noncurrent marketable equity securities accumulated changes in the valuation allowance for decline in market value assessed to be temporary shall not be included in the determination of net income but reflected within the equity section and shown separately.	

(Exhibit continues)

(Exhibit III, cont.)

Caption	German GAAP	Source HGB	U.S. GAAP	Source FAS, APB, ARB
Property, plant, & equipment	As a general rule: valuation at cost Wide range of options for recognition of manufacturing costs Re capitalization of interest, see inventories Extraordinary depreciation required —for corporations if permanent impairment of value is anticipated —in case of premature wear and tear —for noncorporations: even permissible if impairment is only of temporary nature and within a range of "sound business judgment" Re reversal of write-downs in case that related reasons have become void: see Investments	§255 §§253 II 279 I §253 II, IV	As a general rule: valuation at cost Re capitalization of interest, see inventories Extraordinary depreciation required —in case of restricted usage Re reversal of write-downs in case that related reasons have become void: see Investments	APB 6 APB 20 + 30
Intangibles	Only to be recorded as assets by applying the cost method when acquired from third Amortization over the estimated period of benefit With regard to business combinations: disclosure of acquired goodwill as an asset is optional, if capitalized goodwill has to be amortized over a period of up to 15 years	§248 II §253 II §255 IV §7 I EStG	If acquired: recognition as assets by applying the cost method If incurred internally only recognition of assets if they —can be specifically identified —have determinable lives —are not an inherent part in a continuing business and not related to an enterprise as a whole Amortization over the estimated period of benefit up to a maximum of 40 years With regard to business combinations: disclosure of acquired goodwill as an asset is compulsory if the purchase method is applied; maximum amortization period: 40 years In the case that pooling-of-interests method is applied, no goodwill will be recognized since all related assets and liabilities are recorded at historical carrying values	APB 17 APB 16

LIABILITIES

Current Liabilities

	German ref.	German GAAP	US ref.	US GAAP
Accrued liabilities	§249 II §252 I	In trade books presentation of qualifying accruals for future expenses are optional but not permissible for tax purposes. Principle of prudence is established as the basic principle, i.e., valuation and estimates are subject to management's "sound business judgment," basically resulting in the opportunity to set up hidden reserves more easily than under U.S. GAAP	FAS-5, s. 70	Only obligations to third parties resulting from transactions of the past can be accrued; presentation of a true & fair view is the basic principle, i.e., the likelihood of occurrence has to be identified as probable, reasonably possible, or remote; in the case that only a certain range can be applied to an identified probably contingency amount, the amount at the lower edge of the respective range has to be recorded.
Long-term debt (noninterest bearing)	§253 I	General rule: disclosure at face value	APB 21	General rule: disclosure at present value
Other Liabilities				
Pension reserves	§249 I §6a EStG	In most cases application of tax rules (i.e., s. 6a EStG) also for trade books: —discount rate fixed at 6% —no consideration expected future compensation levels influenced by future wage and inflation rates Application of the "claimed when claimable" rule	FAS-87	Computation of net periodic pension cost under consideration of estimated future compensation levels and assumed discount rates which shall reflect the rates at which the pension benefits could be settled in the future; retroactive plan amendments have to be included at the time they have been contractually agreed, i.e., no application of the "claimed when claimable" rule

(Exhibit continues)

(Exhibit III, cont.)

Caption	German GAAP	Source HGB	U.S. GAAP	Source FAS, APB, ARB
PROFIT & LOSS STATEMENT	Option between cost-of-sales method and cost-summary method	§275 I	Cost-of-sales method is compulsory	APB 9
OTHER ISSUES				
Translation of foreign currencies	No legal codification with regard to foreign currency translation methods; according to the principle of prudence no recognition of unrealized gains from translation is possible		Application of the functional currency concept, both gains and losses from translation of foreign currencies have to be recorded	FAS-52
Cash flow statement	Disclosure is optional.		The cash flow statement is an integral part of the financial statements.	FAS-95
CONSOLIDATED ITEMS				
General consolidation policy	Subsidiaries have to be included if —parent owns more than 20% of shares and exercises de facto control, or —parent owns more than 50% of voting shares or has direct control of the composition of the entity's board or via a domination contract Wider range of optional application of the equity method as a substitute for full consolidation; for corporate joint ventures alternative application of both consolidation at equity or proportional consolidation is possible	§§290 I, 271 I §290 II §§311, 295, 296	Generally the condition for a controlling financial interest is ownership of a majority voting interest; exclusion from consolidation only applies in the case that control is only temporary or control does not rest with the majority owner (i.e., for instance, the entity is in legal reorganization, bankruptcy, or operates under public restrictions). Application of the equity method for —Corporate joint ventures and —Investments within a range from 20% to 50% of the voting stock if the investor is able to exercise significant influence	FAS-94 ARB 51
Accounting for goodwill resulting from consolidation	Option for offsetting goodwill from consolidation within the equity section (to be shown separately, if applied)	§309 I	Goodwill from consolidation has to be capitalized and amortized over a maximum period of 40 years	APB 16 + 17

Exhibit IV Comparison of Significant Differences between German GAAP and International Accounting Standards (IAS)

Caption	German GAAP	Source HGB	IAS	Source IAS
ASSETS				
Current Assets				
Deferred charges/ prepaid expenses	Optional capitalization of start-up costs as an accounting convenience, disclosed under a separate caption and amortized over period up to 5 years	§269	Prepaid expenses and deferred income shall be included in other assets and other liabilities, respectively	IAS 5
Deferred tax asset	Effects have to be accounted for under the liability method; recognition of a tax asset is optional for individual financial statements but compulsory for tax assets resulting from consolidation entries; no recognition of a future tax benefit resulting from a loss carryforward in the year the loss has been incurred; only the reversal of deferred tax liabilities is possible to an extent that future tax expenses will be compensated for by the loss carryforward	§§274 II, 306	Option for either applying the deferral method or the liability method; exceptions can be made for timing differences that will not reverse for at least 3 years. Recognition of a future tax benefit resulting from a loss carryforward is permissible in the case that realization of the tax asset is "beyond any reasonable doubt."	IAS 12
Marketable securities	Basically separate valuation of each single item at the lower of cost or market; group valuation possible for homogeneous kinds of securities	§§252 I, 240 IV	Valuation at either market value or the lower of cost or market value, whereby the carrying amount should be determined either on a portfolio basis, in total, or by category of investment, or on an individual investment basis	IAS 25
Accounts receivable, trade	Simultaneous recognition of bad debt allowances and lump sum allowances for general risk of collection permissible	§253 III	Recognition of lump sum allowances not mentioned	

(Exhibit continues)

(Exhibit IV, cont.)

Caption	German GAAP	Source HGB	IAS	Source IAS
Inventories	Wide range of options for capitalization of manufacturing costs between direct and full costs	§255	For manufactured inventories, systematic allocation of those production overhead costs is required that "relate to putting the inventories in their present location and condition."	IAS 2
	Capitalization of interest only in cases of direct relation of interest expense incurred by identified projects, in addition to determination of net realizable value as of balance sheet date allowances due to anticipation of expected future price reductions are optional; for noncorporations, additonal volume of write-downs is available within the range of "sound business judgment."	§253 III	Application of the lower or cost or market principle; net realizable value is determined as the estimated selling price in the ordinary course of business less costs of completion and less costs necessarily to be incurred in order to make the sale	
Noncurrent Assets				
Investments	Application of the cost method; if decrease of value is	§255 §§253 II, 279	Long-term investments should be carried at cost or revalued amounts (i.e., at fair value) or in the case of marketable equity securities, the lower of cost and market value determined on a portfolio basis; reversal of previous extraordinary write-down is compulsory when reasons for write-down have become void; an increase in book value resulting from revaluation should be credited to owner's equity except for write-ups arising from the reversal of a previous decrease in the same investment which was charged to income; for investments in subsidiaries the equity method should be applied if the investor holds 20% or more of the voting stock (if <20%: valuation at cost)	IAS 25
	—nontemporary: write-down is compulsory —temporary: write-down is optional For investments in noncorporations, additional volume of write-downs is optional within the range of "sound business judgment." Reversal of previous extraordinary write-downs when reasons for write-down have become void:	§253 IV		
	• For corporations only compulsory when —write-down was performed in trade books only but disregarded for tax purposes —reasons for write-down permissible for tax purposes only have become void • For noncorporations generally optional	§280 §253 V		IAS 28

Category	German rule	§ reference	IAS rule	IAS reference
Property, plant, & equipment	As a general rule: valuation at cost. Wide range of options for recognition of manufacturing costs. Re capitalization of interest, see inventories	§255	Valuation at either historical cost or at a revaluation amount (both upwards and downwards). An increase in book value resulting from revaluation should be credited to owner's equity and shown separately as revaluation surplus, except that such increase is related to and not	IAS 16
	Extraordinary depreciation required —for corporations if permanent impairment of value is anticipated	§§253 II, 279 I	greater than a decrease arising on devaluation recorded as charged to income; borrowing costs should be capitalized as part of the cost of assets that take a substantial period of time to get them ready for use; amount capitalized should not exceed total borrowing costs of that period. No restrictions with regard to the use of various kinds of depreciation methods as long as they are applied consistently from period to period; extraordinary depreciation required in case of	IAS 23
	—for noncorporations even permissible if impairment is of only temporary nature and within a range of "sound business judgment". Re reversal of write-downs in case that related reasons have become void: see Investments	253 II, IV	premature wear and tear, restricted usage and obsolescence not explicitly covered by IAS	IAS 4
Intangibles	Only to be recorded as assets by applying the cost method when acquired from third parties	§248 II		
	Amortiztion over the estimated period of benefit	§253 II		
	With regard to business combinations: disclosure of acquired goodwill as an asset is optional; if capitalized, goodwill has to be amortized over a period of up to 15 years	§255 IV §7 I EStG	With regard to business combinations: An acquired goodwill should be recognized as an asset, straight-line amortization over its useful life (i.e., generally not longer than 5 years unless a longer period	IAS 22

(Exhibit continues)

(Exhibit IV, cont.)

Caption	German GAAP	Source HGB	IAS	Source IAS
			can be justified—>max. 20 years); write-down of unamortized balance according to results from annual recovery check; in the case that the pooling-of-interests method is applied, no goodwill will be recognized since all related assets and liabilities are recorded at historical carrying values.	
LIABILITIES				
Current Liabilities				
Accrued liabilities	In trade books presentation of qualifying accruals for future expenses are optional but not permissible for tax purposes. Principle of prudence is established as the basic principle, i.e., valuation and estimates are subject to management's "sound business judgment," basically resulting in the opportunity to set up hidden reserves more easily than under IAS	§249 II §252 I	No coverage for accruals set up for determined future expenses under IAS, i.e., the likelihood of occurrence has to be probable and a reasonable estimate of the loss can be made; in case only a certain range can be applied to an identified probable contingency amount, the amount at the lower edge of the respective range has to be recorded	IAS 10
Other Liabilities				
Pension reserves	In most cases application of tax rules (i.e., s. 6a EStG) also for trade books: —discount rate fixed at 6% —no consideration of expected future compensation levels influenced by future wage and inflation rates Application of the "claimed when claimable" rule	§249 I §6a EStG	Accounting for retirement benefit plans is covered by IAS 26 by an overall approach only, i.e., the actuarial present value of promised retirement benefits should be recorded under the terms of the plan using either current or projected salary levels; plan assets shall be carried at fair value; the relationship between the actuarial present value and the net plan assets available for benefits shall be disclosed	IAS 26

PROFIT & LOSS STATEMENT	Option between cost-of-sales method and cost-summary method	§275 I	No prescription of a certain method under IAS, IAS 5 only provides a listing of basic P&L-captions that should be disclosed, e.g., depreciation, unusual charges/credits and significant intercompany transactions	IAS 5
OTHER ISSUES				
Translation of foreign currencies	No legal codification with regard to foreign currency translation methods. According to the principle of prudence, no recognition of unrealized gains from translation is possible.		At each balance sheet date foreign currency monetary items should generally be reported at the closing rate and gains and losses should be recognized; exchange differences on long-term monetary assets may be deferred, except that exchange losses should not be deferred in the case that recurring exchange losses will arise on that item in the future, any cumulative deferred exchange differences must be disclosed	IAS 21
Cash flow statement	Disclosure is optional		The cash flow statement is an integral part of the financial statements	IAS 7

(Exhibit continues)

(Exhibit IV, cont.)

CONSOLIDATION ITEMS

Caption	German GAAP	Source HGB	IAS	Source IAS
General scope of consolidation	Subsidiaries have to be included if —parent owns more than 20% of shares and exercises de facto control, or —parent owns more than 50% of voting shares or has direct control of the composition of the entity's board or via a domination contract Wider range of optional application of the equity method as a substitute for full consolidation; for corporate joint ventures alternative application of both consolidation at equity or proportional consolidation is possible	§§290 I, 271 I §290 II §§311, 295, 296 §310	Generally the condition for a controlling financial interest is ownership of a majority voting interest, exclusion from consolidation applies only in the case that control is only temporary or control does not rest with the majority owner (for instance, the entity is in legal reorganization, bankruptcy, or operates under public restrictions) For joint ventures alternative application of both consolidation at equity or proportional consolidation is available; joint ventures should be accounted for in accordance with IAS 25 (see Investments) if the interest is acquired and held exclusively with a view to its subsequent disposal in the near future or if it operates under long-term restrictions	IAS 27
Accounting for goodwill resulting from consolidation	Option for offsetting goodwill from consolidation within the equity section (to be shown separately, if applied)	§309 I	Goodwill resulting from consolidation should be recognized as an asset; straight-line amortization over its useful life (i.e., generally not longer than 5 years unless a longer period can be justified—>max. 20 years); write-down of unamortized balance according to results from annual recovery check	IAS 22

GREECE

Richard H. Caseley
Price Waterhouse, Athens

1. Background

1.1 Company Law

Before 1920, when Law 2190/1920 was issued, Greek company law was not codified and had not followed developments elsewhere during the twentieth century. Law 2190/1920 was based more or less on foreign legislation of the past century. Requirements for the publication of annual financial statements dated back to 1872, whereas the appointment of auditors had been optional.

Since 1962 there has been a requirement for the formal presentation of financial statements. The provisions of law 2190/1920 and subsequent amendments were codified into a single text in 1963. This text was amended slightly between 1967 and 1980, and to a greater extent with presidential decrees 409/1986 and 498/1987, by means of which the law was harmonized with the provisions of the First, Second, Third, Fourth, Sixth, and Seventh EU Directives. In due course, the law will be completed and harmonized according to the provisions of the Fifth Directive also.

1.2 Tax Law

Income tax in its modern form was introduced to Greece in 1919. The related Law 1640/1919 was based on French standards, modified according to the local economic and social situation. This law was repealed by Law 3323/1955, relating to taxation of individuals, and by Law 3843/1958, relating to taxation of corporations. These two laws have been amended several times and were codified in 1989. In addition, bookkeeping requirements were established by a special law in effect from 1952. This special law constitutes the Code of Books and Records and was last extensively amended with presidential decree 186/1992. The Code of Books and Records specifies the accounting records and relevant documents to be maintained. It also provides rules for the updating of accounting records, balance sheet preparation, certain basic accounting principles, retention of records, and periodic information returns.

1.3 The General Accounting Plan

Companies are obliged to prepare financial statements according to the provisions of the General Accounting Plan (GAP), which took effect in 1987. The GAP is fully harmonized with the Fourth and Seventh EU Directives and certain International Accounting Standards. However, implementation of the GAP, relating to rules other than those referring to the preparation of the financial statements, is obligatory only for companies that are subject to audit by members of the Institute of Certified Auditors (SOE).

All corporations and limited liability companies that fulfill any two of the following three criteria are subject to audit by Certified Auditors:

1. Total assets at least 400 million drachmas (Dr)
2. Annual turnover at least Dr 800 million
3. Average of at least 50 persons employed during the financial year

1.4 Conflict of Regulations

In certain instances there are conflicts between the requirements of the tax legislation and those of company law or the General Accounting Plan. To some extent there is a trend not to record provisions until they materialize since they are not deductible for tax purposes (see also Section 3).

1.5 Accounting and Auditing Professions

The accounting profession in Greece has not yet achieved the level of development found in the United States and most European countries. As described below, the Institute designed to provide qualifications similar to those of a CPA, ACA, WP, or *Expert Comptable* has only recently been established. For this reason, little or no attention has been given to the setting and application of accounting standards. Another factor is that most businesses have been family controlled and, at least until recently, there has been little public interest in quoted shares.

Until 1992 there was no officially recognized independent body of public accountants in Greece. Public accounting was primarily confined to the Institute of Sworn-in-Accountants (SOL). This government-sponsored Institute was established in 1955 for the purpose of training auditors, with the creation of an independent profession as a long-term objective. The auditing profession was liberalized in July 1992 with the establishment of the Institute of Certified Auditors (SOE). The Institute consists of 290 full members who originate from SOL and other auditing firms of the private sector. Admission to SOE is achieved through a combination of examinations and 8 years of professional experience in auditing. The duties and conduct of the auditor are described in general terms in the applicable law.

1.6 Securities Market

At present a stock exchange operates only in Athens; it deals largely in shares and bonds of local corporations (*anonymos eteria*, AE, or *société anonyme*, SA). The shares of 155 such corporations and the bonds of 61 government loans are currently listed on the Athens Stock Exchange. The main registration requirements for shares are as follows:

1. Minimum equity must equal the drachma equivalent of 2.5 million European Currency Units (ECU).
2. Existing share capital is to be increased by at least 25%; all new shares are to be sold through a public subscription.
3. At least one underwriter is required who will guarantee that the issue will be fully subscribed.
4. At least five annual balance sheets must have been published.
5. Operating profits for the past 5 financial years must be satisfactory.

The obligation in item 2 does not apply to companies whose shares are listed on the stock exchange or exchanges in one or more EU member countries. This obligation also does not apply to companies that have resulted from a merger or absorption of companies, on the condition that at least one of the companies involved is already listed on the stock exchange.

The registration requirements for bonds on the stock exchange are as follows:

1. The issuing company must have an equity of at least Dr 500 million.
2. The bond loan must be not less than Dr 20 million, nor must it exceed one half of the company's net equity.

A law enacted in August 1988 includes changes regarding the stock exchange and stock exchange dealings, for the purpose of upgrading and strengthening the capital market. The most important elements of this law are the introduction of stock exchange (stockbroking) companies; the operation of depositories of securities for safekeeping of certificates; the introduction of a parallel capital market; and the provision for the establishment of two new stock exchanges, one of them in Thessaloniki. Stock exchange companies are established as SAs with special permission from the Capital Market Committee. For the establishment and operation of a foreign company, it is additionally required that the foreign company be a member of the stock exchange in its country of origin. The share capital of a stock exchange company must be at least Dr 70 million, fully paid at formation, and consisting purely of cash. A foreign stock exchange company must import capital of at least Dr 70 million.

1.7 Banking System

1.7.1 Central Bank

Whereas the Bank of Greece continues to implement monetary decisions regarding banking and credit facilities in general, there has been some relaxation of controls, for example, regarding interest rates by the commercial banks and foreign exchange rates.

Under the terms of the accession agreement, EU regulations on banking in general will be implemented over a 5-year period, but from January 1993 the regulations applying to the legislative, regulatory, and administrative provisions of the credit institutions have been implemented. Following this implementation, the establishment of branches of banks established in other EU member countries has been allowed, provided that the operation of each branch to be established in Greece is covered by the operation license of the bank in its country of origin and that this is announced officially by the responsible authority of the EU member country to the Bank of Greece.

1.7.2 Commercial Banks

Since the summer of 1985, commercial banks, which are required to invest a large part of their total private deposits in government interest-bearing treasury bills, have been allowed to sell a portion of these bills to the private sector. In March 1985, commercial banks were also allowed to extend housing loans at negotiable interest rates. Until that date, credits for housing loans were available only at the National Mortgage Bank, the Postal Savings Bank, and the Consignments and Loans Fund.

Since the end of 1987, the rates of interest on working capital and long-term loans for acquisition of fixed assets have been freed. In addition, since November 1987 interest rates paid by banks on fixed time deposits have also been freed.

2. The Form and Content of Published Financial Statements

2.1 Disclosure Requirements

Following amendments to corporate legislation, beginning in 1987 the form and content of financial statements were changed to comply with related EU Directives. The annual financial statements include:

- Balance sheet
- Profit and loss account (income statement)
- Profit distribution table
- Appendix (notes to the financial statements)

Attached is a specimen set of published financial statements and auditor's report, in Greek and translated into English. Publishing consolidated financial statements became a legal requirement in 1991.

2.2 Publication

Companies are not required to publish the notes to the financial statements, the notes being filed only with the Ministry of Commerce. The audit report is required to be published, when the auditor is a member of SOE. The financial statements, and audit report if applicable, must be published in two daily newspapers and the official Government Gazette. Some companies, primarily listed ones, also prepare an annual report.

2.3 Layout

Regarding the specimen set of financial statement, it is worth noting the following:

- The layout is in accordance with the General Accounting Plan (see Section 1.3). The alphanumeric references in the various captions are set out in this plan.
- The audit report contains a number of "findings" (equivalent to qualifications). This is not uncommon, and the matters reported are fairly typical, for example, lack of provision for doubtful accounts receivable, depreciation charges, and tax matters.

2.4 Notes to the Accounts

According to corporation legislation, the disclosures required to be made in the Appendix, or notes, are as follows:

- The methods of asset valuation, depreciation, and provisions (see details in Section 3)
- The basis of translation of transactions and balances in foreign currency (see details in Section 3)
- Analysis of investments exceeding 10% of the share capital of investees

- The number and value of shares issued in the year to cover increase of share capital
- The number of any titles issued per category (e.g., preferred shares, convertible bonds)
- Amounts of liabilities due 5 years after the balance sheet date, as well as amounts of liabilities that are secured, mentioning the details of security
- The total amounts of commitments, guarantees, and contingent liabilities not disclosed in the memo accounts, as long as this information is useful for the evaluation of the financial position of the company
- Analysis of sales by activity and geographic area, as long as such activities and areas present essential differences from a sales organization point of view. The Minister of Commerce may approve the nonpublication of this information if he is satisfied that such disclosure might cause damage to the company. This deviation should be mentioned in the Appendix.
- The average number of staff employed during the year by category (e.g., administrative staff, workers). The amounts of salaries, wages, and social security contributions should also be disclosed by category of staff.
- The effect on the results for the year resulting from inappropriate evaluation of current assets for the purpose of saving taxes. If it is anticipated that significant additional taxes will result in following years, detailed explanations should be given.
- Amounts of taxes payable plus any unrecorded significant amounts that are expected to be paid
- Remuneration to members of the board of directors and administrators, as well as any liability to such members who have retired
- Advances and loans given to members of the board of directors and administrators
- The name and the head office of the companies that issue consolidated financial statements in which the company's annual financial statements are or will be included, as well as the location at which the consolidated financial statements are available

- If the company has purchased its own shares, the following should be disclosed:
  — The reason for the purchase
  — The number and nominal value of own shares purchased or transferred during the year, as well as the represented share capital
  — Any amount paid for the acquisition of such shares or collected in case of transfer
- Fees paid in respect of the audit of the financial statements
- Any other information aiming at a more complete understanding of the financial statements

3. Accounting Policies and Practices in Valuation and Income Measurement: Implications for the Analyst

3.1 Group Accounts

3.1.1 Background

Local company regulations have been amended to include consolidated accounts that comply with the Seventh Directive of the EU. The legislation requires any company that qualifies as a parent company and is governed by Greek law to prepare consolidated accounts and related notes thereto, subject to exceeding at least two of the following three size criteria: total consolidated assets, Dr 1,250 million; total consolidated turnover, Dr 2,500; 500 employees. The parent undertaking and all its subsidiaries, regardless of the location of their registered offices, are considered undertakings subject to consolidation. The only companies subject to consolidation are parent undertakings with one or more subsidiary undertakings where the parent or one or more of its subsidiary undertakings is one of the following:

1. A company limited by shares, AE
2. A company with limited liability, E.P.E

3. A company limited by shares partnership, E.E

3.1.2 *Method of Consolidation*

The purchase or acquisition accounting method of consolidation is to be adopted, in accordance with local regulations. Asset and liability items of undertakings whose accounts are consolidated are incorporated in full in the consolidated balance sheet. Income and expenditure of undertakings whose accounts are consolidated are incorporated in full in the consolidated profit and loss statement. Shares in subsidiaries must be set off against the book values of the capital and reserves of those subsidiaries; differences that arise from the set-off must be allocated as far as possible to the relevant items in the consolidated balance sheet. Differences remaining after all set-offs mentioned above must be shown as a separate item in the consolidated balance sheet. If the difference is positive, it should be shown under the heading "Other intangible assets" and can be treated as follows:

1. Carried in the balance sheet as an intangible asset and amortized in equal amounts over a period not exceeding 5 years
2. Written off immediately on acquisition

It is also permissible to eliminate this positive consolidation difference directly against reserves.

If the difference arising on consolidation is a credit balance, it may be shown as a reserve arising on consolidation. It may be transferred partly or wholly to the consolidated profit and loss only if:

1. It corresponds to an expectation, at the date of acquisition, of unfavorable future results in the undertaking, or to the expectation of costs which that undertaking would incur. It may then be transferred to profit and loss when and insofar as this expectation materializes.
2. The difference corresponds to a realized profit.

3.1.3 *Proportional Consolidation*

Proportional consolidation is not provided for in law.

3.1.4 Equity Accounting

In accordance with local regulations, equity accounting is to be used on consolidation for participating interests in associated companies following the criteria in the Seventh EU Directive. When applied for the first time, the participating interest shall be shown in the consolidated balance sheet at its book value, which is to be the lower of cost or market value.

Any difference that arises between the cost of the investment and the proportion of the equity of the associated company may be shown either in the consolidated balance sheet or in the notes to the consolidated financial statements. In the case in which an associated company's assets or liabilities have been valued by methods other than those used for consolidation, they may, for the purpose of calculating the difference mentioned above, be revalued by the methods used for consolidation.

The book value referred to above is to be increased or reduced by the amount of any variation that has taken place during the financial year in the proportion of the associated company's capital and reserves represented by the participating interest, and it will be reduced by the amount of the dividends relating to that participating interest.

3.2 Foreign Currency Translation

3.2.1 Translation of the Financial Statements of Foreign Subsidiaries

Translation to drachmas is performed by using the so-called monetary-nonmonetary method, as follows:

1. Inventories, fixed assets, and marketable securities at historical rates
2. All receivables, cash balances, and payables at closing rates
3. Income and expenses at the year's average rate

Differences arising from the translation of inventories, fixed assets, marketable securities, cash balances, and income and expenses are taken to the income statement currently. For receivables and payables see Section 3.2.2.

3.2.2 *Translation of Foreign Currency-Denominated Assets and Liabilities*

Exchange differences on cash balances are taken to the income statement currently.

Exchange differences on receivables and payables are recorded in separate accounts by currency and nature (short or long term) and are treated as follows:

1. Short- and long-term exchange losses are taken to the income statement currently.
2. Short-term exchange gains are deferred and are taken to the income statement in the following year.
3. Long-term exchange gains are deferred, and after offsetting with any losses in the following year, are taken to the income statement to the extent corresponding to the collection or payment of the receivable or the payable.

Exchange differences on loans or credits for purchases of fixed assets are recorded in separate accounts by loan. After offsetting exchange losses and gains of the same loan, remaining debit balances are recorded as deferred charges and amortized over the period of the loan. Credit balances are also deferred and are taken to the income statement, to the extent corresponding to the loan repaid in each year.

Realized Exchange Differences Exchange differences arising on transactions upon receipt or payment of a receivable or a payable are taken directly to income, except for those arising on the repayment of loans for the purchase of fixed assets, which are matched with unrealized exchange differences and treated as mentioned above.

3.3 Capital and Reserves

Capital must be shown at par value; any premiums thereon should be disclosed separately. Companies may purchase their own shares only under exceptional circumstances (e.g., reduction of share capital, distribution of shares to employees).

Corporate legislation requires that not less than 5% of the annual profits of corporations and limited liability companies be appropriated to a legal reserve until it reaches one-third of the share capital. This reserve may not be distributed. General reserves can be formed freely; their distribution requires approval at annual shareholders' meetings. Both legal and general reserves are taxable.

Companies that carry out productive investments are entitled to tax-deferred reserves.

3.4 Liabilities and Provisions

The presentation of liabilities and provisions in the balance sheet complies with the requirements of the EU Directive for financial statement presentation. Corporate legislation requires that provisions be made for all losses concerning current or prior financial years.

In this connection, companies should make adequate provisions for employee severance pay, bad debts, and so on. In practice, provision for severance pay is not often made, because it is not deductible for tax purposes until it materializes. On the other hand, provision for bad debts is calculated as a percentage of sales. The fact that this provision is deductible for tax purposes may lead to unnecessary provisioning. Users of financial statements need to exercise particular caution in this respect.

3.5 Property, Plant, and Equipment

3.5.1 Valuation

Tangible fixed assets should be valued at historic cost plus improvements; only two departures are allowed:

1. Revaluation according to special legislation: in practice such laws are passed occasionally and provide for obligatory revaluation of land and buildings according to specific indices. There was also one instance of revaluation for machinery, but it was not obligatory. Revaluation applies to both cost and accumulated depreciation. The surplus is transferred to reserves and then capitalized or offset against losses.

2. Devaluation to arrive at the current value of an asset if this devaluation is considered of a permanent nature

3.5.2 Depreciation

Depreciation according to Law 2190 should be based on estimated economic life. Economic rates may be used according to the company's management. However, maximum depreciation rates are prescribed by the law. Accelerated depreciation is also provided under various incentive laws. This depreciation is shown separately in the profit and loss in nonoperating expenses. A company may decide not to depreciate its fixed assets during the year. The relevant tax benefit is deferred, and the useful life of the asset is extended accordingly. Any depreciation in excess of that calculated with the maximum depreciation rates is not recognized as an allowable expense. Deferred taxation as mentioned in Section 3.11 is not accounted for.

3.5.3 Government Grants

According to the General Accounting Plan, government grants relating to the purchase of fixed assets should be credited to a deferred account (reserve) and taken to other income in proportion to the depreciation expense of the fixed assets purchased with the grant.

3.5.4 Interest Charges

Interest charges relating to borrowings for the construction of fixed assets may be written off to income or deferred (capitalized) and amortized over a period of 5 years.

3.6 Assets Whose Services Are Acquired by Means of Leases

According to law, with the lease agreement the lessor is obliged to grant (*a*) the usage of a movable asset to the lessee against a determined rental, and (*b*) the purchase option at the conclusion of the agreement or at a previous stage. The leasing period cannot be less than 3 years.

The accounting treatment is still the one provided by the law, according to which:

1. The lessee records the rentals in operating expenses. Also, an appropriate value for the asset is recorded in both assets and liabilities in memo accounts as third-party property, which are offset upon termination of the lease agreement.

2. The lessor depreciates the value of the asset and takes to income-related expenses such as commissions and legal fees. Also, the value of the asset is recorded in memo accounts as property in the hands of third parties.

In the case of operating leases, no specific disclosures are required.

3.7 Oil, Gas, and Other Mineral Resources

Oil exploration rights belong to the Greek state and may be transferred to private companies only through special government permits.

A special law was enacted specifically to cover the activities of the major drilling consortium in Greece (Law 98/1975). The basis of accounting introduced by this law is in accordance with IAS, except in the following cases:

1. All recoverable petroleum costs that include direct and indirect drilling and facilities costs are capitalized and are amortized against revenue according to fixed percentages. If actual costs exceed the limits, the difference is shown as negative recovery of project development costs. This amount is capitalized and carried forward to future years.

2. Exploration and drilling costs are capitalized and deferred, to be recovered out of future commercial discoveries.

Inventories of hydrocarbons and other mineral resources such as sulfur, even if processed, are not valued for financial statement purposes.

3.8 Intangible Assets

Legally protected intellectual property rights, such as patents and trademarks, are recorded at cost and amortized over the period of their productive use. Deferred charges such as preoperating expenses and research and development costs are either written off as incurred or amortized over 5 years.

3.9 Participations (Equity Investments in Other Companies)

Participations in corporations (*Sociétés Anonymes*) are valued at the lower of cost or market value, or the value in previous financial statements, determined on a portfolio basis; for unincorporated enterprises they are valued at the lower of cost or market value, determined on an individual basis. Differences arising are taken to the income statement currently.

Market price is determined as follows. For quoted shares, market price is the average price of the year's final month. For nonquoted shares of companies that prepare financial statements under the provisions of Law 2190, market price is the book value of these shares, based on the latest published financial statements. For other shares, the market value is considered equal to their historic cost.

3.10 Inventories

3.10.1 Valuation

Inventories are valued at the lower of cost and market (replacement) price. The net realizable value is used when the market value is below the historic cost but in excess of the net realizable value.

Acceptable methods for the determination of the cost are FIFO, LIFO, average, individual, and base stock. In practice, FIFO and average cost are the most usual methods.

3.10.2 Overhead Expenses—Interest Charges

Overhead expenses are allocated to cost to the extent relating to the production (general production expenses, direct distribution cost, etc.). Interest charges are not allocated to cost

3.10.3 Construction Contracts—Percentage of Completion Method

Although the law does not specifically address this matter, it specifies that only profit made at the balance sheet date may be included. On the basis of the interpretation of the law, incomplete constructions should be accounted for according to the stage of completion (i.e., invoices, including profit, should be issued on the basis of an engineer's certificate of completion).

3.11 Taxation

Financial statements are prepared under the provisions of Law 2190. However, accounting is still affected by income tax regulations, although there is a trend toward accounting on an economic basis.

The reported income in the financial statements might differ materially from the taxable income mainly because of the following:

1. Tax deferred reserves provided under various incentive laws
2. Nontaxable income (mainly bank interest)
3. Nonallowable expenses (mainly provisions)
4. Tax losses carried forward
5. Additional taxes and penalties

However, the corporate tax expense of the year is shown separately in the profit distribution table, which also includes any additional taxes assessed by the tax authorities for prior years and item 1, above. Moreover, deferred taxation is not provided for by the local regulations and therefore is not reflected in the financial statements.

3.12 Pensions

Few pension schemes have been implemented in Greece. However, the law provides that all employees and any lawyers on retainer who retire are entitled to a retirement indemnity determined by their status and length of service. Law 2190 provides that this liability be accrued.

Nevertheless, many companies, on the basis of an opinion issued by the Legal Counsel of the State, record an accrual only for the severance pay due to those employees retiring in the following year. Therefore, users of financial statements should be aware of the policy adopted, since the unrecorded liability can be significant.

In the cases of companies providing for the full liability, best estimates based on present data are used instead of actuarial studies. The related expense in either case is not deductible.

3.13 Other

3.13.1 Memo Accounts

Memo accounts are a separate category of accounts that operate dually (as assets and liabilities) in an autonomous accounting system. Memo accounts should include details of the following:

- Third-party property
- Guarantees given and received as security
- Contracts in progress (incomplete portion)
- Various accounts including statistics (untaxed surplus on mergers, tax-free reserve rights, etc.)

4. Expected Future Developments

The regulations for the new institute (SOE) provide that International Standards on Auditing and International Accounting Standards are to be applied. In practice, this is a substantial task, particularly regarding accounting standards in light of prevailing practice described earlier. Considering only the changes in legislation required, it is something that will take several years to achieve.

Company law is also under review, and it is expected that a completely new law will be passed in due course. A new law would aim to remove outdated requirements and introduce provisions to reflect present conditions.

As more and more companies seek a listing on the Athens Stock Exchange, it is expected that reporting and other requirements will become stricter. With the relaxation of exchange controls, there is increasing interest by foreign investors in the Athens Stock Exchange.

The banking system is in a state of change as the Bank of Greece delegates more responsibility to retail banks and regulations are relaxed.

Competition has become more intense, and several small private banks, targeting specific sectors, have been established.

Because Greece is starting from a position somewhat behind most other European countries, in general one can expect to see some significant changes in the years ahead.

Acknowledgment

The author would like to express his appreciation for the valuable assistance and contributions by Vassilis Chaidalis, Dimitris Varvaritis, and Stefanos Arvanitakis, managers with Price Waterhouse.

Useful Addresses

(Temporary address)
Institute of Certified Auditors (SOE)
28 Kapodistriou street
106 82 Athens

Financial Statements

ΑΝΩΝΥΜΟΣ ΓΕΝΙΚΗ ΕΤΑΙΡΙΑ ΤΣΙΜΕΝΤΩΝ "ΗΡΑΚΛΗΣ"
ΑΡ. ΜΗΤΡ. Α.Ε. : 13576/06/Β/86/096
ΓΕΝΙΚΟΣ ΙΣΟΛΟΓΙΣΜΟΣ 31ης ΔΕΚΕΜΒΡΙΟΥ 1992
82η ΕΤΑΙΡΙΚΗ ΧΡΗΣΗ (1 ΙΑΝΟΥΑΡΙΟΥ - 31 ΔΕΚΕΜΒΡΙΟΥ 1992) (ΣΕ ΧΙΛ. ΔΡΧ.)

ΕΝΕΡΓΗΤΙΚΟ

	ΧΡΗΣΕΩΣ 1992			ΧΡΗΣΕΩΣ 1991		
	ΑΞΙΑ ΚΤΗΣΕΩΣ	ΑΠΟΣΒΕΣΕΙΣ	ΑΝΑΠΟΣΒΕΣΤΗ ΑΞΙΑ	ΑΞΙΑ ΚΤΗΣΕΩΣ	ΑΠΟΣΒΕΣΕΙΣ	ΑΝΑΠΟΣΒΕΣΤΗ ΑΞΙΑ
Β. ΕΞΟΔΑ ΕΓΚΑΤΑΣΤΑΣΗΣ						
1. Έξοδα ιδρύσης & πρώτης εγκατάστασης	1.198.549	1.137.340	61.209	1.198.549	1.029.339	169.210
2. Συν/κές διαφορές δανείων για κτήσεις παγίων	10.566.419	9.013.038	1.553.381	10.566.419	7.985.225	2.581.194
3. Τόκοι δανείων κατασκευαστικής περιόδου	3.517.547	3.341.580	175.967	3.517.547	2.989.825	527.722
4. Λοιπά έξοδα πολυετούς απόσβεσης	694.067	619.433	74.634	637.809	595.560	42.249
ΣΥΝΟΛΟ ΕΞΟΔΩΝ ΕΓΚΑΤΑΣΤΑΣΗΣ (Β)	15.976.582	14.111.391	1.865.191	15.920.324	12.599.949	3.320.375
Γ. ΠΑΓΙΟ ΕΝΕΡΓΗΤΙΚΟ						
Ι. Ασώματες ακινητοποιήσεις						
1. Έξοδα ερευνών & ανάπτυξης	105.443	44.820	60.623	76.195	25.607	50.588
ΙΙ. Ενσώματες ακινητοποιήσεις						
1. Γήπεδα-Οικόπεδα	7.756.985	-	7.756.985	4.170.799		4.170.799
2. Ορυχεία-μεταλλεία, λατομεία κτλ.	8.763.980	-	8.763.980	3.832.010		3.832.010
3. Κτίρια & τεχνικά έργα	29.319.429	23.132.838	6.186.591	16.041.550	12.753.415	3.288.135
4. Μηχανήματα-τεχν.εγκατ.& λοιπός μηχαν.εξοπλ.	20.726.484	14.939.578	5.786.906	18.054.060	14.682.205	3.371.855
5. Μεταφορικά μέσα	2.700.622	208.586	2.492.036	447.205	188.684	258.521
6. Έπιπλα & λοιπ. εξοπλ.	361.591	173.125	188.466	284.575	158.983	125.592
7. Ακινητοποιήσεις υπό εκτέλ. & προκαταβολές	1.191.331	-	1.191.331	4.861.713		4.861.713
	70.820.422	38.454.127	32.366.295	47.691.912	27.783.287	19.908.625
ΣΥΝΟΛΟ ΑΚΙΝΗΤΟΠΟΙΗΣΕΩΝ (ΓΙ+ΓΙΙ)	70.925.865	38.498.947	32.426.918	47.768.107	27.808.894	19.959.213
ΙΙΙ.Συμμετοχές & άλλες μακροπρόθεσμες χρηματοοικονομ. απαιτήσεις						
1. Συμμετοχές σε συνδεμένες επιχειρήσεις			1.682.138			1.609.219
2. Συμμετοχές σε λοιπές επιχειρήσεις			42.169			42.169
7. Λοιπές μακροπρόθεσμες απαιτήσεις			606.801			543.495
			2.331.108			2.194.883
ΣΥΝΟΛΟ ΠΑΓΙΟΥ ΕΝΕΡΓΗΤΙΚΟΥ (Γ)			34.758.026			22.154.096
Δ. ΚΥΚΛΟΦΟΡΟΥΝ ΕΝΕΡΓΗΤΙΚΟ						
Ι. Αποθέματα						
1. Εμπορεύματα		81.132			37.952	
2. Προϊόντα έτοιμα & ημιτελή		1.189.275			1.121.986	
3. Παραγωγή σε εξέλιξη		2.446.292			1.820.234	
4. Πρώτες & βοηθ.ύλες-Αναλώσιμα υλ.- αναλ/κά, υλικά συσκευασίας		5.653.478			5.088.353	
5. Προκαταβολές για αγορές αποθεμάτων		160.792	9.530.969		130.907	8.199.432
ΙΙ. ΑΠΑΙΤΗΣΕΙΣ						
1. Πελάτες		11.080.408			9.426.817	
2. Γραμμάτια εισπρακτέα						
- Χαρτοφυλακίου	126.192			145.087		
- Στις τράπεζες για είσπραξη	100			50.944		
- Στις τράπεζες για εγγύηση	368.378	494.670		543.545	739.576	
3. Γραμμάτια σε καθυστέρηση		198.225			186.016	
3α.Επιταγές εισπρακτέες		4.670.368			5.354.472	
5. Βραχυπρόθ.απαιτ.κατά συνδεμ. επιχειρήσεων		7.388.902			7.492.852	
8. Δεσμευμένοι λ/σμοί καταθέσεων		2.820			2.820	
11. Χρεώστες διάφοροι		1.044.767			584.444	
11α.Ελληνικό Δημόσιο		4.918.721			4.409.327	
12. Λογ/σμοί διαχειρίσεως προκαταβολών		43.527	29.842.408		23.432	28.219.756
IV. ΔΙΑΘΕΣΙΜΑ						
1. Ταμείο		84.775			89.089	
3. Καταθέσεις όψεως & προθεσμίας		2.641.997	2.726.772		1.453.542	1.542.631
ΣΥΝΟΛΟ ΚΥΚΛΟΦΟΡΟΥΝΤΟΣ ΕΝΕΡΓΗΤΙΚΟΥ (Δ)			42.100.149			37.961.819
Ε. ΜΕΤΑΒΑΤΙΚΟΙ Λ/ΣΜΟΙ ΕΝΕΡΓΗΤΙΚΟΥ						
1. Έξοδα επόμενων χρήσεων		11.801			7.352	
2. Έσοδα χρήσεως εισπρακτέα		259.059	270.860		72.522	79.874
ΓΕΝΙΚΟ ΣΥΝΟΛΟ ΕΝΕΡΓΗΤΙΚΟΥ (Β+Γ+Δ+Ε)			78.994.226			63.516.164
ΛΟΓΑΡΙΑΣΜΟΙ ΤΑΞΕΩΣ ΧΡΕΩΣΤΙΚΟΙ						
1. Αλλότρια περιουσιακά στοιχεία		118			43	
2. Χρεωστ. λογ/σμοί εγγυήσεων & εμπράγματων ασφαλειών		6.045.057			5.045.747	
3. Απαιτήσεις από αμφοτεροβαρείς συμβάσεις					16.308	
4. Λοιποί λογαριασμοί τάξεως		222.706			227.207	
		6.267.881			5.289.305	

ΣΗΜΕΙΩΣΕΙΣ: α). Επί των γηπέδων, οικοπέδων και εγκαταστάσεων της Εταιρίας υπάρχουν την 31.12.92 προσημφωνα παροχης υποθηκών-προσημειώσεων ύψους δρχ. 2.600 εκατ., που ασφαλίζουν

HERACLES CEMENT COMPANY S.A.
REG. NUMBER 13576/06/B/86/096
BALANCE SHEET AS AT DECEMBER 31, 1992 (82nd Year)
(AMOUNTS IN THOUSANDS OF DRACHMAS)

ASSETS	1992			1991		
	Acquisition value	Depreciation	Written down value	Acquisition value	Depreciation	Written down value
B. FORMATION EXPENSES						
1. Preliminary expenses	1,198,549	1,137,340	61,209	1,198,549	1,029,339	169,210
2. Exchange differences from loans for fix. ass. acquis	10,566,419	9,013,038	1,553,381	10,566,419	7,985,225	2,581,194
3. Construction period loan interest	3,517,547	3,341,580	175,967	3,517,547	2,989,825	527,722
4. Other formation expenses	694,067	619,433	74,634	637,809	595,560	42,249
TOTAL FORMATION EXPENSES (B)	15,976,582	14,111,391	1,865,191	15,920,324	12,599,949	3,320,375
C. FIXED ASSETS						
I. Intangible assets						
1. Research & develop.costs	105,443	44,820	60,623	76,195	25,607	50,588
II. Tangible assets						
1. Land	7,756,985	—	7,756,985	4,170,799	—	4,170,799
2. Mines, quarries etc.	8,763,980	—	8,763,980	3,832,010	—	3,832,010
3. Buildings & techn.works	29,319,429	23,132,838	6,186,591	16,041,550	12,753,415	3,288,135
4. Machinery, techn. installations & other equipm.	20,726,484	14,939,578	5,786,906	18,054,060	14,682,205	3,371,855
5. Transportation equipment	2,700,622	208,586	2,492,036	447,205	188,684	258,521
6. Furniture and fixtures	361,591	173,125	188,466	284,575	158,983	125,592
7. Payments on account & tangible assets in course of construction	1,191,331	—	1,191,331	4,861,713		4,861,713
	70,820,422	38,454,127	32,366,295	47,691,912	27,783,287	19,908,625
TOTAL TANGIBLE AND INTANGIBLE ASSETS (CI+CII)	70,925,865	38,498,947	32,426,918	47,768,107	27,808,894	19,959,213
III. Financial assets						
1. Participating interests in affiliated undertakings			1,682,138			1,609,219
2. Participating interests in other undertakings			42,169			42,169
7. Other financial assets			606,801			543,495
			2,331,108			2,194,883
TOTAL FIXED ASSETS (C)			34,758,026			22,154,096
D. CURRENT ASSETS						
I. Stocks						
1. Merchandise		81,132			37,952	
2. Finished and semi-finished products		1,189,275			1,121,986	
3. Work in progress		2,446,292			1,820,234	
4. Raw and auxiliary materials - consumables - spare parts and packing items.		5,653,478			5,088,353	
5. Payments on account		160,792	9,530,969		130,907	8,199,432
II. Debtors						
1. Trade debtors		11,080,408			9,426,817	
2. Notes receivable						
- In portfolio	126,192			145,067		
- At banks for collection	100			50,944		
- At banks as pledge	368,378	494,670		543,545	739,576	
3. Notes overdue		198,225			186,016	
3a.Cheques receivable		4,670,368			5,354,472	
5. Amounts owed by affiliated undertakings		7,388,902			7,492,852	
8. Blocked Deposits		2,820			2,820	
11. Sundry debtors		1,044,767			584,444	
11a.Greek State		4,918,721			4,409,327	
12. Advances & credits management accounts		43,527	29,842,408		23,432	28,219,756
IV. Cash at bank and in hand						
1. Cash		84,775			89,089	
3. Current and deposit accounts		2,641,997	2,726,772		1,453,542	1,542,631
TOTAL CURRENT ASSETS (D)			42,100,149			37,961,819
E. PREPAYMENTS AND ACCRUED INCOME						
1. Deferred charges		11,801			7,352	
2. Earned income		259,059	270,860		72,522	79,874
TOTAL ASSETS (B+C+D+E)			78,994,226			63,516,164
MEMO ACCOUNTS						
1. Third party asset items			118			43
2. Guarantees and real securities (debit accounts)			6,045,057			5,045,747
3. Bilateral agreements (receivables)			—			16,308
4. Other memo. accounts			222,706			227,207
			6,267,881			5,289,305

Notes: On the Company's land and installations there were preliminary agreements at December 31, 1992 for mortgages - lines of Drs 2,600 m. to secure loan balances of Drs. 2885 m.

20

344 *European Accounting Guide*

ΠΑΘΗΤΙΚΟ

	ΧΡΗΣΕΩΣ 1992		ΧΡΗΣΕΩΣ 1991	
Α. ΙΔΙΑ ΚΕΦΑΛΑΙΑ				
Ι. Κεφάλαιο Μετοχικό				
(50.490.957 μετοχές των 605 δρχ.)				
1. Καταβλημένο		30.547.029		30.547.029
ΙΙ. Διαφορά από έκδοση μετοχών υπέρ το άρτιο		401.642		401.642
ΙΙΙ.Διαφορές αναπροσαρμογής - Επιχορηγήσεις επενδύσεων				
1. Διαφορές από αναπροσαρμογή αξίας συμμετ. & χρεογράφων	396.999		324.104	
2. Διαφορές από αναπροσ. αξίας λοιπών περιουσ. στοιχείων	10.266.185	10.663.184	-	324.104
IV. Αποθεματικά κεφάλαια				
1. Τακτικό αποθεματικό	1.101.227		873.272	
4. Έκτακτα αποθεματικά	5.261.235		5.024.813	
5. Αφορολόγητα αποθεματικά ειδικών διατάξεων νόμων	5.929.118	12.291.580	4.036.610	9.934.695
ΣΥΝΟΛΟ ΙΔΙΩΝ ΚΕΦΑΛΑΙΩΝ (Α)		53.903.435		41.207.470
Β. ΠΡΟΒΛΕΨΕΙΣ ΓΙΑ ΚΙΝΔΥΝΟΥΣ & ΕΞΟΔΑ				
1. Προβλέψεις για αποζημίωση προσωπικού λόγω εξόδου από την υπ.	2.174.575		2.167.270	
2. Λοιπές προβλέψεις	3.973.130	6.147.705	1.664.464	3.831.734
Γ. ΥΠΟΧΡΕΩΣΕΙΣ				
Ι. Μακροπρόθεσμες υποχρεώσεις				
2. Δάνεια τραπεζών		1.981.568		2.198.227
ΙΙ. Βραχυπρόθεσμες υποχρεώσεις				
1. Προμηθευτές	1.587.723		1.764.483	
2. Γραμμάτια πληρωτέα	275.321		641.053	
3. Τράπεζες λ/βραχυπρόθεσμων υποχρεώσεων	6.924.823		6.893.748	
5. Υποχρεώσεις από φόρους - τέλη	1.993.320		1.043.684	
6. Ασφαλιστικοί Οργανισμοί	567.306		487.116	
7. Μακροπρόθεσμες υποχρεώσεις πληρωτέες στην επόμ. χρήση	692.055		648.191	
8. Υποχρ. προς συνδεμένες επιχειρήσεις	76.566		169.038	
10. Μερίσματα πληρωτέα	3.095.416		3.066.043	
11. Πιστωτές διάφοροι	971.467	16.183.997	852.366	15.565.722
ΣΥΝΟΛΟ ΥΠΟΧΡΕΩΣΕΩΝ (Γ)		18.165.565		17.763.949
Δ. ΜΕΤΑΒΑΤΙΚΟΙ Λ/ΣΜΟΙ ΠΑΘΗΤΙΚΟΥ				
2. Έξοδα χρήσεως δουλευμένα	482.521		418.011	
3. Λοιποί μεταβατικοί λ/σμοί	295.000	777.521	295.000	713.011
ΓΕΝΙΚΟ ΣΥΝΟΛ (Α+Β+Γ+Δ)		78.994.226		63.516.164
ΛΟΓΑΡΙΑΣΜΟΙ ΤΑΞΕΩΣ ΠΙΣΤΩΤΙΚΟΙ				
1. Δικαιούχοι αλλότριων περιουσ. στοιχείων		6.267.881		5.289.305
2. Πιστωτ. λογ/μοί εγγυήσεων		118		43
& εμπράγμ. ασφαλειών				
3. Υποχρεώσεις από αμφοτεροβαρείς		6.045.057		5.045.747
συμβάσεις		-		16.308
4. Λοιποί λογ/μοί τάξεως		222.706		227.207
		6.267.881		5.289.305

υπόλοιπα δανείων ύψους δρχ.2.889 εκατ. β) Οι αξίες των γηπέδων, των κτιρίων και των συσσωρευμένων αποσβέσεων των κτιρίων αναπροσαρμόσθηκαν στη χρήση 1992 με βάση τις διατάξεις του Ν. 2065/92.

21

LIABILITIES	1992		1991	
A. CAPITAL AND RESERVES				
I. Share capital of HERACLES GCC				
(50,490,957 shares at Drs.605)...		30,547,029		30,547,029
1. Paid-up capital		401,642		401,642
II. Share premium account				
III. Revaluation reserves - Investment grants				
1. Investment revaluation reserve				
from shares & securities	396,999		324,104	
2. Investment reval. reserve from other assets	10,266,185	10,663,184	—	324,104
IV. Reserves				
1. Legal reserve	1,101,227		873,272	
4. Extraordinary reserve	5,261,235		5,024,813	
5. Tax-free reserves under special laws	5,929,118	12,291,580	4,036,610	9,934,695
TOTAL CAPITAL AND RESERVES		53,903,435		41,207,470
B. PROVISIONS FOR LIABILITIES & CHARGES				
1. Provisions for retirement benefits	2,174,575		2,167,270	
2. Other provisions	3,973,130	6,147,705	1,664,464	3,831,734
C. CREDITORS				
I. Long-term debt				
2. Banks loans		1,981,568		2,198,227
II. Current liabilities				
1. Suppliers	1,587,723		1,764,483	
2. Notes payable	275,321		641,063	
3. Banks short-term liabilities	6,924,823		6,893,748	
5. Litigations for taxes and duties	1,993,320		1,043,684	
6. Insurance organisations	567,306		487,116	
7. Current portion of long-term debt	692,055		648,191	
8. Payables to affiliated companies	76,566		166,038	
10. Dividends payable	3,095,416		3,066,043	
11. Sundry creditors	971,467	16,183,997	852,366	15,565,722
TOTAL CREDITORS (C)		18,165,565		17,763,949
D. ACCRUALS AND DEFERRED INCOME				
2. Accrued expenses	482,521		418,011	
3. Other accrued expenses	295,000	777,521	295,000	713,011
GRAND TOTAL-LIABILITIES (A+B+C+D)		78,994,226		63,516,164
MEMO ACCOUNTS				
1. Beneficiaries of asset item		118		43
2. Guarantees and real securities (credit accounts)		6,045,057		5,045,747
3. Bilateral agreements (amounts owed)		—		16,308
4. Other memo. accounts		222,706		227,207
		6,267,881		5,289,305

to secure loan balances of Drs. 2,889 m b. the value of land and accumulated depreciation has been adjusted for the year in accordance with the provisions of Law N.2065/92.

21

ΚΑΤΑΣΤΑΣΗ ΛΟΓΑΡΙΑΣΜΟΥ ΑΠΟΤΕΛΕΣΜΑΤΩΝ ΧΡΗΣΕΩΣ
31ης ΔΕΚΕΜΒΡΙΟΥ 1992 (1 ΙΑΝΟΥΑΡΙΟΥ - 31 ΔΕΚΕΜΒΡΙΟΥ 1992)
(ΣΕ ΧΙΛ. ΔΡΧ.)

I. Αποτελέσματα εκμετάλλευσης	ΠΟΣΑ ΚΛΕΙΟΜΕΝΗΣ ΧΡΗΣΕΩΣ 1992			ΠΟΣΑ ΠΡΟΗΓΟΥΜΕΝΗΣ ΧΡΗΣΕΩΣ 1991		
Κύκλος εργασιών (πωλήσεις)			63.684.380			56.650.843
ΜΕΙΟΝ: Κόστος πωλήσεων			48.201.956			43.925.149
Μικτά αποτελέσματα εκμετάλλευσης			15.482.424			12.725.694
ΠΛΕΟΝ: Άλλα έσοδα εκμετάλλευσης			135.572			347.638
			15.617.996			13.073.332
ΣΥΝΟΛΟ						
ΜΕΙΟΝ: Έξοδα διοικ. λειτουργίας		2.905.342			2.741.174	
Έξοδα λειτουργ. ερευνών-ανάπτυξης		204.520			162.134	
Έξοδα λειτουργίας διάθεσης		808.974	3.918.836		585.906	3.489.214
Μερικά αποτελέσματα εκμετάλλευσης			11.699.160			9.584.118
ΜΕΙΟΝ: Χρεωστικοί τόκοι & συναφή έξοδα		2.375.427			2.686.624	
ΜΕΙΟΝ: Έσοδα συμμετοχών	516.823			657.973		
Κέρδη πωλήσεως συμμετοχών και χρεογράφων				801.185		
Πιστωτικοί τόκοι	21.689	538.512	1.836.915	4.988	1.464.146	1.222.478
Ολικά αποτελέσματα εκμετάλλευσης (κέρδη)			9.862.245			8.361.640
ΜΕΙΟΝ: Έκτακτα αποτελέσματα						
Έκτακτα & ανόργανα έξοδα	1.585.382			555.777		
Έξοδα προηγούμενων χρήσεων	-			444.943		
Προβλέψεις για έκτακτ.κινδύνους	500.000			-		
Αποσβέσεις συν/κών διαφορών	1.027.813	3.113.195		1.027.813	2.028.533	
Μείον: Έκτακτα & ανόργανα έσοδα		264.964	2.848.231		179.306	1.849.227
			7.014.014			6.512.413
ΜΕΙΟΝ: Απόσβεση προβλέψεων αποζημιώσεως						
προσωπικού λόγω εξόδου από την υπηρεσία			-			117.436
Οργανικά & έκτακτα αποτελέσματα (κέρδη)			7.014.014			6.394.977
ΜΕΙΟΝ: Συνολικές αποσβέσεις		2.296.847			2.737.685	
Μείον: Οι ενσωματωμένες στο λειτουργικό κόστος		2.296.847	-		2.737.685	-
ΚΑΘΑΡΑ ΑΠΟΤΕΛΕΣΜΑΤΑ (ΚΕΡΔΗ) ΧΡΗΣΕΩΣ προ φόρων			7.014.014			6.394.977

ΠΙΝΑΚΑΣ ΔΙΑΘΕΣΗΣ ΑΠΟΤΕΛΕΣΜΑΤΩΝ

	ΧΡΗΣΕΩΣ 1992		ΧΡΗΣΕΩΣ 1991
Καθαρά κέρδη χρήσεως		7.014.014	6.394.977
ΠΛΕΟΝ: Υπόλοιπο κερδών (ζημιών)			
προηγούμενων χρήσεων		-	78.692
Σύνολο		7.014.014	6.473.669
ΜΕΙΟΝ: Φόρος εισοδήματος		1.709.623	567.654
Κέρδη προς διάθεση		**5.304.391**	**5.906.015**
Η διάθεση των κερδών γίνεται ως εξής:			
Τακτικό αποθεματικό		227.955	283.591
Μερίσματα		3.029.457	3.029.457
Διάθεση κερδών στο προσωπικό		160.000	150.000
Έκτακτο αποθεματικό			
- Από απαλλασσόμενα της φορολογίας έσοδα	9.502		
- Από έσοδα φορολ/θέντα κατ΄ειδικό τρόπο	105		
- Από έσοδα φορολογηθέντα	226.815	236.422	
Αφορολόγητο αποθεματικό Ν.1262/1982		-	760.000
Αφορολόγητη έκπτωση Ν.1892/90		947.974	959.817
Αφορολόγητο αποθεματικό Ν.1828/89		702.583	
Αφορολόγητο αποθεματικό κερδών			
από πώληση χρεογράφων		-	723.150
		5.304.391	5.906.015

Η πληρωμή του ανωτέρω μερίσματος δρχ. 60 (εξήντα) κατά μετοχή, θα αρχίσει μετά την έγκριση του παρόντος Ισολογισμού από την Τακτική Γενική Συνέλευση των Μετόχων και σε ημερομηνία που θα ορισθεί από το Διοικητικό Συμβούλιο, με την προσκόμιση της υπ' αριθμ. 4 μερισματαποδείξης.

Λυκόβρυση, 13 Απριλίου 1993

Ο ΠΡΟΕΔΡΟΣ ΤΟΥ ΔΙΟΙΚΗΤΙΚΟΥ ΣΥΜΒΟΥΛΙΟΥ
& ΔΙΕΥΘΥΝΩΝ ΣΥΜΒΟΥΛΟΣ
LORENZO PANZAVOLTA
ΑΡ.ΔΙΑΒ.Ι.175043/23.7.83

Ο ΟΙΚΟΝΟΜΙΚΟΣ ΔΙΕΥΘΥΝΤΗΣ

ΣΩΤΗΡΙΟΣ Ι. ΠΑΠΑΣΠΗΛΙΩΤΟΠΟΥΛΟΣ
Α.829917/63

Ο ΠΡΟΪΣΤΑΜΕΝΟΣ ΤΟΥ ΛΟΓΙΣΤΗΡΙΟΥ

ΧΡΗΣΤΟΣ Α. ΣΤΑΣΙΝΟΠΟΥΛΟΣ
Ι.019339/72

22

PROFIT AND LOSS ACCOUNT
(FOR THE YEAR ENDED DECEMBER 31, 1992)
Expressed in thousands of drachmas

	1992			1991		
Operating Results						
Net turnover			63,684,380			56,650,843
Less: Cost of sales			48,201,956			43,925,149
Gross operating results - profit/(loss)			15,482,424			12,725,694
Plus: Other operating income			135,572			347,638
Total			15,617,996			13,073,332
Less: Administrative expenses		2,905,342			2,741,174	
Research and development costs		204,520			162,134	
Distribution costs		808,974	3,918,836		585,906	3,489,214
Operating results -profit			11,699,160			9,584,118
Less: Interest payable and similar charges		2,375,427			2,686,624	
Less: Income from participating interests	516,823			657,973		
Profits from sale of shares in subsidiaries	–			801,185		
Interest receivable and similar income	21,689	538,512	1,836,915	4,988	1,464,146	1,222,478
Total operating results (profit)			9,862,245			8,361,640
Less: Extraordinary and						
non-operating results	1,585,382			655,777		
Prior years' expenses	–			444,943		
Amortisation of exchange differences	500,000			–		
Amortisation of exchange differences	1,027,813	3,113,195		1,027,813	2,028,533	
Less: Extraordinary and non-operating income		264,964	2,848,231		179,306	1,849,227
			7,014,014			6,512,413
Less : Write off of prior years						
provisions for retirement benefits			–			117,436
Operating and extraordinary results(profit)			7,014,014			6,394,977
Less : Total depreciation		2,296,847			2,737,685	
Less : Depreciation charged to the operating cost		2,296,847			2,737,685	
PROFIT FOR THE YEAR BEFORE TAX			7,014,014			6,394,977

APPROPRIATIONS ACCOUNT

	1992		1991	
Net profit for the year		7,014,014		6,394,977
PLUS: Profit/(loss) brought forward		–		78,692
Total		7,014,014		6,473,669
LESS: Income tax		1,709,623		567,654
Profits for appropriation		5,304,391		5,906,015
Appropriated to :				
Legal reserves		227,955		283,591
Dividends		3,029,457		3,029,457
Staff participation rights		160,000		150,000
Extraordinary reserve arising from				
- Exempt income	9,502			–
- Income otherwise taxed	105			–
- Income subject to income tax	226,815	236,422		–
Tax free reserves arising from				
- L. 1262/1982		–		760,000
- L. 1892/90		947,974		§1
- L. 1828/89		702,583		–
- the sale of securities		–		723,150
		5,304,391		5,906,015

Payment for the above dividend of Drs. 60 (sixty) per share after retention of the fixed asset revaluation tax shall begin after approval of the Balance Sheet at the Ordinary General Meeting of the Shareholders at a date to be fixed by the Board of Directors, upon presentation of coupon No. 4.

Lycovrissi, April 13, 1993

CHAIRMAN OF THE BOARD OF DIRECTORS   FINANCIAL DIRECTOR   HEAD OF ACCOUNTS DEPARTMENT

LORENZO PANZAVOLTA   SOTIRIOS I. PAPASPILIOTOPOULOS   CHRISTOS A. STASSINOPOULOS
PASSPORT NO. 1 175043/23.7.83   A. 829917/63   1. 019339/72

22

_ Ανάλυση των χρεογράφων που κατέχει η Εταιρία την 31.12.92

a. Άμεσες Συμμετοχές σε Συνδεδεμένες Επιχειρήσεις

	Ποσοστό Συμ/χης	Τεμάχια	Αξία Τεμαχίων		Χιλ. Δρχ.
1. ΑΙΓΙΣ ΑΕ	60%	27.082	Δρχ.	1.910	51.726
2. ΑΝΕ ΗΡΑΚΛΗΣ	99,94%	88.949	"	1.000	88.949
3. ΕΜΜΥ ΚΤΙΡΙΑΚΑ ΣΤΟΙΧΕΙΑ ΑΒΕΕ	85,71%	183.276	"	1.000	183.276
4. ΚΑΡΜΟΡ ΕΛΛΑΣ ΕΠΕ	40%	200	"	11.250	2.250
5. ΕΒΙΕΣΚ ΑΕ	87%	1.019.640	"	253	257.967
6. ΑΣΤΗΡ ΜΠΕΤΟΝ ΑΕ	99%	327.579	"	1.051	344.286
7. ΣΚΥΡΟΔΕΜΑ ΕΒΑΕ	99,56%	93.903	"	2.053	192.782
8. ΕΛΛΗΝΙΚΟΝ ΚΕΝΤΡΟΝ ΕΡΕΥΝΩΝ ΤΣΙΜΕΝΤΟΥ ΕΠΕ	90%	90	"	10.000	900
9. ΗΡΑΚΛΗΣ ΣΥΣΚΕΥΑΣΙΑ ΑΕ	65,08%	153.600	"	1.044	160.304
10. ΗΡΑΚΛΗΣ ΔΙΕΘΝΗΣ ΑΕ	90%	9.000	"	1.000	9.000
11. ΕΠΕΝΔΥΣΗ ΣΙΛΟ ΠΟΡΤ ΣΑΙΔ ΑΕ	99%	9.900	"	18.450	182.655
12. HAQL SILO INVESTMENT CO SA	100%	100	S	10.000	51.800
13. ALEXANDRIA SILO INV. CO SA	100%	100	S	30.000	156.047
14. ΑΣΦΑΛΙΣΤΙΚΕΣ ΕΠΙΧΕΙΡΗΣΕΙΣ ΗΡΑΚΛΗΣ ΕΠΕ	5%	1	Δρχ.	10.000	10
15. ΓΡΑΦΕΙΟΡΓΑΝΩΣΗ ΕΠΕ	5%	6	"	17.209	103
16. ΗΡΑΚΛΗΣ ΝΑΥΤΙΚΕΣ ΠΡΑΚΤΟΡΕΥΣΕΙΣ ΕΠΕ	40%	8	"	10.000	80
Μερικό σύνολο					1.682.135

β. Συμμετοχές σε Λοιπές Επιχειρήσεις

	Τεμάχια	Αξία Τεμαχίων		Χιλ. Δρχ.
1. Μετοχές ΣΤΕΓΗΣ ΒΙΟΜΗΧΑΝΙΑΣ	580	Δρχ.	532	309
2. " Τ.Ε.Μ.Ε.Δ.Ε.	650	"	–	
3. " ΠΑΝΑΥΤΙΛΙΑΚΗΣ ΞΕΝΟΔΟΧ. ΕΤΑΙΡΙΑΣ	100	"	–	
4. " Α.Κ.Ε.Τ.(προσωρινοί τίτλοι)	–	"	–	
5. " ΘΕΤΕΚ Α.Ε.	–	"	–	
6. " ΤΡΑΠΕΖΑΣ ΜΑΚΕΔΟΝΙΑΣ-ΘΡΑΚΗΣ	11.428	"	3.545	40.512
7. Ε.Κ.Ε.Π.Υ	–	"	–	100
8. CEMENT MARKETING ASSOSIATION LTD	–	"	–	1.249
				42.170

ΓΕΝΙΚΟ   ΣΥΝΟΛΟ   1.724.305

16

— Analysis of the Company's Investments as at 31.12.92

a. Direct Investments in Associated Enteprises

	Percentage Hollding	Number Of Shares		Total Share Price	Investment Drs.'000
1. AIGIS S.A.	60%	27.082	Drs.	1,910	51,726
2. HERACLES SHIPPING CO S.A.	99.94%	88.949	"	1,000	88,949
3. EMMY-BUILDING ELEMENTS S.A.	85.71%	183,276	"	1,000	183,276
4. CARMOR HELLAS LTD.	40%	200	"	11,250	2,250
5. EVIESK S.A.	87%	1,019,640	"	253	257,967
6. STAR CONCRETE S.A.	99%	327,579	"	1,051	344,286
7. SKYRODEMA S.A.	99.56%	93,903	"	2,053	192,782
8. NATIONAL INSTITUTE RESEARCH IN CEMENT LTD.	90%	90	"	10,000	900
9. HERACLES PACKAGING CO S.A.	65.08%	153,600	"	1,044	160,304
10. HERACLES INTERNATIONAL S.A.	90%	9,000	"	1,000	9,000
11. PORT SAID SILO INVESTMENT CO S.A.	99%	9,900	"	18,450	182,655
12. HAQL SILO INVESTMENT CO SA	100%	100	S	10,000	51,800
13. ALEXANDRIA SILO INV. CO SA	100%	100	S	30,000	156,047
14. HERACLES INSURANCE LTD	5%	1	Drs.	10,000	10
15. OFFICE ORGANISATION LTD.	5%	6	"	17,209	103
16. HERACLES MARITIME AGENCY LTD	40%	8	"	10,000	80
Sub-Total					1,682,135

b. Investments in other Enteprises

	Number Of Shares		Total Share Price	Investment Drs.'000
1. HOME OF INDUSTRY	580	Drs.	532	309
2. T.E.M.E.D.E.	650	"	—	—
3. PANAFTILIAKIS HOTEL COMPANY	100	"	—	—
4. A.K.E.T. (Script Certificate)	—	"	—	—
5. THETEK S.A.	—	"	—	—
6. BANK OF MACEDONIA AND THRACE	11,428	"	3,545	40,512
7. E.K.E.P.Y	—	"	—	100
8. CEMENT MARKETING ASSOSIATION LTD	—	"	—	1,249
				42,170

| GRAND TOTAL | | | | 1,724,305 |

16

– Ανάλυση των Ακινήτων της Εταιρίας την 31.12.92

α. Γήπεδα-Οικόπεδα

1. Οικόπεδο Ευριπίδου 8	Επιφ. m2	453	χιλ. δρχ.	254.882
2. Γήπεδα εργοστασίου ΟΛΥΜΠΟΣ	"	1.558.410	"	811.564
3. Γήπεδα εργοστασίου ΗΡΑΚΛΗΣ ΙΙ	"	714.081	"	1.037.433
4. Οικόπεδα Λυκόβρυσης Αττικής	"	49.354	"	1.261.507
5. Γήπεδα Εγκαταστάσεων Κ. Διανομής	"	256.028	"	4.472.883
6. Λοιπές περιοχές	"	123.270	"	333.319
Σύνολο	Επιφ. m2	2.701.596	χιλ. δρχ.	8.171.588

β. Ορυχεία-Μεταλλεία-Αγροί

1. Αγροί Τροιζηνίας	Επιφ. m2	54.309	χιλ. δρχ.	188.901
2. Αγροί διαφόρων περιοχών	"	4.083.488	"	3.177.898
3. Ορυχεία Πειραιά	"	102.207	"	211.628
4. Ορυχεία Βόλου	"	773.555	"	531.455
5. Ορυχεία Μηλακίου	"	3.387.266	"	3.750.920
6. Ορυχεία λοιπών περιοχών	"	639.176	"	488.575
Σύνολο	Επιφ. m2	9.040.001	χιλ. δρχ.	8.349.377

γ. Κτίρια και Τεχνικά Έργα

1. Κεντρικά Γραφεία	χιλ. δρχ.	1.399.423
2. Εργοστάσιο ΟΛΥΜΠΟΣ	"	13.518.449
3. Εργοστάσιο ΗΡΑΚΛΗΣ ΙΙ	"	11.005.483
4. Εγκαταστάσεις Κ. Διανομής	"	3.334.475
5. Ορυχείο Θήρας	"	61.599
Σύνολο	χιλ. δρχ.	29.319.429

Λυκόβρυση, 13 Απριλίου 1993
ΤΟ ΔΙΟΙΚΗΤΙΚΟ ΣΥΜΒΟΥΛΙΟ

Βεβαιώνεται ότι η έκθεση αυτή είναι εκείνη που αναφέρεται
στο από Απριλίου 1993 πιστοποιητικό ελέγχου.

Αθήνα, 15 Απριλίου 1993

ΟΙ ΟΡΚΩΤΟΙ ΛΟΓΙΣΤΕΣ

ΙΩΑΝΝΗΣ Ν. ΛΑΜΠΡΟΥ
Κ. 227220/77

ΚΩΝ/ΝΑ ΘΩΜΑΪΔΟΥ ΠΑΝΑΓΟΠΟΥΛΟΥ
Η. 215474/62

17

_ The Company's Tangible Fixed Assets as at 31.12.92 are analysed as follows:

a. Land and Sites

1. Building lot 8, Evripidou Str. Athens	Area m2	453	thous. drs.	254,882
2. Site of OLYMPOS plant	"	1,558,410	"	811,564
3. Site of HERACLES II plant	"	714,081	"	1,037,433
4. Site at Lycovrissi, Athens	"	49,354	"	1,261,507
5. Sites of distribution terminals	"	256,028	"	4,472,883
· 6. Other Sites	"	123,270	"	333,319
Total	Area m2	2,701,596	thous. drs.	8,171,588

b. Quarries, Mines and other lands

1. Farmland at Trizinia	Area m2	54,309	thous. drs.	188,901
2. Farmland at other locations	"	4,083,488	"	3,177,898
3. Quarries at Piraeus	"	102,207	"	211,628
4. Quarries at Volos	"	773,555	"	531,455
5. Quarries at Milaki	"	3,387,266	"	3,750,920
6. Quarries at other locations	"	639,176	"	488,575
Total	Area m2	9,040,001	thous. drs.	8,349,377

c. Buildings and Technical Works

1. Head Offices	thous. drs.	1,399,423
2. OLYMPOS plant	"	13,518,449
3. HERACLES II plant	"	11,005,483
4. Distribution terminals	"	3,334,475
5. Quarries in Santorini	"	61,599
Total	thous. drs.	29,319,429

Lycovrissi, 13th April 1993
THE BOARD OF DIRECTORS

It is certified that the above forms part of the short-form
audit report of April 1993

Athens, 15 April,1993

CERTIFIED PUBLIC ACCOUNTANTS OF GREECE

IOANNIS N. LAMBROU   K. THOMAIDOU PANAGOPOULOU
K. 227220/77   H. 215474/62

17

ΠΙΣΤΟΠΟΙΗΤΙΚΟ ΕΛΕΓΧΟΥ ΟΡΚΩΤΩΝ ΛΟΓΙΣΤΩΝ

Προς τους κ.κ. Μετόχους της Ανώνυμης Γενικής Εταιρείας Τσιμέντων "ΗΡΑΚΛΗΣ"

Ελέγξαμε τις ανωτέρω Οικονομικές Καταστάσεις καθώς και το σχετικό Προσάρτημα της Ανώνυμης Γενικής Εταιρείας Τσιμέντων "ΗΡΑΚΛΗΣ" της εταιρικής χρήσεως που έληξε την 31η Δεκεμβρίου 1992. Ο έλεγχός μας, στα πλαίσια του οποίου λάβαμε και γνώση πλήρους λογιστικού απολογισμού των εργασιών των υποκαταστημάτων της εταιρείας, έγινε σύμφωνα με τις διατάξεις του άρθρου 37 του κωδ. Ν.2190/1920 "περί Ανωνύμων Εταιρειών" και τις ελεγκτικές διαδικασίες που κρίναμε κατάλληλες, βάσει των αρχών και κανόνων ελεγκτικής που ακολουθεί το Σώμα Ορκωτών Λογιστών. Τέθηκαν στη διάθεσή μας τα βιβλία και στοιχεία που τήρησε η εταιρεία και μας δόθηκαν οι αναγκαίες για τον έλεγχο πληροφορίες και επεξηγήσεις που ζητήσαμε. Στα βιβλία της εταιρείας έχει τηρηθεί κανονικά λογαριασμός κόστους παραγωγής. Επαληθεύσαμε τη συμφωνία του περιεχομένου της Εκθέσεως Διαχειρίσεως του Διοικητικού Συμβουλίου προς την Τακτική Γενική Συνέλευση των μετόχων, με τις σχετικές Οικονομικές Καταστάσεις. Το Προσάρτημα περιλαμβάνει τις πληροφορίες που προβλέπονται από την παράγρ.1 του άρθρου 43a του κωδ. Ν.2190/1920.

Από τον παραπάνω έλεγχό μας προέκυψαν τα εξής: 1. Οι συναλλαγματικές διαφορές των δανείων και ποιήσεων για κτήσεις πάγιων στοιχείων, που εμφανίζονται στο λογαριασμό ενεργητικού "Έξοδα εγκατάστασης", αποσβέννονται: α) Οι μέχρι 31.12.86, με ετήσιο συντελεστή 10%, τακτική που ακολουθείται πάγιως από του έτους 1982. β) Οι από 1.1.87 και μετά, σύμφωνα με τις νέες διατάξεις του Ν.2190 (άρθρο 43 παρ.3/γ). Αν οι μέχρι 31.12.86 συναλλαγματικές διαφορές αποσβέννονταν ανάλογα με το εξοφλούμενο σε κάθε χρήση τμήμα των δανείων, όπως προέβλεπαν οι ισχύουσες τότε διατάξεις του Κώδικα Φορολογικών Στοιχείων, οι μέχρι 31.12.92 συνολικές αποσβέσεις αυτών θα ήταν μεγαλύτερες κατά δρχ. 1.553 εκατ. με ισόποση μείωση της καθαρής λογιστικής θέσης της εταιρείας, ενώ τα αποτελέσματα της χρήσης 1992 θα είχαν επιβαρυνθεί με ποσό μικρότερο κατά δρχ. 962 εκατ. 2α. Με βάση τις διατάξεις του Ν.2065/1992 έγινε στην χρήση 1992 (την ελεγχόμενη χρήση) αναπροσαρμογή της αξίας κτήσεως των γηπέδων, των κτιρίων και των συσσωρευμένων αποσβέσεων των κτιρίων εξαιτίας της οποίας αυξήθηκε η αξία κτήσεως των γηπέδων και κτιρίων κατά δρχ. 20.183 εκατ. και η αξία των συσσωρευμένων αποσβέσεων των κτιρίων κατά δρχ. 9.917 εκατ. και προέκυψε διαφορά αναπροσαρμογής ποσού δρχ.10.266 εκατ. που καταχωρήθηκε στον λογαριασμό των ιδίων κεφαλαίων Α ΙΙΙ-2 "Διαφορές από αναπροσαρμογή αξίας λοιπών περιουσιακών στοιχείων". Οι αποσβέσεις της χρήσεως 1992 υπολογίσθηκαν επί της νέας αναπροσαρμοσμένης αξίας και είναι μεγαλύτερες από εκείνες που θα προέκυπταν εάν είχαν υπολογισθεί στην αξία πριν την αναπροσαρμογή κατά δρχ. 150 εκ. περίπου. 2β.Η εταιρεία στην παρούσα χρήση σύμφωνα με τον Ν.2065/1992 ελόγισε αποσβέσεις επί των παγίων περιουσιακών στοιχείων με μειωμένους συντελεστές εκείνων τη προηγούμενης χρήσεως με συνέπεια οι αποσβέσεις να εμφανίζονται μειωμένες κατά δρχ. 1.097 εκατ. και το μεγαλύτερο μέρος αυτών δεν φαίνεται ότι σε σχέση με την προηγούμενη χρήση. 3. Μεταξύ των απαιτήσεων περιλαμβάνονται: α) Απαίτηση κατά του πελάτη εξωτερικού "CEMENTONAVIOS" (λογ/σμός ΔΠ/1 "Πελάτες") ύψους δρχ. 3.559 εκατ., οι μετά του οποίου συναλλαγές διακόπηκαν τον Αύγουστο του 1984. Στο ποσό αυτό περιλαμβάνονται και οι μέχρι 31.12.87 τόκοι. Για το ποσό αυτό εκδόθηκε τελεσίδικη απόφαση υπέρ του ΑΓΕΤ ΗΡΑΚΛΗΣ αλλά κατά την Νομική Υπηρεσία της εταιρείας, θεωρείται αμφίβολη η είσπραξή του. Το εν λόγω κονδύλι (δρχ. 3.559 εκατ.) αντικρύζεται κατά δρχ. 1.420 εκ. με τον λογαριασμό Παθητικού (Λογ/σμός Β-2) "Λοιπές Προβλέψεις" και αφορούν συναλλαγματικές διαφορές, μη εισοδοποιηθείσες των δανείων 1988 έως και 1992 από την αποτίμηση του Ξ.Ν. της απαιτήσεως. Σημειώνεται, εξάλλου, ότι δεν λάβαμε απάντηση σε επιστολή που στάλθηκε για την επιβεβαίωση του υπολοίπου αυτού. β) Λοιπές απαιτήσεις ύψους δρχ. 7.289 εκατ. που βρίσκονται σε καθυστέρηση, εκ των οποίων ποσό δρχ. 5.185 εκατ. αφορά εταιρείες κατά συνδεμένων επιχειρήσεων με αρνητική λογιστική καθαρά θέση. Έναντι των απαιτήσεων αυτών η εταιρία, σε αντίθεση με τη προηγούμενη χρήση διενήργησε πρόβλεψη για την πιθανή ζημιά από εισφορελείς απαιτήσεις, σύμφωνα με τον Ν.2065/1992 ύψους δρχ. 500 εκατ. με συνέπεια τα κέρδη της να εμφανίζονται ισόποσα μειωμένα σε σχέση με την προηγούμενη χρήση. γ) Απαιτήσεις κατά του Ελληνικού Δημοσίου δρχ. 4.104 εκατ. που εμφανίζονται στον λογαριασμό ΔΠ 11α και προέρχονται από επιστροφές Φ.Π.Α. (δρχ. 3.627 εκατ.) και λοιπούς φόρους που έχουν παρακρατηθεί (δρχ. 477 εκατ.) και του το μεγαλύτερο μέρος αυτών δεν φαίνεται ότι θα εισπραχθεί μέσα στο 1993 παρόλο που οι απαιτήσεις αυτές είναι ήδη ληξιπρόθεσμες και απαιτητές. δ) Εξάλλου επιδικες απαιτήσεις κατά τρίτων ύψους δρχ. 1.000 εκατ. περίπου για τις οποίες δεν έχει γίνει σχετική εγγραφή στα βιβλία επειδή δεν έχουν τελεσιδικήσει ακόμη. 4. Δεν έχει σχηματισθεί πρόβλεψη για ενδεχόμενες υποχρεώσεις: α) Από ποινικές μήτρες που έχουν επιβληθεί από την Τράπεζα Ελλάδος υπέρ του Δημοσίου, λόγω παραβάσεων νόμων, ύψους δρχ. 1.354 εκατ. Από το εν λόγω ποσό για δρχ. 522 εκατ. η εταιρεία έχει προσφύγει στα Διοικητικά Δικαστήρια και η υπόθεση εκκρεμοδικεί ακόμη. β) Από προσαυξήσεις χαρτοσήμου για χρηματοδοτήσεις προς θυγατρικές εταιρείες. Στα πλαίσια του ελέγχου μας δεν ελέγχθηκαν με τον προσανατολισμό αυτών οι οποίες αφορούσαν στην περίοδο 1981 και εντεύθεν. Για τις χρήσεις 1990 έως και 1992 το ύψος αυτών ανέρχεται σε δρχ. 84 εκατ. περίπου. 5. Δεν έχει σχηματισθεί πρόβλεψη στον Ισολογισμό σε βάρος των αποτελεσμάτων της χρήσεως δρχ. 195 εκατ., που αφορά σε αναδρομική αύξηση τιμής τέφρας ΔΕΗ. 6. Στην από 15.3.93 επιστολή της, η Νομική Υπηρεσία της εταιρείας μάς εγνώρισε ότι διεκδικούνται απο εταιρείες αιγυπτιακής διακόπτων τον λόγω λοιπών περιουσιακών αποζημιώσεις ύψους δρχ. 477 εκατ. περίπου, εις βάρος της ΑΓΕΤ ΗΡΑΚΛΗΣ, που δεν εμφανίζονται στον Ισολογισμό επειδή η έκβαση των εν λόγω διεκδικήσεων κρίνεται αβέβαιη. 7. Η εταιρεία, έως και την προηγούμενη χρήση, σχημάτιζε με όλο το προσωπικό της, πρόβλημα αποζημιώσεων λόγω εξόδου από την υπηρεσία ανεξαρτήτως χρόνου θεμελιώσεως δικαιώματος συνταξιοδοτήσεως. Κατά την παρούσα χρήση η τακτική αυτή άλλαξε και σχηματίστηκε πρόβλημα μόνο για το προσωπικό που θεμελιώνει δικαίωμα συνταξιοδοτήσεως μέχρι το τέλος της επόμενης χρήσης, σύμφωνα με το άρθρο 10 Ν.2065/1992. Αν η πρόβλεψη σχηματιζόταν όπως και στις προηγούμενες χρήσεις το σωρευτικό ύψος της, κατά την ημερομηνία κλεισίματος του Ισολογισμού θα ήταν μεγαλύτερο της εμφανιζόμενης στον Ισολογισμό κατά δρχ. 753 εκατ. Ισόποσα μεγαλύτερη θα ήταν και η επιβάρυνση των Αποτελεσμάτων Χρήσεως.

Δεν τροποποιήθηκε η μέθοδος απογραφής σε σχέση με την προηγούμενη χρήση εκτός των περιπτώσεων των παραπάνω σημειώσεών μας 2α, 2β, 3β και 7.

Οι ανωτέρω Οικονομικές Καταστάσεις προκύπτουν από τα βιβλία και στοιχεία της εταιρείας και, μαζί με το Προσάρτημα, αφού ληφθούν υπ' όψη οι παραπάνω παρατηρήσεις μας, απεικονίζουν, βάσει των σχετικών διατάξεων που ισχύουν και λογιστικών αρχών, οι οποίες έγινε γενικά εφαρμογή και δεν διαφέρουν από εκείνες που η εταιρεία είχε εφαρμόσει στην προηγούμενη χρήση, εκτός περιπτώσεων των παραπάνω σημειώσεών μας 2α, 2β και 3β, την περιουσιακή διάρθρωση και τη χρηματοοικονομική θέση ("οικονομική κατάσταση") της εταιρείας κατά την 31η Δεκεμβρίου 1992 καθώς και τα αποτελέσματα της χρήσεως που έληξε αυτή την ημερομηνία.

Αθήνα, 15 Απριλίου 1993

OI ΟΡΚΩΤΟΙ ΛΟΓΙΣΤΕΣ

ΙΩΑΝΝΗΣ Ν. ΛΑΜΠΡΟΥ   ΚΩΝ/ΝΑ ΘΩΜΑΪΔΟΥ-ΠΑΝΑΓΟΠΟΥΛΟΥ
Κ.227220/77   Η.215474/62

AUDITORS' REPORT

To the Shareholders of "HERACLES" General Cement Co., S.A.

We have audited the above financial Statements of the "HERACLES" GENERAL CEMENT Co., S.A. for the year ended December 31, 1992 and the related Notes to the Accounts. Our examination, within the scope of which we have also obtained a full accounting report of the Company's Branch operations, was made in accordance with the requirements of art. 37 of the Companies' Act (L. 2190) and also in conformity with the standards of auditing accepted by the Institute of Certified Public Accountants of Greece and accordingly included such tests of the accounting records and such other auditing procedures as we considered necessary in the circumstances. We have examined the books of account and records kept by your Company and we obtained all the information and explanations which we needed for the purpose of our audit. A proper production cost account has been kept. No change in the inventory evaluation method has been made as compared with that of the previous year. We have verified that the Directors' report is consistent with the related financial statements. The Notes to the Accounts include the information required by the Companies' Act of Greece (art 43a).

It is noted that: 1) The exchange differences from loans and credits for acquisition of fixed assets which are shown in the Assets under "Formation expenses" are amortised as follows: a) differences to December 31, 1986 at the annual rate of 10%, practice which has been consistently followed since 1982 and b) differences since January 1, 1987 are amortised according to the new provisions of L.2190 (art.43, para. 3c). If the exchange differences to December 31, 1986 were amortised as the loans were repaid, according to the provisions of the Tax Data Code then in force. their total amortisation to December 31, 1992 would be higher by Drs. 1.553 million in which case the Company's book net worth would be lower by the same amount, while the results of the year 1991 would have been charged with an amount lower by Drs. 962 m. 2a) During the year the company's lands and buildings values and accumulated depreciation were revalued in accordance with the provisions of L. 2065/1992. The effect of this was to increase the values of these assets by drs. 20,183 m. and the accumulated depreciation thereon by drs 9,917 m. The resulting net difference from revaluation of drs. 10,266 m. was credited to the capital reserves. The year's depreciation charge was calculated on the revalued values of these assets and as a result they are drs 150 m. more than they would have been had the revaluation not taken place. 2.b) In accordance with L. 2065/1992 the company's 1992 depreciation rates were lower than previous years. As a result the year's depreciation charge was lower by drs. 1,097 m. 3) Among debtors are included: a) a claim of Drs. 3,559 m. against foreign customer "CEMENTONAVIOS" (a/c "Trade debtors", D-II-1) with which the Company has discontinued trading since August 1984. The above amount includes also interest to December 31, 1987. For this claim there is now a final court ruling in favour of Heracles General Cement. There are doubts, however, by the Legal Department whether this claim will be recoverable. Included in the above amount of drs 3,559 million are accumulated exchange differences of drs 1,420 which were not credited to the Profit and Loss accounts of the years 1988-1992 but are included in the Account Other provision (b.2) under Provisions for Liabilities and Charges in the Balance Sheet. Moreover, it is noted that no reply has been received on the request for confirmation of the above balance. b) Other claims totalling Drs. 7,289 m. include an amount of Drs. 5,185 m. which relates to claims against affiliated undertakings with negative book net worth. In contrast to previous years the company has, in accordance with L. 2065/1992, made a provision for drs 500 m. and as a result the company's 1992 profits have corresponding been reduced by an equivalent amount. c) The major part of claims against the Greek State of Drs. 4,104 m., shown in the account D-II-11 and arising from VAT irrefundable (Drs. 3,627 m.) and other taxes withheld (Drs. 477 m.) is unlikely to be collected in 1993 although these claims are due and claimable. d) There are claims (disputed - at law) by the Company against third parties amounting to about drs 1 billion which have not been recorded in the accounting records because the final court ruling is still pending. 4) No provision has been set up for possible obligations arising from: a) Penal clauses totalling Drs. 1,354 m. imposed by the Bank of Greece in favour of the State for violations of currency regulations. In connection with these the Company has appealed to the Administrative Courts for an amount of drs 522 m. The case is still pending. b) Stamp duties for loans obtained since 1981 by subsidiaries. We could not estimate the amounts in respect of these stamp duties. For the years 1990 up to 1992 the amounts of the said stamp duties is about drs. 84 million. 5) No provision has been set up in the Balance Sheet against the year's results of Drs. 195 m. which relates to retroactive increase of the DEH ash. 6) By a letter from the Company's Legal Department dated March 15, 1993 we have been informed that there are claims by Egyptian Companies against Heracles GCC, amounting to drs 4.3 billion drachmas. Because the judicial outcome in respect of these claims is uncertain, no provision for these amounts has been made and therefore they do not appear in the Balance Sheet. 7) The company until 1991 made a provision for employee retirement indemnities based on the total number of employees irrespective of the time retirement. In accordance with article 10 of law 2065/1992, the current year's results have been charged with a provision based only on the employees retiring up to the end 1993. If the provision was made on the same basis as in previous years the amount charged to the Profit and Loss Account would have been more by drs 753m. The Balance sheet related provision would have been correspondingly higher by this amount.

The method of valuation has not changed from previous years except for those cases stated in our notes 2a, 2b, 3b and 7 above.

In our opinion, taking into account the foregoing notes, the above Financial Statements, including the Notes to the Accounts are in agreement with the books and records of the Company, and, give a true and fair view of the Company's assets, liabilities and financial position as at December 31, 1992 and of the results of its operations for the year ended on that date, in conformity with legal requirements and accepted accounting principles applied on a basis consistent with that of the preceding year, except in cases 2a, 2b and 3b noted above.

<table>
<tr><td>JOHN N. LAMBROU
K. 227220/77</td><td>Athens, April 15, 1993</td><td>KON/NA THOMAIDOU-PANAGOPOULOU
H. 215474 92</td></tr>
</table>

23

NOTES TO THE ACCOUNTS
FOR THE YEAR ENDED 31st DECEMBER 1992

The following notes to the Balance Sheet as at 31st December 1992 and the Profit and Loss Account for the year then ended, have been prepared in accordance with the provisions of the Greek Companies Act and the Company's basic accounting policies.

1. **Formation Expenses and Intangible Assets (Companies Act art. 42e parag. 8 and art. 43 parag. 3a, 3c, 3e, 4a, and 4b)**

1.1. Analysis of the changes made during the year in millions of drachmas :

Category	Acquisition cost 31.12.92	Debit in 1992	Depreciation in 1992	Total Depreciation	Written down value 31.12.92
Preliminary expenses	1,199	-	108	1,137	62
Exchange differences on loans for the acquisition of fixed assets up to 31.12.1986	10,567	-	1,028	9,013	1,554
Loan interest during construction	3,518	-	352	3,342	176
Other long - term amortisation exp.	638	56	24	619	75
Sub total	15,922	56	1,512	14,111	1,867
Research costs	76	29	19	45	60
Grand Total	**15,998**	**85**	**1,531**	**14,156**	**1,927**

1.2. Amortisation method:

(a) **Preliminary expenses:** Expenditure incurred up to 31st December 1986 in the form of loan interest during construction periods and research expenditure, is amortised at 10% per annum, while such expenses incurred after that date are amortised at 20% per annum. in conformity with the provisions of the Companies Act. article 43, par. 3a

(b) The rate of amortisation of differences on exchange, arising from loans and credits obtained for the acquisition of fixed assets up to 31st December 1986, is 10% per annum. The rate of amortisation of differences on exchange on liabilities resulting from the acquisition of fixed assets obtained after that date were treated in the books in accordance with the provisions of the Companies Act. art. 43, par. 3c

Thus the 1992 results were charged with Drs. 1,028m. for the amortisation of debit differences on exchange arising up to 31st December. 1986.

2. Tangible Assets (Companies Act art. 42e parag. 8, 43 parag. 5/d, 5/e, and 9 and art 43 a parag. 1/a)

2.1. Analysis of the changes made in the year: .rm 16.00ᵗ

In Drs. million

Fixed asset category	Purchases or own construction	Revaluation	Write-offs or transfers	Depreci-ation in 1992	Increases in depreciation due to revaluation	Adjustments in prior years depreciation
Land	-	3,586	-	-	-	-
Mines - Quarries	1	4,931	-	-	-	-
Buildings - technical works	1,610	11,667	-	453	9,917	-
Machinery etc	2,672	-	-	257	-	-
Transportation equipment	2,268	-	15	32	-	(12)
Furniture etc	77	-	-	14	-	-
Fixed assets under construction etc	3,010	-	6,680	-	-	-
TOTAL	9,638	20,184	6,695	756	9,917	(12)

The acquisition cost, accumulated depreciation and written down value at the beginning and end of the year are shown in the Balance Sheet.

2.2. Tangible fixed assets have been valued at their acquisition cost (historical cost), as amended by subsequent revaluations which have been made in accordance with special laws, plus additions and improvements less depreciation. The 1992 depreciation rates for tangible fixed assets were those provided under Law 2065/1992. Thus for 1992 the depreciation rates used were 60% lower than those provided by Presidential Decree 88/73 used in the previous years. In respect of these lower depreciation rates please refer to note 2.b appearing under the Balance Sheet. The depreciation made has been charged to the 1992 operating costs. No additional depreciation provision or reserve has been provided for the diminution in the value of tangible fixed assets as no such diminution is anticipated.

2.3. During the year the company's fixed assets have been revalued in accordance with the provisions of L. 2065/1992. (Please refer to note 2a appearing below the balance sheet.)

3. Participating Interests (Companies Act art. 43a parag.7c and art. 43a parag. 1b)

3.1. The Company's participations are analysed as follows:

Name	Location	Participation in the capital	Total Equity 31.12.91 Drs.' 000	1991 Profit or loss Drs.' 000
AIGIS S.A.	Lycovrissi Attica	60%	478,304	243,963
HERACLES SHIPPING CO. S.A.	" "	99.94%	1,356,429	453,540
SKYRODEMA S.A.	Neohorouda,Thessal.	99.56%	225,135	73,615
EMMY BUILDING ELEMENTS S.A.	Lycovrissi Attica	85.71%	660,987	642,057
CARMOR HELLAS Ltd	31,N.Phalirou, Ag. Ioannis Rentis	40%	28,152	-
EVIESK,S.A.	Lykovrissi Attica	87%	946,062	318,462
STAR CONCRETE S.A	11 Iras St. Galatsi	99%	317,820	(17,376)
HERACLES PACKAGING CO. S.A.	Lykovrissi Attica	65.08%	(144,379)	(78,303)
HERACLES INTERNATIONAL S.A.	" "	90%	28,947	23,716
PORT SAID SILO INVESTM. CO SA	" "	99%	(236,515)	(33,386)
NATIONAL INSTITUTE RESEARCH IN CEMENT LTD	" "	90%	5,299	1,177
HERACLES MARITIME AGENCY LTD	" "	40%	368	17,313
HAQL SILO INVESTM. CO. S.A.	Panama	100%	(1,000,204)	(7,846)
ALEXANDRIA SILO INVESTMENT CO. S.A.	"	100%	(1,231,294)	(12,825)
HERACLES INSURANCE ENTERPRISES LTD	Lycovrissi Attica	5%	530	20,473
OFFICE ORGANISATION LTD	" "	5%	2,168	588

The above 1991 net results are shown before tax and before profits or losses brought forward. Wherever Group Companies are involved. Parent Company participation below 10% is also shown in the above table.

3.2 Participations in public companies (S.A.), as well as in securities, shares of public companies (S.A.) and all other kinds of securities classified as fixed assets have been valued in accordance with the provisions of the Companies Act art. 43 parag. 6. This valuation also agrees with the tax code. The aggregate value of the participating interest shown in the 1992 Balance Sheet is lower than market value by an amount of Drs. 1,939 m.

4. Stocks (Companies Act art. 43 parag. 7a, 7b and 7c, and art. 43a parag. la, li and lia

4.1. Valuation of stocks and cost of production. Stocks of finished and semi-finished products have been valued at the lower of production cost (historical cost) and the year end net realisable value. In respect of other stocks, each item of stock has been valued at the lower of acquisition cost (historical cost) and market value as at the Balance Sheet date. For the purpose of calculating production or acquisition cost (historical cost) stocks have been valued on a monthly weighted average basis except in the case of materials, spare parts and sacks, for which the successive cumulative balance method has been used.

Included in the production cost as well as the value of raw materials and fuel stocks is the year's depreciation charge for fixed assets which are used in the production process. The depreciation rates used for these assets are those provided in P.D. 88 / 1973 reduced by 60% (see note 2.2 above).

4.2. The stock valuation method has not changed from the previous year.

4.3. The value of stocks appearing in the Balance Sheet is not substantially different from the market value as at 31 December 1992.

5. Receivables

5.1. No loans or advances have been paid to members of the Board of Directors (Companies Act art. 43a parag. l.i.d).

5.2. Receivables and liabilities denominated in foreign currencies have been translated into drachmas, at the official exchange rates ruling at the date of the Balance Sheet (Company's Act art. 43a par.1a.)

The treatment of differences on exchange arising upon payment or translation of foreign currency denominated loans or credits payable and used for the acquisition of fixed assets is stated in par. 11 and 1.2b above

Differences on exchange arising from the valuation of foreign currency denominated receivables and liabilities, other than those stated above, have been recorded and accounted for separately for each currency. Their accounting treatment complies with the provisions of the Companies Act 2190/1920, art. 43, parag. 8b.

5.3. The classification of receivables and liabilities as long term (Companies Act art. 42e. parag. 6). Receivables and liabilities which are to be received or paid after one year from the Balance Sheet date are considered long-term, while those due within a year are considered current.

6. Payments and Accrued Income

These are analysed as follows (Companies Act art. 42e, parag. 12):

	Drs.' 000
6.1 Deferred charges	
(a) Interest on short term loans	3.165
(b) Insurance premiums	8.636
Total	11.801
6.2 Earned income	
(a) Goods in transit	11.556
(b) Other income	247.503
Total	259.059

7. Capital and Reserves

7.1. During 1992, no new shares were issued and thus there was no increase in the Company's share capital. (Companies Act art.43a par. lc).

7.2. At the Balance Sheet date, the Company's share capital consists of 50,490.957 common shares with a nominal value of Drs. 605 each (Companies Act art. 42e, parag. 10 and art. 43a parag. ld and le).

7.3. The Company did not acquire any of its own shares during the year (Companies Act art. 43a, parag. l.i.6).

7.4. In contrast to previous years, this year's calculation of the legal reserves and interim dividends have been based on the net profits of the year after income tax in accordance with the provisions of L.2065/1992. The legal reserve thus calculated amounted to drs. 227,955 thousand and interim dividends drs. 3,029,457 thousand.

26

8. Provisions (Companies Act art. 42e, parag. 14 and art. 43a, parag. la).

Provisions at the Balance Sheet date and their accounting treatment during the current year are analysed as follows:

8.1. Provision for severance payments. In previous years, under the terms of Law 2112, the provision made was based on 40% of the estimated total severance liability payable to all employees irrespective of the time of their retirement. For the current year this was changed by art. 10 parag. 13 of Law 2065/1992 and 100% provision is made only for those employees retiring within a year from the Balance Sheet date.

		Drs.' 000
The accumulated provision for severance payments up to 31st December 1991		2,167,270
Less: Accumulated provisions for severance payments		
- Employees who retired during the year	Ths Drs 145,206	
- Employees retiring in the following year	57,278	202,404
		1,964,786
Plus: Severance payments provision for those retiring in the following year (1993)		209,789
Total provision included under provision for retirement benefits		2,174,575

The year's results have been charged with a retirement provision of drs. 152,511 thousand (209,789 - 57,278). If the company followed the same policy as in previous years, the accumulated provision for this year's balance sheet would have been higher by drs. 752,521 thousand. The year's profits would have been lower by this amount.

8.2. Other provisions

	Drs.' 000
(a) Exchange difference gains arising from the translation of foreign currency denominated claims and liabilities	315
(b) Credit balance of differences on exchange accumulated up to 31st December 1992 and arising from foreign currency translations of overdue claims and liabilities	3,472,635
(c) Provisions for bad and doubtful debts	500,000
(d) Other provisions	180
Total of other provisions	3,973,130

The Company has this year made a provision for bad and doubtful debts. No such provision was made in previous years. The amount of drs 500 millions (against a balance of drs 622 m.) is less than a total amount of drs 10,848 m. required (see Auditor's report note 3).

9. Liabilities, - Mortgages and Charges

9.1. There are no liabilities payable after five years from the Balance Sheet date (Companies Act art. 43a parag. 1f).

9.2. Liabilities for which mortgages and charges have been granted by the Company are analysed as follows (Companies Act art. 42e parag. 14 and art. 43a parag. 1f):

Liability account	Loan balance at 31.12.92 (Drs. thous.)	Mortgages and charges (Drs. thous.)	Type of security
C/II/3 Banks-short-term liabilities	2,889	2,600	preliminary agreement for mortgage
Total	2,889	2,600	

27

9.3. Amounts in respect of other securities, or other guarantees provided by the Company in favour of affiliated companies and or other third parties are analysed in note 11.2 (Companies Act art. 42e par. 9).

9.4. Tax liabilities (Companies Act art. 43a par. 1 i.b).

The Company's books have been audited by the tax authorities up to and including 1981. There are no assessed outstanding tax liabilities for the current or previous years which have not been provided for in the company's books and/or financial statements. Moreover, no significant tax liability assessments are expected to arise in connection with the current or previous years from outstanding tax audits.

10. Accruals and Deferred Income

These are analysed as follows (Companies Act art. 42e, parag. 12):

	Drs. thous.
10.1. Accrued expenses	
(a) Provisions for accrued loan interest	47,730
(b) Accrued expenses of the plants, distribution terminals and head office	729,791
Total	777,521

11. Memo Accounts

The memo accounts shown in the Balance Sheet are analysed as follows (Companies Act art. 42e, parag. 9 and 11)

11.1. Third party assets

Company shares for delivery	21,449
Raw materials of third parties in tons	96,520
Total	117,969

11.2. Guarantees and other securities

The amounts of real sureties provided as security for Company liabilities are shown in parag. 9.2 above. The amounts of other guarantees in favour of or provided by the Company as security for (a) claims by the company (b) company liabilities and (c) liabilities of affiliated companies, are analysed as follows (Companies Act art. 42e, par. 9):

	Drs. thous.	
(a) Guarantees to secure claims of HERACLES GCC	3,235,286	
(b) Guarantees provided by third parties as security for HERACLES GENERAL CEMENT liabilities	1,551,362	
(c) Guarantees provided by the Company to secure liabilities of related companies are as follows:		
AEGIS S.A.	22,485	
EMMY-BUILDING ELEMENTS S.A.	190,000	
EVIESK S.A.	156,043	
HERACLES SHIPPING CO. S.A	1,000	
LAVA, S.A.	259,000	
HERACLES PACKAGING CO. S.A.	157,000	
AMBER, S.A.	203,825	
HAQL SILO INVESTMENT	120,000	
DEPOT AND COORDINATION	149,056	1,258,409
		6,045,057
11.3. Bilateral agreements		
Arising from various agreements	222,706	

11.4. There are no commitments, guarantees or other contingent liabilities arising from agreements or imposed by law which do not appear in the above memo accounts. Similarly there are no liabilities arising from payment of special monthly allowances (i.e. monthly benefits) or commitments to affiliated enterprises (Companies Act art. 43a par. 1g).

28

12. Turnover (Sales)

This is analysed as follows (Companies Act art. 43a, par. 1h):

Turnover in Drs. million

Category of activity	Domestic market	Foreign markets	Total
(a) Sales of products	41,852	17,433	59,285
(b) Sales of other stocks	2,687	211	2,898
(c) Provision of services	1,501	-	1,501
Total	46,040	17,644	63,684

Income from services derives mainly from the invoicing of services offered by company employees posted to subsidiaries.

13. The company's average number of employees and employees cost for wages and salaries, social benefits and allowances are analysed as follows (Companies Act art. 43a parag. Ii):

Staff remuneration and expenses

Type of employee	Number of employees	Salaries and employer's contribution Drs.' 000	Wages Drs.' 000	Total Drs.' 000
Clerical	1,651	10,800,973	-	10,800,973
Manual	348	-	1,947,968	1,947,968
Total	1,999	10,800,973	1,947,968	12,748,941
Social benefits and allowances	-	-	-	317,658
Total	1,999	10,800,973	1,947,968	13,066,599

14. Management and Directors emoluments and remuneration are analysed as follows (Companies Act art. 43a parag. I/i.c):

	Drs.thous.
a) Directors' board attendance fees	29,914
b) Remunerations of members of the Board of Directors for services rendered under special work agreements or assignments	23,517
c) Remuneration of members of the Management (2 General Managers)	30,837
Total	84,268

There are no liabilities or commitments for allowances or other benefits to retired members of the Board or the Management.

15. "Extraordinary and Non-Operating Expenses" and "Extraordinary and Non-Operating Income" are analysed as follows (Companies Act art. 42e parag. 15b):

15.1. Extraordinary and Non-Operating Expenses

	Drs.' 000
(a) Exchange differences	1,369,006
(b) Legal fees - (overseas)	17,473
(c) Prior year expenses	71,716
(d) Land expenses	12,313
(e) Dispatch & demurrage	30,561
(f) Other expenses	84,313
Total	1,585,382

15.2. Extraordinary and Non-Operating Income

	Drs.' 000
(a) Storage expenses	56,345
(b) Insurance refunds	14,500
(c) Despatch and demurrage	12,861
(d) Prior year income	131,797
(e) Other income	49,461
Total	264,964

29

16. Other Information

16.1. Disclosure information required under the following provisions of the Companies Act is non applicable:

    (a) Article 42a, parag. 3 . of L. 2190
    (b) Article 42b, parag. 1, 2, 3 and 4 of L. 2190

16.2. There were no changes, from previous years, in the accounting treatment of assets and liabilities other than those stated in note 2.3 and 8.2 above.

16.3. No financial statements accounting for inflation have been prepared for 1992.

16.4. Consolidated financial statements (Balance Sheet and Profit and Loss Account) for 1992, have been prepared.

Lykovrissi, April 13, 1993
CHAIRMAN OF THE BOARD OF DIRECTORS
AND MANAGING DIRECTOR

LORENZO PANZAVOLTA
PASSPORT NUMBER I 175043/23-7-83

FINANCIAL DIRECTOR   HEAD OF ACCOUNTS
                                                                    DEPARTMENT

SOT. PAPASPILIOTOPOULOS   CH. STASINOPOULOS
      A. 829917/63   I. 019339/72

It is certified that the above Notes to the Accounts (pages 24 up to 34) refer to our short form report of 15 April 1993.

Athens, 15 April 1993.

CERTIFIED PUBLIC ACCOUNTANTS OF GREECE

JOHN N. LAMBROU   KONSTANTINA THOMAIDOU-PANAGOPOULOU
  K. 227220/77   H. 215474/62

ΟΜΙΛΟΣ ΕΤΑΙΡΙΩΝ "ΗΡΑΚΛΗΣ"
12ος ΕΝΟΠΟΙΗΜΕΝΟΣ ΙΣΟΛΟΓΙΣΜΟΣ ΤΗΣ 31ης ΔΕΚΕΜΒΡΙΟΥ 1992 (ΣΕ ΧΙΛ. ΔΡΧ.)

ΕΝΕΡΓΗΤΙΚΟ	ΑΞΙΑ ΚΤΗΣΕΩΣ	ΧΡΗΣΕΩΣ 1992 ΑΠΟΣΒΕΣΕΙΣ	ΑΝΑΠΟΣΒΕΣΤΗ ΑΞΙΑ	ΑΞΙΑ ΚΤΗΣΕΩΣ	ΧΡΗΣΕΩΣ 1991 ΑΠΟΣΒΕΣΕΙΣ	ΑΝΑΠΟΣΒΕΣΤΗ ΑΞΙΑ
Β. ΕΞΟΔΑ ΕΓΚΑΤΑΣΤΑΣΗΣ						
1. Έξοδα ιδρύσης & πρώτης εγκατάστασης	1.298.961	1.237.752	61.209	1.303.504	1.124.256	179.248
2. Συν/κές διαφορές δανείων για κτήσεις παγίων	10.987.364	9.366.098	1.621.266	10.928.842	8.338.285	2.590.557
3. Τόκοι δανείων κατασκευαστικής περιόδου	3.517.547	3.341.580	175.967	3.527.358	2.999.636	527.722
4. Λοιπά έξοδα πολυετούς απόσβεσης	1.150.778	926.964	223.814	1.031.702	808.605	223.097
ΣΥΝΟΛΟ ΕΞΟΔΩΝ ΕΓΚΑΤΑΣΤΑΣΗΣ (Β)	16.954.650	14.872.394	2.082.256	16.791.406	13.270.782	3.520.624
Γ. ΠΑΓΙΟ ΕΝΕΡΓΗΤΙΚΟ						
Ι. Ασώματες ακινητοποιήσεις						
1. Έξοδα ερευνών & ανάπτυξης	138.242	71.252	66.990	107.780	47.815	59.965
ΙΙ. Ενσώματες ακινητοποιήσεις						
1. Γήπεδα-Οικόπεδα	9.326.741	-	9.326.741	4.857.077	-	4.857.077
2. Ορυκεία-μεταλλεία, λατομεία κτλ.	8.763.980	-	8.763.980	3.832.010	-	3.832.010
3. Κτίρια & τεχνικά έργα	32.966.754	26.099.600	6.867.154	18.722.508	14.739.623	3.982.885
4. Μηχανήματα-τεχν.εγκατ. & λοιπός μηχαν.εξοπλ.	24.176.315	17.455.099	6.721.216	21.258.768	17.027.798	4.230.970
5. Μεταφορικά μέσα	10.313.426	4.199.875	6.113.551	7.418.104	3.678.086	3.740.018
6. Έπιπλα & λοιπ. εξοπλ.	757.301	451.556	305.745	622.777	390.096	232.681
7. Ακινητοποιήσεις υπό εκτέλ. & προκαταβολές	1.235.609	-	1.235.609	4.939.060	-	4.939.060
	87.540.126	48.206.130	39.333.996	61.650.304	35.835.603	25.814.701
ΣΥΝΟΛΟ ΑΚΙΝΗΤΟΠΟΙΗΣΕΩΝ (ΓΙ+ΓΙΙ)	87.678.368	48.277.382	39.400.986	61.758.084	35.883.418	25.874.666
ΙΙΙ.Συμμετοχές & άλλες μακροπρόθεσμες χρηματοοικονομ. απαιτήσεις						
2. Συμμετοχές σε εταιρίες εκτός Ομίλου & ίδια μερίδια Ομίλου			548.277			541.647
7. Λοιπές μακροπροθ. απαιτήσεις			612.708			547.383
			1.160.985			1.089.030
ΣΥΝΟΛΟ ΠΑΓΙΟΥ ΕΝΕΡΓΗΤΙΚΟΥ (Γ)			40.561.971			26.963.696
Δ. ΚΥΚΛΟΦΟΡΟΥΝ ΕΝΕΡΓΗΤΙΚΟ						
Ι. Αποθέματα						
1. Εμπορεύματα		46.932			34.061	
2. Προϊόντα έτοιμα & ημιτελή		1.790.899			1.659.881	
3. Παραγωγή σε εξέλιξη		2.580.023			1.862.831	
4. Πρώτες & βοηθ. ύλες-Αναλώσιμα υλ.-ανταλλ. και είδη συσκευασίας		6.518.882			5.924.195	
5. Προκαταβολές για αγορές αποθεμάτων		165.822	11.102.558		160.787	9.641.755
ΙΙ. Απαιτήσεις						
1. Πελάτες		12.268.221			10.561.940	
2. Γραμμάτια εισπρακτέα						
- Χαρτοφυλακίου	138.993			187.465		
- Στις τράπεζες για είσπραξη	100			50.944		
- Στις τράπεζες σε εγγύηση	368.378	507.471		493.545	731.954	
3. Γραμμάτια σε καθυστέρηση		268.594			258.794	
3α.Επιταγές εισπρακτέες		5.363.683			5.574.743	
8. Δεσμευμένοι λ/σμοί καταθέσεων		2.820			2.820	
9. Μακροπροθ. απαιτήσεις εισπρακτ.στην επόμ. χρήση		-			19	
10. Επισφαλείς-Επίδικοι πελάτες και χρεώστες	1.050.661			1.115.967		
Μείον: Προβλέψεις	-	1.050.661		50.449	1.065.518	
11. Χρεώστες Διάφοροι		2.391.424			1.733.661	
11α. Ελληνικό Δημόσιο		4.918.721			4.409.327	
12. Λογαρ. διαχ. προκαταβολών		104.378	26.875.973		73.480	24.402.256
IV. Διαθέσιμα						
1. Ταμεία		99.772			119.068	
3. Καταθέσεις όψεως και προθεσμίας		3.336.937	3.436.709		2.602.023	2.721.091
ΣΥΝΟΛΟ ΚΥΚΛΟΦΟΡΟΥΝΤΟΣ ΕΝΕΡΓΗΤΙΚΟΥ (Δ)			41.415.240			36.765.102
Ε. ΜΕΤΑΒΑΤΙΚΟΙ Λ/ΣΜΟΙ ΕΝΕΡΓΗΤΙΚΟΥ						
1. Έξοδα επόμεν. χρήσης		263.121			198.854	
2. Έσοδα εισπρακτέα		291.355			85.244	
3. Λοιποί μεταβ. λογ/σμοί		141	554.617		28	284.126
ΓΕΝΙΚΟ ΣΥΝΟΛΟ ΕΝΕΡΓΗΤΙΚΟΥ (Β+Γ+Δ+Ε)			84.614.084			67.533.548
ΛΟΓΑΡΙΑΣΜΟΙ ΤΑΞΕΩΣ ΧΡΕΩΣΤΙΚΟΙ			9.714.835			6.881.000

ΣΗΜΕΙΩΣΕΙΣ

1. Σε ορισμένα πάγια περιουσιακά στοιχεία του Ομίλου υπάρχουν προσημφωνα υποθηκών - προσημειώσεων και υποθήκες - προσημειώσεις ύψους 2.968.550 χιλ. δρχ. που ασφαλίζουν υπόλοιπα δανείων συνολικού ποσού 2.996.901 χιλ. δρχ. Επίσης, επί ορισμένων πλοίων και εγκαταστάσεων επ' αυτών έχουν εγγραφεί υποθήκες 15.853.170 χιλ. δρχ. που ασφαλίζουν υπόλοιπα δανείων ποσού 4.493.527 χιλ. δρχ.

2. Οι εταιρίες του Ομίλου με τις διευθύνσεις τους που περιλαμβάνονται στην ενοποίηση είναι:
   α. Εσωτερικού: ΑΓΕΤ ΗΡΑΚΛΗΣ, ΕΒΙΕΣΚ Α.Ε., ΑΝΕ ΗΡΑΚΛΗΣ, ΗΡΑΚΛΗΣ ΔΙΕΘΝΗΣ Α.Ε., ΗΡΑΚΛΗΣ ΣΥΣΚΕΥΑΣΙΑ Α.Ε., ΛΑΒΑ Α.Ε., ΑΜΠΕΡ Α.Ε., ΕΠΕΝΔΥΣΗ ΣΙΛΟ ΠΟΡΤ ΣΑΪΔ Α.Ε., ΓΡΑΦΕΙΟΡΓΑΝΩΣΗ Ε.Π.Ε., ΗΡΑΚΛΗΣ

"HERACLES" GROUP OF COMPANIES
CONSOLIDATED BALANCE SHEET AS AT DECEMBER 31, 1992 (AMOUNTS IN THOUSANDS OF DRS.)

ASSETS	1992 Acquisition value	1992 Depreciation	1992 Written down value	1991 Acquisition value	1991 Depreciation	1991 Written down value
B. FORMATION EXPENSES						
1. Preliminary expenses	1,296,961	1,237,752	61,209	1,303,504	1,124,256	179,248
2. Exchange differences from loans for fixed assets acquisitions	10,987,364	9,366,098	1,621,266	10,928,842	8,338,285	2,590,557
3. Construction period loan interest	3,517,847	3,341,580	175,967	3,527,358	2,999,636	527,722
4. Other formation expenses	1,150,778	926,964	223,814	1,031,702	808,605	223,097
TOTAL FORMATION EXPENSES (B)	16,954,650	14,872,394	2,082,256	15,791,406	13,270,782	3,520,624
C. FIXED ASSETS						
I. Intangible assets						
1. Research & development costs	138,242	71,252	66,990	107,780	47,815	59,965
II. Tangible assets						
1. Land	9,326,741	—	9,326,741	4,857,077	—	4,857,077
2. Mines, quarries etc.	8,763,980	—	8,763,980	3,832,010	—	3,832,010
3. Buildings & technical works	32,966,754	26,099,600	6,867,154	18,722,508	14,739,623	3,982,885
4. Machinery, techn. installat. & other equipm.	24,176,315	17,455,099	6,721,216	21,258,768	17,027,798	4,230,970
5. Transportation equipment	10,313,426	4,199,875	6,113,551	7,418,104	3,678,086	3,740,018
6. Furniture and fixtures	757,301	451,556	305,745	622,777	390,096	232,681
7. Payments on account & tangible assets in course of construction	1,235,609	—	1,235,609	4,939,060	—	4,939,060
	87,540,126	48,206,130	39,333,996	61,650,304	35,835,603	25,814,701
TOTAL TANGIBLE AND INTANGIBLE ASSETS (CI+CII)	87,678,368	48,277,382	39,400,986	61,758,084	35,883,418	25,874,666
III. Financial assets						
2. Participating interests in other undertakings			548,277			541,647
7. Other financial assets			612,708			547,383
			1,160,985			1,089,030
TOTAL FIXED ASSETS (C)			40,561,971			26,963,696
D. CURRENT ASSETS						
I. Stocks						
1. Merchandise		46,932			34,061	
2. Finished and semi-finished products		1,790,899			1,659,881	
3. Work in progress		2,580,023			1,862,831	
4. Raw and auxiliary materials, consumables, spare parts and packing items		6,518,882			5,924,195	
5. Payments on account		165,822	11,102,558		160,787	9,641,755
II. Debtors						
1. Trade debtors		12,268,221			10,551,940	
2. Notes receivable						
- In portfolio	138,993			187,465		
- At banks for collection	100			50,944		
- At banks as pledge	368,378	507,471		493,545	731,954	
3. Notes overdue		268,594			258,794	
3a. Cheques receivable		5,363,683			5,574,743	
8. Blocked Deposits		2,820			2,820	
9. Current portion of long term receivables		—			19	
10. Doubtful trade and other debtors	1,050,661			1,115,967		
Less: Provisions	—	1,050,661		50,449	1,065,518	
11. Sundry debtors		2,391,424			1,733,661	
11a. Greek government		4,918,721			4,409,327	
12. Advances & credits management accounts		104,378	26,875,973		73,480	24,402,256
IV. Cash at bank and in hand						
1. Cash		99,772			119,068	
3. Sight and time deposits		3,336,937	3,436,709		2,602,023	2,721,091
TOTAL CURRENT ASSETS (D)			41,415,240			36,765,102
E. PREPAYMENTS AND ACCRUED INCOME						
1. Deferred charges		263,121			198,854	
2. Earned income		291,355			85,244	
3. Other prepayments & accrued income		141	554,617		28	284,126
GRAND TOTAL ASSETS (B+C+D+E)			84,614,084			67,533,548
MEMO ACCOUNTS			9,714,835			6,881,000

NOTES TO THE CONSOLIDATED 1992 FINANCIAL STATEMENTS:

1. For certain Group fixed assets there are preliminary agreements for mortgages, charges and liens of drs. 2,965,550 thousand to secure loan balances totalling drs. 2,996,901 thousand. There are also mortgages of drs. 15,853,170 thousand registered on ships and installations to secure loan balances totalling drs. 4,493,527 thousand

2. The companies included in the consolidated financial statements are the following:
    a. Domestic: HERACLES GCC SA, EVIESK SA, HERACLES SHIPPING CO. S.A, HERACLES INTERNATIONAL S.A, HERACLES PACKAGING CO. AE, LAVA S.A, AMBER S.A, PORT SAID SILO INVESTMENT S.A, OFFICE

ΠΑΘΗΤΙΚΟ		ΧΡΗΣΕΩΣ 1992		ΧΡΗΣΕΩΣ 1991
Α. ΙΔΙΑ ΚΕΦΑΛΑΙΑ ΟΜΙΛΟΥ				
1. Μετοχικό Κεφάλαιο ΑΓΕΤ ΗΡΑΚΛΗΣ				
(50.497.957 μετοχ. των 605 δρχ.)		30.547.029		30.547.029
2. Διαφορά από έκδοση μετοχών				
υπέρ το άρτιο ΑΓΕΤ ΗΡΑΚΛΗΣ		401.642		401.642
3. Διαφορές αναπροσαρμογής ΑΓΕΤ ΗΡΑΚΛΗΣ				
1. Διαφορές αναπροσαρμογής				
συμμετ. & χρεογράφων	396.999			324.104
2. Διαφορές από αναπροσαρ.				
αξίας λοιπών περιουσιακών στοιχείων	10.939.455	11.336.454		
4. Αποθεματικά ΑΓΕΤ ΗΡΑΚΛΗΣ				
1. Τακτικό αποθεματικό ΑΓΕΤ ΗΡΑΚΛΗΣ	1.101.227		873.272	
2. Έκτακτα αποθεματικά	5.261.235		5.024.813	
3. Αφορολόγητα αποθεματικά				
ειδικών διατάξ. νόμων	5.929.118		4.036.610	
Μείον: Διαφορές ενοποίησης:				
1. Χρεωστική διαφορά ενοπ.	(5.519.870)		(5.721.552)	
2. Πιστωτική διαφορά ενοπ.	3.852.323	10.624.033	3.847.348	8.060.491
5. Υπόλοιπο κερδών (ζημιών) εις νέο				
1. Υπόλ. κερδών εις νέο	2.549.142		1.470.029	
2. Υπόλ. ζημιών εις νέο	(2.903.482)	(354.340)	(1.230.846)	239.183
6. Δικαιώματα μειοψηφίας				
1. Στο Κεφάλαιο	50.141		41.071	
2. Στα αποθεματικά & κέρδη	239.231	289.372	150.304	191.375
ΣΥΝΟΛΟ ΙΔΙΩΝ ΚΕΦΑΛΑΙΩΝ (Α)		52.844.190		39.763.824
Β. ΠΡΟΒΛΕΨΕΙΣ ΓΙΑ ΚΙΝΔΥΝΟΥΣ & ΕΞΟΔΑ				
1. Προβλ. για αποζ. προσωπικού λόγω εξόδ. από υπηρ.	2.630.752		2.592.270	
2. Λοιπές προβλέψεις	4.447.397	7.078.149	2.067.837	4.660.107
Γ. ΥΠΟΧΡΕΩΣΕΙΣ				
Ι. Μακροπρόθεσμες υποχρεώσεις				
2. Δάνεια τραπεζών		4.461.144		3.748.825
ΙΙ. Βραχυπρόθεσμες υποχρεώσεις				
1. Προμηθευτές	1.822.263		1.899.795	
2. Γραμμάτια πληρωτέα	569.686		929.473	
3. Τράπεζες λ/βραχυπρόθεσμων υποχρεώσεων	7.431.406		7.262.545	
4. Προκαταβολές πελατών	182.125		260.225	
5. Υποχρεώσεις από φόρους	2.779.451		2.142.770	
6. Ασφαλιστικοί Οργανισμοί	1.015.720		875.012	
7. Μακροπρόθεσμες υποχρεώσεις				
πληρωτέες στην επόμ. χρήση	929.716		840.389	
10. Μερίσμ. πληρωτ.εκτός Ομίλου	3.132.751		3.103.712	
11. Πιστωτές Διάφοροι	1.412.506	19.275.624	1.153.890	18.467.811
ΣΥΝΟΛΟ ΥΠΟΧΡΕΩΣΕΩΝ (Γ)		23.736.768		22.216.636
Δ. ΜΕΤΑΒΑΤΙΚΟΙ Λ/ΣΜΟΙ ΠΑΘΗΤΙΚΟΥ				
1. Έσοδα επόμενων χρήσεων	517.777		33.722	
2. Έξοδα χρήσεως δουλευμένα	437.200		564.259	
3. Λοιποί μεταβατικοί λ/σμοί	-	954.977	295.000	892.981
ΓΕΝΙΚΟ ΣΥΝΟΛΟ ΠΑΘΗΤΙΚΟΥ (Α+Β+Γ+Δ)		84.614.084		67.533.548
ΛΟΓΑΡΙΑΣΜΟΙ ΤΑΞΕΩΣ ΠΙΣΤΩΤΙΚΟΙ		9.714.835		6.881.000

ΝΑΥΤΙΚΕΣ ΠΡΑΚΤΟΡΕΥΣΕΙΣ Ε.Π.Ε., Γ. ΧΑΤΖΗΚΥΡΙΑΚΟΣ Ν.Ε., Α. ΧΑΤΖΗΚΥΡΙΑΚΟΣ Ν.Ε., ΤΣΙΜΕΝΤΟΚΑΛΗΣ Ν.Ε., ΔΥΣΤΟΣ Ν.Ε., ΠΡΩΤΟΠΟΡΟΣ Ν.Ε., ΘΑΛΑΣΣΟΠΟΡΟΣ Ν.Ε., ΠΟΝΤΟΠΟΡΟΣ Ν.Ε., ΠΟΣΕΙΔΩΝ ΙΙ Ν.Ε., ΒΟΛΟΣ Ι Ν.Ε., ΦΑΕΘΩΝ Ν.Ε., ΙΟΚΑΣΤΗ Ν.Ε., ΝΑΥΣΙΚΑ Ν.Ε., ΑΣΦΑΛΙΣΤΙΚΕΣ ΕΠΙΧΕΙΡΗΣΕΙΣ ΗΡΑΚΛΗΣ Ε.Π.Ε., ΒΙΟΜΗΧΑΝΙΚΑ ΟΡΥΚΤΑ Α.Ε. (Σοφ. Βενιζέλου 49-51, Λυκόβρυση), ΕΚΕΤ ΕΠΕ (Κ.Πατέλη 15, Λυκόβρυση), ΕΜΜΥ ΚΤΙΡΙΑΚΑ ΣΤΟΙΧΕΙΑ ΑΒΕΕ, ΑΓΙΣ Α.Ε. (Ε. Βενιζέλου & Ανδρούτσου 29, Λυκόβρυση). ΑΣΤΗΡ ΜΠΕΤΟΝ Α.Ε., ΛΑΤΟ Α.Ε. (Τέρμα οδού Ηρας, Γαλάτσι), ΣΚΥΡΟΔΕΜΑ ΕΒΑΕ (Νεοχωρούδα, Θεσσαλονίκη).
β. Εξωτερικού: ALEXANDRIA SILO INVESTMENT COMPANY S.A., HERMES COMPANIA NAVIERA S.A., PORT SAID SILO INVESTMENT COMPANY S.A., LOYDIAS COMPANIA NAVIERA S.A., HAQL SILO INVESTMENT COMPANY S.A., MARITIME COMPANY ESPERIDES S.A., DEPOT AND COORDINATION CO. S.A.(Panama) INTERNATIONAL MEDITERRANEAN SHIPPING S.A. (Luxemburg), INTERNATIONAL FLA. (Egypt).

LIABILITIES	1992		1991	
A. CAPITAL AND RESERVES				
I. Share capital of HERACLES GCC				
(50,497,967 shares at Drs. 605)		30,547,029		30,547,029
II. Share premium account				
HERACLES GCC		401,642		401,642
III. Difference from revaluation of				
1. Investment & securities	396,999			324,104
2. Other assets	10,939,455	11,336,454		
IV. Reserves				
1. Legal reserve HERACLES GCC	1,101,227		873,272	
2. Extraordinary reserves	5,261,235		5,024,813	
3. Non taxable reserves under special laws	5,929,118		4,036,610	
Less: Consolidation differences				
1. Debit differences	(5,519,870)		(5,721,552)	
2. Credit differences	3,852,323	10,624,033	3,847,348	8,060,491
V. Profit & Loss carried forward				
1. Profits carried forward	2,549,142		1,470,029	
2. Losses carried forward	(2,903,482)	(354,340)	(1,230,846)	239,183
VI. Minority interests				
1. Share capital	50,141		41,071	
2. Profits & reserves	239,231	289,372	150,304	191,375
TOTAL CAPITAL AND RESERVES		52,844,190		39,763,824
B. PROVISIONS FOR LIABILITIES & CHARGES				
1. Provisions for retirement benefits	2,630,752		2,592,270	
2. Other provisions	4,447,397	7,078,149	2,067,837	4,660,107
C. CREDITORS				
I. Long-term debt				
2. Bank loans		4,461,144		3,748,825
II. Current liabilities				
1. Suppliers	1,822,263		1,899,795	
2. Notes payable	569,686		929,473	
3. Banks short-term liabilities	7,431,406		7,262,545	
4. Customers' advances	182,125		260,225	
5. Obligations for taxes	2,779,451		2,142,770	
6. Insurance organisations	1,015,720		875,012	
7. Current portion of long-term debt	929,716		840,389	
10. Dividends payable	3,132,751		3,103,712	
11. Sundry creditors	1,412,506	19,275,624	1,153,890	18,467,811
TOTAL CREDITORS (C)		23,736,768		22,216,636
D. ACCRUALS AND DEFERRED INCOME				
1. Deferred income	517,777		33,722	
2. Accrued expenses	437,200		564,259	
3. Provisions and accruals	–	954,977	295,000	892,981
GRAND TOTAL LIABILITIES (A–B–C–D)		84,614,084		67,533,548
MEMO ACCOUNTS		9,714,835		6,881,000

ORGANISATION LTD. HERACLES MARITIME AGENCY LTD. G. HADJIKIRIAKOS SHIPPING CO. A. HADJIKIRIAKOS SHIPPING CO. TSIMENTOGLIS SHIPPING CO. DYSTOS SHIPPING CO. PROTOPOROS SHIPPING CO. THALASSOPOROS SHIPPING CO. PONTOPOROS SHIPPING CO. POSEIDON II SHIPPING CO. VOLOS I SHIPPING CO. PHAETHON SHIPPING CO. IOKASTI SHIPPING CO. NAFSIKA SHIPPING CO. HERACLES INSURANCE ENTERPRISES LTD. INDUSTRIAL MINERALS SA. NATIONAL INSTITUTE RESEARCH IN CEMENT LTD. EMMY-BUILDING ELEMENTS SA. AIGIS SA. STAR CONCRETE SA. LATO SA. SKYRODEMA SA.
b. Foreign: ALEXANDRIA SILO INVESTMENT COMPANY SA. HERMES COMPANIA NAVIERA SA. PORT SAID SILO INVESTMENT COMPANY SA (PANAMA). LOUDIAS COMPANIA NAVIERA SA. HAOL SILO INVESTMENT COMPANY SA. MARITIME COMPANY ESPERIDES SA. DEPOT AND COORDINATION CO SA (PANAMA). INTERNATIONAL MEDITERRANEAN SHIPPING SA (LUXEMBOURG). INTERNATIONAL FLAG (EGYPT)

ΚΑΤΑΣΤΑΣΗ ΛΟΓΑΡΙΑΣΜΟΥ ΑΠΟΤΕΛΕΣΜΑΤΩΝ ΧΡΗΣΕΩΣ ΟΜΙΛΟΥ 1992
(ΣΕ ΧΙΛ. ΔΡΧ.)

Αποτελέσματα εκμετάλλευσης		ΧΡΗΣΕΩΣ 1992			ΧΡΗΣΕΩΣ 1991	
Συνολικός κύκλος εργασιών Ομίλου		86.279.181			78.038.206	
Μείον: Ενδοεταιρικός κύκλος εργασιών		14.218.086	72.061.095		14.899.093	63.139.113
Μείον: Κόστος πωλήσεων			53.710.260			48.060.830
Μικτά αποτελέσματα εκμετάλλευσης (κέρδη)			18.350.835			15.078.283
Πλέον: Άλλα έσοδα εκμετάλλευσης			321.249			582.250
Σύνολο			18.672.084			15.630.533
Μείον: Έξοδα διοικ. λειτουργίας		3.582.550			3.233.469	
Έξοδα λειτουργ. ερευνών-ανάπτυξης		225.681			187.884	
Έξοδα λειτουργίας διάθεσης		1.552.778	5.361.009		994.412	4.415.765
Μερικά αποτελέσματα εκμετάλλευσης (κέρδη)			13.311.075			11.214.768
Μείον: Χρεωστικοί τόκοι & συναφή έξοδα		2.652.697			3.132.680	
Μείον: Έσοδα συμμετοχών	4.525			12.872		
Κέρδη από πώληση συμμετοχών						
και χρεογράφων	9.005			801.185		
Τόκοι πιστωτικοί	125.583	139.113	2.513.584	52.471	866.528	2.266.152
Ολικά αποτελέσματα εκμετάλλευσης (κέρδη)			10.797.491			8.948.616
Μείον: Έκτακτα αποτελέσματα						
Έκτακτα & ανόργανα έξοδα	2.545.386			966.470		
Αποσβέσεις συν/κών διαφορών	1.027.813			1.027.813		
Έξοδα προηγούμενων χρήσεων	91.664	3.664.863		509.315	2.503.598	
Μείον: Έκτακτα & ανόργανα έσοδα	827.290			869.812		
Έσοδα προηγούμενων χρήσεων	113.335	940.625	2.724.238	16.436	886.248	1.617.350
			8.073.253			7.331.266
Μείον: Συνολικές αποσβέσεις		2.898.852			3.371.553	
Μείον: Οι ενσωματωμένες στο						
λειτουργικό κόστος		2.778.963	119.889		3.233.806	137.747
Καθαρά κέρδη χρήσης προ φόρων			7.953.364			7.193.519
Μείον: Φόρος εισοδήματος			2.197.264			1.137.546
Καθαρά κέρδη χρήσης			5.756.100			6.055.973
Μείον: Δικαιώματα μειοψηφίας			81.944			64.153
Καθαρά κέρδη χρήσης Ομίλου			5.674.156			5.991.820

Λυκόβρυση, 28 Απριλίου 1993

Ο ΠΡΟΕΔΡΟΣ ΤΟΥ ΔΙΟΙΚΗΤΙΚΟΥ ΣΥΜΒΟΥΛΙΟΥ
ΚΑΙ ΔΙΕΥΘΥΝΩΝ ΣΥΜΒΟΥΛΟΣ ΑΓΕΤ ΗΡΑΚΛΗΣ
LORENZO PANZAVOLTA
ΑΡ.ΔΙΑΒ.Ι.175043/23.7.83

Ο ΟΙΚΟΝΟΜΙΚΟΣ ΔΙΕΥΘΥΝΤΗΣ
ΑΓΕΤ ΗΡΑΚΛΗΣ
ΣΩΤ. Ι. ΠΑΠΑΣΠΗΛΙΩΤΟΠΟΥΛΟΣ
Α.829917/63

Ο ΠΡΟΙΣΤΑΜΕΝΟΣ ΤΟΥ ΛΟΓΙΣΤΗΡΙΟΥ
ΑΓΕΤ ΗΡΑΚΛΗΣ
ΧΡΗΣΤΟΣ Α. ΣΤΑΣΙΝΟΠΟΥΛΟΣ
Ι.019339/72

GROUP PROFIT AND LOSS ACCOUNT (FOR THE YEAR ENDED DECEMBER 31, 1992)
(AMOUNT IN DRS. THOUS.)

Operating Results		1992			1991	
Group net turnover		86,279,181			78,038,206	
Less: Inter-company net turnover		14,218,086	72,061,095		14,899,093	63,139,113
Less: Cost of sales			53,710,260			48,060,830
Gross operating results (profit)			18,350,835			15,078,283
Plus: Other operating income			321,249			552,250
Total			18,672,084			15,630,533
Less: Administrative expenses		3,582,550			3,233,469	
Research and development costs		225,681			187,884	
Distribution costs		1,552,778	5,361,009		994,412	4,415,765
Sub-total of operating results (profit)			13,311,075			11,214,768
Less: Interest payable and similar charges		2,652,697			2,932,680	
Less: Income from participating interests	4,525			12,872		
Profits from sale of securities	9,005			801,185		
Interest receivable	125,583	139,113	2,513,584	52,471	666,528	2,266,152
Total operating results (profit)			10,797,491			8,948,918
Less: Extraordinary results						
Extraordinary and non-operating expenses	2,545,386			996,470		
Amortisation of exchange differences	1,027,813			1,027,813		
Prior years expenses	91,664	3,664,863		509,315	2,533,598	
Less: Extraordinary and non-operating income	827,290			869,812		
Prior years income	113,335	940,625	2,724,238	19,436	889,248	1,617,350
			8,073,253			7,331,266
Less: Total depreciation		2,898,852			3,371,653	
Less: Charged to the operating cost		2,778,963	119,889		3,233,906	137,747
Net profit for the year before taxes			7,953,364			7,193,519
Less: Income tax			2,197,264			1,137,546
Net profit for the year			5,756,100			6,055,973
Less: Minority interest			81,944			64,153
Group net profit for the year			5,674,156			5,991,820

Lycovrissi, April 28, 1993

CHAIRMAN OF THE BOARD OF DIRECTORS AND MANAGING DIRECTOR	FINANCIAL DIRECTOR	HEAD OF ACCOUNTS DEPARTMENT HERACLES GENERAL CEMENT
LORENZO PANZAVOLTA PASSPORT NO. I. 175043/23.7.83	SOTIRIOS I. PAPASPILIOTOPOULOS A. 829917/63	CHRISTOS A. STASINOPOULOS I .019339/.72

44

ΠΙΣΤΟΠΟΙΗΤΙΚΟ ΕΛΕΓΧΟΥ ΟΡΚΩΤΟΥ ΛΟΓΙΣΤΗ

Ελέγξαμε τον ανωτέρω ενοποιημένο ισολογισμό του Ομίλου Εταιρειών ΑΓΕΤ "ΗΡΑΚΛΗΣ", τα αποτελέσματα χρήσεως και το σχετικό προσάρτημα του Ομίλου της ΑΓΕΤ "ΗΡΑΚΛΗΣ", κατά τη χρήση που έληξε την 31η Δεκεμβρίου 1992. Κατά τον έλεγχό μας εφαρμόσαμε τις ελεγκτικές διαδικασίες, τις οποίες κρίναμε κατάλληλες, βάσει των αρχών και κανόνων ελεγκτικής που ακολουθεί το Σώμα Ορκωτών Λογιστών. Ο ανωτέρω ισολογισμός και ο λογαριασμός αποτελεσμάτων χρήσης προέκυψαν από την ενοποίηση των κονδυλίων ενεργητικού, παθητικού και αποτελεσμάτων χρήσης των επι μέρους οικονομικών καταστάσεων των εταιρειών του Ομίλου, που περιλαμβάνονται στη σημείωση Νο 2, η οποία παρατίθεται κάτω από τον ισολογισμό του Ομίλου. Για την ενοποίηση αυτή εφαρμόστηκε η μέθοδος της ολικής ενοποίησης, οι δε κατώτερω παρατηρήσεις αναφέρονται τόσο στον από εμάς έλεγχο της ΑΓΕΤ "ΗΡΑΚΛΗΣ" όσο και από τον έλεγχο των λοιπών εταιρειών του Ομίλου που έγινε από άλλους συναδέλφους του Σώματος Ορκωτών Λογιστών, πλην των αλλοδαπών εταιρειών που δεν μας δόθηκαν σχετικά πορίσματα ελέγχου. Το προσάρτημα περιλαμβάνει τις πληροφορίες που προβλέπονται από το άρθρο 107 του κωδ. Ν.2190/1920.

Από τον έλεγχό μας προέκυψαν τα εξής:

1. Οι συναλλαγματικές διαφορές των δανείων και πιστώσεων για κτήσεις πάγιων στοιχείων, που εμφανίζονται στο λογαριασμό ενεργητικού "Έξοδα εγκατάστασης", αποσβέννονται: α) Οι μέχρι 31.12.86, με ετήσιο συντελεστή 10%, τακτικά που ακολουθείται παγίως από του έτους 1982. β) Οι από 1.1.87 και μετά, σύμφωνα με τις νέες διατάξεις του Ν.2190 (άρθρο 43 παρ.3/γ). Αν οι μέχρι 31.12.86 συναλλαγματικές διαφορές αποσβέννοντο ανάλογα με το εξοφλούμενο σε κάθε χρήση τμήμα των δανείων, όπως προέβλεπαν οι ισχύουσες μέχρι τότε διατάξεις του Κώδικα Φορολογικών Στοιχείων, οι μέχρι 31.12.92 συνολικές αποσβέσεις αυτών θα ήταν μεγαλύτερες κατά δρχ. 1.583 εκατ., με ισόποση μείωση της καθαρής λογιστικής θέσης της εταιρείας, ενώ τα αποτελέσματα της χρήσης 1992 θα είχαν επιβαρυνθεί με ποσό μικρότερο κατά δρχ. 962 εκατ. 2α. Με βάση τις διατάξεις του Ν.2065/1992 έγινε στη χρήση 1992 (την ελεγχόμενη χρήση) αναπροσαρμογή της αξίας κτήσεως των γηπέδων, των κτιρίων και των συσσωρευμένων αποσβέσεων των κτιρίων εξ αιτίας της οποίας αυξήθηκε η αξία κτήσεως των γηπέδων και κτιρίων κατά δρχ. 21.834 εκατ. και η αξία των συσσωρευμένων αποσβέσεων των κτιρίων κατά δρχ. 10.614 εκατ. και προέκυψε διαφορά αναπροσαρμογής ποσού δρχ. 11.220 εκατ. η οποία εμφανίζεται στους του ΠΑΟΗΠΚΟΥ "Α. ΙΔΙΑ ΚΕΦΑΛΑΙΑ" κατά δρχ. 207 εκατ. στον λογ/σμό Α.IV "Διαφορά ενοποίησης" επειδή το εν λόγω ποσό καλύπτει μέρος ζημιών που είχαν προκύψει στις χρήσεις μέχρι 31.12.90 (ημερομηνία δημιουργίας του λογ/σμού "Διαφορές ενοποίησης") κατά δρχ. 22 εκατ. στον λογ/σμό Α.V "Υπόλοιπο κερδών (ζημιών) εις νέο" επειδή το εν λόγω ποσό καλύψε μέρος ζημιών που είχαν προκύψει στις χρήσεις μετά την 31.12.90, κατά δρχ. 52 εκατ. στον λογ/σμό Α.VI "Δικαιώματα μειοψηφίας" και του υπολοίπου της διαφοράς αναπροσαρμογής, κατά δρχ. 10.939 εκατ. κατακωρήθηκε στον λογαριασμό Α III-2 "Διαφορές από αναπροσαρμογή αξίας λοιπών περιουσιακών στοιχείων". 2β. Η αναπροσαρμογή της αξίας κτήσεως των συμμετοχών και τίτλων με κύρια εξ αιτίας εκείνες που θα προέκυπταν εάν είχαν υπολογισθεί στην αξία πριν την αναπροσαρμογή κατά δρχ. 171 εκατ. περίπου. 2β. Ο Όμιλος στην παρούσα χρήση σύμφωνα με τον Ν.2065/1992 ελόγισε αποσβέσεις επι ορισμένων περιουσιακών στοιχείων με μεγαλύτερους συντελεστές εκείνων της προηγούμενης χρήσεως με συνέπεια οι αποσβέσεις επί πλοίων αξίας μειωμένες κατά δρχ. 1.121 εκατ. και τα αποτελέσματα ισόποσα αυξημένα σε σχέση με την προηγούμενη χρήση. 2γ. Δεν έγιναν στην ελεγχόμενη χρήση αποσβέσεις επι πλοίων αξίας κτήσεως δρχ. 200 εκατ. 3. Για ορισμένα πάγια περιουσιακά στοιχεία αλλοδαπών εταιρειών του Ομίλου, που περιλαμβάνονται στην ενοποίηση με συνολική αξία κτήσεως δρχ. 2.502 εκατ. (ισόποσο 11,7 εκατ. δολ. ΗΠΑ) και αναπροσθετή αξία δρχ. 122 εκατ. παραχωρήθηκε, στη χρήση 1980, από τις εν λόγω εταιρείες το δικαίωμα τα αγοραστούν μέχρι 31.12.85 από την αλλοδαπή εταιρεία "CEMENTONAVIOS", αντί τιμήματος ίσου προς το μικρότερο ποσό μεταξύ εκείνου των δρχ. 2.324 εκατ. (ισόποσο 10,8 εκατ. δολ. ΗΠΑ) και εκείνου που θα προσδιορίζοταν και έναν ελεύθερο εκτιμητή κατά τη ημερομηνία άσκησης του δικαιώματος. Στη χρήση 1984 ασκήθηκε το δικαίωμα αυτό, την ενεργούντα του οποίου εμφανίζεται στην ΑΓΕΤ "ΗΡΑΚΛΗΣ", χωρίς να μπορούμε να διαμορφώσουμε γνώμη για τη νομιμότητα του δικαιολογικού αυτού, συνεπεία και τα πάγια τακτικά, με την τρέχουσα τιμή του ξένου νομίσματος τέλους χρήσεως, με συνέπεια η εμφανίζεται, την 31.12.92, αυξημένα τα πάγια του Ομίλου και αντίστοιχα η καθαρή θέση αυτού κατά δρχ. 445 εκατ. Η ξενίαντι ότι οκτώ (8) από τις πιο πάνω αλλοδαπές εταιρείες έχουν διακόψει τις εργασίες τους από τις χρήσεις 1986 και 1987. 7. Δεν έχει σχηματισθεί πρόβλημα στον Ισολογισμό σε βάρος των αποτελεσμάτων της χρήσης συνολικού ποσού δρχ. 328 εκατ. για: α) αναδρομική αύξηση τιμής τέφρας ΔΕΗ δρχ. 195 εκατ. β) για βραδέως κινούμενα αποθέματα δρχ. 40 εκατ., και γ) για το ενδεχόμενο επιβολής χαρτοσήμου και προσαυξήσεων επι ταμιακών διευκολύνσεων των εταιρειών του Ομίλου συνολικού ποσού δρχ. 93 εκατ. περίπου. 8. Χρειωτικές συναλλαγματικές διαφορές, συνολικού ύψους δρχ. 200 εκατ. περίπου, που προέκυψαν κατά την αποτίμηση της 31.12.1992 μακροπρόθεσμων υποχρεώσεων σε ξένο νόμισμα δεν ελήφθησαν υπ' όψη στα αποτελέσματα της χρήσεως σε κρέμεση λογισμού προβλήματος. Έτσι τα αποτελέσματα της παρούσης χρήσεως της παρούσας εμφανίζονται ισόποσα αυξημένα. 9. Στους Μεταβατικούς Λογαριασμούς του Παθητικού Δ-2 "Έξοδα χρήσεως δουλευμένα" αλλά και στους αντίστοιχους λογαριασμούς των δαπανών της χρήσεως, δεν περιλαμβάνεται ποσό δρχ. 60 εκατ. περίπου που αφορά το δεδουλευμένο ποσό μισθώματος πλοίων. 10. Στην από 15.3.1993 επιστολή της, η Νομική Υπηρεσία της ΑΓΕΤ "ΗΡΑΚΛΗΣ" μας εγνώρισε ότι διεκδικούνται από εταιρείες αιγυπτιακών συμφερόντων αποζημιώσεις ύψους δρχ. 4.300 εκατ. περίπου, εις βάρος της "ΑΓΕΤ ΗΡΑΚΛΗΣ" που δεν εμφανίζονται στον ισολογισμό επειδή η έκβαση των εν λόγω διεκδικήσεων κρίνεται αβέβαιη. 11. Ο Όμιλος έχει και την πρακτική και το προσωπικό της, πρόβλεψη αποζημιώσεων λόγω εξόδου και την υπηρεσία ανεξαρτήτου χρόνου θεμελιώσεως δικαιώματος συνταξιοδοτήσεως. Κατά την παρούσα χρήση η τακτική αυτή άλλαξε και σχηματίστηκε πρόβλημα μόνο για το προσωπικό που θεμελίωσε δικαίωμα συνταξιοδοτήσεως μέχρι το τέλος της επόμενης χρήσης, σύμφωνα με το άρθρο 10 Ν.2065/1992. Αν η πρόβλημα σχηματίζοταν όπως και στις προηγούμενες χρήσεις το σωρευμένο ύψος της, κατά την ημερομηνία κλεισίματος του Ισολογισμού θα ήταν μεγαλύτερο του εμφανιζόμενου στον Ισολογισμό κατά δρχ. 1.203 εκατ. Ισόποσα μεγαλύτερη θα ήταν και η επιβάρυνση των Αποτελεσμάτων Χρήσεως. Εν έχων άλλη παρατήρηση στη μέθοδο απογραφής, σε σχέση με εκείνες που αναφέρονται στις περιπτώσεις παραπάνω παρατηρήσεων μας 2α, 2β, 4β και 11. Ο ανωτέρω ενοποιημένος ισολογισμός και η κατάσταση των ενοποιημένων αποτελεσμάτων χρήσεως απεικονίζουν μαζί με το προσάρτημα, με την επιφύλαξη των παρατηρήσεων μας, βάσει των σχετικών διατάξεων που ισχύουν και λογιστικών αρχών, οι οποίες έχουν γίνει γενικά παραδεκτές και δεν διαφέρουν από εκείνες που ο Όμιλος είχε εφαρμόσει στην προηγούμενη χρήση, την περιουσιακή διάρθρωση και τη χρηματοοικονομική θέση ("οικονομική κατάσταση") του Ομίλου κατά την 31η Δεκεμβρίου 1992, καθώς και τα αποτελέσματα της χρήσης που έληξε αυτή τη ημερομηνία.

Αθήνα, 30 Απριλίου 1993

Ο ΟΡΚΩΤΟΣ ΛΟΓΙΣΤΗΣ

ΙΩΑΝΝΗΣ Ν. ΛΑΜΠΡΟΥ
Κ.227220/77

AUDITOR' S REPORT

We have audited the above Consolidated Balance Sheet of the "HERACLES" Group of Companies and the Notes to the Accounts as at December 31, 1992, and the Profit and Loss Account for the year then ended. Our examination was made in conformity with the auditing standards of the Institute of Certified Public Accountants of Greece and accordingly included such tests of the accounting records and such other auditing procedures as we considered necessary in the circumstances. The above Balance Sheet and Profit and Loss Account derived from the combination of the Assets, Liabilities and Profit and Loss Account items of the financial statements of the Group of Companies which are listed in note 2 of the Balance Sheet. No item has been excluded from the consolidation. Except for those foreign companies referred to here below, for which we have not yet received audit reports, the following notes arise both from our audit of HERACLES GCC as well as from the audits, performed by other Certified Public Accountants of Greece, in respect of other Group companies. The information in the Notes to the Accounts comply to the requirements of article 107 of code 2190/1920.

It is noted that:

1) The exchange differences, arising from loans and credits for the acquisition of fixed assets and shown as assets under "Formation expenses", are amortised as follows: a) the differences to December 31, 1986 at 10% p.a. This practice has been consistently followed since 1982. b) The exchange differences since January 1, 1987 are amortised according to the new provisions of L 2190 (art.43, parag. 3c). If the exchange differences up to December 31, 1986 were amortised as the loans were repaid, according to the provisions of the Tax Code then in force, their total amortisation till December 31, 1992 would have been higher and consequently the Net Assets lower, by drs 1,553 millions, while the 1992 profits would have been higher by drs 962 m. 2.a) During the year the company's lands and buildings values and accumulated depreciation were revalued in accordance with the provisions of L. 2065/1992. The effect of this was to increase the values of these assets by drs. 21,834 m. and the accumulated depreciation thereon by drs 10,614 m. The resulting net difference from revaluation of drs. 11,220 m. was credited to the capital reserves accounts as follows: drs. 207 m. in Consolidation Differences (A IV), drs. 22 m. in Profit and Loss carried forward (A V), drs. 52 m. in Minority interests (A VI), and drs. 10,939 m. in Differences From Revaluations Other Assets (A III). The amounts posted to Consolidation Differences (A IV) and Profit and Loss carried forward (A.V) covered losses brought forward from previous years. The year's depreciation charge was calculated on the revalue values of these assets and as a result they are drs 171 m. more than they would have been had the revaluation not taken place. 2.b) In accordance with L. 2065/1992 the company's 1992 depreciation rates were lower that those of previous years. As a result the year's depreciation charge was lower by drs. 1,121 m. and consequently the year's profits were correspondingly higher by this amount. 2.c) No Depreciation was charged on ships with an acquisition value of drs. 200 m. 3) Certain fixed assets belonging to foreign group companies are included in the consolidation at a total acquisition cost of Drs 2,502 m. (or USA $ 11.7m) and written down value of Drs 122 m. Purchase Options up to December 31, 1985, were granted in 1950 to the foreign company CEMENTONAVIOS, by these companies, for a price equal to the lower of Drs 2,324 m. (or USA 10.8 m.) and that which an independent appraiser would have had determined at the date that the option would have been exercised. These options were exercised in 1984 but HERACLES GCC disputes their validity. We cannot foresee the outcome of the relevant legal proceedings. This may prove to be meaningless however for the reasons outlined in our note 4 (a) below. 4) Included in debtors are the following amounts: a) A claim of Drs 4,118 m. against the foreign customer "CEMENTONAVIOS" with whom the Company has discontinued trading since August 1984. The above amount also includes interest up to December 31, 1987. For an amount of Drs. 3,559 millions a final court case ruling was issued in favour of Heracles but according to the Legal Department of Heracles General Cement the recoverability of this amount, as well as the balance of the still pending amount, is doubtful. Included in the amount of drs 4118 m. is an amount of drs. 1,428 m. arising from the foreign currency translation of the amount receivable. This credit difference on exchange has been included in the account Other provisions but was not credited as profit in the Profit and Loss accounts of the years in which it arose. (1988-1992). Furthermore, we have not received a reply to our request for confirmation of the balance of Drs 3,559 m. due to HERACLES GCC. AE. b) Other outstanding claims totalling drs 2,922 m. are also overdue. Against these amounts a provision for bad and doubtful debts amounting to drs 610 m. was made in accordance with Law 2065/1992. As this type of provision was made for the first time and therefore there was a departure from the policy of previous years, the 1992 profits are shown correspondingly lower than they would have otherwise have been. The Group has thus not made a provision for the total overdue claims in 4a and 4b above. c) There are claims against the Greek State amounting to Drs 4,174 m. (account D/II/IIa) in respect of VAT refundable (Drs 3,627 m.) and other taxes withheld (Drs 477 m.). It does not appear that the greater part of these claims will be recovered in 1993 although these claims are already due and payable. d) Also there are disputed claims in favour of Heracles GCC and against third parties, which are pending before the courts, amounting to about one billion drachmas. This amount has not been recorded in the accounting records because the final court decision is still pending. 5. No provision has been made for possible obligations arising from: a) Penal clauses totalling Drs 1,354 m. imposed by the Bank of Greece in favour of the State for violations of currency regulations. In respect of the above, the Group has appealed to the Administrative courts for amounts totalling Drs 522 m. but the court's decision is still pending. b) Claims of third parties amounting to drs 534 m. c) Tax assessments for prior periods amounting to approximately drs 480 m. Appeals against these assessments have been filed with the Administrative courts and it is considered likely that the Group will, in the greater part of this amount, be vindicated. d) From Income tax in respect of prior years, amounting to about drs. 90 million plus penalties. 6. a) Consolidated, but not yet approved by others are the 1992 Financial Statements of nine foreign Group Companies. The assets and liabilities of these companies amount to drs 5,669 m. and drs 10,997 m. respectively. The acquisition costs of the assets of the above companies are consistently translated at the year end rate of exchange and as a result the net worth of these companies is overstated by an amount of drs 445 m. b) It should be noted that eight of the above companies have ceased operations during the years 1986 and 1987. 7. No provision was made in the Balance Sheet and against the year's results for an amount of drs 328 m. in respect of the following: a) Retroactive increases in the cost of ash supplied by DEH (the Public Power Corporation). The extra cost of these increases amount to drs 195m. b) Slow moving inventories amounting to drs 40 m. c) The amount of 93 m. in respect of stamp duties related to credit facilities. 8. Losses amounting to approximately drs 200 m arising from year end foreign currency translations of foreign currency denominated Long Term Liabilities have not been charged to the Profit and Loss Account but have been debited instead to a provisions account. The year's profits are thus overstated by this amount. 9. No provision for accrued expenses (account D 2 in the Balance Sheet) has been made for drs 60 m in respect of the chartering of vessels. The Profit of the year is thus overstated by this amount. 10. By a letter from the Company's Legal Department dated March 15, 1993 we have been informed that there are claims by Egyptian Companies and against Heracles, amounting to about 4.3 billion drachmas. Because the judicial outcome in respect of these claims is uncertain, no provision for these amounts has been made and therefore they do not appear on the Balance Sheet. 11) The Group until 1991 made a provision for employee retirement indemnities based on the total number of employees irrespective of the time of retirement. In accordance with article 10 of law 2065 1992. The current year's results have been charged with a provision based only on the employees retiring upto the end 1993. If the provision was made on the same basis as in previous years the amount charged to the Profit and Loss Account would have been more by drs 1,203m. The Balance sheet related provision would have been correspondingly higher by this amount. Other than those cases referred to in notes 2.a), 2.b), 4.b) and 11 above, there were no other changes from the previous year, in the inventory valuation method. In our opinion, subject to the foregoing notes, the above Consolidated Balance Sheet, the Notes there to, and the Consolidated Profit and Loss Account give a true and fair view of the Group's assets, liabilities and financial position as at December 31, 1992 and of the results of the Group for the year then ended in conformity with legal requirements and accepted accounting principles consistently applied.

Athens, 30 April 1993

Certified Public Accountant of Greece

JOHN N. LAMBROU
K 227220/77

45

ΣΤΟΙΧΕΙΑ ΓΙΑ ΤΟΝ ΕΝΟΠΟΙΗΜΕΝΟ ΙΣΟΛΟΓΙΣΜΟ 1992

1. Οι εταιρίες του Ομίλου που περιλαμβάνονται στην ενοποίηση είναι:

   α. Εσωτερικού: ΑΓΕΤ ΗΡΑΚΛΗΣ, ΕΒΙΕΣΚ Α.Ε., ΑΝΕ ΗΡΑΚΛΗΣ, ΗΡΑΚΛΗΣ ΔΙΕΘΝΗΣ Α.Ε., ΗΡΑΚΛΗΣ ΣΥΣΚΕΥΑΣΙΑ Α.Ε., ΛΑΒΑ Α.Ε., ΑΜΠΕΡ Α.Ε., ΕΠΕΝΔΥΣΗ ΣΙΛΟ ΠΟΡΤ ΣΑΪΔ Α.Ε., ΓΡΑΦΕΙΟΡΓΑΝΩΣΗ Ε.Π.Ε., ΗΡΑΚΛΗΣ ΝΑΥΤΙΚΕΣ ΠΡΑΚΤΟΡΕΥΣΕΙΣ Ε.Π.Ε., Γ. ΧΑΤΖΗΚΥΡΙΑΚΟΣ Ν.Ε., Α. ΧΑΤΖΗΚΥΡΙΑΚΟΣ Ν.Ε., ΤΣΙΜΕΝΤΟΚΛΗΣ Ν.Ε., ΔΥΣΤΟΣ Ν.Ε., ΠΡΩΤΟΠΟΡΟΣ Ν.Ε., ΘΑΛΑΣΣΟΠΟΡΟΣ Ν.Ε., ΠΟΝΤΟΠΟΡΟΣ Ν.Ε., ΠΟΣΕΙΔΩΝ ΙΙ Ν.Ε., ΒΟΛΟΣ Ι Ν.Ε., ΦΑΕΘΩΝ Ν.Ε., ΙΟΚΑΣΤΗ Ν.Ε., ΝΑΥΣΙΚΑ Ν.Ε., ΑΣΦΑΛΙΣΤΙΚΕΣ ΕΠΙΧΕΙΡΗΣΕΙΣ ΗΡΑΚΛΗΣ Ε.Π.Ε., ΒΙΟΜΗΧΑΝΙΚΑ ΟΡΥΚΤΑ Α.Ε. (Σοφ. Βενιζέλου 49-51, Λυκόβρυση), ΕΚΕΤ ΕΠΕ (Κ. Πατέλη 15, Λυκόβρυση), ΕΜΜΥ-ΚΤΙΡΙΑΚΑ ΣΤΟΙΧΕΙΑ ΑΒΕΕ, ΑΙΓΙΣ Α.Ε. (Ε. Βενιζέλου & Ανδρούτσου 29, Λυκόβρυση), ΑΣΤΗΡ ΜΠΕΤΟΝ Α.Ε., ΛΑΤΟ Α.Ε. (Τέρμα οδού Ήρας, Γαλάτσι), ΣΚΥΡΟΔΕΜΑ ΕΒΑΕ (Νεοχωρούδα Θεσσαλονίκη).

   β. Εξωτερικού: ALEXANDRIA SILO INVESTMENT COMPANY S.A., HERMES COMPANIA NAVIERA S.A., PORT SAID SILO INVESTMENT COMPANY S.A., LOYDIAS COMPANIA NAVIERA S.A., HAQL SILO INVESTMENT COMPANY S.A., MARITIME COMPANY ESPERIDES S.A., DEPOT AND COORDINATION CO. S.A. (Panama), INTERNATIONAL MEDITERRANEAN SHIPPING S.A. (Luxemburg), INTERNATIONAL FLAG (Egypt).

2. Η μετατροπή του ξένου νομίσματος που αφορά την αξία κτήσεως των πάγιων στοιχείων των εν λόγω εταιριών γίνεται, κατά πάγια τακτική, με την τρέχουσα τιμή του ξένου νομίσματος τέλους χρήσεως.

3. Συμμετοχές Ομίλου:

   α. Σε εταιρίες εκτός Ομίλου

	ΤΕΜΑΧΙΑ	ΑΞΙΑ
Ε.Τ.Ε.	1.456	6.899.750
ΤΡΑΠΕΖΑ ΜΑΚΕΔΟΝΙΑΣ-ΘΡΑΚΗΣ	11.428	40.511.640
ΚΑΡΜΟΡ ΕΛΛΑΣ ΕΠΕ	200	2.250.000
ΕΚΕΠΥ		100.000
CEMENT MARK ASSOCIATION	1	1.248.973
ΒΙΟΜΗΧΑΝΙΚΗ ΣΤΕΓΗ		308.620
ΔΕΛΤΑ ΟΙΛ ΕΛΛΑΣ ΕΠΕ	400	4.000.000
AXIOS SHIPPING	19	51.580.354
ALFIOS COMPANIA NAVIERA	10	40.993.145
ARMSTOCK CO. SA		351.911.200
EQUITABLE MARINE TRANS. SA		7.724.880
HERACLES OVERSEAS		15.170

   β. Ίδια μερίδια
ΑΓΕΤ ΗΡΑΚΛΗΣ	33.470	8.509.350
Σύνολο		516.023.082

4. Με βάση τις διατάξεις του Ν.2065/1992 έγινε στη χρήση 1992 (την ελεγχόμενη χρήση) αναπροσαρμογή της αξίας κτήσεως των γηπέδων, των κτιρίων και των συσσωρευμένων αποσβέσεων των κτιρίων, εξαιτίας της οποίας αυξήθηκε η αξία κτήσεως των γηπέδων και κτιρίων κατά δρχ. 21.834 εκατ. και η αξία των συσσωρευμένων αποσβέσεων των κτιρίων κατά δρχ. 10.614 εκατ. και αναπτύχθηκε διαφορά αναπροσαρμογής ποσού δρχ. 11.220 εκατ., η οποία εμφανίζεται στους λογ/σμούς ΚΑΘΑΡΑΣ ΘΕΣΕΩΣ (Βλέπε σημείωση Πιστοποιητικού Ορκωτού Λογιστή 2α).

5. Σε ορισμένα πάγια περιουσιακά στοιχεία του Ομίλου υπάρχουν προσημφωνα υποθηκών-προσημειώσεων και υποθήκες-προσημειώσεις ύψους 2.965.550 χιλ. δρχ. που ασφαλίζουν υπόλοιπα δανείων συνολικού ποσού 2.996.901 χιλ. δρχ. Επίσης, επί ορισμένων πλοίων και εγκαταστάσεων επ' αυτών έχουν εγγραφεί υποθήκες 15.853.170 χιλ. δρχ. που ασφαλίζουν υπόλοιπα δανείων ποσού 4.493.527 χιλ. δρχ.

6. Κατά την παρούσα χρήση σχηματίστηκε πρόβλεψη μόνο για το προσωπικό που θεμελιώνει δικαίωμα συνταξιοδοτήσεως μέχρι το τέλος της επόμενης χρήσης, (1993), σύμφωνα με το άρθρο 10 Ν.2065/1992.

7. Ο Όμιλος σε αντίθεση με την προηγούμενη χρήση διενήργησε πρόβλεψη για την πιθανή ζημιά από επισφαλείς απαιτήσεις, σύμφωνα με τον Ν.2065/1992 ύψους δρχ. 615 εκατ.

Λυκόβρυση, 28 Απριλίου 1993

ΤΟ ΔΙΟΙΚΗΤΙΚΟ ΣΥΜΒΟΥΛΙΟ

Βεβαιώνεται οτι η έκθεση αυτή είναι εκείνη που αναφέρεται στο από 30 Απριλίου 1993 Πιστοποιητικό Ελέγχου.

Αθήνα, 30 Απριλίου 1993

Ο ΟΡΚΩΤΟΣ ΛΟΓΙΣΤΗΣ

ΙΩΑΝΝΗΣ Ν. ΛΑΜΠΡΟΥ
Κ.227220/77

INFORMATION IN RESPECT OF THE CONSOLIDATED 1992 FINANCIAL STATEMENTS:

1. The companies included in the consolidated financial statements are the following:

   a. Domestic: HERACLES GCC SA, EVIESK SA, HERACLES SHIPPING CO, S.A., HERACLES INTERNATIONAL S.A., HERACLES PACKAGING CO. S.A., LAVA S.A., AMBER S.A.,PORT SAID SILO INVESTMENT S.A.,OFFICE ORGANISATION LTD, HERACLES MARITIME AGENCY LTD, G. HADJIKIRIAKOS SHIPPING CO, A. HADJIKIRIAKOS SHIPPING CO, TSIMENTOCLIS SHIPPING CO, DYSTOS SHIPPING CO., PROTOPOROS SHIPPING CO, THALASSOPOROS SHIPPING CO, PONTOPOROS SHIPPING CO, PCSEIDON II SHIPPING CO, VOLOS I SHIPPING CO, PHAETHON SHIPPING CO, IOKASTI SHIPPING CO, NAFSIKA SHIPPING CO, HERACLES INSURANCE ENTERPRISES LTD, INDUSTRIAL MINERALS SA., NATIONAL INSTITUTE RESEARCH IN CEMENT LTD, EMMY-BUILDING ELEMENTS SA, AIGIS S.A., STAR CONCRETE S.A., LATO S.A., SKYRODEMA S.A.

   b. Foreign: ALEXANDRIA SILO INVESTMENT COMPANY SA. HERMES COMPANIA NAVIERA SA. PORT SAID SILO INVESTMENT COMPANY SA (PANAMA), LOUDIAS COMPANIA NAVIERA SA. HAQL SILO INVESTMENT COMPANY SA. MARITIME COMPANY ESPERIDES SA, DEPOT AND COORDINATION CO SA (PANAMA), INTERNATIONAL MEDITERRANEAN SHIPPING SA (LUXEMBOURG), INTERNATIONAL FLAG (EGYPT).

2. The foreign currency translations of the fixed assets of foreig subsidiaries is made at the rates of exchange ruling at year end.

3. Group Investments

   a. In other enterprises

	NUMBER OF SHARES	TOTAL INVESTMENT DRS.
NATIONAL BANK OF GREECE	1.456	6.899,750
BANK OF MACEDONIA AND THRACE	11.428	40.511,640
KARMOR HELLAS LTD	200	2.250,000
E.K.E.P.Y.		100,000
CEMENT MARKETING ASSOCIATION	1	1.248,973
HOME OF INDUSTRY		308,620
DELTA OIL HELLAS LTD	400	4.000,000
AXIOS SHIPPING	19	51.550,354
ALFIOS COMPANIA NAVIERA S.A.	10	40.993,145
ARMSTOCK CO. S.A.		351.911,200
EQUITABLE MARINE TRANS S.A.		7.724,880
HERACLES OVERSEAS		15,170

   B. In own shares

HERACLES GENERAL CEMENT CO. S.A.	33.470	8.509,350
Total		516.023,082

4. During the year the company's lands and buildings values and accumulated depreciation were revalued in accordance with the provisions of L. 2065/1992. The effect of this was to increase the values of these assets by drs. 21,834 m. and the accumulated depreciation thereon by drs 10,614 m.. The resulting net difference from revaluation of drs. 11,220 m. was credited to the capital reserves accounts (audit report note 2a).

5. For certain Group fixed assets there are preliminary agreements for mortgages, charges and liens of drs. 2.965,550 thousand to secure loan balances totalling drs. 2.996,901 thousand. There are also mortgages of drs. 15.853,177 thousand registered on ships and installations to secure loan balances totalling drs. 4.493,527 thousand.

6. In accordance with article 10 of law 2065/1992 the current year's results have been charged with a provision based only on the employees retiring upto the end 1993.

7. The group in contrast to previous years has made a provision for bad and doubtful debts in accordance with Law 2065/1992. The total provisions amounted to drachmas 615 m.

Lykobrisi, 28 April 1993

The Board of Directors

We certify that these notese are refered to in our audit report of 30 April 1993

Athens 30 April 1993

Auditor

John N. Lambrou
K. 227220/77

NOTES TO THE CONSOLIDATED ACCOUNTS
FOR THE YEAR ENDED 31st DECEMBER 1992

The following notes to the Consolidated Balance Sheet as at 31st December 1992 and the Consolidated Profit and Loss Account for the year then ended, have been prepared in accordance with the provisions of the Companies Act 2190/1920 and the Company's basic accounting policies.

Consolidation Basis
The financial statements of all Group Companies which include Heracles General Cement Company, the Holding Company, and its subsidiaries, have been consolidated in accordance with the provisions of articles 90-99 of the Companies Act.

Method of Consolidation
The method of integral consolidation has been applied. Incorporated, in the Consolidated Balance Sheet are the companies stated in note 2 to the Balance Sheet and include those subsidiaries whose share capital is owned, directly or indirectly, 100% by Heracles, as well as, the companies listed in note 8.3 in which third parties hold a minority interest.

1. Formation Expenses and Intangible Assets

1.1 Analysis of the changes made during the year, expressed in millions of Drachmas:

Category	Acquisi- tion cost 31.12.91	Debit in 1992	Deprec:- ation in 1992	Total Depre- ciation	Written down value 31.12.92
Preliminary expenses	1,303	(5)	113	1,237	61
Exchange differences on loans for the acquisition of fixed assets up to 31.12.1986	10,567	-	1,028	9,013	1,554
Exchange differences on loans for the acquisition of fixed assets after 31.12.1986	362	59	—	353	68
Loan interest during construction	3,527	(10)	342	3,342	176
Other long - term amortisation expenses	1,032	119	118	927	224
Sub total	16,791	163	1,601	14,872	2,083
Research costs	108	30	23	71	67
Grand Total	16,899	193	1,624	14,943	2,150

1.2 Amortisation method:

(a) Preliminary expenses and expenditure, loan interest during construction periods as well as research expenditure, incurred up to 31st December 1986, is amortised at 10% per annum, while such expenses incurred after that date are amortised at 20% per annum, in conformity with the provisions of the Companies Act article 43, par. 3a.

(b) The rate of amortisation of differences on exchange, arising from loans and credits obtained for the acquisition of fixed assets up to 31st December 1986, is 10% per annum. The rate of amortisation of differences on exchange on said liabilities (whether realised or translated into drachmas at year end) resulting from the acquisition of fixed assets obtained after that date were treated in the books in accordance with the provisions of the Companies Act. article 43, par. 3c. Thus the 1992 results were charged with Drs. 1,028m .for the amortisation of debit differences on exchange arising up to 31st December, 1986 and with Drs. 52m. in respect of amortisation of debit differences on exchange arising after 31st December, 1986. Apart from research and development expenditure the Company has not acquired any other intangible assets.

2. Fixed Assets

The fixed assets are consolidated at the acquisition values as shown in the individual Balance Sheets of Group Companies with the exception of fixed assets of foreign subsidiaries. The financial statements of foreign subsidiaries are expressed in U.S. Dollars and are translated into drachmae at the Bank of Greece rate of exchange (fixing rate) ruling at the date of the Balance Sheet. For each and every company, depreciation has been deducted from the acquisition value. The acquisition values of the fixed assets of Group Companies based in Greece have been consolidated at historical cost as revalued in accordance with the provisions of special laws, plus additions and improvements. Because there was no diminution in the value of tangible assets and no diminution is foreseeable in the future no additional depreciation, provision or reserve has been set aside for this purpose. During 1992 there has been a revaluation in the values of land and buildings as well as in the cumulative depreciation of buildings in accordance with the provisions of L.2065/1992. As a result the values of land and buildings before depreciation increased by drs. 21,834 m. and the accumulated depreciation increased by drs. 10,614 m. The difference of drs. 11,220 m. is shown under Capital and Reserves and specifically are included in the following accounts: drs. 207 m. in Consolidation Differences (A IV), drs. 22 m. in Profit and Loss carried forward (A V), drs. 52 m. in Minority interests (A VI), and drs. 10,930 m. in Differences From Revaluations Other Assets (A III 2).

3. Tangible Assets

31. Analysis of the changes made during the year (in millions of drachmas)

Fixed asset category	Purchases or own construction	Revaluation	Write-offs or transfers	Depreci-ation in 1992	Increases in depreciation due to revaluation
Lands - Mines Quarries	58	9,344	-	-	-
Buildings - technical works	1,754	12,490	-	746	10,614
Machinery etc	2,918	-	-	427	-
Transportation - equipment	2,925	-	30	522	-
Furniture etc	134	-	-	62	-
Fixed assets under construction etc	-	-	(3,671)	-	-
TOTAL	7,789	21,834	(3,641)	1,757	10,614

N.B. The difference between the 1991 & 1992 accumulated depreciation balance and the depreciation of drs. 545 m. charged to the profit and loss account is due to the adjustment of the written down values after depreciation of the assets denominated in foreign currency as a result of foreign currency translations at year end.

4. Participating Interests in Non-Group Companies and Investment in Group Companies.

41. "Participating Interests in Non-Group Companies and Investments in Group Companies" appearing under Fixed Assets include: (a) the acquisition value of shares and participations of non Group Companies and (b. Group Companies' holdings of HERACLES GCC shares. These shares are shown at the lower of acquisition cost or market value.

4.2 Participations in public companies (S.A.), as well as in securities, shares of public companies (S.A.) and all other kinds of securities classified as fixed assets have been valued in accordance with the provisions of the Tax Code. Included in the balance sheet is the acquisition cost of a shareholding in the Armstock Corporation S.A. (note C III 2 of the Auditors Report). This acquisition cost is drs 317 m. higher than the Armstock's current value, based on the last available Armstock Balance Sheet dated 31.12.88. and as calculated under the provisions of the Companies Act 2190/1920. The management of the group legally disputes the accuracy of the Armstock balance sheet and estimates that this company's real value is much higher than the value shown in the Armstock balance sheet.

5. Stocks

5.1 Valuation of stocks and cost of production.

Stocks have been consolidated from the individual Balance Sheets of Group Companies. The value of stocks of raw materials, supplies, spare parts, auxiliary materials, semi-finished products, finished products and other goods, are shown net of intercompany profits and at the lower of acquisition historical cost or market value as at the Balance Sheet date.

5.2. The stock valuation method has not changed from the previous year.

5.3. The value of stocks appearing in the Balance Sheet is not substantially different from market value.

6. Receivables

6.1. No loans or advances have been paid to members of the Board of Directors (Companies Act art. 43a. parag. 1id).

6.2. Receivables and liabilities denominated in foreign currencies have been translated into drachmas, at the official exchange rates ruling at the date of the Balance Sheet. The treatment of differences on exchange arising upon payment or translation of foreign currency denominated loans or credits payable and used for the acquisition of fixed assets is stated in par. 11 and 12b above. Differences on exchange arising from the valuation of foreign currency denominated receivables and liabilities, other than those stated above, have been recorded and accounted for separately for each currency, and the accounting treatment followed complies with the provisions of the Companies Act 2190/1920, art. 43, parag. 8b.

6.3. The classification of receivables and liabilities as long term (Companies Act art. 42e, parag. 6).
Receivables and liabilities which are to be received or paid after one year from the Balance Sheet date are considered long-term, while those due within a year are considered current.

7. Prepayments and Accrued Income

These are analysed as follows :

	Drs. '000
7.1. Deferred charges	
(a) Stamp duty on loan agreements	4,363
(b) Insurance premiums	19,007
(c) Other	239,751
Total	263,121
7.2. Earned income	
(a) Goods in transit	11,556
(b) Commissions	16,602
(c) Other	263,197
Total	291,355

7.3. Accrual

Sundry	141
Total	141

8. Capital and Reserves

8.1. The Total Capital and Reserves appearing in the Consolidated Balance Sheet are those of the parent company.

8.2. Differences on Consolidation

In arriving at Differences on Consolidation, which are shown in the Balance Sheet under shareholders equity, the Group Companies' cost of acquisition of shares and other participations have been set off against the corresponding consolidated companies' shareholders equity which also includes this year's results.

8.3. Minority Interests

The Minority Interest Account (appearing under Shareholders Equity) comprises of the share of third parties in the shareholders' equity of subsidiaries.

Minority interest is applicable in respect of the following Group Companies:

Name of company	Share holding %	Shareholders equity 31/12 92 Drs. '000	Minority Interest Drs. '000
AIGIS, S.A.	40.00 %	723,198	289,279
LATO, S.A.	0.03 %	313,723	94
INTERNATIONAL FLAG CEMENT CO LTD	4.50 %	(753,682)	-
			289,373

9. Provisions

Provisions at the Balance Sheet date and their accounting treatment during year are analysed as follows:

9.1. Provision for severance payments

Please refer to Auditors' Report.

9.2. Other provisions — Drs. '000

	Drs. '000
(a) Exchange difference gains arising from the translation of foreign currency denominated receivables and liabilities	59,829
(b) Credit balance of differences on exchange accumulated up to 31st December 1992 from foreign currency translation of overdue claims	3,734,358
(c) Provision for bad and doubtful debts	615,889
(d) Other provisions	37,321
Total of other provisions	4,447,397

10. Liabilities - Mortgages and Charges

10.1. There are no liabilities expiring after five years from the Balance Sheet date.

10.2. Liabilities for which mortgages and charges have been granted by the Group are analysed as follows:

Liability account	Loan balance at 31.12.92 (Drs. thous.)	Mortgage and charges value (Drs. thous.)	Type of security
- C/I/2 Bank loans-long term	2,996,901	2,965,550	preliminary agreements for mortgages
- C/II/3 Banks short-term liabilities	4,493,527	15,853,170	
Total	7,490,428	18,818,720	

11. Accruals and Deferred Income

These are analysed as follows

	Drs. thous.
11.1 Accrued expenses	
(a) Provisions for 1992 accrued loan interest	51,771
(b) Accrued expenses	868,384
(c) Rents	17,367
(d) DEH. OTE	17,455
Total	954,977

12. Memo Accounts

The memo accounts shown in the Balance Sheet are analysed as follows

	Drs. thous.
(a) Guaranties	7,865,973
(b Other	1,848,862
Total	9,715,835

13.. Turnover (Sales)

Group turnover, after eliminating intercompany balances, amounts to drs. 72,061,095 thousand.

14. The company's average number of employees and employees cost for wages and salaries, social benefits and allowances are analysed as follows:

Staff remuneration and expenses (in thousands of drachmas)

Type of employee	Number of employees	Salaries and employer's contributions	Wages and employer's contributions	Total
Clerical	2,538	15,242,984	-	15,242,984
Manual	763	-	3,099,546	3,099,546
Total	3,301	15,242,984	3,099,546	18,342,530
Social benefits and allowances	-	-	-	401,373
Total	3,301	15,242,984	3,099,546	18,743,903

15. Management and Directors emoluments and remunerations are analysed as follows :

	Drs. thous.
a) Directors' board attendance fees	56,943
b) Remuneration of members of the Board of Directors for services rendered under special work agreement or assignment	23,517
c) Remuneration of members of the Management (2 General Managers)	30,837
Total	111,297

There are no liabilities or commitments for allowances or other benefits to retired members of the Board or the Management.

16. "Extraordinary and Non-Operating Expenses" and "Extraordinary and Non-Operating Income" as well as "Prior Year Expenses" and "Prior Year Inocme" are analysed as follows:

16.1. Extraordinary and Non-Operating Expenses

	Drs. '000
(a) Exchange differences	1,440,625
(b) Legal fees - (overseas)	17,473
(c) Despatch and demurrage	31,653
(d) Other expenses	429,756
(e) Provision for bad and doubtful debts	615,899
(f) Provision for extraordinary events	8,340
(g) Extraordinary losses	1,640
Total	2,545,386

16.2. Extraordinary and Non-Operating Income

	Drs. '000
(a) Exchange differences	172,222
(b) Storage	56,346
(c) Insurance refunds	14,500
(d) Other income	455,523
(e) Commissions, dispatch, demurrage	12,861
(f) Prior year income	27,330
(g) Grants	88,509
Total	827,290

16.3. Prior Year Expenses:

(a) Adjustments to receivables and payables	37,134
(b) Other	54,530
Total	91,664

16.4. Prior year Income

(a) Refunds of custom duties	3,527
(b) Adjustments in provisions	15,118
(c) Other Income	94,690
Total	113,335

17. Other Information

17.1. The methods of valuation of the group have not changed from previous years except those referred to in the Audit Report in relation to fixed assets revaluation.

17.2. No financial statements accounting for inflation have been prepared for 1992.

17.3. Total Group turnover and Group cost of sales was reduced by the intercompany turnover. Intercompany profits or losses, incorporated in year-end inventories and fixed assets arising from purchases, sales or constructions among Group Companies was similarly eliminated.

17.4. Intercompany income from participating interests arising from the distribution of current year interim dividends, or previous year's dividends, has been eliminated.

17.5. Intercompany transactions have been also eliminated from other Profit and Loss Account items.

17.6. The non-distributed profits are shown net of income tax.

17.7. The Consolidated Group net result for the year is shown before any distribution of profits. The accounts 'Difference from consolida_tion' and "Minority Interest" have been accordingly adjusted for distribution of profits .

Lykovrissi, April 28 , 1993

CHAIRMAN OF THE BOARD OF DIRECTORS

LORENZO PANZAVOLTA
PASSPORT NUMBER 1.175043/23.07.83

FINANCIAL DIRECTOR   HEAD OF ACCOUNTS
                                  DEPARTMENT

SOT. PAPASPILIOTOPOULOS   CH. A. STASINOPOULOS
A. 829917/63   I. 019339/72

It is certified that reference to the above Notes to the Accounts (10 pages) is made in our audit report of 30th April 1993.

Athens, 30th April 1993

CERTIFIED PUBLIC ACCOUNTANTS OF GREECE

JOHN N. LAMBROU
K. 227220/77

53

ITALY

Stefano Zambon
University of Padua

1. The Historical and Economic Background of Accounting in Italy

1.1 The Evolution of Accounting Theory: An Introduction

1.1.1 The Origins of Italian Accounting

The Italian tradition of accounting presents some distinctive, but also contradictory, features. In this respect, it is certainly true that this tradition is long-lived, starting from the late Middle Ages, if not from ancient Rome. It is also true, however, that it is not very well known outside Italy, and one could probably say that its Medieval period is by and large more renowned than its recent developments in both theory and practice. In a similar vein, even though Italy is commonly held as the country where the double-entry method of keeping books was first applied, accounting theorizing has been encapsulated from the beginning of this century into a wider conceptual body, called *Economia Aziendale*, so that accounting studies in today's Italy are perceived as belonging academically to a much larger (and messier) discipline regarding organizations' economic profile.

It must be noted that the above-mentioned lack of attention in the international literature to the Italian tradition is, of course, linked to the language barrier, but also to subtle conceptual differences underlying terms and expressions that make Italian accounting theory exceedingly difficult to noninitiates. As extreme examples of this, consider that an appropriate translation in English of *Economia Aziendale* is virtually impossible (the same problem exists, though, with the Dutch *Bedrijfseconomie* and the German *Betriebswirtschaftslehre*), and that *accounting* is used here to translate the Italian word *ragioneria*, even if the former is perhaps wider in terms of concept and content.

Strictly speaking, it would not be fully correct to talk about Italian accounting until 1861, because Italy did not attain political unity until then, hitherto being divided into a number of independent city states (Florence and Tuscany, Milan and Lombardy, Venice, the Papal States, and so on). It is nevertheless reasonable to consider this geographic area from the Middle Ages onward as constituting a single nation having a cultural, linguistic, and artistic identity of its own, this being valid also for accounting.

The emergence and spread of the double-entry bookkeeping technique occurred in Italy between the thirteenth and fifteenth centuries. This method of keeping accounting records was first used, in fact, by Italian merchants (it is still not clear if for the first time in Florence, Genoa, or Venice) and for public accounting purposes (see the accounting registers of the Commune of Genoa dating from the first half of the fourteenth century). However, no books describing such a technique can be found until the end of the fifteenth century. Double entry was, in other words, a technique without systematically stated principles.

In 1494 a Franciscan friar named Luca Pacioli, a mathematician, pupil of Piero della Francesca and Leon Battista Alberti, and close friend of Leonardo da Vinci, published in Venice a book called *Summa de Arithmetica Geometria Proportioni et Proportionalita*, which contains a long section devoted to a description of the principles and functioning of double-entry bookkeeping. Although Luca Pacioli was not the inventor, he was the first systematizer and popularizer of this bookkeeping method, which he saw applied in Venice in a mercantile environment.

In fact, a quick and unclear reference to this method seems to have also been made by a thirteenth century mathematician named Leonardo Fibonacci in his work *Liber Abaci*. Another mathematician, Benedetto Cotrugli, is said to have written in 1458 a short book on double-entry technique titled *Della mercatura e del mercante perfetto*. However, this book was published in Venice (by Giovanni Giuseppi di Ragusa) only in 1573, well after Pacioli's *Tractatus*, which thus appears to be the first comprehensive printed book on the subject matter.

Pacioli described the spread of double-entry bookkeeping over Italy and Europe through the several translations and elaborations of the *Tractatus*, which were made throughout the sixteenth century and, with some improvements and extensions, the seventeenth century.

In particular, from the beginning of sixtenth century, many works were published in Italy on the double-entry technique, but many Italian authors think that no substantial advances in the concept were achieved until around the 1840s. During this period of perceived theoretical decay, double entry could hence be labeled a method in search of conceptual foundations, and the writings thereon a literature without a theory.

1.1.2 Fabio Besta and the Nineteenth Century Theoretical Approaches

From about the first half of the eighteenth century, three main schools of thought developed in Italy in a partially overlapping temporal sequence: the Lombard, the Tuscan, and the Venetian. In the Venetian school of thought are commonly included Fabio Besta, originator of modern accounting in Italy, and Gino Zappa, founder of a new discipline into which accounting has been systematically included in Italy. From this point of view, Zappa could hardly be defined as an accounting scholar according to an Anglo-Saxon perspective, being the initiator and perhaps the main representative of the new disciplinary discourse of *Economia Aziendale*.

It is interesting to note that, in parallel to the development of the mentioned schools, the first Chairs of accounting in Italy (in particular, public accounting) were established in Pavia and Padua in 1839.

Some brief notes on the authors that characterized each of these schools of thought will be given in the following sections, while a somewhat more extensive—though by necessity incomplete—description of Besta's and Zappa's ideas will be provided later in consideration of their profound impact on Italian accounting theory and, to a large extent, practice.

The Lombard School   The beginning of the Lombard School is generally fixed by Italian accounting historians in 1838 with the publication of Lodovico Crippa's work "The Science of the Accounts" (*La Scienza dei conti*), where the author, for the first time in Italy, discussed the nature and the domain of accounting, stating that the science of accounts belongs to the realm of functions linked to business activity.

The second scholar, Francesco Villa, is perceived by Italian historiography as the most important of this school. His main work, published in 1840–1841, is "Accountancy applied to private and public administrative bodies" (*La contabilità applicata alle amministrazioni private e pubbliche*), followed in 1850, by "Elements of administration and accountancy" (*Elementi di amministrazione e contabilità*). Often referred to as the father of Italian accounting, Villa develops the view of accounting as part of a wider administrative process. In fact, in his approach accounting deals with the *azienda* (the basic unit of economic activity), regarding in particular (*a*) the investigation of organizational issues, (*b*) the administration of the economic effects of operations on *azienda*'s overall wealth, and (*c*) the recording of economic transactions. He proposed a theory of accounts based partly on personalist (i.e., on accounts' personification) and partly on materialist (i.e., values) theories. He was appointed Chair of Accounting (of "Science of Governmental Accounting") in 1843 at the University of Pavia.

A further relevant author of this school is Antonio Tonzig, who published the work "Treatise on the science of state accountancy" (*Trattato della scienza di contabilità di Stato*) in 1847.

The Tuscan School The Tuscan school has been comparatively more influenced by the French tradition, especially by the theoretical approaches of the so-called five-accountists (*cinquecontisti*) put forth by the two Degranges. In this sense, the first author of this school, Francesco Marchi—in his 1867 work *I Cinquecontisti, ovvero la ingannevole teorica che viene insegnata negli Istituti Tecnici del Regno e fuori del Regno, intorno al sistema della scrittura a partita doppia, e nuovo saggio per la facile intelligenza e applicazione di quel sistema* ("The Cinquecontisti, or the deceptive theory taught in the Technical Accounting High Schools inside and outside the [Italian] Kingdom, with respect to the system of double entry records, and a new essay aimed at the easy understanding and application of that system")—aimed on the one hand to disprove the *cinquecontisti* theory and on the other hand to draw up a rational theory in order to replace it. Marchi's new theory was the "theory of all personal accounts," which is based on a strong reliance on the personification of accounts, such that to address them always and only as *persons*, no matter whether physical or legal. In this respect, Marchi is to be seen as a developer of previous approaches, especially French ones (Degranges and Vannier).

   Giuseppe Cerboni continued and developed Marchi's work by rational-
izing the latter's concepts and proposing a new method of double-entry
recording, which he called *logismografia*, a word combining the cognate
Greek terms *logismos*, computation, and *logikos*, logical reasoning (see
his 1873 book *Primi saggi di logismografia* ["First essays of
logismography"]). *Logismografia*, as a scientific proposal, reflects the
author's need to investigate the foundations of accounting using a highly
interdisciplinary approach. Accounting discipline is, in fact, divided into a
new partitioning, involving (*a*) the study of the economic administration
of the unit, (*b*) the study of the organization of the firm, (*c*) the process of
computational analysis, and (*d*) the *logismografia* as the method of representing administrative phenomena. *Logismografia* is then part of the accounting discipline broadly conceived, the aim of which is to search for
the "eternal law of administrative mechanics." This search leads Cerboni
to single out some administrative functions (e.g., start-up, executive,
conclusive functions) as procedures or laws generally applicable to all
kinds of businesses. Over the years he tried to enlarge and deepen his
approach in order to arrive at a comprehensive, self-contained theory of
the firm. The classical positivistic intonation of Cerboni's theoretical
construction is clear.

   From a narrower accounting theory point of view, this author pushed
even further the accounts' personification approach, grounding it in legal
roots, wherein the wealth of the firm itself is seen as the "general and
specific sum of rights and duties" of this economic entity. In his opinion,
all the obligations and rights in existence between the various stakeholders
of a business (i.e., proprietor, directors, agents, correspondent firms) are to
be registered in the two classes of general accounts: the owner's (rights
and duties of the owner and individual elements of the firm's wealth) and
the agency's (consignees and correspondents who are debtors or creditors
of owner's assets and liabilities). An idiosyncratic "quadruple entry"
system for keeping accounts is then proposed.

   Cerboni's most important work, "Scientific Accountancy and its relations with the administrative and social disciplines" (*La Ragioneria
Scientifica e le sue relazioni con le discipline amministrative e sociali*),
was published in 1886, and the acceptance of his theories was such that
they were applied to the entire Italian public administration during the

period (1876–1892) in which he remained in office as the State General Accountant (*Ragioniere Generale dello Stato*).

Giovanni Rossi was the third main author of the Tuscan School and supporter of the *logismografia*. In his 1882 work "The economic administrative entity" (*L'ente economico amministrativo*), adopting a unitary and wide approach to accounting (similarly to Cerboni), Rossi addressed his interest toward both the construction of a theory of social entities, which give rise to several classes of economic organizations, and the identification of common vital functions therein, which are—in this scholar's approach—the economic, legal, and administrative ones.

Strictly from the standpoint of accounting theory, Rossi remains within the paradigm of the accounts personification, according to which each element is referred to as a person or personality, of which it represents rights and/or obligations. A particular contribution of this author is his "mathematical theory of accounts," expounded in his "Treatise on the theoretical unitarity of double entry methods" (*Trattato sull'unità teoretica dei metodi di scrittura doppia*), published in 1895, which is based once again on personification theory, and which formulates the basic equation Assets – Liabilities = Equity.

The Venetian School and Fabio Besta (1845–1922)   Fabio Besta took the Chair of Accountancy at the Royal Upper School of Commerce in Ca' Foscari, Venice, in 1872, and held it until 1918. He is universally considered the initiator of modern accounting theory in Italy. He strenuously opposed Giuseppe Cerboni and his followers (the so-called *logismografi*), and proposed new theoretical ideas, which look, interestingly enough, quite similar in many respects to current Anglo-American theoretical approaches to accounting.

Besta's main work, "Accountancy" (*La Ragioneria*), was initially published in 1882–1883 in the form of lecture notes based on his teaching. Its first publication in book form dates from 1909–1910, and the final version, the one usually quoted, was published in 1922.

Besta considers "economic administration" a new discipline, whose subject of interest is the activity of the *azienda*, or the economic unit, which is not a physical or legal subject but is described as "the sum of phenomena, businesses and relationships concerning a given set of capital goods" belonging to a person, a family, or to any other subject, from the individual firm to the state. This new discipline can then be defined as "the governance of phenomena, businesses, and relationships linked with the evolution of an *azienda*'s wealth."

Economic administration consists of three distinct, logical elements, or functions: operations (*gestione*), management (*direzione*), and control (*controllo*). However, the first two functions are so different from one kind of firm to another that, in Besta's opinion, they cannot be studied in a unitary and standardized way. Thus, economic administration remains a sort of general idea, the implementation of which is made impossible by the variety and variability of the economic units (industrial, commercial, financial, and so on).

Only the third function, economic control, that is, accounting, reveals features that are similar, if not identical, in any firm. Therefore, accounting is conceived by Besta as the science of economic control and is placed at the center of his theoretical construction.

The object of this new science should be the element best expressing the firm's value: its current wealth or, perhaps better, the (*a*) value, (*b*) composition, and (*c*) change of firm's assets and equities, which are all assumed as perfectly measurable. Thus, accounting studies become the "science of the economic control" of assets and net wealth. Note that the legal concept of wealth, on which Cerboni's approach was based, is here replaced by an economic concept of wealth, which relies on the valuation of a firm's resources: wealth is nothing but a set of net assets.

Within this theoretical framework, income is a mere sum of gains and losses deriving from the management of the individual elements of the firm's wealth. The valuation nexus hence goes from wealth to income and, as a consequence, from balance sheet to profit and loss account. In fact, a major emphasis is placed on the former statement, which exposes the central phenomenon of the firm's economy (asset and liability values and composition), while the profit and loss account has only a residual, illustrative function (asset-centered accounting system).

In accordance with this framework, Besta proposes an accounting system based on two main characteristics: (*a*) recognition in the accounts of all the values pertinent to the firm, even if they are not objects of legal rights and duties; and (*b*) reporting of all the modifications (of internal and external origin) of the elements from which the wealth measurement derives, by recording in the accounts their value during all the process of their transformation from input value into output value (works-in-progress). This way, one can calculate the value of a firm's wealth at any moment in time by aggregating its individual values. Besta's atomistic-reductionist perspective emerges clearly, according to which each phenomenon can be measured singularly, the income statement being nothing but an aggregation of "partial results" (i.e., changes) associated with specific individual assets.

Characteristic (*a*) implies the "revolutionary" passage from an account personification (see Tuscan school) to a "value-based" theory of accounts (that is, an impersonal or materialist approach, as opposed to the personalist one), according to which accounts refer to objects, to determinable, measurable quantities, in order to keep track of their modifications of value.

Characteristic (*b*) involves the juxtaposition of partial costs and revenues related to a particular production or commercial process. Margins and specialized profit and loss accounts concerning "distinct" firm activities are considered theoretically sound and economically meaningful.

Consistent with the objective of wealth measurement assigned to accounting, the general valuation principle should be the "reproduction cost" (*costo di riproduzione*).

Interestingly, Besta's proposal shows some similarities with today's Anglo-Saxon accounting systems, which in fact allow conceptually both the calculation of partial cost figures via allocation and, thus, the preparation of a "progressive format" income statement.

Besta felt the positivistic climate that was widespread in Italy during the last 30 years of the nineteenth century. Accordingly, he proposed a careful study of the firm's facts, as well as the empirical method as the method of his new "science of economic control." He had many pupils, who became in their turn professors of accounting, such as Vittorio Alfieri, Vincenzo Vianello, Francesco De Gobbis, Pietro D'Alvise, Pietro Rigobon, and Carlo Ghidiglia. His youngest pupil was Gino Zappa, who was to originate what has been somewhat emphatically called in the Italian literature the *Economia Aziendale* revolution.

1.1.3 Gino Zappa and the Twentieth Century Theoretical Approaches

Gino Zappa (1879–1960) Gino Zappa achieved a major breakthrough in Italian accounting theory, even if some of his conceptual roots lie in the Tuscan and Lombard Schools and in Besta's work. Zappa's thought brought about a large body of doctrine and many of his pupils followed and developed his ideas, so that Zappa's school is still considered the dominant one in Italy in conceptual terms.

Only some aspects of Zappa's highly abstract theory can be presented here. Further, it should be borne in mind that these aspects belong to different periods of Zappa's conceptual elaboration, and thus, the present reconstruction could be regarded to some extent as inaccurate from a temporal viewpoint. In fact, Zappa's work extends over a period of nearly 40 years. The main works are the following:

1. "The firm's income. Double entry, accounts and financial statements of commercial firms" (*Il reddito d'impresa. Scritture doppie, conti e bilanci di aziende commerciali*), published in its first edition in two volumes, the first appearing in 1920 and the second in 1929, while an extensively rewritten second edition was published in 1937

2. "New trends in accounting studies" (*Tendenze nuove negli studi di ragioneria*). Inaugural lecture of the 1926–1927 academic year at the Royal Upper School of Commerce of Venice

3. "The productions in the economy of the firms" (*Le produzioni nell'economia delle imprese*), a three-volume work (consisting of more than 2,000 pages), which was published in 1957.

Central to Zappa's conceptual construction is the notion of *azienda*. According to Zappa, the economic profile of any organized human entities (where economic activities take place) could be abstracted from others and be the subject of a new discipline, the *Economia Aziendale*. An *azienda* can be a state, a family, a firm, a charity, and so on; in more general terms, it is the basic unit of production or consumption in its specific space-time context. In this respect, a possible translation of *Economia Aziendale*—but still a problematic one—might be "economics of basic economic units."

For simplicity, in the following we will consider only the category of firms (i.e., the economic units of production).

Zappa conceives of a firm as "an economic coordination in process" (1920–1929). Later he expanded this notion, defining a firm as an "economic institution apt to last through time" (1957). Within this framework, the firm (or, if you like, the *azienda*) is conceived as *decoupled* from all the constituencies having an interest in it (shareholders, workers, creditors, state, managers) and has as its main objective that of its own survival through time. Some of the main characteristics that derive from this conceptual approach are:

- A unitary conception of the firm through time and across space
- A stress on a processual view of the firm in its continuous "becoming"
- A strong systemic view of the firm, which in the evolution of Zappa's thought has been increasingly transforming itself into "a radical holistic position." As a consequence, all the activities within the firm are bound together in a specific "economic combination," within which each element (of the human, technical, economic, and financial kind, including assets and liabilities) loses its individuality to merge into the wider economic coordination.

All this implies an economic unity of all different activities taking place within a firm and, in logical sequence, also of the disciplines that study them. Therefore, *Economia Aziendale* is a unitary knowledge-discipline and consists of the joint, synthetic study of operations (*gestione*), organization (*organizzazione*), and accounting (*rilevazione*).

Within this theoretical framework, income assumes a predominant role, since it represents the result of the entire economic-systemic coordination. It is the emerging property of the system as a whole. If income is the result of the whole firm's co-ordination, then it can be produced only by transactions with external agents. In this respect, the firm is to be seen as a set of coordinated, contracted prices with external parties, from which revenues and costs (i.e., income) originate. On the contrary, internal operations (works-in-progress) could not in principle generate income, as was possible for Besta, since, once again, it is the whole system in its transactions with the environment that produces increases in wealth. Therefore, wealth is generated by, and does not generate, income, and it is not—as for Besta—a set of goods/assets but an abstract fund of values from which income flows and to which it is continuously accrued. An inversion in the valuation nexus therefore takes place (no longer wealth leads to income as for Besta, but income leads to wealth).

In narrower accounting system terms, the profit and loss account thus becomes central within Zappa's theoretical construction, which is called in this respect *sistema del reddito* (income-based accounting system), it being in fact a transaction-rooted approach to income and wealth calculation. Logically, the values of the balance sheet (except for monetary items) are costs and revenues whose underlying operations did not come to an economic end within the reporting period.

Some other accounting implications of this broad theory should be stressed:

1. If income is produced by the continuous and unitary flow of operations, then to interrupt this flow for periodic income calculation is logically, let alone economically, impossible. Thus, the implied income allocations between financial years are only acceptable for practical reasons. The same applies *a fortiori* for *interim* reporting. The only theoretically meaningful measurement of income would be the so-called firm's total life income.

   Financial statements are then a consequence of practical needs, but they are logically flawed and economically indeterminate in their results, owing to the break in the economic continuity of a firm's operations that they imply. In this sense, it is logically possible to draw up different annual reports, as long as valuations may be subjectively calculated according to different practical needs.

2. The accounting system is centered on the profit and loss account, but the latter should assume an *en tableau* and *par nature* format (so-called *a costi, ricavi e rimanenze*) in order to better express the general coordination among the firm's elements and thus the juxtaposition of all costs to all revenues.

   In fact, if the periodic income is to have a possible meaning from the economic standpoint, no partial juxtaposition between some costs and revenues is theoretically sound (e.g., operating income, pre-tax income) nor are any margin determinations (e.g., cost of sales) because of the unity of the whole firm-system. Costs should then be shown by their nature and for their total amount (e.g., salaries, materials costs, financial charges, depreciation allowances) and not be imputed to the processes in which they participated, so to obtain partial cost figures (e.g., cost of sales, administrative costs, manufacturing costs). Incidentally, in terms of Schedule 4 of the British Companies Act 1985, this suggests the use of Format 4 rather than Format 1.

Formats *en liste* and *par destination* of the profit and loss account are instead considered—in Zappa's thought—as overlooking the economic linkages of all the firm's factors and operations. In this respect, the "T format" of the profit and loss account is not primitive and double-entry-dependent, but it is the unique, consistent outcome of a radically holistic position in income determination.

3. Within this unitary conception of the firm, skepticism and circumspection surround unit and partial cost determination, since the allocation of overheads is shown to be logical and economic nonsense and, hence, theoretically impossible. As a consequence, full costs are judged misleading and, above all, cost calculation should be made outside the accounting system, which is aimed only at calculating a transaction-based type of income.

Zappa was in a sense a child of his times. He felt many influences of contemporaneous cultural, social, economic, and philosophical developments. However, he was able to amalgamate them and to apply them to an interdisciplinary object of study, the *azienda*. In particular, from a philosophical perspective, Zappa seems to have derived some of his ideas both from "critical positivism," that is, the extreme phase of the trajectory of the positivistic approach in sciences, and from the "neo-idealism," which dominated by and large the Italian cultural atmosphere from the second decade of the century onward. In the latter respect, the use of unifying concepts, the idea of continuous becoming, and the notion of the partiality of abstractions are likely in fact to be drawn from the Italian neo-idealist philosopher Benedetto Croce.

After Gino Zappa: The Second Part of the Twentieth Century Gino Zappa had many direct and indirect followers. The vast majority of today's accounting professors in Italy are, to different degrees, Zappian or at least have to come to terms with Zappa's theories or influence.

The disciples extended and specialized the fields of investigations, although maintaining in the main Zappa's "imprinting." Among the direct disciples of Zappa are Pietro Onida (the institutionalizer of Zappa's thought), Ugo Caprara (banks and financial institutions), Teodoro D'Ippolito (cost accounting), Giordano Dell'Amore (banks and international trade), Giorgio Pivato (manufacturing firms), Carlo Masini (a developer of Zappa's ideas), Lino Azzini (income dynamics and firm's intertemporal equilibria), Luigi Guatri (marketing and economic value of capital), and Tancredi Bianchi (banks and finance).

All the above-mentioned scholars have been and still are quite influential in the formation pattern of today's young Italian scholars of *Economia Aziendale*. As to accounting, though, the practical relevance of Zappa's ideas—also in respect to the legislation on company annual reports—has probably been fading away, so that at present accounting theory and accounting practice in Italy can be effectively described as two loosely coupled markets.

1.2 Accounting Regulations

In general terms, it must first be pointed out that Italy has a civil law-based legal system, of Roman derivation, and therefore statutes are expected to play a dominant role in regulating commercial subjects, including accounting and related matters. Hence, a concise history of accounting regulation in Italy becomes largely a history of the laws dealing with such a subject.

The most significant steps in the evolution of accounting regulation in Italy—before the 1991 reform—can be briefly summarized as follows.

In 1808, during the period of Napoleon's domination, the French Commercial Code of 1807 was introduced to the Italian Kingdom. Napoleon himself was the King of Italy. After Napoleon's fall in 1815 and the restoration of the previous States in Italy (namely, the Kingdom of Piedmont, the Kingdom of Lombardy and Venice—under Austrian domination—the Duchy of Parma, the Duchy of Ferrara, the Papal States, the Grand Duchy of Tuscany, the Kingdom of Etruria, and the Kingdom of the Two Sicilies), the influence of the French codification was largely preserved, since commercial laws issued by these preunitary states were heavily drawn from the Napoleonic code. Thus, even before the attainment of political unity in 1861, one could say that in Italy there was substantially uniform commercial legislation.

In particular, there were requirements for state authorization to set up a public limited company (*società anonima*), and public surveillance over this category of companies. As to accounting, every merchant was to keep a journal that had been previously numbered, signed, and stamped by commercial courts or the mayor, and to draw up each year a stock-taking to be transcribed in an *ad hoc* book. Accounting books, if regularly kept, could be used as proof in litigations between merchants. The obligation of drawing up financial statements emerged implicitly by the requirement of distributing dividends only from actually realized profits. No rules were given concerning accounting general principles, formats, and year-end valuations, however.

These rules were substantially confirmed by the Italian Commercial Code of 1865, which was promulgated after unification.

It is noteworthy that the mandatory filing of financial statements with the commercial courts and the publication of excerpts from these statements have been required by the *società anonime* since 1864–1865.

The second Italian Commercial Code of 1882 changed some of the previous regulations, abolishing the need for public authorization to set up a *società anonima*, and stating in Article 176 the general principle that the accounts should give with straightforwardness and truth (*evidenza e verità*) the financial situation and the performance results of a company. No detailed rules on formats and valuations were given, though. A legal reserve had to be provided for by transferring to it at least 5% of the net profit for the year, until this reserve reached at least 20% of the share capital (Article 182). As in the 1865 code, dividends could be paid out only from actually realized profits. The 1882 code confirmed the cancellation of public surveillance on *società anonima* (it had already been reduced in scope in 1869). In its place was introduced (by Article 183) a new body in the governance structure of this kind of company, that is, the so-called *Collegio sindacale* composed of *sindaci* (see Section 2.2), to be elected by the members of the company, and whose principal duty was the surveillance of the directors' actions and of respect for the law and the articles of association. Note that since 1882 the concept of a company in Italy automatically embraces the existence of the *collegio sindacale*, which is thus an essential component part thereof.

The 1942 Civil Code (C.C.) took the place of the previous Commercial Code. It regulated company accounts in a more comprehensive way, adding another general principle—with a somewhat similar function of the "true and fair view" formula in the United Kingdom—to that of *evidenza e verità* (which was maintained in this 1942 Civil Code from the 1882 Commercial Code but referred to individual firms), as well as presentation and valuation requirements. According to the then new basic principle of Article 2423 C.C., the balance sheet and the profit and loss account should present with clearness and precision (*chiarezza e precisione*) a company's financial position and results. The formula was intended as a guideline in relation to which specific rules were to be interpreted. It was generally accepted that both *clearness* and *straightforwardness* referred to form and content, while both *precision* and *truth* referred to valuations.

The next article (2424 C.C.) related to "clearness," since it dealt with the balance sheet *minimum* content, indicating the assets and liabilities required to be included therein. The account format was that implicitly indicated by the law for the balance sheet. The 1942 Civil Code did not mention any compulsory contents of the income statement, so that companies were allowed to present quite condensed and unsatisfactory information regarding their performance results.

Valuation rules were given in Article 2425: the historical cost principle was the fundamental one and marked the maximum amount at which fixed assets, both tangible and intangible, were to be stated; inventory was to be valued at the lower of cost and net realizable value. The historical cost basis was usually required in accounting for associates, even when the investor had a substantial interest. No rules were set for liability valuation.

Departures from legal rules were permitted by the last section of Article

2425 Civil Code, only for special reasons (*speciali ragioni*) relating to the company or to a specific asset. Much debate took place on the content and limits of this overriding principle: the simplicity of its form contrasted with its problematic application on practical grounds (see Section 3.1).

Several revaluation laws, permitting the restatement of assets at a higher value than their historical cost, were issued in a nonsystematic way after the 1942 promulgation of the Civil Code. These laws were different in aims, scope, and revaluation mechanisms. Some examples are law-decree no. 436/1946; law-decree no. 49/1948; law no. 74/1952; law no. 576/1975 (the so-called Visentini law); law no. 72/1983 (the so-called Visentini-*bis* law); law no. 408/1990; and law no. 413/1991. The latter two revaluation laws will be discussed in Section 4.1.

A further step in the evolution of financial statement regulation in Italy came with law no. 216 of 1974. This so-called mini-reform of the public limited companies stemmed from both the academic and jurisprudential need to establish that the purpose of financial statements is to give objective information, since this purpose had been severely compromised during the 1960s by secrecy and creative approaches. Hence, the *format* and *minimum* content of the income statement were legally defined and the directors' report with its minimal information to be disclosed introduced. Moreover, a 6-monthly report was required to be produced by listed companies. Some important gaps in Italian accounting legislation, especially related to "clearness" requirements, were thus eventually filled in.

With the same law the National Commission for Companies and the Stock Exchange (*Commissione Nazionale per le Società e la Borsa*, or CONSOB) was set up to monitor quoted companies, and during the ensuing years its power and scope increased (law no. 281 of 1985).

The 1974 law also included the fundamental innovation of the introduction of compulsory external audit for listed companies, which was afterwards regulated in a detailed way by presidential decree no. 136 of 1975. This change may be explained to a great extent by the general unreliability of internal audit performed by *sindaci*, which had been introduced by the 1885 Commercial Code (a *sindaco* is a sort of company institutional auditor, peculiar to the Italian company law tradition—see Section 2.2). This new obligation was welcomed as a significant step toward increasing the legally required information content of the company accounts. Independent auditors had to expressly verify whether the company's financial statements complied with *both* legal rules and *corretti principi contabili* (correct accounting principles—Article 4, section 2, decree no. 136). Confirmation of the equivocal relationship between legal regulation and accounting standards is found in the official "Guidelines for the Auditors' Report" issued by CONSOB in 1983 and updated in 1987. These guidelines do not even tackle the problem. The ambiguity of the requirement for the compulsory audit report to verify compliance with both the legal rules and the correct accounting principles was thus perpetuated at least until 1991 (for more depth see Section 2.3).

Mandatory audit was subsequently extended to other categories of firms, such as newspaper publishers, insurers, and state-owned companies, among a few others.

Progress in ruling consolidated accounts has been much slower. Consolidated financial statements have not, in fact, been traditionally prepared in Italy. Despite the issue in 1983 of standard no. 8, hardly any Italian groups prepared these accounts, apart from the few categories of firms for which consolidated reporting was compulsory. Until 1991, in fact, no *general* legal requirement for group accounts was established in law. Before the Directive's implementation, group accounts were legally required only for certain categories of firms (newspaper publishers, state-owned groups, and so on). Further, the stock exchange regulatory body (CONSOB) could command consolidated reporting for listed companies whenever it was deemed necessary. CONSOB has been using this power since 1983, but in absolute terms only a few Italian groups could possibly be required to file consolidated statements because of the small proportion of the Italian industrial system represented by listed companies. Conversely, some large groups present consolidated accounts on a voluntary basis, especially for supporting bank lending decisions.

Tax legislation strongly affects financial reporting in Italy. Since the 1970s tax distortions of commercial accounts have been common in order to obtain fiscal benefits. At the same time, tax rules, being comparatively more exhaustive, were regarded *de facto* as providing the detail to superimpose on the very general 1942 commercial legislation. This view, which is traditionally referred to as the "single track approach" (*teoria del binario unico*), argues in favor of the tax influence on the annual accounts, so that a sort of dependence of the commercial rules on the fiscal ones occurs (reverse dependence). Accordingly, taxation in Italy affects income measurement in the profit and loss account, with explanations given (but not necessarily until 1993) in the notes. This situation of reverse dependence found a legislative basis from 1973 with the income tax reform (called Visentini reform from the surname of the then Minister of Finance), which linked the tax burden to accounting numbers in a similar way to Germany. This link was confirmed in 1986 by the Consolidated Act on Income Tax (*Testo Unico sulle Imposte sui Redditi*—Presidential Decree no. 917/1986), which includes also a section on Corporation Tax (see Section 3.1).

In recent years accounting regulation in Italy has been undergoing a period of major change. In a short time, relevant aspects of company financial reporting and professional life have been profoundly reshaped, and the process is still going on. The rapidity and magnitude of such a revolution are quite impressive, especially when compared with the relatively unchanging situation that characterized accounting regulation in Italy during the past 15–20 years.

The main contents of this—at least formal—discontinuity concern the formats and principles of the annual accounts of companies and financial institutions (including banks), the generalized introduction of consolidated financial statements, the promulgation of two revaluation laws, and the relationship between commercial and fiscal rules. The accounting profession, too, has been affected by these regulatory changes with regard to access, as well as the qualification of companies' institutional auditors (*sindaci*). Clearly, most of these innovations derive from the close implementation of many of the EU Directives concerning company law (in particular, the Third, Fourth, Sixth, Seventh, Eighth, and Eleventh Directives, and Act no. 1986/633, financial reporting for banks). However, other innovations find their origin in the autonomous trajectory of Italian accounting. (For a comprehensive overview of the recent regulatory innovations in Italian accounting and profession see Figure 1).

The wide scope and importance of the above-mentioned changes seem largely self-evident. In 2–3 years virtually all previous regulation dealing with the technical and professional side of accounting has been swept away and replaced. The detailed contents of this revolution will be described in the following sections.

Figure 1   *Changes in the Italian Regulatory Framework*
of Accounting

Decree no. 127/1991	Implementation of the 4th and 7th EC Directives
Decree no. 87/1992	Implementation of the 11th EC Directive and of EC Act no. 1986/633 (financial reporting for banks and financial institutions)
Decrees no. 408/1990 and no. 413/1991	Revaluation laws
Decrees no. 183/1992 and no. 206/1992	Access to the accounting profession
Decree no. 115/1992	Implementation of EC Act no. 1989/48 (mutual recognition of European professional qualifications)
Decree no. 88/1992	Implementation of the 8th EC Directive: qualification of "institutional" auditors (*sindaci*) and new Register (*Registro*) of the *revisori contabili*
Law-Decree no. 416/1994 (converted into law no. 503/1994)	Amendments to the income statement format and the accounts notes (as in Decree no. 127/1991), and to the income tax law where it deals with accounting valuations

---

1.3 The Accounting Profession

The accounting profession has a long history in Italy. In fact, the first accounting professionals were probably found in Venice at the beginning of the sixteenth century (the *rasonati*, the accountants), with the function of auditing the Doge's expenses. Later in that century (December 11, 1581), the "Council of Ten" issued a decree setting up the College of Auditors (*Collegio dei Rasonati*), whose members had the function of checking and control over the accounts of Venetian state bodies. In order to gain access to this *collegio,* some family and personal requirements, as well as an apprenticeship period of 6 years, were needed (the criteria were laid down by a decree dated June 29, 1596 issued by the Senate), and a professional examination had to be passed. These examinations took place until the fall of the Venice Republic in 1797.

In Milan a College of Accountants (*Collegio dei Ragionieri*) was set up in 1742 by decree of Maria Teresa of Austria. A list of agreed fees (*tariffa*) was also sanctioned.

The first Italian statute regarding the profession of accountant (*ragioniere*) was the regulation published on November 3, 1805 by Prince Eugenio, Viceroy of Italy, in the name of Napoleon I. This regulation set the requirements of sitting for the professional examination and the procedure thereof, the rights and duties of the *Ragioniere*, and the obligation by the local Prefectures to publish a list of the *Ragionieri* who obtained the professional qualification to practice in all the territory of the Italian Kingdom.

The conservative Papal States also recognized the profession of public accountant with the ordinance issued on July 6, 1836 by the Vatican *Congregazione degli Studi* and approved by Pope Gregory XVI.

The *ragionieri* grouped spontaneously in territorially determined bodies called *Collegi.* However, in order to study and analyze the various conceptual and technical problems facing the accounting profession, some academies were also founded. In particular, it is worth mentioning the *Accademia dei Logismofili* (Academy of Logismophiles) set up in Bologna in 1813, and the *Accademia dei Ragionieri* (Academy of Accountants) established in 1868 in Milan. The former, after several transformations, became in the second half of this century the *Accademia Italiana di Economia Aziendale* (Italian Academy of *Economia Aziendale*, AIDEA), which gathers all the Italian university (full) professors dealing with such a subject area.

The first Italian law after unification concerning the accounting profession was issued on June 25, 1865 and was closely followed by a number of decrees regarding access, professional fees, and the required pattern of studies.

In 1879 the first National Congress of Italian Accountants was held in Rome, followed by a series of biennial Congresses. Around the same period many professional journals were launched—especially by members of the Tuscan School—such as *Rivista di Contabilità* (1874), *Il Logismografo* (1877), *Il Ragioniere* (1879), *Il Monitore dei Ragionieri* (1880), *Rivista di Amministrazione e Contabilità* (1881). It is clear that between 1870 and 1890 Italian accountants, together with accounting scholars, were in the process of institutionalizing their competences and knowledge, building on an autonomous and distinct professional discourse.

Law no. 327 of July 15, 1906 set up legally (or legally recognized) the *Collegi dei Ragionieri* on a national scale and established a roll to be held by each *collegio*. New requirements for membership were laid down, and the right to act as public accountants was exclusively attributed to *Ragionieri* belonging to the *collegi*.

Until 1929, the accounting profession in Italy was staffed exclusively by the *ragionieri*. In that year, law no. 588 set up a second accounting profession, the *Dottori Commercialisti*, with duties similar to those of *Ragionieri* but with a separate roll. This development was a result of the creation of the Upper Institutes of Economic and Commercial Sciences (*Istituti Superiori di Scienze Economiche e Commerciali*), which subsequently became Faculties of Economics and Commerce, where subjects such as accountancy (general and applied), business management, and mercantile, banking, and industrial procedures acquired the status of university subjects, whereas previously they had been taught only in the technical high schools for accountants *(Istituti Tecnici per Ragionieri*).

In 1953 two different laws, still enforced, put some order in the accounting profession, definitively recognizing two bodies, the *Dottori Commercialisti* and the *Ragionieri*, with their own autonomous roll, and organized on a territorial scale respectively in *Ordini* and *Collegi*.

In conclusion, the two professional figures dealing with accounting in today's Italy seem to be the result of a historical (and not fully governed) legal and institutional stratification, rather than the outcome of a deliberate governmental plan of attributing different competences and responsibilities to distinct branches of the accounting profession.

1.4 The General Economic Context and the "Accounting Value System"

At a general level, Italian accounting practice is internationally regarded as civil law-based, tax-driven, and conservative-oriented. In addition, textbooks indicate that in Italy listed companies represent a class apart since they must satisfy supplementary accounting rules and requirements (such as a 6-monthly accounting report and the drawing up of consolidated financial statements); that the tradition of the *Economia Aziendale* has exerted a significant influence on accounting practice; and that today a major impetus to change has an exogenous origin (the European Union). All these features have some validity, but they must be located in the context of the Italian economic and social environment; otherwise they risk being simplistic and misleading to a certain extent. In order to approach Italian accounting, further elements must be considered, which are context-specific and sometimes contradictory in character.

In this respect, it should be remembered that the Italian industrial system is, comparatively speaking, small and medium sized (only seven Italian companies are in the Fortune 500). Generally their ownership system is of a closed nature. The two factors are of course interrelated.

On the former factor, it is enough to point out that the largest Italian group in 1992 was the I.R.I., which is state-owned and in the process of being partially privatized, with a turnover of nearly 76,000 billion Italian lire (around $50 billion), followed by FIAT (55,000 billion lire, privately owned) and E.N.I. (50,000 billion lire, state owned). Only four other groups had in 1992 a turnover exceeding 5,000 billion lire (around $3.5 billion). In other words, Italian capitalism is poor, made up of economic dwarfs.

In addition, none of the major privately owned groups have a public company structure since they belong to well-known families. Thus, what we face in Italy is a family capitalism that is not open to share ownership and to external takeovers. In this closed ownership system, an entrepreneur usually makes the most important decisions. This class of firms is generally recognized as the most innovative driving force of Italian industrial capitalism.

In terms of business finance, self-financing and credit financing are traditionally the main sources of funds for Italian firms. As a specific feature of the Italian system, self-financing is carried out largely through the unfunded provisions for the employee severance indemnity. Fiscal advantages, too, are attached to the choice of keeping a low debt/equity ratio, in that debt financing—unlike equity financing—reduces the tax basis for company net worth tax and, via interest expense, also for income taxes.

In correlation with this business finance situation, a relatively small number of companies is traded on the Milan Stock Exchange (around 220), and the largest eight groups capitalize on average more than 80% of the value of the whole listed securities. There is also a junior market in Milan (*Mercato Ristretto*), and nine minor provincial stock exchanges are scattered throughout Italy (e.g., Rome, Turin, Venice, Trieste). Today, as in many other international financial markets, negotiations take place on a continuous basis through computer network devices. As mentioned previously, in 1974 a stock exchange supervisory body, the CONSOB, was set up. As a self-regulating and autonomous body, the CONSOB is today authorized to control the functioning of Italian stock exchanges, to identify the type and content of information to be publicly provided by listed companies (e.g., consolidated financial statements), and to check on the fulfilment of stated requirements. Nevertheless, the role played by the *Borsa* in the Italian economic system is not particularly relevant, and its trends are not always good indicators of the true economic situation.

From this specific capitalistic structure and business financing situation, a series of consequences derive with implications for accounting.

If in this economic context, the firm size tends to be bounded, the number of company members is in principle limited, and entrepreneurs frequently run their own firm, then the external demand for detailed and reliable accounting information is expected to be relatively low; this demand will derive mainly from tax authorities and banks, and often exclusively from the former, since for bank lending decisions either financial statements are not seriously considered or, frequently, ad hoc accounts are prepared. Multiple accounting statements are hence likely to be quite customary in practice.

The demand for independent auditing is also reduced. None or very few shareholders are really outside the company, waiting for financial information thereon. They generally have direct access to the data they need. Accordingly, the general level of disclosure is comparatively quite low and complies essentially only with legal requirements (which increased dramatically after decree no. 127/1991 came into force). Conservatism and information secrecy are recognized as important values in business activity.

As mentioned earlier, Italian accounting regulation has largely been influenced by fiscal rules, due also to the lack of detail, so far, of the Civil Code on the subject. Therefore, as one would expect, the objective of keeping taxable income at the lowest possible amount is, by and large, the leading one for accounting professionals and for the financial directors of companies, especially in the case of small and medium-sized enterprises.

In more general socioeconomic terms, accounting—at least in its official dimension—seems to be perceived by Italian entrepreneurs more as an unavoidable evil than as a potentially fruitful tool for governing a firm's operations. Consistently, from a socioeconomic point of view, accounting practice appears to be perceived in Italy as a sort of Cinderella, being considered a craft that is almost exclusively related to tax purposes and not useful for offering a meaningful view of the economic and financial situation of a firm. Therefore, one might also say that in Italy the ritual dimension of the annual accounts is stressed in comparison with their economic function. In this respect, there is an apparent contradiction between the large spread and volume of accounting practice and the skepticism toward it and the economic significance of its results. It should be borne in mind that Italy has the second largest number of accounting professionals in Europe after the United Kingdom, currently more than 65,000 (without implying, of course, any value judgment on the quality of Italian accounting). In addition, the huge proportion of small and medium-sized firms within the Italian industrial system obviously means that many accounting actions must be performed daily. In contrast, the low confidence in "official" accounting in Italy may be witnessed by the well-known frequent existence of multiple accounts, the substantial disregard for accounting data on the part of banks and even entrepreneurs, and the common inattention paid to financial statements in bankruptcy judgments.

On the whole, then, Italy cannot be considered a valid example of the relationship (if any) between the degree of sophistication and the diffusion of accounting techniques, and a country's socioeconomic development, given that Italy went through two economic booms (in the 1960s and 1980s) without financial information being regarded as significant. Curiously enough (without suggesting any acceptance of the following statement), the 1991 FEE "Survey on Published Accounts" pointed out that Italian annual accounts were not inferior as to quality and level of disclosure than those of other EU member states that had already implemented the Fourth and Seventh Directives.

On the other hand, it is also notable that management accounting techniques appear not to be systematically used in many firms, this probably being related to the scarce appreciation that accounting data have from Italian entrepreneurs and the often practical (rather than university-based) education of the latter.

In the near future the currently ongoing privatization process of large state-owned firms (such as the National Institute of Insurances, Italian Commercial Bank, Italian Credit Bank, Stet, Enel), with the expected vast increase in the number of shareholders and in the demand for accounting information, may bring about a change as to the socioeconomic role and perception of accounting in Italy, even if it is too early to formulate any judgment on any economic and accounting consequences of this process.

2. The Accounting Profession, Audit, and Standards in Today's Italy

2.1 The Accounting Profession

2.1.1 Introductory Aspects

Accounting professionals are an increasingly important phenomenon in Italy from a socioeconomic point of view. Their total number is rapidly increasing, and is now nearly 70,000, around 60% of whom are in practice. Those not in practice usually preserve their professional qualification. The average age is less than 45 years.

The growing importance and social prestige of accounting practitioners are linked to the incredible difficulty of the tax legislation, and to their fundamental role in helping the huge number of small to medium-sized firms carry out their accounting actions and tax obligations. It is customary in Italy for such a firm to have an external professional to look after these aspects, and, in turn, small to medium-sized enterprises are the primary source of business for Italian accountants.

The Italian accounting profession shows a certain number of distinctive features relating to its institutional setting, operational organization, and legal roles.

A clear characteristic of the accounting profession in Italy is that, as mentioned earlier, it is organized into two, approximately equal-sized, bodies, the *Dottori Commercialisti* (the more prestigious one) and the *Ragionieri*. This division is mostly historical (see Section 1.3) rather than deriving from a functional differentiation of professional competences. In fact, the difference between these two categories does not relate to their legally permitted roles, which are quite wide and *de facto* overlapping (accounting, tax and commercial law counseling, *sindaco* activity, management consultancy, judicial expert, bankruptcy trustee, etc.). Moreover, all accounting practitioners have the right to refuse to testify before civil and penal courts (so-called professional secrecy recognized by law no. 507 of 1987). The two bodies are also together in the struggle against the so-called abusivism, that is, the delivery of accounting services by people who do not have the legally required professional qualification. This problem seems to be quite serious, and may damage the image of the accounting profession.

The main *de facto* differentiation between the two accountancy bodies relies today upon the dissimilar paths to qualification (see Figure 2 on page 408). Once the prescribed admission conditions to the bodies have been met, however, the two categories of accountants follow a similar pattern: they may apply for official registration with the respective body and thereafter begin to practice as independent professionals.

Further distinctions between *Dottori Commercialisti* and *Ragionieri* can be summarized as follows. Each body has a specific membership roll (*albo*), which is independently run under the supervision of the Ministry of Justice, the latter exerting control of a general nature over the two professional bodies. Moreover, these are organized in distinct local units called *Ordini* for the *Dottori Commercialisti* and *Collegi* for the *Ragionieri*.

Each body has legally determined fee ranges, chargeable to clients for any of the different roles that it is expected to play (e.g., Presidential decree no. 309/1987 regarding *Dottori Commercialisti*, and Presidential decree no. 348/1987 regarding *Ragionieri*). The *Dottori Commercialisti*'s fees are *in practice* expected to be slightly higher than those of *Ragionieri*'s because more education is required of the former, even if there are not significant differences in the legal fee rates laid down by the two presidential decrees. The application of these fees is looked upon carefully, with particular reference to the stated minimum levels in order to avoid dumping policies among professionals. The two sets of fees are put together, approved, and from time to time, updated by the Ministry of Justice (e.g., Presidential decree no. 645/1994, carrying the revision of the *Dottori Commercialisti* fees, was published in the Official Gazette on November 23, 1994, some 7 years after the last one, while revision of the *Ragionieri*'s is expected at the beginning of 1995).

Another feature of Italian accounting practice is that it is operationally organized in a "studio," that is, the professional's firm for which he or she has single personal liability. Italian studios are in general quite small, and in this respect quite different from Anglo-Saxon accounting firms. One of the reasons for this is that an old law has always hampered professionals in setting up companies or partnerships (in whatever form) aimed at exercising professional activity (Article 2, law no. 1815 of 1939), the only exception allowed being audit (law no. 1966 of 1939). In particular, a further decree states that a legally compulsory audit must be performed through a company or a partnership (Presidential decree no. 136/1975). The rationale for law no. 1815/1939 is that professional performance must remain individually delivered to any client (Article 2232 Civil Code). Clearly, legislators reasoned that the individual nature of the performance would be lost if this were to be provided from within a company or a parthership. As a consequence, Italian accounting professionals are not permitted to exert their activity under any of the latter legal forms and can set up only an "associated studio" between them, that is, a contractual arrangement, if it (*a*) involves at least two formally independent studios, (*b*) does not have external relevance and visibility, (*c*) does not impair the personal characterization of the professional performance, and (*d*) concerns the sharing of profits and expenses and of the cost of fixed assets. Hence, accounting professionals in Italy usually must rely on their individual work (with only some trainees and formally external collaborators) in order to make their own studio grow.

A further distinguishing element of the Italian accounting profession is that there is quite a sharp division between commercial accounting and related legal services such as tax requirements and declarations—which are provided by *Dottori Commercialisti* and *Ragionieri*—and external auditing—which is provided by audit firms. This dichotomy was imposed by the law dealing with legal audit, since any professionals entering an audit firm registered in a special roll with the CONSOB were not allowed to exert professional activity of their own (penultimate section, Article 8, Presidential decree no. 136 of 1975). This rule, though, is now changing (see below). In turn, a *Dottore Commercialista* or a *Ragioniere* cannot perform a legally compulsory audit on his or her own. This work must be carried out by an audit firm, the majority of whose directors and members must be a professional accountant (from 1992 *Revisore contabile*, see below) (Article 8, decree no. 136/1975).

Thus, Italian accountants customarily choose between an individual career in a studio and a career in an audit firm generally registered with the CONSOB, the two paths being exclusive on practical and legal grounds. *Dottore commercialista* and *Ragioniere* are not therefore synonymous with auditors, as in many other countries, but they are accountants carrying out roles other than legal audit. They can perform the so-called voluntary audit, however (see below).

In recent years, the Italian accounting profession has experienced a period of intense change. This is not only because practitioners must cope with the recent innovations in the rules referring to annual accounts (see below), but also because of the current restructuring of some fundamental aspects of the profession. Such modifications deal with (*a*) access to this career, (*b*) the implementation of EU Directive no. 89/48 on the mutual recognition of professional qualifications and the related 3-year academic degrees, and (*c*) the implementation of the EU Eighth Directive regarding the qualification of statutory auditors.

The above-mentioned difference in the paths to qualification as *Dottore commercialista* and *Ragioniere* applied until 1992. Two recent laws, which are still on their way to implementation, made the two paths more similar, while preserving some differences between them (see Figure 2).

At any rate, one may say that in either case there has been an upgrading of the qualification in terms both of the number of years of apprenticeship, and (for the *Ragionieri*) of the minimum educational level. It is fair to say, however, that before the introduction of the new rules the apprenticeship period was *de facto* already in place for the *Dottori Commercialisti* and frequently longer than the then required 2 years for the *Ragionieri*. In the context of the new legal framework, it is likely that the number of *Ragionieri* will progressively decrease in relative terms (they are already marginally the minority of accounting professionals), since the difference between access to their membership roll and to that of *Dottori Commercialisti* (the more prestigious body) has been significantly reduced.

A particular modification of access to the accounting profession comes from the recent implementation in Italy of EU Directive no. 89/48 dealing with the mutual recognition of European professional qualifications (legislative decree no. 115 dated January 27, 1992). According to this decree, in order to get recognition of his or her qualification by Italian law, an EU professional needs to pass an *ad hoc* state exam (Article 6). The transfer exam is periodically run under the supervision of the Ministry of Justice (office no. VII). Even though it does not seem at present that there will be a massive influx of EU accountants to Italy in the near future, it is clear that in the long term the new legal framework might bring about some changes in the composition and qualification of the professionals operating in this country.

The third recent legislative innovation concerning the Italian accounting profession, the one regarding the qualification of statutory auditors, will be illustrated below in the context of the analysis of audit activity (Section 2.2.1).

In the following the most relevant features of the two accountancy bodies will be more closely examined.

2.1.2 Dottori Commercialisti

The first step toward entering the *Dottori Commercialisti* is to graduate in economics and commerce (in general this happens when one is between 23 and 25 years old) with a Faculty of Economics from either a public or a private state-recognized university, after having completed 5 years of

---

Figure 2 *Access to the Accounting Profession in Italy*

Dottori Commercialisti

Before 1995	*Laurea* degree in economics and commerce (4 years) + state exam
From 1995 (Law no. 206/1992)	*Laurea* degree in economics and commerce (4 years) + apprenticeship (3 years) + state exam

Ragionieri

Before 1994	Secondary school degree in accounting (5 years) + apprenticeship (2 years) + qualification exam
From 1994 (Law no. 183/1992)	Secondary school degree in accounting (5 years) + "short" university degree (3 years) + apprenticeship (3 years)* + state exam

---

*For those who hold a full university degree (*laurea*) in economics and commerce or in law, the apprenticeship period is reduced to 2 years.

primary school, 3 years of junior high school, 5 years of any (Italian) high school, and a 4-year university course covering a minimum of 25 subjects including accounting, banking, economics, law (public, civil, commercial, and tax), statistics, and foreign languages. Graduation from the university is attained after an oral presentation, before a Board of Professors formally appointed by the Rector of the University, of a thesis regarding a specific subject included in the candidate's study program.

Until 1994, those who graduated as Doctors in Economics and Commerce could, if they so wished, without any practical apprenticeship, sit for a professional state examination, consisting of written and oral parts, organized twice a year by any university where a Faculty of Economics and Commerce existed. Having successfully passed both parts, such an applicant could apply for membership in the *Ordine dei Dottori Commercialisti*. Now, an apprenticeship period of 2 years after graduation is required before one may sit for the professional exam (see Figure 2).

The body has around 36,000 members at present (it had 25,000 in 1990) and is generally recognized as the most prestigious one. The following offers a brief look at the way the *Dottori Commercialisti* are institutionally structured and at their detailed legal roles.

Ordine dei Dottori Commercialisti The *Ordine dei Dottori Commercialisti* is a recognized legal body that gathers all the *Dottori Commercialisti* of a geographic area and supervises, in a general sense, their professional activity. At present, some 119 *Ordini* are established, virtually in any town where a Tribunal is in existence.

The most important activities of the *Ordine*, apart from that mentioned earlier of keeping the pofessional roll, are the following:

1. Accept new applicants after having ascertained the existence of the required prerequisites
2. Supervise the respect of the professional law by members
3. Report on infringements by nonqualified people practicing
4. Resolve disputes that might arise in connection with fees charged by members to their clients
5. Select members for appointment to the body's National Council
6. Deliver disciplinary sanctions to members

As to the first activity, in order to register with the *Ordine*, an applicant—in addition to having passed the examination referred to above—must fulfil certain requirements, such as having (*a*) Italian citizenship (now one may hold citizenship in one of the European Union member states, see decree no. 115/1992), (*b*) a *laurea* degree in Economics and Commerce from an Italian University, and now (*c*) a minimum 3 years' practical experience in a *Dottore Commercialista*'s studio.

Each *Ordine* maintains two different registers of memberships: (*a*) the roll (*albo*) of practicing *Dottori Commercialisti*; and (*b*) the roll of (temporary) nonpracticing members. Only those in the first *albo* are authorized to pratice as public accountants. There is no particular requirement for transferring from one register to the other.

The professional roles that each *Dottore Commercialista* can perform are set by law no. 1067/1953, which recognized a general competence in commercial, economic, financial, tax, and accounting matters. In particular, the following activities are included among such competencies:

- The administration and liquidation of business concerns, estates and single assets
- Appraisals, surveys, and advice thereon
- Auditing of account books of enterprises and any other inquiry into the reliability of financial statements, accounts, entries, and any other accounting document
- Settlement and liquidation of losses
- Institutional audit as *sindaco* of limited liability companies
- Assistance to judges with respect to the evaluation of assets, liabilities, and so on, in connection with judicial cases
- Bankruptcy trustee

One may observe that the *Dottori Commercialisti* can perform audit activity on their own or with a firm, but—as will be pointed out below—audit must be of only a voluntary type, that is, an audit that is voluntarily undertaken by a company (without being legally obligated to do so).

National Council of *Dottori Commercialisti*   Based in Rome, under the auspices of the Ministry of Justice, the National Council of *Dottori Commercialisti* is the highest authority governing the *Dottori Commercialisti* accountancy body. It is composed of eleven members (consiglieri nazionali), who are elected by the local Ordini and remain in office for a period of 3 years; they may be re-elected subsequently. The activity of consigliere nazionale is not a full-time job, to the extent that it requires generally a one-day trip to Rome once a month to attend the Council meetings.

In the 1970s this National Council promoted the setting up of committees for the preparation of Italian accounting and auditing standards. As mentioned earlier, in 1982 the second accountancy body also joined these committees.

As far as professional ethics is concerned, in 1987 the National Council issued a booklet called "Rules of professional deontology," and in 1988 a second booklet titled "Rules of conduct of *sindaci*" (i.e., company institutional auditors). Under the 1987 rule any form of advertisement for a studio is forbidden to *Dottori Commercialisti*. Moreover, it is stated that a *Dottore Commercialista* may not (*a*) carry out industrial or commercial activities; (*b*) act as a managing director of business enterprises; (*c*) serve simultaneously as consultant and *sindaco*; (*d*) reveal the affairs of his or her clients. It must be said that not all these ethical rules are consistently followed in practice.

Further rules of professional conduct are laid down in the Civil Code—in connection with the independence of *sindaci*—and in the decree governing the legally compulsory audit (this second set of ethical rules apply also to *Ragionieri*).

2.1.3 Accountants and Commercial Experts (Ragionieri e Periti Commerciali)

A school diploma as *Ragioniere e Perito Commerciale* is attained (generally when one is 19 years old) after having attended a business high school and passed a state-run examination. A student's career at that point will have included 5 years of primary school, followed by 3 years of junior high school and 5 years of the above-mentioned high school. The subjects studied in high school will have included accounting, mathematics, and business and company law, but not auditing. Until 1994, after the Diploma, in order to obtain the professional qualification of *Ragioniere* (that of *Perito commerciale* is no longer in use), a candidate had to go through two years of apprenticeship and pass a state examination organized by the local *collegi*. Now he or she must have at least a so-called short university degree (3 years of study) and carry out generally a 3-year apprenticeship before sitting for the professional state examination (see Figure 2).

This body has around 33,000 members at present (it had 25,000 in 1990). The following section offers a brief look at the way in which Ragionieri are institutionally structured.

Collegio dei Ragionieri e dei Periti Commerciali   In a similar way to the *Ordine* for the *Dottori Commercialisti*, the *collegio* is a recognized legal body that gathers all the *Ragionieri* and *Periti commerciali* of a geographic area and supervises in a broad sense their professional activity. It is responsible for keeping and updating the professional roll. At present, 109 *collegi* are established.

The activities of a *collegio* are much the same as those of an *Ordine*. An interesting difference is that each *collegio* runs its own professional qualification examination, which for the *Dottori Commercialisti* is organized by the Faculty of Economics and Commerce. A new applicant must fulfill the same required prerequisites as the *Dottori Commercialisti*.

The professional roles that each *Ragioniere* can perform are set by law no. 1068/1953 and are *de facto* overlapping with those of *Dottori Commercialisti*.

National Council of Accountants and Commercial Experts (*Consiglio Nazionale dei Ragionieri e dei Periti Commerciali*)   The National Council of Accountants and Commercial Experts is the highest authority of the *Ragionieri e Periti Commerciali* accountancy body and is based in Rome, officially under the auspices of the Ministry of Justice. It is composed of eleven members (*consiglieri nazionali*), who are elected by the *collegi* and remain in office for 3 years; they may be re-elected subsequently.

With regard to ethics, in 1983 a "Code of deontological conduct" was issued by the National Council. In essence, these rules are quite similar to those applying to *Dottori Commercialisti*.

2.2   Auditing

2.2.1 General Background

Auditing in Italy is a complex issue because of the legislative maze produced by the different laws that have been ruling this subject for about the past 60 years. At first sight, it can be said that Italian audit is characterized by an evident anomaly. Since 1974–1975 there have been two competing approaches to audit: an institutional-internal one, and an emerging external one. On the one hand, there are the old, established *sindaci*, who make up one of the limited liability company bodies, the *collegio sindacale*, and who are most often accounting professionals (*Dottori Commercialisti* and *Ragionieri*) working on their own.

On the other hand, there is an Anglo-American type of audit, which is performed by companies and professional partnerships. The most important of these are registered with CONSOB (e.g., the Big Six), and as such they are the only ones that can deal with legally compulsory audit, that is, essentially that imposed on listed companies.

The two audits involve carrying out tasks that are in part mutually overlapping and not thoroughly clarified by the law. Even though the law requires that the audit firm inform the *sindaci* of a company about the existence of censurable facts, that is, irregularities that have had a material impact on financial statements, one may assume that the relationships between the two bodies and the two processes aimed at verifying accounts appear in the vast majority of cases as ambiguous and inconsistent or, more likely, nonexistent.

In this perspective, those who were expecting the implementation of the Fourth Directive in Italy (decree no. 127/1991) to extend external audit to medium and large unlisted companies have been proved wrong. On the eve of the implementation of the Fourth Directive, there arose a sharp disagreement between the *Dottori Commercialisti* and *Ragionieri* on the one side—who were much in favor of preserving the role and activity of *sindaci*—and the accountancy firms (mainly the Big Six) on the other side—pressing for an enlargement of independent external audit to all limited liability companies. Each category was, of course, trying to ensure that its form of audit was the one required by the decree. In any event, the two accountancy bodies were successful. In fact, the final text of the decree commands that only the audit by *sindaci* must be performed for all limited liability companies whose share capital exceeds 200 million lire, while external audit is a requirement only for listed companies, newspaper publishers, state-owned companies, and a few others. Therefore, the *status quo ante* on the matter has been essentially maintained. Thus, an important dimension of auditing in Italy is the distinction between a voluntary audit and a legally required one.

In the following a description of the audit context in Italy will be sketched out.

2.2.2 Sindaci and the Collegio Sindacale (Institutional-Internal Audit)

The *collegio sindacale* (the body composed of *sindaci*) is a body of the company that has defined responsibilities toward the company itself, the business community, and society in general (Article 2397–2409 Civil Code). Its presence, when legally required, is a condition of existence of the company itself as a legal person, very much the same as the annual general meeting (*assemblea dei soci*) and the board of directors (*consiglio di amministrazione*). In this sense, the *sindaci* exert a sort of institutional-internal audit.

As already mentioned, the Civil Code requires that all limited liability companies (*società per azioni* and *società a responsabilità limitata*) with a share capital exceeding 200 million lire must appoint, at the annual general meeting, a *collegio sindacale* consisting of three to five members, that is, a president of the body and two to four effective members. Two substitute members are also appointed. In principle, the *sindaci* are appointed for 3 years, but they can be reappointed indefinitely.

Its duties can be summarized as follows (Article 2403 Civil Code):

1. Control the administration of the company
2. Verify general compliance with law and articles of association of the company's operations and the legality of the accounting records
3. Check the correspondence of the balance sheet and income statement with the results of the company's account books
4. Ensure the conformity to legal rules of the financial statement valuations
5. Ascertain every 3 months the amount of petty cash and the existence of company's documents of credit and of the receipts of pledge, custody, or caution from third parties in the company's favor
6. Participate, if the *sindaci* so wish, in the meetings of the board of directors

Only since 1995 (thanks to decree no. 88/1992) has a *sindaco* been allowed to employ an assistant to help perform these activities. This assistant will operate under the *sindaco*'s direction and will be paid by the *sindaco* (Article 2403-*bis* Civil Code).

The Civil Code does not set a minimum number of hours to be spent in audit and controls. The fees are determined by the law in relation to the company's net worth, and in 1985 they were limited in any case to 30 million lire for the president and 20 million for the effective members of the *collegio sindacale*. With the recent legal fees this has been changed.

The audit activity of the *collegio sindacale* results in an annual report (*Relazione del Collegio Sindacale*), which is included in the financial statements and in which this body points out its observations and proposals regarding the regularity of the books, the annual accounts, and their approval by the general meeting. There is no legally prescribed format of the *Relazione del Collegio Sindacale*. In the vast majority of cases, though, this report merely confirms the stated figures and proposes the latter's approval by the general meeting. It is to be noted that financial statements must be signed not only by the members of the board of directors but also by each of the *sindaci*. Since 1994 the *sindaci* have also been required to verify and control the group accounts, if the company for which they are carrying out this function is a parent undertaking (Article 41, decree 127/1991).

Until 1992 officially, but *de facto* until 1995 (i.e., the date of the complete coming into force of legislative decree no. 88/1992), virtually anybody could be eligible for a *sindaco* position, with the consequence that not all the persons carrying out such a function had the appropriate qualification. In most of the cases *sindaci* are accounting professionals.

Since 1995 all *sindaci* must belong to a special register under the supervision of the Ministry of Justice. In fact, as a consequence of the implementation of the Eighth EU Directive in Italy through legislative decree no. 88/1992, from 1995 *only* those who have the qualification of *revisore ufficiale dei conti* (official statutory auditor) can carry out auditing activity and then be appointed *sindaci* of a company.

The professional qualification of *revisore ufficiale dei conti* has quite a long history. In fact, according to a regulation of 1936 (Royal law-decree no. 1548/1936 converted into law no. 517/1937), the *sindaci* who have served for some years (e.g., 5 years for lawyers and engineers; 3 for *Dottori Commercialisti*) and have an indisputable morality could enter—after an undemanding examination by a national committee—the membership (*ruolo*) of the *revisori ufficiali dei conti* (Article 12).

The 1992 decree has now also slightly modified the professional label of *revisore ufficiale dei conti*, which has now become *revisore contabile* (auditor).

In order to join the register (*registro*) of the *revisori contabili* it will be necessary to have at least a "short" university degree in economics, business administration, or law (3 years), to serve an apprenticeship period of 3 years under the guidance of a *revisore contabile*, and to pass a state exam.

As a transitional *régime*, however, those who were previous members of the *Revisori Ufficiali dei Conti*, as well as the *Dottori Commercialisti* and the *Ragionieri* (who have served as a *sindaco* of a company for at least one year), are allowed to be inserted *de jure* in the new register. Therefore, the future level of qualification of the *sindaci* is likely to be higher than beforehand, but it may be also negatively influenced by the presence of inadequately trained members who belonged to the previous membership.

It should also be noted that in this new register there can be inscribed partnerships and limited liability companies between accounting professionals, who hold the qualification of *revisore contabile*, aimed at providing companies with voluntary audit (see below).

The *sindaci* are highly peculiar to the tradition of Italian company law. They are perceived as carrying out functions in the public interest, thus helping to legitimize the company's activity. In addition to the *sindaci*'s not always adequate professional qualification, however, some weaknesses can be pointed out of both the *collegio sindacale* as a company's body and the *sindaco*'s role, which lessen its capability of carrying out an effective audit activity:

1. Its subordinate position toward company's owners, since the latter elect the *sindaci* via their control over the annual general meeting (in this respect, it is a clear case of who controls the controllers)

2. The further reduction of *sindaci*'s independence due to their consultancy activity often rendered for the same company in which they participate in the *collegio sindacale*

3. The limited powers of the *sindaci vis-à-vis* the company's directors

4. The breadth of the *sindaci*'s duties in relation to their scarce resources, which are essentially based on a single person's commitment

5. The poorness of the remuneration granted by law to the *sindaci* role

6. The potentially unlimited number of participations in different

collegi sindacali that a professional may have, with a negative impact on the time, length, and qualitative level of the audit that can be devoted to each of them

Therefore, one might wonder about the significance and incisiveness of the control and role exerted by the *collegio sindacale* in the past and, if no changes occur, in the future (for example, see some of the recent episodes linked to bribery scandals, where the financial statements of big enterprises, which have been found irregular, had been signed by the company's *sindaci*).

It is clear that this type of audit is larger in scope than the accounting-centered one characterizing the Anglo-Saxon tradition, and as such it may be labeled an administrative audit. At the same time, however, it is clear that the *collegio sindacale* does not give rise to an arm's length audit in the sense of the EU Fourth Directive. It essentially represents a formal confirmation of the legitimacy of the company directors' actions. In this perspective, the general assumption in ordinary circumstances is to regard the duties of the *collegio sindacale* as legalistic rather than requiring any value judgment.

Notwithstanding those longstanding concerns, a seeming contradiction referring to this type of audit should be noted—that a body similar to the *collegio sindacale* has been legally extended in 1982 to serve firms controlled by the communes and provinces, and in 1990 to the latter bodies themselves.

2.2.3 The External Independent Audit and the Società di Revisione (Audit Firms)

The activity of external independent audit, similar to the Anglo-Saxon one, can be exerted in Italy under three different legal-institutional forms, which are only partially overlapping. These forms are:

1. *Revisore contabile* (auditor) (legislative decree no. 88/1992)
2. *Società fiduciaria e di revisione* (fiduciary and auditing company) (law no. 1966 of November 23, 1939)
3. *Società di revisione* (audit company) (Presidential decree no. 136 of 1975)

We have already described the evolution of the *revisore contabile* from 1936 to the implementation of the Eighth EU Directive in Italy. In particular, the *revisore contabile* can perform the voluntary audit, that is, an audit that is freely undertaken by companies (which are not bound to do so), and be *sindaco* of a limited liability company. This professional qualification may be attributed to a physical person, a partnership (*società in nome collettivo* or *società in accomandita semplice*) or a limited liability company. In the latter two cases, in order to get the inscription in the *Register*, most of the directors are to be *revisori contabili*, the majority of voting rights must belong to persons having such a qualification, and the objects of the partnership/company (according to their memorandum) must be limited to auditing and company accounting organization. The register is kept under the general supervision of the Ministry of Justice. Of course, the appointment as *sindaco* of a company is reserved only to physical persons. For audit firms already included in the roll of Presidential decree no. 136/1975 (see item 3), registration in the roll of the *revisori contabili* is not required, while audit firms authorized on the basis of law no. 1966/1939 (see item 2) can be inscribed in the roll of *revisori contabili* if they apply for it.

Second, the *società fiduciaria e di revisione* are authorized—according to a law of 1939 that is still in force—by the Ministry of Industry and Commerce to perform the following roles: (*a*) fiduciary administration of third parties' properties; (*b*) company audit and accounting organization; (*c*) shareholder's and bondholder's representation at general meetings.

This kind of firm can take the legal form of partnership or limited liability company (*società per azioni* or *società a responsabilità limitata*), where, in the latter case, one member at least of the board of directors must be a professional (not necessarily an accounting one), the chairman, the managing director, and the majority of the board of directors and of the management are to be Italian (note that in 1939 Italy was still in the fascist era), and the *collegio sindacale* has to be composed of professionals, at least two taken from the accounting professional rolls. The *società fiduciaria e di revisione* can undertake only a voluntary type of audit, as the members of the register of *revisori contabili*.

In a historical perspective, this type of audit firm is important since, after the Second World War, all major international accounting firms opened branches in Italy to carry out their services in accordance with the provisions of the legislation regarding voluntary audit, that is law no. 1966/1939.

As an important part of the so-called mini-reform of the *società per azioni* in 1974 (enacted by law no. 216 of June 7, 1974, which established, *inter alia*, also the CONSOB), Presidential decree no. 136 of March 31, 1975, introduced into Italian company law the requirement for quoted companies to submit their annual accounts to independent audit. The same requirement was later introduced for newspaper publishing companies, state-owned groups, and a few other categories of firms, and from 1994, as already stated, for group accounts.

In order to accomplish this delicate publicly relevant function, it has been deemed appropriate to create a new "special roll" under the supervision and control of CONSOB, which only audit firms with the particular characteristics of professional competence and financial soundness could enter. These audit firms may be set up as partnerships or limited liability companies: in this respect, the most common legal structure of Italian audit firms is that of *società in accomandita semplice* (similar to the U.K. quasi-partnership).

Admission to this special roll is granted when (Article 8 of decree no. 136/1975, as renewed by Article 17 of decree no. 88/1992):

1. Their objects—according to the memorandum—are limited to the auditing and accounting organization of a company, and specifically exclude any other professional activity (e.g., consultancy).

2. The majority of directors and managers or of partners belong to the register of *revisori contabili* (before 1995 they had to be members of one of the Italian accountancy bodies or be a *Revisore Ufficiale dei Conti*, and have at least 5 years' auditing experience or alternatively to have passed a special examination organized by and under the supervision of CONSOB).

3. The majority of their capital is owned by physical persons included in the register of *revisori contabili*; the same qualification is possessed by the majority of the partnership or company members.

4. An insurance guarantee that is judged adequate by CONSOB is available to the audit firm.

Italian subsidiaries of foreign auditing firms may also be registered in the CONSOB special roll, provided that they respect the same requisites set for the other Italian firms.

Before 1995, there could be inscribed in this special roll only firms previously authorized by the Ministry of Industry and Commerce to exert (voluntary) audit activity on the basis of the law no. 1966/1939 (see item 2, above). Moreover, if a firm was a branch of an international audit company, it had to have carried out such activity for at least 10 years. Now all these limitations have been removed by the new version of Article 8 of decree no. 136/1975.

The narrowing of the firm's objects to audit and *accounting organization* stretches itself, until the complete coming into force of decree no. 88/1992 (to be accomplished by the first half of 1995) also to all professionals while working for this type of audit firm, in that one cannot render any professional service on an autonomous basis. The above-mentioned decree no. 88/1992 currently allows this individual delivery of accounting services, thus canceling one of the most acute points of separation between an individual career as an accounting professional in a studio and a career with a *società di revisione* (see Section 2.1.1).

In order to get around the prohibition for a *società di revisione* recorded in the CONSOB special roll to perform any activity other than audit, many firms set up a legally distinct company to deliver consultancy services. Thus, parallel companies did and do come into existence, with no formal linkages with the audit firm, but both having the same name and, in most cases, both depending on the same parent company abroad (examples include the Big Six). Furthermore, this tendency to establish companies different from the audit firm but originating from the latter is likely to increase in the near future because of the new legal possibility for accounting professionals, while being employees of an audit firm to work also on their own. (Of course, this will be possible for these professionals to the extent that they will be allowed by their work contract with the audit firm.)

The audit appointment is given to a firm by the annual general meeting of the company asking to be audited, which should choose, as the CONSOB requires, among three competing proposals from different *società di revisione*. The appointment lasts for 3 years and can be renewed not more than twice (i.e., in total 9 years). It can be assigned again to the same audit firm only after 5 further financial years (Article 2, decree no. 136/1975). In 1994 most of the major Italian groups reshuffled audit appointments.

With regard to the independence of the *società di revisione*, the appointment of an audit firm is incompatible when there are contractual arrangements or participating interests between the latter and the company to be audited, or when partners, directors, *sindaci*, or general managers of an audit firm are related by blood or marriage to their equivalents of the company asking to be audited, or have had connections with the latter in the recently preceeding years by means of a service agreement of any kind, including employee work, or they have served during the same period as director or *sindaco* thereof (Article 3, decree no. 136/1975). Furthermore, partners, directors, *sindaci*, and employees of an audit firm cannot take up, for a period of 3 years after the termination of the audit appointment or of their work relation therewith, any occupation whatsoever with the company that has been audited by their firm.

The outcome of the auditing process is the so-called *relazione di certificazione*, whose translation in English as "auditor's report" is to some extent problematic, since this *relazione* should certify the quality of the accounts audited and not be simply a professional judgment thereon.

In 1983 the CONSOB imposed a compulsory model of this *relazione di certificazione* (which was slightly modified in 1987 and made shorter and more succinct in 1994) to the *società di revisione* when carrying out a legal audit. Beyond the fact of not being easily reconcilable with the standard Anglo-American auditor's reports, this model has been highly criticized because of its rigidity, its relative lack of clarity, its excessive length (criticism now overcome by the 1994 version), and the contradiction between section 3, which is devoted to auditor's comments and remarks, and section 4, where the audit firm expresses its judgment and releases its "certification" of the annual accounts audited, or alternatively does not release the certification and points out the reasons for doing so. In the latter perspective, it should be remembered that there is a legal impossibility in Italy of delivering an auditors' report with any form of qualified opinion on the examined financial statements: in fact it was, and is still, possible for Italian auditors to state only either a fully positive or a fully negative judgment thereon (Article 4, decree no. 136/1975). This legal requirement is likely to force audit firms toward delivering a positive opinion in their reports, provided that the audited accounts comply with the few vague civil rule requirements, even if since 1993 these requirements have been enlarged as a consequence of decree no. 127/1991. In this sense, the *Società di revisione* point out that it does not make sense to address criticisms of a company's annual accounts in section 3 of this compulsory model, while in its section 4 it is not possible to deliver a qualified opinion thereon, as is instead possible in the Anglo-Saxon countries.

By contrast, it is interesting to note that, when carrying out a voluntary audit, the *società di revisione* are free to adopt the *relazione di certificazione* model proposed by auditing standard no. 18, which is quite different from the CONSOB one, and much more similar to that of the Anglo-Saxon environment. In particular, qualified opinions are possible according to this professional model.

Until 1991 audit firms were asked by law to state, in their legal audit report, the compliance of financial statements with the civil rules and the accounting standards *at the same time*. However, the two sets of regulations were not mutually compatible in all cases. As a consequence, some auditors' reports in Italy stressed the conformity of the audited annual accounts to commercial regulation, but some others to the professional standards, despite the explicit request by CONSOB for stating the required double compliance in those reports. With the introduction in 1991 of decree no. 127, this problem has been at least formally solved by stating compliance only with civil code rules (see Section 2.3).

As a legal effect of a *certificazione* delivered in relation to compulsory audit, the approval of the company annual accounts by the ordinary general meeting can be judicially contested only by as many members as represent at least 5% of the share capital, or nominal 100 million lire, if the company share capital exceeds 2 billion lire. CONSOB, too, can contest the approval by the annual general meeting of a financial report.

The legal responsibilities of the audit firm and of its employees, directors, and partners are quite extensive and have a civil, penal, and professional-deontological nature. The sanctions may be heavy and include the cancellation of the guilty audit firm from the CONSOB special roll.

As to the fees of audit firms, there is not at present, as for the *Dottori Commercialisti* and *Ragionieri*, legally determined fees. Audit firms tried to agree among themselves on self-regulation of their fees, but this attempt was opposed by the Authority for Market and Competition, which saw it as going against the rules of free competition. Consequently, Italian *Società di revisione* find themselves without any framework for setting their fees, and some price war among them is said to have begun recently, with a possible risk for the quality of the auditing process in consideration of the lack of any required minimum amount of hours for performing both legal and voluntary audit.

The total turnover of the Italian audit business can be estimated around 600–650 billion lire a year. However, it is remarkable that the number of companies that voluntarily undergo an auditing process (for image and bank financing purposes) is much larger than that of companies for which it is legally required. In fact, the market for voluntary auditing seems to represent in Italy about 70% of the total auditing market (estimate by the Italian Association of Auditors). This could also explain why many audit firms, such as those authorized to operate only according to law no. 1966/1939 (see item 2), can nonetheless survive while remaining outside the business of the legal audit.

Audit firms are grouped into two national associations, which are to some extent rivals: the larger and politically more influential is the *Associazione Italiana Revisori Contabili* (ASSIREVI), the Italian Association of Auditors, which includes the most important 12 Italian audit firms (including the Big Six) for a total turnover as of 1993 year end of 490 billion lire, and 244 partners and 3,500 professionals. The other association is the *Associazione Italiana Società di Revisione* (AIRE), the Italian Association of Audit Firms, which represents 11 audit firms, for a yearly global turnover of around 100–120 billion lire (for contact numbers see the section "Useful Addresses" at the end of this chapter). In Italy this business shows a strong turnover in professional personnel (e.g., in the past 5 years more than 2,500 employees left audit firms associated with ASSIREVI).

In independent external auditing, the international crisis of legitimation and significance hitting auditors and their work is now progressively emerging also in Italy, leaving room for uncertainty and contradictions. In recent years some events clearly revealed the potential weakness of the auditors' report in assessing the soundness of the accounts, seriously shaking public confidence therein. About 3 years ago an audit firm was sued for the first time in Italy. A Milan bank had bought a leasing company with audited financial statements. After purchase, however, a remarkable loss, which had not been indicated in the auditors' report, was discovered. The case was settled out of court. Moreover, at the beginning of 1993 the CONSOB forbade a listed company from renewing its auditing contract with a well-known international firm, since the latter was not able, according to CONSOB, to give enough assurance on the quality of the auditing process. The same position was taken by CONSOB in 1994 with reference to another international audit firm. Furthermore, as a by-product of the 1992 bribery scandal and in the related judicial inquiry, it was revealed that a primary audit firm was being sued and penally investigated in connection with its inability to find any traces of the bribes paid by a large company with audited annual accounts. There have been other cases in which firms with audited financial reports and seemingly in a healthy financial situation revealed instead a very difficult one, because of the illegalities and irregular actions that were operated by the company's board of directors. Neither the audit firms nor the *collegio sindacale* of these companies were able to discover those actions or the bribes paid. CONSOB tried to face this difficult and delegitimizing situation for Italian audit by inviting audit firms and *sindaci* in two 1993 communications to accomplish extra inquires and checks in order to identify and report any possible "censurable facts" linked to bribery payments.

After these events many started questioning—in accordance with the trend in other countries—the true meaning and role of external independent auditing. In light of this situation, several voices have put forward insistent calls for immediate reform.

2.3 Accounting Standards (*Principi Contabili*) and Auditing Standards (*Principi di Revisione*)

For many decades no need was felt in Italy for accounting standards. This was due to the civil law–based legal system, which did and does oblige companies to follow legal rules, and to the strong and lasting resistence of Italian academics to any standardization process of company financial reporting and accounting year-end valuations.

However, law no. 216/1974 imposed compulsory external audit on listed companies, and the following decree (no. 136/1975, Article 4, section 2) required that this legal audit also be performed according to "correct accounting principles." Curiously enough, at the time neither such standards nor any legally or professionally recognized standard-setting body existed. Therefore, the new legal requirements accelerated the preparation of Italian "GAAP."

In fact, auditors began to feel the need for a set of statements that provided the necessary reference for their work. Further, according to some authors, standards were needed in order to contribute to the interpretation and completion of the legal rules, because these latter obviously could not deal with every specific problem concerning accounts.

Some institutions and associations, such as the Ministry for State-owned groups (*Ministero per le Partecipazioni Statali*) and the Association of Italian Public Limited Companies (*Assonime*), started issuing their own accounting standards, trying to legitimize them in their territory of competence. For some years, different sets of standards competed in Italy, until CONSOB made a choice in 1982 in favor of the standards prepared by the accounting professionals, with the backing of the audit firms (see below).

In fact, the National Council of the most authoritative professional body (*Consiglio Nazionale dei Dottori Commercialisti*, CNDC) set up an *ad hoc* committee in 1975 to cope with issues arising from the introduction of compulsory audit. This committee started its activity as a standard setter producing accounting principles (*principi contabili*) related to valuation and presentation criteria. The aim is to offer guidelines for annual accounts and a benchmark for auditing, taking into account authoritative literature, best practice (both national and international), and the EU accounting directives. In 1982, the National Council of the other Italian professional body (*Consiglio Nazionale dei Ragionieri*) joined the standard-setting venture (so the standard setting committee has become appointed by both accountancy bodies—in short CNDCR). Today, this committee is composed of 21 members, of whom 11 are *Dottori Commercialisti* and 10 *Ragionieri*. The chairman is a *Dottore Commercialista*. The majority of members work in their own studio, but some of them come from audit firms. Some academics are also included.

To date, 14 statements have been published (see Figure 3). As a consequence of the criticisms about the slowness with which standards are prepared or updated, a major revision of them is currently in progress in order to take into consideration the new legal framework for accounting originating from decree no. 127/1991 coming into force. The main aim of the revision process is to make standards as close as possible to legal rules and to play an interpretative role of the latter.

Although the accounting standards represented a preliminary step to a rigorous audit, they were perceived as not sufficient since they were partially divergent from the auditors' aims and operating needs. In this respect, in 1975 a second committee was also appointed by the CNDC, which the National Council of *Ragionieri*, as for the accounting standards, joined later. The objective of this second committee was to issue auditing standards (*principi di revisione*) concerning professional ethics, audit planning and procedures, and implications of electronic data processing. To date, twenty audit standards have been issued, dealing with all aspects of the auditing process. In particular, standard no. 18, which was mentioned earlier, regards the auditor's report (*relazione di certificazione*), permitting—as opposed to the CONSOB model—a qualified opinion on the audited accounts. This standard serves as the reference statement for auditor's reports in all voluntary audit activity. At present many auditing standards are undergoing a revision process. At any rate, it is fair to say that, on the whole, Italian audit standards are not materially dissimilar from those commonly used in Anglo-Saxon countries.

Regarding accounting standards, an important feature is that they are not compulsory either in legal or professional terms. They have never been awarded full legal authority: only a short reference to them was made, as already pointed out, in Article 4, section 2, of decree no. 136/1975, according to which the external auditor's report should ensure compliance *at the same time* with correct accounting principles and legal rules.

This requirement, which was a source of ambiguity and operative problems, has recently been cancelled by the new version of Article 4 of decree no. 136/1975 put forth by decree no. 127 of 1991 (Article 23). It is now required that audit should verify the conformity of the accounts *exclusively* to commercial regulation. Even though this legislative intervention might sound like a formal dismissal of accounting standards from any legal relevance, the Ministerial Commentary to decree no. 127/1991 confirmed their technical role of interpretation, and integration, of the legal rules, especially where obscure points persist in the new legal provisions: in other words, they cannot be "creative" with respect to the latter

---

Figure 3 *List of the Italian Accounting Standards*

Jointly issued by the *Consiglio Nazionale dei Dottori Commercialisti* and *Consiglio Nazionale dei Ragionieri*

1. Financial statements: objectives and postulates (1977, but approved in 1975) (Revised in 1994: now Standard no. 11)

2. Formats (1977; revised in 1994: now Standard no. 12)

2. *bis* Interpretations of and clarifications to Accounting Standard no. 2 (1982)

3. Stock valuation (1978; revised in 1994: now Standard no. 13)

4. Tangible assets (1979)

5. Liquid funds and bank overdrafts (1980; revised in 1994: now Standard no. 14)

6. Debtors (1980)

7. Creditors and other liabilities (1981)

8. Investments, participating interests and consolidated accounts (1983)

9. Translation of items in foreign currency (1988)

10. Long-term contracts (1991)

---

since they are not normative sources and have to be subordinated to, and compatible with, the legal requirements. It is in this perspective, in fact, that the above-mentioned revision process of accounting standards is being carried out. Some feel that there is still some room for accounting standards to play an autonomous role in the identification and treatment of the so-called *casi eccezionali* (exceptional circumstances, new Article 2423, section 4, Civil Code), that is, when it is mandatory to depart from legal rules (see Section 3).

On the other hand, their actual acceptance has often been a matter of discretion and discussion, although CONSOB in 1982 indicated that they must be considered a reference (*punto di riferimento*) for listed companies, and suggested, but did not require, their application "where not in contrast with extant law" (*quando non in contrasto con l'ordinamento vigente*, CONSOB Ordinance no. 1079 dated April 8, 1982). The same ordinance stated that for accounting issues not covered by the CNDCR's principles, the IASC standards are relevant for consideration. The low profile taken by CONSOB was probably due to the then expected imminent implementation of the Fourth Directive. As for CNDCR's auditing standards, they were also sanctioned by CONSOB in the 1982 ordinance, but—as opposed to accounting standards—their use was overtly recommended to auditing firms.

In more general terms, however, the significance and effectiveness of these standards within a civil law–based legal system remain problematic. Accounting and commercial law literatures did, and to some extent still do, show an ambivalent attitude toward those statements. It must be remembered that one of the central doctrines of Italian legal scholars is that what really matters is not what practice is (as in the Anglo-Saxon countries), but what practice should be (as in some German legal approaches to accounting). This attitude, of course, opposes the very idea and role of generally accepted accounting standards, since generalized acceptance is not a relevant element in legal terms in Italy.

As a result, Italian accounting standards have always had an uncertain status *vis-à-vis* legal rules, since the latter have been considered preeminent over the former, and they did not clearly specify the standards' role. At present, a legally clear and unequivocal identification of a standard-setting body is also missing.

The contradictory and ambiguous nature of accounting standards in Italy did, and does, influence their scarce application and recognition by professionals and companies. These statements seem in fact very little known and used in economic entities other than large ones. The latter are small in number and not representative of average Italian firms.

2.4 Expected Future Developments Regarding the Accounting Profession and Audit

The future of the accounting profession in Italy will largely depend on the outcome of five challenges, which are highly interrelated:

1. The development of a unitary accounting profession
2. The increase in the degree of acceptance of its standards
3. The reaction to new threatening competing entities and in parallel the success in the struggle against the so-called abusivism
4. Clarification of the *sindaci* roles, also *vis-à-vis* the external independent audit
5. The evolution of the relationship between the accounting profession and audit firms

As to the first challenge, the upgrading of the qualification of accounting professionals in Italy, which is imposed by the new rules, seems to find a correspondance in the growth of their socioeconomic importance. However, the accounting profession remains divided in two competing bodies, with a relative loss of contractual strength and a certain lack of coordination. Since 1929 various attempts have been made to merge the two bodies, without much result. It is most likely that the urgency of this issue will emerge strongly in the near future and that the two bodies will find eventually a compromise in order to reinforce the overall Italian accounting profession.

As to the second challenge, the question of the future role of the accounting standards jointly issued by the two national bodies remains open, especially with reference to all the changes taking place in accounting legislation (see Sections 3 and 4). This issue concerns the capacity of the Italian profession as *an institutional actor* to be able to impose in clearer terms than today its expertise and sociopolitical relevance, to legitimize a wider acceptance and enforcement of its standards. On this matter, the perceived scope and prestige of its professional domain seem to be at stake. Alternatively, the recognition of a specialized knowledge and the social role of Italian accountants risk dependence only upon the individual competences of each of them.

As to the third challenge, in recent years the *Dottore Commercialista* and *Ragioniere* have achieved increased socioeconomic relevance, especially because of the staggering complexity of the tax regulation. Nowadays one might say that the Italian accountant is not, as the Marxists used to say, the slave of the capitalist, but rather a sort of slave of the state since he or she must cope, on behalf of clients, with the new fiscal requirements that are continuously introduced by the government (and of course also to help clients overcome those requirements). However, the recent introduction of the *Centri Autorizzati di Assistenza Fiscale* (CAAF, Authorized Agencies for Fiscal Assistance) (Article 78 of law 413/1991) could take in due course some of the "heavy" fiscal work away from accounting professionals, such as the keeping of account books and the filing of tax declarations of employees and other private citizens (such as pensioners). This might be an opportunity for Italian accountants to expand in the future their presence in different segments of the professional market such as business consultancy.

On the other hand, in their perceived primary market (the accounting one) Italian *Dottori Commercialisti* and *Ragionieri* are fighting an important battle in order to defend their professional territory from the attack of nonqualified practitioners who abusively render accountancy services. The outcome of this struggle is crucial for the very survival and growth of the professional identity of Italian qualified accountants.

As to the fourth challenge, Italians agree that the *collegio sindacale* must be profoundly reformed, but there is no clear consensus so far in what direction (e.g., to increase its administrative control role—to make it similar to a supervisory board—or, alternatively, to increase its internal audit responsibilities. Further, who has to elect it? The company owners or the minorities?). In particular, the relative responsibilities of the *collegio sindacale* and the audit firm, where both are present (e.g., a quoted company), are to be spelled out more clearly, avoiding today's confusion of roles. Moreover, it would be desirable that the relationship between them could be more constructive and go beyond the mere obligation of the audit firm to communicate censurable facts to the *collegio sindacale*, to build up a more solid cooperation between these two entities required to control—from their own specific perspective—a company's operations. In this respect, the government recently proposed a bill according to which the *sindaci* should also perform the role of fiscal police, in that they have to control both the adequacy of fiscal procedures adopted by the company, and their actual implementation (i.e., the company did not evade taxes). Many criticisms and resistences were put forth, and the bill has been retired from Parliament and is under reconsideration. At any rate, the future of the *sindaci* as a company body appears to be central for both the role of the accounting profession within the life of companies and its credibility in social terms.

As to the fifth challenge, this has been in part just discussed with respect to the future possible relationship between *collegio sindacale* and audit firms. However, the issue of the relationship between accounting professionals and audit activity seems to be wider, involving the very shaping of the whole accounting and related services business. As noted earlier, this market was *de facto* (and partially *de jure*) segmented in two bits: accounting and audit, which are separed by two barriers to entry, which explains why a professional has traditionally had to choose between a career in a studio and one in an audit firm. In fact, a professional working in one of these firms could not perform accounting activity on his or her own (old Article 8, decree no. 136/1975), while the *Dottori Commercialisti* and *Ragionieri* were not permitted to enter the business of legal audit, unless operating within one of the firms included in the CONSOB "Special Roll" and having its objects limited to audit services. This practical and to some extent legal dichotomy produced, of course, a situation of tension and professional competition between auditors and professionals, so that *Dottori Commercialisti* and *Ragionieri* of audit firms, though formally included in the same rolls (*albi*) run by the professional local units, were in the main disregarded by the other colleagues and perceived by the latter as not belonging to the same profession.

The first of these barriers to entry has now been removed, with the new version of Article 8 of decree no. 136/1975, which was introduced by decree no. 88/1992, allowing professionals working in audit firms to practice in their own studios. However, the latter barrier is still there, even if the new register of auditors (*revisori contabili*) will admit partnerships and companies between them in order to carry out voluntary audit.

Furthermore, adding to this fluid situation, diffuse calls for reform of the audit activity are being raised today in Italy, even if it is not evident at the moment what direction this process will take. What seems clear is that the outcome of this reform, if it is ever accomplished, is likely to have an impact on the evolution of the delicate relationship between audit firms and the accounting profession. Notwithstanding these legal changes, this relationship appears likely to remaining uneasy in the near future.

3. The Form and Content of Financial Reporting in Italy

3.1 The Current Legal Framework and the Implementation of European Accounting Directives

Several EU Directives have recently been implemented in Italian accounting legislation in order to harmonize it with that of other European countries. In 1991 the Fourth and Seventh Directives on annual and consolidated accounts were together implemented by legislative decree no. 127/1991. One year later the directives on financial reporting of banks and other financial institutions (Directive no. 1986/633 and the Eleventh Directive) (see Figure 1) were implemented. For one of those (the Fourth Directive), Italy was seriously late in its implementation, but for the others, relatively quick progress was made in spite of the surrounding general skepticism.

As a result of these legal changes, accounting regulation in Italy has been largely reshaped. In particular, the rules of decree no. 127/1991 dealing with company accounts have been introduced directly into the Civil Code, Book V, in place of the existing ones, while on the contrary, the rules dealing with consolidated reporting have not been included in the Civil Code and remain external to it. In this case, reference will be made to the relevant articles of decree no. 127/1991.

Today, an Italian (company and group) annual report may be expected to be composed of the following documents:

1. Balance sheet (*stato patrimoniale*)
2. Income statement (*conto economico*)
3. Notes to the accounts (*nota integrativa*)
4. Report on operations (*relazione sulla gestione*)
5. Changes in shareholders' funds statement (*prospetto delle variazioni di capitale netto*)
6. Flow of funds statement (*rendiconto finanziario*)
7. Chairman's statement (*relazione del Presidente*)

8. Directors' report (*relazione del Consiglio di amministrazione*)
9. Auditor's report (*relazione di certificazione*)

Only the first four statements are legally required to be produced by any limited liability company in Italy (primarily *Società per azioni*, or *S.p.A.*—comparable to an English public limited company by shares; *Società a responsabilità limitata*, or *S.r.l.*—comparable to an English private limited company; *Società in accomandita per azioni*, or *S.a.p.a.*—a sort of English quasi-partnership by shares, not much used now). Of course, the auditor's report is also mandatory, where appropriate (e.g., quoted companies, insurances, newspaper publishers; see Section 2.2).

A major innovation relates to the composition of the annual accounts, since the notes (*nota integrativa*) to the latter have become an integral part of the legal concept of financial statements and, hence, are no longer included in the directors' report (now called *relazione sulla gestione*, "report on operations"). Thus, the first three of the above statements are to be considered a single whole from a legal point of view, giving content to the *bilancio d'esercizio* (annual financial statements) (Article 2423, section 1, Civil Code).

Documents from no. 5 to no. 8 are presented on a voluntary basis and generally prepared only by medium to large companies (quoted or not). However, note that presentation of a statement similar to no. 5, that is, a "statement of equity reserve movements" (*prospetto delle riserve*), is compulsory for any limited companies (Article 105, section 7, 1986 Consolidated Act on Income Tax). A further relevant aspect is that neither the European Directive nor Italian law have asked for a flow of funds statement in any form, even though the latter's importance is clearly pointed out by CNDCR's accounting standard no. 2 (see Figure 3), explicitly asking for this statement.

Moreover, it must be considered that listed companies must also produce a 6-month report on operations trends (the so-called *relazione semestrale*). This report is to be drawn up by company directors according to the criteria established by CONSOB and must be made public (Article 2427 Civil Code, section 3).

The figures of the previous accounting period must be shown for each item of the balance sheet and income statement, for both company and group financial reports.

Annual accounts (including consolidated statements) are to be prepared either in lire or in lire and ECU, according to the recently implemented EU Directive no. 90/604 (legislative decree no. 526/1992).

On group acccounting, it should be noted that virtually all Italian large (nonlisted) groups have voluntarily presented consolidated accounts since the second half of the 1980s, while only quoted companies and a few other categories (newspaper publishers, insurance companies, banks, and so on) were legally bound to do so. Quite often consolidated reports are also published in English (see the 1993 Merloni Consolidated Accounts at the end of this chapter), or, sometimes, their English version is the preeminent one. This is the case when Italian companies are listed only on foreign stock exchanges, especially New York (e.g., Luxottica Group, Natuzzi Group). Such situations will probably increase in the future.

As to unlimited liability firms (*Impresa individuale*, sole proprietorship; *Società in nome collettivo*, or *S.n.c.*, comparable to an English conventional partnership; *Società in accomandita semplice*, or *S.a.s.*, a sort of English quasi-partnership), they must prepare only a balance sheet (as a by-product of the annual stock-taking) and an income statement, but they do not have to comply with the formats and rules set for limited companies, except for the year-end valuation criteria that are the same. The general principle to be followed by these firms in the preparation of their accounts is that these shall give with "straightforwardness and truth" the firm financial situation and year's performance (Article 2217, section 2, Civil Code). The unlimited liability firms are not required to make public their annual accounts (no filing with any public institution is required).

An emerging and peculiar aspect of the recent practice of financial reporting in Italy is the accounting treatment of bribes (*tangenti*) paid by firms to public officials in order to gain access to public works. Mention of these "black" monetary outflows started to appear in the notes and directors' reports of some companies in the 1993 accounts.

Another recent—and still much limited—accounting phenomenon in Italy is the publication by some groups (e.g., Fiat, Ibm Italy, Ferruzzi, Enichem, Ciba Geigy Italy) of an environmental report (*bilancio ambientale*), where environmental inputs and outputs (say, consumption of electricity and methane, issuance of polluting substances) of the already existing production activities are accounted for, and plans to improve this relationship are put forth. It is probably too soon to talk about a *greening* of Italian accounting, even though such environmental reports are an interesting development in this direction.

In procedural terms for limited liability entities, the company's annual general meeting (*assemblea dei soci*) must be called within 4 months (or within 6 months, if the memorandum so specifies) from the end of the financial year. At least 30 days (45 days, if a quoted company) before the general meeting, a copy of the company annual accounts (*bilancio d'esercizio*), together with the report on operations and the consolidated accounts (if a parent company of a group), are communicated from the company's directors to the *collegio sindacale* and, if relevant, to the audit firm. At least 15 days before the general meeting a copy of all the above statements, accompanied by the report of the *collegio sindacale* and the auditor's report, if any, are made available to members in the company's registered office. Within 30 days after the approval of company accounts (group accounts are not to be formally approved) by the General Meeting, directors are required to deposit a copy of all the above documents and a copy of the minutes of the meeting in the register of undertakings (*registro delle imprese*), which was recently set up by Article 8 of law no. 580/1993 at the Chambers of Commerce; before 1993 *ad hoc* registers at the Chancery of Tribunals were used) and to mention the occurrence of this deposit in the Official Bulletin of Public and Private Limited Companies (*Bollettino Ufficiale delle Società per Azioni e a Responsabilità Limitata*, BUSARL).

There are two further issues that affect in a relevant way the general form and content of annual accounts in Italy, and hence they must be described somewhat more in depth: (*a*) the Italian approach to the "true and fair view" principle, and (*b*) the relationship between accounting and taxation.

An Italian View of "True and Fair View"   The fundamental principle of the new legislation, which drives in principle the whole drawing up of *both company and group annual accounts* comes, according to the Ministerial Commentary that accompanies decree no. 127/1991, from the British "true and fair view" formula. Accounts are now required to "represent in a true and correct manner" a company's economic and financial situation and the year's results (*rappresentare in modo veritiero e corretto*) (Article 2423 Civil Code, section 2). The Ministerial Commentary on this point states only that this newly phrased principle "seems to be the most exact translation of the expression 'true and fair view' from which the directive norm derives." No definition is given by this official commentary, however, nor by the law, of the actual meaning of this British-derived formula.

In addition to this principle, accounts must also be drawn up with clearness (*chiarezza*).

Additional disclosures and departures from legal rules, when needed to comply with the new fundamental formula of the true and correct representation (*rappresentazione veritiera e corretta*) are *compulsory,* and any relevant explanations thereof must be included in the notes (Article 2423 Civil Code, sections 3 and 4). Any gains from departures from legal rules must not be taken to the income statement but must be "sterilized" from any income effect by being imputed in an *ad hoc* reserve (but this gain will be income taxable, anyway).

It is important to remember that the principles of *rappresentazione veritiera e corretta* and of *chiarezza*, as well as the compulsory additional disclosures and departures from law, apply also to the accounts of groups and financial institutions (Article 29, decree no. 127/1991; and Article 2, decree no. 87/1992).

Since it came into force in 1993, there has been great concern in Italy about how to interpret the true and correct representation formula and about its actual consequences. The transfer of such a context-specific concept from one jurisdiction to another is deemed to be problematic, especially in a legal system, such as the Italian, where a general principle guiding the drawing up of accounts has virtually always existed (see Section 1.2). Because of its importance, and in order to fully appreciate its concrete role in Italian accounting, the evolution of this principle needs to be further analyzed.

In a historical perspective, the original 1942 version of the Civil Code presented two expressions acting as general principles in drawing up annual accounts: these must give with straightforwardness and truth (*evidenza e verità*) (Article 2217) and with clarity and precision (*chiarezza e precisione*) (Article 2423, section 2) the financial situation of a firm and its economic results. Despite these general principles, however, there were a number of legal rules set in the Civil Code dealing with specific year-end valuation criteria, so that the role of those formulas has always been ambiguous and not very much incisive on the whole.

As to departures from legal rules—inherent in the British "true and fair view" formula—they were allowed in Italy by the last section of the original (1942) version of Article 2425 Civil Code, only for special reasons (*speciali ragioni*). Thus, while the meaning of the above-mentioned general legal formulas was sufficiently agreed upon in the literature, this overriding principle has always represented a controversial matter, not least because it introduced a sort of deviance within a legal system that is otherwise strictly civil-law based. The several contrasting opinions about the correct interpretation of *speciali ragioni* may be summarized under two main theoretical headings. One approach interpreted special reasons as specific circumstances regarding the company as a whole, so that, for example, a particular situation of the company could justify exceeding the maximum value prescribed by law. Avoiding a loss either bringing disrepute to the firm or implying a substantial capital reduction (when it is possible to cover it by revaluing an asset) was indicated as an example of special reasons (but a 1983 decision of the Venice Courts was explicitly against the latter interpretation). A second more prevalent approach in the literature deemed that special reasons were to be related to a firm's individual assets. Events changing an asset's economic nature could permit the abandonment of its historical cost and the adoption of a higher and more appropriate value. This was the case for an agricultural site turned into a building site, or that of grazing land transformed into a camping site, or that of land converted into an oil field. It was common opinion that the above formula did not refer to monetary inflation, since it was argued that the question of the impact of this phenomenon on company accounts was periodically addressed by *ad hoc* legislation (the so-called revaluation laws).

In 1983, after a 40-year debate on the role and significance of the special reasons formula, the time was ripe for legal clarification. Article 9 of the revaluation law called *Visentini-bis* (no. 72/1983) stated that special reasons were intended as those requiring departures from legal rules in order to give a faithful picture (*quadro fedele*) of the company's economic and financial situation. The 1983 law drew this formula from the Fourth Directive: *quadro fedele* was in fact the official translation of "true and fair view" in the Italian version of the EU Directive. Therefore, on that occasion, the "true and fair view" concept entered Italian legislation for the first time, almost 10 years before the introduction of decree no. 127/ 1991. The primary intention of the Italian government was probably to state an authoritative interpretation—legally sanctioned—of the special reasons formula in order to clarify its correct application. In this respect, it was probably decided to anticipate in part the Fourth Directive implementation, which at the time was believed to be imminent.

However, this statutory intervention did not solve the problem. "Special reasons" were explained through the use of a new concept, unknown to Italian law, which in turn required clarification. Thus, during the 1980s the dispute on the overriding principle was revived because of the different scholarly reactions to the *quadro fedele* formula. This legal interpretation of "special reasons" was variously considered an innovation or nothing new, a step toward inflation accounting or a barrier in that direction, and so on. Some emphasized that the *quadro fedele* concept, drawn from the Fourth Directive, was incompatible with the Italian civil law tradition, and that this was the reason for misunderstanding. According to one opinion, the *quadro fedele* formula did not differ essentially from the fundamental principle of "clearness and precision" (Article 2423 of the 1942 version of the Civil Code): it would be achieved, in fact, when legal rules were respected. By contrast, it appeared to some that accounting standards could prevail over the principles of law. In this respect, the risk perceived by some legal scholars was that practitioners could be granted too great a flexibility in deciding departures from stated rules, if an interpretation of the *quadro fedele* expression in terms of complete freedom in overcoming valuation limits was to prevail.

In order to avoid the risk of allowing too much flexibility, and not to create confusion with past accounting rules, decree no. 127/1991—in implementing the Fourth Directive—abandoned the *quadro fedele* phrase and enforced the above-mentioned formula *rappresentare in modo veritiero e corretto*. In addition, as already pointed out, the latter was perceived (rightly or wrongly) as closer to the Anglo-Saxon "true and fair view" actual meaning, according to the Ministerial Commentary. Besides, the above formula was intended to prevent the general legal principle of "true and correct representation" being a device to loosen the accounting regulation, as some interpretations of the *quadro fedele* tried to support in earlier times. The clearly persued aim would be now to guarantee information objectivity.

A minimal degree of flexibility is preserved in particular situations. In fact, the overriding principle, which was implied by the special reasons expression in 1942, is maintained and newly phrased in the 1991 legal provisions: departures from civil rules are now *mandatory* in "exceptional cases," which must be intended as *very* rare circumstances concerning primarily the valuation of firm's identified assets (e.g., a change in their economic nature). Further, it is generally agreed that inflation is not an exceptional case and, hence, once again, no Civil Code rule provides for the accounting treatment of this phenomenon.

Paradoxically, the early insertion of the *quadro fedele* concept in 1983 seems then to have determined its rejection and substitution with a more precisely defined and strictly bounded formula, which is consistent with a rigid interpretation of the civil law nature of the Italian legal system.

Despite some optimistic expectations linked to the introduction in Italian accounting of a principle allegedly similar to "true and fair view," however, it appears that the role of any general legal principle (such as "clearness and precision" or "true and correct representation") within the Italian civil legal framework will probably remain limited in practice, because, where specific rules are given, these must be followed (exceptional cases apart). Their application leads then quite automatically—by a sort of legal presumption—to the respect of the stated general principle. From this perspective, the role and scope of application of any general legal principle in Italy are restricted by the existence of *ad hoc* regulations dealing with accounts formats and valuations. As a consequence, this general formula is likely to have some effect only where no detailed legal rule—either of a civil or fiscal nature—is provided (broadly similar to Germany).

To these general considerations, it must be added on more specific grounds the conceptually and legally problematic relationship that the recently implemented principle of "true and correct representation" (Article 2423, section 2, Civil Code) has with the old (1882) but still enforced principle of "straightforwardness and truth" (*evidenza e verità*—Article 2217, section 2, Civil Code). This applies to annual accounts of unlimited liabilities entities, but it cannot be seen—because of the need for a systematic interpretation of the legal framework—as different from the former.

As an ironic result of this situation, the 1882 principle must necessarily have the same meaning and role of the fresh, European-derived formula, considered a major breakthrough in accounting regulation by some Anglo-Saxon scholars!

Accounting and Taxation   Taxation is a factor that influences strongly the drawing up of company accounts in Italy, given that consolidated accounts are tax-neutral for the time being.

Commercial and tax regulations progressively moved closer in the years after 1974 (reform of the income tax, including corporation tax), and they are now probably inextricably intertwined.

Therefore, the scholarly view, which is conventionally identified as the "double track approach" (*teoria del doppio binario*), and according to which there should be a clear independence of the commercial rules from fiscal provisions, has been defeated in practice, even before it was defeated in legal terms. As a consequence of this approach, in fact, tax valuations should be taken into account only for the filing of the annual tax return, and no items of a merely fiscal nature appear in published accounts. It is instead rather clear that a second view more and more prevailed in Italy from the 1970s, the so-called single track approach (*teoria del binario unico*), which establishes an influence of tax rules on commercial accounts, giving rise to a sort of reverse dependence of the latter from the former (see also Section 1.2).

In detail, this result has been caused mainly by the combined effect of two fiscal rules. The first requires that company taxable income is in principle that resulting from the accounting records kept for commercial purposes (Article 52, 1986 Consolidated Act on Income Taxes, T.U.I.R.), while the second rule makes it compulsory for Italian companies to include certain expenses in their profit and loss account in order to deduct them from tax (Article 75, section 4, T.U.I.R.). These provisions give rise to a system of relationships between tax and commercial legislation in accounting that is somewhat similar to that induced by the German *Maßgeblichkeitsprinzip*, that is, the "authoritative principle."

An attempt to overcome the problematic relationship between commercial law and fiscal rules has been made by the original version of decree no. 127/1991, which adopted an odd middle way between the above-mentioned two extreme positions, requiring that the final section of the income statement include adjustments of valuations and provisions both resulting purely from the application of the tax legislation (former items no. 24 and 25 of the income statement format), with a clear attempt to separate the influence of taxation from accounting profit calculation. In this way, however, the intrusion of the tax rules into the Italian commercial accounts was definitively stated and recognized by the Civil Code itself. In other words, there had taken place an institutionalization of the linkage between commercial and tax accounting, which was previously supported only by the joint effect of articles 52 and 74 of the 1986 Consolidated Act on Income Taxes, and which was commonly applied in practice but never overtly set in the Civil Code. As an example, accelerated depreciation exceeding the "correct" amount under the Civil Code's rule had to be shown in the "corrections to valuations that resulted purely from the application of fiscal law" (item no. 24 of the original income statement format). This treatment of accelerated depreciation was similar to that of the French system (*amortissement dérogatoire*). The two lines of fiscal corrections led to a final result that was similar but does not fully overlap with taxable income. This was because, according to most authors and the Ministerial Commentary, only additional charges caused by tax allowances being greater than commercial accounting ones could be entered in these adjustment lines. Where the difference was the other way, that is, the tax allowance was less than the accounting one, the difference could not be included in these two lines, and therefore the reconciliation between the tax profit and the commercial profit was one-sided and partial.

This fiscal section of the income statement format became a source of interpretative problems, its exact use being unclear. Although the intention in the original approach of the 1991 decree to clarify the relationship between commercial and tax laws was in principle commendable, technical problems and cultural resistences arose considering the above-described explicit recognition of the fiscal influence on commercial accounts on the one hand and the stated formal autonomy of commercial accounts from taxation on the other hand (see Article 1 of Parliamentary law no. 69/1990 empowering the Italian government to implement the Fourth Directive). In particular, many firms complained that, given the then new treatment required for accelerated depreciation in the income statement (item no. 24), they could not any longer deduct it—as they did traditionally—from relevant tangible fixed assets, but they had to take this fiscal-derived value to a shareholder funds' provision (a sort of special reserve) titled "accelerated depreciation," and in parallel to account for deferred tax, which is quite uncommon for company accounts in Italy.

As a consequence of this perceived problematic situation, a new rule was issued in August 1994 (Article 2-*bis*, law no. 503/1994), which cancelled the fiscal section in the income statement format (items no. 24 and 25), as well as the "result of the financial year" (item no. 23), which was basically the accounting result before fiscal corrections. The same article stated that it is permitted to operate fiscal corrections to accounting values in company accounts, and that the reasons and amounts of these corrections have to be disclosed in the notes on point no. 14. Incidentally, Article 2-*bis* of law no. 503/1994 cancelled the requirement that consolidation accounts be freed from fiscal interferences existing in company accounts and imposed the requirement that in the notes there should be disclosed the reasons and amounts of these tax-originated values in the group accounts (point 0-*bis* of the notes).

The result of this regulatory change in the relationship between commercial accounts and tax rules is that companies are perfectly allowed to apply the latter in the preparation of the former, and virtually no value nor result in their income statement is now free from fiscal influences, while beforehand the "result of the financial year" (former item no. 23) was relatively unbiased by tax interferences. The "principle of reverse dependence" is thus confirmed, that is, of the dependence of commercial accounting rules on tax rules, so that one could say—ironically—that the former are now completely harmonized with the latter. In a nutshell, the evolution of this relationship went full circle, and Italy went back to the situation existing before decree no. 127/1991.

It must be pointed out, though, that once again the "profit for the year" line does not correspond to taxable income, since a number of fiscal allowances and variations of accounting numbers are carried out by companies directly in their annual tax return (*dichiarazione dei redditi*). In particular, for income tax purposes a 5-year carry-forward of an accounting loss for the financial period is allowed to any limited or unlimited entity (Articles. 5 and 102, Consolidated Act on Income Tax).

It is also noteworthy that the fiscal section of the income statement was in use for the 1993 financial year, and some companies started to treat the fiscal corrections as a sort of reserves in the shareholder funds. Hence, interpretative and technical problems are expected to arise in company accounts relating to year 1994.

On the other hand, it is possible to give a further example of the existing close relationship between fiscal and civil legislation in Italy. In order to make accounts legal from the commercial point of view, the Civil Code requires companies to comply with a great deal of formal requirements, such as the stamping and numbering of the account books (Article 2215 Civil Code). These requirements can also be carried out by the tax authorities and are necessary to legalize accounts from the fiscal standpoint, too.

On the whole, it would then seem possible to state that tax authorities relied to a large extent on accounting numbers for pursuing their own purposes. In quite recent years, however, a trend showing a seemingly contradictory direction has emerged concerning the relationship between taxation and accounting. The large amount of tax evasion and the urgent need to cope with the enlarging public deficit induced the Italian government to adjust its policy and to introduce both a minimum income to be compulsorily declared by a large number of categories of taxpayers in 1992 and 1993, and a series of indices aimed at an artificially determined minimum income (*coefficienti presuntivi di reddito*).

In addition to that, law no. 413 of 1991 granted a taxpayer (e.g., a company) either a fiscal remission, if it spontaneously declared income amounts that did not appear from accounting records, or a significant discount on the due taxes and fines if paid before the definitive sentence of the fiscal court was pronounced. In the former case, companies were allowed to add assets to their balance sheet that were previously omitted and remove assets and liabilities that were "invented." This way, the fiscal remission also had an accounting impact. The amended financial statements resulting from such a process are likely to be a little more realistic but not more internally consistent as to valuations.

So, the Italian fiscal system showed in the recent past a sort of schizophrenic approach to accounting. On the one hand, it is formally based on accounting results, and on the other, it is moving increasingly away from them, linking the tax burden to artificial extraneous parameters and specific negotiations, while preserving the heavy fiscal influence and formalities affecting company accounts. In parallel, it appears also that—from a government perspective—company financial statements are more and more treated merely as an easy tool for tax levying and thus reducing the public deficit, as the recent tax on firms' net worth seems to confirm (law no. 394 of 1992).

Presented on pages 493–533 are two sets of 1993 accounts, group accounts and parent company (individual company) accounts, of the Merloni, so that readers have the opportunity to review both.

In the following the main Italian format and disclosure rules in company and group accounts will be dealt with, although it would be impossible within the framework of this book to cover every particular norm regarding different industries (e.g., insurance) and/or types of companies (e.g., cooperatives).

3.2 The Form and Content of Company Accounts

As already pointed out, the Fourth EU Directive of 1978 on annual accounts was eventually implemented in the Italian Civil Code, with the first part of legislative decree no. 127 dated April 9, 1991. For financial years ending after April 17, 1993, all limited companies are required to produce financial statements that comply with the new legislation. Its *de facto* relevance extended also to 1992 accounts, however, given the already mentioned need for comparative figures.

The company financial statements (*bilancio d'esercizio*) are legally composed, as indicated above, of a balance sheet, an income statement, and notes to the account, accompanied by a report on operations. The detailed contents of each of these documents will be illustrated below.

However, there exists an abridged form of company financial statements (*bilancio in forma abbreviata*), which is allowed for small companies not exceeding—for two consecutive financial years or in the first year of their existence—two of the three size thresholds indicated in Table 1 (Article 2435-*bis* Civil Code).

It is worth observing that these thresholds have been recently updated by decree no. 526/1992 implementing in Italy EU Directive no. 90/604.

These abridged annual accounts consist of a simplified balance sheet format (where only items marked by capital letters and roman numbers must be shown, see Figure 4), a standard income statement, and a reduced number of compulsory notes (seven out of the ordinarily required eighteen disclosures). The report on operations (*relazione sulla gestione*) may be omitted, if some of its information (namely, nos. 3 and 4) are included in the notes. However, decree no. 526/1992 requires small enterprises to *explicitly* show both the depreciation and amortization provisions as deductions from the fixed assets on the face of the balance sheet, and debtors and creditors due beyond next financial year. Note that, on the contrary, for companies that are not small, the net fixed asset figure alone can be shown on the face of the balance sheet, while detail about related depreciation and amortization provisions can be discussed in the notes.

As discussed earlier, the general principle guiding the drawing up of the annual accounts in Italy is now that of "representing in a true and correct manner" the financial situation of a company and its economic results (Article 2423, section 2, Civil Code).

Other general, well-known accounting postulates are specified in the new provisions in order to develop the above fundamental principle: *prudence, accrual, consistency in valuation criteria*, and *going concern* (Article 2423-*bis*, Civil Code). However, these were already applied as common practice and in the main already implicit in the previous law. No particular differences exist with the Anglo-American interpretation of the same postulates.

In the following sections the compulsory legal formats of company accounts and their contents will be analyzed more in detail.

Table 1   *Size Thresholds for Abridged Financial Statements (Article 2435-bis Civil Code)*

Assets (net of depreciation funds)	3.09 billion Italian lira
Sales (net of discounts)	6.18 billion Italian lira
Employees (financial year average)	50

In order to benefit from the special (balance sheet) format and abridged notes and report on operations, the above limits must not be exceeded for two consecutive financial years (or for the first year of life of an undertaking).

3.2.1 Legal Formats and Contents

The minimum contents of financial statements, which had previously been defined by the Civil Code, have now been extended, and *highly rigid formats* (also in the *sequence of items*) prescribed, applying in principle to all companies and groups prevalently performing industrial activity (banks and financial institutions have their own formats, see Section 3.4).

Some flexibility is allowed for modifying the name and the degree of details only of the items that are preceded by Arabic numbers in the balance sheet format, and by small letters in the income statement one (Article 2423-*ter*, Civil Code, see Figures 4 and 5).

It will appear clearly that these formats do not always provide information in a manner suitable for financial analysis and need the analyst's quite complex elaborations to pursue successfully this end.

Balance Sheet (Stato Patrimoniale, Article 2424 Civil Code)   From the options available in the Fourth Directive, Italy has chosen the traditional, horizontal balance sheet format (Article 9 of the directive), with assets on the left and set out apparently in reverse order of liquidity (see Figure 4). In fact, the balance sheet is organized according to the German-based destination principle, which leads to an inappropriate classification according to the Anglo-Saxon approach, which is based on the items' liquidity, since it implies putting items having the same economic nature together. For example, all trade debtors go in the Current Assets section (item C.II. of Assets), independent of their maturity time (maybe beyond the next financial year). This is on the basis that they spring from the same economic process, that is, the trade of the company's (and group's) products. The same applies to debtors having a financial nature that are all to be imputed to Investments (item no. B.III.2. of Assets). Furthermore, the items' liquidity principle of classification is clearly not respected as to liabilities, since, for instance, all creditors must be classified in the same section, without taking into consideration any of their time length to maturity. As a consequence, balance sheet items may be easily misleading to an analyst adopting a mere financial approach.

In the following, a closer look at the sections composing asset and liability sides will be given.

Assets (*Attivo*)   Moving on to the analysis of the individual sections, there appears to be nothing relevant in Section (A) (*Crediti verso soci per versamenti ancora dovuti, con separata indicazione della parte già richiamata*), apart from the facts that (*a*) the amounts of this section are both those that have already been called up and those that are not yet so, and that (*b*) this item should probably be deducted from shareholder funds when carrying out a financial analysis, or put in Current Assets' debtors.

Section (B) (*Immobilizzazioni*) deals with all kinds of fixed assets (B.I: *Immobilizzazioni materiali*; B.II: *Immobilizzazioni immateriali*; B.III: *Immobilizzazioni finanziarie*). As already stated, tangible assets and intangible assets and trade debtors must be shown at their net value (i.e., their respective provisions being deducted). In contrast to some other European countries, it is possible to capitalize research and development costs, as well as advertisement expenses, where relevant. The capitalization of these items hinders the distribution of dividends, however, if the amounts of intangibles capitalized are not counterbalanced by at least an identical amount of available reserves in the shareholder funds. Goodwill (*avviamento*) can be shown in item B.I.5. only if a cost has been incurred by the company and it has been "purchased" to the latter from operations of merger and acquisition. No self-valuation of company brands (*marchi*) is permitted. Equity investments (*partecipazioni*) in other companies are considered fixed assets on the basis of a legal presumption, according to which, if these investments are in associated undertakings, that is, they exceed the 20% of the share capital of the participated company (10% if this is quoted), then these values may be included in section B.III.1. of the balance sheet (since a "significant influence" is attached to them). Note that section B.III.1. was amended in May 1994 by decree no. 315/1994 (Article 6), implementing in Italy EU Directive no. 92/101 regarding the purchase of both own and controlling entities' shares. As a consequence of this regulatory change, item B.III.1.c. has been introduced requiring disclosure of the value of equity investments in parent undertakings. If a company owns an equity investment in another company through a fiduciary firm, then it may write this value under the heading (financial) "debtors" (one of the items in B.III.2.) instead of under the caption "investments" (one of the items in B.III.1).

Figure 4 *Mandatory Balance Sheet Format*
(Article 2424 Civil Code)

1994   1993

ASSETS:
A. Called-up share capital not paid, with a specific note of the amounts already called in
B. Fixed assets:
  I. *Intangible assets:*
    1. start-up costs
    2. research, development, and advertising costs capitalized
    3. patent rights and royalties
    4. brands and licences
    5. goodwill
    6. intangible assets under construction and prepayments [difference on consolidation]*
    7. others
                                    Total
  II. *Tangible assets:*
    1. land and buildings
    2. plant and machinery
    3. fixtures and fittings
    4. other tangible assets
    5. tangible assets under construction and prepayments
                                    Total
  III. *Investments, with a specific note, for each item of debtors,* of amounts receivable within the next financial year:
    1. participating interests in:
      a. subsidiary undertakings
      b. associated undertakings
      c. parent undertakings
      d. other undertakings
    2. debtors:
      a. amounts owed by subsidiary undertakings
      b. amounts owed by associated undertakings
      c. amounts owed by parent undertakings
      d. amounts owed by other undertakings

3. other securities

4. own shares, with a note on their total nominal value

1994   1993

Total

Total fixed assets (B)

C. Current assets:
    I. *Stocks:*
        1. raw materials and consumables
        2. work-in-progress
        3. long-term contract stocks
        4. finished goods and merchandise
        5. prepayments

Total

    II. *Debtors, with a specific note for each item of amounts* due beyond the next financial year:
        1. trade debtors
        2. amounts owed by subsidiary undertakings
        3. amounts owed by associated undertakings
        4. amounts owed by parent undertakings
        5. amounts owed by other undertakings

Total

    III. *Financial assets other than long term:*
        1. participating interests in subsidiary undertakings
        2. participating interests in associated undertakings
        3. participating interests in parent undertakings
        4. participating interests in other undertakings
        5. own shares, with a note also of their total nominal value
        6. other securities

Total

    IV. *Liquid funds:*
        1. cash at bank and in post office accounts
        2. cheques
        3. cash in hand

Total

Total current assets (C)

D. Accrued income and prepayments, with a specific note of discounts on loans

(Figure continues)

(Figure 4, continued)

1994   1993

LIABILITIES:

A. Shareholders' capital:
    I. Called-up share capital
    II. Share premium account
    III. Revaluation reserve
    IV. Legal reserve
    V. Reserve for own shares
    VI. Reserves provided for by the articles
      [Consolidation reserve]*
    VII. Other reserves
      [Capital and reserves of third parties
      (i.e., minority interests)]*
    VIII. Profits (losses) of previous years
    IX. Profit (loss) for the year
                                    Total

B. Provisions for risks and liabilities:
    1. provisions for pensions
    2. provisions for taxes
      [consolidation provision for risks
      and future expenses]*
    3. others
                                        Total

C. Statutory provisions for severance indemnities

D. Creditors, with a specific note for each item of amounts due beyond the next financial year:
    1. debentures
    2. redeemable debentures
    3. bank overdrafts and loans
    4. other loans
    5. prepayments
    6. trade creditors
    7. bills of exchange
    8. amounts owed to subsidiary undertakings
    9. amounts owed to associated undertakings
    10. amounts owed to parent undertakings
    11. taxes
    12. social security
    13. others
                                        Total

1994   1993

E.   Accruals and deferred income, with a specific note of premiums on loans

Memorandum Accounts
1.   List of direct and indirect guarantees, with a specific indication of:
   a.   fiduciary garantees in favor of subsidiary, associated, parent, and group undertakings
   b.   endorsement garantees in favor of subsidiary, associated, parent, and group undertakings
   c.   personal guarantees in favor of subsidiary, associated, parent, and group undertakings
   d.   real property guarantees in favor of subsidiary, associated, parent, and group undertakings
2.   Other memorandum accounts

---

* This item is to be included—where relevant—only in the consolidated balance sheet.

All fixed assets must be devalued only if the loss occurring to them is of a permanent nature; otherwise, they must be maintained at the historic cost. When the reason for which a fixed asset has been devalued ceases, this must be written up again at its original (historic) cost. In Italy, lease capitalization is not permitted, and consequently, operating and financial leasing are treated in the same way, that is, taking the lease rentals to income statement in accordance with the accrual principle.

Section (C) (*Attivo circolante*) includes the values "destinated" to and originating from, the ordinary course of business, such as inventory, trade debtors, short-term securities, and cash (C.I: *Rimanenze*; C.II: *Crediti*; C.III: *Attività finanziarie*; C.IV: *Disponibilità liquide*). A small change in section C.III. was brought about by decree no. 315/1994, which added a new line disclosing the value of current investments in parent undertakings (now item C.III.3.).

In Section (D) (*Ratei e risconti attivi*) note the inclusion of discounts on loans (*disaggio su prestiti*) in "prepayments and accrued income," following the French influence. Discounts on loans should generally be taken to intangible assets for the purposes of financial analysis.

Liabilities (*Passivo*)   Section (A) (*Patrimonio netto*) deals with Share-holders' Capital and Reserves. It is divided into many subsections indicated by a Roman number. They are the following:

I. Called-up share capital	I. *Capitale*
II. Share premium account	II. *Riserva da sovraprezzo azioni*
III. Revaluation reserve	III. *Riserve di rivalutazione*
IV. Legal reserve	IV. *Riserva legale*
V. Reserve for own shares	V. *Riserva per azioni proprie in portafoglio*
VI. Reserves provided for by the articles [Consolidation reserve]	VI. *Riserve statutarie* [*Riserva di consolidamento*]
VII. Other reserves [Capital and reserves of third parties]	VII. *Altre riserve* [*Capitale e riserve di terzi*]
VIII. Profits (losses) of previous years	VIII. *Utili (perdite) portati a nuovo*
IX. Profit (loss) for the year	IX. *Utile (perdita) dell'esercizio*

The items in brackets are to appear only in consolidated accounts. The law does not attribute to them any specific number or identification.

On the individual items, it should be noted that:

- "Called-up share capital" is the amount of capital in issue (paid or not paid) at the end of a financial year.

- "Share premium account" is the reserve where the amount of the issue price over share face value is taken (in Italy shares cannot be issued at a price lower than their nominal value). The amounts of this reserve cannot be distributed before the legal reserve has reached the level indicated below (Article 2431 Civil Code).

- "Revaluation reserve" is the account in which the credit surpluses of the revaluation processes enacted in accordance with the different revaluation laws (see Section 4.1) are written.

- "Legal reserve" is made up of a mandatory annual allowance of 5%

from the profit for the year, until this reserve reaches the amount of 20% of the share capital in issue (Article 2430 Civil Code).

- "Reserve for own shares" is a reserve to be mandatorily provided for when a company buys back own shares: these must be included either in section B.III.4 or in section C.III.5 of Assets, while a nondistributable reserve of the same amount is to be set up with profits of previous years or distributable reserves in the shareholder funds (Article 2357-*ter*, section 3, Civil Code). This reserve has to be maintained as long as the company remains in possession of the shares.

- "Reserves provided for by the articles" are reserves that may be changed only by an *ad hoc* decision of an extraordinary-type of shareholders' general meeting.

- "Consolidation reserve" is an account in which a negative difference between the purchase price of a company and the fair value of its net assets is written to, unless this difference depends on the anticipation of unfavorable trends in the acquired company's future economic results (Article 33, decree no. 127/1991). In the latter case, this difference has to be taken to a "consolidation provision for risks and future expenses" (see below).

- "Other reserves" must be specified one by one; typical examples of reserves falling in this category are "Reserve for credit balances from departures from legal rules according to the true and correct representation principle"; "Reserve for accelerated depreciation" (due probably to disappear as a consequence of the August 1994 change in the relationship between commercial and tax rules; see Section 3.1); "Reserve for public grants"; and "Reserve for gains from the equity method of investment valuation" (see Section 4.1).

- "Capital and reserves of third parties" is an item that in the Anglo-American environment is better known under the label "minority interests" (Article 32, decree no. 127/1991).

- "Profits (losses) of previous years" comprises the amounts of income not yet decided upon by the annual general meeting (note that, with reference to losses, until these are covered, the distribution of dividends is not allowed; Article 2433, section 3, Civil Code).

- "Profit (loss) for the year" corresponds to the amount calculated in the income statement, that is, it includes the dividends to be distributed to shareholders. This implies that shareholder funds in Italian balance sheets are overestimated by the amount of dividends, which is on the contrary usually disclosed as a current liability in British accounts. This derives from a legal approach in Italy to financial statements, according to which they come into existence legally only after the annual general meeting approved them; before that, they are a mere proposal by company directors. Consistently, the amount of dividends is formally decided and approved by the same annual general meeting: only after this decision are dividends existent and distributable. As a consequence, dividends are accounted for as a reserve movement in the financial year subsequent to that which they refer to, and not as a decrease in profit like in Britain (they would then be, in British terms, a prior-year adjustment).

Section (B) (*Fondi per rischi e oneri*) displays the provisions for risks and future expenses, which must have, though, an actual possibility of coming into existence in order to be provided for. In other words, these accounts should not be used with a conservative orientation according to law (Article 2424-*bis*, section 3, Civil Code) but only when there are definite, identifiable contingencies potentially impairing the value of company capital. If a provision refers clearly to a specific asset, however, it has to be directly deducted from the latter. Among the provisions of this section should be mentioned (*a*) the "provision for pensions," which copes with additional pension schemes when they exist at the company or at the industry level; (*b*) "provisions for taxes," which comprises both a provision for tax debits in litigation with tax authorities and a provision for deferred taxes, which is not common in Italian company accounts and anyway not legally required to be disclosed; (*c*) other provision funds, such as the "provision for exchange rate differences," "provision for future manufacturing maintenance," and any other provision for protecting company value from future potential liabilities. As mentioned previously, in consolidated accounts the negative difference between a company purchase price and its net assets—when reasonably relatable to negative future economic events potentially affecting company value—is to be taken to a "consolidation provision for risks and future expenses" to appear in this section of the consolidated balance sheet.

Section (C) (*Trattamento di fine rapporto di lavoro subordinato*) is a one-item section dealing with an Italian legal peculiarity, which is the employee severance indemnity to be paid to each employee when leaving the firm (Article 2120 Civil Code). The amount of the indemnity is linked to the number of years for which the employee has worked for that firm and to his or her position within the organization. In general, it corresponds to the average monthly salary times the number of years worked for the company. In this respect, it must be pointed out that this indemnity is an unfunded provision and tends to assume a large numerical expression in Italian balance sheets, thus being an important context-specific element of the self-financing process of firms (i.e., increase in the cash flow from operating activity).

Section (D) (*Debiti*) exposes all kinds of company creditors: from debenture holders to banks, from trade suppliers to tax authorities and other group undertakings. It is specifically required to disclose the creditor amounts falling due beyond the next financial year. In contrast to the amounts under section (B) of Liabilities, those in this section are certain and acknowledged (e.g., tax debtors in D.11 are due to be paid, while tax amounts included in provision for taxes in C.2 are not definitive or clearly determined).

Section (E) (*Ratei e risconti passivi*) discloses company accruals and deferred income. A specific note on "premiums on loans" is required, but these are not commonly found in practice.

At the foot of the balance sheet memorandum accounts (the so-called *conti d'ordine*) must be disclosed. Their role is to point out off-balance-sheet future risks and obligations, such as guarantees given or received, or commitments to buy and sell. It is noteworthy that in this kind of accounts there can be, and generally there is, exposed the *residual debts for lease operations*.

Income Statement (*Conto Economico*, Article 2425 Civil Code)   From the options available in the Fourth Directive, Italy has chosen the vertical income statement format (Article 23 of the directive). This format is of the *progressive* type (*en liste*) and is based on the cost classification by *nature* (*par nature*) rather than by destination (*par destination*) (see Figure 5).

Figure 5 *Mandatory Income Statement Format*
(Article 2425 Civil Code)

1994   *1993*

A. Value of production:
   1. turnover
   2. change in stocks of finished goods and in work-in-progress
   3. change in long-term contract stocks
   4. own work capitalized
   5. other income, with a specific note of the public "ordinary grants"

Total

B. Production costs:
   6. raw materials and consumables
   7. external services
   8. rents
   9. staff costs:
      a. wages and salaries
      b.   social security costs
      c. statutory severance costs
      d. other pension costs
      e. other staff costs
   10. depreciation and write-offs:
      a. depreciation of intangible assets
      b. depreciation of tangible assets
      c. other amounts written off from fixed assets
      d. amounts written off from current debtors and from liquid funds
   11. change in stock of raw materials, consumables, and merchandise;
   12. provisions for risks
   13. other provisions
   14. other operating charges

Total

Difference between production value and costs (A – B).

C. Income and charges from financial assets:
  15. income from participating interests, with a separate note of that from subsidiary and associated undertakings
  16. other income from financial assets:
      a. income from debtors under fixed assets, with a separate note of that from subsidiary and associated undertakings, and that from parent undertakings
      b. income from fixed asset investments other than participating interests
      c. income from current asset investments other than participating interests
      d. other income from financial assets, with a separate note of that from subsidiary and associated undertakings, and that from parent undertakings
  17. interest and similar charges, with a separate note of those to subsidiary, associated and parent undertakings

  Total (15 + 16 – 17)

D. Changes in value of financial assets:
  18. revaluations:
      a. of participating interests
      b. of fixed asset investments other than participating interests
      c. of current asset investments other than participating interests
  19. write-offs:
      a. of participating interests
      b. of fixed asset investments other than participating interests
      c. of current asset investments other than participating interests

  Total of changes in value (18 – 19)

E. Extraordinary income and charges:
  20. extraordinary income, with a separate note of gains from disposals which cannot be recorded under no. 5
  21. extraordinary charges, with a separate note of losses from disposals which cannot be recorded under no.

(Figure continues)

(Figure 5, continued)

$$1994 \quad 1993$$

14, and of taxes relating to previous financial years

Total of extraordinary items (20 – 21)

Profit or loss before taxation (A – B ± C ± D ± E)

22. taxes on profit

[profit (loss) for the financial year to third parties (i.e., minority interests)]*

23. profit (loss) for the financial year

---

* This item is to be included—where relevant—only in the consolidated income statement.

This German-derived model starts with the "Value of production" and shows some intermediate results, but unfortunately none of them can be easily interpreted as operating income. It is divided into five sections identified by capital letters. In the following a brief description of each section will be given.

Section (A) (*Valore della produzione*, items no. 1–5) is made up of income values deriving from ordinary operations, such as sale and service revenues (*ricavi delle vendite e delle prestazioni*, item no. 1), change in stocks of finished goods and in work-in-progress (*variazioni delle rimanenze di prodotti in corso di lavorazione, semilavorati e finiti*, item no. 2), change in long-term contract stocks (*variazioni dei lavori in corso su ordinazione*, item no. 3), own work capitalized, including financial charges capitalized (*incrementi di immobilizzazioni per lavori interni*, item no. 4), and other income (*altri ricavi e proventi*, item no. 5). In the latter caption must be included a quite wide (and confusing) array of values, such as research and development and advertisement costs capitalized, public grants for interest payments received (to be specifically disclosed), "re-valuations" to historic cost of tangible and intangible fixed assets (see Section B) Assets and Section 4.1), gains from disposals of an "ordinary" nature (which might or might not be exceptional in British terms).

Note that sale and service revenues, as well as costs and expenses, must be disclosed net of any discounts or premiums, respectively, made or received, and from VAT and duties (Article 2425-b*is* Civil Code).

In Section (B) (*Costi della produzione*, items no. 6–14) all "ordinary" costs incurred for the production activity (to be broadly interpreted) are shown (purchases, services, rentals, staff, depreciation and write-offs,

change in stocks of raw materials, consumables and merchandise, allowances for risks, other provisions, and other operating charges). In particular, bad trade debtors allowance is to be put in item no. 10.d., while
provisions for risks and other provisions find a correspondence with
provisions under section (B) of Liabilities. The last, residual item of this
section (*oneri diversi di gestione*) collects a large number of other operating costs, such as taxes other than income tax, realized losses on debtors
and on foreign exchange differences, and losses on "ordinary" disposals
(which again might or might not have an exceptional nature according to
the British definition).

The difference between the total of section (A) and that of section (B)
represents a value close to operating income but not identical to it, considering that interest receivable has not been taken into account and that gains
from and losses on "ordinary" disposals are ambiguous items, which have
not been defined by law.

Section (C) (*Proventi e oneri finanziari*, items no. 15–17) discloses any
kind of revenues and expenses from financial activity, such as dividends
(item no. 15), interest receivable (item no. 16), and interest payable (item
no. 17). It is clear, though, that the balance of this section is rather
equivocal and unhelpful, because of the different management logics
underlying the financial investment policy on the one hand (items no. 15–
16), and the company gearing (leverage) choices on the other hand (item
no. 17).

Section (D) (*Rettifiche di valore di attività finanziarie*, items no. 18–19)
has a quite limited use in practice. Both items refer only to values linked to
financial activity: in particular, item no. 18 to the revaluations (*rivalutazioni*)
to the historic cost of these values after they underwent a previous devaluation; item no. 19 to their write-offs (*svalutazioni*), which are to be
accomplished in any relevant case as to financial values included in
current asset section, and only when facing a lasting loss in their value as
to the financial values in fixed assets. It is interesting to note that, while
item no. 19.a. is due to disclose losses deriving from the equity method in
both company and group financial statements (in accordance with the
conservatism principle), item no. 18.a. is used *only* in the *consolidated*
profit and loss account to show income from the equity method of valuing
associate undertakings. In fact, as mentioned previously, in company
accounts gains arising from this method, when applied to both associate

and subsidiary investment valuation, are to be "sterilized" in *ad hoc* equity reserve.

Section (E) (*Proventi e oneri straordinari*, items no. 20–21) deals with extraordinary values, but no legal definition or list is provided. From the legal text one can deduce only that extrordinary gains on disposals must be included in item no. 20, and extraordinary losses on disposals and taxes relating to previous financial years must be included in item no. 21. In accordance with the Ministerial Commentary (which in turn replicates what is ambiguously stated by Article 29 of the Fourth Directive), extraordinary items consist of income and charges not related to ordinary operations. However, this interpretation clearly does not appear satisfactory and is contrary to both theoretical opinions and practice, which tend to link extraordinary items to their temporal exceptionality or nonrecurrence. Divergent practical applications have therefore taken place, complicating the already difficult process of reinterpreting for financial analysis Italian company (and group) income statements. An emerging scholarly interpretation and the current trend in company accounts seem, however, to lean toward a restriction of the meaning and scope of application of extraordinary items, in parallel with theoretical and practical stances that are already widely adopted in other European countries (such as Germany and the United Kingdom).

After the five above-illustrated sections, the result before taxation is to be calculated, followed by income taxes in item no. 22. No distinction between taxes on ordinary and extraordinary profit is asked for (Italy chose to adopt the option permitted by Article 30 of the Fourth Directive). As pointed out (see Section 3.1), the original version of the income statement format required that items resulting purely from the application of fiscal rules were to be shown. This has been cancelled in the new version of the last lines of the format, according to law no. 503/1994. More simply now, right after income taxes, profit (or loss) for the financial year is to be stated (item no. 23).

In the consolidated income statement, before the last amount representing the group share of group profit (or loss), a further item must be added dealing with the minority interests in group profit or loss (Article 32, section 4, decree no. 127/1991).

Notes to the Accounts (*Nota Integrativa*, Article 2427 Civil Code) Most of the dislosure in Italian company financial statements is now concentrated on the so-called *nota integrativa* (literally, integrating note). Many new disclosures are required in the notes, including details of any departures from legal rules, and the presence of, and quantification of the effects of, valuations induced merely by the tax law. Some are doubtful about the benefits of the increased amount of information because quantity seems to have been given preference over quality. But the new requirements seem to represent a step forward in the level of disclosure in company accounts.

The notes to the accounts have a legally determined minimum contents,which is listed in the following (Article 2427 Civil Code). Note that the order of this list should be in principle respected.

1. Valuation criteria applied to financial statement items and conversion methods of the foreign currency values

2. Fixed asset (tangible, intangible, and financial) movement analysis referred to the financial year, with a specific indication for each of them of their historic cost, previous revaluation amounts, depreciation (or amortization) provisions, write-downs, acquisitions, movement from one category to another, disposals in the financial year, and similar information

3. Composition and amortization criteria of start-up costs, of research and development costs and of advertisement costs capitalized, and reasons for their capitalization and development costs and of advertisement costs capitalized, and reasons for their capitalization

4. Movements in the other assets and liabilities, with particular reference to provisions and employee severance indemnity and the amounts taken to and from them

5. List of participations (equity investments) directly or indirectly (i.e., through a fiduciary firm or intermediary) owned by the company, with an indication for each of the name of the participated company, its registered office, its share capital and shareholder's funds, the profit or loss for the last financial year, the percentage owned, and the book value attributed to this investment;

6. For each relevant item, the amount of debtors and creditors of a residual maturity exceeding 5 years, and the amount of creditors

supported by security on the company's own assets (with specific indication of the nature of these securities)

7. Composition of the balance sheet items "prepayments and accrued income," "accruals and deferred income," "other provisions," as well as "other reserves"

8. For each relevant item, the amount of financial charges capitalized in assets

9. Disclosure on the composition and nature of off-balance-sheet financial commitments and of memorandum accounts, where relevant to appreciate the financial situation of the company and with an indication of those relating to subsidiary, associated, parent, and group undertakings

10. If relevant, the breakdown of sales and service revenues according to categories of activities and to geographic areas

11. Gains from equity investments, indicated in item no. 15 of the income statement format, which are different from dividends received

12. Partitioning of financial interest and similar items, indicated in item no.17 of the income statement format, related to debentures, bank debts, and others

13. Composition of income statement extraordinary items (items no. 20 and 21 of the income statement format)

14. Reasons for the corrections to valuations and allowances resulting purely from the application of fiscal law, and the amounts thereof also compared with the overall corrections to valuations and allowances from the appropriate income statement and balance sheet items (requirement changed by law no. 1 of January 7, 1995)

15. Average number of employees, divided by categories

16. Amount of fees due to directors and *sindaci* (internal-institutional auditors), expressed in an aggregate way for each category

17. Number and nominal value of each category of company shares, and number and face value of the new underwritten shares issued during the financial year

18. Special shares (*azioni di godimento*), convertible debentures, and

similar securities issued by the company, with a specific indication of their number and the rights they grant.

It is easy to observe that the above information can be usefully grouped in four general headings: (*a*) illustration of accounting valuation criteria (point no.1); (*b*) asset and liability movements (points no. 2 and 4, together with the "statement of equity reserve movements" required to any limited companies by fiscal law; see Section 3.1); (*c*) detailed disclosure on particular balance sheet and income statement items (points no. 3, 5–14, 17–18); (*d*) miscellaneous disclosure (points no. 15–16).

It should be recalled that the above list is not exhaustive, since other articles of the Civil Code refer to the need for disclosing in the notes further information, as well as the impact of, and the reasons for, the company adopting a legally allowed option (say, for example, departures from legal rules in "exceptional cases," modifications to mandatory formats, changes in valuation criteria, current cost valuation of stocks, and reasons for exemption from group accounts).

Nevertheless, any other disclosure, which would be appropriate in order to represent in a true and correct way the company's financial position and economic performance, must be *mandatorily* included in the *Nota integrativa* (Article 2423, section 3; see also Section 3.1). Therefore, a generic legal obligation is imposed on companies to provide any additional disclosure in the notes that is relevant to pursue that general objective.

Within the framework of the new Italian accounting legislation, disclosure in the notes is rapidly assuming growing importance. It is also true that this process is likely to be further accelerated because of the aforementioned 1994 change in commercial rules, according to which income statement values deriving merely from the application of tax law must be disclosed in the notes and no longer in the income statement.

Report on Operations (*Relazione sulla Gestione*, Article 2428 Civil Code)   The Report on Operations does not belong to the legal concept of financial statements (*bilancio*), but it must accompany them. *De facto* the *Relazione sulla gestione* is a necessary component of the company's annual report.

According to Article 2428 of Civil Code, this report should (*a*) be prepared by the directors, (*b*) deal with the general situation of the company and the trends of its operations, considered both globally and in the various sectors in which it has operated, also through its subsidiaries; and (*c*) refer especially to company costs, revenues, and investments. At any rate, the following information must be derived from this report:

1. Research and development activities
2. Relationships with subsidiary, associate, parent, and group undertakings
3. Number and nominal value of both company own shares and parent's shares owned at the end of the financial year, also through either a fiduciary undertaking or intermediary, with an indication of the percentage of share capital to which these shares correspond
4. Number and nominal value of both company own shares and parent's shares purchased or disposed of during the financial year, also through either a fiduciary undertaking or intermediary, with an indication of the percentage of share capital that these shares correspond to, of the relative prices, and of the reasons explaining the purchases and disposals
5. Contingencies occurring after the closing of the financial year
6. Foreseeable evolution of the operations

It must be remembered that the Report on Operations may be omitted if a company is allowed to prepare the abridged form of annual accounts (see Section 3.1). In this case, though, the company must provide items 3 and 4 in the notes to the accounts.

Merloni Elettrodomestici S.p.A. 1993 Annual Accounts   At the end of this chapter, after the consolidated financial statements and notes, may be found the 1993 annual accounts of Merloni Elettrodomestici S.p.A., both in Italian and in English.

Merloni Elettrodomestici is family owned but quoted on the Milan and Rome Stock Exchanges. It is the holding company of the Merloni Elettrodomestici group, whose core business is household appliances (refrigerators and freezers, dishwashers and washing machines, ovens and cookers). The group is one of the European market leaders, and its prod-

ucts are marketed under three major brand names: Ariston, Indesit, and
Scholtès. Foreign sales account for 71% of group total revenues.

As can be noted, the structure and sequence of the balance sheet and
income statement follow those set by law and illustrated in the preceding
sections. A few items have been omitted from the compulsory formats,
since it is likely that their value was nil.

Together with these statements, the Merloni Elettrodomestici company
provided also the *nota integrativa* (notes), the *Relazione Sulla Gestione*
(report on operations), the *Relazione del Consiglio di Amministrazione*
(report of Board of Directors), and the *Relazione del Collegio Sindacale*
(internal-insitutional auditors report). However, these documents have not
been reproduced here for reasons of space.

3.3 The Form and Content of Group Accounts

As pointed out earlier (see Sections 1.2 and 3.1), before decree no. 127/
1991 group accounts were required to be presented *only* by groups including listed companies (since the beginning of the 1980s), and by a few other
special categories, such as newpaper publishers, insurance companies,
public utilities, and in general entities receiving public support on an
ordinary basis.

Because of the lack of any specific legislation, the accounting criteria
used were to some extent various: in particular, for quoted companies,
CONSOB recommended explicitly to refer to accounting standards prepared by *Dottori commercialisti* and *Ragionieri* (but interestingly enough
did not recommend the use of standard no. 8 just dealing with consolidated
accounts), and when Italian standards were absent, to the standards issued
by the International Accounting Standards Committee (IASC). However,
for other categories of groups required to draw up consolidated reports, no
clear and consistent regulatory source existed, so that accounting criteria
and methods deriving from Italian professionals, IA.SC and group policies
were mixed together in different proportions. In this respect, it was always
necessary to check carefully which was (were) the source (sources) followed in the preparation of a given set of consolidated accounts.

The implementation of the Seventh Directive through decree no. 127/
1991 introduced in Italy for the first time the *generalized* obligation for

any group of companies to prepare consolidated accounts, starting with reference to the 1994 financial year (to be published, therefore, in the first half of 1995). The introduction of such an accounting technique in an environment that largely lacks experience will probably lead to some practical difficulties. The delay in applying the requirement to relatively small groups (until 1999) should make things easier.

As mentioned previously, the new rules dealing with consolidated reports—in contrast to those regarding company accounts—have not been introduced into the Civil Code. Thus, reference will be made here, if not differently stated, to articles of decree no. 127/1991 (in particular Article 25–43).

In general, all limited liability companies (i.e., *società per azioni, società a responsabilità limitata,* and *società in accomandita per azioni*) that have control over one or more undertakings must prepare group accounts according to stated legal rules (Article 25, section 1). Further, these accounts will apply also to cooperatives and public entities running a commercial activity (Article 25, section 2). They will not, though, apply to sole traders or partnerships, nor to associations or foundations that do not carry out commercial operations. In this respect, there is concern that some smaller corporations might legally structure themselves in a different way (e.g., as partnerships) in order to benefit from such an exception.

As to *exemptions* from consolidated accounts, these will be mandatory only for groups that exceed, for two consecutive financial years or in the first year of their existence, two of the following three size thresholds (Article 27):

1. Total assets 10 billion lire (gross of consolidation adjustments)
2. Turnover 20 billion lire (gross of consolidation adjustments)
3. 250 employees

The limits are transitorily *doubled* until 1999 (Article 46, section 2), with the obvious consequence that only remarkably large groups will need to comply with this requirement. However, in contrast to company accounts, no abridged group accounts are allowed below certain size thresholds. The exemption does not apply if one of the group companies is listed. On the contrary, a nonlisted parent, which is itself controlled by another company, is exempted from preparing group accounts as long as the parent's parent (*a*) owns at least 95% of the former's shares (or, if not, there is not a specific request to do so—at least 6 months before the financial year end—from at least 5% of share capital), (*b*) is in an EU member state, and (*c*) produces consolidated accounts according to Seventh Directive–derived legal rules (it is interesting to note the opposite attitude of Italian legislators on points (*b*) and (*c*) compared with that showed on the same points, say, in France and the Netherlands).

As to *inclusions* in group accounts, the general principle states that a company must be consolidated when it is a subsidiary (*società controllata*) of a parent undertaking. This qualification is determined by the parent's capability to *control* or *exert a dominant influence* (*influenza dominante*) over the subsidiary, through either (*a*) direct or indirect (e.g., a fiduciary company or an intermediary person) possession of voting rights in the ordinary annual general meeting, or (*b*) a "domination" contract or an Article of Association producing a similar effect, or (*c*) agreements with other shareholders (Article 26). Domestic and foreign subsidiaries must be included, irrespective of the legal form and geographic location of the subsidiary. The decree did not take up the option to extend consolidation to companies in which the parent exercises a *de facto* dominant influence thanks only to particular contractual arrangements (e.g., control through market domination). Subsidiaries must be fully consolidated by using the acquisition (purchase) method. No mention is made by law of the merger accounting method (known in the United States as the pooling-of-interests method).

As to *exclusions* from the above general principle, subsidiaries must be excluded from consolidation if they run activities that are so divergent that their inclusion would compromise the "true and correct representation" (Article 28, section 1). In this case, subsidiaries must be accounted for in group accounts by a consolidated account version of the equity method, which is similar to international practice (Article 36, section 1). In fact, these investments may be already valued by this method in the parent company accounts: the relevant difference in consolidated financial statements is that the group's proportion of subsidiary profit can be taken to the income statement (item no. 18.a.), which is not permitted in individual company accounts (as mentioned, it must be written in an *ad hoc* equity reserve).

Subsidiaries may also be *excluded* if they are immaterial, if the parent's actual control is restricted, if they are only temporarily under the control of the parent, or if there is difficulty in obtaining on time or without a disproportionate expense the necessary accounting information (Article 28, section 2).

A company is considered an associate (*società collegata*) if it is under a significant influence (*influenza notevole*) of another company (Article 2357 Civil Code). A significant influence is presumed to exist whether a company controls—directly or indirectly—at least 20% (10% if listed) or more of another company's voting rights. Associates should be accounted for (as for subsidiaries excluded from consolidation on the basis of their strong difference with the rest of the group) by the above-described "consolidated account" version of the equity method (Article 36, section 3). Of course, if the participating percentage goes up to 50%, then the legal presumption is that the participated undertaking becomes a subsidiary.

As to a joint venture, this may be consolidated when (*a*) one of the group companies has a joint control on it together with other members and on the basis of *ad hoc* agreements with them, and (*b*) the participating investment reaches at least 20% (10% if the joint venture is listed) of the share capital of this enterprise. If included in group accounts, joint ventures having such characteristics should be accounted for by proportional consolidation (Article 37), or at any rate, if excluded from group accounts, by the equity method (if they exceed in fact the threshold for being treated as associates). If they do not exceed such a threshold, they must be stated at cost in consolidated financial statements.

Like invidual company accounts, group accounts must comply with the general principle according to which they must represent in a true and correct manner (*rappresentare in modo veritiero e corretto*) the financial situation and the economic results of the whole group (Article 29, section 2). Additional disclosures in the notes are mandatory if this is necessary to give a "true and correct representation" of the group state of affairs. Departures from legal rules are compulsory but to be enacted only in "exceptional" cases (for an illustration of these rules see Sections 3.1 and 3.2). The well-known accounting postulates, such as prudence, consistency through time, uniform accounting policies, and going concern apply also to consolidated accounts.

The date of the group accounts is to be in principle the closing date of the parent company's financial year, alternatively, the date in which the majority of subsidiaries or the most important of them close the financial year may be adopted. If the closing date of a subsidiary is different from that set as a reference for group accounts, then this undertaking is required—with no exceptions allowed—to prepare *ad hoc* interim financial statements (Article 30).

The consolidated formats are those used for individual company accounts (Article 32), of course, suitably amended in some items dealing with minority interests, difference on consolidation, consolidation provision for risks and future expenses, and consolidation reserve, as described above (see Section 3.2).

The disclosures legally required to appear in the notes to the group accounts (*nota integrativa*) are quite similar to those already illustrated with reference to the company annual report. Some adjustments are introduced to take into consideration the nature and the technical preparation of the consolidated accounts (Articles 38 and 39). Examples of these specific indications are principles and criteria of consolidation, and in particular determination and treatment of the difference arising on this process; foreign currency translation methods; chosen closing date of group accounts (if different from the parent's); special adaptations of the formats; list of subsidiaries included in consolidation and of undertakings excluded from it, and their modification through time; when relevant, information needed to keep on ensuring comparability of the figures from one financial year to another.

The report on operations (*relazione sulla gestione*) to be presented together with consolidated financial statements is virtually identical to that described with respect to company accounts.

Further statements and reports (such as, for instance, consolidated flow of funds, Chairman's statement, and changes in shareholders' funds) are voluntary. Before the coming into force of the new legislation, it is fair to say that most of the groups producing consolidated accounts (for legal reasons or on a voluntary basis) used to provide also these supplementary statements. Whether or not this will be so in 1995 remains to be seen, as the first consolidated accounts prepared according to the new legal rules will appear for that year.

Consolidated accounts must be audited by the same body legally due to audit the parent's accounts. Therefore, this can be either its *collegio sindacale* or, if the parent is subject to an external-independent audit by a *società di revisione*, it will be the latter to audit also group financial statements (Article 41, section 3). The control activity and its outcomes must result in an *ad hoc* report that can be either a *Relazione del Collegio Sindacale* (*sindaci* report) in the former case, or a *Relazione della Società di Revisione* (auditors' report) in the latter.

In procedural terms, group accounts follow the same pattern and timing in preparation and presentation to the annual general meeting as the parent company individual accounts (see Section 3.2). However, a fundamental difference is that consolidated financial statements are not to be approved by the parent's shareholders, who can only look over them and not ask for a change or revision of these statements. In fact, only the parent's individual accounts would need the shareholders' endorsement, since on their basis dividend distribution is decided. In parallel with the parent's approved accounts, a copy of the consolidated financial statements, together with the report on operations and the audit report, must be deposited in the Register of Undertakings at the local Chamber of Commerce. Mention of the deposit must be made in the Official Bulletin of Public and Private Limited Companies (BUSARL, Article 42).

As to their technical preparation, group accounts must include all values (assets and liabilities, revenues and costs) relating to subsidiary undertakings (full consolidation method), while intra-group items (debits and credits, revenues and expenses) and unrealized profits must be eliminated (Article 31). The elimination of items can be overlooked if they are immaterial. Intra-group profits can also be maintained in consolidated accounts, if they derive from the company's ordinary operations, are settled at arm's length, and if their elimination would imply disproportionate costs.

A point of major importance in the drawing up and interpretation of group accounts is their relationship with fiscal-based values. As in other European countries, consolidated financial statements are tax-neutral in Italy, since income and net worth taxes are levied on company account figures. Therefore, the EU Seventh Directive required that, where tax-based values have been used in individual company accounts, these shall either be disclosed in the notes or corrected in consolidated financial statements. The original version of Article 31, section 5, of decree no. 127/1991 was clearly moving toward the correction solution, requiring that all company account values resulting purely from the application of fiscal law were to be eliminated in group accounts (a similar approach was taken in France). However, in the recent law no. 503/1994, which was commented upon earlier (see Section 3.1), Article 2-*bis*, section 4, cancelled the just mentioned section 5 of Article 31 and imposed the obligation on groups to disclose in the notes to consolidated accounts "the reasons of corrections to valuations and allowances resulting purely from the application of fiscal law, as well as the amounts thereof compared with the overall corrections to valuations and allowances drawn from the appropriate income statement items." As a consequence, now it is no longer required in Italy to "purify" consolidated financial statements of fiscal interferences, since it is only necessary to give disclosures on this point in the *nota integrativa* (a similar approach has been taken in Germany).

Nevertheless, some commentators noted that the law does not *impose* the nonelimination of the tax-based values in group accounts, and thus, according to the option granted by Article 29, section 5, of the Seventh Directive, the elimination of these values is permitted. This leads the author to forecast a quite chaotic first application in 1995 of the new rules on this point.

The Merloni Elettrodomestici 1993 Group Accounts The Merloni Elettrodomestici 1993 group accounts are provided at the end of this chapter. They comprise the consolidated balance sheet (in Italian and English), the consolidated income statement (in Italian and English), the consolidated statement of changes in shareholders' equity, the consolidated statement of changes in financial position, the notes to the consolidated financial statements, and the auditors' report.

As can be seen, these accounts are a good example of the form and contents of consolidated financial statements before the new rules came into force. It is not possible to provide readers with an example of the new consolidated accounts, given that the first publication of them will take place in the first half of 1995. In this respect, balance sheet and income statement formats have been chosen by the parent and do not correspond—if only marginally—to the now mandatory ones.

In terms of subsidiary consolidation, Merloni Elettrodomestici followed international and Italian practice to include only companies where the group has a direct or indirect control through the majority possession of voting rights (point no. 1 of the notes). Majority holdings that were "inactive or insignificant" have been excluded. Changes in the scope of consolidation are described in detail.

Accounting policies applied are illustrated in point no. 1 of the notes. Note that Merloni, in the absence of Italian legal rules in the subject area, states that it decided to comply with Italian professional standards (at the end of point no. 1 in the notes), though having previously affirmed— somewhat inconsistently—that an effort has been made to bring group accounts into line as far as possible with international accounting standards. The solution to this seeming contradiction relies on Merloni's perception that Italian accounting standards, which are recommended by CONSOB (Merloni is in fact a listed company) are based on the requirements of the I.A.S.C. standards.

Tax-based values have been eliminated. The auditors' report confirms that a "true and fair view" (in fact, the "true and correct representation" principle was not yet legally enforced in 1994 with reference to consolidated accounts) of the group financial and economic situation has been given "in accordance with the accounting principles established by the Italian Accounting Profession."

3.4 The Accounts of Banks and Financial Institutions

Until 1992 Italian accounting regulation of financial companies and banking firms consisted of the 1942 Civil Code and some special provisions related to their particular activity. Legislative decree no. 87 dated January 27, 1992 implemented both the 1986 EU Directive on the annual and consolidated accounts of banks and other financial institutions and the 1989 EU Eleventh Directive on the publication of annual accounts of branches established in a member state but with headquarters outside that state. This double implementation came into force in 1993.

Decree no. 87/1992 provides a special set of rules for the above entities, whereas for the general principles it refers to decree no. 127/1991. The new provisions delegated to the Italian Central Bank, among other things, the authority to precisely define the account contents and formats and to modify them in the future, putting special emphasis on comparability.

With particular reference to formats, the decree states two innovative rules for the Italian context: when possible, substance has to be preferred over form in drawing up company accounts, and the time of settlement has to be given precedence over that of negotiation (Article 7, section 4). These provisions should be particularly meaningful for the presentation of a company's financial situation and the accounting treatment of such innovative financial instruments as interest rate swaps, forward rate agreements, currency swaps, and futures.

The Bank of Italy has chosen a two-sided format for the balance sheet, with assets on the left, set out in order of increasing liquidity. No net worth total is required to be disclosed. A progressive income statement format (*en liste*) has been imposed for credit institutions and a horizontal one for financial companies. As for industrial company accounts, the influence of taxation on accounts is *not* shown in an *ad hoc* section of the income statement, but it is pointed out in the notes. It therefore seems that the relationship between commercial rules and taxation has been treated since the beginning in a clearer, but not necessarily more satisfactory, way by decree no. 87/1992 than by decree no. 127/1991 described in Section 3.1.

As to valuation rules, loans must be presented at their net realizable value. Historical cost is to be used for other assets. In particular, marketable securities, when listed, are valued either at the lower of cost and market value or at market value, the chosen policy being used consistently. Participating interests are valued at historical cost or by the equity method. Provisions for general risks from banking operations, that is, credit interest and exchange risks, are allowed; net adjustments deriving from movements in those provisions are shown on the credit or debit side of the income statement. Only the final outcome of all the transactions in marketable securities, currencies, and other financial instruments is to be taken to the profit and loss account, and no distinction should be made between realized and unrealized results.

Rules for consolidated accounts comply with the Seventh Directive provisions. As for industrial groups, value adjustments that have been made exclusively in application of fiscal law in the individual accounts, can be either eliminated or maintained in consolidated statements (Article 39, decree no. 87/1992).

Branches of banks and financial institutions established in a member state, which are controlled by companies inside the EU, are required to integrate their accounts with those of their parents drawn up in accordance with the accounting regulation of the latter's country. Branches with headquarters outside the EU are allowed to act in the same way only if mutual recognition between the accounting regulation of their parent's country and that of Italy exists. When this is not the case, branches must present, in addition to their own accounts, the balance sheet and income statement of their parent restated according to Italian provisions.

As a final effect of EU pressure, it is interesting to observe that the regulation on mergers and demergers (i.e., Third and Sixth Directives) have been quite recently implemented in Italy (in 1991).

4. Rules, Policies, and Practices of Accounting Valuations in Italy

4.1 Valuations in Company Accounts

In addition to Civil Code and other legal requirements discussed earlier, some more detailed valuation rules were introduced by legislative decree no. 127/1991, with the aim of reducing differences in approach between companies (new Article 2426 Civil Code).

Also of extreme relevance in the Italian environment are the valuation criteria set by fiscal law, which quite often are used in practice as the *actual* legal reference source when individual company accounts are drawn up (in particular, Presidential decree no. 917/1986, the so-called Consolidated Act on Income Taxes, T.U.I.R., which came into force in 1988 and includes a section on corporation tax; since then the decree has received many amendments).

A further normative source on valuations is the accounting standards issued by Italian professionals. These statements are not as authoritative, however, and they are in general considered only when neither tax legislation, nor commercial laws state anything on a given subject area.

In the following some of the most relevant year-end valuations in company accounts will be presented in order to give a comprehensive picture of the contents of the different regulatory sources (Civil Code, tax law, accounting standards) thereon. If the reference to a source is omitted in the description of a given valuation, this implies that either it does not have significantly dissimilar contents from the others or it does not deal with that valuation at all. This is true in particular for professional accounting standards, which are in fact undergoing a revision process at the moment, which aims to make them more similar to the imposed legal criteria.

Incidentally, it should be noted that the decision—when legally and technically possible—of including a value under a heading rather than under another competing one in the balance sheet (e.g., shares can be taken either to "investments" in section B.III.1. or to "securities" in section C.III. of Assets; if their nature is uncertain between trade or finance, debtors can be included either in section B.III.2. or in section C.II. of Assets) is not just a formal one, but it does have profound implications in valuation terms. In fact, to stick with the examples provided above, only to shares in investment section can the equity method be applied, and only items included in fixed assets have to be devalued when a *durable* loss in value takes place: the remaining assets have to be devalued simply when a loss in their value (of a lasting or temporary nature) occurs.

The Legal Definition of Historic Cost   The general principle imposed by Article 2426 Civil Code for asset valuation is the historic cost, which is divided into purchase cost (*costo di acquisto*) and production cost (*costo di produzione*). The same rule specifies also the methods of the respective calculation.

As to purchase cost, assets should be written at the actual cost incurred for their acquisition, increased by all other relevant costs that have been incurred in order to put the asset in the condition of operating (e.g., tax duties, notary expenses, transport costs, installation and running expenses, various fees, nondeductible VAT). To this amount can be added a "reasonable" share of interest payable, but only during the period in which the asset is being (externally) fabricated.

As to production cost, the basis is made up of direct costs, plus a "reasonably" attributable portion of overheads. Also in this case, part of interest payable can be capitalized. The addition of overheads and interest payable to an asset's internal production cost is allowed only during its production period and ceases when it can be utilized by the firm.

Interestingly enough, fiscal law sets a definition of historic cost that is slightly more limiting in scope than that of the Civil Code (Article 76, section 1, T.U.I.R., as recently amended by law-decree no. 416/1994 converted into law no. 503/1994). It permits, in fact, the capitalization of overheads and interests only with reference to tangible and intangible fixed assets. This aspect apart, fiscal rule follows the commercial legislation.

On this point, accounting standard no. 4 provides some technical details useful for implementing the legal indications for calculating historic (purchase and production) costs. In particular, it poses the requirements (which in general are followed in practice) of capitalizing interest on assets only if (*a*) the time period necessary for their production, either internal to the firm or external by the selling entity, is fairly long, and (*b*) interest payable is traceable in a clear way to the acquisition or own production of the asset (e.g., loans that have been taken on just for the purpose of financing either the purchase of the asset or its internal construction).

Tangible Fixed Assets   Tangible assets must be valued at historic cost, according to the described rules. As mentioned previously, they must be devalued only if a *durable* loss in value occurs, but their (historic) cost must be restored when the cause justifying the revaluation ceases.

Tangible assets, whose utilization is temporally limited (e.g., buildings but not land), must be depreciated systematically over their useful (economic) life "in relation to their residual possibility of use." This means that the net value of these assets in the balance sheet should always be "recoverable" through the profitability of the future financial years during which that asset will be providing its economic contribution. The rule also suggests implicitly the preparation of a depreciation plan for each depreciable tangible asset, and the application of the straight line depreciation method. Any change in depreciation method and/or rate must be illustrated and justified in the notes (*nota integrativa*).

It must be remembered that a statement on "tangible (and intangible) asset movements" is to be compulsorily included in point no. 2 of the notes, unless a company is permitted to produce the so-called abridged accounts (*bilancio in forma abbreviata*).

A further aspect of tangible asset valuation according to commercial rules is given by the legal revaluation allowed from time to time by special statutory laws. Considering the peculiarity and the relative frequency, compared with other European countries (e.g., France) of this approach to asset revaluation, it seems appropriate to devote a short section to this topic in order to exemplify the functioning of the last two revaluation laws, the effects of which can still be found in Italian accounts.

Revaluation Laws In addition to the aforementioned changes in accounting rules, two revaluation laws were passed in 1990 and 1991 (law no. 408/1990 and law no. 413/1991). Such a short time lag between the acts is unusual. In the past 40 years only three similar laws were promulgated in Italy (in 1952, 1975, and 1983).

Relating in principle to inflationary periods, an *ad hoc* revaluation law is occasionally issued in Italy in order to allow companies to legitimately overcome the valuation limit of historical cost, without being obliged to justify the new value with reference to "special reasons" (now called "exceptional cases"). In this event, however, the actual reason underlying the promulgation of two revaluation laws is probably to be traced back to the persistent and pressing problem of public debt financing rather than to the inflationary process, which affected the Italian economy in the second half of the 1980s at an average yearly rate of 7–8%. This interpretation is supported by the short time lag between the two acts: the failure of the first voluntary law to meet its objectives in terms of tax inflows may explain the need, after only one year, for a second revaluation law, this time of compulsory application to all firms.

The recent laws resembled each other as to the legal entities involved (all limited liability companies, as well as partnerships and individual businesses) and the taxable nature of the revaluation gains (unlike the laws of 1952, 1975, and 1983). The two laws were dissimilar with reference to the degree of compulsion, scope of application in terms of balance sheet values, revaluation criteria, calculation of the tax burden, and depreciation procedures for tax purposes.

As to the first aspect of differentiation, it has already been noted that the 1990 law could be applied on a voluntary basis, whereas the 1991 law was compulsory. Moreover, the former permitted the revaluation of tangible assets, intangibles legally recognized (such as patents, brands, and licensing rights), and investments in associates and subsidiaries. Conversely, the

1991 law dealt only with buildings and land.

There were differences also in the revaluation methods adopted by the two laws. In the 1990 law the revaluation principle (and limit) was the current value of the asset with regard especially to its value in use to the company, thereby leaving it largely free to choose the most appropriate figure. The resulting credit (revaluation gain) was taxed, if relating to buildings and land, at 16%, and, if relating to other assets, at 20%. The remaining credit had to be allocated to a special revaluation reserve.

The 1991 law imposed a more complex and restrictive revaluation method based on the determination of a maximum amount and a minimum one. Thus, buildings could be revalued up to an amount deriving from the multiplication of their nominal rents by legally defined indices (e.g., 100 for housing estates). The same applied also to land, even though it could be revalued only up to 80% of its "value" calculated according to the described procedure; 38% of the resulting increase, reduced by 1 billion lire, was the minimum amount of the revaluation. The revaluation actually carried out was taxed (at 16%), and the residual credit went to an *ad hoc* reserve. In the 1991 case, companies were thus restricted to a great extent in determining the "fair value" of the assets, given the highly mechanical procedure for establishing both the maximum and the minimum amount of the revaluation.

For 1991, increased depreciation provisions are immediately tax and commercially deductible. For 1990 they are instead completely tax deductible only from the third financial year after that of the revaluation (but they have been deductible since 1990 for commercial regulation purposes).

As a result of the two laws, the annual accounts of Italian companies clearly cannot be said to be drawn up in accordance either with the current value principle or with the historical cost principle. On the contrary, instead of leading to some amelioration in the consistency and quality of the published accounting data, the recent revaluation laws are likely to have produced further distortions by stressing once again the use of the accounts as a tool for collecting financial resources to help with the state's deficit problem.

As to tax rules dealing with tangible fixed assets, they are quite influencial in practice and *de facto* substitute commercial law rules. The T.U.I.R. requires the application of a specific "ordinary tax depreciation rate" (*ammortamento ordinario,* "ordinary depreciation") to each (large) category of tangible assets used in different industries (Article 67). These rates must be reduced by half in the first fiscal year of useful life of an asset and can be reduced by the same percentage every year without a negative tax implication (i.e., it is possible to recover the difference between allowable tax depreciation and actual amount accounted for in one of the following years).

If the intensity of an asset utilization exceeds that normal in an industry, then the "ordinary rate" can be increased (*ammortamento accelerato*). This rate can be doubled in the first 3 years of use of an asset for accelerated depreciation (*ammortamento anticipato*). The amount of tax depreciation exceeding commercial depreciation can be put either in the same provision together with the latter or in an autonomous equity reserve (item no. A.VII. of Liabilities). In order to be deductible, tax depreciation charges must be taken to the income statement ("single track approach," see Section 3.1).

A further tax rule relevant to tangible fixed assets is that requiring their immediate expense to the income statement when being of an amount lower than one million lire. It is also noteworthy that ordinary repairing and maintenance are tax deductible as long as they do not exceed 5% of the original book value (i.e., not depreciated) of depreciable tangible assets as of at the beginning of the financial year.

Intangible Assets   Intangible asset valuation follows in principle the same rules established for tangible assets (historic cost, compulsory devaluation when a durable loss in value occurs, compulsory restoration of historic cost, depreciation principle and method, statement of "intangible asset movements").

Some legal provisions deal specifically with intangibles, however. In particular, the capitalization of research and development, advertising, and business start-up costs is allowable. They must be amortized within 5 years. It is also required that companies having capitalized these categories of intangibles only distribute dividends where available reserves exist in excess of the unamortized amount of these assets.

Goodwill can be written in this section only if a cost has been incurred for its acquisition and with the consensus of the *collegio sindacale.* It must be amortized over 5 years, but it is possible to extend this period a little when goodwill's useful life is estimated to be longer.

Own brand capitalization is not permitted. In order to be tax deductible, fiscal rules state that (*a*) the amortization allowances of royalties, patents, and brands cannot exceed one-third of their book value, (*b*) the amortization period of licences is the same as their contractual or legal length, (*c*) the amortization allowances of goodwill cannot exceed one-fifth of its book value (quite similar to Civil Code rule) (Article 68, T.U.I.R.), (*d*) research and development costs can be either expensed immediately to the income statement or amortized by the straight line method within 4 years, (*e*) advertising and promotion costs can be either expensed immediately to the income statement or amortized by straight line method over 3 years (Article 74, T.U.I.R .). No detailed tax rule is stated for start-up cost amortization: it is considered acceptable for fiscal purposes to use the period fixed by the Civil Code (5 years).

Equity Investments   Equity investments can be valued either at *cost* or by the *equity method*. In the following these approaches will be examined separately.

If the first option is taken, then *historic cost* represents the upper possible limit of valuation. Like tangible and intangible assets, investments must be devalued only when facing a durable loss in value. Their historic cost must be restored as soon as the reason for which they have been devalued ceases to exist.

For tax purposes, investments (apart from those valued by the equity method) have to be considered at a "minimum value" corresponding to the application of LIFO on an annual basis to such investments. Any other valuation method, such as FIFO or weighted average, is acceptable, provided that it leads to a value higher than that according to LIFO. In other words, the same criteria for tax valuing stocks must be applied (see below). Any increase above the historic cost of investments (not allowed, though, by commercial rules) is taxable (Article 54, T.U.I.R.). Losses in value are tax deductible if, and to the extent that, the resulting value of the investment is not lower than the proportion of the investee's shareholder capital emerging from the last approved annual accounts (or not lower than the last 6-month average share price, if the investee company is listed) (Article 66, section 1-*bis*, T.U.I.R.).

Certainly, a major innovation imported by decree no. 127/1991 is the option to use the *equity method* for valuation of investments where the investor has a dominant or significant influence (i.e., it can be applied only to investments included in section B.III.1.a. or B.III.1.b. of Assets). As mentioned in Section 3.3, associates are defined as those over which a company has a significant influence, which is presumed to be the case where 20% or more (10% if the investee company is listed) of the annual general meeting votes can be controlled. If a parent controls the majority of voting rights in, or exerts a dominant influence on, the investee annual general meeting, then this company is to be considered a subsidiary.

Nevertheless, the enforcement of the equity method takes place in a somewhat Italian way. In fact, income from associates must be credited to an undistributable equity reserve in the investor's individual balance sheet and not to the profit and loss statement, insofar as that income corresponds to unrealized gains (realized dividends are instead to be recorded in the income statement). It must be recalled that, according to the Italian interpretation of the realization principle, dividends are realized when already cashed or at least cashable.

The adoption of the equity method in company accounts was, however, limited in 1993 (the first year that the new Civil Code rules were in force), because of the negative tax effects that could follow from the then fiscal rules. In 1994 law-decree no. 416/1994 changed the fiscal attitude toward this valuation method, considering income from subsidiaries and associates—exceeding any previously deducted loss in value—as nontaxable (new 54, section 2-*bis*, T.U.I.R.). This legal innovation should slightly favor the adoption of the equity method, which is not expected to be very wide anyway.

Any loss in value of investments valued by this method is tax deductible within the limits set with reference to investments valued at cost (Article 66, 1-*ter*, T.U.I.R.).

Stocks (Inventories)   The rule of lower of cost (calculated according to the previously discussed guidelines) and net realizable value applies to the valuation of stocks. For valuation at cost, the LIFO method is permitted, as well as the FIFO and weighted average methods. Remarkable is the required indication in the notes of the current cost value of the single categories of stocks, when this is significantly different from that stated in the accounts.

Tax rules are once again quite influencial, stating that stock valuation can be made either at the stock's specific cost or (more frequently in practice) at a "minimum value" that corresponds to the LIFO method applied on an annual basis (so-called *LIFO a scatti*, Article 59, T.U.I.R.). Alternatively, FIFO or weighted average methods can be used, provided they respect the "minimum value" requirement. If in the last month of a financial year the average unit value of stocks is higher than their average current market value, then their tax "minimum value" is determined by multiplying stock physical quantities by their market value.

Noteworthy also is the indication by accounting standard no. 3 (now no. 13) concerning the possible capitalization of interest payable on stocks, when the latter are necessarily subject to a quite long maturity process before being marketable (e.g., some liqueurs such as brandy, or Parmesan cheese, or Parma ham).

Securities   Securities in the Current Asset section (C.III. of Assets) are to be treated at cost, but they have to be devalued whenever they endure any kind of loss in value. Correspondingly, they have to be restored at their historic cost if their (market) value goes up again.

In fiscal terms, securities have to be valued by using the same criteria stated for stocks (either at specific cost or at a "minimum value" corresponding to their LIFO valuation) (Article 61, T.U.I.R.).

Own (or Treasury) Shares   According to the recent legislative decree no. 315/1994 (implementing in Italy EU Directive no. 92/101), own shares in the balance sheet cannot exceed the tenth part of the company's share capital, taking into account any company shares owned by subsidiaries. Own shares are excluded from dividend distribution, and the voting right linked to them is temporarily suspended (Articles 2357 and 2357-*ter* Civil Code).

Own shares must be recorded separately in the balance sheet (items no. B.III.4. and C.III.5. of Assets) and valued at historic cost. While they remain in the possession of the company, a nondistributable equity reserve of an equal amount must be provided for out of profits (item no. A.V. of Liabilities).

Leased Assets   Accounting for financial leasing of assets is a point deliberately not addressed in the new valuation rules, and hence, the practice of taking rents to the income statement and of writing the amount of the residual debt only in the memorandum accounts will probably continue.

Operative leasing must be expensed directly, as in the Anglo-American practice.

Trade Debtors   According to Civil Code rule, trade debtors must be valued at their net realizable value.

Very influential on practice is the tax deductibility limit set with reference to the allowance for bad debts. This allowance is in fact deductible only to the extent that it is lower than 0.5% of the nominal value of debtors as of the end of a financial year. The same fiscal rule also applies to banks and financial institutions, which must take into account in debtors also "off-balance-sheet" operations. This tax deduction is no longer permitted when the overall provision for bad debt has reached 5% of the face value of debtors as of at the financial year end (Article 71, T.U.I.R.).

These limits are at present generating some serious tax problems, especially to banks, since they are considered to be too tight to cover at least in a satisfactory way the amount of bad debts characterizing many Italian businesses in times of recession.

Pensions and Employee Severance (or Termination) Indemnity   In Italy pensions are generally paid by the state or by public entities, from payments made both by companies (in the more relevant part) and by employees, throughout their work life. Thus, no provisions for this are necessary, and the Civil Code requires only that the amounts paid by the company are recorded in accordance with the accrual principle in item no. B.9.b. of the income statement.

Sometimes additional company or group pension schemes exist. In this case, pension costs are provided for in the income statement (item no. B.9.d.) and balance sheet (item no. B.1. of Liabilities).

When employees leave a company, however, for whatever reason, a severance (or termination) indemnity must be paid, and this has to be accrued in the accounts. The annual allowance for each company employee is to be calculated according to legally determined parameters and written in item B.9.c. of the income statement. This allowance has then to be taken to an *ad hoc* provision fund, called *fondo di trattamento di fine rapporto*, in section C of Liabilities. This fund is built up year by year in relation to an employee's salary for the year (see also Section 3.2).

Long-Term Contracts   According to the Civil Code, the percentage of completion method may be used for valuing long-term contracts, but the completed contract method is not excluded either. Technical guidelines for implementation of the two valuation methods can be found in Italian accounting standard no. 10. In most material aspects they do not differ from Anglo-Saxon common practice.

It is important to mention the tax rule on this topic, since it is followed most of the time in practice. T.U.I.R. requires in general the application of the percentage of completion method, with some minor adjustments in favor of the taxpayer, such as the 50% recognition of price increases until they are approved, and an allowance of 2% for unforeseeable contractual risks (Article 60, T.U.I.R.). However, fiscal rule permits also the application of the completed contract method, if requested by the company.

Because of the negative tax effects of the percentage of completion method, Italian practice appears to lean more toward the use of the alternative completed contract method.

Foreign Currency Transactions   There is no rule in the Civil Code on how to translate values in foreign currency within an individual company's own accounts. There is only the requirement to indicate which were the criteria used in the notes (point no. 1).

Conversely, fiscal law deals with such a topic, allowing basically two methods to translate foreign currency items in company accounts:

1. Year-end exchange rate method, with the recognition of gains or losses from the translation process as tax relevant (Article 76, section 2, T.U.I.R.)

2. Historical exchange rate method, with negative translation differences provided for through a yearly tax-deductible allowance in the income statement, which is accrued to an ad hoc fund (*fondo rischi su cambi*, provision for foreign exchange risks) to be decreased when an actual loss or an unexpected gain on foreign exchange occurs (Article 72, T.U.I.R.).

Accounting standard no. 9 is concerned with this topic as well. It states that, if (trade and finance) debtors and creditors expressed in foreign currency are short-term, then they have to be translated using the year-end exchange rate, and the negative and positive translation differences taken to the income statement. It is permitted, though, to defer the recognition of a positive translation difference. If debtors and creditors are long-term, the same rules apply, but when a positive translation difference would emerge there is no option granted, since it must not be recorded in the accounts. A conservative attitude is taken by Italian professionals as to the translation of foreign currency transactions.

Accounting for Tax The generally applied method of accounting for taxes is the "flow-through" method. Accounting for deferred tax in company accounts is very rare.

The income tax burden on limited companies is today around 52.2% of taxable income (36% of state income tax, IRPEG, plus 16.2% of local income tax, ILOR).

A further relevant aspect is the tax credit recognized on company dividends paid to shareholders, which is equal to 36% of the amount distributed, that is, the state income tax levied upon the company.

A 5-year carry forward of accounting losses is allowed to all limited and unlimited entities.

The accounting effects of tax amnesties, which are from time to time granted to Italian taxpayers, should also to be mentioned. The last tax amnesty with accounting implications took place in 1991: in this case law no. 413/1991 granted a taxpayer (e.g., a company) either a fiscal amnesty, in case it declared spontaneously income amounts that did not appear from accounting records, or a significant discount on the incumbent taxes and fines if it paid them before the definitive sentence of the fiscal court was pronounced. In the former case, companies were allowed to add assets to their balance sheet that previously had been omitted and cross out assets and liabilities that were invented. This way, the fiscal amnesty also had an accounting impact. The amended financial statements resulting from such a process, though, are likely to be a little more realistic but not more internally consistent in valuation terms.

Public Grants The Civil Code does not provide any detailed valuation rule as to public grants. The only mention on this point made by the Code is that requiring the inclusion of "ordinary grants" (*contributi in conto esercizio*) in item no. A.5. (as revenue within the value of production) of the income statement. In the main they are contributions given by public authorities, that is, state, regions, provinces, and communes, on a recurrent basis to support the operations of certain kinds of businesses with a general relevance (such as public transportation, newspapers, and utilities). Also, tax law recognizes the "ordinary grants" as revenue (Article 53, T.U.I.R.).

Less clear is the treatment of "capital grants" (*contributi in conto capitale*), that is, of grants given by public authorities in order to assist companies in the expansion and/or strengthening of their production structure. No mention whatsoever of this kind of grant is made in the Civil Code. Accounting standard no. 4 permits two alternative methods of accounting for capital grants:

1. To take them directly to an *ad hoc* equity reserve (A.VII. of the Liabilities)
2. Offset them against the value of the asset whose acquisition they have facilitated, or record them as a provision in the liability side to be progressively decreased in parallel with the asset depreciation process.

Fiscal legislation permits a company to choose if the taxation of capital grants must be done either in just one go when they are cashed or in several years (up to 10) using a straight line partitioning (Article 55, section 3, T.U.I.R.). As an alternative, the same article offers to exempt from taxation 50% of the grant by taking it to a special, nondistributable reserve in shareholders' funds (item no. A.VII. of Liabilities). Needless to say, the latter approach is the one more often used in practice to account for this type of public grant.

Oil, Gas, and Other Mineral Resources   No specific legal provision (neither of commercial nor of fiscal nature) is stated on this point. Also, Italian accounting standards do not mention explicitly such an issue.

4.2 Valuations in Group Accounts

As previously indicated (see Section 3.3), subsidiaries must be fully consolidated by using the accounts of the date when they are consolidated for the first time; moreover, intragroup items and unrealized profits must be completely eliminated (apart from particular cases), and minority interests shown as a part of consolidated shareholders' fund and income. Accounting policies must be uniformly applied to all subsidiary accounts included in the consolidation. Nonconsolidated subsidiaries and associates are to be accounted for by the equity method (however, unlike in the individual company accounts, income from associates must be taken into the income statement). Joint ventures are to be treated by the same method, or by the proportional one if the participating interest in them exceeds 20% (10% if the joint venture is listed). If this interest accounts for less than that percentage, they have to be valued at cost.

It must be remembered that group accounts are tax-neutral in Italy (apart from some cases for VAT purposes), and thus income tax rules disregard such statements.

In principle, the valuation criteria used in subsidiary and parent company individual accounts are transferred to group accounts via the consolidation process; thus, the foregoing analysis (Section 4.1) preserves much of its validity also referring to the latter statements. There are some valuation issues, however, that could be considered specific to consolidated reporting. They are briefly discussed in the following.

4.2.1 Difference on Consolidation

The acquisition (or purchase) method must be applied. "Merger accounting" (in the United States, the pooling-of-interests method) is not allowed (and not even mentioned by decree no. 127/1991).

In this respect, the difference between the cost of acquisition of a subsidiary and the corresponding book equity value of the subsidiary should be first allocated over the latter's individual assets and liabilities probably up to their current value (this benchmark is not specified, though, by the law).

Any residual difference is to be treated according to its sign. If negative, its treatment varies according to the cause. In fact, a negative difference (subsidiary value exceeding the cost of acquisition) must be allocated to an *ad hoc* reserve when deriving from a perceived bargain but classified as a liability representing negative goodwill when caused by negative trading prospects (*fondo di consolidamento per rischi ed oneri futuri*, consolidation provision for future risks and expenses).

A positive difference (acquisition cost exceeding the value of the subsidiary) has to be treated as goodwill (but called *differenza di consolidamento*, difference on consolidation) or, alternatively, written off immediately against group reserves. As mentioned earlier (see Section 4.1), goodwill arising from consolidation, when capitalized, should be amortized over 5 years, but the period may be a little extended if its useful life is reckoned to be longer. Anyway, the consensus of the parent company's *collegio sindacale* (board of internal-institutional auditors) on the recognition of goodwill among group intangible assets, is required.

Foreign Currency Translation   No specific rule is given on foreign currency translation by decree no. 127/1991 or in the Civil Code. Only a need for indicating in the notes the criteria adopted is stated. Nor do Italian accounting standards deal with this topic. Because of the lack of domestic regulatory guidelines, the most authoritative source is probably IAS 21.

Leased Assets   No legal rule allowing for financial lease capitalization is provided. Before decree no. 127/1991 came into force, and because of the lack of a general legal framework, some Italian groups used to capitalize leasing in their accounts. Since financial year 1994, this does not seem to be possible any longer.

Accounting for Taxes   The original version of Article 31, section 5, of decree no. 127/1991 *required* the full elimination in group accounts of all tax-based values written in the individual company statements, tacitly implying the need for providing for deferred taxation. All major Italian groups used to account for deferred tax in their consolidated statements. The recent cancellation of section 5 of Article 31 by law no. 503/1994 *seemed* to have had as a consequence that of *only permitting* the elimination of fiscal interferences in group accounts. In this respect, contradictory treatments of deferred tax *were* expected to arise on the occasion of the first application of the new legal rules on consolidated statements imported by decree no. 127/1991. However, the recent law-decree no. 1 of January 1995 (Article 12, sections 2 and 3) changed once again the treatment of taxes in consolidated financial reporting, getting back to the original approach: now it is *mandatory* to eliminate all fiscal influences and to provide for deferred taxes (no specific method for that is indicated, though). Consequently, the point 0-*bis* of the notes introduced by law no. 503/1994 is no more needed, and hence it has been cancelled.

4.2.2 Merloni Elettrodomestici Valuation Policies

Although the new rules on consolidated reporting had not yet come into force in 1993, it is easy to observe that the Merloni valuation policies in group accounts (but the same would hold also for individual company accounts) reflect in general the regulatory principles and methods discussed above (see point no. 1 in the notes to the Merloni consolidated financial statements).

Nonetheless, it seems relevant to observe that Merloni decided to immediately write off the difference on consolidation against group reserves, and to expose minority interests in a sort of limbo between liabilities and shareholder capital in the balance sheet and outside the profit for the year in the income statement, showing in both choices a strong dependence from Anglo-American practice (especially the British one for the considered aspects).

Accordingly, foreign currency translation follows the closing rate method.

Interestingly enough, stock valuation is made—in contrast to the U.K. practice—by using the LIFO method. Indeed, a change in valuation policy occurred in the parent company individual accounts, since a shift from weighted average cost to the LIFO method occurred. The impact of this change on group profit and net equity is disclosed.

Depreciation is calculated according to rates that are said to be in line with the tax-imposed ones.

Among intangible assets, the Merloni parent company has included, in compliance with particular statutory regulations, costs deriving from early retirements in 1992 (i.e., employees leaving the company before the legally determined age by virtue of a special decree with the aim to sustain the group in recession times), and from the 1991 tax amnesty mentioned above. Both costs are being amortized over 5 years.

Deferred taxes are provided for in group accounts, as well as the "reserve [to be true, provision] for termination indemnities."

"Capital grants" are taken to an equity reserve, while "operating grants" (here referred to as ordinary grants) are expensed directly to the income statement.

Foreign currency transactions are recorded in local currency at the exchange rate ruling at the day when the transaction took place. Foreign exchange (negative or positive) differences, stemming from the comparison of these amounts with year-end exchange rates, are taken to the income statement.

As hinted at earlier, it is likely that Merloni valuation policies, as well as account formats and notes, will face a major discontinuity with reference to the 1994 financial year because of the coming into force of the new rules on consolidated financial statements. If this is true, one might expect a departure to a certain extent from some of the more Anglo-Saxon oriented accounting choices in order to come closer to a more German-like model of consolidated reporting (e.g., treatment of tax items, no capitalization of financial leasing, minorities interests as a component part of shareholders' funds and of profit for the year, proportionate consolidation, account formats).

5. Expected Future Developments

The main expected developments are that the practices of accountants will catch up with, and adapt to, the recent legislative innovations, and that some consensus will emerge, especially on the treatment of tax-based values in individual company and group accounts. Because companies that produced consolidated accounts in the past did so on a voluntary basis, apart from listed companies and a few others, and because of the substantial lack of previous generally accepted rules, there is an inheritance of diversity of practice to be faced in this area.

It must be pointed out, however, that the revolution that has been previously highlighted will impact in a context that has particular characteristics and its own accounting tradition. Change, then, is not likely to be linear or painless, since it will probably be influenced by the dynamics of a context that seems resistent to change and tends to show quite a strong accounting inertia.

In this respect, whether the recent innovations in the Italian accounting regulatory framework will actually mean a new era in this country's financial reporting is a matter largely still to be discovered. One could say that Italian accounting will surely end up formally changed and probably ameliorated in certain areas such as disclosure and group accounts, but, on the other hand, the actual depth of the innovations may be questioned. The described discontinuities do not seem likely to lead to a radical change in the Italian socioeconomic foundations of accounting, which will probably continue to be inspired for a certain period by the same fiscal, conservative, and secrecy criteria.

However, three events of a more general nature might in the near future have a substantial impact not just on accounting practices, but also on their socioeconomic role and perception. These are the general tax reform, the ongoing privatization process—leading to a substantial increase in the number of shareholders—and the setting up of small secondary interconnected stock exchange markets (*Borse regionali*) to be run in a decentralized way at a regional level and hopefully to be entered in due course by many of the small and medium-sized, entrepreneurial-based firms characterizing the Italian economic system.

On the accounting legislative front, it is extremely unlikely that there will be any radical new regulation in the short to medium term, even if small but significant regulatory changes still take place (e.g., law no. 503/1994).

Useful Addresses

Consiglio Nazionale dei Dottori Commercialisti
Via Poli, 29
00187 Roma
Italy
Tel. +39-6-675861
Fax +39-6-67586349/67586348

Consiglio Nazionale dei Ragionieri e Periti Commerciali
Via Paisiello, 24
00198 Roma
Italy
Tel. +39-6-8415123/8541354
Fax +39-6-8417829

Associazione Italiana Revisori Contabili (ASSIREVI)

Via Vincenzo Monti, 16
20123 Milano
Italy
Tel. +39-2-436950
Fax +39-2-437326

Associazione Italiana Società di Revisione (AIRE)
Via Donizetti, 30
20100 Milano
Italy
Tel. +39-2-783339
Fax +39-2-76005079

Ministero di Grazia e Giustizia (Ministry of Justice)
Ufficio VII: Libere Professioni
Via Arenula
00100 Roma
Italy
Tel. +39-6-68851
Fax +39-6-6833611 (Ufficio VII)

Accademia Italiana di Economia Aziendale (AIDEA)
Via Garibaldi, 3
40124 Bologna
Italy
Tel. +39-51-227683/227684
Fax +39-51-226012

Merloni Elettrodomestici

Consolidated financial statements as of 31st December 1993

The accompanying notes to the financial statements are an integral part of the schedules published on pages 36-41.

Stato patrimoniale consolidato
al 31 dicembre 1993

Attività

(milioni di lire)	1993	1992
Attività a breve termine		
Cassa e banche	89.230	21.498
Titoli a reddito fisso	5.841	6.281
Crediti:		
Clienti ed effetti attivi	586.400	434.966
Consociate	15.309	8.077
Anticipi a fornitori	7.730	4.625
Altri	53.868	73.044
	663.307	**520.712**
Fondo svalutazione crediti	(31.774)	(18.349)
	631.533	**502.363**
Rimanenze di magazzino	212.176	189.480
Depositi cauzionali, ratei e risconti attivi	8.640	12.735
Totale attività a breve termine	**947.420**	**732.357**
Attività immobilizzate		
Immobilizzazioni finanziarie:		
Partecipazioni, netto	15.577	43.210
Impieghi finanziari	77.278	69.800
	92.855	**113.010**
Immobilizzazioni tecniche:		
Terreni e fabbricati	211.184	153.934
Impianti, macchinari e attrezzature	431.160	342.831
Mobili e macchine d'ufficio	43.179	33.767
Automezzi	20.738	18.351
	706.261	**548.883**
Fondi di ammortamento	(334.621)	(264.347)
	371.640	**284.536**
Beni immateriali e costi pluriennali, in corso di ammortamento	29.047	34.477
Totale attività immobilizzate	**493.542**	**432.023**

Totale attività	**1.440.962**	**1.164.380**

Passività e patrimonio netto

(milioni di lire)	1993	1992
Passività a breve termine		
Quota corrente dei finanziamenti a medio e lungo termine	13.966	13.313
Banche conto corrente	15.839	20.718
Anticipazioni bancarie	124.681	29.330
Debiti:		
Fornitori	470.491	399.373
Consociate	24.821	5.480
Anticipi da clienti	23.133	16.586
Altri	86.759	61.322
	605.204	**482.761**
Ratei e risconti passivi	43.269	36.018
Fondo oscillazione cambi	7.585	10.097
Fondo garanzia prodotti	13.055	9.178
Fondo imposte correnti	14.306	6.795
Totale passività a breve termine	**837.905**	**608.210**
Passività a medio-lungo termine		
Debiti a medio-lungo termine	174.293	182.899
Fondo imposte differite	17.988	16.068
Altri fondi non correnti	7.696	8.024
Fondo plusvalenze differite	–	422
Fondo trattamento di fine rapporto	74.620	66.927
	274.597	**274.340**
Prestito obbligazionario	57.255	57.855
Totale passività a medio-lungo termine	**331.852**	**332.195**
Quota di patrimonio netto appartenente ad azionisti di minoranza	22.404	391
Patrimonio netto		
Capitale sociale	91.502	91.502
Riserva legale	2.690	2.504
Fondo sovrapprezzo azioni	18.145	18.145
Contributi in conto capitale	60.205	66.305
Altre riserve, netto	26.577	30.919
Effetto cumulativo della conversione dei bilanci in valuta	17.122	12.659
Utile netto d'esercizio	32.560	1.550
Totale patrimonio netto	**248.801**	**223.584**
Totale passività e patrimonio netto	**1.440.962**	**1.164.380**

Consolidated balance sheet as of 31st December 1993
Translation from original Italian version

Assets

(millions of Italian lire)	1993	1992
Current Assets		
Cash and banks	89,230	21,498
Marketable securities	5,841	6,281
Receivables:		
Trade accounts and notes	586,400	434,966
Affiliated companies	15,309	8,077
Advances to suppliers	7,730	4,625
Others	53,868	73,044
	663,307	**520,712**
Allowance for doubtful accounts	(31,774)	(18,349)
	631,533	**502,363**
Inventories	212,176	189,480
Guarantee deposits, accrued income and prepayments	8,640	12,735
Total current assets	**947,420**	**732,357**
Non current assets		
Financial assets:		
Investments	15,577	43,210
Long-term financial assets	77,278	69,800
	92,855	**113,010**
Property, plant and equipment:		
Land and buildings	211,184	153,934
Machinery and equipment	431,160	342,831
Office furniture and fixtures	43,179	33,767
Vehicles	20,738	18,351
	706,261	**548,883**
Accumulated depreciation	(334,621)	(264,347)
	371,640	**284,536**
Intangible assets and deferred charges	29,047	34,477
Total non current assets	**493,542**	**432,023**
Total assets	**1,440,962**	**1,164,380**

Liabilities and shareholders' equity

(millions of Italian lire)	1993	1992
Current Liabilities		
Current portion of medium and long-term debt	13,966	13,313
Bank overdrafts	15,839	20,718
Bank advances	124,681	29,330
Payables: Trade accounts	470,491	399,373
Affiliated companies	24,821	5,480
Advances from customers	23,133	16,586
Other	86,759	61,322
	605,204	**482,761**
Accrued liabilities and deferred income	43,269	36,018
Reserve for exchange losses	7,585	10,097
Product warranty reserve	13,055	9,178
Accrued income taxes	14,306	6,795
Total current liabilities	**837,905**	**608,210**
Long-term liabilities		
Medium and long-term debt	174,293	182,899
Deferred income taxes	17,988	16,068
Other non-current provisions	7,696	8,024
Deferred capital gains	–	422
Reserve for termination indemnities	74,620	66,927
	274,597	**274,340**
Convertible bonds	57,255	57,855
Total long-term liabilities	**331,852**	**332,195**
Minority interests	22,404	391
Shareholders' equity		
Share capital	91,502	91,502
Legal reserve	2,690	2,504
Additional paid-in capital	18,145	18,145
Capital grants	60,205	66,305
Other reserves, net	26,577	30,919
Cumulative translation adjustment	17,122	12,659
Net income for the year	32,560	1,550
Total shareholders' equity	**248,801**	**223,584**
Total liabilities and shareholders' equity	**1,440,962**	**1,164,380**

Conto economico consolidato al 31 dicembre 1993

Ricavi

(milioni di lire)	1993	%	1992	%
Vendite nette mercato nazionale	470.471	26,8	450.749	34,5
Vendite nette mercato estero	1.247.060	71,1	818.866	62,7
Ricavi diversi	37.432	2,1	36.987	2,8
Totale ricavi	**1.754.963**	100,0	**1.306.602**	100,0

Costi e spese

(milioni di lire)	1993	%	1992	%
Acquisti ed altri costi	952.074	54,3	673.450	51,5
Salari, stipendi ed altri costi del personale	296.282	16,9	242.212	18,5
Ammortamenti	62.912	3,6	53.260	4,1
Spese generali, amministrative e di vendita	350.077	19,9	259.986	19,9
Variazioni di magazzino	(7.896)	(0,4)	15.270	1,2
	1.653.449	94,2	**1.244.178**	95,2
Utile operativo	**101.514**	5,8	**62.424**	4,8
Oneri e (proventi) diversi				
Oneri finanziari, al netto	43.224	2,5	35.254	2,7
Proventi da partecipazioni, al netto	(538)	–	579	–
Altri oneri, al netto	18.441	1,1	21.746	1,7
	61.127	3,5	**57.579**	4,4
Utile prima delle imposte e della quota parte degli azionisti di minoranza	**40.387**	2,3	**4.845**	0,4
Imposte sul reddito	(16.086)	(0,9)	(3.291)	(0,3)
Risultato di pertinenza degli azionisti di minoranza	8.259	0,5	(4)	–
Utile netto d'esercizio	32.560	1,9	1.550	0,1

Consolidated income statement as of 31st December 1993
Translation from original Italian version

Revenues

(millions of Italian lire)	1993	%	1992	%
Domestic sales	470,471	26.8	450,749	34.5
Foreign sales	1,247,060	71.1	818,866	62.7
Other	37,432	2.1	36,987	2.8
Total revenues	**1,754,963**	100.0	**1,306,602**	100.0

Costs and expenses

(millions of Italian lire)	1993	%	1992	%
Purchases and other costs	952,074	54.3	673,450	51.5
Wages, salaries and other personnel costs	296,282	16.9	242,212	18.5
Depreciation and amortization	62,912	3.6	53,260	4.1
General, selling and administrative expenses	350,077	19.9	259,986	19.9
Inventory change during the year	(7,896)	(0.4)	15,270	1.2
	1,653,449	94.2	**1,244,178**	95.2
Operating margin	**101,514**	5.8	**62,424**	4.8
Other (income) expense				
Interest expense, net	43,224	2.5	35,254	2.7
Investment income, net	(538)	–	579	–
Other expense, net	18,441	1.1	21,746	1.7
	61,127	3.5	**57,579**	4.4
Profit before income taxes and minority interests	**40,387**	2.3	**4,845**	0.4
Income taxes	(16,086)	(0.9)	(3,291)	(0.3)
Minority interests	8,259	0.5	(4)	–
Net income for the year	32,560	1.9	1,550	0.1

Analisi delle variazioni nel patrimonio netto consolidato avvenute nell'esercizio chiuso al 31 dicembre 1993

(milioni di lire)	Capitale sociale	Riserva legale	Sovrapprezzo azioni, contributi in conto capitale ed altre riserve al netto	Effetto cumulativo di conversione	Utile netto d'esercizio	Totale patrimonio netto
Saldi iniziali al 31 dicembre 1991	**91.502**	**2.154**	**110.500**	**(3.836)**	**11.747**	**212.067**
Riparto utile consolidato d'esercizio 1991		350	11.397		(11.747)	–
Differenza fra costo di acquisizione e quote di patrimonio netto di società controllate e collegate acquisite nell'esercizio			(11.878)			(11.878)
Differenza fra costo di acquisizione e patrimonio netto di società fusa nell'esercizio			(15.614)			(15.614)
Rivalutazioni monetarie			4.107			4.107
Contributi per investimenti			21.183			21.183
Distribuzione dividendi			(4.326)			(4.326)
Variazioni dell'effetto cumulativo della conversione dei bilanci in valuta				16.495		16.495
Utile netto d'esercizio					1.550	1.550
Saldi al 31 dicembre 1992	**91.502**	**2.504**	**115.369**	**12.659**	**1.550**	**223.584**
Riparto utile consolidato esercizio 1992		186	1.364		(1.550)	
Distribuzione Dividendi			(2.146)			(2.146)
Differenza fra costo di acquisizione e quota di patrimonio netto di società controllate e collegate acquisite nell'anno			(9.309)			(9.309)
Utilizzo riserve per il pagamento dell'imposta patrimoniale della Capogruppo per l'anno 1992			(1.131)			(1.131)
Contributi per investimenti			780			780
Variazioni dell'effetto cumulativo della conversione dei bilanci in valuta				4.463		4.463
Utile netto d'esercizio					32.560	32.560
Saldi al 31 dicembre 1993	**91.502**	**2.690**	**104.927**	**17.122**	**32.560**	**248.801**

Consolidated statement of changes in shareholders' equity as of 31st December 1993
Translation from original Italian version

(millions of Italian lire)	Share capital	Legal reserve	Additional paid-in capital, capital grants and other reserves	Cumulative translation adjustment	Net income for the year	Total shareholders' equity
Balance at 31st December 1991	**91,502**	**2,154**	**110,500**	**(3,836)**	**11,747**	**212,067**
Allocation of 1991 income		350	11,397		(11,747)	–
Difference between purchase cost and the Group's share of equity in subsidiaries and associated companies acquired during the year			(11,878)			(11,878)
Difference between purchase cost and the Group's share of equity in the company merged during the year			(15,614)			(15,614)
Monetary revaluations			4,107			4,107
Investment grants			21,183			21,183
Dividends paid			(4,326)			(4,326)
Translation adjustment				16,495		16,495
Net income for the year					1,550	1,550
Balance at 31st December 1992	**91,502**	**2,504**	**115,369**	**12,659**	**1,550**	**223,584**
Allocation of 1992 income		186	1,364		(1,550)	
Dividends paid			(2,146)			(2,146)
Difference between purchase cost and the Group's share of equity in subsidiaries and associated companies acquired during the year			(9,309)			(9,309)
Utilization of reserves to pay the parent company's 1992 capital taxes			(1,131)			(1,131)
Investment grants			780			780
Translation adjustment				4,463		4,463
Net income for the year					32,560	32,560
Balance at 31st December 1993	**91,502**	**2,690**	**104,927**	**17,122**	**32,560**	**248,801**

Rendiconto finanziario consolidato al 31 dicembre 1993

Fonti di finanziamento

(milioni di lire)	1993	1992
Fondi generati dalla gestione:		
Utile netto d'esercizio	32.560	1.550
Rettifiche relative alle voci che non determinano movimenti di capitale circolante netto:		
Ammortamenti operativi	62.912	53.260
Ammortamenti finanziari	1.857	–
Quota di trattamento fine rapporto maturata nell'esercizio	12.707	11.204
Capitale circolante netto generato dalla gestione reddituale	**110.036**	**66.014**
Alienazione partecipazioni	19.812	131
Valore netto contabile dei cespiti alienati	1.704	38.084
Finanziamenti a lungo termine ricevuti nell'esercizio	53.506	150.818
Accantonamenti al fondo imposte differite	3.126	4.410
Incremento della quota di patrimonio netto degli azionisti di minoranza	22.013	–
Contributi in conto capitale registrati nell'esercizio	780	21.183
Incremento della riserva di rivalutazione ex lege 413/91 per crediti d'imposta	–	760
Effetto delle variazioni dei cambi sulle attività e passività a medio e lungo termine e sul patrimonio netto consolidato	–	10.537
Totale	**210.977**	**295.674**

Impieghi

(milioni di lire)	1993	1992
Impieghi finanziari	7.478	3.930
Incremento delle partecipazioni in società non consolidate	4.023	8.748
Investimenti in immobilizzazioni tecniche	80.509	78.744
Effetto dell'applicazione dei criteri contabili previsti dallo IAS 17 nelle immobilizzazioni tecniche	4.205	–
Incrementi dei beni immateriali e dei costi pluriennali	4.311	10.444
Trasferimento delle quote correnti dei finanziamenti a medio e lungo termine ed estinzioni anticipate	69.234	78.534
Rimborsi e conversioni del prestito obbligazionario	600	1.000
Utilizzo e trasferimento delle quote correnti del fondo imposte differite	1.569	6.956
Decremento degli altri fondi non correnti	697	–
Decremento del fondo plusvaslenze differite	422	2.127
Pagamenti per trattamento di fine rapporto	5.836	10.885
Decremento della quota di patrimonio netto degli azionisti di minoranza	–	6.599
Distribuzione dividendi	2.146	4.326
Utilizzo riserve per l'imposta patrimoniale della Capogruppo	1.131	–
Effetto netto delle variazioni del campo di consolidamento	36.787	505
Effetto delle variazioni dei cambi sulle attività e passività a medio e lungo termine e sul patrimonio netto consolidato	6.661	–
Totale	**225.609**	**235.883**
Aumento (diminuzione) del capitale circolante netto	**14.632**	**59.791**

Consolidated statement of changes in financial position as of 31st December 1993
Translation from original Italian version

Sources of funds

(millions of Italian lire)	1993	1992
Funds generated by operations:		
Net income for the year	32,560	1,550
Adjustments not involving outlay of working capital:		
Fixed asset depreciation	62,912	53,260
Financial amortization	1,857	–
Provision for termination indemnities	12,707	11,204
Working capital generated by operations	**110,036**	**66,014**
Sale of investments	19,812	131
Net book value of property sold	1,704	38,084
Long-term loans arranged during the year	53,506	150,818
Provision for deferred income taxes	3,126	4,410
Increase in minority interests	22,013	–
Capital grants recorded during the year	780	21,183
Increase in revaluation reserve (Law 413/91) as a result of tax credits	–	760
Currency adjustment on translation of foreign non-current assets and liabilities and consolidated shareholders' equity	–	10,537
Total	**210,977**	**295,674**

Application of funds

(millions of Italian lire)	1993	1992
Financial investments	7,478	3,930
Increase in investments in non-consolidated companies	4,023	8,748
Additions to property, plant and equipment	80,509	78,744
Effect of applying IAS 17 (accounting for leases) to property, plant and equipment	4,205	–
Increase in intangible assets and deferred charges	4,311	10,444
Portion of medium and long-term debt transferred to current liabilities and early repayments	69,234	78,534
Reimbursement and conversion of bonds	600	1,000
Utilization of reserve for deferred income taxes and transfer of current portion	1,569	6,956
Decrease in other non-current reserves	697	–
Decrease in reserve for deferred capital gains	422	2,127
Payments of termination indemnities	5,836	10,885
Decrease in minority interests	–	6,599
Dividends paid	2,146	4,326
Utilization of reserves to cover the parent company's capital taxes	1,131	–
Net effect of changes in the scope of consolidation	36,787	505
Currency adjustment on translation of foreign non-current assets and liabilities and consolidated shareholders' equity	6,661	–
Total	**225,609**	**235,883**
Increase (decrease) in working capital	**14,632**	**59,791**

**Dimostrazione degli aumenti (diminuzioni) delle attività e passività
a medio/lungo termine e del patrimonio netto derivanti dalle variazioni
del campo di consolidamento**

(milioni di lire)	1993	1992
Immobilizzazioni, al netto	47.267	24.669
Beni immateriali e oneri pluriennali	326	73
Partecipazioni	(11.944)	17.951
Fondo trattamento fine rapporto dipendenti	(1.167)	(3.329)
Finanziamenti a medio-lungo termine	(6.475)	(31.244)
Fondo imposte differite	(363)	(649)
Altri fondi non correnti	(166)	–
Utilizzo riserve per copertura disavanzo da fusione ICE Srl	–	15.614
Effetto sulle riserve delle variazioni delle quote di possesso	9.309	–
Totale	**36.787**	**23.085**

Variazione del capitale circolante netto

(milioni di lire)	1993	1992
Aumento (diminuzione) delle attività a breve		
Cassa e banche	67.732	9.378
Titoli a reddito fisso	(440)	(5.330)
Crediti	129.170	70.341
Rimanenze di magazzino	22.696	(1.812)
Depositi cauzionali, ratei e risconti attivi	(4.095)	(4.379)
	215.063	**68.198**
Aumento (diminuzione) delle passività a breve		
Quota corrente dei finanziamenti a medio e lungo termine	653	(50.854)
Banche conto corrente	(4.879)	–
Anticipazioni bancarie	95.351	(33.785)
Debiti	122.443	82.844
Ratei e risconti passivi	7.251	(1.859)
Fondo garanzia prodotti	3.877	536
Fondo oscillazione cambi	(2.512)	10.097
Fondo imposte correnti	7.511	1.428
	229.695	**8.407**
Aumento (diminuzione) del capitale circolante netto	**14.632**	**59.791**

Increase (decrease) in non-current assets and liabilities and shareholders' equity due to changes in the scope of consolidation

(millions of Italian lire)	1993	1992
Property, plant and equipment, net	47,267	24,669
Intangible assets and deferred charges	326	73
Investments	(11,944)	17,951
Reserve for termination indemnities	(1,167)	(3,329)
Medium/long term loans	(6,475)	(31,244)
Reserve for deferred taxes	(363)	(649)
Other non-current reserves	(166)	–
Equity reserves used to cover ICE Srl merger deficit	–	15,614
Effect on reserves of changes in ownership percentages	9,309	–
Total	**36,787**	**23,085**

Changes in working capital

(millions of Italian lire)	1993	1992
Increase (decrease) in current assets		
Cash and banks	67,732	9,378
Marketable securuties	(440)	(5,330)
Receivables	129,170	70,341
Inventories	22,696	(1,812)
Guarantee deposits, accrued income and prepayments	(4,095)	(4,379)
	215,063	68,198
Increase (decrease) in current liabilities		
Current portion of medium and long-term debt	653	(50,854)
Bank overdrafts	(4,879)	–
Bank advances	95,351	(33,785)
Payables	122,443	82,844
Accrued liabilities and deferred income	7,251	(1,859)
Product warranty reserve	3,877	536
Reserve for exchange losses	(2,512)	10,097
Accrued income taxes	7,511	1,428
	229,695	8,407
Increase (decrease) in working capital	**14,632**	**59,791**

*Notes to the consolidated financial
statements as of 31st December 1993*
Translation from original Italian version

1. Basis of consolidated financial statements

The consolidated accounts include the financial statements of Merloni Elettrodomestici Spa, the parent company, and of Italian and foreign subsidiaries in which the company has direct or indirect control, except for majority holdings which are inactive or insignificant.

The subsidiaries included in the consolidated financial statements at 31st December 1993 are listed below:

Subsidiaries included in the consolidated financial statements	Country	Activity	Share capital (Currency)	Percentage ownership Group	
				direct	indirect
Merloni Ariston International sa	Luxembourg	Holding	US$ 86,000,000	99.9	-
Merloni Electrodomésticos sa	Spain	Trading	Pts 400,000,000	-	99.9
Merloni Domestic Appliances Ltd	UK	Trading	£ 11,501,000	-	99.9
Merloni Electroménager sa	France	Trading	FF 65,000,000	-	99.9
Merloni Electrodomésticos sa	Portugal	Production	Esc. 2,356,495,000	-	99.2
Merloni Overseas Ltd	Cayman Islands	Finance	Lire 1,270,500	-	99.9
Merloni Huishoudapparaten nv	Holland	Trading	Hfl 1,000,000	-	99.9
Merloni Pts Ltd	UK	Trading	£ 1,000	-	99.9
R.T.C. International Ltd	UK	Trading	£ 50,000	-	99.9
Scholtès sa	France	Production	FF 70,000,000	-	99.6
Scholtès ag	Switzerland	Trading	SF 50,000	-	99.6
Scholtès Nederland bv	Holland	Trading	Hfl 175,000	-	99.6
Scholtès Luxembourg Sarl	Luxembourg	Trading	LF 500,000	-	99.6
Scholtès GmbH	Germany	Trading	DM 50,000	-	99.6
Scholtès Warenhandelsgesmbh	Austria	Trading	Ats 250,000	-	99.6
Scholtès Ireland Ltd	Ireland	Trading	£Eire 5,000	-	99.6
Sodemac sa	France	Services	FF 670,000	-	66.9
Fabrica Portugal sa	Portugal	Production	Esc. 1,750,000,000	-	76.3
Pekel Teknik Sanayi Ve Ticaret as	Turkey	Production	Tl 300,000,000,000	54	-
Pekel Dayanikly Tuketim Mallari Pazarlama aa	Turkey	Trading	Tl 17,000,000,000	54	-
Belimovel Construcoes Lda	Portugal	Finance	Esc. 2,400,000	-	80
Hevdove Ltd	Ireland	Finance	£Eire 102	-	99
Merloni Financial Services	Luxembourg	Finance	Lire 2,500,000,000	99,9	0.1
Merloni Electrodomésticos de Integ	Spain	Trading	Pts 80,000,000	-	51

During the year, the following changes in the scope of consolidation occurred:
• Merloni Elettrodomestici Spa exercised its option to acquire another 29% of the Turkish companies Pekel Teknik a.s. and Pekel Pazarlama a.s.

At the time of exercising these options, the parent company subscribed to its own share of the increase in capital of the two companies.

As for the increase in share capital of Pekel Teknik a.s., the rights were also taken up by Philco Italia Spa (5%).

Subsequently, Philco Italia Spa's interests in these two companies were purchased.

As a result of this transaction, Merloni Elettrodomestici Spa's shareholding in the two companies amounts to 54%.

Lastly, in accordance with its institutional purposes, SIMEST Spa purchased 10% of the share capital of Pekel Teknik a.s. from Merloni Elettrodomestici Spa. In conformity with the repurchase agreement relating to this interest, signed by the parties and described in Note 11, the investment has been consolidated at 54%.

• Merloni Ariston International sa purchased from IPE (Investimentos e Partecipacoes do Estado sa) its shareholding in Fabrica Portugal sa. Merloni Ariston International's investment therefore passed from 49.8 to 76.3%.

At the same time, IPE's 20% interest in Belimovel sa has been acquired, raising Merloni Ariston International's shareholding to 80%.

Due to these transactions, these two companies have been fully consolidated (previously Fabrica Portugal sa was consolidated at equity, Belimoval sa at cost).

• Merloni Elettrodomestici Spa sold its investment in Smeg Spa. This 30% investment was previously valued using the equity method.

• Merloni Elettrodomestici Spa acquired 20% of Argentron sa of Buenos Aires. The significant influence of the parent company over the commercial, technical and purchasing activities of Argentiron suggested that this investment should be valued at equity.

• During the year, a new company was set up in Spain, Merloni Electrodomésticos de Integrar sa, in which the Spanish subsidiary Merloni Electrodomésticos sa holds 51% of the share capital.

• Within the ambit of a program designed to better integrate the European commercial structures of the Group, all assets and liabilities of Scholtès UK Ltd and Merloni Blue Air bv were spun off and transferred to Merloni Domestic Appliances Ltd and Merloni Huishoudapparaten bv respectively.

These operations have not led to the liquidation of the above-mentioned companies, which are dormant and have therefore been excluded from the consolidation.

Merloni Blue Air bv's name has been changed to Merloni International Trading bv.

• Lastly, during the latter part of the year, Merloni Elettrodomestici Spa set up Merloni Financial Services sa with head office in Luxembourg, subscribing to its entire share capital.

The financial statements used in the consolidation are those for the

Annual
Report 1993

year ended 31st December 1993, as approved by the shareholders of the individual companies, or those prepared by the respective Boards of Directors for their shareholders' approval, suitably reclassified to bring them into line, as far as possible, with international accounting standards.

Where necessary, the accounts have been adjusted to eliminate provisions made for purely fiscal purposes and to standardize the accounting principles with those of the parent company which are consistent with those recommended by CONSOB (the Italian regulatory commission for the stock exchange) based on the requirements of the I.A.S.C., the International Accounting Standards Committee.

Summary of significant accounting principles

The more significant accounting policies used to prepare the consolidated financial statements are summarized as follows:

Principles of consolidation and foreign currency translation:

- Assets and liabilities of consolidated companies are included in the consolidated financial statements on a line-by-line basis by eliminating the carrying value of the investment against the net equity of the companies concerned.

- The difference between purchase cost and net equity of shareholdings at the date of purchase is booked directly to consolidated net equity.

- Minority interests in shareholders' equity and net income are shown separately in the consolidated balance sheet and statement of income.

- All unrealized profits on intercompany transactions are eliminated on consolidation, together with payables, receivables and all transactions among companies included in the consolidation area.

- Financial statements of subsidiaries denominated in foreign currencies have been translated into lire as follows: assets and liabilities at the exchange rate in effect at 31st December 1993; revenues and costs, as well as other income and expenses, at the average exchange rate for the year; shareholders' equity accounts at historical exchange rates.
Translation differences between closing shareholders' equity at historical rates and at year-end rates are booked directly to equity, together with differences between the net income at average rates and the net income translated into Italian lire at year-end rates.
The figures for foreign subsidiaries and affiliates operating in countries with high inflation rates reflect the adjustments made to apply international principles for accounting for inflation (I.A.S. no. 29).

Marketable securities

Securities are valued at the lower of cost or market.

Receivables and allowance for doubtful accounts

Receivables are shown at face value and adjusted to their estimated realizable value by the allowance for doubtful accounts.

Inventories

Inventories are stated at the lower of purchase or production cost, determined using the LIFO method, or their estimated realizable value determined by reference to market conditions. All Group companies follow more or less the same valuation method.

Obsolete or slow moving inventory is written down considering the extent to which it can be used or sold.

During the year, the parent company changed its valuation method from the average cost for the year to the LIFO method with annual layers, as this represents one of the three criteria acceptable under the new statutory rules.

If the inventory at 31 December 1993 had been valued at the average cost for the year, it would have been higher by around Lire 2,400 million; the net profit for the year and shareholders' equity would therefore have been greater by around Lire 1,250 million, net of the tax effect.

Investments

Investments in non-consolidated companies over which the Group exercises significant management influence (but not majority control), are valued using the equity method.

Other non-controlling investments or those with limited activities are shown at cost, and are only adjusted in the event of a reduction in share capital or permanent loss in the value of the investment.

Property, plant and equipment and accumulated depreciation

Property, plant and equipment are stated at conferral value or cost, revalued as appropriate, as explained in Note 7. Depreciation is calculated on a straight-line basis by applying the following rates, reflecting the estimated useful lives of the assets, which for Italian companies are generally in line with those permitted for tax purposes:

Annual
Report 1993

Buildings and temporary constructions	from 1.5% to 10%
Machinery and equipment	from 10% to 33%
Office furniture and fixtures	from 5% to 25%
Vehicles	from 15% to 30%

Ordinary repairs and maintenance are expensed.

Accounting for leases

The effects of a sale and leaseback operation arranged in previous years by a subsidiary which merged with the parent company in 1990 have been treated in the consolidation in accordance with I.A.S. 17.

Intangible assets and deferred charges

Intangible assets and deferred charges refer mainly to the Ariston, Indesit and Scholtès trademarks, as well as to expenses for increases in share capital, bond issues, loans, patents, new product design, software and plant restructuring costs.

Trademarks are amortized on a straight-line basis, taking into account their estimated useful life (10 years) or the period for which they may be used, while other intangible assets are amortized on a straight-line basis for periods generally not exceeding five years.

As allowed by special Italian statutory regulations, the parent company has also deferred over five year costs deriving from early retirements in 1992 and from the tax amnesty. Application of the alternative accounting principle would have increased net profit by around Lire 600 million and reduced the consolidated shareholders' equity by around Lire 1,600 million, net of the tax effect, where applicable.

Accrued income taxes

The balance includes accruals recorded by the consolidated companies on the basis of a realistic estimate of taxable income for the year. In addition, the consolidated financial statements include the effect of deferred taxes resulting from consolidation adjustments and from timing differences between the taxable profits and those shown in the accounts used for consolidation purposes.

Any equalization tax on dividends is accounted for, at the time of payment, out of retained earnings.

Reserve for termination indemnities

This reserve covers the liability of Italian companies to pay index-linked indemnities to all personnel on termination of employment, in accordance with local laws and collective labour contracts.

Termination indemnities paid by some foreign companies in accordance with local laws and practice are charged to the income statement when payment is made.

Product warranty reserve

This represents an estimate of costs (labour and materials) for free after-sales service on products sold under warranty.

Capital grants

Capital grants for the purchase of property, plant and equipment are booked to shareholders' equity at the moment the company becomes certain of their collection.

Operating grants for the year are taken to income.

Capital grants received by the parent company during the year are shown net of deferred taxes, in accordance with the new fiscal regulations.

Foreign currency transactions

Receivables and payables, along with related costs and revenues, are recorded in local currency at the exchange rate in effect on the day the transaction takes place.

The effect of adjusting foreign currency receivables and payables to year-end exchange rates is included in the consolidated statement of income, as are the exchange gains and losses realized during the year, except for those receivables and payables that are hedged. For such transactions, the exchange rates indicated in the hedging contracts are used.

Revenue recognition

Revenues from the sale of products are recognized when the transfer of goods is effected, which usually occurs on shipment.

Explanation added for translation into English

The consolidated financial statements and related notes have been transla-

Annual
Report 1993

ted into English from the original Italian version. These financial statements have been prepared in accordance with accounting principles established by the Italian Accounting Profession which may differ from those in other countries.

2. Cash and banks, marketable securities, bank overdrafts and advances

The increase of Lire 90 billion in short-term bank borrowings is offset by the Lire 61 billion increase in cash and banks, due to a temporary imbalance between cash collections and payments, and also reflects the consolidation of Fabrica Portugal sa, Pekel Tknik as and Pekel Pazarlama as.

Marketable securities are short-term Government bonds.

The lines of credit granted by banks at 31st December 1993 are summarized below:

(millions of Italian lire)	Credit lines	Utilized
Bank overdrafts	73,600	15,839
Bank advances	439,600	124,681
Total	**513,200**	**140,520**

These credit lines are generally unsecured.

3. Receivables

The balance as at 31st December 1993 is made up as follows:

(millions of Italian lire)		
Trade accounts and notes:		
Italy	240,346	
Foreign countries	346,054	586,400
Affiliated companies:		
Argentron sa	8,894	
Philco Italia Spa	3,489	
Sofarem	1,517	
Merloni Hausgeräte GmbH	791	
Others	618	15,309
Advances to suppliers		7,730
Other receivables		53,868
		663,307
less: Allowance for doubtful accounts		31,774
Total		**631,533**

"Other receivables" includes Lire 20,960 million for capital grants requested under Law 219/81. The fact that these grants were not collected during the year is essentially due to organizational and administrative problems of the public entities, caused by the liquidation of the special section and the transfer of its duties to the Ministry of Industry. As these problems have now been clarified following the issuance of the implementation regulations, it should be possible to collect this grant in 1994.

The significant increase in the allowance for doubtful accounts is mainly due to the consolidation of Pekel Pazarlama as.

4. Inventories

Inventories include the following main categories:

(millions of Italian lire)	
Raw materials	60,933
Work in process	9,524
Spare parts	16,362
Finished goods	125,357
Total	**212,176**

Finished goods include goods invoiced but not shipped at the date of these financial statements. As in the previous year, the related net revenues will be recognized at the date of shipment in accordance with the matching principle.

5. Investments

As of 31st December 1993, the principal investments not included in the consolidation are:

(millions of Italian lire)	Percentage of shares owned	Carrying value
Investments accounted for using the equity method		
Philco Italia Spa	48.33	8,653
Necchi Compressori Srl	15.00	4,085
Appliance Trading Int.Inc.	99.90	(2,863)
Argentron sa	20.00	2,986
Merloni Blue Air bv	99.90	893
Investments accounted for at cost		
Controlling interests:		
Merloni Indesit Haztartastechnikai Kft	99.00	149
Merloni Indesit Polska Sp.Z O.O	100.00	110
Merloni Indesit Bulgaria Srlu	100.00	40
Merloni Indesit Domaci Elektrospotrebice Sro	100.00	60
Ice Componenti Spa	100.00	200
Other investments:		
Akros Spa	0.18	701
Other minor investments	–	563
Total investments		**15,577**

Annual
Report 1993

The foreign investments mentioned above, valued at cost even if controlling interests, have not been consolidated as they were set up recently, so their business activities to date are not material.

During the year, the 30% investment in Smeg Spa was sold. This sale resulted in a gain of Lire 200 million.

The Milan Court has revoked the precautionary confiscation of 1,800,000 shares in Philco Italia Spa, owned by the parent company. This action was taken as a result of a bankruptcy claim made by certain creditors of the company which sold these shares to Merloni Elettrodomestici Spa. Subsequently the Court declared that the insolvency status did not exist anymore, as the company had in the meantime become solvent.

Aggregate key financial data in 1993 for significant investments are as follows:

(millions of Italian lire)	
Revenues	383,773
Net loss	(1,966)
Total assets	**341,029**
Total shareholders' equity	**70,621**

6. Long-term financial assets

Long-term financial assets (Lire 77,278 million) represent certificates of deposit in Italian lire held by a foreign subsidiary, which the company expects to collect gradually over future years.

A portion amounting to Lire 7,000 million was deposited as a guarantee for a loan granted in 1993 by Banco di Napoli, Frankfurt, to Merloni Partecipazioni & Servizi Srl. The interest rate on this amount is the same as on other loans.

7. Property, plant and equipment

Parent company

Fixed assets are shown at their conferral value or at cost if acquired subsequent to the contribution. Buildings were revalued by 9,000 million lire under Law no. 72/83 (of which 450 million lire is still to be depreciated at 31st December 1993) and by 16,123 million lire under Law no. 413/91 (of which Lire 11,501 million is still to be depreciated at 31st December 1993) and by 7,163 million to cover the deficit deriving from the merger of ICE Srl into Merloni Elettrodomestici Spa.

Fixed assets are encumbered by mortgages and liens to guarantee loans (Note 11).

Foreign companies

The fixed assets of certain foreign companies were revalued in previous years and in 1993 for about Lire 7,000 million under laws specifically permitting revaluation.

Certain fixed assets resulting from acquisitions are shown at market value based on independent appraisals of the companies concerned.

The revaluation reserve is shown under consolidated shareholders' equity.

The fixed assets of Pekel Teknik as and Pekel Pazarlama as, were restated by applying the accounting principles for inflation (IAS no. 29).

The amount of the respective revaluations is shown net of exchange adjustments under the related reserve within consolidated shareholders' equity.

8. Intangible assets and deferred charges

The balance as at 31 December 1993 is made up of:

- Costs for the purchase of the Indesit and Scholtès trademarks and for the concession of the Ariston trademark (expiring in 2006) granted by Merloni Termosanitari Spa for Lire 15,930 million;

- Costs for the early retirement of employees of the parent company incurred in 1992 and deferred as allowed by Decree Law 364/92 for Lire 1,260 million;

- Charges for the tax amnesty requested by the parent company in 1992 for Lire 1,085 million. Deferral of these charges is allowed by Decree Law 298/92;

- Expenses related to bond loans, mortgages, patents, restructuring costs of production facilities and other deferred charges for Lire 10,772 million.

The net increase for the year amounts to Lire 2,712 million and the related amortization to Lire 8,142 million.

9. Product warranty reserve

The balance shown in the consolidated balance sheet (Lire 13,055 million) has been provided to cover after-sales service costs on products sold with a guarantee of one or more years.

These expenses have been estimated on the basis of an historical analysis of costs incurred in prior years.

10. Accrued income taxes

The accrued income taxes (Lire 14,306 million) cover the short-term liability for income taxes payable based on a realistic estimate of the amount due, taking into account local tax rates and any exemptions available under local tax laws. The reserve for deferred taxes (Lire 17,988 million) reflects the provision

for residual gains that arose in the current and prior years deriving from the sale of assets, and from consolidation adjustments that mainly take into consideration the effect of reversing accelerated depreciation and other adjustments necessary to align the accounting principles of subsidiaries with those of the parent company.

The accounts of certain foreign subsidiaries have been subject to review by the local tax authorities. Management believes that settlement of the outstanding years will not result in significant liabilities over and above the amounts accrued. At 31st December 1993, certain subsidiaries had carry-forward tax losses of Lire 26,300 million. In 1993, as in previous years, the Group benefited from the use of tax losses accumulated by certain subsidiaries in previous years, and from tax-exempt income.

No tax has been provided for on the retained earnings of foreign subsidiaries as the company considers such earnings to be permanently invested.

11. Medium and long-term debt

Outstanding loans at 31st December 1993 are as follows:

Bank	(millions of Italian lire)
Secured loans	
Istituto Mobiliare Italiano-Rome	4,872
Mediocredito Regionale delle Marche - Ancona	5,656
Isveimer - Naples	15,636
BNL - CECA	5,860
Various banks under Law 1329/65 (Sabatini)	10,590
Lordex France	2,714
Cepme France	92
Pool of French credit institutions	6,257
	51,677
Unsecured loans	
Ministry of Industry, Commerce and Trade - Rome	4,481
BNL - BEI	430
Swiss Bank Corp.Int.Ltd.	47,161
Banco di Napoli-Frankfurt	70,278
B.PARISBAS - LISBON	5,207
Lordex - Francia	2,918
	130,475
Total loans	**182,152**
Other medium-term debt	6,107
Total medium and long-term debt	**188,259**
Current portion	(13,966)
Medium and long-term debt, net of current portion	**174,293**

The loans are generally reimbursable in six-monthly instalments up to the end of the year 2000 and are guaranteed by mortgages on the fixed assets of the companies or by guarantees issued by Fineldo Spa and financial institutions.

Loans in foreign currencies are covered against currency fluctuation risks by the reserve for exchange losses.

Other medium-term loans include a loan from SIMEST Spa (a company operating on foreign markets that supplies technical assistance and administrative, organizational and finance services) under a contract whereby the parent company sold to SIMEST 10% of its share in Pekel Teknik as for Lire 5,975 million, which does not include any part of the majority premium.

The sale contract also includes a guaranteed obligation to repurchase the above 10% by 31st December 1996, at the higher of the sale price or the corresponding value of net equity.

SIMEST will exercise the voting rights relating to the shares in its possession in accordance with instructions from Merloni Elettrodomestici Spa.

Consequence to the above, in the consolidated financial statements the holding in Pekel Teknik a.s. amounts to 54%, while the debt of Lire 5,975 million to SIMEST has been classified under medium-term loans.

In view of the plans to invest heavily in plant expansion, requests are being made to various financial institutions for low interest loans (about Lire 20,000 million) which, if obtained, would include some outright grants.

12. Bonds

These refer to the outstanding bonds issued in 1989 by Merloni Overseas Ltd. (9% per annum, 20,000 bonds with a nominal value of 5,000,000 lire each), convertible from 1989 onwards into a maximum of 19 million ordinary shares and 19 million non-convertible savings shares of the parent company, offered to the public in conjunction with the increase in share capital of Merloni Elettrodomestici Spa. The duration is 10 years.

During 1993, no conversions occurred and Merloni Overseas Ltd. acquired bonds for a nominal value of 600 million lire, cancelling the certificates.

Merloni Overseas Ltd has announced its intention to reimburse this bond in advance (see Note 18) and therefore all related charges have been amortized during 1993.

13. Other non-current provisions

This item includes principally the amount of Lire 6,845 million set aside by the parent company against charges deriving from the early retirement of personnel in 1992 and 1993.

**Annual
Report 1993**

14. Shareholders' equity

Share capital and reserves

Share capital, subscribed and paid-in, is represented by the share capital of the parent company, Merloni Elettrodomestici Spa, and consists of 91,501,930 shares of par value 1,000 lire each, of which 80,985,265 ordinary shares and 10,516,665 non-convertible savings shares.

Consolidated shareholders' equity at 31st December 1993 includes reserves of Lire 1,533 million which are in suspense for tax purposes and will be subject to taxation only in the event of distribution or utilization other than to cover losses.

For settlement of the tax on net equity for 1993, the parent company will utilize reserves available at the moment of payment.

This is permitted under the special fiscal regulations instead of booking this amount to the 1993 income statement, as required by the established accounting principles.

The alternative accounting treatment would have resulted in a reduction of net income for the year and of shareholders' equity by Lire 1,200 million.

Cumulative translation adjustment

This balance represents the effect of the translation into lire of financial statements denominated in foreign currencies. Following the provisions of I.A.S. 21, such adjustments are included in shareholders' equity (Note 1).

Reconciliation with the parent company's financial statements

The reconciliation of consolidated shareholders' equity and net income with those of Merloni Elettrodomestici Spa is as follows:

Increase (Decrease) (millions of Italian lire)	Shareholders' Equity	Net income for the year
Per Merloni Elettrodomestici Spa financial statements	**195,804**	**7,975**
Effect of consolidation of subsidiary and affiliated companies	41,868	2,635
Elimination of intercompany profits in inventory	(3,271)	(2,150)
Adjustments of values and accruals made by the parent company solely in application of fiscal regulations Reversal of accelerated depreciation provided in excess of the fixed assets' estimated useful lives by the parent company and certain subsidiaries (net of tax effect)	6,300	16,000
Writedown of investments	8,100	8,100
Per consolidated financial statements	**248,801**	**32,560**

15. Other income	The item includes:

- Lire 9,814 million of proceeds from the sale of raw materials;

- Lire 19,479 million for recovery of various costs;

- Lire 686 million for design know-how charged to third parties.

16. Other net charges	This amount includes mainly reorganization costs for early retirement and severance incentives (around Lire 7,500 million), exchange losses (around Lire 5,500 million) principally attributable to Pekel Teknik as and Pekel Pazarlama as, as well as expenses for the social security amnesty requested by the parent company (around Lire 2,500 million).

17. Outstanding litigation, capital commitments and contingent liabilities	Bills of exchange at banks (discounted or for collection) not yet due on 31st December 1993 amounted to about Lire 2,700 million. Capital commitments for new investments totalled about Lire 27,000 million at the same date.

The company has an outstanding dispute with INPS the result of which, considering the opinion of counsel, should not give rise to significant liabilities.

At the year end, the parent company had issued guarantees to financial institutions and third parties for Lire 65,893 million, and in turn received guarantees for Lire 47,088 million, of which Lire 35,552 million from Assicurazioni Generali and Banco di Napoli to guarantee the amount received under Law 219/81 in relation to the plants of Indesit Srl, now merged.

In addition, the parent company has further commitments under currency hedging contracts for about Lire 278,000 million.

No provision has been made for any liabilities that could result from the settlement of outstanding litigation, as they are considered insignificant.

Merloni Elettrodomestici Spa has contractual agreements to refinance some of its foreign subsidiaries.

18. Subsequent events	During the opening months of 1994, the reorganization of foreign holdings, which began in December, continued with the setting up of Merloni Financial Services and the purchase by Merloni Ariston International of the investment companies Merloni Overseas and Hevdove; this will allow the new company to concentrate on financial management of the Group. In order to provide this company with adequate resources, in March Merloni Elettrodomestici Spa authorised and subscribed to the entire increase in capital to Lire 10 billion.

As for the concentration and protection of the Indesit trademark,

Merloni Financial Services sa acquired, on the basis of an appraisal prepared by an independent expert, the Indesit Elettronica trademark from Merloni Partecipazioni & Servizi Srl (a related company).

In Spain, in order to strengthen market penetration and fully exploit all synergies, the company acquired a further 39% of Merloni Electrodomésticos de Integrar, increasing the investment in this company to 90%.

In order to strengthen and internationalize the commercial organization supporting non-EC countries, a new branch of Merloni International Trading bv was opened in Lugano.

Further, the purchase of 33% of Merloni Progetti Spa (a related company) for Lire 17,556 million has been finalized. The amount paid was determined on the basis of an appraisal carried out by a leading international firm.

Merloni Progetti Spa designs and manufactures plant mainly for the construction of domestic appliances using Merloni Elettrodomestici know-how and technologies; the purchase of a significant interest will improve the coordination of its activities, take full advantage of all possible synergies and avoid skills being dispersed outside the Group.

Lastly, on 16th February 1994, Merloni Overseas announced the early reimbursement, after only four years, of the bond convertible into Merloni Elettrodomestici ordinary and savings shares, which had an initial value of 100 billion lire.

Redemption of the bonds, which is possible under the issue regulations, is possible due to the performance of Merloni Elettrodomestici stock. Our shares have exceeded 130% of their original placement value and touched 150% during the last few days of February.

Converting the loan will substantially reduce the group's financial costs and debt/equity ratio.

In January and February, 972 debentures with a nominal value of L. 4,860,000,000 were converted into 895,024 ordinary shares and 895,024 savings shares of Merloni Elettrodomestici.

On the strength of that conversion, as of 1st March 1994 our share capital amounted to L. 93,291,978,000, represented by 93,291,978 shares with a par value of 1,000 lire each: 81,880,289 ordinary and 11,411,689 savings shares.

Although the general economy is still dominated by recession, the group plans to go ahead with its expansion policy. This policy is designed to take advantage of all opportunities that might appear, thanks to our recognised ability to adapt rapidly to the changing needs of the market, with customer service as our main objective. The early months of 1994 have shown that the Merloni group is performing in line with forecast.

ARTHUR
ANDERSEN

Arthur Andersen & Co. s.a.s.

Via Campania 47
00187 Roma

RELAZIONE DELLA SOCIETA' DI REVISIONE

Agli azionisti della
Merloni Elettrodomestici S.p.A.

Abbiamo assoggettato a revisione contabile il bilancio consolidato della
MERLONI ELETTRODOMESTICI S.p.A. e sue controllate al 31 dicembre 1993.

Il nostro esame è stato svolto secondo gli statuiti principi di revisione e,
in conformità a tali principi, abbiamo fatto riferimento ai corretti principi
contabili enunciati dai Consigli Nazionali dei Dottori Commercialisti e dei
Ragionieri e, ove mancanti, dall'International Accounting Standards Committee
(IASC).

Lo stato patrimoniale, il conto economico ed il rendiconto finanziario
consolidati presentano a fini comparativi i valori dell'esercizio precedente.
Per il nostro giudizio sul bilancio consolidato dell'esercizio precedente si
fa riferimento alla nostra relazione emessa in data 29 marzo 1993.

A nostro giudizio, il sopramenzionato bilancio consolidato nel suo complesso è
stato redatto con chiarezza e rappresenta in modo veritiero e corretto la
situazione patrimoniale e finanziaria e il risultato economico della Merloni
Elettrodomestici S.p.A. e delle sue controllate per l'esercizio chiuso al 31
dicembre 1993, in conformità a corretti principi contabili.

ARTHUR ANDERSEN & Co. s.a.s.

Gianandrea Faccini
(Socio accomandatario)

Roma, 25 marzo 1994

Sede Legale: Via della Moscova 3 20121 Milano
Reg Soc 297992 7540 42 CCIAA 960046
Cod Fisc 02466670581 Part Iva 09869140153

Milano Roma Torino Treviso Genova Bologna
Napoli Verona Firenze Parma Brescia Padova Bari

ARTHUR ANDERSEN

Arthur Andersen & Co. s.a.s.

Via Campania 47
00187 Roma

AUDITORS' REPORT

(TRANSLATION FROM THE ORIGINAL ISSUED IN ITALIAN)

To the Shareholders of
Merloni Elettrodomestici S.p.A.

We have audited the consolidated financial statements of MERLONI
ELETTRODOMESTICI S.p.A. and subsidiaries as of and for the year ended December
31, 1993.

Our examination was made in accordance with established auditing standards
and, in compliance with those standards, we have made reference to the
accounting principles established by the Italian Accounting Profession and, in
the absence thereof, to those issued by the International Accounting Standards
Committee (I.A.S.C.).

The consolidated balance sheet and statements of income and changes in
financial position present prior year amounts for comparative purposes. For
our opinion on the prior year's consolidated financial statements reference
should be made to our auditors'report dated March 29, 1993.

In our opinion, the above-mentioned consolidated financial statements, taken
as a whole, have been prepared clearly and give a true and fair view of the
financial position of Merloni Elettrodomestici S.p.A. and subsidiaries as of
December 31, 1993 and the results of its operations for the year then ended in
accordance with the accounting principles established by the Italian
Accounting Profession.

ARTHUR ANDERSEN & Co. s.a.s.

Gianandrea Faccini - Partner

Rome, Italy
March 25, 1994

Sede Legale: Via della Moscova 3 20121 Milano
Reg Soc 297992 7540 42 CCIAA 960046
Cod Fisc 02466670581 Part Iva 09869140153

Milano Roma Torino Treviso Genova Bologna
Napoli Verona Firenze Parma Brescia Padova Bari

MERLONI ELETTRODOMESTICI SPA

Sede legale: V.le A. Merloni - 45, 60044 Fabriano
Capitale sociale: Lire 93.291.978.000 i.v.
Iscritta alla Cancelleria del Tribunale di Ancona
Reg. Soc. 9677

Bilancio al 31 dicembre dell'esercizio   1993   1992
(importi in Lire Italiane)

STATO PATRIMONIALE

ATTIVO

	1993	1992
A) Crediti verso soci per versamenti ancora dovuti	0	0
B) Immobilizzazioni		
I- *Immobilizzazioni immateriali:*		
costi di impianto e di ampliamento	127.813.950	292.871.255
diritti di brevetto industriale e diritti di		
utilizzazione delle opere dell'ingegno	68.980.006	77.413.583
marchi e licenze	15.819.255.137	18.004.805.994
altre	11.887.744.224	17.400.185.092
Totale	27.903.793.317	35.775.275.924
II- *Immobilizzazioni materiali:*		
terreni e fabbricati	88.629.076.114	83.226.403.131
impianti e macchinario	83.078.120.141	63.545.100.269
attrezzature industriali e commerciali	30.762.710.437	26.264.287.269
altri beni	9.411.183.360	6.772.646.518
immobilizzazioni in corso e acconti	17.534.632.932	16.438.633.284
Totale	229.415.722.984	196.247.070.471
III- *Immobilizzazioni finanziarie:*		
partecipazioni in:		
imprese controllate	123.397.793.700	84.068.201.201
imprese collegate	7.513.742.933	21.212.539.014
altre imprese	851.886.000	851.886.000
crediti:		
verso imprese collegate	549.800.000	549.800.000
Totale	132.313.222.633	106.682.426.215
Totale immobilizzazioni (B)	*389.632.738.934*	*338.704.772.610*
C) Attivo circolante		
I- *Rimanenze:*		
materie prime, sussidiarie e di consumo	32.813.403.713	33.152.120.783
prodotti in corso di lavorazione e semilavorati	5.753.706.303	5.210.152.413
prodotti finiti e merci	59.897.627.049	61.983.148.512
Totale	98.464.737.065	100.345.421.708

13

MERLONI ELETTRODOMESTICI S.p.A.
Registered office: V.le A. Merloni - 45, 60044 Fabriano
Authorised capital: Lire 93.291.978.000 (fully paid)
Registered at the Tribunal of Ancona
Company Register no. 9677

FINANCIAL STATEMENTS AS OF 31 DECEMBER **1993**   **1992**
(amounts in Italian Lira)

BALANCE SHEET

ASSETS

A. Called up share capital not paid

B. Fixed assets

  I- *Intangible assets:*
   start-up costs
   patent rights and royalties
   brands and licences
   others

     Total

  II- *Tangible assets:*
   land and buildings
   plant and machinery
   fixtures and fittings
   others
   tangible assets under construction and prepayments

     Total

  III- *Investments:*
   participating interests in:
    subsidiary undertakings
    associate undertakings
    other companies
   debtors:
    amounts owed by associate undertakings

     Total
     Total fixed assets (B)

C. Current assets

  I- *Stocks:*
   raw materials and consumables
   work in process
   finished goods and merchandise

     Total

II-	*Crediti:*		
	verso clienti	275.559.963.132	244.139.034.987
	(di cui esigibili oltre il 1994 L. 1.418.916.545)		
	verso imprese controllate	107.773.401.737	129.332.788.706
	verso imprese collegate	13.350.463.795	9.107.443.178
	verso altri	38.551.135.072	58.120.153.804
	(di cui esigibili oltre il 1994 L. 302.482.459)		
	Totale	435.234.963.736	440.699.420.675
III-	*Attività finanziarie che non costituiscono immobilizzazioni:*	0	0
IV-	*Disponibilità liquide:*		
	depositi bancari e postali	60.110.580.648	10.791.706.517
	danaro e valori in cassa	134.226.793	209.221.033
	Totale	60.244.807.441	11.000.927.550
	Totale attivo circolante (C)	*593.944.508.242*	*552.045.769.933*
D) Ratei e risconti		*2.071.543.888*	*2.505.998.468*
	TOTALE	*985.648.791.064*	*893.256.541.011*

STATO PATRIMONIALE

PASSIVO		1993	1992
A) Patrimonio netto			
I-	Capitale sociale	91.501.930.000	91.501.930.000
II-	Riserva da soprapprezzo delle azioni	18.145.170.000	18.145.170.000
III-	Riserve di rivalutazione	0	404.336.032
IV-	Riserva legale	894.033.287	894.033.287
V-	Riserva per azioni proprie in portafoglio	0	0
VI-	Riserve statutarie	0	0
VII-	Altre riserve	77.287.749.524	64.857.006.521
VIII-	Utili (perdite) portati a nuovo	0	0
IX-	Utile (perdita) dell'esercizio	7.975.129.223	(4.330.703.837)
	Totale	*195.804.012.034*	*171.471.772.003*
B) Fondi per rischi e oneri			
	per imposte	17.081.428.509	9.159.660.142
	altri.	14.541.044.872	14.600.316.793
	Totale	*31.622.473.381*	*23.759.976.935*
C) Trattamento di fine rapporto di lavoro subordinato		*72.525.195.835*	*66.926.520.232*

II- *Debtors:*
   trade debtors
   (of which L. 1,418,916,545 fall due beyond 1994)
   amounts owed by subsidiary undertakings
   amounts owed by associate undertakings
   amounts owed by other undertakings
   (of which L. 302,482,459 fall due beyond 1994)

   Total

III- *Financial assets other than long term:*

IV- *Liquid funds:*
   cash at bank and in the post accounts
   cash in hand

   Total
   Total current assets (C)

D.   **Accrued income and prepayments**

   TOTAL

BALANCE SHEET

LIABILITIES

A.   **Shareholders' capital**

   I-   Called up share capital
   II-   Share premium account
   III-   Revaluation reserve
   IV-   Legal reserve
   V-   Reserve for own shares
   VI-   Reserves provided for by the articles
   VII-   Other reserves
   VIII-   Profits (losses) of previous years
   IX-   Profit (loss) for the year

   Total

B.   **Provisions for risks and liabilities**

   provisions for taxes
   others

   Total

C.   **Statutory provisions for severance indemnities**

D) Debiti

debiti verso banche	193.729.813.770	165.593.783.215
(di cui esigibili oltre il 1994 L. 117.394.469.394)		
debiti verso altri finanziatori	30.644.905.956	23.281.844.374
(di cui esigibili oltre il 1994 L. 27.396.782.624)		
acconti	9.015.714.915	16.527.164.358
debiti verso fornitori	371.066.780.216	332.962.160.611
debiti rappresentati da titoli di credito	10.589.525.336	13.321.451.753
(di cui esigibili oltre il 1994 L. 6.172.707.660)		
debiti verso imprese controllate	5.792.772.160	15.520.322.097
debiti verso imprese collegate	7.754.553.507	4.497.776.081
debiti verso controllanti	120.993.300	425.250
debiti tributari	14.156.807.795	6.386.471.912
debiti verso istituti di previdenza e sicurezza sociale	10.569.508.925	7.676.816.700
altri debiti	31.245.337.952	44.120.996.639
Totale	*684.686.713.832*	*629.889.212.990*
E) Ratei e risconti	*1.010.395.982*	*1.209.058.851*
TOTALE	*985.648.791.064*	*893.256.541.011*

CONTI D'ORDINE

Elenco garanzie dirette e indirette:		
fideiussioni a favore di imprese controllate	65.892.702.680	67.148.906.280
garanzie reali a favore di terzi	32.023.759.682	65.603.762.650
altri conti d' ordine	459.621.451.680	225.740.128.052
TOTALE	557.*537.914.042*	*358.492.796.982*

15

D.   Creditors

bank overdrafts and loans
  (of which L. 117,394,469,394 fall due beyond 1994)
other loans
  (of which L. 27,396,782,624 fall due beyond 1994)
prepayments
trade creditors
bills of exchange
  (of which L. 6,172,707,660 fall due beyond 1994)
amounts owed to subsidiary undertakings
amounts owed to associate undertakings
amounts owed to holding companies
taxes
social security
others

Total

E.   Accruals and deferred income

TOTAL

MEMORANDUM ACCOUNTS

List of direct and indirect guarantees:
  fiduciary garantees in favor of subsidiary undertakings
  real property guarantees in favor of third persons
  other memorandum accounts

TOTAL

CONTO ECONOMICO	1993	1992
A) Valore della produzione		
1) ricavi delle vendite e delle prestazioni	1.120.388.360.671	951.524.103.638
2) variazioni delle rimanenze di prodotti in corso di lavorazione, semilavorati e finiti	(1.541.967.573)	(12.695.250.696)
3) variazioni dei lavori in corso su ordinazione	0	0
4) incrementi di immobilizzazioni per lavori interni	0	1.839.535.917
5) altri ricavi e proventi	2.396.313.493	13.434.830.183
(di cui contributi in conto esercizio per L. 87.327.732)		
Totale	*1.121.242.706.591*	*954.103.219.042*
B) Costi della produzione		
6) per materie prime, sussidiarie, di consumo e di merci	586.324.179.588	488.350.207.877
7) per servizi	196.474.061.264	170.595.901.993
8) per godimento di beni di terzi	7.456.002.442	8.806.502.936
9) per il personale:		
salari e stipendi	131.009.759.942	122.622.608.098
oneri sociali	39.595.926.323	36.990.812.838
trattamento di fine rapporto	11.431.734.601	11.204.001.414
altri costi	4.634.400.619	4.327.569.239
10) ammortamenti e svalutazioni:		
ammortamento delle immobilizzazioni immateriali	7.497.033.939	7.735.486.559
ammortamento delle immobilizzazioni materiali	33.100.300.319	29.090.742.803
svalutazione dei crediti compresi nell'attivo circolante e delle disponibilità liquide	2.125.675.875	2.175.171.672
11) variazioni delle rimanenze di materie prime, sussidiarie, di consumo e merci	338.717.070	2.154.954.755
12) accantonamenti per rischi	860.000.000	665.000.000
13) altri accantonamenti	0	0
14) oneri diversi di gestione	12.555.192.448	11.071.122.805
Totale	*1.033.402.984.430*	*895.790.082.989*
Differenza tra valore e costo della produzione (A-B)	*87.839.722.161*	*58.313.136.053*
C) Proventi e oneri finanziari		
15) proventi da partecipazioni	10.640.414.876	355.000.000
(di cui da collegate L. 10.630.414.876)		
16) altri proventi finanziari:		
da crediti iscritti nelle immobilizzazioni	320.999.715	243.659.917
(di cui da collegate L. 75.306.566)		
da titoli iscritti nell'attivo circolante che non costituiscono partecipazioni	0	93.750.000
proventi diversi dai precedenti	23.159.348.708	15.274.905.503
17) interessi e altri oneri finanziari	51.278.872.802	70.383.132.510
Totale	*(17.158.109.503)*	*(54.415.817.090)*

PROFIT AND LOSS ACCOUNT   **1993**   **1992**

A)   **Value of production**

   1)   turnover
   2)   change in stocks of finished goods and in work in progress
   3)   change in long-term contract stocks
   4)   own work capitalised
   5)   other income
        (of which public grants for interest payments L. 87,327,732)

              Total

B)   **Production costs**

   6)   raw materials and consumables
   7)   external services
   8)   rents
   9)   staff costs
          wages and salaries
          social security costs
          statutory severance costs
          other staff costs
   10) depreciation and write-offs
          depreciation of intangible assets
          depreciation of tangible assets
          amounts written off from current debtors and from liquid funds
   11) change in stock of raw materials, consumables and merchandise
   12) provisions for risks
   13) other provisions
   14) other operating charges

              Total
              Difference between production value and costs (A-B)

C)   **Income and charges from financial assets**

   15) income from participating interests
        (of which L. 10,630,414,876 from associate undertakings)
   16) other income from financial assets:
          income from debtors under fixed assets
          (of which L. 75,306,566 from associate undertakings)
          income from current asset investments other than participating interests
          other income from financial assets
   17) interest and similar charges

              Total

D) Rettifiche di valore di attività finanziarie

18)	rivalutazioni	0	0
19)	svalutazioni		
	di partecipazioni	1.756.258.169	0
	Totale delle rettifiche (18-19)	*(1.756.258.169)*	*0*

E) Proventi e oneri straordinari

20)	proventi	2.509.163.873	11.111.483.230
21)	oneri	13.478.129.281	15.370.862.498
	Totale delle partite straordinarie (20-21)	*(10.968.965.408)*	*(4.259.379.268)*
	Risultato prima delle imposte (A-B+C+D+E)	*57.956.389.081*	*(362.060.305)*
22)	Imposte sul reddito dell'esercizio	22.571.120.500	3.968.643.532
23)	*Risultato dell'esercizio*	*35.385.268.581*	*(4.330.703.837)*
24)	Rettifiche di valore operate esclusivamente in applicazione di norme tributarie	8.100.000.000	0
25)	Accantonamenti operati esclusivamente in applicazione di norme tributarie	19.310.139.358	0
26)	*Utile (perdita) dell'esercizio*	*7.975.129.223*	*(4.330.703.837)*

Il presente bilancio è conforme alle scritture contabili.

17 Marzo 1994

p. Il Consiglio di Amministrazione

Il Presidente
Vittorio Merloni

Il Collegio Sindacale

Giorgio Venturini

Valeriano Balloni

Mario Ninno

17

D) **Changes in value of financial assets**

18)   revaluations

19)   write-offs
of participating interests

Total of changes in value (18-19)

E) **Extraordinary income and charges**

20)   extraordinary income
21)   extraordinary charges

Total of extraordinary items (20-21)

Profit before taxation (A-B+C+D+E)

22)   Taxes on profit

23)   *Result of the financial year*

24)   Corrections to valuations that result purely from the application of fiscal law
25)   Provisions resulting purely from the application of fiscal law

26)   *Profit (loss) for the financial year*

These financial statements are in conformity with the accounting records of the company.

17 March 1994

The Chairman of the Board of Directors

Vittorio Merloni

The Board of Statutory Auditors

Giorgio Venturini

Valeriano Balloni

Mario Ninno

LUXEMBOURG

Gerd H. Gebhard
Chartered Accountant, Luxembourg

1. Background

1.1 Introduction

The Grand Duchy of Luxembourg lies at the very heart of Europe, nestled between Belgium, Germany, and France. It covers 2,586 square kilometers and has 395,200 inhabitants, of whom 30.3% (119,700) are foreigners.[1]

Luxembourg is a constitutional monarchy and a member of the European Community. A number of EC institutions are located in Luxembourg, including the Court of Justice, Court of Auditors, European Investment Bank, and Secretariat of the European Parliament. French, German, and Luxembourgish are the official languages, French being most widely used in administration.

Between 1952 and 1988 the composition of the gross domestic product changed dramatically, as can be seen in the following table:

	1952 (%)	1988 (%)
Agriculture and mining	13.5	2.4
Industry and construction	52.1	32.3
Trade and services	34.4	65.3

Although ARBED, Luxembourg's large steel manufacturer, remains by far the largest private-sector employer, it is the growth of banking and financial services that has marked the economic development and the international reputation of the Grand Duchy.

There are 213 banks, 1041 investment funds, and about 10,700 holding companies registered in Luxembourg. The majority are owned by foreign companies or individuals. Legally, the administration of such banks and investment funds must be situated in Luxembourg, ensuring near full employment in the Grand Duchy. The government encourages and supports all investment from abroad. Government aid is available for investment in manufacturing and for certain services. No particular restrictions affect foreign investment, in respect to the type of investment, its ownership, or the flow of funds.

Luxembourg has had close economic and political links with its neighbors for a long time, and this is reflected in the development of its accounting conventions and practices.

1.2 Historical Background

The Commercial Code of 1807 determines the contents of the basic accounting records that must be kept by each enterprise. These are a journal for day-to-day transactions and such registers of assets and liabilities as will enable annual accounts to be drawn up.

Another Napoleonic legacy is the system of registration of commercial transactions and the capital taxation of companies. In fact, the annual taxation of the capital of a company (*taxe d'abonnement*) has been abolished for all commercial companies. It remains the only periodic charge to taxation for investment funds (at 0.06% of net assets) and holding companies (at 0.20% of capital).

The Company Law of 1915 is based on Belgium's Company Law of 1913. Belgian case law and academic doctrine is referred to if a question of interpretation arises. Luxembourg's Company Law was modified in 1933 to introduce private limited companies and, in the 1980s, to adopt the EU Directives.

Before the adoption of the Fourth Directive on company accounts, there were no specific regulations relating to the form or content of annual financial statements, other than that they had to consist of a balance sheet and a profit and loss account. Financial information produced was shaped by the requirements of the tax authorities. The resultant accounts consisted of "some lines of vague and imprecise headings with numbers against them."[2]

1.3 Legal and Regulatory Framework

1.3.1 Implementation of EU Directives

Rules on the preparation of accounts entered the statute book with the implementation of the EU Directives on the harmonization of accounting information:

- Law of May 4, 1984: Fourth Directive on company accounts, their contents, format, and valuation of balances
- Law of June 28, 1984: Introduction of audits by independent professional accountants
- Law of July 11, 1988: Seventh Directive on consolidated accounts

The new section 13 to the August 10, 1915 Company Law closely follows the structure and text of the Fourth Directive, with subsequent amendments for the implementation of the Seventh Directive.

Most of the options given to member states in the Directives have been maintained, for the benefit of preparers of accounts in Luxembourg. This is in line with government policy to provide businesses with the most liberal environment possible.

The new law applies only to the following types of companies:

- *Société anonyme* (S.A.) (public limited company)
- *Société à responsiblité limitée* (S.à.r.l) (private limited company)
- *Société en commandite par actions* (partnership limited by shares).

Special rules apply to banks, investment funds and insurance companies. The *Institut Monétaire Luxembourgeois* (IML) supervises banks and investment funds. Luxembourg has implemented the rules of the Bank Accounts Directive, which banks have had to comply with since 1993. The financial statements of investment funds are set out in the Law of March 30, 1988, which provides the whole framework of this important industry for the Grand Duchy.

The *Commissariat des Assurances* regulates the insurance sector. The provisions of the third generation insurance Directives as well as the Insurance Accounts Directive are expected to be fully implemented in the near future. Currently special provisions apply to the accounts of insurance companies.

1.3.2 Special Regimes

Audit and publication requirements have been reduced for small and medium-sized companies. In order to qualify as small or medium-sized, a company must not exceed at least two of the following three criteria (amounts in Luxembourgian francs, LF):

	Medium-sized	*Small*
Total assets	LF 372 million	LF 93 million
Turnover	LF 745 million	LF 186 million
Number of employees	250 employees	50 employees

If the criteria are exceeded for two consecutive years, then the company will change its classification.

Special account formats may be used by holding companies; see Section 2.4.

1.3.3 Accounting Standards

The Luxembourg Institute of Auditors (*Institut des Réviseurs d'Entreprises*, or IRE) has legal authority to issue accounting standards by itself. It has, in fact, not used this mandate but is seeking to set up a body of parties concerned with accounting and audit regulation to develop standards. In practice, international accounting standards are generally followed, except where they contradict Luxembourgian law

2. Audit and Publication

2.1 Statutory Auditor

According to the Company Law of 1915, every company must appoint a *commissaire aux comptes* (usually translated as a statutory auditor). The statutory auditor is charged with the ongoing supervision and management of the audit of the annual accounts. The results of the audit must be presented in a report to the shareholders at the annual general meeting.

The statutory auditor, whether person or legal entity, need not be professionally qualified nor independent of the company. He or she is an officer of the company, elected at the annual general meeting for up to 6 years. He or she has unlimited rights of access to company records and to information from the directors.

The law prescribes that the statutory auditor must receive a statement of affairs every 6 months and the annual accounts 1 month before the annual general meeting, in order to report on them at least 2 weeks before the meeting.

The law of May 4, 1984 introduced the requirement for an independent professional audit of large and medium-sized companies and also abolished the office of the statutory auditor for such companies. In practice, a large number of small companies are audited by professional accountants acting as their statutory auditors.

2.2 *Réviseur d'Entreprises*

The law of June 28, 1984 established the profession of *réviseurs d'entreprises* (independent auditor). The audit of large and medium-sized companies, banks, and investment funds must be carried out by a *réviseur d'entreprises*.

A number of other services are also reserved for the profession:

- Audit of consolidated accounts
- Audit of certain financial intermediaries and insurance companies
- Report if shares are issued for consideration other than cash by a public company
- Report on merger and demerger proposals.

The *réviseur d'entreprises* must be professionally qualified. A university degree, 3 years' practical training, and two examinations are required. Authorized auditors from other EC countries may be admitted after taking conversion examinations in Luxembourg.

Upon authorization by the Ministry of Justice, each *réviseur* becomes a member of the *Institut des Réviseurs d'Entreprises*. The Institute represents the profession externally and exercises disciplinary control over the conduct of its members.

The *réviseur d'entreprises* carries out his or her work for a company under a contract for services and is elected at the AGM, usually for a term of 1 year.

The auditor of a bank is appointed by the board of directors, and for investment funds the law stipulates appointment "by the fund." For banks, investment funds, and insurance companies, the appointment of the auditor is subject to approval by the relevant supervisory authority.

2.3 Publication

A full set of accounts (balance sheet, profit and loss account, notes, and directors' report) and the report of the auditors must be filed with the registrar of the commercial court within 1 month of the AGM approving the accounts. The fact of their filing will then be published in the official gazette, the *Memorial*.

By law the shareholders are entitled to receive only the balance sheet, profit and loss account, and the report of the statutory auditor. They need not be furnished with the notes, the directors' report, or the report of the *réviseur d'entreprises*. This anomaly is the result of the old publication requirements of 1915 not having been updated for the new definition of annual accounts in the law of May 4, 1984.

Exemptions available for small and medium-sized companies are summarized in Table 1.

2.4 Holding Companies

Holding companies are an important feature of the financial services sector in Luxembourg. There were nearly 10,700 holding companies registered in Luxembourg at the end of 1992. It should be noted that a holding company is subject to the same rules and regulations as all other companies, except for its liability to taxation and the restrictions on its activities related to the tax benefits it enjoys.

This section deals only with the classic Luxembourg holding company, based on the law of July 31, 1929. A second type of holding company was created by the implementation of the EU Directive on the taxation and distribution within groups of companies, referred to as SOPARFI. Dividend payments within the same group of companies and certain capital gains on the sale of shares are exempt from tax in the hands of the receiving company, subject to certain conditions (*Schachtelprivileg*). The exemption is available to all fully taxable companies, whether they are trading companies holding some investments or pure holding company vehicles.

An advantage over the 1929 holding company lies in the fact that SOPARFI are technically fully taxable and may thus benefit from double

TABLE 1 *Publication Exemptions for Small and Medium-sized Companies*

	Information to Shareholders		Information to Outsiders—Publication	
	Medium-sized	*Small*	*Medium-sized*	*Small*
Balance sheet	In full	Abbreviated	Some detail omitted	Abbreviated
Profit and loss account	Abbreviated	Abbreviated	Abbreviated	Not published
Notes to the accounts	In full	Abbreviated	Some detail omitted	Abbreviated
Directors' report	In full	In full	Published in full	Not published
Auditors' report	*Réviseur d'entreprises*	Statutory auditor	Published	Not published

tax agreements. Legally, SOPARFI are treated as normal companies, and they are subject to the normal audit and reporting requirements.

2.4.1 Definition

A holding company may have as its object only the acquisition and management of investments in other enterprises. Such investments include shares, bonds, loans to companies in which a significant interest is held, the holding of patents, and the granting of licenses. Holding companies may not engage in industrial or commercial activities. There are, however, no specified minimum or maximum amounts that must be invested.

Holding companies are supervised by the *Administration de l'Enregistrement et des Domaines*. There is no specific authorization requirement for a new holding company. It may commence its activities as soon as it is formed.

2.4.2 Taxation

Holding companies are exempt from taxation of their income and capital in Luxembourg, except for the two registry taxes indicated below. They do not have to deduct withholding taxes from dividends or interest paid but cannot obtain relief for withholding taxes suffered. Double taxation treaties concluded by the Grand Duchy generally do not apply to holding companies.

Holding companies are subject to the following taxes:

- Capital duty at the rate of 1% on the capital contributed to the company on formation or when the capital is increased.
- Registry tax at the rate of 0.2% per annum on the value of the shares of the company. The value is one of the following:
  —the stock exchange price (if shares are quoted)
  —the paid-in capital and share premium
  —ten times the dividend paid for the previous year, if such dividend exceeded 10% of the paid-in capital

2.4.3 Capital Requirements

The capital requirements of a holding company are as follows:

- Minimum subscribed capital LF 1,250,000.
- All shares must be at least 25% paid.
- Paid-in capital must be at least LF 1,000,000.
- Creditors, excluding bonds, may not exceed three times subscribed capital.
- Bonds issued may not exceed ten times paid-in capital.

There must be at least three directors and one statutory auditor. Two shareholders are required for the formation of the company. Neither officers nor shareholders need be Luxembourg residents.

2.4.4 Accounting Requirements

Holding companies are invariably classified as small companies because:

- They are not allowed to pursue any industrial or commercial activity, and therefore have no turnover.

- No Luxembourg holding company is known to have more than fifty employees.

Small companies do not have to be audited by a *réviseur d'entreprises*.

The Fourth Directive gave member states the option to implement special accounts formats for holding companies and similar institutions. The grand ducal regulation of 29 June 1984 introduced the simplified format of balance sheet and profit and loss account for holding companies as shown on pages 553–554.

3. Accounting Principles and Practices

3.1 Basic Principles

The basic principles governing the annual financial statements of companies are those laid down by the Fourth Directive. They are summarized below in the order in which they appear in the law.

3.1.1 Statement of Affairs

Every business must prepare an annual statement of affairs (*l'inventaire*), which must include all assets and amounts receivable and payable. The rules of the Commercial Code of 1807 were amplified in 1986 to include the requirement that double-entry bookkeeping be used and financial statements be prepared.

3.1.2 Annual Accounts

The annual accounts are made up of:

- Balance sheet
- Profit and loss account
- Notes

Directors' and auditor's reports are also required. With the exception of the auditor's report, the directors are responsible for all these documents.

3.1.3 True and Fair View

The accounts must be prepared in such a way as to give a true and fair view of the state of affairs of the company. The information given in the accounts must be free from ambiguities and must be consistent from year to year. Assets and liabilities, expenses and revenues, respectively, may not be netted. All items must be evaluated separately. Consistency means that items in the accounts are described and presented in the same manner and are evaluated by using the same principles from one year to the next. Any material changes of description or in valuation method must be justified and explained in the notes.

3.1.4 Accounting Concepts

The accounts must be prepared according to the following concepts:

- Going concern assumption
- Accruals/matching concept
- Prudence concept

3.1.5 Reporting Basis

The accounts are to be expressed in nominal monetary terms. At present, inflation accounting is not permitted, even though the government is empowered by law to introduce it. It is thought unlikely that this option will be exercised in the near future.

3.1.6 Valuation Basis

Historical cost accounting is the basic method of valuation. The historical cost of an asset represents its maximum value in the balance sheet. Revaluations (upward) are not permitted.

3.1.7 Formats

The balance sheet and the profit and loss account must be drawn up in one of the formats prescribed by law. See pages 550–552 for an example of a balance sheet and profit and loss account.

3.2 Foreign Currencies

The accounts of a company may be expressed in any freely convertible currency. There is no requirement to use the national currency, the Luxembourg franc. Any statutory amounts (e.g., size criteria) are calculated by reference to the Luxembourg franc, as is the liability to taxation.

The restatement of shareholders' funds from one year to the next will give rise to differences in the tax charge on the basis of financial and tax accounts, respectively, as will the calculation of allowable depreciation based on historical costs in Luxembourg francs. There are no specific rules relating to foreign currency translation in the Fourth Directive or in Luxembourg law.

3.3 Financial and Tax Accounts

The valuation of assets in the financial accounts is binding for the tax accounts. This principle is the same as the one established in German tax law (*Maßgeblichkeitsprinzip*). Thus, allowable depreciation for tax purposes is limited to the depreciation charged in the financial accounts. If the depreciation charged is in fact in excess of the economically sensible rate of amortization (in order to reduce the tax liability), then this must be explained in the notes to the accounts.

3.4 Valuation

Again, the basic principles of valuation are those commonly followed throughout the EC.

3.4.1 Fixed Assets

Fixed assets are depreciated over their useful lives on a systematic basis. All assets must be shown net of their related depreciation. Depreciation need not be charged on assets with an indefinite useful life.

Fixed assets must be written down if the value to be attributed to them is lower than the current book value and the reduction in value is expected to be long-term. Investments must be written down in all cases. If the reason for the write-off ceases to apply, the amount written off must be reinstated via the profit and loss account to the level at which it would have been recorded in the books under normal depreciation policy

3.4.2 Current Assets

Current assets are valued at the lower of cost or market value, equivalent to net realizable value. Actual cost, average cost, LIFO, and FIFO may be used to determine cost. The use of net realizable value, LIFO, and FIFO may not be accepted by the tax authorities, however, and thus may generate deferred tax balances.

3.4.3 Liabilities

Loans are normally stated at the amount due. If the amount received is lower, the difference may be capitalized and written off over the term of the loan.

Provisions are defined as known or probable liabilities that are known as to their nature but not as to their precise amount or due date.

3.5 Specific Accounting Practices

3.5.1 Format

The law leaves the choice of the format of the accounts open to each company. The balance sheet is usually in account form, showing gross assets and liabilities.

The profit and loss account may be shown by using the analysis of operating profit by function (i.e., the traditional Anglo-Saxon method, showing gross profit, distribution costs, and administrative expenses) or by type of income and expenses (e.g., raw materials, staff costs)

The first note to the accounts will normally give general information about the company and its principal activities. The second note relates to accounting policies, and the remainder follow the order in which items appear in the accounts.

3.5.2 *Share Capital Not Paid In*

Share capital not paid in must be shown, whether or not it has been called up, and be stated in the notes. At the same time, the capital subscribed must be shown in full on the liabilities side of the balance sheet.

3.5.3 *Formation Expenses*

Expenses arising relating to the incorporation or development of the company may be capitalized as formation expenses. Professional fees and taxes on capital issued are the most common items under this heading. Formation expenses must be written off within 5 years. Dividends may be distributed only to the extent that distributable reserves and available profits exceed unamortized formation expenses.

3.5.4 *Research and Development Costs*

Research and development costs may be capitalized and normally must be written off over 5 years. Their nature and reasons for adopting a longer period of amortization must be explained in the notes to the accounts. Dividend distributions are subject to the same restrictions as formation expenses.

3.5.5 *Goodwill*

Goodwill is determined after the allocation of fair values to the assets of the business acquired or in the first consolidation. It should be written off over 5 years. Longer periods of amortization must be explained in the notes to the accounts.

3.5.6 *Accruals and Prepayments*

Prepayments and deferred income are shown separately in the balance sheet, but accrued income and accrued expenses are to be included in debtors and creditors, respectively.

3.5.7 Legal Reserve

A legal reserve must be accumulated by public companies. Five percent of the annual profit must be allocated to this reserve, until it reaches 10% of the subscribed capital. The legal reserve may not be distributed.

3.5.8 Profit for the Year

The profit (or loss) for the year is to be shown in the balance sheet before appropriations. The annual general meeting votes on the appropriation proposed in the directors' report. Proposed dividends are not charged to the profit and loss account and are not included in liabilities.

3.6 Consolidation

The implementation of the Seventh Directive introduced the requirement to produce consolidated accounts. These were previously only required of banks under the regulations of the IML.

In principle, every company owned at least 50% by another company must be consolidated into group accounts. Some exemptions are available, however. Consolidations are normally by the acquisition method, but in certain circumstances merger accounting is permitted.

Associated companies and joint ventures (with a participation of at least 20% and up to 50%, respectively) may be consolidated on a proportional basis under certain conditions. Otherwise, equity accounting must be used.

Notes

1. Statistical data taken from *Luxembourg in figures*, published by STATEC, the government statistical office. All data as of December 31, 1992, unless otherwise indicated.

2. Berna/Leclerc (1984), *Les nouveaux comptes sociaux des societes de capitaux luxembourgeoises,* p. 9, Luxembourg (translated from the French original).

Useful Addresses

Institut des Reviseurs d'Entreprises
7 rue Alcide de Gasperi
BP 1362, Kirchberg
Luxembourg 1615
Tel- +437 484

Ordre des Experts Comptables
Luxembourgeois
7 rue Alcide de Gasperi
BP 1362, Kirchberg
Luxembourg 1615
Tel: +437 484

Financial Statements

Standard Accounts Format

BILAN ACTIF	*BALANCE SHEET ASSETS*
Capital souscrit non versé dont appelé	Capital subscribed, unpaid of which called up
Frais d'établissement	Formation expenses
Actif immobilisé	Fixed assets
Immobilisations incorporelles	Intangible assets
Frais de recherche et de développement	Research and development costs
Concessions, brevets, licences, marques, ansi que droits et valeurs similaires	Concessions, patents, licences, trademarks and similar rights and assets
Fonds de commerce	Goodwill
Acomptes versés	Payments on account
Immobilisations corporelles	Tangible assets
Terrains et constructions	Land and buildings
Installations techniques et machines	Plant and machinery
Autres installations, outillage et mobilier	Other fixtures and fittings, tools and equipment
Acomptes versés et immobilisations en cours	Payments on account and assets under construction
Immobilisations financières	Financial assets
Parts dans des entreprises liées	Shares in affiliated undertakings
Créances sur des entreprises liées	Amounts due from affiliated undertakings
Participations	Participating interests
Créances sur des entreprises avec lesquelles la société a un lien de participation	Amounts due from undertakings with which the company is linked by virtue of participating interests
Titres ayant le caractère d'immobilisations	Other fixed asset investments
Autres prêts	Other loans
Actions propres	Own shares
Actif circulant	Current assets
Stocks	Stocks
Matières premières et consommables	Raw materials and consumables
Produits en cours de fabrication	Work-in-progress
Produits finis et marchandises	Finished goods
Acomptes versés	Payments on account
Créances	Debtors
Créances résultant de ventes et prestations de services	Trade debtors
Créances sur des entreprises liées	Amounts due from affiliated undertakings
Créances sur des entreprises avec lesquelles la société a un lien de participation	Amounts due from undertakings with which the company is linked by virtue of participating interests

Autres créances	Other debtors
Valeurs mobilières	Securities
Parts dans des entreprises liées	Shares in affiliated undertakings
Actions propres	Own shares
Autres valeurs mobilières	Other securities
Avoirs en banques, avoirs en compte de chèques posteaux, chèques et encaisse	Cash at bank and in hand
Comptes de régularisation	Prepayments
Perte de l'exercice	Loss for the period

PASSIF   *LIABILITIES*

Capitaux propres	Shareholders' funds
Capital souscrit	Subscribed capital
Primes d'émission	Share premium
Réserve de réévaluation	Revaluation reserve
Réserves	Reserves
Réserve légale	Legal reserve
Réserve pour actions propres	Capital redemption reserve
Réserve statutaires	Reserves provided for by the articles of the company
Autres réserves	Other reserves
Résultats reportés	Profit brought forward
Provisions pour risques et charges	Provisions for liabilities and charges
Provisions pour pensions et obligations similaires	Pension provisions
Provisions pour impôts	Provision for taxation
Autres provisions	Other provisions
Dettes	Creditors
Emprunts obligataires	Debenture loans
Dettes envers des établissements de crédits	Amounts due to banks
Acomptes récus	Payments on account received
Dettes sur achats et prestations de services	Trade creditors
Dettes représentées par des effets de commerce	Bills of exchange
Dettes envers des entreprises liées	Amounts due to affiliated undertakings
Dettes envers des entreprises avec lesquelles la société a un lien de participation	Amounts due to undertakings with which the company is linked by virtue of participating interests
Autres dettes	Other creditors
Comptes de régularisation	Deferred income
Bénéfice de l'exercice	Profit for the period

COMPTE DE PROFITS ET PERTES	*PROFIT AND LOSS ACCOUNT*
Montant net du chiffre d'affaires	Turnover
Variation du stock de produits finis et en cours de fabrication	Change in stocks of finished goods and work-in-progress
Travaux effectués par l'entreprise pour ellemême et portés à l'actif	Own work capitalized
Autres produits d'exploitation	Other operating income
Charges de matières premières et consommables	Raw materials and consumables
Autres charges externes	Other external charges
Frais de personnel	Staff costs
Salaires et traitements	Wages and salaries
Charges sociales avec mention séparée de celles couvrant les pensions	Social security, with indication as to amounts in respect of pensions
Corrections de valeur sur frais d'établissement et sur immobilisations corporelles et incorporelles	Depreciation and amortization of formation expenses, tangible and intangible assets
Corrections de valeur sur éléments de l'actif circulant dans la mesure où elles dépassent les corrections de valeur normales au sein de l'entreprise	Exceptional value adjustments to current assets
Autres charges d'exploitation	Other operating charges
Produits provenant de participations avec mention séparée de ceux provenant d'entreprises liées	Income from investments, with indication of income from affiliated undertakings
Produits provenant d'autres valeurs mobilières et de créances de l'actif immobilisé avec mention séparée de ceux provenant d'entreprises liées	Income from other securities and other fixed assets, with indication of income from affiliated undertakings
Autres intérêts et produits assimilés avec mention séparée de ceux provenant d'entreprises liées	Other interest and similar income, with indication of income from affiliated undertakings
Corrections de valeur sur immobilisations financières et sur valeurs mobilières faisant partie de l'actif circulant	Value adjustments of investments and securities included in current assets
Intérêts et charges assimilées avec mention séparée de ceux concernant des entreprises liées	Interest and similar charges, with indication of amounts paid to affiliated undertakings
Impôts sur le résultat provenant des activités ordinaires	Tax on profit from ordinary activities
Résultat provenant des activités ordinaires après impôts	Profit/loss from ordinary activities after taxation
Produits exceptionnels	Extraordinary income
Charges exceptionnelles	Extraordinary charges
Résultat exceptionnel	Profit/loss from extraordinary items
Impôts sur le résultat exceptionnel	Tax on profit/loss from extraordinary items
Autres impôts ne figurant pas sous les postes ci-dessus	Other taxes
Résultat de l'exercice	Profit/loss for the period

Holding Company Accounts

BILAN ACTIF	BALANCE SHEET ASSETS
Capital souscrit non versé, dont appelé	Subscribed capital not paid up of which called up
Frais d'établissement	Formation expenses
Actif immobilisé	Fixed assets
Immobilisations incorporelles	Intangible assets
Immobilisations corporelles	Tangible assets
Immobilisations financières	Financial assets
Actif circulant	Current assets
Créances	Debtors
Valeurs mobilières	Investments
Avoirs en banque, compte chèques postaux, chèque et encaisse	Cash at bank, on postal cheque accounts and in hand
Comptes de regularisation	Prepayments
Perte de l'exercice	Loss for the period

BILAN PASSIF	LIABILITIES
Capitaux propres	Capital and reserves
Capital souscrit	Subscribed capital
Primes d'émission	Share premium
Réserve de réévaluation	Revaluation reserve
Réserves:	Reserves:
Réserve légale	Legal reserve
Réserve pour actions propres ou parts propres	Capital redemption reserve
Réserves statutaires	Reserve provided for by the statute of the company
Autres réserves	Other reserves
Résultat reportés	Profit/loss brought forward
Provisions pour risques et charges	Provisions for liabilities and charges
Dettes	Creditors
Emprunts obligataires	Debenture loans (bonds)
Autres dettes	Other creditors
Comptes de régularisation	Deferred income
Bénéfice de l'exercice	Profit for the period

COMPTE DE PROFIT ET PERTES	PROFIT AND LOSS ACCOUNT

Charges

    Corrections de valeur sur éléments d'actifs
    Intérêts et charges assimilées
    Autres charges
    Bénéfice de l'exercice

Produits

    Produits de l'actifs immobilisé
    Produits provenant de l'actif circulant
    Produits exceptionnels

Produits

    Produits de l'actifs immobilisé
    Produits provenant de l'actif circulant
    Produits exceptionnels
    Perte de l'exercice

Expenses

    Value adjustments on assets
    Interest and similar charges
    Other charges
    Profit for the period

Income

    Income from fixed assets
    Income from current assets
    Extraordinary income
    Loss for the period

Income

    Income from fixed assets
    Income from current assets
    Extraordinary income
    Loss for the period

THE NETHERLANDS

Martin N. Hoogendoorn

Moret Ernst & Young, University of Amsterdam and Limperg Institute, Amsterdam

1. Background

1.1 The Accounting and Auditing Profession

The Dutch accounting and auditing profession began to develop in the last decades of the nineteenth century. Early accountants were primarily bookkeepers, but soon the function of independent auditor of financial accounts became a necessity, as the separation between ownership and management of limited liability companies, which gained importance in the years 1890–1910, created the need for the independent and professional judgment of an auditor. In the course of time, accountants started to perform other duties, like internal auditing, governmental auditing, and advising management on internal control and accounting matters.

In 1895 the Netherlands Institute of Accountants (NIVA) was founded. One of its purposes was to create statutory rules for the accounting profession. A bill was drawn up in 1900, but it did not receive parliamentary reading.

In 1918, the Minister of Education, Arts and Sciences established a committee to prepare a new bill, which was published in 1920. The accounting profession was unenthusiastic, mainly because the degree of government interference embodied in the bill was considered too drastic. The belief that the new law would involve high governmental expenditure in a period of economic crisis was the main reason that this bill also did not receive a parliamentary reading.

Further bills were drawn up in 1930 and again in 1939. The 1939 bill was discussed in Parliament but not accepted. Finally, a committee established in 1956 produced a bill that led to the Chartered Accountants Act (*Wet op de Registeraccountants*) in 1962. This law became partially effective in 1963 and fully effective in 1967.

The Chartered Accountants Act reserved the auditing of financial statements for what are known as *registeraccountants* (RA, chartered accountants whose names are entered in a register). An RA is automatically a member of the public professional body, created by this law, the Dutch Institute of Chartered Accountants (NIVRA, *Nederlands Instituut van Registeraccountants*).

Another related group of accountants was created in 1974, when the *Accountants-Administratieconsulenten* Act came into effect: the *accountant-administratieconsulent* (AA). Comparable to the NIVRA, but with a lower official status, is the NOVAA, *Nederlands Instituut van Accountants-Administratieconsulenten*. The AA was not authorized to certify accounts but provided only other services, for example, implementing and maintaining accounting records, reviewing the manner in which records are kept, preparing financial statements, analyzing and interpreting (in explanatory reports) the data extracted from a company's records, and providing data and advice in connection with such data. The RA provides for such services as well, but the main function of the RA has always been the audit of financial statements and providing specific audit-related services. The traditional field of the AA is the small and medium-sized company; the traditional field of the RA is the large and medium-sized company.

The adaptation of Dutch law to the EC Eighth Directive, regulating the accounting profession, was used to reorganize the division of labor between RAs and AAs. The new Act of 1993 accepted both RAs and AAs as statutory auditors. Both categories will have the right to audit financial statements regardless the size of the company. However, the level of education will remain different, resulting in a continued difference in level of knowledge. Therefore, although is officially entitled to do so, an AA will normally not audit the financial statements of a large company.

The education and examination of AAs will be on the minimum level required by the Eighth Directive. This will result in more education than the current level of education. In particular, AAs currently do not need to know the audit process.

The education and examination of RAs will remain on the currently high academic level, which goes beyond the requirements of the Eighth Directive. Traditionally, the education and examination of RAs can be obtained by way of a university course or by courses organized by the NIVRA.

The university-based course is offered at universities with an economics faculty. The first step is to obtain a business economics degree by completing a full-time course that takes about 5 years. The final step is a part-time postgraduate course taking 2 or 3 years, during which candidates are usually employed by public accounting firms.

The NIVRA courses are available only on a part-time basis. Students start these courses after finishing normal high school or the higher economic and administration schools. They attend evening and day classes. It normally takes between 8 and 12 years to complete the full program of courses leading to RA qualification. Since 1994 the NIVRA has cooperated with Nijenrode University. The RA education program is under the faculty of Information Management and will lead not only to an RA qualification but also to the *doctorandus* degree, as does full-time business economics study at universities.

Currently, there is no practical training requirement. However, following the Eighth Directive, beginning in 1999 all RAs and AAs should have received 3 years of practical training.

1.2 Statutory Accounting Rules

The first statutory accounting rule was published in 1928 (Article 42 of the Commercial Code): the rule contained some requirements for limited liability companies for preparing the assets side of the balance sheet. There were no requirements for the liabilities side, nor for the income statement.

This situation lasted for more than 40 years, during which time, however, there were several discussions about the desirability of introducing further rules, especially in view of developments in the United States and the United Kingdom. Employers published working papers (in 1955 and 1962), as did the scientific committees of political parties (in 1959 and 1962). All these working papers recommended additional rules be promulgated.

Many companies, primarily large companies listed on the Amsterdam Stock Exchange, voluntarily followed the specific recommendations. In the period from 1928 to 1970, however, it was management itself that primarily decided whether or not to follow the suggestions for improving financial reporting. Some companies used the freedom provided by the law and confined themselves to minimal reporting.

A radical change took place in 1970. In that year, the first Act on Financial Reporting was published, becoming effective on May 1, 1971. The bill was prepared by a committee of the Ministry of Justice, which had been working on it from 1960 to 1965. Preparation of the bill and subsequent parliamentary debates took a further 5 years. The act embodied some general rules for preparing financial statements. It applied to limited liability companies (*naamloze venootschap*, NV), private companies (*besloten vennootschap*, BV), cooperative associations (*coöperatie*), and mutual guarantee associations (*onderlinge waarborgmaatschappij*)

The main consideration that governed accounting policies in the formulation of the act was that they should be generally acceptable, and that financial statements should give a true and fair view (i.e., a view that makes possible a sound judgment by users of the financial statements). The act also contained provisions for the publication of financial statements and the administration of justice. The provision relating to the administration of justice offered interested parties the opportunity to complain about financial statements to the Company Division of the Court of Appeal, with the possibility of further appeal to the Supreme Court. These rules were created as an alternative to creating a supervisory authority like the U.S. Securities and Exchange Commission. Departures from statutory rules should be referred to in the auditor's report.

The Act on Financial Reporting was incorporated into the Dutch civil code in 1976 (Book 2, Title 6), with only minor changes in the requirements. More important was the transition from Title 6 to Title 8 because of the adaptation of the Dutch accounting requirements to the Fourth EC Directive. This transition became effective on January 1, 1984. The main differences between Title 6 and Title 8 are:

- Title 8 has more detailed rules, especially concerning the format of the balance sheet and the income statement and concerning the information to be given in the notes to the accounts.
- Title 8 requires an indication of the basic valuation rules of historical cost and current value, although the general rule still is that of using generally acceptable accounting policies.
- Title 8 introduces what are known as legal reserves (or statutory reserves).
- There are stricter rules on the publication of the financial statements.

- The mandatory audit requirements are extended. (Because of a transitional arrangement, this rule did not become effective for 5 years.)

Two government orders were published in connection with Title 8: one on the formats of the balance sheet and the income statement, and the other on the application of the current value concept. Title 8 became Title 9 on January 1, 1989.

The statutory accounting rules had to be adapted once again because of the Seventh EC Directive on consolidated accounts. The amendment was published in November 1988 and became effective on January 1, 1990. Preparing consolidated accounts had been mandatory since the 1970 Act on Financial Reporting so the practical consequences of adaptation to the Seventh Directive were only minimal.

Further minor changes included simplifications and clarifications of existing requirements, and these became effective on March 1, 1990. The most recent changes concern adaptation to the EC Bank Directive and the EC Insurance Companies Directive: Title 9 was extended on March 17, 1993 by a new section on accounting by banks and on September 16, 1993 by a new section on accounting by insurance companies. The rules for banks are effective for all statutory years beginning on or after January 1, 1993. The rules for insurance companies are effective for all statutory years beginning on or after January 1, 1995.

One of the elements requiring special attention is the use of the current value concept in the Netherlands. The theory of current values (replacement values) was developed by Theodore Limperg in the 1930s, a period of rapid inflation. This theory had great impact on accounting thought in the Netherlands. The first company adopting the current value system in its primary accounts was Philips, in 1953. Current value accounting has always been considered a generally acceptable accounting principle in the Netherlands, and it is explicitly mentioned in the current statutory accounting rules.

Recently, however, almost all companies that had adopted the current value accounting system returned to the historical cost system, including Philips in 1992. The main reason for this development is international harmonization: in most other countries the historical cost system is the only acceptable system for the primary accounts. Notwithstanding this development, many companies still value part of their fixed assets at current value (for instance, property), and many companies provide supplementary accounts on the basis of current value accounting.

The practical application of the current value concept is discussed in more detail in Section 3.5 below.

The financial statements for tax purposes are based on tax law. The general requirement is that taxable income should be calculated on the basis of sound business practice (*goed koopmanschap*). Although sound business practice is equivalent to generally accepted accounting principles in the commercial financial statements (except for certain specific tax rules), there is no direct relationship between the two sets of financial statements. In this way, it is possible to use a certain accounting policy in the commercial statements and to use another policy in the statements for tax purposes. The practical implications are discussed in more detail in Section 3.11 below.

Companies listed on the Amsterdam Stock Exchange are required to disclose information in accordance with the Stock Exchange Regulations (*Fondsenreglement*), in addition to other requirements discussed here. For stock exchange flotations and new issues, a prospectus should be published that fairly presents the state of affairs of the issuing organization as of the balance sheet date of the last financial year for which annual accounts have been published. The prospectus should also contain information on events of special significance that have taken place after the balance sheet date. Other information, for instance, 3 years of comparative figures and certain forecasts, should be included. Listed companies should make available to the public their biannual and annual accounts and their directors' report, prepared in accordance with generally acceptable accounting principles and giving a true and fair view. As a rule, consolidated and unconsolidated data should be provided. The annual accounts must be audited, the biannual accounts need not. Listed companies are obliged to keep the public informed of any major developments that may have a significant effect on the price of their securities.

1.3 Accounting Standards

In the explanatory statement to the 1970 Act on Financial Reporting, the Ministry of Justice expressed its expectation that the business community and auditors, because of the main statutory rule that accounting policies should be generally acceptable, would survey the accounting policies used and examine the general acceptability of those accounting polices. The Dutch Institute of Chartered Accountants (NIVRA), the joint employers' organizations (*Raad van Nederlandse Werkgeversverbonden*), and the Trade Union Federation (*Overleorgaan Vakcentrales*) fulfilled this expectation by setting up the Tripartite Accounting Standards Committee (*Tripartiete Overleg*) in 1971. This committee published opinions on the Act of Financial Reporting (*Beschouwingen naar aanleiding van de Wet op de Jaarrekening van Ondernemingen*). As the title "opinions" suggests, these "standards" were informal and therefore not very effective.

This may be the main reason for replacing the *Tripartiete Overleg* by the *Raad voor de Jaarverslaggering* (Council for Annual Reporting; hereafter referred to as RJ) in 1980. The tripartite structure was maintained and adapted: the RJ consisted of representatives of the providers of information (the employers), representatives of the auditors of information (the accounting profession, NIVRA), and representatives of the users of information (employees and financial analysts). The government is not represented in the RJ. The RJ replaced the opinions by Guidelines for Annual Reporting (*Richtlijnen voor de Jaarverslaggering*).

These guidelines have a more formal character and should be regarded as authoritative pronouncements to be taken into consideration by producers of financial statements in choosing generally acceptable accounting policies and in presenting a true and fair view. The guidelines have no legislative status but may be considered an important frame of reference by the auditor in evaluating financial statements and by the Company Division of the Court of Appeal in arriving at its decisions.

Departures from the guidelines are not referred to in the auditor's report. The guidelines incorporate as far as possible the accounting standards of the International Accounting Standards Committee and those opinions of the Company Division of the Court of Appeal (and the Supreme Court) that have a general application. In general, the Dutch accounting guidelines are of an Anglo-Saxon nature (emphasizing the true and fair view, and with a dominant emphasis on "economic substance" rather than "legal form"), but they have generally developed independently of accounting standards in the United States and the United Kingdom.

Summarizing, the current frames of reference for accounting (concerning commercial financial statements) in the Netherlands are (in decreasing order of importance):

1. Civil Code (Title 9) and related government orders
2. Case Law (Company Division of the Court of Appeal, Supreme Court)
3. Guidelines of the RJ
4. International Accounting Standards
5. Other authoritative sources, such as literature and generally accepted practice

Wherever article numbers are used throughout this chapter, they refer to the latest version of Title 9. Reference is also made to the guidelines of the RJ (for instance, "RJ 4.20. 103" means that the requirement or recommendation is included in the guidelines of the RJ chapter 4.20, paragraph 103). References to the RJ guidelines are updated to issue no. 13 (November 1993).

1.4 Auditing Standards and the Auditor's Report

The Dutch auditing profession is fully autonomous in setting the standards required to meet legal audit requirements. Historically, the profession has avoided detailed guidance to public accountants on auditing principles and procedures. Dutch audit philosophy was mainly to be found in literature.

In 1973, a Code of Conduct for RAs was published by the NIVRA. This code set standards for ethical behavior, impartiality, secrecy, independence, the auditor's report, accepting engagements, and so on.

In the 1970s, the NIVRA started issuing ad hoc opinions on various topical subjects and interpretations of its Code of Conduct, but it was not until 1985 that the NIVRA started working on a comprehensive set of auditing guidelines (*Richtlijnen voor de Accountantscontrole*). The contents of these guidelines are highly influenced by the Union des Experts Comptables (UEC) Auditing Statements and the International Federation of Accountants (IFAC) International Auditing Guidelines.

The structure and the wording of the auditor's report have been changed recently, partly in order to follow international developments in this respect. An auditor who has audited financial statements in accordance with generally accepted auditing standards can express the following opinions.

1. An unqualified opinion. This opinion is given when an auditor is convinced that the financial statements give a true and fair view of the financial position and financial results.

2. An opinion with limitation (a qualified opinion). This opinion is given in two situations:
   —In the case of uncertainties of material importance in the audit
   —In the case of objections of material importance to the annual accounts

3. A disclaimer of opinion. This opinion should be given in the situation of uncertainties of fundamental importance in the audit.

4. An adverse opinion. This opinion is used in the situation of objections of fundamental importance to the annual accounts.

As can be inferred from the various alternatives, the distinction between *material* and *fundamental* is important. There are, however, no strict criteria for differentiating between the two. So, in practice, this is an important element of professional judgment.

The standard wording of the unqualified opinion is:

> We have audited the financial statements of xxx (company name) in xxx (place of business) for the year xxx. We conducted our audit in accordance with auditing standards generally accepted in the Netherlands. In our opinion, these financial statements give a true and fair view of the financial position of the company at xxx (balance sheet date) and of the result for the year then ended and also comply with other Dutch legal requirements for financial statements.

As can be seen, the standard wording includes a reference to the compliance with Dutch legal requirements for financial statements. Generally speaking, these legal requirements are those mentioned in Title 9 (see Section 1.2). No reference is made to the guidelines of the RJ (see Section 1.3).

When financial statements are not in compliance with legal requirements, the departure should be mentioned in the auditor's report. A departure can be compatible with giving a true and fair view and, therefore, with an unqualified opinion. If the departure leads to financial statements not giving a true and fair view, an opinion with limitation or an adverse opinion should be given, depending on whether the objection is of a material or a fundamental nature.

In addition to the standard wording given above, additional information in the form of an emphasis of matter can or should be given. An emphasis of matter is mandatory in the case of a serious uncertainty as to the going concern status of the company. In this case, an additional paragraph is added at the end of the report, of which the standard wording is:

> Without qualifying our opinion above, we draw attention to note xxx, which refers to the uncertainty as to the company's ability to continue as a going concern. It is not impossible, however, that in the long term the company will be able to continue operating as a going concern. The financial statements have therefore been prepared on a going concern basis.

An emphasis of matter is nonmandatory in other cases. It is used to draw the reader's attention to an important matter, for instance, to a possible claim for which no provision is made in the balance sheet.

There are also standard wordings for the other opinion, which will not be fully reproduced here. For the opinion with limitation it is essential that the words "subject to" are used when the cause of the limitation is the uncertainty in the audit, and that the words "except for" are used when the cause of the limitation is the objection to the annual accounts. For the disclaimer of opinion, it is essential to use the words "unable to form an opinion as to whether the financial statements give a true and fair view." The disclaimer might include a negative assurance, stating that the audit did not reveal any errors or omissions in the financial statements. For the adverse opinion, the words "these financial statements do not give a true and fair view" should be used.

The auditors' report need not be addressed, the assumption being that the report is meant for any potentially interested party. The report can be signed by either an individual in his or her name or in the firm's name, or both, if applicable. The report is dated to indicate that the effect on the financial statements of post-balance sheet events until that date is included in the opinion. Preferably, the date of the audit report is the same as the date of the annual accounts.

2. The Form and Content of Published Financial Statements

2.1 Content of the Annual Report

The annual report includes the executive directors' report on the financial statements and certain other information

2.1.1 Executive Directors' Report

The executive directors' report gives a fair review of the position at balance sheet date and of the development of the business during the financial year. In addition, this report contains information in respect of:

- Significant post-balance sheet events
- Likely future developments, with particular attention to capital expenditure, financing and employment, and to the circumstances on which future net turnover and profitability depend
- Activities in the field of research and development.

The executive directors' report may not be at variance with the financial statements.

2.1.2 Financial Statements

The financial statements comprise the balance sheet, the income statement, the notes, and other prescribed information. There are two different sorts of financial statements: the legal entity's own financial statements and the consolidated financial statements. Specific information concerning the content of the legal entity's own financial statements is given in Section 2.2 below, and information concerning the content of consolidated financial statements is given in Section 2.3 below. The requirements for preparing and publishing the legal entity's and consolidated financial statements are discussed in Section 2.4 below.

As part of the notes, many companies publish a statement of source and application of funds or, recently, a cash flow statement. It is not obligatory to include such a statement, with the exception that the Stock Exchange Regulations require it for new companies to be listed. The new guideline of the RJ of November 1993 (RJ 4.20) recommends that companies include a cash flow statement, based on the principles of IAS 7 (revised).

2.1.3 Other Data

Certain other information must be included in the annual report (in a separate section, normally called "other data"). Included with this supplementary information (Article 392) is:

- The auditor's report
- The profit appropriation clauses of the articles of association
- The appropriation of the profit or the treatment of the loss or, if these have not yet been adopted, the relevant proposal
- The names of holders of special controlling rights arising from the articles of association, as well as the nature of these rights
- The number of profit-sharing certificates including similar rights
- Post-balance sheet events having material financial consequences, and their significance; the existence of branches, the names of the countries in which these branches are established, and their trading name (when this name differs from that of the reporting entity)

2.2 The Content of the Legal Entity's Own Financial Statements

The provision regarding the object of the financial statements (Article 362 (1)) reads:

> The financial statements shall in accordance with generally acceptable accounting principles furnish such information as to enable a responsible

opinion to be formed regarding the financial position and the profit and loss and, to the extent that the nature of financial statements permits, regarding the solvency and liquidity of the corporate body.

We summarize this object as follows: the financial statements shall give a true and fair view.

The balance sheet shall present the financial position and the income statement shall present the profit or loss in a fair, consistent and clear manner (Articles 362 (2) and (3)).

Should the true and fair view so demand, it is the company's duty to include information in addition to that which is legally required. Should this be necessary for presenting a true and fair view, the company is obliged to depart from the special requirements laid down in or pursuant to the law. The reasons shall then be stated as far as necessary, with mention of the impact on the financial position and on the profit or loss (Article 362 (4)).

In preparing the financial statements, the general principles of going concern, consistency, accrual, prudence, substance over form, and materiality apply (Articles 362 (5), 363 (3), 384 (2), 384 (3)). Significant accounting policies should always be disclosed (Article 384 (5)). Furthermore, corresponding figures for the preceding period should be shown in the balance sheet and the income statement (Article 363 (5)). Where necessary in the interest of comparability, that figure must be adjusted and the change resulting from the adjustment must be explained. These general principles are in line with IAS 1. The revenue recognition rules of IAS 18 are covered by these general principles as well.

The foregoing general principles are part of the statutory accounting rules. From a general point of view, it is important to mention also the publication by the RJ in May 1992 of the Dutch translation of the International Accounting Standards Committee (IASC) Framework for the Preparation and Presentation of Financial Statements. The translation has been published as an exposure draft, with the intention that it will be accepted as the conceptual framework underlying Dutch accounting.

In preparing the balance sheet and income statement, a company should follow one of the standard formats for the layout of accounts, prescribed by governmental decree as a consequence of the EC's Fourth Directive.

For the balance sheet, two standard formats are available: a horizontal format (with assets on the left and liabilities on the right), and a vertical format (with assets at the top and liabilities at the bottom, with a separate reference to working capital).

For the income statement, there are four standard formats, differing from each other in the horizontal layout (seldom used) versus the vertical layout, and in the functional classification of costs (cost of sales, distribution expenses, general administrative expenses) versus the classification of costs by category (wages and salaries, social security expenses, raw materials and consumables, amortization and depreciation).

Examples of some formats are given in Section 2.5 below. Further requirements concerning the classification of items are discussed in Section 3.

Important disclosure items, specified in the statutory accounting rules, not relating to the classification of items, include the following (if applicable):

1. General
    —Any (additional) information required for giving a true and fair view (Article 362 (4))
    —The principles underlying the valuation of the assets and liabilities and the determination of the financial results in relation to each item (Article 384 (5)), including the methods of calculating depreciation and amortization (Article 386 (2)); furthermore, if applicable, the information that interest is included in the asset value (Article 388 (2)) and whether and in what way, in connection with revaluation, allowance has been made for the effect of taxation on the financial position and results (Article 390 (5))
    —Changes in accounting policies and in the layout of the balance sheet and income statement, the well-founded reasons for the change, and the significance for the financial position and results (Article 363 (4) and 384 (6))
    —A reconciling statement of movements in each of the fixed asset items (tangible, intangible, and financial) during the financial year (including acquisitions, disposals, revaluations, depreciation, downward value adjustments, and rectifications thereof) (Article 368 (1))
    —Relating to each fixed asset item held at the balance sheet date, the cumulative total of any revaluation and the cumulative total

of amounts written off and the downward value adjustments (Article 368 (2))

—Any major financial commitments entered into by the legal entity for a number of years to come and not shown in the balance sheet, with separate disclosure of commitments to group companies (Article 381);

—The average number of employees of the legal entity during the financial year, broken down in a manner compatible with the way the business is organized (Article 382)

—The aggregate amount of remuneration, including retirement benefit costs, and other payments, of the present and former executive board members and, separately, of the present and former supervisory board members, except when this amount is attributable to one natural person (Article 383 (1))

—The amount of loans, advances, and guarantees granted by the legal entity, its subsidiaries, or its consolidated companies for the benefit of the executive and supervisory board members of the legal entity, with specific disclosure of the amounts receivable, the rate of interest, the most important other terms, and the repayments during the financial year (Article 383 (2))

2. Intangible assets:

—Explanatory notes to capitalized incorporation and share expenses and research and development costs (Article 365 (2))

—If goodwill is amortized over a period longer than 5 years, the period of amortization together with the reasons why it is in excess of 5 years (Article 386 (3))

3. Tangible assets:

—A limited right (*in rem* or *in personam* of permanent enjoyment in or in respect of tangible fixed assets (Article 366 (2))

4. Financial fixed assets:

—The name, principal place of business, and proportion of the issued capital of any company to which it, alone or together with subsidiaries, has furnished or has caused to be furnished at least 20% of the issued capital, on its own account, and of any company in which it is fully liable as a partner for its debts to creditors (Article 379 (1))

—Relating to the same companies as mentioned above, the amount of shareholders' equity and the result for the latest financial year for which financial statements are available (unless certain conditions are met) (Article 379 (2))

—The name and principal place of business of the company managing the group to which it belongs and of any company consolidating the financial statements of the legal entity in its published consolidated financial statements, as well as the name and place of office where copies may be obtained (at no more than cost) (Article 379 (3))

5. Current assets:

—For each group of receivables classified under current assets: the amount becoming due and payable after more than one year (Article 370 (2))

—The extent to which securities are not at the legal entity's free disposal (Article 371 (2))

—The extent to which bank and postal giro (bank) balances are not at the legal entity's free disposal (Article 372 (2))

6. Shareholders' equity:

—A statement showing the movements in the shareholders' equity during the financial year, stating additions and disposals subdivided by item according to their nature (Article 378 (1))

—The issued share capital and the paid-in capital or paid-in and called-up capital (Article 373 (2)), broken down into classes of shares (Article 378 (2))

—The book value of and the movements in a legal entity's own shares or depositary receipts thereof (treasury shares)

—As treasury shares may not be capitalized but should be deducted from the shareholders' equity (see Section 3.3 below), the item of the shareholders' equity from which the acquisition cost or book value thereof has been deducted (Article 378 (2))

—For a public limited liability company: every acquisition and disposal for its own account of treasury shares (and depositary receipts thereof), with reasons for the acquisition, the number, par value, and agreed price of the shares involved in each transaction, and the proportion of the capital that they represent (Article 378 (3))

— The way in which payment for shares, demandable or voluntarily deposited during the financial year, has been effected, and the substance of contracts, underlying payments on shares otherwise than in cash (Article 378 (3))

7. Provisions:

   —A precise definition of the provisions and an indication, as far as possible, to what extent the provisions are regarded as long term (Article 374 (3))

   —If the legal entity has accepted liability for the debts of others, or is still at risk in respect of discounted bills of exchange or checks: obligations arising from these commitments in accordance with the form of security furnished, insofar as no provisions have been made for them in the balance sheet; commitments entered into for the benefit of group companies must be disclosed separately (Article 376)

8. Liabilities

   —For each category of debt, the amount becoming due and payable after more than 1 year, with an indication of the interest rate and with separate disclosure of the amount becoming due and payable after more than 5 years (Article 375 (2))

   —The amount that must be repaid within 1 year on loans classified under liabilities with a term of more than 1 year (Article 375 (6))

   —For each category of debt, the amount and nature of any collateral and, to the extent necessary for giving a true and fair view, those liabilities for which the company (conditionally or unconditionally) has committed itself to encumber or not to encumber its assets to provide collateral (Article 375 (3))

   —The amount of debts that have been subordinated to all other debts and an explanation of the nature of any such subordination (Article 375 (1))

—For convertible loans, the terms of conversion (Article 375 (7)); any major commitments entered into for a number of years to come and not shown in the balance sheet, such as those arising out of long-term contracts (Article 381)

9. Turnover:
    —If the legal entity is divided into various industry sectors, the extent to which each type of activity has contributed to net turnover (Article 380 (1))
    —The breakdown of net turnover by the various geographic areas in which the legal entity supplies goods and services (Article 380 (2)). (A breakdown of results and assets employed, as required in IAS 14. is not required in the Netherlands, although the RJ recommends that large companies provide a breakdown of operational results (RJ 271. 616)

In general, the disclosures as mentioned in IAS 5 are required in the Netherlands as well, partly in the form of layout requirements for the balance sheet and the income statement. Some requirements of IAS 5, like disclosure of significant intercompany transactions, are not stated in the statutory rules but in the accounting guidelines (RJ 1.19.304; the related party disclosures of IAS 24 are incorporated in RJ 1.19 as well). Many more disclosure requirements are formulated by the RJ. We will summarize some of them in Section 3, but to give a complete description of them would exceed the scope of this chapter.

2.3 The Content of Consolidated Financial Statements

Consolidated financial statements are the financial statements integrating assets, liabilities, income, and expenses of legal entities and partnerships constituting a group or a part of a group. A group is defined as those companies that form an economic unity under common control; a group company is any company in the group.

In accordance with Article 362 (1), consolidated financial statements should give a true and fair view of the (part of the) group (Article 405). In IAS 27 the term grou*p company* is not used. The equivalent term is *subsidiary*. In the Netherlands a subsidiary has a specific meaning, which is somewhat different from a (subordinate) group company. A subsidiary is not a group company unless it is under the control of the holding company; but in practice both terms are normally equivalent. When prepared, the consolidated financial statements are officially included in the notes to the legal entity's (i.e., the holding company's) own financial statements (Article 406 (1)). In practice, the consolidated financial statements are considered to be of primary importance, and they are normally presented before the legal entity's own statements.

Included in the consolidated statements are the legal entity (holding company) itself and its (sub)group companies (Article 406 (1,2)). Subsidiaries not belonging to the group (see above) as well as some group companies (see below) are not included in the consolidated accounts; in that case they are normally valued at net asset value (which is a variant of the equity method, see Section 3.1 below).

If, because of a major difference in its activities, consolidation of a group company would conflict with the true and fair view, its financial statements or, when applicable, its consolidated financial statements, must be disclosed separately in the notes. Important but invisible consequences of this separate disclosure must be elucidated (Article 406 (3)). Furthermore, consolidation is not required for data (Article 407 (1)):

- Of group companies whose total significance is negligible
- Of group companies whose financial data can be obtained only or estimated at disproportionate costs, or with great delay
- Of group companies that are held to be sold

In comparison with IAS 27 there is one important point of difference concerning the scope of consolidation: IAS 27 does not allow exclusion from consolidation of group companies with dissimilar business activities.

The legal entity may itself be excluded from consolidation when it has no activities other than managing and financing group companies and participations, and when the management of group companies takes place under the terms of a joint operating agreement with another legal entity not included in the consolidated statements (Article 407 (3)).

In the case of joint ventures, the financial data may be included in the consolidated financial statements in proportion to the interest held in it, if this meets the legal requirement of a true and fair view (Article 409).

Proportional consolidation is not acceptable in other cases. If joint ventures are not consolidated, they are normally accounted for using the equity method.

The requirements mentioned in Section 2.2 above regarding the content of the legal entity's own financial statements apply to the consolidated financial statements as well, with a few exceptions (Article 410 (1)). The most important exceptions are:

- Shareholders' equity is not specified, and the specific disclosures concerning this item are not given; however, disclosure of the interest of third parties in the consolidated equity and result is required, and differences between equity and result in the legal entity's own and in the consolidated statements should be elucidated (Article 411)

- The information mentioned above concerning financial fixed assets is not disclosed; however, specific information must be given concerning the group companies, including disclosure of the companies for which the reporting legal entity has accepted liability for their debts (Article 414)

- The information concerning remuneration of board members and loans, advances and guarantees granted by the legal entity to board members is not given (Article 401(1))

- Inventories need not be specified if this would require disproportionate costs due to special circumstances (Article 410(2)).

Accounting policies are normally the same as those used in the legal entity's own financial statements; different principles may be used only for valid reasons, which are to be disclosed in the notes (Article 410(3)).

The balance sheet date of the consolidated financial statements must correspond with the balance sheet date of the legal entity's own financial statements. On no account may consolidated statements be drawn up by using information determined more than three months before or after the group's balance sheet date (Article 412).

Specific consolidation procedures such as the elimination of intragroup balances and transactions and the application of uniform accounting policies are not elaborated upon in law, but on this point practice is equivalent to IAS 27.

2.4 Obligations to Prepare and Publish the Annual Report

As indicated above, the annual report includes (in its most extended form) the executive directors' report, the legal entity's own financial statements, the consolidated financial statements, and certain other information. In this section we will identify the obligations concerning the preparation and publication of the annual report. These requirements apply to the companies mentioned in Section 1.2 above.

A limited liability company (NV) and private company (BV) are required to prepare their annual reports within 5 months of the balance sheet date (cooperative associations and mutual guarantee associations have 6 months). The annual report must be approved within 6 months of the balance sheet date (cooperative associations and mutual guarantee associations have 7 months) and must be published within 8 days of approval. The annual general meeting can extend the time limit for preparing/ approving the annual report, by a maximum of 6 months (cooperative associations and mutual guarantee associations: 5 months). If the accounts are not approved within 2 months of the latest possible (extended) date of preparing the annual report, the board of directors must file a draft set of accounts with the annotation that the accounts have not yet been approved. In all cases the annual report must be published not later than 13 months after the balance sheet date; if they are not, the company commits an economic offense.

Publication of the annual report is realized by filing the annual report at the Company Registry. The accounts must be signed by all executive and supervisory directors. Certain parts of the report may be excluded from filing, provided they are available for inspection at the office of the company and a copy is provided on request; this fact must then be reported to the Company Registry.

In principle, every NV and is obliged to prepare, as a part of the annual report, its own financial statements, subject to the exceptions mentioned below. In addition, a legal entity managing a group of companies, alone or together with another group company, must include consolidated financial statements in the notes to its own financial statements, combining the financial statements of its group companies together with its own financial statements. If the legal entity is not managing the whole group, but only part of the group, it must present consolidated financial statements as well, which are to include group companies of which it exercises dominant control (Article 406).

Consolidated statements need not be prepared if all of the following apply (Article 407 (2)):

- The company is small (see below).
- None of the companies involved is listed.
- The company is not a credit institution.
- No notices of objection have been lodged with the legal entity within 6 months of commencement of the financial year by at least 10% of the members or by holders of at least 10% of the issued share capital.

A legal entity that is considered to be the head of a part of a group is exempted from preparing consolidated accounts if all of certain conditions are met. The most important conditions (Article 408) are that the shareholders are in agreement; that the accounts of the company and of the companies to be consolidated are included in the consolidated statements of a larger part of the group; and that these consolidated statements are prepared in accordance with the EC Seventh Directive, or, when this Directive does not apply, in a similar way. The legal entity must disclose in its own financial statements that the exemption is applied. This regulation is equivalent to that in IAS 27.

A legal entity is exempted from preparing full own accounts if all of certain conditions are met. The most important conditions (Article 403) are that simplified statements are prepared; that the shareholders are in agreement; that the accounts are included in the consolidated accounts of an EC-based group (prepared in accordance with the Seventh Directive); and that the company preparing the consolidated accounts has guaranteed the liabilities of the company being exempted.

For any entity, if the financial data of a legal entity have been included in its consolidated financial statements, the legal entity's own profit and loss account need disclose as a separate item only the income from participating interests after taxes (Article 402). The application of this provision must be disclosed in the notes to the consolidated financial statements.

The obligations to prepare and publish the annual report differ according to the size of the company (as does the question of whether the accounts need to be audited). There are three size categories: small companies, medium-sized companies, and large companies.

A small company is a company, not engaged in insurance or banking, that satisfies at least two of the following three criteria:

1. The value of the assets on the basis of historical cost accounting does not exceed 5 million florins (Fl)
2. The net turnover (sales) for the year does not exceed Fl 10 million.
3. The average number of employees during the year is less than 250.

A medium-sized company is a company not engaged in insurance or banking and not being a small company that satisfies at least two of the following three criteria:

1. The value of the assets on the basis of historical cost accounting does not exceed Fl 20 million.
2. The net turnover (sales) for the year does not exceed Fl 40 million.
3. The average number of employees during the year is less than 250.

A large company is a company that is neither a small company nor a medium-sized company.

The above criteria are based on consolidated amounts, including all group companies that would have been consolidated if consolidated statements had been prepared. The criteria are subject to periodic adjustment. A company moving up or down from one category to another continues to be subject to the legal requirements for its previous category during the year in which its status changes.

A large company is required to prepare and publish:

- An executive directors' report
- A full balance sheet and notes thereto
- A full income statement and notes thereto
- Full other information, including the auditor's report

A medium-sized company is required to prepare:

- An executive directors' report
- A full balance sheet and notes thereto
- A condensed income statement and notes thereto
- Full other information, including the auditor's report

A medium-sized company is required to publish the same information, with the following exceptions:

- Only a condensed and not a full balance sheet need be published.
- Not full but only limited other information need be published, including the auditor's report.

A small company is obliged to prepare:

- An executive directors' report
- A condensed balance sheet and notes thereto
- A condensed income statement and notes thereto
- Limited other information (no auditor's report)

A small company is required to publish only a condensed balance sheet and notes thereto. An executive directors' report, an income statement, and other information need not be published. Furthermore, a small company is never required to prepare consolidated accounts.

Only large and medium-sized companies are required to have their accounts audited.

2.5 An Example of Published Financial Statements

An example of a published set of financial statements is shown on pages 633-660. We reproduce parts of the annual report for the year 1993, published by a large, 92-year-old chemical company in the Netherlands, DSM. We reproduce from the official English language version as well as from the original Dutch version.

The annual report is sixty-four pages long, with the following elements:

- Some principal data (consolidated)
- Foreword

- Report by the Managing Board of Directors, subdivided into:
  —General review
  —Dividend
  —Financial results
  —Balance-sheet profile
  —Prospects
  —Safety, health, and the environment
  —Personnel and organization
  —Research and development
  —Review by business segment (Hydrocarbons & Polymers, Base Chemicals and Fine Chemicals, Resins & Plastic Products, Energy & other activities)
- Report by the Supervisory Board of Directors to the shareholders
- Corporate organization
- Financial statements
- Other information
- Quarterly financial data
- Some key data in ECUs and U.S. dollars
- DSM figures since 1986
- Principal operating companies and minority interests
- Sales centers
- Information on DSM shares

Reproduced at the end of this chapter are:

1. The consolidated balance sheet at 31 December 1993 (after profit appropriation) in the original Dutch version
2. The consolidated balance sheet at December 31, 1993 (after profit appropriation) in the English version
3. The consolidated 1993 statement of income in the Dutch version
4. The consolidated 1993 statement of income in the English version

5. The consolidated 1993 statement of cash flows in the Dutch version
6. The consolidated 1993 statement of cash flows in the English version
7. The accounting policies, in the English version
8. The notes to the consolidated financial statements, in the English version
9. The legal entity's own balance sheet at December 31, 1993, and its own 1993 statement of income, in the Dutch and English versions
10. The notes to the legal entity's own balance sheet, in the English version
11. The other information, including auditor's report, in the English version

The excerpts from the DSM annual report should be studied in light of the following short clarifications and comments.

2.5.1 Consolidated Balance Sheet

DSM has adopted a horizontal layout, with separate balance sheet totals for assets on the one hand and group equity and liabilities on the other hand. The numbers in brackets refer to the notes.

If the vertical layout had been used, the current liabilities would have been deducted from the current assets, presenting a separate working capital amount. The long-term liabilities, provisions, equalization account (for an explanation: see Section 3.5.3 on government grants) and group equity would then have been presented at the bottom of the balance sheet, in that order and without a total amount.

2.5.2 Consolidated Income Statement

DSM applies the vertical layout, with a classification of costs by category. The majority of cost elements are identified not in the income statement but in the notes (included in "other operating costs," note 15).

2.5.3 Classification

The classification of assets, liabilities, revenues and expenses in the consolidated balance sheet and income statement is in conformity with Dutch law and can be found in the financial statements of other companies as well. A difference between companies might be that some subclassifications (for instance inventories, provisions) are given either in the balance sheet or in the notes to the balance sheet (as in the DSM financial statements).

2.5.4 Statement of Cash Flows

DSM recently changed from a statement of source and application of funds to a statement of cash flows. The changes in cash are subdivided into operating activities, investing activities, and financing activities. The indirect method is applied, adjusting the net result by changes in balance sheet amounts to arrive at the net cash provided by operating activities. In note 19 a reconciliation is made of certain balance sheet movements and items in the statement of cash flows.

2.5.5 Legal Entity's Balance Sheet

The layout of the legal entity's balance sheet does not differ from the consolidated one. However, the layouts of the two income statements do differ. As indicated in Section 2.4 above, the legal entity whose financial data are included in the consolidated statements is allowed to prepare a simplified own income statement, showing only as a separate item the income from participating interests after taxes. The application of this provision (Article 402) is disclosed in the general note to the consolidated statements.

As indicated in Section 2.3 and further explained in Section 3.1 below, the accounting policies in the consolidated financial statements and in the legal entity's own financial statements are normally the same. This can be illustrated in the annual report of DSM by comparing stockholders' equity and net result in both statements: the amounts in both statements are equal.

2.5.6 Accounting Policies

Accounting policies regarding the scope of consolidation show that status as a group company is decisive for being included in the consolidated financial statements. Other accounting policies will be discussed in more detail in Section 3.

2.5.7 Notes

The notes to the consolidated financial statements and to the legal entity's own balance sheet show several of the disclosure items mentioned in Sections 2.2 and 2.3.

In notes 1, 2 and 3, the reconciling statements of movements in each of the fixed asset items during the financial year are given. The classification and statement of movements of shareholders' equity is partially given in the notes to the consolidated accounts (note 7) and fully in the notes to the legal entity's own balance sheet (note 5).

The obligatory breakdown of net sales by division and by region is given in note 12 of the consolidated statements. The geographic break-down is presented by origin as well as by destination. Note 16 shows the breakdown of the operating profit by division, and note 2 of the consolidated statements shows a geographic breakdown of capital expenditure and the book value of tangible assets at year end. These breakdowns are not obligatory.

The commitments not shown in the balance sheet are disclosed in note 11 of the consolidated statements and in note 8 of the legal entity's own balance sheet. In Section 3 reference will be made to some more notes.

2.5.8 Other Information

Other information includes, among other things, the auditor's report. The auditor's report covers the parent company and group accounts of DSM for the year 1993, following the standard form and wording laid down by the NIVRA (see Section 1.4 above). The auditors, Moret Ernst & Young, attest that the financial statements give "a true and fair view" (in Dutch, "*een getrouw beeld*") of the financial position and the result.

3. Accounting Policies and Practices in Valuation and Income Measurement: Implications for the Analyst

3.1 Group Accounts

The general content of group accounts is discussed in Section 2.3 above. As indicated in Section 2.3, the group accounting policies are normally the same as those in the legal entity's own financial statements. This normally means that equity accounting is used in the legal entity's own financial statements in the same way as in the consolidated statements. As a consequence, in the Netherlands, equity and income in the legal entity's own financial statements are normally the same as those in the consolidated statements, as is the case with DSM. A notable exception is Unilever, the large Dutch-British company. Unilever does not use equity accounting in its own legal entity financial statements. This is without doubt a consequence of applying British accounting rules, in which equity accounting is used only in group accounts.

For participations with significant influence, Dutch law allows equity accounting not to be used in the legal entity financial statements only when there are well-founded reasons (Article 389 (8)). International entanglement, such as with Unilever, is considered to be such a well-founded reason, as is the use of Article 408 in not preparing consolidated accounts (see Section 2.4).

The use of equity accounting in the legal entity's financial statement is obligatory for all enterprises in which the investor exercises significant influence on business and financial policy. These investments comprise subsidiaries (group companies), associated companies, and joint ventures. It is irrelevant whether or not the investments are consolidated. In the consolidated statements the same principle applies, with the difference, of course, that group companies are consolidated.

The method of equity accounting has several variants (Article 389; RJ 2.03.2):

1. The *net asset value* method: the investor must determine the net asset value of its investment by valuing assets, provisions, and

liabilities of the company in which it participates and by calculating its financial results by means of the same method as that applied to its own assets, provisions, liabilities, and financial results.

2. The *visible equity* method: the investor does not use its own method of valuing assets, provisions, liabilities, and financial results, but uses the method that is used by the company itself, as shown in its own financial statements.

3. The *equity method on the basis of cost*: the investor values its investment at cost and adjusts this value by the amount of its share in the retained profits and other reserve movements of the company in which it participates. Usually, no adjustment is made to the investor's share in the financial results for amortization of goodwill.

In all variants, the income statement reflects the investor's share in the results of operations of the investee.

The *net asset value* method is the principal method. The *visible equity* method is allowed when insufficient information is available to the legal entity to determine the net asset value. The *equity method on the basis of cost* normally should not be used.

Except for the last variant, application of the equity method leads to a separate identification of goodwill. Because of the equivalence between the legal entity's financial statements and the consolidated statements, goodwill is shown in both statements in the same way.

In IAS 27 and 28, the term *equity accounting* has a specific meaning, namely, what is called above "the equity method on the basis of cost," with the difference that adjustments are made for amortizing goodwill. An important difference with IAS 27 and 28 is that in the Netherlands the investments in which the investor has a significant influence may not be accounted for by using the cost method. According to the cost method the investment is recorded at cost and the income statement reflects the dividends received from profits distributed. The cost method can be acceptable in other cases, however (see Section 3.9 below).

The DSM accounting policy for financial fixed assets is the *net asset value* method (the share in equity is determined in accordance with DSM Group policies).

3.1.1 Goodwill

Positive goodwill, paid on the acquisition of a participation, can be accounted for in the following ways:

- It can be capitalized under intangible fixed assets and amortized (Articles 365, 386 (3), 389 (6))
- It can be charged directly to the income statement (shown separately) (Article 389 (6))
- It can be charged directly to the reserves (shown separately) (Article 389 (6)

If goodwill is capitalized and amortized, the amortization will have to be charged to the income statement. The period of amortization is the estimated useful life. If amortization takes place over a period greater than 5 years, that longer period should be disclosed, together with an explanation of why the period is longer. A periodic evaluation of the future economic benefits of goodwill in relation to its capitalized amount is required. In case of a permanent decline in value, an additional write-off will be required (RJ 2.03.221).

In practice, most companies charge the goodwill direct to the reserves, as does DSM. This practice is no longer allowed in IAS 22 (revised), which contains the requirement to capitalize goodwill and amortize it and not to take it directly to the reserves (immediate write-off to income would be acceptable, but only in the case that goodwill is not offset by future economic benefits).

For negative goodwill, there is only one general rule (Article 389 (7)): it is accounted for by a direct addition to the revaluation reserve, as far as there are no disadvantages connected with the acquired company. Any possible disadvantages would have to be taken into account, for instance, by creating a provision for reorganization expenses.

The immediate allocation of negative goodwill to the revaluation reserve is not in line with IAS 22 (revised), which requires it to be treated as deferred income.

Recently, some companies began to identify hidden assets in the goodwill paid on acquisitions. Examples are publishing rights, brands, and copyrights on music and databases. These assets are excluded from goodwill and separately accounted for as intangible assets (and amortized over their expected useful lives, which are sometimes considered to be indefinite or indeterminable).

These recent developments with intangible assets have created the need for a revision of the existing RJ Guideline 2.01. In that respect, the RJ published a Consideration, in which it indicated that capitalizing publishing rights and comparable intangible assets might be the preferable alternative. The Consideration took into account the arguments for and against not amortizing intangible assets, but no position was taken whatsoever. The intention is to include definitive views in a revised guideline.

For the method of accounting for business mergers or combinations, there are no definite rules for opting between purchase accounting (or acquisition accounting) and pooling of interests accounting (or merger accounting). In the majority of cases, however, purchase accounting is used. There are only a few cases known in which pooling of interests accounting has been used; in all these cases there was a merger involving an exchange of shares between more or less equal sized companies. This is equivalent to the situation envisaged in IAS 22.

3.2 Foreign Currency Translation

In dealing with foreign subsidiaries and associated companies, a distinction is made between foreign entities and direct foreign operations. (RJ. 1.03.913). In drawing up their financial statements, for each of their foreign participating interests investors should classify their operations either as foreign entities or as direct foreign operations. Nonconsolidated foreign investments should always be regarded as foreign entities. For practical reasons, it is acceptable to group all foreign-based operations in one of the two categories, on the basis of the nature of the more important of those foreign operations (RJ 1.03.914).

In IAS 21, a similar distinction is made, and "direct foreign operations" are defined as "foreign operations that are integral to the operations of the reporting enterprise. A difference with IAS 21 is that the option to group all foreign-based operations into one category for practical reasons is not available.

Foreign currency translation can also play a role in foreign currency transactions of the reporting entity itself. While the translation of foreign entities and direct foreign operations is discussed in Sections 3.2.1 and 3.2.2, respectively, the foreign currency transactions are discussed in Section 3.2.3.

3.2.1 Foreign Entities

A foreign entity is a type of foreign operation in which the foreign-based activities take place independently and where there are few or no connections between the cash flows arising from those activities and those of the investor (RJ 1.03.913).

In translating the assets and liabilities of foreign entities, the closing rate should be used, that is, the rate of exchange ruling at the balance sheet date. The resulting translation difference in relation to the shareholders' equity of (the net investment in) the foreign entity at the beginning of the accounting period should be taken directly to the investor's reserves (RJ 1.03.916/7), either to a separate foreign exchange equalization reserve or to the general reserves (other reserves). DSM accounts for the translation differences in its "other reserves" (note 5 to the legal entity's own balance sheet).

Income statement accounts should be translated either at the closing rate or at average rates for the period. If the individual items from the income statement of the foreign entity are translated at average rates for the period, net income may be translated either likewise at the average rate or at the closing rate (RJ 1.03.919). DSM has applied average rates.

To the extent that the intragroup receivables and liabilities are in effect an expansion or contraction of the net investment in a foreign entity, the exchange differences arising on those receivables and liabilities should be taken directly to the reserves as well (RJ 1.03.921).

Furthermore, if a loan has been contracted in a foreign currency in order to finance or provide a hedge against the net investment, the exchange differences arising on the loan should also be taken directly to the reserves, to the extent that they are effective as a hedge against the exchange differences arising from the net investment (RJ 1.03.922). In its accounting policies, DSM mentions the situation of loans for hedging purposes.

These requirements are equivalent to those set by IAS 21, with the exception that income statement accounts and the resulting net income should be translated at average rates (or actual rates).

3.2.2 Direct Foreign Operations

A direct foreign operation is defined as a foreign-based activity that is not a foreign entity. In such cases, the investor will look at the foreign activities primarily from its own currency point of view, because the investor regards the foreign subsidiary's assets and liabilities as its own (RJ 1.03.913). In the case of translating direct foreign operations, the temporal method is prescribed.

When current values are applied, the assets and liabilities of a direct foreign operation should be translated at the closing rate. The difference arising from this translation should be regarded as part of the revaluation, in sofaras it relates to items for which a revaluation reserve has been created. The translation difference should be regarded as part of the income from ordinary operations, insofar as it relates to other items (RJ 1.03.923).

When historical cost accounting is applied, the assets, liabilities, income, and expenditure of direct foreign operations should be translated as if they directly form part of the financial statements of the investor. This means that fixed assets and stocks are to be translated at the rates ruling on the dates on which the valuation of the relevant item is based (historical rates) and other assets and liabilities at closing rates. Translation differences should be shown in the income statement as part of the result on ordinary operations (RJ 1.03.924/6).

In the income statement, items related to balance sheet items that have been translated at historical rates should likewise be translated at historical rates. The other income statement items should be translated at settlement rates or at average rates (RJ 1.03.925). These requirements are equivalent to those of IAS 21.

3.2.3 Foreign Currency Transactions

Transactions in foreign currencies that have been settled during the accounting period should be reported in the financial statements at the settlement rate (RJ 1.03.906). Where transactions have not been settled by the balance sheet date, the liabilities arising from those transactions should be carried in the balance sheet at the closing rate, except where forward transactions have been concluded as a hedge against the difference on exchange. Where exchange differences on long-term or short-term receivables or liabilities have been hedged by forward transactions, it is preferable to value those receivables or liabilities at the relevant forward rate (RJ 1.03.907), as does DSM.

The exchange gains and losses on short-term transactions and the exchange losses on long-term transactions should be taken to income in the period in which they arise. Exchange gains on long-term transactions are preferably accounted for in the same way, but it is also acceptable to allocate the gains over the period remaining to maturity. In that case the unallocated portion of such differences is shown in the balance sheet as a deferred gain. Subsequent exchange losses on long-term transactions in the same currency are deducted from this deferred gain (RJ 1.03.908/10). In the case of forward transactions that have been concluded as a hedge, the difference between the spot rate and the forward rate should be allocated over the duration of the forward transaction. (RJ 1.03.911).

There is one important difference between the Dutch rules and IAS 21 (revised): IAS 21 does not allow any deference of losses or gains, which is more restrictive than the Dutch rules.

3.3 Capital and Reserves

Shareholders' equity is specified only in the legal entity's financial statements, not in the consolidated statements, as can be illustrated in the DSM annual report. The legal specification (Article 373 (1)) is:

1. Issued share capital
2. Share premium (paid-in surplus)
3. Revaluation reserves
4. Other legally required reserves (subdivided according to their nature)
5. Statutory reserves
6. Other reserves
7. Retained profits

Some of these elements of shareholders' equity will be discussed in the following paragraphs.

3.3.1 *Issued Share Capital*

If the issued share capital has not been paid up, the legal specification starts with the paid-in capital or, if payments have been called, the capital paid in and called up. In these cases, the issued share capital is mentioned in the notes (Article 373 (2)).

It is possible for an NV or BY to purchase its own paid-up shares (or depositary receipts thereof), provided that the following four cumulative conditions are met (presented here in simplified form):

- The capital and reserves after purchase amount to no less than the called-up portion of the company's issued share capital, plus legal and statutory reserves;
- The nominal amount of the shares to be acquired does not exceed 10% (NV) or 50% (BV) of the issued capital.
- The articles of association allow the acquisition.
- The annual general meeting has authorized the executive directors to make the acquisition.

Article 373 (3) stipulates that the company's share capital may not be reduced by the amount of its own shares purchased. Furthermore, according to Article 385 (5), own shares may not be shown as assets. Therefore, the purchase price of the acquired own shares normally must be deducted from the other reserves (RJ 2.41.107) as is done by DSM (see note 5 to the own balance sheet). If the shares of the company are held by a subsidiary, the value attributed to the interest in the subsidiary should be reduced by the acquisition price of the shares (Article 385 (5)). If that subsidiary is a group company, the reduction normally should be made in full, irrespective of the interest in the subsidiary (RJ 2.03.116).

3.3.2 *Revaluation Reserve*

A revaluation reserve is formed if assets and liabilities are valued at current value. When a company revalues an asset (at a higher amount), the company must carry in the balance sheet a revaluation reserve equal to the difference between the book value before and after the revaluation (Article

390 (1)). The revaluation reserve may be converted into share capital (Article 390 (2)).

Downward value adjustments reduce the revaluation reserve. Where the revaluation reserve is insufficient, the reduction in value is charged to the income statement (Article 387 (5)) and shown separately (RJ 2.41.221). The revaluation reserve may not be reduced below the sum of the revaluations included in the reserve in respect of assets that are still held by the company at the balance sheet date (Article 390 (3)). This is called the minimum position of the revaluation reserve (the unrealized revaluation).

The revaluation reserve must be reduced to the extent that the amounts transferred thereto are no longer necessary for the implementation of the valuation method adopted and for the object of the revaluation (Article 390(3)). This can be the case, for instance, when the financial structure is considered to be an integral part of the valuation system (gearing adjustment), so that the changes in value financed by capital other than equity are recognized in the income statement when realized (RJ 2.41.225).

Any reductions of the revaluation reserve that are taken to the income statement (for instance upon realization of the revaluation), are to be shown separately (Article 390 (4)). Realization of the revaluation can also lead to a transfer from the revaluation reserve to the other reserves.

The notes must disclose whether and in what way allowance has been made for the effect of taxation on revaluations (Article 390 (5)).

3.3.3 Legally Required Reserves

The aforementioned minimum position of the revaluation reserve is a legally required reserve. Other legal reserves include, among others:

- A reserve for capitalized incorporation and share issue expenses and the capitalized research and development costs (Article 365 (2));
- A reserve for undistributed profits of subsidiaries and associated companies accounted for under the equity method, unless the profits can be distributed on the authority of the company and received without limitations (Article 389 (4)). DSM has indicated that no legal reserve for retained profits is required (see note 5 to the own balance sheet).

592 Europeanseable Accounting Guide

The reserves may be created on an item-by-item basis or collectively for similar items (RJ 2.41.217 and they may be created as a charge against the profit appropriation account or against the free reserves (other reserves, retained profits). DSM creates its legal reserve against its other reserves (see note 8 to the own balance sheet). Reductions of the legal reserves (for instance, because of amortization of the capitalized costs or the distribution of profits) can also be credited to the free reserves or included in profit distribution (RJ 2.41.215). Legal reserves are mandatory, and they are intended to protect creditors against excessive profit distributions to shareholders.

3.3.4 Other Reserves and Retained Profits

Other reserves and retained profits are what are known as free reserves, and are normally disclosed together. A point at issue is whether direct movements in other reserves (bypassing the income statement) are allowed. The basic principle in the Netherlands is that of an all-inclusive income statement, with the only acceptable direct movements in shareholders' equity being the result of share issues, share reductions, dividend payments charged to the free reserves, and revaluations based on the current value method. However, several exceptions to this general rule prevail. As described in Section 3.2 above, a direct movement is required in the case of some foreign exchange translations. A direct movement in the other reserves is allowed for the following items (RJ 2.41.211):

- Goodwill (see Section 3.1)
- Adjustments to the provision for deferred tax liabilities resulting from changes in tax rates but only as far as related to deferred tax on revaluation
- The consequences of a financial reorganization under which creditors and shareholders surrender some or all of their rights, accompanied by the writing off of a loan
- Losses resulting from the destruction of assets (e.g., owing to a disaster), which it would have been impossible or unusual to insure against
- Losses resulting from nationalization, unexpected capital levies, or similar forms of expropriation

- The cumulative effect of changes in accounting policies (see Section 3.13.1)

The direct movements should be made net of tax.

In general, the IASC follows a stricter all-inclusive income statement approach. As far as IAS 8 is interpreted in a way that all unusual items should be included in net income, the foregoing rules of the RJ are in conflict with IAS 8.

3.4 Liabilities and Provisions

In the balance sheet, a distinction is made among provisions, long-term debts, and short-term debts.

The term liabilities refers to all three elements. Liabilities not presented in the balance sheet are either contingent liabilities or *pro memoria* liabilities. Furthermore, part of the liabilities are the accruals and deferred income, normally classified as a part of short-term debts. One element of deferred income, however, the equalization account for investment grants, is normally classified separately between shareholders' equity and provisions (see Section3.5 below), as is the case in the DSM financial statements.

A contingent liability is an obligation to pay or to render a performance to another party, in the event that a third party fails to meet its obligations or an obligation to bear the losses of other third parties (RJ 2.51.102). These contingent liabilities may not be shown in the balance sheet (RJ 2.65.101) but have to be disclosed (see Section 2.2 above, concerning Article 376).

A *pro memoria* liability is the liability arising from a contract under which both performance and consideration are due to take place after the balance sheet date (RJ 2.51.103). This liability is normally not included in the balance sheet, but when there are financial commitments for a number of years to come, they must be disclosed (see Section 2.2 above, concerning Article 381; see also RJ 2.65.2).

3.4.1 Debts

Debts should be carried under liabilities and may not be offset against assets for the financing of which debt has been contracted (RJ 2.51.106).

A debt that has to be paid or that will become due and payable not more than one year after it has come into existence is to be considered a short-term debt. If the agreed period for payment is longer, the debt will be of a long-term nature (RJ 2.51.107).

Debts are normally valued at face value.

3.4.2 Accruals and Deferred Income

Accruals and deferred income are normally classified under short-term debts. These items are a consequence of using the matching principle, and may be (RJ 2.62.102):

- Amounts received in advance for income to be recognized in subsequent periods, for instance, subscriptions and membership fees
- Amounts still to be paid after the balance sheet date relating to expenses imputed to a period that has elapsed, such as telephone costs, energy costs, and current interest on debts.

3.4.3 Provisions

According to Article 374 (1) the balance sheet shall show provisions against:

1. Liabilities and losses, the amount of which is uncertain at the balance sheet date but which can be reasonably estimated
2. Risks existing at the balance sheet date in respect of expected liabilities or losses, whose size can be reasonably estimated
3. Costs that will lead to an expense in a subsequent financial year, provided that a part of these costs originated before the balance sheet date and that the provision is intended to allocate costs evenly over a number of years

   The provision under item 3 is a cost-smoothing provision. Regarding items 1 and 2, it is clear that not every uncertainty will provide grounds for making a provision.

Such grounds will exist only when two conditions are satisfied (RJ 2.53.105):

- There are concrete, specific risks, that is, risks attaching to particular assets or liabilities, or attaching to particular business activities. No provision is to be made for the general risk inherent in entrepreneurial activity.
- The risks must exist on the balance sheet date. They must arise from events that took place before the balance sheet date, from acts performed before that date or from commitments entered into before that date.

The general criteria for recognizing provisions under items 1 and 2 are the same as those for recognizing contingent losses in IAS 10.

A reduction in the value of an asset may not be expressed by creating a provision (Article 374 (2)). Provisions related to specific assets, for instance, provisions for stock obsolescence and bad debts, should be accounted for in the balance sheet as a deduction from the assets concerned (RJ 2.53. 103). Other provisions should be shown separately in the balance sheet on the liabilities side. The use of the term *reserve* for provisions is not acceptable; reserves are part of equity (RJ 2.53.107).

The notes must indicate, where possible, to what extent the provisions are regarded as long term (Article 374 (3)). A provision is regarded as long term when settlement is expected to take place after one year (RJ 2.53.110).

Provisions should be valued at face value, except for pension and similar provisions and provisions for deferred taxation (see Section 3.11 and 3.12 below) (RJ 2.53.111). The amount of a provision can be determined by using the static method or the dynamic method.

In applying the static method, the best possible estimate is made of the cash value of current liabilities and risks. When the company is running a (large) number of similar risks, the estimate may be made collectively. Otherwise, the estimate is made on an item-by-item basis (RJ 2.53.115).

In applying the dynamic method, the addition to the provision is calculated on the basis of a percentage of the amount of a related item. An example is the addition to the provision of bad debts as a percentage of sales effected in the period under review. A periodic examination of the validity of the underlying assumptions (for instance, the percentage used) will be essential (RJ 2.53.113/114).

Provisions must be subdivided (in the balance sheet or in the notes) according to the nature of the liabilities, losses, and costs for which they are made, and they must be precisely defined in accordance with their nature (Article 374 (3)). Article 374 (4) states that in any case, separate disclosure must be made of:

- Provisions for tax liabilities (hereafter called provisions for deferred taxation) that may arise after the financial year but which are chargeable to that financial year or to a preceding financial year, including a provision for taxation that may arise from a valuation at above purchase price or production costs
- Provisions for pension commitments

In addition to the legal distinction, the RJ identifies (RJ 2.53.9):

- Provisions related to early retirement of personnel and other release schemes (RJ 2.53.4)
- Provisions for specific assets
- Guarantee provisions
- Provisions for contract risks
- Provisions for risks from disputes and legal actions
- Provisions for cleaning environmental pollution
- Provisions for major maintenance
- Provisions for uninsured risks
- Provisions for costs related to the discontinuation of operations
- Provisions for redundancy payments
- Provisions for disability payments

Several of these provisions are shown in the DSM annual report (note 9 to the consolidated financial statements).

We will not elaborate on these individual provisions, except for the provisions for deferred taxation and the provisions for pension commitments, which are discussed in Sections 3.11 and 3.12 below.

3.5 Property, Plant, and Equipment

Article 366 (1) identifies the following separate categories of tangible fixed assets:

1. Land and buildings
2. Plant and machinery
3. Other operating fixed assets, such as technical and office equipment
4. Fixed assets under construction, and payments on account
5. Tangible fixed assets not used in the production process (for instance dwellings for management and personnel and tangible fixed assets held as investments)

3.5.1 Valuation

The general principle of valuation is stated in Article 384 (1): in choosing a principle for the valuation of an asset and for the determination of the financial results, the company should be guided by the rules of Article 362. The general rule of Article 362 (1) is discussed in Section 2.2 above: financial statements should give a true and fair view. Article 384 (1) identifies two suitable bases for tangible fixed assets: historical cost (i.e., purchase price or production cost) and current value.

The purchase price of an asset is the price at which it was acquired. The term *production cost* is applicable to assets produced by the company, and it comprises the purchase price of the raw materials and consumables used and the other expenses attributable to the production of those assets. The production cost may include a reasonable proportion of the indirect costs and the interests on debts over the period attributable to the production of the asset (Article 388 (2)). If interest is included in the valuation of the assets, this must be stated in the notes. The foregoing is in line with IAS 16 and IAS 23, although specific rules on the capitalization of borrowing costs are lacking.

The current value of an asset is arrived at by means of the Asset Valuation Decree, which contains rules on the content, limits, and method of application in financial statements of the valuation of assets at current value. The current value of an asset can be the replacement value, the recoverable amount, or the net realizable value (RJ 103.203).

The replacement value is defined as the amount required to acquire or produce as a replacement for the existing asset another asset of equal significance economically for the operation of the business.

The recoverable amount is defined as the value, at the time of valuation, of net turnover attributable to the asset that may be generated by operating the business in which the asset is employed or for which it is intended.

The net realizable value is defined as the amount for which the asset can be sold to best advantage, net of the costs still to be incurred.

If replacement of the tangible fixed asset may reasonably be assumed, the relevant current value is the replacement value. Otherwise, the relevant current value is the recoverable amount if the asset will still be employed for the operation of the business, and the net realizable value if the asset will no longer be employed.

The choice between the valuation principles of historical cost (purchase price or production cost) and current value is in principle a free one. However, if the balance sheet and the income statement have been drawn up on the basis of historical cost, it should be considered whether the information on the basis of current value must be given in the notes per item (or heading) of the balance sheet and the income statement in order to give the true and fair view required (RJ 1.03.403). The information to be provided resembles that mentioned in IAS 15. DSM applies the principle of historical cost but provides limited supplementary data based on current value (see note 2 to the consolidated statements).

If the balance sheet has been drawn up on the basis of current value, the income statement should be based on current value as well (RJ 1.03.408). It is recommended (but not required) that there be the same uniformity between balance sheet and income statement in the case when the balance sheet has been drawn up on the basis of historical cost (RJ 1.03.408).

In IAS 16 (revised), property, plant, and equipment should be valued at either historical cost or at a revalued amount, with a preference for the first basis. Valuation in the context of a comprehensive system reflecting the effects of changing prices is allowed according to IAS 15. In the Netherlands there is only the basic choice between valuation at historical cost and at current value. When current value accounting is applied, revaluation should take place on a consistent basis. Incidental revaluation is not normally allowed. However, although the RJ suggests application of current value either to all tangible fixed assets and stocks or to none, in practice some companies carry part of the fixed assets at current value and part at historical costs. When the current value system is applied to a specific asset, however, revaluation takes place systematically.

When the current value principle is applied, changes in the current value are recognized in the revaluation reserve. The rules governing the revaluation reserve are discussed in Section 3.3 above.

Article 401 (2) states that investments, including investment properties, held by an investment company may be valued at market value. The market value of investment properties is considered to be equal to the net realizable value. The investment company may also apply the general rules of Article 384, including valuation at historical cost.

3.5.2 Depreciation

Depreciation and amortization must be applied irrespective of the results for the financial year. The methods of calculating depreciation and amortization must be stated in the notes (Article 386 (1,2)). Depreciation should take place on a consistent basis, taking into account the expected useful life, the estimated residual value, and the decline in value of the performance potential of the asset (Article 386 (4); RJ 2.02.216).

The depreciation method for tax purposes can be different from that for commercial purposes, for instance, accelerated depreciation for tax purposes and straight-line depreciation for commercial purposes. Differences are taken to the provision for deferred taxation (see Section 3.11 below).

The valuation basis for depreciation for tax purposes is historical cost. Depreciation on the basis of current value is not allowed. These differences may or may not be taken to the provision for deferred taxation (see also Section 3.11).

The depreciation guidelines are in line with IAS 16 (revised).

In addition to consistent depreciation, when valuing the tangible fixed assets at historical costs, it may be necessary to recognize other reductions in the value of the asset. Pursuant to Article 387 (4), it is mandatory to recognize a reduction in the value where this reduction is expected to be permanent. The lower value to be taken into account is either the net realizable value or the recoverable amount, but not the replacement value (RJ 2.02.224). The value adjustments must be charged to the income statement and shown separately. The charge must be reversed as soon as the value ceases to be reduced (Article 387 (5)).

Special write-downs for tax purposes in excess of what would be justifiable for commercial purposes may not be included in commercial financial statements.

3.5.3 Grants

Government grants related to tangible fixed assets (investment grants) may not be credited direct to shareholders' equity but should be either included separately as an equalization account under liabilities or deducted from the invested amount itself (RJ 3.01. 107/109). The equalization account is normally classified between shareholders' equity and provisions (see the DSM balance sheet).

Each year, a part of the equalization account should be released to the income statement. This part should be calculated consistently with due regard to the way in which the expenditure for which the subsidy has been granted is itself accounted for in the financial statements (RJ 3.01.111).

If the subsidy is deducted from the invested amount, the yearly depreciation amounts are automatically lowered.

Account should be taken of any grant to be reimbursed.

Although the investment grant facility was abolished in 1988, the financial statements are still affected by grants received in the past. The accounting for government grants is in line with IAS 20.

3.6 Assets Whose Services Are Acquired by Means of Leases

In accounting for leases, a distinction is made between finance leases and operating leases. A finance lease is a form of financing in which the legal ownership of the asset generally remains with the lender (lessor), while the economic risks are borne entirely or almost entirely by the borrower (lessee). In the case of an operating lease, the economic risks are borne by the lessor. In practice, there are a number of hybrid forms. The terms of the contract as a whole determine whether the accounting method for finance leases or the accounting method for operating leases should be used (RJ 1.05. 121/124). Some general guidelines for determining the existence of economic ownership are given in RJ 1.05.125, which states that economic ownership in principle exists where:

- The lessee will be entitled, during or immediately after the expiration of the period for which the lessor has committed himself, to purchase the asset at a price substantially below its market value; or

- The lessor has committed himself for a period of approximately the same duration as the economic life of the asset; or
- The lessee has committed himself for a shorter period than the economic life of the asset but has been granted an option at a considerably lower rental for the ensuing period up to approximately the end of the economic life of the asset

The accounting method for finance leases is for the lessee to capitalize the leased asset and to show the lease commitments as liabilities. Valuation should take place at the price that would have been paid in the event of a cash payment. If the cash price is not known, it is assumed to be the present value of the installments, excluding service charges. The interest rate to be applied should include a factor for credit risk. A proportion of the installment is accounted for as repayment of the lease commitment. The capitalized lease asset should be depreciated in line with the other tangible assets (RJ 2.02.220). It should be stated in the balance sheet or in the notes that the company is the economic but not the legal owner (RJ 1.05.125). In note 11 to the consolidated financial statements of DSM, the amount of capitalized leased assets is disclosed.

The accounting method for operating leases is for the lessor to capitalize the leased asset. An operating lease can never give rise to the leased items being carried as an asset in the balance sheet of the lessee. Where the legal entity has entered into commitments involving substantial sums of money for rather long periods, however, this should be disclosed in the notes (see *pro memoria* liabilities in Section 3.4 above) (RJ 1.05.126). In note 11 to the DSM consolidated financial statements, the amount of long-term commitments concerning, among others, operating leases is disclosed.

The requirements for both operating and finance leases are in line with IAS 17, although in the Netherlands there are no specific requirements for lessor accounting or accounting for sale and leaseback transactions.

3.7 Oil, Gas, and Other Mineral Resources

In the Netherlands, there are no specific requirements for oil and gas accounting. Therefore, in principle, there is a free choice between the full cost method and the successful-efforts method in accounting for exploration costs. The Royal Dutch/Shell company uses the successful-efforts method.

3.8 Intangible Assets

Article 365 distinguishes the following categories of intangible fixed assets:

1. Incorporation and share issue expenses
2. Research and development costs
3. Expenses related to concessions, licenses, and intellectual property rights
4. Cost of goodwill, acquired from third parties
5. Prepayments on intangible fixed assets

In addition to the intangible assets referred to in the law, there may be others such as brand names, publishing rights, and computer software. These assets are also included separately under intangible fixed assets (RJR 2.01.l03). DSM identifies "pre-operating and start-up expenses" as a special category.

The problem of accounting for goodwill was discussed in Section 3.1. If expenses referred to under items 1 and 2 above are capitalized, explanatory notes should be furnished and a legal reserve should be formed for the amounts at which these costs are capitalized (see Section 3.3 above) (Article 365(2)).

Intangible fixed assets are only shown in the balance sheet if there is a well-founded expectation that the future yields from these assets allow sufficient scope for amortization (RJ 2.01.108). Intangible assets cannot be valued at a price higher than the amount of expenditure or the price paid, with allowance being made for amortization (RJ 2.01.109).

Research and development costs meet the criteria for capitalization only if (RJ 2.01.111):

- The product or process is (accurately) defined and the costs to be allocated can be determined separately

- The technical feasibility of the product or process is proven
- The management has decided to introduce the new product or process and bring it on to the market or to start using it
- There is a clear indication of a future market for the product or process, or— if it is to be used internally instead of being sold—its usefulness to the company can be proved
- Sufficient funds are available or can reasonably be expected to become available for completion of the process and for the marketing (or the internal use) of the product or process.

Costs of research (basic research work) will very often not qualify for capitalization. In IAS 9 research costs may never be capitalized, which is a stricter rule. The general criteria for capitalization of development costs in IAS 9 are similar to the above-mentioned criteria.

The total amount of the costs of research and development charged to the results for the financial year should be disclosed (RJ 2.01.123).

Intangible assets should be amortized consistently. Amortization in proportion to the sale or the use of the product or process also meets this requirement. When the future yields do not allow sufficient scope for consistent amortization, the intangible asset must be written down to its recoverable amount by means of exceptional amortization (RJ 2.01.113). Incorporation and share issue expenses, and cost of research and development should be amortized over a maximum period of five years from their date of origin (Article 386 (3)).

3.9 Participating Interests

Equity investments in other companies can be divided into three categories:

1. Participations in companies in which the investor exercises significant influence on business and financial policy
2. Participations in companies in which the investor does not exercise the significant influence indicated above
3. Equity investments that are not considered to be participations

An equity investment is considered to be a participation if there is a durable link between both companies and if the investment is undertaken for the purpose of the company's own activities (Article 24c (l)). To make it easier to ascertain whether a relationship of participation exists or not, the law has introduced a statutory assumption of participation. If the company or a subsidiary, alone or together with a subsidiary or group company, provides at least 20% of the issued capital, the existence of a participation is assumed. This statutory assumption may be refuted.

There is also a statutory assumption related to the question as to whether significant influence is exercised on the invested company. Significant influence is assumed if the company or one or more of its subsidiaries, alone or together, are authorized to cast 20% or more of the votes of members, partners, or shareholders at their own discretion. The statutory assumption in the foregoing paragraph was 20% of the issued capital; this statutory assumption is 20% of the voting rights. Normally, a significant influence will be assumed for all or most of the participations.

The applicable accounting method differs for the three types of equity investments.

Participations in which the investor exercises significant influence are accounted for by using the equity method, as described in Section 3.1 above (Article 389(1)). Recall that in legal entity accounts, investments in subsidiaries are accounted for by using the equity method (see Section 3.1 above). DSM uses the equity method for all its participations.

Participations in which the investor does not exercise significant influence are accounted for by using the cost method or the current value method (Article 384 (1)). In both cases, only the dividends declared are reflected in the income statement. The cost method implies valuation of the investment at purchase price, without making adjustments for amortization of goodwill. The current value method implies valuation at current value, but it is unclear how the current value of a participation should be measured.

Equity investments which are not considered to be participations can be classified as long-term investments (an element of the financial fixed assets in the balance sheet, as with DSM) or as short-term investments (an element of the investment category under current assets). The long-term investments may be valued at historical cost or at current value, while the short-term investments must be valued at the lower of historical cost and market value (net realizable value) (Article 384 (1)). If, in the case of the short-term investments, the market value is higher than the balance sheet value, the market value should be disclosed in the notes (RJ 2.13.108)

Notwithstanding the specific statutory rules, the RJ allows the possibility of marketable securities to be valued at higher market value, including the unrealized gains in the income statement (RJ 2.13.107/110). However, valuation at higher market value requires the use of Article 362 (4) (see Section 2.2), according to which the company is obliged to depart from the special requirements laid down in the law, should this be necessary for presenting a true and fair view. The reasons for applying Article 362 (4) should be disclosed, as well as the impact on the financial position and the profit or loss.

The above mentioned Dutch rules are generally in line with IAS 25, which allows current investments to be carried at either market value or the lower of cost or market value. A difference is that current investments that are not marketable securities may not be carried at market value.

3.10 Inventories

Article 369 distinguishes four categories of inventory:
1. Raw material and consumables
2. Work in progress
3. Finished goods and goods for resale
4. Payments on account of inventories

The valuation of inventories is similar to that of tangible fixed assets: Article 384 (1) allows the choice between historical cost and current value. The following specific rules for inventories apply:

- Similar components of inventories may be valued on the basis of weighted average prices or by the FIFO method, the LIFO method, or some similar method, such as the base stock method (Article 385 (2))
- If the LIFO method, or a similar method is used, the current value of the inventory should either be shown in the balance sheet or disclosed in the notes (RJ 2.11.212).

- If the inventories are valued at historical cost and the market value (net realizable value) is lower, a downward value adjustment to the lower market value should be made (Article 387 (2)); where an exceptional reduction in the value of inventories in the near future is foreseeable, this may be taken into account (Article 387 (3)).

- The recoverable amount may not be used in determining the current value of inventories; the only alternative to the replacement value is the net realizable value, to be used when replacement is not anticipated, or when the net realizable value is lower than the replacement value (RJ 1.03.2; Asset Valuation Decree).

The valuation for tax purposes does not affect the valuation for accounting purposes.

The historical cost rules for inventories are in line with IAS, although the base stock method is not explicitly forbidden in the Netherlands.

DSM values raw materials and consumables at the historical purchase prices plus additional costs or, if lower, at the price on the purchase market plus additional costs. Work in progress and finished products are valued at manufacturing cost or at the lower net realizable value. Products for which the manufacturing cost cannot be calculated because of shared cost components are stated at net realizable price after deduction of a margin.

Accounting for work in progress under long-term contracts (construction contracts) depends on the possibility of making a reliable estimate of the outcome of the contract (RJ 2.11.406). When a reliable estimate can be made, the percentage of completion method should be applied. Otherwise, application of the completed contract method is required. The percentage of completion method requires revenue (including allocated profit) and costs incurred to be recognized by reference to the stage of completion of the contract activity at the balance sheet date. The completed contract method recognizes revenue and costs incurred only at the completion of the contract. Under both methods, expected losses should be taken into account immediately.

An important difference with IAS 11 (revised) exists in case no reliable estimate can be made of the outcome of the contract. IAS 11 then requires the recognition of revenue to the extent of costs incurred that are recoverable and the recognition of costs as an expense in the period when incurred. This is known as the percentage of completion method with zero profit. This method is not allowed in the Netherlands. The required method in the Netherlands in these cases, the completed contract method, however, is not allowed by IAS 1 (revised).

3.11 Taxation

In the Netherlands there is a distinction between calculating reported income and taxable income. The calculation of reported income is based on the principles outlined so far and is directed at presenting a true and fair view.

Taxable income is calculated on the basis of rules identified in tax law and is directed at determining a fair tax charge.

One basic rule in tax law is that in calculating taxable income the principles of accounting for reporting purposes should be used, except when different specific rules are given. One of these specific rules is that tangible fixed assets should always be depreciated on the basis of historical cost; depreciation on the basis of current value is not allowed. With the exception of these specific rules, it is possible for reported income and taxable income to be the same, and this will often be the case with smaller companies. However, it is also possible for the different income concepts to diverge. Larger companies normally choose that option. The general situation is that in those cases, the prudence concept plays a much more important role in calculating taxable income than it does in calculating reported income. Therefore, taxable income will normally be lower than reported income, and a provision for deferred taxation is included on the liabilities side of the balance sheet.

3.11.1 Deferred Tax Liabilities

The provision for deferred taxes should be presented separately, either in the balance sheet or in the notes, as in the DSM financial statements (Article 374 (4)). Valuation of deferred taxes at either nominal value or present value is acceptable (RJ 2.53.510).

Tax allocation should be made on the basis of the fully comprehensive method (full provision). Partial tax allocation (partial provision) is not allowed (RJ 2.53.509). The liability method should be used to calculate the deferred tax liability (RJ 2.53.515). Until 1992 the deferral method was also allowed.

A tax liability can be accrued for taxes payable on the distribution of retained earnings of subsidiaries and associated companies. However, there is no obligation to do so (RJ 2.03.504).

In general, the above rules are in line with IAS 12 (and ED 33), although valuation of deferred taxes at present value is not discussed in IAS 12.

Although the disclosure by DSM is not unambiguous, the group seems to state deferred taxes at nominal value, applying the "fully comprehensive" method and the liability method.

3.11.2 Deferred Tax Assets

The general rule is that deferred tax assets should be recognized to the extent that it is reasonable to expect future profits for tax purposes to be sufficient to offset the deferred tax debits (RJ 2.53.512). Deferred tax assets are always recognized if there are deferred tax credits (provisions) that can be set off against the debits. However, deferred tax credits either arising from revaluations to current cost or disputed by tax authorities may not be taken into account for this purpose.

The general rule also applies to deferred tax debits attributable to a tax loss carryforward (RJ 2.53.520). Needless to say, the carryforward period should in that case be taken into account. As stated earlier, the carryforward period is 8 years. There is a carryback period of 3 years. Carryback does not give rise to a deferred tax asset, but to a tax receivable.

When deferred tax debits and credits are of the same duration, the net figure may be shown in the balance sheet when they relate to the same tax group (RJ 2.53.512). The amount of tax loss carryforward not accounted for in the balance sheet should be disclosed separately (RJ 2.53.5.13).

There is a significant difference between the above rules and IAS 12 (and ED 33). In the case of tax loss carryforwards, IAS 12 states that the potential tax saving may be recognized only if there is assurance beyond a reasonable doubt that future profits will be sufficient to allow the benefits of the loss to be realized. The criterion of the RJ is that there must be no reason to doubt that future profits will be sufficient, which is less restrictive than "assurance beyond any reasonable doubt." When there is no reason to doubt, or there is enough assurance, the RJ states that a deferred tax asset *should* be recognized, whereas IAS 12 only *allows* the recognition of a deferred tax debit. The IASC's revision of deferred tax accounting is expected to bring its rules closer in line with those of the RJ while on the aspect of deferred tax assets, both IAS 12 and ED 33 seem to be in conflict with the IASC's conceptual framework.

3.11.3 Deferred Taxes and Current Value Accounting

The deferred tax resulting from the application of current value accounting is not normally a timing difference but a permanent difference, as tax law does not allow depreciation on the basis of current value. This means that part of the depreciation costs in the financial statements are not accepted in calculating taxable income. This extra tax charge may be accounted for by charging it to equity (revaluation reserve) or to the income statement (RJ 2.53.533).

Apart from accounting for this extra tax charge, there is the option to present in the balance sheet at the moment of revaluation a deferred tax provision charged to the revaluation reserve, but there is no obligation to do so (Article 390 (5)). ED 33 includes both options as well but prefers the recognition of a deferred tax liability. Upon realization of the deferred tax (by depreciation), the deferred tax provision, if identified, is either added to the revaluation reserve again (when the extra tax is charged to the income statement) or reduced against the extra tax payment (in which case the extra tax charge is charged to equity) (RJ 2.53.533).

3.12 Pensions

In the Netherlands the usual systems of accruing pension entitlements are (RJ 2.53.301):

1. Average pay system: for each completed year of service, a future pension amounting to a certain percentage of the wage in that year is granted.
2. Final pay system: for each completed year of service a future pension amounting to a certain percentage of the wage at the time of retirement is acquired.

Mixed forms of these two systems are not uncommon.

When a pension scheme is being introduced or improved, pension entitlements are sometimes granted in respect of past service as if the new scheme had been applicable from the commencement of the service. The ensuing liability is called back-service (or past-service) liability (RJ 2.53.302).

If a legal entity operating in the Netherlands makes legally enforceable commitments towards its employees in the matter of retirement benefits, under the Pension Funds and Savings Funds Act those commitments are in general required to be covered by a life insurance company, a company pension fund, or an industry-wide pension fund (RJ 2.53.303).

There are only a number of cases in which the Pension Funds and Savings Funds Act permits the legal entity to provide funds to cover pension entitlements itself. One example is the case of retirement benefits for directors who are also major shareholders.

Funding must take place by means of the advance funding system, which implies that the funds are provided during the employee's active working life (RJ 2.53.304).

In the Netherlands, there are no specific rules governing the financial statements of pension funds, comparable to IAS 26.

In valuing the provisions for pension commitments, a choice may be made between the static method and the dynamic method (see Section 3.4 above) (RJ 2.53.306). In either case, valuation should be at present value (or discounted value). There are no requirements for the interest rate to be used in discounting. There is only the recommendation to give an indication of the interest rate used (RJ 2.53.323).

Retirement benefits are normally determined by using an accrued benefit valuation method and not a projected benefit valuation method (with some exceptions, mentioned below). IAS 19 (revised) prefers the first one.

3.12.1 Back-service

In the case of unconditional back-service entitlements, the back-service must be accounted for as it arises. When they have not already been financed, such commitments should be shown in the balance sheet, valued in accordance with actuarial principles (RJ 2.53.311). The same holds for awards made by the company, at its own expense, to former employees, of pensions or pension supplements that are deemed to be irrevocable (RJ 2.53.312).

IAS 19 (revised) requires the allocation of back-service costs consistently over a period not exceeding the expected remaining working lives of the participating employees. This method is not allowed in the Netherlands for unconditional back-service entitlements.

As indicated in note 9 to the consolidated statements of DSM, the provision for pensions includes past-service commitments.

3.12.2 Conditional Entitlements

Conditional entitlements, not giving rise to legally enforceable pension rights, should be disclosed in the annual accounts, although it is recommended that they be included in the balance sheet under "provisions for pension commitments" (RJ 2.53.314).

The same holds for entitlements to be granted on the basis of a company's firm intention to make legally enforceable pension arrangements (RJ 2.53.315).

It is permitted to account for anticipated back-service related to future periodic and functional wage increases (RJ 2.53.317). General wage increases that can reasonably be expected at some future date may be recognized only when the dynamic method is applied, to the extent that this will ensure an acceptable distribution of liabilities over the years. As indicated above, it is not allowed to spread past back-service evenly over future years.

Provision for possible deficits in a company pension fund that can legally be claimed from the company should be made in the balance sheet (RJ 2.53.318). If there is a backlog in the financing, surpluses shown by the company pension fund may be taken into account, provided and to the extent that they may reasonably be expected to reduce the company's liabilities.

In the case of industry-wide pension funds, it is recommended that the company provide for its share in the deficits; if not, the relevant amount should be disclosed in the notes (RJ 2.53.320/324).

In the case of an early retirement scheme, a provision should be made for the liability that arises (RJ 2.53.405). The provision should be made for all employees who have already opted for the scheme for the entire period, for employees who under the existing scheme are entitled to opt for early retirement but have not yet done so, and for other employees who are not yet entitled to exercise that option but who will be able to do so while the existing scheme is in operation.

3.13 Some Other Topics

In this section we will discuss four other important topics:

1. Changes in accounting policies
2. Extraordinary items
3. Post-balance sheet events
4. Specific industry rules

3.13.1 *Changes in Accounting Policy*

One of the basic principles in preparing financial statements is that of consistency. The consistency principle means that changes in accounting policies normally should not be made. Changes, relating to the presentation of financial statements and to the principles of valuation and income determination, however, may be made when there are justified reasons for doing so (Articles 363 (4), 384 (6)). A basic justified reason is to present a better true and fair view by using the new accounting policy.

Changes should, if possible, be accounted for retrospectively, that is, as if the new policy had always been in use. The resulting cumulative effect may be accounted for either as an immediate adjustment of shareholders' equity or as an extraordinary item in the income statement (RJ 1.06.113/ 117). There is a preference for the first method. The effect of the change on shareholders' equity and on net income should be disclosed (RJ 1.06.121). The comparative figures for the year before should be adjusted to the new policy, irrespective of the method in accounting for the cumulative effect (RJ 1.06.118). The adjustment of the comparative figures is made only to retain comparability, and it does not formally adjust the previous year's financial statements. Adjustment of historical summaries is recommended but not required (RJ 1.06. 119).

In general, there is agreement between these Dutch requirements and IAS 8.

3.13.2 Extraordinary Items

Article 377 (1) requires that, among other things, income and expense arising from ordinary activities, and extraordinary income and expense be shown separately in the income statement. In Article 377 (7), extraordinary income and expense are defined as income and expense arising otherwise than in the ordinary course of the company's business. According to the RJ (2.71.205), the frequency of occurrence is important in this respect. Possible examples are:

- Insurance payments, to the extent that they differ from the book value of the assets lost
- Gains/losses on the disposal of participating interests
- Changes arising from reorganizations or related to discontinuity
- Special provisions, such as those for litigation

Examples of extraordinary items are given in note 18 to the consolidated statements of DSM. Income and expenses that are substantially larger in volume than is usual for the enterprise, but that nevertheless arise from its ordinary operations, should not be regarded as extraordinary income and expense (RJ 2.71.207).

The cumulative effect of a change in accounting principle, when accounted for in the income statement, is always an extraordinary item.

The concept of extraordinary items in IAS 8 (revised) differs substantially from that in the Netherlands. Although the definition of an extraordinary item according to IAS 8 resembles that of Article 377, the interpretation is different. The examples mentioned above would probably never be an extraordinary item according to IAS 8. Examples IAS 8 mentions are gains and losses from the expropriation of assets and from an earthquake.

3.13.3 Post-Balance Sheet Events

For post-balance sheet events a distinction can be made between (RJ 4.03.104):

- Information that becomes known after the balance sheet date and provides further details of the actual position at the balance sheet date; this information should be accounted for when the annual accounts are drawn up (changing the balance sheet and income statement, when necessary); and

- Particulars that become known after the balance sheet date and that give no further information on the actual situation at the balance sheet date; these particulars should not be accounted for in the financial statements, unless they raise doubt about the going-concern assumption; if these particulars have important financial consequences, they should be disclosed in the section on other data (see Section 2.1 above).

These requirements are in line with IAS 10.

3.13.4 Specific Industry Rules

The Dutch civil code contains specific industry rules for insurance companies, credit institutions, and investment companies. Those companies normally must use the general principles of Title 9, with some specific additions.

Insurance Companies   The current regulation for insurance companies is included in Article 399. According to this article, an insurance company, among others, may base the valuation of its investments and its technical provisions on principles that are regarded as acceptable for the insurance industry, even where they differ from historical cost or current value (Article 399(3)). New regulations, in force from 1994 on, will be included in articles 427–446. Generally speaking, all options in the EC Insurance Directive have been included in Dutch law. It would be beyond the scope of this chapter to go into detail in this respect.

Besides the rules for financial reporting to shareholders, policyholders, and the general public, there are separate rules for giving detailed financial information to the Insurance Supervisory Authority (*Verzekeringskamer*).

Banks   For banks, the new regulation, in force from 1993 on, is included in Articles 415–426 and in the Bank Accounting Decree. For banks the same holds as for insurance companies: generally speaking, all options in the EC Bank Directive have been included in Dutch law. Again, we will not go into detail, with the exception of discussing the current regulation of the provision for general banking risks. Historically, this so-called provision was a hidden reserve, called VAR. It was not disclosed separately in the balance sheet or in the notes, but included in liabilities.

Article 424 now states that banks may include a fund for general banking risks in the balance sheet immediately under the item provisions, whenever this is required for reasons of prudence on account of the particular risks associated with banking. The balance of additions to and withdrawals from this fund is to be shown as a separate item in the profit and loss account. This part of the former VAR is no longer a hidden reserve, as the amount and the additions and withdrawals are disclosed.

As a transitional provision, banks may, whenever this is required for reasons of prudence on account of the particular risks associated with banking, understate the value of investments not held as fixed assets or forming part of the dealing portfolio, and of loans and advances to credit institutions and customers by at most 4% of the cost or lower market value or, in the case of loans and advances to credit institutions and customers, of the book value. This part of the former VAR is still a hidden reserve, even more hidden than in the old VAR, as additions to the VAR were always to be disclosed, which is not the case with movements in the understatement of the value. The transitional provision will be in force until the financial year commencing on or after January 1, 1998. However, in 1995 the ending of the transitional provision in 1998 will be evaluated as to its desirability. This might lead to a postponement.

Banks are also required to give detailed information to the Dutch Central Bank. The Dutch Central Bank will publish additional detailed accounting and disclosure rules in this respect, which go beyond the general rules in Dutch law. In their reporting to the Central Bank, banks are required to follow these detailed rules. In their reporting to shareholders, clients, and the general public, however, they are only restricted by the requirements in the law.

Investment Companies   Financial reporting rules for investment companies are of a general nature and are included in Article 401. An investment company may value its investments at market value (Article 401 (2)) Losses in market value since the preceding balance sheet date need not be charged to the profit and loss account, provided that they are set off against reserves; gains in market value may be added to the reserves. The amounts involved must, however, be disclosed in the balance sheet or in the notes (Article 401 (2)).

4. Expected Future Developments

As described in the foregoing sections, the Netherlands has a tradition of financial reporting aimed at presenting a true and fair view—a good insight into financial position and results. The impact of tax law on financial reporting is minimal. This tradition resembles that of the IASC and of practice in the United Kingdom and the United States. The basic idea of presenting a true and fair view is deep-seated and will certainly not change in the near future.

One of the important differences with practice in the United Kingdom and the United States is the less powerful role of the accounting standard-setting body. Companies may deviate from published accounting standards when they consider it to be acceptable for presenting a true and fair view, and they need not disclose the deviation as part of the notes to their financial statements. This is one of the reasons why Nobes and Parker (Comparative International Accounting, 1991) consider Dutch accounting to be "extremely judgmental" and state: "International and EC harmonization notwithstanding, Dutch accounting is still *sui generis*" (p. 229). The *sui generis* aspect has also to do with the traditional impact of current value accounting as an element of presenting a true and fair view. The isolated position of Dutch accounting is vividly described in Zeff, Camfferman, and Van der Wel (*Company Financial Reporting*, North-Holland, 1992)

There are, however, indications that in the future Dutch accounting will be gradually more influenced by international harmonization. Some of these indications are the following:

1. The call for less flexibility in applying accounting standards and the call for adoption of IASC standards as much as possible (see Zeff, Camffelman and Van der Wel, as well as the proceedings of the conference on the future of financial reporting in the Netherlands: *Financial Reporting in the Nineties, Regulation and Innovation at a Crossroads*, Kluwer Bedrijfswetenschappen, 1992).

2. The near abolition of the use of the current value accounting system in the primary statements, as a consequence of the worldwide use of historical cost accounting

3. The use of some FASB accounting standards by multinationals, like Royal Dutch/Shell and Philips; examples are the use of FAS-106 on pensions and FAS 95 on cash flow statements.

4. The literal translation of the IASC Conceptual Framework, with the intention of considering this to be the Dutch Conceptual Framework as well

5. The fact that one of the most recent Dutch accounting standards, that on cash flow statements, is strongly and explicitly based on IAS 7 (revised)

These indications might be the forerunners of Dutch accounting adapting to the international community.

Useful Address

Nederlands Institut van Registeraccountants
AJ Ernstraat 55 1083 GR
Postbus 7984
1008 AD Amsterdam
Netherlands
Tel: +(20) 464 046
Fax: +(20) 44 3131

Appendix A: Comparisons with IASC Standards and U.S. GAAP

1. International Accounting Standards

The following International Accounting Standards correspond in all material respects with the requirements in the Netherlands:

- IAS 1 Disclosure of Accounting Policies
- IAS 4 Depreciation Accounting
- IAS 5 Information to be Disclosed in Financial Statements
- IAS 10 Contingencies and Events Occurring after the Balance Sheet Date
- IAS 13 Presentation of Current Assets and Current Liabilities
- IAS 15 Information Reflecting the Effects of Changing Prices
- IAS 16 Property, Plant, and Equipment
- IAS 18 Revenue
- IAS 20 Accounting for Government Grants and Disclosure of Government Assistance
- IAS 23 Borrowing Costs
- IAS 24 Related Party Disclosures

  The following International Accounting Standards do not fully correspond with the requirements in the Netherlands (only the most important differences between the IASC regulations and the Dutch requirements are explained):

- IAS 2 Inventories

  IAS 2 forbids the use of the base stock method. This method is not explicitly forbidden in the Netherlands.

- IAS 7 Cash Flow Statements

  IAS 7 requires the inclusion of a cash flow statement as an integral part of the financial statements. In the Netherlands such a requirement does not exist, except for companies that are newly listed on the Amsterdam Stock Exchange

- IAS 8 Net Profit or Loss for the Period, Fundamental Errors and Changes in Accounting Policies

  As far as IAS 8 is interpreted in a way that all unusual items should be included in net income, IAS 8 is in conflict with the Guidelines of the RJ

The Netherlands **619**

which allow certain items to be directly recognized in a shareholders' equity.

Furthermore, the concept of extraordinary items in IAS 8 is substantially more restrictive than in the Netherlands.

- IAS 9 Research and Development Costs

IAS 9 never allows research costs to be capitalized. In the Netherlands capitalization is allowed, but only when the general conditions for capitalization are met, which will seldom be the case for research costs.

- IAS 11 Construction Contracts

In case no reliable estimate can be made of the outcome of the contract, IAS 11 (revised) requires the recognition of revenue to the extent of costs incurred that are recoverable and the recognition of costs as an expense in the period when incurred. This method is not allowed in the Netherlands. When no reliable estimate can be made, the completed contract method should be applied, which method is not allowed according to IAS 11 (revised).

- IAS 12 Accounting for Taxes on Income

In the Netherlands, valuation at present value is allowed, which is not discussed in IAS 12. In the case of tax loss carryforwards, IAS 12 states that the potential tax saving may be recognized only if there is assurance beyond reasonable doubt that future profits will be sufficient to allow the benefits of the loss to be realized. In the Netherlands, there must be no reason to doubt that future profits will be sufficient, which is less restrictive than "assurance beyond any reasonable doubt." When there is no reason to doubt, or there is enough assurance, a deferred tax asset should be recognized in the Netherlands, whereas IAS 12 only allows the recognition of a deleted tax debit.

- IAS 14 Reporting Financial Information by Segment

A breakdown of profit/loss and assets employed, comparable to the breakdown of net turnover as discussed above, is not required in the Netherlands, contrary to IAS 14.

- IAS 17 Accounting for Leases

In the Netherlands, there are no specific requirements concerning lessor accounting and accounting for safe and leaseback transactions.

- IAS 19 Retirement Benefit Costs

In IAS 19, it is required to allocate back service costs systematically over a period not exceeding the expected remaining working lives of the participating employees. This method is not allowed in the Netherlands: in the case of unconditional back service entitlements, immediate recognition is required.

- IAS 21 The Effects of Changes in Foreign Exchange Rates

  The RJ allows all foreign-based operations to be grouped in one category for practical reasons, which is not allowed by IAS 21. IAS 21 requires income statement accounts and the resulting net income to be translated at average rates (or actual rates), while in the Netherlands the income statement items or only the resulting net income may be translated at closing rates. In the Netherlands, exchange gains on long-term transactions may be deferred, which is not allowed in IAS 21. Finally, in the case of forward contracts, IAS 21 requires that the difference between the spot rate and the forward rate is allocated over the duration of the forward transaction; in the Netherlands immediate recognition in income is acceptable in the case of loss.

- IAS 22 Business Combinations

  IAS 22 requires positive goodwill to be capitalized and amortized, while Dutch law allows goodwill to be written off direct to reserves. Dutch law requires negative goodwill to be accounted for in a revaluation reserve when it results from a lucky buy. This method is not allowed by IAS 22, which requires this amount to be treated as deferred income.

- IAS 25 Accounting for Investments

  IAS 25 allows current investments to be carried at either market value or the lower of cost or market value. In the Netherlands, current investments that are not marketable securities must be carried at the lower of cost or market value.

- IAS 26 Accounting and Reporting by Retirement Benefit Plans

  No specific rules exist in the Netherlands. However, the general rules of pension accounting apply (IAS 19).

- IAS 27 Consolidated Financial Statements and Accounting for Investments in Subsidiaries

  IAS 27 does not allow exclusion from consolidation of group companies with dissimilar business activities, but Dutch law does allow exclusion when consolidation of the group company would conflict with the true and fair view. According to IAS 27, investments in subsidiaries may be accounted for in the legal entity's own financial statements by using the cost method. In the Netherlands, valuation according to the equity method is required.

- IAS 28 Accounting for Investments in Associates

According to IAS 28, investments in associates may be accounted for in the legal entity's own financial statements by using the cost method. In the Netherlands, valuation according to the equity method is required.

- IAS 29 Financial Reporting in Hyperinflationary Economies

  No specific rules exist in the Netherlands.

- IAS 30 Disclosures in the Financial Statement of Banks and Similar Financial Institutions

  In the Netherlands, a fund for general banking risks may be recognized in the balance sheet but must then be disclosed. Furthermore, until 1998, a hidden reserve with a maximum of 4% of some specified assets may be taken into account as understatement of the value.

- IAS 31 Financial Reporting of Interests in Joint Ventures

  When reporting interests in joint ventures in the consolidated statements of a venturer, IAS 31 prefers the use of proportionate consolidation. The equity method is an allowed alternative treatment. In the Netherlands, both methods are allowed, without a preference for proportionate consolidation.

The following International Accounting Standards are no longer operative:

- IAS 3 Consolidated Financial Statements (superseded by IAS 27 and IAS 28)
- IAS 6 Accounting Responses to Changing Prices (superseded by IAS 15)

2. U. S. GAAP

An in-depth comparison between the requirements in the Netherlands and U. S. Generally Accepted Accounting Principles (U.S. GAAP) would be too lengthy. A general difference is the level of detail of the requirements: the U.S. requirements are far more detailed than those in the Netherlands. In this section we limit ourselves to a short description of some of the most important differences.

Most requirements in the United States are laid down in:

- The Statements of Financial Accounting Standards (FAS) of the Financial Accounting Standards Board (FASB)
- The Opinions of the Accounting Principles Board (APB), the predecessor of the FASB
- The Accounting Research Bulletins (ARB) of the Committee on Accounting Procedure (CAP), the predecessor of the APB.

1. The companies to be included in the consolidated statements

   U.S. GAAP (FAS-94) requires consolidation of all majority-owned subsidiaries. In the Netherlands, group companies must be excluded from consolidation when this would conflict with the true and fair view.

2. Research and development costs

   In the Netherlands, research and development expenses may be capitalized when certain conditions are met. In the United States (FAS-2), these expenses should always be charged to income when incurred, except for expenses related to computer software (FAS-86).

3. Valuation of tangible fixed assets

   U.S. GAAP (APB Opinion No. 6) requires valuation on the basis of historical costs. In the Netherlands, valuation at current value is acceptable as well.

4. Goodwill

   U.S. GAAP (APB Opinion No. 17) requires goodwill to be capitalized and amortized over the expected useful economic life. The maximum period of amortization is 40 years.

   In the Netherlands, capitalization and amortization is an acceptable policy. Amortization should take place on the basis of the expected useful life. A maximum period of amortization is not defined. However, goodwill may also be charged directly to shareholders' equity and this policy is the dominant policy in practice. A direct charge to shareholders' equity is not allowed in the US.

5. Valuation of inventories

   U.S. GAAP (ARB No. 43) requires valuation on the basis of historical costs. In the Netherlands, valuation at current value is acceptable as well.

6. The provision for pensions

   In the Netherlands, the provision is normally calculated on the basis of current wages, without taking into account future wage increases. U.S. GAAP (FAS-106) requires future wage increases to be taken into account.

   Another difference is the discount rate used. In Dutch practice, a discount rate of 4% is mostly used. In the United States, the discount rate reflects the expected market yield, which is considerably higher than 4%.

   In the Netherlands, unconditional back service must be accounted for as it arises. According to U.S. GAAP, such back services are to be recognized during the remaining working life of the employee.

7. Changes in accounting policy

In most cases, U.S. GAAP (APB Opinion No. 20) requires recognition of the cumulative effect of the accounting change in net income. This is allowed in the Netherlands as well, although a preference exists for immediate recognition in shareholders' equity and adjustment of the comparative figures.

Appendix B: EU Directives and Dutch Legislation

1. The Fourth Directive and Dutch Legislation

In this section an overview is given of the options of the Fourth Directive and of the choices that are made in the Netherlands. First, the option will be stated, then the choice made, including the related article numbers in Title 9 or the governmental decrees (article numbers mentioned as such in the "choice" section relate to Title 9; article numbers stated in the "option" section relate to the Fourth Directive). The phrase "option adopted" means that the free choice in the Fourth Directive is a free choice in Dutch law as well.

Option 1. The balance-sheet and profit and loss account items that are preceded by arabic numerals may be combined in the interests of clarity. However, items so combined must be dealt with separately in the notes on the accounts (Article 4(3)(b)).

Choice. Option adopted (combination is allowed) (Governmental Decree on the Standard Chart of Accounts, Article 8).

Option 2. Where the figures and items in the balance sheet and in the profit and loss account are not comparable with the corresponding figures for the preceding financial year, the later figures may be adjusted. Any adjustment of the figures must be disclosed in the notes on the accounts, with relevant comments (Article 4(4)).

Choice. Adjustment is required (Article 363(5)).

Option 3. Member states may authorize or require the layout of the balance sheet and the profit and loss account to be adapted to include the appropriation of profit or the treatment of loss (Article 6). Where the appropriation of profit or the treatment of loss appears in the annual accounts, it need not be disclosed separately (Article 50).

Choice. Option adopted (Governmental Decree on the Standard Chart of Accounts, Article 11).

Option 4. For the presentation of the balance sheet, Member states may prescribe a layout in account form (Article 9) or in vertical form (Article

10) or they may allow companies to choose between the two forms (Article 8).

Choice. Companies are allowed to choose between the two forms (Governmental Decree on the Standard Chart of Accounts, Article 1).

Option 5. The following options are available for showing capital (Article 9, Assets A and D II 5, Liabilities A 1; Article 10 A, D 115 and L 1):

(a) Subscribed capital to be shown on the liabilities side under A I or L 1. The subscribed capital unpaid must then be shown under A on the assets side. The portion of subscribed capital called must be disclosed.

(b) The part of the capital called is to be shown on the liabilities side under A I or L 1, with the amounts of subscribed and paid-up capital being shown separately. Under those circumstances, the part of the capital called but not yet paid is to be shown on the assets side, either under A or under D II ("Debtors") 5.

Choice. Alternative (b) is required (Article 373 (2)).

Option 6. Formation expenses (Article 9, Assets B; Article 10 B):

(a) These expenses may be shown as an asset. They must be written off within a maximum period of 5 years. If such expenses have not been completely written off, there are restrictions on the distribution of profits. The amounts entered under "formation expenses" must be explained in the notes on the accounts (Article 34).

(b) In the event of such expenses appearing as an asset, they may be shown either under B or as the first item under "Intangible assets" (CI).

Choice. The option under (a) is adopted, with the expenses to be indicated as "incorporation and share issue expenses" (Article 365 (1, 2) and 386 (3)). Concerning (b) the item is required to be shown as the first item of intangible assets (Article 365 and the formats included in the Governmental Decree on the Standard Chart of Accounts).

Option 7. Concessions, patents, licenses, trademarks, and similar rights and assets may be shown as assets even if they were created by the undertaking itself (Article 9, Assets C12(b);Article 10 C I 2(b)).

Choice. They may only be shown as assets as far as expenditures to third parties are made (Article 365 (2)).

Option 8. Research and developments costs.

(a) These costs may be shown as assets (Article 9, Assets C I 1; Article 10 C 1 1). The amounts entered must be explained in the notes on the accounts (Article 37 (1) and Article 34).

(b) Where they are shown as an asset they may either be written off within a maximum period of 5 years or in exceptional cases (the reasons for which must be disclosed in the notes on the accounts) within a longer period (Article 37 (1)) EC Directives and Dutch legislation 223

(c) In exceptional cases (the reasons for which must be disclosed in the notes on the accounts), derogations from the restrictions on the distribution of profits during the depreciation period may be allowed (Article 37 (1)).

Choice. The option under (a) is adopted (Article 365 (1)). Concerning (b) the maximum period is always 5 years (Article 386 (3)). The option under (c) is not adopted: derogations from the restrictions on the distribution of profits are never allowed (Article 36S (2)).

Option 9. Goodwill may be systematically written off over a limited period exceeding 5 years, provided that this period does not exceed the useful economic life of the asset and is disclosed in the notes on the accounts together with the reasons for so doing (Article 37 (2)).

Choice. Option adopted (Article 386 (3)).

Option 10. Own shares may be shown as an asset. If they represent fixed assets, they are to be shown on the assets side under C III 7 or, if they represent current assets, under D III 2. It is specifically prohibited for them to be shown in items other than those prescribed (Article 13 (2)). Furthermore, in the case of public limited companies a transfer to reserve must be made on the liabilities side (Article 9, Liabilities A IV 2 or Article 10 L IV 2).

Choice. Option not adopted. Own shares should be subtracted from shareholders' equity (Article 378 (2)).

Option 11. Prepayments and accrued income.

(a) These are to be shown either under E or under "Debtors" in D 116.

(b) Income which is not due until after the expiration of the financial year in question may be included in "Debtors" (Article 18).

Choice. Both options adopted (Governmental Decree on the Standard Chart of Accounts, Article 12 (1)).

Option 12. Accruals and deferred income.

(a) These are to be shown either under D or K or are to be included in "Debtors" under C 9 and I 9.

(b) Where they represent charges that will be paid only in the course of a subsequent financial year, they may be included in "Creditors" (Article 21).

Choice. Both options adopted (Governmental Decree on the Standard Chart of Accounts, Article 12 (2)).

Option 13. A loss for the financial year may be shown either on the assets side under or on the liabilities side in "Capital and reserves" under A VI or L VI (profit or loss for the financial year).

Choice. Loss to be shown on the liabilities side in "Capital and reserves" (Article 373 (1), formats in the Governmental Decree on the Standard Chart of Accounts).

Option 14. A profit for the financial year may be shown on the liabilities side either under E or in "Capital and reserves" under A VI or L VI (Profit or loss for the financial year).

Choice. Profit to be shown on the liabilities side in "Capital and reserves" (Article 373 (1), formats in the Governmental Decree on the Standard Chart of Accounts).

Option 15. Provisions for pensions and similar obligations are to be shown either on the liabilities side in the balance sheet under B 1 or J 1 or are to be disclosed in the notes on the accounts (Article 43 (1) (7)).

Choice. Companies may choose either alternative (Article 374 (4)), Governmental Decree on the Standard Chart of Accounts, Article 8 (1)).

Option 16. Commitments by way of guarantee that are not to be shown as liabilities must be shown either at the foot of the balance sheet or in the notes on the accounts (Article 14).

Choice. Option adopted (Article 376; no specific requirement; disclosure in the notes is the regular case).

Option 17. Movements in the various fixed asset items and, if necessary, formation expenses (see Option No. 6) are to be shown in the balance sheet or in the notes on the accounts (Article 15 (3) (A)).

Choice. A reconciliation statement is required and is automatically shown in the notes (Article 368).

Option 18. The percentage required for the presumption of a participating interest may be set lower than a share of 20% of the capital of another undertaking (Article 17). Such an option also exists for the obligation to disclose details of such undertakings in the notes on the accounts (Article 43 (1) (2)).

Choice. Presumption is set at 20% or more (Article 24c); 20% is also the criterion in disclosing details of undertakings (Article 379).

Option 19. Provisions may be created to cover certain charges (Article 20 (2)).

Choice. Option adopted (Article 374).

Option 20. For the presentation of the profit and loss account, member states may prescribe the total costs procedure or the turnover costs procedure (both in account or vertical form), or may permit companies to choose between all or part of the layouts in question (Articles 22–26).

Choice. All options adopted; all presentations are allowed (Governmental Decree on the Standard Chart of Accounts, Article 1 (1)).

Option 21. For the disclosure of taxes on the profit or loss, the following option is available regarding the prescription of separate items (Article 30):

First solution:

Taxes on the profit or loss on ordinary activities; profit or loss on ordinary activities after taxation; extraordinary profit or loss;

Taxes on the extraordinary profit or loss; other taxes not shown under the above items; n profit or loss for the financial year.

Second solution:

Profit or loss on ordinary activities; extraordinary profit or loss;

Taxes on the profit or loss; taxes not included under the above items; profit or loss for the financial year.

In the event of the second solution being adopted, the notes on the accounts must disclose the extent to which the taxes on the profit or loss affect the profit or loss on ordinary activities and the extraordinary profit or loss.

Choice. First solution is required (formats in the Governmental Decree on the Standard Chart of Accounts).

Option 22. Valuation other than on the basis of purchase price or production cost (Article 33)

(a) valuation by the replacement value method for tangible fixed assets with limited useful economic lives and for stocks, or

(b) valuation by methods designed to take account of inflation, or

(c) revaluation of tangible fixed assets and financial fixed assets

(d) valuation by the equity method for holdings on the basis of which a dominant influence is exercised (Article 59).

In cases (a), (b), and (c), the method used must be disclosed in the notes on the accounts, a revaluation reserve must be created, and a comparison must be provided with valuations based on the purchase price and production cost methods.

Choice. Choice (a) is allowed (Article 384 (1)) but not (b) and (c), (c) being interpreted as occasional revaluation; systematic revaluation takes place in the context of the replacement value (or current cost) system. Concerning (d), the equity method is required for holdings in which a significant influence (which is less influential than having dominant influence) is exercised (Article 389 (1)).

Option 23. Value adjustment may be made to financial fixed assets so that they are valued at a lower figure on the balance sheet date (Article 35 (1) (c) (aa)). These value adjustment must be charged to the profit and loss account or disclosed in the notes on the accounts.

Choice. Option adopted (Article 387 (4)).

Option 24. Exceptional value adjustments may be made in respect of fixed and current assets for taxation purposes. The amounts of such adjustments and the reasons for making them must be indicated in the notes on the accounts (Article 35 (1)(d), Article 39 (1)(e)).

Choice. Option not adopted (exceptional value adjustments for taxation purposes not allowed, although this is not stated directly in the statutory regulations; as stated in Chapter 5 (see Section 3.4), income for tax purposes is independent of income for reporting purposes).

Option 25. A reasonable proportion of the costs that are only indirectly attributable to the product in question may be added into the production costs to the extent that they relate to the period of production (Article 35 (3) (b) and Article 39 (2)).

Choice. Option adopted (Article 388 (2)).

Option 26. Interest on capital borrowed to finance the production of fixed assets may be included in the production costs. The inclusion of such interest under "Assets" must be disclosed in the notes on the accounts (Article 35 (4)).

Choice. Option adopted (Article 388 (2)).

Option 27. Interest on capital borrowed to finance the production of current assets may be included in the production costs. The inclusion of such interest under "Assets" must be disclosed in the notes on the accounts (Article 39 (2)).

Choice. Option adopted (Article 388 (2)) 74 (4), Governmental Decree on the Standard Chart of Accounts, Article 8 (1)).

Option 28. Exceptional value adjustments may be made in respect of current assets to take account of future fluctuations in value. The amount of such adjustments must be disclosed separately in the profit and loss account or in the notes on the accounts. (Article 39 (l)(c)).

Choice. Option adopted (Article 387 (3)).

Option 29. The purchase price or production cost of goods of the same category may be calculated on the basis of weighted average prices according to various methods (Article 40 (1)). The method used must be disclosed in the notes on the accounts (Article 43 (1) (l)). Where such a valuation differs materially from that based on the market value, the amount of that differences must likewise be disclosed in the notes on the accounts (Article 40 (2)).

Choice. Option adopted (Article 385 (2)); method to be disclosed in the notes (Article 384 (5)). There is no separate requirement in law to disclose material differences between book value and market value of inventory. However, such a requirement is included in the Guidelines for Annual Reporting of the RJ (2.11.505).

Option 30. Where the amount repayable on account of any debt is greater than the amount received, the difference may be shown as an asset. It must be shown separately in the balance sheet or in the notes on the accounts and must be written off no later than the time of repayment of the debt (Article 41).

Choice. Option adopted (Article 375 (S)).

2. The Seventh Directive and Dutch Legislation

Seventh Directive Article	*Choice of the Netherlands*
1(1) (d) (aa)	Required if necessary to give a true and fair view
1(1) (d) (bb)	Not introduced
1(2)	Required only if necessary to give a true and fair view

4(2)	Only NVs, BVs, Cooperative Associations and Mutual Guarantee Companies are required to prepare consolidated accounts.
5	Exempt if no group exists (i.e., in the case of a passive holding company)
6	Not exempt; not permitted to ignore consolidation adjustments; size criteria not increased
7(2) (b)	Exempt subject to conditions. The intermediate parent must not: (1) have any of its securities listed; (2) have any bearer securities outstanding; (3) be a bank, financial institution, or insurance company. (4) Its shareholders must all have formally agreed to the exemption. (5) Its obligations must be guaranteed by the entity preparing the consolidated accounts for the group to which it belongs.
9(1)	Not required
9(2)	Not required
11(1)	Exemption depends on parent outside Community preparing audited consolidated accounts in a manner equivalent to that required by the Directive.
11(3)	As above
12(1)	Required if necessary for a true and fair view
15(1)	Not permitted
16(5)	None defined
16(6)	No additional information required; any may be given
17(2)	Permitted; circumstances not defined
19(1) (b)	Date not defined, but goodwill must be calculated at date of acquisition
20(1)	Permitted but not required (mergers normally take the form of "fusions" in which one legal entity disappears).
26(1) (c)	Proportional eliminations permitted only under conditions of joint venture relations
26(2)	Not permitted
27(2)	Closing date of parent should be within 3 months (ear-

	lier or later) of the date of the date of the consolidated accounts
28	Permitted, not required
29(2) (a)	Not required but not forbidden
29(5)	Not applicable
30(2)	Permitted
32(1)	Permitted, subject to a true and fair view being given, and powers over the jointly owned subsidiary being jointly exercised
33(2) (c)	Method described in Article 33(2) (b) required, that is, at an amount equivalent to the proportion of the associated undertaking's capital and reserves represented by the participating interest, with the difference between that amount and the book value (normally cost) being disclosed separately.
33(2) (d)	Not required; no specific rules
33(3)	Required
34(5)	Allowed for holding of less than 20%
34(12)&(13)	Aggregate remuneration of executive directors and aggregate remuneration of supervisory board members, loans to executive directors and aggregate loans to supervisory board members must be disclosed.
35(1)	Permitted. Reference to separate information must be made in the notes.
36(2) (d)	Required
39(1)&(2)	Not required or permitted
39(3)	Permitted
40(1)	Excluded (banks and other financial institutions are covered by Directive 86/635/EEC)
40(2)	Not excluded
41(3)	Not adopted
41(5)	Not excluded
49(2)	Not adopted

DSMN.V.
Accounting policies

Consolidation

The consolidated financial statements include DSM N.V. and the Group companies in which DSM holds, directly or indirectly, more than 50% of the voting capital or in which DSM, owing to supplementary regulations, has a decisive say in matters of management and financial policy. The consolidated financial statements further cover the financial data of companies in which DSM N.V. has an interest of 50% or less and which rank as Group companies on account of their operations being interwoven with other activities of the Group. The assets, liabilities and results of these companies are wholly consolidated. Minority interests in the Group's equity and income are stated separately.

Companies whose activities bear no relation to those of the Group are not included in the consolidated statements.

Goodwill, which is determined at the time of acquisition as the amount paid in excess of DSM's share in the net asset value of the company acquired, is charged direct to shareholders' equity.

The results of companies acquired in the course of the year are incorporated into the consolidated statement of income as from the takeover date. Results of companies sold are included in the accounts up to the date of sale.

A list of affiliated companies, drawn up in conformity with Book 2 of the Dutch Civil Code, articles 379 and 414, has been filed at the Trade Registry in Heerlen.

Translation of foreign currencies

Commercial transactions expressed in foreign currencies are stated in the accounts of the local companies at the relevant day rates or at forward rates if forward contracts have been concluded in connection with those commercial transactions.

Balance sheet items in foreign currencies are translated at spot rates as at the balance sheet date or at the original forward rate if the exchange risks attaching to the relevant receivables and liabilities have been hedged through forward transactions. As a rule, exchange rate differences are taken to the statement of income.

Assets and liabilities of foreign participations are translated at the spot rates prevailing at balance sheet date, while the items of the statements of income of foreign participations are translated at the average exchange rates of the period under review. Exchange rate differences arising from translation of the equity invested in these companies are taken to Other reserves. The same applies to exchange-rate differences arising from foreign currency loans in so far as such loans hedge the currency-exchange risk associated with foreign Group companies.

Intangible fixed assets

Intangible fixed assets are stated at cost less amortization calculated on a straight-line basis. Concessions and permits are amortized in 10 years, licences and patents in 4 years, pre-operating and start-up expenses in 6 years. Pre-operating and start-up expenses included under this heading relate exclusively to large projects.

Tangible fixed assets

Tangible fixed assets are carried at cost less depreciation calculated on a straight-line basis or at recoverable value, if this is permanently lower. Office buildings are generally depreciated in 30 years, other buildings in 20 years, plant and machinery in 10 years. For large projects, interest expense during construction is capitalized.

Investments relating to oil and gas recovery are grouped under tangible fixed assets. Costs of proven oil and gas reserves are capitalized from the moment development is decided upon. Costs which in the past were charged to the statement of income but which afterwards appear to relate to items that will be used as production tools in a project to be developed are then capitalized. Depreciation is determined on the basis of the production quantities in relation to proven reserves.

Financial fixed assets

Consolidated participations are valued according to DSM Group policies.

Valuation of non-consolidated companies is based on DSM's share in these companies' equity, in principle determined in accordance with DSM Group policies. Results are determined on the same basis.

Long-term receivables are shown at face value, where necessary after deduction of a value adjustment. Other securities are valued at cost or at recoverable value or market value, if this value is lower.

Inventories

Raw materials and consumables are valued at cost, i.e. historical purchase prices plus additional costs. If the price on the purchase market at balance sheet date or during the time of consumption of existing inventories is lower, valuation is effected at the lower market value plus additional costs. If necessary, an allowance for obsolete inventories is made.

Work in progress and finished products are valued at manufacturing cost, where necessary less an allowance for obsolescence. Internal storage costs, selling expenses and interest charges are not taken into account in determining manufacturing cost. Where the market selling price at balance sheet date or during the time of sale of existing inventories is lower than manufacturing cost, valuation is based on the net realizable price. Products for which the manufacturing cost cannot be calculated because of shared cost components are stated at net realizable price after deduction of a margin.

Unrealized intercompany results are eliminated in the valuation of inventories.

Receivables
Receivables are stated at face value less an allowance for doubtful debts. Also included is the portion of receivables forming part of the financial fixed assets that falls due within one year.

Cash
Items hereunder are stated at face value.

Provisions
Provisions are shown at face value, except the provision for pension obligations, which is determined on the basis of present cash value by actuarial methods.

Liabilities
These are stated at face value. Amounts payable within one year on long-term liabilities are included under Current liabilities.

Operating income
Net sales comprises the income from the supply of goods and services to third parties less discounts and sales taxes.

Change in inventories of finished products and work in progress relates to the difference in value between opening and closing inventories.

Own work capitalized relates to internally generated fixed assets included under Operating costs.

Sundry includes DSM's share in the net result of Energie Beheer Nederland BV.

Operating costs
Operating costs are calculated on a historical cost basis. Intra-group supplies are allocated at competitive prices.

Investment grants are credited to the operating result (Other operating costs) in proportion to the depreciable life of the assets concerned. Premiums and grants not yet credited to the operating result are carried in the Equalization account.

Corporate tax
This item covers taxes currently payable or receivable for the year under review, as well as deferred tax liabilities. Matured tax liabilities of loss-making Group units are withdrawn from the Provision for deferred taxes.

Results of non-consolidated companies
The share in results of non-consolidated companies is determined in proportion to the respective holdings owned by the Group in the year under review, after deduction of applicable taxes.

Geconsolideerde balans (na resultaatbestemming)

Activa

in miljoenen guldens	ultimo 1993		ultimo 1992	
vaste activa				
immateriële vaste activa (1)	53		54	
materiële vaste activa (2)	5 210		5 315	
financiële vaste activa (3)	637		678	
		5 900		6 047
vlottende activa				
voorraden (4)	1 230		1 445	
vorderingen (5)	2 146		2 079	
liquide middelen (6)	791		1 116	
		4 167		4 640
totaal		10 067		10 687

Passiva

in miljoenen guldens	ultimo 1993		ultimo 1992	
groepsvermogen (7)				
eigen vermogen	4 089		4 252	
belang van derden	72		69	
		4 161		4 321
egalisatierekening investeringspremies (8)		184		241
voorzieningen (9)		1 500		1 443
langlopende schulden (10)		2 161		2 048
kortlopende schulden (11)		2 061		2 634
totaal		10 067		10 687

Consolidated balance sheet as at December 31 <small>(after result appropriation)</small>

Assets

ƒ million	1993		1992	
fixed assets				
intangible fixed assets (1)	53		54	
tangible fixed assets (2)	5 210		5 315	
financial fixed assets (3)	637		678	
		5 900		6 047
current assets				
inventories (4)	1 230		1 445	
receivables (5)	2 146		2 079	
cash (6)	791		1 116	
		4 167		4 640
total		10 067		10 687

Group equity and liabilities

ƒ million	1993		1992	
group equity (7)				
shareholders' equity	4 089		4 252	
minority interests' share	72		69	
		4 161		4 321
equalization account (8)		184		241
provisions (9)		1 500		1 443
long-term liabilities (10)		2 161		2 048
current liabilities (11)		2 061		2 634
total		10 067		10 687

Geconsolideerde winst- en verliesrekening

in miljoenen guldens		1993		1992
netto-omzet (12)	8 040		8 907	
andere bedrijfsopbrengsten (13)	72		293	
som der bedrijfsopbrengsten		8 112		9 200
afschrijvingen (14)	-744		-706	
andere bedrijfslasten (15)	-7 459		-8 212	
som der bedrijfslasten		-8 203		-8 918
bedrijfsresultaat (16)		-91		282
financiële baten en lasten (17)		-134		-122
resultaat uit gewone bedrijfsuitoefening voor belastingen		-225		160
belastingen resultaat uit gewone bedrijfsuitoefening		126		49
resultaat niet-geconsolideerde deelnemingen		43		48
resultaat uit gewone bedrijfsuitoefening na belastingen		-56		257
buitengewoon resultaat na belastingen (18)		-58		-22
groepsresultaat na belastingen		-114		235
belang van derden		-4		-11
nettoresultaat		-118		224

Consolidated statement of income

ƒ million	1993		1992	
net sales (12)	8 040		8 907	
other operating income (13)	72		293	
total operating income		8 112		9 200
amortization and depreciation (14)	-744		-706	
other operating costs (15)	-7 459		-8 212	
total operating costs		-8 203		-8 918
operating result (16)		-91		282
balance of financial income and expense (17)		-134		-122
result from ordinary activities before taxation		-225		160
tax on result from ordinary activities		126		49
results of non-consolidated companies		43		48
result from ordinary activities after taxation		-56		257
extraordinary result after taxation (18)		-58		-22
group result after taxation		-114		235
minority interests' share in result		-4		-11
net result		-118		224

Overzicht van kasstromen

in miljoenen guldens		1993		1992
Bedrijfsactiviteiten				
nettoresultaat	-118		224	
herleiding naar middelen uit bedrijfsactiviteiten:				
- afschrijvingen	744		706	
- resultaat op desinvesteringen	-37		-16	
- winstinhouding bij				
niet-geconsolideerde deelnemingen	19		14	
- mutatie bedrijfskapitaal *	337		24	
- mutatie egalisatierekening	-50		-10	
- mutatie voorzieningen	-55		-59	
- uitkering dividend	-49		-196	
- overige mutaties	-7		38	
middelen uit bedrijfsactiviteiten		784		725
Investeringsactiviteiten				
investeringen in:				
- immateriële vaste activa	-16		-12	
- materiële vaste activa	-672		-1 040	
verwerving van geconsolideerde deelnemingen	-56		-8	
opbrengst verkochte materiële vaste activa	28		35	
verkoop van geconsolideerde deelnemingen	91		56	
financiële vaste activa:				
- verwervingen en kapitaalstortingen	-28		-31	
- opbrengst verkochte deelnemingen	85		25	
- mutatie leningen u/g	-17		33	
middelen aangewend voor investeringsactiviteiten		-585		-942
Financieringsactiviteiten				
opname leningen	295		465	
aflossing leningen o/g	-110		-253	
mutatie schulden aan kredietinstellingen	-748		218	
ingekochte eigen aandelen	39		3	
middelen uit financieringsactiviteiten		-524		433
mutatie liquide middelen		-325		216

* mutatie bedrijfskapitaal:				
- voorraden	233		66	
- vorderingen	52		-22	
- kortlopende schulden (excl. leningen,				
schulden aan kredietinstellingen en dividend)	52		-20	
	337		24	

Zie toelichting 19 op pagina 49.

Statement of cash flows

f million	1993	1992
Operating activities		
net result	-118	224
adjustments to reconcile net result to		
net cash provided by operating activities:		
- amortization and depreciation	744	706
- revenue from divestments	-37	-16
- profit retention at non-consolidated companies	19	14
- change in working capital*	337	24
- change in equalization account	-50	-10
- change in provisions	-55	-59
- dividends paid	-49	-196
- other changes	-7	38
net cash provided by operating activities	784	725
Investing activities		
investments in:		
- intangible fixed assets	-16	-12
- tangible fixed assets	-672	-1 040
acquisitions of consolidated companies	-56	-8
proceeds from sale of tangible fixed assets	28	35
sale of consolidated companies	91	56
financial fixed assets:		
- acquisitions and capital payments	-28	-31
- proceeds from sale of participations	85	25
- change in loans granted	-17	33
net cash used in investing activities	-585	-942
Financing activities		
loans taken up	295	465
redemption of loans taken up	-110	-253
changes in liabilities to credit institutions	-748	218
own shares purchased	39	3
net cash provided by financing activities	-524	433
change in cash	-325	216
* specification of change in working capital:		
- inventories	233	66
- receivables	52	-22
- current liabilities (excl. loans, liabilities to credit institutions and dividend payable)	52	-20
	337	24

See note 19 on page 49.

Notes to the consolidated financial statements

General

Unless stated otherwise, all amounts are in millions of guilders.

In conformity with Book 2 of the Dutch Civil Code, article 402, a condensed statement of income has been included in the DSM N.V. accounts.

As a result of acquisitions made in 1993, the financial results relating to the fine-chemicals activities of Bristol-Myers Squibb GmbH (Germany) and to the joint venture DSM Kenkyo EPP Ltd. (Hong Kong) were consolidated for the first time. In addition, Curver Rubbermaid Kft. was consolidated for the first time in the statement of income because DSM obtained a majority share in this company at the end of 1992.

The following companies/activities were sold: BV Computer Centrum Nederland (Netherlands), NVCP BV (Netherlands), Pixley Richards Inc. (USA), and Daniel Products Company (USA). The sale of the retail activities of Agrarische Unie-Vulcaan BV (Netherlands) was completed in 1993.

(1) Intangible fixed assets

	total	concessions and permits	licences and patents	pre-operating and start-up expenses
balance at January 1, 1993				
cost	118	3	50	65
amortization	64	1	36	27
book value	54	2	14	38
changes in book value:				
- capital expenditure	16	-	3	13
- amortization	17	-	7	10
	-1	-	-4	3
balance at December 31, 1993				
cost	134	3	53	78
amortization	81	1	43	37
book value	53	2	10	41

(2) Tangible fixed assets

	total	land and buildings	plant and machinery	other fixed assets	in course of reali- zation or prepaid	not used for operational purposes
balance at January 1, 1993						
cost	13 520	2 071	9 275	1 033	1 038	103
depreciation	8 205	812	6 544	742	43	64
book value	5 315	1 259	2 731	291	995	39
changes in book value:						
- capital expenditure	672	21	191	17	443	.
- acquisitions	36	21	14	1	.	.
- put into operation	.	75	839	41	-955	.
- depreciation	-727	-80	-535	-111	.	-1
- deconsolidations	-81	-25	-8	-47	-1	.
- disposals	-19	-8	-6	-3	-1	-1
- exchange rate differences	13	2	9	.	2	.
- other	1	-3	21	3	-22	2
	-105	3	525	-99	-534	0
balance at December 31, 1993						
cost	13 874	2 137	10 254	884	502	97
depreciation	8 664	875	6 998	692	41	58
book value	5 210	1 262	3 256	192	461	39

Included is an amount of ƒ 16 million (31 December 1992: ƒ 10 million) for assets acquired under financial lease agreements. The related commitments are included under Other liabilities.

A geographic breakdown of capital expenditure on tangible fixed assets and their book value is given below:

	capital expenditure		book value of tangible fixed assets at December 31	
	1993	1992	1993	1992
Netherlands	525	889	4 090	4 178
other EU countries	96	88	677	670
	621	977	4 767	4 848
rest of Europe	7	4	29	27
North America	42	56	400	427
rest of the world	2	3	14	13
total	672	1 040	5 210	5 315

Approximate current value

The book value of the tangible fixed assets on the basis of current value is approximated at ƒ 6.3 billion (31 December 1992: ƒ 6.3 billion). The depreciation charge on this basis amounts to ƒ 0.8 billion (1992: ƒ 0.8 billion).

40

(3) Financial fixed assets

	total	non-consolidated companies		other securities	other receivables
		share in equity	loans		
balance at January 1, 1993	678	576	4	3	95
changes:					
- share in result	43	43	-	-	-
- dividends	-61	-61	-	-	-
- acquisitions and capital payments	28	16	-	12	-
- advances	37	-	11	-	26
- disposals	-65	-65	-	-	-
- redemptions	-20	-	-	-	-20
- transfer to current receivables	-15	-	-	-	-15
- exchange rate differences	14	13	-	-	1
- other	-2	4	-1	-	-5
balance at December 31, 1993	637	526	14	15	82

(4) Inventories

	1993	1992
raw materials and consumables	305	357
work in progress	72	77
finished products	853	1 011
total	1 230	1 445

(5) Receivables

	1993	1992
trade accounts receivable	1 327	1 407
receivable from non-consolidated companies	57	69
investment grants	29	44
other receivables	677	500
deferred items	56	59
total	2 146	2 079

(6) Cash

	1993	1992
deposits	666	972
cash, bank, giro	125	144
total	791	1 116

(7) Group equity

	total	shareholders' equity	minority interests' share
balance at January 1, 1993	4 321	4 252	69
acquisition price of own shares purchased	65	65	-
	4 386	4 317	69
changes:			
- net result for 1993	-114	-118	4
- dividend	-56	-54	-2
- exchange rate differences	-13	-12	-1
- goodwill	-18	-18	-
- other	-8	-10	2
	4 177	4 105	72
acquisition price of own shares purchased	-16	-16	-
balance at December 31, 1993	4 161	4 089	72

For a breakdown of shareholders' equity, the reader is referred to the DSM N.V. financial statements.

(8) Equalization account

balance at January 1, 1993	241
changes:	
- new claims	3
- released to the statement of income	-37
- other	-23
balance at December 31, 1993	184

42

(9) Provisions

	1993	1992
pensions	42	34
deferred taxes	256	184
self-insurance fund	173	182
restructuring and renovation costs	354	376
other provisions	675	667
total	1 500	1 443

The provisions can largely be regarded as long term.

The major portion of the pension liabilities is covered by independent pension funds. The Provision for pensions concerns the pension commitments and past service commitments which the company has kept under its own control.

The Provision for deferred taxes reflects the balance of future fiscal liabilities resulting from, among other things, timing differences between equity calculated on the basis of DSM accounting principles and equity determined for tax purposes.

An annual allocation is carried to the Self-insurance fund provision for internal insurance of objects. This allocation roughly equals the amount of the premiums which would be owing in the case of external insurance. Damage cases, if and in so far as covered by the internal insurance, are charged against this provision.

The Provision for restructuring and renovation costs concerns reorganization of industrial operations and renovation of assets.

Included in Other provisions are some items relating to, among other things, cost equalization, guarantee obligations and early retirement of personnel.

(10) Long-term liabilities

	1993	1992
debenture loans	1 197	1 294
private loans	955	737
other liabilities	9	17
total	2 161	2 048

This item includes an amount of ƒ 3 million (31 December 1992: ƒ 3 million) in subordinated loans contracted by subsidiaries of DSM N.V. and subordinated to all liabilities owing to third parties by these subsidiaries.

For private loans, an amount of ƒ 82 million (31 December 1992: ƒ 115 million) has been furnished, mainly in mortgage collateral. Moreover, agreements governing loans with a residual amount at 31 December 1993 of ƒ 2,003 million, of which ƒ 110 million of a short-term nature (31 December 1992: ƒ 1,670 million, of which ƒ 3 million short-term) contain clauses restricting the provision of securities.

Of the total long-term liabilities as at 31 December 1993. ƒ 928 million had a remaining term of more than five years. Of this amount, ƒ 300 million relates to debenture loans. ƒ 624 million to private loans and ƒ 4 million to other liabilities.

The schedule of repayment of long-term liabilities is as follows:

- 1995	350
- 1996	547
- 1997 and 1998	336
- 1999 through 2003	818
- after 2003	110
	2 161

The repayments scheduled for 1994, totalling f 177 million, are included under Current liabilities.

Breakdown of long-term liabilities by currency:

	1993	1992
Dutch guilders	1 331	1 109
US dollars	564	631
German marks	195	216
other currencies	71	92
total	2 161	2 048

On balance, Long-term liabilities increased by f 113 million owing to the following changes:

balance at January 1, 1993	2 048
changes:	
- loans taken up	295
- transfer to current liabilities	-177
- extra redemptions	-40
- exchange rate differences	38
- other	-3
balance at December 31, 1993	2 161

Debenture loans

		1993	1992
4 3/8% CHF loan	1988-1995	149	149
6 1/2% convertible personnel loan	1989-1994	-	23
14 3/4% AUD loan	1990-1994	-	110
7 3/4% CHF loan	1991-1995	126	126
10 3/8% CAD loan	1991-1996	209	196
8 1/2% USD loan	1991-1996	291	272
2% SEK loan	1991-1997	56	52
1 1/2% ITL loan	1991-1997	66	66
9% NLG loan	1992-1999	300	300
total		1 197	1 294

A number of the above-mentioned loans were converted into loans in different currencies or with different interest types by means of swaps.

The average effective interest rate on long-term liabilities in 1993 amounted to 8.1%.

The total confirmed credit facilities open to DSM N.V. in the long term amounted to approximately S 300 million as at 31 December 1993 (31 December 1992: $ 300 million).

(11) Current liabilities

	1993	1992
debenture loans and private loans	176	64
credit institutions	333	1 078
received in advance on orders	3	6
suppliers and trade credits	693	745
notes and cheques due	33	24
owing to non-consolidated companies	44	34
taxes and social security	103	94
pensions	8	5
dividend payable	54	49
other liabilities	434	376
deferred items	180	159
total	2 061	2 634
of which interest-bearing	510	1 148

Commitments not appearing from the balance sheet

Outstanding orders for projects under construction amount to ƒ 53 million (31 December 1992: ƒ 197 million). Guarantee obligations on behalf of non-consolidated companies and third parties amount to ƒ 66 million (31 December 1992: ƒ 36 million). Further, there are long-term financial obligations relating to rents, operational lease, etc. amounting to a total of ƒ 178 million (31 December 1992: ƒ 188 million).

(12) Net sales

Net sales, showing a decrease of 9.7% relative to 1992, can be broken down as follows
by business segment:

	1993	%	1992	%
Hydrocarbons & Polymers	3 499	43.5	3 561	40.0
Base Chemicals & Fine Chemicals	2 292	28.5	2 897	32.5
Resins & Plastic Products	2 409	30.0	2 660	29.9
Energy & other activities	176	2.2	203	2.3
total supplies	8 376	104.2	9 321	104.7
intra-group supplies	336	4.2	414	4.7
total	8 040	100.0	8 907	100.0

The following is a geographic breakdown of net sales:

By origin

	1993	%	1992	%
Netherlands	4 960	61.7	5 551	62.3
other EU countries	1 715	21.3	2 026	22.8
	6 675 ·	83.0	7 577	85.1
rest of Europe	87	1.1	39	0.4
North America	1 243	15.5	1 273	14.3
rest of the world	35	0.4	18	0.2
total	8 040	100.0	8 907	100.0

By destination

	1993	%	1992	%
Netherlands	1 107	13.8	1 453	16.3
other EU countries	4 491	55.8	4 964	55.7
	5 598	69.6	6 417	72.0
rest of Europe	447	5.6	414	4.6
North America	1 231	15.3	1 189	13.4
rest of the world	764	9.5	887	10.0
total	8 040	100.0	8 907	100.0

(13) Other operating income

	1993	1992
change in inventories of finished products and work in progress	-139	26
own work capitalized	24	36
sundry	187	231
total	72	293

(14) Amortization and depreciation

	1993	1992
amortization and depreciation of intangible and tangible fixed assets	735	690
other changes in value of intangible and tangible assets	9	16
total	744	706

(15) Other operating costs

	1993	1992
raw materials and consumables	3 829	4 285
work subcontracted and other external expenses	1 857	2 025
wages and salaries	1 447	1 521
pension charges	47	78
other social charges	309	336
sundry	-30	-33
total	7 459	8 212

Wages and salaries relate to the following average workforce totals by business segment:

	1993	1992
Hydrocarbons & Polymers	5 428	5 552
Base Chemicals & Fine Chemicals	4 274	4 755
Resins & Plastic Products	8 218	8 714
Energy & other activities	3 601	4 255
total	21 521	23 276

(16) Segmentation of operating result

The table below shows a breakdown by business segment of the operating result:

	1993	1992
Hydrocarbons & Polymers	-183	-53
Base Chemicals & Fine Chemicals	-105	80
Resins & Plastic Products	14	71
Energy & other activities	183	184
total	-91	282

(17) Financial income and expense

	1993	1992
interest income	39	51
interest expense	-179	-177
other	6	4
total	-134	-122

An amount of ƒ 35 million was deducted from interest expense (1992: ƒ 25 million) on account of capitalized interest expense during construction.

(18) Extraordinary result after taxation

	1993	1992
extraordinary income	27	170
extraordinary expense	-89	-230
taxes	4	38
total	-58	-22

Extraordinary income related to revenues from the sale of activities. Extraordinary expense mainly related to provisions made for restructuring and renovation costs.

(19) Notes to the Statement of cash flows

The Statement of cash flows is drawn up on the basis of a comparison of the balance sheets as at 1 January and 31 December. Changes that do not involve cash flows, such as currency exchange rate changes, revaluations and transfers to other balance-sheet items, are eliminated.

Changes in working capital due to the acquisition or sale of consolidated companies are included under Investment activities.

Most of the changes in the Statement of cash flows can be traced back to the detailed statements of changes for the balance-sheet items concerned. For those balance-sheet items for which no detailed statement of changes is included, the table below shows the link between the change according to the balance sheet and the change according to the Statement of cash flows:

	working capital*	provisions	interest-bearing debt**
balance at year-end 1992	2 086	1 443	3 196
balance at year-end 1993	1 878	1 500	2 671
balance-sheet change	-208	57	-525
adjustments:			
exchange rate changes	-17	-2	-41
acquisition/sale of consolidated companies	-7	-7	-
transfers, etc.	-105	-103	3
adjusted balance-sheet change	-337	-55	-563
change in cash flow	337	-55	-563

* inventories and receivables less interest-free current liabilities and dividend payable.
**long-term liabilities and interest-bearing current liabilities.

The Statement of cash flows has been changed compared with 1992; it no longer includes a separate item 'other changes'. From now on changes in cash flow will be classified exclusively under the following three headings:
- net cash provided by operating activities
- net cash used in investing activities
- net cash provided by financing activities
For the sake of comparison, the figures for 1992 have been changed accordingly.

Quarterly financial data

1993	ƒ million	quarter				year
		1st	2nd	3rd	4th	
	net sales	2 102	2 093	1 903	1 942	8 040
	operating result	19	2	-45	-67	-91
	financial income and expense	-37	-36	-34	-27	-134
	result from ordinary activities before taxation	-18	-34	-79	-94	-225
	tax on result from ordinary activities	20	34	35	37	126
	result of non-consolidated companies	7	7	8	21	43
	result from ordinary activities after taxation	9	7	-36	-36	-56
	extraordinary result after taxation	-	0	-18	-40	-58
	result after taxation	9	7	-54	-76	-114
	minority interests' share in result	-3	-3	2	0	-4
	net result	6	4	-52	-76	-118
	per share in guilders					
	result from ordinary activities after taxation	0.25	0.19	-1.00	-0.99	-1.55
	net result	0.17	0.12	-1.45	-2.12	-3.28

1992	ƒ million	quarter				year
		1st	2nd	3rd	4th	
	net sales	2 433	2 468	2 075	1 931	8 907
	operating result	140	133	46	-37	282
	financial income and expense	-32	-30	-33	-27	-122
	result from ordinary activities before taxation	108	103	13	-64	160
	tax on result from ordinary activities	-11	-10	26	44	49
	results of non-consolidated companies	7	16	6	19	48
	result from ordinary activites after taxation	104	109	45	-1	257
	extraordinary result after taxation	-	5	10	-37	-22
	result after taxation	104	114	55	-38	235
	minority interests' share in result	-4	-4	-2	-1	-11
	net result	100	110	53	-39	224
	per share in guilders					
	result from ordinary activities after taxation	2.96	3.03	1.25	-0.03	7.13
	net result	2.85	3.06	1.49	-1.08	6.22

Balans van DSM N.V. (na resultaatbestemming)

Activa

in miljoenen guldens	ultimo 1993		ultimo 1992	
vaste activa				
materiële vaste activa (1)	60		61	
financiële vaste activa (2)	5 099		6 171	
		5 159		6 232
vlottende activa				
vorderingen (3)	3 215		2 618	
liquide middelen (4)	471		219	
		3 686		2 837
totaal		8 845		9 069

Passiva

in miljoenen guldens	ultimo 1993		ultimo 1992	
eigen vermogen (5)				
- aandelenkapitaal	720		720	
- agio	199		199	
- overige reserves	3 170		3 333	
		4 089		4 252
egalisatierekening investeringspremies		4		5
voorzieningen (6)		902		910
langlopende schulden (7)		1 903		1 728
kortlopende schulden (8)		1 947		2 174
totaal		8 845		9 069

Winst- en verliesrekening van DSM N.V.

in miljoenen guldens	1993	1992
resultaat deelnemingen (na belastingen)	-343	38
overige resultaten	225	186
nettoresultaat	-118	224

DSM N.V. balance sheet as at December 31 (after result appropriation)

Assets

f million	1993		1992	
fixed assets				
tangible fixed assets (1)	60		61	
financial fixed assets (2)	5 099		6 171	
		5 159		6 232
current assets				
receivables (3)	3 215		2 618	
cash (4)	471		219	
		3 686		2 837
total		8 845		9 069

Shareholders' equity and liabilities

f million	1993		1992	
shareholders' equity (5)				
- share capital	720		720	
- share premium account	199		199	
- other reserves	3 170		3 333	
		4 089		4 252
equalization account		4		5
provisions (6)		902		910
long-term liabilities (7)		1 903		1 728
current liabilities (8)		1 947		2 174
total		8 845		9 069

DSM N.V. statement of income

f million	1993	1992
results of consolidated and non-consolidated companies (after taxation)	-343	38
other results	225	186
net result	-118	224

Notes to the balance sheet

General
Unless stated otherwise, all amounts are in millions of guilders.

For the accounting policies, please refer to pages 34 and 35.

(1) Tangible fixed assets

This item mainly relates to land and buildings. Capital expenditure amounted to ƒ 2 million, while the depreciation charge was ƒ 3 million. Cost of tangible fixed assets as at 31 December 1993 was ƒ 86 million; accumulated depreciation amounted to ƒ 26 million.

(2) Financial fixed assets

	total	consolidated companies		non-consolidated companies	other securities	other receivables
		share in equity	loans	share in equity		
balance at January 1, 1993	6 171	4 049	1 701	350	1	70
changes:						
- share in result	-343	-346	-	3	-	-
- dividend	-559	-557	-	-2	-	-
- acquisitions and capital payments	55	55	-	-	-	-
- capital adjustment	-708	-708	-	-	-	-
- advances	874	-	866	-	-	8
- disposals	-92	-29	-	-63	-	-
- redemptions	-140	-	-134	-	-	-6
- transfer to receivables	-177	-	-163	-	-	-14
- goodwill	-3	-3	-	-	-	-
- exchange rate differences	13	-13	26	-	-	-
- other	8	38	-30	-	-	-
balance at December 31, 1993	5 099	2 486	2 266	288	1	58

(3) Receivables

	1993	1992
receivable from consolidated companies	2 595	2 168
receivable from non-consolidated companies	39	45
other receivables	581	405
total	3 215	2 618

(4) Cash

	1993	1992
deposits	37	74
cash, bank, giro	434	145
total	471	219

(5) Shareholders' equity

	total	share capital	share premium account	other reserves
balance at January 1, 1993	4 252	720	199	3 333
acquisition price of own shares purchased	65	-	-	65
	4 317	720	199	3 398
changes:				
- net result for 1993	-118	-	-	-118
- dividend	-54	-	-	-54
- exchange rate differences	-12	-	-	-12
- goodwill	-18	-	-	-18
- other	-10	-	-	-10
	4 105	720	199	3 186
acquisition price of own shares purchased	-16	-	-	-16
balance at December 31, 1993	4 089	720	199	3 170

Share capital
The authorized DSM N.V. capital at 31 December 1993 amounted to *f* 2.5 billion, divided into 62,500,000 ordinary shares of *f* 20 each, 5 priority shares of *f* 20 each, and 62,499,995 preference shares of *f* 20 each. Of these, 36,017,783 ordinary and 5 priority shares have been issued and fully paid up, so that the total paid-up share capital as at 31 December 1993 stood at *f* 720 million.

Options
Certain groups of employees have been granted options on DSM N.V. shares. Each option entitles the holder to one ordinary share of *f* 20. The life of the options is 5 years.

	issued	outstanding as at Dec. 31, 1993	exercise price	exercise period
1989	251 588	138 310	*f* 137.36	up to and incl. 1994
1990	80 600	80 600	*f* 115.20	up to and incl. 1995
1991	92 600	26 700	*f* 89.30	up to and incl. 1996
1992	92 500	83 000	*f* 97.20	up to and incl. 1997
1993	93 400	25 600	*f* 76.00	up to and incl. 1998

Convertible bonds
DSM has issued personnel debentures which are convertible into ordinary shares until 1 March 1994 at a conversion price of *f* 107.70. Conversion of all personnel debentures still outstanding at 31 December 1993 would mean a conversion into 200,970 ordinary shares.

Share premium account
The share premium account can be regarded as wholly free of tax.

Purchased own shares
DSM has purchased own shares, on the one hand as a possible means of (partial) financing of acquisitions and on the other for use when share options are exercised or personnel debentures are converted. In 1993 67,800 shares, at an average acquisition price of *f* 118.95, were used for the latter purpose. In addition, 350,000 shares, at an average acquisition price of *f* 118.56, were sold.

As at 31 December 1993, DSM N.V. and its subsidiaries possessed 134,222 purchased own shares (nominal value *f* 2.7 million, or 0.4% of the issued capital) at an average acquisition price of *f* 117.34. The purchased own shares were charged against Other reserves at acquisition price.

Legal reserve for retained profits

Since the profits retained in DSM N.V.'s consolidated and non-consolidated companies can be distributed and received in the Netherlands without restriction, no Legal reserve for retained profits is required.

(6) Provisions

This item can be broken down as follows:

	1993	1992
deferred taxes	203	114
self-insurance fund	131	130
restructuring and renovation costs	251	310
other provisions	317	356
total	902	910

(7) Long-term liabilities

This item relates entirely to debenture loans and private loans. Of the total amount of long-term liabilities outstanding at 31 December 1993, ƒ 837 million had a remaining term of more than five years.

The repayment schedule for long-term liabilities is as follows:

- 1995	301
- 1996	508
- 1997 and 1998	257
- 1999 through 2003	731
- after 2003	106
	1 903

The repayments scheduled for 1994 are included under Current liabilities.

In agreements governing loans with a residual amount of ƒ 2,003 million, of which ƒ 110 million concerns short-term loans (31 December 1992: ƒ 1,667 million, all of them long term) clauses have been included which restrict the provision of securities.

(8) Current liabilities

	1993	1992
debenture loans and private loans	132	5
credit institutions	358	1 079
owing to consolidated companies	1 099	828
taxes and social security	3	-
dividend payable	54	49
other liabilities	274	201
deferred items	27	12
total	1 947	2 174

Commitments not appearing from the balance sheet
Guarantee obligations on behalf of non-consolidated companies and third parties amount to ƒ 76 million (31 December 1992: ƒ 39 million). DSM N.V. has declared in writing that it accepts several liability for debts arising from acts-in-law of a number of consolidated companies. These debts are included in the consolidated balance sheet.

The other guarantees on behalf of subsidiary companies amount to ƒ 32 million (31 December 1992: ƒ 37 million).

Manpower
DSM N.V. employed on average 19 people (1992: 20).

Remuneration for Members of the Managing Board and the Supervisory Board of DSM N.V.
In the financial year under review, remuneration (including pension costs and other commitments) and pension benefits for members and former members of the Managing Board of DSM N.V. amounted to ƒ 4.5 million (1992: ƒ 4.6 million). Members of the Supervisory Board received a fixed remuneration totalling ƒ 0.7 million (1992: ƒ 0.6 million).

Heerlen, 2 March 1994

Managing Board

S.D. de Bree
R.E. Selman
A.P. Timmermans
L.J.A.M. Ligthart

Supervisory Board

H.H.F. Wijffels
L.M. Kretzers
G.M.V. van Aardenne
M. Epema-Brugman
L.A. Geelhoed
A.C. Helfrich
M.G. Kikken
C.J. van der Klugt
J.K.T. Postma
F.W. Rutten
W.J.L. Spit
H. Vredeling

Overige gegevens

Resultaatbestemming

Volgens artikel 32 van de Statuten van de Vennootschap kan op voorstel van de Raad van Bestuur onder goedkeuring van de Raad van Commissarissen de Algemene Vergadering besluiten het verlies te delgen ten laste van het uitkeerbare deel van het eigen vermogen.

Voorgesteld wordt om aan het nettoresultaat de volgende bestemming te geven:

	1993	1992
ten laste van/ten gunste		
van de reserves	-118	80
uitkering dividend	-	144
	-118	224

Volgens artikel 33 van de Statuten van de Vennootschap kan op voorstel van de Raad van Bestuur, dat is goedgekeurd door de Raad van Commissarissen en door de Prioriteit de Algemene Vergadering besluiten tot uitkeringen aan houders van gewone aandelen ten laste van het uitkeerbare deel van het eigen vermogen.

Voorgesteld wordt ten laste van de algemene reserve een uitkering beschikbaar te stellen van ƒ 54 miljoen, overeenkomend met ƒ 1,50 per aandeel.

Accountantsverklaring

Wij hebben de jaarrekening 1993, waarvan de geconsolideerde jaarrekening deel uitmaakt, van DSM N.V. te Heerlen gecontroleerd. Onze controle is verricht in overeenstemming met algemeen aanvaarde controlegrondslagen.
Wij zijn van oordeel, dat deze jaarrekening een getrouw beeld geeft van de grootte en de samenstelling van het vermogen op 31 december 1993 en van het resultaat over 1993 en ook overigens in overeenstemming is met de wettelijke bepalingen inzake de jaarrekening.

Heerlen, 2 maart 1994

Moret Ernst & Young Accountants

Bijzondere statutaire rechten

Stichting Prioriteitsaandelen DSM

Er zijn vijf prioriteitsaandelen van ƒ 20. Deze zijn geplaatst bij de Stichting Prioriteitsaandelen DSM gevestigd te Heerlen (de Prioriteit). Aan de Prioriteit komen onder meer de volgende statutaire bevoegdheden toe:

- goedkeuring van bestuursbesluiten tot uitgifte van aandelen en tot vaststelling van het deel van de winst dat wordt gereserveerd;
- goedkeuring van voorstellen van het bestuur tot wijziging van de statuten of tot ontbinding van de vennootschap;
- vaststelling van de bezoldiging van commissarissen.

Het bestuur van de Prioriteit bestaat uit 5 personen waarvan de voorzitter en twee andere bestuursleden worden benoemd door de Minister van Economische Zaken; de overige twee bestuursleden zijn de voorzitter van de Raad van Commissarissen en de voorzitter van de Raad van Bestuur van de vennootschap.
De bestuurders zijn:

Drs. T.C. Braakman, Voorzitter
Prof. Mr. L.A. Geelhoed
Drs. J.K.T. Postma
Drs. H.H.F. Wijffels
Ir. S.D. de Bree.

Minder dan de helft van de stemmen kan worden uitgebracht door personen die tevens bestuurder van de vennootschap zijn.

Stichting Preferente Aandelen DSM

In oktober 1989 is de Stichting Preferente Aandelen DSM opgericht. Krachtens de statuten van DSM kunnen 62 499 995 stuks preferente aandelen worden uitgegeven. De uit te geven aandelen kunnen bij de Stichting worden geplaatst teneinde bescherming te bieden tegen een overval.
De bestuursleden zijn:

Mr. A.G. Maris, Voorzitter
Drs. F.A. Maljers
Drs. H.H.F. Wijffels.

De Stichting is onafhankelijk van de vennootschap.

Other information

Appropriation of the result

According to art. 32 of the DSM N.V. Articles of Association the General Meeting may, at the proposal of the Managing Board of Directors and subject to the approval of the Supervisory Board of Directors, decide to settle the loss to the debit of the distributable part of the shareholders' equity.

It is proposed to appropriate the net result as follows:

	1993	1992
charged against/appropriated to the reserves	-118	80
dividend	-	144
	-118	224

According to art. 33 of the DSM N.V. Articles of Association the General Meeting may, at the proposal of the Managing Board of Directors and subject to the approval of the Supervisory Board of Directors and the DSM Priority Shares Foundation, decide to make payments to holders of ordinary shares to the debit of the distributable part of the shareholders' equity.

It is proposed to make a payment of ƒ 54 million or ƒ 1.50 per share, to be charged against the general reserve.

Auditors' report

We have audited the financial statements, including the consolidated financial statements, of DSM N.V., Heerlen, for the year ended December 31, 1993. We conducted our audit in accordance with auditing standards generally accepted in the Netherlands.

In our opinion, these financial statements give a true and fair view of the financial position of DSM N.V. at December 31, 1993 and of the result for the year then ended and also comply with the other Dutch legal requirements for financial statements.

Heerlen, March 2, 1994

Moret Ernst & Young Accountants

Special statutory rights

DSM Priority Shares Foundation

There are five priority shares of ƒ 20 each, held by DSM Priority Share Foundation, Heerlen, whose statutory powers include:

- sanctioning of Board resolutions concerning the issue of shares and the portion of the profit to be appropriated to reserves;
- sanctioning of Board proposals for modification of the Articles of Association or dissolution of the company;
- fixing of the remuneration for supervisory directors.

The Foundation is administered by a committee of five members, the chairman and two other members of which are appointed by the Minister of Economic Affairs, the other two members being the chairmen of DSM's Supervisory and Managing Boards of Directors. The committee members are:

T.C. Braakman, chairman
L.A. Geelhoed
J.K.T. Postma
H.H.F. Wijffels
S.D. de Bree.

Fewer than half of the votes can be cast by members who are also managers of the company.

DSM Preference Shares Foundation

The DSM Preference Shares Foundation was established in October 1989. By virtue of DSM's Articles of Association, 62,499,995 preference shares can be issued. Shares thus issued can be placed with the Foundation in order to provide protection against a hostile bid. The committee members are:

A.G. Maris, chairman
F.A. Maljers
H.H.F. Wijffels.

The Foundation is independent of DSM N.V.

PORTUGAL

Leonor Fernandes Ferreira
Universidade Técnica de Lisbõn

1. Background

1.1 Brief History

Portugal occupies an area slightly greater than 88,500 square kilometers in the southwest corner of Europe, bordering Spain. The territory of Portugal includes, in addition, two groups of islands in the Atlantic: the archipelagos (3,600 square kilometers) of Madeira and the Azores.

In 1993 the resident population of Portugal was approximately 9.4 million, with a density of 292 persons per square mile. More than one-third of the population lives in towns of more than 10,000 inhabitants, the largest being Lisbon and Oporto, with 2.1 and 1.6 million inhabitants, respectively. From a demographic point of view, the Portuguese population is relatively young compared with those of other European countries.

The official language is Portuguese, which is also spoken in Brazil and in the former Portuguese territories in Africa.

The monetary unit is the escudo (Esc or $), made up of 100 centavos. In everyday usage 1,000 escudos are commonly referred to as a *conto*.

1.1.1 Political Institutions

The Portuguese monarchy survived until 1910, when it was succeeded by the republic that has lasted until today, albeit with a number of changes. The present constitution dates from 1976, with major revisions made in 1982 and 1988, and may be described as a form of parliamentary democracy. The constitution was substantially revised in June 1989 to permit, among other things, full privatization of those firms nationalized in the 1970s. The institutions of sovereignty are the presidency, the assembly (Parliament), and the government, headed by the prime minister. The role of the presidency has been a matter of debate. Under the original 1976 constitution there was a strong presidency, so that the country was not a pure parliamentary democracy but was described as "semi-presidential." The powers of the president were substantially reduced in subsequent constitutional revisions, which resulted in the present parliamentary democracy.

Portugal is a member of the United Nations, the International Monetary Fund, the World Bank, the Organization of Economic Cooperation and Development, and the North Atlantic Treaty Organization, as well as being a party to the General Agreement on Tariffs and Trade. Last but not least, Portugal became a member of the European Community in 1986.

1.1.2 The Economy

The Portuguese economy is that of an industrialized country, in which the tertiary sector (services and distribution) produces the largest contribution to the gross national product, followed by the secondary sector (manufacturing). The primary sector (agriculture, fisheries, extraction, etc.) contribute the lowest share of the GNP, and this situation has tended to become more marked in recent years.

The importance of the public sector in the economy remains considerable, although the tendency in recent years has been toward a sustained reduction. This tendency became conspicuous with the beginning of the process of privatization in 1988.

The economically active population of the country represents approximately one-third of the total. As far as the sectors of the economy are concerned, the pattern is much the same as in the other European countries, namely a marked reduction in the percentage of people employed in the primary sector, with a shift to the secondary and tertiary sectors, with the latter receiving the major share. The percentage of people employed has risen, especially among women.

The average wage level in Portugal is currently the lowest for the European Union. The rate of inflation, as measured by the consumer price index, is at a level 2% to 3% in excess of the EU average, and this makes it one of the government's main preoccupations.

Portugal's trade balance has, for some years, been consistently in deficit. Its main trading partners are France, Germany, the United Kingdom, and Spain for exports and Germany, France, and Spain for imports.

Portugal's exports are composed mainly of textiles, cork products, and footwear.

Most business in Portugal is conducted on the basis of sole proprietorship or limited companies, either private (*limitadas* or *sociedades por quotas*) or public (*sociedades anónimas*), some of the latter having a stock exchange listing.

1.1.3 The Financial System

The Portuguese financial system, with the opening of the banking sector to private initiative in 1984 and the entry into the EC in 1986, has undergone a major liberalization and a deregulation of capital, financial, and money markets and has become much more dynamic. Since 1987, the central bank (Bank of Portugal) has introduced a number of financial instruments in order to increase liquidity. These include various types of term deposits, medium-term treasury bonds with maturities of between 18 months and 10 years, and interest rates fixed by tender. There has also been legislation authorizing mortgage bonds and asset management companies (which are authorized to manage both real estate and financial assets), among other things.

Recently, changes have occurred in the legal frame of the financial markets, with government approval of the *Regime Geral das Instituições de Crédito e Sociedades Financeiras*, due to the effort of harmonization of Portugal in the EU.

Financial institutions in Portugal may be classified into two large groups (according to the *Regime Geral das Instituições de Crédito e Sociedades Financeiras*):

1. Credit institutions (*instituições de crédito*), those legally authorized to create means of payment, including the Central Bank, the commercial banks, and the special credit institutions, such as leasing companies, factoring companies, investment companies, and stock exchange dealing companies.

2. Other financial institutions (*sociedades financeiras*), which, although having no credit function, attract savings to be applied in financial activities, such as investment funds, pension funds management companies, and asset management companies. The latter

manage both real estate and financial assets on behalf of individuals and corporate entities and are incorporated under a specific legal form that authorizes them to do so (similar to the *Sociétés Civiles Financières et Immobilières* in France).

To sum, the increases in the number and type of institutions operating in the market, together with the development of "secondary banking" activities, have accelerated the entire process of change, stimulating competition. From the rapid expansion of investment companies and leasing companies via the creation of new financial instruments that allow both enterprises and individuals to put their savings to work, to the remarkable recovery of the capital market starting in 1986, a clear and progressive liberalization of the system is evident.

In 1991 the Stock Exchange Regulation Entity was created (*Código do Mercado de Valores Mobiliários*) in order to develop and supervise both the Lisbon and the Oporto Stock Exchanges. Its functions also include the supervision of the primary market (new issues, disclosures, etc.), as well as authorization for the introduction of new products, such as options, futures, and derivatives, and in general, supervision of all the financial intermediaries.

As far as the foreign exchange market is concerned, with the introduction of the quotation of spot and forward rates, the gradual internationalization of the escudo, and the imminent introduction of new products such as options, flexibility and liberalization are among the government's main concerns.

Foreign investment in Portugal is not subject to any kind of approval. Dividends and capital gains may be repatriated from Portugal. Activities in which foreign investment is not allowed include telecommunications, air and rail transport, ports and airports, armaments, and the treatment and distribution of water. In general, foreign investments in corporations being privatized may not exceed 25% of the share being offered.

1.1.4 The Legal Environment

The legal system is a structured hierarchy of laws, with the most important, the constitution (*Constituição da República Portuguesa*) as the basis. In descending order of priority, the other sources of law are *leis* passed by

Parliament (the *Assembleia da República*), *decretos-lei* of the government, *decretos-regulamentares*, and *portarias* issued by ministries, and *despachos normativos* and *despachos* signed by secretaries of state.

The legal environment that is relevant to accounting in Portugal comprises the commercial code, the body of tax law, stock market regulations, and the Official Accounting Plan, which has legal backing (see Section 3, below). In general, Portugal is a country in which accounting principles require legal expression or backing in order to be valid. There is no tradition of accounting principles gaining general acceptance through recognition by the accounting profession. The past 20 years have had a particular significance, not only for Portugal's economic and political life, but also for accounting.

The Official Accounting Plan currently in force was established by Decree-Law No. 410/89, dated November 21, 1989 and Decree-Law No. 238/91, dated July 2, 1991. The form and content of financial statements are also regulated by the Companies Law (*Código das Sociedades Comerciais*), under Decree-Law No. 262/86, dated September 2, 1986. Public filing requirements generally are stated in the companies law and specifically in the commercial register law (*Código do Registo Comercial*), Decree-Law No. 403/86, dated December 3, 1986, and by *Lei Sapateiro* the Stock Exchange Regulation, Decree-Law No. 142-A/91, dated April 10, 1991. Statutory audit requirements are established in the Companies Law and in the Decree-Law No. 422-A/93, dated December 30, 1993.

By the beginning of 1994, the first eight EU directives had been enacted into law, although it is too early to assess their impact on the business community.

1.2 The Accounting Background

According to the noted scholar Fernando Gonçalves da Silva, Portuguese accounting history may be divided into four periods. The first period lasted from the foundation of the Portuguese nation in 1143 until the end of the fifteenth century. Portugal became a leading maritime and trading country in the fifteenth century, so this first period saw the beginning of Portugal's maritime greatness. In spite of Portugal's trading links with the Italian republics, however, it would seem that the accounting techniques used in Portugal remained at a primitive level.

The second period included the sixteenth and seventeenth centuries and the first half of the eighteenth century. The sixteenth century saw Lisbon become the center of a vast empire, one of the world's leading ports and commercial centers. Portugal's role as an imperial power received a setback in 1680, however, when the country was invaded by Philip II of Spain, and Portugal remained under Spanish domination for 60 years. Portugal lost much of its empire, including almost all its Asian possessions, to the Spanish and the Dutch, although it retained enormous territories in Brazil and Africa, as well as some outposts in Asia. It was during this period that the use of Venetian-style double-entry bookkeeping in Portugal became apparent. Surviving examples can be seen in the records of the India Company (*Casa da India*) and the Monastery of Alcobaça (*Mosteiro de Alcobaça*). Little is known, however, regarding the extent to which such methods were used at the time. There are no books on accounting in Portuguese, either original works or translations, dating from this period, nor were any legal requirements for accounting introduced in Portugal.

The third period started with the ministry of Sebastião José de Carvalho e Melo (Minister of Finance and the future Marquis of Pombal) in 1750, and lasted until the early twentieth century. Under Pombal's ministry, efforts were made to lay down a legal structure for trade and commerce, including accounting. In 1755, a Royal Decree created a trade association (*Junta de Comércio*), and in 1756, there followed ordinances concerning mercantile books and the statutes of the Hall of Commerce (*Aula de Comércio*), which were to play a lasting role in the teaching of accounting and business methods. The first accounting texts in Portuguese appeared in 1758 and 1764. However, Gonçalves da Silva comments that the lack of education and the inertia of the businessmen of the period were such that reforms introduced by Pombal were neither as rapid, nor as profound, nor as durable as the Marquis had intended.

In the following century, commercial codes were introduced by Ferreira Borges (1786–1838) in 1833 and by Veiga Beirão (1841–1916) in 1888, under the influence of contemporary French commercial codes. These included requirements for the keeping of books of account and other records. Some of the provisions of the 1888 code are still in force today. Such provisions include the obligation to keep a journal, a ledger, and a balance sheet book (inventory), which must be written up within 90 days and retained for 10 years. The pages of these books must bear the official stamp of the authorities.

The fourth period began in the late 1920s. At this time, accounting was recognized in Portugal as a body of knowledge having a relationship with business economics and the theory of the firm. Several influential books on accounting were published by Portuguese authors, as well as translations of foreign classics by such authors as Schmalenbach, Zappa, and Dumarchey and the appearance of a journal, *Revista de Contabilidade e Comércio* (*Review of Accounting and Commerce*) which began publishing in 1933 and continues today. A professional body, the *Sociedade Portuguesa de Contabilidade*, was founded, and specialized accounting courses began to be taught in high schools. The inclusion of accounting in university curricula was slower to gain acceptance, but in due course it began to make its appearance in economics faculties and in some law faculties.

For much of this time, Portugal's economic development, perhaps even more than that of Spain, lagged behind that of her northern neighbors in Europe. For the first third of the nineteenth century, dynastic wars involving the Spanish, French, and British took place on Portuguese soil, with disastrous consequences for Portugal's economy. Brazil became independent in 1822, but the maintenance and administration of the vast African territories remained a dominant consideration, which in the present century became more and more burdensome, impeding the modernization of the country's economy and political institutions.

Almost until the end of the third quarter of the present century, while Western Europe in general enjoyed a crucial period of economic growth and modernization, the economic and political fate of Portugal was under the control of an authoritarian regime dating back to the 1930s. This regime lacked the political will to face up to the inevitable issues of decolonization abroad and democratization at home and remained locked in an increasingly vain attempt to retain African territories whose size was quite disproportionate to the resources of the nation. Resources that could otherwise have been applied to the development of Portugal's economy were thus absorbed in colonial administration and, increasingly, in wasteful colonial wars. This was associated with the persistence of archaic structures and methods in the industrial sector, cushioned by privileged positions in colonial markets.

Nevertheless, in the decade before the oil price crisis of 1973, Portugal achieved rapid growth in GDP, averaging more 7%. As it turned out, however, the postponement of decolonization in Africa and of democratization at home meant that the Portuguese economy had, to some extent, been living on borrowed time.

Therefore, to Gonçalves da Silva's four periods, one is tempted to add a fifth, since certain developments during the past 20 years have had a particular significance, not only for Portugal's economic and political life, but also for Portuguese accounting. During this later period, Portugal relinquished its overseas territories in Africa, notably those in Angola and Mozambique, thus ending the colonial administration and wars that had taken such a heavy toll of its resources. Turning toward Europe, Portugal has become established among the western European democracies and, since January 1986, has been a member state of the European Community, with all that such membership entails for the country's economic orientation and its accounting and financial reporting practices. In particular, the influences of French ideas and practices, already important in the commercial codes of the nineteenth century, have been especially significant in the field of accounting.

Before joining the EC, Portugal had already embarked on the modernization of its financial accounting practices under the influence of French ideas. In fact, during the period 1970–1973, that is to say, before the 1974 revolution, a study had been undertaken under the aegis of the Directorate General of Taxes in the Ministry of Finance, with the objective of producing proposals for accounting modernizations with a view to achieving greater equity in the taxation of company profits. This study identified the French 1957 *Plan Comptable Général* as a suitable model.

To the impact of the 1973 oil price crisis were added those of the political revolution of 1974 and the negative short-term effects of decolonization. The change in political regime was followed by a period of political instability and doctrinaire socialist measures of a nature unpropitious for economic development. The decolonization resulted in the loss of privileged markets and the repatriation of about 700,000 settlers, which entailed a sudden 7% increase in population.

In spite of these difficulties, Portugal's rate of GDP growth averaged 3.3% from 1973 to 1980. The economy, however, was plagued by inflation of more than 20% per annum, budget deficits, and unemployment. It was therefore ill-equipped to confront the second oil price crisis in the early 1980s. In particular, this resulted in current account deficits on the order of 10.5% of GDP during 1980–1982, which in turn led to unacceptable levels of foreign debt. In order to contain these problems, the government was forced to sacrifice economic growth, which fell to zero in 1983 and –2% in 1984.

The political and economic history of Portugal since the 1950s has not been without its implications for accounting development. Whereas the need for improvements in accounting was recognized in the early 1970s, the various endeavors to introduce reforms were constantly overtaken by political events until the early 1980s. Thus, on the one hand, the state of accounting development indicated by Portugal's 1977 Official Accounting Plan may be considered comparable to that in France 20 years earlier, when the *Plan Comptable 1957* made its appearance. On the other hand, the pursuit of the proposed accounting reforms was effectively delayed for about 6 years.

The process of modernizing Portuguese accounting regulation took a step forward in 1976 with the law establishing the Accounting Standards Commission (*Comissão de Normalização Contabilística*, or CNC), and with the issuing of the first Official Accounting Plan (*Plano Oficial de Contabilidade*, POC) in the decree-law of February 7, 1977. This signified the official adoption of the institutional model for accounting regulation suggested by the Finance Ministry study group, namely the French model. This model involves a standard-setting body attached administratively to the Ministry of Finance, with powers to lay down a national accounting plan, the provisions of which are given legal force in the form of decrees or decree-laws.

At the same time, although the law creating the CNC was issued in 1976, the decree specifying its structure and powers did not appear until October 1980, and the members of the Commission were not appointed until June 1983. Thus, the political and economic vicissitudes of the 1970s and early 1980s have made the creation of a modern institution for accounting regulation in Portugal a protected affair, spread over some 12 or 13 years. They also resulted in the temporary demise of industrial and financial groups, so that consolidated accounts were hardly called for until new industrial groups emerged. This helps to explain the delay in implementing the Seventh Directive.

In November 1989, a revised version of the POC was issued to give effect to the EC Fourth Directive. Sometime later, in July 1991, a revised version of the POC was issued to give effect to the EC Seventh Directive. This latter has been applied to the annual and group accounts for financial years beginning in 1991. French influence is beginning to lose its importance, as the international standards, mainly from Anglo-Saxon countries, are gaining more and more followers.

The required annual accounts are the balance sheet, the profit and loss account, and the annex (notes). Companies below certain size criteria may present abridged financial statements. These annual accounts, together with the management's report and, if appropriate, the auditor's report, must be made public by being deposited with the Commercial Registry.

The layout of the accounts of certain kinds of companies differs from those in the POC. This happens with banks and other financial institutions for which accounting rules are issued by the Bank of Portugal (*Banco de Portugal*) and also with insurance companies, whose accounting principles, procedures, and financial reports depend on the Insurance Institute of Portugal (*Instituto de Seguros de Portugal*).

1.2.1 The Structure, Membership, and Powers of the CNC

The Ministry of Finance regulation dated April 3, 1987 set out the current powers, structure, and functions for the CNC.

Powers of the CNC   The CNC is empowered to ensure the process and improvement of national accounting standardization, and specifically:

1. To promote studies necessary to establish accounting principles, concepts, and procedures to be considered generally accepted
2. To carry out projects concerned with updating, amending, and interpreting the POC
3. To steer the development of sectorial accounting plans or to comment on and approve those developed by other bodies
4. To comment on draft laws with repercussions on company accounting

5. To respond to inquiries made by companies concerning the implementation or interpretation of the POC

6. To participate in international meetings where matters relating to accounting standardization are to be discussed, with the objective of issuing a technical opinion

Structure of the CNC   The CNC has a president, a general council, and an executive committee. The president is designated by the minister of finance and must be generally recognized as being professionally and intellectually competent. The chairman of the executive committee may act as vice-president of the CNC.

The president has the power to represent the CNC in its relations with the government and with international bodies and may delegate this power to other CNC members or be accompanied by them. He or she also chairs the general council and attends meetings of the executive committee at the request of the latter or its chairman.

The general council is the deliberative body that represents at national level the various groups interested in accounting standardization. In addition to the president, it consists of 33 members, drawn from government departments, professional associations, the Bank of Portugal, and from universities and industry.

The powers of the General Council are:

1. To advise the Minister of Finance on accounting principles, concepts, and procedures as set out in items 1, 2, and 3, above

2. To approve the annual plan of activities and the program of research to be carried out by the executive committee or by working groups

The general council meets normally once a quarter, and a quorum consists of at least 12 members. Decisions are made by a simple majority of those present, with the president also having a vote.

The executive committee has 11 members, chosen from the members of the General Council for a renewable period of 3 years. The chairman of this committee is elected by the general council by secret ballot. The other 10 members are chosen to represent the various constituencies mentioned above.

The executive committee carries out work laid down by the general council. It sets up working groups and coordinates their activities, decides on the submission of draft proposals from the working groups to the General Council, prepares annual activity programs and budgets for submission annually to the General Council, and arranges the publication of periodic reports, the preparation of which will be entrusted to working groups.

The executive committee meets regularly four times a month, and also on the special request of its chairman. The required quorum is six, including the chairman (or his deputy), who also has a vote.

Working groups are composed of a member of the executive committee, who acts as coordinator, plus other members of the executive committee or of the general council, plus external assessors chosen for their special qualifications in order to ensure the quality or appropriateness of the work. The members of working groups are selected by the executive committee.

The Opinions of the CNC   Since 1987 the CNC has been preparing opinions *(Directrizes Contabilísticas)*. Some of them already have been approved by the General Council of the CNC and have been published in the official journal. In some cases they include information to amplify and explain items in the POC. In other cases they provide information that is not in the POC. Contrary to what happened with the official accounting plan (POC), however, these opinions are not laws, being only approved by the general council of the CNC and not by any ministry. Currently, there are 15 opinions. Table 1 lists them and their dates of approval.

1.2.2 The Accounting and Auditing Professions

In common with certain other European countries (e.g., Belgium), Portugal has separate professions, and not just separate professional bodies, for accounting and auditing. The accounting profession consists of técnicos de contas. Before the reform they were registered with the Ministry of Finance. To be eligible for registration, they had to hold a university degree (in law or economics), or have gained 5 years' practical experience, before taking the técnicos de contas professional examinations. Either

TABLE 1 *CNC Opinions (Directrizes Contabilísticas)*

Opinion Number	Date Published	Description
1/91	January 16, 1992	Accounting for business combinations
2/91	January 16, 1992	Accounting of assets received through donation
3/91	March 4, 1992	Accounting for long-term contracts
4/91	March 4, 1992	Accounting for concession contracts
5/91	March 4, 1992	Accounting for costs and revenues from the bingo game
6	March 30, 1993	Elimination of profits and losses resulting from transactions between undertakings included in a group
7	March 30, 1993	Accounting for research and development expenses
8	March 30, 1993	Clarification on the contents of *Resultados Transitados* account (preceding years income not appropriated and/or losses carried forward), in what concerns not usual and of great significance regularizations
9	March 30, 1993	Accounting for investments in subsidiaries and associated companies in the individual accounts of the undertaker company
10	March 30, 1993	Transitional procedures for leasing contracts accounting
11	March 30, 1993	Intracommunitary Value Added Tax accounting
12	March 30, 1993	The accounting concept of goodwill
13	April 5, 1994	The concept of fair value
14	April 5, 1994	Cash-flow statements
15		Shares' redemption and amortization (still in draft form)
16		Rental agreements (still in draft form)

route to qualification involved passing theoretical courses in financial accounting, cost accounting, and taxation.

Under Portuguese tax law, company accounts prepared for tax purposes must be signed by an accountant who is also responsible for keeping the company's financial records in one centralized location. As a result of the 1989 fiscal reform, it is no longer necessary for an accountant to be a registered *técnicos de contas* in order to sign a company's tax return, provided he or she is named the company's official accountant in its statutory declaration of commencement of activities.

There is no officially recognized professional organization of accountants, but there are several professional associations. The oldest of these is the *Sociedade Portuguesa de Contabilidade*, founded in the 1930s, but the most influential is the *Associação Portuguesa de Técnicos de Contas* (APOTEC). A third body is the *Associação Portuguesa de Contabilistas*, and a fourth body is the *Câmara dos Técnicos de Contas*. Membership numbers vary among these associations. For example, APOTEC, the largest, has about 7000 members.

The auditing profession consists of Revisores Oficiais de Contas, (ROCs), statutory auditors registered with the Ministry of Justice and belonging to the Chamber of Registered Statutory Auditors (*Câmara dos Revisores Oficiais de Contas*). The latter is the officially recognized professional body for auditors, while the associations of professional accountants have no such official recognition (although their qualification is officially recognized, as described above). In order to be registered as a statutory auditor, it is necessary to hold a relevant university degree (the same as for registered accountants) or a technical college accounting diploma, followed by a 3-year apprenticeship and passing a written and oral examination. In December 1993 the new legal regime of auditing professionals was approved (Decree-law 422-A/93, published in the Official Journal on December, 30, 1993) regulates the auditing profession in Portugal. This is in line with the Eighth EC Directive and was effective on January 1, 1994.

The accounting and auditing profession has not been an important group in anticipating the application in Portugal of international accounting rules. Neither the accounting nor the auditors' professional bodies have developed a set of accounting principles and procedures that are considered generally accepted by the companies. French influences, however, are becoming less important as Anglo-Saxon standards gain more and more followers.

TABLE 2 *Technical Recommendations of the CROC*

CROC Number	Date Published	Description
1	April 1986	Auditing of the financial statements and other published reports
2	August 1986	Influence of initial balances on the final balances to be verified
3	February 1987	Verification of the application of the principle of consistency
4	August 1987	Influence of tax rules on the statutory audit
5	January 1988	Auditing of intermediate financial statements
6	May 1988	Annual report on statutory auditing carried out
7	October 1988	Auditing of nonmonetary paid-up capital
8	January 1991	Auditing of accounts that include comparative figures relating to the previous year
9	September 1991	Statutory audit of consolidated accounts
10	December 1991	Information and qualifications on the statutory audit
11	April 1992	Auditing of prospective financial information

The Official Auditors Chamber (*Câmara dos Revisores Oficiais de Contas*, or CROC) has issued a set of technical recommendations that guide auditing practice (Table 2).

The audit obligation is applicable to all companies that exceed certain size limits, to listed companies, and to financial institutions and insurance companies. Auditors are appointed for a minimum of 3 years and a maximum of 9 years. Companies with stock listed on the Portuguese Stock Exchange are subject to an additional audit, according to the stock exchange regulations now in force. In the case of companies not subject to statutory audit, shareholders owning 5% of the capital stock can demand the appointment of auditors. Auditors in Portugal are members of a professional body and must be registered in the Official Auditors Chamber (CROC), which is responsible for issuing standards and undertaking disciplinary measures.

As for auditing, Portuguese corporations (*Sociedade Anónima*, SA) and private limited companies (Ldas) must appoint a statutory board of auditors (*conselho fiscal*), the size and composition of which depend on the size and legal form of the company. All SAs must have a three member audit board, one of whom is the company's *revisor oficial de contas* (ROC), unless the share capital is less than 20 million escudos, in which case a single ROC may act as auditor. For private companies above a certain size as specified in the law implementing the EC Fourth Directive, the same applies as in the case of an SA (50 employees, net assets of 180 million escudos, and sales turnover of 370 million escudos). For smaller Ldas, no statutory audit is required. Although only one member of the statutory board of auditors need be professionally qualified, the following restrictions apply to all members.

No member of the statutory board of auditors may:

- be a director or employee of the company, or receive any special benefits from it;
- be a director, employee or audit board member of the company's parent or subsidiary companies or of any company which is in a position to controlor be controlled by the company because of any special contractual obligations;
- be a shareholder, owner or employee of any company carrying out in its own name any of the functions or subject to the restrictions described above;
- perform any functions in a compeititor company;
- have a close family relationship with persons in any of the preceding categories;
- be legally incapacitated from carrying out public duties.

In addition to the statutory audit, a number of the largest Portuguese companies employ international accounting firms to carry out an independent audit in accordance with international auditing standards.

Regarding nonstatutory auditing, there has been a significant increase in demand for international auditors in Portugal, both from state-owned companies, especially those under the privatization process, and from private companies, whether for merger, acquisitions, financing, and stock exchange purposes, or, generally, for greater credibility of their financial statements.

The fees of auditors in Portugal are calculated in terms of the number and size of an individual ROC's customer companies, according to a *points* system, under which each company is attributed a certain number of points (ranging form 0 to 8) and calculated on the basis of its total assets and total revenues. Each individual (ROC) has an allocation of 48 points, which may not be exceeded. This system was designed to ensure independence.

2. The Form and Content of Published Financial Statements

Accounts are always published in Portuguese, although some companies—primarily subsidiaries of foreign concerns—present bilingual financial reports.

The requirements of the POC are based on those of the EC Fourth Directive and thus encompass the balance sheet, profit and loss statement, and annex (notes to the financial statements); there is no requirement for statements of sources and applications of funds or of cash flows. The POC presents a statement of sources and applications of funds, however, and recently the CNC issued Opinion No. 14/93 concerning the cash-flow statements and providing models of presentation. Until 1990, companies in Portugal had not been required to publish group accounts, although they have been permitted to file tax returns on a group basis since 1988. This situation has changed as a result of the extension of the POC in July 1991 to include requirements for consolidated accounts as set out in the Seventh Directive. These have applied to financial statements for years beginning on or after January 1, 1991. Details are given in Section 3.4 below.

Companies with shares listed in the Portuguese Stock Exchanges must disclose, additionally, a mid-year balance sheet and profit and loss account, as well as forecasts for the assets and cash-flow for the year.

A specimen set of Portuguese financial statements (consolidated accounts) is included as an appendix to this chapter.

2.2 Balance Sheet Format and Contents

The POC opted for the horizontal format provided in the Fourth Directive. With regard to content, the POC gives a highly detailed version (*Balanço Analítico*), in which most lines of the balance sheet correspond to a single two- or three-digit account code within the national chart of accounts. There is also a summarized version (*Balanço Sintético*), in which most lines correspond to a combination of account codes and that may be used by smaller enterprises, that is, those that during the past two successive years have not exceeded two of the following three size criteria (from the Companies Law): 50 employees; turnover 370 million escudos; total assets 180 million escudos.

The appendix provides the detailed format, with the description of line items in Portuguese and English. It may be noted that three columns are provided for the current year's balance sheet figures: these are for the gross values of assets, provisions for depreciation or amortization, and net values, respectively.

2.3 Profit and Loss Statement Format and Contents

Of the four formats offered by the Fourth Directive, the POC opts for the horizontal format, classified by nature, with expenses and losses on the left-hand side and revenues and income for the year on the right. This is the most traditional of the four, and the one that, generally speaking, discloses least to the financial analyst, omitting the subtotals that are of interest for analytical purposes. However, the Portuguese format provides a number of these in a *résumé* at the bottom of the statement and in some of the notes to the accounts (see the appendix).

As with the balance sheet, as far as contents are concerned, the full version (*Demonstração de Resultados Analítica*) is relatively detailed, and smaller enterprises may produce a more succinct version (*Demonstração de Resultados Sintética*). The difference between the level of detail in the two versions is much less than in the case of the balance sheet, however.

The profit and loss account format requires intermediate income balances to be calculated and presented. These balances are calculated in accordance with the step-by-step approach to income calculation.

The POC also provides a vertical format by function, based on that given in the Fourth Directive. This may be produced in addition to the required horizontal format but cannot replace it.

2.4 The Annex

The annex (*Anexo ao Balanço e à Demonstração de Resultados*) required by the POC has been designed to meet the requirements of the Fourth Directive. It includes information intended to amplify and explain items in the financial statements, as well as other information that does not appear in the financial statements but could be useful for the reader or be relevant to the financial position of the enterprise. The POC emphasizes that the quality of the financial information given by companies is dependent on the content of the notes.

The contents of the annex are too numerous to list here in detail. The most significant items contained in it are the following:

1. Any departure from the requirement of the POC in exceptional cases in order to show a true and fair view and the reasons for such departure

2. Any items in the balance sheet or profit and loss statement that are not comparable with those of the previous year, with an explanation

3. The valuation principles and methods of calculating depreciation and provisions

4. Exchange rates used to translate amounts originally expressed in foreign currency for inclusion in the balance sheet and profit and loss statement

5. Accounting methods used in order to obtain tax benefits:

    a. The use of asset valuation principles different from those referred to above

    b. Depreciation in excess of what is economically justified

    c. Extraordinary provisions (write-downs) against assets

6. Situations having an impact on future taxation

7. Comments on organization costs and research and development costs and on goodwill and other intangibles if amortized over more than 5 years

8. Supplementary schedules on fixed assets, including intangibles, property, plant, and equipment and financial fixed assets

9. Further information on fixed assets, such as interest capitalized during the year, revaluation, breakdown by sector of activity, and other analyses relevant for tax or EC purposes

10. A list of subsidiaries, associated companies, and participations in which the parent company holds at least 10% of the capital (Associated companies and participations that are not required to publish their financial statements may be omitted.)

11. Information on investments in other companies included in negotiable securities if they have a carrying value amounting to more than 5% of the working capital of the reporting entity

12. Analysis of assets held on account of restricted funds, for example, pension funds

13. For working capital items:

    a.   The total difference by category of asset between book value and market value, if material

    b.   In the case of items stated at a book value below the lower of cost or market value, the reasons for this

    c.   Indication of and reasons for any extraordinary provisions for loss of value

14. The global value of inventories belonging to the entity but not in its possession

15. The overall value of debts for each category of receivables

16. Details of advances or loans to members of the board of directors or the audit board of the company

xx

3. Accounting Principles in Portugal

Portuguese accounting principles are promulgated in the POC (Official Accounting Plan). Given the tax orientation of Portuguese financial accounting, however, tax rules are also influential in certain areas of accounting, such as those for fixed assets and provisions. The basic bookkeeping requirements are laid down in the Commercial Code.

Banks and financial institutions are subject to a separate set of accounting requirements. The POC was drawn up in light of the EC Fourth and Seventh Directives, which do not apply to banks and financial institutions. The latter are subject to the 1986 Directive on the financial statements of credit and financial institutions. An accounting plan applicable to the financial sector drawn up in light of the 1986 Directive exists and has been applied since January 1, 1990. This accounting plan is the responsibility not of the CNC but of the Bank of Portugal.

The financial statements of insurance companies are also regulated by a sectorial plan that was prepared by the Instituto de Seguros de Portugal.[1]

3.2 The Official Accounting Plan—General

As already noted, the current version of the Official Accounting Plan (POC) was published in October 1989 and was modified and amended in July 1991 to attend to the requirements of the Seventh EC Directive on group accounts. It is perhaps noteworthy that the publication took the form of a document annexed to a decree-law approved by the Council of Ministers and not simply by the Finance Ministry, a fact that may indicate the national importance attributed to such a document. The contents are as follows:

1. Introduction
2. General considerations
3. Objectives and qualitative characteristics of financial information
4. Accounting principles
5. Accounting rules for specific classes of items
6. Balance sheet formats and contents

7. Profit and loss statement format and content
8. Notes to the balance sheet and the profit and loss statements
9. Statement of sources and application of funds
10. Overall chart of accounts
11. Detailed code of accounts
12. Explanatory notes on the operation of certain accounts
13. Group accounts methods and procedures
14. Group financial statements format and contents

3.3 Detailed Consideration of the Official Accounting Plan

3.3.1 The Introduction

The introduction to the POC makes clear that the November 1989 POC is a revision of the original 1977 version. The reasons for the revision were as follows: compliance with EC Directives; to take the opportunity to introduce some improvements and clarifications in light of 12 years' experience, for example, titles of accounts; and to remove some minor differences between Portuguese accounting and internationally accepted principles (IASC), for example, accounting for leased assets.

The CNC decided to keep the changes to a minimum in order to facilitate matters for both accountants and users.

3.3.2 General Considerations

The section on general considerations explains the reasons for the changes being introduced and provides justifications for the options exercised under the Fourth Directive. It also provides a number of legal definitions, for example, regarding related companies and provisions.

Portuguese law (POC) makes the following distinctions between different categories of related companies:

Group companies: Those companies that belong to a range that includes the mother company and the subsidiaries (those holding more than 50% the voting capital of another)

Associated companies: When one company holds 20% or more and no more than 50% of the voting capital of another and can not be considered either a mother company or a subsidiary

Participations: When one company does not meet the conditions required to be a group company or an associated company

A *group* is defined as including subsidiaries but not associated companies and participations.

The Business Companies Code defines totally controlled and simply controlled subsidiaries as follows:

Totally controlled subsidiaries: When one company holds 90% or more of the voting capital of another, either directly or indirectly

Simply controlled subsidiaries: When one company holds a majority of the voting capital of another, either directly or indirectly, or over which it exercises control by other means

3.3.3 Objectives and Qualitative Characteristics of Financial Information

This section of the POC sets out certain general ideas and is mainly a brief summary of those expressed in the FASB's Statements of Financial Accounting Concepts (SFAC) 1 and 2, regarding the objectives and qualitative characteristics of financial statements.

Objectives   Financial statements should be suitable for making rational economic decisions and hence contributing to the functioning of efficient capital markets and the accountability of management.

User groups that are specifically cited are investors, lenders, workers, suppliers and other creditors, government and other official authorities, and the public in general. The responsibility for preparing and presenting financial statements is laid on management and, in particular, on the board of directors (these responsibilities are set out in detail in the company law). It is stated that users of financial statements will be better able to analyze the capacity of the firm, in terms of the timing and certainty of the cash flows it may generate, if they are provided with information that focuses on its financial position, results of operations, and changes in financial position.

Qualitative Characteristics   The essential quality of financial statement information is understandability by users, and its usefulness depends on three characteristics: relevance, reliability, and comparability. The definitions of these three characteristics given in the POC are derived from those in SFAC 2. The POC states that these characteristics, together with concepts, principles, and accounting rules, make it possible that general purpose financial statements may give a true and fair view of the firm's financial position and results of operations.

3.3.4 Fundamental Accounting Principles

The principles of continuity, consistency, accruals, and prudence included in the POC are similar to those stated in the EC Fourth Directive. This directive also refers to the use of the cost (or entry price) basis of accounting for assets but specifically allows the use of current cost as a member state option. The wording of the POC is somewhat different: it requires the use of "costs of acquisition or production, either in nominal or in constant escudos." This suggests that current purchasing power accounting would be legally acceptable in Portugal, but the acceptability of current cost accounting is more doubtful. (See under Fixed Assets, below.)

The principle of substance over form requires operations to be accounted for with regard to their substance and financial reality and not merely their legal form. With regard to the treatment of finance leases, in the beginning, finance leases were accounted for in the assets of the lessor company. The latest version of the POC was adapted to the Anglo-Saxon model, in which the located goods are accounted for in the assets of the lessee company.

The principle of materiality requires financial statements to show all the items that are relevant and may affect evaluations or decisions by interested users.

3.3.5 Accounting Rules for Specific Classes of Items

Financial accounting in Portugal has traditionally been tax-oriented, so that an important influence of accounting practice in the sphere of valuation and income measurement is the body of decree-laws and decrees dealing with the calculation of taxable profit and with tax treatments that are mandatory if certain tax allowances are to be obtained. Notwithstanding the fundamental principles enunciated in the POC, if the accounting treatment required to obtain a tax benefit differs from that which is consistent with the POC, it is the former that will prevail (although the POC requires the difference to be disclosed in the notes to the financial statements—see Section 2, above). On the other hand, Portuguese tax law does not set out to provide anything approaching a comprehensive set of accounting guidelines.

The main task of the POC has been to promote the standardization of accounting terminology and classification. Its contribution to valuation and income measurement has been much slighter. In all fairness, it should be said that much the same is true of its model, the French *Plan Comptable* Générale (PCG). However, the latter has been supplemented by a body of accounting principles enunciated by the French *Conseil National de la Comptabilité* (CNC), as well as by technical recommendations by the official French professional accounting body, which only recently began to have a counterpart in Portugal through the Opinions issued by the CNC. These facts need to be borne in mind when considering the rules for valuation and income measurement set out in the 1989 POC, which are described below.

Liquid Assets   Liquid assets in foreign currencies should be accounted for at closing rates, and unrealized exchanges gains and losses are taken to profit and loss and reported in the section "Financial Expenses and Income."

Negotiable securities are to be treated according to the criteria set out for inventories, as far as these are applicable.

Amounts Due from Third Parties   In the case of amounts in foreign currencies, unrealized exchange gains or losses are generally to be dealt with in the same way as those on liquid assets. There are exceptions, however. In the case of medium- and long-term loans, unrealized exchange gains should be deferred if there are reasonable expectations that the gain may be reversed. In the case of exchange differences on financing for fixed assets, it is permitted to impute the exchange differences to the cost of the fixed assets only during the period in which the fixed assets are acquired or in the course of construction.

When the amount of loans payable exceeds that of corresponding loans receivable, the net unrealized difference on exchange may be treated as a deferred charge.

As in the case of other provisions, those for risks and charges (losses) should not exceed what is necessary.

Inventories   The valuation basis for inventories is the cost of acquisition or production except if this exceeds the market price, in which case the latter is to be used (the principle of the lower of cost or market value). The cost of acquisition includes the purchase price and any expenditure incurred directly or indirectly to place the item in its present state and location. The cost of production includes that of raw materials, direct labor, variable manufacturing costs plus fixed manufacturing costs necessarily incurred to produce the item and place it in its present state and location. Fixed manufacturing costs can be imputed to cost of production, taking account of the normal capacity of the means of production. Costs of distribution or of general administration and financial costs are not to be incorporated in cost of production.

Obsolescence, physical deterioration, a fall in price, or analogous factors are to be dealt with according to the principle of the lower of cost or market value.

By-products, scrap, and other such items are valued, in the absence of better criteria, at their net realizable value.

Market price is to be understood as replacement cost for goods acquired for production, and as net realizable value for goods acquired for sale.

The following cost-flow conventions are permitted: specific cost, weighted average, FIFO, LIFO, and standard cost. Standard cost may be used if it is checked and, if necessary, adjusted in accordance with accepted accounting principles. Adjustments should be made to take account of confirmed variances.

In the case of agricultural, livestock, and forestry operations, if the determination of production cost is too difficult, the following criterion may be used in valuing inventory: net relizable value less the normal profit margin. The same criterion may also be used in the extractive and fishing industries.

Merchandise inventories in retail sales establishments, when the variety of such items is great, may also be valued at net selling price less the profit margins included in such prices. Cash and carry establishments that predominantly sell small quantities of each type of merchandise to small retailers may also be considered retail sales establishments for the present purpose.

In the case of work-in-process under long-term contracts, either the percentage of completion method or the completed contract method may be used.

Raw materials and consumables may be accounted for by using the base stock method at a fixed quantity and value, provided the following conditions are satisfied: they turn over frequently; they represent an overall value of relatively little importance for the business; and there are no significant variations in quantity, value, or composition.

Fixed Assets   Fixed assets are to be valued at cost of acquisition or production. Such cost is to be determined by using the same principles as those for inventories. However, it may include financial costs associated with the financing of fixed assets, insofar as these are incurred during the period in which the fixed asset was in the course of purchase or production. In the case in which parts of an asset in the course of construction come into service at different dates, financial costs should cease to be imputed to each part as soon as it comes into service.

Fixed assets having a limited useful life must be written off systematically over that life.

The POC refers to the capitalization of finance leases, in the detailed comments on Class 4 of the Chart of Accounts. It is envisaged that finance leases will be capitalized using the approach of the IAS 17/FAS-13, but the implementation of this was delayed pending the revision of the accounting plan applicable to financial institutions until January 1, 1994.[1]

In the case of financial fixed assets, if at the balance sheet date the market value of such an asset is less than its book value, the latter may be reduced accordingly by using the appropriate account. This provision should be reversed as soon as the loss of value ceases to be confirmed.

The item investments include undertakings in group companies, associated companies, and others, as well as bonds and other securities held for more than one year. It also includes land and property (real estate) held as a financial investment.

It is important to note that this item does not include own shares (which are recorded in the liabilities side of the balance sheet, in the equity).

The equity method is also valid, as an option, for the valuation of group and associated companies undertakings, according to the most recent version of POC, dated July 1991.

Also, in a few cases, the increase of the nominal capital of the participated company through the incorporation of reserves is recorded in the asset of the participating company up to the nominal value of the percentage of capital held.

In the case of tangible or intangible fixed assets, whether or not they have a limited useful life, if at the balance sheet date their value is less than the corresponding book value, and it is expected that this loss of value will be permanent, a write-off equal to the loss of value should be made. This exceptional depreciation should be reversed if the reason for its being made no longer applies.

Organization costs and research and development costs may be capitalized but must normally be written off over a maximum of 5 years. Departures from this must be disclosed in the notes.

Goodwill and short-term lease premiums should be written off over a maximum period of 5 years, but this period may be prolonged, provided it does not exceed the asset's useful life.

Although the fundamental accounting principles described in Section 4 of the POC envisage the use of cost in terms of "constant escudos," nothing further is said about this in the POC's rules for fixed assets. The tax law, however, permits the revaluation of fixed assets by using coefficients based on the consumer price index (see Section 3.5.3, below), so one may suppose that the reference to the use of constant escudos in Section 4 of the POC is intended to bring this within the ambit of accounting principles.

Accruals and Deferrals   The POC uses the deferred accounts to record revenues and expenses that arise in one accounting period but that will be allocated to the profit and loss account in a different period. They are specific kinds of assets and liabilities (prepayments, deferrals, and accruals) and are not the same as ordinary creditors or debtors.

On the assets side, the deferred item is subdivided into revenues received in advance and deferred charges. The POC requires deferred charges to appear before liquid assets, at the foot of the balance sheet. Examples include, among others, interest to be received on long-term receivables, discounts arising on bond issues, and redemption premiums on bond issues.

On the liabilities side, the deferred item is subdivided into prepaid expenses and accrued expenses of the current year that will be paid in the future. The POC requires accrued expenses to appear at the bottom of the liabilities side of the balance sheet. These items include interest to be paid and insurance premiums received in advance.

3.4 Group Accounts

With regard to consolidated accounts, the most recent amendment to the Official Accounting Plan, approved on July 2, 1991, made it mandatory for all groups controlled by a parent company to consolidate. Some groups are exempted, however, for reasons of size or because they belong to consolidated larger groups with parent companies in EC member countries. In any case, the parent companies of listed groups must always present their consolidated annual accounts.

Provisions implementing the requirements of the Seventh Directive regarding the audit and publication of consolidated accounts, and laying down requirements for an annual management report on group activities, are included in the legislation already published.

Regulations on group accounts were added to the POC, in the revision of July 1991, as Chapter 13, "Methods and Procedures for Group Accounting," and Chapter 14, "Group Financial Statements."

3.4.1 Scope of Application

The scope of application is the same as that laid down in the Seventh Directive. SAs and Ldas must prepare consolidated accounts, subject to criteria stated below. The size criteria below which an entity is exempted from the requirement, provide it has not exceeded two out of the three during two successive financial years, are: total assets: 1,500 million escudos; total turnover: 3,000 million escudos; number of employees: 250. These size exemptions do not apply to groups, however, if one or more of their member companies are listed on any EC stock exchange.

The Seventh Directive's exemption of subgroups, when the ultimate "parent" company prepares consolidated accounts under EC Seventh Directive, also applies, subject to the same conditions. The general rule is that subsidiaries are to be consolidated by using full consolidation and associated companies included by using the equity method. Proportional consolidation may be used for joint ventures as an alternative to the equity method. The method of full consolidation mentioned in the POC is the "acquisition" or "purchase" method described in the Directive.

As required by the Seventh Directive, subsidiaries must be excluded from consolidation if their activities are of such a different nature from those of the rest of the group that their inclusion would militate against a true and fair view. In such cases, the equity method should be used.

An optional exclusion exists on grounds of materiality; however, the materiality of companies excluded under this rule must be considered as a whole, not individually. A further optional exclusion exists in the case of subsidiaries in foreign countries over which the group's control is restricted by the policies of the governments of those countries. A subsidiary may also be excluded from consolidation if it is impossible to obtain any accounts from it without disproportionate expense or undue delays. Subsidiaries may also be excluded if the interest in them is held on a short-term basis only.

3.4.2 Methods and Procedures for Group Accounts

According to Chapter 13 of the POC, the following points are to be considered when preparing consolidated accounts:

Consolidated Financial Statements   Consolidated financial statements should comprise a balance sheet, a profit and loss statement, and notes to the accounts (annex), and these documents should make up a composite whole. The preparation of a statement of sources and applications of funds is also recommended, although the POC does not provide any format for it. The methods and procedures of consolidation must be applied consistently from one financial year to the next.

Objective of Group Accounts   The objective is to give a true and fair view of the assets, liabilities, financial position, and profit or loss of the undertakings included in the consolidation taken as a whole. The annex should be used to disclose information related to this objective.

Date of Group Accounts   The group accounts should be drawn up as of the same date as the annual accounts of the parent undertaking, except that another date may be considered in order to take account of the largest number or the most important of the undertakings included in the consolidation.

Changes in the Scope of the Consolidation   If the composition of the undertakings included in the consolidation has changed significantly in the course of a financial year, additional information must be given (in either the balance sheet or the annex) in order to provide the necessary comparability.

Consolidation Method   The full or global method is the rule in the case of subsidiaries. This is the line-by-line method, with assets, liabilities, income, and expense being included in full and with minority interests (*interesses minoritários*) being shown where appropriate. (See below for the treatment of associated companies).

Valuation Criteria   Valuation criteria should conform to the criteria laid down by the POC (as described above) and be the same as those used in the annual accounts of the parent undertaking. If necessary, consolidating adjustments should be made to the figures of companies being consolidated in order to meet these criteria.

Differences in Taxes   Account shall be taken in the consolidated financial statements of any difference arising on consolidation between the tax *chargeable* for the financial year and for the preceding financial years and the amount of tax p*aid* or *payable* in respect of those years.

Eliminations   The POC follows Article 26 of the Seventh Directive and requires elimination of debts and claims between undertakings included in the consolidation, of income and expense relating to transactions between those undertakings, and of profits and losses from such transactions included in the book values of assets. The "prudence principle" applies; also, derogation from the need to eliminate may be accepted if elimination would involve undue expense or if the transaction giving rise to the profit or loss originated outside the group.

3.4.3 Associated Companies

The proportional consolidation, as in a number of countries, is reserved for joint ventures.

According to the POC, the method of proportional consolidation (line-by-line) may be used if an undertaking included in a consolidation manages another undertaking jointly with one or more undertakings not included in that consolidation. In that case, the inclusion of that other undertaking in the consolidated accounts may be in proportion to the rights in its capital held by the undertaking included in the consolidation.

3.4.4 Transitional Provisions

According to the POC, when a participating interest in an undertaking is first included in a consolidation, the amount to be included in the consolidated balance sheet is equal to the capital and reserves of the undertaking, and the difference between that amount and the book value of the participating interest in the parent's accounts (i.e., goodwill) should be disclosed separately within the equity capital in the consolidated balance sheet at the relevant date. The treatment of goodwill according to the POC was given in Section 3.3.5.

3.4.5 Structure of Group Financial Statements

As already noted, the group financial statements consist of a consolidated balance sheet, consolidated statement of profit and loss, and an annex (together with a funds statement if the recommendation given in the POC is followed). The required formats of these statements are essentially the same as those for the parent company (legal entity or "social") accounts, except that items relating to minority interests may appear in the group accounts.

3.5 The Impact of Tax Rules on Financial Accounting

3.5.1 Taxable Income

Traditionally, accounting in Portugal has been highly influenced by tax regulations. Indeed, the 1977 POC was quite related to the tax authorities and was designed more to facilitate tax inspections and to justify a company's income tax (because the basis for calculation of the tax is the income/profit from the accounting books) more than to disclose information to shareholders and to the public on the company's financial situation and operations report.

This tax orientation continued with the Companies Income Tax Code of 1988 that provides a set of rules for the valuation and recording of items in order to assess the taxable income.

In some cases, the tax rules do not differ from the accounting rules and only give more detail to them. For example, the tax treatment of inventories is the same in all material respects as that laid down in the POC, except for the matter of provisions for obsolescence, where the tax rules are much more detailed.

In other cases, the tax rules are opposite the accounting laws. This is the case for the depreciation of goodwill. The POC requires it to be written off, normally over 5 years but if explained in the notes up to 20 years. However, depreciation and other write-downs of goodwill are not tax deductible.

Portuguese tax rules affect financial accounting in the following areas: inventory valuation, revaluation of fixed assets, depreciation of fixed assets, provisions for loss of value of assets, confidential expenses, pension funds, and donations for cultural purposes.

Taxable income is based broadly on the net equity change during the tax period. It is the net result for the year shown in the financial statements, excluding capital increases, revaluation reserves, some equity increases, dividends, and capital decreases. For income tax computations, accounting income is subject to adjustments, namely, charges not accepted if above certain limits (including donations for cultural, scientific, and humanitarian purposes, depreciation, and provisions for doubtful debts and obsolete inventories), charges not accepted at all (such as real estate tax, fines related to infringement of laws, confidential expenses), and value adjustments (such as 95% of dividends from investments in subsidiaries and associated companies).

The adjusted accounting result is then reduced by the previous 5 years' losses brought forward. Adjustments related to tax incentives and tax credits from international bilateral tax agreements are also taken into consideration.

Deferred taxes are not accounted for under the POC, but all relevant situations that impact future taxes must be disclosed in the notes to the financial statements.

3.5.2 Inventory Valuation

The tax treatment of inventories is the same in all material respects as that laid down in the POC, except for the matter of provisions for obsolescence, where the tax rules are much more detailed (see under "Provisions" below).

3.5.3 Revaluation of Fixed Assets

The net book value of tangible operating fixed assets held on December 31, 1978, could be revalued on the basis of a set of prescribed price coefficients. This is optional, but in order to obtain the tax benefit of the additional depreciation, the revaluation and the additional depreciation thereon must be shown in the accounts. The first law permitting this expired in 1979, but since then a number of laws of limited duration have been introduced that allow revaluation of fixed assets by using prescribed price coefficients. The coefficients are based on the consumer price index and are published annually by the Ministry of Finance. However, only 60% of the additional annual depreciation is deductible for tax purposes, although all of the additional depreciation must be shown in the accounts.

3.5.4 Depreciation of Fixed Assets

Depreciation may be based on either the straight line or the declining balance method, but not the sum of years' digits method. For many categories of asset, the maximum and minimum straight-line depreciation rates are specified by the tax law, the minimum rates being 50% of the maxima. Some representative rates are given in Table 3. If companies charge less than the minimum rate, the difference is not allowable for tax purposes.

If the declining balance method is used, the corresponding straight-line rates are increased by the following coefficients: for useful lives of less than 5 years, 1.5; for useful lives of 5 or 6 years, 2.0; for useful lives of more than 6 years, 2.5.

Under some circumstances, companies may charge additional depreciation in respect of intensive use of assets. "Intensive use" is defined as using the assets for two or more shifts per day. Article 9 of the decree of January 12, 1990 allows the normal maximum rates to be increased by 25% in the case of two shifts, and 50% for more than two shifts. There are restrictions

---

TABLE 3   *Selected Percentage Depreciation Rates*

Buildings	
Commercial and administrative	2
Industrial	5
Hotels, restaurants, etc.	5
Fixtures	
Water, electrical, compressed air, refrigeration, and telephones	10
Machinery	
Electronic machines	20
Typewriters and other office machinery	20
Machine tools	
Light	20
Heavy	12.5
Vehicles	
Light	25
Heavy	20

The rates are generic for the assets indicated. In addition, there are a large number of rates for assets specific to particular industries (percentage).

on allowable depreciation for light vehicles (cars), the maximum depreciable value being 4 million escudos. For fixed assets of small value (less than 20,000 escudos), on the other hand, 100% write-off in the year of acquisition is allowable.

3.5.5 Provisions for Loss of Value of Assets

Financial Fixed Assets and Negotiable Securities   The treatment of financial fixed assets and negotiable securities required by the POC is not acceptable for tax purposes, as provisions for amortization or loss of value in respect of them are not tax-deductible, even though they may be required in order to give a true and fair view. For financial sector enterprises, such as banks and insurance companies, there are special tax rules, and in any case the accounting rules are not those in the POC.

Bad Debts   The tax law lays down the maximum allowable provisions for bad debts, on the basis of the age of the debts, varying from 25% for debts between 6 months and 1 year old to 100% for debts over 2 years old. To take full advantage of the tax deductions, it must be demonstrated that all reasonable efforts have been made to collect the items.

If a debtor is declared bankrupt during the year, amounts owed by that debtor are treated as losses for tax purposes and do not need to be provided for via the provisions account.

If a debtor holds 10% or more of the creditor company's share capital or is a company in which the creditor holds 10% or more of the share capital, then no bad debts provision is tax deductible. No bad debts provisions are tax deductible on accounts of amounts owed by government agencies.

Inventories   Deductible provisions for inventories are limited to the difference between the cost of acquisition or production and market value at the balance sheet date if lower. Market value is replacement cost for raw materials and selling price for finished goods. A special case exists for publishing companies, which may write off old editions that have been in stock for more than 2 years.

Goodwill   The POC requires goodwill to be written off, normally over 5 years, but over up to 20 years if this is explained in the notes. Amortization or other write-downs of goodwill are not tax deductible, however.

3.5.6 Pension Funds

In what refers to pensions, tax deduction is only allowed if the pension fund is not managed by the contributing company.

Costs of employers' contribution to employee pension funds, voluntary insurance of employees and similar expenses are tax deductible up to a maximum of 15% of salary costs.

3.5.7 Confidential Expenses

Confidential expenses (those authorized by management but not supported by business documents such as invoices, in other words, expenses of an undivulged nature) are subject to a 10% income tax in addition to normal taxation; this tax is payable even if the company pays no normal income tax or reports losses.

3.5.8 Donations for Cultural Purposes

Tax deductions in respect of donations for cultural purposes are limited to 0.2% of the turnover for the financial year, unless the recipient is the government or one of its agencies or branches, in which case the limit does not apply.

4. Expected Future Developments

The developments in Portuguese financial accounting and reporting that have been described in this chapter are related to the economic and political development of the country itself during the past 20 years. They also include a number of recent major changes resulting from Portugal's membership in the European Union and its implementation of the Fourth, Seventh, and Eighth Directives. These changes will need to be digested before any further significant developments can be expected. In general, the distinction between tax accounting and financial reporting has now been made, and one may anticipate the further development of financial reporting as an aid to financial analysis.

Portugal has influenced the taxation and accountancy concepts (and tax and accounting income concepts) adopted by the African Portuguese speaking countries, such as Angola, Mozambique, Guinea-Bissau, and Cabo Verde. Accounting and tax regulation in force in those African countries were inspired in Portuguese versions of the POC and income tax codes. The interchange with Brazil also has been quite important.

It is likely that while for the moment most people still associate annual accounts with taxation, perceptions will change in the longer term and group accounts will come to take on a much higher profile.

The main expected development would be that the practices of accountants will catch up with the legislative developments, and some consensus will emerge on the treatment such of items as leasing, goodwill, and deferred taxation in group accounts.

The forces that influence the disclosures of financial information by Portuguese companies have been mainly the legal environment, the tax regulation, and the stock exchange regulation. The influence of the accounting and auditing professions has not been important. International influence, traditionally from France, is being replaced by influence from the Anglo-Saxon countries and IAS, which are gaining more and more followers.

Notes

1. During 1982, the Bank of Portugal approved the first accounting plan (published in the Official Journal on September, 29, 1982) to be followed by Portuguese leasing companies. That plan set out the valuation rules and a chart of accounts. The 1982 accounting plan was recently replaced by another one, to apply from January 1, 1994 (*Carta- circular n° 71/N-DSB*, November 21st).

2. Companies incorporated in Portugal, and Portuguese branches of foreign companies, are subject to income tax on the results computed on 12 months ending on December 31. The tax year may be changed in special cases after the approval of the tax authorities.

Financial Statements of Companhìa Portuguesa Rádio Marconi, S.A.

BALANÇOS EM 31 DE DEZEMBRO DE 1993 E 1992

ACTIVO	Notas	1993 Activo Bruto	1993 Amortiz. Provisões	1993 Activo Líquido	1992
IMOBILIZADO					
Imobilizações Incorpóreas	10				
Despesas de Instalação		417 659	229 291	188 368	69 473
Desp. Invest. Desenvolvimento		29 325	17 584	11 741	5 602
Propr. Indúst. e Outros Direitos		313 642	195 070	118 572	111 772
Trespasses		37 500	37 500		9 375
Imobilizações em Curso		421 433		421 433	184 674
		1 219 559	479 445	740 114	380 896
Imobilizações Corpóreas	10				
Terrenos e Recursos Naturais		2 962 275		2 962 275	2 962 275
Edifícios e Outras Construções		8 758 888	511 816	8 247 072	8 363 834
Equipamento Básico		48 154 982	31 428 902	16 726 080	18 009 742
Equipamento de Transporte		167 744	120 017	47 727	42 477
Ferramentas e Utensílios		1 045 761	704 250	341 511	258 245
Equipamento Administrativo		4 171 486	2 928 857	1 242 629	1 697 416
Imobilizações em Curso		1 616 258		1 616 258	1 668 922
Adiant. P/Conta Imob. Corpóreas		7 642		7 642	18 821
		66 885 036	35 693 842	31 191 194	33 021 732
Investimentos Financeiros					
Partes Capital Empresas do Grupo	10/16	9 157 858	223 600	8 934 258	6 612 677
Empréstimos a Empresas do Grupo	10	4 424 885	963 496	3 461 389	1 894 212
Partes Capital Empr. Associadas	10/16	2 365 017		2 365 017	3 512 548
Títulos e Outras Aplic. Financeiras	10/16	1 280 664	771 786	508 878	846 587
Outros Empréstimos Concedidos					1 250 000
Adiant. P/Conta Invest. Financeiros	10	710 529		710 529	101 708
		17 938 953	1 958 882	15 980 071	14 217 732
CIRCULANTE					
Existências					
Mercadoria/Mat. Primas e Subsid.		81 515		81 515	88 871
		81 515		81 515	88 871
Dívidas de Terceiros a Médio e Longo Prazo					
Clientes C/C		715 558	150 000	565 558	
Outros Devedores		748 047	570 000	178 047	67 265
		1 463 605	720 000	743 605	67 265
Dívidas de Terceiros a Curto Prazo					
Clientes C/C		9 283 366	743 146	8 540 220	10 281 457
Clientes de Cobrança Duvidosa	23	6 521 478	5 756 254	765 224	790 759
Empresas do Grupo		3 255 750	125 970	3 129 780	3 335 147
Empresas Assoc. e Participadas		1 801 669	1 749 517	52 152	2 652 615
Restantes Accionistas		11 479		11 479	18 900
Adiantamentos a Fornecedores		2 644		2 644	25 726
Estados e Outros Entes Públicos					12
Outros Devedores	23	1 322 854	255 202	1 067 652	1 280 358
		22 199 240	8 630 089	13 569 151	18 384 974
Títulos Negociáveis					
Acções/Obrig./Outros Títulos		319 119	109 864	209 255	301 162
Outras Aplicações Tesouraria		2 525 000		2 525 000	
		2 844 119	109 864	2 734 255	301 162
Depósitos Bancários e Caixa					
Depósitos Bancários		196 512		196 512	292 271
Caixa		12 152		12 152	16 557
		208 664		208 664	308 828
Acréscimos e Diferimentos	49				
Acréscimos de Proveitos		185 339		185 339	199 089
Custos Diferidos		130 700		130 700	143 852
		316 039		316 039	342 941
TOTAL das AMORTIZAÇÕES			36 173 287		
TOTAL das PROVISÕES			11 418 835		
TOTAL do ACTIVO		113 156 730	47 592 122	65 564 608	67 114 401

(Valores em Milhares de Escudos)

BALANCE SHEET AS OF 31 DECEMBER 1993 AND 1992

ASSETS	Notes	1993 Gross Assets	1993 Depreciation Provisions	1993 Net Assets	1992
FIXED ASSETS					
Intangible Fixed Assets	10				
Installation costs		417 659	229 291	188 368	69 473
Research an development costs		29 325	17 584	11 741	5 602
Industrial property and other rights		313 642	195 070	118 572	111 772
Property transfers/goodwill		37 500	37 500		9 375
Fixed assets in progress		421 433		421 433	184 674
		1 219 559	479 445	740 114	380 896
Tangible Fixed Assets	10				
Real estate/Natural resources		2 962 275		2 962 275	2 962 275
Buildings and other premises		8 758 888	511 816	8 247 072	8 363 834
Basic equipment		48 154 982	31 428 902	16 726 080	18 009 742
Transport equipment		167 744	120 017	47 727	42 477
Tools and instruments		1 045 761	704 250	341 511	258 245
Administrative equipment		4 171 486	2 928 857	1 242 629	1 697 416
Fixed assets in progress		1 616 258		1 616 258	1 668 922
Prepayments on tangible fixed assets		7 642		7 642	18 821
		66 885 036	35 693 842	31 191 194	33 021 732
Financial Assets					
Investments in companies of the group	10/16	9 157 858	223 600	8 934 258	6 612 677
Loans to companies of the group	10	4 424 885	963 496	3 461 389	1 894 212
Investments in subsidiaries	10/16	2 365 017		2 365 017	3 512 548
Securities and other financial investments	10/16	1 280 664	771 786	508 878	846 587
Other loans granted					1 250 000
Prepayments on financial assets	10	710 529		710 529	101 708
		17 938 953	1 958 882	15 980 071	14 217 732
CURRENT ASSETS					
Stocks and raw materials		81 515		81 515	88 871
		81 515		81 515	88 871
Medium and Long Term Debtors					
Customers current account		715 558	150 000	565 558	
Other debtors		748 047	570 000	178 047	67 265
		1 463 605	720 000	743 605	67 265
Short term debtors					
Customers current account		9 283 366	743 146	8 540 220	10 281 457
Doubtful debts	23	6 521 478	5 756 254	765 224	790 759
Companies of the group		3 255 750	125 970	3 129 780	3 335 147
Subsidiary and participated companies		1 801 669	1 749 517	52 152	2 652 615
Other shareholders		11 479		11 479	18 900
Prepayments to suppliers		2 644		2 644	25 726
State and other public utilities					12
Other debtors	23	1 322 854	255 202	1 067 652	1 280 358
		22 199 240	8 630 089	13 569 151	18 384 974
Marketable					
Shares/ Bonds/ other securities		319 119	109 864	209 255	301 162
Other short investments		2 525 000		2 525 000	
		2 844 119	109 864	2 734 255	301 162
Cash and Banks					
Bank deposits		196 512		196 512	292 271
Cash		12 152		12 152	16 557
		208 664		208 664	308 828
Accruals and deferrements	49				
Accrued income		185 339		185 339	199 089
Deferred costs		130 700		130 700	143 852
		316 039		316 039	342 941
TOTAL DEPRECIATION			36 173 287		
TOTAL PROVISIONS/WRITE-OFFS			11 418 835		
TOTAL ASSETS		113 156 730	47 592 122	65 564 608	67 114 401

(Amounts expressed in thousand of escudos)

BALANÇOS EM 31 DE DEZEMBRO DE 1993 E 1992

CAPITAL PRÓPRIO e PASSIVO	Notas	1993	1992
CAPITAL PRÓPRIO			
Capital	35	15 600 000	15 600 000
Acções Próprias:	35		
Valor Nominal		(663 918)	(882 000)
Descontos e Prémios		(2 601 226)	(1 792 646)
Ajust. Partes Capital em Fil. Assoc.	10	2 081 000	
Reservas de Reavaliação	39	6 484 139	6 484 139
Reservas:			
Reservas Legais	40	5 744 825	6 153 054
Outras Reservas	40	15 421 732	12 471 959
		42 066 552	38 034 506
Resultados Líquidos		4 168 173	3 671 221
Total do Capital Próprio		46 234 725	41 705 727
PASSIVO			
Provisões p/ Riscos e Encargos:			
Provisões p/ Pensões	50	3 351 000	3 609 963
Provisões p/ Impostos		178 603	215 620
Outras Prov. p/ Riscos e Encargos	50	1 542 875	1 380 000
		5 072 478	5 205 583
Dívidas a Terceiros a Médio e Longo Prazo			
Dívidas a Instituições de Crédito	51	2 431 472	9 364 091
		2 431 472	9 364 091
Dívidas a Terceiros a Curto Prazo			
Dívidas a Instituições de Crédito	51	2 713 521	2 877 118
Fornecedores C/C		578 875	1 226 452
Fornecedores c/ Fact. Reconh. e Conferência		112 331	113 256
Empresas do Grupo		23 908	258 218
Empresas Assoc. e Participadas		4 103	
Restantes Accionistas		47 323	60 983
Outros Empréstimos Obtidos			
Fornecedores de Imobilizado C/C		835 815	777 857
Estado e Outros Entes Públicos	52	2 256 448	490 334
Clientes C/C com Saldos Credores		1 752 949	1 590 254
Outros Credores	53	861 412	1 669 940
		9 186 685	9 064 412
Acréscimos e Diferimentos	54		
Acréscimos de Custos		1 687 425	1 341 303
Proveitos Diferidos		951 823	433 285
		2 639 248	1 774 588
Total do Passivo		19 329 883	25 408 674
TOTAL do CAPITAL PRÓPRIO e do PASSIVO		65 564 608	67 114 401

(Valores em Milhares de Escudos)

BALANCE SHEET AS OF 31 DECEMBER 1993 AND 1992

EQUITY AND LIABILITIES	Notes	1993	1992
SHAREHOLDERS' EQUITY			
Issued share capital	35	15 600 000	15 600 000
Own shares	35		
Face value		(663 918)	(882 000)
Premiums and discounts		(2 601 226)	(1 792 646)
Adjust. in the % of Investments in Subsidiaries	10	2 081 000	
Revaluations reserves	39	6 484 139	6 484 139
Reserves:			
Legal reserves	40	5 744 825	6 153 054
Other reserves	40	15 421 732	12 471 959
		42 066 552	38 034 506
Net Profit		4 168 173	3 671 221
Total Shareholders' Equity		46 234 725	41 705 727
LIABILITIES			
Provisions for liabilities and charges			
Provisions for retirements benefits	50	3 351 000	3 609 963
Provisions for corporation tax		178 603	215 620
Other provisions	50	1 542 875	1 380 000
		5 072 478	5 205 583
Medium and Long Term Creditors			
Bank loans and overdrafts	51	2 431 472	9 364 091
		2 431 472	9 364 091
Short Term Creditors			
Amount owed to credit institutions	51	2 713 521	2 877 118
Suppliers/current account		578 875	1 226 452
Other suppliers/invoices received		112 331	113 256
Group companies		23 908	258 218
Subsidiary companies		4 103	
Other shareholders		47 323	60 983
Other Loans			
Fixed assets suppliers/current account		835 815	777 857
State and other public utilities	52	2 256 448	490 334
Trade creditors		1 752 949	1 590 254
Other creditors	53	861 412	1 669 940
		9 186 685	9 064 412
Accruals and deferred income	54		
Accrued charges		1 687 425	1 341 303
Deferred income		951 823	433 285
		2 639 248	1 774 588
Total Liabilities		19 329 883	25 408 674
TOTAL SHAREHOLDER'S EQUITY and LIABILITIES		65 564 608	67 114 401

(Amounts expressed in thousands of escudos)

DEMONSTRAÇÃO DE RESULTADOS PARA OS EXERCÍCIOS FINDOS EM 31 DE DEZEMBRO DE 1993 E 1992

CUSTOS e PERDAS	Notas	1993		1992	
Fornecimentos e Serviços Externos					
Subcontractos Telecomunicações		17 225 801		14 786 694	
Serviços de Telecomunicações		2 967 714		2 060 072	
Fornecimentos e Serviços		3 571 511	23 765 027	3 859 750	20 706 516
Custos com Pessoal	55				
Renumerações		5 949 503		5 580 817	
Encargos Sociais/ Pensões		756 854		505 431	
Encargos Sociais/ Outros		1 588 050	8 294 407	2 043 213	8 129 461
Amortizações do Imob. Corp. e Incorpóreo	10	4 993 904		4 488 324	
Provisões	34	1 766 225	6 760 129	140 000	4 628 324
Impostos	56	413 869		57 870	
Outros Custos e Perdas Operacionais		105 440	519 308	492 658	550 528
(A)			39 338 872		34 014 829
Custos e Perdas Financeiros	45				
Perdas em Empresas do Grupo e Associadas		1 197 155			
Amortiz. Provisões Aplic. e Inv. Financeiros		690 819		669 690	
Diferenças de Câmbio Desfavoráveis		2 282 714		1 436 290	
Juros e Custos Similares		526 371	4 697 059	1 383 543	3 489 524
(C)			44 035 931		37 504 353
Custos e Perdas Extraordinários	46		3 745 627		2 308 446
(E)			47 781 558		39 812 799
Impostos S/ Rendimento do Exercício	52		2 750 000		2 019 000
(G)			50 531 558		41 831 799
RESULTADO LÍQUIDO do EXERCÍCIO			4 168 173		3 671 221
			54 699 731		45 503 021

PROVEITOS e GANHOS					
Prestação de Serviços	44				
Serviços-Telecomunicações Principais		45 461 525		39 324 172	
Serviços-Telecomunicações Secundários		1 032 360	46 493 885	838 965	40 163 137
Trabalhos para a Própria Empresa		265 104		360 036	
Proveitos Suplementares		1 037 524		1 348 611	
Subsídios à Exploração		96 327		35 155	
Outros Proveitos Operacionais		945	1 399 900	11 620	1 755 422
(B)			47 893 785		41 918 559
Proveitos Financeiros	45				
Ganhos em Empresas do Grupo e Associadas		865 778			
Rendimento de Participações de Capital		528 932		293 348	
Rendimento de Tit. Negociáveis/Outras Aplicações		669 804		893 366	
Diferenças de Câmbio Favoráveis		2 857 472		1 258 317	
Outros Juros e Proveitos Similares		102 375	5 024 361	10 518	2 455 549
(D)			52 918 146		44 374 108
Proveitos e Ganhos Extraordinários	46		1 781 585		1 128 912
(F)			54 699 731		45 503 021

RESUMO				
Resultados Operacionais	(B) - (A) =		8 554 913	7 903 730
Resultados Financeiros	(D-B) - (C-A) =		327 302	(1 033 974)
Resultados Correntes	(D) - (C) =		8 882 215	6 869 755
Resultados Antes Impostos	(F) - (E) =		6 918 173	5 690 221
Resultado Líquido do Exercício	(F) - (G) =		4 168 173	3 671 221

(Valores em Milhares de Escudos)

PROFIT AND LOSS ACCOUNT AS OF 31 DECEMBER 1993 AND 1992

Costs and losses	Notes	1993		1992	
Third party services					
Subcontracts Telecommunications		17 225 801		14 786 694	
Telecommunications Services		2 967 714		2 060 072	
Services and Supplies		3 571 511	23 765 027	3 859 750	20 706 516
Staff Costs	55				
Wages and Salaries		5 949 503		5 580 817	
Social Security Costs/Pensions Funds		756 854		505 431	
Social Security/Welfare		1 588 050	8 294 407	2 043 213	8 129 461
Depreciation on Assets	10	4 993 904		4 488 324	
Provisions	34	1 766 225	6 760 129	140 000	4 628 324
Taxes	56	413 869		57 870	
Other operating costs and losses		105 440	519 308	492 658	550 528
(A)			39 338 872		34 014 829
Interest payable and similar charges	45				
Losses from Group Companies and Subsidiaries		1 197 155			
Write-offs on Investments		690 819		669 690	
Exchange Rate Losses		2 282 714		1 436 290	
Other Financial Costs		526 371	4 697 059	1 383 543	3 489 524
(C)			44 035 931		37 504 353
Extraordinary costs and Losses	46		3 745 627		2 308 446
(E)			47 781 558		39 812 799
Taxes on Profit	52		2 750 000		2 019 000
(G)			50 531 558		41 831 799
NET PROFIT FOR the FINANCIAL YEAR			4 168 173		3 671 221
			54 699 731		45 503 021

INCOME					
Services Supplied	44				
Services Supplied-Main Telecommunications		45 461 525		39 324 172	
Services Supplied-Secondary Telecommunications		1 032 360	46 493 885	838 965	40 163 137
Own Work		265 104		360 036	
Other income		1 037 524		1 348 611	
Subsidies		96 327		35 155	
Other operating Income		945	1 399 900	11 620	1 755 422
(B)			47 893 785		41 918 559
Financial Income	45				
Profits from Group Companies and Subsidiaries		865 778			
Income From Share Capital Holdings		528 932		293 348	
Income from Marketable Securities and other Investments		669 804		893 366	
Exchange Rate Gains		2 857 472		1 258 317	
Other interest and Similar Income		102 375	5 024 361	10 518	2 455 549
(D)			52 918 146		44 374 108
Extraordinary Income	46		1 781 585		1 128 912
(F)			54 699 731		45 503 021

SUMMARY			
Operational Profits	(B) - (A) =	8 554 913	7 903 730
Financial Profit	(D-B) - (C-A) =	327 302	(1 033 974)
Current Profit	(D) - (C) =	8 882 215	6 869 755
Profit Before Tax	(F) - (E) =	6 918 173	5 690 221
Net Profit	(F) - (G) =	4 168 173	3 671 221

(Amounts expressed in thousands of escudos)

DEMONSTRAÇÃO DOS FLUXOS DE CAIXA DO ANO FINDO EM 31 DE DEZEMBRO DE 1993 (método indirecto)

	1993

ACTIVIDADES OPERACIONAIS

Resultado Líquido do Exercício	4 168 173

Ajustamentos:

Amortizações	4 993 904
Provisões	3 084 036
Resultados Financeiros	943 906
Diminuição das Dívidas de Terceiros	1 421 285
Diminuição das Existências	7 356
Aumento das Dívidas a Terceiros	466 174
Diminuição dos Proveitos Diferidos	67 385
Aumento dos Acréscimos de Proveitos	13 750
Diminuição dos Custos Diferidos	300 626
Aumento dos Acréscimos de Custos	346 121
Ganhos na Alienação de Imobilizações	(1 231 895)
Perdas na Alienação de Imobilizações	15 435
Trabalhos para a Própria Empresa	(265 104)

Fluxos das Actividades Operacionais (1)		14 331 154

ACTIVIDADES DE INVESTIMENTO

Recebimentos Provenientes de:

Investimentos Financeiros	1 463 931	
Imobilizações Corpóreas	1 787 230	
Subsídios de Investimento	358 451	
Juros e Proveitos Similares	853 431	
Dividendos	38 787	4 501 830

Pagamentos Respeitantes a:

Investimentos Financeiros	1 529 329	
Imobilizações Corpóreas	3 685 461	
Imobilizações Incorpóreas	301 768	5 516 558

Fluxos das Actividades de Investimento (2)		(1 014 728)

ACTIVIDADES DE FINANCIAMENTO

Recebimentos Provenientes de:

Empréstimos Obtidos	1 762 147	
Venda de Acções Próprias	3 680 714	5 442 861

Pagamentos Respeitantes a:

Empréstimos Obtidos	10 595 035	
Juros e Custos Similares	449 498	
Dividendos	2 372 984	
Aquisição de Acções Próprias	3 035 740	16 453 257

Fluxos das Actividades de Financiamento (3)		(11 010 396)

Variação de Caixa e Seus Equivalentes (4) = (1 + 2 + 3)	2 306 030
Efeito das Diferenças de Câmbio	118 806
Caixa e seus Equivalentes no Início do Período	308 828
Caixa e seus Equivalentes no Fim do Período	2 733 664

(Valores em Milhares de Escudos)

CASH FLOW AS OF 31 DECEMBER 1993 (Indirect Method)

	1993
OPERATIONAL ACTIVITIES	
Net Profit For the Year	4 168 173
Adjustments:	
Depreciation	4 993 904
Provisions	3 084 036
Financial Profits	943 906
Reduction in Debtors	1 421 285
Reduction in Stocks	7 356
Increase in Creditors	466 174
Reduction in Deferred Income	67 385
Increase in Accrued Income	13 750
Reduction in Deferred Costs	300 626
Increase in Accrued Charges	346 121
Capital Gains on the Sale of Fixed Assets	(1 231 895)
Capital Losses on the Sale of Fixed Assets	15 435
Work for Own Assets	(265 104)
Total Cash Flow from Operational Activities (1)	14 331 154
INVESTMENT ACTIVITIES	
Income From:	
Financial Investments	1 463 931
Tangible Fixed Assets	1 787 230
Investment Subsidies	358 451
Interest and Other Similar Income	853 431
Dividends	38 787
	4 501 830
Payments Relating to:	
Financial Investments	1 529 329
Tangible Fixed Assets	3 685 461
Intangible Fixed Assets	301 768
	5 516 558
Cash Flow from Investment Activities(2)	(1 014 728)
FINANCING ACTIVITIES	
Income From:	
Loans	1 762 147
Sale of Own Shares	3 680 714
	5 442 861
Payments relating to:	
Loans	10 595 035
Interest and Other Similar Charges	449 498
Dividends	2 372 984
Acquisitions of Own Shares	3 035 740
	16 453 257
Cash Flow from Financing Activities (3)	(11 010 396)
Changes in Cash Flow and its Equivalent(4) = (1 + 2 + 3)	2 306 030
Exchange Rate Differences	118 806
Cash Flow and its Equivalent at the Start of the Period	308 828
Cash Flow and its equivalent at the end of the Period	2 733 664

(Amounts expressed in thousand of escudos)

NOTES TO THE CASH FLOW STATEMENT AS OF 31 DECEMBER 1993

1. Aquisition or Sale of Subsidiaries

The amounts involved were not relevant.

2. Breakdown of the Cash and Similar items

The amounts relating to "Marketable Securities" are net of Provisions which amounted to 109, 864 thousand escudos as

(Amounts expressed in thousand of escudos)

	1993	1992
Cash	12 152	16 557
Demand Deposite	196 512	292 271
Cash Equivalents	2 525 000	
Cash and Similar Items	2 733 664	308 828
Other deposit:		
Marketable Securities	209 255	301 162
Balance Sheet Cash and Banks	2 942 919	609 990

of 31 December 1993 and to 70, 029 thousand escudos as of 31 December 1992.

3. Non Monetary Financial Activities

There was an international short term credit line of 1 million escudos. As of 31 December 1993, 17.7 million escudos had been used.
Marconi has not used other credit lines offered by the banks.

4. Breakdown of Cash Flow by Activity and Geographical Areas

The "Income" and "Payments" amounts stated in this note are not comparable to those described in Note nr.44 to the financial statements as of 31 December 1993.
Income and Payments in the Cash Flow statement are stated at net value but include VAT.

5. Other Information

There is no other relevant information necessary to understand the Cash Flow Statement.

NOTES TO THE FINANCIAL STATEMENTS AS OF DECEMBER 31, 1993

(All values reported in the notes with no indication of monetary unit are stated in thousands of escudos)

(Amounts expressed in thousand of escudos)

	Internal Market	External Market	Total
Income:			
Main Telecommunications			
Services	6 983 985	33 120 415	40 104 400
Secondary Services	281 277	447 961	729 238
	7 265 262	33 568 376	40 833 638
Payments:			
Main Telecommunications			
Services	316 703	7 008 461	7 325 164
Secondary Services	6 267	291 112	297 379
	322 970	7 299 573	7 622 543
TOTAL	6 942 292	26 268 803	33 211 095

1. Intruductory Note

Activity

Companhia Portuguesa Rádio Marconi, S.A. ("The Company") was awarded an exclusive concession contract by the Portuguese Government to run national and international telecommunication systems in Portugal. The original concession contract expired in 1966. It was then renewed twice, firstly up to 31 December 1991 and after that up until 31 December 2001.
Under the terms of the concession contract, the net profit for the year is allocated as follows:
- 5% for legal reserve
- 7% of the share capital as first dividend
- 25% of the balance remaining after the first two appropriations for the State
- the remaining net balance - to be decided by the Annual General Meeting.

Note Numbers

The notes presented below are in compliance with the numbering laid down by the Official Accounting Plan. The missing numbers refer to notes which are neither applicable nor relevant to the financial statements.

3. Main Accounting Principles and Policies

a) Accounting Principles

The financial statements were prepared in accordance with the accounting principles laid down in the Official Accounting Plan. Thus, they were prepared using the historical cost accounting principle, except for the change in revaluation of tangible fixed assets, and in conformity with the generally accepted accounting principles applied consistently, continuously and on an accrual and conservative basis.

b) Intangible Fixed Assets

These are stated at cost and the respective depreciation is calculated using the straight line method at a 33.33% rate.

c) Tangible Fixed Assets

These are stated at cost or revaluation value, in accordance with current legislation. The last revaluation was carried out under the terms of Decree-Law Nr.264/92 of 24 November and stated in the 1991 accounts.

All major repairs and improvements are capitalized. All maintenance and repair costs are stated as costs in the financial year in which they were incurred.

Depreciation is calculated using the straight line method on the revaluation or acquisition value in order fully to depreciate the value of the assets by the end of the expected useful life or by the end of the concession contract, whichever is more appropriate, as can be seen from the following table:

	Annual Depreciation Rate
Building and other premises (which will not be handed back to the State at the end of the concession period)	2 e 5
Basic equipment	
Stations and premise Radioelectric	18,75
Satellite stations	6,66 - 9,09
Submarine Cables	5 - 9,09
Transport equipment	25
Tools and Instruments	25
Administrative equipment	12,5 - 25

d) Financial Investments

Financial investments in companies of the group or subsidiaries are calculated using the Equity method, and are initially stated at cost. This figure is adjusted by the value corresponding to the percentage in net profits or other charges in the Shareholder's Equity of aforementioned companies respectively. Profits channelled to subsidiaries, as dividends or profits, are deducted from the value of the financial investment at the date of the operation.

The remaining financial investments are stated at cost. Provisions have been set up to cover potential losses. Income is stated in the profit and loss account for the respective year.

In accordance with current legislation the Company prepares the consolidated accounts of the Marconi Group.

e) Financial Leasing

Equipment on lease as well as payments are not stated in the Balance Sheet. Payments on leased equipment are stated in the Profit and Loss Accounts.

f) Stocks

Stocks are stated at average cost which is lower than the respective market value.

g) Foreign Currency

All assets and liabilities in foreign currency are stated in Escudos at the exchange rate in force at 31 December 1993.

Exchange rate losses or gains caused by changes in the exchange rates at the date of the operations, at the date of payments received or at the Balance Sheet date are stated as Costs or Income in the Profit and Loss Account.

h) Marketable Securities

These are stated at cost. A provision is set up to cover potential losses. Income is stated in the profit and loss account for the respective financial year, except in the case of dividends from shares, which are only stated when received.

i) Own Shares

These are stated at cost. The cost of the sales of own shares is calculated on a F.I.F.O. basis. Capital gains from the sale of own shares are stated in free reserves.

j) Pensions and Medical Treatment

The Company has its own Social security regime - "Caixa de Previdência do Pessoal da Companhia Portuguesa Rádio Marconi" - an independent body part of the Public Social Security system.

The Company and its staff make regular payments, which vary according to the wages and salaries paid to the employees, in accordance with applicable legislation. The Company's Social Security Fund pays the staff's retirement pensions.

The Company also pays its staff retirement and survival pensions as a complement to retirement pensions paid by Social Security (it also pays pensions to the widows/widowers of retired employees).

In accordance with an actuarial study undertaken in 1991, the Company set up provisions to cover existing liabilities and delivered regular payments from 1987 onwards to a Pension Fund. As a result, all liabilities are now fully covered.

In accordance with regulations in force, the Company also contributes towards the costs of Medical Treatment and prescription drugs, which are stated as costs in the Profit and Loss Account for the respective financial year (see note55).

k) Traffic Revenue and Costs

Traffic revenue and costs referring to the last quarter of the financial year are normally based on estimated values, which are then corrected in the following year after the final figures have become available. Usually these changes are not significant.

l) Research and Development

General Research and Development costs are stated in the profit and loss account for the year in which they were incurred. Research and Development costs related to specific projects are capitalized as intangible fixed assets.

m) Accruals and Deferrements

The Company includes in this account the following transactions:

- Expenses and Revenues, from several financial years, which are stated as Costs and Income for each one of those financial years at their respective value;
- Subsidies granted for the acquisition of tangible fixed assets are stated as Deferred Income and included in the Profit and Loss Account. The amount is in proportion to the depreciation on subsidized tangible Fixed Assets;
- Holiday pay already earned but not yet paid;
- Interest payments overdue and not yet paid.

4. Exchange Rates Used

The exchange rates used to state the foreign currency accounts in Portuguese escudos were those published by the Bank of Portugal as of 31 December 1993.

7. Company Staff

The average number of people working for the company at the 1993 year end was 1283.

8. Setting Up and Research and Development Costs

Setting up costs include costs related with shares issues and the costs of studies and projects related to company organization.

Given the high level of technology on which the company's activities are based, all research and development costs are stated as costs in the financial year (1993: 608 million escudos) with the exception of costs relating to specific projects which are capitalized as intangible fixed assets.

10. Tangible and Intangible Fixed Assets and Financial Investments

Changes in tangible fixed assets, intangible fixed assets and financial investments, their respective depreciation and provisions are described in the following table:

DEPRECIATION

Items	Initial Balance	Increases	Transfers and Write-offs	Final balance
Intangible fixed assets				
Setting up costs	103 652	139 219	13 580	229 291
Research and development costs	7 809	9 775		17 584
Industrial property and other rights	215 295	104 547	124 772	195 070
Transfers of property/goodwill	28 124	9 376		37 500
	354 880	262 917	138 352	479 445
Tangible fixed assets				
Building and other premises	342 328	169 488		511 816
Basic telecommunications equipment	30 743 552	3 817 726	3 132 376	31 428 902
Tranport equipment	117 252	25 962	23 198	120 017
Tools and instruments	538 918	177 380	12 048	704 250
Administrative equipment	2 441 348	540 431	52 922	2 928 857
	34 183 398	4 730 987	3 220 544	35 693 842

GROSS ASSETS

Items	Initial Balance	Increases	Sales	Tranfers and Write-offs	Final Balance
Intangible fixed assets					
Setting up Costs	173 125	258 113		13 580	417 658
Research and Development Costs	13 411	15 915			29 325
Industrial Property and Other Rights	327 067	111 348		124 772	313 642
Tranfers of Property/Goodwill	37 500				37 500
Intangible Fixed assets in Progress	184 673	236 759			421 433
	735 776	622 135		138 352	1 219 559
Tangible fixed assets					
Real Estate and Natural Resources	2 962 275				2 962 275
Buildings and Other Premises	8 706 162	52 726			8 758 888
Basic telecommunications equipment	48 753 293	2 584 994	3 121 350	61 955	48 154 982
Transport equipment	159 729	41 331	29 326	3 991	167 743
Tools and instruments	797 163	262 057	11 345	2 114	1 045 761
Administrative equipment	4 138 765	110 409	67 857	9 830	4 171 487
Fixed assets in Progress	1 668 922	1 294 171		1 346 835	1 616 258
Prepayments on tangible fixed assets	18 821	7 597		18 776	7 642
	67 205 130	4 353 285	3 229 878	1 443 501	66 885 036

FINANCIAL INVESTMENTS AND PROVISIONS

Items	Initial balance	Asset equivalent effect	Increases	Sales	Transfers and Write-offs	Final Balance
Financial Investments						
Share Capital - Group Subsidiaries	6 612 677	2 651 909	16 908	(147 344)	23 708	9 157 858
Share Capital - Other Subsidiaries	3 512 548	(902 286)	542	(207 000)	(38 787)	2 365 017
Other financial investments	2 725 794		10 430	(1 250 000)	(205 560)	1 280 664
Financial loans - Companies of the Group	1 894 212		2 465 673		65 000	4 424 885
Prepayments on financial investments	101 708		710 529	(13 000)	(88 708)	710 529
	14 846 939	1 749 623	3 204 082	(1 617 344)	(244 347)	17 938 953
Provisions	629 207		1 332 735		(3 060)	1 958 882
	14 217 732					15 980 071

a) Basic equipment includes submarine cables, satellites and radio electric systems as well as the respective land, buildings and premises and also capital contributions to international satellite telecommunications organizations (Intelsat, Eutelsat and Inmarsat). These investments are stated as tangible fixed assets as they might be transferred to the State at the end of the concession period, and so are fully depreciated at the end of the same period.

Basic equipment is as follows:

	Gross Value	Depreciation	Net Value
Station and Premises Conventional Radioelectric	10 753 949	7 439 741	3 314 208
Satellites	17 842 423	12 828 864	5 013 559
Submarines cables	19 558 610	11 160 297	8 398 313
	48 154 982	31 428 902	16 726 080

b) The Company agreed to convey the operation of the ATLAS submarine cable system, the net value of which is included in basic equipment and amounts to approximately 390.038 thousand escudos.

c) As indicated in Note 3 (c), the Company decided fully to depreciate assets at the end of the expected useful life or at the end of the concession period, whichever is more appropriate. However, as regards stations and satellite and submarine cable premises the concession period is shorter than the expected useful life period of the respective assets. As a result depreciation for the year has been increased by approximately 273.199 thousand escudos in relation to the depreciation which would have been stated had the assets been depreciated at the end of their expected useful life.

d) As a result of the application of the Equity method, the "Adjustments to Share Capital" and the "Investments in Share Capital" accounts increased respectively by 2,081,000 thousand escudos and 1,750,753 thousand escudos. Profits for the year fell by 330,247 thousand escudos.

The most significant contribution to this profit was the 850,000 thousand escudo loss made by TMN - Telecomunicações Móveis Nacionais, S.A., and the 580,000 thousand escudo profit made by SGPS - Comunicações and other international telecommunications companies.

The application of the Equity method as of 31 December 1993 (Profits and Shareholders' Equity), was done on the basis of the latest figures known for each of the companies at the year end.

e) The value of "tangible work in progress" corresponds to the acquisition of capacity on submarine cable systems (1,331,134 thousand escudos) and to the development of community projects in the field of intangible Research and Development (approximately 400 million escudos).

f) The value of the sale of tangible fixed assets corresponds to the sale of basic telecommunications equipment which has already been fully depreciated.

12. Revaluation of Tangible Fixed Assets

Tangible fixed assets as of 31 December 1991 have been revaluated in compliance with the terms of decree-law 264/92 of 24 November.

13. Historical Cost of Tangible Fixed Assets

Detailed below is a comparison between the book value and the historical cost value of fixed assets:

Items	Historical Costs	Revaluations	Book Value
Tangible fixed assets			
Land and natural resources	1 168 525	1 793 750	2 962 275
Building and other premises	8 002 946	244 126	8 247 072
Basic telecommunications equipment	9 422 437	7 303 643	16 726 080
Transport equipment	41 477	6 250	47 727
Tools and instruments	307 952	33 560	341 512
Administrative equipment	977 285	265 344	1 242 629
	19 920 622	9 646 673	29 567 295

14. Other Information Concerning Fixed Assets

The Company operates mainly in the field of telecommunications. Accordingly, no fixed assets are allocated to other activities.

Fixed assets abroad amount to approximately 3.812.303 thousand escudos. The participation in international telecommunication organizations (Intelsat, Eutelsat and Inmarsat) and participations in consortia of submarine cables with no landing points in Portugal should be emphasized.

The net value, as of 31 December 1993, of fixed assets which are to be handed back to the State, under the terms of article18 of the Concession Contract, is 17,948,728 thousand escudos.

15. Financial Leasing

Fixed assets do not include any equipment on lease. As of 31 December 1993 the Company had the following payments to make on leased equipment.

Year	Amount
1994	651 908
1995	420 752

16. Financial Investments

As of 31 December 1993 the Company held shares in the following companies:

[Notes 16–22, containing details of financial investments, are omitted.]

3. Securities and Other Financial Investments

Other Holdings

Centrel - Gestão e Comparticipações, S.A.	678.772
Promindústria, S.A.	351.864
Others	250.028
	1.280.664
Provisions	(771.786)
	508.878

(a) This Company was set up on 25.08.93
(b) Includes the indirect investment through SGPS - Comunicações, Lda
(c) This company is in liquidation
(d) Profits and shareholders' equity are for the 1992 financial year

23. Doubtful Debts

Doubtful debts as of 31 December 1993 amount to 6.521.478 in the doubtful debts account and 475.529 in the Other Debtors account.

25. Debts from and to the Staff

Staff debts amounted to 168.212 thousand escudos as of 31 December 1993.

29. Long Term Creditors

There are no outstanding long term creditors beyond five years.

31. Financial Commitments

As of 31 December 1993 the contractual liabilities on the purchase of fixed assets amounted to 247.028 thousand escudos, over and above liabilities amounting to 1.072.660 thousand escudos (note 15).

32. Company Liabilities Not Stated in the Balance Sheet

Bank Guarantees	4 258 775
Other Guarantees	1 149 060
	5 407 835

34. Provisions

The increase in provisions for the financial year are stated as follows:

Items	Initial Balance	Increases	Transfers and Write-offs	Used Up	Final balance
Provisions for marketable securities	70 029	39 835			109 864
Provisions for doubtful debts	6 814 954	2 010 862	524 528	(255)	9 350 089
Provisions for financial investments	629 207	448 300	884 435	(3 060)	1 958 882
Provisions for liabilities and charges	5 205 583	1 312 875	(1 408 963)	(37 017)	5 072 478
	12 719 773	3 811 872	0	(40 332)	16 491 313

The increase in provisions for the financial year are stated as follows:

Provisions for the financial year	1 766 225
Extraordinary profits (Note 46)	1 354 828
Financial profits (Note 45)	690 819
	3 811 872

35. to 38. Equity

The company's equity capital as of 31 December 1993,has been fully paid in and is represented by 15.600.000 shares of 1.000 escudos each. The State holds 50.036% of the share capital of the company through CN - Comunicações Nacionais, SGPS, S.A., corresponding to 7.805.644 shares. The Company holds 663.918 own shares corresponding to 4,26% of the capital and the changes during the financial year were as follows:

	Number of Shares	Value
Initial balance	882 000	2 674 646
Acquisitions	633 918	3 035 740
Sales	(852 000)	(2 445 242)
Final balance	663 918	3 265 144

Sales during the year are discribed below:

Sale price	3 680 714
Cost price- FIFO	2 445 225
Free reserves - increase (Note 40)	1 235 489

Based upon the 1993 year end share price the total value of own suares is approximately 3 426 420 thousand escudos.

39. Revaluation Reserves

The Company revalued its tangible fixed assets in compliance with the relevant legal provisions. The most recent revaluation took place in 1992, under the terms of Decree-law nr.246/92 of 24 November. During the year there was no movement in this account and so the balance as of December 31st is the same as it was on January 1st 1993 (6.484.139thousand escudos). These reserves may only be used for capital increases.

	Initial balance	Increase	Reduction	Final balance
Capital adjustments		2 081 000		2 081 000
Legal reserves	6 153 053	774 060	1 182 288	5 744 825
	6 153 053	2 855 060	1 182 288	7 825 825
Other reserves				
Free reserves	12 471 959	5 862 440	2 912 667	15 421 732
Net profit of the financial year	3 671 221	4 168 173	3 671 221	4 168 173
	22 296 233	12 885 673	7 766 176	27 415 730

40. Movement in the Remaining Equity Accounts

In compliance with the law and the Articles of Association, 5% of annual profits has to be transferred to "legal reserves" until that value reaches at least 20% of the equity capital. This reserve may only be used for capital increases. The movement in free reserves for the financial year was as follows:

Balance as of January 1, 1993	12 471 959
Allocation of 1992 profits	1 122 503
Tranferred from reinvested reserves	1 182 288
Transferred from acquisition of own share reserves	(590 498)
Sale of own shares (Note 35)	1 235 480
Balance as of December 31, 1993	15 421 732

43. Remuneration of the Governing Bodies

The remuneration paid to members of the Company's governing bodies was as follows:
- 48.138 thousand escudos for the Board of Managing Directors,
- 5.435 thousand escudos for the Audit Board

44. Services Supplied

Services supplied	Internal Market	External Market	Total
Main telecommunications services			
Telephone	4 556 344	32 846 999	37 403 343
Telex, Telegraphy and Data communication	28 544	1 286 134	1 314 678
Radio and TV broadcasting	593 265	2 072 160	2 665 425
Mobile communications	106 300	391 959	498 259
Equipment rentals	2 139 541	595 767	2 735 308
Others	569 165	275 347	844 512
	7 993 159	37 468 366	45 461 525
Secondary services			
Submarine cable	224 453	722 737	947 190
Satellites		50 616	50 616
Others	34 554		34 554
	259 007	773 353	1 032 360
Total	8 252 166	38 241 719	46 493 885

45. Financial Profits

Sources	Financial Years 1993	1992	Sources	Financial Years 1993	1992
Interest paid	457 912	1 103 206	Interest received	669 804	893 366
Losses from Group Companies/subsidiaries	1 197 155		Capital gains from Group Companies/ Subsidiaries	865 778	
Investments/Write-offs	690 819	669 690	Capital gains from Group holdings	528 932	293 348
Exchange rate losses	2 282 714	1 436 290	Exchange rate gains	2 857 472	1 258 317
			Discounts from sight payments	6 479	1 865
Losses from the sale of short term investments	13 217	21 550	Capital gains on the sale of short term investments		435
Other financial losses and costs	55 242	258 787			
Financial profit	327 302	(1 033 974)	Other financial income	95 895	8 218
	5 024 361	2 455 549		5 024 361	2 455 549

46. Extraordinary Profits

Sources	Financial Years 1993	1992	Sources	Financial Years 1993	1992
Donations	23 840	15 308	Taxes returned	4 965	9 076
Bad debts		428	Debt collections	468	
Losses from fixed assets and stocks	15 435	542 934	Gains on fixed assets	1 231 895	98 466
Fines and penalties	51	1 148	Gains from contract penalties	39 844	
Increase in provisions and depreciation	1 354 828	1 693 642	Decrease in provisions and depreciation		133 347
Adjustments relating to previous financial years	42 347	53 332	Adjustments related to previous years	14 830	124 223
Other costs and extraordinary losses	2 309 126	1 654	Other extraordinary income	489 583	763 800
Extraordinary profits	(1 964 042)	(1 179 534)			
	1 781 585	1 128 912		1 781 585	1 128 912

The "Increase in provisions and depreciation" account includes an amount of approximately 754 million escudos referring to a provision set up with a view to defferring for the life time of the contract the capital gains from a "Leaseback" operation. The 600,828,000 escudo difference refers to extraordinary provisions set up to cover "Bad debts" and "Other Risks and Charges".

The "Other costs and extraordinary losses" account includes an amount of 675 million escudos referring to Redundancy Pay and payments made during the year to the Company's Pension Fund (1,250 million escudos), to cover liabilities already transferred to the Fund.

The "Gains on fixed assets" account includes an amount of 1,131 million escudos referring to the Capital gains on the sale of equipment, already fully paid back, from a "leaseback" operation related to the provision mentioned above.

The "Other extraordinary income" account includes an amount of 426,781,000 escudos (note 51) referring to the cancellation of the surplus on the Corporation tax estimate for the 1992 financial year.

49. Accruals and Deferred Costs (Assets)

Accrued Revenues	
Interest receivable	34 339
Other	151 000
	185 339

Deferred costs

Pluriannual maintenance	80 633
Other	50 067
	130 700
	316 039

Pluriannual maintenance is stated as cost for a three year period.

50. Provision for Liabilities and Charges

(a) Provisions for Pensions

The Company has committed itself to pay its staff supplementary Retirement and Survival Pensions, both for current and retired staff.

The Company, as of 31 December 1993, had Liabilities with Supplementary Retirement Pensions for staff retired before 31 December 1987 and with Survival Pensions for survivors of retired staff that passed away before 31 December 1988. As of 1 January 1994, Liabilities with Survival Pensions for survivors of retired staff that passed away before 31 December 1988 were transfered to the Pension Fund.

The Company's Liabilities with the Retirement Fund and Survival pensions were calculated on the basis of actuarial studies, carried out by an independent body, referring to 31 December 1993. The technical criteria used, which was more conservative and prudent than in previous years, was as follows: Actuarial Method - estimated "unit credit"; Mortality table - PF 60/64; Handicap table - Swiss Re; Actuarial technical rate - 4%; Long Term interest rate - 9% per annum; Salary growth rate - 7% per annum; and Pension growth rate - 5% per annum.

The aforementioned actuarial study also took into consideration the new Social Security regime, as described in Decree-Law Nr.329/93, and current staff turnover. Whenever staff leave the Company before the retirement age, they will not be entitled to retirement Pensions.

According to this actuarial study the Company's liabilities, as of 31 December 1993, were as follows:

Pension Fund Liabilities:

Liabilities with present staff	2 629 000
Liabilities with current pensioners	2 423 000
Liabilities with current survivors	1 728 000
	6 780 000

Company Liabilities:

Liabilities with current pensioners	1 587 000
	8 367 000

These liabilities, as of 31 December 1993, are fully covered by the existing provisions (3 351 000 thousand escudos) and Pension Fund (the market value of the fund portfolio as of 31 December 1993 was 5 016 425 thousand escudos).

The change in the Pension Fund account in the year ended 31 December 1993 was as follows:

Balance as of 31 December 1992	3 087 371
Contributions during the financial year	1 250 000
Pensions Payments	(50 690)
Income From the Fund	729 744
Balance as of 31 December 1993	5 016 425

(b) Provisions for sundry risks

The change in the financial year was as follows:

Balance as of 1 January	1 380 000
Tranfers from "Provision for Corporation Tax"	(1 150 000)
Increase	1 312 875
Balance as of 31 December 1993	1 542 875

This provision includes an amount of 356 million escudod referring to special benefits (reflecting the number of years worked for the Company) paid when staff reach retirement age.

51. Bank Loans and Overdrafts

Foreign currency loans	
medium and long Trem (less than 5 years)	2 431 472
Foreign currency loans	
short therm	2 481 597
Demand deposits - Credit Balance	231 924
	2 713 521
	5 144 99

Foreign currency loans will be paid back in their respective currencies and the amounts outstanding as of 31 December 1993 are as follows:

	Foreign Currency	In thousands of escudos
US Dollars USD	19 356 918	3 422 535
ECU's XEU	7 558 410	1 490 534
		4 913 069

52. State and Other Public Utilities

Income tax	2 750 000
Pre-payments and retentions	1 038 318
	1 711 682
Sundry	544 766
	2 256 448

The change in the "income tax" account was as follows:

Initial balance	28 124
Recovered	398 657
Annulment (Note 46)	(426 781)
Estimated taxes for the year	2 750 000

Pre-payments and retentions	(1 115 826)
Final Balance	1 634 174

53. Other Creditors

This account includes the following:

Participation in European Community Projects	250 403
Guarantees Given	286 736
Submarine Cable Creditors	80 255
Others	244 018
	861 412

54. Accruals and Deferred Income (Liabilities)

Accrued charges	
Holidays and holiday allowance	676 825
Space segment	381 779
Variable income	323 915
Staff's participation in the profits	119 000
Other charges to be paid	185 906
	1 687 425
Deferred income	951 823
	2 639 248

The "Deferred income" account includes an amount of 451,154 thousand escudos referring to the adjustment to the payment of the national extension for the 1993 incoming and outgoing traffic. This amount is currently being negotiated with Telecom Portugal.

55. Staff Costs

This account includes the following:

Salaries and Wages	5 949 503
Welfare benefits	
Retired pensions and survival pensions	364 593
Extraordinary payment by Marconi to the National Health System for pensions	392 261
	756 854
Welfare benefits/others	1 588 050
	8 294 407

The "Welfare benefits/others" account includes an amount of 550,080 thousand escudos referring to Medical Treatment and prescription drug costs.

In accordance with the current collective wage agreement in force, the Company makes an one - off payment (based on the number of years worked for the Company) whenever staff reach retirement age. This special benefit amounted to 91,510 thousand escudos in the 1993 financial year and was stated in the Profit and Loss Account under "Wages and Salaries".

56. Direct Taxation

This includes approximately 346.322 thousand escudos, corresponding to the radiocommunication service rates charged by the Instituto de Comunicações de Portugal.

SUPLEMENTARY DOCUMENTS

SHAREHOLDER POSITION OF
THE MEMBERS OF THE GOVERNING BODIES

	Nr. Shares held as of 31.12.92	Nr. Shares purchased in 1993	Nr. Shares sold in 1993	Nr. Shares as of 1.12.93
Gonçalo Manuel Bourbon Sequeira Braga	96			96
Carlos Maria Cunha Horta e Costa				
José Augusto Soares Pinto da Silva	23			23
Armando Manuel Salvador Mendes Madeira				
Abílio Ança Henriques				
Pedro José Rodrigues Pires de Miranda				
Mário Martins Adegas (a)				
Carlos Manuel Ruivo de Carvalho				
Crisóstomo Aquino de Barros				
Maria da Conceição Gamboa Abecassis Manzanares Pinto da Silva (b)	20			20

(a) Member of the Audit Board who is also a member of the Board of Managing Directors appointed by the shareholder Banco Espirito Santo e Comercial de Lisboa who holds 5 000 shares
(b) Spouse

Stock Options (1)

Chairman of the Board of Managing Directors - 1	3314
Members of the Board of Managing Directors - 2	5676
Total	8990
% of Capital	0,000576282

(1) Stock options for the 1989, and 1991 financial years. This regime has been suspended by the 1993 Annual General Meeting without prejudice to existing rigths.

AUDIT BOARD REPORT

. . . .

1993 Financial Year

. . . .

To the shareholders,

1. In accordance with the law and the Articles of Association, the Audit Board of Companhia Portuguesa Rádio Marconi S.A., hereby submits its report and opinion on the Annual Report, Balance Sheet, the Profit and Loss Account, the respective Notes and the Cash Flow statement presented by the Board of Managing Directors for the year ended 31 December 1993.

2. The report of the Board of Managing Directors, including the statement by the Chairman, describes in a detailed way the activities carried out by the Company and the constraints it faced at all levels.

In 1993 the Company improved its performance in comparison to the previous year. There was an increase in "Services Supplied", financial profits and a reduction in bank loans. As a result, Net Profits for the year increased, in spite of increased payments made to the Pension Fund.

3. As usual and in accordance with its responsibilities the Audit Board studied the company's activity with the utmost care. It examined all the documents presented, and the information which it requested and also held regular contacts with the Board of Managing Directors from whom it always obtained the best cooperation.

The Board also analysed the Report prepared by the Certified Public Accountant who is a member of this Audit Board, in compliance with the provisions laid down by Company law; that report is an integral part of this Report and Opinion.

4. The Audit Board also analysed the Legal Certification of Accounts submitted by the same Certified Public Accountant and in relation to which the Board expresses its agreement. The Audit Board - which is grateful to the reference made to it in the Report of the Board of Managing Directors - therefore recommends that: a) the report of the Board of Managing Directors and the Financial Statements for the 1993 financial year be approved; b) the proposal for the allocation of profits presented by the Board of Managing Directors also be approved.

Lisbon, 25 February 1994.

The Audit Board

Legal Certification of accounts

. . . .

Introduction

1. I have examined the financial statements of Companhia Portuguesa Rádio Marconi S.A. consisting of the Balance Sheet as of December 31, 1993, the Profit and Loss Account for the year then ended and the respective Notes to the accounts and the Cash flow statement and the respective notes. Total Assets amounted to 65,564,608 thousand escudos, Shareholders' Equity to 46,234,725 thousand escudos and Net Profits to 4,168,173 thousand escudos.

Responsabilities

2. The Board of Managing Directors of the Company is responsible for preparing the financial statements which should present a true and fair view of the financial situation of the company and the result of its operations. The Board is also responsible for implementing generally accepted accounting principles and maintaining an adequate internal control system.

3. It is my responsibility to issue an independent and professional opinion based on the examination of the Company's Financial Statements.

Scope

4. The audit was conducted in accordance with the technical standards for the Legal Audit of Accounts as approved by the Chamber of Official Auditors which require that an audit must be planned and carried out in such a way as to provide a reasonable guarantee as to whether the financial information contains important distortions or not. The audit thus includes:

- a random examination of the relevant evidence supporting the figures in the financial statements and the assessment of the decisions made by the Board of Managing Directors in the preparation and presentation of the financial statements;
- an examination of the adoption of adequate accounting procedures according to the circumstances and to whether these are in conformity with generally accepted accounting principles consistently applied in relation to the previous year;
- an assessment of whether the adequate financial statements were presented.

5. The audit which was carried out allows me to issue an opinion on the financial statements.

Opinion

6. In my opinion these financial statements present a true and fair view of the financial situation of Companhia Portuguesa Rádio Marconi, S.A., as of 31 December 1993, and the result of its operations and cash flow for the year then ended, in accordance with generally accepted accounting principles.

Lisbon, 25 February 1994

Carlos Ruivo de Carvalho

**To the Shareholders and Board of Managing Directors
of Companhia Portuguesa Rádio Marconi, S.A.**

(Amounts expressed in thousands of Escudos)

. . . .

1. We have examined the financial statements of Companhia Portuguesa Rádio Marconi S.A. as of December 31, 1993, the Profit and Loss Account and the Cash-Flow Statement for the year then ended, and the corresponding Notes. The preparation of these financial statements is the responsibility of the Board of Managing Directors of the Company. Our responsibility is to issue an opinion based on our audit on these financial statements.

2. Our audit was conducted in accordance with generally accepted accounting principles which require that an audit be planned and carried out in such a way as to provide a reasonable guarantee that the financial statements do not contain important distortions. An audit includes a random examination of the relevant evidence supporting the financial statements, and the assessment of the decisions made by the Board of Managing Directors, in the preparation and presentation of the financial statements. Likewise, an audit also includes an examination of the adoption of adequate accounting procedures, according to the circumstances and the adoption of adequate financial statements. In view of the examination which we carried out and the reports of the other chartered accountants on the subsidiary companies, it is our conviction that our audit provides a reasonable basis for the presentation of our opinion.

3. The financial statements of the Company as of December 31, 1992, used for comparison with the 1993 statements, were examined by other auditors, who issued an opinion without reservations, as of February 19, 1993. Our opinion is expressed solely with regard to the financial statements as of December 31, 1993.

4. The Financial Statements pertain just to the Company, although the "Financial Investments" account has already been consolidated through the equity method, in accordance with Accounting Guideline nr.9. Consequently, the impact of the subsidiaries profits and shareholders equity has already been stated in net profits and shareholders equity, as of December 31, 1993, but not the impact of the straight line method , wich led to an increase in assets and liabilities (including minority interests) of aproximately 14 000 000 escudos. Most of the subsidiaries Financial Statements and most of the other information used in the process, were audited by other independent auditors and, as a result, our opinion was based on aforementioned information.

5. In our opinion based on our audit and the reports of the other auditors, the financial statements mentioned in the preceding paragraph 1 give a true and fair view of the financial position of Companhia Portuguesa Rádio Marconi S.A., as of December 31, 1993, as well as profits of its operations and its cash-flow statement for the year then ended, in accordance with generally accepted accounting principles.

6. During the 1993 financial year, the Company increased provisions by approximately 3,800,000,000 escudos. This increase in provisions is mainly due to the supplementary retirement pension payments, losses from financial investments and doubtful debts.

7. Following the restructuring process of the telecommunications sector in Portugal, the impact of the decisions taken on the future operations and financial situation of the Company is not yet known. As of the date of this report, those facts and decisions are not yet known with precision, and the annexed financial statements also do not include any kind of adjustments arising from the aforementioned process.

Lisbon, 24 February 1994

Arthur Andersen

Arthur Andersen

Report of the External Auditor

(Amounts expressed in thousands of Escudos)

. . . .

Scope

1. In accordance with paragraph d), nr.1 of article 341 of the stock exchanges code,we hereby present our Audit Report on the Accounts and the financial situation relating to the financial information contained in the financial statements of Companhia Portuguesa Rádio Marconi, S.A. which include the Report of the Board of Managing Directors , the Balance Sheet as of December 31,1993, the Profit and Loss account and the Cash Flow statement for the year then ended and the respective notes to the accounts.

Responsabilities

2. The Board of Managing Directors of the Company is responsible for preparing the consolidated financial information contained in the Company's financial statements. As external Auditors we are responsible for examining whether the financial information is in accordance with international auditing guidelines,as required by the stock exchanges code,with the aim of issuing an independent opinion on that information,based on our audit.

Examination Made

3. Our Audit was conducted in accordance with the technical standards for the Legal Audit of Accounts as approved by the Chamber of Official Auditors which require that an audit ·be planned and carried out in such a way as to provide a reasonable guarantee that the financial statements do not contain important distortions. An Audit includes a random examination of the relevant evidence supporting the financial statements and the assesment of the decisions made by the Board of Managing Directors in the preparation and presentation of the financial statements.Likewise, an Audit also includes,an examination of the adoption of adequate accounting procedures, according to the circumstances and to whether these are in accordance with generally accepted accounting principles consistently applied in relation to the

previous year, and of the adoption of adequate financial statements.

Our Report includes examination of the Report of the Board of Managing Directors and whether that report is in accordance with the remaining financial information included in the Company's financial statements .

In view of the examination which we carried out and the reports of the other Chartered Accountants on the subsidiary companies it is our conviction that our audit provides a reasonable basis for the presentation of our opinion.

The financial statements of the Company as of December 31,1992, used for comparison with the 1993 statements ,were examined by other auditors,who issued an opinion without reservations as of February 19,1993. Our opinion is expressed solely with regard to the financial statements as of December 31,1993.

Opinion without Reservations with Emphasis

4. In our opinion, based on our audit and the reports of the other Chartered Accountants, the financial information contained in the Company's Financial Statements mentioned in the preceding paragraph 1: - give a true and fair view of the financial position of Companhia Portuguesa Rádio Marconi and its subsidiaries, as of 31 December 1993, and the profits of its operations and its cash-flow statements for the year then ended, in accordance with generally accepted accounting principles; and - are consistently applied in relation to the previous year as laid down by the Stock Exchange Code.

5. Notwithstanding the opinion expressed in the preceding paragraph, we draw your attention to the following situation:
- During the 1993 financial year, the Company increased provisions by approximately 3,800,000,000 escudos. This increase in provisions is mainly due to the supplementary retirement pension payments, losses from financial investments and doubtful debts.

- Following the restructuring process of the telecommunications sector in Portugal, the impact of the decisions taken on the future operations and financial situation of the Company and its subsidiaries is not yet known. As of the date of this report, those facts and decisions are not yet known with precision, and the annexed financial statements also do not include any kind of adjustments arising from the aforementioned process.

Lisbon, 24 February 1994

Carlos Freire, Carlos Loureiro & Associados, SROC
Represented by Carlos Manuel Pereira Freire

CONSOLIDATED ACCOUNTS

Consolidation Principles

Introduction

Consolidation of the Accounts of the Marconi Group was carried out in compliance with the provisions laid down under decree-law nr. 238/91 of July 2, 1991 and in accordance with the consolidation standards and accounting principles of the Official Accounting Plan.

In 1993 the Consolidation included 31 companies. Of the 31 companies, 25 were consolidated using the straight line method and 6 were consolidated using the equity method.

Consolidation Boundaries

The following table details all the companies included in the consolidation. the consolidation methods used in each company of the Group and the respective percentages of holdings and consolidation.

MARCONI GROUP
COMPANIES CONSOLIDATED IN THE 1993 FINANCIAL YEAR
(Consolidation Boundaries)

Company	Method of Consolidation	% of Ownership	Real % Ownership
MARCONI S.A.	PARENT CO.		
SGPS COMUNICAÇÕES	STRAIGHT LINE	100.00	100.00
TELESOSOTTO	EQUITY	45.00	45.00
VOICE PROCESSING	STRAIGHT LINE	85.00	85.00
REGISTRADE	STRAIGHT LINE	88.74	88.74
INFONET	STRAIGHT LINE	51.00	44.47
CONTACTEL	STRAIGHT LINE	51.00	51.00
DIRECTEL	STRAIGHT LINE	60.00	60.00
DIRECTEL MACAU	STRAIGHT LINE	80.00	49.99
CTM	EQUITY	28.00	28.00
GUINÉ TELECOM	STRAIGHT LINE	51.00	51.00
CST S. TOMÉ	STRAIGHT LINE	51.00	51.00
TDC	STRAIGHT LINE	33.33	33.33
TMN	EQUITY	33.33	33.33
CPRM ÁSIA	STRAIGHT LINE	99.99	99.99
MATRIX ÁSIA	EQUITY	22.22	22.22
CPRM BRASIL	STRAIGHT LINE	99.99	99.99
CPRM EUROPA	STRAIGHT LINE	98.70	98.70
CPRM NORTH AMERICA	STRAIGHT LINE	100.00	100.00
SATCOM	STRAIGHT LINE	100.00	100.00
KENIA POSTEL DIRECTORIES	STRAIGHT LINE	60.00	36.00
DIRECTEL - CABO VERDE COMUNIC.	STRAIGHT LINE	60.00	36.00
TIME SHARING	STRAIGHT LINE	45.57	45.56
TELEMATICA	STRAIGHT LINE	100.00	61.88
SGPS - SISTEMAS DE INFORMAÇÃO	STRAIGHT LINE	100.00	100.00
CRS	EQUITY	49.94	30.90
REALMARC	STRAIGHT LINE	100.00	100.00
SIMARC	STRAIGHT LINE	100.00	100.00
BURGO FUNDIÁRIA	EQUITY	33.33	33.33
COSMOS	STRAIGHT LINE	100.00	100.00
TRAÇA ANTIGA	STRAIGHT LINE	70.00	69.99

BALANÇO CONSOLIDADO EM 31 DE DEZEMBRO DE 1993 E 1992

Activo	Actv. Bruto	1993 Amort./Prov.	Actv. Líquido	1992
Imobilizado				
Imobilizações Incorpóreas:				
Despesas de Instalação	801 921	433 623	368 298	589 323
Despesas Invest. e Desenvolvimento	475 283	171 081	304 202	204 468
Propried. Industrial Outros Direitos	422 578	239 864	182 714	239 343
Trespasses	67 236	37 500	29 736	33 855
Imobilizações em Curso	442 433		442 433	184 673
Diferenças de Consolidação	467 944	105 783	362 161	483 174
	2 677 395	987 851	1 689 544	1 734 836
Imobilizações Corpóreas:				
Terrenos e Recursos Naturais	3 283 695		3 283 695	3 283 695
Edifícios e Outras Construções	15 502 611	626 233	14 876 378	14 398 581
Equipamento Básico	54 847 832	33 763 815	21 084 017	21 790 662
Equipamento de Transporte	421 930	280 290	141 640	157 290
Ferramentas e Utensílios	1 099 119	747 115	352 004	274 749
Equipamento Administrativo	4 971 733	3 284 953	1 686 780	2 141 629
Outras Imobilizações Corpóreas	106 118	77 205	28 913	43 330
Imobilizações em Curso	3 156 632		3 156 632	2 704 369
Adiantam. P/Conta Imobiliz. Corpóreas	14 440		14 440	83 078
	83 404 110	38 779 611	44 624 499	44 877 383
Investimentos Financeiros:				
Partes Capital Empr. Associadas	7 194 331	124 893	7 069 438	6 089 170
Partes Capital Out. Empr. Participadas	2 086 931	1 334 178	752 753	508 377
Títulos e Out. Aplic. Financeiras	2 377		2 377	1 381 686
Outros Empréstimos Concedidos	703 311	650 942	52 369	1 879 323
Adiantamento P/Conta Investimentos Financeiros	710 529		710 529	
	10 697 479	2 110 013	8 587 466	9 858 556
Existências:				
Mat. - Primas, Subsidiárias e de Consumo	101 025	1 767	99 258	135 734
Produtos e Trabalhos em Curso	78 543		78 543	290 028
Mercadorias	801 887	4 202	797 685	854 153
	981 455	5 969	975 486	1 279 915
Dívidas de Terceiros - Médio e Longo Prazo:				
Clientes, C/C	715 558	232 204	483 354	0
Outros Devedores	684 046	570 000	114 046	67 265
	1 399 604	802 204	597 400	67 265
Dívidas de Terceiros - Curto Prazo:				
Clientes, C/C	13 313 191	1 132 988	12 180 203	13 409 507
Clientes - Títulos a Receber	128		128	2 764
Clientes de Cobrança Duvidosa	6 581 185	5 756 254	824 931	1 534 443
Empresas Associadas/Participadas	5 249 547	1 256 654	3 992 893	1 702 027
Adiantamentos a Fornecedores	39 298		39 298	39 745
Adiant. a Fornecedores de Imobilizado	3 079		3 079	1 408
Estado e Outros Entes Públicos	400 481		400 481	346 153
Outros Devedores	2 075 679	908 124	1 167 555	2 804 812
	27 662 588	9 054 020	18 608 568	19 840 859
Títulos Negociáveis:				
Outros Títulos Negociáveis	322 900	109 864	213 036	347 043
Outras Aplicações de Tesouraria	2 540 718		2 540 718	0
	2 863 618	109 864	2 753 754	347 043
Depósitos Bancários e Caixa:				
Depósitos Bancários	772 064		772 064	1 103 752
Caixa	30 786		30 786	37 063
	802 850	0	802 850	1 140 815
Acréscimos e Diferimentos:				
Acréscimos de Proveitos	336 548		336 548	342 012
Custos Diferidos	506 898		506 898	634 876
	843 446	0	843 446	976 888
Total de Amortizações		39 767 462		
Total de Provisões		12 082 070		
Total do Activo	131 332 545	51 849 532	79 483 013	80 123 560

(Valores em Milhares de Escudos)

CONSOLIDATED BALANCE SHEET AS OF 31 DECEMBER 1993 AND 1992

Assets	1993 Gross Assets	1993 Depreciations Provisions	1993 Net Assets	1992
Fixed Assets				
Intangible fixed assets:				
Setting up costs	801 921	433 623	368 298	589 323
Research and development costs	475 283	171 081	304 202	204 468
Industrial property and other rights	422 578	239 864	182 714	239 343
Goodwill/property transfers	67 236	37 500	29 736	33 855
Fixed assets in progress	442 433		442 433	184 673
Differences in consolidation	467 944	105 783	362 161	483 174
	2 677 395	987 851	1 689 544	1 734 836
Tangible fixed assets:				
Real state and natural resources	3 283 695		3 283 695	3 283 695
Buildings and other premises	15 502 611	626 233	14 876 378	14 398 581
Basic equipment	54 847 832	33 763 815	21 084 017	21 790 662
Transport equipment	421 930	280 290	141 640	157 290
Tools and instruments	1 099 119	747 115	352 004	274 749
Administrative equipment	4 971 733	3 284 953	1 686 780	2 141 629
Other tangible fixed assets	106 118	77 205	28 913	43 330
Fixed assets in progress	3 156 632		3 156 632	2 704 369
Pre-payments on tangible fixed assets	14 440		14 440	83 078
	83 404 110	38 779 611	44 624 499	44 877 383
Financial investments:				
Investments in subsidiaries	7 194 331	124 893	7 069 438	6 089 170
Investments in other participated companies	2 086 931	1 334 178	752 753	508 377
Securities and other financial investments	2 377		2 377	1 381 686
Other loans granted	703 311	650 942	52 369	1 879 323
Pre-payment on financial investments	710 529		710 529	
	10 697 479	2 110 013	8 587 466	9 858 556
Stocks:				
1st raw materials	101 025	1 767	99 258	135 734
2nd products and work in progress	78 543		78 543	290 028
3rd Merchandise	801 887	4 202	797 685	854 153
	981 455	5 969	975 486	1 279 915
Medium and long term debtors:				
Customers-current account	715 558	232 204	483 354	0
Other debtors	684 046	570 000	114 046	67 265
	1 399 604	802 204	597 400	67 265
Short term debtors:				
Customers - current account	13 313 191	1 132 988	12 180 203	13 409 507
Customers - receivables	128		128	2 764
Doubtful debtors	6 581 185	5 756 254	824 931	1 534 443
Subsidiaries and participated companies	5 249 547	1 256 654	3 992 893	1 702 027
Pre-payments to suppliers	39 298		39 298	39 745
Pre-payments to suppliers of fixed assets	3 079		3 079	1 408
State and other public utilities	400 481		400 481	346 153
Other debtors	2 075 679	908 124	1 167 555	2 804 812
	27 662 588	9 054 020	18 608 568	19 840 859
Marketable securities:				
Other marketable securities	322 900	109 864	213 036	347 043
Other short terms investments	2 540 718		2 540 718	0
	2 863 618	109 864	2 753 754	347 043
Cash and banks:				
Bank deposits	772 064		772 064	1 103 752
Cash	30 786		30 786	37 063
	802 850	0	802 850	1 140 815
Accruals and deferred payments:				
Accrued income	336 548		336 548	342 012
Deferred costs	506 898		506 898	634 876
	843 446	0	843 446	976 888
Total depreciation		39 767 462		
Total provisions		12 082 070		
Total assets	131 332 545	51 849 532	79 483 013	80 123 560

(Thousands of escudos)

BALANÇO CONSOLIDADO EM 31 DE DEZEMBRO DE 1993 E 1992

Capital Próprio e Passivo	1993	1992
Capital Próprio:		
Capital	15 600 000	15 600 000
Acc. (quotas) Próprias Valor Nominal	(663 918)	(885 781)
Acções (quotas) Próprias - Desc./ Prem.	(2 601 226)	(1 781 446)
Diferenças de Consolidação	(63 789)	(643 342)
Ajust. Partes Capit. Filiais Associadas	2 085 440	(1 137 154)
Reservas de Reavaliação:	6 484 139	6 484 139
Reservas		
Reservas Legais	5 744 825	6 153 053
Outras Reservas	14 847 567	14 430 411
Diferenças de Câmbio	902 830	15 563
Resultados Transitados		
Subtotal	42 335 868	38 235 443
Resultados Líquidos do Exercício	4 078 199	4 033 037
Total do Capital Próprio	46 414 067	42 268 480
Interesses Minoritários	2 066 397	1 522 833
Passivo:		
Provisões para Riscos e Encargos:		
Provisões para Pensões	3 351 000	3 609 963
Provisões para Impostos	178 603	217 318
Outras Provisões Riscos e Encargos	1 687 093	1 389 749
	5 216 696	5 217 030
Dívidas a Terceiros - Médio Longo Prazo	8 937 446	10 117 130
Dívidas a Terceiros - Curto Prazo:		
Dívidas a Instituições de Crédito	3 649 686	8 233 288
Fornecedores, C/C	1 986 696	2 183 756
Fornecedores - Fact. Recep. Conferência	182 267	251 069
Fornecedores - Títulos a Pagar	170 216	261 371
Empresas Participadas e Participantes	414 208	2 040 328
Adiantamentos de Clientes	6 319	5 038
Outros Empréstimos Obtidos	177 434	0
Fornecedores de Imobilizado, C/C	982 633	1 357 714
Estado e Outros Entes Públicos	2 582 791	875 026
Clientes C/C	1 986 499	1 514 346
Outros Credores	1 176 949	1 789 074
	13 315 698	18 511 010
Acréscimos e Diferimentos:		
Acréscimos de Custos	2 034 700	1 784 448
Proveitos Diferidos	1 498 009	702 629
	3 532 709	2 487 077
Total Passivo	31 002 549	36 332 247
Total Capit. Propr. Minorit. Passivo	79 483 013	80 123 560

(Valores em Milhares de Escudos)   (As notas anexas fazem parte integrante destas demonstrações consolidadas)

CONSOLIDATED BALANCE SHEET AS OF 31 DECEMBER 1993 AND 1992

Equity and Liabilities	1993	1992
Shareholders' Equity:		
Share capital	15 600 000	15 600 000
Own shares- face value	(663 918)	(885 781)
Own shares-premiums and discount	(2 601 226)	(1 781 446)
Differences in consolidation	(63 789)	(643 342)
Adjustment in the % of investments in subsidiaries	2 085 440	(1 137 154)
Revaluation reserves:	6 484 139	6 484 139
Reserves		
Legal reserves	5 744 825	6 153 053
Other reserves	14 847 567	14 430 411
Differences in exchange rates	902 830	15 563
Profits brought forward		
Subtotal	42 335 868	38 235 443
Net profit for the financial year	4 078 199	4 033 037
Total shareholders' equity	46 414 067	42 268 480
Minority interests	2 066 397	1 522 833
Liabilities:		
Provisions for liabilities and charges:		
Provisions for retirement benefits	3 351 000	3 609 963
Provisions for corporation tax	178 603	217 318
Other provisions	1 687 093	1 389 749
	5 216 696	5 217 030
Medium and long term creditors	8 937 446	10 117 130
Short term creditors:		
Bank loans	3 649 686	8 233 288
Suppliers - currente account	1 986 696	2 183 756
Suppliers - invoices received	182 267	251 069
Suppliers - securities to be paid	170 216	261 371
Subsidiaries and participating companies	414 208	2 040 328
Customers pre-payments	6 319	5 038
Other loans	177 434	0
Fixed assets suppliers-current account	982 633	1 357 714
State and other public utilities	2 582 791	875 026
Trade creditors	1 986 499	1 514 346
Other creditors	1 176 949	1 789 074
	13 315 698	18 511 010
Accruals and deferrements:		
Accrued charges	2 034 700	1 784 448
Deferred income	1 498 009	702 629
	3 532 709	2 487 077
Total Liabilities	31 002 549	36 332 247
Total Shareholders' Equity, Liabilities and minority interests	79 483 013	80 123 560

(Thousands of escudos)

(The following notes are part of the consolidated financial statements)

DEMONSTRAÇÕES DE RESULTADOS CONSOLIDADOS - 31 DE DEZEMBRO DE 1993 E 1992

	1993		1992	
Custo das Mercadorias Vendidas e Consumidas				
Mercadorias	1 343 708		1 615 695	
Matérias	6 037	1 349 745	122 144	1 737 839
Fornecimentos e Serviços de Terceiros				
Subcontratos de Tráfego	20 698 716		16 290 541	
Fornecimentos e Serviços	6 179 094	26 877 810	7 281 449	23 571 990
Custos com Pessoal				
Remunerações	7 444 508		7 047 048	
Encargos Sociais / Pensões	756 854		505 431	
Encargos Sociais / Outros	2 100 702	10 302 064	2 625 216	10 177 695
Amortizações Imobilizado Corpóreo / Incorpóreo	6 345 748		5 505 217	
Provisões	1 990 602	8 336 350	387 758	5 892 975
Impostos	427 976		83 723	
Outros Custos Operacionais	300 350	728 326	524 830	608 553
(A)		47 594 295		41 989 052
Custos e Perdas Financeiras				
Perdas relativas a Empresas Associadas	886 008		281 863	
Amortizações Prov. Aplic. e Invest. Financeiros	465 652		669 691	
Diferenças de Câmbio Desfavoráveis	2 419 354		1 636 544	
Outros Juros e Custos Similares	1 146 529	4 917 543	2 205 055	4 793 153
(C)		52 511 838		46 782 205
Custos e Perdas Extraordinários		4 639 502		2 471 811
(E)		57 151 340		49 254 016
Imposto s/ Rendimento do Exercício		2 806 429		2 021 182
(G)		59 957 769		51 275 198
Interesses Minoritários		(156 502)		(213 270)
Resultado Consolidado Líquido do Exercício		4 078 199		4 033 037
PROVEITOS E GANHOS		63 879 468		55 094 965
Vendas:				
Mercadorias	1 576 391		1 575 032	
Produtos	342 929	1 919 320	835 445	2 410 477
Prestação de Serviços:				
Telecomunicações	48 593 902		42 461 673	
Cabos / Satélites e Outros	3 744 207	52 338 109	1 894 644	44 356 317
Subsídios à Exploração	122 150		189 292	
Proveitos Suplementares	797 196		1 477 321	
Trabalhos para Própria Empresa	535 482		598 757	
Outros Proveitos Operacionais	1 153	1 455 981	67 956	2 333 326
(B)		55 713 410		49 100 120
Ganhos de Participações de Capital:				
Relativos a Empresas Associadas / Outras		1 991 943		1 357 413
Rendim. Títulos Negociáveis e Outras Aplicações	239 687		490 927	
Diferenças de Câmbio Favoráveis	2 976 503		1 328 251	
Outros Juros e Proveitos Similares:	558 827	3 775 017	525 800	2 344 978
(D)		61 480 370		52 802 511
Proveitos e Ganhos Extraordinários		2 399 096		2 292 454
(F)		63 879 466		55 094 965

Resumo:		1993	1992
Resultados Operacionais	(B) - (A)	8 119 115	7 111 068
Resultados Financeiros	(D-B) - (C-A)	849 417	(1 090 762)
Resultados Correntes	(D) - (C)	8 968 532	6 020 306
Resultados antes Impostos	(F) - (E)	6 728 126	5 840 949
Result. Consol. Líq. c/ Interes. Min. Exerc.	(F) - (G)	3 921 697	3 819 767

(As notas anexas fazem parte integrante destas demonstrações consolidadas)   (Valores em Milhares de Escudos)

CONSOLIDATED PROFIT AND LOSS ACCOUNT 1993 FINANCIAL YEAR

	1993		1992	
Costs of goods sold and consumed				
Stocks	1 343 708		1 615 695	
Materials	6 037	1 349 745	122 144	1 737 839
Supplies and third party services				
Sub-contracts-traffic	20 698 716		16 290 541	
Services supplied	6 179 094	26 877 810	7 281 449	23 571 990
Staff costs				
Wages and salaries	7 444 508		7 047 048	
Social security costs/pension funds	756 854		505 431	
Social security costs/ welfare	2 100 702	10 302 064	2 625 216	10 177 695
Depreciation	6 345 748		5 505 217	
Provisions	1 990 602	8 336 350	387 758	5 892 975
Taxes	427 976		83 723	
Others operating costs	300 350	728 326	524 830	608 553
(A)		47 594 295		41 989 052
Interest payable and similar charges				
Losses of subsidiary companies	886 008		281 863	
Investment write-offs	465 652		669 691	
Exchange rate losses	2 419 354		1 636 544	
Other financial costs	1 146 529	4 917 543	2 205 055	4 793 153
(C)		52 511 838		46 782 205
Extraordinary costs and losses		4 639 502		2 471 811
(E)		57 151 340		49 254 016
Taxes on profit		2 806 429		2 021 182
(G)		59 957 769		51 275 198
Minority interests		(156 502)		(213 270)
Consolidated net profit for the financial year		4 078 199		4 033 037
INCOME	**63 879 468**		**55 094 965**	
Sales:				
Goods	1 576 391		1 575 032	
Products	342 929	1 919 320	835 445	2 410 477
Supply of services:				
Telecommunications	48 593 902		42 461 673	
Cable satellites and others	3 744 207	52 338 109	1 894 644	44 356 317
Operation subsidies	122 150		189 292	
Additional income	797 196		1 477 321	
Work for own assets	535 482		598 757	
Other operating income	1 153	1 455 981	67 956	2 333 326
(B)		55 713 410		49 100 120
Income from capital holdings in:				
Subsidiaries/Others		1 991 943		1 357 413
Income from marketable securities and other investments	239 687		490 927	
Favourable exchange rate differences	2 976 503		1 328 251	
Other interest and similar income:	558 827	3 775 017	525 800	2 344 978
(D)		61 480 370		52 802 511
Extraordinary gains and income		2 399 096		2 292 454
(F)	**63 879 466**		**55 094 965**	
Summary:				
Operational profit (B) - (A)		8 119 115		7 111 068
Financial profit (D-B) - (C-A)		849 417		(1 090 762)
Current profit (D) - (C)		8 968 532		6 020 306
Profit before tax (F) - (E)		6 728 126		5 840 949
Consolidated net profit/with minority interest of the financial year (F) - (G)		3 921 697		3 819 767

(The following notes are part of the consolidated financial statements)

(Thousands of escudos)

DEMONSTRAÇÃO DOS FLUXOS DE CAIXA DO ANO FINDO EM 31 DE DEZEMBRO DE 1993

MÉTODO INDIRECTO

ACTIVIDADES OPERACIONAIS — 1993

RESULTADO LÍQUIDO do EXERCÍCIO	4 078 199
AJUSTAMENTOS:	
Amortizações	6 343 122
Provisões	3 441 183
Resultados Financeiros	396 083
Aumento das Dívidas de Terceiros	(2 010 721)
Diminuição das Existências	298 460
Aumento das Dívidas a Terceiros	108 134
Diminuição dos Proveitos Diferidos	(32 913)
Aumento dos Acréscimos de Proveitos	5 464
Diminuição dos Custos Diferidos	(159 497)
Aumento dos Acréscimos de Custos	250 252
Ganhos na Alienação de Imobilizações	(1 301 047)
Perdas na Alienação de Imobilizações	189 003
Trabalhos para a Própria Empresa	(464 203)
Fluxos das Actividades Operacionais (1)	11 141 519

ACTIVIDADES DE INVESTIMENTO
RECEBIMENTOS PROVENIENTES DE:

Investimentos Financeiros	2 477 137	
Imobilizações Corpóreas	2 040 984	
Subsídios de Investimento	735 591	
Juros e Proveitos Similares	958 342	6 212 054

PAGAMENTOS RESPEITANTES A:

Investimentos Financeiros	2 686 852	
Imobilizações Corpóreas	3 955 888	
Imobilizações Incorpóreas	237 720	6 880 460
Fluxos das Actividades de Investimento (2)		(668 406)

ACTIVIDADES DE FINANCIAMENTO
RECEBIMENTOS PROVENIENTES DE:

Empréstimos Obtidos	8 153 161	
Venda de Acções Próprias	3 680 714	11 833 875

PAGAMENTOS RESPEITANTES A:

Empréstimos Obtidos	13 916 447	
Juros e Custos Similares	943 885	
Dividendos	2 372 984	
Aquisição de Acções Próprias	3 035 740	20 269 056
Fluxos das Actividades de Financiamento (3)		(8 435 181)

Variação de Caixa e Seus Equivalentes (4)=(1+2+3)	2 037 932
Efeito das Diferenças de Câmbio	164 821
Caixa e Seus Equivalentes no Início do Período	1 140 815
Caixa e Seus Equivalentes no Fim do Período	3 343 568

(Valores em Milhares de Escudos)

ANEXO À DEMONSTRAÇÃO DOS FLUXOS DE CAIXA DO ANO FINDO EM 31 DE DEZEMBRO DE 1993

1. Aquisição ou Alienação de Filiais
Não existem operações materialmente relevantes.
2. Decomposição dos Componentes de Caixa e Seus Equivalentes

	1993	1992
Numerário	30 786	37 063
Depósitos bancários imediatamente mobilizáveis	772 064	1 103 752
Equivalentes e Caixa	2 540 718	
	3 343 568	1 140 815
Outras disponibilidades Títulos negociáveis	213 036	347 043
Disponibilidades constantes do balanço	3 556 604	1 487 858

Os valores apresentados neste mapa relativos à rúbrica de Títulos Negociáveis estão líquidos de provisões que, em 31 de Dezembro de 1993, ascenderam a 109 864 milhares de Escudos e em 31 de Dezembro de 1992 apresentavam um montante de 70 029 milhares de Escudos.
3. Actividades Financeiras Não Monetárias
Em 31 de Dezembro de 1993 a Empresa-Mãe tinha utilizado 17,7 milhões de Escudos de uma linha de financiamento externo de curto prazo pelo valor global de 1000 milhões de Escudos.
Não existe formalização, por parte da Empresa-Mãe, para utilização de outras linhas de crédito oferecidas pelos bancos.
4. Repartição na Empresa-Mãe dos fluxos de caixa por ramos de actividade e zonas geográficas.

	Mercado Interno	Mercado Externo	Total
RECEBIMENTOS			
Serv. de Telec. Principais	6 983 985	33 120 415	40 104 400
Serv. Secundários	281 277	447 961	729 238
PAGAMENTOS			
Serv. de Telec. Principais	316 703	7 008 461	7 325 164
Serv. Secundários	6 267	291 112	297 379
	322 970	7 299 573	7 622 543
TOTAL GERAL	6 942 292	26 268 803	33 211 095

Os recebimentos e pagamentos evidenciados no âmbito dos fluxos de caixa estão considerados numa base líquida de custos e proveitos e incluem valores de IVA.
5. Outras Informações
Por não haver disponibilidade de algumas das informações, por parte das empresas do Grupo, tomaram-se como base as informações da Empresa-Mãe.

CASH FLOW AS OF 31 DECEMBER 1993

INDIRECT METHOD

	1993
OPERATIONAL ACTIVITIES	
NET PROFIT FOR THE YEAR	4 078 199
ADJUSTMENTS:	
Depreciation	6 343 122
Provisions	3 441 183
Financial Profits	396 083
Increase in Debtors	(2 010 721)
Reduction in Stocks	298 460
Increase in Creditors	108 134
Reduction in Deferred Income	(32 913)
Increase in Accrued Income	5 464
Reduction in Deferred Costs	(159 497)
Increase in Accrued Charges	250 252
Capital Gains on the Sale of Fixed Assets	(1 301 047)
Capital Losses on the Sale of Fixed Assets	189 003
Work for Own Assets	(464 203)
Total Cash Flow from Operational Activities (1)	11 141 519

INVESTMENT ACTIVITIES		
INCOME FROM:		
Financial Investments	2 477 137	
Tangible Fixed Assets	2 040 984	
Investment Subsidies	735 591	
Interest and Other Similar Income	958 342	6 212 054
PAYMENTS RELATING TO:		
Financial Investments	2 686 852	
Tangible Fixed Assets	3 955 888	
Intangible Fixed Assets	237 720	6 880 460
Cash Flow from Investment Activities (2)		(668 406)

FINANCING ACTIVITIES		
INCOME FROM:		
Loans	8 153 161	
Sale of Own Shares	3 680 714	11 833 875
PAYMENTS RELATING TO:		
Loans	13 916 447	
Interest and other Similar Charges	943 885	
Dividends	2 372 984	
Aquisition of Own Shares	3 035 740	20 269 056
Cash Flow from Financing Activities (3)		(8 435 181)

Changes in Cash Flow and its Equivalent (4)=(1+2+3)	2 037 932
Exchange Rate Differences	164 821
Cash Flow and its equivalent at the start of the period	1 140 815
Cash Flow and its equivalent at the end of the period	3 343 568

(Amounts expressed in thousands of escudos 1993)

NOTES TO THE CASH FLOW STATEMENT AS OF 31 DECEMBER 1993

1. Aquisition or sale of asubsidiaries
The amounts involved were not relevant

2. Breakdown of the cash and similar items

	1993	1992
Cash	30 786	37 063
Demand Deposits		
Cash Equivalents	772 064	1 103 752
Cash and Similar Items	2 540 718	
	3 343 568	1 140 815
Other Deposits		
Marketable Securities	213 036	347 043
Balance Sheet		
Cash And Banks	3 556 604	1 487 858

The amouts relating to "Marketable Securities" are not of Provisions which amounted to 109 864 thousand escudos as of 31 December 1993 and to 70 029 thousand escudos as of 31 December 1992.

3. Non-Monetary Financial Activities
There was an international short term credit line of 1 000 million escudos. As of 31 December 1993, the Parent Company had used 17,7 million escudos.
The Parent Company has not used other credit lines offered by the banks.

4. Breakdown in the Parent Company of Cash Flow by Activity and Geographical Areas

Income and Payments in the Cash Flow statement are stated at the net value but include VAT.

	Internal Market	External Market	Total
Incomes			
Main Telecommunications			
Services	6 983 985	33 120 415	40 104 400
Secondary Services	281 277	447 961	729 238
PAYMENTS			
Main Telecommunications			
Services	316 703	7 008 461	7 325 164
Secondary Services	6 267	291 112	297 379
	322 970	7 299 573	7 622 543
TOTAL	6 942 292	26 268 803	33 211 095

5. OtherInformation
As some information from some of the companies of the Group was not avaible, data from the Parent Company was used.

10. DIFFERENCES IN CONSOLIDATION

The balance in the "Differences in Consolidation" account, as of December 31, 1993, was as follows:

	1993	1992
In Shareholder's Equity	(63 789)	(643 342)
In intangible Fixed Assets	467 944	515 547

The main differences from one year to the other were found in the following companies:

	In Shareholders' Equity	In intangible Fixed assets
Estereofoto	(80 599)	(20 122)
Geometral	(55 505)	-
Globalsis	(19 994)	(165 497)
IN	(23 908)	-
Mobitel-Brasil	-	(76 150)
Registrade	-	291 488
Simarc	(80 545)	-
Softlog	(51 423)	-
Time Sharing	(116 384)	-
TSI	(41 750)	(74 906)
Voice-Processing	(86 125)	-

The differences in consolidation stated in a "shareholders' Equity" item correspond to differences between the value of investments and the percentage in the shareholders' Equity of the subsidiaries, at the time of the first consolidation or whenever changes occur to the level of investment in that subsidiary.

The differences in consolidation stated in a separate item in the Intangible Fixed Assets account correspond to the positive differences between the acquisition value and the percentage in the Shareholders' Equity of the subsidiaries. The respective value is depreciated in a 5 year period.

14. CHANGES IN THE COMPANIES INCLUDED IN CONSOLIDATION

In relation to the previous year the following companies were not included in consolidation:

a) Companies closed down:
Soflog, TSI, Dados e Ideias, IN e TBD;

b) Companies sold:
Dynargie, Geotrânsito, Risfomento e Marconi-SVA;

c) Companies for which no data is available:
Mobitel;

d) Companies which are being sold:
Estereofoto e Geometral;

e) The amounts involved were not relevant in terms of consolidation:
AF, Marcsat.

In view of the significant changes in the consolidation boundaries, in relation to the previous year, and in order to make notes 27, 42, 44, 45 and 46 comparable, the same companies were used in the two years, i.e., only the companies included in the consolidation boundaries of 1993 were considered.

21. FINANCIAL LIABILITIES

As of 31 December 1993, the contractual liabilities on the purchase of fixed assets amounted to 620 116 thousand escudos, as well as liabilities with the lease of equipment, amounting to 1 121 660 thousand escudos.

As of 31 December 1993, Parent Company's liabilities with current pensioners amounted to 1 587 000 thousand escudos.

22. CONTINGENT LIABILITIES

Bank guarantees	10 714 985
Other guarantees given	1 149 060

23. MAIN ACCOUNTING PRINCIPLES

a) Intangible fixed assets
These are valued at cost. Depreciation is carried out at a 33.33% rate with the exception of "Differences in consolidation" which is depreciated at a 20% rate.

Guiné -Telecom and CST revaluated their fixed assets as of 31 December 1993.

Guiné - Telecom revaluated its Financial Statements at the average exchange rate of the Peso in relation to the Escudo.

CST revaluated its Financial Statements at the average exchange rate of the Dobra in relation to the Escudo.

CPRM Brasil revaluated its Financial Statements at the average exchange rate of the Cruzeiro in relation to the Escudo.

b) Tangible fixed assets
Tangible fixed assets are valued at cost plus the value of the revaluation carried out.

Depreciation is calculated through the straight line method on the value of the revaluation or the cost of acquisition in order to fully depreciate all assets at the end of their expected useful life or by the end of the concession contract, whichever is more appropriate.

c) Financial investments
Financial investments in companies of the Group or subsidiaries are initially stated at cost. This figure is adjusted by the value corresponding to the percentage in its Shareholders' Equity in compliance with the Equity Consolidation method described in the Official Accounting Plan (item 5.4.3).

The remaining financial investments are stated at cost. In some cases a provision has been set up to cover potential losses.

d) Stocks
Stocks are valued at average cost.

e) Foreign currency
Foreign currency operations are stated at the exchange rate in force at the date of the operation. Receivables, payables, and foreign currency deposits are stated in Escudos at the exchange rate in force at the end of the year and the respective exchange rate differences are stated in the profit and loss account.

The financial statements of the companies located abroad are converted into escudos at the following exchange rates: equity at the historical exchange rate, profits at the average exchange rate, and the remaining accounts at the exchange rate in force at the end of the year.

f) Marketable securities
These are stated at cost. A provision is set up to cover potential losses. Income is stated in the profit and loss

account for the respective financial year, except in the case of dividends from shares, which are only stated when received.

g) Own shares

These are stated at cost and the cost of sales is determined on a FIFO basis. Capital gains on the sale of these shares are stated in free reserves.

h) Pensions and Medical Treatment

The Parent Company has its own Social security regime - "Caixa de Previdência do Pessoal da Companhia Portuguesa Rádio Marconi" - an independent body part of the Public Social Security system.

The Parent Company and its staff make regular payments, which vary according to the wages and salaries paid to the employees, in accordance with applicable legislation. The Company's Social Security Fund pays the staff's retirement pensions.

The Parent Company also pays its staff retirement and survival pensions as a complement to retirement pensions paid by Social Security (it also pays pensions to the widows/widowers of retired employees).

In accordance with an actuarial study undertaken in 1991, the Parent Company set up provisions to cover existing liabilities and delivered regular payments from 1987 onwards to a Pension Fund. As a result, all liabilities are now fully covered.

In accordance with regulations in force, the Parent Company also contributes towards the costs of Medical Treatment and prescription drugs, which are stated as costs in the Profit and Loss Account for the respective financial year (see note 55).

i) Traffic revenue and costs

Traffic revenue and costs referring to the last quarter of the financial year are normally based on estimated values, which are then corrected in the following year after the final figures have become available.

j) Research and Development

General Research and Development costs are stated in the profit and loss account for the year in which they were incurred. Research and Development costs related to specific projects are capitalized as intangible fixed assets.

k) Accruals and Deferrements

This account includes the following transactions:

- Expenses and Revenues, from several financial years, which are stated as Costs and Income for each one of those financial years at their respective value;

- Subsidies granted for the acquisition of tangible fixed assets are stated as Deferred Income and included in the Profit and Loss Account. The amount is in proportion to

the depreciation on subsidized tangible Fixed Assets;

- Holiday pay already earned but not yet paid;
- Interest payments overdue and not yet paid.

l) Financial Leasing

Equipment on lease as well as payments are not stated in the Balance Sheet. Payments on leased equipment are stated in the Profit and Loss Accounts.

m) Consolidation principles

As a rule , companies in which Marconi holds more than 50 % of the capital or controls the management were consolidated using the straight line method.The balances and the significant transactions between companies included in the consolidation were not considered. The amount corresponding to third party holdings and profits is stated as "Minority interests".

Companies in which Marconi holds more than 20 % but less than 50 % of the capital ,or does not control the management were consolidated using the equity method.In this method the value of "financial investments" is adjusted in accordance with the percentage of the equity capital held in the company. Consolidated net profits is the sum of all the profits of the companies of the group net of all the necessary consolidation adjustments.

24. FOREIGN CURRENCY EXCHANGE RATES

The exchange rates used at the end of the year, to convert the accounts of the companies located abroad, were those published by the Bank of Portugal as at 31 December 1993.

25. SETTING UP COSTS, RESEARCH AND DEVELOPMENT COSTS

Setting up costs and current research and development costs are stated in the Profit and Loss Account for the year.

Research and development costs related to specific projects are stated in intangible fixed assets.

27. CHANGES IN FIXED ASSETS, DEPRECIATION, AND PROVISIONS

The changes in intangible and Tangible Fixed Assets, Financial Investments and respective Depreciation and Provisions as of December 31, 1993, were as follows:

The Parent Company contributes significantly to the "Fixed Assets" account. Specially important aspects related with the Parent Company are:

CHANGES IN FIXED ASSETS DEPRECIATION, AND PROVISIONS

Gross assets	Initial Balance	Revaluation	Increase	Sale	Transfers and Write-offs	Final Balance
Intangible Fixed assets						
Setting up costs	509 136	3 215	324 151	0	13 580	822 922
Research and development costs	232 720	32 652	323 057	0	113 147	475 282
Industrial property and other costs	430 477	0	181 599	0	189 498	422 578
Property transfers/Goodwill	37 500	0	37 111	0	7 375	67 236
Fixed assets in progress	332 663	0	236 759	0	147 990	421 432
Prepayments on intangible fixed assets	0	0	0	0	0	0
Differences in consolidation	0	0	0	0	0	0
Total	1 542 496	35 867	1 102 677	0	471 590	2 209 450
Tangible fixed assets						
Real state and natural resources	3 283 695	0	0	0	0	3 283 695
Buildings and other premises	15 128 715	152 863	421 233	196 505	3 695	15 502 611
Basic equipment	52 702 207	1 136 794	4 175 289	3 122 305	44 153	54 847 832
Transport equipment	367 778	44 372	63 387	35 178	18 429	421 930
Tools and instruments	838 728	12 847	264 636	11 345	5 747	1 099 119
Administrative equipment	4 739 712	40 827	319 906	78 482	50 230	4 971 733
Tare and containers	0	0	0	0	0	0
Other tangible fixed assets	79 382	26 062	674	0	0	106 118
Fixed assets in progress	2 588 324	9 170	2 113 464	0	1 554 326	3 156 632
Prepayments on tangible fixed assets	78 993	0	12 293	0	76 846	14 440
Total	79 807 534	1 422 935	7 370 882	3 443 815	1 753 426	83 404 110
Financial Investments						
Percentage capital in subsidiaries	10 741 596	1 749 572	891 728	996 442	647 020	11 739 434
Loans to subsidiaries	2 434 899	0	4 098 195	0	(65 000)	6 598 094
Percentage capital in other companies	5 946 255	715 986	412 899	216 880	85 100	6 773 160
Loans to other companies	0	0	3 000	0	0	3 000
Securities and other financial assets	2 741 603	0	10 430	1 250 815	205 561	1 295 657
Other loans granted	0	0	0	0	0	0
Fixed assets in progress	0	0	0	0	0	0
Prepayments - financial investments	126 108	0	780 529	13 000	88 708	804 929
Total	21 990 461	2 465 558	6 196 781	2 477 137	961 389	27 214 274

DEPRECIATION AND PROVISIONS

Items	Initial Balance	Revaluation	Increases	Transfers and Write-offs	Final Balance
Intangible fixed assets					
Setting up costs	312 260	34 114	225 158	137 909	433 623
Research and Development costs	109 208	0	163 271	101 398	171 081
Industrial property and other rights	225 780	0	129 791	115 707	239 864
Property tranfers/Goodwill	28 124	0	9 376	0	37 500
Fixed assets in progress	0	0	0	0	0
Differences in consolidation	12 167	0	93 616	0	105 783
Total	687 539	34 114	621 212	355 014	987 851
Tangible fixed assets					
Real state and natural resources	0	0	0	0	0
Buildings and other premises	633 914	12 703	189 549	209 933	626 233
Basic equipment	31 942 608	362 322	4 597 406	3 138 522	33 763 815
Transport equipment	218 854	22 381	73 544	34 490	280 289
Tools and instruments	566 985	5 345	187 110	12 325	747 115
Administrative equipment	2 682 775	19 208	670 351	87 382	3 284 953
Tare and containers	0	0	0	0	0
Other tangible fixed assets	44 831	12 176	20 199	0	77 205
Fixed assets in progress	0	0	0	0	0
Prepayments on tangible fixed assets	0	0	0	0	0
Total	36 089 966	434 136	5 738 160	3 482 652	38 779 611
Financial investments					
Securities and other financial investments	0	0	0	0	0
Other loans granted	683 017	0	(32 075)	0	650 942
Total	683 017	0	(32 075)	0	650 942

a) Basic equipment includes submarine cables, satellites and radio electric systems as well as the respective land, buildings and premises and also capital contributions to international satellite telecommunications organizations (Intelsat, Eutelsat and Inmarsat). These investments are stated as tangible fixed assets as they might be transferred to the State at the end of the concession period, and so are fully depreciated at the end of the same period.

Basic equipment is as follows:

	Gross Value	Depreciation	Value Net
Station and Premises			
Conventional Radioelectric	10 753 949	7 439 741	3 314 208
Satellites	17 842 423	12 828 864	5 013 559
Submarine Cables	19 558 610	11 160 297	8 398 313
	48 154 982	31 428 902	16 726 080

b) The Parent Company agreed to convey the operation of the ATLAS submarine cable system, the net value of which is included in basic equipment and amounts to approximately 390.038 thousand escudos.

c) The Parent Company decided fully to depreciate assets at the end of the expected useful life or at the end of the concession period, whichever is more appropriate. However, as regards stations and satellite and submarine cable premises the concession period is shorter than the expected useful life period of the respective assets. As a result depreciation for the year has been increased by approximately 273.199 thousand escudos in relation to the depreciation which would have been stated had the assets been depreciated at the end of their expected useful life.

d) As a result of the application of the Equity method, the "Adjustments to Share Capital" and the "Investments in Share Capital" accounts increased respectively by 2,081,000 thousand escudos and 1,750,753 thousand escudos. Profits for the year fell by 330,247 thousand escudos.

The most significant contribution to this profit was the 850,000 thousand escudo loss made by TMN - Telecomunications Móveis Nacionais, S.A., and the 580,000 thousand escudo profit made by SGPS - Comunications and other international telecommunications companies.

The application of the Equity method as of 31 December 1993 (Profits and Shareholders' Equity), was done on the basis of the latest figures known for each of the companies at the year end.

e) The value of "tangible work in progress" corresponds to the acquisition of capacity on submarine cable systems(1,331,134 thousand escudos) and to the development of community projects in the field of intangible Research and Development (approximately 400 million escudos).

f) The value of the sale of tangible fixed assets corresponds to the sale of basic telecommunications equipment which has already been fully depreciated.

33. DEBTS TO THIRD PARTIES ONLY DUE AFTER A 5 YEAR PERIOD

Debts to third parties which are only due after a 5 year period amount to 1.075.185 thousand escudos.

39. REMUNERATIONS OF THE GOVERNING BODIES

Remunerations paid to the Governing Bodies of the parent company were as follows:

- 48.138 thousand Escudos for the Board of Managing Directors,
- 4.814 thousand escudos for the Audit Board

41. REAVALUATION OF TANGIBLE ASSETS

The revaluations carried out in Portugal were made in compliance with the legal diplomas. Other annual monetary and Fixed Assets revaluations of companies in Brazil, Guiné and S.Tomé and Príncipe were undertaken.

42. REVALUATION OF FIXED ASSETS

a) Net of depreciation

Items	Historic Cost a)	Revaluation a) b)	Revaluated Book Value
Tangible fixed assets			
Real state and natural resources	1 425 482	1 858 492	3 283 974
Buildings and other premises	12 661 965	395 101	13 057 066
Basic equipment	12 085 397	9 449 913	21 535 311
Transport equipment	101 605	117 458	219 063
Tools and equipment	312 196	67 248	379 444
Administrative equipment	1 126 644	355 722	1 482 367
Tare and containers	0	0	0
Other fixed assets	28 840	73 888	102 728
Total	27 742 130	12 317 824	40 059 954

b) Includes successive revaluations

44. FINANCIAL INCOME AND FINANCIAL COSTS

Income and Gains	Financial Year 1993	Financial Year 1992
Interest received	668 387	1 057 977
Profits from subsidiaries and associated companies	1 385 033	848 903
Income from real state	378	
Capital gains from subsidiary companies		
Capital gains from other associated companies	606 910	498 730
Exchange rate gains	2 976 503	1 315 890
Prompt payment discounts	8 031	3 768
Capital gains from sale of short term investments	12 230	8 095
Other income and financial gains	109 488	17 357
Total	**5 766 960**	**3 750 720**

Costs and Losses	Financial Year 1993	Financial Year 1992
Interest paid	978 564	1 676 914
Losses from subsidiary and associated companies	886 008	281 866
Depreciation of investments in real estate		
Provisions for financial assets	465 652	1 099 661
Exchange rate losses	2 419 354	1 637 979
Prompt payment discounts given	54 605	27 380
Losses from the sale of short term investments	13 217	21 550
Other costs and financial losses	100 143	284 404
Financial profits	849 417	(1 279 034)
Total	**5 766 960**	**3 750 720**

45. CONSOLIDATED EXTRAORDINARY PROFIT AND LOSS ACCOUNT

Income and Gains	Financial Year 1993	Financial Year 1992
Tax refunds	6 715	9 076
Debt collection	468	
Gains from stocks		247 007
Profits from real state	1 301 047	1 066 768
Benefits from contractual penalties	39 844	1 666
Reduction in depreciation and provisions	4 506	137 577
Corrections in relations to previous financial years	207 130	273 920
Other extraordinary income	839 386	801 188
Total	**2 399 096**	**2 537 202**

Costs and Losses	Financial Year 1993	Financial Year 1992
Donations	26 172	16 350
Bad debts	7 027	1 109 878
Losses in stocks		12 867
Losses from real state	189 003	622 016
Fines and penalties	1 302	4 434
Increases in depreciation and provisions	1 489 478	178 590
Corrections relating to previous years	372 575	278 737
Other extraordinary losses and costs	2 553 945	196 590
Extraordinary profits	(2 240 406)	117 740
Total	**2 399 096**	**2 537 202**

46. PROVISIONS

The changes in the Accumulated Provisions Accounts, as of December 31, 1993, were as follows:

Accounts	Initial Balance	Increase	Reduction	Final Balance
Provisions for Short term investments	70 029	39 835	0	109 864
Provisions for Doubtful debts	7 194 190	2 307 699	(447 869)	9 054 020
Provisions for Liabilities and charges	5 238 617	1 424 059	(1 445 980)	5 216 696
Provisions for financial investments	629 207	750 562	730 244	2 110 013
Total	**13 132 043**	**4 522 155**	**(1 163 605)**	**16 490 593**

47. Considering the transitory nature, as laid down in D.L. 410/89 of 21 November of leased equipment, only the lease payments were stated as costs in the financial year.

49. In spite of all the efforts undertaken to obtain essential data to prepare consolidated accounts, it was not possible to collect some of the final figures for some of the tables of these notes. Provisional data was used instead. However the amounts involved are not relevant.

50. PARENT COMPANY - CAPITAL

The Parent Company's share Capital as of December 31,1993, has been fully paid in and is represented by 15 600 000 shares of 1000 escudos each. The state holds 50.036 % of the share capital of the Parent Company through CN-Comunicações Nacionais, SGPS, SA, corresponding to 7 805 644 shares. The Parent Company holds 663 918 own shares corresponding to 4.26 % of the capital .

51. a) Accruals and Deferred Costs (Assets)

Accrued Revenues

Interest Receivable	38 959
Other	297 589
	336 548

Defered Costs

Pluriannual Maintenance	121 956
Other	384 942
	506 898
	843 446

b) Accruals and Deferred Payments (Liabilities)

Accrued Costs

Insurance Premiums	530
Remunerations	797 600
Interest Payable	1 236 570
	2 034 700

Deferred Income

Interest	104 449
Investment Subsidies	662 412
Other	731 148
	1 498 009
	3 532 709

52. PROVISION FOR LIABILITIES AND CHARGES

a) Provisions for Pensions	3 351 000
b) Provisions for sundry risks	1 865 696
	5 216 696

53. PROVISIONS FOR PENSIONS

The Parent Company has committed itself to pay its staff supplementary Retirement and Survival Pensions, both for current and retired staff.

The Parent Company, as of 31 December 1993, had Liabilities with Supplementary Retirement Pensions for staff retired before 31 December 1987 and with Survival Pensions for survivors of retired staff that passed away before 31 December 1988. As of 1 January 1994, Liabilities with Survival Pensions for survivors of retired staff that passed away before 31 December 1988 were transfered to the Pension Fund.

The Parent Company's Liabilities with the Retirement Fund and Survival pensions were calculated on the basis of actuarial studies, carried out by an independent body, referring to 31 December 1993. The technical criteria used, which was more conservative and prudent than in previous years, was as follows:

Actuarial Method - estimated "unit credit"; Mortality table - PF 60/64; Handicap table - Swiss Re; Actuarial technical rate - 4%; Long Term interest rate - 9% per annum; Salary growth rate - 7% per annum; and Pension growth rate - 5% per annum.

The aforementioned actuarial study also took into consideration the new Social Security regime, as described in Decree-Law Nr.329/93, and current staff turnover. Whenever staff leave the Parent Company before the retirement age, they will not be entitled to retirement Pensions.

According to this actuarial study the Company's liabilities, as of 31 December 1993, were as follows:

Pension Fund Liabilities	
Liabilities with present staff	2 629 000
Liabilities with current pensioners	2 423 000
Liabilities with current survivors	1 728 000
	6 780 000
Parent Company Liabilities	
Liabilities with current pensioners	1 587 000
	8 367 000

These liabilities, as of 31 December 1993, are fully covered by the existing Parent Company provisions (3,351,000 thousand escudos) and Pension Fund (the market value of the fund portfolio as of 31 December 1993 was 5,016,425 thousand escudos).

The change in the Pension Fund account in the year ended 31 December 1993 was as follows:

Balance as of 31 December 1992	3 087 371
Contributions during the financial year	1 250 000
Pension payments	(50 690)
Income from the fund	729 744
Balance as of 31 December 1993	5 016 425

54. BANK LOANS AND OVERDRAFTS

Short term bank loans	3 649 686
Long and medium term bank loans	8 188 761
	11 838 447

55. STATE AND OTHER PUBLIC UTILITIES

Income Tax	1 586 419
Income Tax Retention	147 088
VAT	291 808
Other	156 995
	2 182 310

56. OTHER CREDITORS

Unpaid subscriptions	129 509
Others	1 047 440
	1 176 949

COMPANHIA PORTUGUESA RÁDIO MARCONI, S.A AUDIT BOARD REPORT

Consolidated Accounts of the Marconi Group for the 1993 Financial Year

To the Shareholders,

1. In accordance with the law and the Articles of Association, the Audit Board of Companhia Portuguesa Rádio Marconi S.A., hereby submits its report and opinion on the Consolidated Balance Sheet and Profit and Loss Account of the Marconi Group for the year ended 31 December 1993. The report of the Board of Managing Directors of the Parent Company describes in detail the problems facing the group and refers the most interesting issues; in spite of that, the present report regarding the Consolidated Financial Statements highlights some interesting information. Particularly important is the restructuring of the group with a view to concentrating business in the field of telecommunications hand in hand with the development of information services. Some of the most important aspects should also be emphasized, such as:

a) the maintenance of a balanced financial structure as can be seen from the most important indicators;

b) the dominant position which the Parent Company continues to hold in the Group, as can be seen from its share in the equity capital;

c)the net profit of the Parent Company, slightly above that of the Group due to better operating and extraordinary profits. The Audit Board also analysed the Legal Certification of Accounts submitted by the Certified Public Accountant member. Finally, mention should be made of the drawbacks arising from the current legal framework governing the presentation of consolidated accounts as regards the time limits established, which are clearly not adjusted to company activity. The Audit Board of Companhia Portuguesa Radio Marconi, S.A., (Parent Company) therefore recommends that the Consolidated Financial Statements of the respective Group for the 1993 financial year be approved.

Lisbon, 11 March 1994

The Audit Board

LEGAL CERTIFICATION OF THE CONSOLIDATED ACCOUNTS

Introduction

1. I have examined the financial statements of the Group, the Parent Company of which is Companhia Portuguesa Rádio Marconi S.A. consisting of the Balance Sheet as of December 31, 1993, the Profit and Loss Account for the year then ended and the respective Notes to the accounts and the Cash flow statement and the respective notes. Total Assets amounted to 65,564,608 thousand escudos, Shareholders' Equity to 46,234,725 thousand escudos and Net Profits to 4,168,173 thousand escudos.

Responsabilities

2. The Board of Managing Directors of the Company is responsible for preparing the financial statements which should present a true and fair view of the financial situation of the company and the result of its operations. The Board is also responsible for implementing generally accepted accounting principles and maintaining an adequate internal control system 3. It is my responsibility to issue an independent and professional opinion based on the examination of the Company's Financial Statements.

Scope

4. The audit was conducted in accordance with the technical standards for the Legal Audit of Accounts as approved by the Chamber of Official Auditors which require that an audit must be planned and carried out in such a way as to provide a reasonable guarantee as to whether the financial information contains important distortions or not.
5. The audit which I have carried out allows me to issue an opinion on the Consolidated financial statements.

Opinion

6. In my opinion these financial statements present a true and fair view of the financial situation of the Group, the Parent Company of which is Companhia Portuguesa Rádio Marconi, S.A., as of 31 December 1993, and the result of its operations and cash flow for the year then ended, in accordance with generally accepted accounting principles.

Lisbon, 11 March 1994

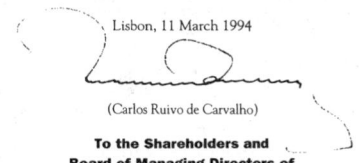

(Carlos Ruivo de Carvalho)

To the Shareholders and Board of Managing Directors of Companhia Portuguesa Rádio Marconi, S. A.
(Amounts expressed in thousands of escudos)

1. We have examined the financial statements of Companhia Portuguesa Rádio Marconi S.A. (The Company) and subsidiaries as of December 31, 1993, the Profit and Loss Account and the Cash-Flow Statement for the year then ended, and the corresponding Notes. The preparation of these financial statements is the responsibility of the Board of Managing Directors of the Company. Our responsibility is to issue an opinion based on our audit on these financial statements.
2. Our audit was conducted in accordance with generally accepted accounting principles which require that an audit be planned and carried out in such a way as to provide a reasonable guarantee that the financial statements do not contain important distortions. An audit includes a random examination of the relevant evidence supporting the financial statements, and the assessment of the decisions made by the Board of Managing Directors, in the preparation and presentation of the financial statements. Likewise, an audit also includes an examination of the adoption of adequate accounting procedures, according to the circumstances and the adoption of adequate financial statements. In view of the examination which we carried out and the reports of the other chartered accountants on the subsidiary companies, it is our conviction that our audit provides a reasonable basis for the presentation of our opinion.
3. The consolidated financial statements of the Company and its subsidiaries as of December 31, 1992, used for comparison with the 1993 statements, were examined by other auditors, who issued an opinion without reservations, as of February 19, 1993. Our opinion is expressed solely with regard to the consolidated financial statements as of December 31, 1993.
4. In our opinion, based on our audit and the reports of the other auditors, the consolidated financial statements mentioned in the preceding paragraph 1 give a true and fair view of the consolidated financial position of Companhia

Portuguesa Rádio Marconi S.A. and its subsidiaries, as of December 31, 1993, as well as consolidated profits of its operations and its consolidated cash-flow statement for the year then ended, in accordance with generally accepted accounting principles.

5. During the 1993 financial year, the Company increased provisions by approximately 3 800 000 000 escudos. This increase in provisions is mainly due to the supplementary retirement pension payments, losses from financial investments and doubtful debts.

6. Following the restructuring process of the telecommunications sector in Portugal, the impact of the decisions taken on the future operations and financial situation of the Company and its subsidiaries is not yet known. As of the date of this report, those facts and decisions are not yet known with precision, and the annexed financial statements also do not include any kind of adjustments arising from the aforementioned process.

Lisbon, 24 February 1994

Arthur Andersen.

Arthur Andersen

Report of The External Auditor
(Amounts expressed in thousands of escudos)
. . . .

Scope

1. In accordance with paragraph d),nr.1 of article 341 of the stock exchanges code,we hereby present our Audit Report on the Consolidated Accounts and the consolidated financial situation relating to the financial information contained in the financial statements of Companhia Portuguesa Rádio Marconi,AS. which include the Report of the Board of Managing Directors , the consolidated Balance Sheet as of December 31,1993, the consolidated Profit and Loss account and the Cash Flow statement for the year then ended and the respective notes to the consolidated accounts.

Responsabilities

2. The Board of Managing Directors of the Company is responsible for preparing the consolidated financial information contained in the Company's financial statements. As external Auditors we are responsible for examining whether the financial information is in accordance with international auditing guidelines,as required by the stock exchanges code,with the aim of issuing an independent opinion on that information,based on our audit.

Examination Made

3. Our Audit was conducted in accordance with the technical standards for the Legal Audit of Accounts as approved by the

Chamber of Official Auditors which require that an audit be planned and carried out in such a way as to provide a reasonable guarantee that the financial statements do not contain important distortions. An Audit includes a random examination of the relevant evidence supporting the financial statements and the assesment of the decisions made by the Board of Managing Directors in the preparation and presentation of the financial statements.Likewise ,an Audit also includes,an examination of the adoption of adequate accounting procedures, according to the circumstances and to whether these are in accordance with generally accepted accounting principles consistently applied in relation to the previous year, and of the adoption of adequate financial statements.

Our Report includes examination of the Report of the Board of Managing Directors and whether that report is in accordance with the remaining financial information included in the Company's financial statements .

In view of the examination which we carried out and the reports of the other Chartered Accountants on the subsidiary companies it is our conviction that our audit provides a reasonable basis for the presentation of our opinion.

4. The consolidated financial statements of the Company and its subsidiaries as of December 31,1992, used for comparison with the 1993 statements ,were examined by other auditors,who issued an opinion without reservations as of February 19,1993.Our opinion is expressed solely with regard to the consolidated financial statements as of December 31,1993.

Opinion without Reservations with Emphasis

5. In our opinion, based on our audit and the reports of the other Chartered Accountants, the financial information contained in the Company's Financial Statements mentioned in the preceding paragraph 1: - give a true and fair view of the consolidated financial position of Companhia Portuguesa Rádio Marconi and its subsidiaries, as of 31 December 1993, and the consolidated profits of its operations and its consolidated cash-flow statements for the year then ended, in accordance with generally accepted accounting principles; and are consistently applied in relation to the previous year as laid down by the Stock Exchange Code.

6. Notwithstanding the opinion expressed in the preceding paragraph, we draw your attention to the following situation:

- During the 1993 financial year, the Company increased provisions by approximately 3,800,000,000 escudos. This increase in provisions is mainly due to the supplementary retirement pension payments, losses from financial investments and doubtful debts.

- Following the restructuring process of the telecommunications sector in Portugal, the impact of the decisions taken on the future operations and financial situation of the Company and its subsidiaries is not yet known. As of the date of this report, those facts and decisions are not yet known with precision, and the annexed financial statements also do not include any kind of adjustments arising from the aforementioned process.

Lisbon, 24 February 1994

Carlos Freire, Carlos Loureiro & Associados, SROC
Represented by Carlos Manuel Pereira Freire

TEXT FROM THE MINUTES - TO COMPLY WITH PARAGRAPH e), NUMBER 1 OF ARTICLE 341 OF THE STOCK EXCHANGE CODE

On March 30, 1994, at 10 o'clock, at the Conference Center in the Company head office, Avenida Álvaro Pais, 2, in Lisbon, the Annual General Meeting of Shareholders of Companhia Portuguesa Rádio Marconi S.A. was held. Shareholders with shares deposited or registered, under the terms of article 13 of the Articles of Association, representing 61.37% of the share capital were present, as can be seen by the list of presences which is annexed to the relevant documents. Under item 2 of the Agenda, a proposal for allocation of profits presented by the Board of Managing Directors was approved. The proposal was as follows: Under the terms of article 38 of the Company's Articles of Association, the Board of Managing Directors proposes the following allocation of profits:

Net Profits of the 1993 Financial Year:		4 168 173 218$
Allocations		
Legal Reserve		
(5% of 4 168 173 218$)	208 408 661$	
First Dividend		
(7% of 15 600 000 000$)	1 092 000 000$	1 300 408 661$
		2 867 764 557$
State's Share of Profits		
(25% of 2 867 764 557$)		716 941 139$
		2 150 823 418$
Second Dividend		865 000 000$
Free Reserves		1 285 823 418$
Total dividends To Be Paid Out		
First Dividend	1 092 000 000$	
Second Dividend	865 000 000$	1 957 000 000$

The proposal for allocation of profits was approved by 78 056 votes in favour, 17 014 votes against and 13 abstentions.

REPUBLIC OF IRELAND

Niall W. Deasy
Coopers & Lybrand, Chartered Accountants
Dublin

1. Background

1.1 Introduction

The development and codification of accounting and financial reporting requirements in the Republic of Ireland has been greatly influenced by the development of Irish company law for two particular reasons. In the first instance Irish company law is the basic body of regulatory requirements for by far the greatest number of incorporated businesses in the Republic of Ireland and, as such, the provisions of this body of law—in particular, its accounting provisions—have the widest application in the Republic of Ireland. Second, the Irish accountancy profession's response to the accounting and financial reporting requirements of this body of law have served to complement and add to the legislation and in doing so have served to provide the basis for further development in Irish company law.

Whereas other forms of incorporation of business occur in the Republic of Ireland (such as friendly societies, building societies, credit unions, agricultural and other forms of co-operative societies), none of the various bodies of legislation governing those businesses has had as marked an influence on the manner of organization of Irish business activity and on the accounting and financial reporting requirements of Irish business as has been provided by Irish company law.

For these reasons, this section primarily consists of a short overview of the development of Irish company law, with particular reference to the accounting and financial reporting requirements it imposes on Irish businesses. The section also contains background information on the Irish accountancy profession and the audit requirements imposed on businesses in the Republic of Ireland.

1.2 The Development of Company Law in the Republic of Ireland

The development of Irish company law can be said to have occurred in three distinct phases in recent history, as follows:

- Up to 1921 (Before 1921 all Irish company law, together with other statute law applicable to Ireland, was enacted in London.)
- From 1921 to 1973 (Over the period from 1921 to 1973 many changes occurred in Irish company law that were largely based on changes in company law in Britain.)
- Since 1973 (The Republic of Ireland joined the European Economic Community in 1973, and many of the changes in Irish company law in the interim have arisen from compliance with the requirements of the EEC's harmonization of company law Directives.)

1.3 The Companies Act of 1963

The most significant statute in company law in the Republic of Ireland until recent times was the Companies Act of 1963 (the 1963 act), which had its origins in the recommendations of the Cox Committee on the reform of company law. The 1963 act embodied many of the provisions of the English Companies Act of 1948 and certain of the recommendations of the Jenkins Committee, which reported in Britain shortly after the Cox Committee reported in the Republic of Ireland. Whereas the structure and content of the 1963 act and the English 1948 act are quite similar, if not exactly the same for many provisions, there are enough differences between the content of the two acts to suggest that it would not be prudent to assume that a knowledge of the content of one of these acts automatically provides a knowledge of the content of the other act .

1.4 Post-1963 Act Legislation

Since the 1963 act, the following principal laws affecting companies have been enacted in the Republic of Ireland:

1. The European Communities (Companies) Regulations of 1973 implemented certain aspects of the EEC's First Directive, which were applicable to the Republic of Ireland. The significant matters involved were the protection of third parties in regard to *ultra vires* transactions and the publication of information about the company.

2. The Companies (Amendment) Act of 1983 implemented the EEC's Second Directive, which introduced the designation *public limited company* (or plc) for public companies with limited liability. This act sets out requirements for the minimum authorized share capital of public companies and for the payment of such share capital. The act also sets out requirements for the maintenance of capital of companies and requires the company's auditor to report whether or not a *financial situation* has arisen in the company's balance sheet at its balance sheet date (a financial situation occurs if the balance sheet discloses net assets that are less than the 50% of the company's issued share capital). The act also defined the nature of distributable profits.

3. The Companies (Amendment) Act of 1986, which implemented the EEC's Fourth Directive was a significant addition to the body of Irish company law. The core provisions of this act were the requirement for prescriptive formats for profit and loss accounts and balance sheets of all companies and the requirement for Irish private companies to file their accounts with the Registrar of Companies, thereby making these available for public inspection. The content of this act is reviewed in more detail in the following paragraphs.

4. The Companies (Amendment) Act of 1990, enacted in August 1990, introduced a new legal mechanism for the rescue or reconstruction of ailing, but potentially viable, companies. The key feature of the act is the power to appoint an examiner to a company and the placement of that company under the protection of the court for a period of 3 months (which may be extended on application to the court). If the examiner believes the company can be saved, then the examiner is required to produce a draft rescue plan for submission to shareholders and creditors and, if agreed, to the court for confirmation. If the court confirms the plan it becomes binding on those concerned.

5. The Companies Act of 1990, enacted in December 1990, sets out a series of significant additional requirements for Irish companies that in the main are concerned with expanding the responsibilities of directors of companies and include provisions permitting companies to acquire or buy back their own share capital. The content of this act is also reviewed in the following paragraphs.

6. In 1992 the provisions of two European Communities (EC) Council Directives with implications for financial reporting were brought into Irish law by means of statutory instruments. They were:

   —Statutory Instrument No 201 of 1992 ("European Communities [Companies: Group Accounts] Regulations, 1992"), which brought into Irish law the provisions of the EC Council Directive on the preparation of Group Accounts.

   —Statutory Instrument No 294 of 1992 ("European Communities [Credit Institutions: Accounts] Regulations, 1992"), which brought into Irish Law the EC Council Directive on the content of annual accounts and on the preparation of consolidated accounts of banks and other financial institutions. This statutory instrument also brings into force the Council directive on the publication of accounts of branches of credit institutions that operate in the Republic of Ireland but that are incorporated outside the state.

7. In 1993 the provisions of two further EC Directives with implications for financial reporting were introduced into Irish law, once again by means of statutory instrument. They were:

   —Statutory Instrument No 395 of 1993 ("European Communities [Branch Disclosures] Regulations, 1993"), which gave effect to the EC's Council Directive dealing with the disclosure requirements of branches established within the state of certain types of company that are governed by the law of another state.

   —Statutory Instrument No 396 of 1993 ("European Communities [Accounts] Regulations, 1993"), which gave effect to the EC's Council Directive, which provides for unlimited companies and partnerships (where all the members or partners have limited liability) to produce and file accounts under the same rules as if they were limited companies.

1.5 The Companies (Amendment) Act of 1986

The key provisions of the Companies (Amendment) Act of 1986 ("the 1986 act"), which, as already indicated, implemented the Fourth Directive, may be summarized as follows:

1. The act specifies the form and content of profit and loss accounts and balance sheets of companies, including footnotes to these financial statements.

2. The act differentiates large, medium, and small companies, with large and medium-sized companies being required to publish (by means of filing with the Registrar of Companies) both profit and loss account and balance sheet. Disclosures for medium-sized companies are slightly less onerous than for large companies. Small companies are required to publish only their balance sheet.

3. The act requires that all limited companies incorporated in the Republic of Ireland file their annual accounts (modified as per item 2, above) with their Annual Returns with the Registrar of Companies in Dublin Castle. This requirement applies to dormant companies and to unlimited companies. In the case of branches of non-Irish incorporated companies, the annual accounts of these companies should be filed.

4. If a private company has a parent company registered in another member state of the European Community (the EC), then that parent company's consolidated accounts may be filed in lieu of the subsidiary company's accounts. The principal requirements in this instance include:

   a. All of the subsidiary company's shareholders must consent to not filing the company's accounts, at the Annual General Meeting (AGM) following the financial year.

   b. The parent company must irrevocably guarantee all the liabilities of the subsidiary for the financial year.

   c. The annual accounts of the company must be consolidated in the parent company's consolidated accounts, which in turn should note the fact that the guarantee has been given.

      d. A copy of the parent company's guarantee must be attached to the company's annual return, together with a statement that the company has availed itself of the exemption, a declaration that all members have consented to the exemption and a copy of the parent company's consolidated accounts. (Note, this exemption does not apply to banks or insurance companies).

  5. The act requires that accounts filed with the Registrar of Companies give a true and fair view.

The 1986 act applied in respect of a company's accounting periods commencing after December 31, 1986, which in practice meant that the act's requirements were applicable in the first instance for financial years ended December 1987.

1.6 The Companies Act of 1990

The Companies Act of 1990 ("the 1990 act") was enacted in December 1990, and its provisions may be summarized as follows:

  1. Investigation of Company's Affairs—The act empowers the court to appoint inspectors to investigate a company's affairs on the application of various interested parties; previously this power lay with the Minister of Industry and Commerce alone. In addition, the Minister is empowered to investigate the ownership of a company, and if there is difficulty finding out the relevant information regarding those shares (or debentures), the Minister is empowered to impose restrictions on those shares (or debentures).

  2. Transactions Involving Directors—The act imposes wide-ranging obligations on directors (or shadow directors, that is, a person or persons in accordance with whose instructions the directors are accustomed to act) in respect of certain of their transactions with companies and sets out value thresholds for those transactions. Greater disclosure of details of transactions involving directors is also required than previously (by the 1963 act).

  3. Disclosure of Interests in Shares—The act imposes a duty on directors and secretaries of companies to disclose their beneficial

interests in the share capital of a company where the beneficial interest exceeds 5% of the issued share capital of the company (including in this context the interest of parties connected with them). The act also addresses the issue of parties acting in concert and imposes separate disclosure obligations on such parties.

4. Insider Dealing—The act makes it illegal to deal in securities where an individual is in possession of inside information; in consequence, the act has implemented the EC Directive on Insider Dealing.

5. Winding Up and Related Matters—The act strengthens the provisions of the 1963 act in regard to winding up and related matters and imposes increased accountability requirements on company officers.

6. Disqualifications and Restrictions for Directors and Other Officers—The act empowers the court to impose the penalty of disqualification from future directorships (or restrictions thereon) for directors of insolvent companies that have been wound up. The restriction, which can run up to 5 years, is that any company with which that individual becomes involved must have a minimum issued share capital of 20,000 Irish pounds (£) (£100,000 in the case of a public limited company).

7. Receivers—The act contains some important new provisions in the role and duties of receivers, including a new duty on receivers to obtain the best price reasonably obtainable in disposing of assets.

8. Accounts and Audit—The act strengthens the obligation to keep proper books of account and includes provisions to extend the auditor's obligations (regarding forming an opinion on proper books of account) and for strengthening the auditor's hand in dealing with the company (through penalties for misleading auditors). The part of the act dealing with these issues has implemented the requirements of the EC's Eighth Directive, while the remaining requirements of the Directive were implemented by statutory instrument in 1992.

9. Acquisition of Own Shares and Shares in Holding Company—The act empowers companies to acquire their own shares (or shares in

their holding company) either by cancellation on redemption or by holding the redeemed shares as treasury shares.

10. Investment Companies—The act provides for the establishment of variable capital companies that must be authorized by the Central Bank.

Commencement orders for the key provisions of the 1990 act were fixed for various dates over 1990 to 1992.

1.7 Statutory Instrument No. 201 of 1992

Statutory Instrument No. 201 of 1992 (European Communities [Companies: Group Accounts] Regulations, 1992) ("the 1992 Group Accounts Regulations") brings into Irish law the EC Council Directive on preparation of consolidated or group accounts. The regulations address such matters as:

1. The format and content of group accounts and the notes to the accounts

2. The definition of a subsidiary undertaking

3. The circumstances and conditions under which companies may be exempted from the requirement to produce group accounts

4. Matters to be included in the directors' report of a parent undertaking and the disclosure of the ultimate parent company in the accounts of subsidiary companies

These regulations apply to financial years beginning on or after September 1, 1992.

1.8 Statutory Instrument No. 294 of 1992

Statutory Instrument No. 294 of 1992 (European Communities [Credit Institutions: Accounts] Regulations, 1992) brings into Irish law the EC Council Directive on the annual accounts and consolidated accounts of banks and other financial institutions and certain other matters. The more significant requirements of these regulations include:

1. The publication within the State of the accounts of branches of credit and financial institutions operating within the State that are incorporated outside the State
2. The format and content of the group accounts of these institutions and the content of the directors' report
3. The accounting treatment and disclosures to be provided in regard to subsidiary and associated undertakings and for joint ventures

These regulations apply to financial years beginning on or after January 1, 1993.

1.9 Statutory Instrument No. 395 of 1993

Statutory Instrument No. 395 of 1993 (European Communities [Branch Disclosures] Regulations, 1993) imposes a similar disclosure of information requirement on branches to that which Irish company law already imposes on subsidiary companies. The requisite information must be returned to the Registrar of Companies in Dublin in (or accompanied by) prescribed forms.

These regulations came into effect on February 1, 1994.

1.10 Statutory Instrument No. 396 of 1993

Statutory Instrument No. 396 of 1993 (European Communities [Accounts] Regulations, 1993) provides that unlimited companies and partnerships, where all the members or partners have limited liability, must produce and file accounts under the same requirements as are laid down for limited companies. This requirement applies for accounting periods beginning on or after January 1, 1994.

These regulations also provide for the following size criteria for companies to come into effect on January 1, 1994:

	Small *(Not Exceeding)*	*Medium* *(Not Exceeding)*
Total assets (fixed & current)	£1.5 million	£6.0 million
Turnover	£3.0 million	£12.0 million
Average number of employees	50	250

1.11 The True and Fair View Requirement

A central feature of the accounting requirements expressed in Irish company law is that companies' accounts must give a true and fair view. This requirement is expressed in the 1963 act (which is viewed as the principal act in the present corpus of Irish company law), in the 1986 act, which effected the requirements of the Fourth Directive, and, more recently, in certain aspects of the 1990 act. In addition to the requirements of Irish company law, the work of the Accounting Standards Committee (ASC) in the development of Statements of Standard Accounting Practice (SSAPs) up to 1990, and the subsequent work of the Accounting Standards Board (ASB) in the development of Financial Reporting Standards (FRSs) has emphasized the relevance and significance of the true and fair view requirement. In consequence, all of the significant forms of business organization in the Republic of Ireland (which would include friendly societies, building societies, credit unions, agricultural, and other co-operative societies, in addition to limited companies) would recognize the true and fair view requirement as being the primary accounting requirement for financial reporting purposes, if that requirement had not already been imposed by their governing statutes.

From a developmental standpoint, the Irish accounting profession has been closely associated with the work of both the ASC and the ASB by virtue of the involvement of the Institute of Chartered Accountants in Ireland (ICAI) in the standard-setting process. ICAI, which is the largest body of professional accountants in Ireland, was a founding member of ASC and fully participated in ASC's development program from its inception. After the establishment of the independent Accounting Standards Board (ASB) in 1990, in succession to ASC, ICAI continues to act as the body with responsibility for promulgating accounting standards in the Republic of Ireland.

1.12 Organization of the Accounting Profession in the Republic of Ireland

The largest body of professionally qualified accountants in the Republic of Ireland is the Institute of Chartered Accountants in Ireland (ICAI), which has a total membership of 8,500 (as of July 1994) of which 4,000 are partners or employees in public practices and 4,500 are involved in industry, commerce, and the public sector. ICAI's membership in the Republic of Ireland is 5,300 members (the remainder being outside Ireland), of which 2,300 are members in practicing offices and 3,000 are members in industry, commerce, and the public sector. The other significant bodies of accountants in the Republic of Ireland are:

- The Chartered Institute of Management Accountants (CIMA)—The membership of CIMA's Republic of Ireland Division is 1,200, almost all of whom are involved in industry, commerce, and the public sector, when due account is taken of CIMA members who are also members of the other accounting bodies in the Republic of Ireland.
- The Chartered Association of Certified Accountants (ACCA)—The membership of ACCA's Irish Region (which includes Northern Ireland) is 2,100 members, of which 1,500 are involved in industry, commerce, and the public sector and 600 in the auditing profession.
- The Institute of Certified Public Accountants in Ireland—The membership of ICPAI is approximately 1,100 members, of which some 550 are engaged in the auditing profession, with the balance engaged in industry, commerce, and the public sector.

ICAI together with CIMA, ACCA, and ICPAI make up the Consultative Committee of Accounting Bodies—Ireland (CCAB-I) and through this organization promulgate the views of the Irish accounting profession on issues of importance to the profession.

1.13 Entry to the Irish Accountancy Bodies

Accountancy students who wish to become members of ICAI must:

- Be either university graduates or have attained a school leaving standard equivalent to that required for entry to university
- Enter into and complete a training contract that will provide for practical training in a recognized training establishment, which in most instances will be a firm of practicing chartered accountants. The duration of the training contract will depend on whether the student is a business graduate or otherwise.
- Undertake part-time education and take professional examinations during the period of the training contract, culminating in a final

admitting examination. The numbers of examinations to be passed
before the final admitting examination will depend on the student's
third level educational attainments.

The standards of education of members of ICAI are such as permit
reciprocity of recognition of membership with the Institutes of Chartered
Accountants in England and Wales, and of Scotland.

Accountancy students who wish to become members of CIMA or
ACCA follow a training, education, and examination program consistent
with that applied by those bodies to their students in the United Kingdom.
Students who wish to become members of ICPAI can enter the accountancy profession both through firms of accountants in public practice and
through industry, commerce, and the public sector in Ireland.

1.14 Audit Requirements in the Republic of Ireland

The 1963 act requires that the accounts of all companies incorporated
under the provisions of the Irish Companies Act be audited annually. This
requirement applies to virtually all other forms of business in the Republic
of Ireland through various governing statutes, the most significant exception being that of incorporated businesses organized as partnerships (unless, that is, all of the partners in the partnership have limited liability, in
which case an annual audit is required).

The working practices and procedures adopted by the auditing profession in the Republic of Ireland are those prescribed by the Auditing
Practices Committee (APC) and its successor body (established in 1991),
the Auditing Practices Board (APB). Auditors' reports incorporating true
and fair view opinions issued in the Republic of Ireland state that the audit
has been conducted in accordance with Auditing Standards issued by the
Auditing Practices Board. ICAI was a founding member of APC and
promulgated APC's Auditing Standards and Guidelines in the Republic of
Ireland. It retains its significant involvement in the standard-setting process carried out by APC's successor body, APB, by virtue of its involvement in the selection of members of APB and by its contribution to the
standard-setting process and to the promulgation of standards.

Auditors of limited liability companies are appointed under the provisions of the Companies Acts and are, in effect, automatically reappointed annually thereafter, unless the auditors indicate in advance that they do not wish to be reappointed (in which case the notice filed with the Companies Office must contain a statement to the effect that there are no circumstances connected with the resignation that should be brought to the attention of the shareholders or, alternatively, a statement of the circumstances should be provided) or a resolution for their dismissal is advised to shareholders after giving appropriate notice. Similar provisions apply for auditors of other forms of business organization in the Republic of Ireland.

Irish company law requires that auditors be members of a recognized accounting body. This requirement is met by membership of one of the following:

- The Institute of Chartered Accountants in Ireland
- The Institute of Chartered Accountants in England and Wales
- The Institute of Chartered Accountants of Scotland
- The Chartered Association of Certified Accountants
- The Institute of Certified Public Accountants in Ireland

1.15. Example of an Auditors' Report in the Republic of Ireland

An example of an auditors' report (without qualification) prepared in accordance with the requirements of Irish company law, and incorporating requirements expressed in the Statement of Auditing Standards titled "Auditors' Reports on Financial Statements," is provided in Appendix B. It will be seen from this example that there are three separate sections in the auditors' report dealing with:

1. The respective responsibilities of directors and auditors
2. The basis of the auditor's opinion
3. The auditors' opinion on the financial statements

The statement of the respective responsibilities of the directors and auditors is for the purpose of distinguishing the responsibilities of both of these parties concerning the preparation of the financial statements and the expression of the auditor's opinion on those statements. If the directors' responsibilities are described elsewhere in the financial statements or in the information accompanying those statements (such as in the Directors' Report), then this section of the auditor's report should cross reference to them.

If, however, they are not so included or the description of the directors' responsibilities is not adequate, then the auditors are required to include an appropriate description of these responsibilities in this section of their audit report.

The section dealing with the basis of the auditors' opinion should explain the basis of the opinion and should identify the auditors' compliance with Auditing Standards in the course of their work, briefly explain the audit process, and indicate that the auditors' work was so planned as to give them reasonable assurance that the financial statements are free from material misstatement.

The final section of the auditors' report sets out the auditors' opinion on the financial statements that the auditors have examined. It will be seen from the following example that the key reporting issue for auditors is whether the accounts under examination show a true and fair view of the results and state of affairs (or financial position). The audit report in Appendix B also shows that many of the auditor's reporting requirements in the Republic of Ireland are similar to those required under company law in the United Kingdom, except that the Irish company law requires affirmative comment in respect of each matter for report, in contrast with the exception basis of reporting required in the United Kingdom. It should also be noted (as mentioned earlier) that Irish company law requires auditors to report (in their audit report) whether or not a financial situation existed at the company's balance sheet date (see Section 2.1.1). This requirement applies to all companies in the Republic of Ireland and is in contrast with the obligation imposed by U.K. Company Law, which requires directors to take action when a financial situation occurs in the case of public limited companies only.

The key reporting requirement for auditors of other forms of business organization in the Republic of Ireland is, in general, fundamentally the same as for limited companies in that the key issue is whether the accounts being reported on show a true and fair view of results and state of affairs (or financial position).

2. The Form and Content of Published Financial Statements in the Republic of Ireland

2.1 The Form and Content of Published Financial Statements

This section focuses on disclosure (rather than measurement) considerations applicable to entities preparing financial statements in the Republic of Ireland. Emphasis is placed on the requirements laid down in the Irish Companies Acts and Financial Reporting Standards (including Statements of Standard Accounting Practice), which are the principal sources of both accounting disclosure (and measurement) requirements in the Republic of Ireland.

In Appendix B to this chapter are the published consolidated financial statements of Bord Telecom Eireann (BTE) for the year ended March 1994. These financial statements have been included to illustrate the issues discussed. BTE's annual report and financial statements won the Chartered Accountants Annual Award for annual reports of businesses registered in the Republic of Ireland on a number of occasions in the past, and so they may be viewed as an example of the standard of best practice in published Irish financial statements.

The content of the core elements of BTE's 1993/1994 financial statements is described in the following paragraphs.

2.1.1 Auditors' Report

The report of the auditors on BTE's 1993/94 financial statement is set out on page 794 in the specimen financial statements. A feature of the auditors' statutory reporting requirements in the Republic of Ireland is that each of the matters to be reported on under the requirements of the Companies Acts must be expressly stated in the auditors' report. The matters to be reported upon by auditors, all of which are expressed in the opinion segment of the auditors' report, are as follows:

- Whether all required information and explanations required for the purposes of the audit have been obtained
- Whether proper books of accounts have been maintained by the company

- Whether the financial statements are in accordance with the books of account
- Whether the financial statements give a true and fair view of the company's profit or loss and of its state of affairs per its balance sheet (in compliance with Irish company law) and of its total recognized gains and losses (in accordance with professional reporting standards)
- Whether the financial statements have been properly prepared in accordance with the Companies Acts and the 1992 Group Accounts Regulations
- Whether the information given in the directors' report is consistent with the financial statements
- Whether the holding company's balance sheet discloses a financial situation that would require the convening of an extraordinary general meeting (a financial situation arises in circumstances in which the company's net assets amount to half or less of the company's called-up share capital).

The respective responsibilities of directors and auditors are addressed at the beginning of the auditors' report, from which it will be seen that directors' responsibilities are described separately in a stand-alone Statement of Directors' Responsibilities. The basis of the auditors' opinion is set out in the middle segment of the auditors' report.

2.1.2 Accounting Policies

The group's accounting policies are set out in the first two pages of the publication (pages 796 and 797 in the specimen financial statements) and are included in compliance with the requirements of SSAP 2 (Disclosure of Accounting Policies).

Section 5 of the Companies Act 1986 requires that the company's financial statements be prepared in accordance with the fundamental accounting principles, namely the going concern, consistency, prudence, and accruals principles. In addition, the 1986 act prohibits set-offs of amounts of assets and liabilities (unless there is a legal right to do so) and income and expenditure.

Section 6 of the 1986 act permits directors to depart from the fundamental accounting principles required by Section 5 if there are special reasons for doing so. However, if they do so they must provide particulars of the departure, the reasons for the departure, and its effect on the company's profit and loss account and balance sheet in a note to the financial statements.

Paragraph 44 of the schedule to the 1986 act requires that if a change in accounting policy occurs, then the corresponding amounts for the previous year should be adjusted to ensure comparability. In addition, particulars of any such adjustment and of the reasons for it must be provided in the financial statements.

Notable accounting policies in BTE's financial statements are those in respect of:

- Basis of Consolidation
- Foreign Currencies
- Tangible Assets
- Grants
- Leased Assets
- Stocks
- Deferred Taxation
- Pensions

2.1.3 Group Value Added Statement

The Group Value Added Statement (on page 798 in the specimen financial statements) identifies the amount of value added generated by the business and its application over the various parties associated with the company, in this instance employees, government, and providers of capital. There are no statutory provisions in Irish company law requiring the inclusion of this statement in a company's annual report or financial statements, and only a minority of companies in the Republic of Ireland publish it.

2.1.4 Group Profit and Loss Account and Group Balance Sheet

The group profit and loss account and the group balance sheet are consolidated financial statements in both instances (pages 799 and 800 in the specimen financial statements) and are required both by the provisions of the Irish Companies Acts and by Financial Reporting Standard 2 (Accounting for Subsidiary Undertakings) (FRS2). The principles involved in the preparation of consolidated accounts and embodied in FRS2 are described in more detail in Section 3.1.

2.1.5 Balance Sheet of the Company

The balance sheet of the holding company (page 801 in the specimen financial statements) must be published as part of the company's annual financial statements.

2.1.6 Format and Content of Profit and Loss Account and Balance Sheets

The format and content of the group profit and loss account and of the group balance sheet and the balance sheet of the holding company comply with the detail specified in the 1986 act and the 1992 Group Accounts Regulations (see Section 1.7) for the format and content of these statements.

2.1.7 Group Cash Flow Statement

Although the Irish Companies Acts do not require that a company's financial statements include a cash flow statement, Financial Reporting Standard 1 (Cash Flow Statements) (FRS1) requires that such a statement be prepared for all entities other than those companies that are deemed to be small companies for the purposes of filing financial statements with the Registrar of Companies (size criteria for such companies are set out in Section 1.10). The cash flow statement (page 802 in the specimen financial statements) in BTE's financial statements complies with the disclosure requirements set out in FRS1.

2.1.8 Notes to the Financial Statements

The notes to BTE's financial statements (pages 804–819 in the specimen financial statements) illustrate many of the disclosures specified under the information requirements laid down for companies in the 1986 act and the 1992 Group Accounts Regulations.

The notes to BTE's financial statements deal with:

1. Turnover—Turnover is analyzed over the company's various classes of business, in accordance with the provisions of paragraph 41 of the schedule to the 1986 act.

2. Operating Costs—This analysis, among other things, provides details of items for which specific disclosures are required, such as staff costs and auditors' and directors' remuneration.

3. Interest Payable and Similar Charges—This note analyses interest payable over the various segments of the company's loan portfolio (in accordance with the provisions of paragraph 39(2) of the schedule to the 1986 act) and also discloses exchange differences.

4. Tax on Profit on Ordinary Activities—Details are provided in this note of the incidence of taxation on the company's business activities (see Section 3.11) and of required disclosures regarding deferred taxation (see Section 3.11.3).

5. Tangible Assets—Movements on fixed assets in terms of cost and depreciation are set out in this note and are separately disclosed over the parent company and the group (see Section 3.5). Disclosure is also provided of details of tangible assets acquired under finance leases (see Section 3.6) and of capital grants (see Section 3.5.2).

6. Financial Assets—Details of the holding company's investment in its subsidiary and related companies, as required under the Irish Companies Acts, are provided in this note (see Section 3.9).

7. Stocks—Details of the make-up of stocks (inventories) are provided in this footnote for both the consolidated and holding company balance sheet (see Section 3.10).

8. Debtors—Details of the make-up of debtors (receivables) are provided for both the consolidated and holding company balance sheet and also of the amounts of group balances in the case of the holding company.

9. Loans and Other Debt—This note provides an analysis of consolidated and holding company loans and other debt as required by the

1986 act; the repayment time analysis is also a specific 1986 act requirement (see Section 3.4).

10. Other Creditors—This note discloses the amounts of trade and other creditors analyzed by reference to the holding and consolidated balance sheets and also of the amounts of group balances for the parent balance sheet (see Section 3.4).

11. Share Capital—The disclosure requirements of the 1986 act referable to the company's share capital are set out in this note (see Section 3.3).

12. Group and Related Companies—Details of the company's subsidiary and related companies as required by the 1986 act are provided in this note.

13. Profits on Ordinary Activities—In that the holding company's profit and loss account is not published separately, this note discloses the profit on the ordinary activities of the holding company.

14. Employees—This note provides the analysis of the average number of persons employed by the group by reference to their various categories as required by the 1986 act.

15. Pensions—This note provides disclosures relative to the company's pension scheme (see Section 3.12).

16. Contingent Liabilities and Capital Commitments—These notes provide details of the group's contingent liabilities and capital commitments (see Sections 3.4.2 and 3.4.3).

17. Approval of Financial Statements—This note identifies the date at which the financial statements were approved by the Board of Directors of the company.

2.1.9 Financial Reporting Standard 3 (Reporting Financial Performance)

Financial Reporting Standard 3 (FRS 3) expanded the requirements for reporting the financial performance of companies and for the content of companies' financial statements. The requirements of the standard are applicable for accounting periods ending on or after June 22, 1993.

The principal features of this standard are:

1. It requires increased disclosures of financial performance by means of changes in the format of the profit and loss account and by means of the presentation of additional financial statements that include summaries and reconciliations of key data.

2. It requires that the results of continuing and discontinued operations be separately identified in the profit and loss account.

3. It requires that any significant profits or losses arising on termination of an operation, or costs arising from a fundamental reorganization or restructuring of profits or losses on the disposal of fixed assets be separately disclosed in the profit and loss account.

4. It redefines extraordinary items, albeit in an extremely restrictive manner.

5. It requires that earnings per share (EPS) be calculated on the profits attributable to the ordinary shareholder of the company after accounting for minority interests, extraordinary items, preference shares (if any), and other appropriations in respect of preference shares.

FRS 3 supersedes SSAP 6 (Extraordinary Items and Prior Year Adjustments) and amends SSAP 3 (Earnings per Share).

Implementation of the requirements of FRS 3 in BTE's financial statements has occurred in the following manner:

1. Continuing Operations—There is a statement at the end of the profit and loss account (page 799) to the effect that all of the company's results are in respect of continuing operations.

2. Additional Financial Statements and Reconciliations—New financial statements and data are set out on page 803 in the specimen financial statements dealing with:

   — The Statement of Total Recognized Gains and Losses, which facilitates users seeing all recognized gains and losses arising in any accounting period being brought together in a single statement

— The Note of Historical Cost Profits or Losses, which is memorandum information for the purpose of showing the difference between the reported results and the historic results that would otherwise have arisen if there had not been a revaluation of fixed assets

— The Reconciliation of Movements in Shareholders' Funds, which brings together the results for the period with all other changes in shareholders' funds during the period under review

The specimen set of published financial statements for 1993/1994 may be found in Appendix B at the end of this chapter.

2.2 Segmental Disclosure

The requirements governing segmental disclosures in the Republic of Ireland are contained in the Companies (Amendment) Act of 1986 (the 1986 act), in the Stock Exchange's regulations, and in Statement of Standard Accounting Practice 25 (Segmental Reporting).

2.2.1 Companies (Amendment) Act of 1986

The 1986 act requires that a company's turnover be analyzed over:

1. Class of business, where in the directors' opinion the company has carried on two or more classes of business that differ substantially from each other
2. Geographic markets, where in the directors' opinion the company has supplied markets that differ substantially from each other

This analysis need not be provided, however, if the directors are of the opinion that the disclosure of such information would be seriously prejudicial to the interests of the company. If this exemption is availed of, however, the lack of disclosure of such information must be disclosed.

Finally, immaterial amounts of turnover may be included with another class of business or geographic market for the purposes of this analysis.

2.2.2 Standard Accounting Practice

SSAP 25 requires that where an entity has two or more classes of business or operates in two or more geographic segments it should disclose the following information for each class of business and geographic segment:

- Turnover
- Result before taxation, minority interest, and extraordinary items
- Net assets

The standard permits nondisclosure of this information if, in the opinion of the directors, such disclosure would be seriously prejudicial to the interests of the reporting entity. Any such omission must be stated.

3. Accounting Policies and Practices in Valuation and Income Measurement: Implications for the Analyst

3.1 Group Financial Statements

The requirement to produce consolidated financial statements for groups of companies in the Republic of Ireland is expressed in Company Law (principally in the 1992 Group Accounts Regulations, see Section 1.7) and FRS2. Note that FRS 2 applies to all parent undertakings, whether or not they are incorporated and whether they are public or private companies.

3.1.1 Subsidiary Undertakings

An undertaking is a parent undertaking of another undertaking (a subsidiary undertaking) if any of the five following conditions apply:

1. The parent holds a majority of the voting rights in the undertaking.
2. The parent is a member of the undertaking and has the right to appoint and remove directors holding a majority of the voting rights at board meetings.

3. The parent (whether or not it has a shareholding) has the right to exercise a dominant influence over the undertaking by virtue of the provisions of its Memorandum and Articles of Association or in a control contract.

4. The parent is a member of the undertaking and controls alone (by virtue of an agreement with other shareholders) a majority of voting rights in the undertaking.

5. The parent has a participating interest in the undertaking and

   • Actually exercises a dominant influence over it, or,
   • The parent and the undertaking are managed on a unified basis.

The common feature of the criteria set out above is that of control by the parent (or by the parent and its subsidiaries) over the subsidiary undertaking.

3.1.2 Exclusion of Subsidiary Undertakings

The overriding principle is that a parent should not consolidate a subsidiary that it does not control. FRS2 specifically requires that subsidiary undertakings be excluded from consolidation in the following circumstances:

1. If the parent's control over the subsidiary is subject to severe long-term restrictions

2. Where the group's interest is held exclusively with a view to subsequent resale and the subsidiary undertaking has not previously been consolidated in the consolidated financial statements prepared by the parent

3. Where the subsidiary's activities are so different from those of other subsidiary undertakings that its inclusion would be incompatible with the obligation to show a true and fair view. FRS2 notes that it will be exceptional for exclusions to arise under this category, and in particular it emphasizes that this exclusion does not apply merely because the subsidiary undertakings are involved in different businesses or are dealing with different products and services.

Two other considerations are worth noting, namely:

1. FRS2 permits the exclusion of a subsidiary undertaking if its inclusion is not material for a true and fair view. However, two or more subsidiaries may be excluded only if, taken together, they are not material.
2. Unlike Irish company law, FRS2 does not permit exclusion of a subsidiary's undertaking from the consolidated financial statements on the grounds of undue delay or disproportionate expense.

Where a subsidiary is excluded from the consolidation, then certain information about the results and balance sheet of that subsidiary will still be required to be included in the notes to the financial statements.

3.1.3 Exemption from Consolidation Requirement

Three situations exist under the provisions of FRS2 and Irish company law, where a parent may be exempt from the consolidation requirement:

1. Parents of small or medium-sized groups (small or medium in this context as defined in Irish company law, see Section 1.10)
2. Intermediate parents (where the parents are registered in an EC member state), namely, parents that are in turn subsidiaries of another parent
3. Parents, all of whose subsidiaries are permitted or required to be excluded from consolidation

3.1.4 Consolidated Financial Statements

FRS 2 requires parents preparing financial statements that are to show a true and fair view to prepare them in the form of consolidated financial statements in which appropriate adjustments will be made to:

- The results of subsidiary companies to ensure uniformity of application of accounting policies throughout the group
- Eliminate intergroup balances and unrealized intergroup profits and losses

In addition, it will be necessary to ensure that any outside or minority interests in the share capital, reserves, and results of the group are appropriately disclosed.

Whereas Section 149(5) of the Companies Act of 1963 provides that preacquisition reserves of a subsidiary company may not be distributed, the section also goes on to permit that "where the directors and the auditors are satisfied and so certify that it would be fair and reasonable and would not prejudice the rights and interests of any person," then the preacquisition profits of an acquired company may be treated in a manner other than in accordance with this general provision.

3.1.5 Merger Accounting

Since the enactment of the 1992 Group Accounts Regulations, merger accounting is permissible under Irish company law subject to compliance with a number of conditions, in particular that:

- At least 90% of the acquired undertakings' shares are held by the investing undertaking or its subsidiaries, and
- No more than 10% of the consideration for the acquisition is for cash.

Note that where merger accounting is to be adopted, if a goodwill amount arises in the course of an acquisition there is no provision for merger relief under Irish company law.

3.1.6 Coterminous Year Ends for Subsidiaries

Regulation 26 of the 1992 Group Accounts Regulations requires that group financial statements be drawn up as of the same date as the annual financial statements of the parent undertaking. Notwithstanding this requirement, however, the regulation also permits consolidation of the financial statements of a subsidiary undertaking where these have a year end date not more than 3 months before the parent's year end date.

3.1.7 Accounting for Goodwill

Where the purchase of a subsidiary is accounted for as an acquisition, any amount of goodwill arising as a result of the transaction (the amount of goodwill being the difference between the fair value of the consideration and the aggregate amount of the fair values of the net assets acquired), in accordance with the provisions of SSAP 22, may be accounted for either by way of:

- Immediate write-off against reserves, or
- Amortization on a systematic basis by reference to its estimated useful economic life.

Negative goodwill should be credited to reserves.

3.1.8 Goodwill in the Balance Sheet

Under the provisions of the 1986 act, if goodwill is to be carried forward in the balance sheet, then it should be included under intangible fixed assets and disclosure should be made of the following:

- Cost, accumulated depreciation, and net book value amounts at the beginning and end of the accounting period in each instance
- The amount of goodwill amortized through the profit and loss account for the year

The 1986 act also provides that financial statements disclose the period over which the amount of goodwill will be written off and the reason for selecting this period.

3.1.9 Equity Accounting

Under the provisions of SSAP 1, an associated company is a company in which an investing company:

- Has an interest that is effectively that of a partner in a joint venture or consortium, and
- Is in a position to exercise significant influence over the company in which the investment is made, or
- The investment is long term, and the investing company can exercise significant influence over the company in which the investment has been made.

Significant influence involves participation in (but not necessarily control over) the financial and operating policies of the company in which the investment has been made. Board representation is indicative of such participation (but not necessarily conclusive). A 20% or more shareholding would be indicative of significant influence.

The concept of a related company under the provisions of the 1986 act is similar to, although not precisely the same as, that of an associated company under SSAP 1.

SSAP 1's accounting requirements for associated companies provide that:

- The investing group's profit and loss account should include its share of the associated company's pretax profits, tax charge, extraordinary items, and post-tax profit
- The investing group's balance sheet should include the cost of its investment in the associated companies, together with its share of the postacquisition reserves of the associated companies

The 1986 act sets out specific disclosures in respect of associated companies, as regards, among other things, details of the associated company, the investing company's shareholding in it, and amounts owed to, or by, the associated company.

3.2 Foreign Currency Translation

Paragraph 44 of Part IV to the Schedule to the Companies Act of 1986 requires that the basis on which amounts denominated into foreign currencies have been translated into Irish currency for the purposes of inclusion in a company's financial statements should be disclosed. Paragraph 13 of the Schedule to the 1992 Group Accounts Regulations requires that the basis on which various items are translated be stated in the financial statements.

The provisions of SSAP 20—which sets out the basis of accounting for foreign currency translation—govern the manner in which foreign currency denominated amounts are translated for the purposes of preparing an entity's financial statements. The provisions of this SSAP deal with accounting considerations referable to both consolidated financial statements and financial statements of individual companies.

3.2.1 Consolidated Financial Statements

The provisions of SSAP 20 in regard to preparing consolidated financial statements that include a foreign subsidiary (or an associated company or branch) may be summarized as follows:

- Normally either the closing rate or the net investment method is used for translating the foreign entity's financial statements for consolidation purposes.
- Exchange differences arising on the translation of the opening net investment at the closing exchange rate should be accounted for as a movement on reserves.
- Profit and loss account items should be translated at either the closing rate or at the average rate for the accounting period. If the average rate is used, the difference between the profit and loss account translated at the average rate and at the closing rate should be accounted for as a movement on reserves.
- Balance sheet items should be translated at the closing rate.

The SSAP permits that the temporal rate method may be used where a business's trade is more dependent on the investing companies' economic environment than that of its own reporting currency.

Also, where foreign currency borrowings have been used to finance a group's equity investment in a foreign enterprise, exchange gains or losses on those borrowings may be accounted for through reserves and offset against exchange differences arising on the retranslation of net investment. If this approach is to be applied, however, the relationship between the investing company and the foreign enterprise must justify the use of the closing rate method.

3.2.2 Individual Companies

The SSAP's provisions in regard to preparing the financial statements of individual companies may be summarized as follows:

- All items (assets, liabilities, revenues, or costs) denominated in a foreign currency should be translated at the rate of exchange applicable at the date on which the transaction took place. An average rate is acceptable in lieu of this approach if rates do not fluctuate significantly. If a rate for a transaction is fixed (such as by contracting for a specific rate or by covering the rate by way of a forward contract), then the fixed rate may be used.

- Monetary assets and liabilities denominated in foreign currencies at the balance sheet date should be translated by using the closing rate or, alternatively, at the rate that is fixed contractually for these items. Normally, no subsequent translations should be made once nonmonetary assets have been translated and recorded.

- Exchange differences arising on settled transactions and on unsettled short-term monetary items should be reported as part of the results of the period. If they result from transactions that are deemed to be extraordinary (or exceptional), then they should be reported as part of the extraordinary (or exceptional) item.

- Exchange differences arising on unsettled long-term monetary items should also be recognized in the profit and loss account. In exceptional cases, however, where there are doubts about the convertibility or marketability of the currency in question, then it will be necessary to consider, on the grounds of prudence, whether the amount of the gain (or the amount by which exchange gains exceed past exchange losses on the same items) should be restricted.

- The closing rate method may be used to translate the value of an equity investment where foreign currency amounts have been used to finance or hedge the amount of the investment, provided the following conditions apply:
  — Exchange differences arising from the borrowings may be offset only to the extent of exchange differences arising from the equity investment in any accounting period.
  — The foreign currency borrowings used for offset purposes should not exceed the total amount of cash that the equity investment or investments are expected to generate;
  — The accounting treatment adopted should be applied consistently

If the above circumstances apply, then the exchange difference on the borrowing should be taken directly to reserves and offset, as a reserve movement, against any exchange difference arising on the translation of the amount of the equity investment.

SSAP 20 requires the following disclosures in financial statements:

- The methods used in translating the financial statements of foreign enterprises and treatment accorded to exchange differences
- The net amount of exchange gains and losses on foreign currency borrowings less deposits identifying separately the amount offset in reserves and the net amount accounted for in the profit and loss account
- The net movement on reserves arising from exchange differences

3.3 Capital and Reserves

The 1986 act requires disclosure of the amounts of a company's authorized and issued share capital in its financial statements, together with supporting details of that share capital. For redeemable shares, the 1986 act requires that details be provided regarding the basis and timing of the redemption process. Financial Reporting Standard 4 (Capital Instruments) [FRS4] specifies additional disclosure requirements regarding shares, in particular regarding the terms and conditions applicable to them.

The 1990 act permits companies to repurchase their own shares, provided the company's articles of association so permit. Any repurchase must be from distributable profits or from the proceeds of an issue of new shares.

The 1963 and 1986 acts, among other things, require that reserves be treated in the following manner:

1. Retained Profits—Retained profits should be accumulated and identified as the balance on the profit and loss account in the company's balance sheet. These profits are normally available for distribution by way of dividend.
2. Revaluation Reserves—If a surplus (or deficit) arises from a revaluation of the book value of fixed assets, then it should be separately identified in the company's balance sheet as a "revaluation reserve." Such reserves, being unrealized in nature, are not available for distribution by way of dividend.

3. Share Premium Account—If a company issues shares at a premium over their nominal value, then the amount of that premium must be separately identified in the company's balance sheet. It is permitted to write off against this premium:

—Preliminary expenses incurred in incorporating the company

—Expenses, commissions, or discounts incurred in connection with the issue of the shares (or debentures)

—Any premium arising on the redemption of preference shares

All movements on reserves should be separately identified in the company's financial statements over opening and closing balances and transfers to or from other reserves.

As a general rule, realized profits or surpluses (net of unrealized losses) may be distributed by way of dividend, whereas unrealized profits or surpluses may not be so distributed.

3.4 Liabilities and Provisions

The balance sheet formats specified in the 1986 act require that creditors be separately quantified and identified in the balance sheet by reference to:

* Creditors that are in respect of amounts due within one year of the balance sheet date, and
* Creditors that are in respect of amounts due after more than one year from the balance sheet date.

Amounts of creditors under each of the above headings must be analyzed and disclosed in the company's balance sheet or related notes over the following headings:

* Debenture loans
* Bank loans and overdrafts
* Payments received on account
* Trade creditors
* Bills of exchange payable
* Amounts owed to group companies

- Amounts owed to related companies
- Other creditors, including tax and social welfare
- Accruals and deferred income

For all items included under the heading "Creditors" in the balance sheet, the 1986 act requires that the following information be disclosed:

- The aggregate amount of items included in creditors that are repayable other than by installments after 5 years from the balance sheet date
- The aggregate amount of items in creditors repayable by installments after 5 years from the balance sheet date
- The amounts of debts that have been secured and the nature of the security given
- The fact that any charges exist on the company's assets to secure the debts of the other parties

FRS4 requires that the 1986 act's disclosure requirements for analysis of maturity of debt be expanded to disclose (in addition to the above) amounts falling due between 2 and 5 years from the balance sheet date.

3.4.1 Provisions for Liabilities and Charges

In addition to the creditors' amounts listed above, the 1986 act requires separate disclosure in a company's balance sheet (under the heading "Provisions for Liabilities and Charges") of the following items:

- Pensions and similar obligations
- Taxation, including deferred taxation
- Other provisions

3.4.2 Contingent Liabilities

The 1986 act also requires that the nature and amount of any contingent liabilities that have not been provided for be disclosed in a company's balance sheet. If security has been given for such a liability, this should also be disclosed.

3.4.3 Commitments

The 1986 act requires the following disclosures of commitments entered into by a company:

- Capital Commitments—Amounts contracted for but not provided for and the total amount of capital expenditure authorized but not contracted for must be stated.
- Pension Commitments—Particulars of the amounts of pension commitments provided for and not provided for must be disclosed.
- Other Financial Commitments—Particulars of any other financial commitments that have not been provided for and are relevant to assessing a company's state of affairs must be disclosed.

3.5 Property, Plant, and Equipment

The Companies Act of 1986 requires that fixed assets comprising property, plant, and equipment be disclosed in a company's balance sheet under the heading "Tangible Fixed Assets" at the net book value (which is cost or valuation less accumulated depreciation) of those assets. Details of such assets must be analyzed over the headings:

- Land and buildings
- Plant and machinery
- Fixtures, fittings, tools, and equipment
- Payments on account and assets in the course of construction

All movements in cost or valuation of these assets during the year (opening, closing balances, additions, and disposals) and also the amount of depreciation of these assets must also be disclosed.

3.5.1 Accounting for Fixed Assets

The rules for accounting for cost or valuation or depreciation of the assets may be summarized as follows:

1. Cost may be either the purchase price or the production cost of the fixed asset. The purchase price of an asset will be the actual price paid for the asset, and the amount may be increased by any expenses incurred in acquiring the asset. The production cost of the asset will comprise the cost of the raw materials and consumables used in producing the asset, together with a reasonable proportion of the costs indirectly incurred in the production of the asset. Interest on capital relative to the financing of the production of the asset may be included in the production of the asset, but if it is, the amount included must be disclosed in a note to the accounts.

2. The value of a tangible fixed asset may be the market value of a fixed asset as of the date of its valuation or the current cost of the asset. Any surplus or deficit arising from the revaluation of a fixed asset must be transferred to a revaluation reserve, which must be separately disclosed in the company's balance sheet. (It should be noted that while it is permitted to reduce the balance on the revaluation reserve—if, in the opinion of the directors, the amount is no longer necessary for the accounting policies followed by the company—the amount may be transferred to the profit and loss account only if it represents realized profit). The application of alternative accounting rules to investments is discussed in Section 3.9, and the principles set out there are also applicable where fixed assets are included in a balance sheet at a valuation.

3. Depreciation of a fixed asset must be calculated on a basis that will write off the purchase price or production cost of the asset, less the amount of any estimated residual value, over the period of the asset's useful economic life. If the fixed asset is included on the basis of a valuation, then the amount of the valuation will form the basis for the depreciation charge rather than the purchase price or production cost of that asset.

3.5.2 Government Grants

In accordance with the provisions of SSAP 4, government grants received in respect of fixed assets acquired by a company must be credited to the profit and loss account over the expected useful life of the asset to which the grant relates. This accounting requirement may be implemented by one of the following methods:

- Carrying the amount of the grant as a deferred credit in the balance sheet and amortizing the amount thereof annually to the profit and loss account. The net book amount of this credit at any time would be the total amount of the grant received less the amount of accumulated amortization amounts transferred to the profit and loss account.
- If the deferred credit approach is adopted, the net credit amount deferred should be disclosed separately in the balance sheet, but it should not be included as part of shareholders' funds.
- Alternatively, the amount of the purchase price or production cost of the fixed asset should be reduced by the amount of the capital grant and the net resulting cost amount depreciated over the asset's useful economic life.

The amended version of SSAP No. 4 (issued in July 1990) states that on the basis of legal advice received, the option to deduct government grants from the purchase price (or production cost) of fixed assets is not available to companies governed by the 1986 act.

Any contingency to repay grants should be disclosed in the company's accounts.

3.5.3 Investment Properties

SSAP 19 ("Accounting for Investment Properties") defines an investment property as a completed or developed property that is "held for its investment potential" and whose rental income is negotiated on an arm's-length basis. Exceptions to this definition are owner-occupied properties, with the concept of owner occupied having groupwide application in groups of companies.

The provisions of SSAP 19 for accounting for such properties may be summarized as follows:

- Investment properties should be included in the balance sheet at their open market value and should not be depreciated (leasehold properties with 20 years or less to run are an exception and should be depreciated over the remaining unexpired term of the lease).

- Where investment properties make up a significant part of a company's total assets, the properties should be valued annually, but every 5 years the valuation should be completed by an external valuer.
- Changes in the value of the portfolio of investment properties should be accounted for through an investment revaluation reserve.
- The carrying value of the investment properties and the investment revaluation reserve should be displayed prominently in the accounts, together with either the name of or qualifications of those who completed the valuation of the properties and the basis of the valuation. If the person is an employee of the company, this fact should also be disclosed.

Paragraph 6 of the schedule to the 1986 act requires that any fixed asset that has a useful economic life must be depreciated over the term of that life. However, the act also imposes an overriding requirement that financial statements shall give a true and fair view of results and balance sheet position, and this consideration permits the application of the provisions of SSAP 19. It should be noted that the 1986 act requires details of this departure from the act and the reasons therefor to be disclosed in the company's financial statements. Note also in this context that Urgent Issues Task Force Abstract 7 (True and Fair Override Disclosures) states that where a true and fair view override is being evoked, this should be stated clearly and unambiguously in the financial statements (together with the particulars of any such departure, the reasons for the departure, and its effect).

3.5.4 Deferred Taxation

Writing down the value of fixed assets for tax purposes is calculated by reference to the rates and bases permitted by the Revenue Commissioners for tax computation purposes. The rates used have varied over time, and the basis on which they are calculated is (mainly) the diminishing balance basis. In these circumstances it is extremely unlikely that a company's depreciation rates and bases of calculation will produce a depreciation charge that equates with the amount of capital allowances permitted for tax computation purposes.

In the more likely event of a value difference materializing between the net book value of fixed assets and their corresponding written down value for tax purposes, consideration will have to be given to the need for providing for deferred taxation in respect of the amount of the difference arising.

There is no need to accelerate depreciation write-downs in the financial statements in excess of the normal depreciation charge in order to obtain an entitlement to write-offs for tax purposes.

Other significant timing differences can arise from provisions made in the financial statements that only become deductible for tax purposes when the expenditure (or event) is actually incurred.

3.6 Assets Whose Services Are Acquired by Means of Leases

Accounting for assets acquired by means of leases in the Republic of Ireland—whether they are formal leases or hire purchase contracts—is based on the principles laid down in SSAP 21, "Accounting for Leases and Hire Purchase Contracts." Under the provisions of this SSAP, leases are categorized into finance leases and operating leases, as follows:

- A finance lease is a lease in which the lessee has substantially all the risks and rewards associated with the ownership of the asset but not the legal title (substantial in this context is normally 90% or more of the fair value of the leased asset).
- An operating lease is a lease other than a finance lease but usually involves the lessee paying for the rental of an asset for a period that is substantially less than its useful economic life, while the lessor retains most of the risks and rewards of ownership.

The accounting provisions of SSAP 21 require that assets acquired under finance lease contracts be accounted for in the lessee's financial statements, usually at the cost of the asset acquired with the lessee's financing obligations in respect of that asset being included as a liability in those financial statements. The accounting rules for these leases (in the lessee's books) may be summarized as follows:

- The fixed asset acquired should be included in the lessee's balance sheet at fair value (usually cost), which amount should be depreciated over the shorter of the term of the lease or the asset's useful life. If the financing contract is a hire purchase contract, however, then the asset should be depreciated over its useful life.
- A liability should be recorded for the present value of the minimum lease payments under the terms of the financing lease, which amount is derived by discounting these payments by the interest rate implicit in the lease. Subsequent rental payments should be analyzed between the amount required to reduce the lease obligation (which should be accounted for against that liability) and the amount of the finance charge (which should be charged to the profit and loss account).

3.6.1 Disclosures Required in Lessee's Accounts

For assets acquired under finance leases, the following disclosures are required:

- The gross value amounts of assets held under finance leases, together with related accumulated depreciation, should be disclosed over each major class of asset, together with the amount of the current period depreciation charge applicable to those assets (which should also be analyzed by major class of asset). Alternatively, if owned and leased fixed assets are merged in the financial statements, then the net book value of the leased assets and the current period depreciation charge relevant to them should be disclosed.
- Finance lease obligations (net of finance charges) should be separately disclosed from other obligations and liabilities. The total amount involved should be analyzed over the amount payable in the year following the balance sheet date, the amount payable in the 2nd to 5th year following and the amount payable after 5 years from the balance sheet date.
- The total amount of the finance charges allocated to the period covered by the financial statements should be disclosed.
- The amounts of any finance lease commitments entered into at the balance sheet date but whose inception occurred after the year end should be disclosed.

- The accounting policy adopted should be disclosed.

For assets acquired under operating leases, the following disclosures are required:

- Total operating lease rentals charged to the profit and loss account for the period should be disclosed, analyzed over payments related to hire of plant and machinery and for other operating leases.
- Payment commitments under the terms of the operating leases should be disclosed and analyzed over the following year's payment, the amounts to be paid over years 2 to 5 after the balance sheet date and amounts payable after 5 years from the balance sheet date. All of these amounts should be analyzed between payments applicable to land and buildings and payments under other operating leases.
- The accounting policy adopted in regard to such leases should be disclosed.

3.7 Oil, Gas, and Other Mineral Resources

There are no specific provisions in Irish company law regarding the manner of accounting for oil, gas, and other mineral exploration and development activities. Guidance on the appropriate approach to be adopted for oil and gas exploration and development activities is set out in two SORPs published by the Oil Industry Accounting Committee and franked by ASC. The Accounting Standards Board (ASB) has not yet issued guidance on accounting for mineral exploration and development costs.

The recommended practice required by the SORP for accounting for oil and gas exploration and development activities should be either the full cost or successful efforts/methods as set out in the SORP. Whichever method is adopted should be applied consistently by all companies within a group.

3.7.1 Full Cost Accounting

Full cost accounting requires:

- All costs incurred in exploration and development of oil and gas resources should be capitalized.

- All such capitalized expenditures should be recorded within cost pools (which should normally be country-sized or larger).
- The basis on which cost pools are established should be disclosed as an accounting policy.
- All expenditure carried forward within each pool should be depreciated on a unit-of-production basis by reference to quantities.
- A ceiling test should be carried out at the balance sheet date to determine whether the net book values of the capitalized costs are recoverable against anticipated future net revenues.
- Proceeds from the full or partial disposal of a property should be credited to the relevant cost pool.
- Full cost pools expenditures should be classified in the balance sheet as "tangible assets," whereas any expenditures related to exploration activities but held outside full cost pools should be classified as "intangible assets—exploration expenditure."

3.7.2 Successful Efforts Accounting

The successful efforts approach to accounting for such expenditures requires the following:

- While exploration expenses should be capitalized in the first instance, pending determination, they should be written off if commercial reserves are not established.
- General expenditures should be capitalized only where they relate to activities for which costs are also being capitalized.
- Capitalized expenditures should be written off on a unit-of-production basis by reference to quantities.
- Ceiling tests should be carried out at the balance sheet date to assess whether the net book value of the costs is recoverable against future net revenues.
- Proceeds from the full or partial disposal of a property should be credited either to the relevant cost center or capitalized cost as appropriate.
- Pending evaluation, exploration expenditures should be classified as "intangible assets—exploration expenditure" and reclassified as "tan-

gible assets" when the existence of commercial reserves is established.

The SORP dealing with disclosures about oil and gas exploration and production activities requires the following matters to be disclosed relative to such activity:

- The method of accounting for oil and gas activities, including the accounting policies applied in respect of accounting for preproduction costs, amortization of capitalized costs, ceiling tests, decommissioning costs, deferred taxation, turnover, and royalties
- The aggregate amount of capitalized costs and related depreciation or amortization analyzed by reference to proven and unproven properties and also by geographic areas
- Preproduction costs and the results of operations of exploration and development activities, in total and by geographic area
- The net quantities of a company's interest in proved developed and undeveloped reserves as of the beginning and end of each accounting period and by geographic area

3.8 Intangible Assets

The schedule to the 1986 act requires that intangible assets be included in a company's balance sheet if either they were acquired for valuable consideration (and are not required to be shown as goodwill; see below) or the assets involved were created by the company itself. Intangible assets must be disclosed over the headings as prescribed in the 1986 act:

- Development costs
- Concessions, patents, licenses, trademarks, and similar rights and assets
- Goodwill
- Payments on account

The 1986 act requires that an amount may be included under the heading "Development Costs" only in special circumstances (which are not specified in the act), in which case the period of write-off of these costs, and the reasons for capitalizing them, must be disclosed. It should be noted that research costs are not included in the list of items to be disclosed, although the information that is required to be disclosed to supplement the profit and loss account includes the amount of any expenditure on research and development in the financial year and the amount committed for R&D for future years (Section 43(4) of the schedule to the 1986 act). If the directors conclude that this information would be prejudicial to the interests of the company, however, then it need not be disclosed, but the fact that it has not been disclosed must be stated. It should also be noted that Section 13(d) of the 1986 act requires that the directors' report contain information concerning the company's research and development activities (and those of its subsidiaries, if applicable).

Goodwill amounts may be included only to the extent that the goodwill is acquired for valuable consideration.

Intangible assets must be accounted for and depreciated in the same manner as specified for tangible fixed assets. Hence, these assets may be accounted for at cost (purchase price or production cost less any estimated residual value) or at current cost (with the exception of goodwill), and they must be depreciated in such a manner as to write off the amount of cost over its useful life. All movements on such assets during the year must be disclosed regarding cost or valuation and depreciation over the relevant component headings.

SSAP 13 requires that development expenditures meet the following criteria if they are to be capitalized and written off over future accounting periods:

- The project must be a clearly defined project, and the expenditure involved must be separately identifiable.
- The technical feasibility and commercial viability of the project must be reasonably certain.
- Any additional development costs to be incurred must be aggregated with costs incurred to date and production and selling costs, the total of which must reasonably be expected to be covered by related future revenues.
- Adequate resources exist or are reasonably expected to be available to complete the project.

The accounting policy adopted for accounting for R&D costs must be disclosed, together with details of movements on the account.

3.9 Participations (Equity Investments in Other Companies)

The balance sheet formats provided for in the 1986 act require that equity investments in subsidiary or associated companies shall be disclosed in a company's balance sheet under the heading "financial assets" in the fixed assets segment of the balance sheet or under "investments" in current assets, depending on the nature of the investment involved.

Such investments are accounted for as follows:

1. The cost of the investments may be recorded by reference to historical cost accounting rules or by reference to alternative rules provided for under the 1986 act.

2. Cost, in a historical cost context, represents the actual price paid for the investment, together with any expenses incurred incidental to its acquisition.

3. Under the alternative accounting rules, such investments may be included at a market value determined as of the date of the last valuation, or at a value that the directors deem to be appropriate in the circumstances of the company. (If the latter approach is used, then the method of valuation adopted and the reasons for adopting it must be disclosed). The investments may also be included at their current cost.

4. If there has been a diminution in the value of the investment, a provision may be made in respect of the amount of the diminution. If, however, the diminution is expected to be permanent, then a provision must be made in respect of that diminution. Any such provision must be charged to the profit and loss account and disclosed in the company's accounts.

5. Where an investment is held as a current asset, the value of the investment must be written down to its net realizable value if there has been a reduction in the value of the investment below its acquisition price. On the other hand, if the reasons for which the

write-down occurred no longer apply, then the write-down provision may be written back to the extent that it is no longer necessary.

6. If a surplus arises as a result of a valuation of an investment, it must be taken to a revaluation reserve in the company's balance sheet. Amounts may be transferred to the profit and loss account from the revaluation reserve only if they represent realized profit. It will be necessary to charge the profit and loss account with the amount by which a deficit on a revaluation exceeds the amount of any surpluses in the revaluation account.

7. The 1986 act requires disclosures of:

—Any movements in amounts of investments held as fixed assets

—The amounts of investments in listed securities analyzed over investments listed on a recognized stock exchange and other investments

—The market value of the listed investments

3.10 Stocks/Inventories

Paragraphs 10 and 11 of the schedule to the 1986 act require that current assets—and thereby stocks/inventories—be valued at the lower of purchase price (or production cost) or net realizable value. Paragraph 14 of the schedule defines the purchase price of an asset as being the actual price paid for the assets, together with any expenses incidental to its acquisition. The production cost of an asset is defined as the purchase price of the raw materials and consumables used in producing the asset, together with the amount of the costs incurred in producing the asset and a reasonable proportion of indirect overheads and interest on capital to the extent that these items relate to the period of production of the asset. Distribution costs may not be included in these calculations.

The purchase price or production cost of inventories may be determined by reference to any of the following methods:

- First in, first out (FIFO)
- The weighted average price
- Any other method similar to the FIFO and weighted average method

In addition to the above, paragraph 19(5) of the schedule to the Companies Act of 1986 permits stocks to be included in the balance sheet at current cost.

It will be noted that the above listing does not include the last in, first out (LIFO) stock valuation method or the base stock method of valuation.

Stocks must be disclosed on the face of the company's balance sheet and must be analyzed over the following:

- Raw materials and consumables
- Work-in-progress
- Finished goods and goods for resale
- Payments on account

Paragraph 15(4) of the schedule to the 1986 act provides that if the purchase price or production cost of stocks in the company's balance sheet materially differs from the replacement cost of these assets, then the difference will be disclosed in the company's financial statements.

3.10.1 Long-Term Contracts

With regard to the issue of accounting for long-term contracts (which are defined as contracts that usually exceed a period of one year and that are for the design, manufacture, and construction of a single substantial asset or for the provision of a service), SSAP 9 requires that:

- Where the outcome of a contract can be determined with reasonable certainty, the attributable profit should be calculated on a prudent basis and reflected in the company's financial statements, as should the amount of related turnover.
- The amount by which recorded turnover exceeds the amounts of payment on account should be described as "amounts recoverable on contracts" and separately disclosed in the amount of total debtors.
- The balance of payments on account—that is, the excess amount remaining having matched the payments on account with turnover and offset against long-term contract balances—should be described as "payments on account" and separately disclosed within creditors.

- There should be separate disclosure within the amount of stocks/ inventories in the balance sheet of the costs that have been incurred in long-term contracts, net of amounts transferred to cost of sales and after deducting foreseeable losses and payments on account not matched with turnover. The amount determined on this basis should be described as "long-term contract balances" within the amount of stocks. There should also be separate disclosures of the amounts of net cost less foreseeable losses and applicable payments on account.
- If the provision or accrual for foreseeable losses exceeds the costs incurred (after transfers to cost of sales), the excess amount should be included in the provisions for either liabilities and charges or creditors, as appropriate.

3.10.2 Accounting Policy

The accounting policies that have been used to determine the amounts of cost and net realizable value of stocks should be disclosed. In the case of long-term contracts, the accounting policies disclosed should describe the bases adopted for determining turnover, attributable profit, and foreseeable losses.

3.11 Taxation

3.11.1 Profit and Loss Account Disclosures Required

Paragraph 40 of the schedule to the 1986 act requires that companies disclose the following in regard to taxation charges in their financial statements:

1. The basis on which the tax charge on its profits is computed, whether the tax charge consists of corporation tax, income tax, or any other tax on the company's profits and whether the amount is payable within or outside the State
2. Particulars of any special circumstances that affect the tax liability arising on the company's profits, income, or capital gains, whether for the current year or for succeeding financial years

3. The amount of the charge for corporation tax, income tax, and other taxation on profits or capital gains, so far as charged to revenue, including tax payable outside the State on profits (distinguishing where practicable between corporation tax and other taxation)
4. The tax relative to the profit or loss on ordinary activities and the tax relative to any extraordinary profits or losses earned by the company

In addition to the above, FRS3 requires that the tax applicable to profits or losses arising on sale or termination of an operation, costs of a fundamental restructuring or reorganization, and profits or losses on disposal of fixed assets should be attributed to these items in the note to the financial statements showing the make-up of the tax charge.

The tax charge on the results of the ordinary activities of the business could, among other things, involve disclosure of the following components:

1. Rate of corporation tax
2. Corporation tax charge
3. Capital gains tax
4. Income tax
5. Any other tax on profits
6. Tax attributable to franked investment income
7. Irrecoverable advance corporation tax (ACT)
8. Overseas taxation, relieved and unrelieved (distinguishing corporation tax and other taxes)
9. Deferred taxation (including any adjustments arising from changes in tax rates and allowances)

In the rare circumstances of an extraordinary item, the tax charge arising on any extraordinary profit or loss should be separately disclosed, usually by means of a footnote disclosure having netted off the charge against the amount of the extraordinary item on the face of the profit and loss account.

3.11.2 Balance Sheet Disclosures

The 1986 act requires that any provision for taxation other than deferred taxation be disclosed. Accordingly, the company's balance sheet should disclose details of amounts due at its balance sheet date in respect of corporation tax, income tax, capital gains tax, value added tax, social welfare, and any other tax.

Notwithstanding the comment in paragraph 33 of the schedule to the 1986 act, implying that deferred taxation may not have to be disclosed, it should be remembered that SSAP 15 requires a disclosure of the deferred taxation balance and analysis of its major components. Further, the balance sheet formats required under the 1986 act require that the amount of deferred taxation be included under the heading "Taxation" in the section of the balance sheet dealing with "Provisions for Liabilities and Charges."

3.11.3 Deferred Taxation

Deferred taxation—which is the tax attributable to timing differences between the company's reported results and its results as computed for tax purposes—is computed for Irish companies' financial statements under the provisions of SSAP 15 by the liability method, which requires the deferred tax provision to be calculated at the rate at which it is estimated the eventual tax liability will actually be paid (see also Section 3.5.4). SSAP 15 also provides that:

- A deferred tax provision (or asset) should not be accounted for where it is probable that a liability (or asset) will not crystallize.
- The amount of any unprovided deferred taxation should be disclosed in a note to the financial statements, as should the amount of the deferred tax balance and its major components (for both the current period and the cumulative amount) and any transfers to and from the deferred tax balance.

3.12 Pensions

Paragraph 36(4) of the schedule to the 1986 act requires that particulars of a company's pension commitments be disclosed in its balance sheet either by way of analysis of the total provision or by way of separate disclosure if no provision has been made for the commitment. Separate disclosure is also required of a pension commitment that relates wholly or partly to pensions payable to the company's past directors.

In addition to the above, paragraph 36(5) of the schedule requires disclosure of the following information regarding a company's pension scheme:

- The nature of every pension scheme operated by the company, indicating whether or not each scheme is a defined benefit or a defined contribution scheme
- Whether each scheme is externally funded or internally financed
- Whether professional actuarial advice is obtained in respect of pension costs and liabilities and, if so, the date of the most recent relevant actuarial valuation
- Whether (and where) any such actuarial valuation is available for public inspection

The 1986 act also requires that the profit and loss account disclose the amount of pension costs incurred in respect of the company's employees during the financial year. The Companies Act of 1963 requires disclosure of the total amount of directors' and past directors' pensions, other than pensions provided under a scheme in which contributions are substantially adequate for the maintenance of the scheme. In addition, the 1963 act requires disclosure of contributions paid in respect of directors' pension schemes as a separate item within the disclosure of directors ' emoluments.

In addition to the above, Statement of Standard Accounting Practice 24 (Accounting for Pension Costs) (SSAP 24) sets out additional disclosure requirements relative to pension costs and pension schemes.

3.13 Accounting Standards Currently Operative in the Republic of Ireland

A listing of Accounting Standards currently operative in the Republic of Ireland (both SSAPs and FRSs) is given in Appendix A.

4. Future Developments

For the foreseeable future, it would appear that influence on changes in company law in the Republic of Ireland will come from the European Community. This section reviews those EC measures that have yet to be legislated for and that are expected to be enacted over the next few years.

4.1 Twelfth Directive

The Twelfth Directive provides for companies to be incorporated with only one shareholder (as opposed to the present minimum requirement of two shareholders) and has, as yet, to be legislated for in the Republic of Ireland.

4.2 Insurance Accounts Directive

The Insurance Accounts Directive concerns the published financial statements of insurance companies and applies (with appropriate modifications) the Fourth and Seventh Directives to the insurance industry.

The Fourth Directive was concerned with setting down a true and fair requirement for results and financial position and with the standardization of company accounts formats. The Seventh Directive addressed the accounting requirements of groups of companies. The Insurance Accounts Directive seeks to apply similar requirements for the published financial statements of insurance companies. The provisions of this directive are intended to take effect for financial years beginning on January 1, 1995.

4.3 Company Law Review Group

In February 1994, the Irish government set up a company law review group to examine and make recommendations on various aspects of Irish company law, specifically including such topics as the provisions relating to examinerships, investigations, and insider dealing. Other topics include addressing the recommendations of the Ryan Commission (which reported on the expectations of users of published financial statements) and the needs of smaller businesses. The review group has also been asked to examine the need for a Commercial Court and the possibility of consolidating all Irish company law.

4.4 Accounting Standards

The Institute of Chartered Accountants in Ireland (ICAI) will continue to maintain close liaison with the Accounting Standards Board (ASB) and will promulgate the ASB's financial reporting standards in the Republic of Ireland after incorporating appropriate modifications to reflect legal differences.

Appendix A: Financial Reporting in the Republic of Ireland

Accounting Standards Currently in Force (July 1994)

Statements of Standard Accounting Practice (SSAPs)

1. Accounting for associated companies (to be read in conjunction with the Interim Statement on Consolidations)
2. Disclosure of accounting policies
3. Earnings per share (amended by FRS 3)
4. Accounting for government grants
5. Accounting for value-added tax
8. The treatment of taxation under the imputation system (Appendix 3 ROI)
9. Stocks and long-term contracts in progress
12. Accounting for depreciation
13. Accounting for research and development
15. Accounting for deferred taxation
17. Accounting for post-balance sheet events
18. Accounting for contingencies
19. Accounting for investment properties
20. Foreign currency translation

21. Accounting for leases and hire purchase contracts
22. Accounting for goodwill
23. Accounting for acquisitions and mergers
24. Accounting for pension costs
25. Segmental reporting

Financial Reporting Standards (FRSs)

1. Cash flow statements
2. Accounting for subsidiary undertakings
3. Reporting financial performance
4. Capital Instruments
5. Reporting the substance of transactions

Urgent Issues Task Force Abstracts

UITF Foreword

3. Treatment of goodwill on disposal of a business
4. Presentation of long-term debtors in current assets
6. Accounting for postretirement benefits other than pensions
7. True and fair view override disclosures
9. Accounting for operations in hyperinflationary economies
10. Disclosure of Directors' share options (not mandatory)

Appendix B: Financial Statements

Report of the Directors

The Directors submit their tenth annual report, together with the audited financial statements for the year ended 31 March, 1994, which are prepared under the requirements of the Companies Acts, 1963 to 1990

1. Financial Year
The financial year comprises the 52 weeks ended 31 March, 1994.

2. Principal Activity
The Group's principal activity is the supply of telecommunications services in the Republic of Ireland.

3. Results
The financial results for the year are set out in the Group Profit and Loss Account on page 38.

4. Review of the Business and Future Developments
A review of the business and future developments of the Group is contained in the Chairman's Statement and Chief Executive's Review included in the annual report.

5. Dividends
An interim dividend of IR£10m was paid on 23 December, 1993. The Directors propose the payment of a final dividend of IR£18m in respect of the year ended 31 March, 1994.

6. Health and Safety
A comprehensive safety statement which meets the requirements of The Safety, Health and Welfare at Work Act, 1989 has been developed. The Company has a full time Safety Group which advises all sectors of the Company on matters of safety, occupational health and hygiene. During the year, more than 2,000 employees underwent training on a range of safety courses. Also, the Company supported a broad range of events throughout the organisation promoting safety at work.

7. Research and Development
The Group's research and development activities are summarised in the Chief Executive's Review.

8. Directors
The directors of the Company are listed on page 59.

9. Directors' Interests in Shares in the Company
According to the Register of Directors and Secretaries, neither the Company Secretary nor any Director has any interest in the Share Capital of the Group during the year under review.

10. Corporate Governance
The Directors have carefully considered the Code of Best Practice published in December 1992 by the Cadbury Committee on the Financial Aspects of Corporate Governance ("the Code") and following a review of the Company's established procedures, the Board concluded that the company substantially complies with the seventeen paragraphs of code currently in force and have determined an action plan to ensure fuller compliance where feasible within the next financial year.

11. Group and Related Companies
The information required by Section 158 of the Companies Act, 1963 is shown in Note 18 to the financial statements.

12. Auditors
The auditors, Coopers & Lybrand, Chartered Accountants and Registered Auditors, have indicated their willingness to continue in office in accordance with Section 160 of the Companies Act, 1963.

Signed on behalf of the Board
Ronald J. Bolger
Charles Mulligan   *Directors*
20 July, 1994

Report of the Auditors

To the members of Bord Telecom Eireann

We have audited the financial statements on page 35 to 58.

Respective Responsibilites of Directors and Auditors

As described on page 34, the company's directors are responsible for the preparation of the financial statements. It is our responsibility to form an independent opinion, based on our audit, on those statements and to report our opinion to you.

Basis of Opinion

We conducted our audit in accordance with Auditing Standards issued by the Auditing Practices Board. An audit includes examination, on a test basis, of evidence relevant to the amounts and disclosures in the financial statements. It also includes an assessment of the significant estimates and judgements made by the directors in the preparation of the financial statements, and of whether the accounting policies are appropriate to the company's circumstances, consistently applied and adequately disclosed.

We planned and performed our audit so as to obtain all the information and explanations which we considered necessary in order to provide us with sufficient evidence to give reasonable assurance that the financial statements are free from material misstatement, whether caused by fraud or other irregularity or error. In forming our opinion we also evaluated the overall adequacy of the presentation of information in the financial statements.

Opinion

In our opinion, the financial statements give a true and fair view of the state of affairs of the Company and the Group as at 31 March,1994 and of the profit, total recognised gains and losses and cash flows of the Group for the year then ended and have been properly prepared in accordance with the Companies Acts, 1963 to 1990 and European Communities (Companies: Group Accounts) Regulations, 1992.

We have obtained all the information and explanations we consider necessary for the purposes of our audit. In our opinion, proper books of account have been kept by the Company. The financial statements are in agreement with the books of account.

In our opinion, the information given in the directors' report on page 32 is consistent with the financial statements.

In our opinion, the balance sheet on page 40 does not disclose a financial situation which, in terms of the Companies (Amendment) Act, 1983, would require the convening of an Extraordinary General Meeting of the Company.

Coopers & Lybrand
Chartered Accountants
and Registered Auditors

20 July, 1994

Statement on Directors' Responsibilities

The Board is responsible by law for keeping
proper accounting records which disclose at any
time the financial position of the Company and
the Group. The Board is also responsible for
overall management of the Company and the
Group including strategy policy and reporting.
In discharging these mandates the Board pays
particular attention to economic and regulatory
issues, marketing strategy, investment
programmes, financial performance and
personnel matters. Company law requires the
Directors to prepare financial statements for
each year which give a true and fair view of the
state of affairs of the Company and the Group
and of the profit for the period. In preparing
those financial statements the Board ensures:
· the selection of suitable accounting policies
  and their consistent application;
· judgements and estimates that are
  responsible and prudent;
· applicable accounting standards have been
  followed, subject to any material departures
  disclosed and explained in the financial
  statements;
· the preparation of the financial statements
  on the going concern basis unless it is
  inappropriate to presume that the Group will
  continue in business.

The Board is also responsible for safeguarding
the assets of the Company and the Group and
hence for taking reasonable steps for the
prevention and detection of fraud and other
irregularities.
The Board meets at least ten times a year, has
five permanent committees and appoints other
committees as necessary.

Accounting Policies

I. Authority

Bord Telecom Eireann (The Irish Telecommunications Board) was established by the Postal and Telecommunications Services Act, 1983. The financial statements of the Company have been prepared to comply with the Companies Acts, 1963 to 1990 and with Section 33 (2) of the Postal and Telecommunications Services Act, 1983.

2. Basis of Consolidation

The Group financial statements comprise a consolidation of the financial statements of the Company and of its subsidiaries. The financial statements are prepared in accordance with the historical cost convention modified by the valuation of land and buildings, excepting those held on a short leasehold basis. Related companies are accounted for under the equity method of accounting.

3. Turnover

Turnover comprises the value of all services provided and equipment sold to third parties, exclusive of value added tax.

4. Goodwill

Goodwill represents the excess of the consideration paid for the acquisition of shares in subsidiary companies over the fair value of their separable net assets.

Goodwill on acquisition of subsidiaries is written off against reserves in the year of acquisition.

5. Foreign Currencies

Transactions designated in foreign currencies are translated into Irish Pounds at the rate of exchange ruling at the transaction date. Assets and liabilities denominated in foreign currencies are translated at the rates ruling at the Balance Sheet date, or rates of exchange contracted for under various currency management instruments, with the resulting gain or loss being dealt with through the Profit and Loss Account.

6. Tangible Assets

Tangible assets are stated at historical cost or valuation less accumulated depreciation. Land and buildings, excepting those held on a short leasehold basis, are stated at a valuation, the basis of which is depreciated replacement cost or open market value as appropriate.

Depreciated replacement cost is the gross replacement cost of fixed assets less depreciation based on that cost and on the age of the assets.

Plant and equipment assets, stated at a valuation, comprise assets taken over on Vesting Day (1 January, 1984) which are stated at valuations determined, as at that date, by the Minister for Communications.

Cost in the case of network services comprises expenditure up to and including the last distribution point before customers' premises and includes contractors' charges, materials, direct labour, related overheads and interest incurred in financing the construction of tangible assets.

Accounting Policies
(continued)

6. Tangible Assets (continued)
Depreciation

Depreciation is provided on tangible assets (excluding land) on a straight line basis so as to write off their historical costs or valuations over their estimated useful lives. The estimated useful lives assigned to tangible assets are as follows:

	Years
Buildings	60
Network Services –	
Transmission Equipment	
Duct	40
Cable	10-20
Radio and Repeater Equipment	11-35
Exchanges	10-20

7. Grants
Non-repayable grants are accounted for as deferred income, a portion of which is amortised to the Profit and Loss Account at the same rate as the related assets are depreciated.

8. Leased Assets
The capital cost of assets acquired under finance leases is included in tangible assets and written off over the shorter of the lease term or the estimated useful life of the asset. The outstanding capital element of the lease obligations is included in loans and other debt, while the interest is charged to the Profit and Loss Account over the primary lease period.

9. Stocks
Stocks comprise consumable items, stores which may be used in the construction or maintenance of plant and goods held for resale. Stocks are stated at the lower of cost and net realisable value.

Cost includes invoice price, import duties and transportation costs.

Net realisable value is calculated as cost less provision for damaged, deteriorated, obsolete and unusable items.

10. Deferred Taxation
Deferred taxation is provided, using the liability method, in respect of all timing differences between profits stated in the financial statements and profits computed for taxation purposes except where, in the opinion of the directors, the timing differences are not expected to reverse in the foreseeable future.

11. Pension costs
The pension entitlements of employees arising from their service with the Group, are secured by contributions from the Group and the employees to separately administered superannuation schemes. The contributions are based on the advice of a professionally qualified actuary and are included as staff costs in the Profit and Loss Account.

Pension costs in respect of the Group's defined benefit schemes are charged in the Profit and Loss Account on a basis which spreads the cost of pensions over the service lives of employees in the schemes.

Group Value Added Statement

For the year ended 31 March 1994

	1994 IR£'000	1993 IR£'000
Value added generated		
Turnover (exclusive of VAT)	871,258	813,767
VAT	163,800	125,723
	1,035,058	939,490
Add: Staff costs capitalised	30,638	32,679
Share of profits/(losses) of related companies	514	169
	1,066,210	972,338
Less: Cost of materials & services utilised		
(exclusive of recoverable VAT)	226,872	187,617
VAT recoverable	46,561	44,714
	273,433	232,331
	792,777	740,007
Application of value added		
Net compensation of employees (Including pension contributions)	232,631	222,886
Government		
- Payroll taxes	76,254	72,618
- Dividends	28,000	26,000
- Corporation tax	12,336	11,971
- VAT	117,239	81,009
- Rates	16,027	14,578
	249,856	206,176
Other Providers of Capital		
- Interest and currency cost	92,745	102,062
- Currency realignment cost	-	44,400
	92,745	146,462
Minority interests	1,431	1,315
Provision for future investment		
- Depreciation	176,898	152,517
- Retained profit for the financial year	39,216	10,651
	216,114	163,168
	792,777	740,007

Directors
Ronald J. Bolger
Charles Mulligan

The notes on pages 35 and 36 and 43 to 58 form part of these financial statements.
Auditors' report page 33.

Group Profit and Loss Account

For the year ended 31 March 1994

	Notes	1994 IR£'000	1993 IR£'000
Turnover	2	871,258	813,767
Operating costs	3	521,146	465,020
Contribution on ordinary activities		350,112	348,747
Depreciation		176,898	152,517
Operating profit		173,214	196,230
Interest payable and similar charges	4	92,745	102,062
		80,469	94,168
Exceptional item - Currency realignment cost		-	44,400
		80,469	49,768
Share of profits of related companies		514	169
Profit on ordinary activities before taxation		80,983	49,937
Tax on profit on ordinary activities	5	12,336	11,971
Profit on ordinary activities after taxation		68,647	37,966
Minority interests		(1,431)	(1,315)
Profit attributable to group shareholders		67,216	36,651
Dividend paid and proposed	6	28,000	26,000
Retained profit for the financial year		39,216	10,651
Retained by:			
Holding company		40,245	10,339
Subsidiaries		(450)	1,163
Related companies		(579)	(851)
		39,216	10,651

The movements on reserves are shown in note 16 to the financial statements.
All of the Group's turnover and operating profit relate to continuing activities.

Directors
Ronald J. Bolger
Charles Mulligan

The notes on pages 35 and 36 and 43 to 58 form part of these financial statements.
Auditors' report page 33.

Group Balance Sheet
At 31 March 1994

	Notes	1994 IRS'000	1993 IRS'000
Assets employed			
Fixed assets			
Tangible assets	7	1,535,268	1,558,432
Financial assets	8	5,406	6,068
		1,540,674	1,564,500
Current assets			
Stocks	9	19,813	22,002
Debtors	10	161,636	136,999
Cash at bank and in hand		80,396	132,930
		261,845	291,931
Creditors: Amounts falling due within one year			
Loans and other debt	11	161,983	83,606
Other creditors	12	234,131	233,358
Proposed dividend		18,000	-
		414,114	316,964
Net current liabilities		(152,269)	(25,033)
Total assets less current liabilities		1,388,405	1,539,467
Financed by			
Creditors: Amounts falling due after more than one year			
Loans and other debt	11	846,484	1,027,280
Other creditors		36,915	32,915
		883,399	1,060,195
Provision for liabilities and charges	13	23,577	34,736
Capital grants	14	40,203	43,723
Capital and reserves			
Called up share capital	15	335,315	335,315
Revenue reserves	16	36,944	2,134
Revaluation reserve	16	60,923	56,751
		433,182	394,200
Minority interests		8,044	6,613
		1,388,405	1,539,467

Directors
Ronald J. Bolger
Charles Mulligan

The notes on pages 35 and 36 and 43 to 58 form part of these financial statements.
Auditors' report page 33.

Balance Sheet of the Company
At 31 March 1994

Assets employed	Notes	1994 IR£'000	1993 IR£'000
Fixed assets			
Tangible assets	7	967,688	928,142
Financial assets	8	68,665	62,088
		1,036,353	990,230
Current assets			
Stocks	9	15,398	17,337
Debtors	10	146,937	129,953
Cash at bank and in hand		22,480	18,508
		184,815	165,798
Creditors: Amounts falling due within one year			
Loans and other debt	11	15,600	9,229
Other creditors	12	250,869	308,070
Proposed dividend		18,000	–
		284,469	317,299
Net current liabilities		(99,654)	(151,501)
Total assets less current liabilities		936,699	838,729

Financed by	Notes	1994	1993
Creditors: Amounts falling due after more than one year			
Loans and other debt	11	392,897	324,852
Other Creditors		34,000	30,000
		426,897	354,852
Provision for liabilities and charges	13	21,200	32,000
Capital grants	14	40,203	43,723
Capital and reserves			
Called up share capital	15	335,315	335,315
Revenue reserves	16	67,195	31,523
Revaluation reserve	16	45,889	41,316
		448,399	408,154
		936.699	838,729

Directors
Ronald J. Bolger
Charles Mulligan

The notes on pages 35 and 36 and 43 to 58 form part of these financial statements.
Auditors' report page 33.

Group Cash Flow Statement

For the year ended 31 March 1994

	Notes	1994 IR£'000	1993 IR£'000
Net cash inflow from operating activities	17(a)	351,317	345,629
Net cash outflow from return on investments and servicing of finance			
Net interest paid	17(b)	(91,048)	(98,930)
Dividends paid		(10,000)	(41,000)
		(101,048)	(139,930)
Net cash outflow from investing activities	17(c)	(171,159)	(149,661)
Taxation paid	17(d)	(16,540)	(13,687)
		(187,699)	(163,348)
Net cash inflow before financing		62,570	42,351
Net cash (outflow)/inflow from financing	17(e)	(120,239)	67,720
(Decrease)/Increase in cash and cash equivalents	17(f)	(57,669)	110,071

Directors
Ronald J. Bolger
Charles Mulligan

The notes on pages 35 and 36 and 43 to 58 form part of these financial statements.
Auditors' report page 33.

Group Statement of Total Recognised Gains and Losses

For the year ended 31 March 1994

	1994	1993
	IR£'000	IR£'000
Profit attributable to group shareholders`	67,216	36,651
Currency translation differences	(234)	—
Unrealised surplus on revaluation of properties	—	56,751
Total recognised gains relating to the year	66,982	93,402

Note of Historical Cost Profits and Losses

The reported profit on ordinary activities before tax is IR£81.0m

If account were taken of the impact of assets carried at valuation this amount would be reduced by IR£4.6m (1993: nil) to produce a historical cost profit on ordinary activities before tax of IR£76.4m. The historical cost profit retained after taxation and dividends would be IR£34.6m.

Reconciliation of Movements in Shareholder Funds

	1994	1993
	IR£'000	IR£'000
Profit attributable to group shareholders`	67,216	36,651
Dividends	(28,000)	(26,000)
Retained profit for the financial year	39,216	10,651
Surplus on valuation	—	56,751
Currency translation differences	(234)	— ,
Net addition to shareholders' funds	38,982	67,402
Shareholders' funds at beginning of year	394,200	326,798
Shareholders' funds at end of year	433,182	394,200

The notes on pages 35 and 36 and 43 to 58 form part of these financial statements. Auditors' report page 33.

Notes to the Financial Statements

1. Segmental Information

There are no significant segments within the Group's operations which would warrant separate disclosure of segmental information.

2. Turnover	1994	1993
	IR£'000	IR£'000
Telephone income		
Rental	**162,629**	151,479
Traffic	**503,325**	506,592
Connection fees	**17,111**	17,537
Income from overseas telecommunications agencies	**77,276**	42,263
Total telephone income	**760,341**	717,871
Private circuits	**31,399**	30,176
Switched data and other network services	**13,855**	13,866
Total telecommunications services	**805,595**	761,913
Other income	**65,663**	51,854
	871,258	813,767

3. Operating Costs	1994	1993
	IR£'000	IR£'000
Staff costs		
Wages & salaries	**264,828**	253,192
Social welfare costs	**6,449**	6,315
Pension costs	**37,608**	35,997
	308,885	295,504
Staff costs capitalised	**(30,638)**	(32,679)
Net staff costs	**278,247**	262,825
Charges by overseas telecommunications agencies	**60,644**	31,640
Other operating costs	**182,255**	170,555
	521,146	465,020

Operating costs include:-	1994	1993
	IR£	IR£
Auditors' remuneration	**237,585**	236,000
Directors' remuneration		
For services as directors	**62,500**	50,012
Other emoluments	**196,811**	190,048
Compensation for Loss of Office	**-**	34,349

The Directors deem the individuals noted at page 59 to be officers of the company for the purposes of S.43 of the Companies Act 1990. No transactions took place with these officers during the year.

Notes to the
Financial Statements

4. Interest Payable and Similar Charges

	1994 IRS'000	1993 IRS'000
On loans and other debt repayable wholly within five years		
Loans	53,513	66,594
Leases	2,887	2,835
On loans and other debt not wholly repayable within five years		
Loans	34,698	31,256
Leases	3,462	3,253
Total interest payable	94,560	103,938
Less: Interest receivable	(5,991)	(5,806)
Net interest payable	88,569	98,132
Exchange (gains)/losses arising on foreign currency borrowings		
Realised	(37)	1,780
Unrealised	12,722	(3,646)
Hedging contracts	(8,509)	5,796
	92,745	102,062

5. Tax on Profit on Ordinary Activities

	Note	1994 IRS'000	1993 IRS'000
Advance corporation tax		9,333	8,667
Deferred taxation	13	(359)	(349)
Corporation taxation		2,710	2,942
Share of taxation of related companies		652	711
		12,336	11,971

There is no further taxation arising on the result for the year because of the Group's cumulative tax losses and capital allowances. Deferred taxation is dealt with at note 13.

Notes to the
Financial Statements

6. Dividends Paid and Proposed	1994 IRS'000	1993 IRS'000
Ordinary dividends:		
Paid: interim dividend of 2.98p per share (1993: 7.75p)	10,000	26,000
Proposed: final dividend of 5.37p per share (1993: nil)	18,000	-
	28,000	26,000

7. Tangible Assets

(a) Group	Land & Buildings IRS'000	Plant & Equipment IRS'000	Total IRS'000
Cost or Valuation			
Cost	16,699	1,405,461	1,422,160
Valuation	244,839	816,484	1,061,323
At 1 April 1993	261,538	2,221,945	2,483,483
Additions	2,929	160,742	163,671
Disposals	(4,952)	(10,172)	(15,124)
At 31 March 1994	259,515	2,372,515	2,632,030
Cost	19,506	1,558,232	1,577,738
Valuation	240,009	814,283	1,054,292
Accumulated Depreciation			
At 1 April 1993	3,364	921,687	925,051
Charge for year	7,324	175,403	182,727
Disposals	(1,006)	(10,010)	(11,016)
At 31 March 1994	9,682	1,087,080	1,096,762
Total Net Book Value at 31 March 1994	249,833	1,285,435	1,535,268
Total Net Book Value at 1 April 1993	258,174	1,300,258	1,558,432

Notes to the Financial Statements

7. Tangible Assets (continued)

(b)

The Depreciation charged in the Group profit and loss account is net of capital grants amortised during the year (see note 14) as follows:

	1994 IRS'000	1993 IRS'000
Depreciation	182,727	158,035
Amortisation of capital grants	(5,829)	(5,518)
	176,898	152,517

(c) Company

	Land & Buildings IRS'000	Plant & Equipment IRS'000	Total IRS'000
Cost or Valuation			
Cost	11,535	827,301	838,836
Valuation	158,727	439,119	597,846
At 1 April 1993	170,262	1,266,420	1,436,682
Additions	2,669	154,930	157,599
Disposals	(3,956)	(4,869)	(8,825)
At 31 March 1994	168,975	1,416,481	1,585,456
Cost	14,181	979,563	993,744
Valuation	154,794	436,918	591,712
Accumulated Depreciation			
At 1 April 1993	1,791	506,749	508,540
Charge for year	3,984	110,070	114,054
Disposals	(10)	(4,816)	(4,826)
At 31 March 1994	5,765	612,003	617,768
Total Net Book Value at 31 March 1994	163,210	804,478	967,688
Total Net Book Value at 1 April 1993	168,471	759,671	928,142

Notes to the
Financial Statements

7. Tangible Assets (continued)

(d)

A valuation of properties owned by Bord Telecom Eireann and its subsidiary Irish Telecommunications Investments plc, excepting those held on a short leasehold basis, was carried out by Hamilton Osborne King, Estate Agents, Auctioneers and Valuers, as at 31 March 1993. This valuation valued those assets on a depreciated replacement cost basis or open market value as appropriate.

The historical cost of the property assets shown at valuation amounts to:

	Group IR£'000	Company IR£'000
Cost	203,409	121,024
Accumulated Depreciation	29,043	16,030
Net Book Value	174,366	104,994

(e)

Included in plant and equipment taken over on Vesting Day are amounts of expenditure incurred in the connection of customers' premises to the last distribution point which were capitalised by the former Department of Posts and Telegraphs at IR£170m and which are being written off on a straight line basis over the ten year period to 31 March 1994. Since Vesting Day such expenditures are charged to the profit and loss account as incurred.

(f)

Included in tangible assets is plant and equipment acquired under finance leases as follows:-

	Group 1994 IR£'000	Group 1993 IR£'000	Company 1994 IR£'000	Company 1993 IR£'000
Cost	127,698	126,769	116,697	106,898
Accumulated depreciation	26,233	29,061	24,576	24,000
Depreciation charge for the year	9,543	8,524	8,697	8,103

Notes to the
Financial Statements

8. Financial Assets

(a) **Group**

Shares in related companies - unlisted	Shares IR£'000	Advances IR£'000	Total IR£'000
At beginning of year	4,428	1,640	6,068
Additions	820	-	820
Share of losses	(333)	-	(333)
Repayments	(309)	(840)	(1,149)
At end of year	4,606	800	5,406

(b) **Company**

	Subsidiaries		Related Companies		Total
	Shares IR£'000	Advances IR£'000	Shares IR£'000	Advances IR£'000	IR£'000
At beginning of year - unlisted	30	57,221	4,050	787	62,088
Additions	2,000	4,544	820	-	7,364
Repayments	-	-	-	(787)	(787)
At end of year - unlisted	2,030	61,765	4,870	-	68,665

(c)

Telecom Eireann Information Systems Limited, Eircable Limited and Eirtrade Limited, wholly owned subsidiaries of the Company, have availed of the filing exemption available under Section 17 of the Companies (Amendment) Act, 1986, whereby they will annex the financial statements of the Group to their annual returns.

9. Stocks

	Group		Company	
	1994 IR£'000	1993 IR£'000	1994 IR£'000	1993 IR£'000
Network development and maintenance stocks	8,478	8,828	6,378	6,745
Consumable and other stocks	11,335	13,174	9,020	10,592
	19,813	22,002	15,398	17,337

Notes to the
Financial Statements

10. Debtors

	Group		Company	
	1994	1993	1994	1993
	IR£'000	IR£'000	IR£'000	IR£'000
Trade debtors	126,718	105,746	109,824	101,469
Prepayments and accrued income	34,439	30,640	34,389	25,368
Amounts owed by Subsidiary companies	-	-	2,754	2,587
Amounts owed by Related companies	228	341	(53)	373
Other debtors	251	272	23	156
	161,636	136,999	146,937	129,953

All amounts above fall due within one year.

11. Loans and Other Debt

Payable	Within 1 Year IR£'000	Between 2 & 5 Years IR£'000	After 5 Years IR£'000	Total IR£'000
Group				
Loans	145,225	392,876	370,122	908,223
Finance leases	9,923	60,769	22,717	93,409
Overdrafts	6,835	-	-	6,835
At 31 March 1994	161,983	453,645	392,839	1,008,467
At 1 April 1993	83,606	555,001	472,279	1,110,886
Company				
Loans from Subsidiaries	-	319,450	-	319,450
Finance leases	9,157	55,311	18,136	82,604
Overdrafts	6,443	-	-	6,443
At 31 March 1994	15,600	374,761	18,136	408,497
At 1 April 1993	9,229	307,204	17,648	334,081

Notes to the
Financial Statements

11. Loans and Other Debt (continued)

Included in the above are amounts:	Group		Company	
	1994	1993	1994	1993
	IR£'000	IR£'000	IR£'000	IR£'000
Wholly repayable within 1 year	115,153	47,761	8,675	3,052
Wholly repayable within 5 years	441,188	516,279	357,453	288,227
Repayable by instalments, not wholly repayable within 5 years:				
within 5 years	60,086	75,018	25,033	25,605
after 5 years	76,110	95,956	17,336	17,197
Repayable, otherwise than by instalments, due after 5 years	315,930	375,872	-	-
	1,008,467	1,110,886	408,497	334,081

Loans and other debt are denominated in the following currencies:

	'000	IR£'000
Irish Punts	463,578	463,578
ECU's	38,881	31,253
Deutsche Marks	576,195	240,131
Dutch Guilders	90,302	33,497
Belgian Francs	2.900,000	58,669
Swiss Francs	124,674	61,561
French Francs	475,839	58,051
Japanese Yen	3,794,733	19,930
Pounds Sterling	29,863	30,863
Luxembourg Francs	540,506	10,934
TOTAL		1,008,467

The capital value of the loans and other debts has been fully hedged into Irish Pounds.

The Minister for Finance has guaranteed loans included in the above table at 31 March 1994 to the extent of IR£366.0m (1993: IR£462.3m). Bord Telecom Eireann has also guaranteed loans of its subsidiary, Irish Telecommunications Investments plc of IR£527.2m (1993: IR£557.8m), and Telecom Eireann Information Systems Limited of IR£3m (1993: nil).

Notes to the Financial Statements

12. Other Creditors

Amounts falling due within one year	Group 1994 IR£'000	Group 1993 IR£'000	Company 1994 IR£'000	Company 1993 IR£'000
Trade creditors	56,839	30,689	55,324	28,625
Amounts owed to Group Companies	-	-	61,327	122,693
Accruals and deferred income	143,428	161,361	103,644	118,779
PAYE	4,714	4,336	4,637	4,245
PRSI	1,040	865	990	816
VAT	16,007	19,507	15,614	19,245
Advance corporation tax	9,333	13,667	9,333	13,667
Corporation tax	2,770	2,933	-	-
	234,131	233,358	250,869	308,070

13. Provision for Liabilities and Charges

	Group Deferred Taxation IR£'000	Group Pension Provision IR£'000	Total IR£'000	Company Pension Provision IR£'000
At beginning of year	2,736	32,000	34,736	32,000
Reclassified	-	(10,800)	(10,800)	(10,800)
Profit and Loss Account	(359)	-	(359)	-
At end of year	2,377	21,200	23,577	21,200

Deferred taxation arises from the utilisation of capital allowances of IR£2.51m (1993: IR£2.88m) and losses forward of IR£0.14m (1993: IR£0.15m) in a subsidiary company.

Further provision for deferred taxation is not required because, in the opinion of the directors, unprovided timing differences are unlikely to reverse in the forseeable future. The full potential liability for deferred taxation is as set out below.

	Group 1994 IR£'000	Group 1993 IR£'000	Company 1994 IR£'000	Company 1993 IR£'000
Capital allowances	227,313	221,589	36,798	49,711
Losses forward	(42,136)	(68,969)	-	-
Advance corporation tax	(48,334)	(39,001)	(48,334)	(39,001)
	136,843	113,619	11,536	10,710

Notes to the
Financial Statements

14. Capital Grants

Group and Company	1994	1993
	IR£'000	IR£'000
Received		
At beginning of year	60,914	60,019
Received during year	2,309	895
At end of year	63,223	60,914
Amortisation		
At beginning of year	17,191	11,673
Amortisation to profit and loss account	5,829	5,518
At end of year	23,020	17,191
Net book value at end of year	40,203	43,723

15. Called Up Share Capital

	1994	1993
	IR£'000	IR£'000
Authorised Ordinary Shares of IR£1 each	500,000	500,000
Issued and Fully Paid	335,315	335,315

16. Reserves

Group

	Revaluation Reserve	Revenue Reserves
	IR£'000	IR£'000
At beginning of year	56,751	2,134
Retained profit for the financial year	-	39,216
Transfers on realisation of revalued assets	4,172	(4,172)
Exchange adjustments	-	(234)
At end of year	60,923	36,944

Company

At beginning of year	41,316	31,523
Retained profit for the financial year	-	40,245
Transfers on realisation of revalued assets	4,573	(4,573)
At end of year	45,889	67,195

No provision has been made for any tax liability that would arise if these revalued property assets were disposed of at their revalued amounts.

Notes to the
Financial Statements

17. Amounts in Group Cash Flow Statement

Amounts included in the group cash flow statement are reconciled or analysed as follows:-

(a) Net Cash Flow from Operating Activities

	1994	1993
	IRS'000	IRS'000
Operating profit	**173,214**	196,230
Depreciation	**176,898**	152,517
Decrease in stock	**2,189**	495
Decrease in creditors	**21,297**	7,444
Increase in debtors	**(17,047)**	(11,057)
Decrease in other creditors	**(5,000)**	–
Exchange loss on translation of a related company	**(234)**	–
Net cash inflow from operating activities	**351,317**	345,629

(b) Analysis of Net Interest Paid

Interest received	**7,452**	4,235
Interest paid	**(93,713)**	(97,294)
Interest element of finance lease payments	**(4,787)**	(5,871)
Net interest paid	**(91,048)**	(98,930)

(c) Analysis of Net Cash Flow From Investing Activities

Payments to acquire tangible fixed assets	**(173,797)**	(149,163)
Investment in related companies	**(820)**	(1,740)
Advances to related companies	**–**	(353)
Repayments from Related Companies	**1,149**	700
Capital grants received	**2,309**	895
Net cash outflow from investing activities	**(171,159)**	(149,661)

(d) Taxation Paid

Advance Corporation Taxation	**13,667**	13,667
Corporation Taxation	**2,873**	20
	16,540	13,687

**Notes to the
Financial Statements**

17. Amounts in Group Cash Flow Statement (continued)

(e) **Analysis of Net Cash Flow from Financing**

	1994	1993
	IR£'000	IR£'000
Repayment of loan capital	**(460,186)**	(926,401)
Additions to loan capital	**322,995**	978,548
Capital element of finance lease additions	**26,132**	25,592
Capital element of finance lease payments	**(9,180)**	(10,019)
Net cash inflow/(outflow) from financing	**(120,239)**	67,720

The net movement on the loans and finance leases during the year is accounted for by the net cash outflow from financing as per above and an adverse exchange rate movement of IR£14.188m (1993 IR£50.602m)

(f) **Analysis of Changes in Cash and Cash Equivalents during the Year**

	1994	1993	1992	Change in Year	
				1994/93	1993/92
	IR£'000	IR£'000	IR£'000	**IR£'000**	IR£'000
Cash at bank and in hand	**80,396**	132,930	21,917	**(52,534)**	111,013
Bank overdraft	**(6,835)**	(3,203)	(9,420)	**(3,632)**	6,217
	73,561	129,727	12,497	**(56,166)**	117,230

The total net cash outflow of IR£56.166m is comprised of the decrease in cash and cash equivalents as per the cash flow statement of IR£57.669m and the surplus arising on translation of foreign exchange denominated deposit accounts of IR£1.503m.

Notes to the
Financial Statements

18. Subsidiary and Related Companies

	Interest in Ordinary Shares at 31 March 1994	Business	Registered Office and Country of Incorporation
Subsidiary Companies			
Irish Telecommunications Investments plc (ITI plc)	100%	Telecommunications Financing and Treasury Management.	La Touche House, International Financial Services Centre, Custom House Docks, Dublin 1, Ireland.
Telecom Eireann Information Systems Limited	100%	Marketing and Installation of Telecommunications Customer Equipment.	114 St Stephen's Green West, Dublin 2, Ireland.
Eircable Limited	100%	Investment Holding Company.	Merrion House, Merrion Road, Dublin 4, Ireland.
Telecom Ireland (U.S.) Limited	100%	Marketing of Telecom Services in U.S.A.	114 St Stephen's Green West, Dublin 2, Ireland.
Eirtrade Limited	100%	Provision of Electronic Trading Services.	114 St Stephen's Green West, Dublin 2, Ireland.
ITI International Finance Limited (Subsidiary of ITI plc)	100%	Provision of Treasury Management and Consultancy Services.	La Touche House, International Financial Services Centre, Custom House Docks, Dublin 1, Ireland.
ITI Hungary Consulting KFT (Subsidiary of ITI plc)	100%	Provision of Treasury Management and Consultancy Services.	Ordogorum Lejto 32/a, Budapest, Hungary.
Cablelink Limited (Subsidiary of Eircable Limited)	60%	Construction and Operation of Cable and MMDS Television Systems.	10 Pembroke Place, Ballsbridge, Dublin 4, Ireland.
Cablelink Waterford Limited (Subsidiary of Cablelink Limited)	60%	Cable & MMDS Television Systems.	10 Pembroke Place, Ballsbridge, Dublin 4, Ireland.
Cablelink Galway Limited (Subsidiary of Cablelink Limited)	60%	Cable & MMDS Television Systems.	10 Pembroke Place, Ballsbridge, Dublin 4, Ireland.

Notes to the
Financial Statements

18. Subsidiary and Related Companies (continued)

	Interest in Ordinary Shares at 31 March 1994	Business	Registered Office and Country of Incorporation
Subsidiary Companies (continued)			
Little Bird Ventures Seven Limited (Subsidiary of Cablelink Limited)	60%	Film Investment.	10 Pembroke Place, Ballsbridge, Dublin 4, Ireland.
Eirpage Limited	51%	Marketing of Radio Paging Service.	Anglesea House, Donnybrook, Dublin 4, Ireland.
Related Companies			
Telecom PhoneWatch Limited	50%	Installation, Monitoring and Maintenance of Residential Security Systems.	114 St Stephen's Green West, Dublin 2, Ireland.
INET Limited	50%	Managed Network Provider.	50 Dawson Street, Dublin 2, Ireland.
Golden Pages Limited	49%	Directory Publishing.	St. Martins House, Waterloo Road, Dublin 4, Ireland.
Broadcom Eireann Research Limited	45%	Broadband Telecommunications Research and Development.	6 Fitzwilliam Square, Dublin 2, Ireland.
Minitel Communications Limited	30%	Provision of Videotex Services and Terminals.	I.P.C. House, Shelbourne Road, Ballsbridge, Dublin 4, Ireland.
Investel Rt (Related company of ITI plc)	21.1%	Telecommunications Capital Financing and Treasury Management.	Krisztina Korut, 6-8 Budapest, Hungary.

Notes to the
Financial Statements

19. Profit on Ordinary Activities Attributable to Bord Telecom Eireann

An amount of IR£68.2m (1993: IR£36.3m) of the consolidated profit attributable to the shareholders of Bord Telecom Eireann has been dealt with in the financial statements of the Company. A separate Profit and Loss Account for the Company has not been prepared because the conditions laid down in Section 3(2) of the Companies (Amendment) Act, 1986 have been satisfied.

20. Employees

The average number of persons employed by the Company and its subsidiaries during the year was as follows:-

	Group		Company	
	1994	1993	1994	1993
Managerial	1,354	1,354	1,316	1,319
Clerical	1,712	1,737	1,611	1,648
Technical	7,873	7,952	7,766	7,862
Operator Services	1,665	1,789	1,665	1,789
Other	465	481	460	481
	13,069	13,313	12,818	13,099

21. Pensions

(a)

The Group's pension commitments are funded through separately administered Superannuation Schemes and are of a defined benefit nature. The Group's contributions of IR£37.6m (1993: IR£36.0m) in respect of the year to 31 March 1994 are at an average rate of 15.9% of pensionable emoluments as advised by the Actuaries to the Schemes.

The last Triennial Actuarial Valuation of the principal Scheme was carried out as at 1 June 1992 by Mercer Fraser Pension and Investment Consultants Limited who are actuaries to the Scheme (but are neither officers nor employees of the Group).

The actuarial method used involved determining an appropriate future Company contribution rate designed to fund the projected liabilities of the Scheme (related to service subsequent to 1 January 1984) over the remaining working lifetime of the current members. The primary financial assumption underlying the actuarial valuation was that the Scheme's investments will earn a real rate of investment return, over and above salary inflation and pension increases, of 2% per annum. At the date of the last triennial actuarial valuation the market value of the pension Scheme assets was IR£375.2m and the actuarial valuation of the assets was sufficient to meet 97% of the value of the Schemes accrued liabilities (making due allowance for future increases in salaries and pensions). The actuarial report is available for inspection by the members of the Scheme.

Notes to the Financial Statements

21. Pensions (continued)

(b)

Included in creditors is IR£40.8m payable to the Superannuation Scheme in respect of the capital value of additional liabilities related to completed early retirement programmes. This amount, by agreement with the Trustees of the Superannuation Scheme, will be paid in equal instalments over the next six years together with a commercial rate of interest thereon.

(c)

The payment of pension entitlements in respect of certain persons who were members of the staff of the Department of Posts and Telegraphs and who retired or died before the Vesting Day (1 January 1984) has been delegated to the Company by the Minister for Finance under Section 46 of the Postal and Telecommunications Services Act, 1983. Payments made by the Company in accordance with the delegation are made out of the Superannuation Fund and the costs are the liability of the Minister for Finance who is also liable in respect of the pension entitlements arising from pre-Vesting Day reckonable service of staff who transferred from the Department to the Company on Vesting Day and who subsequently retired or died. The amount of the liability of the Minister for pre vesting service and the manner of discharge by him of the liability has been recently agreed by the Minister for Finance.

22. Contingent Liabilities

At the balance sheet date there were no contingent liabilities or guarantees in respect of which material losses are expected.

In the normal course of business, the Group has entered into contracts involving the exchange or purchase and sale of foreign currencies. No material losses are expected in respect of these transactions other than losses for which provision has been made in the financial statements.

23. Capital Commitments

Capital commitments approved by the Board at the balance sheet date amounted to approximately IR£187.0m for the Group and Company, of which IR£131.8m was contracted. Capital commitments at 31 March 1993 amounted to approximately IR£182.4m.

24. Approval of Financial Statements

The financial statements were approved by the Board of Directors on 20 July 1994.

SPAIN

Francisco J. Martinez
Price Waterhouse, Madrid

1. Background

1.1 A Brief History of Accounting Regulation in Spain

The history of accounting practice in Spain can be traced back to the Middle Ages. In the early modern period, the huge volume of trade with Spain's vast overseas empire gave rise to an impressive quantity of accounting records, examples of which may be seen in an archive in the city of Seville. In more modern times, official regulations were established in the early decades of the nineteenth century, when the Commercial Code of 1829 laid down some rules for the formalities of account-keeping but imposed no obligations in regard to annual financial reporting. Certain changes were introduced during the following decades, and particularly by the revised Commercial Code of 1885, Heading III. The rules contained in the latter still mainly concerned the formal aspects of accounting, although some financial reporting requirements were imposed for limited companies.

The Commercial Code of 1885 essentially remains in force as the basis of commercial rules in Spain, although it has been modified in many aspects. In addition, the enactment of laws and bylaws has produced additional developments.

In general, the development of financial reporting and auditing in Spain remained slow and patchy until the stimulus provided by the need to comply with European Community Directives, and other international pressures, brought about comprehensive reform beginning in the late 1980s.

In 1951 a new Companies Act came into force, with the aim of regulating the main aspects of the business affairs of companies. Chapter VI of the act introduced some accounting rules, but these rules were quite brief and limited. More complete coverage had to await the first General Accounting Plan published in 1973 (PGC-73); excluding certain special situations, however, use of the plan was optional.

The PGC-73 was based on the French Accounting Plan of 1959. Its regulations were excessively rigid and more concerned with the content of the accounts from the point of view of taxation than with meaningful reflection of the economic situation of a company. The definition and the accounting principles were poor, and the plan skated over such important issues as leasing, deferred taxation, pensions, and exchange rate differences. Certain sectorial accounting plans were issued to deal with problems in specific sectors.

Companies continued to prepare their financial statements in accordance with the principles generally accepted by custom, taking into account some or all of the pronouncements of the General Accounting Plan of 1973.

In 1979, a private association called the Spanish Association of Accounting and Business Administration (*Asociación Española de Contabilidad y Administración de Empresas*, AECA; see Section 2.6.2, below) was set up. This body worked to develop certain pronouncements on accounting matters, which were taken in many instances as a guide, given the lack of official regulation.

The promulgation in 1989 of the law known as the Commercial Reform Act 19/1989 (*Ley 19/1989 de Reforma Mercantil y Adaptación a las Directivas de la CEE*), was the vehicle to introduce commercial reform into the Spanish rules in line with those in force in the European Community and to adopt the Directives in accounting matters. A change was introduced to the Commercial Code of 1885 to provide the necessary legal environment.

In summary, until recently, accounting regulations in Spain were characterized by the paucity of their appearance in official texts. The basic commercial legislation—the Commercial Code of 1885 and the Companies Act 1951—hardly made any mention of these matters and did not even set out the basic principles with which accounting was supposed to comply. The General Accounting Plan of 1973 included certain basic principles but inconclusively and without obligation. Generally speaking, there was a lack of definition of regulations concerning the preparation and presentation of company accounts, which were not required to be made public, except in the case of companies listed on the stock exchange.

1.2 Present Accounting Rules

The commercial and accounting regulations introduced by the Commercial Reform Act 19/1989 led to a new set of rules, which constitute the framework for all current commercial and accounting rules. The most significant are the Legislative Royal Decree 1564/1989, the General Accounting Plan of 1990 (PGC-90), and the rules for Consolidation of Annual Accounts, issued in December 1991.

The Legislative Royal Decree 1564/1989, which contains the adapted text of the Companies Act of 1989 (*Texto Refundido de la Ley de Sociedades Anónimas*), in force since January 1, 1990, now provides wide and comprehensive control of accounting practices and completes the criteria and regulations for the preparation and presentation of accounting information in the annual financial statements. With respect to generally accepted international accounting practices, these can be considered advances.

As a provisional measure, it was permitted that the accounts closed at June 30, 1990 could be prepared in accordance with the previous regulations.

Because the regulations in force until December 31, 1989 were not very complete, as we have already stated, we shall refer from now on to the requirements of the new legislation, which affects annual accounts closed from July 1, 1990.

The General Accounting Plan of 1990 (PGC-90) was issued in December 1990 by Royal Decree 1643/1990. The PGC-90 is obligatory for financial years commencing from January 1, 1991 for all companies, whatever their size or legal standing, with respect to accounting principles, valuation rules, and the information to be given in the annual accounts.

Although the Companies Act of 1989 gives a number of accounting rules and a full detail of accounting principles, the PGC-90 is richer in descriptions and interpretations. The latter is therefore the real source of the standards required to implement the Companies Act of 1989, in the sense of ensuring that the annual accounts fulfill the legal obligation to give a true and fair view (*imagen fiel*).

In the following sections, we give details of both sets of requirements—the legal ones and those included in the PGC-90.

The rules for Consolidation of Annual Accounts, issued in December 1991 by Royal Decree 1815/1991, in order to amplify the provisions of the

Commercial Reform Act of 1989, which imposed an obligation to prepare consolidated accounts for financial years ending after January 1, 1991. These rules were the last big step in bringing Spanish accounting practice into line with international practice.

PGC-90 is a general text, and many of the rules contained in it need to be interpreted and clarified in order to be properly applied. For this purpose, the ICAC has developed and published several documents that provide the interpretations that must be followed by companies in the preparation of their accounts and by the auditors in their review. These interpretations relate, among other things, to tangible fixed assets, intangible fixed assets, general information to be disclosed in the accounts, accounting for taxation, and so on.

Some sectorial accounting plans have been issued to cover specific matters in the related sectors, for example, building and construction and sporting companies or associations. Others are in preparation and will be issued in the near future.

1.3 The Auditing Profession

Until quite recently, auditing had no specific coverage under Spanish legislation. There was no general obligation to submit accounts to be reviewed by an auditor. The only exception was that the accounts of companies listed on the Stock Exchange were supposed to be reviewed by members of the Institute of Sworn Auditors (*Instituto de Censores Jurados de Cuentas*, ICJC), which performed reviews that were generally more restricted than audits according to international practice. The ICJC was founded in 1943 and received legal recognition in the Companies Act of 1951, but its professional effectiveness was limited not just by the restricted nature of the work carried out by its members, but also by weak enforcement by the authorities of such requirements as there were.

With the publication of the Auditing Act 19/1988, which came into force on July 16, 1988, a state body was set up to regulate company accounting and auditing: the Institute of Accounting and Auditing (*Instituto de Contabilidad y Auditoría de Cuentas*, ICAC), which is attached to the Ministry of Finance and Treasury. At the same time, an Official Register of Auditors (*Registro Oficial de Auditores de Cuentas*, ROAC) was also established, and all auditors are now required by law to be registered with the ROAC. In addition to the members of the ICJC, two other professional bodies were set up during the 1980s, whose members are eligible for registration with the ROAC.

In March 1990, the ICAC published the Technical Auditing Standards, with which all auditors must comply. They are similar to the International Auditing Standards.

The Auditing Act 19/1988 established compulsory audits for the following companies for any financial year beginning after July 16, 1998:

1. Those having their securities listed on any stock exchange
2. Those making public issues of debentures
3. Those generally involved in financial intermediation
4. Those governed by the Private Insurance Regulation Act (within limits pending definition at this date by the government)
5. Those receiving subsidies or aid, or undertaking work for the state, or providing services or supplies to the latter (within limits still pending definition by the government)
6. Any other companies within the limits determined by the laws that govern them.

Point 6 has already been covered for limited companies by the Commercial Reform Act of 1989, which states that an audit is compulsory for the accounts of all companies, except those that qualify for an abridged balance sheet. As a result, an audit must be performed for the accounts of every company meeting the requirements and limits set out in Section 2.1.5 (Abridged Balance Sheet) below. Similar considerations apply to Point 4.

Within the scope of the audit, the auditor will also review whether or not the accounting information contained in the management report agrees with the annual accounts and the accounting books.

In addition to normal auditing, auditors are required by the Companies Act of 1989 to carry out special reviews of certain situations with regard to companies' legal operations. Such reviews are regulated by the ICAC, which has issued certain standard rules to be followed by auditors in such cases. Some of these special legal reviews are the following:

- Increases in share capital made by capitalization of reserves
- Report on fair value of shares in increases of capital share in case of total or partial removal of the right to preferential share subscription
- Reductions of share capital to reflect losses
- Mergers of companies
- Issues of convertible bonds

The ICAC has issued several documents to regulate auditing practice. Some of the most relevant relate to those referring to the special legal review just mentioned, materiality limits, the form and content of audit reports, relations between auditors, and subsequent events review.

2. The Form and Content of Annual Accounts

2.1 Presentation of Accounting Information

As generally described above, accounting practice in Spain is regulated by the Commercial Code of 1885, the Companies Act of 1989, the Commercial Reform Act of 1989, the General Plan of Accounting 1990 (PGC-90), and the rules for Consolidation of Annual Accounts set out in Royal Decree 1815/1991 of December 1991 (amplifying the provisions of the Commercial Reform Act). In the following paragraphs we will analyze the presentation requirements.

2.1.1 General Requirements

The new legislation contains certain general requirements, most of them introduced for the first time into Spanish practice. We present a list of them in general form:

- Preparation and content of annual accounts

- Structure of annual accounts
- Types of annual accounts
- The management report
- Publication of annual accounts
- Compulsory audit
- Consolidation of the annual accounts of groups of companies

2.1.2 Preparation and Content of Annual Accounts

Annual financial statements are in respect of the accounts at the close of the financial reporting period, which may not exceed 12 months. The year end can be any date of the year, although the most common date is December 31. A management report and a proposal for the appropriation of the profits must also be prepared.

The annual accounts consist of the balance sheet, the profit and loss account, and the notes (*la memoria*), all forming one whole. They must be worded clearly and must truthfully reflect the net worth, the financial position, and the profits and losses of the company. In the case of limited companies, the notes also include a statement of sources and application of funds.

These documents must be signed by all the directors. If any signature is absent, this fact must be indicated on each of the documents, and the reasons must be stated.

Whenever the application of legal provisions is insufficient to give a true and fair view, additional information is to be provided in order to obtain this. In exceptional cases, if the application of a legal provision on accounting matters is incompatible with the true and fair view, such provision will not be applicable. In such cases, mention should be made in the notes, stating the causes and the effects on the net worth, the financial situation, and the profit and loss of the company.

2.1.3 Structure of the Annual Accounts

The Companies Act of 1989 requires that the annual accounts be structured as in the example shown in Appendix A at the end of this chapter.

The entries making up each of the documents should appear separately. However, more detailed subdivisions may be made, or new entries included, provided that they comply with the established structure. Grouping may also be made under arabic numbers whenever necessary for the sake of clarity, and provided that the amount involved is not large, in which case such figures should be shown separately in the notes.

In addition to the figures for the closing financial year, each of the entries in the balance sheet, profit and loss account, and the statement of sources and application of funds must indicate the figures for the immediately preceding financial year. Whenever these amounts are not comparable, the amounts from the earlier financial year should be adjusted. In any event, any problems of comparison and adjustments of the amounts should be indicated in the notes, with explanations as appropriate. As a provisional arrangement, during the first financial year closed after July 1, 1990, it was not necessary to present comparative figures in the statement of sources and application of funds.

Legal provisions prohibit offsetting between asset and liability headings. Balance sheet and profit and loss entries showing nil balances in the present financial year and in the preceding year will not be shown in the aforementioned documents.

2.1.4 The Notes (la Memoria)—Concept and Content

La Memoria is a new concept within Spanish accounting doctrine, which replaced the former "notes to the financial statements." Previously, many companies prepared and published another document, called the "commercial report," which contained accounting, commercial, and management information. The present document is much more generous in terms of information and much more detailed in its analysis. However, the previous document contained nonaccounting information, in many cases with respect to future projects, which do not now form part of the annual report. Nevertheless, much of this information is not altogether lost, as it may be given in the management report (see Section 2.1.6 below).

Conceptually, *la memoria* completes, expands, and comments on the balance sheet and profit and loss account. It must contain all the information considered necessary for adequate interpretation of the annual accounts.

The information required in *la memoria* according to the PGC-90 is wider in scope than that demanded under the Commercial Reform Act of 1989 and the Companies Act of 1989.

The requirements of each set of regulatory texts are given below.

Requirements of the Commercial Reform Act of 1989 and the Companies Act of 1989   In addition to what has been mentioned in the preceding paragraphs, the annual report should contain the following information:

1. Valuation rules applied to the items in the annual accounts
2. Calculation methods used for provisions on assets
3. The procedure used to calculate the exchange rate for items expressed in foreign currency
4. The names and addresses of the companies in which an important participation is held, that is, the direct or indirect possession of a minimum of 3% of the capital of a company. The fraction of the capital held will also be stated, in addition to the amount of capital and reserves and the profit and loss for the previous financial year.
5. The number and nominal value of each type of share of the company
6. The statement of sources and applications of funds
7. The existence of bonds, convertible securities and securities, and other rights, stating the number and extent of the rights so granted
8. The amount of debts having a remaining duration of more than 5 years.
9. The amount of debts actually secured, with an indication of the form and type
10. The overall amount of guarantees committed with third parties
11. Separate mention of existing commitments with respect to pensions
12. Analysis of the net turnover by categories of activity and geographic markets
13. The average number of employees in the current financial year according to category, as well as itemized staff expenses

14. The difference between the accounting results and those earmarked for taxation purposes, indicating the future tax charge

15. The difference between the tax charge allocated in respect of the present and previous financial years and that already paid or to be paid

16. The overall amount of salaries, allowances, and all types of remuneration earned during the financial year by directors, as well as the obligations contracted in terms of pensions or life assurance in respect of former or present staff

17. Overall information with respect to advances and credits granted to staff, stating interest rates, essential facts, and amounts eventually repaid, as well as obligations assumed by the company on their behalf in the form of guarantees

18. Movements of items included under fixed assets, as well as establishment costs. Additions, withdrawals and conveyances, corrections of accrued value, and any rectifications made during the year should be shown separately by category of fixed asset.

19. If the payment of a dividend on account is approved, an accounting statement, prepared by directors and showing the existence of sufficient liquidity

20. Justification for the amortization of goodwill over a period of more than 5 years (if applicable)

Mention of items 4 and 12 may be omitted, this being indicated in the annual report, whenever, owing to their nature, serious prejudice might be caused to the company by their disclosure.

In the event that an abridged annual report may be prepared (see the conditions under Section 2.1.5, Abridged Memoria, below), it is only necessary to include the information contained in items 1–5, 16, and 18–20. The statement of sources and application of funds need not be included.

Requirements of the PGC-90   As mentioned previously, the General Accounting Plan of 1990 is more demanding with respect to the presentation of information in the annual accounts, because in addition to the requirements listed above, it requires the following information to be included in the annual report:

1. The proposed distribution of profits for the year
2. The valuation rules applied, including an exhaustive list of the criteria to be applied for each category of assets and liabilities
3. With respect to fixed assets:
   - Goods possessed under a leasing agreement: cost at source, length of contract, years expired, contributions paid in previous years and in the current year, pending contributions, and value of the purchase option
   - In the case of significant items of intangible fixed assets, information concerning their use, expiration date, and period of depreciation
4. Company commitments with respect to purchases and foreseeable financing sources, as well as company commitments with respect to the sale of any type of asset
5. Other information concerning leases, insurance, lawsuits, attachments, and other similar situations that might affect the assets of the company
6. Additional information concerning tangible fixed assets:
   - Details of the updating of the value of tangible fixed assets
   - Useful lives of the assets or depreciation ratios used
   - The characteristics, gross value, and accrued depreciation of elements acquired from group companies
   - Investments located outside Spanish territory
   - Capitalized interest and exchange differences
   - Amount of elements not subject to the operation
   - Amount of totally written-off items that are technically obsolete or not in use
   - Items subject to guarantees and reversion
   - Subsidies and donations received
7. Point 4 relating to the Commercial Reform Act of 1989 and the

Companies Act of 1989 is expanded as follows:

- Separation of group companies and associates, the latter being those in which a significant participation is held (20%, or 3% if listed on the Stock Exchange), without forming part of the group
- The activities undertaken by each of the group companies
- Analysis of extraordinary items in the profit and loss account
- Dividends received during the financial year
- An indication as to whether or not the shares are listed on the Stock Exchange, and if so, the average quotation for the last quarter and at the close of the financial year
- The same information for associated companies
- Securities given in guarantee
- Fixed income securities maturing in each of the next 5 years and the remainder, separated according to group companies, associates, and others
- Securities given in foreign currency
- The amount of interest due and not collected
- The average rate of the yield of the fixed income securities

8. Nontrade debits and credits, distinguishing between short- and long-term, foreign currency, exchange difference cover, maturities in each of the next 5 years, guarantees, and so on.

9. With respect to inventory, a breakdown of the following:
   - Firm purchase and sale commitments, as well as future contracts
   - Limitations in availability
   - Stocks appearing under assets at a fixed value

10. With respect to equity:
   - Increases and decreases in equity
   - Movement of own shares, number held, final destination of same and amount of the related reserve
   - Details concerning capital increases underway, with respect to

number of shares, nominal value, issue premium, rights and restrictions, etc.

- Amount of capital authorized by the General Meeting of Shareholders to be floated by the company directors and period of authorization.
- Restrictions on the availability of reserves
- Any part of the capital held by another company, directly or through its affiliates, which is more than 10%.

11. Discount lines and policies granted to the company
12. Debentures and bonds outstanding
13. With respect to taxation:

- Negative assessments (tax losses) pending compensation, with indication of time limits and conditions
- The nature and type of applicable and pending tax incentives, as well as commitments acquired in connection with same

14. Relevant subsequent events (following the close of the financial year)
15. A funds flow statement (*cuadro de financiacion*)

In the event that an abridged annual report may be prepared (see conditions under 2.1.5, Abridged *Memoria* (Notes), it is only necessary to give the additional information included under items 1, 2, and 8. The funds flow statement need not be included.

2.1.5 Types of Annual Accounts

Companies must prepare their annual accounts according to what can be called the normal pattern. The structures required under the Commercial Reform Act of 1989 and the Companies Act of 1989 are those indicated in Appendix A in Spanish and English.

The PGC-90 requires the preparation of more detailed models, indicated in Appendix B.

Both the Commercial Reform Act of 1989 and the Companies Act of 1989, as well as the PGC-90, allow the preparation of summarized annual accounts, which are known as "abridged accounts," in the case of small companies and under certain conditions.

Abridged Balance Sheet   An abridged balance sheet may be prepared if at least two of the following circumstances prevail on the closing date of the accounting period for two consecutive years:

- Total assets of no more than 230 million pesetas
- Net annual turnover of less than 480 million pesetas
- Average number of employees no more than 50 during the accounting period

Section 2.2.2 below indicates the required content of the abridged balance sheet.

Abridged Profit and Loss Account   An abridged profit and loss account may be prepared if at least two of the following circumstances prevail on the closing date of the accounting period for two consecutive years:

- Total assets of no more than 920 million pesetas
- Net annual turnover of less than 1,920 million pesetas
- Average number of employees no more than 250 during the accounting period

Section 2.2.2 below indicates the required content of the abridged profit and loss account.

Abridged *Memoria* (Notes)   Abridged *memoria* may be prepared by any company qualifying for an abridged balance sheet. The required minimum information was given in Section 2.1.4 above.

2.1.6 The Management Report

The management report is a new document under Spanish legislation, although, owing to its similarity to the old "commercial report" as indicated in Section 2.1.4, it is not entirely new to commercial practice.

Under the new legislation, the management report is seen as a document separate from the annual accounts, compulsory for all companies, regardless of size and the type of annual accounts presented, and should be prepared by the directors of the company at the same time as the annual accounts.

The management report includes the following:

1. A true indication of the evolution of the business and the position of the company
2. Important events occurring after the close of the financial year
3. Research and development activities carried out by the company
4. Acquisitions and disposals of own shares:
   - Reasons for the acquisitions and disposals during the financial year
   - The number and nominal value of shares acquired and disposed of during the financial year, plus the fraction of capital they represent
   - Consideration received for the shares acquired or disposed of on a payment basis
   - The number and nominal value of all own shares acquired and held by the company itself or by an intermediary, plus details of the fraction of capital they represent

The management report must be examined by the auditors under the terms established in Section 1.3. It must be filed, together with the annual accounts, as indicated in the following section.

2.1.7 Publication of Annual Accounts

An important new requirement of the Commercial Reform Act of 1989 concerns the publication of annual accounts. The maximum time for approval by the general meeting of shareholders is 6 months from the closing date of the accounting period. After approval, the annual accounts, together with the management report and the auditors' report, must be filed in the Mercantile Register of the city in which the company has its registered office, within a maximum period of 1 month. The Register may , then provide such information to anyone who requests it.

According to information from the Mercantile Registers, the number of companies filing their annual accounts is increasing every year.

Although it is still too early to reach final conclusions, it would appear that the new accounting rules are being introduced quickly into routine accounting practice and that the standardization of rules and models of accounts is resulting in published accounts of a good quality. This was one of the main objective of the reforms.

2.2 Model of Financial Statements since 1990

2.2.1 General Information

As we have already mentioned, regulation of accounting matters before the reforms of the late 1980s—in effect, until January 1, 1990—was incomplete. In general, there were no extensive information requirements. Accounts were prepared with the precision expected by virtue of accepted accounting practices.

Models of the balance sheet, profit and loss account, and statement of sources and applications of funds, as laid down by the PGC-90, are shown in Appendix B, in both Spanish and English, at the end of this chapter. Additionally, a specimen set of financial statements is appended, also in Spanish and English.

2.2.2 Model of Abridged Accounts since 1990

Both the Companies Act of 1989 and PGC-90 coincide with respect to the models of the abridged balance sheet and profit and loss account, which consists of presenting the information specified in the full models under roman numerals without the further detail specified under arabic numerals.

2.3 Consolidated Annual Accounts

2.3.1 Overview

In the past, consolidation of the accounts of groups of companies was not compulsory and was only required in respect of certain types of companies, for example, financial entities. With the publication of the Commercial Reform Act of 1989, it became compulsory to prepare annual consolidated accounts for all accounting periods ending after December 31, 1990.

The Commercial Reform Act did not specify the model to be followed for the annual group accounts, although it did specify general standards in respect of the structure and content of the consolidated annual report. However, in December 1991 the rules for Consolidation of Annual Accounts were issued by Royal Decree 1815/1991.

2.3.2 General Definitions

Consolidated accounts are considered to be an accounting tool to present the financial results and position of a group but do not have legal implications or tax effects. There exists a scheme for consolidated corporation tax returns that can be applied in certain circumstances but that follows different principles from the consolidation for financial reporting purposes, in that only companies in which 90% or more of the share capital is held by the group can be included.

Under Spanish legislation, a group of companies exists when a Spanish company (the parent company) is in such a relationship with one or more other companies (the subsidiaries) that the parent company has control of the majority of the voting rights in a general meeting of shareholders.

To calculate the real control held by the parent company, all direct and indirect control must be considered, and own shares held by the company and shares without voting rights must be deducted (the Spanish Companies Act allows the issue of shares having only financial rights and no voting rights).

The rules have provided some transitory exemptions allowing small groups not to prepare annual consolidated accounts. The limits defined relate to the following figures for the group:

- Total assets less than 2,300 million pesetas
- Net annual turnover less than 4,800 million pesetas
- Average number of employees less than 500 during the accounting period

There is another exemption (as provided in the Seventh Directive), when the parent company of a group is a subsidiary of a company in another European Union member state, which effectively presents its consolidated accounts. In other words, in those circumstances it is not necessary to prepare the consolidated accounts of a Spanish subgroup. For the exemption to apply, certain circumstances must occur and some formal requirements must be observed.

In general terms, Spanish consolidation principles are now in line with principles generally accepted internationally.

2.3.3 *Methods of Consolidation*

Three methods have been defined to consolidate different kinds of investment of the parent company:

1. Full consolidation (*Integración global*),
2. Equity method (*Puesta en equivalencia*)
3. Proportional consolidation (*Consolidación proporcional*)

Subsidiaries effectively controlled by the parent company must be consolidated by using the full consolidation method (line-by-line consolidation). Such a treatment implies the integration of all the assets and liabilities, income and expenses of the subsidiaries with the accounts of the parent company, recognizing the minority interest, and recording separately the goodwill arising on first consolidation of each subsidiary.

Investments in which the parent company has a significant influence must be consolidated by the equity method. A significant influence is defined as existing, in the absence of evidence to the contrary, when a participating interest is held greater than 20% of the voting shares (or 3% for listed companies).

The proportional consolidation method may be used for investments in which the parent company participates in a joint venture with other groups, and they are managed jointly. This method is not obligatory, and the parent company may choose this method or the equity method.

2.3.4 *Accounting Principles and Policies*

The accounting principles and policies to be used in consolidated accounts do not differ from the general accounting principles and policies. The only differences are those derived from the consolidation process.

When performing the process of consolidation, the following steps should be observed in all three methods:

- *Homogeneización*, or the application of the same (homogeneous) accounting principles and policies and dates of closing, that is, those of the parent company, to the accounts of all group companies. In addition, assets and liabilities of acquired companies are restated at their fair values (v*alor de mercado*)
- *Agregación*, or addition of the resultant "homogeneous" accounts
- *Eliminaciones*, or the elimination of the investments of the parent company together with the equity of the subsidiaries; any profits or losses, balances, dividends, and so on, existing from intragroup operations

Goodwill (when positive) is accounted for as an intangible asset and amortized against the profit and loss account over a 10-year period. If the period is longer than 5 years, specific disclosure of the justification should be included in the annual accounts. A periodic evaluation of the future economic benefits related to the goodwill is required. Negative goodwill is accounted for as a liability, that is, either as a deferred credit to be amortized back to income or as a provision for future reorganization expenses or losses of the acquired company.

Because the other accounting principles and policies used in consolidated accounts are similar to the general rules, we refer the reader to the relevant paragraphs in Section 3.

2.4 Breakdown: Geographic or by Activity

Both the Commercial Reform Act of 1989 and the Companies Act of 1989, as well as the General Accounting Plan of 1990, stipulate that the annual report should include a breakdown of the net turnover figure according to categories of activity and by geographic markets. No further information is given as to the scope of this analysis.

As stated in the regulations, the aforementioned requirements may be omitted when, owing to their nature, they could cause prejudice to the company. No further information or clarification is given regarding the conditions for this exception or of the causes that would be considered acceptable.

As we may note from many annual reports, this information is generally shown in published accounts. The descriptions included are sufficient to provide a general indication of the activities of companies.

2.5 Legal or Institutional Requirements

2.5.1   Legal Requirements

As previously mentioned, the legal requirements for the preparation and presentation of annual accounts are basically those stipulated by the Commercial Reform Act of 1989 and the Companies Act of 1989. In addition, the General Accounting Plan 1990 provides a precise interpretation of the requirements of the Commercial Reform Act, and thus it is advisable to follow its pronouncements. The Commercial Reform Act states that, when the legal provisions are insufficient to ensure a true and fair view *(imagen fiel)*, they shall be extended as necessary in order to reach the desired objective.

Furthermore, with the publication of the PGC-90, a set of transitional regulations came into force that affect a considerable number of companies in Spain. (For further details, see Section 3.2.)

2.5.2   Institutional Requirements: The Accounting Profession and the Stock Exchange

Until the new regulations came into effect, accounting practice was guided by the pronouncements of the Spanish Association of Accounting and

Business Administration (*Asociación Española de Contabilidad y Administración de Empresas*, AECA), a private body made up of professionals and experts in accounting and business administration. Its pronouncements are of an advisory nature and are neither binding nor compulsory but do represent a consensus of opinion on different situations given by leading professionals and are therefore obviously a model to be followed.

To date, the AECA has published the documents listed below and is in the process of reviewing them in order to adapt them, where necessary, to the new legal situation. The documents issued are of a varied nature, but the most relevant for the purpose of this work are those referring to accounting practice, which are the following:

1. Principles and standards of accounting in Spain
2. Accounting principles for tangible fixed assets (including a supplement)
3. Accounting principles for intangible fixed assets and deferred expenses
4. Accounting principles for the treatment of exchange differences in foreign currency
5. Accounting principles for suppliers, creditors, and other accounts payable
6. Accounting principles for customers, debtors, and other accounts receivable
7. Accounting principles for accruals and prepayments and collections and deferred payments
8. Accounting principles for stocks
9. Accounting principles for corporation tax
10. Accounting principles for equity
11. Accounting principles for provisions, contingencies, and events subsequent to the closing of the financial statements
12. Accounting principles for accrued income
13. Accounting principles for income
14. Accounting principles for the reversion fund (a provision for the return of assets to the state)

Companies whose shares are listed on the Stock Exchange must prepare and present their annual accounts according to the requirements of the Commercial Reform Act of 1989 and the Companies Act of 1989.

3. Accounting Principles and Policies in Valuation and Income Measurement

The following section presents the most important principles to be observed in dealing with the different items or sections of the annual accounts. Mention should be made of the transitory provisions that came into effect with the publication of the PGC-90, which are explained in the following section and which are applicable in general terms to all accounting periods closed after June 30, 1990 (see Section 3.2).

3.1 Transitory Provisions

1. In the valuation of the different items making up net worth in accordance with the new regulations, the adjustments of the values of the assets and liabilities in the annual accounts closed during the first accounting period in which the General Accounting Plan is applied will be made using the reserve accounts for the balancing entries. (It should be remembered that PGC-90 can be applied voluntarily from July 1, 1990.)

2. The sectoral adaptations of the old General Accounting Plan will remain in force for all aspects that are not contrary to present legislation.

3. Losses in respect of exchange differences activated before January 1, 1990 should be written off within a period of 3 years following the accounting period closed after June 30, 1990.

4. Companies with deficits on their provisions for pensions, being the funds invested in the employer company, should systematically endow the respective provisions until such deficit is covered, within the following time limits, starting from the commencement of the first accounting period that closes after June 30, 1990:

    a. In the case of provisions in respect of pensions created at the commencement of the said accounting period: 7 years

    b. In the case of provisions in respect of pensions not created at the commencement of the said accounting period: 15 years

5. For the first accounting period for which the PGC-90 is applicable, if leasing arrangements exist, the lessee company may choose between:

    a. Recording the outstanding amounts as of that date according to the criterion used in previous accounting periods (i.e., showing the amounts as an expenditure for the financial year and not including the goods under assets or recognizing them under liabilities)

    b. Applying the valuation standards of the PGC-90, and including the goods under assets and recognizing the liability, as retroactive from the commencement of the contract. The difference arising in the different criteria will be recorded in the reserve accounts after deduction of tax

    Where there are several contracts in force, the same option selected should be used for all of them.

6. For the first accounting period after June 30, 1990, the comparative figures of the previous financial year may be disclosed in the statement of sources and applications of funds.

In addition to those just described, another provision was published that provided a separate tax accounting framework independent of that for financial reporting, which until then had been tied completely to tax accounting requirements. This is not the place to analyze it, but it is appropriate to know of its existence and its publication with the same legal status as PGC-90.

3.2 Accounting Policies and Valuation Rules

The most important accounting policies and valuation rules included in PGC-90 are given below.

3.2.1 Statement of Accounting Principles

1. The valuation rules laid down are in conformity with the stated accounting principles, and a complete description is included for each component of the annual accounts.
2. Application of the valuation rules is compulsory.

3.2.2 Tangible Fixed Assets

1. Valuation:
   a. At acquisition price or production cost
   b. If acquired free of charge, at salable value
   c. Additional or complementary investments will be incorporated into the cost of the fixed asset.
2. Acquisition price:
   a. Acquisition price includes the amount invoiced by the supplier and additional expenses involved until it is in working order.
   b. Financial expenses incurred in the asset's acquisition or production (intercalated interest) may be included, with an indication of the amount in the annual report.
   c. Taxes related to the purchase will only be considered as costs if they cannot be recovered from the Public Treasury.
3. Production cost:
   a. Acquisition price of raw materials and components and directly imputable costs
   b. Indirect cost that may be reasonably assigned to the period of manufacture
   c. Intercalated interest may be included, indicating the amount in the annual report.
4. Salable value:
   a. The price one would be prepared to pay, bearing in mind the condition of the goods
   b. Will generally be arrived at according to the going concern concept

5. Corrections in the value of tangible fixed assets:

   a. Systematic depreciation in terms of useful life, considering also conditions of use and obsolescence

   b. Downwards value adjustments

   c. Use will be made of provisions in the event that it is considered that the loss of value could be reversible.

   d. In the event of the cessation of the relevant circumstances, the provision will cease to exist.

   e. If the loss of value is irreversible, the decrease in the value of the goods will be debited directly to the asset account.

3.2.3 Specific Standards Applicable to Tangible Fixed Assets

The following specific standards apply to tangible fixed assets.

1. Building land: cost includes preparation expenses, as well as the demolition of buildings and the costs involved in inspections and preparation of plans before acquisition.

2. Buildings: cost includes permanent installations and professional taxes and fees. The value of the land should be disclosed separately.

3. Technical installations, machinery, and equipment: include all costs until start-up.

4. Tools and utensils: if included with plant and machinery, the criteria used for the latter will be applied.

   a. If the above do not form part of any machinery and their useful life is estimated at less than a year, they should be charged to expenses. If they last for more than one year, the annual regularization (restatement of assets in accordance with tax laws) is recommended, by means of a physical inventory.

   b. Patterns used for mass production are considered to be fixed assets and should be depreciated according to their useful life. If they are used only for isolated manufacturing operations, they are not considered part of the inventory.

5. Work carried out on the fixed asset itself: the expenses will be

debited to the fixed asset and credited as income at the year end under the heading "work carried out by the company for fixed assets."

6. Renewal, expansion, or improvement: these items will be capitalized if they represent an increase in capacity, productivity, or a lengthening of the useful life, if it is possible to estimate the net value of the elements that should be written off owing to replacement.

3.2.4 Intangible Fixed Assets

1. Intangible fixed assets will be valued at acquisition price or production cost.
2. The rules regarding depreciation and provisions in respect of tangible fixed assets are applicable to the extent that they do not contradict Subsection 3.2.5 below.

3.2.5 Specific Rules with Respect to Intangible Fixed Assets

The following specific rules apply to intangible fixed assets.

1. Research and development expenses:
   a. Research and development expenses will be considered as expenses of the accounting period in which they occur.
   b. Research and development expenses may be capitalized if they comply with the following conditions:
      - They are individualized according to project and with specifically established costs that can be allocated over time.
      - There are justifiable reasons for believing in the success and economic and commercial profitability of the project in question.
   c. The amounts capitalized should be amortized over a period of not more than 5 years. If any doubts arise as to the project, an immediate write-off to the profit and loss should be made.
   d. The amounts included under this heading restrict the possibility

of distributing dividends, as they reduce the available reserves by an amount equal to their net balance.

2. Industrial property rights (e.g., patents): these include research and development expenses when the patent is obtained, inclusive of registration charges.

3. Goodwill:

   a. Goodwill can be included only if acquired for valuable consideration.

   b. Goodwill should be written off systematically over the period of contribution, which should not exceed 10 years. If the period exceeds 5 years, mention should be made in the annual report.

4. Transfer rights:

   a. Transfer rights may be included only if acquired for valuable consideration.

   b. Transfer rights should systematically be written off over the period during which such rights contribute to the flow of income.

5. Software:

   a. Programs prepared by the company will only be capitalized in the event that their use is anticipated over various accounting periods.

   b. In no event may maintenance costs of the application be included under assets.

   c. The rules applicable to research and development expenses are applied.

6. Leased assets (in Spain, as in a number of EU member states, leased assets are considered intangibles):

   a. To be included under assets when, because of economic conditions, there is no reasonable doubt that the purchase option will be exercised.

   b. The contra credit, including the value of the purchase option, is recorded under liabilities. The interest should be considered as an expense to be distributed over the accounting periods covered by the lease contract by using a financial criterion (e.g., the liability is the present value of the stream of lease payments at a given rate of interest, and each periodic lease payment is divided between notional repayment of principal and interest on the beginning-of-period balance of principal outstanding).

c. Depreciation should be calculated over the useful life of the leased asset.

7. Sale and lease-back: If the economic conditions of the sale, in connection with the subsequent leasing back of the asset disposed of, imply that this is a method of financing, the lessee should account for the transaction as a financial lease, as follows:

a. Transfer the net book value of the asset from fixed assets to leased assets (included under intangibles)

b. Recognize under liabilities the total debt, that is, the present value of the lease payments plus the purchase option

c. Any difference will be allocated to profit and loss over the duration of the lease.

3.2.6 Establishment Costs

1. Establishment costs are to be valued at the acquisition price or production cost of the asset in question.

2. Treatment as expenses involved in the constitution and increase of capital will be given to the following items arising at such times:

a. The fees of lawyers, notaries, and registrars

b. The printing of annual reports, bulletins, and share certificates

c. Taxes

d. Advertising

e. Commissions and placement costs

3. The following related items will be considered as establishment costs:

a. fees

b. traveling and prior study expenses

c. launching advertising

    d. hiring, training and distribution of personnel

4. Establishment costs should be systematically written off over a period of not more than 5 years.

5. Distributable reserves in an amount equal to the net balance of establishment costs must be transferred to nondistributable reserves.

3.2.7 Expenses to be Distributed over Various Accounting Periods

Expenses to be distributed over various accounting periods include the following.

1. Expenses involved in the arrangement of debts:
   a. Should be valued at acquisition cost or production cost
   b. Should be treated as expenses of the respective accounting period
   c. If capitalized exceptionally, should be written off within the same period as the aforementioned debts, in accordance with the financing plan
2. Expenses of the nature of deferred interest:
   a. Discount on issue or premium on redemption of a debt
   b. To be amortized as provided for over the maturity of the debt

3.2.8 Negotiable Securities

1. Valuation:
   a. Short- or long-term securities, or fixed or variable income securities, will be valued at their acquisition price upon subscription or purchase.
   b. The said price will include the expenses inherent in the operation, and the following should be borne in mind:
      - The cost of the rights of preferential subscription will be included in the purchase price.

- The dividends due and the interest payable that are not part of the repayment value of the security will not be considered as forming part of the price.

c. When rights are sold, their cost will reduce that of the securities.

d. The cost of the rights sold will be determined by applying generally accepted valuation formulas following a prudent criterion and bearing in mind the valuation adjustments recorded in the accounts.

e. The system to be applied in the valuation of the investments will be that of the average weighted price or cost.

2. Valuation adjustments:

a. In the case of listed securities, the valuation will be the lower of cost or market value.

b   If market value is lower, a provision should be made, the amount of which could reduce even more the net book value, if prevailing circumstances made it advisable.

c   Market price is the lower of the average quotation for the last quarter and that of the day of the closing of the balance sheet. In the event of any interest that distorts the comparison, such interest should be considered for all purposes.

d. If the securities are not listed, they should appear at acquisition cost. When the acquisition cost exceeds rational valuation criteria accepted in practice, a provision must be recorded against this value.

e. In the latter case, the net equity value should be considered after being corrected for any potential surplus derived from fixed assets, when proved.

f. The same criteria will be applied to participations in the capital of group companies or associates, with provisions being made to reflect the evolution of the equity of the investee company, even though listed securities are involved.

3.2.9 Own Shares

1. Own shares are to be valued as set in Section 3.3.8.
2. When own shares are amortized, the difference between the acquisition cost and par value, being positive or negative, must be recorded against reserves.
3. Profits or losses from sales of own shares will be credited or charged as extraordinary items of profit or loss, in accounts established for this purpose.

3.2.10 Nontrade Credits

1. Nontrade credits are to be valued according to the amount made available. The difference between this amount and the nominal value, which represents the interest charged, will be entered as financial income over the maturity term.
2. Balances from the sale of fixed assets will be valued at sales price, discounting the interest included in the nominal value of the credit.
3. The accrued interest, whether due or not, will be credited in consideration of the due date and will be recognized in accordance with the respective accruals.
4. Provisions for bad debts should be recorded as considered necessary.

3.2.11 Nontrade Debts

1. Nontrade debts should be included at repayment value. The difference between this value and the amount received will be shown in the assets and will be written off in accordance with a financial criterion.
2. Debts from fixed assets will be shown at nominal value. Any interest included in the nominal value and not included in the fixed asset will be treated in accordance with point 1, above.

3. Credit amounts will be shown exclusively according to the amount of the drawdown.

3.2.12 *Customers, Suppliers, Trade Debtors, and Creditors*

1. Customers, suppliers, trade debtors, and creditors will be included at nominal value.
2. The interest included in the nominal value will be considered as income or expenses to be distributed over various accounting periods.
3. The necessary provisions will be set up in consideration of the risk of possible bad debts.

3.2.13 *Stocks (Inventories)*

1. Valuation: at acquisition price or production cost
2. Acquisition price: price included on the invoice plus additional costs until the goods are in the warehouse, including taxes imposed on the sale if such taxes are not recoverable from the public treasury.
3. Production cost: acquisition price of raw materials and consumables, plus costs directly imputable and a reasonable part of the indirect costs in the period of manufacture.
4. Valuation adjustments: a provision will be made in the event of a reversible depreciation of the acquisition price or production cost, considering the market value or completion value of the goods in question.
5. Market value is understood as:
    a. In the case of raw materials, the lesser of replacement cost and net completion value
    b. In the case of commodities and finished products, the completion value, less the respective trade taxes
    c. For work in progress, the completion value of the finished product, less costs to complete and marketing costs

6. Products subject to a definitive future sale will not be the object of an evaluative correction, if the price obtained is sufficient to cover all the historical costs as well as those still pending to be incurred during that particular operation.

7. If the articles cannot be identified, the method of the average weighted price of cost will be applied in general. Other methods, such as FIFO, LIFO, or similar methods, are also acceptable.

8. In exceptional cases the stocks can be valued at an overall fixed rate, if:

   • They are constantly renewed

   • Their overall value and composition do not vary significantly

   • Their overall value is not material for the company

3.2.14 Foreign Exchange Differences

Generally, the items originally denominated in foreign currency should be included in the annual accounts by using the exchange rate in force on the date of acquisition, on the date they were included in the net worth, or on the date of the transaction, as applicable.

Other specific provisions are as follows:

1. Tangible and intangible fixed assets: depreciation should be calculated according to the value obtained as above.

2. Stocks:

   a. The rule will be applied individually for each transaction and will be separate from the method of valuation applied.

   b. The calculation of the market value for the purpose of the closing provision will be made, should such be the case, by applying the quotations and exchange rates in force at that date.

3. Securities: the value at closing may not exceed the result of applying the exchange rate at that date to the market quotation.

4. Treasury: at close, all items should reflect current exchange rates, the resulting exchange differences being treated as profit or loss for the accounting period.

5. Credits and debits:

  a. At close, credits and debits should be valued at the exchange rate in force at that moment, exclusively with respect to the part without exchange cover.

  b. Any resulting differences will be classified according to maturity and currency, and in the latter case, it is permitted to group together currencies convertible in Spain that show a similar performance on the market.

  c. The net balance resulting from the above grouping:

  • If positive (profit), it should be treated as a deferred credit under "Income to be distributed over various accounting periods" (but see item d, below).

  • If negative (loss), it should be charged to the profit and loss account.

  d. Unrealized positive differences may be credited to the profit and loss account if they are in respect of groups for which losses have been recorded in previous accounting periods, and up to said amount.

  e. Income deferred in this way will be applied to profit and loss as:

  • The items causing them become due

  • Negative exchange differences for equal or greater amounts are recognized

6. Special regulations:

  a. Exchange differences should not be considered as a correction of the value of the fixed assets, except in the case of long-term financing for the purchase of a fixed asset (which in this case would be considered part of the cost of the fixed asset, subject to a general ruling in this respect), provided the following are complied with:

  • That the debt has been unmistakably to acquire a specific identifiable fixed asset

  • That the period of installation is more than 12 months and the exchange rate difference occurs before start up.

- That the resulting amount does not exceed the market or replacement value of the fixed asset
  b. Special regulations may be issued for specific industries or sectors.

3.2.15 Value Added Tax

1. Nondeductible value added tax (VAT) (even in the case of internal consumption) will form part of the acquisition cost of the goods acquired.
2. In the case of companies subject to pro rata arrangements, the valuation will not be altered by the final regularization (restatement of assets in accordance with tax laws) applicable.

3.2.16 Corporation Tax

1. Differences will be considered to exist between the accounting net income and the taxable income (taxable base) in the event of the following cases:
   a. Definitional (permanent) differences in expense and income
   b. Temporary differences in the allocation of expense and income
   c. The admission for tax purposes of compensation for negative taxable bases from previous accounting periods (tax loss carry-forwards)
2. Differences may be classified as:
   a. Permanent: differences not reverting in subsequent periods, excluding the compensatable losses
   b. Temporary: based on differences in the temporary criteria of allocation, reversing in subsequent periods
   c. Losses compensated for tax purposes
3. The expense to be recorded will be calculated on the profit or loss before tax, corrected by the permanent differences. The respective tax rate will be applied to this amount, and the allowances and

deductions (not payments on account) will be deducted from the resulting quota.

4. Therefore, the deductions and allowances from the quota will be considered as a reduction of the tax accrued in the year.

5. Temporary differences and compensated losses will not be taken into consideration when determining the expense for corporation tax purposes.

6. The items resulting from the temporary differences will be stated, according to each case, as assets or liabilities (advance or deferred tax) in the balance sheet (but see item 7, below). For valuation purposes, the rate actually in force during the accounting period should be used, the appropriate corrections being made to the value in the accounting period in which the quota is modified.

7. Advance taxes by way of temporary differences or compensatable tax losses (advance tax assets) may only be recognized in the accounting sense when their future realization is reasonably assured, and will be immediately withdrawn should any doubts arise in this respect.

8. The deductions and allowances from the quota may be considered as deferred income and be subject to a reasonable time apportionment.

3.2.17 *Purchases and Other Expenses*

Purchases of commodities and goods for resale follow the rules given below:

1. The following items will be charged net of deductible VAT:
    *   Purchase expenditures
    *   Transportation
    *   Tax on acquisitions

2. Discounts, etc. included in the invoice will be deducted from the amount of the purchase.

3. Discounts, etc. for prompt payment, whether or not they are in-

cluded in the invoice, will not be deducted and will be treated as financial income.

4. The following discounts or credit notes will be recorded as a shown below:
   - Those that are based on reaching a specific number of transactions, in one account
   - In another, distinct account, the credit notes in respect of quality defects, delivery times, and other similar reasons

5. Containers to be returned to suppliers that are charged in invoices by the latter will be recorded by reducing the balance payable and using a separate account, and the amount that the company keeps for its use (deteriorated or lost containers, etc.) will be allocated to expenses.

With respect to service costs, the aforementioned regulations will apply, with the exception of containers.

3.2.18 Sales and Other Income

The sale of goods will be treated in accordance with the following rules:

1. The sales figure will not include the taxes imposed.
2. The following will be entered in distinct expense accounts:
   - Expenses inherent to sales
   - Transportation of sales for the account of the company
3. Discounts will be accounted for as follows:
   - Those included in the invoice that are not for prompt payment will be deducted from the sales figure.
   - Those granted for prompt payment will be classified as financial expenses.
   - Those based on a volume of activity to be reached will be recorded as expenses.
   - Goods returned for quality defects, delivery times, or other

similar reasons will be registered as returns.

4. Containers to be returned to suppliers that are charged in invoices by the latter will be recorded by reducing the balance to be collected and using a separate account, and the amount that the customer keeps for its use (deteriorated or lost containers, etc.) will be allocated to income.

Income from the sale of services will be registered in the same way, with the exception of containers (see item 4, above).

3.2.19 Contributions to Pension Funds

1. Accrued expenses will be included.
2. They will be based on estimates, carried out according to actuarial calculations.
3. They are considered internal funds, which are invested in the employer company.
4. Their object is to cover legal or contractual obligations.
5. The financial yields generated in their favor may be applied as contributions.

3.2.20 Capital Subsidies

1. Capital subsidies will be valued according to the amount granted when they are of a nonrefundable nature.
2. They will be considered as nonrefundable if:
   a. The conditions established for the granting of such subsidies have been complied with; or
   b. There are no doubts as to future compliance.
3. They will be allocated to the profit and loss for the accounting period in proportion to the depreciation of the assets financed by the subsidy.

4. Expected Future Developments

The process of harmonization with European practice might now be considered complete, because the recent reforms of Spanish commercial and company law have resulted in a highly developed environment for accounting. The commercial and accounting legislation is recent, however, and the implementation of many rules is still in process. Some committees nominated by the *Instituto de Contabilidad y Auditoría de Cuentas* are currently working to issue documents on accounting policies and interpretations, and others are working on sectorial plans to adapt the general rules to the specific requirements of sectors.

Spanish companies have made great efforts to adapt their account systems to the rules to which we have referred in this chapter, and in a very short time. The fruits of these efforts are now evident and are making Spanish accounting practice modern, transparent, and generally useful.

Useful Address

Instituto de Auditores-Censores Jurados de Cuentas de España
General Arrando, 9
Madrid 28010
Spain

Tel.: +(1) 446 0354
Fax: +(1) 447 1162

Appendix A: Required Structures of the Balance Sheet and the Profit and Loss Account, According to the Companies Reform Act of 1989 and the Companies Act of 1989

BALANCE—ACTIVO
A) Accionistas (socios) por desembolsos
   no exigidos
   Total A . . . .
B) Inmovilizado
   I   Gastos de establecimiento
   II Inmovilizaciones inmateriales
      1. Gasos de investigación y
         desarrollo
      2. Concesiones, patentes, licencias,
         marcas y similares
      3. Fondo de comercio
      4. Anticipos
   III Inmovilizaciones materiales
      1. Terrenos y constucciones
      2. Instaliaciones técnicas y
         maquinaria
      3. Otras instalaciones, utillaje y
         mobiliario
      4. Anticipos e inmovilizaciones
         materiales en curso
   IV.Inmovilizaciones financieras
      1. Participaciones en empresas del
         grupo
      2. Créditos a empresas del grupo
      3. Participaciones en empresas
         asociadas
      4. Créditos a empresas asociadas
      5. Valores que tengan carácter de
         inmovilizaciones renta fija
      6. Otros créditos
      7. Acciones propias
   Total B . . . .
C) Activo circulante
   I   Accionistas por desembolsos
       exigidos
   II Existencias
      1. Materias primas y consumibles

      2. Productos en curso de
         fabricación
      3. Productos terminados y
         mercancias
      4. Anticipos

BALANCE SHEET—ASSETS
A) Shareholders (partners) per non-
   required disbursements
   Total A . . . .
B) Fixed Assets
   I.   Start-up expenses
   II. Intangible fixed assets
      1. Research and development costs

      2. Concessions, patents, licences,
         trademarks and similar
      3. Goodwill
      4. Advances
   III.Tangible fixed assets
      1. Land and buildings
      2. Technical installations and
         machinery
      3. Other installations, equipment
         and furniture
      4. Advances and tangible invest-
         ments under way
   VI.Financial fixed assets
      1. Participations in companies of
         the group
      2. Credits to companies of the
         group
      3. Participations in associated
         companies
      4. Credits to associated companies
      5. Fixed income securities
      6. Other credits
      7. Own shares
   Total B . . . .
C) Current assets
   I.   Shareholders per required disburse-
        ments
   II. Stocks
      1. Raw materials and consumer
         goods
      2. Products being manufactured

      3. Finished products and merchan-
         dise
      4. Advances

III Deudores
1. Clientes por ventas y prestaciones de servicios
2. Empresas del grupo, deudores
3. Empresas asociadas, deudores
4. Otros deudores
IV Valore mobiliarios
1. Participaciones en Sociadades del grupoes de empresas del grupo
2. Particpaciones en empresas asociadas
3. Acciones propias
V Tesorería
VI ajustes por periodificación
Total C . . . .
TOTAL GENERAL (A + B+ C) . . .

BALANCE—PASIVO
A) Fondos propios
I Capital suscrito
II Prima de emisión
III Reserva de revalorización
IV Reservas
1. Reserva legal
2. Reservas para acciones propias
3. Reservas estatutarias

4. Otras resevas
V Resultados ejercicios anteriores
VI Resultado del ejercicio (beneficio o pérdida)
Total A . . . .
B) Provisiones para riesgos y gasios
1. Provisiones para pensiones y obligaciones similares
2. Provisiones para impuestos
3. Otras provisiones
4. Fondo de reversión

Total B . . . .
C) Acreedores a largo plazo
1. Emisiones de obligaciones, separando convertibles
2. Deudas con entidades de crédito
3. Anticipos recibiods por pedidos
4. Deudas por compras o prestaciones de servicios

III.Debtors
1. Customers per sales and services rendered
2. Group companies—debtors
3. Associated companies—debtors
4. Other debtors
IV.Securities
1. Participations in companies of the group

2. Participations in associated companies
3. Own shares
V. Treasury
VI.Accruals and pre-payments
Total C . . . .
GENERAL TOTAL (A + B + C) . . .

BALANCE SHEET—LIABILITIES
A) Equity
I. Subscribed capital
II. Share premium
III.Revaluation reserve
IV.Reserves
1. Legal reserve
2. Reserves for own shares
3. Statutory reserves (created in accordance with a company's own bylaws)
4. Other reserves
V. Profit or loss from previous years
VI.Profit or loss for the year
Total A . . . .
B) Provisions for risks and expenses
1. Provisions for pensions and similar obligations
2. Provisions for taxes
3. Other provisions
4. Reversion fund (a provision for the return of assets to the State)
Total B . . . .
C) Long-term creditors
1. Issues of debentures, separating convertible ones
2. Debts with credit entities
3. Advances received by orders
4. Debts by purchases or services rendered

5. Deudas representadas en efectos de comercio
6. Deudas con Sociedades del grupo
7. Deudas con empresas asociadas al grupo
8. Otras deudas
Total C . . . .
D) Acreedores a certo plaza
  1. Emisiones de obligaciones, separando convertibles
  2. Deudas con entidades de crédito
  3. Anticipos recibiods por pedidos
  4. Deudas por compras o prestaciones de servicios
  5. Deudas representadas en efectos de comercio
  6. Deudas con Sociedades del grupo
  7. Deudas con empresas asiciadas al grupo
  8. Otras deudas
Total D . . . .
TOTAL GENERAL (A + B+ C +D) . .

5. Debts represented by trade bills
6. Debts with companies of the group
7. Debts with companies associated with the group
8. Other debts
Total C . . . .
D) Short-term creditors
  1. Issues of debentures, separating convertible ones
  2. Debts with credit entities
  3. Advances received by orders
  4. Debts by purchases or services rendered
  5. Debts represented by trade bills
  6. Debts with companies of the group
  7. Debts with companies associated with the group
  8. Other debts
Total D . . . .
GENERAL TOTAL (A + B + C + D) .

CUENTA DE PERDIDAS Y GANACIAS—DEBE
A) GASTOS
  1. Reducción de existencias de productos terminados y en curso de fabricación
  2. Aprovisionamientos
    a) Consumo de materias primas y mercancias
    b) Otros gastos externos
  3. Gasos de personal
    a) Sueldos, salarios y asimilados
    b) Cargas sociales, separando pensiones
  4. Dotaciones para amortizaciones de inmovilizado
  5. Otros gastos de explotación
  6. Dotaciones para provisiones y amortizaciones de valores mobiliarios
  7. Intereses y gastos asimilados
  8. RESULTADO DE LAS ACTIVIDADES ORDINARIAS
  9. Gastos extraordinarios

PROFIT AND LOSS ACCOUNT—DEBIT
A) EXPENDITURES
  1. Reduction of stock of finished products and work in progress
  2. Supplies
    a) Consumption of raw materials and merchandise
    b) Other external expenditure
  3. Personnel expenses
    a) Salaries, wages and similar
    b) Staff welfare expenses, separating pensions
  4. Fixed asset depreciation transfers
  5. Other operating expenses
  6. Transfers to the provision and depreciation of securities
  7. Interest and similar expenses
  8. RESULTS OF NORMAL ACTIVITIES
  9. Extraordinary expenditures

10.Impuesto sobre sociedades
11.Otros impuestos
12.RESULTADO DEL EJERCICIO (BENEFICIOS)

CUENTA DE PERDIDAS Y GANANCIAS—HABER
B) INGRESOS
1. Importe neto de la cifra de negocios
2. Aumento de las existencias de productos terminados y en curso de fabricación
3. Trabajos efectuados por la empresa para el invocilizado
4. Otros ingresos de explotición
5. Ingresos de particpaciones
   a) En empresas del grupo
   b) En empresas asociadas
   c) En empresas fuera del grupo
6. Ingresos de otros valores mobiliarios y créditos del activo inmovilzado
   a) De empresas del grupo
   b) De empresas asociadas
   c) De empresas fuera del grupo
7. Otros intereses e ingresos asimilados
   a) De empresas del grupo
   b) De empresas asociadas
   c) Otros intereses
8. RESULTADO DE LAS ACTIVIDADES ORDINARIAS
9. Ingresos extraordinarios
10.RESULTADO DEL AJERCICIO (PERDIDAS)

10.Corporations Tax
11.Other taxes
12.RESULTS FOR THE YEAR (PROFITS)

PROFIT AND LOSS ACCOUNT— CREDIT
B) INCOME
1. Net amount of turnover
2. Increase in stocks of finished products and work in progress
3. Work undertaken by the company for fixed assets
4. Other income from operations
5. Income from participations
   a) In group companies
   b) In associate companies
   c) In companies outside the group
6. Income from other securities and fixed asset credits
   a) From group companies
   b) From associate companies
   c) From companies outside the group
7. Other comparable interest and income
   a) From group companies
   b) From associated companies
   c) Other interest
8. PROFITS FROM NORMAL ACTIVITIES
9. Extraordinary income
10.PROFIT (LOSS) FOR THE FINANCIAL YEAR

Appendix B: Model of Accounts According to the 1990 General Accounting Plan (in Spanish and English)*

Balance—Activo

A) Accionistas (socios) por desembolsos no exigidos
  Total A . . . .
B) Inmovilizado
  I   Gastos de establecimiento
  II Inmovilizaciones inmateriales
    1. Gastos de investigación y desarrollo
    2. Concesiones, patentes, licencias, marcas y similares
      2 a) Adquiridos a título oneroso
      2 b) Creados por la empresa
    3. Fondo de comercio
    4. Derechos de traspaso
    5. Aplicaciones informáticas
    6. Anticipos
    7. Provisiones
    8. Amortizaciones
  III Inmovilizaciones materiales
    1. Terrenos y construcciones
    2. Instalaciones técnicas y maquinaria
    3. Otras instalaciones, utillaje y mobiliario
    4. Anticipos e inmovilizaciones materiales en curso
    5. Otro inmovilizado
    6. Provisiones
    7. Amortizaciones
  IV Inmovilizaciones financieras
    1. Participaciones en empresas del grupo
    2. Créditos a empresas del grupo
      2 a) Valores de empresas del grupo
      2 b) Otros créditos a empresas del grupo
      2 c) Créditos por intereses
    3. Participaciones en empresas asociadas

Balance Sheet—Assets

A) Shareholders (partners) per non-required disbursements
  Total A . . . .
B) Fixed assets
  I.   Establishment costs
  II. Intangible fixed assets
    1. Research and development costs
    2. Concessions, patents, licences, trademarks and similar
      2.a) Acquired by consideration
      2.b) Created by the company
    3. Goodwill
    4. Transfer rights
    5. Computer applications
    6. Advances
    7. Provisions
    8. Depreciations
  III Tangible fixed assets
    1. Land and buildings
    2. Technical plant and machinery
    3. Other installations, tools and furniture
    4. Advances and fixed assets in course of construction
    5. Other fixed assets
    6. Provisions
    7. Depreciation
  IV Investments
    1. Participations in group companies
    2. Credits to group companies
      2.a) Securities of group companies
      2.b) Other credits to group companies
      2.c) Credits from interest
    3. Participations in associated companies

---

*   Editors' Note. A specimen set of financial statements is shown in Appendix C, which follows the detailed formats required by the new Spanish General Accounting Plan.

4. Créditos a empresas asociadas
    4 a) Valores de empresas asociadas
    4 b) Otros créditos a empresas asociadas
    4 c) Créditos por intereses
5. Valores que tengan carácter de inmovilizaciones
    5 a) Participación en capital
    5 b) Valores de renta fija
    5 c) Intereses de valores de renta fija
6. Otros créditos
    6 a) Principal de crédito
    6 b) Créditos por intereses
7. Depósitos y fianzas entregados a largo plazo
8. Provisiones
    8 a) De empresas del grupo
    8 b) De empresas asociadas
    8 c) De otros valores mobiliarios
    8 d) De insolvencias
V Acciones propias
Total B . . . .

C) Gastos a distribuir en varios ejercicios

Total C . . . .

D) Activo circulante
  I. Accionistas por desembolsos exigidos
  II Existencias
    1. Comerciales
    2. Materias primas y otros aprovisionamientos
    3. Productos en curso y semiterminados
    4. Productos terminados
    5. Subproductos, residuos y materiales recuperados
    6. Anticipos
    7. Provisiones
  III Deudores
    1. Clientes por ventas y prestaciones de servicios
    2. Empresas del grupo, deudores

4. Credits to associated companies
    4.a) Securities of associated companies
    4.b) Other credits to associated companies
    4.c) Credits from interest
5. Securities having the nature of investments
    5.a) Participations in capital
    5.b) Fixed income securities
    5.c) Interest on fixed income securities
6. Other credits
    6.a) Credit principal
    6.b) Credit from interest
7. Long-term deposits and guarantees
8. Provisions
    8.a) Of group companies
    8.b) Of associated companies
    8.c) Of other investments
    8.d) For bad debts
V Own shares
Total B . . . .

C) Expenses to be distributed over various accounting periods
Total C . . . .

D) Current Assets
  I Shareholders per required disbursements
  II Inventory
    1. Commercial
    2. Raw materials and other supplies
    3. Work in progress and semicompleted
    4. Finished products
    5. By-products, scrap and recovered materials
    6. Advances
    7. Provisions
  III Debtors
    1. Customers for sales and services rendered
    2. Group companies, debtors

3. Empresas asociadas, deudores	3. Associate companies, debtors
4. Deudores varios	4. Miscellaneous debtors
5. Personal	5. Personnel
6. Administraciones Públicas	6. Public Administrations
7. Provisiones	7. Provisions

IV Inversiones financieras temporales
1. Participaciones en empresas del grupo
2. Créditos a empresas del grupo
2 a) Valores y créditos de empresas del grupo
2 b) Créditos por intereses de empresas del grupo
3. Participaciones en empresas asociadas
4. Créditos a empresas asociadas
4 a) Valores y créditos de empresas asociadas
4 b) Créditos por intereses de empresas asociadas
5. Cartera de valores a corto plazo
5 a) Participaciones en capital
5 b) Valores de renta fija
5 c) Intereses de valores de renta fija
6. Créditos
6 a) Principal de créditos
6 b) Créditos por intereses
7. Depósitos y fianzas entregados a corto plazo
8. Provisiones
8 a) De empresas del grupo
8 b) De empresas asociadas
8 c) De valores mobiliarios
8 d) De insolvencias

V Acciones propas a corto plazo
VI Tesorería
VII Ajustes por periodificación

Total D . . . .

TOTAL GENERAL (A + B + C + D)
. . . .

IV Temporary financial investments
1. Participations in group companies
2. Credits to group companies
2.a) Securities and credits of group companies
2.b) Credits from interest from group companies
3. Participations in associated companies
4. Credits to associated companies
4.a) Securities and credits of associated companies
4.b) Credits from interest from associated companies
5. Short-term securities portfolio
5.a) Participations in capital
5.b) Fixed income securities
5.c) Interest from fixed income securities
6. Credits
6.a) Credits principal
6.b) Interest from credits
7. Short-term deposits and guarantees
8. Provisions
8.a) Of group companies
8.b) Of associated companies
8.c) Of securities
8.d) For bad debts

V Own shares short-term
VI Treasury
VII Accruals and pre-payments

Total D . . . .

GENERAL Total (A + B + C + D)
. . . .

Balance—Pasivo	**Balance Sheet—Liabilities**
A) Fondos proprios	A) Equity
I Capital suscrito	I Subscribed capital
II Prima de emision	II Share premium
III Reserva de revalorización	III Revaluation reserve
IV Reservas	IV Reserves
1. Reserva legal	1. Legal reserve
2. Reservas para acciones propias	2. Reserves for own shares
3. Reservas para acciones de la sociedad dominante	3. Reserves for shares of the dominant company
4. Reservas estatutarias	4. Legal reserves
5. Otras reservas	5. Other reserves
V Resultados ejercicios anteriores	V Results from previous accounting periods
1. Remanente	1. Retained earnings
2. Resultados negativos de ejercicios anteriores	2. Loss from previous accounting periods
3. Aportaciones de socios para compensación de pérdidas	3. Contributions from partners to compensate losses
VI Pérdidas y ganancias (beneficio o pérdida)	VI Profits and/or losses
VII Dividendo a cuenta entregado en el ejercicio	VII Dividend on account paid during the accounting period
Total A	Total A . . . .
B) Ingresos a distribuir en varios ejercicios	B) Income to be distributed over various accounting periods
1. Subvenciones de capital	1. Capital grants
2. Diferencias positivas en cambio	2. Positive exchange rate differences
3. Otros ingresos a distribuir en varios ejercicios	3. Other incomes to be distributed over various accounting periods
Total B	Total B . . . .
C) Provisiones para riesgos y gastos	C) Provisions for risks and expenditures
1. Provisiones para pensiones y obligaciones similares	1. Provisions for pensions and similar liabilities
2. Provisiones para impuestos	2. Tax provisions
3. Otras provisiones	3. Other provisions
4. Fondo de reversión	4. Reversion fund (N.B.: a provision for the return of assets to the State)
Total C	Total C . . . .
D) Acreedores a largo plazo	D) Long-term creditors
I Emisiones de obligaciones	I Issues of debentures
1. Obligaciones no convertibles	1. Non-convertible debentures
2. Obligaciones convertibles	2. Convertible debentures

3. Otras deudas representadas en valores negociables
II Deudas con entidades de crédito
III Deudas con empresas del grupo y asociadas
  1. Deudas con empresas del grupo
  2. Deudas con empresas asociadas
IV Otros acreedores
  1. Deudas representadas por efectos a pagar
  2. Otras deudas
    2 a) Deudas transformables en subvenciones
    2 b) Proveedores de inmovilizado
    2 c) Otros
  3. Fianzas y depositos recibidos a largo plazo
V Desembolsos pendientes sobre acciones no exigidos
  1. De empresas del grupo
  2. De empresas asociadas
  3. De otras empresas
Total D . . . .
E) Acreedores a corto plazo
  I Emisiones de obligaciones
    1. Obligaciones no convertibles
    2. Obligaciones convertibles
    3. Otras deudas representadas en valores negociables
    4. Intereses de obligaciones y otros valores
  II Deudas con entidades de crédito
    1. Préstamos y otras deudas
    2. Deudas por intereses
  III Deudas con empresas del grupo y asociadas a corto plazo
    1. Deudas con empresas del grupo
      1 a) Préstamos y otras deudas
      1 b) Intereses de deudas
    2. Deudas con empresas asociadas
      2 a) Préstamos y otras deudas
      2 b) Intereses de deudas
  IV Acreedores comerciales
    1. Anticipos recibidos por pedidos
    2. Deudas por compras o prestaciones de servicios

3. Other debts represented by negotiable securities
II Debts with credit entities
III Debts with group companies and associates
  1. Debts with group companies
  2. Debts with associate companies
IV Other creditors
  1. Debts represented by bills payable
  2. Other debts
    2.a) Debts convertible into subsidies
    2.b) Suppliers of fixed assets
    2.c) Others
  3. Guarantee deposits and deposits received long-term
V Disbursements pending on nondemandable shares
  1. From group companies
  2. From associate companies
  3. From other companies
Total D . . . .
E) Short-term creditors
  I Issues of debentures
    1. Non-convertible debentures
    2. Convertible debentures
    3. Other debts represented by negotiable securities
    4. Interest on debentures and other securities
  II Debts with credit entities
    1. Loans and other debts
    2. Debts from interest
  III Short-term debts with group companies and associates
    1. Debts with group companies
      1a) Loans and other debts
      1b) Interest on debts
    2. Debts with associate companies
      2a) Loans and other debts
      2b) Interest on debts
  IV Trade creditors
    1. Advances received on orders
    2. Debts in respect of purchases or services rendered

3. Deudas representadas por efectos a pagar
V Otras deudas no comerciales
1. Administraciones Públicas
2. Deudas representadas por efectos a pagar
3. Remuneraciones pendientes de pago
4. Otras deudas
5. Fianzas y depósitos recibidos a corto plazo
VI Provisiones para operaciones de tráfico
VII Ajustes por periodificación

Total E . . . .

TOTAL GRAND
(A + B + C + D + E) . . . .

3. Debts represented by bills payable
V Other non-trade debts
1. Public Administration
2. Debts represented by bills payable
3. Accrued wages and salaries

4. Other debts
5. Short-term guarantees and deposits received
VI Provisions for trading operations

VII Accruals and pre-payments

Total E . . . .

GENERAL Total
(A+B+C+D+E) . . . .

Cuenta de Pérdidas y Ganancias—Debe

A) Gastos

1. Reducción de existencias de productos terminados y en curso de fabricación
2. Aprovisionamientos
   a) Consumo de mercancías
      a1) Compras
      a2) Variación de existencias
   b) Consumo de materias primas y otras materias consumibles
      b1) Compras
      b2) Variación de existencias
   c) Otros gastos externos
3. Gastos de personal
   a) Sueldos, salarios y asimilados
   b) Cargas sociales
      b1) Cargas sociales
      b2) Aportaciones y dotaciones para pensiones
4. Dotaciones para amortizaciones de inmovilizado
5. Variación de las provisiones de circulante
   a) Variación de provisiones de existencias
   b) Variación de provisiones y pérdidas de créditos incobrables
      b1) Fallidos
      b2) Variación de provisión para insolvencias
   c) Variación de otras provisiones de tráfico
6. Otros gastos de explotación
   a) Servicios exteriores
   b) Tributos
   c) Otros gastos de gestión corriente.

I. Beneficios de Explotación
   (Bl + B2 + B3 + B4 − Al − A2 − A3 − A4 − A5 − A6)

7. Gastos financieros por deudas a largo plazo
   a) Con empresas del grupo
   b) Con empresas asociadas
   c) Con terceros
8. Otros gastos financieros y gastos asimilados

Profit and Loss Account—Debit

A) Expenses

1. Reduction of stocks of finished products and work in progress
2. Supplies
   a) Merchandise consumption
      a1) Purchases
      a2) Change in stock
   b) Consumption of raw materials and other consumer materials
      b1) Purchases
      b2) Change in stock
   c) Other external expenses
3. Staff expenses
   a) Salaries, wages and similar
   b) Staff welfare expenses
      b1) Staff welfare expenses
      b2) Pension contributions
4. Contributions towards repayment of fixed assets
5. Changes in provisions for assets

   a) Changes in inventory provisions

   b) Changes in provisions and losses from bad debts
      b1) Bad debts
      b2) Changes in provision for bad debts
   c) Changes in other trade provisions
6. Other operating expenses
   a) Outside services
   b) Taxes
   c) Other normal business expenses

I. Operating Profits
   (Bl + B2 + B3 + B4 − Al − A2 − A3 − A4 − A5 − A6)

7. Financial expenses in respect of long-term debts
   a) With group companies
   b) With associated companies
   c) With third parties
8. Other financial expenses and similar expenses

a) Por deudas con empresas del grupo
b) Por deudas con empresas asociadas
c) Por deudas con terceros y gastos asimilados
d) Pérdidas de inversiones financieras temporales
9. Variación de las provisiones de inversiones financieras
   a) De valores mobiliarias y de créditos a largo plazo
   b) De valores mobiliarios y de créditos a corto plazo
10. Diferencias negativas de cambio

II. Resultados Financieros Positivos
(B5 + B6 + B7 + B8 – A7 – A8 – A9 – A10)

III. Beneficios de las Actividades Ordinarias
(AI + AII - BI – BII)
11. Variación de las provisiones de inmovilizado inmaterial y material
12. Pérdidas procedentes del inmovilizado
13. Pérdidas por operaciones con acciones y obligaciones propias
14. Gastos extraordinarios
15. Gastos y pérdidas de otros ejercicios

IV. Resultados Extraordinarios Positivos
(B9 + B10 + B11 + B12 + B13 – A11 – A12 – A13 – A14 – Al5)

V. Beneficios Antes de Impuestos
(AIII + AIV – BIII – BIV)
16. Impuesto sobre sociedades
17. Otros impuestos

VI. Resultado del Ejercicio (Beneficios)
(AV – A16 – A17)

a) In respect of debts with group companies
b) In respect of debts with associated companies
c) In respect of debts with third parties and similar expenses
d) Losses of temporary financial investments
9. Changes in provisions for financial investments
   a) In respect of securities and long-term credits
   b) In respect of securities and short-term credits
10. Losses owing to exchange rates

II. Financial Profits
(B5 + B6 + B7 + B8 – A7 – A8 – A9 – A10)

III. Profits from Normal Activities

(AI + AII – BI – BII)
11. Changes in provisions for intangible and tangible fixed assets
12. Losses originating from fixed assets

13. Losses as a result of operations with own shares and debentures
14. Extraordinary expenses
15. Expenses and losses with respect to other accounting periods

IV. Extraordinary Profits
(B9 + B10 + B11 + B12 + B13 – A11 – A12 – A13 – A14 – Al5)

V. Pre-Tax Profits
(AIII + AIV – BIII – BIV)
16. Corporation taxes
17. Other taxes

VI. Profits for the Financial Year
(AV – A16 – A17)

Cuenta de Perdidas y Ganancias— Haber

B) Ingresos
   1. Importe neto de la cifra de negocios
     a) Ventas
     b) Prestaciones de servicios
     c) Devoluciones y "rapplels" sobre ventas
   2. Aumento de las existencias de productos terminados y en curso de fabricación
   3. Trabajos efectuados por la empresa para el inmovilizado
   4. Otros ingresos de explotación
     a) Ingresos accesorios
     b) Subvenciones
     c) Exceso de provisiones para riesgos y gastos

I. Perdidas de Explotacion
$(A1 + A2 + A3 + A4 + A5 + A6 - B1 - B2 - B3 - B4)$
   5. Ingresos de participaciones en capital
     a) En empresas del grupo
     b) En empresas asociadas
     c) En empresas fuera del grupo
   6. Ingresos de otros valores mobiliarios y créditos del activo immovilizado
     a) De empresas del grupo
     b) De empresas asociadas
     c) De empresas fuera del grupo
   7. Otros intereses e ingresos asimilados
     a) De empresas del grupo
     b) De empresas asociadas
     c) Otros intereses
     d) Beneficios en inversiones financieras temporales
   8. Diferencias positivas de cambio

II. Resultados Financieros Negativos
$(A7 + A8 + A9 + A10 - B5 - B6 - B7 - B8)$

III. Perdidas de las Actividades Ordinarias

Profit and Loss Account—Credit

B) Income
   1. Net amount of turnover
     a) Sales
     b) Services rendered
     c) Returns and recalls on sales
   2. Increase in stocks of finished product and work in progress
   3. Work carried out by the company for fixed assets
   4. Other income from operations
     a) Non-trading income
     b) Subsidies
     c) Excess of provisions for risks and expenses

I. Operating Losses
$(A1 + A2 + A3 + A4 + A5 + A6 - B1 - B2 - B3 - B4)$
   5. Income from participations in capital
     a) In group companies
     b) In associate companies
     c) In groups outside the group
   6. Income from other securities and fixed asset credits
     a) From group companies
     b) From associate companies
     c) From companies outside the group
   7. Other comparable interest and income
     a) From group companies
     b) From associate companies
     c) Other interests
     d) Profits in temporary investments
   8. Positive exchange differences

II. Financial Losses
$(A7 + A8 + A9 + A10 - B5 - B6 - B7 - B8)$

III. Losses from Normal Activity

(BI + BII – AI – AII)
9. Beneficios en enajenación de inmovilizado
10. Beneficios por operaciones con acciones y obligaciones propias
11. Subvenciones de capital transferidas al resultado del ejercicio
12. Ingresos extraordinarios
13. Ingresos y beneficios de otros ejercicios

IV. Resultados Extraordinarios Negativos
(A11 + A12 + A13 + A14 + A15 – B9 – B10 – B11 – B12 – B13)
V. Perdidas Antes de Impuestos
(BIII + BIV – AIII – AIV)
VI. Resultado del Ejercicio (Perdidas)
(BV + A16 + A17)

CUADRO DE FINANCIACION— APLICACIONES
1. Recursos aplicados en las operaciones
2. Gastos de establecimiento y formalización de deudas
3. Adquisiciones de inmovilizado
   a) Inmovilizaciones inmateriales
   b) Inmovilizaciones materiales
   c) Inmovilizaciones financieras
      c1) Empresas de grupo
      c2) Empresas asociadas
      c3) Otras inversiones financieras
4. Adquisición de acciones propias
5. Reducciones de capital
6. Dividendos
7. Cancelación o traspaso a corto plazo de deuda a largo plazo
   a) Empréstitos y otros pasivos análogos
   b) De empresas del grupo
   c) De empresas asociadas
   d) De otras deudas

(BI + BII – AI – AII)
9. Profits from disposal of fixed assets
10. Profits from operations involving own shares and debentures
11. Capital subsidies transferred to the profits for the year
12. Extraordinary income
13. Income and profits from other years

IV. Extraordinary Losses
(A11 + A12 + A13 + A14 + A15 – B9 – B10 – B11 – B12 – B13)
V. Losses Before Tax
(BIII + BIV – AIII – AIV)
VI. Profits (Losses) for the Financial Year
(BV + A16 + A17)

FUNDS FLOW STATEMENT— APPLICATIONS
1. Resources applied in operations
2. Establishment and debt formalization expenses
3. Acquisitions of fixed assets
   a) Intangible fixed assets
   b) Tangible fixed assets
   c) Investments
      c.a) Group companies
      c.2) Associated companies
      c.3) Other financial investments
4. Acquisition of own shares
5. Capital reductions
6. Dividends
7. Cancellation or short-term conveyance of long-term debt
   a) Borrowings and other similar liabilities
   b) Of group companies
   c) Of associated companies
   d) Of other debts

e) De proveedores de inmovilizado y otros	e) Of suppliers of fixed assets and others
8. Provisiones para riesgos y gastos	8. Provisions for risks and expenses

TOTAL APLICACIONES	TOTAL APPLICATIONS
EXCESO DE ORIGENES SOBRE APLICACIONES	EXCESS OF SOURCE OVER APPLICATION
(AUMENTO DE CAPITAL CIRCULANTE)	(INCREASE OF WORKING CAPITAL)

CUADRO DE FINANCIACION— ORIGENES	FUNDS FLOW STATEMENT— SOURCES
1. Recursos procedentes de las operaciones	1. Resources from operations
2. Aportaciones de accionistas a) Ampliación de capital b) Compensación para pérdidas	2. Contributions by shareholders a) Capital increase b) Compensation for losses
3. Subvenciones de capital	3. Capital grants
4. Deudas a largo plazo a) Empréstitos y otros pasivos análogos b) De empresas del grupo c) De empresas asociadas d) De otras empresas e) De proveedores de inmovilizado y otros	4. Long-term debts a) Borrowings and other similar liabilities b) Of group companies c) Of associated companies d) Of other companies e) Of suppliers of fixed assets and others
5. Enajenación de inmovilizado a) Inmovilizaciones inmateriales b) Inmovilizaciones materiales c) Inmovilizaciones financieras c1) Empresas del grupo c2) Empresas asociadas c3) Otras inversiones financieras	5. Disposal of fixed assets a) Non-tangible fixed assets b) Tangible fixed assets c) Investments c1) Group companies c2) Associated companies c3) Other financial investments
6. Enajenación de acciones propias	6. Disposal of own shares
7. Cancelación anticipada o traspaso a corto plazo de inmovilizaciones financieras a) Empresas del grupo b) Empresas asociadas c) Otras inversiones financieras	7. Advance cancellation or short-term conveyance of investments a) Group companies b) Associated companies c) Other financial investments

TOTAL ORIGENES	TOTAL SOURCES

Appendix C: Extract from the 1993 Annual Report of Telefónica de España, S.A. and Grupo Telefónica, Including a Set of Specimen Financial Statements

Telefónica de España, S.A. y Grupo Telefónica.

En millones de pesetas	Telefónica (Compañía Matriz)		Grupo Consolidado	
ACTIVO	**1993**	**1992**	**1993**	**1992**
A. ACCIONISTAS POR DESEMBOLSOS NO EXIGIDOS	-	-	-	1
B. INMOVILIZADO	3.343.388	3.365.365	3.436.855	3.409.276
I. Gastos de Establecimiento	162	359	226	503
II. Inmovilizaciones Inmateriales (Nota 5)	55.520	41.609	63.207	50.778
Gastos de investigación y desarrollo	50.454	36.500	48.812	36.415
Arrendamiento financiero	-	-	3.505	4.759
Otro inmovilizado inmaterial	30.670	19.345	38.863	25.678
Amortizaciones	(25.604)	(14.236)	(27.973)	(16.074)
III. Inmovilizaciones Materiales (Nota 6)	3.181.505	3.216.689	3.172.110	3.211.231
Terrenos y construcciones	438.189	403.197	441.443	406.830
Instalaciones técnicas y maquinaria	116.795	111.478	129.800	122.393
Instalaciones telefónicas	4.538.490	4.308.549	4.502.870	4.275.703
Mobiliario, utillaje y otros	113.059	103.854	127.986	114.406
Inmovilizaciones materiales en curso	250.007	325.061	249.356	329.974
Anticipos de inmovilizaciones materiales	16.589	30.804	14.977	30.352
Materiales de instalación	16.605	24.013	16.605	24.013
Amortizaciones	(2.308.229)	(2.090.267)	(2.310.927)	(2.092.440)
IV. Inmovilizaciones Financieras (Nota 7)	106.201	106.708	201.312	146.764
Participaciones en empresas del grupo	84.055	81.919	-	-
Participaciones en empresas asociadas	11.578	11.676	151.679	82.352
Otras participaciones	17.437	16.328	28.330	58.757
Créditos a empresas del grupo	1.060	2.014	-	-
Otros créditos	795	1.200	22.057	3.560
Depósitos y fianzas entregados a largo plazo	1.077	911	1.405	4.354
Provisiones	(9.801)	(7.340)	(2.159)	(2.259)
C. FONDO DE COMERCIO DE CONSOLIDACION (Nota 7.8)	-	-	48.236	13.226
D. GASTOS A DISTRIBUIR EN VARIOS EJERCICIOS (Nota 8)	224.113	203.486	225.589	205.811
E. IMPUESTOS ANTICIPADOS A LARGO PLAZO (Nota 10)	13.616	-	14.109	-
F. ACTIVO CIRCULANTE	328.977	348.316	377.094	378.838
I. Accionistas por desembolsos exigidos	-	-	22	-
II. Existencias	3.832	5.019	16.505	18.552
Existencias	3.832	5.019	17.074	19.576
Anticipos	-	-	400	193
Provisiones	-	-	(969)	(1.217)
III. Deudores	317.323	329.144	332.841	337.400
Clientes (Nota 11)	288.378	273.452	308.964	293.739
Empresas del grupo, deudores	11.165	7.127	-	-
Empresas asociadas, deudores	751	131	4.359	778
Deudores varios	38.001	45.080	43.970	42.080
Personal	9.498	9.041	10.047	9.492
Administraciones públicas (Nota 18)	6.726	20.876	8.703	22.666
Provisiones para insolvencias (Nota 11)	(30.429)	(20.356)	(36.288)	(25.044)
Provisiones deudores varios	(6.767)	(6.207)	(6.914)	(6.311)
IV. Inversiones Financieras Temporales	1.201	6.449	11.804	7.115
Créditos a empresas del grupo y asociadas	1.080	-	-	242
Cartera de valores a corto plazo	121	-	11.167	2.768
Otros créditos	-	6.449	637	4.105
V. Tesorería	5.031	3.789	7.996	5.909
VI. Ajustes por periodificación	1.590	3.915	7.926	9.862
TOTAL GENERAL (A+B+C+D+E+F)	**3.910.094**	**3.917.167**	**4.101.883**	**4.007.152**

Telefónica de España, S.A. and Telefónica Consolidated Group.

In million pesetas	Parent Company		Consolidated group	
ASSETS	1993	1992	1993	1992
A. Subscribed shares not paid-in (unrequested payments)	-	-	-	I
B. Long term assets	3 343 388	3 365 365	3 436 855	3 409 276
I. Cost of new equity capital	162	359	226	503
II Intangible assets (Note 5)	55 520	41 609	63 207	50 778
Research and development expenses	50 454	36 500	48 812	36 415
Finance leasing	-	-	3 505	4 759
Other intangible assets	30 670	19 345	38 863	25 678
Accumulated amortization	(25 604)	(14 236)	(27 973)	(16 074)
III. Fixed assets (Note 6)	3 181 505	3 216 689	3 172 110	3 211 231
Land and buildings	438 189	403 197	441 443	406 830
Technical installations and machinery	116 795	111 478	129 800	122 393
Telephone installations	4 538 490	4 308 549	4 502 870	4 275 703
Furniture, equipment and other	113 059	103 854	127 986	114 406
Construction in progress	250 007	325 061	249 356	329 974
Advance payments for fixed assets	16 589	30 804	14 977	30 352
Installation equipment	16 605	24 013	16 605	24 013
Accumulated depreciation	(2 308 229)	(2 090 267)	(2 310 927)	(2 092 440)
IV. Investments (Note 7)	106 201	106 708	201 312	146 764
Investments in group companies	84 055	81 919	-	-
Investments in associated companies	11 578	11 676	151 679	82 352
Other investments	17 437	16 328	28 330	58 757
Credits to group companies	1 060	2 014	-	-
Other credits	795	1 200	22 057	3 560
Long-term deposits and financial guarantees	1 077	911	1 405	4 354
Depreciation Reserve	(9 801)	(7 340)	(2 159)	(2 259)
C. Goodwill on consolidation (Note 7.8)	-	-	48 236	13 226
D. Deferred expenses (Note 8)	224 113	203 486	225 589	205 811
E. Long term prepaid taxes (Note 10)	13 616	-	14 109	-
F. Current assets	328 977	348 316	377 094	378 838
I. Subscribed shares not paid-in	-	-	22	-
II Inventories	3 832	5 019	16 505	18 552
Inventories	3 832	5 019	17 074	19 576
Advances	-	-	400	193
Provisions	-	-	(969)	(1 217)
III. Accounts receivable	317 323	329 144	332 841	337 400
Subscribers and customers (Note 11)	288 378	273 452	308 964	293 739
Group companies	11 165	7 127	-	-
Associated companies	751	131	4 359	778
Sundry accounts receivable	38 001	45 080	43 970	42 080
Personnel	9 498	9 041	10 047	9 492
Taxes receivable (Note 18)	6 726	20 876	8 703	22 666
Reserve for bad debts (Note 11)	(30 429)	(20 356)	(36 288)	(25 044)
Reserve for sundry accounts receivable	(6 767)	(6 207)	(6 914)	(6 311)
IV. Short term investments	1 201	6 449	11 804	7 115
Credits to group companies	1 080	-	-	242
Short-term securities portfolio	121	-	11 167	2 768
Other credits	-	6 449	637	4 105
V. Cash and banks	5 031	3 789	7 996	5 909
VI. Prepayments	1 590	3 915	7 926	9 862
Total Assets (A+B+C+D+E+F)	3 910 094	3 917 167	4 101 883	4 007 152

Balances de Situación al 31 de diciembre

PASIVO	Telefónica (Compañía Matriz) 1993	1992	Grupo Consolidado 1993	1992
A. Fondos propios (Nota 12)	1.397.712	1.376.751	1.437.055	1.392.005
I. Capital suscrito	469.735	463.480	469.735	463.480
II. Prima de emisión	43.067	33.467	43.067	33.467
III. Reserva de revalorización	653.780	653.780	649.316	649.316
IV. Reservas	169.394	142.004	201.671	164.860
Reserva legal	57.796	49.406	57.796	49.406
Otras reservas	111.598	92.598	92.125	84.306
Reservas de consolidación (Nota 7.9)	-	-	20.653	14.112
Diferencias de conversión de consolidación	-	-	31.097	17.036
V. Resultados de ejercicios anteriores	86	121	86	121
VI. Pérdidas y ganancias del grupo	84.837	83.899	96.367	80.761
Pérdidas y ganancias	84.837	83.899	81.771	73.831
Pérdidas y ganancias de empresas asociadas	-	-	20.177	9.391
Pérdidas y ganancias atribuibles a los socios externos	-	-	(5.581)	(2.461)
VII. Dividendo a cuenta entregado en el ejercicio	(23.187)	-	(23.187)	-
B. Socios externos (Nota 12.2)	-	-	41.798	31.044
C. Ingresos a distribuir en varios ejercicios (Nota 13)	54.765	58.723	55.326	58.732
Subvenciones de capital	49.860	46.983	49.860	46.983
Diferencias positivas en cambio (Nota 9)	-	8.861	44	8.870
Otros ingresos a distribuir	4.905	2.879	5.422	2.879
D. Provisiones para riesgos y gastos (Nota 14)	216.094	211.813	231.775	215.796
E. Impuestos diferidos a largo plazo (Nota 10)	53.003	52.904	57.131	56.016
F. Acreedores a largo plazo	1.529.151	1.593.504	1.569.568	1.610.878
I. Emisiones (Nota 15)	685.614	696.811	708.440	722.284
Obligaciones y bonos no convertibles	679.494	658.999	681.345	660.823
Obligaciones y bonos convertibles	-	28.063	9.300	37.363
Otras deudas en valores negociables	6.120	9.749	17.795	24.098
II. Deudas con entidades de crédito (Nota 16)	540.494	602.800	681.881	690.728
III. Deudas con empresas del grupo y asociadas (Nota 17)	122.403	103.586	-	18.565
IV. Otros acreedores	180.040	178.656	179.161	178.975
Otras deudas	132.497	147.677	131.618	147.996
Deudas representadas por efectos a pagar	47.543	30.979	47.543	30.979
V. Desembolsos pendientes sobre acciones no exigidos (Nota 7)	600	11.651	86	326
De empresas del grupo	600	11.351	-	-
De empresas asociadas	-	300	-	300
De otras empresas	-	-	86	26
G. Acreedores a corto plazo	659.369	623.472	709.230	642.681
I. Emisiones (Nota 15)	167.267	130.225	167.271	122.991
Obligaciones	118.671	17.362	118.666	17.546
Otras deudas en valores negociables	32.631	96.759	32.631	89.327
Intereses de obligaciones y otros valores	15.965	16.104	15.974	16.118
II. Deudas con entidades de crédito (Nota 16)	59.197	127.751	87.815	153.818
Préstamos y otras deudas	47.426	115.574	74.717	140.694
Deuda por intereses	11.771	12.177	13.098	13.124
III. Deudas con empresas del grupo y asociadas (Nota 17)	41.459	68.265	19.358	25.626
Deudas con empresas del grupo	24.326	44.132	-	-
Deudas con empresas asociadas	17.133	24.133	19.358	25.626
IV. Acreedores comerciales	179.470	134.416	211.046	165.676
Anticipos recibidos por pedidos	-	-	6.016	5.001
Deudas por compras o prestación de servicios	118.059	93.717	140.403	117.670
Deudas representadas por efectos a pagar	61.411	40.699	64.627	43.005
V. Otras deudas no comerciales	195.149	142.118	205.592	152.851
Administraciones públicas (Nota 18)	71.516	41.237	75.372	45.297
Otras deudas no comerciales (Nota 19)	123.633	100.881	130.220	107.554
VI. Ajustes por periodificación	16.827	20.697	18.148	21.719
Total General (A+B+C+D+E+F+G)	**3.910.094**	**3.917.167**	**4.101.883**	**4.007.152**

Balance sheets at December 31

LIABILITIES AND SHAREHOLDERS' EQUITY	Parent Company		Consolidated group	
	1993	1992	1993	1992
A. SHAREHOLDERS' EQUITY (Note 12)	1 397 712	1 376 751	1 437 055	1 392 005
I. Share premium	469 735	463 480	469 735	463 480
II Share premium	43 067	33 467	43 067	33 467
III. Revaluation reserve	653 780	653 780	649 316	649 316
IV. Reserves	169 394	142 004	201 671	164 860
Legal reserve	57 796	49 406	57 796	49 406
Other reserves	111 598	92 598	92 125	84 306
Consolidation reserve	-	-	20 653	14 112
Differences on foreign currency translation for consolidation	-	-	31 097	17 036
V. Unappropriated profit	86	121	86	121
VI. Group profit and loss	84 837	83 899	96 367	80 761
Profit for year	84 837	83 899	81 771	73 831
Profit from associated companies			20 177	9 391
Profit attributed to outside shareholders	-	-	(5 581)	(2 461)
VII. Interim dividend	(23 187)	-	(23 187)	-
B. OUTSIDE SHAREHOLDERS' INTERESTS (Note 12.2)	-	-	41 798	31 044
C. DEFERRED INCOME (Note 13)	54 765	58 723	55 326	58 732
Capital grants	49 860	46 983	49 860	46 983
Deferred unrealized exchange gains (Note 9)	-	8 861	44	8 870
External contributions not repayable	4 905	2 879	5 422	2 879
D. PROVISIONS FOR RISKS AND EXPENSES (Note 14)	216 094	211 813	231 775	215 796
E. LONG TERM DEFERRED TAXES (Note 10)	53 003	52 904	57 131	56 016
F. LONG TERM CREDITORS	1 529 151	1 593 504	1 569 568	1 610 878
I. Debentures, bonds and other issues (Note 15)	685 614	696 811	708 440	722 284
Debentures and non-convertible bonds	679 494	658 999	681 345	660 823
Debentures and convertible bonds	-	28 063	9 300	37 363
Other negotiable documents issued	6 120	9 749	17 795	24 098
II Debts with financial institutions (Note 16)	540 494	602 800	681 881	690 728
III. Debts with group and associated companies (Note 17)	122 403	103 586	-	18 565
IV. Other accounts payable	180 040	178 656	179 161	178 975
Other debts	132 497	147 677	131 618	147 996
Notes payable	47 543	30 979	47 543	30 979
V. Uncalled subscriptions on shares (Note 7)	600	11 651	86	326
Group companies	600	11 351	-	-
Associated companies	-	300	-	300
Other companies	-	-	86	26
G. SHORT TERM CREDITORS	659 369	623 472	709 230	642 681
I. Debentures, bonds and other issues (Note 15)	167 267	130 225	167 271	122 991
Debentures	118 671	17 362	118 666	17 546
Other negotiable documents issued	32 631	96 759	32 631	89 327
Interest on debentures and other negotiable documents	15 965	16 104	15 974	16 118
II Debts with financial institutions (Note 16)	59 197	127 751	87 815	153 818
Loans and other debts	47 426	115 574	74 717	140 694
Interest due	11 771	12 177	13 098	13 124
III. Debts with group and associated companies (Note 17)	41 459	68 265	19 358	25 626
Group companies	24 326	44 132	-	-
Associated companies	17 133	24 133	19 358	25 626
IV. Trade creditors	179 470	134 416	211 046	165 676
Advance payments received on orders	-	-	6 016	5 001
Debts for purchases and services rendered	118 059	93 717	140 403	117 670
Notes payable	61 411	40 699	64 627	43 005
V. Other non-trade debts	195 149	142 118	205 592	152 851
Taxes payable (Note 18)	71 516	41 237	75 372	45 297
Other (Note 19)	123 633	100 881	130 220	107 554
VI. Accruals	16 827	20 697	18 148	21 719
TOTAL LIABILITIES AND SHAREHOLDERS' EQUITY (A+B+C+D+E+F+G)	**3 910 094**	**3 917 167**	**4 101 883**	**4 007 152**

67

Telefónica de España, S.A. y Grupo Telefónica.   **Cuenta**

En millones de pesetas	Telefónica (Compañía Matriz)		Grupo Consolidado	
DEBE	**1993**	**1992**	**1993**	**1992**
GASTOS				
Reducción de existencias	-	-	2.268	1.908
Aprovisionamientos	-	-	63.067	58.395
Compras	-	-	33.210	31.227
Trabajos realizados por otras empresas	-	-	29.857	27.168
Gastos de personal (Nota 23.2)	408.103	392.736	448.402	429.626
Dotaciones para amortizaciones de inmovilizado	372.401	341.903	374.259	343.179
Material	360.674	334.833	361.506	335.183
Inmaterial	11.368	6.210	12.260	6.820
Gastos amortizables	359	860	493	1.176
Variación de las provisiones de tráfico	24.115	16.769	25.816	18.787
Variación de créditos incobrables	22.077	15.855	22.432	16.353
Variación de otras provisiones de tráfico	2.038	914	3.384	2.434
Otros gastos de explotación	149.560	156.665	159.050	141.186
Servicios exteriores de empresas del grupo	21.755	33.646	-	-
Servicios exteriores	93.427	87.507	106.164	104.444
Tributos	23.871	22.260	23.981	22.976
Otros gastos de gestión corriente	10.507	13.252	28.905	13.766
I.BENEFICIOS DE EXPLOTACION	365.279	338.889	369.726	346.965
Gastos financieros por deudas con empresas del grupo	8.816	9.598	-	-
Gastos financieros por deudas con empresas asociadas	-	-	38	12
Otros gastos financieros por deudas	194.308	189.963	208.694	202.286
Amortización de gastos de formalización de deudas	4.952	5.462	4.954	5.810
Variación de las provisiones de inversiones financieras	-	-	25	2
Diferencias negativas de cambio (Nota 9)	27.243	12.411	28.631	12.802
II.RESULTADOS FINANCIEROS POSITIVOS	-	-	-	-
Participación en pérdidas de empresas puestas en equivalencia	-	-	3.467	2.924
Amortización del fondo de comercio de consolidación	-	-	4.798	808
III.BENEFICIOS DE LAS ACTIVIDADES ORDINARIAS	140.151	144.529	153.294	139.317
Variación de las provisiones de inmovilizado	4.436	11.306	1.974	9.874
Pérdidas procedentes del inmovilizado	19.956	29.589	20.062	30.661
Pérdidas por enajenación de sociedades consolidadas	-	-	205	107
Gastos y pérdidas extraordinarias (Nota 23.3)	16.683	12.058	19.164	12.559
IV.RESULTADOS EXTRAORDINARIOS POSITIVOS	-	-	-	-
Resultado atribuido a los socios externos (beneficios)	-	-	5.620	2.554
V.RESULTADO ANTES DE IMPUESTOS	107.468	99.724	121.212	94.459
Impuesto sobre beneficios (Nota 22)	22.631	15.825	24.845	13.698
VI.RESULTADO DEL EJERCICIO (BENEFICIOS)	**84.837**	**83.899**	**96.367**	**80.761**

de Pérdidas y Ganancias para los Ejercicios terminados el 31 de diciembre

HABER	Telefónica (Compañía Matriz)		Grupo Consolidado	
	1993	1992	1993	1992
INGRESOS				
Ventas netas a empresas del grupo (Nota 23.1)	17.256	8.638	-	-
Ventas netas y prestaciones de servicios (Nota 23.1)	1.202.828	1.146.058	1.297.437	1.208.938
Aumento de existencias	-	-	2.980	3.561
Trabajos de la empresa para el inmovilizado	75.742	68.920	109.103	103.929
Otros ingresos de explotación	23.632	23.346	33.068	23.618
Ingresos accesorios y otros de gestión corriente	23.479	22.852	32.620	22.738
Subvenciones	153	494	318	726
Exceso de Provisiones de riesgos y gastos	-	-	130	154
I.PÉRDIDAS DE EXPLOTACION	-	-	-	-
Ingresos de participaciones en capital	6.717	20.587	1.456	1.084
En empresas del grupo	5.270	19.331	-	-
En empresas asociadas	25	181	25	-
En otras empresas	1.422	1.075	1.431	1.084
Ingresos de otros valores y créditos	3.474	2.487	6.381	3.234
En empresas del grupo	322	438	-	-
En empresas asociadas	-	-	570	-
En otras empresas	3.152	2.049	5.811	3.234
Diferencias positivas de cambio	-	-	2.695	363
II.RESULTADOS FINANCIEROS NEGATIVOS	225.128	194.360	231.810	216.231
Participación en b° de emp. puestas en equivalencia	-	-	23.643	12.315
III.PÉRDIDAS DE LAS ACTIVIDADES ORDINARIAS	-	-	-	-
Beneficios en enajenación de inmovilizado	809	254	5.011	322
Beneficios por enajenación de particip. soc. consol.	-	-	-	35
Subvenciones de capital (Nota 13)	5.377	3.693	5.377	3.693
Ingresos extraordinarios (Nota 23.3)	2.206	4.201	4.516	6.754
IV.RESULTADOS EXTRAORDINARIOS NEGATIVOS	32.683	44.805	26.501	42.397
Resultado atribuido a los socios externos (pérdidas)	-	-	39	93
V.PÉRDIDAS ANTES DE IMPUESTOS	-	-	-	-
VI.RESULTADO DEL EJERCICIO (PÉRDIDAS)	-	-	-	-

Telefónica de España, S.A. and Telefónica Consolidated Group.

In million pesetas	Parent Company		Consolidated group	
DEBIT	1993	1992	1993	1992
EXPENSES				
Reduction in inventories	-	-	2 268	1 908
Supplies	-	-	63 067	58 395
Other purchases	-	-	33 210	31 227
Purchases from other companies	-	-	29 857	27 168
Personnel costs (Note 23.2)	408 103	392 736	448 402	429 626
Depreciation and amortization	372 401	341 903	374 259	343 179
Tangible	360 674	334 833	361 506	335 183
Intangible	11 368	6 210	12 260	6 820
Expenses	359	860	493	1 176
Trade provisions	24 115	16 769	25 816	18 787
Variation in provision for doubtful accounts receivable	22 077	15 855	22 432	16 353
Variation in other provisions	2 038	914	3 384	2 434
Other operating expenses	149 560	156 665	159 050	141 186
Subsidiary companies external services	21 755	33 646	-	-
External services	93 427	87 507	106 164	104 444
Taxes	23 871	22 260	23 981	22 976
Other operating expenses	10 507	13 252	28 905	13 766
I.OPERATING PROFIT	365 279	338 889	369 726	346 965
Financial expenses with subsidiary companies	8 816	9 598	-	-
Financial expenses with associated companies	-	-	38	12
Other financial expenses	194 308	189 963	208 694	202 286
Amortization of costs of formalizing debts	4 952	5 462	4 954	5 810
Variation in provisions for investments	-	-	25	2
Losses on exchange (Note 9)	27 243	12 411	28 631	12 802
II FINANCIAL INCOME	-	-	-	-
Participation in losses of associated companies	-	-	3 467	2 924
Amortization of goodwill on consolidation	-	-	4 798	808
III.PROFIT FROM NORMAL OPERATIONS	140 151	144 529	153 294	139 317
Variation in investments provision for investments in group companies	4 436	11 306	1 974	9 874
Losses on fixed assets	19 956	29 589	20 062	30 661
Losses on disposal of investment in consolidated companies	-	-	205	107
Extraordinary expenses (Note 23.3)	16 683	12 058	19 164	12 559
IV.EXTRAORDINARY NET PROFIT	-	-	-	-
Profit attributed to the shareholders' interests	-	-	5 620	2 554
V.PROFIT BEFORE TAX	107 468	99 724	121 212	94 459
Corporate income tax (Note 22)	22 631	15 825	24 845	13 698
VI.NET PROFIT FOR YEAR	84 837	83 899	96 367	80 761

Profit and loss accounts for years ended december 31, 1993 and 1992

CREDIT	Parent Company		Consolidated group	
	1993	1992	1993	1992
INCOME				
Net sales to group companies (Note 23.1)	17.256	8.638	-	-
Net sales and services rendered (Note 23.1)	1.202.828	1.146.058	1.297.437	1.208.938
Increase in inventories	-	-	2.980	3.561
Work carried out by Company on own fixed assets	75.742	68.920	109.103	103.929
Other operating income	23.632	23.346	33.068	23.618
Sundry trade income	23.479	22.852	32.620	22.738
Grants	153	494	318	726
Excess provision for risk and expenses	-	-	130	154
I.OPERATING LOSS	-	-	-	-
Income from shareholdings	6.717	20.587	1.456	1.084
Group companies	5.270	19.331	-	-
Associated companies	25	181	25	-
Other companies	1.422	1.075	1.431	1.084
Income from other negotiable documents and credits	3.474	2.487	6.381	3.234
Group companies	322	438	-	-
Associated companies	-	-	570	-
Other companies	3.152	2.049	5.811	3.234
Gains on exchange	-	-	2.695	363
II.FINANCIAL LOSS	225.128	194.360	231.810	216.231
Participation in profit of companies consolidated by the equity method	-	-	23.643	12.315
III.LOSS ON NORMAL OPERATIONS	-	-	-	-
Profit on sales of fixed assets	809	254	5.011	322
Profit on sales of shareholdings in consolidated companies	-	-	-	35
Capital grants (Note 13)	5.377	3.693	5.377	3.693
Extraordinary income (Note 23.3)	2.206	4.201	4.516	6.754
IV.EXTRAORDINARY LOSS	32.683	44.805	26.501	42.397
Profit attributed to the shareholders' interests	-	-	39	93
V.LOSS BEFORE TAX	-	-	-	-
VI.NET LOSS FOR YEAR	-	-	-	-

CUADRO DE FINANCIACION CONSOLIDADO EJERCICIO 1993 Y 1992

APLICACIONES	1993	1992	ORIGENES	1993	1992
1. Recursos aplicados en las operaciones	-	-	1. Recursos procedentes de las operaciones	602.317	597.806
2. Gastos de establecimiento y Form. de deudas	1.854	5.810	2. Aportaciones de los accionistas:		
			a) Ampliaciones de capital	6.255	1
3. Adquisición de inmovilizado:			b) Primas de emisión de acciones	9.600	-
a) Inmovilizaciones inmateriales	24.896	19.774	c) Participaciones de socios minoritarios	584	-
b) Inmovilizaciones materiales	374.920	435.556			
c) Inmovilizaciones financieras	64.640	10.663	3. Ingresos diferidos	11.805	17.669
d) Anticipos a proveedores	(13.680)	17.077			
e) Materiales de instalación	(5.502)	(13.128)	4. Impuestos diferidos a largo plazo	161	-
			5. Deudas a largo plazo	145.881	343.629
4. Impuestos anticipados largo plazo.	2..866	-	6. Enajenación de inmovilizado:		
			a) Inmovilizaciones inmateriales	-	2
5. Dividendos	79.827	31.517	b) Inmovilizaciones materiales	12.465	8.671
			c) Inmovilizaciones financieras	15.829	4.780
6. Recursos aplic. por adquis. de participaciones	490	12.872			
			7. Provisiones y gastos a distribuir.	1.716	-
7. Cancelación o traspasos deudas a L.P.	326.665	224.824			
			8. Aumento del circulante por enajenación de		
8. Provisiones	22.664	135.225	participaciones	-	328
9. Impuestos diferidos	586	343			
10. Disminución del circulante por enajenación			9. Aumento del circulante por Incorporación de		
de participaciones	204	-	filiales	10.053	1.457
11. Variación del circulante por diferencias con-					
versión	4.530	-			
Total Aplicaciones	**884.960**	**880.533**	**Total Orígenes**	**816.666**	**974.343**
Exceso de Orígenes sobre Aplicaciones			**Exceso de Aplicaciones sobre Orígenes**		
(Aumento del Capital Circulante)	**-**	**93.810**	**(Disminución del Capital Circulante)**	**68.294**	**-**
	884.960	**974.343**		**884.960**	**974.343**

VARIACIONES DEL CAPITAL CIRCULANTE CONSOLIDADO

AUMENTOS DEL CAPITAL CIRCULANTE	1993	1992	DISMINUCIONES DEL CAPITAL CIRCULANTE	1993	1992
1. Accionistas por desembolsos exigidos	22	-	1. Accionistas por desembolsos exigidos	-	40
2. Existencias	-	-	2. Existencias	2.047	1.867
3. Deudores	-	49.482	3. Deudores	4.559	-
4. Acreedores	-	43.052	4. Acreedores	70.121	-
5. Acciones propias	-	-	5. Acciones propias	-	-
6. Inversiones financieras temporales	4.688	5.770	6. Inversiones financieras temporales	-	-
7. Tesorería	2.088	-	7. Tesorería	-	803
8. Ajustes por periodificación	1.635	-	8. Ajustes por periodificación	-	1.784
Total	**8.433**	**98.304**	**Total**	**76.727**	**4.494**
Variación del Capital Circulante	**68.294**	**-**	**Variación del Capital Circulante**	**-**	**93.810**
	76.727	**98.304**		**76.727**	**98.304**

Note: The parent company statement of source and application of funds has been omitted.

STATEMENT OF SOURCE AND APPLICATION OF FUNDS PER CONSOLIDATED GROUP AT DECEMBER 31

APPLICATION	1993	1992	SOURCES	1993	1992
1. Funds applicated to operations	-	-	1. Funds provided by operations	602 317	597 806
2. Establishment costs and cost of formalizing debts	1 854	5 810	2. Contributions from shareholders:		
			a) Capital increases	6 255	1
3. Acquisition of long-term assets:			b) Share premiums	9 600	-
a) Intangible assets	24 896	19 774	c) Participations of minority shareholders	584	-
b) Tangible fixed assets	374 920	435 556			
c) Long term investments	64 640	10 663	3. Deferred income	11 805	17 669
d) Advances to suppliers	(13 680)	17 077			
e) Installation materials	(5 502)	(13 128)	4. Long term deferred taxes	161	-
			5. Long term liabilities	145 881	343 629
4. Long term prepaid taxes.	2 866	-	6. Sale of long-term assets:		
			a) Intangible fixed assets	-	2
5. Dividends	79 827	31 517	b) Tangible fixed assets	12 465	8 671
			c) Long-term investments	15 829	4 780
6. Funds used on acquisition of participations	490	12 872			
			7. Provision and deferred expenses	1 716	-
7. Cancellations or transfer to short-terms					
of long-term liabilities	326 665	224 824	8. Funds used by sales of participation	-	328
8. Provision	22 664	135 225			
9. Deferred tax	586	343			
10. Decrease in working capital due to disposal			9. Increase of working capital by acquisition		
of subsidiary companies	204	-	of new subsidiaries companies	10 053	1 457
11. Variation of working capital due to					
differences in currency translation	4 530	-			
Total applications	**884 960**	**880 533**	**Total sources**	**816 666**	**974 343**
Excess of sources over applications			**Excess of applications over sources**		
(Increase in working capital)	**-**	**93 810**	**(Decrease in working capital)**	**68 294**	**-**
	884 960	**974 343**		**884 960**	**974 343**

CHANGES IN WORKING CAPITAL PER CONSOLIDATED GROUP

INCREASE IN WORKING CAPITAL	1993	1992	DECREASE IN WORKING CAPITAL	1993	1992
1. Shareholders for uncalled share capital	22	-	1. Shareholders for uncalled share capital	-	40
2. Inventories	-	-	2. Inventories	2 047	1 867
3. Accounts receivable	-	49 482	3. Accounts receivable	4 559	-
4. Accounts payable	-	43 052	4. Accounts payable	70 121	-
5. Own shares	-	-	5. Own shares	-	-
6. Short term investments	4 688	5 770	6. Short term investments	-	-
7. Cash and banks	2 088	-	7. Cash and banks	-	803
8. Prepayments and accruals	1 635	-	8. Prepayments and accruals	-	1 784
Total	**8 433**	**98 304**	**Total**	**76 727**	**4 494**
Changes in working capital	**68 294**	**-**	**Changes in working capital**	**-**	**93 810**
	76 727	**98 304**		**76 727**	**98 304**

La conciliación entre el saldo de la cuenta de pérdidas y ganancias y los recursos procedentes de las operaciones es la siguiente:

	COMPAÑIA MATRIZ		CONSOLIDADO	
	1993	1992	1993	1992
Pérdidas y ganancias (Beneficios)	84.837	83.899	96.367	80.761
Pérdidas y ganancias socios externos	-	-	5.581	2.461
Pérdidas y ganancias empresas asociadas	-	-	(20.176)	(9.391)
			81.772	73.831
MÁS:				
Dividendos sociedades puestas en equivalencia	-	-	7.849	6.267
Amortización del inmovilizado	372.401	341.903	374.259	343.179
Amortización gastos de formalización de deudas	4.952	5.462	4.954	5.810
Amortización fondo de comercio de consolidación	-	-	4.798	808
Provisión depreciación inversiones financieras	2.530	1.949	68	519
Diferencias negativas en cambio	27.122	9.066	27.157	9.086
Provisión constitución fondo de pensiones	-	12.531	-	12.731
Dotación fondo seguro colectivo	4.038	8.965	4.038	9.492
Planta desmontada no amortizada	29.250	35.101	29.250	35.355
Provisión ajuste inventario	1.906	9.357	1.906	9.357
Provisión para responsabilidades	3.113	-	3.113	-
Intereses diferidos	69.600	58.406	70.072	58.964
Impuestos diferidos y otros	-	31.321	-	27.836
Amortización gastos COOB 92 y EXPO 92	1.784	5.738	1.784	5.738
Inmovilizado material e inmaterial	-	-	208	188
Dotación financiera y complemento pasivos	18.381	9.040	18.381	9.040
Dotación otras provisiones	-	-	2.370	-
Provisión déficit activos	4.128	-	4.128	-
Pérdidas enajenación sociedades consolidadas	-	-	205	-
MENOS:				
Beneficio enajenación inmovilizado financiero	564	145	4.767	162
Beneficio enajenación inmovilizado material	9.539	5.621	9.539	5.682
Subvenciones en capital	5.377	3.693	5.377	3.693
Impuestos diferidos y anticipados a largo plazo	10.226	-	10.289	-
Otros	4.026	767	4.023	858
Recursos procedentes de las operaciones	**594.310**	**602.512**	**602.317**	**597.806**

Recursos aplicados por adquisición o enajenación de participaciones:

Efectos sobre el capital circulante	Adquisiciones		Enajenaciones	
	1993	1992	1993	1992
Inversión financiera compradora y cambio criterio consolidación	(988)	-	-	-
Inmovilizaciones inmateriales	-	(3.522)	136	396
Inmovilizaciones materiales	199	(3.525)	32	677
Inmovilizaciones financieras	1	-	32	46
Fondo de comercio	426	(7.595)	-	46
Socios externos	(61)	-	(197)	-
Diferencias de cambio	-	2.371	-	-
Provisiones	(9.472)	-	-	-
Pasivos a largo plazo	(158)	12.872	(2)	(309)
Pérdidas enajenación participaciones	-	-	(205)	-
Capital circulante	**(10.053)**	**601**	**(204)**	**856**
Precio de adquisición o enajenación de las participaciones	**490**	**12.872**	**1**	**328**

The reconciliation net profit to funds provided by operations:

	PARENT COMPANY		CONSOLIDATED	
	1993	1992	1993	1992
Net profit for the year	84 837	83 899	96 367	80 761
Net profit attributed to the shareholders' interests	-	-	5 581	2 461
Net profit attributed to the associated companies	-	-	(20 176)	(9 391)
			81 772	73 831
ADDITIONS:				
Dividends from associated companies	-	-	7 849	6 267
Depreciation	372 401	341 903	374 259	343 179
Amortization	4 952	5 462	4 954	5 810
Amortization of Consolidation Goodwill	-	-	4 798	808
Reserve for deterioration in value of long term investments	2 530	1 949	68	519
Exchange losses	27 122	9 066	27 157	9 086
Provision for pension fund	-	12 531	-	12 731
Charge on collective endowment insurance	4 038	8 965	4 038	9 492
Dismantled plant non amortized	29 250	35 101	29 250	35 355
Provision adjustment inventories	1 906	9 357	1 906	9 357
	3 113	-	3 113	-
Deferred interest	69 600	58 406	70 072	58 964
Deferred taxes and other	-	31 321	-	27 836
Amortization of COOB92 and Expo 92	1 784	5 738	1 784	5 738
Lost on sale of intangible fised assets	-	-	208	188
Financial provision and liabilities compliments	18 381	9 040	18 381	9 040
Charge on other provisions	-	-	2 370	-
Provision for deficit of current employees	4 128	-	4 128	-
Losses on disposal of consolidated companies	-	-	205	-
REDUCTIONS:				
Profit on sale of long term investment	564	145	4 767	162
Profit on sale of fixed assets	9 539	5 621	9 539	5 682
Capital grants	5 377	3 693	5 377	3 693
Deferred and prepaid taxes	10 226	-	10 289	-
Outside contributions refundable and other	4 026	767	4 023	858
Funds provided by operations	**594 310**	**602 512**	**602 317**	**597 806**

Sources applied for purchases or sales of participations:

Effects on working capital	Purchases		Sales	
	1993	1992	1993	1992
Purchaser financial investment and consolidated change criteria	(988)	-	-	-
Intangible assets	-	(3 522)	136	396
Tangible assets	199	(3 525)	32	677
Investments	1	-	32	46
Goodwill	426	(7 595)	-	46
Minority interest	(61)	-	(197)	-
Exchange differences	-	2 371	-	-
Provisions	(9 472)	-	-	-
Long term Liabilities	(158)	12 872	(2)	(309)
Losses on sales of consolidated companies	-	-	(205)	-
Working capital	**(10 053)**	**601**	**(204)**	**856**
Purchase or sale price of participations	**490**	**12 872**	**1**	**328**

Edificio Price Waterhouse
Paseo de la Castellana, 43
28046 Madrid

Juan Bravo, 3 b
28006-Madrid

Price Waterhouse

  AUDIBERIA

Informe de auditoría de cuentas anuales

A los Accionistas de Telefónica de España, S.A.

1. Hemos auditado las cuentas anuales de Telefónica de España, S.A., y las cuentas anuales consolidadas de Telefónica de España, S.A. y sus filiales al 31 de diciembre de 1993 y 1992, que comprenden los balances de situación, las cuentas de pérdidas y ganancias y las memorias correspondientes a los ejercicios anuales terminados en dichas fechas, cuya formulación es responsabilidad de los administradores de la sociedad. Nuestra responsabilidad es expresar una opinión sobre las citadas cuentas anuales en su conjunto, basada en el trabajo realizado de acuerdo con las normas de auditoría generalmente aceptadas, que requieren el examen, mediante la realización de pruebas selectivas, de la evidencia justificativa de las cuentas anuales y la evaluación de su presentación, de los principios contables aplicados y las estimaciones realizadas. Nuestro trabajo sobre las cuentas anuales consolidadas de Telefónica de España, S.A. y sus filiales, en lo relativo a la participación de las sociedades del grupo mencionadas en la Nota 1.2., se basa en los informes de sus auditores.

2. Como se indica en la Nota 1 de la Memoria, Telefónica se encuadra dentro del grupo de empresas de tarifas reguladas, cuyas peculiaridades permiten que la imputación de ingresos y gastos responda no solamente a la aplicación del criterio del devengo sino también a la consideración del momento en que un determinado concepto de ingreso y/o gasto es computado como parte de la estructura tarifaria. Sobre esta base, la recuperabilidad de los importes invertidos o diferidos en los activos de la compañía, en especial, las diferencias de cambio dependerán de la adecuada consideración futura, en las tarifas, de estas partidas.

3. En nuestra opinión, basada en nuestra auditoría y en los informes de otros auditores, las cuentas anuales adjuntas expresan, en todos los aspectos significativos, la imagen fiel del patrimonio y de la situación financiera de Telefónica de España, S.A. y de su grupo consolidado al 31 de diciembre de 1993 y 1992 y de los resultados de sus operaciones y de los recursos obtenidos y aplicados durante los ejercicios anuales terminados en dichas fechas y contienen la información necesaria y suficiente para su interpretación y comprensión adecuada, de conformidad con principios y normas contables generalmente aceptados que guardan uniformidad con los aplicados en el ejercicio anterior.

4. El informe de gestión adjunto del ejercicio 1993, contiene las explicaciones que los administradores consideran oportunas sobre la situación de la sociedad, la evolución de sus negocios y sobre otros asuntos y no forma parte integrante de las cuentas anuales. Hemos verificado que la información contable que contiene el citado informe de gestión, concuerda con la de las cuentas anuales del ejercicio 1993. Nuestro trabajo como auditores se limita a la verificación del informe de gestión con el alcance mencionado en este mismo párrafo, y no incluye la revisión de información distinta de la obtenida a partir de los registros contables de la Sociedad.

Price Waterhouse Auditores, S.A.

Inscrita en el ROAC con número S0242

Augusto San Segundo Ontín
Socio-Auditor de Cuentas

25 de marzo de 1994

Audiberia
Osorio, Navarro y Cía, S.R.C.
Inscrita en el ROAC con número S0677

Alfonso Osorio Iturmendi
Socio-Auditor de Cuentas

Edificio Price Waterhouse
Paseo de la Castellana, 43
28046 Madrid

Juan Bravo, 3 b
28006-Madrid

 *Price Waterhouse*

 AUDIBERIA

Free translation from the original in Spanish

Independent auditor's report on the annual accounts

To the Shareholders of Telefónica de España, S.A.

1. We have audited the annual accounts of Telefónica de España, S.A. and the consolidated annual accounts of Telefónica de España, S.A. and its subsidiaries at December 31, 1993 and 1992 consisting of the balance sheets, the profit and loss accounts and the notes for the years then ended, whose preparation is the responsibility of the company's management. Our responsibility is to express an opinion on the aforementioned annual accounts as a whole, based on our audit work carried out in accordance with generally accepted auditing standards, which included selected substantive tests of the underlying records of the annual accounts, an assessment of their presentation and of the accounting principles and the estimates applied. Our work on the consolidated annual accounts of Telefónica de España, S.A. and subsidiaries, insofar as it relates to the participation in the group companies mentioned in Note 1.2, is based on the examination and report of other auditors.

2. As indicated in Note 1 to the annual accounts, Telefónica falls within the group of regulated entities whose peculiarities permit that income and expenses may be attributable to each period not only on the accrual basis but also when the related specific concepts of revenue and cost are computed as part of the approved tariffs. On this basis, the recovery of the amounts invested or included in the assets of the Company, particularly deferred exchange differences, will depend upon the adequate future consideration, in tariffs, of recovery of these concepts.

3. In our opinion, based on our examination and on the reports of other auditors, the attached annual accounts present fairly, in all material respects, the shareholders' equity and financial position of Telefónica de España, S.A. and the consolidated group at December 31, 1993 and 1992, the financial results of their operations and the consolidated resources obtained and applied for the years ended on those dates, and they contain the necessary and relevant information in order to adequately interpret and understand them, in conformity with generally accepted accounting principles consistently applied.

4. The accompanying Director's Report for 1993 contains the information that management considers relevant to the company's situation, the evolution of their business and of other matters which do not form an integral part of the annual accounts. We have verified that the accounting information contained in the aforementioned Director's Report coincides with that of the annual accounts for 1993. Our work as auditors is limited to verifying the Director's Report within the scope already mentioned in this paragraph and it does not include the review of information other than that obtained from the company's accounting records.

Price Waterhouse Auditores, S.A.

ROAC Member nº S0242

Augusto San Segundo

March 25, 1994

Audiberia
Osorio, Navarro y Cía, S.R.C.
ROAC Member nº S0677

Alfonso Osorio Iturmendi

Annual accounts of Telefonica de España, S.A. and of Telefonica consolidated group

NOTE 1 - OPERATIONS AND GENERAL INFORMATION

1.1 Parent company

a) Telefónica de España, S.A. (Telefónica or "the Company") is a commecial corporation which was incorporated in Madrid on April 19, 1924. Its main corporate purpose is to provide and operate all types of public and private telecommunication services, and to this purpose, is the State's licensee for the supply of certain public services, according to the Contract of Consession undersigned with the State's Administration on December 26, 1991.

b) Concession

In accordance with the New State Contract and the standing legislation in telecommunications, some of these services are rendered in a monopoly arrengement, while others are supplied by Telefónica in a regime of either free or restricted competition.

The New State Contract also gives Telefónica the right to maintain the overall financial balance of the contract in accordance with Article 74 and related provision of the State Contract Law.

c) Regulation of tariff

As the concessionaire of public services, and according to the afforementioned contract, Telefónica is submitted to regulated prices and to a tariff regime; the tariff regulations for services will allow the principle of universality for the supply of basic services and the overall financial balance of the concession to be safeguarded. For that purpose, within the framework of costs and effective management of the productive resources of the concessionaire company, the tariff regulations must ensure that Telefónica can cover both its operating expenses and the requirements for reserves and capital contributions, in the context of an alignment of the tariff structure to that of costs.

d) Tax regime

According to the Telefónica Taxation Law 15/1987 of July 30, 1987 and Royal Decree 1334/1988 of November 4, 1988, from January 1, 1988 Telefónica is subject to the general tax regulations for State taxes. As regards local taxes, Telefónica is required to pay local property taxes but other local and Autonomous Community taxes are substituted by an annual payment equivalent to two per cent of gross invoiced income.

By Ministerial Order dated December 27, 1989 Telefónica obtained authorization from the Spanish tax authorities to file consolidated income tax returns for the years 1990, 1991 and 1992. Such authorization is subject to compliance with certain requirements established by current legislation (Royal Decree Law 15/1977 of February 25, 1977 and Law 18/1982 of May 26, 1982).

Consolidation group changes

The new corporations which have been added to the group are Inversiones Hispano-Chilenas, B.V. (Holland); Telecartera, S.A.; Telefónica Servicios Avanzados de Información, S.A.; Telefónica Gestión de Sistemas, S.A.; Gestión y Operación de Redes, S.A.; Radiored Uno, S.A.; Radiored, S.A.; Radiored Barcelona, S.A.; Radiored Valencia, S.A.; Radiored Málaga-Costa del Sol, S.A. The group has disposed of the company Servicios Telefónicos Auditex, S.A., the associated companies Semiconductores, S.A. and Ecomyf, S.A. (previously Efecom, S.A.). Consolidates for the first time Casiopea, Re, S.A. and Telefónica Romanía (Rumania) by the full consolidation method, and Venworld Telecom, C.A. by the equity consolidation method.

NOTE 2 - BASES OF PRESENTATION OF THE ANNUAL ACCOUNTS

a) The attached annual accounts have been presented in accordance with the accounting principles stipulated by current legislation, approved by Royal Decree 1643/1990 of September 20, 1990 and by Law 19/1989 of July 25, 1989 of partial reform and adaptation of Commercial Law to European Community Standards refering to Corporations and the specifical regulation which applies, in order to present fairly, the shareholders financial position and the results of the operations and they have been prepared on the basis of the accounting records of Telefónica, and its group companies, at December 31, 1993 and 1992.

The Directors who have formulated the annual accounts estimate that the accounts of the year ended will be approved by the General Meeting of Shareholders without material changes. The comparative accounts at December 31, 1992 had been approved by the General Meeting of Shareholders on April 16, 1993.

Accounts payable are classified at the time they are contracted according to their maturity dates. Long term accounts payable are reclassified as short term when their due date is less than 12 months away. These accounts are recorded at their reimbursement value except for debentures and zero coupon bonds which are shown in the balance sheet at their issue value plus accrued interest.

b) Data comparison

Due to the fact that installation equipments are presented as fixed assets, the variation in provision for obsolescence of inventories which covers their devaluation, appears as extraordinary expenses in the paragraph "Variation in provisions for fixed assets". There has been an adaption of the amount of 1992, in which year this amount was shown in the paragraph "Variation in provisions for current assets".

c) All figures contained in the documents comprising the financial statements, balance sheet, profit and loss account and notes thereto, are expressed in millions of pesetas.

NOTE 3 - DISTRIBUTION OF PROFITS

The Directors propose to the Shareholders General Meeting the distribution of the parent company's profit, aggregating the final dividend and voluntary reserve amounts, according to the following:

BASIS OF DISTRIBUTION

Profit for year	84 837
Surplus	86
Total available for distribution	**84 923**

DISTRIBUTION

Interim dividend of 5% for each of the shares numbered 1 to 927,496,319 payable as from February 17, 1994	23 187
Complementary dividend of 7.4% for each of the shares numbered 1 to 939,470,820, pending approval	34 761
Dividend	57 948
Legal reserve	8 484
Final dividend and voluntary reserve	18 400
Surplus	91
Total proposed distribution	**84 923**

INTERIM DIVIDEND

The Board of Directors, on December 22, 1993, and in accordance with the financial information made available to them, agreed, as article 216 of the Corporations outstanding, the distribution of a 1993 interim gross dividend of 25 Ptas for each of the outstanding shares, numbered 1 to 927,496,319, from which the applicable tax will be withheld.

Budget status - Annual liquidity Budget

Anticipated cash receipts for the period 1/1/94 to 31/12/94	1 674 273
Anticipated payments for the period 1/1/94 to 31/12/94	1 606 629

Accounting to justify an interim dividend distribution (forecast at January 27, 1993).

Profit January 1, 1993 to November 30, 1993	79 999
Surplus 1992	86
Previous' years losses	-
Compulsory reserves provision	(8 000)
Distributable profit	72 085
Proposed interim dividend	23 187

Financial position (Forecast at January 27, 1993)
Funds available for distribution

Cash and banks	5 521
Short term investments	29 845
Available credits	106 621
Proposed interim dividend	(23 187)
Difference	118 800

NOTE 4 - SIGNIFICANT ACCOUNTING PRINCIPLES

4.1 Accounting principles

The most significant accounting principles applied in the preparation of the financial statements are as follows:

a) Cost of new equity capital

Costs of issuing shares for the conversion of bonds,. and expenses incurred to increase share capital are stated at cost and are amortized on a straight line basis over a period of five years from the date of each capital conversion, or increase.

b) Intangible assets and amortization

Intangible assets include costs incurred in developing new product lines that can be marketed or used in the Company's own telephone network. Costs of completed projects having a possibility of commercial or industrial use are amortized over a period of five years while costs of unsuccessful projects are deducted immediately.

This heading also includes the value of rights acquired for the use of outside equipment and installations and the cost of licences for the use of software for an indefinite period, which are amortized on a straight line basis over a period of 25 and 3 years, respectively.

c) Fixed assets and depreciation

Additions to fixed assets are valued at acquisition cost plus installation cost, which includes direct labor and materials together with allocable share of indirect costs.

The annual depreciation charge is calculated by the straight line method based on the estimated useful lives of the assets. The estimated useful lives are as follows:

TYPES OF FIXED ASSETS	YEARS OF USEFUL LIFE	
	PARENT COMPANY	CONSOLIDATED
Buildings	40	40
Technical installations and machinery	13 - 18	13 - 18
Exchange equipment	10 - 20	10 - 20
Transmission equipment	5 - 15	5 - 15
Local and domestic long distance networks	8 - 25	8 - 25
User equipment and other installations	4 - 8	4 - 8
Other installations, equipment and furniture	5 - 10	5 - 10

Maintenance and repair costs not representing extensions or improvements are expensed when incurred.,

In 1993 new technical studies of the useful lives have been made to adequate the amortization to the estimated depreciation of the fixed assets. These new studies are in line with the sector's fiscal percentages and have resulted in an increase of the depreciation charge for 1993 of 8,645 million pesetas. In these cases in which the useful life is under fiscal percentages, a special amortization plan has been obtained from the Inland Revenue.

d) Long term investments - net shareholdings in companies

Long term investments are stated at cost, including related acquisition expenses and, where applicable, the cost of the subscription rights. Capital losses compared with book value are charged against results; these losses are calculated on the basis of the respective underlying net equity values of the investments as shown by the financial statements of each company. Dividends are accounted for as income when received, and capital gains on the sale of shares are accounted for as income in the year in which they are realized.

e) Deferred expenses

Deferred expenses comprise:

a) Costs of formalizing debts: valued at their realizable value and are amortized on the same basis as their respective principal amounts.

b) Interest on notes payable: reflects the difference between the issue price and repayment value of notes with maturity exceeding one year. The interest is charged to results by the accrual method.

c) Differences on foreign exchange: (see Note 4.j).

d) Annex 91 suppliers: expenses of supply contracts, with deferred payment terms of three years, entered into with the principal Telefónica suppliers. These expenses are amortized over the same period.

e) Complements for retired personnel (deficit): reflects the difference between the present value of complementary annuities to Telefónica's retired personnel calculated on an 8% annual interest, and the provision applied for this purpose. They are amortized by the straight line method over a period of 15 years (Note 19).

f) Deferred expenses for the amortization of the deficit of current employees at 1992: according to the rebalancing plan at December 31, 1992, the difference between the contribution amount for the pension plan and the amount debited in the profit and loss account to amortize the deficit for current employees of 1992 in 28 years was included in this paragraph. With the actual rebalancing plan, this provision is considered unnecessary, having cancelled the total amount of this provision of December 1992 (See note 20).

f) Inventories:

Inventories and stocks are valued at their weighted average cost. Provisions for obsolescence are stated according to the age and rotation of inventories, in order to record its real depreciation.

g) Capital grants

Capital grants are stated at their nominal amounts and are charged to income on a straight-line basis over a maximum period of 10 years, which does not differ significantly from the useful lives of the assets linked to these grants. Sources for the grants are:

• Official Agencies, Autonomous Communities, Local and Regional Administrations, for the extension of the telephone services to rural areas.

• The European Economic Community, for the promotion and development of telecommunication activities among companies in the sector.

• In all cases, Telefónica Group companies fulfill all the requirements to receive the grants.

h) Retirement pensions and collective endowment insurance

The retirement pensions of Telefónica's personnel are cared for by the Social Security.

In accordance with the statutory collective agreement, retired personnel at June 30, 1992, receive a non revaluable pension complement chargeable to Telefónica as detailed in note 20.

Until June 30, 1993 current personnel had the chance to enlist the Pension Plan unfolded through the offer of June the 30, 1992, ratified by the employees on September 17, 1992, contained in the statutory collective agreement with the workers representatives. The description of the commitments assumed and the accounting principles applied are explained in note 20.

According to the terms of the agreement, personnel who have not joined the Pension Plan at June 30, 1993 can remain on the Collective Endowment Insurance. For this consideration, charges are made based on a percentage of the regulatory salary indexes, calculated in accordance actuarial studies (Note 21).

i) Corporate income tax

Corporate income tax is charged against the corresponding year. The timing differences between the amount to be paid and the total charged on the profit and loss account are considered prepaid or deferred taxes according to their nature.

j) Valuation of foreign currency accounts

In accordance with the Third Transitory Disposition of Royal Decree 1643/90 of December 20, unrealized foreign exchange losses as of December 31, 1989, have been amortized over a period of three years (1990 to 1992) limited to the maturity date of each transaction.

As a result of the coming into effect of the Order of the Ministry of Economy an Resources dated March 12th 1993 concerning the accounting treatment of currency exchange differences for regulated companies (BOE number 64; March 16th 1993) there has been a change in the treatment of exchange differences losses have been lineally distributed, for each loan, according to the period of maturity. The fiscal year's profit and loss account reflects exclusively for each transaction the unrealized losses, accumulated lineally from their origin to year end. The remainder of the negative differences corresponding to future years, will be included as "deferred expenses" and lineally distributed to maturity.

Positive differences are deferred, until their realization, under the heading "Deferred income".

The tax treatment for exchange differences is the same as last year's, and are included as taxable income when materialized.

k) Income and expenses

Income and expenses are accounted for on an accrual basis, at the time the corresponding goods and services are purchased or rendered regardless of the time when they are paid for.

However, according to the prudence concept, only profits realized at year end have been accounted for, while foreseeable risks and losses, even if remote, are recorded when they become known.

4.2 Principles of consolidation

a) The Telefónica Group consolidates, by the full consolidation method, the financial statements of its subsidiary companies, companies in which it owns or controls a majority of the votes and in which it has the capacity to nominate the majority of the board members. The multi-group companies, in which Telefónica owns 50% of its share capital and voting rights, are consolidated by the proportional integration method.

The consolidated subsidiary companies, together with their trade names, registered addresses, percentage ownership and operations, are listed in Notes 1.2 and 7.

b) Transactions between companies in the Group and intercompany balances at year end are eliminated on consolidation, as well as sales and profit included in invoices to Telefónica for telephone installations from subsidiary and associated companies, recognizing those results as the installations are being amortized.

c) As regards the annual accounts of associated companies (that is, those companies outside the Telefónica Group on which Telefónica has a financial investment and an ability to influence its management to a large extent) investments and results for each company are accounted for by the equity method, making adjustements on the basis of the underlying equity as calculated from the balance sheets and profit and loss accounts at each year end.

Associated companies, together with their trade names, registered addresses, percentage ownership and operations, are listed in Notes 1.3 and 7.

d) Stock ownership in other companies (minority-interest companies) is tracted as investment and accounted for at cost.

Ownership in minority-interest companies is set forth in Notes 1.3 and 7.

e) The amount paid for the acquisition of companies in excess of their book value at the purchase date is accounted for as consolidation goodwill, which is amortized over a period of five or ten years depending on the period of recovery of each of the investments.

f) For companies located in countries with high rates of inflation, local currency financial statements are translated to US dollars by applying the year-end rate of exchange to the financial statements adjusted for inflation at December 31, 1993.

g) The financial statements of other companies located abroad have been translated to pesetas by translating the assets and liabilities at the year-end rates of exchange, capital and reserves at historical rates and income and expenses at the average rates for the year. The difference between applying the foregoing bases of translation and applying the year-end exchange rate is presented under the heading, "Differences on foreign currency translation for consolidation".

h) The consolidated annual accounts do not include the fiscal effect of the incorporation of the foreign subsidiaries reserves to the parent company consolidated financial statements, due to the fact that reserves have not been transferred and will not be distributed at the end of the period, and will be used as a financing source of the foreign subsidiaries to reduce their endowment.

i) The financial statements of individual companies have been prepared homogeneously following the accounting principles listed in Note 4.1.

NOTE 5 - INTANGIBLE ASSETS

The movement during the year is as follows:

	PARENT COMPANY				CONSOLIDATED				
	Research and development expenses	Licences for indef. use of software	Other intangible assets	Total	Research and development expenses	Leasing	Licences for indef. use of software	Other intangible assets	Total
Balance at December 31, 1991	25 498	9 530	1 246	36 274	26 075	5 080	10 241	3 117	44 513
Additions	11 002	7 408	1 161	19 571	10 433	321	7 718	1 302	19 774
Additions of TLD	-	-	-	-	-	-	-	3 522	3 522
Reductions	-	-	-	-	-	276	-	66	342
Disposal of Ecotel	-	-	-	-	93	245	-	156	494
Transfers	-	-	-	-	-	(121)	-	-	(121)
Balance at December 31, 1992	36 500	16 938	2 407	55 845	36 415	4 759	17 959	7 719	66 852
Additions	13 954	10 645	680	25 279	12 398	41	11 920	1 167	24 896
Reductions	-	-	-	-	1	8	72	35	116
Transfers	-	-	-	-	-	(1 140)	-	-	(1 140)
Disposal of Audiotex	-	-	-	-	-	147	-	1	148
Exchange rate variation and others	-	-	-	-	-	-	-	836	836
Balances at December 31, 1993	50 454	27 583	3 087	81 124	48 812	3 505	29 177	9 686	91 180

The movement on amortization is as follows:

	PARENT COMPANY				CONSOLIDATED				
	Research and development expenses	Licences for indef. use of software	Other intangible assets	Total	Research and development expenses	Leasing	Licences for indef. use of software	Other intangible assets	Total
Balance at December 31, 1991	2 571	4 583	872	8 026	3 012	556	4 874	1 339	9 781
Additions	2 102	3 999	109	6 210	2 127	324	4 176	193	6 820
Reductions	-	-	-	-	-	56	-	96	152
Disposal of Ecotel	-	-	-	-	-	43	-	54	97
Transfers	-	-	-	-	-	(278)	-	-	(278)
Balance at December 31, 1992	4 673	8 582	981	14 236	5 139	503	9 050	1 382	16 074
Additions	5 116	6 129	123	11 368	4 867	221	6 376	796	12 260
Reductions	-	-	-	-	-	5	9	-	14
Transfers	-	-	-	-	(15)	(416)	15	-	(416)
Disposal of Audiotex	-	-	-	-	-	-	-	12	12
Exchange rate variation and others	-	-	-	-	(214)	-	-	295	81
Balances at December 31, 1993	9 789	14 711	1 104	25 604	9 777	303	15 432	2 461	27 973
Net intangible assets	40 665	12 872	1 983	55 520	39 035	3 202	13 745	7 225	63 207

NOTE 6 - TANGIBLE ASSETS

6.1 The details of fixed assets and accumulated depreciation are as follows:

PARENT COMPANY

	Balance at 12.31.91	Additions	Reductions	Balance at 12.31.92	Additions	Reductions	Balance at 12.31.93
Land and buildings	349 255	54 078	136	403 197	35 289	297	438 189
Technical installations and machinery	102 156	11 424	2 102	111 478	8 895	3 578	116 795
Exchange equipment	1 349 879	134 740	35 996	1 448 623	86 828	50 971	1 484 480
Transmission equipment	638 032	97 133	7 008	728 157	82 424	14 742	795 839
Local and domestic long distance networks	1 727 291	197 088	64 643	1 859 736	186 907	71 341	1 975 302
Subscriber equipment and other installations	253 922	35 667	17 556	272 033	42 502	31 666	282 869
Furniture, office and other equipment	88 554	15 359	59	103 854	9 667	462	113 059
Total fixed assets in service	4 509 089	545 489	127 500	4 927 078	452 512	173 057	5 206 533
Net movement on:							
Construction in progress	449 774	(122 441)	2 272	325 061	(74 661)	393	250 007
Advances to suppliers of fixed assets	13 154	17 650	-	30 804	(14 215)	-	16 589
Stock Installation equipment	44 891	(20 878)	-	24 013	(7 408)	-	16 605
Total fixed assets	5 016 908	419 820	129 772	5 306 956	356 228	173 450	5 489 734

The movement on accumulated depreciation is as follows:

PARENT COMPANY

	Balance at 12.31.91	Additions	Reductions	Balance at 12.31.92	Additions	Reductions	Balance at 12.31.93
Buildings	74 504	8 204	76	82 632	9 393	21	92 004
Technical installations and machinery	44 174	7 489	1 474	50 189	7 607	2 738	55 058
Exchange equipment	592 633	102 311	16 764	678 180	125 999	40 464	763 715
Transmission equipment	262 163	46 459	4 857	303 765	54 964	8 841	349 888
Local and domestic long distance network	672 792	117 645	51 828	738 609	116 759	60 157	795 211
Subscriber sets and other related installation	166 667	39 437	16 870	189 234	30 861	30 129	189 966
Furniture, office and other equipment	34 405	13 288	35	47 658	15 091	362	62 387
Total accumulated depreciation	1 847 338	334 833	91 904	2 090 267	360 674	142 712	2 308 229
Total net fixed assets	3 169 570	84 987	37 868	3 216 689	(4 446)	30 738	3 181 505

							CONSOLIDATED
	Balance at 12.31.91	Additions	Reductions	Balance at 12.31.92	Additions	Reductions	Balance at 12.31.93
Land and buildings	353 754	53 896	820	406 830	35 947	1 334	441 443
Technical installations and machinery	110 614	14 909	3 130	122 393	11 339	3 932	129 800
Exchange equipment	1 337 786	134 770	35 996	1 436 560	85 823	50 979	1 471 404
Transmission equipment	632 184	96 912	7 008	722 088	82 127	14 750	789 465
Local and domestic long distance networks	1 711 457	197 433	64 643	1 844 247	185 410	71 326	1 958 331
Subscriber equipment and other installations	251 647	38 717	17 556	272 808	42 612	31 750	283 670
Furniture, office and other equipment	98 400	16 937	931	114 406	15 124	1 544	127 986
Total fixed assets in service	**4 495 842**	**553 574**	**130 084**	**4 919 332**	**458 382**	**175 615**	**5 202 099**
Net movement on:							
Construction in progress	446 829	(114 361)	2 494	329 974	(80 219)	399	249 356
Advances to suppliers of fixed assets	13 275	17 198	121	30 352	(15 375)	-	14 997
Stock Installations equipment	46 498	(22 485)	-	24 013	(7 408)	-	16 605
Total fixed assets	**5 002 444**	**433 926**	**132 699**	**5 303 671**	**355 380**	**176 014**	**5 483 037**

The movement on accumulated depreciation is as follows:

							CONSOLIDATED
	Balance at 12.31.91	Additions	Reductions	Balance at 12.31.92	Additions	Reductions	Balance at 12.31.93
Buildings	75 131	8 348	83	83 396	9 614	110	92 900
Technical installations and machinery	46 109	8 178	1 780	52 507	8 645	2 885	58 267
Exchange equipment	590 724	101 243	15 557	676 410	125 002	40 464	760 948
Transmission equipment	261 142	45 981	4 098	303 025	54 564	8 841	348 748
Local and domestic long domestic distance network	670 026	116 865	52 247	734 644	115 830	60 157	790 317
Subscriber sets and other related installation	165 596	39 140	17 384	187 352	30 945	30 236	188 061
Furniture, office and other equipment	40 201	15 682	777	55 106	17 480	894	71 686
Total accumulated depreciation	**1 848 929**	**335 437**	**91 926**	**2 092 440**	**362 080**	**143 587**	**2 310 927**
Total net fixed assets	**3 153 515**	**98 489**	**40 773**	**3 211 231**	**(6 700)**	**32 421**	**3 172 110**

6.2 Fully depreciated fixed assets at December 31 are as follows:

	PARENT COMPANY		CONSOLIDATED	
	1993	1992	1993	1992
Land and buildings	-	-	-	-
Technical installations and machinery	15 771	5 304	16 698	5 304
Exchange equipment	105 558	74 200	105 558	74 200
Transmission equipment	145 098	121 161	145 098	121 161
Local and domestic long distance networks	94 600	48 234	94 600	48 234
Subscriber and other installations	97 163	86 071	97 163	86 071
Furniture, office and other equipment	15 578	9 676	19 104	11 939
Totals	**473 768**	**344 646**	**478 221**	**346 909**

6.3 The investment budget for 1994 amounts to 484,651 million pesetas (476,416 in Telefónica) of which 437,015 million pesetas (430,594 in Telefónica) will be invested in tangible assets 37,636 million pesetas (35,822 in Telefónica) in intangible assets and the remainder largely in investments in companies. The continued and long-term nature of Telefonica's investments indicates that a part of this budget is related to the completion of projects initiated in previous'years.

6.4 Telefonica's fixed assets used to provide telephone services may not be mortgaged, except when an authorization of the Government Delegate exists.

6.5 At December 31, 1993 there were assets totalling 6,985 million pesetas regulated by Decree Law 19/1961 and Law 61/1978 which regulate the tax benefits obtained from the reduction of the withholding tax rates on the interest on the loans and borrowings.

6.6 Telefónica Group companies are insured against possible risks on fixed assets used in operations, with the exception of the deductibles applicable to local and domestic long distance networks and subscriber equipment, for which self-insurance reserves have been made.

6.7 The revaluations of balances made by the parent company up to 1987 (year of last revaluation) have had the following movement for the years shown:

	FROM 1946 TO 1985		1986		1987		TOTAL		
	Fixed assets	Accum. deprec.	Fixed assets	Accum. deprec.	Fixed assets	Accum. deprec.	Fixed assets	Accum. deprec.	Revaluation reserve
Land	23 140	-	-	-	6 901	-	30 041	-	30 041
Buildings	58 061	14 545	-	-	35 221	10 489	93 282	25 034	68 248
Power equipment	24 367	11 373	2 697	1 222	4 461	2 378	31 525	14 973	16 552
Exchange equipment	408 892	180 280	38 078	15 098	57 672	20 312	504 642	215 690	288 952
Transmission equipment	131 107	84 187	11 759	6 922	8 170	3 909	151 036	95 018	56 018
Local and domestic long distance networks	535 420	287 030	56 905	20 718	56 620	24 003	648 945	331 751	317 194
Subscriber equipment and other installations	31 757	40 936	-	-	(35 910)	(13 287)	(4 153)	27 649	(31 802)
Total	**1 212 744**	**618 351**	**109 439**	**43 960**	**133 135**	**47 804**	**1 455 318**	**710 115**	**745 203**

The effect of these revaluations on the annual depreciation charge was Ptas 44,959 million (Ptas 45,671 million in 1992).

6.8 The useful lives of the various elements of Telefonica's fixed assets are calculated based on technical studies by the Company, which are revised regularly on the basis of technological development and renewal programs. These useful lives are shown in Note 4.c).

6.9 Inventories are shown net of reserve for obsolescence. The total reserve in Telefónica amounts to 6,669 million pesetas (7,844 million pesetas in 1992). The charge to the reserve in 1993 based on estimates made, was 1,906 million pesetas (9,357 million pesetas in 1992).

NOTE 7. INVESTMENTS

7.1 The composition and movements with respect to investments, together with the reserve for depreciation, were as follows:

PARENT COMPANY

a) Movement on investments:

	Balance at 12.31.91	Additions	Reductions	Transfers	Balance at 12.31.92	Additions	Reductions	Transfers	Balance at 12.31.93
Investments in Group companies	81 382	1 034	183	(314)	81 919	2 476	340	-	84 055
Investments in associated companies	14 405	2 163	-	(4 892)	11 676	383	481	-	11 578
Other investments	11 211	2 811	2 900	5 206	16 328	7 828	6 719	-	17 437
Loans to Group Companies	-	2 014	-	-	2 014	20	974	-	1 060
Loans to employees	1 642	179	621	-	1 200	112	517	-	795
Guarantees and deposits	774	261	124	-	911	464	298	-	1 077
Total	109 414	8 462	3 828	-	114 048	11 283	9 329	-	116 002

b) Movement on reserve for depreciation

	Balance at 12.31.91	Additions	Reductions	Transfers	Balance at 12.31.92	Additions	Reductions	Transfers	Balance at 12.31.93
Investments in Group companies	4 490	33	685	(27)	3 811	378	783	-	3 406
Investments in associated companies	266	2 169	102	27	2 360	2 990	191	-	5 159
Other investments	636	533	-	-	1 169	78	11	-	1 236
Total	5 392	2 735	787	-	7 340	3 446	985	-	9 801

c) Movement on payments pending on shares

	Balance at 12.31.91	Additions	Reductions	Transfers	Balance at 12.31.92	Additions	Reductions	Transfers	Balance at 12.31.93
Investments in Group companies	27 252	114	16 015	-	11 351	-	10 751	-	600
Investments in associated companies	1 490	300	1 490	-	300	-	300	-	-
Total	28 742	414	17 505	-	11 651	-	11 051	-	600
Total Investments	75 280	5 313	(14 464)	-	95 057	7 837	(2 707)	-	105 601

CONSOLIDATED

a) Movement on investments:

	Balance at 12.31.91	Additions	Reductions	Transfers	Balance at 12.31.92	Additions	Reductions	Transfers	Balance at 12.31.93
Investments in associated companies	61 516	752	54	20 138	82 352	72 242	12 133	9 218	151 679
Other investments	51 791	6 999	3 435	3 402	58 757	11 408	6 885	(34 950)	28 330
Other loans	2 315	1 388	1 047	904	3 560	19 449	940	(12)	22 057
Guarantees and deposits	4 456	327	153	(276)	4 354	527	3 475	(1)	1 405
Total	120 078	9 466	4 689	24 168	149 023	103 626	23 433	(25 745)	203 471

b) Movement on reserve for depreciation

	Balance at 12.31.91	Additions	Reductions	Transfers	Balance at 12.31.92	Additions	Reductions	Transfers	Balance at 12.31.93
Other investments	1 597	574	71	159	2 259	222	239	(83)	2 159
Total	1 597	574	71	159	2 259	222	239	(83)	2 159

c) Movement on payments pending on shares

	Balance at 12.31.91	Additions	Reductions	Balance at 12.31.92	Additions	Reductions	Balance at 12.31.93
Investments in associated companies	1 490	300	1 490	300	-	300	-
Other investments	33	-	7	26	60	-	86
Total	1 523	300	1 497	326	60	300	86

7.6 The subsidiary companies listed on the Stock Exchange are the following:

			Share price			
			Year-end		Average last quarter	
Subsidiary Companies	Currency	Stock Exchange	1993	1992	1993	1992
Amper_____	Peseta	Madrid	142	170	167	190
CTC (CHILE) _____	Peso chileno	Santiago/New York	2 550	1 315	2 156	1 228
Entel (CHILE) _____	Peso chileno	Santiago	4 910	2 120	3.463	1 989
TASA (ARGENTINA)	Peso argentino	Buenos Aires/New York y Portal	7.28	0.3133	5.66	0.2832

7.7 The provisions of Article 86 of the Corporations Law have been complied with the acquisitions of shareholdings during the year.

7.8 The composition of goodwill on consolidation is as follows at December 31:

	Balance at 12.31.91	Additions	Reductions	Transfers	Balance at 12.31.92	Additions	Balance at 12.31.93
Companies consolid. by the full consolid. method	180	7 595	72	(108)	7 595	426	8 021
Companies consolid. by the equity method	7 732	80	31	108	7 889	39 382	47 271
Total	7 912	7 675	103	-	15 484	39 808	55 292
Accumulated amortization							
Companies consolid. by the full consolid. method	36	27	25	(38)	-	907	907
Companies consolid. by the equity method	1 439	781	-	38	2 258	3 891	6 149
Total	1 475	808	25	-	2 258	4 798	7 056
Goodwill pending amortization	6 437	6 867	78	-	13 226	35 010	48 236

7.9 The consolidation reserve consists of the following at December 31:

	Balance at 12.31.91	Additions	Reductions	Balance at 12.31.92	Additions	Reductions	Balance at 12.31.93
Companies consolid. by the full consolid. method	5 881	3 766	2 934	6 713	3 548	1 162	9 099
Companies consolid. by the equity method	1 415	8 032	2 048	7 399	7 164	3 009	11 554
Total	7 296	11 798	4 982	14 112	10 712	4 171	20 653

NOTE 8. DEFERRED EXPENSES

The balances and amortization schedule are as follows:

PARENT COMPANY

					Maturities		Balance 12.31.93	Balance 12.31.92
	1994	1995	1996	1997	1998	Subsequent		
Debt formalization expenses _____	5 240	3 940	3 475	2 718	1 947	3 707	21 027	21 901
Exchange losses _____	9 628	9 438	8 743	7 786	6 273	15 311	57 179	19 473
Interest on long term notes _____	4 540	4 372	3 946	3 388	3 741	4 474	24 461	29 055
Interest on commercial notes _____	1 127	4	-	-	-	-	1 131	3 134
Financing Annex 91 contract _____	6 845	3 516	25	-	-	-	10 386	15 264
Liabilities Compliments (deficit) _____	8 143	8 143	8 143	8 143	8 143	69 214	109 929	113 756
Deferred Expenses deficit assets amortization	-	-	-	-	-	-	-	903
Total	35 523	29 413	24 332	22 035	20 104	92 706	224 113	203 486

CONSOLIDATED

					Maturities		Balance 12.31.93	Balance 12.31.92
	1994	1995	1996	1997	1998	Subsequent		
Debt formalization expenses _____	5 242	3 941	3 477	2 720	1 948	3 712	21 040	22 845
Exchange losses _____	9 628	9 438	8 743	7 786	6 273	15 311	57 179	19 473
Interest on long term notes _____	4 540	4 372	3 946	3 388	3 741	4 474	24 461	29 055
Interest on commercial notes _____	655	4	-	-	-	-	659	3 134
Interest on leasing operat. and other _____	718	469	247	119	89	293	1 935	1 381
Financing Annex 91 contract _____	6 845	3 516	25	-	-	-	10 386	15 264
Liabilities Cumpliments déficit _____	8 143	8 143	8 143	8 143	8 143	69 214	109 929	113 756
Deferred Expenses deficit assets amort.	-	-	-	-	-	-	-	903
Total	35 771	29 883	24 581	22 156	20 194	93 004	225 589	205 811

NOTE 9. DEFERRED EXCHANGE DIFFERENCES

Due to new criteria adopted in 1992 (Note 4.j) unrealized exchange losses have been deferred amounting to 57,179 million pesetas which would have resulted in an increase of expenses in the profit and loss account.

The composition of the balance and amortization schedule are as follows:

<table>
<tr><td></td><td colspan="7"></td><td colspan="2">PARENT COMPANY</td></tr>
<tr><td></td><td></td><td></td><td></td><td></td><td colspan="2">Maturities</td><td>Balance at</td><td>Balance at</td></tr>
<tr><td></td><td>1994</td><td>1995</td><td>1996</td><td>1997</td><td>1998</td><td>Subsequent</td><td>12.31.93</td><td>12.31.92</td></tr>
<tr><td>Deferred realized exchange losses</td><td>9 628</td><td>9 438</td><td>8 743</td><td>7 786</td><td>6 273</td><td>15 311</td><td>57 179</td><td>19 473</td></tr>
<tr><td>Deferred unrealized exchange gains</td><td>-</td><td>-</td><td>-</td><td>-</td><td>-</td><td>-</td><td>-</td><td>(8 861)</td></tr>
<tr><td>Total</td><td>9 628</td><td>9 438</td><td>8 743</td><td>7 786</td><td>6 273</td><td>15 311</td><td>57 179</td><td>10 612</td></tr>
<tr><td></td><td colspan="7"></td><td colspan="2">CONSOLIDATED</td></tr>
<tr><td></td><td></td><td></td><td></td><td></td><td colspan="2">Maturities</td><td>Balance at</td><td>Balance at</td></tr>
<tr><td></td><td>1994</td><td>1995</td><td>1996</td><td>1997</td><td>1998</td><td>Subsequent</td><td>12.31.93</td><td>12.31.92</td></tr>
<tr><td>Deferred realized exchange losses</td><td>9 628</td><td>9 438</td><td>8 743</td><td>7 786</td><td>6 273</td><td>15 311</td><td>57 179</td><td>19 473</td></tr>
<tr><td>Deferred unrealized exchange gains</td><td>-</td><td>-</td><td>-</td><td>-</td><td>(19)</td><td>(25)</td><td>(44)</td><td>(8 870)</td></tr>
<tr><td>Total</td><td>9 628</td><td>9 438</td><td>8 743</td><td>7 786</td><td>6 254</td><td>15 286</td><td>57 135</td><td>10 603</td></tr>
</table>

Details of the charges to expenses for the year:

	PARENT COMPANY		CONSOLIDATED	
	1993	1992	1993	1992
For Repayment of loans	6 241	5 528	7 624	5 919
Deferred losses O.M. March 12, 1993 (Note 4.j)	22 642	6 864	22 642	6 864
Services charges in foreign currency and other	(1 640)	19	(1 635)	19
Total	27 243	12 411	28 613	12 802

NOTE 10. LONG TERM PREPAID AND DEFERRED TAXES

The balance detail is as follows:

	PARENT COMPANY		CONSOLIDATED	
	1993	1992	1993	1992
Long term prepaid taxes				
Currency exchange differences	10 328	-	10 328	-
Complementary pensions for retired employees	1 342	-	1 342	-
Pension plan for current employees	1 946	-	1 946	-
Other	-	-	493	-
Total	13 616	-	14 109	-
Long term deferred taxes				
Tax regulations amortization	47 021	48 347	48 598	50 416
Collective endowment insurance	579	-	579	-
Consolidation adjustments	5 403	4 557	-	-
Intragroup adjustments	-	-	7 954	5 600
Total	53 003	52 904	57 131	56 016

NOTE 11. ACCOUNTS RECEIVABLE FROM CUSTOMER

The balance detail at December 31, is as follows:

	PARENT COMPANY		CONSOLIDATED	
	1993	1992	1993	1992
Service billed				
Customers	108 554	108 227	129 140	128 514
Former subscribers	28 255	18 807	28 255	18 807
Accounts pending classification	1 951	1 908	1 951	1 908
	138 760	128 942	159 346	149 229
Unbilled (Telefónica)	149 618	144 510	149 618	144 510
	288 378	273 452	308 964	293 739
Provision for bad debts	(30 429)	(20 356)	(36 288)	(25 044)
Total	257 949	253 096	272 676	268 695

The balance of public customers accounts amounts to 84,131 millions pesetas (83,447 millions pesetas in 1992).

During the 1993 year cancelled bad debts amounted to 11,119 million pesetas. (7,767 million pesetas in 1992).

88

NOTE 12. SHAREHOLDERS' EQUITY

12.1 The amount and movements in shareholder's equity during the years ended at December 31 1992 and 1993, were as follows:

PARENT COMPANY

	1991	Distribution of 1991 profit	Other movements ·	1992	Distribution of 1992 profit	Other movements	1993
Stated capital	463 479	-	1	463 480	-	6 255	469 735
Capital surplus	33 467	-	-	33 467	-	9 600	43 067
Revaluation and reserve	653 780	·	-	653 780	-	-	653 780
Legal reserve	41 321	8 085	-	49 406	8 390	-	57 796
Voluntary reserve	74 498	18 100	-	92 598	19 000	-	111 598
Unappropriated retained earnings	150	(29)	-	121	(35)	-	86
Profit for year	80 847	(80 847)	83 899	83 899	(83 899)	84 837	84 837
Interim dividend	(23 174)	23 174	-	-	-	(23 187)	(23 187)
Total	**1 324 368**	**(31 517)**	**83 900**	**1 376 751**	**(56 544)**	**77 505**	**1 397 712**

CONSOLIDATED

	1991	Distribution of 1991 profit	Other consolidated movements	1992	Distribution of 1992 profit	Other consolidated movements	1993
Stated capital	463 479	-	1	463 480	-	6 255	469 735
Capital surplus	33 467	·	-	33 467	-	9 600	43 067
Revaluation and reserve	649 316	-	-	649 316	-	-	649 316
Legal reserve	41 321	8 085	-	49 406	8 390	-	57 796
Voluntary reserve	52 920	18 100	13 286	84 306	8 887	(1 068)	92 125
Reserve in consolidation	7 296	23 400	(16 584)	14 112	6 975	(434)	20 653
Unappropriated retained earnings	150	(29)	-	121	(35)	-	86
Profit for year	104 247	(104 247)	80 761	80 761	(80 761)	96 367	96 367
Interim dividend	(23 174)	23 174	-	-	-	(23 187)	(23 187)
Differences on foreign currency translation for consolidation	1 251	-	15 785	17 036	-	14 061	31 097
Total	**1 330 273**	**(31 517)**	**93 249**	**1 392 005**	**(56 544)**	**101 594**	**1 437 055**

All the outstanding shares of Telefónica are fully subscribed and paid, and they are bearer shares of 500 pesetas par value each.

The shares are quoted on the four Spanish stock exchanges as well as in Frankfurt, London, Paris, Tokyo and New York. At December 31, 1993 the State held approximately 31.86% of the shares (32.28% in 1992). Under current legislation the foreign ownership in Telefónica cannot exceed in total 25% of the share capital.

The movement on share capital has been as follows:

	Number of shares	Par value	Characteristics of issue Price as a percentage of par value	Cash
At December 31, 1991	926 958 077	463 479	-	-
Capital increase January 1992	1 074	1	184.950%	1
At December 31, 1992	926 959 151	436 480	-	-
Capital increase May 1993	537 168	268	214.976%	577
Capital increase July 1993	2 148	1	250.536%	3
Capital increase September 1993	220 237	110	245.704%	270
Capital increase October 1993	675 754	338	246.200%	832
Capital increase November 1993	11 041 984	5 521	255.898%	14 218
Capital increase December 1993	34 378	17	259.204%	45
At December 31, 1993	939 470 820	469 735		

The above capital increase was made in connection with the conversion of bonds on the London stock exchange.

The General Meeting of Shareholders held on June 15, 1990 gave power to the Board of Directors to issue additional shares during a period not exceeding five years without further notice to and approval of the shareholders, to a maximum share capital of 695,218 million pesetas.

12.2 Outside shareholders' interests

These interests refer to the stake of minority shareholders in the ownership of and last year's results for the following companies:

1992

Company	% Minority participation	Net equity	Differences on foreigncurrency translation	Results	Total
AUDIOTEX	49	41	-	156	197
MAPTEL	24	39	-	(15)	24
SINTELAR	25	19	12	79	110
. INTERNACIONAL	23.78	20,454	5 307	2 239	28 000
T.H.M.	1	8	-	2	10
TL.D. Puerto Rico	21	2 703	-	-	2 703
		23 264	5 319	2 461	31 044

1993

Company	% Minority participation	Net equity	Differences on foreigncurrency translation	Results	Total
AUDIOTEX	-	-	-	-	(1)
MAPTEL	24	24	-	(25)	(1)
SINTELAR	25	3	25	246	274
T. INTERNACIONAL	23.78	22 491	9 661	5 138	37 290
T.H.M.	0.68	6	-	1	7
T.L.D. Puerto Rico	21	2 703	626	(212)	3 117
GESTIRED	49	34	-	(14)	20
PUBLIGUIAS	45	325	34	470	829
TELEFONICA ROMANIA	40	273	-	(16)	257
TELECARTERA	20	12	-	(7)	5
		25 871	10 346	5 581	41 798

Beginning in fiscal year 1992 the Telefónica Consolidated Group owns 50% of Sietel, S.A. and Cleon, S.A., which are consolidated by the proportional method and therefore do not generate outside shareholders. Telefónica has purchased an additional 4,45% of T.H.M., Control Electrónico Integrado, S.A. Tepesa owns the other 1% (Tepesa is owned by T.H.M. in 31.78%). For the Companies located abroad outside shareholders' interests include the differences on foreign currency translation.

12.3 Movement of outside shareholders' interests:

	1991	Addition of companies	Profit or loss	Diferencces on foreign currency translation	Other movements	Dividends paid	Disposals of companies	1992
Audiotex	41	-	156	-	-		-	197
Maptel	39	-	(15)	-	-		-	24
Sintelar	19	-	79	12	-		-	110
T. Internacional	20 959	-	2 239	5 007	(205)		-	28 000
T.L.D. Puerto Rico	-	2 703	-	-	-		-	2 703
T.H.M.	46	-	2	-	-		(38)	10
Total	21 104	2 703	2 461	5 019	(205)	-	(38)	31 044

	1992	Addition of companies	Profit or loss	Diferencces on foreign currency translation	Other movements	Dividends paid	Disposals of companies	1993
Audiotex	197	-	-	-	-	-	(197)	-
Gestired	-	34	(14)	-	-	-	-	20
Maptel	24	-	(25)	-	-	-	-	(1)
Publiguias	-	325	470	34	-	-	-	829
Sintelar	110	-	246	13	-	(95)	-	274
T. Internacional	28 000	-	5 138	4 354	(202)	-	-	37 290
T.L.D. Puerto Rico	2 703	-	(212)	626	-	-	-	3 117
Telefónica Romania	-	273	(16)	-	-	-	-	257
Telecartera	-	12	(7)	-	-	-	-	5
T.H.M.	10	-	-	-	(3)	1	-	7
Total	31 044	644	5 580	5 027	(205)	(96)	(197)	41 798

Other movements of Telefónica Internacional reflect the portion ascribed to the outside shareholders of the variation in the consolidation reserve caused by the incorporation of Cointel to the Group.

NOTE 13. DEFERRED INCOME

13.1 The composition of deferred income at December 31 is as follows:

	PARENT COMPANY		CONSOLIDATED	
	1993	1992	1993	1992
Capital grants	49 860	46 983	49 860	46 983
Deferred unrealized exchange gains (Note 9)	-	8 861	44	8 870
External contributions not repayable	4 905	2 879	5 422	2 879
Total	**54 765**	**58 723**	**55 326**	**58 732**

13.2 The movement on capital grants in the parent company is as follows:

	Balance 12.31.91	Additions	Amortizat.	Balance 12.31.92	Additions	Amortizat.	Balance 12.31.93
From official organisations, autonomous communities and local government bodies	13 019	6 301	1 506	17 814	2 873	2 110	18 577
From European Economic Community:							
STAR Program	15 847	6 672	1 698	20 821	347	2 367	18 801
FEDER Program	4 084	1 658	409	5 333	2 052	575	6 810
IRTA Program	498	1 561	50	2 009	1 163	206	2 966
Other	581	455	30	1 006	1 819	119	2 706
Total	**34 029**	**16 647**	**3 693**	**46 983**	**8 254**	**5 377**	**49 860**

NOTE 14. PROVISIONS FOR RISKS AND EXPENSES

The composition of the balances at December 31 is as follows:

									PARENT COMPANY
	1991	Provisions for year	Applicat.	Add. Transfers	1992	Provisions for year	Applicat.	Add. Transfers	1993
Self insurance for damages in plant	3 051	-	444	-	2 607	-	690	-	1 917
For contingencies (Note 20)	51 098	-	-	(51 098)	-	-	-	-	-
For contribution to employee benefit systems (Note 20.2)	18 829	-	-	(18 829)	-	-	-	-	-
For establishing pensions (Note 20)	76 615	12 531	89 146	-	-	-	-	-	-
Provision for rebalancing plan	-	-	-	-	-	4 128	-	813	4 941
For Pensioners' integrating cost in Social Security System	-	-	-	55 683	55 683	3 113	-	-	58 796
For endowment (Note 21)	52 886	8 965	37 651	(112)	24 088	4 038	5 805	-	22 321
For complementary pensioners annuity	-	5 127	7 717	132 025	129 435	10 089	15 870	4 465	128 119
Total	**202 479**	**26 623**	**134 958**	**117 669**	**211 813**	**21 368**	**22 365**	**5 278**	**216 094**

									CONSOLIDATED
	1991	Provisions for year	Applicat.	Add. Transfers	1992	Provisions for year	Applicat.	Add. Transfers	1993
Self insurance for damages in plant	3 660	179	640	(3)	3 196	55	784	9 233	11 700
For contribution to employee benefit systems (Note 20.2)	19 613	10	8	(19 615)	-	-	-	-	-
For establishing pensions (Note 20)	76 765	12 731	89 201	-	295	247	101	-	441
Provision for rebalancing plan	-	-	-	-	-	4 128	-	813	4 941
For Pensioners' integrating cost in Social Security System	-	-	-	55 683	55 683	3 113	-	-	58 796
For endowment (Note 21)	52 886	8 965	37 651	(112)	24 088	4 038	5 805	-	22 321
For complementary pensioners annuity	-	5 127	7 717	132 025	129 435	10 089	15 870	4 465	128 119
For contingencies and other provision	53 081	338	8	(50 312)	3 099	2 068	104	394	5 457
Total	**206 005**	**27 350**	**135 225**	**117 666**	**215 796**	**23 738**	**22 664**	**14 905**	**231 775**

NOTE 15 - DEBENTURES, BONDS AND OTHER ISSUES

15.1 Composition and movements are as follows:

PARENT COMPANY

	Debentures and bonds in local currency		Debentures and bonds in foreign currency			
	Non-convertible	Convertible and/or exchangeable	Non convertible	Convertible and/or exchangeable	Commercial paper	Total
Balance 12/31/91	597 744	-	6 381	22 561	128 365	755 051
New issues	95 220	-	-	-	273 754	368 974
Repayments, conversions and exchanges	(67 870)	-	-	-	(295 611)	(363 481)
Revaluations and other movements	44 163	-	723	5 502		50 388
Balance 12/31/92	669 257	-	7 104	28 063	106 508	810 932
New issues	86 677	-	-	-	101.588	188.265
Repayments, conversions and exchanges	(10 606)	-	(7 936)	(29 242)	(169 345)	(217 129)
Revaluations and other movements	52 837	-	832	1 179		54 848
Balance 12.31.93	798 165	-	-	-	38 751	836 916
Detail of maturities						
Long term	679 494	-	-	-	6 120	685 614
Short term	118 671	-	-	-	32 631	151 302
Accrued interest net yet payable	15 965	-	-	-	-	15 965

CONSOLIDATED

	Debentures and bonds in local currency		Debentures and bonds in foreign currency			
	Non-convertible	Convertible and/or exchangeable	Non convertible	Convertible and/or exchangeable	Commercial paper	Total
Balance 12/31/91	599 603	-	6 381	22 561	117 422	745 967
New issues	95 220	9 300	-	-	273 754	378 274
Repayments, conversions and exchanges	(67 523)	-	-	-	(295 611)	(363 134)
Revaluations and other movements	43 965	-	723	5 502	17 860	68 050
Balance 12.31.92	671 265	9 300	7 104	28 063	113 425	829 157
New issues	86 699	-	-	-	101 588	188 287
Repayments, conversions and exchanges	(10 790)	-	(7 936)	(29 242)	(169 345)	(217 313)
Revaluations and other movements	52 837	-	832	1 179	10 878	65 726
Balance 12.31.93	800 011	9 300	-	-	56 546	865 857
Detail of maturities:						
Long term	681 345	9 300	-	-	17 795	708 440
Short term	8 666	-	-	-	32 631	151 297
Accrued interest net yet payable	15 974	-	-	-	-	15 974

15.2 There are two commercial paper issue programs in Telefónica, as follows:

	Balance limit	Par value	Method of acquisition
Public issues	200 000 millones	500 000 pesetas	Monthly competitive bids
Company and institutional issues	200 000 millones	100 millones minimo	Operations

15.3 The details of the debentures and bonds of the consolidated Group outstanding at December 31. 1993 are as follows.

Issue		Interest %	Total	1994	1995	1996	1997	1998	Subsequent
Debentures									
June 1984	Zero coupon	14.8556	10 151	10 151	-	-	-	-	-
June 1986	Variable	11.6500	14 807	-	-	-	-	-	14 807
July 1987	Variable	10.2500	798	-	-	-	798	-	-
January 1988		12.5000	28 447	-	-	-	-	28 447	-
May 1989		12.2500	2 022	-	-	2 022	-	-	-
July 1989		12.0000	10 180	-	-	-	-	-	10 180
December 1989	Variable	7.7278	4 800	800	800	800	800	800	800
January 1990		12.0000	71	-	-	-	-	-	71
February 1990 Series A		12.6000	9 351	-	-	-	-	-	9 351
February 1990 Series B		12.6000	1 367	-	-	-	-	-	1 367
February 1990 Series C		12.6000	626	-	-	-	-	-	626
February 1990 Series D	Zero coupon	12.8896	10 170	-	-	-	-	-	10 170
February 1990 Series E	Zero coupon	12.8531	3 317	-	-	-	-	-	3 317
February 1990 Series F	Zero coupon	12.5793	368	-	-	-	-	-	368
June 1990	Zero coupon	14.0081	47 647	-	47 647	-	-	-	-
July 1990	Zero coupon	14.4358	47 784	-	-	47 784	-	-	-
December 1990	Zero coupo	13.5761	29 342	-	-	-	-	-	29 342
January 1991		12.0000	20	-	-	-	-	-	20
February 1991 Serie A		14.2500	30 000	-	-	-	-	30 000	-
February 1991 Serie B	Zero coupon	14.4676	44 040	-	-	-	-	44 040	-
March 1991	Zero coupon	14.4813	7 340	-	-	-	-	5 872	1 468
Private issue April 1991		14.2500	20 000	-	-	-	-	20 000	-
April 1991 Series A		13.5000	10 000	-	-	-	-	-	10 000
April 1991 Series B	Zero coupon	13.6659	28 299	-	-	-	-	-	28 299
A September 1994	Zero coupon	9.8749	45 648	45 648	-	-	-	-	-
B September 1996	Zero coupon	10.0000	42 042	-	-	42 042	-	-	-
C September 1998	Zero coupon	10.1250	31 351	-	-	-	-	31 351	-
D September 2001	Zero coupon	10.2500	42 234	-	-	-	-	-	42 234
January 1992		12.0000	257	-	-	-	-	-	257
January 1992		12.0000	220	-	-	-	-	-	220
A November 1995		10.0625	14 058	-	14 058	-	-	-	-
B November 2000		10.0625	20 439	-	-	-	-	-	20 439
C November 2002		10.0625	19 315	-	-	-	-	-	19 315
A October 1996		7.7500	900	-	-	900	-	-	-
B October 2000		8.0000	5 507	-	-	-	-	-	5 507
C October 2004		8.2500	8 002	-	-	-	-	-	8 002
B.I.F.E. Bank		9.8500	22	-	-	-	-	11	11
Bonds									
November 1985		11.7500	3 383	-	3 383	-	-	-	-
January 1988	Zero coupon	10.0000	2 067	2 067	-	-	-	-	-
October 1989		12.7500	20 000	-	-	20 000	-	-	-
September 1990		14.2500	60 000	60 000	-	-	-	-	-
November 1990		14.0625	600	-	-	-	600	-	-
November 1990	Variable	9.2075	400	-	-	-	400	-	-
January 1991	Variable	9.2075	1 370	-	-	-	1 370	-	-
February 1991		13.9375	3 440	-	-	-	3 440	-	-
February 1991	Variable	9.2075	400	-	-	-	400	-	-
April 1991	Zero coupon	14.5154	67 185	-	-	-	-	-	67 185
April 1991		12.3750	10 160	-	-	-	10 160	-	-
April 1991	Variable	9.2075	300	-	-	-	300	-	-
May 1991		12.3750	4 437	-	-	-	4 437	-	-
July 1991	Variable	9.2075	5 100	-	-	-	5 100	-	-
July 1992	Zero coupon	14.5154	4 889	-	-	-	-	-	4 889
February 1992		11.1875	1 470	-	-	-	1 470	-	-
November 1992		12.9375	400	-	-	-	400	-	-
April 1993		12.2500	21 000	-	-	-	21 000	-	-
May 1993		11.7500	2 468	-	-	-	2 468	-	-
Total Issues			800 011	118 666	65 888	65 764	100 927	160 521	288 245

15.4 Debentures and zero coupon bonds are presented on the Balance Sheet at their issue price plus interest accrued through December 31 of the stated year.

The schedule of the maturities and percentage of repayment of the debentures and zero coupon bonds is as follows:

ISSUE	DUE DATE OF AMORTIZATION	% REPAYMENT	ACTUAL VALUE	REPAYMENT VALUE
Debentures				
June 1984	07.05.1994	400 000	10 151	10 889
February 1990 serie D	02.26.2000	336 154	10 170	21 447
February 1990 serie E	02.26.2005	613 338	3 317	12 776
February 1990 serie F	02.26.2010	1 069 470	368	2 503
June 1990	06.22.1995	192 610	47 647	57 783
July 1990	07.20.1997	257 000	47 784	77 100
December 1990	12.28.2005	675 000	29 342	135 000
February 1991 serie B	02.28.1998	257 500	44 040	77 250
March 1991	03.01.1998	257 729	1 468	2 577
March 1991	06.01.1998	266 659	1 468	2 667
March 1991	09.01.1998	275 899	1 468	2 759
March 1991	12.01.1999	285 353	1 468	2 854
March 1991	03.01.1999	295 022	1 468	2 950
April 1991 serie B	04.17.2001	360 000	28 299	72 000
A September 1994	09.18.1996	132 715	45 648	48 828
B September 1996	09.18.1996	161 135	42 042	54 459
C September 1998	09.18.1998	196 531	31 351	49 401
D September 2001	09.18.2001	265 543	42 234	89 687
Bonds				
January 1988	01.26.1994	177 156	2 072	2 086
April 1991 zero coupon	04.15.1999	295 740	67 185	137 519
July 1991 zero coupon	07.15.1999	295 740	4 889	10 351
			463 879	872 886

15.5 Additional information

	PARENT COMPANY		CONSOLIDATED	
	1993	1992	1993	1992
Interest expenses	93 900	84 844	93 923	84 875
The amounts from the issues subject to tax benefits are as follows:				
Debentures in local currency	-	2 834	-	2 834
Debentures in foreign currency	-	30 061	-	30 061

The average cost of the debentures and bonds outstanding is 12.22% for 1993 (12.57% in 1992).

15.6 The Eurobonds issue at Frankfurt's stock market of 100 million german marks was amortized on its maturity date on May 1993. The issue of convertible bonds at London's stock market of 200 million US dollars has been cancelled by premature amortization of 83.53 million US dollars and by conversion of 116,46 million US dollars in ordinary shares of Telefónica.

The issue in US dollars gives the holders the right, within the established periods, to convert the debentures into ordinary shares of the Company, according to the terms and conditions of the issue.

15.7 In October 1993 there was an issue of 105,000 million pesetas (which may be increased to 150 million pesetas). These will be subscribed over a one-year period. At December 31, 1993, 14,409 debentures had been subscribed for.

NOTE 16. DEBTS WITH CREDIT ENTITIES

16.1 As mentioned in Note 2 a), these accounts are classified in the balance sheet according to their maturity dates. The balances at December 31 are as follows:

	PARENT COMPANY						CONSOLIDATED					
	1993			1992			1993			1992		
	Long term	Short term	Total	Long term	Short term	Total	Long term	Short term	Total	Long term	Short term	Total
Notes payable at face value	52 950	10 365	63 315	63 315	365	63 680	52 950	10 365	63 315	63 315	4 784	68 099
Loans and credits	179 300	31 160	210 460	258 241	115 209	373 450	220 075	40 760	260 835	331 861	131 318	463 179
Loans in foreign currency	308 244	5 901	314 145	281 244	-	281 244	408 856	23 592	432 448	295 552	4 592	300 144
Total	540 494	47 426	587 920	602 800	115 574	718 374	681 881	74 717	756 598	690 728	140 694	831 422

16.2 The years of maturity of the debts are as follows:

							PARENT COMPANY
						Maturities	Balance at
	1994	1995	1996	1997	1998	Subsequent	12.31.93
Notes payable	10 365	365	15 365	365	1 314	35 541	63 315
Loans and credits	31 160	11 724	8 402	32 656	25 250	101 268	210 460
Loans in foreign currency	5 901	19 053	44 252	27 464	42 269	175 206	314 145
Total	47 426	31 142	68 019	60 485	68 833	312 015	587 920

							CONSOLIDATED
						Maturities	Balance at
	1994	1995	1996	1997	1998	Subsequent	12.31.93
Notes payable	10 365	365	15 365	365	1 314	35 541	63 315
Loans in foreign currency	23 592	19 074	48 311	35 582	69 799	236 090	432 448
Loans and credits	40 760	12 337	8 995	33 300	42 183	123 260	260 835
Total	74 717	31 776	72 671	69 247	113 296	394 891	756 598

16.3 Additional information:

							PARENT COMPANY				CONSOLIDATED	
	Financial expenses		Accrued interest		Average interest rate		Financial expenses		Accrued interest			
	1993	1992	1993	1992	1993	1992	1993	1992	1993	1992		
Loans in foreign currency	31 794	25 308	8 165	5 449	6.99	7.50	39 947	25 308	8 400	5 551		
Loans and credits	33 872	45 681	3 606	6 728	13.13	13.42	34 308	52 480	4 698	7 573		
Notes payable	4 595	4 111	-	-	13.40	13.34	4 595	4 111	-	-		

16.4 Loans and credit facilities accounts reflect only the accounts actually borrowed. Unused facilities are disclosed in Note 24.

16.5 At December 31, 1993 a total of 52.243 million pesetas in foreign currency loans is eligible for the tax benefits established by Decree Law 19/1961 and Law 61/1978.

16.6 Details of Telefónica Group loans denominated in foreign currency from financial institutions are as follows:

		1993		1992
Foreign currency	Amount	Exchange rate	Amount	Exchange rate
US dollars	412.8	142.356	325.0	114.795
German marks	325.5	82 358	205.5	71.036
Swiss francs	422.5	96.382	422.5	78.681
Dutch florins	258.9	73.615	258.9	63.227
Japanese yen	38 520.6	1.27388	45 520.6	0.92131
French francs	649.9	24.251	649.9	20.849
ECUs (XEU)	804.5	159.439	804.4	138.581
Pesetas (ESP) (*)	12 750.0	1.000	12 750.0	1.000

(*) This amount includes the disposition in pesetas of a multicurrency loan originally authorized in ECUs by the European Investment Bank.

16.7 Loans denominated in foreign currency include the following:

• The Company has multi-option financial facility for 250 million US dollars represented by Telefónica's certificates in Euronotes with maturities of less than six months. When they become due, Telefónica can opt to:
a) issue new Euronotes;
b) use the credit facility to refinance the amounts due; or
c) repay the notes without using such credit facility.

• Details of Loans from the European Investment Bank, authorized through the Official Credit Institute are as follow:

Year	Per value	Maturity	Grace period	Amortization	Interest rate	Option
1988	XEU 1 200 MM	15 years	5 years	20 semestres	Fixed for the first 5 years, variable 5th - 10th	Multicurrency
1992	Pts 12 500 MM	15 years	5 years	20 semestres	10.95% fixed for first 6 years, variable next 9 years	-
1992	XEU 150 MM	15 years	5 years	20 semestres	Quarterly variable	-
1992	JPY 19 500 MM	10 years	5 years	10 semestres	Semianual variable	-
1992	NLG 82.1 MM	10 years	5 years	10 semestres	Quarterly variable	-

NOTE 17 - DEBTS WITH GROUP AND ASSOCIATED COMPANIES

The detail at December 31, 1993 is as follows:

| | PARENT COMPANY | | | | | | CONSOLIDATED | | | | | |
| | 1993 | | | 1992 | | | 1993 | | | 1992 | | |
	Long term	Short term	Total	Long term	Short term	Total	Long term	Short term	Total	Long term	Short term	Total
Loans	118 975	-	118 975	83 436	-	83 436	-	-	-	-	-	-
Purchases and services:												
From Group companies	-	24 142	24 142	-	43 948	43 948	-	-	-	-	-	-
From Associated companies	-	17 133	17 133	18 565	24 133	42 698	-	19 358	19 358	18 565	25 626	44 191
Corporation Tax	3 428	184	3 612	1 585	184	1 769	-	-	-	-	-	-
Total	122 403	41 459	163 862	103 586	68 265	171 851	-	19 358	19 358	18 565	25 626	44 191

The loans consist of:

a) A loan from the European Investment Bank, authorized in 1991 through the subsidiary Telefónica y Finanzas, S.A., (Telfisa) for 600 million ECUs. An amount of 500 million ECUs of the loan facility was used in 1991 in four different currencies. The loan is for a period of 15 years with a grace period of five years. Thereafter the loan is repayable in 20 equal semi-annual installments. The loan bears interest at rates varying quarterly.

b) A further loan from the European Investment Bank granted in 1993 through Telfisa of 300 million ECUS to be used in pesetas, of an equivalent amount of 38,700 million pesetas. In 1993 the first disposal of 20,000 million pesetas has been made, with a 15 year period of maturity, with a 5 year grace period, and to be amortized in 19 yearly payments and variable quarterly interest rate.

c) A commercial loan facility with the subsidiary Telefónica North America Inc., for up to 125 million US dollars and with maturity in 1997. The loan facility has been used in full. The funds for this loan were raised with commercial paper issued in the USA by the subsidiary and guaranteed by Telefónica

NOTE 18 - TAXES PAYABLE:

The details of the balances at December 31 are as follows:

| | PARENT COMPANY | | CONSOLIDATED | |
	1993	1992	1993	1992
Taxes payable and recoverable				
Payroll withholding taxes	7 649	7 370	8 375	8 144
Value added tax	21 254	11 374	21 998	13 168
Dividend and interest at withholding taxes	933	457	1 130	669
Corporate income tax	18 595	-	19 099	363
Local government taxes	1 172	2 609	1 180	2 613
Social Security Contributionsl	21 913	19 427	22 745	20 123
Foreign taxes	-	-	845	217
Total	71 516	41 237	75 372	45 297
Taxes recoverable:				
Payments on account of corporate income tax:				
Tax withhold from income at source	1 235	49	2 553	1 014
Payments on account on consolidate corporate income tax returns	346	760	346	760
Payments on account on individual income tax returns	-	-	2	-
Taxes surcharges and Social Security payments recoverable	542	579	553	914
Corporate income tax-consolidated 1990	1 128	2	1 128	2
Taxes paid in advance	739	16 602	767	16 698
V.AT pending deduction	2 736	2 884	2 736	3 142
Foreign taxes	-	-	618	136
Total	6 726	20 876	8 703	22 666

NOTE 19 -OTHER ACCOUNTS PAYABLE

This heading comprises the following amounts:

| | PARENT COMPANY | | CONSOLIDATED | |
	1993	1992	1993	1992
Remuneration payable	18 656	17 877	20 939	20 751
Exchange of telephone services	14 491	14 270	14 491	14 270
Guarantee deposits	7 899	9 721	7 899	9 721
Expenses accrued and due	39 451	32 107	39 523	32 107
Dividends payable	23 201	7 647	23 201	7 647
Institución Telefónica de Previsión	(8 846)	(343)	(8 846)	(343)
Sundry creditors	28 781	19 602	33 013	23 401
Total	123 633	100 881	130 220	107 554

NOTE 20 - PENSIONS

20.1 Up to the time of the publication of the Order from the Ministry of Labour and Social Security dated December 30th 1991 (published in the Spanish Official Bulletin nº 1, January 1st 1992) which stated that active employees and pensioners at that time under the Institución Telefónica de Previsión (ITP) would be integrated into the Social Security general regime from January 1st 1992 onwards, Telefónica personnel had benefited from a social welfare system provided by I.T.P. Therefore since January 1st 1992, Telefónica and its employees have been contributing to the Social Security system for the coverage previously provided by the I.T.P., and payments to the latter have ceased.

The I.T.P., which is currently being liquidated in accordance with the resolution by the General Office of Insurance pursuant to which the dissolution order of July 10th 1992 was published, was a mutual employee benefit fund created under the Ley de Montepíos y Mutualidades de Previsión Social dated December 6th 1941 and its Regulations of May 26th 1943. It was, therefore, an independent legal entity and, as such, was governed by its own regulations approved by the Subsecretariat of Social Security on January 28th 1977.

20.2 In accordance with the dissolution Order previously mentioned, the resolution reached by the General Office of Planning and Economic Organization of Social Security on May 25th 1992 stated that the cost of integration of retired personnel would amount to 130 683 million pesetas.

Based on this ministerial order the liquidators of I.T.P. proceeded to pay 65 000 million pesetas to the Social Security, retaining an additional 10 000 million pesetas as provisions to cover the payments to be made on behalf of the Social Security. Of the retained amount 4 154 million pesetas remained and was transferred to the Social Security by the liquidators in July 1993.

The 55 683 million pesetas remaining for the previously mentioned overall total cost of 130 683 million pesetas will be paid over a ten year period. Over the first two years only interest will be paid, amortizing over the remaining eight years the principal amount with its corresponding interest.

Payment of the interest for the two-year grace period was made by the I.T.P. liquidators in yearly payments of 4 455 million pesetas, the first of which was made in December 1992 and the second in December 1993.

Annual payments of 9 690 million pesetas will be made over the remaining eight years in December of each year. The first of such payments will be made in December 1994.

Once I.T.P. has been liquidated, Telefónica de España, S.A. will be obligated to cover the difference between the total cost of 130 683 million pesetas and the liquidation value of I.T.P. This difference is estimated at 58 796 million pesetas for which a corresponding provision has been made (note 14).

20.3 Telefónica, which presented an offer on June 30th 1992 that was accepted by the employees on September 17th of the same year, reached a collective statutory agreement with the union representatives.

The most significant term of the agreement involves the creation of a Pension Plan under the Law 8/1987 of June 8 for Pension Schemes and Funds with the following points:

a) An employment system pension Plan.

b) Defined contribution.

c) Obligatory contributions by participating employees.

d) Financial capitalization on an individual basis.

e) The Promoter contributes 6.87% of the participating employees' basic salary. For personnel who joined Telefónica after June 30th 1992, the contribution is 4.51% of their basic salary.

f) The direct contribution of the participating employee will be a minimum 2.2% of his basic salary.

g) Entitlements for past services were recognized to a maximum amount of 237 696 million pesetas. Employees who chose not to join the Plan during the one year period on beginning July 1st 1992 (the date on which the scheme came into force) have no rights regarding entitlements for past services and therefore the amount previously mentioned for these consolidated entitlements decreased in the corresponding amount.

h) The financing of consolidated rights would be carried out, as deemed necessary, through provisions already accounted for in the amount of 121 350 million pesetas. The effective transfer of this amount would be made not later than the year 2002 applying an effective annual interest rate of 6.7% in accordance with the Rebalancing Plan.

The remaining deficit, up to a maximum of 116 346 million pesetas, would be financed over twenty eight years pursuant to the Rebalancing Plan not yet approved by the General Office of Insurance. The effective annual interest rate for the financing of this deficit will be 6% with payments to be made at the beginning of each month.

i) The plan became effective July 1st 1992. The time period stipulated for incorporation into the Plan was the one year period beginning that date, although there may be, at a future date, additional incorporation periods in accordance with the law and with no recognition of consolidated rights for past services.

20.4 66 158 employees had joined the Plan as of December 31 1993. In accordance with actuarial calculations the consolidated rights for these employees amount to 228 118 million pesetas. The final amount will depend on the outcome of certain individual situations currently under study, although these should not cause any significant changes.

20.5 During the fiscal year a new Rebalancing Plan has been drafted to comply with General Office of Insurance regulations. The draft has not been approved yet, but in essence it would result in a two-year acceleration of the transfer of the provisions for the consolidated rights, whose transfer would therefore be made not later than the year 2000.

In accordance with the conditions laid down for incorporation to the Plan, transfers of 33 130 million pesetas have been made as follows:

Transferred in 1992	9 153
Transferred in 1993	23 977
Corresponding to 1992 for those employees who joined the Plan in 1993 with backdated rights in accordance with the 1st Transitory Provision of Telefónica's Pension Plan's regulation	1 445
Corresponding to 1993	22 532
	33 130
Pending transfer for the adjustment of the Rebalancing Plan	1 110
Total	**34 240**

The existing debt will be amortized following a systematic plan in accordance with the Rebalancing Plan. The provision made for 1993 amounts to 4 128 million pesetas (in 1992 the figure was 813 million pesetas).

At the end of the fiscal year the total figure for consolidated rights liabilities pending transfer to the Plan amounted to 215 145 million pesetas, for which provisions amounting to 107 757 million pesetas have been made. The Promoter's contribution for 1993 totalled 16 566 million pesetas (6 231 million pesetas in 1992).

20.6 One of the agreements within the overall solution to the Company's social welfare scheme was reached on July 8th, 1992 with the employees' representatives in relation with the supplementary pension to be received by those employees who retired on or before June 30th 1992.

In short, this agreement states that Telefónica will pay to those pensioners covered by ITP on June 30. 1992 and those employees who would have been recognized as pensioners, a complementary amount equivalent to the difference between the State pension received from Social Security up to July 1st 1992 and that which corresponds to, or would have corresponded to, had it been recognized by, the ITP.

The aforementioned supplementary payments, once quantified, will be fixed, to be received for life, and not revisable. Upon death of the employee the spouse recognized as such before June 30th 1992 is entitled to 60% of the payment.

NOTE 21 - COLLECTIVE ENDOWMENT INSURANCE

At December 31st 1993 Telefónica had provisions totalling 22 321 million pesetas to cover liabilities accrued in accordance with actuarial calculations. These provisions will be used to cover the payments to be made to retired personnel under 65 who have not been entitled to endowment insurance and will also cover the 7 056 current employees who have chosen not to join the Pension Plan and who will be entitled to the endowment insurance once they reach the age of 65.

Telefónica has made provisions of 4 038 million pesetas for this purpose charged to 1993 results (in 1992 this figure was 8 965 million pesetas). The payments made throughout 1993 amounted to 5 805 million pesetas (the figure for 1992 was 5 444 million pesetas).

NOTE 22 - TAXATION

The years open to inspection for the main taxes are:
- Corporate income tax:1988 through 1992.
- Corporate income tax for companies filing a consolidated tax return: 1990 through 1992.
- Local government taxes: 1988 through 1993.
- Value added tax: 1988 through 1993.
- Capital transfer tax: 1988 through 1993.
- Dividend and interest withholding taxes: 1988 through 1993.
- Payroll withholding tax: 1988 through 1993.

RECONCILIATION OF PROFIT BEFORE TAX PER ACCOUNTS OF TELEFONICA AND TAXABLE INCOME:

	Increase	Decrease	
Profit before tax			107 468
PERMANENT DIFFERENCES:	4 195	1 583	2 612
Adjusted profit per accounts			110 080
TIMING DIFFERENCES:			
Originating in present year	32 748	1 654	31 094
Originating in previous year	13 463	4 052	9 411
Taxable income			150 585
Individual Taxable income rest of tax group			2 534
Intra group eliminations			
Fixed assets sales			(4 123)
Dividends			(2 651)
Taxable Income (Tax Group)			146 345

CORPORATE INCOME TAX:

	Accrued	Deferred	Prepaid	Telefónica	Payable Group
Rate of 35%: :					
On adjusted profit per accounts	38 528	(4 133)	10 044	-	-
On taxable income	-	-	-	52 705	51 221
Deductions:					
Double taxation relief	(2 614)	-	-	(2 614)	(2 338)
Allowances	(360)	-	-	(360)	(360)
Investment tax credits	(13 014)	3 899	(13 547)	(30 460)	(29 928)
Employment	-	-	-	-	-
Total deductions	22 540	(234)	(3 503)	19 271	18 595
Taxes paid abroad and other	1 730				
Repercussion for consolidated tax	(974)				
Surplus of provisions corporate income tax 92	(665)				
	22 631				

RECONCILIATION OF PROFIT BEFORE TAX PER CONSOLIDATED ACCOUNTS AND TAXABLE INCOME:

Profit before tax per accounts	121 212

PERMANENT DIFFERENCES:

Individual corporations	2 537
Losses on foreign governments	(3 497)
Losses on associated companies	(20 176)
Eliminations included on consolidation and not included on corporate income tax report	2 203
Amortization of goodwill on consolidation	4 798
Deduction of taxable losses	(323)
Losses of non tax consolidating companies	205
Adjusted profit per accounts	**106 959**

TIMING DIFFERENCES:

Individual corporations increase	47 133
Individual corporations decrease	(7 049)
Profit of transparent corporations 1992	3 662
Profit of transparent corporations 1993	(3 145)
Taxable income	**147 560**

CORPORATION TAX	Accrued	Payable	Deferred	Prepaid
Rate of 35% :				
On adjusted profit per accounts	37 436	-	(4 407)	10 079
On taxable income	-	51 646	-	-
Deductions:				
Double taxation relief	(2 338)	(2 338)	-	-
Allowances	(360)	(360)	-	-
Investment tax credits	(13 201)	(29 849)	3 377	(13 547)
total	21 537	19 099	(1 030)	(3 468)
Taxes paid abroad	3 308			
total	24 845			

There are carry-over investment tax credits which were not applied due to insufficient tax liabilities in the following amounts: 1989, 18.008 million pesetas; 1990, 30.180 million pesetas; 1991, 27.977 million pesetas; 1992, 19.000 million pesetas; and 1993, 19.248 million pesetas. As a result of the prescription of the term of application. 12.945 million pesetas of 1988 have been cancelled. They have profitted of fiscal deductions for reinvestment totalling 537 million pesetas.

Timely differences have derived from: 22.642 million pesetas, of exchange differences caused by keeping a cash fiscal criteria; 13.463 million pesetas of reversion of tax regulation amortization applied on previous years; 5.561 million pesetas of the Pension Fund rebalancing plan (surplus over payments); 3.016 million pesetas of spare provision of the Pension Plan for 1992; 2.511 million pesetas of charges for complement of retired personnel (surplus over payments); 1.874 million pesetas of provision charges for depreciation of investments as a result of applying the fiscal standard of deduction on the following year; 1.654 million pesetas of payments for collective insurance endowment (surplus of payments over charges for provision); 4.052 million pesetas of reverted prepaid taxes of 1992.

Advance payments of the Group for corporate income tax, amount to 346 million pesetas and the withholding tax to 1.235 million pesetas.

NOTE 23- INCOME AND EXPENSES

23.1 The distribution of sales by products is as follows:

Concepts	PARENT COMPANY 1993	1992
Subscribed payments	276 280	253 751
Transmission of data and images	112 433	115 669
National automatic service	579 671	539 564
Operator trunk calls	3 271	2 861
International service	132 672	135 005
Marine portable service	32 754	25 989
Advertising	15 007	12 806
Connection fees	43 930	44 014
Marketing of terminals and other	24 066	25 037
Operating income	**1 220 084**	**1 154 696**

Concepts	CONSOLIDATED 1993	1992
Parent company	1 220 084	1 154 696
International Telephone Group	18 338	1 767
Other subsidiaries	161 106	156 395
Intra - group sales	(102 091)	(103 920)
Total	**1 297 437**	**1 208 938**

23.2 The numbers of employees by category and personnel costs are as follows:

AVERAGE NUMBER OF EMPLOYEES: Category	PARENT COMPANY 1993	1992	CONSOLIDATED 1993	1992
General management	1 141	1 129	1 482	1 155
University graduates and special technicians	4 007	3 941	5 277	5 302
Personnel with higher education degrees and technicians	6 640	6 726	7 994	8 106
Personnel in charge and operators of internal plant	18 225	18 240	18 240	18 240
Personnel in charge and operators of external plant	20 755	21 079	20 835	21 079
Applications operator and data processing assistants	732	1 080	732	1 080
Administrative personnel	10 702	10 482	12 727	12 237
Subscribed service personnel	3 510	3 467	3 709	3 722
Operation personnel	5 923	6 031	5 923	6 031
Warehouse, office and garage personnel	1 757	1 798	1 757	1 801
Auxiliary personnel	975	965	982	971
Manual workers	--	--	3 297	2 807
Other personnel	22	30	1 101	1 271
Total	**74 389**	**74 968**	**84 056**	**83 802**

PERSONNEL COSTS: Concepts	PARENT COMPANY 1993	1992	CONSOLIDATED 1993	1992
Salaries and wages	302 599	292 661	334 097	318 288
Pensions Funds	18 022	24 065	18 233	24 470
Social Security and other expenses	87 482	76 010	96 072	86 868
Total	**408 103**	**392 736**	**448 402**	**429 626**

23.3 The following is an analysis of extraordinary income and expenses:

EXTRAORDINARY INCOME Concept	PARENT COMPANY 1993	CONSOLIDATED 1993
Reversion of fixed assets contributions for COOB 92 and EXPO 92	881	881
Indemnities for breach of contract	533	533
Insurance compensation	146	146
Complementary income tax report	161	849
Miscellaneous	485	2 107
Total	**2 206**	**4 516**

EXTRAORDINARY EXPENSES	PARENT COMPANY	CONSOLIDATED
Concept	1993	1993
Pension complements	8 292	9 130
Donations	1 080	1 080
Sponsorship costs of COOB 92, EXPO 92 COM 92 and XACOBEO 93	1 784	1 784
Irrecoverable costs of rejected projects	405	405
Charge on provision for contingencies	3 113	3 113
Complementary income tax report	1 138	1 369
Expenses for exhibitions and other functions	614	615
Miscellaneous	257	1 668
Total	**16 683**	**19 164**

NOTE 24 - OTHER INFORMATION

24.1 Compensation of Directors

The total amount paid to Telefónica's directors during the year 1993 for salaries, wages and expense allowances was 125 million pesetas.

The 4 members of the Board of Directors who are Telefónica's employees have joined the Pension Plan in the same conditions as the rest of the employees. The contributions to the annual cost towards the Pension Fund of these 4 members for 1993 amount to 2.272,328 pesetas.

Telefónica did not grant any loans or credits in favor of the members of the Board of Directors.

24.2 Unused credit facilities:

	PARENT COMPANY		CONSOLIDATED	
	1993	1992	1993	1992
Unused long term credit facilities	32 079	4 682	126 693	85 224
Other credit facilities (floating credit lines)	62 000	21 627	62 000	21 627
Short term credit facility	31 965	12 189	41 946	30 085
Total	**126 044**	**38 498**	**230 639**	**136 936**

24.3 Commitments:

Guarantees for financial operations	75 073	75 201	85 579	2 795
Guarantees granted to employees	2 646	2 924	2 646	6 603

Guarantees for financial operations include primarily guarantees given by the Company to its subsidiary and participated companies to secure their operations with third parties.

NOTE 25- SUBSEQUENT EVENTS

25.1 Loans in foreign currency

In January 1994, the following loans have amortized in advance:

a) Loan of the European Bank of Investments, granted through the I.C.O. in 1989, with a maturity of 15 years, used in 3 multi-currencies, 52.4 million ECU'S, 61.7 million dutch florins, and 46.6 million swiss francs.

b) Loan of the Swiss Bank granted in 1990 of 75 million US dollars, with a maturity of 8 years, to be amortized by a single payment and variable interest rate from 3 to 6 months.

25.2 Foreign operations

a) In January 1994 the COCELCO consortium, in which Telefónica's group participates in 35%, has obtained the license to operate through mobile technology in the west region of Colombia.

b) In February 1994, through public licitation, the Telefónica Group was the successful bidder of 35% of the equity of the peruan companies CPT and ENTEL, which control 95% of the telecommunication market in Perú. The requirements are included in the privatization document. The bidded amount totals 2.002 million of US dollars for the aforementioned adjudication.

UNITED KINGDOM

Michael J. Mumford
Lancaster University Management School
Lancaster LA1 4YX, United Kingdom

1. Background

1.1. History: Development of Company Law from 1844

The practice of forming companies in Britain, whether by Royal Charter or by parliamentary statute, goes back several centuries. The use of companies in Britain grew substantially, however, only after the 1844 Companies Act made it easy to form a company by a simple process of registration. After the 1855 Companies Act, it became possible for the first time to form a company in which the shareholders enjoyed limited liability for the debts of the company.

From 1844, company law in Britain has set the basic framework that compels companies to prepare financial accounts, and (with certain exceptions, as in the case of many smaller "exempt private" companies, between 1907 and 1967) to publish these accounts by filing them on public record with the Registrar of Companies. The situation in Britain contrasts with that in the United States, where the requirement to publish accounts laid down by the 1933 and 1934 Securities Acts was imposed on listed companies alone. The Companies Acts in Britain lay down regulations for all registered companies.

The 1844 Companies Act required companies to prepare (and present each year to an annual meeting of shareholders) a balance sheet, which was to be audited (although not by a professional accountant). The law did not specify what information was to be contained in the balance sheet, nor did it require an income statement. The 1856 Companies Act had the effect of raising the quality of disclosure by specifying the various headings of assets and liabilities that were to be disclosed, but it made disclosure and audit voluntary on the part of the company. Companies were to adopt a set of rules for their conduct (their "Articles of Association"), and a standard set of Articles (which later came to be known as "Table A")

913

was set out in the act and deemed to apply to any company that had not specifically agreed on some alternative set. Table A last appeared in the 1948 Companies Act; no reference was made to it in the 1985 act, which consolidated existing company law, but it still exists in regulations published by the Department of Trade and Industry (the government department responsible for companies regulation).

The 1900 Companies Act once again made an audit mandatory for all registered companies, although by this date many of the most important classes of business enterprise (such as railways, banks, insurance companies, and utilities) were covered by their own separate legislation, which required accounts to be published in more detail than for the general run of companies.

The 1907 Companies Act made a distinction between public companies and private companies. Such a distinction survives, although the 1980 Companies Act made important changes to the definitions of each class (discussed further in Section 1.2.1). The 1929 Companies Act for the first time required the publication of a profit and loss account, and in addition it provided a definition of a subsidiary company, since intercompany holdings were by then common in Britain. Despite this, there were no effective provisions for group accounts until the 1947 Companies Act (consolidated in the 1948 Companies Act). The 1947 act raised the standards of reporting substantially, both by requiring group accounts to be published in addition to the accounts of the holding company and also by raising disclosure levels.

The Companies Acts of 1967 and 1976 both made some useful minor reforms to company disclosure. In many ways more important, however, was the outcry that followed certain widely reported financial scandals in 1968, leading to the creation in 1969 of the Accounting Standards Steering Committee (the ASSC). Until this time, disclosure laws had demanded that information be published under general categories of information, but there was very little guidance as to how the information was to be produced. In particular, the law was carefully worded to allow practically any valuation conventions that the directors chose to adopt. The annual report and accounts were, as they continue to be, the responsibility of the directors. Now, however, with the establishment of the ASSC, the British accountancy profession was moved for the first time to set detailed standards to guide companies in the preparation of their accounts. The ASSC later became the Accounting Standards Committee (the ASC), replaced in 1990 by the Accounting Standards Board (the ASB). The distinctions are considered in Section 1.4.

Companies Acts in 1980 and 1981 reflected a new and important force in British companies legislation—membership of the European Community (now the European Union). Several of the major company law directives were already in draft form before Britain became a member in 1973, but some vigorous negotiations on the part of the British profession led to further changes, introducing, for example, reference to a "true and fair view," whereas European regulations were otherwise expressed in more precise legal terms.

By 1981 there were company law provisions currently in force in Britain from the 1948, 1967, 1976, 1980, and 1981 Companies Acts, to name only the major statutes, together with many other lesser provisions in other laws passed over several decades. The 1985 Companies Act consolidated current company law. This act is now the basic statute in the area, amended in some significant ways by the 1989 Companies Act and by lesser provisions elsewhere. In the rest of this chapter, the 1985 and 1989 Companies Acts are usually referred to simply as "the 1985 act" and "the 1989 act," respectively.

1.2 Explanatory Background to the Authority of Standards

1.2.1 Legal Background

Britain has no written constitution. The law itself comprises three elements:

1. Those statutes that have been passed by government
2. The decisions of the courts, either specifically on the matter decided or, with lesser authority, as a matter merely discussed by the court by way of *obiter dicta* not involving a final decision
3. A body of "common law," which is deemed to exist and to be capable of recognition by the courts, even though it has not yet been stated orally or in writing

To a large extent the regulations governing registered companies are framed in the Companies Acts, as summarized above (and described further below).

On a number of questions affecting accountants, however, the law is not clear. The nature and authority of "generally accepted accounting principles" is a good example. There are references to the need for accounts to show a "true and fair view" (see Section 1.4.1), but the term is not defined in statute law, nor are clear guidelines available in the form of decided case law. The existence of accounting standards is recognized in Section 256 of the 1985 act, as amended by Section 19 of the 1989 act, which also empowers the relevant minister to prescribe regulations to recognize standard-setting bodies. It is reasonable to assume that accounting standards (analyzed in more detail in Section 1.4.2) constitute strong authority, but their precise status is not defined by statute or in any detail by the courts. There is a further complication in that the courts concerned might differ in their views, depending on whether action is brought within Britain or before the European Court of Justice. Different legal traditions of interpretation arise in each case.

This is all in marked contrast with the state of the law in the United States, where the Securities and Exchange Commission has the authority to lay down detailed rules for drawing up published accounts for listed companies. In Britain no such formal legal powers to lay down detailed accounting rules have been defined. Neither the Department of Trade and Industry nor the accounting profession sets accounting standards enforceable directly through the courts, even though departure from standards may need to be defended by the company concerned (see Section 1.4). Thus, the American term *Generally Accepted Accounting Principles* has a meaning that is more clearly defined than it is in Britain (indeed, although the term *accounting principles* appears in the 1985 Companies Act, the expression *GAAP* has not been generally used in Britain until recently; the London office of Ernst and Young published a comprehensive survey under the title "UK GAAP" in 1989, since which time use of the term has grown).

Whereas certain provisions are laid down by law and by established practice, a great deal is left to the discretion of company directors to decide, usually on the advice of professional accountants. Even though there is a legal obligation on all companies to have directors, there is no requirement that any director shall be designated a "finance director," with special authority over accounting matters, nor is there any requirement that the board of directors shall include a qualified accountant among its numbers—although in fact this is usually the case with public companies. (By contrast, each company must have a company secretary and an auditor, both of whom in the case of public companies must be members of a recognized professional body, specified in the Companies Acts.)

In the mid-1990s, of the 1.3 million companies registered in Britain, the overwhelming majority are "private" companies. There are only about 11,000 "public" companies, out of which about 2,000 are listed on the International Stock Exchange (as the London Stock Exchange is now known).

Until 1980, all companies were public companies unless they met the specific requirements that made them private companies. These were, basically, that the company had no more than 50 members (stockholders) and that it restricted its right to transfer its shares. Any company that was not registered as a private company was automatically a public company, of which there were until 1980 some 16,000. Under the 1980 Companies Act, the definitions were altered (and the number of public companies fell to about 8,000). Now companies are automatically private unless they meet the specific requirements that make them public. These are, basically, that the company's memorandum of association (the document that defines the existence of the company) states that it is to be a public company and that it has a share capital of not less than £50,000 (of which not less than £12,500 is to be paid up). Only public companies may have their securities listed; the minimum paid-up share capital of listed companies under the rules of the International Stock Exchange is £250,000.

Most of the material in this chapter is devoted to public companies, since these include all the companies whose securities are traded on the financial markets.

1.3 Accounting Standards: Present Conditions

1.3.1 *Statute Law*

The major accounting provisions of the 1985 Companies Act appear in Part VII of the act, in Sections 221–262. It is possible to read the original

1985 Companies Act without being aware of the changes made by the 1989 act. The relevant sections, with amendments noted, are summarized in Table 1.

The revised Section 262 (3), inserted into the 1985 act by Section 22 of the 1989 act (and expanded by paragraph 91 of Schedule 4) describes how "realized" profits and losses are to be defined in Part VII of the act and refers to "principles generally accepted," although it leaves this latter phrase undefined.

The 1989 act gave rise to a new Financial Reporting Council with the duty of overseeing the work of its three offshoots: the Accounting Standards Board (ASB), which replaced the ASC from June 1990, an Urgent Issues Task Force (UITF), and a Review Panel to consider departures from accounting standards and secure compliance (see Section 1.4 below).

The new Section 256(1), inserted by Section 19 of the 1989 act, contains the following provision in interpreting Part VII of the act (see Section 2.1 below):

> In this part "accounting standards" means statements of standard accounting principle issued by such body or bodies as may be prescribed by regulations.

Regulations laid down under the act have given the ASB this formal recognition, although in fact the ASB chose to use the name Financial Reporting Standards in place of the former Statements of Standard Accounting Practice. It remains possible for the Secretary of State to increase the formal authority of the ASB, its UITF, and the Review Panel still further in the future, by way of Statutory Instruments (which, unlike Acts of Parliament, do not require full debate by both Houses of Parliament).

Presumably, Statements of Standard Accounting Practice (SSAPs), that is, accounting standards issued between 1970 and 1990 by the ASC, and Financial Reporting Standards (FRSs), accounting standards issued by the ASB since 1990, are generally accepted by the accounting profession; however, it is unclear from the statutes just what status is enjoyed by the set of SSAPs and FRSs (listed below), and how the status of SSAPs has been altered under the 1989 Companies Act (see Section 1.4.1 below). There are certainly cases in which the provisions of existing SSAPs seem to conflict with practices permitted by the Companies Acts, for example, in the valuation of inventories (see Section 3.10.1 below) where the act permits the use of methods that SSAP 9 forbids.

TABLE 1 *Changes Introduced by the 1989 Companies Act*

S. 221 [S. 2] Companies must keep sufficient accounting records.

S. 222 [S. 2] These records must be available to the company's officers, and (in the case of a public company) kept for at least 6 years. The old 1985 S. 223, dealing with penalties for noncompliance, is now included in the revised S. 222.

S. 223–225 (S. 224–226) [S. 3] Company's financial year and accounting reference date.

S. 226 (S. 227 and part of S. 228) [S. 4] Duty to prepare annual accounts for the company in accordance with Schedule 4 of the act.

S. 227–230 (part of S. 228, S. 229-230) [S. 5] Duty to prepare group accounts in accordance with Schedule 4 of the act if the company is a parent company, with exemption for parent companies included in the accounts of larger groups.

S. 231 [S. 6] Disclosure in notes to the accounts of the details of related undertakings.

S. 232 (S. 232-234) [S. 6] Disclosure of directors' emoluments as set out in Schedule 6.

S. 233 (part of S. 235) [S. 7] Approval and signing of accounts.

S. 234 (part of S. 235) [S. 8] Directors' report as set out in Schedule 7.

S. 235–237 (S. 236–237) [S. 9] Auditors' report and duties.

S. 238–240 (S. 238–240, 246 & 254-255) [S. 10] Publication of accounts and members' rights to obtain copies.

S. 241–244 (S. 241–244) [S. 11] Directors' duty to lay and deliver accounts.

S. 245–245C (S. 245) [S. 12] Correction of defective accounts.

S. 246–250 (S. 247–251) [S. 14] Dormant companies.

S. 251 [S. 15] Power for directors to issue summary financial statements (in the case of listed companies).

S. 252–253 [S. 16] Rights for private company to dispense with laying of accounts before members.

S. 254 [S. 17] Exemptions for unlimited companies.

S. 255 (S. 257–262) [S. 18] Accounts of special category companies (in general, banking and insurance companies).

S. 256 [S. 19] The role of accounting standards.

S. 257 (S. 256) [S. 20] Power for the Secretary of State to alter accounting regulations.

S. 258 [S. 21] Definitions of parent and subsidiary undertaking.

S. 259–262 [S. 22] Definitions of the term *undertaking*, of *participating interest* and other matters.

Note: The former section numbers of the 1985 act are shown in parentheses, if they have been altered, and the sections of the 1989 act that have inserted these alterations are shown in square brackets.

1.4 The Accounting Standards Board, Urgent Issues Task Force, and Financial Reporting Review Panel

As noted, the former Accounting Standards Committee enjoyed a status that was loosely defined in company law. Created in 1970 as a result of financial scandals in the late 1960s, its major source of authority arose from its implicit recognition by law and from its position as a subcommittee of the Consultative Committee of Accountancy Bodies (the CCAB), comprising the six major U.K. professional accounting bodies (see Section 1.4.4 below). Its method of operation reflected this. The councils of each of the CCAB bodies had to adopt each SSAP before it could be issued in final form by the CCAB (although the power of veto was only used once in 20 years). It was up to the six bodies individually to enforce standards on their own members.

After the Dearing Report was issued in 1988, the government made major changes to the standard-setting process. An independent Financial Reporting Council was set up, consisting of about 30 members, each appointed in an individual capacity, of whom roughly half are from the accountancy profession and half from elsewhere, including government. Its members serve on a part-time basis, full meetings of the Council usually taking place twice a year. The executive functions are discharged by the ASB, the UITF, and the Review Panel.

The chairman and research director of the ASB serve full time, together with a technical staff mainly on short-term contracts, and a further seven part-time members of the Board. The ASB has the authority to publish standards in its own name. Its due process includes publishing exposure drafts and standards for comment, often after a discussion paper. Although the CCAB bodies are invited to comment, they have no veto. Enforcement is no longer left to the CCAB bodies.

The UITF is, constitutionally, a committee of the ASB. Its main role is "to assist the ASB in areas where an accounting standard or a Companies Act provision exists (including the requirement to give a true and fair view), but where unsatisfactory or conflicting interpretations have developed or seem likely to develop." The UITF forms a view within the framework of the law and existing ASB statements, and the stated views of the UITF are normally accepted by the ASB as having similar authority to its own. In case of any conflict, the ASB's views prevail.

The Financial Reporting Review Panel was set up one year later than the FRC and ASB. Its duties are outlined briefly at the end of the next section (Section 1.4.1).

Three features of the ASB's policies are worth particular note.

1. It has specifically stressed the need for accounting standards to lay down matters of principle rather than detailed legal prescriptions. It has also stated its wish to reduce the emphasis placed by analysts on a single "bottom line" accounting profit figure. (See also Section 1.4.6 on "Substance over Form".)

2. It has developed an explicit "conceptual framework," unlike its predecessor the ASC, in the form of a "Statement of Principles" published in 1994. This is discussed further in Section 4.1.

3. Greater distinction has come to be made, both in statute law and accounting standards, between larger and smaller companies. The old ASC held to the principle that disclosure standards might reasonably distinguish between large and small companies on the basis of size criteria, but recognition and valuation principles were universal. The ASB has never accepted the latter principle, and it has always been more concerned with public, particularly listed, companies. It is likely that separate accounting principles will develop for large and small companies. However, as noted earlier, this chapter is also concerned almost entirely with larger companies, so the issue is not pursued further here.

1.4.1 The True and Fair View

It is considered important by the British accounting profession that Section 226(2) of the 1985 act specifies:

The balance sheet shall give a true and fair view of the state of affairs of the company as at the end of the financial year; and the profit and loss account shall give a true and fair view of the profit or loss of the company for the financial year.

This implies that there exists such a thing as a "true and fair view," which can be recognized and shown by the accounts quite distinctly from the result that arises when accepted accounting principles are applied, as laid down in Schedule 4 of the 1985 act. In other words, the generally accepted principles are not sufficient to provide a "true and fair view," even though the accounts are required by law to present one. Section 226(4) reinforces this point:

> Where compliance with the provisions of that Schedule, and the other provisions of this Act as to the matters to be included in a company's individual accounts or in notes to those accounts, would not be sufficient to give a true and fair view, the necessary additional information shall be given in the accounts or in a note to them.

(Section 227 similarly requires group accounts to show a true and fair view of the affairs of the group.) Abstract 7 of the Urgent Issues Task Force (1992) sets out the information that must be disclosed when a company invokes this provision of the 1985 act. What is lacking is guidance as to the criteria for defining such a "true and fair view," and for recognizing when it is lacking. Given that accepted accounting principles must be used in any case, why does the act anticipate that such principles might be insufficient, particularly when augmented by the "other matters" required by the Act, referred to in Section 226(4)?

In 1993 the ASB published its "Foreword to Accounting Standards," which contains the statement (paragraph 16):

> Accounting standards are authoritative statements of how particular types of transaction and other events should be reflected in financial statements and accordingly compliance with accounting standards will normally be necessary for financial statements to give a true and fair view.

In an appendix to this foreword, an opinion of leading counsel (Hon. Mrs. Justice Arden) sets out her support for this statement, although it is made plain that the final arbiter must still be the court. There has still been no case to test the court's view since the 1989 Companies Act established the FRC and its satellite bodies. But as Judge Arden points out in her opinion, there is an increasingly strong presumption that since 1989 accounts that comply with standards present a true and fair view, and any departure requires specific justification. She quotes Schedule 4 paragraph 36A of the 1985 act (as amended by the 1989 act):

> It shall be stated whether the accounts have been prepared in accordance with applicable accounting standards and particulars of any material departure from those standards and the reasons for it shall be given.

Clearly the Review Panel reviews cases of noncompliance, for which purpose it is specifically authorized by the Secretary of State under the (revised) 1985 act. Some of these cases it identifies for itself (usually as a result of qualified audit reports or reported nondisclosure in company statements themselves), but more often they are referred to the Review Panel by individual or corporate third parties (including press commentators).

This review function gives the Review Panel powers to act as a form of quasi-judicial tribunal. In most cases it discusses matters privately with the company concerned rather than calling upon its formal powers to refer to matter to the Secretary of State or to the courts with a request that the court should order the defective accounts to be corrected (under Section 245 of the 1985 act). On the minority of occasions when the Review Panel has made a public statement on a concluded case, the company concerned has always complied with the panel's suggested treatment, and reference to the court has not been necessary. Since 1993, the panel has been more explicit in its public statements about the precise section of the 1985 Companies Act or the accounting standard at issue.

1.4.2 Statements of Standard Accounting Principle (SSAPs) and Financial Reporting Standards (FRSs)

Accounting principles evolve over time, and there is always the likelihood that new financial conditions and problems will arise in the future for which existing accounting principles present no satisfactory treatment. The need for SSAPs 4, 5, 8, 11, 20, 21, and 24 (listed below) all arose from changes in the business environment. Moreover, current accounting conventions exclude many aspects of economic importance to the business, such as the state of its order book, the technical knowledge of its staff and their ideas for new products, markets, and processes, potential sources of credit, and so on. Businesses are too complex for it to be possible to report every aspect of their affairs, but this makes it impossible to prescribe exactly what matters will be significant to readers from one year to the next. Hence, it is not possible to lay down exactly what will be necessary to convey a true and fair view.

Even though the precise legal status of SSAPs and FRSs is unclear, they are extensively used by company directors in preparing their accounts and by their professional staff, advisers, and auditors. Auditors also have a set of "accepted auditing standards," laid down by the CCAB Auditing Practices Board (although, just as with *GAAP*, the term *GAAS*, widely used in the United States, is not normally used in Britain). These auditing standards mainly describe established ways of handling difficult decisions that face auditors. As valuable as they are as a guide to auditor behavior, accepted auditing standards tend to leave to SSAPs and FRSs the resolution of many of the more difficult conceptual questions, such as "How does the realization principle work in this unfamiliar context?", "What is profit?", "How should joint costs be allocated and matched against revenues?", and "How should new financial instruments be accounted for?"

The list of SSAPs issued in Britain between 1970 and 1990 and FRSs since 1990 is a useful guide to those issues that accountants have needed to address as problem areas (see Table 2): The accounting standards can be divided into three groups—those that deal with disclosure issues; those that deal with uncontroversial new problems, sometimes including circumstances in which the standard requires an arbitrary choice; and those that affect the "bottom line" reported profit figure. Little controversy has arisen either with the first group, including SSAPs 3 and 18 and FRS 1, or the second group, including SSAPs 4 and 5, and they have been generally observed. By contrast, SSAPs 9 and 12, which are in the third group, have produced much disagreement, and there are many cases in which they have been disregarded. Historically, enforcement in these cases has been a major problem. The greatest pressure on accountants formerly came from the possibility of a court action, for example, against the auditor for negligence after a company's insolvency. Setting up the Review Panel in 1992 added a powerful new force for compliance in the case of listed companies.

1.4.3 EU Directives

The company law directives of the European Union have been adopted in British company law as they have fallen due. Britain claims a good record of compliance; thus, the Second Directive was implemented in the 1980 Companies Act, the Fourth Directive in the 1981 Companies Act, the Seventh and Eighth Directives in the 1989 Companies Act, and various

TABLE 2   SSAPs and FRSs Issued 1970–1994

SSAP 1 Associated companies

SSAP 2 Disclosure of accounting policies

SSAP 3 Earnings per share

SSAP 4 The accounting treatment of government grants

SSAP 5 Accounting for value added tax

SSAP 6[a] Extraordinary items and prior year adjustments

SSAP 7[a] Accounting for changes in the purchasing power of money

SSAP 8 The treatment of taxation under the imputation system

SSAP 9 Stocks and long-term contracts

SSAP 10[a] Statements of source and application of funds

SSAP 11[a] Accounting for deferred tax

SSAP 12 Accounting for depreciation

SSAP 13 Accounting for research and development

SSAP 14[a] Group accounts

SSAP 15 Accounting for deferred taxation

SSAP 16[a] Current cost accounting

SSAP 17 Accounting for post balance sheet events

SSAP 18 Accounting for contingencies

SSAP 19 Accounting for investment properties

SSAP 20 Foreign exchange translation

SSAP 21 Accounting for leases and hire purchase contracts

SSAP 22 Accounting for goodwill

SSAP 23 Accounting for acquisitions and mergers

SSAP 24 Accounting for pensions costs

SSAP 25 Segmental reporting

FRS 1 Cash flow statements

FRS 2 Accounting for subsidiary undertakings

FRS 3 Reporting financial performance

FRS 4 Capital instruments

FRS 5 Reporting the substance of transactions

FRS 6 Acquisitions and mergers

FRS 7 Fair values in acquisition accounting

[a] SSAPs 6, 7, 10, 11, 14, and 16 are no longer in force.

other provisions have been made elsewhere to anticipate directives while they were still in draft form.

Some members of the accounting profession in Britain are concerned about potential conflict between European regulations for financial reporting and those of the International Accounting Standards Committee (IASC). Britain tends to view corporate financial reporting rather differently than do some other European countries, taking a view much more similar to that in the United States, Canada, and Australia. Different philosophical traditions underlie the mainland European and international debates, although a degree of common understanding has grown over the years through such forums as the OECD Working Group on Accounting Standards.

The IASC (and its parent, the International Federation of Accountants, IFAC) tend, like British standard-setters, to take a utilitarian view of accounting disclosure, in which companies are expected to meet the information needs of groups of external decision makers (although in fact these groups and their decision models are poorly defined, and their supposed needs are linked only loosely to any standards set). When examined more closely, the "user needs" argument tends to collapse into mere rhetoric. Little empirical support is actually cited by standard-setters to show how the required information actually matches up with user needs. On the other hand, published accounts are seen as having a particularly important role to play in financial markets; equity capital is typically raised through the stock market, rather than through investment bankers, and the need for price-sensitive information to be published accurately and rapidly to all potential market transactors underlies much of the Anglo-American thinking about disclosure. Pressure for International Accounting Standards (IASs) originates largely from the perceived need for investors in worldwide securities markets to be able to make comparisons among companies reporting under different disclosure regulations.

1.4.4 The British Auditing Profession

The legal framework that regulates the auditing profession in Britain is set out in the 1985 Companies Act, Part XI, Chapter V (i.e., Sections 384–394) as amended by the 1989 Companies Act, Part II (i.e., Sections 24–54).

There are six major professional bodies of accountants, which co-ordinate many of their activities through a voluntary joint committee formed in 1970, the Consultative Committee of Accountancy Bodies (CCAB). The six tend to have different functional specialties, histories, and training traditions.

The authority to sign audit reports is restricted to those members of the ICAEW, ACCA, ICAS, and ICAI (see Table 3) who hold practicing certificates from their professional bodies, together with a number of practitioners who were authorized to audit under previous companies acts and who are now members of a separate Authorized Practitioners Association. Individuals and firms that meet the requirements to act as auditors are called "Registered Auditors," and they are supervised by their respective professional bodies.

Attempts to rationalize the British accountancy profession have been made ever since professional bodies first appeared in the nineteenth century. Many mergers have taken place, but an attempt to secure the merger of the six main bodies failed in 1970, after which the CCAB was itself formed to help produce some unity of purpose and policy. Other attempts since 1970 to merge some or all of the bodies have also so far failed.

From an auditing perspective, the most important CCAB committees have been the Accounting Standards Committee (until superseded by the

TABLE 3   *CCAB Bodies Showing Those Qualified to Audit under the Companies Acts*

Name	Membership	Audit?
Institute of Chartered Accountants in England and Wales (ICAEW)	110,000	Yes
Chartered Association of Certified Accountants (ACCA)	45,000	Yes
Chartered Institute of Management Accountants (CIMA)	36,000	No
Institute of Chartered Accountants of Scotland (ICAS)	14,000	Yes
Institute of Chartered Accountants in Ireland (ICAI)	9,000	Yes
Chartered Institute of Public Finance and Accountancy (CIPFA)	11,000	No

Accounting Standards Board, which stands outside the accounting profession) and the Auditing Practices Board (the status of which as an independent body is less autonomous than that of the ASB, since its business is more specifically concerned with the technical performance of auditors).

Relations are close and amicable between the Accounting Standards Board and the Auditing Practices Board and their respective international counterparts, the International Accounting Standards Committee and the International Auditing Practices Committee. Care is taken to ensure consistency between the standards that they each produce. Where conflict arises, the U.K. accounting and auditing standards prevail in Britain.

Despite some debate over the subject, the standard form of audit report in Britain takes a short form, generally just stating the basis for the audit opinion and confirming both that the audit has been completed in accordance with auditing standards and that the accounts show a true and fair view of the state of affairs of the company at its balance sheet date and of the profits for the period then ended. Statements are published both by the auditors and by the directors setting out their respective responsibilities in respect of the accounts. (Examples are shown with the accounts of Bunzl plc on pages 1004–1024.)

The question of the legal liability of the auditor is contentious. Although the audit report is presented by the auditors to the shareholders in general meeting, and attached to the annual report and accounts circulated and published, the auditor is in a contractual relationship only with the company and owes a common law duty of care to the shareholders only as a class. This still raises the possibility that the auditor owes a wider duty of care to other parties, although it appears that the courts take a narrow view. The subject is highly controversial, however, and the legal position is still not fully resolved.

1.4.5 *Company Finance and the Stock Market*

The main source of finance of British companies is retained earnings. The proportion of new capital raised from this source tends to vary with the state of the economy, but in aggregate it constitutes about 65% of the liabilities on corporate balance sheets. Long-term finance tends to come from stockholders, either from the proceeds of new stock issues or in the form of retained profits. Short-term finance tends to come from the banking sector. Banks in Britain have been reluctant to take major equity holdings since the nineteenth century, in contrast to the investment banking traditions of Japan and continental Europe. The banking sector is quite highly developed, with well-traded markets for all forms of security.

The heavy reliance of British companies on the stock market for long-term finance has resulted in a strong emphasis on published financial information for the use of investors. Unlike the United States, where the SEC has a prime responsibility to protect the interests of stock market investors, financial markets in Britain are largely self-regulating. The International Stock Exchange, like most of the other markets, is constituted as a private body run by its own membership, in this case the brokers who deal in stocks and shares. Whereas the government takes a close interest in the operations of financial markets, this is mainly channeled through the Bank of England, which as the government's banker has a special responsibility for financial affairs, playing an important role informally in overseeing self-regulation. Thus, the Accounting Standards Board reports to a Financial Reporting Council (the FRC), and it is quite natural for appointments to the chair of the FRC to be nominated jointly by the Governor of the Bank of England and the Secretary of State for Trade and Industry.

The Stock Exchange itself takes responsibility in Britain for supervising the rules for listing securities, which include the procedures for admission to listing and continuing obligations to regulate the conduct of companies after listing. The main source of information is the Stock Exchange "Yellow Book" a loose-leaf book that is updated at frequent and irregular intervals (for example, in 1993). The Stock Exchange is also one of the leading supporters of the City of London's "Panel on Take-overs and Mergers," whose offices are located in the Exchange and which publishes the "City Code on Take-overs and Mergers." The Stock Exchange is concerned to ensure that price-sensitive information about listed securities is made publicly available to all parties promptly, fairly, and accurately. Because this clearly includes accounting information, in the case of listed companies, Stock Exchange requirements must be heeded alongside statute law and FRC regulations. Stock Exchange requirements often go beyond the others, for example, in requiring the publication of half-yearly (unaudited) accounts covering the first 6 months of each financial year.

Although the Stock Exchange plays an important role in the regulation of listed companies, it has acquired a reputation for inactivity in enforcing accounting standards. Companies listed in the United Kingdom can at present file accounts with the Stock Exchange even though they do not comply with SSAPs and lack a clean audit report. This contrasts with the SEC in the United States, which would not accept accounts for filing if either condition were not fulfilled. The Stock Exchange is moving toward more active monitoring of filed accounts, including reference to the Review Panel.

1.4.6 Substance over Form

There has long been conflict between substance and form in British corporate reporting, particularly in respect of off-balance-sheet financing. To some degree the conflict is between the legal and accounting professions, with the lawyers tending to look to strict legal form and the accountants looking to substance. While it is beyond doubt that the courts have the authority to decide what is meant by a "true and fair" view in any particular set of circumstances, in practical terms it is mainly left to accountants to develop and apply the relevant rules, and it is clear that the ASB regards the exercise of professional judgment in relation to accounts to rest with the accounting profession rather than lawyers (a view exemplified in the treatment of assets in FRS 5). Thus, while the law insists that distributions can be made only out of "realized" profits, it is in practice left to accountants to decide what realization is to mean. Thus, for example, it seems to be legitimate for a company to realize profits on an asset by selling it to another company in the same group—perhaps a subsidiary—provided that there is a genuine transaction at no more than a fair market price. (Note that for the purposes of determining distributable profits it is the accounts of the individual company that matter, not group accounts. Unrealized intergroup profits must still be removed from group accounts. Thus, the parent company may be able to declare dividends larger than reported group profits.)

Taxation plays a much looser role in relation to published company accounts in Britain than it does in most other European countries. The income figures that appear in published accounts are regarded by the

Inland Revenue as the starting point for adjustments to arrive at the taxable profit. It is virtually impossible to reconcile, by using the information provided in published accounts, the amount of a company's current tax charge with its reported profit figures.

It used to be thought that taxation was an area in which form always dominated over substance, so that the strict letter of the law could be relied upon to prevail. However, the courts have held that transactions that were set up merely as devices to avoid tax could be set aside by looking through the form to the underlying purpose. The application of the principle of substance over form to tax matters has since been questioned, however, and there exists an uneasy tension in this area, as in so many others.

1.4.7 *The Cadbury Report on the Financial Aspects of Corporate Governance*

The Cadbury Committee (so named after its chairman, Sir Adrian Cadbury) was set up in May 1991 by the FRC and the accountancy profession, together with the Stock Exchange, to review "the financial aspects of corporate governance," with specific reference to listed companies. Its final report in December 1992 set out a 19-point Code of Best Practice. From mid-1993 it became mandatory under the Stock Exchange Listing Agreement for reporting companies to state their compliance with the Code and explain any noncompliance; auditors "review" compliance with these requirements in areas in which relatively objective evidence can be secured. The Code includes the following main provisions: companies were to establish effective audit committees within 2 years; directors' contracts were to be limited to a maximum of 3 years; interim reports were to be expanded to include balance sheets, and were to be subject to "review" by the auditors (not a full audit); nonaudit fees paid to auditors were to be disclosed and rotation of audit partners formalized to increase independence; and directors were to publish a statement each year declaring that the company's system of internal control is sound and that the company is a going concern. Emphasis was placed in particular on the role of nonexecutive directors (at least three) to act as independent monitors of board performance, with special responsibilities for the nomination of directors, remuneration, and the audit committee.

2. The Form and Content of Published Financial Statements

2.1 Companies Act Schedules and "Formats"

The 1985 Companies Act, Part VII (Sections 221–262 of the act) provides regulations governing accounts and audit. The 1989 Companies Act, Part I (Sections 1–23) amends the 1985 act in some important ways.

Schedules 4–10 of the 1985 act, amended quite extensively by the 1989 act, are printed at the end of the act and set out further details, covering the following matters:

- Schedule 4—the form and content of the accounts
- Schedule 4A—the form and content of group accounts
- Schedule 5—disclosure of information: related undertakings
- Schedule 6—disclosure of information: emoluments and other benefits of directors and others
- Schedule 7—the matters to be dealt with in the directors' report
- Schedule 8—the accounts that may be filed by companies qualifying as small or medium sized
- Schedule 9—the form and content of "special category" accounts, which are, in general, the accounts of banking and insurance companies
- Schedule 10—the matters to be dealt with in the directors' report attached to "special category" accounts
- Schedule 10A—parent and subsidiary undertakings: supplementary provisions

Note that the schedules are still known by the numbers given to them by the 1985 act, even though they have been amended by the 1989 act.

2.1.1 Schedule 4 Formats

Schedule 4 of the 1985 act lays down formats for the presentation of the balance sheet and profit and loss account, as discussed below.

The Balance Sheet   The schedule contains two alternative formats for the balance sheet, which differ in order. Format 1 is designed for the presentation of a balance sheet in vertical form, beginning (in contrast with American practice) with fixed assets and continuing with current assets before external liabilities and provisions are deducted to produce the components of stockholders' equity. Format 2 is designed for the older two-sided form of presentation, which in Britain traditionally presented liabilities on the left and assets on the right. It is now less commonly used, but assets are now to appear on the left and liabilities on the right. There is little difference in content except for the way that Format 1 separates into different places the creditors falling due within one year from those falling due in one year or more.

The Profit and Loss Account   The profit and loss account formats also differ according to whether they present a vertical or two-sided format. Format 1 requires the following items:

1. Turnover
2. Cost of sales
3. Gross profit or loss
4. Distribution costs
5. Administration expenses
6. Other operating income
7. Income from shares in group companies
8. Income from shares in related companies
9. Income from other fixed asset investments
10. Other interest receivable and similar income
11. Amounts written off investments
12. Interest payable and similar charges
13. Tax on profit or loss on ordinary activities
14. Profit or loss on ordinary activities after taxation
15. Extraordinary income
16. Extraordinary charges

17. Extraordinary profit or loss
18. Tax on extraordinary profit or loss
19. Other taxes not shown under the above items
20. Profit or loss for the financial year

Format 3 requires the above items, but in two-sided form.

Format 2 requires the following items:

1. Turnover
2. Change in stocks of finished goods and in work in progress
3. Own work capitalized
4. Other operating income
5. (*a*) Raw materials and consumables; and (*b*) other external charges
6. Staff costs: (*a*) wages and salaries; (*b*) social security costs; and (*c*) other pension costs
7. (*a*) Depreciation and other amounts written off tangible and intangible fixed assets; and (*b*) exceptional amounts written off current assets
8. Other operating charges

(Items 9–22 of Format 2 are identical to items 7–20 of Format 1.)

Format 4 presents the same headings as Format 2, only in two-sided form.

2.1.2 Group Accounts

Section 277 of the 1985 Companies Act, amended by Section 5 of the 1989 Companies Act, requires that any parent company shall, as well as preparing individual accounts, prepare group accounts. These comprise a consolidated balance sheet dealing with the state of affairs of the parent company and its subsidiary undertakings and also a consolidated profit and loss account dealing with the profit and loss of the parent company and its subsidiary undertakings. It is also required by FRS 1 (although not by law) to present a group cash flow statement. Under Section 5(4), however, the parent company does not usually need to publish its own separate profit and loss account but merely the consolidated profit and loss account. Small companies are exempt from the need to prepare group accounts under Section 248 of the 1985 act.

The 1989 Companies Act (elaborated in some areas by FRS 2) significantly altered the definition of the terms *parent* and *subsidiary*. The usual rule under the old legislation was that a company was a parent if it owned more than 50% of the shares in another company, its subsidiary. There was also an alternative rule that made it a parent if it was a member of the subsidiary and controlled the composition of its board of directors, even though it might not own more than 50% of its shares. Shares in the subsidiary that are not owned by the parent company are described as the "minority interest." Under the new legislation, the rules were extended. Now the law relates to "undertakings" that might include not only companies but also unincorporated entities. Moreover, the main criterion is now whether control is exercised. It is even possible for a parent undertaking to own no shares at all in the subsidiary (e.g., where it controls shares through a trust), and this requires the inclusion of the subsidiary in consolidated accounts even though no income comes directly to the parent. (This makes the use of the term *minority* to describe the outside shareholding rather odd, since here the "minority" would own all of the shares.)

When a company does not exercise control over another undertaking but still exercises a significant influence over it, the relationship may well give the company a "participating interest" under Section 22 of the 1989 act. Since 1970 there has been a requirement under SSAP 1 for what were then called "associated companies" to be treated differently from subsidiaries and from other investments in shares. These former rules are now reflected closely in the 1985 Companies Act, but the term *associated company* is replaced by the term *related company*, and since 1989 by *related undertaking*. The participating interest is presumed to arise where a company owns 20% or more of the shares in another undertaking. (Because it is described as having shares, this suggests the other undertaking is a company, but a partnership, for example, could also have shares.)

There are thus three tiers of intercompany investment: (*a*) where a company owns a controlling interest in a subsidiary; (*b*) where it holds a participating interest and over which it exercises significant influence; and (*c*) where it holds an interest too small to give it significant influence.

As stated above, Case *a* normally leads to the preparation of consolidated accounts, and is discussed in Section 3.1 below. Cases *b* and *c* are discussed in more detail in Section 3.9 below.

2.1.3 Additional Statements Required by FRS 3, and the "Operating and Financial Review"

FRS 3 seeks to make the income statement more informative. Not only does it require a fuller analysis of the results from continuing operations distinct from discontinued operations, but it also requires presentation of a "Statement of Total Recognized Gains and Losses" (to eliminate movements direct to reserves, by-passing the income statement), a "Note of Historical Cost Profits and Losses" (where any assets or liabilities are carried at values different from historical cost), and a "Reconciliation of Movements in Shareholders' Funds." (See the specific accounts, page 1001.)

Since publication of the Cadbury Report, the ASB has required listed companies to include a yearly Operating and Financial Review, somewhat similar to that required in the United States.

2.2 A Specimen Set of Published Financial Statements

Shown on pages 998–1018 is a specimen set of accounts for a British company, Bunzl plc, for the year ended December 31, 1993. These are preceded by a directors' report, conforming to the headings set out in the Companies Act, and a 5-year financial summary (common but not obligatory). The statutory accounts comprise the group's consolidated profit and loss account, group balance sheet and group cash flow statement, the parent company's own balance sheet, the statement of accounting policies, and notes to the accounts. There follows a list of principal subsidiaries, the auditors' report, and (not obligatory) the main dates in the financial calendar. Bunzl plc does not have a full listing in the United States; however, it has a number of U.S. investors and so it also shows its consolidated profit and loss account and balance sheet converted into U.S. dollars, although prepared under U.K. generally accepted accounting principles.

2.3 Main Features of the 1993 Bunzl Accounts

The set of accounts reproduced here excludes almost half the volume contained in the published annual report. In particular, it does not reproduce the Chairman's Statement, nor the Chief Executives' reviews of the five principal operating divisions. These latter statements fall outside the basic minimum requirements of the Companies Acts, although most listed companies in Britain provide them.

Note that the group's 5-year summary reveals 1993 to have been a good year, with turnover up by 16% on 1992, and operating profit up by 12.5%. Profit for the financial year is even more sharply up, with a rise in earnings per share from 5.6p to 8.3p.

One of the major features of FRS 3, "Reporting Financial Performance," is its stress on the need to separate in the profit and loss account the results of continuing operations (including acquisitions) from those of discontinued operations. As a minimum, such an analysis must include the turnover and operating profit attributable to each of these two main classes. One effect of this has been to remove substantial amounts of past turnover and profits from the 5-year analysis. In the case of Bunzl, the trend of sales, in particular, is markedly different, depending upon whether "total sales" or "continuing" sales are observed.

Immediately following the Consolidated Cash Flow Statement, there appears a page setting out the three statements required by FRS 3 (see Section 2.1.3).

Dividends have been raised modestly. There is no requirement to publish a figure showing the maximum amount that legally can be paid out by way of dividend. Company law is complex in this area, but it is important to bear in mind that distributable profits are defined on the basis of the accounts of the company that pays the dividend and not the consolidated accounts of the group. Thus, the item "Movements on Reserves" shown in Note 21 indicates retained group profits of £84.5 million at the end of 1993, but the parent company Bunzl plc only shows £45.0 million (of which £10.3 million is described at the foot of Note 21 as not being available for distribution). Nevertheless, dividends of £17.3 million paid and proposed by Bunzl are less than the dividends receivable from subsidiaries of £27.7 million for the year, while group retained profits themselves rose over the year from £66.6 million to £84.5 million. Note 21 also comments that the "special reserve" of £177.2 million in the parent company balance sheet is not distributable. It is worth remembering that British practice is to show dividends declared in the year (out of earnings), whether they have been paid already or remain to be paid as a "final dividend" for the year (included in accounts payable at the year end).

At the end of the Directors' Report is an analysis of ordinary shareholdings, showing sizes of holdings and also types of holder. This is common practice among listed companies but not obligatory. Bunzl is typical of British listed companies in having a large fraction of private individuals among its total number of shareholders (80%), but their holdings represent only a small fraction of the company's equity (5%).

One of the effects of FRS 3 was to reduce drastically the number of items reported as "extraordinary items" in the profit and loss account. As is currently the case in most British companies, no such items are reported in 1993.

The consolidated balance sheet shows (again in Note 21) a credit balance of £16.2 million within its reserves under the heading "merger reserve." This includes £14.7 million written off during 1993 by way of goodwill on acquisitions. To date there is no obligation for purchased goodwill to be written off against revenue earnings. Note 21 observes that £201.9 million has been "written off" by the end of 1993, but it is safe to assume that this has all been charged against reserves rather than profits.

The term *merger reserve* has no statutory force, but it is generally used where merger relief has been claimed under Section 131 of the 1985 Companies Act (see Section 3.1.1) following a pooling of interests in which at least 90% of the equity in another company has been acquired. The purpose of Section 131 is to relieve acquiring companies from the need to create a "Share Premium Account" (a compulsory reserve where shares are issued for a consideration greater than their nominal value). Such a share premium account could otherwise be needed to record the "fair value" of shares issued above nominal value where these have been used to buy the capital of another company.

2.4 Important Notes to the 1993 Bunzl Accounts

Note 1 shows the segmental analysis of sales, operating profit, and net operating assets for the years 1993 and 1992. As required by SSAP 25, the total figure for net operating assets is reconciled to the net assets shown in the consolidated balance sheet.

Note 2 shows an analysis of net operating costs broken down into rather greater detail between continuing operations, acquisitions, and discontinued operations than the minimum requirements of FRS 3.

Note 5, "Taxation," shows, as required by SSAP 15, the charge for U.K. and overseas taxes on income for the year, supplemented by an amount for deferred tax. As usual with U.K. companies, it is not possible to determine exactly how the tax charges have been computed, nor to reconcile them with the income figures shown.

In accordance with the current provisions of SSAP 15, deferred tax must be provided only to the extent that it is expected that an actual liability or asset will crystallize in some future period. However, paragraph 34 of SSAP 15 requires U.K. reporting companies to show by way of a note "the amount of any unprovided deferred tax in respect of the period...analyzed into its major components." Thus, it is possible to calculate the amount that would have been charged on a "full provision" (or "comprehensive allocation") basis. Bunzl does not specifically show such a figure, but it is possible to deduce the relevant movement in reserves (see Notes 19 and 22). U.K. companies also show how much would appear in the accumulated "deferred taxation provision" if provision were made on a comprehensive basis; in Bunzl's case this is obtained by adding the upper and lower halves of Note 22, which also points out that no provision is made for any potential corporation tax liability on unrealized revaluation surpluses in respect of properties where it is expected that those properties will be held for the foreseeable future.

Note 25 shows that the company's pension schemes were overfunded. It is reported toward the bottom of Note 21 that "cumulative unrealized profits of £10.3m (1992: £11.2m) relating to pension costs have been included in the profit and loss account." This is not regarded as distributable, and none has been included in the earnings for the year.

Contingent liabilities (Note 24) shows that substantial parent company guarantees have been given for group company bank borrowing.

The Bunzl accounts provide an example of good British practice; further points are noted in Section 3 below.

3. Accounting Policies and Practices in Valuation and Measurement

It was noted earlier that Sections 226, 227, and 256 of the 1985 act (as inserted by Sections 4, 5, and 19 of the 1989 act) map out the role of accounting standards by reference to Schedule 4 of the act. Schedule 4 includes, in Parts I to VII, a great deal of information within forty dense pages. This is particularly true of Part II, "Accounting Principles and Rules."

Whereas most companies in Britain publish their accounts using historical costs, that is, on the basis set out in Part II, Section B, of the "Historical Cost Accounting Rules," they also have the power to elect to use current value accounting rules, as set out in Part II, Section C, "Alternative Accounting Rules." Previous Companies Acts have generally tried to avoid restricting the power that directors have to use any of a variety of valuation bases in preparing their accounts, and the 1985 act seeks to preserve their discretion. The 1985 act now states that fixed assets must be valued at either their purchase price or production cost, or otherwise (under the "Alternative Accounting Rules") at current value (which includes both current market value and also "current costs," a term discussed in greater detail shortly). These Alternative Accounting Rules specify that, where the Rules are adopted, all intangible fixed assets except for goodwill should be valued at their "current cost."

Companies thus have discretion whether to use the usual historical cost valuation rules and show the original purchase price or production costs of their tangible fixed assets or to adopt the Alternative Accounting Rules, whether for some or all of their fixed assets, and to revalue them to some subsequent market value or "current cost."

No rule determines how often a fixed asset must be revalued, or if it is to be revalued at all. The rules for valuing investments are even more broadly permissive. They may be valued "on any basis which appears to the directors to be appropriate in the circumstances of the company" (1985 Act, Schedule 4 Part II, paragraph 31 (3)(b)). (See also Section 3.5 below for further discussion of the valuation of property, plant, and equipment, Section 3.8 for intangible fixed assets, and Section 3.9 for fixed asset investments, that is, equity investments in other companies that are not subsidiaries.)

The term *current cost* used in the Alternative Accounting Rules has a special meaning, arising out of 14 years of debate between about 1970 and 1984 over how to present accounts under conditions of inflation. In 1974 there was apparent consensus among accountants for the use of general price level adjusted historical costs (called in Britain "current purchasing power" or "constant purchasing power," abbreviated as CPP accounting). However, just as the CCAB bodies were adopting SSAP 7, "Changes in the Purchasing Power of Money," in 1974, the government set up its own Committee on Inflation Accounting. In 1975 this committee published its report (known as the Sandilands Report), which totally rejected the use of general price adjusted accounts and recommended instead a rather complex alternative, to be known as current cost accounting (CCA).

CCA is basically a replacement cost system, but it rejects the idea of using current replacement costs for valuing all assets since, it was argued, there are some assets in any balance sheet that are unlikely to be replaced, which should then be valued at the higher of their net realizable value and their discounted net present value. There were several attempts to produce a workable standard, but eventually a set of CCA rules was put into effect in 1980 in a temporary SSAP, "Current Cost Accounting." These rules were discontinued after a 3-year experimental period.

The set of rules in SSAP 16 was designed to show in a supplementary income statement a figure for "CCA profit" attributable to stockholders after maintaining intact the physical operating capacity of the business. Beginning with the historical cost profit figure, a supplementary CCA profit and loss account showed additional charges required to bring up to current cost levels the cost of goods sold and the year's provision for depreciation. In addition, there was an extra charge to maintain monetary working capital at a real level, thus showing an entity's CCA operating profit after maintaining the firm's operating capability intact. Finally, SSAP 16 included a complex "gearing adjustment" designed to show the share of the additional charges above those that were attributable to assets financed by loan capital (and thus not necessary to maintain the physical capital financed by stockholders' capital).

A handbook of guidance on CCA was published in 1985; however, few companies now use CCA. The main exception is the group of newly privatized utilities that must negotiate with regulatory bodies over price fixing, and thus have to justify their prices. These companies use CCA for this purpose, to reduce their reported profits and increase their capital employed. The only significant company that still publishes its financial accounts on a CCA basis is British Gas.

3.1 Group Accounts

By the 1985 Companies Act Section 227(3) (as amended by the 1989 act Section 5), a company that is a parent company shall, as well as preparing individual accounts, prepare group accounts:

> The accounts shall give a true and fair view of the state of affairs as at the end of the financial year, and the profit or loss for the financial year, of the undertakings included in the consolidation as a whole, so far as concerns members of the company.

The group accounts must comply with the provisions of Schedule 4A with regard to form and content, as set out in Schedule 2 to the 1989 act. In fact, the formats are virtually the same for consolidated accounts as for individual company accounts. The 1989 act made some important changes to the law on group accounts, in particular by broadening the definition of a group as required by the European Seventh Directive, so that the key criterion is now control rather than ownership. It is now possible for certain partnerships and unincorporated joint ventures to come within consolidation requirements, so the statute now refers not to subsidiary "companies" but to subsidiary "undertakings."

Small and medium-sized groups are now exempt from the requirement to file group accounts by Sections 248–249 of the 1985 act (as amended by Section 13 of the 1989 act). Similarly, a company that is a subsidiary of a parent company within any European Union state is exempt from the need to file group accounts.

The U.K. profession has an accounting standard (FRS 2) on group accounts. This is quite short, and it adds some guidance to the statute law. FRS 5 further broadens the definition of a subsidiary undertaking to include "quasi subsidiaries," based on wider definitions of control.

3.1.1 Methods of Consolidation

The acquisition, that is, purchase, method is generally used to prepare group accounts, in which the cost of acquiring control of a subsidiary is compared with the fair value of assets acquired at that time. Merger (i.e., pooling) is used under certain conditions, discussed further in Section 3.1.4 and does not involve the use of fair values. Where the purchase is effected by the use of nonmonetary assets (usually by the issue of shares) these assets are to be valued at their fair value unless the pooling method is used. This typically means that the shares are deemed to be issued at a value in excess of par, so that a share premium or paid-in surplus arises. There is no statutory guidance as to the meaning of fair value, but it means open market value both for the consideration given and the assets acquired. In general, this means valuing securities at their open market value on the day that the offer becomes unconditional; any other nonmonetary assets given as consideration will be valued at their realizable value or, if they are to be replaced, at their replacement cost. Assets and liabilities acquired should be identified and valued by using the acquirer's accounting policies and should employ the lower of current replacement cost at the date of acquisition and the amounts recoverable from the ownership of the assets (by sale or use). The ASB insists in its FRS 7, "Fair Values in Acquisition Accounting," that the calculation of fair value at acquisition should not take into account any provisions for future operating losses or reorganization costs (including plant closure costs) that may follow the acquisition. Any such future costs must be expensed against future earnings, not written off against any reserves (such as share premium on new issues of stock) created at the time of the acquisition. The difference between the cost of the acquisition and the value acquired is regarded as "goodwill" in the consolidated accounts.

Profits made by subsidiaries before takeover are regarded as part of the equity acquired; profits made after takeover are treated as part of group profits, after deduction of any amount due to minority stakeholders in the subsidiary. Unrealized intercompany profits within the group are eliminated from group accounts, whether on current or fixed assets transferred.

Several areas of group accounting practice are uncertain under current British practice; for example, it is not clear whether the elimination of unrealized intercompany profits within the group means in principle removing the whole profit recorded by the supplying member of the group or whether it is only necessary to eliminate that part that relates to the group while allowing that part relating to minority shareholders to remain. Suppose a 75% owned subsidiary has realized £100,000 of profits on the sale of goods still held within the group. Is it necessary to mark down the inventory by £100,000 or by £75,000? Viewing the group as a single business entity dictates the first treatment, but a strict proprietary view might say that there is no reason why the minority shareholders' interest should be reduced by £25,000 as well as the group's share of £75,000. In practice, 100% elimination is usually adopted, since the group accounts are not prepared for the benefit of minority shareholders (who look instead to their company's own separate set of accounts). This treatment is consistent with a requirement of FRS 2 that insists that no goodwill should be attributed to the minority interest.

3.1.2 Proportional Consolidation

Although proportional consolidation has never been adopted for use in preparing group accounts in Britain, its use was suggested in Exposure Draft (ED) 50 in 1990 for use in the case of unincorporated joint ventures. The same treatment was advocated in the 1990 ASB "Interim Statement: Consolidated Accounts." A 1994 ASB discussion paper, "Associates and Joint Ventures," formally rejects proportional consolidation for joint ventures (termed "strategic alliances"), whether incorporated or not. But the "expanded equity method" proposed has much the same results, except with more disclosure.

Some responses to ED 50 argued against this on the grounds that the full consolidation of joint ventures would be more informative, but proportional consolidation has become accepted practice since then. Until the 1989 Companies Act, it was not essential to report any more about unincorporated joint ventures than the cost of the investment and the income actually received.

3.1.3 Goodwill

The accounting treatment of goodwill is still a matter of controversy in Britain. For several years, under SSAP 22 companies had the option either to write off goodwill by amortization against income or to write it off (eliminate it) against reserves, the latter being presented as the preferred treatment. ED 47 "Accounting for Goodwill" proposed that goodwill should be written off over its expected life, not to exceed 20 years except where, in unusual circumstances, reasons can be established for it to be written off over up to 40 years. Whereas the rules under SSAP 22 used to prefer elimination against reserves, without specifying which reserves could be used for the purpose, the ASB is considering the prohibition of this in its future accounting standard on the subject. The matter is bound to be tested at some stage in the courts. It has been normal treatment to use any reserve for eliminating goodwill, unless there is specific prohibition by law (as in the case of the share premium account and, probably, any revaluation reserve). The Bunzl accounts presented in the appendix to this chapter show goodwill written off against the merger reserve; you will see that this leaves a credit balance separately reported in note 21 to the accounts.

It is not permissible to capitalize self-generated goodwill, for example, value created by advertising products or training employees. SSAP 22, paragraph 28 specifically rules out the inclusion of nonpurchased goodwill in the balance sheets of companies or groups.

In the case of purchased goodwill, an intangible asset may arise either in the group accounts on consolidation or in the books of the acquiring company after transfer of the assets of the company acquired when it is not proposed to operate the acquired company as a subsidiary. Rather than buying the equity capital of another company, it is often the practice in Britain to buy just the assets, thus avoiding any residual risks and claims such as product indemnity liabilities that may attach to the other party. The problem of accounting for intangibles in company accounts is discussed further in Section 3.8. The more common problem arises in the case of goodwill on consolidation.

The ASB has expressed its preferred view that goodwill on consolidation should be written off against profits over a limited period. The profits that must be used for the purpose are the group profits arising after consolidation and not the profits of the parent company. Because profits available for dividend are defined in terms of the accounts of an individual company and not the group accounts, the restriction placed on the parent is limited. There is, however, a considerable risk that group profits will appear lower than the parent's distributable profits where large amounts of goodwill are be written off the former only. The issue is one of some importance in Britain, where takeover activity is relatively high. The

SSAP 22 rules for goodwill accounting were broadly permissive; if the rules are altered to require write-off against profits, it may deter takeovers, produce renewed opposition to the Accounting Standards Board, and lessen the attractions of the British capital market.

3.1.4 Pooling

Merger accounting (i.e., pooling) was permitted by SSAP 23, where companies came together without material resources leaving the group on acquisition. Similar principles appear in FRS 6, "Acquisitions and Mergers." There is some potential confusion, since provisions described as being for merger relief have appeared separately in both SSAP 23 and FRS 6 and also in the 1985 and 1989 Companies Acts (now in the amended Section 131 of the 1985 act). Note that the criteria in the act are different from those in either SSAP 23 or FRS 6.

The merger provisions in Section 131 are intended to relieve companies that make an acquisition by a new issue of shares from the need to set up a share premium account (i.e., a form of compulsory, nondistributable reserve that represents the excess of issue consideration over nominal value). Section 131 allows companies to value the shares given as consideration at their nominal value and not at fair market value, thus avoiding, entirely or in part, the need to create a share premium account. Section 131 also allows them to value the assets acquired at those values at which they were carried in the books of the former owner, which helps to limit the amount that needs to appear as goodwill.

In fact, it is often the case that acquisitive companies that are able to claim merger relief actually use acquisition accounting for those very same deals. Instead of showing a credit to "share premium account," however, they credit "merger reserve" with the excess of fair value over nominal value of shares issued. This merger reserve is then regarded as a proper place to write off goodwill on acquisition. In some cases, the debit balance shows that goodwill written off exceeds the credit balance created. (Indeed, this has been true of Bunzl plc in past years.) The resulting debit balance is then deducted from other credit balances shown under equity.

The merger criteria in SSAP 23 and FRS 6 do not have quite the same coverage. It would be reasonable to assume that merger accounting under

SSAP 23 or FRS 6 would have to be applied in all cases where merger relief is obtained under Section 131. This is not the case, however; indeed, SSAP 23 and FRS 6 do not permit merger accounting in certain cases where Section 131 has permitted "merger relief." The conditions for merger accounting are defined more narrowly.

3.1.5 Related Undertakings

Group accounts do not merely incorporate the financial affairs of subsidiary companies. There are other investments in the equity capital of other companies that need to be reported. Accounting for "related undertakings" arises when the shareholding is more than 20% but less than 50% of the shares in another company (or, less frequently, when substantial influence is exercised over its policies even though the percentage shareholding falls outside the 20%–50% limits). There may also be investments in other companies that give ownership of less than 20% of share capital. Both these types of investment will be considered in Section 3.9.

3.2 Foreign Currency Translation

SSAP 20 addresses the translation of foreign currencies in two stages. First the financial statements are prepared for the individual companies within the group, and any transactions conducted in foreign currency are translated. Then, as a second stage, consolidated accounts are prepared for the group as a whole, with translation of the complete financial statements of foreign enterprises that are part of the group.

3.2.1 Foreign Currencies in Individual Company Accounts

Foreign currency transactions are translated into the home currency of each company at the exchange rate ruling at the date of the transaction. At the balance sheet date, monetary assets and liabilities that are denominated in a foreign currency are translated at the closing rate as of that date. Nonmonetary assets are not restated but left at the conversion rate ruling as of the date they were originally recorded.

Differences on exchange are included in the profit and loss account for the year, as ordinary items except for any gain or loss arising from translation of an extraordinary item (which will be included as part of the extraordinary item). In the case of long-term monetary items, exchange gains and losses are usually taken into the profit or loss for the year; however, where there are doubts about the convertibility or marketability of the currency concerned, it may be prudent to defer recognizing such gains if the item is not yet due for settlement.

Special rules apply under SSAP 20, where investment in a foreign enterprise is financed by foreign borrowings, so that the investment is effectively "hedged" against exchange risks. In such cases, and in variants that have a similar effect, exchange gains and losses may be passed through reserves rather than the profit and loss account of individual companies.

3.2.2 Foreign Currencies in Group Accounts

Once the accounts for the individual enterprises have been drawn up in local currency, it is time to prepare the consolidated accounts, normally in the currency of the country in which the parent company is based. As SSAP 20, paragraph 13 states:

> The method used to translate financial statements for consolidation purposes should reflect the financial and other operational relationships which exist between an investing company and its foreign enterprises.

The standard refers to "foreign enterprises" here, rather than related companies, since the rules relate not only to subsidiaries but also to associates and even foreign branches (which may be closely integrated into the activities of the investing company or may be quite autonomous).

The closing rate/net investment method is normally used. The investment in the foreign enterprise is represented by the net worth held by the parent, rather than by the individual assets and liabilities. Such investment will usually take the form of a holding of equity capital, but it may also be in the form of a long-term loan.

The foreign enterprise will probably have its own local borrowings, which will be repaid without having an impact on its parent overseas. The balance sheet will be translated by using the exchange rate at the balance sheet date. On the other hand, when it comes to translating items in the profit and loss account, it is permissible to choose either the closing rate or an average rate for the year, provided that whichever is selected is used consistently from one year to the next. Exchange gains or losses arising on transactions carried out by the investing company or the foreign enterprises will appear in its own profit and loss account before consolidation. But differences on exchange that arise in the course of preparing the consolidated accounts should be taken to reserves, not to the profit and loss account.

SSAP 20 recognizes that sometimes the business activities of a foreign enterprise are so closely linked to those of the investing company that the use of the closing rate/net investment method would be misleading. In such cases it is permissible to use the temporal method (broadly, using the translation methods for the individual company referred to in Section 3.2.1).

The Bunzl accounts show a statement of the company's policy on foreign exchange translation in its Statement of Accounting Policies (item (f) "foreign currencies").

3.3 Capital and Reserves

3.3.1 Share Capital

The Companies Acts specify in detail the information that must be shown in respect of share capital, both in the balance sheet and in notes to the accounts.

3.3.2 Reserves

For many years company directors in Britain had discretion to use the term *capital reserve* to describe any credit balances that the directors regarded as nondistributable, including unrealized revaluation surpluses. The term *revenue reserve* is used to describe profits that could in principle be regarded as available for distribution. The designations were terms of art rather than matters of strict legal precision, conventional terms that enabled directors to signal to shareholders and others just how much might be distributed as future dividends (revenue reserves) and how much needed to be retained in the business, either as a matter of legal necessity (e.g., in the form of "share premiums," which cannot by law be distributed) or as a matter of sound business practice.

The 1948 Companies Act made specific reference to "capital" and "revenue" reserves, as well as defining what was meant by "provisions" and "reserves." These definitions have disappeared from later Companies Acts, which is a pity since they were quite helpful. Current usage is summarized below.

Common terminology used in Britain distinguishes among:

1. Expenses for a period, recorded in the books when the supplier's invoice was received

2. Accruals, the cost of which can be determined quite accurately, even though no invoice has yet been received and recorded

3. Provisions, which are estimates of costs for the current period, even though they cannot be determined with substantial accuracy

4. Reserves, which do not relate to costs of the current period but represent sums set aside out of the profits of the period to provide for future growth or for unknown contingencies

In addition to the figures that appear in the accounts, there may also be estimates shown by way of notes to the accounts to reflect contingent liabilities, those that fall due to be met if some event comes about beyond the control of the company (see also Section 3.4 below).

Although the term *capital reserves* is no longer in use, companies may set up accounts called "general reserves" or "asset replacement reserves" if they wish to earmark some part of the retained profits for permanent retention in the company. These accounts may be shown in the balance sheet formats under the heading "Reserves provided for by the articles of association." Any credit balance on the "profit and loss account" can usually be regarded as potentially distributable, although in many companies the balance is in fact too large for it to be distributed without harming the operations of the business. Moreover, such a balance does not necessarily represent the maximum amount that legally could be distributed (see Section 3.3.5 below). Retained profits are usually the major source of capital, averaging more than 65% among British companies. (In the Bunzl accounts, it represents only 35% of net assets in the consolidated balance sheet and considerably less in the parent company balance sheet.) "Revaluation reserves" will be discussed briefly in Section 3.3.7.

3.3.3 Ordinary Earnings and Extraordinary Items

Another important distinction was made formerly between "ordinary" and "extraordinary" earnings, as reported in the income statement. SSAP 6, "Extraordinary Items and Prior Year Adjustments," published in 1974 and revised in 1986, gave rise to a great deal of difficulty, mainly because of the imprecise definitions of the terms used and the fact that "extraordinary items" were taken into the income statement after the ordinary earnings figure used to calculate earnings per share (EPS) under SSAP3. (Further reference is made to SSAP3 in Section 3.13.3.) SSAP 6 relied on a distinction between persistent and transient earnings. By contrast, FRS 3 seeks separate disclosure of earnings from discontinued and continuing activities.

FRS 3 redefined extraordinary items so that they virtually disappeared from financial reports. The major component of extraordinary items used to be gains and losses on the disposal of fixed assets. Such gains and losses are now disclosed separately on the face of the profit and loss account after operating profit and before interest. It is no longer permitted to deal with them "below the line" in calculating EPS.

"Prior year adjustments" can arise under FRS 3 when changes are made in accounting policies or when fundamental errors relating to former periods are corrected. Prior period adjustments should be accounted for by restating the comparative figures for the preceding period in the primary statements and notes, and adjusting the opening balance of reserves for the cumulative effect. The cumulative effect of the adjustments should also be noted at the foot of the statement of total recognized gains and losses of the current period. The effect of prior period adjustments on the results for the preceding period should be disclosed where practicable.

3.3.4 Provisions for Taxation

Although taxation will be discussed in greater detail in Section 3.11, it is appropriate at this point to refer to two specific points. The first is that the estimated charge for corporation tax on the earnings of a year appears in the income statement, with a corresponding provision being made in the balance sheet. The amount is not known exactly at this stage: there may be various adjustments to make before a final assessment is agreed with the Inland Revenue. Moreover, there is a long time delay before the mainstream corporation tax is liable to be paid over to the authorities. It is common for two tax liabilities to be outstanding at any one balance sheet date—an amount due for payment in more than one year's time in respect of the estimated tax assessment on the current year's profit, and a further amount due for payment quite soon in respect of the tax assessment on the previous year's profits.

The second point worth noting is that dividends in Britain are "declared" out of the net profits of a particular year, being proposed by the directors to the shareholders at a general meeting held after the year end to consider the results of the year. Thus, a balance sheet will usually show an amount payable in respect of the proposed dividend (often the second such dividend out of the year's earnings, with an earlier "interim" dividend paid during the course of the accounting period). Because dividend payments involve payment also of a withholding tax called "advance corporation tax" (ACT), which can usually be recovered many months later against the mainstream corporation tax assessment when this falls due for payment, there can be quite large amounts of recoverable ACT paid to the Inland Revenue within 3 months or so of the dividends being declared, waiting to be offset against subsequent corporation tax assessments. Section 3.11 explains the U.K. corporate tax system.

3.3.5 Distributable Profits

It is not easy to determine the amount currently available for distribution by way of dividends. This area of law is governed by Part VIII of the 1985 Companies Act, which goes beyond the scope of this chapter. The published accounts do not show the quantum of profit that is potentially distributable, which is, broadly speaking, restricted to accumulated realized profits less accumulated realized losses of the company (not the group).

3.3.6 Redemption of Shares

It is possible for a company to repurchase its own ordinary shares (common stock) as well as preferred shares, under certain conditions laid down in Sections 159–181 of the 1985 act. The capital of the company must be preserved, however, so that a transfer of an equal amount must be made out of distributable profits to the credit of a "capital redemption reserve," unless redemption of the shares is to be paid from the proceeds of a new share issue. Shares that are redeemed are canceled and not reissued: there is no "treasury stock."

3.3.7 Revaluation Reserves

The term revaluation reserve is used specifically for unrealized surpluses on the revaluation of fixed assets. When such assets are eventually disposed of, it used to be the practice that the amount of revaluation surplus relating to the asset disposal was transferred out of the revaluation reserve and put (plus any book profit or less any loss on the sale) to the credit of the profit and loss account as an extraordinary item. Since FRS 3 was issued in 1992, practice has changed. The profit or loss on disposal to be reported in the profit and loss account is now the difference between the net sale proceeds and the net carrying amount at which the asset appeared in the books immediately before sale (whether this was at historical cost, less depreciation, or at valuation). This means that the revaluation reserve can now include credit balances in respect of past revaluations of assets that have been disposed of.

It must be added that FRS 3 also requires a note to explain any difference between the profit and loss actually disclosed for the year and the figure that would have resulted "on an unmodified historical cost basis."

3.4 Liabilities and Provisions

In common with U.S. practice, British companies use accrual accounting in which income realization principles first determine the timing of revenues, and costs are then matched to produce a figure for profit or loss. SSAP 2, "Disclosure of Accounting Policies," set out in 1971 a brief statement of four fundamental accounting concepts, the going concern concept, the accruals or matching concept, the consistency concept, and the prudence concept. They also appear now in paragraphs 9–15, Schedule 4 of the 1985 act. It is worth noting that sales revenues are recorded in Britain at figures that exclude value added tax (VAT). SSAP 5 lays down the standard treatment of VAT, which is generally excluded both from sales revenue and also from costs unless the VAT on inputs cannot be recovered.

The term *provision* is used to describe an expense of the period in which the amount cannot yet be determined with substantial accuracy. Accumulated charges for depreciation used to be known also as provisions for depreciation, since the amount charged depends on the unexpended future life of the assets concerned; however, it is now common practice to refer to accumulated depreciation.

Contingent liabilities are less certain than provisions. They would give rise to an expense only if some uncertain future event were to take place, with a reasonable likelihood that it will not. For example, if a claim is made against the company under warranty where the company contests liability, the chances of incurring costs may depend on the outcome of a court hearing (particularly since in Britain the losing party usually must pay the legal costs of both sides). The probability of the event occurring is sufficiently low that no definite provision is made in the current accounts, but it is sufficiently probable for it to be necessary to give information on it, by way of a note to the accounts, to give a true and fair view. SSAP 18, "Accounting for Contingencies," lays down accounting rules in more detail.

Appropriations of profit, for example, to allow for future growth, do not give rise to liabilities or provisions (except in the sense that all equity capital, including retained earnings, represents a liability of the company to its stockholders).

One additional type of disclosure required by the 1985 act (Schedule 4, paragraph 50) falling outside the above categories is the note of future capital commitments authorized by the directors, divided into those for which contracts have been signed and those for which contracts have not yet been signed. (See, for example, the foot of note 10 of Bunzl's accounts.) While this does not show the time scale over which the commitments extend, the information is valuable both in the context of the trend of net earnings and in assessing the liquidity of the company.

3.5 Property, Plant, and Equipment

The 1985 act Section 262(1) (as inserted by the 1989 act, Section 22) states that fixed assets are "assets of a company which are intended for use on a continuing basis in the company's activities, and 'current assets' means assets not intended for such use." Fixed assets may be tangible or intangible, and they include investments in other undertakings. The 1985 act continues a long tradition of legislation that leaves unspecified how fixed assets are to be valued and how depreciation is to be charged, but it insists that disclosure be made of the cost or valuation used to record the book value of the assets, the charge for depreciation in the current year, and the aggregate depreciation expensed to date on the assets recorded.

There is no single SSAP dedicated to the treatment of fixed assets as a class, but SSAP 12, "Accounting for Depreciation," explicitly requires depreciation to be charged on fixed assets, while SSAP 13 deals with fixed assets used for research and development, SSAP 19 deals with accounting for investment properties, and SSAP 22 deals with goodwill. Intangible fixed assets are discussed in Section 3.8, and investments in Section 3.9.

It was pointed out in the discussion of the historical cost vs. alternative valuation rules, at the beginning of Section 3, that most companies in Britain publish their accounts on the basis of historical cost, although if they wish they can choose to use Alternative Accounting Rules. These Alternative Accounting Rules allow all intangible fixed assets *except for goodwill* to be valued at their current cost. Tangible fixed assets may be valued either at current cost or, alternatively, at a market value determined at the date of their last valuation. For many years statute law has been more permissive still, and most British companies present fixed assets at a mixture of cost, past valuations, and current valuations.

Previous companies acts have generally tried to avoid restricting the power of directors to use any of a variety of valuation bases in preparing their accounts, and the 1985 act seeks to preserve some degree of discretion to directors. The 1985 act states that fixed assets must either (*a*) be valued at their purchase price or production cost, or (*b*) be shown, under the Alternative Accounting Rules, at some current value.

The Alternative Accounting Rules allow tangible fixed assets to be valued either at current cost or at a market value determined at the date of their last valuation. There is no rule that determines how often a fixed asset must be revalued or if it is to be revalued at all. The ASB, as shown in its 1993 discussion paper "The Role of Valuation in Financial Reporting," clearly favors a move to using current values throughout the accounts. However, it recognizes on pragmatic grounds that it would be impractical to move too fast. It therefore supports the use of the present modified historical cost system. In order to address what it describes as "some of the existing anomalies," the discussion paper proposed new standards to require:

1   The revaluation of properties (excluding fixed assets specific to the business)
2.   The revaluation of quoted investments
3.   The revaluation of stock of a commodity nature and long-term stock where a market of sufficient depth exists

Subject to this, SSAP 12 (on fixed asset depreciation) obviously contemplated the possibility of fixed asset revaluation: it states (SSAP 12, paragraph 5) that it "does not prescribe how frequently assets should be revalued but, where a policy of revaluing assets is adopted, the valuation should be kept up to date." Any method of calculating depreciation is acceptable, provided it allocates the charge "as fairly as possible to the periods expected to benefit from the asset's use" (SSAP 12, paragraph 8). The rules for valuing investments have to date been even more broadly permissive. Under the Companies Acts, investments may be valued "on any basis which appears to the directors to be appropriate in the circumstances of the company" (1985 act, Schedule 4, Part II, paragraph 31 (3)(b)).

ED 51, "Accounting for Fixed Assets and Revaluations" (1990), recognized that the Companies Act requires fixed assets to be valued either at purchase price or at production cost or under the Alternative Accounting Rules. The ED proposed, however, that, even without departing from historical cost, revaluations should be permitted, provided that once such a policy is adopted the assets concerned should be revalued (at open market value) at intervals of not more than 5 years. The ASB is clearly sympathetic to this.

The calculation of the purchase price of a fixed asset includes those costs incidental to the shipment and installation of the asset. In the case of production costs of assets made by the company, these may include "a reasonable proportion of the costs incurred by the company which are only indirectly attributable to the production of that asset, but only to the extent that they relate to the period of production" (1985 act, Schedule 4, paragraph 26(3)(a)). Interest costs may also be included (see Section 3.5.4).

SSAP 12 requires that depreciation be charged over the life of any fixed asset whose life is of limited duration, including property. Depreciation must be charged even if the market value of such an asset increases. An exception is made under SSAP 19 in the case of investment properties. Despite the specific requirement of SSAP 12 that property be depreciated (unless it is investment property, which excludes buildings occupied either by the company or by others in the same group), it used to be quite common for companies with large property investments to ignore this requirement. Supermarkets, hotels, and similar buildings kept in a good state of repair were previously often not depreciated; the stated reason in the accounts was usually that the open market value of the property was rising faster than any deterioration in its fabric. Practice changed in this area after 1993, with the Review Panel exerting pressure on a number of large companies with major property assets.

3.5.1 Departures from Historical Cost

Some controversy has existed over the proper accounting treatment of the depreciation of fixed assets where they have been revalued. When SSAP 12 was first issued in December 1977, it was not explicit whether the amount of depreciation charged in the income statement had to be based on the revalued amount or merely on the original cost, with any extra depreciation being charged against reserves. This treatment (often called split depreciation) was favored by some companies and their accountants.

The current version of SSAP 12 is insistent:

> The accounting treatment in the profit and loss account should be consistent with that used in the balance sheet. Hence the depreciation charge in

> the profit and loss account for the period should be based on the carrying amount of the asset in the balance sheet, whether historical cost or revalued amount. The whole depreciation charge should be reflected in the profit and loss account. (SSAP 12, paragraph 16)

This question of depreciation is linked with three others: (*a*) the effect of revising the estimated residual lives of fixed assets; (*b*) the need to write down fixed assets in the event of a permanent diminution in their value; and (*c*) the treatment of gains and losses on disposal. These are discussed briefly in turn.

The effect of revising the estimated residual lives of fixed assets is usually that the firm will write off the unamortized book value over the remaining life as newly estimated. Only if "future results would be materially distorted" should there be an adjustment to the accumulated provision for depreciation for years before the new estimate (SSAP 12, paragraph 18).

The need to write down fixed assets in the event of a permanent diminution in their value may arise perhaps as a result of obsolescence or because of a fall in demand for a product. The net book value should be written down immediately to the estimated "recoverable amount," that is to say the lower of (*a*) the net realizable value of an asset held for resale or (*b*) the amount expected to be produced by an asset in its future use as a fixed asset. The latter figure, in particular, is ill-defined. It might be the cash flows produced by the asset (although not normally discounted), or it might include some definition of net profits. If it is judged to be necessary to reduce the asset value, the write-down will be against current earnings. If it turns out that the reasons for making such a write-down cease to apply, it may be reversed to the extent that it is no longer necessary, with a credit to the profit and loss account.

The treatment of gains and losses on disposal involves further controversy. For those who seek consistent application of historical cost rules, the realized gain or loss on sale of fixed assets compares sale proceeds with the depreciated historical cost. If a fixed asset had been revalued, the revaluation surplus would have been taken to the credit of a revaluation reserve as an unrealized profit until the time of disposal. On sale, this is reversed, so that the surplus will enter into the calculation of the realized profit or loss on disposal.

As noted earlier, however, profit or loss on disposal of fixed assets must now be calculated as the difference between any sale proceeds and the carrying value of the asset in the books, whether this is at historical cost less depreciation or at a revaluation (FRS 3, paragraph 21).

Any transfer out of revaluation reserve on disposal of a redundant asset should be shown as a movement on reserves and not included in the profit or loss on sale of the fixed asset. FRS 3, paragraph 27, requires a "statement of total recognized gains and losses" to follow the profit and loss account if there are any gains or losses or other transfers to or from reserves for the year that do not appear in the profit and loss account. This is explicitly to include (paragraph 56) any unrealized gain "such as a revaluation surplus on fixed assets."

Accordingly, the FRS requires, as a primary statement, a statement of total recognized gains and losses to show the extent to which shareholders' funds have increased or decreased from all the gains and losses recognized in the period. It follows from this perspective that the same gains and losses should not be recognized twice (for example, a holding gain recognized when a fixed asset is revalued should not be recognized a second time when the revalued asset is sold).

This means, of course, that there will be greater disjunction between reported operating profits for the year and the amount that becomes legally distributable during the year. This latter figure is strictly defined as being realized. Since revaluation gains may now bypass the profit and loss account entirely and be transferred straight to profit and loss *reserves* (even though depreciation must be charged against operating profits on the relevant basis), realized revaluation gains now miss being reported in profits at all.

3.5.2 Relationship between Accounting Depreciation and Tax Allowances

There is no relationship between the book value of assets and their tax treatment (although a temporary exception to the rule is noted in Section 3.5.4); indeed, the amount charged by way of depreciation is unlikely to be the amount allowed for taxation by way of capital allowances. The Inland Revenue publishes its own scale of allowances for use with the cost of fixed assets in making an assessment of taxable profits.

3.5.3 *Government Grants*

The treatment of government grants is addressed in SSAP 4, "The Accounting Treatment of Government Grants." The intention is that any grants from government (whether a local or the national government or the European Union) should be credited to income at the time any relevant costs are being debited. In the case of fixed assets, this means that the grant will serve to reduce the cost of using the asset year by year over its life (and not be taken as a credit in full to income in the year the grant was made or paid). SSAP 4 requires grants in respect of fixed assets to be treated as a deferred credit, to be released bit by bit as depreciation is charged. It does not permit the grant to be taken off the cost of the fixed asset so that a lower depreciation charge arises in that way. However, there is some controversy over whether the 1985 act, Schedule 4, necessarily requires the SSAP 4 treatment; some companies evidently deduct grants from the cost of fixed assets on the grounds that only the net amount really represents "cost."

3.5.4 *Interest*

The treatment of interest on fixed assets is addressed in the 1985 act, Schedule 4, paragraph 26(3)(b), where it is stated that there may be included in the production cost of an asset "interest on capital borrowed to finance the production of that asset, to the extent that it accrues in respect of the period of production." There is no obligation to capitalize interest and considerable freedom to decide how to do so. Such capitalization will lessen current charges to income but increase later depreciation charges by inclusion of interest in the cost of the asset.

Generally there is little connection between the profit or loss figure published in the income statement and the profit or loss figure used in the assessment of corporation tax. There were several years, however, in which the accounting treatment effectively determined the tax treatment of interest capitalization. In a 1966 case it was decided that the Inland Revenue was within its rights to disallow interest as a business expense in the current year where it had been capitalized as part of the costs of buildings. In a 1977 case, however, the Inland Revenue subsequently decided to change its view, and it inserted an amendment into the 1981 Finance Act (S. 38) in order to reverse the rule.

3.5.5 Investment Properties

Investment properties are covered by SSAP 19, after the requirement of SSAP 12 to depreciate freehold buildings had produced extensive disagreement. SSAP 19 requires investment properties to be carried at open market value, not necessarily appraised by a professional appraiser (valuer) but accompanied by details of the names and qualification of valuers, the bases used, and a statement whether the valuation is by an employee or officer of the company. Valuation surpluses should be taken to an "investment revaluation reserve," but any deficit greater than the balance on this reserve should be written off against income. No charge should be made for depreciation on such properties, except for properties held on lease.

FRS 3, paragraph 66 observes:

> Investment companies as defined in section 266 of the Companies Act 1985 (Companies Act investment companies) have special legal provisions regarding the recording of unrealized capital losses, with the result that their profit and loss accounts are not comparable with those of other reporting entities. In the case of such investment companies all recognized gains and losses of a capital nature should be shown only in the statement of total recognized gains and losses leaving the profit and loss account to be confined to profits available for distribution.

3.6 Leased Assets

SSAP 21, "Accounting for Leases and Hire Purchase Contracts" (August 1984) obliges companies that lease assets under a "finance" lease to treat the assets as though they were owned rather than leased. Hire purchase transactions are in most cases analyzed in the same way as leases. The definition of a finance lease is set out below. Any other lease is an operating lease, under which the asset does not appear in the books of the lessee, but the lease payments are shown in the income statement as they accrue. From the point of view of the lessor, the asset remains on the balance sheet and will be depreciated accordingly.

Operating leases create little difficulty. All that is necessary is that the amounts payable under the lease are allocated to the proper time periods in which the assets are used. On the other hand, until 1984 it was believed that substantial asset leasing enabled lessee companies to hold assets "off balance sheet," giving a view of their capital employed that, even if true, was not fair. SSAP 21 was passed after some controversy; it represents an example of substance dominating over form, since it requires a company to show an asset hired under a finance lease as if it were owned rather than merely leased.

SSAP 21 defines a finance lease as one "that transfers substantially all the risks and rewards of ownership of an asset to the lessee." This is normally presumed to be the case if, at the outset, the present value of the minimum lease payments (including any initial payment) amounts to 90% or more of the fair value of the leased asset.

Under a finance lease the asset is valued by the lessee either at the discounted present value of the expected payments or at fair value. The latter is more logical. The discount rate under the former method is the implicit rate that equates the payments with their fair value at the start; there is little point in working out this discount rate in order to discount the payments back to yield the figure for fair value. The book value of the asset will then be depreciated over its expected life as if it had been purchased outright, taking into account any terminal residual value to be paid or received under the agreement. At the same time, a liability will be recorded of the value of the loan taken out to "buy" the asset, the loan being paid off over the life of the asset. The actual payments under the finance lease will, of course, exceed the depreciation charges, the difference representing the financing costs involved. SSAP 21 permits these financing costs to be written off against revenues, apportioned either by an actuarial method (representing a constant percentage on the outstanding balance of the loan), or on a sum of the digits or straight-line basis. The choice is basically arbitrary.

From the point of view of the lessor, the rules determining whether a lease is an operating or a finance lease are applied quite independently of how they have been applied by the lessee. (For example, the lessor may be aware of the actual cost of the asset leased, whereas the lessee may have a different idea of the fair value.) Under a finance lease, the lessor must separate the cost of the investment made in the leased asset from the "gross earnings" to be received under the lease. These "gross earnings" are the total minimum lease payments (including any initial payment and any unguaranteed residual value accruing to the lessor) less the cost of the leased asset (net of any grants receivable). The principle is that the gross earnings will be allocated on an actuarial basis to produce a constant percentage return on the net investment in the asset, reduced year by year by a proportion of rental income received.

Disclosure of leased assets by the lessee is required by SSAP 21 as follows:

1. Policies adopted
2. Operating lease expenses for the period, divided between those for the hire of plant and machinery and all other operating leases (including property)
3. Aggregate finance charges for the period in respect of finance leases
4. Aggregate depreciation for the period on assets held either under finance leases or hire purchase contracts
5. Gross amount and accumulated depreciation in respect of each major class of asset held either under finance leases or hire purchase contracts
6. Future obligations in respect of finance leases and hire purchase contracts (which may be combined with other obligations), divided into those payable (*a*) in the next year, (*b*) in 2 to 5 years inclusive, and (*c*) in more than 5 years
7. Operating lease commitments for payments to be made in the next year alone in respect of operating leases still to run (*a*) for no more than one year, (*b*) for 2 to 5 years, and (*c*) for more than 5 years
8. Commitments authorized but not yet started should be shown as a note under the 1985 Act, Schedule 4, paragraph 50

Disclosure of leased assets by the lessor is required by SSAP 21 as follows:

1. Policies adopted
2. Rentals receivable in the period from operating leases and (separately) from finance leases

3. Net investment in finance leases and (separately) hire purchase contracts

4. The cost of assets bought to be leased out either under finance leases or hire purchase contracts (these assets, once leased out, will be shown under "debtors" and hence will usually need to be divided between amounts due within 1 year and amounts due in more than 1 year)

5. Gross amount and accumulated depreciation in respect of each major class of asset held for the purpose of hiring under operating leases

FRS 5 notes that a leasing transaction may form only part of a larger series of transactions; in such a case it may be necessary to comply with both standards. (In case of conflict, it is likely that FRS 5 should take precedence.)

3.7 Oil, Gas, and Mineral Reserves

In Britain an active Oil Industry Accounting Committee (OIAC) has taken the initiative in drafting several Statements of Recommended Practice (SORPs), which have been approved (franked) by the Accounting Standards Committee. The Accounting Standards Board has announced that it will authorize certain bodies to issue their own (industry) accounting standards, and the oil and gas industry has made a start in setting its own standards.

The four oil industry SORPs are "Disclosures about Oil and Gas Exploration Activities" (April 1986), "Accounting for Oil and Gas Exploration and Development Activities" (December 1987), "Accounting for Abandonment Costs" (June 1988), and "Accounting for Various Financing, Revenue and Other Transactions of Oil and Gas Exploration and Production Companies" (January 1991). Reference should be made to these for matters of detail.

Both "full cost" and "successful efforts" methods are permitted in Britain, by SORP 2. "Cost pools" are defined geographically but will not normally cover an area smaller than a complete country. Each cost pool recorded by a full cost company will be regarded as a separate fixed asset, but each field, well, or license cost center recorded by a successful efforts company will be an individual fixed asset of that company. This is significant, for example, in deciding whether to write down the value of a fixed asset in order to reflect a permanent diminution in its value (as required by the 1985 Companies Act). Interest on capital employed may be capitalized up to the start of production.

The OIAC is unhappy with the use of historical cost accounts but reluctant to drop them in favor of current value or discounted cash flow data. Instead, it urges supplementary disclosure to guide users as to the quantities of proven reserves and similar factual information. A 1990 discussion paper "Accounting for the Value of Discovered Reserves of Oil and Gas" still expressed the view that "a comprehensive system of Value Accounting which encompasses a Profit and Loss Account and Balance Sheet, whether as primary or supplementary accounts, appears to be undesirable" (p. 40). The caution of the OIAC is understandable in light of the number of international operators in the industry who might be thought ready to flee to more welcoming shores if regulation becomes too oppressive in Britain. On the other hand, there is still an incentive for companies with a good financial history to want high reporting standards if they are to persuade investors to commit their funds.

3.8 Intangibles (Excluding Goodwill on Consolidation)

Some discussion has already appeared in Section 3.5 of the valuation of fixed assets, which in general includes intangible and tangible fixed assets as well as investments. The 1985 act states that fixed assets must be valued either at their purchase price or production cost or, alternatively, under the Alternative Accounting Rules, at some current value. The Alternative Accounting Rules allow all intangible fixed assets except for goodwill to be valued at their current cost.

A 1990 ASC exposure draft, ED 52, discussed the treatment of intangible fixed assets. It specifically excluded four types of asset: development expenditure, covered by SSAP 13; leases of tangible assets, covered by SSAP 21; goodwill, then covered by SSAP 22 and now subject to new ASB deliberations; and investments, the subject of ED 55. The 1993 ASB discussion paper "Goodwill and Intangible Assets" sought to capture purchased intangibles within the heading of goodwill, which cannot be revalued upwards under the Alternative Accounting Rules and which the ASB wants to see either eliminated against reserves on acquisition (the goodwill being carried as a negative balance on the balance sheet—a "dangling debit") or capitalized and amortized against earnings (normally over 20 years). The discussion paper argues that the distinction between goodwill and other intangibles "is often one of labeling rather than substance." Although apparently tempted by the idea of valuing intangibles at current market value, the discussion paper accepts that this would not be practicable. However, management is encouraged to give details of the nature and estimated value of intangible benefits included within the figure for goodwill by way of a note to the accounts, as well as qualitative details in the Operating and Financial Review (see Section 2.1.3).

Under the 1985 Companies Act, intangible property rights can generally be shown on the balance sheet, including purchased trademarks, patents, and so on. Indeed, SSAP 22, "Accounting for Goodwill," formerly seemed to encourage this in paragraph 13:

> Separable net assets may include identifiable intangibles such as those specifically mentioned in the balance sheet formats in the Companies Act 1985, i.e. "concessions, patents, licenses, trade marks and similar rights and assets"; other examples include publishing titles, franchise rights and customer lists. (This list of examples is not intended to be comprehensive.) Identifiable intangibles such as these form part of the separable net assets which are recorded in an acquiring company's accounts at fair value, even if they were not recorded in the acquired company's accounts.

There is full agreement that internally generated intangibles should not be capitalized on the balance sheet but any expenditure written off as an expense against earnings.

Development costs must be shown under a separate heading in the balance sheet formats. Given the severe restrictions set in SSAP 13 for carrying forward research and development (R&D) expenditure, the development costs referred to here represent just that small fraction of development costs that can be capitalized. The rules on distributable profits also treat R&D expenditure quite cautiously; any such expenditure is treated as a realized expense unless strict rules are observed for carrying some part of development costs forward.

3.9 Equity Investments in Other Companies

It was noted in Section 3.1.5 that equity investments in other companies do not necessarily make those companies subsidiaries. The first SSAP produced by the Accounting Standards (Steering) Committee in Britain was on the subject of "Associated Companies"; SSAP 1 was originally issued in 1971 and amended in 1974 and 1982. This distinguished among three levels of investment relationships in other companies:

1. Subsidiaries (where more than 50% of the shares are owned or where control is exercised)
2. Associates (where between 20% and 50% of shares are owned or where significant influence is exercised)
3. Other investments where the degree of influence is less, usually because the participating interest is too small

FRS 2 follows the 1985 Companies Act very closely in defining parent and subsidiary undertakings in terms of control. It moves away from the criteria set out in SSAP 1, which define the three levels of investment in terms of percentages of shares owned, although these percentages may still be useful in identifying the extent of control and significant influence. The 1994 ASB Discussion Paper "Associates and Joint Ventures" suggests new definitions of both the terms *participating interest* and *significant influence*, apart from introducing the new expression, *strategic alliances*. Where the equity method is still to be used, the Discussion Paper urges that more information should be given (under an "expanded equity method," which discloses the investor's share of turnover, dividends retained, results for the year, and total assets and liabilities). Far greater judgment will be required if the terms of the Discussion Paper are adopted in a forthcoming FRS to replace SSAP 1.

3.9.1 Subsidiaries

Subsidiaries are listed in the annual report of the parent company, and their financial results are normally consolidated in group accounts. Under certain circumstances the parent company is exempt from the need to include a particular subsidiary in group accounts. The EC Seventh Directive on group accounts was embodied in the 1989 Companies Act, which restricted the right to exemption to the minimum possible under the Directive. Thus, under Section 229(3) and (4) of the 1985 act (as amended by Section 5 of the 1989 act), a subsidiary shall be excluded from consolidation because of severe long-term restrictions over the parent's right of control, or because the subsidiary is held exclusively with a view to resale, or because the activities of the subsidiary are so different from those of the group that consolidation would be incompatible with presenting a true and fair view. The wording of the last of the conditions is obscure in the act; it really applies only if the subsidiary is bound to report its affairs under separate legislation, for example, as a bank or insurance company. Group accounts were discussed in Section 3.1.

3.9.2 Associated Companies

SSAP 1 requires that associates be accounted for on the "equity" basis. That is to say, the cost of the investment will be shown in the books of the holding company (or the group accounts, if prepared) as a fixed asset, and whenever the associate reports profits or losses, the holding company takes its share into its own accounts (or its group accounts). This means that the balance on the investment account shows the total amount currently invested in the associate, both at the time of the initial purchase and also by way of any subsequent retained profits (and reduced by any losses). When a dividend is declared, this is credited to the investment account (since less profit is retained in the associate), and debited to accounts receivable until paid.

If the value of the investment is believed to have fallen permanently below the level at which it is shown in the accounts, the value in the accounts must be written down.

3.9.3 Other Investments

Where the holding in the other enterprise consists of a holding of shares too small to confer substantial influence, the investment will be shown by the holding company in its accounts at cost. No income from the investment will be shown until a dividend is declared, when it will be credited to the income statement and included among receivables

There is some uncertainty over the proper treatment of investments in joint ventures. In Section 3.1.2 it was noted that ED 50 and the ASB "Interim Statement: Consolidated Accounts" proposed proportional consolidation for joint ventures, and the 1994 Discussion Paper "Associates and Joint Ventures" refines this. The 1985 act seems to imply that joint ventures are to be defined in terms of joint *management*. The ASB suggests that joint *control* is a more valuable criterion.

A new FRS is expected to require companies to disclose the nature of any relationship in which transactions are not at arm's length. There has been controversy over the extent of the disclosure required; it appears that the identity of any such counterparty (excluding members of the same group of undertakings) needs to be revealed, together with the aggregate level of business during the financial year with that party.

3.9.4 A Note on the General Rules for Valuing Investments

The rules for valuing investments are even more broadly permissive than the rules for valuing other assets, except that the book value will not normally be increased once it has been recorded at the fair value of consideration given. This may be valued "on any basis which appears to the directors to be appropriate in the circumstances of the company" (1985 act, Schedule 4, Part II, paragraph 31 (3)(b)).

3.10 Inventories

SSAP 9 addresses the issue of valuing inventories (called "stocks" in Britain) and long-term contracts. The rules applying to long-term contracts are complex and specialized; they are summarized in Section 3.10.5.

3.10.1 Valuation Bases

Inventories are normally valued at cost or net realizable value, whichever is lower, unless the alternative valuation rules are being used, in which case stocks may be valued at current cost. According to SSAP 9, the comparison of cost and net realizable value should be done for each item of stock separately, unless this is impractical. In this context, "cost" is defined as either purchase price or direct costs of inputs plus any related production overhead that can be allocated to the goods produced or processed. The methods of identifying the costs of goods sold and the remaining inventory generally use certain simplifying conventions, rather than attempting to trace the specific movement of individual stock items. Thus, FIFO and weighted averages are both commonly used, and other bases are occasionally found, such as the base stock method (a method that assumes some basic constant level of stock is included in inventory at the same cost from period to period). Neither LIFO nor the base stock method is approved in SSAP 9, but there is some conflict between this and Schedule 4, paragraph 27, of the 1985 act, which permits any inventory valuation method. However, companies in Britain do not use LIFO because, although permitted by the 1985 act, its use is not allowed for tax purposes.

The 1985 Companies Act states that all current assets are to be treated alike regarding valuation, but of course receivables are actually valued at invoice price (less any provision for bad debts). This point is important in relation to long-term contracts, discussed in Section 3.10.5.

Inventories will be presented in the accounts subdivided into:

1. Raw materials and consumables
2. Work in progress
3. Finished goods and goods for resale
4. Payments on account

Although SSAPs require that the basis used for valuing inventories must be stated, and used consistently from one period to another, there is considerable variation in the amount of detail about inventory methods provided by companies in their statement of accounting policies.

3.10.2 Special Write-Downs for Tax

Although LIFO is not normally used by British companies because it is not allowed for tax purposes, this does not mean that the tax assessment is made on the reported net profit figure published in the accounts. In Britain, negotiations with the Inland Revenue over the tax assessment for the period may well begin with a copy of the draft accounts, but there are many items that might well be treated differently in the assessment of income for tax purposes.

3.10.3 Departures from Historical Cost

Departures from historical cost are allowed only downward where net realizable value is below cost and not upward. Upward revaluation would imply recognizing some element of profit on the goods before it was realized by being sold and invoiced to the customer (see also Section 3.10.5, however). This general rule is liable to be disregarded in certain specialized lines of business such as banking and commodity dealing, where the practice of "marking to market" is now well established in respect of dealing portfolios that have a ready market. In effect, the profit is treated as realized in these cases even though a particular buyer has not yet been identified.

3.10.4 Treatment of Overheads

The inclusion of production overheads in inventory valuation presents some difficulties in practice. There is likely to be some arbitrary judgment involved in estimating what to include in production overhead and then in how to apply this to production. SSAP 9, Appendix 1, paragraph 8, indicates that overhead allocation is to be based on the company's "normal" level of activity, which serves, if anything, to increase rather than to limit the area of discretion.

There is also the unresolved matter of whether interest may be included in defining the cost of inventory. In practice, this is more likely to present a problem in the context of long-term contracts and fixed assets, but the possibility exists in the case of inventory also.

3.10.5 Work-in-Progress under Long-Term Contracts

In 1988 the ASC revised SSAP 9 to correct anomalies that had arisen between the original version (issued in May 1975) and the 1981 Companies Act. The special rules relating to work-in-progress under long-term contracts are designed to permit profits to be recognized before the completion of the contract, which by definition could take years.

Long-term contracts are assessed individually, and the related profit is estimated by comparing turnover with related costs as the activity continues over the years, both terms being interpreted "in a manner appropriate to stage of completion of the contracts, the businesses and the industries in which they operate" (SSAP 9, paragraph 8). Disclosure is required to distinguish between costs and revenues.

If, and only if, it is considered that the outcome of the contract can be foreseen with reasonable certainty before its conclusion, attributable profit may be calculated on a prudent basis and included in current earnings, reflecting the proportion of work carried out to date and taking into account any "known inequalities of profit in the various stages of the contract" (SSAP 9, paragraph 9). If the outcome cannot be foreseen with reasonable certainty, no profit should be anticipated. If a loss is expected, the whole loss should be recognized as soon as it is foreseen, in accordance with the prudence concept (SSAP 9, paragraph 11).

SSAP 9, Appendix 3, provides further guidance on the treatment of long-term contracts. Paragraph 84 observes that "The classification of an 'amount recoverable on contracts' within debtors is a somewhat unfamiliar concept which needs careful attention." As noted in Section 3.10.1, the classification makes all the difference whether this current asset can be valued as stock (and thus at the lower of cost or net realizable value) or as debtors (i.e., receivables), which may be valued to include realized profits.

Interest may be included in defining the cost of work-in-progress under long-term contracts, as discussed in Section 3.5.4.

3.11 Taxation

When the Accounting Standards Committee began to discuss taxation (Exposure Draft 11 was issued in 1973), it apparently never questioned the possibility that taxes borne by a corporation on its profits could be regarded as a distribution of those profits to the community, as one of the parties interested in its progress. Rather, it followed the U.S. precedent and treated tax charges as an expense of running the business, even though tax charges bear virtually no relationship to input costs associated with producing revenues.

The abrupt adoption of U.S. tax accounting practices relates specifically to the treatment of deferred taxation. Before we examine this issue, however, there are particular forms of tax that appear in the accounts of British companies and that need to be explained.

3.11.1 Corporation Tax

After 1965, companies were liable to pay taxes on their net profits, by way of "corporation tax." The system of corporation tax was amended substantially with effect from April 1973 to introduce the "imputation system" in place of the "classical system." The principle was to keep company earnings from being taxed twice (once as company profits and again when distributed to stockholders as dividends as had been the case under the classical system).

The basic principle is quite simple. When a cash dividend payment is made to stockholders, withholding tax becomes payable by the company to the revenue in respect of the amount involved. Under the imputation system, this tax can be offset within certain limits against corporation tax levied on the taxable profits of the corporation. It also funds a tax credit, which the shareholder can use as partial payment of personal tax on individual income. For basic rate income tax–paying shareholders, the imputation system abolished the double taxation of dividends and was more neutral in respect of dividend distribution decisions than was the classical system. In practice, this concept of neutrality has been eroded because stockholders who are not liable to pay income tax at the basic rate (low income individuals, charities, pension funds, and some companies) are able to reclaim from the Inland Revenue the full value of the tax credit. This has created constant pressure from such shareholders for high payout ratios, and the benefits available have contributed to a substantial growth of institutional shareholding in the United Kingdom, at the expense of direct personal holders for whom the tax advantages are much lower. At the time of writing, the long-term future of the present system is in some doubt.

After the introduction of the imputation system, SSAP 8 came into force to provide guidance over the treatment of taxation in the accounts of companies.

3.11.2 Advance Corporation Tax

In practice, for "large" companies (i.e., those with annual taxable profits currently exceeding £1.25 million), the rate of corporation tax is generally set higher than the basic rate of income tax. If profits of, say, £10 million are subject to corporation tax at, say, 33%, but dividends are taxed at a standard rate of 20%, the effect of a full distribution is that there will be two payments of tax by the company—one will be the payment made within 14 days of the end of the calendar quarter in which the cash dividend is paid, known as Advance Corporation Tax (ACT), amounting to £6.7 million/4 = £1.675 million (at the tax rates applicable in the year to April 5, 1995); the other will be the remaining amount of the full corporation tax bill of £3.3 million charged on the £10 million of taxable profit, namely the £1.625 million (i.e., £3.3 million minus £1.675 million). This final corporation tax payment is called mainstream corporation tax (MCT).

The date of payment of the dividend determines the rate of ACT payable in respect of it. An ACT payment may be offset by a subsequent MCT liability to the extent of the ACT rate on the taxable profit. Any excess, or surplus, ACT may be carried back for relief against MCT bills for the previous 6 years (taking the earlier years first), or it may be carried forward indefinitely for relief against a future MCT bill, subject in each case to the limitation for relief for the period in question.

Each company in a group is separately assessed for corporation tax on its profits, although special rules allow some reliefs to be transferred between companies in groups in certain circumstances, and where a holding company and its minimum 51% subsidiary jointly so elect an intercompany dividend payment need not incur an ACT liability.

It can be complicated (indeed, often impossible) to identify from published accounts how much is currently owing to the revenue and how much ACT is prepaid at any point in time. There is a time delay between the date of dividend payments out of profits for the year and the rather later date of the assessment and payment of corporation tax. Mainstream corporation tax for an accounting period ending after September 30, 1993 is automatically due under "pay and file" rules 9 months from the end of the accounting period.

Franked investment income, or FII, is dividend income from another company paid out of earnings already subjected to corporation tax. Such income is not taxed in the hands of the receiving company (to avoid double taxation of the same income).

Many companies have insufficient taxable profits to be able to offset the whole of their ACT against mainstream corporate tax and, where the situation is unlikely to change in the foreseeable future, the "unrelieved ACT," which results will need to be written off against income. The effect of this is that the company loses the benefit of the imputation system and effectively suffers a tax burden as a result of the distribution that would not have arisen if the profit had been retained in the company.

Under U.K. tax law, a "scrip" dividend (i.e., a stock dividend in which stockholders choose to receive additional shares of stock in place of cash) does not attract ACT. Such a dividend is attractive to companies that have unrelieved ACT, for example, those that because of tax relief on foreign earnings have insufficient U.K. corporation tax against which to recover ACT on cash dividends. Scrip dividends have become increasingly popular in the 1990s, partly because they retain funds in the hands of the company, partly because they allow investors to increase their holdings without incurring brokers' charges, and partly because they save payment of ACT at the date when the dividend is paid. Even where the company has no unrelieved ACT, the use of scrip dividends may well serve to defer payment to the Inland Revenue for several months, and the consequent retention of cash in the company is in many respects similar to, but simpler than, the making of a mini "rights" issue of new stock to achieve a similar effect.

3.11.3 Deferred Taxation

Accounting for deferred tax was proposed in ED 11 in 1973 and appeared in SSAP 11 in 1975. There was virtually no discussion of the need for deferred taxation in the United Kingdom; debate centered on two particular matters of detail—whether to defer on the liability method or the deferral method and whether to provide for deferred tax on a full or on a partial basis (discussed below). Apart from one or two fairly mild protests, the principle of treating tax as an expense to be "matched" to relevant revenues (rather than as an appropriation of profits, in accordance with traditional British views) was taken for granted. Clearly, the treatment of deferred tax came to Britain from the United States, where the view was well established that taxation was a charge on business (rather than on the owners of the business). The effect is to reallocate the tax effects of an accounting event in order to place those tax effects in the appropriate accounting period.

Deferred tax arises only when an event (either an item of income or an expense) is treated for accounting purposes as arising in some time period (or several) and treated for the purposes of tax assessment in some other period (or periods). Cases in which an event appears in the accounts but has no tax effect, or where it has a tax impact but no accounting impact, do not give rise to deferred tax. Only where tax treatment arises in periods other than the accounting treatment is it possible for deferred tax to arise. The effect of the item on the tax charge (which may mean a saving in the current tax charge or an increase) is reallocated to conform to the accounting treatment. Thus, for example, an item of expense (say, interest on capital used in expanding a building) is allowed as an expense for tax purposes in the year ended December 31, 1995 but is not written off in the income statement for that year. Instead, it is capitalized and included as part of the building cost, depreciated over the next 40 years. A timing difference arises between the two treatments. Under deferred tax, the tax benefit would not be taken to the credit of the 1995 income statement but to the credit of a deferred tax account. It would then be released slowly to the credit of income over the 40 years' life of the building, offsetting part of the depreciation cost. Thus, after 40 years the timing differences would have fully reversed, and the interest expense would have been written off under both systems.

SSAP 11 produced strong opposition after 1975. Companies often found themselves with huge credit balances on the deferred tax account, typically because they were usually able to write off capital expenditure for tax purposes faster than they depreciated the assets in the income statement. These produced accumulations of deferred tax credits, growing faster than any "reversals" could reduce them.

SSAP 15 in 1978 reduced the impact of deferred tax so that it had to be provided for only where it was reasonably clear that the aggregate timing differences accumulated in any year would actually be reversed in aggregate in one or more future years.

SSAP 15 was revised in 1985 so that only the "liability" method of calculating the deferred tax provision can now be used. This means that the yearly adjustment to the deferred tax account, passing through the income statement, will be based on the tax liabilities that are expected to arise foreseeably over the next few years. Thus, for example, if an asset is revalued in the accounts by, say, £500,000 and this amount is expected to be realized on sale in the next few years, the credit to revaluation reserve of £500,000 will be reduced by the expected tax charge on that gain at the rate of corporation tax in force at the end of the year. If in subsequent years this tax rate changes, the credit to the deferred tax account will be adjusted accordingly.

3.12 Pensions

Some SSAPs have been drafted to meet new problems arising in the U.K. business environment, such as company taxation under the imputation system and accounting for value added tax. In other cases, SSAPs have followed existing U.S. practice, for example, in providing for deferred taxation. In the case of accounting for pension costs, British practice has developed in response to both pressures. From the 1960s onward, increasing numbers of British companies began providing pension schemes for the majority of their employees (not, as previously, for just their senior executives); as these schemes developed, problems of accounting for their cost were recognized in Britain as they had been in the United States from the 1950s.

The relevant U.K. standard, SSAP 24, was published in May 1988 after several years of discussions. The standard follows U.S. precedent in the sense that it seeks to match pension costs as an expense against the revenues produced at the time that the employees were working for the company. Previously, British companies had generally shown the cost of pensions as they were paid by the company. If pensions were included with current payroll costs, this meant that these costs might be shown as expenses several years—perhaps many years—after the former employees had ceased to work for the company. It was to repair this breach in the matching principle that SSAP 24 was adopted.

By comparison with U.S. requirements in FAS-87 and FAS-88, U.K. regulations are still pretty permissive. On the other hand, U.K. practice presents certain institutional features that do not arise in the United States. The most obvious of these is the occurrence of "defined contribution" schemes, which began to appear in the late 1980s. Most British (and all American) schemes are "defined benefit" schemes. (The Bunzl accounts show some relevant detail in note 25.) The pension rights of employees are laid down as part of their contracts of employment and are specified as a particular pattern of benefits to be received on retirement (with modified rights arising if the employee leaves the employment of the company before retirement age). The pension benefits to be paid in each year of retirement are normally set as a fraction of the wage or salary received in the last year of employment or as an average of the last 3 years' employment. It is the employer's responsibility to make sure that funds are available to pay the pension (and any associated rights) after the employee retires. Contributions into the scheme may be made by both employees and employer or by the employer alone.

The main feature of the defined contribution scheme is that the risk attaching to funding the pension is left primarily with the employee; contributions will be made into the scheme by employees and employer, or by the employer alone, but it is left to each individual employee to make sure that the proceeds are used to buy an annuity or to make some other suitable arrangement, whatever the proceeds of the scheme may prove to be at the date of retirement.

Pension schemes have generally been set up in Britain in the form of a trust, with aims specifically to provide employee pension benefits. Trustees are appointed either by the company alone or jointly by the company and employees (often through the employees' trade union representatives). The payments have been made to the trust, which has then invested them either externally, for example, with an assurance company, or internally by holding a stake in the assets of the company. Since 1992 it has been illegal to hold more than 5% of the current market value of the resources of the scheme at any one time invested in employer-related investments (i.e., in assets of the parent company or its associates).

The Social Security Act of 1990 laid down requirements for some degree of index-linking of pension schemes for inflation. As in most other areas, this act will present problems first for the actuary to the pensions scheme. It is only when the scheme is currently seen to be underfunded or overfunded that major accounting policy decisions must be made, arising from the need to decide whether to spread the effects over a number of years or to take the full impact into the current income statement.

3.12.1 Schemes Funded Externally

It has, of course, been possible for an assurance company to provide pension services to the company and its employees on a defined benefit basis. Although the assurance company, through its own actuarial staff, could then make its own estimates of the likely pension costs in future years and arrange that the necessary funds will be provided, it is in fact generally the case that the company retains responsibility for ensuring the adequacy of the scheme.

More commonly, the trustees of the company pensions scheme run their own investment portfolio, buying actuarial advice as needed to ensure that the pensions fund is being maintained at an adequate level to meet future needs. Given the necessary economies of scale offered by a large number of employees, such a trustee scheme can employ its own expert professional staff. From the viewpoint of the employees, there may be some degree of risk when the pension trust is run by the management of their own company, relying on obscure and complex powers set out in a lengthy trust deed. There have been cases, particularly in the context of takeover bids, where the status of the pension trust and its substantial assets has been found to be unclear. The position of individual employees can also be left rather vague, even when there is little doubt that the pension scheme as a whole is well run and fully funded.

3.12.2 Schemes Funded Internally

Until 1992 it was possible for a pension trust to invest all of its funds in the company itself; indeed, it is legitimate for the trustees to receive, say, equity shares in the company rather than payments in cash. There are obvious disadvantages to this, particularly in that the portfolio held by the pension scheme is all in one security and not diversified, as finance theory requires. In the case of a pension fund, indeed, the problem of the undiversified portfolio is even worse: if the company fails, the employees lose not only income from current employment but their pensions too.

3.12.3 Defined Contribution Schemes

The idea of the defined contribution scheme seems to have been a political statement by the Conservative government in power during the 1980s, as part of its measures to encourage popular capitalism and wider holdings of equity shares. Individuals were to carry responsibilities for managing their own financial affairs, including the need to seek actuarial and investment advice to provide a pension portfolio for their old age. In principle, there are obviously economies of scale in obtaining professional advice for all employees collectively, through the pension scheme, rather than leaving it to individual employees to make their own arrangements.

From an accounting point of view, however, a defined contribution scheme has the great advantage that as soon as the agreed-upon contributions are paid into the scheme and shown as expenses in the accounts, the problem of accounting for pension costs ceases forthwith. The problems of defined benefits schemes are much greater, mainly because the actuarial risks need to be taken into account every year in deciding whether the benefits currently accruing to employees are being fully met by payments into the scheme. The next section, therefore, addresses only defined benefit schemes.

3.12.4 Defined Benefit Schemes

Uncertainties arise over many different variables under defined benefit schemes. How many employees are currently in the pension scheme? How long have they been with the company? How long will they stay before either retiring or leaving? What will be their likely final level of pay before retiring? What pensions or withdrawal rights do they enjoy under the scheme in either case? For how many years will they draw a pension after retirement? Do they have other rights, for example, for payments to be made to their estate in the event that they die while in service? Will the surviving spouse and dependents enjoy rights? Will rights be automatically indexed for inflation? Is there provision for any *ex gratia* increase in benefits for past, present, or future employees? What earnings can be expected on the pensions fund meanwhile?

SSAP 24 requires that "the actuarial valuation method and assumptions used for accounting purposes should satisfy the accounting objective" (paragraph 18), that is to say, the objective of making full provision over the employees' service lives for the expected costs of their pensions. This stated accounting objective is not, in fact, sufficient to produce a single, identifiable accounting treatment of pension costs. Instead, there are many different working assumptions that can legitimately be made. One important implication of making actuarial assumptions central to the accounting treatment, however, is that the treatment of pension costs becomes one of the few areas in which discounting is used under accepted British accounting principles.

SSAP 24 attempts to make a basic distinction between regular pension costs and variations in cost. The division between regular costs and variations in cost is fairly arbitrary in practice. The distinction means that regular costs are charged against current income, while variations in cost are generally spread over "the expected remaining service lives of the current employees in the scheme after making suitable allowances for future withdrawals" (paragraph 23). As a short-cut method, variations in cost may alternatively be spread over a period representing the average remaining service lives. Limited exceptions to this principle may arise (*a*) where substantial numbers of employees leave the pension scheme, (*b*) where pensions effects arise from a reorganization accounted for as an extraordinary item, and (*c*) under exceptional circumstances where a significant additional cost arises to the scheme that has not been allowed for in the actuarial assumptions. Under these three exceptional circumstances, prudence requires a write-off over a shorter time.

The practical effect of SSAP 24 is that analysts can now have some picture of the existence of a pension scheme and whether or not it is currently being fully funded. It is not generally possible for the effects of overfunding or underfunding to be taken to the income statement in a single year, or even over a short period of years.

An Abstract of the Urgent Issues Task Force (UITF 6, November 1992) extends the principles of SSAP 24 to noncash pension benefits.

3.13 Other Standards

3.13.1 Segmental Reporting

Reporting on the activities of the different segments of a company's business can often present problems of arbitrary allocation of costs and revenues between activities. After all, the reason for combining several activities in one company is typically that significant economies of scale exist in the exploitation of one or more common inputs. There is no way to allocate joint inputs in a way that is not arbitrary. In the rare cases of companies that are "pure" conglomerates, in which the activities are entirely independent and held as a portfolio, there is no economic logic for the company. Market investors could presumably have produced their own portfolios to give them just the same benefits.

Companies have been required to disclose segmental information in Britain for more than 20 years, even though this may well include some arbitrariness. Segmental disclosure in Britain is regulated at three levels—company law, stock exchange listing rules, and professional SSAPs. The 1967 Companies Act first required that turnover and profit before tax be analyzed in the directors' report into two or more classes when, in the opinion of the directors, these items differed substantially from one another. It also required the value of exports to be reported. The 1981 Companies Act increased these disclosure requirements. Now turnover and profits were to be split (in notes to the accounts) by principal export markets, unless the directors considered such a split would present a serious risk to the interests of the company (Schedule 4, paragraph 55, 1985 act). The emphasis is on the destination of sales, rather than sources of supply.

The Stock Exchange Listing Agreement requires an analysis by geographic region, of turnover and contribution to trading results relating to trading operations carried on by the company outside Britain and Ireland. "Contribution to trading results" might be defined differently from "profit before tax" as required by the 1985 act; moreover, the emphasis is on the countries in which business activity originates (for example, the manufacturing units from which sales originate, rather than the markets they supply). Both the 1985 act and the Listing Agreement require only geographic analysis, not line of business results. Companies often report both, however.

SSAP 25, "Segmental Reporting," was issued in June 1990. It extends segmental reporting requirements, both by requiring more information and also by extending the coverage of the requirements to all public companies (whether listed or not) as well as a few large private companies (see below). ED 45, which preceded SSAP 25, aroused controversy over the proposal that companies should disclose the basis on which transfer prices were set between segments. This requirement does not appear in SSAP 25. ED 45 also proposed limiting its scope to public companies and "large" private companies rather than applying (as do virtually all other SSAPs) to all those entities required to present a true and fair view; this limitation of coverage was adopted in order to aid acceptance of the regulation and to protect smaller companies.

Thus, the higher disclosure standards required by SSAP 25, over and above those set by company law, apply only to

1. Public limited companies
2. Holding companies that have a public company as a subsidiary
3. Banking and insurance companies
4. Private companies that exceed any two or more of the following criteria, set at 10 times the size criteria for defining medium-sized companies by Section 248 of the 1985 act. (It is likely that only 150 or so private companies will meet these criteria, out of a million private companies on the register, and out of some 16,000 estimated by the Department of Trade and Industry to be medium sized.)

FRS 3, paragraph 53 states:

> It is important for a thorough understanding of the results and financial position of a reporting entity that the impact of changes on material components of the business should be highlighted. To assist in this objective, if an acquisition, a sale or a termination has a material impact on a major business segment the FRS requires that this impact should be disclosed and explained.

SSAP 25 seeks to advise directors how to determine segments. Schedule 4, paragraph 55(2) of the 1985 act specifically states: "In this paragraph 'market' means a market delimited by geographical bounds." SSAP 25 is a little ambiguous as to how far it seeks to go beyond the act, but it certainly suggests to directors a number of factors that are more than merely geographic. Directors should consider how far different classes of business

1. Earn returns on investment out of line with the remainder of the business; or
2. Are subject to different degrees of risk; or
3. Have experienced different growth rates in the past, or have different potentials for growth in the future.

Factors that should be considered include the nature of products or services supplied and the markets for them, the nature of production processes, distribution channels for products, the way in which activities are organized by the company, and any distinctive legislative requirements relating to parts of the business. These clearly suggest an analysis by different lines of business, rather than geographic areas. However, the latter are also considered important, particularly where economic climates are regarded as notably expansionist or restrictive, where political regimes are unusually unstable, where exchange controls are restrictive, or where exchange rates fluctuate widely. Geographic proximity is not the overriding consideration in grouping territories into a single segment.

Whereas great judgment is left to the directors, SSAP 25 suggests that a segment will normally be considered significant if it contributes 10% or more of the total entity's third party turnover, or profits, or total net assets.

Segmental disclosure should show turnover, both by source and by destination, if they differ materially, divided between sales to external customers and sales to other segments of the company or group. Similarly, segmental disclosure should show operating results, which may be defined as profits or as contribution to profits (depending how far joint costs are allocated to segments) and net assets employed. Recognizing the problems that arise in practice, SSAP 25 leaves some latitude for directors to define these terms in a manner that suits their company.

The provisions are intended, of course, to produce information that goes beyond (indeed, well beyond) that available in the accounts of the holding company, or the group accounts (in which, for example, intercompany sales are eliminated). It is perhaps odd that, having required that consolidated accounts be prepared to aggregate the results of a group of companies, regulators should also require disaggregation of the results in a form of analysis that may sometimes reflect the distinct constitution of group companies or, alternatively, may cut right across the boundaries of separate group companies.

3.13.2 *Cash Flow Statements*

SSAP 10 formerly required that reporting entities with a turnover or income of more than £25,000 a year should present a statement of source and application of funds, going beyond the minimum requirement of statute law. SSAP 10 laid down a standard method for preparing such a statement, derived from the income statement and balance sheet information. SSAP 10 was replaced in 1991.

FRS 1, "Cash Flow Statements," followed U.S. practice in SFAS 95 (1987) and adopted a statement of cash flows rather than a statement of changes in working capital and liquid assets.

FRS 1 requires the publication of a cash flow statement with all financial statements intended to give a true and fair view of financial position and profit or loss, except for small companies as defined in Section 246 of the 1985 act (currently, sales below £2.8 million; balance sheet total below £1.4 million; no more than 50 employees), wholly owned subsidiaries of companies presenting an FRS 1 group cash flow statement, building societies, and mutual life assurance companies.

The cash flow statement can be prepared on either a direct or an indirect basis, that is to say, either as a summary of the cash book or derived indirectly from the opening and closing balance sheets and income statement (together with the notes). A statement reconciling the operating profit shown in the accounts with the operating cash flow figure (see below) is required under FRS 1.

Cash flows are grouped under five headings:

1. Operating cash inflow/outflow (reconciled to the operating profit before charging depreciation or interest)
2. Returns on investment and servicing of finance invested in or by the company/group (including dividends)
3. Taxation actually paid (not accrued) in the year
4. Investing expenditure on fixed assets and businesses, together with the proceeds of sales of such assets
5. Financing activities (proceeds of issues and costs of redemptions of stocks and bonds for cash)

The statement finishes with a balance representing the increase or decrease of cash or cash equivalents. The opening and closing balances will be reconciled with the corresponding figures in the balance sheets. FRS 1 has been criticized for separating investment in operating fixed assets from other expenditure on current operations. A number of U.K.

companies have presented two different explanations of their cash flows in the same set of accounts. The ASB has been reviewing FRS 1 in 1994.

The use of published accounts to assess liquidity is still rather limited, however. The commonly used liquidity ratio comparing current assets with current liabilities gives little indication of the urgency with which those liabilities need to be met; inventories are valued at cost, rather than the realizable values they are expected to yield; the accounts give little sign how far assets of the company are charged by way of security for loans received; and finally, the accounts give no clue how far the company has available to it potential sources of liquidity, for example, in the form of overdraft facilities (for which guarantees may be forthcoming, from directors personally or from other trading partners, etc.)

3.13.3 Earnings per Share

SSAP 3 requires disclosure, going beyond the legal minimum of earnings per share. The SSAP also requires that a fully diluted earnings per share figure is to be shown if the exercise of existing conversion rights and options would reduce the basic EPS figure by 5% or more. The Bunzl accounts show, in note 7, that full dilution would not reduce EPS by as much as 5%.

One of the major aims of FRS 3 was to lessen the emphasis placed on the bottom line earnings figure in the income statement. The ASB also reduced the use of extraordinary items below the line and, hence, outside the definition of earnings for use in investment analysis. In 1993 the Institute of Investment Management and Research (IIMR) published new guidelines that set out ways to calculate a new "headline" earnings figure before extraordinary items (since the institute maintained that FRS 3 caused unnecessary volatility of earnings) and a new figure for sustainable earnings suitable as a basis for forecasts and EPS ratios. The Financial Times has adopted the use of the IIMR's headline earnings.

3.13.4 Post Balance Sheet Events

SSAP 17 requires disclosure of events that take place after the date of the year end but before the date on which the directors approve the accounts for publication. Both dates must be published. Briefly, if the event shows additional evidence of conditions already existing at the balance sheet date not reflected by the accounts, the accounts will have to be adjusted if the new evidence is material. If the conditions did not exist at that date, but disclosure would still be necessary in order for the reader to reach a proper understanding of the financial situation, disclosure will be made by way of a note.

3.13.5 Research and Development Expenditure

It is worth commenting again that research and development expenditure is treated quite conservatively in British accounts, both by law and under SSAP 13 (see also the comment in Section 3.8). Costs are written off against current income except for development expenditure that is pretty clearly going to be recouped.

3.13.6 Complex Financial Instruments

The fear of creative accounting has troubled the British accounting profession for many years, and some widely publicized allegations of manipulation have appeared in the press, accounting journals, newspapers, and books. Alert financial journalists perform an important job in watching for unorthodox accounting practices and reporting them widely. An annual survey of the accounts of 300 major British companies is published by the Institute of Chartered Accountants in England and Wales; this includes informed commentary on developing issues.

A major field for creative accounting was complex financial instruments. This presented opportunities to manipulate items on both the asset and liability side of the balance sheet. The ASB responded with two accounting standards in 1994. FRS 4, "Capital Instruments," concentrates on the liabilities side of the balance sheet. In particular, it aims to dispel ambiguities over the treatment of liabilities as debt, minority interests, or stockholders' funds. It does this by relying largely on the legal form of the financial instrument issued. The standard also prescribes the treatment of finance costs.

Capital instruments are defined as any means of raising finance, whether or not the consideration given for its issue takes the form of cash and whether or not the instrument is a transferable security or a contract between as few as two parties. FRS 4 distinguishes between equity shares (basically, those with unlimited rights to participate in profits or surplus on winding up), nonequity shares (those with some, but limited, participation rights), and other liabilities. It excludes only (*a*) warrants issued to employees under employee share schemes; (*b*) leases, which should be accounted for in accordance with SSAP 21; and (*c*) equity shares issued as part of a business combination that is accounted for as a merger.

The effect of the standard is to limit what can be shown as equity. Thus, the conversion of debt should not be anticipated, but convertible debt should be reported within liabilities and the finance cost should be calculated on the assumption that the debt will never be converted. The amount attributable to convertible debt should be stated separately from that of other liabilities. Capital instruments should be reported within shareholders' funds only if they contain no obligation at all (even contingent) to transfer economic benefits.

As for valuing debt, immediately after issue debt should be stated at the amount of the net proceeds. The finance costs of debt should be allocated to periods over the term of the debt at a constant rate on the carrying amount. All finance costs should be charged in the profit and loss account, except in the case of investment companies. The carrying amount of debt should be increased by the finance cost in respect of the reporting period and reduced by payments made in respect of the debt in that period.

The practice of treating finance costs on an annuity basis seems to be an ingrained feature of the ASB's thinking; there is little theoretical justification for making this choice when, for example, there is no corresponding requirement to depreciate fixed assets on a similar pattern. A definite rule, even if arbitrary, however, may serve to limit alternative treatments for monitoring and contracting.

FRS 5, "Reporting the Substance of Transactions," adopts the principle that the substance of transactions should dominate over their legal form. FRS 5 deals as much with assets as with liabilities. It begins by referring to the "Statement of Principles," Chapter 3, in its definition of assets and liabilities:

> Assets are rights or other access to future economic benefits controlled by an entity as a result of past transactions or events.
> Liabilities are an entity's obligations to transfer economic benefits as a result of past transactions or events.

FRS 5 says that "where a transaction results in an item that meets the definition of an asset or liability, that item should be recognized in the balance sheet if there is sufficient evidence of the existence of the item (including, where appropriate, evidence that a future inflow or outflow of benefit will occur), and the item can be measured at a monetary amount with sufficient reliability." There are also rules for the "derecognition" of assets and liabilities, concerned with the removal of items from the balance sheet. FRS 5 discusses this only in the context of assets but makes a distinction among complete derecognition, no derecognition, and partial derecognition. Basically, an asset is derecognized when a transaction means the transfer of an asset to another party, together with all the significant benefits and risks relating to that asset. Partial recognition arises where, after a transaction to buy or sell an asset, some residual risks or benefits remain with the seller.

FRS 5 may impact on other standards, for example, SSAP 21 if a lease transaction is only part of a larger series of transactions.

FRS 5 also introduces an extension of the definition of subsidiary undertaking in the 1985 Companies Act. It adds the concept of the quasi-subsidiary (see Section 3.1 above).

4. Expected Future Developments

4.1 The Future Development of the Accounting Standards Board Arising from Its Conceptual Framework Project

As a result of criticism of the haphazard development of accounting standards, the Accounting Standards Board produced a "Statement of Principles" in an attempt to define a conceptual framework that would form an underlying basis for accounting and financial reporting. The principle is that a definitive written theory of accounting should exist to enable objective and comprehensive testing of practical problems against it.

The development of a framework has been attempted in the United States, Canada, and Australia, with varying degrees of success. The International Accounting Standards Committee has issued its own version, titled "Framework for the Preparation and Presentation of Financial Statements," which forms a basis for parts of the statement of principles.

The stated objectives of the Statement of Principles are (*a*) to assist the ASB in reviewing existing statements and developing future standards, (*b*) to help to reduce the number of alternative accounting treatments, (*c*) to assist the preparers and auditors of financial statements, and (*d*) to assist the users in interpreting the information contained in the financial statements. The Statement of Principles is not, and does not replace, any specific accounting standard; it is intended to serve as a guide in the preparation and revision of standards. The explicit intention is that the Statement of Principles will apply to the financial statements of all commercial and manufacturing organizations in both public and private sectors.

The Statement of Principles comprises seven chapters, on

- Objectives of financial statements, where the need of the various users is discussed
- Qualitative characteristics of financial information, which outlines primary or relevant characteristics and secondary characteristics, which include comparability and understandability
- Elements of financial statements, where the essential components of each statement are identified
- Recognition, which outlines criteria for inclusion of items in the financial statements
- Measurement in financial statements, which deals with the method of valuation of assets and discusses various bases
- Presentation of financial Information, which reinforces the need for a structured presentation that takes into consideration the level of detail presented
- The reporting entity, where the principles largely mirror the existing provisions of FRS 2 for the accounting treatment of subsidiary companies

It is clear that the Accounting Standards Board is building upon a line of conceptual thinking that stresses user needs for information that is "decision relevant." Within Britain, this is identified by using current market values for financial reporting. The Statement of Principles is largely concerned with making a case to justify this preference for current values, which appeared earlier in its 1993 discussion paper "The Role of Valuation in Financial Reporting." This latter paper compared three policy alternatives: strict historical cost, full-scale current value accounting, and the evolutionary development of the present modified historical cost system. Pragmatically, the ASB recommended the last of these alternatives.

4.1.2 Valuation Conventions

A state of uneasy tension exists at present between the existing historical cost valuation conventions, used by the vast majority of British companies, and current proposals for reform. Existing practices are based largely on historical cost conventions of income realization and cost matching (using a mixture of historical transactions costs and *ad hoc* occasional revaluations at the choice of directors). Proposals for new standards usually have been judged according to whether they appear consistent with established views on accruals accounting. There has been relatively little agreement, however, over the basic purposes of financial reporting, so it has been quite difficult to resolve conflicts of opinion as they have arisen over inconsistencies in the complex set of rules.

The rhetoric of reformers has tended to be conducted in utilitarian terms, with proponents claiming that some new proposal would meet user needs more fully than previous methods. Little empirical evidence has been adduced to support any such arguments, however. Moreover, the ASC lacked a conceptual framework, although it was often urged to develop one. Right from the beginning of its life, there were signs that the new Accounting Standards Board was going to attempt to establish the validity of a new set of concepts.

Proposals to alter the sequence and significance of subheadings on the published income statement, effectively abolishing the distinction between extraordinary and exceptional items, have been aired. There are also clear and persistent signs from the ASB and others that active encouragement to increase the extent of current value reporting, rather than historic cost reporting, is firmly on the agenda. Reactions within (and without) the United Kingdom to these moves remain to be seen, but an interesting and important debate is in prospect.

4.2 The Auditing Practices Board

Another area that is somewhat unclear is the future relationship between the CCAB bodies and the Auditing Practices Board, set up as a replacement for the Auditing Practices Committee. A major concern in setting up the Accounting Standards Board (APB) was the lack of authority of the old Accounting Standards Committee, and this in its turn tended to impugn the authority of the old Auditing Practices Committee.

Auditing derives its authority from different sources from those underlying accounting standards, and there is good reason for the CCAB to keep its direct line of authority over auditing standards, even though the new APB is constituted with a greater measure of independence. Auditors need to be able to compare their actions with those of their peers, particularly if challenged in the courts. This means that they must be able to cite established good practice, rather than producing a reasoned statement of abstract principles. Moreover, the auditor derives more authority from the law than the accountant preparing a set of accounts.

A reasonably happy division of responsibility has long existed, whereby auditors rely on established precedent (as laid down in auditing standards) in carrying out their duties, while both they and accountants who prepare accounts look to accounting standards to set out the more general statements of principle that underlie a "true and fair" view. Arguably, the latter type of standard is more abstract and depends for its success upon public acceptance to a greater extent than auditing standards. Hence the need for the ASB to report to a Financial Reporting Council on which sit a substantial number of senior nonaccountant business figures. By the same token, the APB has less need to make friends with the business world outside accountancy; it draws formal authority of its own from other sources.

4.3 Future Directions

4.3.1 The Stresses of International Harmonization

The United Kingdom is pulled in two different directions by conflicting demands for the harmonization of financial reporting, from the European Union in one direction and from the International Accounting Standards Committee in the other.

As suggested earlier in this chapter, the United Kingdom has complied promptly with European Directives on Company Law as these have fallen due, and as a full member of the European Union, there is little doubt about the authority of Community law over U.K. company affairs. The European Court has already shown that it can be effective in enforcing European legal principles where these conflict with national laws (for example, where U.K. law failed to protect women's rights to equal employment).

On the other hand, the United Kingdom has also been quite prominent in its support for the IASC. The IASC has always had to rely on informal means of persuasion to secure support for international standards. Within national jurisdictions, statute law usually lays down requirements that company accounts be audited, and sometimes it prescribes in detail the contents of those accounts and the rules governing valuation and display. In the case of the IASC, however, there is no comparable set of international regulation to back its call for harmonized reporting.

Traditionally, the IASC's main function has been to help Third World countries by setting broad, general accounting standards that they could adopt for use internally, without the need· for them to set up their own standard-setting machinery. Whereas some countries have looked to a single developed country (often the United States, Britain, or France) as a guide, the IASC's standards have been formally adopted in a number of countries. At the end of the 1980s, however, its focus changed.

Pressure built during the 1980s for the IASC to bring some measure of harmonization into the accounting reports of companies listed on the stock markets of more than one country. There are good economic reasons for investors to want to be able to compare the results of companies that report under different jurisdictions, and economies of scale would be secured for investors operating in world financial markets.

There are some wide disparities in reporting rules among European countries at present, particularly between Germany and the United Kingdom. It thus might seem unlikely that European harmonization will be achieved within the next 20 years. By contrast, the IASC has been offered support from many sources, including the International Organization of Stock Commissions (IOSCO) and the European Commission itself.

At the end of the day, however, the pressure toward European harmonization is propelled not merely by strong economic incentives towards unified markets (financial and nonfinancial): it also has in place a framework of legal authority to give effective power to its policies. It will presumably prevail, just as a skilled professional will usually prevail over an amateur in a long-drawn-out contest.

4.3.2 The Possible Effects of Crisis Conditions

Britain is one of the most politically stable countries in the world, despite 25 years of strife in Northern Ireland. Its population and its political institutions seem to resist change, even though the nature of British society has been altered deeply by new technologies and social pressures over the decades. Corporate reporting practice, however, has been affected in the past by the whiff of scandal, even though such scandal tends to be kept away from popular view. One of the major effects of a possible crisis of confidence, for example, if there were a major corporate collapse or financial scandal, would probably be pressure for greater government control in the form of a U.K. Securities and Exchange Commission. Australia has set a precedent in another major Commonwealth country, with the former National Companies and Securities Commission reconstituted in a tougher form as the Australian Securities Commission in early 1991.

Financial pressure from economic recession produced large numbers of company bankruptcies in the years after 1989. (The term *bankruptcy* is not in fact correct to use in relation to companies in Britain, since it is used specifically for personal financial failure: insolvent companies may be put into receivership, administration, or winding-up, but they are not strictly bankrupt since this implies different legal procedures.) There was also a steep fall in stock market prices. Both events produced pressure on the accountancy profession, since disappointed investors tend to use accountants as scapegoats, partly because of a wish to recoup financial losses and partly because the expectations gap is all the more evident when companies with apparently clean accounts suddenly fail.

If there were to be a crisis of investor confidence, then, it would be likely to produce:

1. Greater pressure for a tighter legal framework of regulation, probably including some form of British securities and exchange commission

2. A move away from self-regulation in the areas of accountancy and audit, insolvency, and financial advisory services, where at present recognized professional bodies operate to administer the general framework of the law

3. Higher compliance and monitoring costs (tending toward U.S. levels)

4.3.3 New Patterns of Corporate Financing

There is also some criticism in Britain, as in the United States, of reliance by companies upon financial markets to raise capital, rather than relationship banking, as is more common in Germany and Japan. Particularly in the case of innovative, high-technology companies, it is sometimes argued that the most important information about the future financial success of a company is far too confidential for disclosure to market transactors: this would merely reveal the company's strategy to potential competitors (especially to those located in countries that have lower disclosure rules).

Although it is reasonable to assume the semi-strong efficiency of capital markets, these markets can only respond to published data. This line of criticism arises from conflicting evidence about the comparative merits of market competition and more protected policies toward competitive innovation. Whereas this debate presents profound implications for corporate financial reporting, as well as for other aspects of corporate disclosure, it is still too early to predict the outcome.

Acknowledgments

The author acknowledges with thanks the help of David Williams and David Matthews of Bunzl plc, Barry Shippen, Roger Mace, and the Technical Department of the Chartered Association of Certified Accountants (ACCA), in particular David Harvey for checking the accuracy of the technical details in this chapter. Any errors that may remain are, of course, the responsibility of the author alone.

Useful Addresses

United Kingdom

Institute of Chartered Accountants in England and Wales
Chartered Accountants' Hall
Moorgate Place
London EC2P 2BJ
Tel: +(071) 920 8100
Fax: +(071) 920 0547

Institute of Chartered Accountants of Scotland
27 Queen Street
Edinburgh EH2 1LA
Tel: +(031) 225 5673
Fax: +(031) 225 3813

Chartered Association of Certified Accountants
29 Lincoln's Inn Fields
London WC2A 3EE
Tel: +(071) 242 6855
Fax: +(071) 831 8054

Chartered Institute of Management Accountants
63 Portland Place
London W1N 4AB
Tel: +(071) 637 2311
Fax: +(071) 631 5309

Chartered Institute of Public Finance and Accountancy
3 Robert Street
London WC2N 6BH
Tel: +(071) 895 8823
Fax: +(071) 895 8825

International Accounting Standards Committee
167 Fleet Street
London EC4A 2ES
Tel: +(071) 353 0565
Fax: +(071) 353 0562

United States of America

International Federation of Accountants
540 Madison Avenue
New York, NY 10022

Tel: +(212) 486 2446
Fax: +(212) 751 1614

Financial Statements of Bunzl plc

		Notes	1993 £m	1992 £m
Consolidated Profit and Loss Account	for the year ended 31 December 1993			
	Sales			
	Continuing operations		**1,463.5**	1,289.4
	Acquisitions		**41.6**	
			1,505.1	1,289.4
	Discontinued operations		**14.4**	20.6
	Total sales	1	**1,519.5**	1,310.0
	Net operating charges	2	**(1,455.5)**	(1,253.1)
	Operating profit			
	Continuing operations		**61.6**	55.5
	Acquisitions		**1.0**	
			62.6	55.5
	Discontinued operations		**1.4**	1.4
	Total operating profit	1	**64.0**	56.9
	Profit/(loss) on sale of fixed assets used in continuing operations		**0.2**	(3.8)
	Profit/(loss) on sale of discontinued operations	3	**1.1**	(1.4)
	Profit on ordinary activities before interest		**65.3**	51.7
	Net interest payable	4	**(9.5)**	(11.3)
	Profit on ordinary activities before taxation		**55.8**	40.4
	Taxation on profit on ordinary activities	5	**(20.5)**	(16.9)
	Profit on ordinary activities after taxation		**35.3**	23.5
	Profit attributable to minorities		**(1.0)**	(0.7)
	Profit for the financial year		**34.3**	22.8
	Dividends paid and proposed	6	**(17.3)**	(16.4)
	Retained profit		**17.0**	6.4
	Earnings per share	7	**8.3p**	5.6p

Movements on consolidated reserves are shown in Notes 11 and 21.
The Accounting Policies and Notes on pages 33 to 48 form part of these Accounts.

as at 31 December 1993	Notes	1993 £m	1992 £m
Consolidated Balance Sheet			
Fixed assets			
Tangible assets	10	**134.3**	131.8
Associated undertakings	11	**7.3**	9.1
Investments	12	**2.0**	1.7
		143.6	142.6
Current assets			
Stocks	13	**152.1**	140.4
Debtors: amounts falling due within one year	14	**230.8**	215.5
Debtors: amounts falling due after more than one year	14	**23.3**	25.6
Investments	15	**7.8**	6.2
Cash at bank and in hand		**12.0**	14.7
		426.0	402.4
Current liabilities			
Creditors: amounts falling due within one year	16	**244.9**	237.6
Net current assets		**181.1**	164.8
Total assets less current liabilities		**324.7**	307.4
Creditors: amounts falling due after more than one year			
7 per cent. Convertible Unsecured Loan Stock 1995/97	17	**24.9**	24.9
Other creditors falling due after more than one year	17	**32.0**	28.3
		56.9	53.2
Provisions for liabilities and charges	19	**29.4**	33.5
Net assets		**238.4**	220.7
Capital and reserves			
Called up share capital	20	**105.9**	102.4
Share premium account	21	**14.7**	0.4
Revaluation reserve	21	**5.2**	6.9
Merger reserve	21	**16.2**	30.9
Profit and loss account	21	**84.5**	66.6
Attributable share of associated undertakings' reserves	11	**6.3**	8.1
Shareholders' funds		**232.8**	215.3
Minority interests		**5.6**	5.4
		238.4	220.7

Approved by the Board of Bunzl plc on 21 March 1994

A P Dyer, Chairman
D M Williams, Finance Director

The Accounting Policies and Notes on pages 33 to 48 form part of these Accounts.

	Notes	1993 £m	1992 £m
for the year ended 31 December 1993			

Consolidated Cash Flow Statement

	Notes	1993 £m	1992 £m
Net cash inflow from operating activities	27	**69.6**	84.7
Returns on investments and servicing of finance			
Interest received		**4.4**	3.2
Interest paid		**(14.8)**	(13.9)
Dividends paid		**(9.0)**	(15.4)
Dividends paid to minority shareholders		**(0.3)**	(0.2)
Dividends received from associated undertakings		**0.9**	0.9
Other movements		**(0.4)**	0.4
Net cash outflow from returns on investments and servicing of finance		**(19.2)**	(25.0)
Tax paid		**(18.8)**	(5.4)
Investing activities			
Purchase of tangible fixed assets		**(24.2)**	(20.1)
Sale of tangible fixed assets		**3.9**	4.0
Purchase of businesses	9	**(5.7)**	(6.2)
Sale of businesses		**–**	6.7
Sale of investments		**–**	0.9
Other movements		**(6.3)**	(4.9)
Net cash outflow from investing activities		**(32.3)**	(19.6)
Net cash (outflow)/inflow before financing		**(0.7)**	34.7
Financing activities			
Decrease in short term deposits with original maturity of more than 90 days		**–**	14.6
(Decrease)/increase in short term loans with original maturity of more than 90 days		**(18.6)**	21.2
Increase/(decrease) in long term loans		**5.4**	(77.6)
Shares issued for cash		**1.0**	–
Net cash outflow from financing	28	**(12.2)**	(41.8)
Decrease in cash and cash equivalents	29	**(12.9)**	(7.1)

Cash flows are stated at the average exchange rates for the year. For the purpose of calculating these cash flows the opening and closing balance sheets have been retranslated at the average exchange rates for the year. As a result the movements cannot be ascertained from the figures shown in the consolidated balance sheets.

for the year ended 31 December 1993	Consolidated 1993 £m	1992 £m
Consolidated Statement of Total Recognised Gains and Losses		
Profit for the financial year	34.3	22.8
Currency translation differences on foreign currency net investments	(1.6)	9.4
Total recognised gains and losses for the year	32.7	32.2

for the year ended 31 December 1993	Consolidated 1993 £m	1992 £m
Note of Historical Cost Profits and Losses		
Reported profit on ordinary activities before taxation	55.8	40.4
Realisation of property revaluation gains of previous years	1.0	0.5
Downward revaluation of fixed assets held for disposal	–	4.2
Adjustment of depreciation to historical cost basis	0.2	0.1
Historical cost profit on ordinary activities before taxation	57.0	45.2
Historical cost profit for the year retained after taxation, minority interests and dividends	18.2	11.2

for the year ended 31 December 1993	Consolidated 1993 £m	1992 £m
Reconciliation of Movements in Shareholders' Funds		
Profit for the financial year	34.3	22.8
Dividends	(17.3)	(16.4)
Scrip dividend adjustment	0.1	0.9
Goodwill written off	(14.7)	(1.0)
Issue of share capital	17.8	0.1
Currency translation and other movements	(2.7)	9.4
Net addition to shareholders' funds	17.5	15.8
Opening shareholders' funds	215.3	199.5
Closing shareholders' funds	232.8	215.3

as at 31 December 1993	Notes	1993 £m	1992 £m
Company Balance Sheet			
Fixed assets			
Tangible assets	10	**12.1**	12.9
Investments	12	**107.5**	92.1
		119.6	105.0
Current assets			
Debtors: amounts falling due within one year	14	**190.3**	163.8
Debtors: amounts falling due after more than one year	14	**94.1**	107.1
Investments	15	**–**	0.4
		284.4	271.3
Current liabilities			
Creditors: amounts falling due within one year	16	**28.6**	26.4
Net current assets		**255.8**	244.9
Total assets less current liabilities		**375.4**	349.9
Creditors: amounts falling due after more than one year			
7 per cent. Convertible Unsecured Loan Stock 1995/97	17	**24.9**	24.9
Other creditors falling due after more than one year	17	**0.1**	0.2
		25.0	25.1
Provisions for liabilities and charges	19	**7.1**	8.6
Net assets		**343.3**	316.2
Capital and reserves			
Called up share capital	20	**105.9**	102.4
Share premium account	21	**14.7**	0.4
Revaluation reserve	21	**0.5**	0.5
Special reserve	21	**177.2**	177.2
Profit and loss account	21	**45.0**	35.7
		343.3	316.2

Approved by the Board of Bunzl plc on 21 March 1994

A P Dyer, Chairman
D M Williams, Finance Director

The Accounting Policies and Notes on pages 33 to 48 form part of these Accounts.

Accounting Policies

a Basis of preparation
The Accounts have been prepared under the historical cost convention, as modified by the revaluation of land and buildings, and have been prepared in accordance with applicable UK Accounting Standards. In order to give a true and fair view, the provisions of the Companies Act 1985 have been departed from as described in Note 21 to the Accounts.

b Comparative figures
Following the issue of the Accounting Standards Board's Financial Reporting Standard 3 — 'Reporting Financial Performance', the prior year comparative figures have been restated. The principal impact of the restatement is to analyse sales and operating profit between continuing operations, acquisitions made during the current year and discontinued operations and also to reclassify certain items. For the purposes of the 1992 results, operating profit of £1.4m has been reclassified from extraordinary items to operating profit from discontinued operations and a loss on sale of discontinued operations of £1.4m has been reclassified from extraordinary items to 'profit/(loss) on sale of discontinued operations'. The downward revaluation of fixed assets held for disposal of £4.2m, previously shown as a movement in the revaluation reserve, is now shown within 'profit/(loss) on sale of fixed assets used in continuing operations'. £0.5m of revaluation credits, previously taken to operating profit, are now shown as a reserve movement. The net effect of these changes to the 1992 results is a £4.7m decrease in earnings and a 1.1p reduction in earnings per share.

c Basis of consolidation
The consolidated Accounts incorporate the assets and liabilities of the Company and its subsidiary undertakings at 31 December 1993 and their results for the periods during 1993 in which they were part of the Group. The consolidated Accounts include the Group's share of the results and net assets of associated undertakings owned during the financial year. Associated undertakings are those in which the Group holds a substantial shareholding and over which it is able to exercise significant influence.

Goodwill, being the excess of the costs of interests acquired over the fair value of net tangible assets, is fully written off against reserves on acquisition. On disposal of a business, any goodwill on acquisition is transferred from reserves to the face of the profit and loss account in determining the profit or loss on disposal.

d Investments in subsidiary undertakings
Where the merger relief provisions of the Companies Act 1985 apply, investments of the Company are accounted for on the basis of the nominal value of shares issued as purchase consideration.

e Discontinued operations
A business is classified as a discontinued operation if it is clearly distinguishable, has a material effect on the nature and focus of the Group's activities, represents a material reduction in the Group's operating facilities and either its sale is completed or, if a closure, its former activities have ceased permanently prior to the approval of the Accounts.

f Foreign currencies
The results of overseas subsidiary and associated undertakings have been translated into pounds sterling at average exchange rates. Assets and liabilities denominated in foreign currencies have been translated at year-end exchange rates, except where a forward exchange contract has been arranged when the contracted rate is used. The Brazilian financial statements have been adjusted to reflect current price levels before translation.

Exchange differences on the retranslation of opening net worth in overseas subsidiary and associated undertakings, net of related foreign currency borrowings and foreign currency hedging contracts, together with differences arising from the use of average and year-end exchange rates, have been taken to reserves. Other exchange differences are taken to the profit and loss account.

g Fixed assets
Freehold and leasehold land and buildings are included at cost or valuation on an open market existing use basis, prepared at regular intervals by qualified valuers. All other assets are included at historical cost, less accumulated depreciation. The profit or loss on sale of tangible fixed assets is calculated by reference to the carrying value of the assets.

h Depreciation
Fixed assets are depreciated over their estimated remaining useful lives at the following annual rates applied to original cost or subsequent valuation less estimated residual value:

Buildings	2% or life of lease if shorter
Plant and machinery	5 – 35%
Fixtures, fittings and equipment	4 – 35%

Depreciation is not provided on freehold land.

i Sales
Sales are net sales invoiced to third parties, excluding inter company transactions, sales by associated undertakings and sales taxes.

j Stocks
Stocks are valued at the lower of cost (on a first in, first out basis) and net realisable value. For work-in-progress and finished goods, cost includes an appropriate proportion of labour and overheads.

k Deferred taxation
Deferred taxation arises from differences in the treatment of certain items for accounting and taxation purposes and is accounted for on the liability method. Provision is made to the extent that it is probable that a liability or asset will crystallise in the foreseeable future.

l Pension benefits
The Group operates both defined benefit and defined contribution pension schemes throughout the world. The funds of the principal schemes are administered by trustees, are held independently from the Group and are not included in the Accounts. Contributions paid to defined benefit schemes operated by the Group are based upon the recommendations of qualified actuaries and are charged against profits on a systematic basis over the expected remaining service lives of participating employees. Independent actuarial valuations of defined benefit schemes are made approximately every three years. Contributions paid to defined contribution schemes are charged to the profit and loss account in the period in which they arise.

		Sales		Operating profit		Net operating assets	
1 Segmental analysis	1993 £m	1992 £m	1993 £m	1992 £m	1993 £m	1992 £m

Business segment

	1993 £m	1992 £m	1993 £m	1992 £m	1993 £m	1992 £m
Paper and Plastic Disposables	**724.1**	565.2	**40.6**	31.6	**116.3**	97.5
Fine Paper	**341.3**	337.8	**6.0**	12.9	**100.9**	100.8
Building Supplies	**239.0**	206.6	**4.2**	0.7	**51.9**	52.0
Cigarette Filters	**114.5**	102.3	**11.4**	10.3	**32.2**	34.8
Plastic Products	**86.2**	77.5	**8.8**	6.3	**50.9**	47.9
Corporate activities			**(8.4)**	(6.3)	**31.9**	32.8
Continuing operations	**1,505.1**	1,289.4	**62.6**	55.5	**384.1**	365.8
Discontinued operations	**14.4**	20.6	**1.4**	1.4	**0.9**	4.6
Group total	**1,519.5**	1,310.0	**64.0**	56.9	**385.0**	370.4

Country of operation

	1993 £m	1992 £m	1993 £m	1992 £m	1993 £m	1992 £m
UK	**281.5**	254.8	**16.8**	15.5	**98.0**	99.0
Rest of Europe	**222.7**	231.0	**1.4**	9.1	**61.9**	65.6
US	**933.8**	757.8	**47.7**	35.1	**170.5**	150.6
Rest of the world	**81.5**	66.4	**6.5**	3.5	**22.7**	22.4
Corporate activities			**(8.4)**	(6.3)	**31.9**	32.8
Group total	**1,519.5**	1,310.0	**64.0**	56.9	**385.0**	370.4

Geographical market supplied

	1993 £m	1992 £m
UK	**227.4**	204.0
Rest of Europe	**239.6**	251.0
US	**949.8**	771.1
Rest of the world	**102.7**	83.9
Group total	**1,519.5**	1,310.0

Reconciliation to consolidated balance sheet

	1993	1992
Net operating assets as above	**385.0**	370.4
Interest bearing cash and investments	**12.9**	11.8
Interest bearing debt (Note 18)	**(119.3)**	(121.5)
Dividends and corporate taxes (Notes 14 and 16)	**(20.4)**	(12.7)
Provisions for deferred taxation and discontinued operations (Note 19)	**(19.8)**	(27.3)
Net assets	**238.4**	220.7

2 Net operating charges	Continuing operations 1993 £m	Acquisitions 1993 £m	Discontinued operations 1993 £m	Total 1993 £m	Continuing operations 1992 £m	Discontinued operations 1992 £m	Total 1992 £m
Changes in stocks of finished goods and work-in-progress	(6.3)	0.7	1.0	(4.6)	(8.2)	1.5	(6.7)
Purchases of finished goods and goods for resale	1,004.6	30.8	–	1,035.4	881.7	1.6	883.3
Raw materials and consumables	86.0	0.9	6.5	93.4	80.0	8.4	88.4
Own work capitalised	(1.6)	–	–	(1.6)	(1.0)	–	(1.0)
Staff costs	172.5	5.0	3.2	180.7	155.1	4.5	159.6
Depreciation	18.1	0.2	–	18.3	16.5	0.2	16.7
Auditors' remuneration	1.4	–	–	1.4	1.3	–	1.3
Hire of plant and machinery and operating lease costs	9.9	0.4	–	10.3	8.6	0.2	8.8
Property rentals	16.8	0.7	0.3	17.8	15.0	–	15.0
Other operating expenses	102.4	1.9	2.0	106.3	87.5	2.8	90.3
Share of profits of associated undertakings	(1.9)	–	–	(1.9)	(2.6)	–	(2.6)
Net operating charges	**1,401.9**	**40.6**	**13.0**	**1,455.5**	1,233.9	19.2	1,253.1

Net operating charges include reorganisation costs of £1.5m (1992 : £nil) in respect of the withdrawal from the Fine Paper operations in Southern Italy. Other operating expenses include £0.1m (1992 : £0.1m) for non-audit work performed by the Company's auditors and their associates.

3 Profit/(loss) on sale of discontinued operations

The profit of £1.1m in 1993 is the result of the release of the remaining provisions set up to cover losses relating to the disposal of the Transportation business in 1989.

The loss of £1.4m in 1992 was a charge to set up provisions for the costs relating to the disposal of the business of Wycombe Marsh Paper Mills Ltd.

4 Net interest payable

	Consolidated 1993 £m	1992 £m
Interest receivable		
On bank deposits and unlisted investments	4.1	2.8
Income from listed investments	0.3	0.2
Total interest receivable	4.4	3.0
Interest payable		
On loan capital, bank loans, overdrafts and other borrowings:		
Repayable within five years, not by instalments	(13.6)	(13.8)
Repayable within five years, by instalments	(0.1)	(0.2)
Repayable wholly or partly in more than five years	–	(0.1)
Finance lease charges	(0.2)	(0.2)
Total interest payable	(13.9)	(14.3)
Net interest payable	(9.5)	(11.3)

Interest payable includes a credit of £nil (1992 : £0.3m) for discount on deferred proceeds from the disposal of businesses.

Notes to the Accounts

5 Taxation	Consolidated 1993 £m	1992 £m
UK corporation tax at 33% (1992 : 33%)	**1.2**	11.3
Overseas taxes	**16.1**	8.0
Deferred taxation transfers:		
Accelerated capital allowances	**0.3**	(1.0)
Pension arrangements and other timing differences	**3.4**	(0.3)
Credit for overseas tax	**(1.4)**	(2.8)
	19.6	15.2
Associated undertakings	**0.8**	1.3
Total taxation for year	**20.4**	16.5
Credited to other reserves	**0.1**	0.4
Taxation on profit on ordinary activities	**20.5**	16.9

Deferred taxation not accounted for is £0.2m (1992 : £1.7m) in respect of accelerated capital allowances and £0.2m (1992 : £(0.2)m) in respect of other timing differences.

6 Dividends paid and proposed	Per share 1993	1992	Total 1993 £m	1992 £m
Interim paid 2 January 1994	**1.8p**	1.8p	**7.6**	7.3
Proposed final payable 1 July 1994	**2.3p**	2.2p	**9.7**	9.1
	4.1p	4.0p	**17.3**	16.4

7 Earnings per share	1993	1992
Earnings per share calculated by dividing earnings of £34.3m (1992 : £22.8m) by 415,107,112 (1992 : 408,773,287), the weighted average of ordinary shares in issue, are:	**8.3p**	5.6p

The 1992 reported earnings per share have been restated as explained in paragraph b of the Accounting Policies on page 33.

The dilution in earnings per share, after taking account of the exercise of all outstanding options and the shares that would be issued on conversion of the 7 per cent. Convertible Unsecured Loan Stock 1995/97, would be less than 5%.

Notes to the Accounts

9 Acquisitions	1993 £m	1992 £m
Assets/(liabilities) acquired:		
Fixed assets and investments	2.4	0.8
Stocks	7.3	2.2
Debtors	13.3	2.8
Creditors	(11.9)	(0.9)
Net bank overdrafts	(0.2)	(0.5)
Deferred taxation	0.2	–
Provisions for liabilities and charges	(3.8)	–
Minority interest acquired	0.2	0.3
	7.5	4.7
Goodwill	14.7	1.0
Consideration	22.2	5.7
Satisfied by:		
Shares allotted	16.7	–
Cash	5.5	5.7
	22.2	5.7

The principal acquisitions made during 1993 were the purchase in April of the assets of Grossman Paper Company, a US distributor of paper and plastic disposables and the purchase in August of Automatic Catering Supplies Ltd, a UK distributor of catering supplies.

On acquisition the net assets/(liabilities) of the businesses acquired were accounted for under the acquisition method of accounting and were adjusted to reflect their fair values to the Group. Fixed assets were reduced by £0.1m, debtors were reduced by £0.1m, creditors were increased by £0.5m and a provision of £3.8m was established to provide for future reorganisation costs.

The net outflow of cash and cash equivalents in respect of the acquisition of businesses was:

	1993 £m	1992 £m
Cash consideration	5.5	5.7
Net bank overdrafts of businesses acquired	0.2	0.5
Net outflow of cash and cash equivalents in respect of the acquisition of businesses	5.7	6.2

In the period following acquisition Automatic Catering Supplies Ltd produced a £1.5m net cash inflow from operating activities and a £2.5m net cash outflow from financing activities. In the period following acquisition Grossman Paper Company produced a £0.6m net cash inflow from operating activities and a £0.2m net cash outflow from the servicing of finance.

In the 7 months preceding the date of acquisition Automatic Catering Supplies Ltd made an operating profit of £0.8m. In its previous financial year, January 1992 to December 1992, its operating profit was £2.5m. Grossman Paper Company made an operating loss of £0.6m in the 8 months preceding acquisition and an operating loss of £0.1m in its previous financial year, August 1991 to September 1992.

10 **Tangible assets**	Land and buildings £m	Plant and machinery £m	Fixtures fittings and equipment £m	Total £m
Consolidated:				
Cost or valuation				
Beginning of year	69.8	114.9	38.9	223.6
Acquisitions less divestments	1.0	3.4	1.4	5.8
Additions	3.2	14.4	6.6	24.2
Disposals and adjustments	(2.1)	(7.6)	(3.2)	(12.9)
Currency translation movement	(1.2)	(0.7)	(0.1)	(2.0)
End of year	70.7	124.4	43.6	238.7
Depreciation				
Beginning of year	6.0	62.9	22.9	91.8
Acquisitions less divestments	–	2.4	1.0	3.4
Charge in year	1.9	11.0	5.4	18.3
Disposals and adjustments	(1.6)	(4.5)	(2.3)	(8.4)
Currency translation movement	0.1	(0.7)	(0.1)	(0.7)
End of year	6.4	71.1	26.9	104.4
Net book value at 31 December 1993	**64.3**	**53.3**	**16.7**	**134.3**
Net book value at 31 December 1992	63.8	52.0	16.0	131.8

The net book value of fixed assets includes assets held under finance leases and hire purchase contracts totalling £1.2m (1992 : £1.1m). Accumulated depreciation of these assets amounts to £1.3m (1992 : £1.2m).

The net book value of fixed assets at 31 December 1993 comprised:

	Land £m	Freehold buildings £m	Long leasehold £m	Short leasehold £m	Plant and machinery £m	Fixtures fittings and equipment £m	Total £m
Consolidated:							
At cost	1.4	4.5	2.3	6.7	124.4	43.6	182.9
At valuation in 1992	15.8	36.7	2.5	0.8	–	–	55.8
Cost or valuation	17.2	41.2	4.8	7.5	124.4	43.6	238.7
Depreciation	–	(1.8)	(1.3)	(3.3)	(71.1)	(26.9)	(104.4)
Net book value at 31 December 1993	**17.2**	**39.4**	**3.5**	**4.2**	**53.3**	**16.7**	**134.3**

The historical cost and the related depreciation of the tangible fixed assets are:

	Land and buildings £m	Plant and machinery £m	Fixtures fittings and equipment £m	Total £m
Historical cost	75.4	124.4	43.6	243.4
Depreciation	(16.3)	(71.1)	(26.9)	(114.3)
Net book value at 31 December 1993	**59.1**	**53.3**	**16.7**	**129.1**
Net book value at 31 December 1992	56.9	52.0	16.0	124.9

	1993 £m	1992 £m
Future capital expenditure		
Commitments not provided for	**1.1**	3.2
Expenditure authorised but not contracted for	**3.6**	1.2
	4.7	4.4

10 Tangible assets (continued)	Land £m	Freehold buildings £m	Short leasehold £m	Fixtures fittings and equipment £m	Total £m
Bunzl plc:					
Cost or valuation					
Beginning of year	3.5	9.2	1.0	1.1	14.8
Additions	–	–	0.4	0.3	0.7
Disposals and adjustments	–	(1.3)	(1.0)	(0.6)	(2.9)
End of year	3.5	7.9	0.4	0.8	12.6
Depreciation					
Beginning of year	–	–	0.9	1.0	1.9
Charge in year	–	–	–	0.2	0.2
Disposals and adjustments	–	–	(0.9)	(0.7)	(1.6)
End of year	–	–	–	0.5	0.5
Net book value at 31 December 1993	**3.5**	**7.9**	**0.4**	**0.3**	**12.1**
Net book value at 31 December 1992	3.5	9.2	0.1	0.1	12.9

11 Associated undertakings	Consolidated 1993 £m	1992 £m
Share of post-acquisition reserves at beginning of year	8.1	7.8
Share of current year profit after taxation	1.1	1.3
Dividends paid in the year	(0.9)	(0.9)
Currency translation and other movements	(2.0)	(0.1)
Share of post-acquisition reserves at end of year	6.3	8.1
Cost of investments	1.0	1.0
Investment in associated undertakings	7.3	9.1

The principal associated undertaking is shown on page 48. All associated undertakings were unlisted in 1993.

12 Investments held as fixed assets	Unlisted £m	Listed £m	Total £m
Consolidated:			
Beginning of year at cost less provisions	1.4	0.3	1.7
Additions and transfers	0.3	–	0.3
End of year at cost less provisions	**1.7**	**0.3**	**2.0**
Market value at 31 December 1993		0.3	
Market value at 31 December 1992		0.3	

The listed investments at 31 December 1993 are listed on stock exchanges outside the UK.

	Investments in subsidiary undertakings £m
Bunzl plc:	
Beginning of year at cost less provisions	92.1
Additions and transfers	15.4
End of year at cost less provisions	**107.5**

The investments in subsidiary undertakings at 31 December 1993 are stated net of provisions of £3.4m (1992 : £3.4m). Principal subsidiary undertakings are listed on page 48.

		Consolidated	
13 Stocks		1993 £m	1992 £m
Raw materials and consumables		9.4	9.7
Work-in-progress		2.6	2.9
Finished goods and goods for resale		140.1	127.8
		152.1	140.4

	Bunzl plc		Consolidated	
14 Debtors	1993 £m	1992 £m	1993 £m	1992 £m
Amounts falling due within one year				
Trade debtors	0.1	0.4	196.2	179.2
Amounts owed by subsidiary undertakings	189.9	163.1	–	–
Other debtors	–	–	14.9	13.5
Prepayments and accrued income	0.3	0.3	13.1	12.8
Corporate taxes	–	–	6.6	10.0
	190.3	163.8	230.8	215.5
Amounts falling due after more than one year				
Amounts owed by subsidiary undertakings	73.2	88.1	–	–
Pension fund prepayment	15.5	16.8	19.6	21.0
Advance corporation tax recoverable	3.3	–	–	–
Other debtors	2.1	2.2	3.5	4.3
Corporate taxes	–	–	0.2	0.3
	94.1	107.1	23.3	25.6
	284.4	270.9	254.1	241.1

	Bunzl plc		Consolidated	
15 Investments held as current assets	1993 £m	1992 £m	1993 £m	1992 £m
Investments in subsidiary undertakings	–	0.4	–	–
Short-term deposits	–	–	7.8	6.2
	–	0.4	7.8	6.2

	Bunzl plc		Consolidated	
16 Creditors	1993 £m	1992 £m	1993 £m	1992 £m
Amounts falling due within one year				
Loans and overdrafts (Note 18)	–	–	62.8	68.8
Payments received on account	–	–	0.4	0.8
Trade creditors	0.1	0.1	116.8	101.6
Amounts owing to subsidiary undertakings	3.8	8.8	–	–
Dividend proposed	17.3	9.1	17.3	9.1
Corporate taxes	4.5	5.0	9.9	13.9
Other taxation and social security contributions	0.1	0.1	6.7	8.0
Other creditors	–	–	7.0	7.6
Accruals and deferred income	2.8	3.3	24.0	27.8
	28.6	26.4	244.9	237.6

Notes to the Accounts

17 Creditors	Bunzl plc 1993 £m	1992 £m	Consolidated 1993 £m	1992 £m
Amounts falling due after more than one year				
7 per cent. Convertible Unsecured Loan Stock 1995/97 (Note 18)	24.9	24.9	24.9	24.9
Other creditors falling due after more than one year				
Other loans (Note 18)	0.1	0.1	31.6	27.8
Accruals and deferred income	–	0.1	0.4	0.5
	0.1	0.2	32.0	28.3
	25.0	25.1	56.9	53.2

18 Loans and overdrafts	Bunzl plc 1993 £m	1992 £m	Consolidated 1993 £m	1992 £m
Falling due after more than one year				
Wholly repayable within five years				
7 per cent. Convertible Unsecured Loan Stock 1995/97	24.9	24.9	24.9	24.9
Other loans repayable within five years	0.1	0.1	30.2	26.0
	25.0	25.0	55.1	50.9
Repayable by instalments				
Instalments due within five years	–	–	0.5	0.5
Instalments due after more than five years	–	–	0.3	0.4
	–	–	0.8	0.9
Obligations under finance leases	–	–	0.6	0.9
Loans falling due after more than one year	25.0	25.0	56.5	52.7
Loans falling due within one year	–	–	62.8	68.8
Total loans and overdrafts	25.0	25.0	119.3	121.5
The total borrowings are repayable:				
Within one year	–	–	62.8	68.8
Between one and two years	–	–	0.7	25.9
Between two and five years	25.0	25.0	55.5	26.4
After more than five years	–	–	0.3	0.4
	25.0	25.0	119.3	121.5
Obligations under finance leases included above are repayable:				
Within one year	–	–	0.5	0.4
Between one and five years	–	–	0.6	0.9
	–	–	1.1	1.3

The aggregate of bank loans and overdrafts is £93.7m (1992 : £95.6m). Loans amounting to £2.0m (1992 : £4.0m) are secured by either fixed or floating charges on various assets of the relevant companies.

Loans wholly repayable within five years include £29.2m drawn under a bilateral facility maturing on 2 January 1998 at variable interest rates linked to Deutschmark LIBOR. Other loans are at various market rates.

£24.9m of 7 per cent. Convertible Unsecured Loan Stock 1995/97 remains outstanding and is convertible up to 31 May 1995 at the option of the holder into 13,691,626 ordinary shares at a conversion rate of 75.7p nominal of ordinary share capital per 550p of loan stock. The stock is redeemable at par at the Company's option between 1 July 1995 and 1 July 1997.

19 Provisions for liabilities and charges	Bunzl plc 1993 £m	Bunzl plc 1992 £m	Consolidated 1993 £m	Consolidated 1992 £m
Pensions	–	–	3.2	3.2
Discontinued operations	3.3	4.8	7.6	15.1
Deferred taxation (Note 22)	2.0	2.7	12.2	12.2
Other	1.8	1.1	6.4	3.0
	7.1	8.6	29.4	33.5

Movements	Pensions £m	Discontinued operations £m	Deferred taxation £m	Other £m	Total £m
Beginning of year	3.2	15.1	12.2	3.0	33.5
Acquisitions	–	–	(0.2)	3.8	3.6
Charge/(release) in year	0.3	(1.1)	3.7	0.7	3.6
Amounts utilised or transferred in year	(0.1)	(6.4)	(3.5)	(0.8)	(10.8)
Currency translation movement	(0.2)	–	–	(0.3)	(0.5)
End of year	3.2	7.6	12.2	6.4	29.4

20 Share capital	1993 £m	1992 £m
Authorised: 550 million (1992 : 550 million) ordinary shares of 25p each	137.5	137.5
Issued and fully paid ordinary shares of 25p each	105.9	102.4

Number of ordinary shares in issue		
Beginning of year	409,408,257	408,314,845
Issued during year – loan stock conversions	1,099	14,565
– option exercises	1,093,328	109,849
– scrip dividends	58,039	968,998
– acquisition of Automatic Catering Supplies Ltd	12,984,497	–
End of year	423,545,220	409,408,257

Details of share options granted and exercised during 1993 and those outstanding at 31 December 1993 under the Company's Savings-Related Share Option Scheme (1981), the Sharesave Scheme (1991), the Senior Executive Share Option Scheme and the Executive Share Option Scheme (No. 2) are set out below:

Scheme	1993 Grants Number	1993 Grants Price (p)	1993 Exercises Number	1993 Exercises Price (p)	Outstanding options at 31.12.93 Number	Outstanding options at 31.12.93 Price (p)
Savings-Related Scheme (1981)	–	–	59,175	68.0-126.0	1,377,274	68.0-133.0
Sharesave Scheme (1991)	659,210	102.0-119.0	17,469	72.0- 78.0	2,404,271	72.0-119.0
Senior Executive Scheme	–	–	100,000	84.0	1,483,140	84.0-149.0
Executive Scheme (No. 2)	2,204,516	115.6-148.0	916,684	84.0-124.8	9,845,041	84.0-249.0
	2,863,726		1,093,328		15,109,726	

The outstanding options are exerciseable at various dates up to September 2003. The adoption of a new executive scheme will be proposed at the forthcoming Annual General Meeting. Full details are contained in a separate letter from the Chairman to shareholders.

21 Movements on reserves

Consolidated:

	Share premium account £m	Revaluation reserve £m	Merger reserve £m	Profit and loss account £m
Beginning of year	0.4	6.9	30.9	66.6
Premium on exercise of share options	0.8	–	–	–
Premium on issue of shares	13.5	–	–	–
Scrip dividend adjustment	–	–	–	0.1
Realised revaluation surplus	–	(1.0)	–	1.0
Goodwill written off	–	–	(14.7)	–
Dividends from associated undertakings	–	–	–	0.9
Transfers	–	(0.2)	–	0.2
Currency translation movement	–	(0.5)	–	(0.2)
Retained profit (excluding associated undertakings)	–	–	–	15.9
End of year	**14.7**	**5.2**	**16.2**	**84.5**

Currency (losses)/profits of £(0.3)m (1992 : £2.4m) relating to foreign currency exchange contracts and borrowings to finance investment overseas have been included within the currency translation movement in the profit and loss account.

Included within the merger reserve is £177.2m, being the special reserve of the Company.

As at 31 December 1993 the cumulative amount of goodwill written off in respect of acquisitions, net of goodwill attributable to subsidiary undertakings disposed of or closed, was £201.9m (1992 : £187.2m).

Bunzl plc:

	Share premium account £m	Revaluation reserve £m	Special reserve £m	Profit and loss account £m
Beginning of year	0.4	0.5	177.2	35.7
Premium on exercise of share options	0.8	–	–	–
Premium on issue of shares	13.5	–	–	–
Scrip dividend adjustment	–	–	–	0.1
Loss for the year before dividends receivable	–	–	–	(1.2)
Dividends receivable from subsidiary undertakings	–	–	–	27.7
Dividends paid and proposed	–	–	–	(17.3)
End of year	**14.7**	**0.5**	**177.2**	**45.0**

As permitted by Section 230 of the Companies Act 1985, the profit and loss account of the Company has not been separately presented in these Accounts.

As permitted under paragraph 15 of Schedule 4 to the Companies Act 1985, the directors consider it appropriate to depart from paragraph 12(a) of Schedule 4 to the Companies Act 1985, having implemented SSAP24 – 'Accounting for pension costs'. As a result, cumulative unrealised profits of £10.3m (1992 : £11.2m) relating to pension costs have been included in the profit and loss account. This amount is not considered to be distributable. The amount of unrealised profit included in the results for the year is £nil (1992 : £0.1m).

The special reserve arose from the cancellation of the share premium account in 1987 and 1988 and at the present time is not considered to be distributable.

22 **Deferred taxation**	Bunzl plc 1993 £m	1992 £m	Consolidated 1993 £m	1992 £m
Accelerated capital allowances	**0.4**	0.4	**3.9**	3.8
Pension provisions and other timing differences	**4.8**	5.3	**14.8**	11.4
Advance corporation tax recoverable	**(3.2)**	(3.0)	**(6.5)**	(3.0)
	2.0	2.7	**12.2**	12.2

The potential liability for deferred taxation not provided above is:

	Bunzl plc 1993 £m	1992 £m	Consolidated 1993 £m	1992 £m
Accelerated capital allowances	**(0.1)**	–	**1.4**	1.0
Other timing differences	–	–	**(0.6)**	(0.2)
Capital gains on disposal of properties	–	–	**7.5**	8.8
	(0.1)	–	**8.3**	9.6

No provision has been made for potential corporate taxation on the unrealised revaluation surpluses in respect of properties which are expected to be held for the foreseeable future.

24 **Contingent liabilities**	Bunzl plc 1993 £m	1992 £m	Consolidated 1993 £m	1992 £m
Bills discounted	–	–	**2.8**	2.5
Bank guarantees	**86.9**	82.5	**10.9**	1.5
Other items	–	–	**7.5**	10.4

The bank guarantees of the Company include £86.5m (1992 : £82.4m) of guarantees provided on behalf of subsidiary undertakings. Other items principally comprise trade and other guarantees.

25 Pensions

As permitted by SSAP 24, the pension fund surpluses arising in the principal UK defined benefit schemes were included in the balance sheet on the implementation of the standard. Subsequent valuations have shown further actuarial surpluses in the UK schemes. The regular pension cost of the principal UK defined benefit schemes is offset by amortisation of the additional surpluses over the average remaining service lives of current employees.

The net pension cost for the Group was £7.4m (1992 : £5.0m) of which £5.6m (1992 : £2.8m) was in respect of principal defined benefit schemes, which provide benefits based on final pensionable salary, and is assessed in accordance with the advice of independent qualified actuaries.

The results of the most recent actuarial valuations of the principal defined benefit schemes were:

	UK	US
Date of most recent valuations	6 April 1991	1 January 1993
Method used	Projected unit method	Projected unit method
Main assumptions:		
Investment return/return on assets per annum	9.5%	8%
Salary increases per annum	7.5%	8% up to age 40 and 5% for ages over 40
Market value of investments at last valuation date	£47.8m	£8.1m
Level of funding, being the actuarial value of assets expressed as a percentage of the accrued service liabilities	120-123%	94-109%

The Group operates other schemes overseas in accordance with local practice and legislation. Some of these schemes are externally funded, whilst others are internally funded, the amount set aside being shown in provisions for liabilities and charges.

26 Operating lease commitments

	Land and buildings 1993 £m	Other 1993 £m	Land and buildings 1992 £m	Other 1992 £m
At 31 December the Group had the following annual commitments under non-cancellable operating leases:				
Expiring within one year	2.4	2.2	1.9	1.5
Expiring between two and five years	8.2	5.7	10.6	6.0
Expiring after five years	11.3	0.3	7.6	1.8
	21.9	8.2	20.1	9.3

27 Reconciliation of operating profit to net cash inflow from operating activities

	Consolidated 1993 £m	1992 £m
Operating profit	64.0	56.9
Adjustments for non cash items:		
Depreciation	18.3	16.7
Share of profits of associated undertakings	(1.9)	(2.6)
Profit on divestments	–	(0.5)
Others	0.2	(1.8)
Working capital movement:		
Stocks	(3.5)	8.6
Debtors	(6.9)	(0.5)
Creditors	(0.6)	7.9
Net cash inflow from operating activities	**69.6**	84.7

28 Analysis of changes in financing	Consolidated 1993 £m	1992 £m
Beginning of year	**199.1**	211.4
Net cash outflow from financing	**(12.2)**	(41.8)
Shares issued for non-cash consideration (Note 9)	**16.7**	–
Currency translation movement	**1.3**	29.5
End of year	**204.9**	199.1

Financing comprises share capital and share premium, loans and finance lease obligations due after more than one year and loans due within one year with an original maturity of more than 90 days of £28.3m (1992 : £44.1m), less short term deposits with an original maturity of more than 90 days of £0.5m (1992 : £0.5m).

29 Analysis of changes in cash and cash equivalents	Consolidated 1993 £m	1992 £m
Beginning of year	**(4.3)**	(0.1)
Net decrease in cash and cash equivalents	**(12.9)**	(7.1)
Currency translation movement	**2.0**	2.9
End of year	**(15.2)**	(4.3)

Cash and cash equivalents comprise cash at bank and in hand, short term deposits with an original maturity of less than 90 days of £7.3m (1992 : £5.7m) held as current assets, less loans and overdrafts due within one year with an original maturity of less than 90 days of £34.5m (1992 : £24.7m).

Statement of Directors' Responsibilities

Company law requires the directors to prepare financial statements for each financial year which give a true and fair view of the state of affairs of the Company and the Group and of the profit or loss for that period. In preparing those financial statements, the directors are required to:

- select suitable accounting policies and then apply them consistently;

- make judgements and estimates that are reasonable and prudent;

- state whether applicable accounting standards have been followed, subject to any material departures disclosed and explained in the financial statements;

- prepare the financial statements on a going concern basis unless it is inappropriate to presume that the Group will continue in business.

The directors are responsible for maintaining proper accounting records which disclose with reasonable accuracy at any time the financial position of the Company and to enable them to ensure that the financial statements comply with the Companies Act 1985. They have general responsibility for taking such steps as are reasonably open to them to safeguard the assets of the Group and to prevent and detect fraud and other irregularities.

Auditors' Report

To the Members of Bunzl plc:
We have audited the Accounts on pages 28 to 48.

Respective responsibilities of directors and auditors
As described above, the Company's directors are responsible for the preparation of the Accounts. It is our responsibility to form an independent opinion, based on our audit, on those Accounts and to report our opinion to you.

Basis of opinion
We conducted our audit in accordance with Auditing Standards issued by the Auditing Practices Board. An audit includes examination, on a test basis, of evidence relevant to the amounts and disclosures in the Accounts. It also includes an assessment of the significant estimates and judgements made by the directors in the preparation of the Accounts and of whether the accounting policies are appropriate to the Group's circumstances, consistently applied and adequately disclosed.

We planned and performed our audit so as to obtain all the information and explanations which we considered necessary in order to provide us with sufficient evidence to give reasonable assurance that the Accounts are free from material misstatement, whether caused by fraud or other irregularity or error. In forming our opinion we also evaluated the overall adequacy of the presentation of information in the Accounts.

Opinion
In our opinion the Accounts give a true and fair view of the state of affairs of the Company and the Group at 31 December 1993 and of the profit of the Group for the year then ended and have been properly prepared in accordance with the Companies Act 1985.

KPMG Peat Marwick
Chartered Accountants
Registered Auditors
London

21 March 1994

	1993 £m	1992 £m	1991 £m	1990 £m	1989 £m
Group Five Year Summary **Sales**					
Continuing operations	**1,505.1**	1,289.4	1,264.2	1,242.5	1,194.2
Discontinued operations	**14.4**	20.6	236.3	373.6	705.8
Total sales	**1,519.5**	1,310.0	1,500.5	1,616.1	1,900.0
Operating profit					
Continuing operations	**62.6**	55.5	51.4	55.4	60.7
Discontinued operations	**1.4**	1.4	(7.7)	(3.0)	13.0
Total operating profit	**64.0**	56.9	43.7	52.4	73.7
Profit/(loss) on sale of fixed assets	**0.2**	(3.8)	0.3	(0.4)	3.6
Reorganisation of continuing operations	**–**	–	(13.3)	–	(11.1)
Profit/(loss) on sale of discontinued operations	**1.1**	(1.4)	(10.3)	(13.7)	(62.3)
Profit on ordinary activities before interest	**65.3**	51.7	20.4	38.3	3.9
Net interest payable	**(9.5)**	(11.3)	(9.3)	(5.4)	(15.2)
Profit on ordinary activities before taxation	**55.8**	40.4	11.1	32.9	(11.3)
Taxation on profit on ordinary activities	**(20.5)**	(16.9)	(15.3)	(15.4)	(23.3)
Profit on ordinary activities after taxation	**35.3**	23.5	(4.2)	17.5	(34.6)
Profit attributable to minorities	**(1.0)**	(0.7)	(0.4)	(0.9)	(1.7)
Profit/(loss) for the financial year	**34.3**	22.8	(4.6)	16.6	(36.3)
Dividends paid and proposed	**(17.3)**	(16.4)	(16.3)	(24.1)	(24.1)
Dividends per share	**4.1p**	4.0p	4.0p	5.9p	5.9p
Earnings per share	**8.3p**	5.6p	(1.1)p	4.1p	(8.9)p
Shareholders' funds per share	**55.0p**	52.6p	48.9p	52.7p	57.3p
Net assets employed					
Fixed assets	**143.6**	142.6	140.8	148.5	155.9
Net current assets and other liabilities	**94.8**	78.1	64.9	72.1	84.7
Net assets	**238.4**	220.7	205.7	220.6	240.6
Financed by:					
Shareholders' funds	**232.8**	215.3	199.5	215.2	233.7
Minority interests	**5.6**	5.4	6.2	5.4	6.9
	238.4	220.7	205.7	220.6	240.6

The prior year comparative figures have been restated as explained in paragraph b of the Accounting Policies on page 33.

OTHER EUROPEAN COUNTRIES EXCLUDING FORMER COMECON MEMBER STATES: OVERVIEW

At first glance it may appear that the countries included in this section have little or nothing in common, except that none was incorporated into the group of states having centrally planned economies under the domination of the Soviet Union (COMECON).

In terms of the history and origins of their financial reporting practices, there is obviously some truth in this view. This is not to say that interrelationships do not exist. A number of attempts have been made over the years by the Nordic countries to develop active cooperation, and Turkish accounting developments have been strongly influenced by Swiss practice. Interrelationships also exist with other countries now in the European Union, of course. In particular, the influence of German thinking from the early part of the twentieth century can be seen to permeate much of the background to many later developments.

If the individual chapters of this section are considered from a slightly detached viewpoint, however, then a common thread clearly emerges. This relates to the momentum and direction of change. It is clear that the content and general thrust of the IASC and its work are having, and are expected to continue to have, a significant influence on the thinking and developments in these countries. Perhaps even more important, however, is the influence of developments *within* the EU. There is a clear tendency in the discussions presented here, and in recent developments and expected future changes, for movement toward the philosophy and practices inherent in the Fourth and Seventh EC Directives. The speed and strength of movement obviously vary, as would be expected, given the quite different historical and legal starting points. Political considerations are also relevant.

It is increasingly clear that the European Union, whatever its shortcomings, is the dominant pole of attraction for countries in (and even bordering on) the continent of Europe. For the countries in this section, this means that they are very likely either to become member states of the EU or to enter into some form of economic association with it. This, in turn, implies that they will seek progressively to make their accounting practices compatible with EU requirements.

AUSTRIA

Walter Lukas
Ernst & Young, Vienna

1. Background

1.1 Historical Development

The history of Austrian accounting law dates from July 1, 1863, when the General Commercial Code (*Allgemeines Handelsgesetzbuch*, AHGB) was introduced. This code of law was drawn up by the delegates of the states of the German Confederation, among which was Austria. German commercial law then developed further with the enactment of the German Commercial Code (*Deutsches Handelsgesetzbuch,* dHGB) on January 1, 1900. Whereas this piece of legislation did in fact contain reference to the principles of proper accounting, it did not define these principles in any detail. The objective of this approach was to leave room for further development of the principles of proper accounting by prudent and honorable businessmen, which explains why even today these rules still meet the needs of modern business life. After the annexation of Austria by Germany in 1938, dHGB was introduced in Austria as part of the measures aimed at achieving unification of law.

Another step of critical importance in the development of accounting law was the passing in 1937 of the German Corporation Law (*Deutsches Aktiengesetz,* dAktG), which was also designed to serve the purpose of unification of law. Even after the reestablishment of the Republic of Austria in 1945, this law remained in force unchanged until December 31, 1965. The Austrian Corporation Law (*Osterreichisches Aktiengesetz* 1965, OAktG) only "Austrified" the dAktG 1937, the substance of which was left essentially unchanged.

The significance of dAktG 1937 (and, subsequently, of OAktG 1965) with respect to accounting was that some of the provisions concerning accounting constituted a legal interpretation of the provisions of the 1938 Commercial Code (*Handelsgesetzbuch,* HGB), which are applicable to all businesses. The HGB did not contain any specific rules regarding valuation or the layout of the balance sheet and the profit and loss statement. Therefore, provisions applicable to *Aktiengesellschaften* (corporations) had to be adopted.

In view of this fact, a review of dAktG was required to determine to what extent its provisions had already become accepted principles of proper accounting and, thus, binding on all businesses required to prepare accounts. Wherever gaps had been left in the law, they were filled in a continuous process of further development of the principles of proper accounting, which thus became an integral part of the legal system.

Because Austria was seeking to establish closer relations with the European Community (EC), and part of the existing body of law was considered obsolescent, a process of fundamental reorganization of accounting law began in the mid-1980s, resulting specifically in a reform of the HGB. It must be noted that Austria is not yet a member of the EC and thus under no statutory obligation to comply with EC Directives. Because of her geographic situation, close economic ties with other European countries, and frequently similar legal traditions, however, Austria is nevertheless seeking to develop her legal system in increasing conformity with EC legislation. In 1994 Austrian entry into the EC was finally agreed upon, subject to national approval.

1.2 Present Law and Reforming Efforts

The accounting regulations previously in force had relatively early origins, Austria not having adopted adjustments that had in the meantime been implemented in other countries. This situation was addressed by the *Rechnungslegungsgesetz* (RLG), aimed at achieving concurrence with the adjustments of accounting regulations that had been implemented by the countries of the European Community.

Regarding the position of new Austrian legislation with respect to EC regulations, it may be said in brief that it conforms in principle to EC Directives. The *Rechnungslegungsgesetz* was passed by the National Council (the Lower House of the Austrian Parliament) on June 28, 1990 and promulgated by Issue 192 of the *Federal Law Gazette*, dated July 31, 1990.

Pursuant to RLG Article XI paragraph 1, the provisions of the RLG were applicable to all fiscal years starting after December 31, 1991. The provisions governing group accounting are applicable as of 1994. RLG

Article X paragraph 11 provided that the new provisions may be applied to earlier fiscal years, provided that the entire set of rules is applied, not only those containing the more favorable provisions.

The main areas where reforms were implemented are registered merchants (*Vollkaufleute*, merchants who have been entered in the commercial register as such, particularly including all commercial companies), corporations, consolidated financial statements, and annual audits, which will be commented on in more detail below, together with significant aspects of tax law, which is based on the 1988 tax reform.

1.3 The Effects of Tax Law

Apart from the obligation to draw up a commercial balance sheet, persons carrying on a trade or business who are required by law to keep accounts and to close accounts at regular intervals must prepare, for the purpose of profit computation, at the end of a business year a statement of their business assets and liabilities, in accordance with the commercial principles of adequate and orderly accounting. This also applies to persons carrying on a trade or business who keep books and who close accounts on a voluntary basis.

The principle of authoritativeness of the commercial balance sheet with regard to the tax balance sheet arises from the Income Tax Act (*Einkommensteuergesetz*, EStG) Section 5. According to this principle, the commercial financial statements are the authoritative basis for tax accounts. The values entered in the commercial balance sheet must also be used for the tax balance sheet, unless tax law specifically requires that other values be shown.

The "reversed authoritative principle" means that in practice the commercial balance sheet is based on the tax balance sheet; that is, the commercial balance sheet is prepared to suit the desired appearance of the tax balance sheet. HGB section 208 will result in a statutory, if limited, form of "reversed authoritativeness," limited to tax concessions. Such concessions currently include special depreciation (EStG 1988, section 8, paragraph 2), write-down to the going value of foreign participation and lendings (EStG 1988, section 6, subparagraph 7), and tax concessions for capital expenditure (EStG 1988, sections 10, 12, and 13). Pursuant to HGB section 205, such items must be disclosed as "untaxed reserves."

The 1993 tax reform, effective January 1, 1994, eases the tax burden on businesses. Trade income tax (12.5%) and property tax have been eliminated; the corporate income tax rate (previously 30%) has been increased to 34%; the total effective tax rate on corporate income has therefore been reduced from 39% to 34%. However, some of the special investment allowances previously available have been reduced or even abolished (e.g., EStG 1988, section 9).

2. General Accounting Regulations

The general regulations applicable to all registered merchants are contained mainly in HGB sections 189–216 as amended by RLG, with special emphasis on proper accounting practices.

2.1 General Requirements

Pursuant to HGB section 189, paragraph 1, accounts must be kept in such a way that they convey to a competent third party a general understanding of the business transactions and the position of an enterprise within reasonable time. They must furthermore allow reconstruction of the origins and transactions of accountable events. The obligation of registered merchants to prepare financial statements and, as a result, to use double-entry bookkeeping, arises from section 124 of the Federal Tax Code (*Bundesabgabenordnung*, BAO).

2.2 Inventory

The results of taking stock are inventory listings showing all asset and liability items with a description of kind, quantity, and value. The inventory must show all asset and liability items that must be disclosed in the balance sheet. The content and scope of inventory, therefore, depend on the quantity of asset items that must be shown and the volume of debts that must be entered as liabilities.

Inventory listings must be drawn up when a business is started and at the close of every fiscal year. The following inventory principles must be complied with in this context:

- The principle of completeness requires that the inventory show all assets and liabilities that are attributable to the merchant in legal and/or commercial terms. Nothing may be omitted, and no fictitious items may be added.

- The principle of itemized recording and valuation is laid down in HGB section 191, paragraph 1. Each asset item and each liability item must be listed and valued individually.

- The principle of correctness applies to kind, quantity, and value of the asset items and liabilities to be listed.

- According to the principle of correctness in terms of kind, the asset items and liabilities listed must be described appropriately in order to avoid deception.

- The principle of correctness in terms of quantity requires that quantities listed in the inventory are given as accurately as possible. Absolute accuracy of quantity statements is, of course, not possible, because errors of counting, weighing, and measuring can never be ruled out completely.

- The principle of correctness in terms of value requires that quantities listed are valued correctly. This principle is generally complied with when asset items are valued at acquisition or production cost and liabilities are valued at the repayable amount. If there are reasons for a decline in value, a lower value must be estimated.

- The principle of nonarbitrariness prohibits arbitrary exploitation of the scope of discretion available in making estimates. The value chosen must be a value that any competent third party, taking into account all the facts and circumstances underlying the estimate, would be willing to confirm as being justified.

- The principle of verifiability requires that all a competent third party may need for reconstructing the quantities and values shown in the inventory must be documented. The principle of clarity, as laid down in HGB section 190 paragraph 2, is also applicable to the inventory. Inventory listings must be comprehensible and clear. Single inventory items must be described unambiguously and appropriately. If required, quality designations must also be provided.

2.3 Principles Relating to the Preparation of Balance Sheets

When starting a business, the merchant has the obligation to prepare an opening balance sheet (HGB section 193, paragraph 1) and to prepare an annual financial statement (HGB section 193, paragraph 2) after each fiscal year. Pursuant to HGB section 193, para 3., the length of any fiscal year must not exceed 12 months.

Annual financial statements must be prepared within the first 9 months of the fiscal year following the previous fiscal year. The financial statements comprise the balance sheet and the profit and loss statement. This rule applies to registered merchants in general, without taking into account any supplementary requirements applicable to corporations. In preparing balance sheets, the following disclosure rules must be observed:

- The regulations applicable regardless of legal status do not contain any detailed rules regarding balance sheet organization and disclosure requirements.
- HGB section 195 can be regarded as the general guideline, requiring a clear and easy-to-read presentation of information, which should afford as true a view as possible of assets and profit position. In contrast to HGB section 222, paragraph 2, this addresses only the knowledge that a merchant would generally have and does not generally require the provision of reliable insight. There is, moreover, no requirement concerning reliable insight into the financial standing.

The regulations determining what items may or must be shown as assets and liabilities comprise in essence the following provisions:

- Under HGB section 195, paragraph 1, the rule of completeness requires that the annual financial statement must be based on all business transactions having an effect on the financial position and the profit position of the enterprise. Any contracts entered into with respect to which none of the contracting parties has yet started any work or performed any services, and which have not developed unfavorably for the enterprise preparing the balance sheet and which will not result in any negative effects on the enterprise—so-called pending business—need not be included in the balance sheet.

- HGB section 196, paragraph 2, prohibits offsetting of items shown on the assets side against items shown on the liabilities side.

- Pursuant to HGB section 197, promotion and formation expenses, the cost of equity in capital procurement, and self-provided intangible assets must not be shown in the balance sheet. In contrast to previous balance sheet practices, new limitations have been imposed with respect to the last of these three categories, as a result of which capitalization of intangible assets acquired without payment—such as software or know-how—is no longer permitted.

- Capitalization of starting, extension, and reorganization expenses is optional under HGB section 198, paragraph 3. Depreciation, in any case, must be based on the principle of conservatism (HGB section 201, paragraph 1, subparagraph 4, and section 210).

- Capitalization of original goodwill is not permitted. Under HGB section 203, paragraph 5, goodwill is the market value of a going concern that exceeds the balance sheet value of assets and is a reflection of expected future benefits. Goodwill that is acquired against payment must therefore be capitalized. Capitalization of derivative goodwill is optional under HGB section 203, paragraph 5. For commercial purposes, goodwill must be distributed according to a schedule over the fiscal years during which it is expected to be utilized. Under HGB section 225, paragraph 4, corporations are required to show derivative goodwill in their schedule of assets.

- Under HGB section 198, paragraphs 5 and 6, and following sections, the accrued and deferred items to be shown are limited to transitory items (expenses prepaid and income received) in the narrow sense and are thus used to apportion payment transactions that constitute expenses or income of future periods. Receivables deferred and expenses accrued, and thus a merchant's own arrears and those of third parties, must be shown as other liabilities or other receivables. Any income that is payable only after the closing date, and any expenses incurred before the closing date with the related cash outflows occurring only after that date, must be shown under receivables and payables, respectively. Such items may therefore be shown in the balance sheet only if they can be classified as asset or liability items. Under HGB section 225, paragraphs 3 and 6, corporations are required to provide supplementary comments in that respect in the annex.

- Under RLG, redemption discounts and capital procurement costs may be shown under accrued and deferred items and can be amortized according to a schedule of annual installments. Such an apportionment, however, is permissible only in respect of expenses that are directly connected with the procurement of outside funds in terms of materiality and time.

- Liability reserves (i.e., provisions) must be shown strictly on the liabilities side. Whereas a definition of the concept of liability reserves is not provided, HGB section 198, paragraph 8, lists types of provisions that must be made. On the basis of the wording of HGB section 198, paragraph 8, such provisions are mandatory, no right of option being allowed.

2.4 Valuation Requirements

The following section presents an outline of valuation requirements that now no longer form part of the accounting regulations applicable to corporations but are contained in the body of requirements that are applicable to all merchants. The aim of these requirements is to ensure a true and fair view of the position of an enterprise.

HGB section 201, paragraph 1, subparagraph 1 requires adherence to the principle of continuity in valuation. The valuation method applied in preparing the previous annual financial statement must be retained to ensure the highest possible measure of comparability of statements.

For the computation of values, any valuation or depreciation method may be used that is in compliance with proper accounting principles. Once chosen, such methods must then be applied consistently. Under HGB section 201, paragraph 3, any departure from the principle of continuity in valuation is permissible only under special circumstances. Such circumstances would have to be of a substantial nature, such as statutory changes or a major reorganization of the enterprise. Balance sheet policy alone does not constitute a valid reason.

In addition, HGB section 201, paragraph 1, subparagraph 2 lays down the principle of continuity in business operations—the going concern principle. It is this principle on which is based the valuation of asset items that are used up or realized in the course of business operations, provided it is not rendered inapplicable by actual circumstances or prevailing law. If the assumption that an enterprise will continue to exist is justified, liquidation values must not be shown in the annual financial statement, unless it would appear that there is a serious danger that under special circumstances business operations could not be continued. In the event of plans to close down an enterprise, or when continuation is rendered impossible by legal reasons, application of the HGB valuation rules is no longer permissible.

Pursuant to HGB section 201, paragraph 1, subparagraph 2, the assumption of continuing operations must also be departed from when a continuation of operations is rendered impossible by physical circumstances. In view of the impossibility of formulating clear and verifiable facts and conditions under which the standard assumption is no longer applicable, any departure from the assumption of continuity in business operations can arise only as the result of a subjective assessment.

Another major principle is that of individual valuation, pursuant to HGB section 201, paragraph 1, subparagraph 3, which prohibits the offsetting of falls in the value of individual asset items or provisions against value increases in other asset items or expected receivables by summary treatment.

The principle of conservatism (HGB section 201, paragraph 1, subparagraph 4) furthermore requires that the assets side may show only profits that actually have been realized by the closing date. The liabilities side, on the other hand, must show all foreseeable risks and losses incurred until the closing date, even if such risks or losses became known only between the closing date and the day on which the financial statement was finally drawn up. For balance sheet purposes, nonrealized profits and losses are therefore treated according to the principle of imparity, that is, in different ways.

The central elements of the valuation provisions now in force are the following:

- The concept of acquisition cost (HGB section 203, paragraph 2) is now defined by law.

- The same applies by analogy also to the concept of production cost (HGB section 203, paragraph 3). Fundamental departures from past practices must be pointed out, however.

- The scope of discretion in valuation has been largely eliminated by fixing the value for the purpose of capitalization on the basis of direct cost, raw material cost, and production overheads.

- Capitalization of general administrative expenses and special distribution expenses is no longer permissible.

- Interest payable on outside funds—pursuant to HGB section 236, paragraph 1, subparagraph 2, corporations are required to disclose such information in the annex—may be capitalized (HGB section 206, paragraph 3). Under certain conditions (HGB section 206, paragraph 3) a reasonable portion of administrative and distribution expenses in respect of long-term production contracts may be capitalized also. This is applicable to long-term production contracts with a production period extending over more than 12 months.

Another central element in asset valuation (HGB section 203), which is particularly emphasized, is the requirement of strict adherence to the depreciation schedule in depreciating assets (HGB section 204, paragraph 1). Corrections of the elements of depreciation fixed in the year of acquisition may be made only under special circumstances. Under HGB section 204, paragraph 2, extraordinary depreciation of depreciable assets is mandatory in the case of a presumed permanent decline in value. In the case of fluctuations in value that are presumed to be only temporary, there is a right of option. The so-called moderated lowest value principle must be applied. Computation of the lower value must be based on the assumption of continuing business operations (HGB section 201, paragraph 1, subparagraph 2) and the possibility of using the asset in business operations (HGB section 204, paragraph 2).

Pursuant to HGB section 204, paragraph 3, any non-writing-up of assets must be disclosed in the annex. In the case of corporations, it must be noted that the written-up amount must not increase distributable profit (HGB section 235) in the year of writing-up.

With regard to current assets, the so-called strict lowest value principle applies. According to this principle, acquisition or production costs must or may be subject to extraordinary write-offs if the value allocable to such asset items is lower at the balance sheet date. Such write-offs must be effected regardless of the expected duration of any decline in value.

Another aspect that must be taken into account is better insight gained by the time the financial statement is drawn up. In addition, any losses over and above the position as of the date of the balance sheet may be anticipated (HGB section 207, paragraph 2) if required in light of reasonable commercial judgment, in order to avoid the necessity of depreciations in the near future.

HGB section 211, paragraph 2, provides a general description of the valuation principles to be applied to so-called liability reserves, including actuarial principles as applicable. The law does not prescribe any specific computation method, nor does it contain rules regarding single computation elements.

Liability reserves are provisions in the balance sheet for liabilities existing at the balance sheet date, or expenses commercially attributable to the closing period, which, while not being fixed yet by reason and/or amount, have their commercial origins in the closing period. The amounts of such provisions must be estimated according to proper accounting principles. Noncash capital contributions, donated items, and withdrawals are shown at present value (HGB section 202), taking into account, however, the possibility of actual utilization of such asset items within the enterprise.

3. Special Provisions Applicable to Corporations

Corporations are subject to the supplementary provisions contained in HGB sections 221–243 and sections 277–283. The obligation of corporations to draw up balance sheets arises under BAO section 124. Corporations are registered merchants by virtue of their legal status.

3.1 General

The information presented in this section applies to corporations (Aktiengesellschaft, or AG, similar to American stock corporations, and Gesellschaft mit beschränkter Haftung, or Ges.m.b.H., similar to American close corporations), as well as to some types of partnerships formed under commercial law. It is applicable to partnerships when the general partner is a corporation that has no natural person (HGB section 221, paragraph 3) acting as general partner with the right of representation.

The special provisions applicable to corporations relate to the following areas:

- Requirements concerning annual financial statements, including layout of balance sheet and income statement
- Rules on the information to be provided in the annex and the situation report
- Disclosure requirements

The reporting requirement thus includes the annual financial statements and the situation report, with the financial statements made up of the balance sheet, the profit-and-loss statement, and the annex.

The provisions that will be discussed in detail below are in essence based on the general norm contained in HGB section 222, paragraph 2, which requires that the annual financial statement should provide a true and fair view of the assets and liabilities, the financial and the profit position of a business. This fundamental standard applies generally in the absence of any special rules and in the event of doubts concerning interpretation and application of single rules, or when gaps in the law must be closed.

The additional requirement of a true and fair presentation of the financial position refers specifically to the indication of the due dates of receivables and payables.

3.2 Classification by Size

The first distinction that must be drawn between the different types of corporation is that between "big" and "small" businesses. Statutory requirements vary depending on the size of a business. Under HGB section 221 paragraph 1, "small" corporations are businesses that exceed not more than one of the three following limits:

- A balance sheet total of 200 million schillings (Sch)
- Sales revenues in the 12 months before the closing date of Sch 300 million
- 300 employees on a yearly average; the average number of employees is determined on the basis of the number of employees on the last days of the respective months of the previous calendar year.

If two or more of the above three limits are exceeded, a business will be classified as a "big" corporation.

Differences in size and type of corporation are reflected in different legal requirements, the most important of which are outlined below.

- With one exception, the size of a corporation has no effect on the application of the provisions relating to the balance sheet and the profit and loss statement. The provision concerning the creation of statutory reserves is applicable only to AGs and "big" Ges.m.b.H.s.
- With respect to the annex HGB section 242, which provides some relief from the statutory requirements for small businesses, must be noted.
- There are no differences in statutory requirements as far as the situation report is concerned.
- Under HGB section 268, the obligation to have the annual financial statement and the situation report audited applies to AGs and "big" Ges.m.b.H.s. The audit obligation extends equally to some other Ges.m.b.H.s, namely those that are required by law or under their internal constitution to have a supervisory board, even if the Ges.m.b.H. is a "small" one in terms of the law.

3.3 Balance Sheet Layout

Another rule contained in the supplementary provisions for corporations relates to balance sheet layout. Balance sheet layout is governed by HGB section 224, paragraph 2, which prescribes the format shown in the example on pages 1052–1057 and requires adherence to particular principles.

HGB section 223, paragraph 1, prescribes the principle of balance sheet continuity. Once chosen, the form of presentation, specifically the layout of subsequent balance sheets and profit and loss statements, must be retained. To ensure the highest possible measure of comparability, moreover, the law requires that the figures of the previous year be shown, rounded to Sch 1,000. This provides a better picture of changes in the situation of a business. The only time that the figures of the previous year need not be shown (RLG Article X, paragraph 4) is the first time the law is applied. Whenever the amounts shown are not comparable, this fact must be noted and commented on in the annex. This applies also when an amount shown for a previous year has been adjusted.

HGB section 223, paragraph 4, permits further breakdown of items, provided that the prescribed layout is adhered to. When an asset or a liability falls under several balance sheet items, reference to such other items must be made (HGB section 223, paragraph 5) under the item under which the asset or the liability is actually shown, or a note must be included in the annex, if this is required to render the annual financial statement clear and comprehensible.

Section 223, paragraph 6, permits summary of the balance sheet items marked by Arabic numerals and the items of the profit and loss statement that are marked by letters. Pursuant to HGB section 223, paragraph 7, blank items need not be included except where this is required for comparison with the previous year.

HGB section 223, paragraph 8, permits a modified balance sheet layout and renaming of the items of the balance sheet and the profit and loss statement that are marked by Arabic numerals if this is required—owing to any special characteristics of a corporation—to enable preparation of a clear and comprehensible annual financial statement.

HGB section 223, paragraph 3, contains provisions for enterprises engaged in several branches of business, to which different rules regarding balance sheet layout apply.

3.4 The Core Items of the Balance Sheet

Following the outline of the general principles of balance sheet layout, the core items of a balance sheet are discussed below.

Assets (asset items, prepaid expenses, deferred income). Under HGB section 198, paragraph 1, asset items include fixed asset and current asset items. Fixed assets comprise tangible assets and similar items, as well as intangible assets such as franchises, industrial property rights and licenses, and goodwill. No exact definition is provided by the law. For tangible assets, no breakdown is required into residential buildings on the one hand and commercial or plant buildings on the other. Pursuant to HGB section 225, paragraph 7, the value of land must be either noted in the balance sheet or given in the annex. With respect to financial assets, the disclosure of participating interests must be specially noted. HGB section 228, paragraph 1, defines the concept of *participating interest*. The criteria specified by the definition may be satisfied, however, even at lower participation quotas. The existence of a participating interest is currently assumed when a holding amounts to at least 25% of the shares of a business.

The item "loans" must be included in the balance sheet (HGB section 227). This item is used to report receivables with a term of at least 5 years. The valuation principle applicable to such loans is not the strict lowest value principle, as applicable to current assets, but the moderated lowest value principle that is used for fixed assets. According to the moderated lowest value principle, any presumed temporary only decline in value may be accounted for by extraordinary write-off. A write-off *must* be made only in the case of a presumed permanent decline in value.

With regard to the item "investments held as fixed assets," the definition contained in HGB section 198, paragraph 2, must be noted. The synonymous description "loan stock rights of fixed assets" permits the listing under this item of shares in partnerships or corporate shares that neither constitute a participating interest as defined by HGB section 228, paragraphs 1 and 2, nor are evidenced by certificates. This includes, among others, shares in a Ges.m.b.H., shares in cooperatives, and capital contributed to limited partnerships, which—while falling under the definition of fixed assets—are not participating interests in the terms of HGB section 228, paragraphs 1 and 2.

With respect to the inclusion in the balance sheet of leasing contracts, the following distinctions are made: when the asset leased is attributed to the lessor, the rental payments constitute operating income for the lessor (*Einkommenssteuerrichtlinien,* EStR, income tax regulations, section 2, paragraph 7). When the leased asset is used by the lessee for business or professional purposes, rental payments made will be treated as the lessee's operating or advertising expense.

When the asset is attributed to the lessee, it must be capitalized by the lessee at acquisition or production cost. The acquisition or production cost shown may be the cost incurred by the lessor.

When movable items or buildings are leased, a distinction is required as to whether or not this constitutes a case of special leasing. Assets leased under special leasing arrangements are attributed to the lessee. Special leasing contracts are for goods that are made to suit the lessee's special requirements and which upon expiration of the contractual rental period can be put to regular and meaningful commercial use only by the original lessee.

With respect to the treatment for balance sheet purposes of low-value fixed assets, HGB section 226, paragraph 3, provides the following rights of option:

- The assets may be treated as retirements in the same year in which they are acquired, which means that identical amounts are shown in the "additions" column, in the "retirements" column, and in the "depreciation charge" column of that fiscal year. Accumulated depreciation, of course, need not be shown for assets that are treated as retirements.
- Low-value fixed assets are retired at the end of their useful life. This means that in the year of acquisition identical amounts are shown in the "additions" and "depreciation charge" columns of that fiscal year and under "accumulated depreciation." At the end of the useful life, the amount is removed both of acquisition or production costs and accumulated depreciation.

Pursuant to HGB section 226, corporations must prepare a so-called fixed asset movements schedule to be attached to the annex or to the balance sheet, which is an itemized schedule showing the development of the items "expenditure for starting, extending, and reorganizing business operations," intangible assets, tangible and financial assets.

This schedule is to provide to the recipient of the annual financial statements information on the development of the book values of every item. The basis used is not the book values shown at the previous balance sheet date but original acquisition or production costs. This type of representation is called the *direct gross method*. A third party reading the annual financial statement thus gains an insight into the full amount of funds invested in fixed assets.

3.5 Profit and Loss Statement Layout

The rules relating to the layout of the profit and loss statement are contained in HGB section 231 and the following sections. (See the example on pages 1048–1051.) The law prescribes the format to be followed and, depending on the business's size, the minimum reporting requirements. Use of the report form (vertical) has recently become mandatory. Presentation of the profit and loss statement in account form (two-sided) is no longer permissible.

The report form allows structuring of the income statement by summarizing materially related items and improvement of readability by showing subtotals. It furthermore enables clear differentiation between calculation of profit and utilization of profit. The types of charges, income, and subtotals to be shown, and the order in which they are to be listed in the profit and loss statement, are also prescribed. In preparing the income statement, one of two alternative methods may be used: the expenditure style of presentation (HGB section 231, paragraph 2) or the cost sales style of presentation (HGB section 231, paragraph 3).

The expenditure style of presentation shows on the income side gross performance, which consists of:

- Revenue from sales
- Inventory changes in finished goods and work in progress
- Work performed by the undertaking for its own purposes and capitalized

Revenue from sales includes only revenue earned from normal business operations—proceeds from the sale of products and goods that are typical of the business concerned, or from the performance of services that are typical of the business concerned. The proceeds from the disposal of atypical goods or the rendering of atypical services must be shown under "other operating income" or, if "extraordinary" in terms of the law, under "extraordinary income." The sales revenue shown is net revenue, that is, net of any reductions such as discounts, bonuses, rebates, and net of value added tax.

Changes in inventory in finished goods and work in progress may be a result of movements in inventory quantity or inventory value.

"Work performed by the undertaking for its own purposes and capitalized" consists of fixed assets that were manufactured by and are used in the business, and must be shown in the balance sheet. This item must also be used to report charges for the start-up and any subsequent extensions of business operations if the reporting corporation chooses to make use of the capitalization option.

The charges side shows the expenses associated with gross performance as defined above. Total expenditure is broken down into cost of raw materials and consumables, staff expenses, and depreciation charges.

The cost sales style of presentation shows on the income side only part of the gross performance of a fiscal year: sales revenue. The charges side therefore shows only those expenses that are associated with the quantity sold. This cost of sales is broken down into:

- Production costs
- Distribution costs
- Administrative costs

It must be noted in this context that if the cost sales style of presentation is used, comments on a number of items must be included in the annex (HGB section 237, paragraph 4). Regardless of the style of presentation selected, the general layout principles to be adhered to pursuant to HGB section 223 are the same as those that must be followed in drawing up the balance sheet. Moreover, the gross principle as laid down in HGB section 196 applies, prohibiting balancing of expense and income items.

Both the expenditure style of presentation and the cost sales style of presentation show subtotals called "profit or loss on ordinary activities" and "extraordinary profit or loss." The cost sales style of presentation shows an additional subtotal, "gross profit from sales." The "profit or loss on ordinary activities" can be broken down into the "operating profit or loss" and the "financial profit or loss." The operating profit or loss, however, cannot be interpreted as "profit or loss from activities that are typical of the undertaking," as it is influenced by income expenses that may be atypical of the undertaking, belongs to other periods and is considered extraordinary, and is reported under "other operating income" and "other operating charges." "Other operating income" includes, among other things:

- Income from the disposal of fixed assets
- Income from the dissolution of provisions
- Income from the sale of securities forming part of the current assets

"Other operating charges" includes, among other things:

- Losses from the disposal of fixed or current assets
- Donations
- Expenses for damages

The financial profit or loss is the balance of income and charges from financial investments and group affiliations. Income basically consists of dividends and other profit shares, as well as interest earned on financial assets and credit balances at banks. Financial charges mainly comprise write-off from financial assets, write-off from securities forming part of current assets, and interest paid on borrowings.

The item "extraordinary profit or loss" shows the balance of income and charges in respect of operations that, pursuant to HGB section 233, paragraph 1, are outside the ordinary scope of business of an undertaking.

3.6 Notes to the Accounts

Apart from the profit and loss statement, an annex must be provided for the disclosure of certain information. The obligation to draw up an annex extends to all corporations, regardless of their legal status or size. Pursuant to HGB section 222, the annex forms an integral part of the annual financial statement. Its objective is to supplement the balance sheet and the profit and loss statement by conveying a true and fair view of the position of a business with respect to assets and liabilities, the financial position, and the profit position.

The annex consists of the following parts:

- HGB section 236 requires notes on the balance sheet and the profit and loss statement, specifically with respect to the major closing items, reference to the methods used in balance sheet preparation, and valuation and disclosure of any changes in valuation
- HGB section 237 requires the provision of supplementary information on the balance sheet and the profit and loss statement
- HGB section 238 prescribes the information to be provided in respect of affiliated enterprises

- HGB section 239 prescribes the information to be supplied in respect of corporate agents and employees
- HGB section 240 prescribes the information to be submitted by AGs

Under HGB section 222 paragraph 2, additional information may be included in the annex if, owing to special circumstances, the annual financial statement should fail to provide a true and fair view of the overall situation of an enterprise. It must also be noted that pursuant to HGB section 242, some relief is granted to small corporations from the statutory requirements concerning the volume of information to be reported in the annex.

There are no specific provisions concerning the organization of the annex. It must conform to the general norm prescribed by HGB section 222 paragraph 2. Any information given must be presented in a meaningful way to be of real use to readers of the balance sheet.

3.7 Situation Report

The situation report required under HGB section 243 must be clearly distinguished from the annex. It does not form part of the financial statement, but exists in its own right.

Under HGB section 243 the situation report is required to describe the projected development of the enterprise, its research and development activities, and its future commercial position, in a manner that provides a true and fair view of actual conditions. The law prescribes only the minimum contents of the situation report.

The situation report must show the trend of business in the course of the closing year, with special reference to events that are not directly reflected by the annual financial statement but are of major significance in assessing the commercial position of an enterprise.

3.8 Publicity Requirements

The disclosure requirements for AGs are defined by law (HGB section 277) as the duty to submit the annual financial statement and other records to the main commercial register of the corporation. Submission of the statement is the responsibility of the management board and must be effected within 13 months of the balance sheet date.

Under HGB sections 278 and 279, the disclosure requirements applicable to small AGs and big Ges.m.b.H.s are graduated. Their statements need not be published—a notice announcing submission of the statements to the commercial register is sufficient. Some relief from the statutory requirements is granted to small AGs, which are allowed to summarize certain items (HGB section 278, paras 1 and 2). The disclosure requirements for group accounts are contained in HGB sections 277 and 279, with only a few exceptions relating to the exemption of subsidiaries from the disclosure obligation. The form and content of the required records is prescribed by HGB section 281.

It must be noted that the statements must be published in accordance with the applicable formal requirements. Regarding the obligation under HGB section 282 of the court administering the commercial register to examine annual financial statements, there is no such ex-officio obligation. The court will inspect the records for completeness and adherence to formal requirements only upon application.

4. Regulations Applicable to Group Accounts

The obligation of corporations to prepare group accounts arises from HGB sections 244–267. These regulations enter into force as of 1994. The most important provisions are presented below. An example of group accounts is presented on pages 1058–1065.

The obligation to draw up group accounts arises from HGB section 244. Group accounts must be prepared in the case of parent-subsidiary relationships. Such a relationship is deemed to exist in the case of unified management by the parent company and the existence of a "control relationship." Under HGB section 244 paragraph 1, group accounts must be drawn up under the so-called concept of unified management, if the enterprises of a group are subject to unified management by a corporation—the parent—having its seat in Austria, and if the parent company has a participating interest in these enterprises—the subsidiaries (HGB section 228). The legal status of the subsidiaries is of no relevance in this context.

Participating interests, as defined by HGB section 228, paragraph 1, are investments in other enterprises made with the intention to benefit the operations of the parent by creating a permanent link with the subsidiary. When such a parent-subsidiary relationship exists in respect of a joint undertaking, such an undertaking must also be included in the group accounts.

Under the so-called control concept (HGB section 244, paragraph 2), group accounts and a group situation report must also be drawn up when the parent holds a participating interest in one or several other enterprises, as regulated by HGB section 228, and enjoys the following rights with respect to such enterprises, that is, subsidiaries:

- Majority of voting rights under HGB section 244, paragraph 2, subparagraph 1; or
- Right to appoint corporate agents under HGB section 244, paragraph 2, subparagraph 2; or
- Right of control under a contract or articles of incorporation under HGB section 244, paragraph 2, subparagraphs 3 and 4; or
- Agreement regulating the exercise of voting rights under HGB section 244, paragraph 2, subparagraph 4.

HGB section 244, paragraphs 1 and 3, furthermore require that the parent must be a corporation or a partnership under commercial law, with a corporation as the general partner and having no natural person as general partner with the right of representation.

Under HGB section 250 paragraph 1, group accounts have to consist of the group balance sheet, the group profit and loss statement, and the group annex, all forming one unit. The accounts must be clear and informative and, under HGB section 250 paragraph 2, must convey a true and fair view of a group's assets and liabilities, its financial position and its profit position.

Pursuant to HGB section 250 paragraph 3, group accounts must show the assets and liabilities as well as the financial and profit position of the enterprises, covered in a manner as if all the enterprises were one single enterprise. The general principles applicable to group accounts are the following:

- Clarity and readability
- A true and fair view
- The fiction of legal unity
- Continuity in consolidation methods

Group accounts are subject to the same regulations of HGB section 251 as apply to the parent's individual financial statement.

Pursuant to HGB section 253, group annual accounts are required to constitute a summary of the parent's and the subsidiaries' annual financial statements. This section furthermore lays down the principle that for the purpose of group consolidation the investment of the parent in a subsidiary must be replaced in the balance sheet by the subsidiary's balance sheet assets, untaxed reserves, provisions, liabilities, and deferred and accrued items. This rule applies to the extent to which the law applicable to the parent allows inclusion of these items in the balance sheet, and as long as other regulations do not provide otherwise. This type of consolidation is termed "full consolidation."

The assets, liabilities, deferred and accrued items, as well as the income and expenses of the enterprises covered by the group accounts must be fully accounted for, regardless of the fact that they may already have been included in the annual financial statement prepared by these enterprises, unless this is not allowed under the balance sheet law applicable to the parent or disclosure in the balance sheet is optional. Rights of option with regard to the balance sheet that are available under the law applicable to the parent may be exercised in drawing up the group accounts, regardless of whether or not such rights have already been exercised by the enterprises covered by group accounts in drawing up their balance sheets.

Under HGB section 263, a simplified type of consolidation may be used for participating interests that must not or need not be accounted for by full consolidation but with respect to which an enterprise covered by the group accounts exercises a controlling influence. Such enterprises are called *affiliated* or *associated* enterprises. A controlling influence is deemed to exist if a holding amounts to at lease 25% of the shares of such an enterprise.

A participating interest in an affiliated enterprise must be shown in the group balance sheet either at book value or at the amount corresponding to the share held in the affiliated enterprise's net worth. This so-called equity method compares the book value of the participating interest against the proportionate share in the net worth of the enterprise. Any difference found is then examined to determine whether it is a result of hidden reserves, goodwill, or equity shown on the liabilities side. Depending on the type of method used, the book value either will be retained or the value of the interest is fixed at the value of the proportionate equity capital. The method used must be disclosed in the group annex (HGB section 264, paragraph 1, subparagraph 2, sentence 4). This type of consolidation is applied mostly to holdings of minority interests.

Another type of consolidation is quota consolidation (HGB section 262). It is used mainly for joint undertakings in which none of the partners has a direct or indirect share amounting to more than half the capital and with respect to which the equity method (HGB section 263) is not applied. Quota consolidation is permissible if a parent or subsidiary covered by group accounts is managing another enterprise jointly with one or several enterprises not covered by this group's accounts. This type of consolidation is applied most frequently to so-called joint undertakings. Quota consolidation is not allowed, however, if the requirements for full consolidation pursuant to HGB section 244 are satisfied.

The exemption of small groups from group accounting requirements is regulated by HGB section 246. A parent will be exempted from the obligation to prepare group accounts if certain size limits are not exceeded. The limits concern balance sheet total, revenue from sales, and number of employees. The size criteria will be tightened step by step. The current criteria are as follows:

- Balance sheet total less than Sch 500 million
- Revenue from sales less than Sch 1,000 million
- Number of employees employed on a yearly average less than 1,000

After a transition period of 2 years, that is, effective 1996, the limits are to be reduced to a balance sheet total of Sch 300 million, revenue from sales of Sch 500 million, and 500 employees.

Exemption will be granted if two of the three criteria are satisfied at the closing date and in the course of the year preceding it.

Foreign currency translation, which is of significance particularly in consolidating foreign undertakings, is not specifically regulated by law.

The guiding principle is that a true and fair view of assets and liabilities, the financial position, and the profit position should be provided. The valuations of assets and liabilities as of the balance sheet date are therefore translated at the exchange rate or rates prevailing at that date. Translation differences may be shown as a special item under other charges in the profit and loss statement, affecting the result of the closing period. Alternatively, they may be shown under equity on the liabilities side of the balance sheet, without effect on the income statement.

The group annex forms part of the group accounts. It contains notes on the group balance sheet and the group profit and loss statement (HGB section 265) as well as further information required (HGB section 266).

The group situation report (HGB section 267) corresponds to the situation report on the annual financial statement. It comments furthermore on the trend of business and highlights events of particular significance that occurred within the period allowed for preparation of the group accounts, as well as the expected development of the group and research and development.

The rules governing the auditing of annual financial statements that are discussed below are also applicable to group accounts.

5. Regulations Concerning the Auditing of Annual Financial Statements

The rules with respect to the auditing of annual financial statements are contained in HGB sections 268–276. The obligation to have annual financial statements audited arises from HGB section 268. The annual financial statements and situation reports of AGs, big Ges.m.b.H.s. and other Ges.m.b.H.s., which by law or under their shareholders' agreement have to have a supervisory board, must be subjected to such audits.

Audits are performed by certified public accountants and firms of certified public accountants. Ges.m.b.H.s. may also be audited by sworn accountants and auditing companies. Under HGB section 270, paragraph 1, the auditors of annual financial statements are appointed by the shareholders. The auditors of group accounts are appointed by the shareholders of the parent. Important reasons precluding the appointment of potential auditors in this context are enumerated in HGB section 271.

Pursuant to HGB section 269, paragraph 1, the auditor has to examine whether the annual financial statement was prepared in conformity with statutory requirements and the provisions of the shareholders' agreement or articles of incorporation.

Accounts are included in the audit pursuant to HGB section 269, paragraph 1. Balance sheet, profit and loss statement, and the annex are subject to a full audit with respect to completeness, correct valuation, and correct identification of the single items. The situation report is subject only to a limited audit. Taken as a whole, it must not render an untrue view of the situation of the enterprise.

The audit report (HGB section 273) contains comprehensive written comments on the performance of the audit of the annual financial statement and the results thereof. Unfavorable changes vis-à-vis the previous year and substantial losses sustained by a corporation require explanation.

The certification of the annual financial statement reflects the final result of the audit. Provided that no objections are raised, the certification must be worded as prescribed in HGB section 274.

6. Future Developments

Pan-European harmonization will not have any substantial effects on present Austrian accounting law. Current regulations will have to be modified only slightly when Austria joins the EC. Any developments beyond that time are all but impossible to forecast, but it may well be assumed that the accounting rules currently in force will not undergo any major changes within the next 5 or 10 years.

Financial Statements

Individual Company Financial Statements (from an Austrian AG, 1994)

Gewinn- und verlustrechnung (für die Zeit vom 1. Jänner 1996 bis 31. Dezember 1994

1. Umsatzerlöse
2. Erhöhung oder Verminderung des Bestands an fertigen un unfertigen Erzeugnissen sowie an noch nicht abrechenbaren Leistungen
3. Sonstige betriébliche Erträge
   Erträge aus dem Abgang vom und der Zuschreibung zum Anlagevermögen mit Ausnahme der Finanzanlagen (Z 10)
   a) Erträge aus der Auflösung von Rückstellungen
   b) Übrige
4. Materialaufwand und Aufwendungen für bezogene Leistungen
5. Personalaufwand
   a) Löhne
   b) Gehälter
   c) Aufwendungen für Abfertigungen und Pensionen
   d) Aufwendungen für gesetzlich vorgeschriebene Sozialabfaben sowie vom Entgelt abhängige Abgaben und Pflichtbeiträge
   e) Sonstige Sozialaufwendungen
6. Abschreibungen auf immaterielle Vermögensgegenstände und Sachanlagen
7. Sonstige betriebliche Aufwendungen
   a) Steuern, soweit sie nicht unter Z 15 fallen
   b) Übrige
8. Ordentliches Betriebsergebnis
9. Erträge aus Beteiligungen
10. Zinsenerträge, Wertpapiererträge und ähnliche Erträge (davon aus verbundenen Unternehmen S 432.899,43)
    Erträge aus dem Abgang von und der Zuschreibung zu Finanzanlagen
11. Aufwendungen aus Beteiligungen
12. Zinsen und ähnliche Aufwendungen (davon betreffend verbundene Unternehmen S 4.929.636,65)
13. Finanzergebnis
14. Ergebnis aus der gewöhnlichen Geschäftstätigkeit
15. Steuern vom Einkommen und vom Ertrag
16. Jahresüberschuß/Jahresfehlbetrag
17. Auflosung unversteuerter Rücklagen
    Auflösung von Kapitalrücklagen
18. Zuweisung zu unversteuerten Rücklagen
19. Gewinnvortrag aus dem Vorjahr
20. Bilanzgewinn

	1996			1990
S		S		TS
		1.456.500.674,25		1.373.438
	./.	149.013,--`	+	19.849
-,--				2.015
1.086.200,--				300
18.206.489,26		19.292.689,26		7.635
	./.	744.125.490,02	./.	748.668
126.245.793,52			./.	116.969
138.516.727,12			./.	123.328
21.414.747,--			./.	7.959
66.862.353,22			./.	63.309
6.873.486,10	./.	359.913.106,96	./.	6.575
	./.	50.658.265,68	./.	52.371
4.710.679,50			./.	7.602
235.560.579,61	./.	240.271.259,11	./.	337.278
	+	80.676.228,74	./.	60.822
		6.774.513,51		11.352
		21.407.061,82		19.968
		-,--		21
	./.	7.600.000,--		-
	./.	45.318.770,95	./.	35.753
	./.	24.737.195,62	./.	4.412
	+	55.939.033,12	./.	65.234
		1.785.822,--		1.842
	+	57.724.855,12	./.	63.392
		2.970.742,41		897
		-,--		78.300
	./.	14.519.347,--	./.	22.109
		529.494,02		6.833
		46.705.744,55		529

Profit and loss account (as for the period January 1 to December 31, 1994

1. Revenue from sales
2. Inventory changes in finished goods and work in progress as well as services not yet chargeable
3. Other operating income gains on disposal and appreciation writeup of fixed assets excluding financial assets
   a) Gains from retransfer of accrued liabilities
   b) Other
4. Raw materials and consumables and other external charges
5. Staff cost
   a) Wages
   b) Salaries
   c) Severance payments, retirement plans
   d) Social Security levies and remuneration-dependent charges and compulsory contributions
   e) Other welfare expenditure
6. Value adjustments in respect of intangible and tangible assets
7. Other operating expenses
   a) Taxes, excepting those falling under point 15
   b) Other
8. Operating profit or loss
9. Income from participating interests
10. Interest receivable, income from other investments and similar income (with S 432.899,43 of this amount derived from affiliated undertakings)
    Gains on disposal and appreciation writeup of financial assets
11. Expenses from participating interests
12. Interest and similar expenses (including S 4.929.636,65 paid to affiliated undertakings)
13. Financial profit or loss
14. Profit or loss on ordinary activities
15. Taxes on income
16. Net profit or loss for the financial year
17. Retransfer of untaxed reserves
    Retransfer of capital reserves
18. Allocations to untaxed reserves
19. Balance-sheet profit carried forward from the previous year
20. Balance sheet profit

1996		1990	
S	S	TS	
	1.456.500.674,25	1.373.438	
	./. 149.013,--	+ 19.849	
-,--		2.015	
1.086.200,--		300	
18.206.489,26	19.292.689,26	7.635	
	./. 744.125.490,02	./. 748.668	
126.245.793,52		./. 116.969	
138.516.727,12		./. 123.328	
21.414.747,--		./. 7.959	
66.862.353,22		./. 63.309	
6.873.486,10	./. 359.913.106,96	./. 6.575	
	./. 50.658.265,68	./. 52.371	
4.710.679,50		./. 7.602	
235.560.579,61	./. 240.271.259,11	./. 337.278	
	+ 80.676.228,74	./. 60.822	
	6.774.513,51	11.352	
	21.407.061,82	19.968	
	-,--	21	
	./. 7.600.000,--	-	
	./. 45.318.770,95	./. 35.753	
	./. 24.737.195,62	./. 4.412	
	+ 55.939.033,12	./. 65.234	
	1.785.822,--	1.842	
	+ 57.724.855,12	./. 63.392	
	2.970.742,41	897	
	-,--	78.300	
	./. 14.519.347,--	./. 22.109	
	529.494,02	6.833	
	46.705.744,55	529	

Bilanz (zum 31. Dezember 1994)*

AKTIVA

A. ANLAGEVERMÖGEN

  I. Immaterielle
  Vermögensgegenstände
    Konzessionen, gewerbliche Schutzrechte und ähnliche Rechte und Vorteile
    sowie daraus abgeleitete Lizenzen

  II. Sachanlagen

    1. Bebaute Grundstücke und Bauten auf fremden Grund

    2. Unbebaute Grundstücke

    3. Maschinen und maschinelle Anlagen

    4. Werkzeuge, Betriebs- und Geschäftsausstattung

    5. Umweltschutzeinrichtungen

    6. Geleistete Anzahlungen und Anlagen in Bau

  III. Finanzanlagen

    1. Beteiligungen, davon Anteile an verbundenen Unternehmen

    2. Werpapiere des Anlagevermögens

B. UMLAUFVERMÖGEN

  I. Vorräte

    1. Roh-, Hilfs- und Betriebsstoffe

    2. Unfertige Erzeugnisse

    3. Fertige Erzeugnisse und Waren

    4. Geleistete Anzahlungen

  II. Forderungen und sonstige
  Vermögensgegenstände

    1. Forderungen aus Lieferungen und Leistungen

    2. Forderungen gegen verbundene Unternehmen

    3. Sonstige Forderungen und Vermögensgegenstände

  III. Wertpapiere und Anteile Sonstige Wertpapiere und Anteile

  IV. Kassenbestand, Schecks, Guthaben bei Banken

C. RECHNUNGSABGRENZUNGSPOSTEN

*Comparatives omitted.

historische Anschaffungs- werte	kumulierte Abschreibungen	Buchwert 31.12.1994
S	S	S
11.558,954,57	9.156.233,25	2.402.721,32
209.833.241,98	112.161.919,94	97.671.322,04
4.579.391,87	0,00	4.579.391,87
277.804.912,08	186.915.701,08	90.889.211,00
134.583.404,32	87.783.120,32	46.800.284,00
13.704.475,42	8.997.591,42	4.706.884,00
9.195.429,10	0,00	9.195.429,10
132.325.470,77	0,00	132.325.470,77
18.045.676,01	1.075.362,28	16.970.313,73
811.630.956,12	406.089.928,29	405.541.027,83
126.006.369,47		
36.114.558,00		
97.855.058,90		
7.216.404,44	267.192.390,81	
247.020.266,26		
46.581.178,69		
115.791.876,66	409.393.321,61	
	80.080.000,00	
	97.097.610,81	853.763.323,23
		6.046.807,73
		1.265.351.158,79

Balance sheet (as at December 31, 1994)*

A. FIXED ASSETS

I. Intangible assets

Concessions, industrial property rights and similar rights and advantages as well as licences thereof

II. Tangible assets

1. Land together with buildings thereon and buildings on land owned by others
2. Land without buildings
3. Machinery and equipment
4. Tools, fixtures, furniture and office equipment
5. Pollution control devices
6. Advances on fixed assets and construction in progress

III. Financial assets

1. Participating interests, including shares in affiliated undertakings
2. Investments held as fixed assets

B. CURRENT ASSETS

I. Stocks

1. Raw materials and supplies
2. Work in process
3. Finished goods and goods for resale
4. Payments on account

II. Accounts receivable and other assets

1. Accounts receivable
2. Accounts due from affiliated undertakings
3. Other accounts receivable and assets

III. Investments

Other investments and shares

IV. Cash on hand, checks, cash at bank

C. PREPAID EXPENSES AND DEFERRED CHARGES

* Comparatives omitted.

Historical costs	Accumulated depreciation	Book value as at 31.12.1994
S	S	S
11.558,954,57	9.156.233,25	2.402.721,32
209.833.241,98	112.161.919,94	97.671.322,04
4.579.391,87	0,00	4.579.391,87
277.804.912,08	186.915.701,08	90.889.211,00
134.503.404,32	87.783.120,32	46.800.284,00
13.704.475,42	8.997.591,42	4.706.884,00
9.195.429,10	0,00	9.195.429,10
132.325.470,77	0,00	132.325.470,77
18.045.676,01	1.075.362,28	16.970.313,73
811.630.956,12	406.089.928,29	405.541.027,83
126.006.369,47		
36.114.558,00		
97.855.058,90		
7.216.404,44	267.192.390,81	
247.020.266,26		
46.581.178,69		
115.791.876,66	409.393.321,61	
	80.080.000,00	
	97.097.610,81	853.763.323,23
		6.046.807,73
		1.265.351.158,79

			Buchwert 31.12.1994
PASSIVA	S	S	S

A. EIGENKAPITAL
  I. Grundkapital   100.000.000,00
  II. Gewinnrücklagen

1. Gesetzliche Rücklage	13.100.000,00		
2. Andere Rücklagen	23.834.515,87	36.934.515,87	
III. Bilanzgewinn		46.705.744,55	183.640.260,42

B. UNVERSTEUERTE RÜCKLAGEN
  1. Bewertungsreserve auf Grund
     von Sonderabschreibungen   98.293.896,56
  2. Sonstige unversteuerte
     Rücklagen   47.016.039,85   145.309.936,41

C. STILLE EINLAGEN GEMÄSS BETEILIGUNGSFONDSGESETZ   125.290.362,00

D. RÜCKSTELLUNGEN
  1. Rückstellungen für
     Abfertigungen   39.658.752,00
  2. Rückstellungen für
     Pensionen   22.019.361,00
  3. Steuerrückstellungen   15.226.000,00
  4. Sonstige Rückstellungen   71.844.843,43   148.748.956,43

E. VERBINDLICHKEITEN
  1. Verbindlichkeiten gegenüber
     Banken   389.452.664,79
  2. Verbindlichkeiten aus
     Lieferungen und Leistungen   99.263.312,122
  3. Verbindlichkeiten aus der
     Annahme gezogener Wechsel
     und der Ausstellung eigener
     Wechsel   23.149.309,18
  4. Verbindlichkeiten gegenüber
     verbundenen Unternehmen   69.911.499,27
  5. Sonstige Verbindlichkeiten   80.584.858,17   662.361.643,53

                               1.265.351.158,79

"Die Buchfürung und der Jahresabschluß entsprechen nach unserer pflichtgemäßen Prüfung den gesetzlichen Vorschriften. Der Jahresabschluß vermittelt unter Beachtung der Grundsätze ordnungsmäßiger Buchführung ein möglichst getreues Bild der Vermögens-, Finanz- und Ertragslage der Gesellschaft. Der Lagebericht steht im Einklang mit dem Jahresabschlus."

Wien, am 28. März 1995

Sud-Ost Treuhand Aktiengesellschaft
Wirtschaftsprüfungs- und
Steuerberatungsgellschaft

| | | Book value as at 31.12.1994 |
LIABILITIES	Sch	Sch	Sch

A. EQUITY CAPITAL

I. Capital stock — 100.000.000,00

II. Revenue reserves
1. Legal reserve — 13.100.000,00
2. Other reserves — 23.834.515,87 — 36.934.515,87

III. Balance sheet profit — 46.705.744,55 — 183.640.260,42

B. UNTAXED RESERVES

1. Valuation reserve from special depreciation allowances — 98.293.896,56
2. Other untaxed reserves — 47.016.039,85 — 145.309.936,41

C. DORMANT EQUITY HOLDINGS UNDER BETEILIGUNGSFONDSGESETZ (EQUITY FUND ACT) — 125.290.362,00

D. PROVISIONS FOR LIABILITIES AND CHARGES

1. Provisions for severance payments — 39.658.752,00
2. Provisions for pensions — 22.019.361,00
3. Provisions for taxation — 15.226.000,00
4. Other provisions — 71.844.843,43 — 148.748.956,43

E. LIABILITIES

1. Due to bands — 389.452.664,79
2. Accounts payable — 99.263.312,122
3. Notes payable — 23.149.309,18
4. Liabilities due to affiliated undertakings — 69.911.499,27
5. Other liabilities — 80.584.858,17 — 662.361.643,53

1.265.351.158,79

"We have duly examined the accounts and the annual financial statements and have found them to be in compliance with statutory provisions. The annual financial statements have been prepared in accordance with proper accounting principle and give a true and fair view of the assets and liabilities and the financial an profit position of the undertaking the situation report is consistent with the financial statements."

Vienna, as at March 28, 1995

Sud-Ost Treuhand Aktiengesellschaft
Wirtschaftsprüfungs- und
Steuerberatungsgellschaft

KONZER-GEWINN- UND VERLUSTRECHNUNG
für das Geschäftsjahr 1994

	TATS	TATS	*Mio* ATS '93
1. Umsatzerlöse		33,888,259	32,180.00
2. Erhöhung des Bestands an fertigen und un-fertigen Erzeugnissen sowie an noch nicht abrechenbaren Leistungen		−581,465	3,450.00
3. Im Anlagevermögen berücksichtigte Eigen-leistungen		80,969	74.60
4. Sonstige betriebliche Erträge			
(a) Erträge aus dem Abgang vom Anlagever-mögen mit Ausnahme der Finanzanlagen			
(b) Erträge aus der Auflösung von Rückstel-	510,919		167.50
lungen	1,688,581		1,247.10
(c) Ubrige	1,335,763	3,535,263	1,274.40
5. Materialaufwand und Aufwendungen für bezogene Leistungen		−15,127,101	−17,584.50
6. Personalaufwand			
(a) Löhne	−3,425,916		−3,373.00
(b) Gehälter	−5,727,864		−56,610.90
(c) Aufwendungen für Abfertigungen	−401,820		−511.90
(d) Aufwendungen für Pensionen	−275,895		−197.00
(e) Aufwendungen für gesetzlich vorgeschriebene Sozialabgaben sowie vom Entgelt abhängige Abgaben und Pflichtbeiträge	−2,154,881		−2,090.70
(f) Sonstige Sozialaufwendungen	−241,203	−12,227,579	−185.10
7. Abschreibungen auf immaterielle Vermögens-gegenstände und Sachanlagen			
(a) Normalabschreibungen	−1,123,316		−1082.40
(b) außerplanmäßige Abschreibungen	−12,439	−1,135,755	−29.30
8. Sonstige betriebliche Aufwendungen			
(a) Steuern, soweit sie nicht unter Steuern vom Einkommen und Ertrag fallen	−161,575		−167.40
(b) Ubrige	−8,447,734	−8,609,309	−7,597.70
9. Zwischensumme aus Z 1 bis 8 (Betriebserfolg)		−176.718	−36.30

CONSOLIDATED PROFIT AND LOSS ACCOUNT
for the year ended December 31, 1994

		TATS	TATS	Mio ATS '93
1.	Revenue from sales		33,888,259	32,180.00
2.	Increase in finished goods and work in progress as well as services not yet chargeable		−581,465	3,450.00
3.	Own work capitalized		80,969	74.60
4.	Other operating income			
	(a) Other operating income gains on disposal and appreciation writeup of fixed assets	510,919		167.50
	(b) Gains from transfer of accrued liabilities	1,688,581		1,247.10
	(c) Other	1,335,763	3,535,263	1,274.40
5.	Raw materials and consumables and other external charges		−15,127,101	17,584.50
6.	Staff cost			
	(a) Wages	−3,425,916		−3,373.00
	(b) Salaries	−5.727,864		−5,610.90
	(c) Severance payments	−401,820		−511.90
	(d) Retirement plans	−275,895		−197.00
	(e) Social security levies and remuneration-dependent charges and compulsory contributions	−2,154,881		−2,090.70
	(f) Other welfare expenditure	−241,203	−12,227,579	−185.10
7.	Value adjustments in respect of intangible and tangible assets			
	(a) Normal depreciation	−1,123,316		−1,082.40
	(b) Extraordinary depreciation	−12,439	−1,135,755	−29.30
8.	Other operating expenses			
	(a) Taxes, excepting those falling under point 15	−161,575		−167.40
	(b) Other	−8,447,734	−8,609,309	−7,597.70
9.	Z1–8 (Operatlng profit or loss)		−176,718	−36.30

	TATS	*Mio* *ATS '93*
9. Zwischensumme aus Z 1 bis 8 (Betrieb- serfoig)	−176,718	−36.30
10. Erträge aus Beteiligungen	18,132	20.40
11. Erträge assoziieter Unternehmen	8,508	21.50
12. Zinsenerträge, Wertpapiererträge und ähn- liche Erträge (davon aus verbundenen Unter- nehmen 808.087 TATS)	2,422,813	2,066.50
13. Erträge aus dem Abgang von und der Zu- schreibung zu Finanzanlagen	18,582	2.30
14. Aufwendungen aus Beteiligungen (davon außerplanmäßige Abschreibungen für ver- bundene Unternehmen 39.224 TATS)	−307,657	−250.00
15. Aufwendungen assoziierter Unternehmen	−33,470	−12.90
16. Abschreibungen auf sonstige Finanzanlagen und auf Wertpapiere des Unlaufvermögens	−88.213	−25.60
17. Zinsen und ähnliche Aufwendungen (davon betreffend verbundene Unternehmen 78,745 TATS)	−1,234,903	−1,194.80
18. Zwischensumme aus Z 10 bis 17 (Finanzerfolg)	803,792	627.40
19. Ergebnis der gewöhnlichen Geschäftätigkeit	627,074	591.10
20. Außerordentliche Erträge	90,874	591.10
21. Außerordentliche Aufwendungen	−541,596	−251.00
22. Außerordentliches Ergebnis	−450,722	−69.50
23. Steuern vom Einkommen und vom Ertrag	−173,034	−169.80
24. Jahresüberschuß	3,318	351.80
25. Auflösung von Ausgleichsposten aus der Erstkonsolidierung	0	905.20
26. Auflösung von Gewinnrücklagen	209,226	−1,230.60
27. Konzernfremden Gesellschaftern zustehender Gewinn/Verlust	30,479	−8.20
28. Gewinn- bzw. Verlustvorgrag aus dem Vorjahr	−193,025	90.10
29. Bilanzgewinn	49,998	108.30

		Mio
	TATS	*ATS '93*
9. Z1–8 (Operatlng profit or loss)	−176,718	−36.30
10. Income from participating interests	18,132	20.40
11. Gains relating to enterprises in which participations are held	8,508	21.50
12. Interest receivables, income from other investments and similar income (with 808.087 TATS of this amount derived from affiliated undertakings)	2,422,813	2,066.50
13. Gains on disposal and appreciation writeup of financial assets	18,582	2.30
14. Expenses of participating interests (including 39.224 TATS for extraordinary depreciation for affiliated undertakings)	−307,657	−250.00
15. Expenses relating to enterprises in which participations are held	−33,470	−12.90
16. Depreciation on other financial assets and on investments of current assets	−88,213	−25.60
17. Interest and similar expenses (including 78.745 TATS paid to affiliated undertakings)	−1,234,903	−1,194.80
18. Z10–17 (Flnancial profit or loss)	803,792	627.40
19. Profit or loss on ordinary activities	627,074	591.10
20. Extraordinary gains	90,874	181.50
21. Extraordinary expenses	−541,596	−251.00
22. Extraordinary result	−450,722	−69.50
23. Taxes on income	−173,034	−169.80
24. Net profit or loss for the financial year	3,318	351.80
25. Release of adjustment items from initial consolidation	0	905.20
26. Release of revenue reserves	209,226	−1,230.60
27. Minorities' share of profit/loss	30,479	−8.20
28. Balance-sheet profit or loss carried forward from the previous year	−193,025	90.10
29. Balance-sheet profit	49,998	108.30

KONZERNBILANZ
zum 31. Dezember 1994

			Mio
AKTIVA	*TATS*	*TATS*	*ATS '93*
A. Aufwendungen für das Ingangsetzen, Erweitern und Umstellen elnes Betriebes		425	0.30
B. Anlagevermögen			
I. Immaterielle Vermögensgegenstande	304.290		336.70
II. Sachanlagen	6,084,065		6,128.70
III. Finanzanlagen	2,059,031	8,447,386	2,340.60
C. Umlaufvermögen			
I. Vorräte			
1. Roh-, Hilfs- und Betriebsstoffe	1,096,884		1,159.80
2. Unfertige Erzeugnisse abzüglich Erhaltene	6,183,123		4,178.50
Anzahlungen	–4,373,186	1,809,937	0.00
3. Fertige Erzeugnisse	820,466		778.20
4. Handelswaren	93,020		132.40
5. Noch nicht abrechenbare Leistungen abzüglich	10,485,738		13,159.70
Erhaltene Anzahlungen	–8,961,957	1,523,781	0.00
6. Geleistete Anzahlungen abzüglich Erhaltene	1,880,936		1,317.80
Anzahlungen	–711,455	1,169,481	6,513,569	0.00
II. Forderungen und sonstige Vermögensgegenstände			
1. Forderungen aus Lieferungen und Leistungen	6,814,646		6,787.90
2. Forderungen gegen verbundene Unternehmen	10,207,395		8,075.80
3. Forderungen gegen Unternehmen, mit denen ein Beteiligungsverhältnis besteht	67,916		66.50
4. Sonstige Forderungen und Vermögengsgegenstände	2,160,573	19,250,530	2,409.80
III. Wertpapiere und Anteile (Sonstige Anteile)		6,375,266	6,083.20
IV. Kassenbestand, Schecks, Guthaben bei Banken			
1. Kassenbestand	51,200		49.10
2. Schecks	29,835		24.80
3. Guthaben bei Banken	1,815,740	1,896,775	2,351.50
D. Rechnungsabgrenzungsposten		99,272	118.00
		45,583,223	55,499.30

CONSOLIDATED BALANCE SHEET
at December 31, 1994

ASSETS	TATS	TATS	Mio ATS '93
A. Expendlture relating to the start-up, expansion, and reorganization of operations		425	0.30
B. Fixed Assets			
I. Intangible Assets	304,290		336.70
II. Tangible Assets	6,084,065		6,128.70
III. Financial Assets	2,059,031	8,447,386	2,340.60
C. Current Assets			
I. Stocks			
1. Raw materials and supply	1,096,884		1,159.80
2. Work in process less advance payments	6,183,123 −4,373,186	1,809,937	4,178.50 0.00
3. Finished goods	820,466		778.20
4. Goods for sale	93,020		132.40
5. Services not yet chargeable less advance payments	10,485,738 −8,961,957	1,523,781	13,159.70 0.00
6. Payments on account less advance payments	1,880,936 −711,455	1,169,481	6,513,569	1,317.80 0.00
II. Accounts receivable and other assets			
1. Accounts receivable	6,814,646		6,787.90
2. Accounts due from affiliated undertakings	10,207,395		8,075.80
3. Accounts receivable from enterprises in which participations are held	67,916		66.50
4. Other accounts receivable and assets	2,160,573	19,250,530	2,409.80
III. Investments		6,375,266	6,083.20
IV. Cash on hand, checks, cash at bank			
1. Cash on hand	51,200		49.10
2. Checks	29,835		24.80
3. Cash at bank	1,815,740	1,896,775	2,351.50
D. Prepaid and deferred expenses		99,272	118.00
		45,583,223	55,499.30

PASSIVA

	TATS	TATS	Mio ATS '93
A. Eigenkapital			
I. Grundkapital	650,000		650.00
II. Kapitalrücklagen			
1. gebundene	1,175,896		198.30
2. nicht gebundene	0		501.10
Ill. Gewinnrücklage	1,767,689		2,669.20
IV. Bilanzgewinn	49,998		108.30
V. Ausgleichsposten für Anteile in Fremd- besitz	896,757	4,540,340	96.30
B. Zuschüsse		43,657	47.70
C. Einlagen stiller Gesellschafter		35,000	10.00
D. Rückstellungen			
1. Rückstellung für Abfertigungen	1,973,178		1,920.40
2. Rückstellung für Pensionen	1,004,724		1,100.10
3. Steuerrückstellungen	678,051		585.40
4. Sonstige Rückstellungen	11,626,209	15,282,162	11,195.90
E. Verbindlichkeiten			
1. Anleihen	262,320		313.50
2. Hypothekarschulden	2,053		2.10
3. ERP-Kredite	542,083		505.70
4. Andere langfristige Verbindlichkeiten	482,669		559.60
5. Verbindlichkeiten gegenüber Banken	7,155,416		7,814.40
6. Erhaltenen Anzahlungen auf Bestellungen	7,030,385		19,555.80
7. Verbindlichkeiten aus Lieferungen und Leistungen	3,612,788		4,216.40
8. Verbindlichkeiten aus der Annahme gezogener Wechsel und der Ausstellung eigener Wechsel	80,817		321.10
9. Verbindlichkeiten gegenüber verbundenen Unternehmen	1,577,477		945.10
10. Verhindlichkeiten gegenüber Unternehmen, mit denen ein Beteiligungsverhältnis besteht	55,502		58.00
11. Sonstige Verbindlichkeiten	1,831,410	22,632,920	2,036.80
F. Rechnungsabgrenzungsposten		49,144	88.10
		42,583,223	55,499.30
Eventualverbindlichkeiten		2,240,408	11,585.00

LIABILITIES

	TATS	TATS	Mio ATS '93
A. Equity capital			
I. Capital stock	650,000		650.00
II. Capital reserves			
1. fixed	1,175,896		198.30
2. other	0		501.10
III. Revenue reserves	1,767,689		2,669.20
IV. Balance sheet profit	49,998		108.30
V. Minority shareholders' interests	896,757	4,540,340	96.30
B. Subsidies		43,657	47.70
C. Dormant equity holdings		35,000	10.00
D. Provisions for liabilities and charges			
1. Provisions for severance payments	1,973,178		1,920.40
2. Provisions for pensions	1,004,724		1,100.10
3. Provisions for taxation	678,051		585.40
4. Other provisions	11,626,209	15,282,162	11,195.90
E. Liabilities			
1. Loans	262,320		313.50
2. Mortgage loan	2,053		2.10
3. ERP-loans	542,083		505.70
4. Other long-term liabilities	482,669		559.60
5. Due to banks	7,155,416		7,814.40
6. Trade orders' advance payments	7,030,385		19,555.80
7. Accounts payable	3,612,788		4,216.40
8. Bills of exchange payable (drawn and accepted)	80,817		321.10
9. Liabilities due to affiliated undertakings	1,577,477		945.40
10. Payable to enterprises in which participations are held	55,502		58.00
11. Other liabilities	1,831,410	22,632,920	2,036.80
F. Prepaid and deferred expenses		49,144	88.10
		42,583,223	55,499.30
Contingent liabilities		2,240,408	11,585.00

FINLAND

Salme Näsi
Associate Professor of Accounting
University of Oulu

Kari Kankaanpää
Research Assistant
University of Tampere, Finland

1. Background—A Brief History of Accounting in Finland from the Nineteenth Century to the Present Day

The roots of bookkeeping in Finland stretch back to the fourteenth and fifteenth centuries; even double-entry bookkeeping goes back as far as the seventeenth century. It was only in the second half of the nineteenth century, however, that bookkeeping was established by legislation in Finland.

Between 1809 and 1917 Finland was an autonomous Grand Duchy of the Tsarist Empire. In the first half of this period, Finland was one of the most remote and impoverished countries in Europe. In the second half, the ideas of liberalism and entrepreneurial freedom began to spread into the country. Industrialization and urbanization began, and the country's economic life diversified and expanded. Storekeeping in the countryside became legal in 1859, and the number of merchants (storekeepers), both in urban communities and in the countryside, rose rapidly from 1860 until 1913 and the First World War.

Bookkeeping obligations at that time were based on the bankruptcy regulations prescribed in 1868. Bookkeeping mainly served the business proprietor himself in recording his receivables, debts, and assets. It was not considered necessary to distinguish between the proprietor's private assets and those belonging to his business. Bookkeeping was designed to keep the business proprietor's property separate from that of other businesses and households.

The first share companies act, which included some general bookkeeping and auditing requirements, was passed in 1895. This law precipitated the development of the accounting and auditing professions in Finland.

Several factors contributed to the development of financial accounting practices in the first two decades of the twentieth century: rapid growth in the number of corporations and co-operatives, inflation caused by the First World War, and new legislation on company income taxation passed after Finland gained its independence in 1917. The profit and loss calculation (measurement of net income or net loss) became a central function of bookkeeping at that time.

Financial accounting in Finland is governed by specific bookkeeping legislation. The first such law, the Law on Bookkeeping Obligation (*Laki kirjanpitovelvollisuudesta*) was passed in 1925. Only a few years later, in 1928, the Law on the Publication of Financial Statements (*Laki tilinpäätösten julkisuudesta*) was passed. The legislation did not define the form and content of financial statements but left it to the individual companies. The static balance equation theory (assets = liabilities + equities) formed the fundamental basis of accounting at that time, contradicting the profit calculation function of bookkeeping. The balance sheet, therefore, was the primary financial statement.

Bookkeeping legislation was reformed in 1945. Wartime had increased state control over the economy, and one consequence of this control was the need for greater uniformity in companies' disclosure practices. Companies now had to follow, in form and content, a model for financial statements set out in the new legislation. The 1945 Bookkeeping Law was still static by nature, being based on asset accounting even though the main function of accounting was seen as the calculation of the profit of the accounting period. Given this contradiction, a dynamic "expenditure-revenue theory of bookkeeping" was outlined and demonstrated in Finland during the 1940s and 1950s, especially by Professor Martti Saario, the originator of the theory.

The expenditure-revenue theory of bookkeeping is coherently based on the realization principle for the recording of business transactions. There are three kinds of transactions: expenditures (associated with the acquisition of resources, factors of production), revenues (associated with the sale of goods and services), and monetary transactions (payments). The closing accounts are a matter of profit calculation, the core of which is divided into two parts:

1. The division of revenues into expenses and profit
2. The division of expenditures into expenses and *aktiva* (i.e., the division of expenditures between the profit and loss account and the balance sheet)

The second division is the most difficult and crucial task in annual profit calculation.

Through the balance sheet some expenditures are transferred to later years to be covered by later revenues. In the income statement, the aim is to match expenditures against corresponding revenues, that is, to follow the matching principle in annual profit measurement. According to the conservatism concept, all expenditures that are no longer expected to generate revenues must be written to the profit and loss statement as expenses. The matching principle is theoretically clear, but in practice it is not so simple. Depreciations of noncurrent asset were dependent on future revenue expectations.

It took almost 20 years before the new theory and way of thinking were officially sanctioned in legislation. The 1968 Company Income Tax Law (*Elinkeinotuloverolaki*, EVL) and the 1973 Bookkeeping Law and Statute (*Kirjanpitolaki ja -asetus*) were in line with the expenditure-revenue theory. Thanks to this legislation, profit calculation has undoubtedly enjoyed a primary role in financial accounting for the past 20 years in Finland. The profit and loss statement represents the company's result and its composition. According to the matching principle, depreciations depend on annual revenues. More generally, measurement of the annual result has had a great degree of flexibility (not only for depreciations but also for reserves and provisions) to allow targeted results to be achieved.

Tax accounting rules have always had a strong effect on financial accounting practices in Finland. Taxation is tied to bookkeeping; that is, deductions and allowances are tax deductible provided that corresponding entries have affected the profit calculation in the financial statements. For example, when depreciations of fixed assets are made, it has been usual to make the maximum depreciations permitted by tax law whenever the result has made this possible. During the past 10 years, however, listed companies have presented planned depreciations of their fixed assets in line with international practice, the recommendations of the Helsinki Stock Exchange, and the single change made in 1985 to bookkeeping legislation.

The balance sheet has been of secondary importance in dynamic accounting thinking. It has been interpreted as a transfer account through which sums are transferred to the following accounting period. The balance sheet, however, does show the financial position of the company at the moment when accounts are closed.

By the time the law based on the theory described above was passed in 1973, there was an awareness that the internationalization of Finnish business life and the need for harmonization in disclosure practices would soon lead to a new phase of accounting reform. In the 1980s most Finnish parent companies began to include a set of secondary financial statements prepared according to international accounting standards (IAS) in their annual reports. This "double-accounts system" was costly for companies, and it led to a lively debate about the need for international harmonization of Finnish financial accounting regulations. A government committee was appointed in 1989 to consider the reform of bookkeeping legislation to establish international harmonization and comparability of financial statements. New regulations were issued in December 1992, and they will be followed in bookkeeping and disclosure practice beginning in 1993–1994. The EU's Fourth and Seventh Company Law Directives have strongly guided Finnish reform work. Finnish regulations concerning consolidated financial statements were included in the companies legislation. In this reform group, accounting regulations were included in their own chapter in bookkeeping legislation.

The Share Companies Act (*Osakeyhtiölaki*, abbreviated OYL) of 1978 still provides some additional regulations on individual company and group accounting and disclosure. In addition to the legislature, important authorities giving regulations and recommendations on financial accounting and reporting in Finland are the Commission of Bookkeeping (*Kirjanpitolautakunta*), a legal institution affiliated with the Ministry of Trade and Industry, and the authorized public accountants' organizations, in particular the Association of Auditors (*KHT-yhdistys*), authorized by the Chamber of Commerce and a member of IASC.

2. Accounting Policies and Practices in Individual Companies' Accounts: The Form and Content of Published Financial Statements

2.1 Introduction

The latest reform in accounting legislation, consisting of the Bookkeeping Act (abbreviated KPL) and the Bookkeeping Statute (abbreviated KPA), both passed December 23, 1992, was a response to the increased internationalization of Finnish companies. Another reason, of course, was Finland's aim of integrating into the European Union. New regulations meant a step toward harmonization of Finnish accounting practice with the EU's Fourth and Seventh Company Law Directives and also with IAS standards. The expenditure-revenue theory has so far been retained as the fundamental basis for accounting legislation and practice, even though certain individual regulations may undermine the theoretical foundations of Finnish financial accounting.

According to Finnish accounting theory (expenditure-revenue theory), the main purpose of financial accounting is to calculate profit for the accounting period and to determine the maximum amount payable as dividends to shareholders. Expense items on the profit and loss statement (or income statement) have followed a specific order of priority, based on Saario's cost priority theory proposed in 1949. The most prominent expense items to be deducted from sales revenues are materials and supplies, external services, personnel expenses, and other variable costs and expenses. Listed below these are fixed costs and expenses: personnel expenses, rents and other fixed costs of the period. Operating expenses are followed by depreciation according to plan. Financial incomes and expenses, extraordinary incomes and expenses, differences in depreciation in excess of plan, change in voluntary provisions, and income taxes are added to and subtracted from the operating profit. The residual, "profit for the financial year," is attributable to the shareholders.

In addition to profit calculation, the information needs of all stakeholders were also taken into consideration when authorities reformed Finnish accounting regulations. New regulations taking effect from 1992 include the *true and fair view* concept, which emphasizes the informative nature of disclosure. Financial statements should give a true and fair view of the results of operations and the financial position of the company. The inclusion of this principle in law represents a significant change to the spirit of Finnish financial accounting, based as it is on the calculation of profit to be distributed. In practice, the true and fair view requirement has been interpreted in Finland to mean voluntary disclosure of supplementary information in the notes if the true and fair view requirement is not otherwise fulfilled.

Accounting legislation sets the minimum requirements for information in the profit and loss statement, balance sheet, and notes. In addition to these statements, larger Finnish corporations must prepare, in accordance with the Share Companies Act (1978), a statement of changes in financial position, a funds statement, or a statement of cash flows at an aggregate level and publish it in their annual report.

2.2 The Form and Content of the Profit and Loss Statement

2.2.1 Sales Revenues

The first item in the standard Finnish profit and loss statement is turnover (net sales), which represents the revenue resulting from goods delivered and services rendered in the course of the ordinary activities of the company. Sales adjustments usually are not disclosed, and thus net sales are given in the profit and loss statement. As an exception to the realization principle, it is possible to classify income from a project that is carried out over a prolonged period of time as revenue, on the basis of the degree of completion of the project. Following the matching principle, costs are also deducted from revenues according to the degree of completion of the project. This new method of periodization can be applied, for example, to construction, shipbuilding, and machinery contracts with a long completion time. The change (decrease or increase) in stocks of finished goods of a manufacturer and the acquisition cost of assets manufactured for a company's own use are either subtracted from or added to net sales. Of course, this procedure is also contradictory to Finnish accounting theory and its realization principle.

2.2.2 *Variable and Fixed Expenses*

The most recent legislation contains two alternative formulas for companies' profit and loss statements: a formula that classifies the company's operating expenses into two categories, variable and fixed, and a formula that separates expenses according to the company's activities (KPL 1§ and 2§). The first "nonactivity-based" alternative will probably be the most common. Accounting legislation, however, allows operating expenses to be presented in the first formula without being divided into variable and fixed costs. This is likely to be the most common practice, particularly in companies that have subsidiaries overseas and must prepare consolidated statements using foreign financial information.

As a rule, inventories are valued by using variable purchasing and manufacturing costs. Product costs thus contain only variable expenditures, all other expenditures being expensed as period costs. It is also possible, however, to include fixed purchasing and manufacturing costs in inventory values, provided that their amount is relatively important. This possibility is primarily intended for large companies that need to present financial information in an internationally comparable way. In this case, the presentation of expenses in the profit and loss statement as two groups, variable and fixed, is infeasible. FIFO and the lower of cost or market principle are generally followed in inventory valuation. Changes in inventories (other than of finished goods of manufacturers) are presented in connection with material, supplies, and goods purchases.

2.2 *Depreciations*

Regulations concerning depreciation expenses of tangible assets (e.g., property, plant, and equipment) and other long-term expenditures (e.g., research and development) are few in Finnish bookkeeping legislation. Before 1993 the main rule was that the expenditure (acquisition cost) of a long-lived asset was to be capitalized (i.e., recorded as an asset on the balance sheet) and allocated as depreciation expenses over the periods in which the asset is in use. According to the 1992 regulations, firms must present depreciations systematically according to a plan. This method was to have been adopted at the latest in 1995 (KPL 16 §).

The Company Income Tax Law (1968, abbreviation EVL) prescribes the maximum rates of depreciation for fixed assets and other long-term expenditures (EVL 30-45 §). These rates vary depending on the nature of the item. For many categories of assets, particularly machinery and equipment, the depreciation rates in the income tax legislation may be higher than those estimated by using a systematic depreciation method over the asset's economic life (i.e., the straight-line method or declining balance method). The difference between the expense according to plan and that permitted by tax legislation is therefore recognized as an appropriation of income in the profit and loss statement for the period (KPL 19 §). An item called "depreciation in excess of plan" means that the amount of planned depreciation has been lower than the tax allowance for fixed assets and other long-term expenditures. The difference is recorded as an "extra" expense in bookkeeping because taxation is linked to accounting.

Detailed information about planned and booked depreciation must be given in financial statements or in the notes. The groups of assets and corresponding depreciation expenses are intangible assets and rights, buildings and structures, machinery and equipment, and other tangible assets. The various fixed asset items are reported in the balance sheet at their acquisition cost, less depreciation according to plan. Total accumulated depreciation in excess of plan is shown separately under provisions in the balance sheet (KPL 20§).

The maximum depreciation rate for buildings, depending on their use, ranges from 4% to 20% (EVL 34 §). For machinery and equipment the rate is 30% (EVL 30 §). The method applied here is an accelerated depreciation method known as the declining balance method by which the maximum percentages are applied against declining book values.

The cost of tangible assets with a service life 3 years or less (e.g., tools) is usually recorded as an expense for the acquisition year. This practice is also based on income tax legislation (EVL 33 §).

Expenditures on intangible assets (such as patents, trademarks, operating licenses, copyrights, and data processing programs) are usually allocated by using the straight line method of depreciation, based on a maximum service or life span of 10 years. This practice is also based on the tax regulations (EVL 37 §).

Some regulations concern capitalization and amortization of intangible assets in tax legislation, but the Share Companies Act (1978) gives exact rules for depreciation. Goodwill must be allocated in 5–20 years (OYL 11. 3 § 1), and other long-standing expenditures, such as R&D, market research, and technical consultation expenditures, if capitalized, are to be amortized by 20% annually.

2.2.4 Changes in Provisions

According to the 1973 accounting legislation and company income tax legislation (EVL), provisions and reserves in Finland were made for future expenditures and losses, for example, for future investments and bad debts. "Reserves" offered a way of achieving the desired profit level and minimizing taxes. One of the most common reserves was the inventory reserve. This was always used for smoothing results and was permissible both in accounting and tax legislation. Forming an inventory reserve meant that the company transferred, in addition to the cost of goods sold, "extra" inventory expenses to the profit and loss statement, even though the practice was contrary to the expenditure-revenue theory of bookkeeping and its matching concept. Only large corporations had to disclose their inventory reserves; smaller companies could keep them secret.

International comparability called for open disclosure of reserves and changes in the whole Finnish system. EU Directives require provisions to be made in the accounts as liabilities and charges for all those clearly definable losses and debts that, at the date of the balance sheet, are either likely to be incurred or certain to be incurred but uncertain with respect to the amount or date on which they will arise. The same practice became mandatory in Finland with the 1992 regulations.

According to the 1992 bookkeeping legislation, provisions are divided into two categories: obligatory provisions and voluntary reserves. Future expenses that the company is bound to pay but that no longer generate a corresponding revenue must be recorded as an expense and an obligatory provision formed. The same practice is applied to future losses that seem obvious at the date of closing the books. These obligatory provisions are not shown separately on the profit and loss statement; they are included in the corresponding expenses. Some examples of obligatory provisions are warranty, complaint, indemnity, and guarantee provisions. The total pension liability also must be deducted from revenues and shown as an obligatory provision on the balance sheet by December 31, 2000. At present, uncovered pension liabilities are usually presented only in the notes.

"Change in voluntary reserves" is an appropriation item that affects results and is shown in the profit and loss statement before income taxes. Voluntary reserves are tax-related; increases in reserves decrease the profit and taxes of the accounting period under consideration and vice versa. The accounting legislation names voluntary reserves (e.g., investment and operations reserves), but in taxation they were mostly abolished by the 1992 tax reform (see Section 2.3.5 on provisions).

2.2.5 Financial Income and Expenses, Extraordinary Income and Expenses, Taxes

Financial income and expenses are always presented as their own group, after the operating profit or loss. They include dividend and interest income, interest and other financial expenses, and value adjustments of financial investments. Extraordinary income and expense items (e.g., revenue from the sale of a profit center or business area) are presented after financial income and expenses.

Taxes and interest expenses are considered as profit distribution items according to the expenditure-revenue theory of bookkeeping. Like expenses, these items are subtracted from revenue to give the net profit, the amount distributable to shareholders. Income and property taxes should include, according to good accounting practice, the total accrual-based amount of taxes calculated for the accounting period. However, Finnish companies are also allowed to record taxes by debiting the company's unrestricted shareholders' equity. Therefore, taxes listed on the income statement do not necessarily show the real amount of taxes accrued during the accounting period. Further information about the total amount of taxes and how they have been dealt with in the accounts ought to be found in the notes.

2.3 The Form and Content of the Balance Sheet

According to Finnish accounting theory, the balance sheet is treated primarily as a "transfer account" between two accounting periods, even though it is used to display the financial position of the accounting entity at the moment of closing the accounts.

In the 1992 legislation (KPA 7 §) there is a common balance sheet formula for all types of firms. This new formula is highly compatible with the EU directives concerning balance sheet form and content. Assets on the left-hand side of the balance sheet follow the liquidity order, the most liquid assets being at the end. Assets include fixed assets and other long-term investments, valuation items, and stocks and financial assets. The right-hand side of the balance sheet lists financial sources used to acquire the assets or to pay for the expenditures shown on the left-hand side. These sources are divided into four groups: equity capital, provisions, valuation items, and liabilities. They follow the order of pay-back of different types of capital, short-term debts with the shortest pay-back times being at the end.

2.3.1 Fixed Assets and Other Long-Term Investments

Intangible assets include capitalized expenditures, such as set-up and organizing expenditures, purchased goodwill, and research and development. Depreciation rules concerning these assets were considered in Section 2.2.3.

The book value on the balance sheet of a tangible fixed asset describes the difference between the acquisition cost and accumulated depreciation according to plan. The services of assets that are acquired by means of leases are not presented as assets on the Finnish balance sheet. In legislation there is no difference between financial and operating leases. It is, however, expected that the Commission of Bookkeeping will issue new guidelines concerning the bookkeeping and disclosure practice of leasing agreements.

Financial accounting focuses on the cost of assets rather than on their market value. Finnish accounting legislation allows exceptions to this rule if the fair market value of a fixed asset (such as land, buildings, and stocks) is permanently and significantly higher than its net book value. Legislation then allows the company to revalue the asset up to its estimated market value (KPL 18 §). This revaluation of an asset, however, has no effect on the profit and loss statement and on the measured result of the entity. Depreciation is always based on the acquisition cost, not on the revalued book value of an asset. Revaluation should be separately disclosed in the footnotes to the financial statements. The revaluation reserve must be cancelled if the conditions for revaluation have changed.

In bookkeeping, revaluation involves debiting the asset account in question (or alternatively a special debit-side revaluation account) and crediting the "contra-asset" account "revaluation." On the right-hand side of the balance sheet revaluations are included in "valuation items." In corporations, however, revaluations increase shareholders' restricted equity. This equity item is known as the revaluation fund *(Arvonkorotus-rahasto)*.

2.3.2 Valuation Items

Exchange losses of foreign currency loans, if capitalized, can be included under valuation items. If the loan falls due in a year, then the exchange loss should be deducted from revenues immediately.

2.3.3 Stocks and Financial Assets

Stocks are stated at their variable cost, but fixed acquisition and manufacturing costs may be included in inventory values if they are significant. The FIFO method and concept of conservatism are applied in valuation.

Financial assets consist of receivables, financial securities, and cash on hand and in bank accounts. According to the accounting legislation, the rate of translation of receivables, as well as debts and other obligations denominated in foreign currencies, should not exceed the rate of exchange prevailing on the balance sheet date. This is the rule, and all exceptions should be disclosed in the financial statements or in the notes.

2.3.4 Equity Capital

Equity capital of corporations is to be divided, according to the Share Companies Act, into restricted and distributable (nonrestricted) equity.

The distinction is made between restricted and nonrestricted equity capital to clearly define those funds distributable to shareholders. The same division should also be applied when the consolidated balance sheet is prepared. Share capital and other paid-up capital (share premium), retained profits in the so-called reserve fund, and the revaluation fund mentioned above, all belong to restricted equity, which cannot be paid out as cash dividends. Distributable equity, that is, unappropriated retained earnings and net profit for the period, form the maximum amount available to be paid as dividends. Changes in equity capital must be disclosed in the statements or in the notes.

2.3.5 Provisions

"Provisions" on the right-hand side of the balance sheet are listed between equity capital and valuation items. They include the accumulated depreciation difference and voluntary and obligatory provisions (see Section 2.2.4).

According to the Bookkeeping Act (KPL 17 §), voluntary provisions can be made for future investments, bad debts, inventories, and so on. The company tax reform of 1992 abolished almost all voluntary provisions. Formation of most of the voluntary provisions (e.g., inventory provision) was prohibited after 1992. Provisions formed earlier will be taxed at the latest in 1997.

Voluntary provisions and the accumulated depreciation difference in excess of plan are untaxed reserves. According to the "one set of books" concept, these provisions must be recorded in bookkeeping to qualify for tax benefits. Provisions result in a lower annual profit, lower taxable income, and naturally lower taxes. As a matter of fact, provisions are partly liabilities (deferred income taxes) and partly shareholders' equity, depending on the current income tax rate. In Finnish disclosure practice voluntary provisions or untaxed reserves are shown as separate items in the company's balance sheet. In group accounts the disclosure practice is usually different.

Any future expenses that the company is bound to pay and any future losses that seem obvious at the time of closing the books must be recorded as expenses and obligatory provisions formed.

2.3.6 *Liabilities*

Liabilities are divided into noncurrent (long-term) and current, the latter falling due within one year from the date of the balance sheet. The short-term portions of long-term debts that are due within one year are also disclosed as current liabilities in the balance sheet. Employee pensions are often organized through pension insurance companies or pension foundations. Pension loans in noncurrent liabilities mean that the company has borrowed the money paid as pension insurance back from insurance companies and foundations.

It is recommended that pension liabilities be included on an accrual basis in the profit and loss statement and that uncovered pension liabilities be presented the same way as all other long-term debts in the balance sheet. If the total pension liability is not recorded on an accrual basis, then the total liability and any uncovered part must be included in the notes to the balance sheet. Pension liabilities must be charged in full against income no later than December 31, 2000.

2.4 Assets and Liabilities Denominated in Foreign Currencies in Financial Statements

According to Finnish accounting legislation, foreign currency denominated assets and liabilities are converted into Finnish marks by using the closing exchange rates (average rate on the closing day) supplied by the Bank of Finland. If receivables or liabilities will mature after one year or later then they can be valued by using their historical exchange rate (rate of agreement day, KPL 15 § 2). If the exchange rate for a foreign receivable, liability, or other obligation has been fixed by an agreement, then this fixed rate can be used in conversion. The principle that has been followed when determining exchange rates for foreign receivables or liabilities must be explained in the financial statements or in the notes, if the rate used is not that of the closing date (i.e., determined by the Bank of Finland, KPL 21 § 11).

All exchange differences (gains and losses) realized during the accounting period must be included in the profit calculation of the accounting period in question. Unrealized exchange gains and losses can also be recorded in a way that affects the result. The conservatism concept should, however, be followed when recording unrealized exchange gains.

3. Accounting Policies and Practices for Group Accounts

3.1 The Regulations of Group Accounts

All regulations concerning the consolidated financial statements of Finnish companies were included in the Share Companies Act passed in 1978. Since the 1982 accounting period, consolidated statements have been compulsory. There were quite a few paragraphs on the subject in the Share Companies Act, so various accounting authorities have issued guidelines, recommendations, and instructions as to how to prepare consolidated statements. Such instructions were issued by the KHT-Association of Auditors in 1980, by the Commission of Bookkeeping, affiliated with the Ministry of Trade and Industry in 1981, and by the Board of Directors of the Helsinki Stock Exchange Co-operative in 1987. The 1992 bookkeeping regulations now include general instructions for consolidated accounts (KPL 22a-22d § and KPA 19-19b§). The Ministry of Trade and Industry later issued a resolution for the preparation of consolidated accounts (*Kauppa- ja teollisuusministeriön päätös konsernitilinpäätöksen laatimisesta*, October 22, 1993, abbreviation KTMp), and the Commission of Bookkeeping has issued general instructions for consolidated accounts (*Kirjanpitolautakunta, Yleisohje konsernitilinpäätöksen laatimisesta*, November 1, 1993).

3.2 The Scope and Purpose of Group Accounts

By international standards Finnish consolidated financial statements have until now covered only a part of the economic entity called a group. Companies that operate in any legal form apart from a limited liability company have not usually been consolidated. Similarly, associated companies have not been combined in consolidated accounts. The 1992 accounting regulations changed this situation.

In Finnish legislation the definition of a concern relationship is based on the group's *exercise of control*, this concept being applied in the same way as in the EU's Seventh Directive and international accounting standards. A company (a subsidiary) is consolidated if more than 50% of its

equity voting rights are held by another company (the parent) either
directly or through its subsidiaries. Consolidation is applied to all kinds of
business companies: limited liability companies, general and limited partnerships, and co-operatives, for both parent companies and subsidiaries.
One-person businesses and small groups, depending on their size as measured by net sales, balance sheet total, or the number of employees, do not
have to prepare consolidated accounts.

Associated companies, that is, companies in which the investing group
or company has the ability to exercise *significant influence* (an interest of
20–50% of equity voting rights), are to be included in the consolidated
accounts by using the equity method (KPL 22c §, 5 and 6, KPA 19 §).

Consolidated financial statements serve three purposes. The first purpose is presentation of *the net result and the financial position of the whole
economic entity* (the consolidated group). The second, very important,
purpose is to *present the nonrestricted equity of the group* since it indicates
the maximum amount available for cash dividends from the parent company. The third purpose, and main principle to be followed in consolidation, is to give *a true and fair view of the group* with respect to its financial
position and profitability. The main users of group accounting information
are existing and potential owners and creditors, together with other stakeholders.

3.3 Methods Applied in Producing Consolidated Financial Statements

Consolidated financial statements are prepared by combining the separate
financial statements of the parent company and its subsidiaries and then
eliminating all transactions between members of the group. The Finnish
parent company and its domestic subsidiaries prepare financial statements
according to Finnish accounting, tax, and company legislation. The problem is how to combine the statements of foreign subsidiaries that are based
on accounting policies and practices differing, at least to some extent,
from the Finnish system.

Another problem is how to provide information to foreign stakeholders
who are not familiar with the Finnish accounting system. For this reason
many of the largest international Finnish companies have prepared consolidated financial statements according to the IAS 27 standards. The

latest accounting legislation reform in 1992 was meant to harmonize the Finnish practice with international (especially European) practices.

Consolidated companies should have the same accounting period (KPL 22c § 3) and similar accounting systems. All intercompany transactions should be recorded in their own special accounts to enable reliable and simple elimination when consolidated financial statements are prepared.

3.3.1 Elimination of Intercompany Transactions

Intercompany transactions, that is, intercompany sales, purchases, profit distribution, and unrealized internal gross margins are to be eliminated from the consolidated income statement. Mutual receivables, debts, and intercompany ownership of shares are to be eliminated from the consolidated balance sheet. Eliminations are carried out in Finnish consolidated statements by using generally known techniques.

3.3.2 Elimination of Internal Ownership

The parent company's investment in a subsidiary's stock is an internal matter and must therefore be eliminated from the consolidated balance sheet. The purchase or acquisition method is recommended in Finnish regulations and is usually applied in capital consolidation (KTMp 8.1 §). Under some conditions, the pooling method can also be used (KTMp 10 §). Internal ownership is eliminated by setting off the purchase price of the subsidiary shares in the books of the acquiring company against the acquiring company's share of shareholders' equity on the subsidiary's balance sheet at the date of acquisition. Elimination is primarily carried out by using the share capital or other restricted capital of the subsidiary; only as a secondary option is nonrestricted capital used.

If the parent company purchased the subsidiary's stock at a price higher than the shareholders' equity (assets minus liabilities and reserves) on the subsidiary's balance sheet at the time of acquisition, then the difference is called consolidation *aktiva*. In the consolidated statements this *aktiva* is handled by first estimating the fair value of the subsidiary's identifiable assets (e.g., estimated at present acquisition cost or selling price). The consolidation *aktiva* is then divided between these assets, any remainder being shown as an intangible asset, "goodwill," on the consolidated balance sheet.

The consolidation *aktiva* is amortized according to the depreciation plan of the particular assets under consideration. The remaining goodwill must be written off in group accounts over the accounting period during which it gives benefits. According to the Share Companies Act (OYL chapter 11, 3 § 1), the amortizing period for goodwill is 5–20 years. The recommendation is 5 years, but if the goodwill will benefit the company for more than 5 years then the amortizing period can be longer, up to 20 years. The reason for extending the amortizing period must appear in the notes.

In contrast to consolidation *aktiva* a *consolidation passiva* may arise. This will be the case if the purchase price of the subsidiary shares is smaller than the acquiring company's share of the subsidiary's shareholders' equity at the date of acquisition. The *consolidation passiva* should be divided between the balance sheet items that have generated the *passiva*. The remaining excess of consolidated *passiva* is called *consolidation reserve*. The consolidation reserve is shown on the right-hand side of the consolidated balance sheet as a separate item under provisions and is transferred into the consolidated profit and loss statement in subsequent accounting periods according to the conservatism and matching principles.

3.4 Separation of Minority Interests

The consolidated income statement must show the annual profit of the group after minority interests in subsidiaries' results. The group's shareholders' equity must therefore be shown on the consolidated balance sheet with minority ownership at subsidiaries as its own item. Besides equity and results, it is recommended that minority shares in voluntary provisions and depreciations in excess of plan (taking deferred taxes into account) also be separated. Minority interest can be based on direct ownership in subsidiaries or on indirect ownership when subsidiaries own shares of each other.

3.5 Consolidation of Associated Companies

An associated company relationship is based on the concepts of significant influence and notable ownership. The former means an ability to influence economic and operational decision making and 20–50% of the equity voting rights. The latter means ownership of at least 20% of the equity.

Equity accounting or the one-line consolidation method is applied when associated companies are included in the consolidated accounts. Equity accounting means that the investment in the associated company's shares is corrected by the investor's share of undistributed profits (or losses) of the associated company, calculated cumulatively since the establishment or acquisition of the associated company. It is possible to leave an associated company out of consolidation if it does not affect the true and fair view of the results and financial position of the group. Information on why associated companies are not included and the effects of this decision on the result and equity of the group should be included in the notes.

Minority interests in subsidiaries, as well as the parent company's share of results and ownership in associated companies, should be presented separately as consolidated income statement and balance sheet information.

3.6 Translation of Foreign Subsidiary Statements

The use of closing exchange rates of the Bank of Finland (average rates on the closing day) is recommended for translating the financial statements of foreign subsidiaries into Finnish marks. Profit and loss accounts can also be translated by using the average rate of the accounting period (average of the rates on the last day of each month). Other well-known methods can also be used, providing that the consolidated financial statements still give a true and fair view of the result and financial position of the group.

According to the conservatism concept, any significant change for the worse in exchange rates occurring between the date of the balance sheet and the preparation date of the financial statements must be taken into account as an obligatory provision in the consolidated financial statements, unless this was already done in the companies' own financial statements.

Translation differences, that is, differences caused by different exchange rates at the moment of acquisition of foreign subsidiary shares and at the date of the balance sheet and arising when internal ownership is eliminated, are commonly entered in shareholders equity, either as nonrestricted equity or divided between restricted and nonrestricted according to the composition of the subsidiary's equity on the date of acquisition.

Exchange differences that arise in the preparation of consolidation statements should be handled according to the conservatism concept. Exchange losses can be recorded either as an expense in the consolidated profit and loss statement or as a valuation item in the consolidated balance sheet. It is recommended that exchange gains be recorded as a valuation item in the consolidated balance sheet.

3.7 Changes in Financial Position

Consolidated groups, and individual companies as well, that have more than two million Finnish markka restricted equity or more than 500 employees (during the last two accounting periods) must prepare and publish a statement on "changes in financial position" in their annual report. In 1983 the Bookkeeping Commission issued general instructions on how to prepare this statement, on either a "cash flow" or "net working capital flow" basis. In each case the sources and applications of funds must be disclosed. Sources are income, loans, and equity financing, and applications are investments, repayment of capital, and distribution of profit. No standard form is required for the presentation of the consolidated statement of changes in financial position, but the Association of Authorized Public Accountants has expressed recommendations as to how it should be prepared.

3.8 The Auditor's Report

Auditors' reports as published in Finnish annual reports are formal and uninformative from a user's viewpoint. Audit and its development have been under public discussion in Finland, both because of the EU's Eighth Directive and because of recent bankruptcy cases. A special law for auditing is currently under review.

4. Expected Future Developments

Further developments, and some interesting difficulties, can be expected as Finnish accounting seeks to come to terms with European Union accounting harmonization (and vice versa).

Following are the financial statements of KONE Corporation (the Finnish parent company, established in 1910) and the KONE Group (main business sectors: vertical transportation, industrial and dockside materials handling, and wood handling in pulp and paper mills; products manufactured in several countries in Europe, North and South America and Asia).

KONE Annual Report 1993

Accounting Principles

Scope of consolidation

The consolidated accounts include the parent company and those companies in which the parent company held directly or indirectly more than 50% of the voting power at the end of the year. Subsidiaries acquired during the financial year have been included in the consolidated financial statements from the date of acquisition. Holdings in housing and real estate companies which are insignificant in relation to the size and scope of the KONE Group, and the consolidation of which is unnecessary in order to give a true and fair view of the group's result and financial position, have not been included in the consolidated financial statements.

Investments in associated companies have been accounted for in the consolidated financial statements under the equity method. An associated company is a company in which the parent company holds, directly or indirectly, 20–50% of the voting power and has, directly or indirectly, a participating interest of at least 20%.

Method of drawing up accounts

Intercorporate transactions have been eliminated in the consolidated financial statements.

Intercorporate ownerships have been eliminated by deducting the amount of each subsidiary's equity at the time of acquisition from the acquisition cost of its shares. The difference between the acquisition cost and the subsidiary's equity at the time of acquisition has been entered, where applicable, under fixed and intangible assets. The remainder of the difference has been shown as goodwill.

The KONE Group's share of the profit or loss of an associated company is shown in the consolidated statements of income as a separate item. The depreciation of the goodwill arisen from the acquisition of the shares of associated companies is included in goodwill depreciation. The dividends received from the associated companies are not included in the consolidated statement of income. The Group's share of the associated companies' shareholders equity at the date of acquisition, adjusted by changes in the associated companies' equity after the date of acquisition, is shown in the balance sheet under 'shares and participating interests'. The goodwill arisen from the acquisition of the shares of associated companies is shown under 'goodwill'.

Investments in other companies are stated at cost. The book value of investments has been reduced, when necessary, to estimated net realizable value.

In certain countries, tax legislation allows allocation to be made to untaxed reserves. These allocations are not subject to taxation on condition that the corresponding deductions have also been made in the accounts. In the consolidated financial statements the yearly allocations (reserves as well as the difference between the depreciation according to plan and depreciation accepted by tax laws) have been added to net income, excluding the change in the calculative deferred tax liability. The deferred tax liability is determined from the accumulation of untaxed reserves. The accumulation of untaxed reserves, excluding the calculative deferred tax liability, is included in the shareholders' equity in the consolidated balance sheet. Accumulated deferred tax liability is shown as a separate liability item in the consolidated balance sheet.

The taxes shown in the consolidated statement of income include income taxes to be paid on the basis of local tax legislation as well as the effect of the yearly change in the deferred tax liability, determined from the untaxed reserves by using the current tax rate. Tax credits related to intercompany dividends or dividends from the associated companies have been deducted from taxes in the consolidated statement of income.

Minority shares are shown as a separate item in the consolidated statement of income and balance sheet. The minority share in the statement of income is calculated from the income before allocation to untaxed reserves but after taxes adjusted by the change in the calculative deferred tax liability. The minority share in the balance sheet is calculated from the sum of shareholders' equity and accumulation of untaxed reserves, from which the calculative deferred tax liability has been deducted.

Conversion of foreign subsidiary financial statements

The financial statements of foreign subsidiaries have been converted into Finnish marks at the rates current on the last day of the year. Translation differences resulting from converting the shareholders' equity of foreign subsidiaries have been included in 'other restricted equity' under shareholders' equity.

Foreign currency items and exchange differences

Receivables and liabilities in foreign currencies have been valued at the rate current at the end of the year. Receivables and liabilities covered by forward contracts have been valued at contract rates. Realized exchange rate differences as well as exchange rate gains or losses resulting from the valuation of receivables and liabilities, have been entered in the statement of income. The exchange rate differences resulting from forward contracts and foreign currency loans which are designated as hedges on net investments in foreign subsidiaries have been matched against the translation differences and entered under restricted equity in the balance sheet.

Revenue recognition

Revenue from goods sold and services rendered is recognized on completion of the delivery. This principle is also applied to long-term projects.

Research and development costs

Research and development costs are charged to income during the year in which they are incurred.

Pension settlements and costs

Pensions are generally handled for KONE companies by outside pension insurance companies. A small number of pensions are handled by the pension fund within the parent company. The pension fund within the parent company is fully funded.

Valuation of inventories

Raw materials and supplies are valued at standard costs. Semimanufactures have been valued at variable production costs. Work in progress includes direct labor and material costs as of 31 December, as well as a proportion of indirect costs related to production and installation of orders included in work in progress.

Valuation and depreciation of fixed assets

Fixed assets are stated at cost. In addition, certain land and buildings can be stated at revalued amounts. A predetermined plan is used in carrying out depreciation of fixed assets. This predetermined depreciation plan has been charged for acquisitions from 1 January, 1993 and thereafter. Depreciation is based on the estimated useful economic life of various assets as follows:

—Buildings	5–40 years
—Machinery and equipment	4–10 years
—Goodwill	5–20 years
—Other intangible assets	4–20 years

Provisions for liabilities and charges

Future expenses to which companies have committed themselves and which will produce no future income are charged against income as provisions for liabilities and charges. The same concerns those future losses which are certain to be realized.

Statement of changes in financial position

Changes in financial position are presented as cash flows classified by operating, investing and financing activities. The effects of changes in exchange rates has been eliminated. The items in the Cash Flow Statement have the following content:

—'Cash' consists of cash at bank and in hand.
—'Cash flow' signifies the increase of decrease in cash.
—'Investing activities' consist of the purchase of fixed assets an the proceeds from the sale of fixed assets.
—'Financial activities' consist of increases in share capital, dividends paid, proceeds from borrowing, repayments of amounts borrowed, bank deposits and investments, granted loans and swap agreements.
—Cash flows of other than investing or financing activities belong to operating activities.

The Formulas of the Profit and Loss Statement (KPA 1§, Formula 1) and the Balance Sheet (KPA 7 §) in Finland (in Finnish and in English)

The Profit and Loss Statement

Liikevaihto
Valmistevarastojen lisäys (+) tai
  vähennys (-)
Valmistus omaan käyttöön (+)
Liiketoiminnan muut tuotot

Muuttuvat kulut:
  Aineet, tarvikkeet ja tavarat:
  Ostot tilikauden aikana
  Varastojen lisäys (-) tai
    vähennys (+)
  Ulkopuoliset palvelut
  Henkilöstökulut
  Muut muuttuvat kulut =
Myyntikate

Kiinteät kulut:
  Henkilöstökulut
  Vuokrat
  Muut kiinteät kulut
Käyttökate

Poistot käyttöomaisuudesta ja muista
  pitkävaikutteisista menoista =

Liikevoitto (-tappio)

Rahoitustuotot ja -kulut
  Osinkotuotot
  Korkotuotot pitkäaikaisista
    sijoituksista
  Muut rahoitustuotot
  Korkokulut
  Muut rahoituskulut
  Poistot sijoituksista
*Voitto (Tappio) ennen satun-
naiseriä, varauksia ja veroja*

Satunnaiset tuotot ja kulut:
  Satunnaiset tuotot
  Satunnaiset kulut
*Voitto (Tappio) ennen varauksia ja
veroja*

Poistoeron lisäys (-) tai vähennys (+)

Vapaaehtoisten varausten lisäys (-)
  vähennys (+)
Välittömät verot
Tilikauden voitto (tappio)

Net Sales
Change in stocks in finished
  goods (increase +; decrease -)
Own work capitalized (+)
Other operating income

Variable costs and expenses:
  Materials, supplies and goods
  Purchases during the period
  Changes in inventories
    (increase -; decrease +)
  External services
  Personnel expenses
  Other variable costs and expenses =
Gross profit or loss

Fixed costs and expenses:
  Personnel expenses
  Rents
  Other fixed costs and expenses
*Profit from operations before
  depreciations*

Depreciation according to plan from
  fixed assets and other long-term
  investments =
Operating profit (loss)

Financial income and expenses
  Dividend income
  Interest income from long-term
    investments
  Other financial income
  Interest expense
  Other financial expense
  Value adjustments of investments
*Profit (Loss) before extraordinary
  items, appropriations and taxes*

Extraordinary income and expense:
  Extraordinary income
  Extraordinary expense
*Profit (Loss) before appreciations
  and taxes*

Depreciation in excess of plan (+)
  less than plan (-)

Changes in voluntary provisions   tai
  (increase -) (decrease +)
Income taxes
Profit (Loss) for the financial year

The Balance Sheet

VASTAAVAA	ASSETS

Käyttöomaisuus ja muut pitkäaikaiset sijoitukset

Fixed assets and other long-term investments

Aineettomat hyödykkeet
Perustamis- ja järjestelymenot
Tutkimus- ja kehittämismenot
Aineettomat oikeudet
Liikearvo
Muut pitkävaikutteiset menot
Ennakkomaksut

Intangible assets
Start-up and organizing expenses
Research and development costs
Intangible rights
Goodwill
Other long-term expenditures
Advances paid

Aineelliset hyödykkeet
Maa-ja vesialueet
Rakennukset ja rakennelmat
Koneet ja kalusto
Muut aiheelliset hyödykkeet
Ennakkomaksut ja
   keskeneräiset hankinnat

Tangible assets
Land and water
Buildings and structures
Machinery and equipment
Other tangible assets
Advances paid and unfinished
   supplies

*Käyttöomaisuusarvopaperit
   ja muut pitkäaikaiset sijoitukset*
Osakkeet ja osuudet
Lainasaamiset
Muut sijoitukset

*Fixed securities and other long
   term investments*
Shares and participation certificates
Loans receivable
Other investments

Arvostuserät

Valuation items

Vaihto-ja rahoitusomaisuus

Stocks and financial assets

Vaihto-omaisuus
Aineet ja tarvikkeet
Keskeneräiset tuotteet
Valmiit tuotteet/ tavarat
Muu vaihto-omaisuus
Ennakkomaksut

Stocks
Materials and supplies
Semifinished products
Finished products/goods
Other stocks
Advances paid

Saamiset
Myyntisaamiset
Lainasaamiset
Siirtosaamiset
Muut saamiset

Receivable
Trade receivable
Loans receivable
Prepaid expenses
Other receivable

Rahoitusomaisuusarvopaperit
Osakkeet ja osuudet
Muut arvopaperit
Rahat ja pankkisaamiset

Financial securities
Shares and participation certificates
Other securities
Cash on hand and in bank

VASTATTAVAA	SHAREHOLDERS EQUITY AND LIABILITIES
Oma pääoma	*Equity capital*
Osake-, osuus-ja muu niitä vastaava pääoma	Share capital or other paid-up capital
Muu oma pääoma	Share premium and other capital reserves
Edellisen tilikauden voitto/tappio	Profit/loss for the previous accounting period
Tilikauden voitto/tappio	Profit/loss for the accounting period
Varaukset	*Provisions*
Kertynyt poistoero	Depreciation in excess of plan
Vapaaehtoiset varaukset	Voluntary provisions
Investointivaraukset	Provisions for investments
Muut varaukset	Other provisions
Pakolliset varaukset	Obligatory provisions (for liabilities and charges)
Arvostuserät	*Valuation items*
Vieras pääoma	*Liabilities*
Pitkäaikainen	*Long-term debt*
Joukkovelkakirjalainat	Bonds
Vaihtovelkakirjalainat	Convertible bonds
Lainat rahoituslaitoksilta	Loans from financial institutions
Eläkelainat	Pension loans
Saadut ennakot	Advances received
Ostovelat	Trade creditors
Muut pitkäaikaiset velat	Other long-term debt
Lyhytaikainen	*Short-term debt*
Lainat rahoituslaitoksista	Loans from financial institutions
Eläkelaina	Pension loans
Saadut ennakot	Advances received
Ostovelat	Trade creditors
Rahoitusvekselit	Notes payable
Siirtovelat	Accrued liabilities
Muut lyhytaikaiset velat	Other short-term debt

Consolidated Balance Sheet

	31.12.1993	31.12.1992
Assets		
Fixed assets and other long-term investments		
Intangible assets and goodwill (Note 5)	1,395,023	1,514,589
Tangible assets		
Land (Note 6)	163,736	158,560
Buildings (Note 7)	769,582	774,827
Machinery and equipment (Note 8) 903,169	958,292	
Advance payments	10,940	27,469
	3,242,450	3,433,737
Fixed securities and other long-term assets		
Shares and participating interests (Note 9)	96,055	114,204
Valuation items		
Current assets		
Inventories		
Raw materials, supplies and	574,935	672,205
semi-manufactured goods		
Work in progress	1,926,632	1,721,244
Advance payments	41,921	47,941
Advance payments received	(1,908,427)	(1,603,923)
	635,061	837,467
Receivables		
Accounts receivable	2,441,364	2,539,920
Loans receivable (Note 10)	322,521	230,726
Deferred assets (Note 11)	490,619	484,517
Bills receivable	89,447	64,407
	3,343,951	3,319,570
Financial securities and cash (Note 12)	896,888	1,422,180
	4,875,900	5,579,217
	8,214,405	**9,127,158**

Shareholders' Equity and Liabilities

		31.12.1993	31.12.1992
Shareholders' equity			
Restricted capital			
Share capital		302,431	302,431
Other restricted equity		60,985	70,273
Non-restricted capital			
Retained earnings		1,962,755	1,743,467
Profit for the period		287,131	278,706
	Note 14	2,613,302	2,394,877
Minority shares		29,726	20,775
Provisions	Note 15	448,278	395,251
Deferred tax liability		249,015	262,150
Valuation items			
Liabilities			
Long-term debt			
Loans from financial institutions		928,489	917,700
Pension loans		301,919	450,786
Other long-term debt		6,461	12,216
	Note 16	1,236,869	1,380,702
Current liabilities			
Long-term debt due within one year		162,169	268,810
Accounts payable		814,389	804,044
Bills payable		67,735	94,267
Accruals	Note 17	1,601,960	1,559,590
Other current liabilities	Note 18	990,962	1,946,692
		3,637,215	4,673,403
Total liabilities	Note 19	5,571,377	6,711,506
		8,214,405	**9,127,158**

Consolidated Statement of Income
(A short formula; all specifications are made in notes)

	1.1.–31.12.1993	1.1.–31.12.1992
Turnover/Net sales[1]	10,812,570	11,279,352
Costs and expenses (Note 1)	9,933,881	10,235,087
Depreciation according to plan (Note 2)	414,473	401,123
Operating profit (loss)	**464,216**	**643,142**
Share of associated companies' profits	24,402	25,462
Financial income and expenses (Note 3)	(160,450)	(211,922)
Profit (loss) before extraordinary **items, appropriations, and taxes**	**328,168**	**456,682**
Extraordinary income and expenses	101,858	
Profit (loss) before appropriations **and taxes**	**430,026**	**456,682**
Taxes (Note 4)	(141,215)	(176,729)
Profit (loss) for the financial year before the minority share	288,811	
Minority share	(1,680)	(1,247)
PROFIT (LOSS)	**287,131**	**278,706**

[1] Change in stocks of finished goods and work in progress', 'Own work capitalized' and 'Other operating income' are added to or subtracted from the net sales to get a figure describing the total volume of operations of the firm.

Consolidated Statement of Cash Flows

	1993	1992
Cash receipt from customers	11,069	11,411
Cash paid to suppliers and employees (9,872)	(10,177)	
Cash flow from financial items	(83)	(206)
Cash flow from taxes and other items (44)	(201)	
Cash flow from operating activities 1, 070	**828**	
Capital expenditure	(306)	(579)
Proceeds from sale of fixed assets 99	50	
Fixed assets of new subsidiaries	(16)	(15)
Fixed assets of sold subsidiaries	84	—
Cash flow from investing activities (139)	**(544)**	
Cash flow after investing activities 931	**284**	
Change in current creditors (net)	(1,131)	(108)
Change in long-term debt (net)	(137)	(12)
Dividends paid	(59)	(59)
Other financing activities	352	(223)
Cash flow from financing activities (975)	**(403)**	
Change in net cash	**(44)**	**(119)**
Cash and bank (December, 31)	311	343
Exchange difference	(12)	(39)
Cash and bank (January, 1)	343	423
Change in net cash	**(44)**	**(119)**

Reconciliation of net income to cash flow from operating activities

	1993	1992
Net income	287	279
Depreciation	414	401
Other adjustments	2	0
Income before change in working capital	703	680
Change in receivables	166	(141)
Change in payables	273	423
Change in inventories	(72)	(135)
Cash flow from operating activities	1,070	828

Notes on the Consolidated Financial Statements
(Parentheses are used to indicate negative figures in tables.)

Consolidated statement of income

1. Cost and expenses
   The costs and expenses were spread as follows:

	1993	1992
Materials and supplies	3,665.7	4,095.5
Salaries of boards of directors and managing directors	61.5	60.2
Wages and other salaries	2,842.3	2,866.0
Other personnel expenses	1,596.3	1,558.4
Other expenses	1,768.1	1,655.0
Total	**9,933.9**	**10,235.1**

The consolidated statement of income includes a FIM 56.7 increase in the provision for liabilities and charges in 1993.

2. Depreciation

	1993	1992
Intangible assets and goodwill	183.4	169.0
Buildings	49.0	50.8
Machinery and equipment	182.1	181.3
Total	**414.5**	**401.1**

3. Financial income and expenses

	1993	1992
Dividends received	2.0	2.1
Interest received	227.7	254.4
Interest paid	(417.2)	(436.9)
Other financial income and expenses	27.0	(31.5)
Total	**(160.5)**	**(211.9)**

4. Income taxes
   Income taxes were composed of the following items.

	1993	1992
Local income taxes of group companies166.5	166.6	
Change in the calculative deferred tax liability	(13.1)	22.8
Tax credits related to dividends	(12.2)	(12.7)
Total	**141.2**	**176.7**

Consolidated balance sheet

5. Intangible assets and goodwill

Goodwill

	1993	1992
Acquisition cost (January 1)	1,143.4	1,030.8
Increase	14.9	93.3
Decrease	(38.9)	—
Accumulated depreciation	(492.3)	(405.7)
Total (December 31)	**627.1**	**718.4**

Other intangible assets

	1993	1992
Acquisition cost (January 1)	1,321.5	1,203.3
Increase	40.2	89.9
Decrease	—	—
Accumulated depreciation	(593.8)	(497.0)
Total (December 31)	**767.9**	**796.2**

Other intangible assets primarily consist of maintenance contracts acquired in connection with the acquisition of subsidiaries.

6. Land

	1993	1992
Acquisition cost (January, 1)	159.6	146.8
Accumulated revaluation	10.0	10.0
Increase	3.6	4.5
Decrease	(9.5)	(2.7)
Total (December 31)	**163.7**	**158.6**

7. Buildings

	1993	1992
Acquisition cost (January, 1)	1,004.3	934.3
Accumulated revaluation	178.1	178.1
Increase	47.4	82.7
Decrease	(13.1)	(17.8)
Accumulated depreciation	(447.1)	(402.5)
Total (December 31)	**769.6**	**774.8**
Residual value of revaluation	105.4	109.9

8. Machinery and equipment

Goodwill

	1993	1992
Acquisition cost (January 1)	2,032.2	1,733.0
Increase	196.0	301.8
Decrease	(53.1)	(44.8)
Accumulated depreciation	(1,271.9)	(1,031.7)
Total (December 31)	**903.2**	**958.3**

9. Shares and participating interests

	1993	1992
Total (January 1)	114.2	96.7
Change in the share in associated companies	4.5	12.2
Increase	1.1	17.7
Decrease	(23.8)	(12.4)
Depreciation	—	—
Total (December 31)	**96.0**	**114.2**

The asset value of the shares in associated companies consists of the Group's proportion of the associated companies' shareholders' equity at the acquisition date, adjusted by any variation in the associated companies' shareholders' equity after the acquisition.

10. Loans receivable

Swap agreements at net value totaling FIM 655.0 million (562.3) have been deducted from loans receivable.

11. Deferred assets
Deferred assets include the following items:

	1993	1992
Sales and value added taxes	80.2	53.1
Interest income	44.7	104.0
Income taxes	75.7	67.4
Other receivables	290.0	260.0
Total	**490.6**	**484.5**

12. Financial securities and cash

	1993	1992
Cash at bank and in hand	310.7	343.2
Short-term deposit	193.7	358.0
Other marketable securities	392.5	721.0
Total	**896.9**	**1,422.2**

13. Receivables
Receivables falling due after one year:

	1993	1992
Accounts receivable	8.0	9.3
Loans receivable	89.4	126.0
Total	**97.4**	**135.3**

Receivables from associated companies:

	1993	1992
Advance payments	2.9	1.6
Accounts receivable	6.2	3.0
Loans receivable	137.2	3.4
Deferred asset	20.9	17.2
Bills receivable	0.5	0.9
Total	**167.7**	**26.1**

14. Changes in shareholders' equity in 1993

	Share capital	Other restricted equity	Retained earnings	Profit for the year	Total equity
January, 1	302.4	70.3	2,022.2	—	2,394.9
Revaluations	—				
Translation differences		(9.3)			(9.3)
Dividend			(59.4)		(59.4)
Profit for the year			287.1		287.1
December 31	302.4	61.0	1,962.8	287.1	2,613.3

Other restricted equity includes translation differences of FIM (-41.1) million (-31.8). The accumulation of untaxed reserves, excluding the calculative deferred tax liability, totaled FIM 530.5 million (598.6). Accumulated untaxed reserves are not distributable equity.

15. Provisions for liabilities and charges

	1993	1992
Provisions for guarantees	127.3	121.3
Provisions for product liability claims	67.1	64.5
Provisions for business reorganizing	36.7	22.1
Provisions for loss contracts	82.9	38.5
Other provisions	134.3	148.9
Total	448.3	395.3

16. Long-term debt
    Pension loans consist of loans from insurance companies against pension insurance payments to them.

    Long-term debt falls due as follows:

	FIM mill.	%
1995	254.2	20.6
1996	111.0	9.0
1997	585.1	47.3
Later	286.6	23.2

17. Accruals

	1993	1992
Sales and value added taxes	145.0	146.5
Income taxes	110.2	88.0
Wages, salaries and personnel expenses	597.1	596.7
Pension commitments	250.2	226.5
Interest	67.6	83.4
Other items	431.8	418.5
Total	1,601.9	1,559.6

18. Other current liabilities

	1993	1992
Bank overdrafts	175.7	330.5
Current bank loans	610.4	1,396.2
Commercial papers	204.9	220.0
Total	991.0	1,946.7

19. Liabilities owed to associated companies
    The consolidated balance sheet includes liabilities owed to associated companies as follows:

	1993	1992
Accounts payable	53.7	60.6
Other current liabilities	5.2	0.8
Total	58.9	61.4

20. Contingent liabilities and pledged assets

	Group		Parent Company	
	1993	1992	1993	1992
Endorsements	—	3.5	—	—
Assets pledged to secure loans				
Group and parent company	334.4	452.9	204.5	256.4
Subsidiaries			1.0	1.0
Pledged assets	305.8	329.9	185.0	202.5
Guarantees				
Subsidiaries			2,056.0	2,347.7
Associated companies	42.8	11.0	42.8	11.0
Others	160.2	29.0	157.5	2.0
Leasing liabilities				
Falling due in the next year	45.5	35.4	3.0	3.0
Falling due after 1 year	57.6	51.6	3.2	2.7
Other liabilities	17.8	69.0	—	—
Total	964.1	982.3	2,653.0	2,826.3

Parent Company: Statement of Income

		31.12.1993	**31.12.1992**
Turnover/Net sales[1])	(Note 1)	1,824,406	1,482,119
Costs and expenses	(Note 2)	(1,789,352)	(1,486,078)
Change in inventories		26,393	60,798
Depreciation according to plan	(Note 3)	(109,913)	(85,244)
Operating profit (loss)		(48,466)	(28,405)
Financial income and expenses	(Note 4)	359,686	474,077
Profit (loss) before extraordinary items, appropriations, and taxes		311,220	445,672
Extraordinary items	(Note 5)	52,421	15,571
Profit (loss) before appropriations and taxes		363,641	461,243
Depreciation difference	(Note 6)	32,636	(11,467)
Change in voluntary provisions	(Note 7)	26,334	67,438
Taxes		(27,014)	(34,545)
PROFIT (LOSS)		395,597	482,669

[1] 'Change in stocks of finished goods and work in progress', 'Own work capitalized' and 'Other operating income' are added to or subtracted from the net sales to get a figure describing the total volume of operations of the firm.

Parent Company: Balance Sheet

ASSETS		**31.12.1993**	**31.12.1992**
FIXED ASSETS AND OTHER LONG-TERM INVESTMENTS			
Intangible assets	Note 8	4,522	4,212
Tangible assets			
Land	Note 9	21,920	22,331
Buildings	Note 10	168,997	210,491
Machinery and equipment	Note 11	185,708	211,685
Fixed securities and other long-term assets			
Shares in subsidiaries	Note 12	1,647,539	1,521,116
Other stocks and shares	Note 13	56,782	62,118
		2,085,468	2,031,953
VALUATION ITEMS			
CURRENT ASSETS			
Inventories			
Raw materials, supplies and semi-manufactured goods		62,618	67,529
Work in progress	Note 14	341,427	310,123
Advance payments		23,824	19,164
		427,869	396,816

Receivables	Note 15		
Accounts receivable		414,086	296,783
Loans receivable	Note 16	329,026	585,207
Deferred assets	Note 17	153,947	100,044
		897,059	982,034
Financial securities and cash Note 18	608,747	565,600	
TOTAL CURRENT ASSETS		**1,933,675**	**1,944,450**
		4,019,143	**3,976,403**

SHAREHOLDERS' EQUITY AND LIABILITIES		**31.12.1993**	**31.12.1992**
SHAREHOLDERS' EQUITY			
Restricted capital			
Share capital		302,431	302,431
Reserve fund		66,661	72,945
Non-restricted capital			
Retained earnings		1,203,605	780,354
Net income		395,597	482.669
	Note 19	1,968,294	1,638,399
UNTAXED RESERVES	Note 20	315,307	390,757
PROVISION FOR LIABILITIES AND CHARGES	Note 21	14,022	—
VALUATION ITEMS			
LIABILITIES	Note 22		
Long-term debt	Note 23		
Outstanding loans		336,513	699,524
Pension loans		267 161	339 530
Other long-term debt		2,806	6,373
		606,480	1,045,427
Current liabilities			
Long-term debt due within one year	Note 24	472,515	146,035
Bank overdrafts		9,929	73,507
Advances received		565,244	382,676
Accounts payable		182,535	116,529
Accruals	Note 25	191,513	183,073
Other current liabilities		93,304	—
		1,115,040	901,820
TOTAL DEBT		1,721,520	1,947,247
		4,019,143	3,976,403

Parent Company: Statement of Cash Flows

Cash receipt from customers	1,901,265	1,664,733
Cash paid to suppliers and employees	(1,705,544)	(1.496,226)
Cash flow from financial items	338 792	470,245
Cash flow from taxes and other items	(7,601)	(2,215)
CASH FLOW FROM OPERATING ACTIVITIES	526,912	636,537
Capital expenditure	(224,984)	(520,486)
Proceeds from sale of fixed assets	38,793	2,853
CASH FLOW FROM INVESTING ACTIVITIES	(186,191)	(497,633)
CASH FLOW AFTER INVESTING ACTIVITIES	340,721	138,904
Change in current creditors (net)	(43,795)	67,079
Change in long-term debt (net)	(438,947)	(94,108)
Dividends paid	(59,418)	(59,418)
Other financing activities	197,929	(80,716)
CASH FLOW FROM FINANCING ACTIVITIES	(344,231)	(167,163)
CHANGE IN NET CASH	(3,510)	(28,259)
Cash and bank (31st December)	27,246	30,756
Cash and bank (1st January)	30,756	59,015
CHANGE IN NET CASH	**(3,510)**	**(28,259)**

RECONCILIATION OF NET INCOME TO CASH FLOW FROM OPERATING ACTIVITIES

NET INCOME	395,597	482,669
Depreciation	109,913	85,244
Other adjustments	(58,970)	(55,971)
INCOME BEFORE CHANGE IN WORKING CAPITAL	446,540	511,942
Change in receivables	(164,271)	64,909
Change in payables	271,036	120,484
Change in inventories	(26,393)	(60,798)
CASH FLOW FROM OPERATING ACTIVITIES	526,912	636 537

Notes on the Parent Company Financial Statements

(Parentheses are used to indicate negative figures in tables and the previous year's figures in text.)

Statement of income

1. Sales
   Sales to subsidiaries totalled FIM 716.1 million (678,3) corresponding to a share of 39 % (46 %) of net sales.

2. Cost and expenses

Costs and expenses were spread as follows:

	1993	1992
Materials and supplies	883.4	632.9
Salaries of boards of directors and managing directors	3.3	2.7
Wages and other salaries	311.6	320.9
Other personnel expenses	196.2	180.3
Other expenses	394.9	349.3
Total	1,789.4	1,486.1

3. Depreciation

	1993	1992
Intangible assets and goodwill	3.0	2.7
Buildings	13.5	16.0
Machinery and equipment	43.2	44.5
Investments and intangibles	50.2	22.0
Total	109.9	85.2

4. Financial income and expenses

	1993	1992
Dividends received from subsidiaries	361.1	440.8
Other dividends received	1.7	2.2
Interest received from subsidiaries	34.7	81.6
Other interest received	57.3	110.6
Interest paid to subsidiaries	(56.0)	(77.2)
Other interests paid	(60.0)	(87.8)
Other financial income and expenses	(20.9)	(3.8)
Total	**359.7**	**474.0**

5. Extraordinary items

	1993	1992
Capital gains	26.2	—
Group contribution received	33.3	24.5
Group contribution granted	(7.1)	(8.9)
Total	52.4	15.6

6. Depreciation difference

Depreciation difference was spread by asset category as follows (Increases in depreciation difference are indicated by parentheses. Figures not in parentheses indicate a decrease in depreciation difference.)

	1993	**1992**
Buildings	13.7	5.6
Machinery and equipment	18.9	(17.1)
Total	32.6	(11.5)

The change in building depreciation difference includes a FIM 6.3 million debit from revaluations related to incorporations.

7. Changes in voluntary provisions (untaxed reserves)

The impact of allocations to untaxed reserves on net income was as follows (Increase in untaxed reserves are indicated by parentheses. Figures not in parentheses indicate a decrease in untaxed reserves.):

	1993	**1992**
Reserve for inventories	—	(14.8)
Reserve for operations	3.0	2.8
Reserve for doubtful accounts	15.0	3.0
Reserve for investments	—	70.0
Other reserves	(6.7)	—
Total	26.3	67.4

Balance sheet

8. Intangible Assets

	1993	**1992**
Acquisition cost (January 1)	13.2	9.8
Increase	3.4	3.6
Decrease	—	(0.2)
Accumulated depreciation	(12.1)	(9.0)
Total (December 31)	4.5	4.2

9. Land

	1993	**1992**
Acquisition cost (January 1)	12.3	12.2
Accumulated revaluation	10.0	10.0
Increase	—	0.1
Decrease	(0.4)	—
Total (December 31)	21.9	22.3

10. Buildings

	1993	1992
Acquisition cost (January 1)	—	220.5
	216.2	
Accumulated revaluation	160.3	160.3
Increase	1.5	4.3
Decrease	(29.5)	—
Accumulated depreciation	(183.8)	(170.3)
Total (December 31)	169.0	210.5
Residual value of revaluation	75.4	78.3

11. Machinery and equipment

	1993	1992
Acquisition cost (January 1)	601.9	567.4
Increase	34.9	50.7
Decrease	(17.7)	(16.2)
Accumulated depreciation	(433.4)	(390.2)
Total (December 31)	185.7	211.7

12. Shares in subsidiaries

	1993	1992
Total (January 1)	1,521.1	1,104.5
Increase	184.3	432.2
Decrease	(7.8)	—
Transfer form other shares	—	6.5
Depreciation	(50.1)	(22.1)
Total (December 31)	1,647.5	1,521.1

13. Other stocks and shares

	1993	1992
Total (January 1)	62.1	57.6
Increase	1.3	11.0
Decrease	(6.6)	—
Transfer to shares in subsidiaries	—	(6.5)
Depreciation	—	—
Total (December 31)	56.8	62.1

14. Work in progress

The amount of fixed costs relating to the production and installation of products included in work in progress was FIM 10.0 million.

15. Receivables

Receivables falling due after one year:

	1993	**1992**
Accounts receivable	0.5	6.4
Loans receivable	9.5	8.9
Deferred assets	0.7	0.3
Total	10.7	15.6

Receivables from group companies

	1993	**1992**
Accounts receivable	29	0.5
	207.7	
Loans receivable		304.9
	523.2	
Deferred assets	79.8	35.7
Total	675.2	766.6

Receivables from associated companies

	1993	**1992**
Accounts receivable	2.6	2.1
Loans receivable	2.2	1.9
Total	4.8	4.0

16. Loans receivable

Swap agreements in the net amount of FIM 40.1 million (38.2) have been deducted from loans receivable.

17. Deferred assets
Deferred assets include the following items:

	1993	**1992**
Sales and value added taxes	35.2	27.9
Interest income	15.2	24.1
Income taxes	—	9.0
Other receivables	103.5	39.0
Total	153.9	100.0

18. Financial securities and cash

	1993	**1992**
Cash at bank and in hand	27.2	30.7
Short-term deposit	189.0	194.4
Other marketable securities	392.5	340.5
Total	608.7	565.6

19. Changes in shareholders' equity in 1993

	Share capital	Reserve fund	Retained earnings	Profit for the year	Total equity
January 1	302.4	72.9	1,263.0	—	1,638.3
Revaluations	—	(6.2)	—	—	(6.2)
Dividend	—	—	(59.4)	—	(59.4)
Profit for the year	—	—	—	395.6	395.6
December 31	302.4	6.7	1,203.6	395.6	1,968.3

The total number of shares, with a nominal value of FIM 50 per share, is 6,048,612. Of these, 2,250 shares (representing a combined nominal value of FIM 112,500) have been redeemed for the company, leaving the shareholders 6,046,362 shares of which 1,045,482 are 'A' shares and 5,000,880 are 'B' shares.

20. Untaxed reserves

	1993	1992
Cumulative depreciation difference, buildings	(42.6)	(12.1)
Cumulative depreciation difference, machinery and equipment	130.4	149.0
Reserve for inventories	89.8	89.8
Reserve for guarantees	13.7	28.6
Reserve for doubtful accounts	—	15.0
Reserve for operations	117.3	120.4
Other reserves	6.7	—
Total	315.3	390.7

Reserves are in conformance with those permitted under the Company Income Tax Law (EVL). The reserve for inventories is 22.2% of total inventories. The reserve for operations corresponds to 30 per cent of salaries and wages paid during the financial year and subject to withholding tax. Other reserves correspond to 2/3 of fixed costs included in work in progress.

21. Provisions for liabilities and charges

	1993	1992
Provisions for guarantees	11.0	—
Other provisions	3.0	—
Total	14.0	—

22. Liabilities owed to group and associated companies

Liabilities owed to group companies:

	1993	1992
Outstanding loans	251.6	496.6
Advanced received	7.5	17.3
Accounts payable	80.8	42.3
Accruals	15.1	20.1
Other current liabilities	93.3	—
Total	448.3	576.3

Liabilities owed to associated companies:

	1993	1992
Advances received	6.5	0.1
Accounts payable	0.5	2.2
Accruals	—	0.4
Total	7.0	2.7

23. Long-term debt
Long.-term debt falling due after five years:

	1993	1992
Outstanding loans	10.2	4.3
Pension loans	199.8	254.0
Total	210.0	258.3

24. Long-term debt falling due within one year

	1993	1992
Outstanding loans	32.1	111.3
Pension loans	24.4	25.7
Other long-term debt	16.0	9.0
Total	72.5	146.0

25. Accruals

	1993	1992
Sales and value added taxes	—	1.1
Income taxes	3.7	4.5
Wages, salaries and personnel expenses	87.5	68.1
Interest	26.9	49.2
Other items	73.4	60.2
Total	191.5	183.1

Board of Directors' Proposal to the Annual General Meeting

The KONE group of companies' distributable equity is FIM 1,719.4 million. The parent company's distributable equity from the previous year is FIM 1,203,605,208.60 and profit from 1993 is FIM 395,597,397.75 for the total of FIM 1,599,202,606.35.

The Board of Directors proposes to the Meeting that a dividend of FIM 9 be paid on each of the 1,045,482 A shares, and FIM 10 on each of the 5,000,880 B shares, for a total of FIM 59,418,138. The Board of Directors further proposes that the rest (FIM 1,539,784,468.35) be retained and carried forward.

It is also proposed that the dividends for 1993 be payable as from 8 March 1994.

Helsinki, 11th February, 1994

(Names of members of Board of Directors; 6 members)

Auditors' Report

We have examined the closing of the books, the accounts and the administration of KONE Corporation and the consolidated financial statements of the KONE group of companies for the year 1993 in accordance with generally accepted auditing standards.

PARENT COMPANY

The financial statements, showing a profit of FIM 395,597,397.75, have been prepared in accordance with regulations in force.

We propose that the Income Statement and the Balance Sheet be adopted and that the members of the Board of Directors and the President be discharged from the responsibility for the year 1993.

We agree with the Board of Directors' proposal concerning the disposal of the year's profit.

THE KONE GROUP OF COMPANIES

The consolidated financial statements have been prepared in accordance with regulations in force.

The consolidated distributable shareholders' equity has been determined in accordance with prevailing requirements.

We propose that the Consolidated Income Statement and the Consolidated Balance Sheet for the year 1993 be adopted.

Helsinki, 11th February, 1994

Names of Authorized Public Accountants (2)

ICELAND

Stefan Svavarsson
University of Iceland and
L.E. Ltd. representing
Arthur Andersen & Co. S.C.

1. Background

1.1 Introduction

An island in the North Atlantic Ocean, Iceland is about 103,000 square kilometers in size and has a population of 260,000. The capital, Reykjavík, is located in the southwest part of the island. Approximately 160,000 people live in the capital and the neighboring municipalities. The island was settled in the late ninth century by Norwegians, although there are also some indications that Irish monks lived in the country at that time.

Iceland became a fully independent republic in 1944, when it terminated its union with Denmark. Previously, the country had been granted limited home rule in 1874, becoming an autonomous state with monarchial ties to Denmark in 1918. At the time Iceland became a fully independent nation, it had been under Norwegian and Danish rule for almost seven hundred years. The parliament of Iceland, Althingi, was established in 930, making it the oldest parliament in the world.

The main economic activities of the country have been based on agriculture and fisheries. Major technological advances in these areas resulted in marked improvements in living conditions after the turn of the century. The economy has gradually changed from the two basic industries to a more modern industrial structure.

The present economy is based primarily on the use of renewable natural resources—that is, the fishing banks, hydroelectric and geothermal power, and the grassland that supports the livestock industry. The economy depends largely on fisheries and fish processing, even though the relative share of fisheries in the occupational distribution is small. Currently, fisheries and fish processing account for some 12% of the labor force, whereas the services sector, government services, and commerce account for 21%, 18%, and 14%, respectively. About 5% of the labor force is engaged in agriculture. The fisheries sector accounts for some 80% of all exports, and the exports are 33% of the gross domestic product.

Most companies in Iceland are small; somewhere between 200 and 300 companies employ 60 or more people. The majority of companies are closely held, but interest in public companies has increased since the stocks and bonds market opened in the early 1980s. At the end of 1993 the approximate value of bonds outstanding plus the capitalization of the stock market was 200 billion Icelandic krona (IKr) ($1 = 73 IKr).

Three commercial banks operate in Iceland, two of which are state owned. By far the largest bank is Landsbanki Íslands (National Bank of Iceland), which had outstanding loans in excess of IKr 62 billion at the end of 1992, accounting for 39% of total bank loans. The investment funds had total outstanding loans in the amount of IKr 200 billion at the end of 1992.

1.2 Historical Background

Iceland's cultural and historical ties with the other Nordic countries have greatly influenced its economic and legal environment. In fact, most of the laws governing business operations have been based on similar laws in the other Nordic countries, particularly Denmark. A brief review of the historical developments will clarify this.

1.2.1 Bookkeeping Act

Iceland's first public document on accounting was a directive from the King of Denmark in 1787. This document described briefly which accounting records were to be kept by individuals engaged in business. The first Act on Bookkeeping (*Bókhaldslög*) was enacted in 1911. It included a fairly detailed description of the accounting records that were to be used. Additionally, the law stipulated that companies were to prepare a balance sheet at the end of every fiscal year; no mention was made of a profit and loss account.

Technical advances in accounting records maintenance led to revisions in the bookkeeping law in 1938 and again in 1968. The bookkeeping law of 1938 allowed assets to be stated at their market value; this was probably the first rule issued on financial reporting in Iceland. In practice, however, companies seldom used the rule.

The current law on bookkeeping was passed in 1968. For the first time, legislation specified a number of rules concerning the recording and valuation of financial statement items. This law was based mainly on similar law in Denmark and Norway. The Bookkeeping Act of 1968 introduced two important accounting concepts. First, the annual accounts were to be prepared in conformity with good accounting practice. Second, the accounts should give a fair representation of the operating activities of companies; oddly enough, that phrase applied only to the profit and loss account.

The Bookkeeping Act of 1968 has been changed only once since it was enacted. A revision of the law in 1991 set up the Accounting Standards Board. Currently, a committee is working on changing the Bookkeeping Act in connection with Iceland's becoming a member of the European Economic Area (EEA).

1.2.2 Companies Act

The first Companies Act (*Hlutafélagalög*) was enacted in 1921. The act was almost silent on accounting. The only requirements of the law were that an annual statement of revenues and expenses be prepared as well as a balance sheet.

The current law, enacted in 1978, was based on a common project in the Nordic countries to harmonize the legal environment for limited liability companies. Previously, all the other Nordic countries had passed legislation based on this project. This law was a major event in the development of accounting in Iceland. The chapter on accounting is a literal translation of the Danish act. Certain changes were made to this act in 1989, when the law was revised; thus, today the law better reflects the peculiarities of financial reporting in Iceland. The provisions on accounting in the Companies Act will be described in some detail in Section 3.1.

1.2.3 Tax Act

As in many countries, the Tax Act (*Lög um tekju- og eignarskatt*) has greatly influenced financial reporting in Iceland. Until quite recently, the income concept of the tax law was synonymous with accounting income. In fact, the accounting reports of companies were a mere by-product of the tax return. This gradually changed, particularly after the enactment of the Companies Act of 1978 and the Tax Act in the same year. The provisions of the Tax Act that have influenced financial reporting will be explained below, particularly the provisions dealing with inflation.

Before 1978 the tax law was based largely on the historical cost concept of accounting. Several revisions to the law, however, allowed revaluation of fixed assets. Curiously enough, fixed assets were to be stated at their estimated selling price when the net worth tax was calculated. Despite this explicit requirement, tax authorities silently consented to the cost concept for the purpose of levying the net worth tax. Additionally, the tax law allowed for several other corrections because of the effects of inflation. They were partial adjustments that were, in fact, inadequate to deal with the problem, both for tax and accounting purposes.

2. Publication and Auditing

In this section the legal requirements for the publication of annual accounts as well as auditing requirements will be discussed briefly.

2.1 Publication of Annual Accounts

According to the Companies Act, the annual accounts of certain companies must be filed with the Registrar Office of Limited Liability Companies. Before 1989, when the law was revised, all limited liability companies, regardless of size, were obliged to file their annual accounts. Since the revision, only those companies whose shares are available to the general public must file their annual accounts with the Registrar Office. At its discretion, the Registrar Office can also require individual companies to file their annual accounts. The filed accounts should conform to the provisions of the Companies Act as described in the next section. Additionally, the Registrar Office must be furnished with the directors' report and auditor's report. The annual accounts should show the date that the accounts were approved at the general shareholders' meeting and how the profits are to be allocated.

The Iceland Stock Exchange in Reykjavík has been operating since 1986. For the first few years it was run under the auspices of the Central Bank of Iceland, but since July 1, 1993, the exchange is independently operated. The operating rules of the Exchange are in conformity with EEC directives for the listing of public companies. The board of directors of the Exchange is responsible for overseeing its operations, including the trading of shares of listed companies. Additionally, the Bank Inspectorate of the Central Bank has monitoring duties. At the end of 1993, only about 50 companies were trading their shares through the Exchange or on the over-the-counter market.

The Stock Exchange has issued some requirements for the publication of annual accounts; they all conform to the requirements of the law and good accounting practice as described in the next section. The Exchange has the authority to issue specific rules on accounting but has not done so to date. One requirement of the Exchange in this regard is the inclusion of a cash flow statement in the annual accounts, which is not a requirement of the law; good accounting practice, however, calls for such a statement. Listed companies must file their annual accounts with the Exchange; such accounts must be audited. Additionally, the Exchange requires, at a minimum, semiannual statements, but more frequent publication of interim statements is recommended. The interim statements need not be audited.

Finally, the annual accounts of companies owned and operated by the national government or municipalities must be published and made available to the public.

2.2 Auditing

The current law regarding State Authorized Accountants was enacted in 1976. To qualify as a State Authorized Accountant, one must fulfill the following requirements:

- An applicant for the professional examinations must have graduated from the Department of Business Administration of the University of Iceland with a major area of specialization in accounting and auditing, or have received comparable education from other institutions of higher learning.

- An applicant, after having successfully completed the above educational requirements, must work for an auditing firm for a minimum period of 3 years.
- To receive a certificate as a State Authorized Accountant, issued by the Minister of Finance, an applicant must successfully complete four examinations with a minimum score of 75% on each test. The tests are in accounting practice, accounting theory, auditing, and taxation.

The Companies Act requires that certain companies' annual accounts be audited by State Authorized Accountants if one of the following conditions exists:

- The share capital of a company is 15 times greater than the minimum amount, which must be paid to establish a limited liability company (The minimum amount of share capital is IKr 400,000 stated in terms of the price level in 1989. This amount is indexed so that the minimum amount changes with general price level movements. Companies established before 1989 are exempt from this requirement.)
- The number of employees exceeds 100
- Total liabilities and owners' equity exceeds 200 times the minimum amount required to establish a limited liability company

In addition, many other accounting entities must be audited by State Authorized Accountants. Various laws govern the operation of the relevant entities. For example, pension funds, insurance companies, commercial banks, savings banks, and municipalities are required by law to have their annual accounts audited by professional accountants.

3. Accounting Principles and Practices

As indicated earlier, financial reporting in Iceland is based primarily on the Companies Act, the Income Tax Act, and opinions of the accounting profession. In this section the influence of each of these factors, including a comment on the newly established Accounting Standards Board, will be discussed in some detail.

3.1 Companies Act

The basic requirements of the Companies Act as adjusted by the amendment of 1989 are summarized below.

3.1.1 Annual Accounts

According to the Companies Act of 1978 the annual accounts should contain a balance sheet, profit and loss account, and directors' report. This definition of the annual accounts was changed in 1989 to eliminate the directors' report but to include notes accompanying the annual accounts.

The Companies Act does not require the inclusion of a fund flow statement, but the accepted practice is to include such a statement. Through the 1980s the fund flow statement was based on the working capital concept, but today the cash flow format prevails in annual accounts.

The Companies Act requires the preparation and publication of consolidated annual accounts. The law is silent, however, on the principles to be used in the preparation of such statements, except that they should conform to good accounting practice. The accounting profession has not issued an opinion on consolidated annual accounts. Both the purchase and poolings methods are found in practice.

3.1.2 Basic General Requirement of the Companies Act

Annual accounts of limited liability companies must conform to specific provisions of the Companies Act. The Act includes a format for the presentation of the balance sheet and, to some extent, the profit and loss account, as well as rules of substance for valuation. The act permits deviations from the presentational requirements to the extent that such deviations conform with good accounting practice. This is generally interpreted to mean that good accounting practice must be within the limits of the law. In practice, however, many instances of noncompliance exist. The argument for such deviation is that fair representation of the financial affairs of companies must override the specific requirements of the law, which, if followed, would prevent such representation.

3.1.3 *Basic Valuation Principle*

The basic valuation principle of assets is the lower of original cost or real value (market value). Current assets must be stated at original cost, but the law allows for a higher valuation of such assets to the extent that good accounting would permit. The same is true of fixed assets, but the requirements are more detailed. The law, however, does not include a definition of original cost, except to state that improvements of fixed assets should be capitalized.

The basic provision of the law is that fixed assets cannot be stated at a higher value than book value from the previous accounting period. The law allows for a deviation from this valuation principle in certain cases, as will be discussed below.

To the extent that the book value of a fixed asset is higher than its real value, and such a difference is not of a temporary nature, a company must decrease the book value of the respective asset. If the book value has previously been revalued, as explained below, the write-down of a fixed asset can be charged to the revaluation account under owners' equity. Otherwise it must be charged to the profit and loss account. The accounting profession does not agree that this requirement of the law is in conformity with good accounting practice in the country.

If the real value of fixed assets is materially higher than the book value from the previous accounting period, a company can increase the book value of fixed assets and credit the increase to a revaluation account under owners' equity. The law does not further explain procedures for a revaluation process. The accounting profession recommends, however, that this option to increase the book value of fixed assets be implemented within the limits of good accounting practice. The profession has issued an opinion on this matter, and the fundamental revaluation principle is based on restated historical cost. Some instances of other revaluation methods exist, but the primary revaluation rule is restated historical cost. The profession feels that the annual restatement of fixed assets is in conformity with the general provision of the Companies Act concerning the revaluation of fixed assets.

3.1.4 *Depreciation of Fixed Assets*

According to the provisions of the Companies Act, fixed assets must be depreciated annually. The general requirement is that such depreciation should be adequate to cover the deterioration of fixed assets due to use and other reasons. A company can stop charging depreciation on fixed assets to the profit and loss account if the previous charges are considered adequate. The accounting profession's opinion is that this option does not conform to good accounting practice; the writer is not aware, however, of this option being used. Additionally, the law states that fixed assets must be depreciated even though such depreciation may lead to a loss in the profit and loss account.

The Companies Act does not specify which method of depreciation should be used. The straight-line method is by far the most common method. It is also safe to say that the rates being used are based on the provisions of the Tax Act. This practice is gradually changing, however, and companies are using rates that take into account the estimated expected deterioration of fixed assets.

3.1.5 *Format of Annual Accounts*

As indicated previously, the Companies Act requires a certain format for the annual accounts. The headings of the balance sheet should be current assets, fixed assets, other assets, current liabilities, long-term liabilities, untaxed reserves, and owners' equity. The law specifies what should be shown in each of these categories, and this format more or less is used in practice. According to the law, this format must be used, but deviations from it are permitted if in conformity with good accounting practice. The accounting profession has recommended certain changes in the format, as will be explained below.

Certain items must be shown separately in the profit and loss account. The law requires that the following items at a minimum, be indicated in the income category:

- Sales from regular operations
- Dividends received from subsidiary companies and others
- Interest income
- Gain on net monetary items
- Gain on sale of assets
- Extraordinary items

The law also requires specific disclosure of the following items among expenses:

- Expenses from regular operations
- Interest expenses
- Depreciation and other write-downs of assets
- Losses on net monetary items
- Loss on sales of fixed assets
- Extraordinary items
- Tax on net income and net worth

The accounting profession has recommended a certain format for the profit and loss account, which allows for subtotals important in reading the statement.

3.1.6 Other Specific Disclosure Rules of the Law

The Companies Act deals specifically with the substance and format of various issues. The main items will be discussed briefly here.

Goodwill. When a company purchases another concern, and the purchase price is in excess of the real value of the purchased assets and assumed liabilities, a company can capitalize the excess if it can be regarded as goodwill. This probably means that the excess must be attributable to superior earning power in order to be classified as goodwill. The law specifies that the goodwill purchased must be amortized over a period not to exceed 10 years.

Research and development costs. According to the Companies Act research and development expenditure can be capitalized if the expenditure is of material and nontemporary value. For the same reason, expenditure for other intangible assets can be capitalized. Such costs would include, but not be limited to, technical and commercial assistance and market research. These costs must be amortized over a period of 5 years, except where a longer period of amortization would be in conformity with good accounting practice.

Investments. Investments in debt and equity securities should be recorded at original cost or market value, whichever is lower. The provision of the law concerning investments in shares and bonds of publicly listed companies is vague. Some interpret it to mean that market valuation of such assets is possible, with the resulting changes in valuation being charged or credited to the profit and loss account. At any rate, such a market valuation is acceptable, at least for financial investment companies.

Revaluation account. As indicated, fixed assets can be revalued. The law provides that the increase in book value be credited to a separate revaluation account under owners' equity. The Companies Act restricts the use of such a revaluation. The following entries are acceptable under the law:

- Indexation (bonus issue) of share capital
- Indexation of legal reserves
- Restatement of untaxed reserves
- Gain on net monetary items
- Write-down of previously revalued fixed assets
- Restatement of the retained earnings account to adjust for general price changes

A few words to explain these entries are called for. According to the provisions of the Tax Act, share capital can, at the option of the general shareholders, be revalued to reflect general price level changes from the dates of payment of such shares. The purpose is to allow cash dividends to be paid on the real value of the money paid for the shares issued; cash dividends are declared as a percentage of stated share capital. The law requires that a certain percentage of profits be allocated to legal reserves. The minimum balance should be 25% of share capital, and it normally takes a few years to reach that stage. If share capital is increased with a bonus issue of shares (free shares), the legal reserve account is increased correspondingly. If a company has used the tax deferral options of the Tax Act, such as extra depreciation, the balances of such deferrals must be restated for general price level changes. The counterbalancing entry for the gain (or loss) on monetary items that are recognized in the profit and loss account is charged or credited to the revaluation account. Finally, the retained earnings account can be restated to the price level at the date of the balance sheet; the corresponding entry is charged to the revaluation account or credited to that account in case of a deficit balance.

3.1.7 Notes to the Annual Accounts

A separate paragraph in the Companies Act stipulates which notes are to be included in the annual accounts of limited liability companies. The following is a summary of the main requirements of the law:

1. Share ownership in other companies, including information on the ownership percentage as well as the names of the companies in question

2. Information on the methods used to account for inflation

3. Specification of fixed assets, including information on the official assessment values and insurance values of buildings

4. Pension obligations to the extent that such obligations have not been included in the annual accounts

5. Information on the effects of changes in the valuation methods of assets and liabilities

6. Information on the tax position of a company, including information on the tax benefits of operating losses carried forward

7. Information on commitments and contingent liabilities, including information on the amount of debt that is secured by assets. Information on assets and liabilities denominated in foreign currency or linked to an index must also be provided.

8. Information on assets and liabilities relating to transactions between subsidiaries and/or their parent company

3.1.8 Directors' Report

The Companies Act requires a specific report by the directors of limited liability companies. At a minimum, the report shall include information on the number of employees, total salaries and wages, bonuses paid to directors, and the percentage share of those shareholders who hold shares in excess of 10%. The report shall also contain the proposal of the board of directors for the payment or nonpayment of dividends. Additionally, the directors' report shall provide information on the financial condition and operating results of the company to the extent that such information is relevant but not included in the balance sheet and profit and loss account. The company, however, can opt not to divulge such information if to do so would be to the company's competitive disadvantage.

3.2 The Tax Act

Enacted in 1978, the current Tax Act has since been revised on several occasions. This act takes into account the effects of general inflation on the measurement of operating performance and financial position; the act is based on the general purchasing power model of accounting. It was necessary to change the Tax Act in 1978 to take into consideration the effects of inflation. Previously, partial adjustments were made to combat the effects of inflation on accounting measurements. During the 1970s the general rate of inflation was approximately 40% per annum, so there was a great need to abandon the historical cost model of accounting for tax purposes. During the 1980s the comparable rates of inflation were about 30% per annum on the average. Currently, however, the rates of inflation are much lower, with the average for the first few years of the 1990s being lower than 5%. Despite this recent trend, the inflation model of the tax law is still intact.

Throughout the 1970s the Tax Act was used for both tax and financial reporting. In fact, most companies made no distinction between tax and financial accounting. Obviously, therefore, the provisions of tax acts have greatly influenced the content of annual financial accounts. Given the inflation rates in Iceland through the 1970s, it is obvious that financial reporting was not of great value, since it was based on the conventional wisdom of accounting, that is, the historical cost principle. The Tax Act of 1978 had great impact on the quality of financial reporting. It is, therefore, informative to examine the most important provisions of the Tax Act to see how they influenced annual accounts. The following four subsections explain the fundamental issues.

3.2.1 Restatement of Fixed Assets

The Tax Act of 1978 took effect in 1979. The act provides for the cost of fixed assets to be restated on the basis of average changes in the construction cost index between the year of reporting and the previous year. This method of calculating the changes in price levels was changed in 1991; now the restatement factor is based on changes in the same index during the year of reporting. This index was chosen because it was commonly used for sundry restatement calculations, and it also adequately reflects general price level movements.

In 1979 the cost of fixed assets purchased before that year was retroactively restated to the price level in 1979. From then on the restatement of fixed assets has been performed as follows:

1. The cost of fixed assets is not restated during the year of purchase, regardless of when within the year of purchase the assets were acquired.
2. The book value of fixed assets at the beginning of a year is annually restated, and such restatement is credited to the revaluation account; both the restated original cost at the beginning of a year and accumulated depreciation are restated.
3. The book value of fixed assets sold during a year is restated, regardless of when within the year the assets were sold.

According to the law, probably for the sake of simplicity, a full year's depreciation is to be taken during the year of purchase of fixed assets, and no depreciation is to be recorded during the year of sale, regardless of when within the year the respective assets were purchased or sold. Depreciation is charged to the profit and loss account on the basis of the restated historical cost.

3.2.2 Gain or Loss on the Sale of Fixed Assets

If fixed assets are sold during a year, the calculation of gain or loss on the sale is based on the restated historical cost. Gain or loss is based on the selling price, on the one hand, and the book value of the asset sold on the other hand. The book value is the book value at the beginning of the year of sale, restated for general price changes during the year of sale. As indicated above, no depreciation is charged during the year of sale. The same calculation also applies to the sale of investments in the shares of other companies. The basic purpose is to tax only real income on the sale of fixed assets.

3.2.3 *Indexation on Monetary Items and Foreign Exchange Differences*

According to the Tax Act, indexation on monetary assets and liabilities must be credited or charged to the profit and loss account. The law also provides that assets and liabilities linked to a domestic index be stated in terms of the price level at the balance sheet date. The corresponding increases (or decreases) in the book value of the respective items are to be charged or credited to the profit and loss account.

The same also applies to assets and liabilities denominated in foreign currency. The exchange rate differences are charged or credited to the profit and loss account. The law requires that the value of foreign assets and liabilities be calculated with the rates of exchange prevailing on the date of the balance sheet.

3.2.4 *Gain or Loss on Net Monetary Position*

The Tax Act provides that the effects of general inflation on monetary items be calculated in the following fashion. The calculation is based on the net monetary position of a company at the beginning of the year of reporting. If monetary assets exceed monetary liabilities, a loss is recognized, and conversely, a gain is indicated if monetary liabilities exceed monetary assets. For this purpose, the same index is used as for the restatement of fixed assets. For example, if monetary liabilities exceed monetary assets by IKr 10 million, and the average change in the construction cost index was 20%, the gain on net monetary position would be IKr 2 million. This gain is recognized in computing taxable income, and it is debited to the revaluation account. Conversely, a loss on the net monetary position is credited to the revaluation account and charged to the profit and loss account.

In calculating the net monetary position, inventories are treated as a monetary asset. This practice recognizes that the cost of goods sold needs to be adjusted during inflationary periods. All monetary assets are included in this calculation, but to the extent that a company may have used its option to defer income tax payments and written down the nominal value of debtors outstanding by 5%, the assets have to be adjusted for such tax deferral allocation. On the liabilities side, all items are included, except for the estimated taxes on income and net worth at the end of the previous period. Finally, loans to and from company directors are excluded from this calculation if such assets and liabilities are non-interest-bearing or have abnormally low interest rates.

In summary, the purposes of calculating the net price level adjustment on monetary items are as follows:

- To recognize the loss of holding monetary assets of fixed amounts
- To recognize the gain of owing liabilities of fixed amounts
- To eliminate the indexation of assets and liabilities that are linked to a domestic index
- To eliminate the foreign exchange differences on assets and liabilities denominated in a foreign currency
- To allow for a correction of the cost of goods sold on the basis of the inventory level at the beginning of the reporting period

The accuracy of this calculation of the gain or loss on monetary items depends on how representative the beginning balance of the monetary position of a particular company is for the remainder of the year of reporting. Again, as was indicated in connection with the restatement of fixed assets, the lawmakers opted for a simple rule for this calculation. Both simplifications can lead to an overstatement or understatement of the operating performance of a company; this, therefore, can lead to over- or undertaxation. The accounting profession recognized these errors and recommended a more precise model for financial statement purposes. The next subsection will describe this model in some detail.

3.3 The Influence of the Accounting Profession

With the increased demand for a higher quality of financial reporting, the accounting profession recognized the need for more uniformity in accounting. Therefore, the accounting profession set up a Committee on Accounting Procedure (*Reikningsskilanefnd*) in 1976. The bylaws of the Association of State Authorized Accountants (FLE) state that the committee is responsible for issuing recommendations on accounting.

Before the 1980s, the law, particularly on taxation, had the greatest impact on financial reporting. In fact, the annual accounts were more or less identical with the substance of the tax returns of companies. This emphasis on the tax law gradually began to change in the late 1970s through the efforts of the accounting profession. The single most important event that changed the emphasis was the enactment of the Companies Act of 1978, but the Tax Act, oddly enough, was also instrumental in raising the quality of financial reports, because it allowed for better methods to deal with inflation. A brief summary of the most important documents issued by the Committee on Accounting Procedure follows. The committee opted to issue opinions rather than firm recommendations as required by the bylaws of the profession. Partly, this was a result of the experimental stage that the profession felt prevailed in financial accounting.

The following summary shows that the accounting profession has been the primary force in making financial reports comply with the general provision of the Companies Act, that is, fair representation, and thus, divorcing financial accounting income from tax income.

3.3.1 The Format Statement of 1980

The Committee's first opinion in 1980 has probably influenced financial reporting in Iceland more than any other document on accounting. Basically, the opinion suggested a new format for the presentation of annual accounts that were based on the new Companies and Tax acts. The new format was widely accepted; in fact, many not-for-profit organizations adopted the format even though it may not always have been appropriate. The sample annual accounts at the end of the chapter illustrate this format.

The new format, for the most part, conforms to the presentational requirements of the Companies Act. This is, at least, true for the balance sheet and the notes, which became more common than before. The format for the profit and loss account was based on the one-page format with various subtotals, which became popular in Icelandic accounts in the early

1970s; this format is not required by the Companies Act, but the act does specify that certain items be shown separately, as explained previously.

It is noteworthy that the Committee's recommendation did not follow certain requirements of the law. For example, the Companies Act specified that transfers to and from untaxed reserves were to be expensed (or credited) to the profit and loss account. The committee, however, did not recommend such a format, since it felt that the overriding requirement of the law, that is, fair presentation of operating performance, could not be achieved if such allocations to tax reserves were entered in the profit and loss account. The Companies Act was changed on this point to conform with practice in 1989 when the law was revised.

The Committee on Accounting Procedure suggested that interest income and expenses be shown separately in the profit and loss account. Under this heading came also the indexation on bonds payable, exchange rate fluctuations, and the price level adjustment on monetary items. The purpose was to show separately in the profit and loss account the net real cost of interest to companies. With that presentation, however, it would have been more appropriate to classify the price level adjustment for inventories with the cost of goods sold under operating expenses. That, however, was generally not done; some accountants included that information in the notes accompanying the annual accounts.

3.3.2 *The Opinion on Price-Level Corrections*

As indicated, the Tax Act of 1978 was responsible for a major improvement in the calculation of profits and net worth over the period before 1979. Actually, it is safe to say that accounting reports in Iceland in the 1970s, excluding 1979, were quite misleading because they were based on the historical cost model during periods of hyperinflation. Even though the new Tax Act raised the quality of accounting reports, however, the accounting profession realized that the tax model was rather simple and could lead to errors of reporting operating performance and net worth. For that reason, the Committee on Accounting Procedure issued an opinion on price level corrections in 1982. This opinion was revised in 1985 to make the concepts of profit and net worth more precise. Most large and medium-sized companies in Iceland adhere to these recommendations. Some companies, however, do not use the committee's recommendations. In effect, then, there are two different concepts of operating performance being used, and both are considered good accounting practice; one is in conformity with the law, whereas the other is based on the accounting profession's recommendations. The following is a summary of the committee's recommendations:

- Nonmonetary assets are stated in terms of the purchasing power of the monetary unit as of the balance sheet date. This means that the cost of fixed assets is restated from the price level at the date of purchase to the price level at the date of reporting.

- Depreciation is recorded in the profit and loss account at the mid-period price level, but accumulated depreciation in the balance sheet is stated in terms of the price level at the date of the balance sheet.

- The gain or loss on the net monetary position is based on the monetary position at the beginning of the year of reporting as well as the ending balance, taking into consideration the changes in that position during the accounting period. The gain or loss on monetary items is calculated to report the net effect of inflation on monetary items in terms of the purchasing power of the monetary unit at the average price level for the operating period.

- The cost of goods sold shall be calculated by taking into consideration the effects of inflation on stocks. The cost of goods sold shall include a price level correction in order to state the expense item in terms of mid-period prices. Stocks in the balance sheet shall be restated to the price level as of the balance sheet date.

- A reconciliation shall be made between the owners' equity at the beginning of the year of reporting and the balance in the owners' equity accounts at the end of the reporting period. Such a reconciliation shall be presented in the notes accompanying the annual accounts in terms of the monetary unit at the price level as of the date of the balance sheet.

- The Committee on Accounting Procedure recommended that the monetary value of the share capital be shown in the annual accounts in terms of the measuring unit on the balance sheet date. The excess of total owners' equity over that amount would represent the undistributed remaining profits of a company; and conversely, if share capital restated is in excess of total owners' equity, the difference would represent a net accumulated deficit as of the balance sheet date.

As can be deduced from these rules, no profit is recognized in the profit and loss account unless a company is able to maintain the real purchasing power of its owners' equity, that is, when general price level movements have been considered.

As indicated, most companies adhere to the committee's recommendations. In several cases, however, companies have opted to restate the cost of fixed assets in terms of changes in specific prices rather than general prices. Additionally, some companies have used a concept of capital maintenance, which relies on an operating capacity concept of profit rather than the financial capital concept.

3.3.3 Other Opinions of the Accounting Profession

The Committee has issued several other opinions. As far as possible, these opinions have been based on the standards issued by the International Accounting Standards Committee. The Association of State Authorized Accountants is a member of that international body. The committee has also issued opinions on matters that are peculiar to the Icelandic accounting environment. The following is a list of issues with which the committee has dealt:

- Presentation of financial accounts (1980)
- Accounting for the effects of inflation (1982/85)
- Fund flow statements; working capital and cash (1986)
- Accounting for financing leases (1987)
- Accounting for investments in stocks and bonds (1988)
- Accounting for the divergence between exchange rate fluctuations and general inflation (1989)
- Accounting for interim financial statements (1990)
- Accounting for prior period adjustments, extraordinary items, and accounting principles changes (1990)
- Accounting for inventories of fish processing plants (1990)

- Accounting for fishing quotas (1991)
- Accounting for investments of investment companies (1991)
- Accounting for certain items in the accounts of municipalities (1991)
- Accounting for income taxes (1991)

3.3.4 *The Accounting Standards Board*

At the end of 1991 the Parliament of Iceland (Althingi) passed a law adding a new provision to the Bookkeeping Act of 1968. With this change of the law, an Accounting Standards Board was established which has the responsibility for issuing standards on financial accounting. The board has five members, nominated by the Association of State Authorized Accountants (one member), the Department of Business Administration of the University of Iceland (one member), and the Chamber of Commerce (one member). One member is appointed by the Minister of Finance, and the fifth member is the Auditor General of Iceland.

In the first months of 1994, the board did not formally issue a regulation on accounting, but an exposure draft on the basic principles and concepts of financial accounting was published. At the time of writing, it had not yet been approved by the board.

4. Future Developments

In January 1993 the Parliament of Iceland approved a proposal by the government that Iceland become a member of the European Economic Area (EEA). The EEA agreement stipulates that Iceland must adopt the directives issued by the EEC. Such adoption means that Icelandic annual accounts must conform with the Fourth Directive. At the time of writing it was not clear when, or in fact whether, Iceland will change from its current accounting practices; there is some period of adjustment for this transition.

Useful Addresses

Association of State Authorized Accountants,
Ármúla 27,
Reykjavík,
Iceland
Tel. 354-1-688188

Accounting Standards Board
c/o Stefán Svavarsson,
University of Iceland,
Reykjavík,
Iceland
Tel. 354-1-694500
Fax 354-1-26806

Financial Statements

Financial accounts of Johan Rönning hf (Ltd.)
(Medium sized company in Iceland)

Auditor's report
We have audited the annual accounts of Johan Rönning hf for 1993. The annual accounts consist of a profit and loss account, balance sheet and cash flow statement as well as accompanying notes. The audit was performed in conformity with generally accepted auditing standards and included all checking of the accounting records that we considered necessary.

In our opinion the annual accounts are in conformity with requirements of the law and the bylaws of the company and present fairly the operating results and cash flows for 1993 and the balance sheet as at the end of that year in conformity with generally accepted principles of accounting in Iceland.

Reykjavík, March 14th 1994

Löggiltir endurskoðendur hf
representing
Arthur Andersen & Co. S.C.

Directors' report
(Minimum requirements of the law)

The year 1993 was the 60th operating year of the company. Net income amounted to 22 million ISK after deducting a charge for back taxes in the amount of 11 million ISK. The owners' equity amounted to 175 million ISK at the end of 1992, but at the end of 1993 owners' equity amounted to 191 million ISK, which is 46% of total assets.

The company employed 25 people during the year, and total salaries amounted to 53 million ISK. Two shareholders own 80% of the outstanding shares.

The board of directors proposes that a 15% cash dividend be paid for 1993 in the amount of 2 million ISK.

Notes to the annual accounts
(A summary of the main notes)

Accounting principles

1. The effects of general price level movements on the operation and financial position of the company have been calculated and entered into the accounts. The following policies are used for this purpose:

> * The historical cost of fixed assets is restated annually to account for changes in general prices. For this purpose the construction cost index is used. During 1993 this index rose by 3.11%. The increase in the book value of fixed assets after this restatement is credited to the revaluation account.

> * Depreciation of fixed assets is based on the restated historical cost and is calculated on a straight line basis. Depreciation is recorded in the profit and loss account at mid-period prices, whereas accumulated depreciation is shown at the year-end price level.

* Monetary assets and liabilities linked to a domestic index or denominated in a foreign currency are stated at the price level or prevailing rate of exchange at the end of the year. The corresponding increases or decreases in the asset or liability accounts are recorded in the profit and loss account under financial income and (expense).

* The effects of general price level changes on the monetary assets and liabilities are calculated and recorded in the accounts. For this purpose stocks are treated as monetary assets. The calculation is based on the net monetary position of the company at the beginning of the year and at the end of the year, taking into consideration changes in that position during the year. Since the company was in a net positive position, meaning that monetary assets exceeded liabilities, the company recognizes a loss on the net monetary position. The net loss can be analysed as follows (in '000 ISK):

Inflation correction on stocks	2.080
Inflation adjustment on monetary items	(192)
	1.888

2. The accrued pension obligation of the company has been recorded. The amount is based on actuarial calculation, and the expected future cash outlays are discounted at 3% per annum. The discount rate represents the rate of return on high quality bonds in excess of future estimated changes in salaries levels.

3. The company recognizes a deferred tax obligation. At the end of 1993 the timing differences in depreciation are more than negated by the pension obligation charges; therefore, the deferred taxes payable at the end of 1992 in the amount of 9 million ISK have been dissolved. The tax court decided in 1993 that pension charges are deductible when paid; the company, however, had accrued such obligations for both tax and accounting purposes.

Changes in owners' equity

4. The owners' equity amounted to 175 million ISK at the end of 1992 which is equivalent to 180 million ISK at the end of 1993. At the end of 1993 owners' equity amounted to 191 million ISK, and the increase of 11 million ISK during the year can be analysed as follows (figures are in '000 ISK):

	As per financial accounts	Year-end prices 1993
Owners' equity at beginning of 1993	174.703	180.044
Purchase of treasury stock	(9.997)	(10.297)
Net income for the year	22.380	22.763
Cash dividends	(1.950)	(1.950)
Restatement of fixed assets and		
loss on monetary position	5.424	--
	190.560	190.560

5. The changes in the separate owners' equity accounts can be further analysed as follows (figures are in '000 ISK):

	Share capital	Legal reserves	Revaluation account	Retained earnings	Total
Balance at January 1st	17.837	5.586	17.200	134.081	174.704
Restatement of fixed assets			3.536		3.536
Restatement of retained earnings			(5.129)	5.129	0
Loss on monetary position			1.887		1.887
Purchase of treasury stock	(1.177)		(8.820)		(9.997)
Net income for the year				22.380	22.380
Cash dividends				(1.950)	(1.950)
	16.660	5.586	8.674	159.640	190.560

| Rekstrarreikningur árið 1993 | | | Profit and loss account for 1993 |
| Tölur eru í þúsundum króna | | | Figures are in '000 ISK |

Rekstrartekjur	1993	1992	Operating revenues
Hrein vörusala	499.035	486.915	Net sales
Aðrar tekjur	18.527	21.074	Other income
	517.562	507.989	
Rekstrargjöld			**Operating expenses**
Kostnaðaverð seldra vara	357.691	351.303	Cost of goods sold
Laun og tengd gjöld	57.839	60.631	Salaries and related expenses
Húsnæðiskostnaður	15.160	7.727	Cost of operating buildings
Sölukostnaður	18.945	18.245	Selling expenses
Stjórnunarkostnaður	16.752	17.575	Administrative expenses
Afskriftir	7.117	7.965	Depreciation
	473.504	463.446	

Hagnaður af rekstri án vaxta	44.058	44.543	Operating income before interest

Fjármunatekjur og (fjármagnsgjöld)			Financial income and (expenses)
Vaxtagjöld, verðbætur			Interest expense, indexation
og gengismunur	(7.042)	(5.266)	and exchange rate losses
Vaxtatekjur, verðbætur			Interest expense, indexation
og gengismunur	16.962	19.544	and exchange rate gains
Reiknaðar tekjur peningalegra liða	193	125	Net gain on monetary position
	10.113	14.403	

Hagnaður fyrir skatta	54.171	58.946	Net income before taxes

Skattar			Taxes
Tekjuskattur	17.031	23.202	Income tax
Eignarskattur	3.071	1.959	Net worth tax
	20.102	25.161	

Hagnaður fyrir óreglulega liði	34.069	33.785	Net income before extraordinary items

Óreglulegar tekjur og (gjöld)			Extraordinary income and (expense)
Skattalegt hagræði vegna sameiningar	0	13.580	Tax benefit from merger
Skattar vegna fyrri tímabila	(11.689)	0	Prior period taxes based on tax court decision
Afskrifuð hlutabréf	0	(10.254)	Share investment writtten off
	(11.689)	3.326	

Hagnaður ársins	22.380	37.111	Net income for the year

Efnahagsreikningur				Balance sheet
Tölur eru í þúsundum króna				Figures are in '000 ISK

Eignir		1993	1992	Assets
Veltufjármunir				**Current assets**
Bankainnstæður		51.580	33.763	Bank deposits
Markaðsverðbréf		35.120	17.139	Marketable securities
	Handbært fé alls	86.700	50.902 Total cash	
Viðskiptakröfur		92.889	95.644	Debtors
Aðrar kröfur		28.787	35.090	Other receivables
Birgðir		63.521	75.657	Stocks
		271.897	257.293	
Fastafjármunir				**Fixed assets**
Fasteignir		104.461	65.616	Buildings
Vélar		16.617	16.095	Equipment
Eignarhlutir í félögum		15.119	12.757	Share investments
Aðrar langtímaeignir		6.000	8.660	Other long-term assets
		142.197	103.128	
Eignir alls		414.094	360.421	**Total assets**

1140 *European Accounting Guide*

31. desember 1993
Tölur eru í þúsundum króna

as at December 31st 1993
Figures are in '000 ISK

Skuldir og eigið fé	1993	1992	Liabilities and owners' equity
Skammtímaskuldir			**Current liabilities**
Viðskiptaskuldir	62.578	65.446	Trade creditors
Aðrar skammtímaskuldir	46.051	21.981	Other short-term debt
Ógr. áætlaðir skattar	20.260	2.629	Accrued taxes payable
Ógr. úthlutaður arður	2.499	2.676	Dividends payable
Afborganir langtímaskulda á næsta ári	11.954	11.463	Current maturities on long-term debt
	143.342	104.195	
Langtímaskuldir			**Long-term debt**
Gengisbundin lán	0	2.020	Foreign exchange loans
Verðtryggð lán	37.984	26.921	Indexed loans
Eftirlaunaskuldbinding	54.162	55.466	Pension obligation
Tekjuskattsskuldbinding	0	8.579	Deferred taxes payable
	92.146	92.986	
Afborganir á næsta ári	11.954	11.463	Current maturities
	80.192	81.523	
Eigið fé			**Owners' equity**
Hlutafé	16.660	17.836	Share capital
Lögbundinn varasjóður	5.586	5.586	Legal reserve
Endurmatsreikningur	8.674	17.201	Revaluation account
Óráðstafað eigið fé	159.640	134.080	Retained earnings
	190.560	174.703	
Skuldir og eigið fé alls	414.094	360.421	**Total liabilities and owners' equity**

Sjóðstreymi 1993
Tölur eru í þúsundum króna

	1993	1992
Handbært fé frá rekstri		
Hagnaður fyrir skatta	54.171	58.946
Rekstrarliðir sem ekki hreyfa handbært fé:		
Afskriftir	7.117	7.965
Verðbætur á langtímalán	3.473	1.841
Afskrifuð hlutabréf	850	0
Reiknuð gjöld vegna verðlagsbreytinga	1.887	763
	67.498	69.515
Breyting rekstrartengdra liða:		
Skammtímakröfur, lækkun (hækkun)	3.397	(13.524)
Birgðir, lækkun	12.136	1.201
Skammtímaskuldir, hækkun (lækkun)	971	(7.812)
	84.002	49.380
Greiddir skattar	(1.959)	(1.666)
	82.043	47.714
Fjármunahreyfingar		
Breytingar á eignarhlutum	(2.884)	(4.854)
Keyptar vélar	(4.311)	(1.869)
Keyptar fasteignir	(38.963)	(13.528)
Aðrar breytingar	8.320	(16.076)
	(37.838)	(36.327)
Fjármögnunarhreyfingar		
Tekin langtímalán	15.863	11.986
Keypt eigin hlutabréf	(9.997)	(1.177)
Greiddar afborganir langtímaskulda	(11.597)	(15.609)
Greiddur arður	(2.676)	(2.424)
	(8.407)	(7.224)
Aukning á handbæru fé	35.798	4.163
Handbært fé 1. janúar	50.902	46.739
Handbært fé í árslok	86.700	50.902

Cash flow for 1993
Figures are in '000 ISK

Cash flow from operating activities
Net income before taxes
Items not affecting cash
Depreciation
Indexation on long-term loans
Share investment written off
Net loss on total monetary position

Changes in short-term items
Debtors, decrease (increase)
Stocks, decrease
Short-term debt, increase (decrease)

Taxes paid

Investing activities
Changes in share investment
Purchase of equipment
Investment in building
Other changes in long-term assets

Financing activities
New long-term loans
Purchase of treasury stock
Repayment of long-term loans
Cash dividends

Increase in cash
Cash balance at January 1st
Cash balance at year-end

NORWAY

Atle Johnsen
Norwegian School of Economics and Business Administration, Bergen
Aasmund Eilifsen
Norwegian School of Economics and Business Administration, Bergen

1. Background

1.1 Introduction

Financial reporting in Norway is regulated by legislation. Accounting legislation is modest and may best be characterized as constituting a legal framework for accounting principles to be applied in practice. The basic principle of accounting legislation in Norway is the general requirement that annual accounts shall be prepared in accordance with good accounting practice.

Good accounting practice is a dynamic concept, allowing practice to develop as economic conditions change and business firms undertake new kinds of transactions and face new accountable events. In this dynamic setting, accounting theory and research, both domestic and international, are intended to guide good practice.

A legal framework rather than detailed rules leaves room for the exercise of professional judgment. Inherent in Norwegian accounting legislation is an implicit conceptual framework, which may best be described as historical cost accounting theory. The basic concepts and principles of this theory underlie good accounting practice and govern professional judgment in a given situation. Good accounting practice, therefore, means compliance with basic accounting principles and the legal framework as well as general acceptance.

Interpretation of the concept of good accounting practice has challenged parties interested in financial reporting (the Accounting Advisory Council, the Norwegian Institute of State Authorized Public Accountants, the Norwegian Society of Financial Analysts, and the Accounting Committee at the Oslo Stock Exchange) to express their opinions. In 1989 the Norwegian Accounting Standards Board was established under the initiative of the Oslo Stock Exchange and the Norwegian School of Economics and Business Administration. Given the limited resources available in Norway, it was considered desirable to pool the competence and resources of interested parties into one body and thus pave the way for better standards.

In 1990 the Ministry of Finance appointed the Accounting Act Committee to draft proposals to revise existing accounting legislation. Important issues to be addressed are continued adherence to a legal framework versus detailed legal rules, the role and legal status of standard setting, alternative valuation principles to historical cost, and harmonization with EC Directives. The main report from the Accounting Act Committee will be completed in 1994, and new accounting legislation will be effective from the beginning of 1996.

In 1992 the Accounting Act Committee submitted an important subreport on accounting for income taxes. Primarily as a consequence of the Tax Reform of 1992, which changed the relationship between financial reporting and tax accounting, the accounting legislation was changed to introduce deferred tax liabilities and assets into Norwegian financial statements beginning in 1992.

Finally, in 1994, the Norwegian Accounting Standards Board initiated another major accounting reform by issuing a preliminary standard on pension costs.

1.2 Accounting Legislation

1.2.1 Historical Development

The first legal rules for bookkeeping in Norway go back to 1874, when certain kinds of businesses were required to keep accounts for the protection of creditors. The law did not regulate valuation or financial statements, but the bookkeeping rules were in force for more than a hundred years. The Tax Act of 1911 stipulated that taxable income be calculated on the basis of accounting income. The Tax Act Committee, therefore, simultaneously drafted a proposal for an Accounting Act that included valuation rules, but it was never enacted. Another curiosity worth mentioning is the requirement of the Trade Act of 1935 that assets be valued at "true value."

In 1959 the Accounting Act Committee was appointed. Although the Accounting Act was enacted almost 20 years later, in 1977, and adapted to later changes in companies legislation, the report of the Accounting Act Committee is the foundation of Norwegian accounting legislation and is an implicit conceptual framework for the interpretation of good accounting practice.

Traditionally, accounting rules have been formulated in companies legislation. The first Joint-Stock Companies Act of 1910 adopted the concept of prudence in valuation by requiring the preparation of annual accounts in accordance with "orderly and prudent business practice." The next Joint-Stock Companies Act of 1957 strengthened the regulation of accounts by including valuation rules and rules on specification of financial statements. Parent companies were also required to prepare a consolidated balance sheet. For the present debate on the general requirements to annual accounts, it is of interest to note a requirement in the law to draw up the income statement to present correctly the results of the company's operations and the law permitting departure if disclosed.

The Nordic Council decided in 1962 to harmonize companies legislation, and a common Nordic proposal was drafted. The Norwegian version was published in 1970.

1.2.2 Present Accounting Legislation

The third Joint-Stock Companies Act was enacted in 1976. This law includes a chapter on annual accounts. Without doubt, the common Nordic accounting rules are influenced by the Report of the Accounting Act Committee in Norway. The Accounting Act was enacted one year later, in 1977. The Accounting Act also applies to joint-stock companies except for the chapter on annual accounts. The regulation of annual accounts in the two laws is similar, and the inclusion of accounting rules in the Joint-Stock Companies Act is, in fact, unnecessary.

The legislation on annual accounts includes valuation rules, contents and format of financial statements, consolidated financial statements, supplementary information, and disclosure in the board of directors' report. The valuation rules are general rules for current and fixed assets, respectively, and shall apply to all assets. Special valuation rules apply to intangible assets like goodwill and the costs of research and development;

treasury stocks; discount, costs incurred in connection with the arrangement of borrowings, and losses on long-term liabilities; and the cost of equity financing. For the items involved, the special rules modify the general valuation rules.

Current assets shall be measured at the lower of cost or fair value. *Fair value* is defined as net realizable value, unless another value is appropriate according to good accounting practice. An exception allows income recognition for long-term manufacturing contracts as work on a contract progresses. Fixed assets shall be measured at cost. Depreciation is required according to a rational depreciation plan. If the fair value of a fixed asset is lower than the carrying amount, and the reason for the impairment of value is other than temporary, a write-down of the asset is required if it is necessary according to good accounting practice. Except for long-term receivables, the law does not allow reversal of a previous write-down in the case of a subsequent increase in value. Although the legislation basically prohibits writing up of fixed assets, they may be written up under certain restrictions.

1.2.3 Legal Framework

The legislation on annual accounts does not contain a detailed set of rules and can best be characterized as constituting a legal framework. The basic principle that annual accounts shall be prepared in accordance with good accounting practice leaves room for professional interpretation and application of theory and international accounting principles. It also allows dynamic practice in a changing environment. The general requirement that preparation must be in accordance with good accounting practice, however, is not an overriding principle. Practice also must be in accordance with the individual rules. Some specific rules explicitly permit departure, however, if such a departure is in accordance with good accounting practice, notably the definition of fair value for current assets and the format rules of the financial statements.

Changes of accounting principles and methods violating the written law must be accompanied by changes in legislation. A time-consuming process, legislation delays the evolution of financial reporting in Norway. The primary objective of updating the legal framework was neglected by the Ministry of Trade, which was more concerned with enlarging the domain of legal regulation. Since 1987 the Ministry of Finance has been in charge of the accounting legislation.

1.3 Implicit Conceptual Framework

Inherent in accounting legislation is an implicit conceptual framework. The foundation of financial accounting in Norway is historical cost theory. The Report of the Accounting Act Committee published in 1962 contains a discussion of the concepts of historical cost accounting, which also underlie the valuation rules in the law. In recent years many controversial questions have been raised for which no direct answers are to be found, either in legislation or in recommendations or standards. The Oslo Stock Exchange has taken a strong position in favor of interpretation and application of concepts of the implicit conceptual framework. This view has been controversial, however. Lawyers and accountants who have limited familiarity with accounting theory have argued that the Oslo Stock Exchange has gone too far in that direction.

Historical cost accounting is often more appropriately described as transaction-based accounting. The reason is that transactions are the basis for recognition and measurement. Determination of when a transaction occurs or whether a transaction has occurred at all is crucial for revenue recognition. Substance and economic reality, rather than legal form, shall be accounted for. It has been the experience of the Oslo Stock Exchange that agreements for the sale of buildings, property, and ships often include elements changing the economic reality of the transaction, and the stock exchange has issued guidelines to ensure that financial statements report the substance. The guidelines published in the annual Accounting Bulletins deal with agreements for sale and leaseback, exchange of assets, sale and repurchase agreements, and sales subject to various options.

The treatment of executory contracts is related to the concept of transactions. Executory contracts usually are not recorded. The Oslo Stock Exchange has encouraged listed companies in the shipping sector to adopt a practice of recognizing shipbuilding contracts as assets and liabilities. Besides providing useful information about business risk, the recognition of contracts would be in accordance with fundamental definitions of transactions, assets, and liabilities.

Measurement of the transaction price is of vital importance to the historical cost system. The consideration in a sale transaction, the cost in a purchase transaction, or the consideration in an equity capital transaction basically is the fair value of the consideration at the transaction date. For interest-free credit sales, the Accounting Advisory Council has stated that the nominal amount be discounted if the effect is material. This statement has raised the consciousness of the time value of money in accounting. Several accounting standards now mandate discounting when it is appropriate.

The Accounting Act Committee of 1959 stated that the primary function in accounting is measurement of periodic income. The focus on income determination requires proper matching of expenses with revenues. The matching concept is a key element in the conceptual framework. Examples of important interpretations of the matching concept are an opinion of the Oslo Stock Exchange on expense recognition of maintenance costs and a statement from the Accounting Advisory Council on decommissioning costs.

The concept of prudence should be interpreted in the context of uncertainty. This means one should be conservative in making estimates under conditions of uncertainty to avoid overstating assets or income and understating liabilities or expenses. It does not imply the creation of hidden reserves. Efforts to eliminate and reduce risk, like hedging, basically should be reflected in the financial statements. A well-known application of prudence is the principle of lower of cost or market value.

Other concepts inherent in the legislation are the consistency concept, the all-inclusive income concept, and the assumption of going concern. *Consistency* means consistent application of principles and methods from one period to the next. As a corollary, if a change is made, the fact of the change and its effect should be disclosed. To ensure comparability, consistency over time should be combined with uniformity in application of principles and methods. The *all-inclusive income concept* requires that all items that have an effect on equity, other than contributions from and contributions to owners, should be included in the income statement of the current period. Exceptions are adjustments resulting from so-called fundamental accounting reforms, which should be reported by adjusting opening retained earnings.

The present state of accounting regulation in Norway, characterized by a legal framework, including the concepts of good accounting practice and standard setting at an early stage, makes the implicit conceptual framework and authoritative interpretations of it the most important part of the regulations.

1.4 Good Accounting Practice

The report of the Accounting Act Committee explained the concept of *good accounting practice* and proposed that the concept be introduced in legislation to replace the old term "orderly and prudent business practice." Although the new accounting legislation was not enacted until 1976 and 1977, the Norwegian Institute of State Authorized Public Accountants in 1970 started to work on recommendations for good accounting practice. This professional accountancy body published 17 recommendations from 1978 to 1988. The recommendations purported to be no more than guides to good practice. Several recommendations were prepared in close cooperation with the Norwegian School of Economics and Business Administration. The recommendations included important areas like foreign currency, leasing, and write-down of fixed assets. Interpretation of the concept of good accounting practice has also provoked other parties interested in financial reporting to express their opinions. The Ministry of Trade (later the Ministry of Finance) appointed an Accounting Advisory Council to issue statements on good accounting practice. The Norwegian Society of Financial Analysts has issued guidelines for the preparation and analysis of financial statements. Since the middle of the 1980s the Accounting Committee at the Oslo Stock Exchange has taken a leading role by reviewing the annual reports of the listed companies and by publishing Accounting Bulletins. In 1985 the Oslo Stock Exchange appointed an ad hoc committee to issue a recommendation for equity accounting and propose changes in legislation making possible the application of the equity method. The committee had a broad composition of representatives, including preparers of financial statements, financial analysts, and professional accountants, as well as members of the Accounting Committee of the Oslo Stock Exchange. Another broadly composed ad hoc committee was appointed two years later to issue a recommendation on accounting for business combinations.

The experience with broadly representative committees to issue recommendations to good accounting practice covering controversial and important areas was a major step in the direction of establishing a standard-setting body. The field of those involved was radically widened, better and more diversified expertise was available, and the Oslo Stock Exchange gave the recommendations authoritative support.

1.5 Norwegian Accounting Standards

The Norwegian Accounting Standards Board (NASB) was established in 1989 for the purpose of publishing financial accounting standards. Behind the standard-setting body are the following organizations: The Oslo Stock Exchange, the Norwegian School of Economics and Business Administration, the Norwegian Institute of State Authorized Public Accountants, the Norwegian Association of Registered Accountants, the Norwegian Society of Financial Analysts, and the Norwegian Association of MBA Graduates. This cooperation provides access to a wide range of resources and competence, as well as ensuring that a broad range of views and interests are reflected in published standards.

The standard-setting process involves development of exposure drafts, which are submitted to a wide range of bodies for comment. The comments received are evaluated before a preliminary standard, which has the status of recommended practice, is published. The Oslo Stock Exchange has encouraged the listed companies to take the lead in adopting exposure drafts and preliminary standards in their financial statements. Final standards are published only after the preparers and users of financial statements have obtained practical experience with the preliminary standards and have had the opportunity to comment on their experience to the NASB. In 1992 the NASB published three final standards: NAS 1, Inventory, NAS 2, Long-term Manufacturing Contracts, and NAS 3, Contingencies and Post-Balance Sheet Events. Although standards have no legal status, the Oslo Stock Exchange has stated in *Accounting Bulletin 1992* that listed companies are expected to apply Norwegian Accounting Standards.

In addition to the final standards, the NASB has issued preliminary standards on extraordinary items, income taxes, investments in associated companies and subsidiaries, interests in joint ventures, and pension costs.

Current projects include financial instruments, revenue recognition, related party transactions, segment information, the cash flow statement, and an update of recommendations on good accounting practice.

At the inception the NASB faced some strategic decision problems. Ideally, the new body should begin by issuing a statement of basic concepts and principles as did the ASB in Britain. In practice, the Board considered the substantive problems existing in financial reporting to be quite serious. The review of annual reports conducted by the Accounting Committee at the Oslo Stock Exchange revealed an urgent need for specific standards. The all-volunteer Norwegian standard-setting body, without a research staff of its own, does not have the resources to explore as does the ASB or the FASB. The standards therefore must be short and not very detailed. In arriving at conclusions, the standard setters have in their minds the implicit conceptual framework inherent in the legislation. They also rely on foreign standards, research reports, and literature.

1.6 The Internationalization of Financial Reporting

The internationalization of Norwegian business and the globalization of the capital markets contribute to the necessity of internationalization of financial reporting. Norwegian companies listed on foreign stock exchanges must report in accordance with foreign or International Accounting Standards (IAS). At the Oslo Stock Exchange, the investments of foreign investors account for almost 30% of the total market value. This also calls for the application of international accounting principles. The Oslo Stock Exchange encourages disclosure of IAS or U.S. GAAP information as supplements in the annual reports of Norwegian companies. This type of information may be presented in different forms: Complete financial statements with notes, income statement and balance sheet with disclosure of the accounting principles applied, or reconciliation of income and equity under Norwegian and international accounting principles.

The annual report of Norsk Hydro is an interesting example of the internationalization of financial reporting in Norway. Hydro is listed in Oslo, on other European stock exchanges, and since 1985 on the New York Stock Exchange. Besides the disclosure requirements following from listings, it is of primary concern for Hydro to present financial information for the main areas of business on a comparable basis with other companies operating internationally. Hydro presents two sets of consolidated financial statements, one prepared in accordance with Norwegian accounting legislation and good accounting practice, the other prepared in accordance with U.S. GAAP. The individual financial statements for the parent company are prepared in accordance with Norwegian accounting principles only. The editorial layout of the annual report has been subject to changes to facilitate comparability for investors. Hydro now presents the two sets of consolidated financial statements accompanied by common notes. The notes include disclosures required by U.S. GAAP, as well as disclosures in accordance with Norwegian requirements, and are an integral part of both sets of financial statements. The description of accounting principles applies to both sets, and differences are specified. The final note, summarizing and explaining the main differences, provides a reconciliation of income and equity under Norwegian and U.S. accounting principles. Other financial information, including information for the industry segments, is presented in accordance with U.S. GAAP.

With a view toward the internationalization of financial reporting, the NASB will work for harmonization of accounting standards. The Board applauds the IASC's comparability project and overall improvement process. Of even greater importance from the perspective of the NASB is the establishment of international cooperation among national standard setters. This has taken the form of annual meetings and working groups addressing key areas. The idea of developing a common conceptual basis on which national standard setting bodies can issue their own accounting standards seems promising and should help lead to a prospective harmonization.

1.7 The Relationship between Financial Accounting and Tax Accounting

Fundamentally, the preparation of financial statements according to the valuation rules in the accounting legislation and good accounting practice should be independent of the computation of taxable income. Accounting income, however, has been the basis for the computation of taxable income. Special tax rules developed to meet particular objectives have usually resulted in a figure for taxable income that was lower than that for accounting income. The positive differences have been recognized as untaxed reserves in the Nordic format of financial statements. The dependence of taxable income on accounting income has had adverse effects on accounting practice, both in terms of the application of accounting principles and the making of accounting estimates.

The Tax Reform Committee in 1989 proposed a taxable-income concept independent of accounting income. In addition to specific measurement rules, two basic principles for income measurement were proposed, a realization principle and a nondeduction principle for "provisions according to good accounting practice." The basic principles were not defined or explained. The most serious weakness of the proposed set of rules for income measurement was the elimination of the fundamental concept of matching.

The enacted Tax Reform of 1992 kept the dependence on accounting income but included the nondeduction rule for "provisions according to good accounting practice." This apparent inconsistency has caused uncertainty in the arena of tax reform.

From an accounting point of view, computation of taxable income will still affect the application of accounting principles and the making of accounting estimates, even if the specific measurement rules of the tax code have limited the scope of the latter. Tax reform has caused negative differences between accounting income and taxable income that cannot be handled in the Nordic format of financial statements. In line with the subreport on accounting for income taxes from the Accounting Act Committee, the accounting legislation was changed in 1992 to introduce deferred tax liabilities and assets into financial statements. The NASB simultaneously published a preliminary accounting standard for income taxes.

1.8 Auditing

The Auditing Act of 1964 and the 1976 Joint-Stock Companies Act set out the legal requirements for external auditing and the auditing profession. On behalf of the Ministry of Finance, the Banking, Insurance and Securities Commission supervises the profession and licenses auditors. In addition, the Ministry has appointed an Auditing Advisory Council. A Norwegian auditor is either state authorized or registered. A state authorization is needed to conduct auditing in listed and larger-sized companies.

The Norwegian Institute of State Authorized Public Accountants acts as the professional body. The Institute publishes rules of professional ethics and issues the national auditing standards, closely following the content in the International Auditing Standards. As already mentioned, the state-authorized auditors have been strongly involved in developing good accounting practice and take an active part in the standard-setting process within the NASB. The Big 6 international auditing firms employ about 60% of the approximately 1,350 state-authorized auditors. The Norwegian School of Economics and Business Administration runs the national graduate program in accounting and auditing, which lasts 15 months. The candidates enrolled in the program hold an MBA degree (i.e., they have completed 4 years of study in business administration) or have passed the examinations required for registered auditors. In addition to passing rigorous examinations in the program, the candidates need two years of practical training to become eligible for state authorization.

Registered auditors are trained during three years at regional colleges. The Norwegian Association of Registered Accountants organizes the approximately 2,400 registered auditors.

The Joint-Stock Companies Act requires all joint-stock companies to engage a state-authorized or registered auditor. The Auditing Act specifies the same requirement for other businesses, other than small personal ones. A state authorization is required for the auditing of joint-stock companies that have more than 200 employees, all listed companies, and some companies in specific fields like insurance and financial services.

The audit report is presented at the shareholders' annual meeting and included in the annual corporate report. Basically, the audit report confirms that auditing has been conducted in accordance with the regulations and good auditing practice and includes an opinion on the compliance of the company's accounts with legal requirements and good accounting practice.

The Auditing Act Committee, appointed in 1994, is revising the set of national auditing regulations, with the specific aim of bringing the legislation in line with the EC Directives, which will be effective in Norway from the beginning of 1996.

2. The Form and Content of Published Financial Statements

The legal annual accounts comprise the income statement and the balance sheet, including the notes, the board's report, and, if required by law, consolidated statements, constituting a composite whole. All statements must include comparative figures for the past year. Listed companies, companies with total assets exceeding NOK 10 million, or more than 200 employees (i.e., "large-sized companies") must comply with more extensive disclosure rules, most significantly, to prepare a statement of changes in financial position and interim reports.

2.1 The Format of the Income Statement

The primary focus of financial reporting in Norway is information about earnings and its components. The introductory paragraph to the legal format of the income statement is a general requirement with respect to the presentation of the components of earnings.

The format of the income statement is vertical, grouping revenues and expenses (including gains and losses) as operating, financial, or extraordinary. The main groups and income concepts in the statement are:

- Operating revenues and expenses
- Operating income
- Financial items
- Ordinary income (income before extraordinary items)
- Extraordinary items
- Income before taxes
- Income taxes
- Earnings (income for the year)

Income before taxes is either ordinary, that is, net operating and financial items, or extraordinary.

The preliminary NAS on extraordinary items is restrictive. Extraordinary items are material income and expenses deriving from events and transactions distinct from, or only incidentally related to, the business's ordinary activities and expected to occur irregularly. Consequently, any gains or losses related to the sale of fixed assets are normally classified as part of ordinary income. Following the all-inclusive income concept more strictly than the international standards, the effects of changes in accounting principles and correction of a fundamental error that relates to prior periods are included in the income statement and classified as extraordinary. However, the effect of the introduction of a fundamental accounting reform is adjusted directly to the opening retained earnings. The standard enjoys wide acceptance by the listed companies.

2.2 The Format of the Balance Sheet

The balance sheet is of the classic two-sided form, assets on the left side, arranged from cash to fixed assets, and grouped into current and noncurrent. Liabilities are arranged and grouped correspondingly.

The presentation of equity in the individual financial statements of a company is related to the regulation of capital and reserves and restrictions on dividends and other distributions in the companies legislation. To facilitate this regulation, the equity presented in the balance sheet is divided into restricted and unrestricted capital. Restricted capital includes paid-in capital in excess of par value, part of retained earnings, and the revaluation reserve. This presentation of equity is not applied in the consolidated balance sheet (see Section 2.5). The Accounting Advisory Council has proposed a division of equity into paid-in capital and retained earnings.

Any noncapitalized pensions liabilities, mortgages, and guarantees must be specified in the extension of the balance sheet.

In addition to the main groups in the income statement and the balance sheet, the format rules include a detailed subdivision of the items. During the past decade it has become customary practice to combine items. The format rules have been interpreted to allow the combination of items, where such combination makes for greater clarity, provided that the items so combined are dealt with separately in the notes.

2.3 The Notes

The notes are an integral part of the financial statements. Legislation sets the specific minimum disclosure requirements. However, the listed companies have increasingly expanded the information given in notes. This development is driven by the general legal requirement for the board's report to provide information, not given in the financial statements, of importance for assessing the company's financial position and income.

Most listed companies now describe thoroughly the accounting principles applied in their financial statements. The Oslo Stock Exchange has strongly encouraged this evolution and has in several Accounting Bulletins made recommendations on the disclosure of accounting policies.

Although the legislation requires only so-called large-sized companies to prepare a statement of changes in financial position, other companies often present such a statement voluntarily. However, there is no specific legal layout of the statement. In the late 1980s practice adopted a cash flow statement. This innovation, influenced by the FASB, was recommended by the financial analysts and the Oslo Stock Exchange. Listed companies now commonly present the cash flow statement immediately after the two basic financial statements.

2.4 The Board of Directors' Report

The board of directors' report should provide information of importance for assessing the company's financial position and income not included in the financial statements and notes. This basic requirement for the content of the report reflects the fact that the report is an integral part of the annual accounts and is vital for the disclosure. Disclosure should also be made of post-balance-sheet events that do not affect the condition of assets or liabilities at the balance sheet date but are of importance for making the financial statements useful.

For the parent company in a group, the report focuses on the group as an economic entity.

2.5 Consolidated Financial Statements

The objective of reporting consolidating financial statements is to present the companies in the group as if they were an economic entity. A group exists if a company, the parent company, has control of another company, the subsidiary. Control is defined in the legislation to exist if a company has a majority of the shareholders' voting rights or through ownership or agreement exercises dominant influence and has a considerable stake in operating income.

Consolidated financial statements comprise the consolidated income statement and the consolidated balance sheet, including the notes. The legislation requires the preparation of consolidated financial statements to be in accordance with good accounting practice and requires the legal formats to be used, suitably amended. The latter permits simplified presentation of equity in the consolidated balance sheet. Basically, the valuation rules for the individual statements apply to the consolidated statements, as does the implicit conceptual framework, implying uniform rules to be used for the whole group. The legal requirement of the consolidated statements to be a summary of the individual statements of the group has been interpreted to mean application of the same principles used in the individual statements, for the parent company as well as for each subsidiary. In fact, when different acceptable principles are used, the statements should not be changed before consolidation.

The effect on accounting income of the conformity requirement in the tax legislation, although reduced by the tax reform, can be an incentive to use other principles of valuation in the consolidated statements, where tax is not relevant. It is common knowledge that the Accounting Act Committee will consider the member state option in Article 29 of the Seventh Directive to permit other principles of valuation in the consolidated statements.

Specific legislation on the consolidation of financial statements, being quite modest, also requires intercompany transactions and unrealized gains to be eliminated and any noncontrolling interest's part of the group's equity to be presented separately in the balance sheet. The 1988 recommendation on accounting for business combinations (see Section 3.7) supplements the legal framework and has strongly influenced consolidation practice.

For the listed companies there has been a development in focusing on the consolidated statements. The individual statements of the parent company are now commonly prepared in accordance with minimum requirements and presented as secondary to the consolidated statements of the group. The Oslo Stock Exchange has encouraged this development.

2.6 Additional Content in the Annual Reports

Some companies, notably the listed ones, present financial highlights, key figures, summaries of five or more years' data, and various financial ratios in the annual reports. Financial summaries for segments according to line of business or market are disclosed by the listed companies, typically reporting figures like net sales, operating income, ordinary income, and total assets. Different definitions are encountered and practice varies. The Oslo Stock Exchange has imposed some structure on companies' reporting by segments and disclosure of key figures. The NASB has a current project on segment information. The Norwegian Society of Financial Analysts has issued guidelines for the preparation of various ratios for analysis of financial statements.

3. Accounting Policies and Practices in Valuation and Income Measurement

3.1 Current Assets

The accounting legislation applies the lower of cost or market principle to all current assets. For current investments, any unrealized losses are therefore recognized as expense. However, current securities may be valued on an aggregate portfolio basis if the securities are managed as one portfolio with respect to risk and return. The Oslo Stock Exchange has requested the companies to supplement the legal minimum specifications in the notes with the market values of the securities. The portfolio principle is controversial, and some argue that it results in losses being offset against unrealized gains.

Legislation defines fair value as net realizable value, unless another value is appropriate according to good accounting practice. NAS 1, Inventory, prescribes net realizable value to be the appropriate value for inventory. The standard defines net realizable value as estimated future selling price in the ordinary course of business, less estimated costs of disposal and completion. Each item of inventory is normally valued separately. The cost of manufactured goods is variable costs plus some elements of fixed costs. FIFO or weighted averages are recommended for the calculation of cost of goods sold.

NAS 2, Long-term Manufacturing Contracts, recommends that revenue and related costs be recognized in the income statements as the contract activity progresses, often referred to as the percentage of completion method. The standard sets the specific terms for the application. In the case of considerable uncertainty as for profit and completion, the standard recommends the method with a zero estimate of profit. Although the general valuation rules allow the completed contract method, its use is discouraged.

3.2 Long-Term Investments

Long-term investments are usually carried at cost. A decline in value, other than temporary, is recognized as expense if it is necessary according to good accounting practice. Good accounting practice is interpreted to allow valuation on an aggregate portfolio basis if appropriate. When a long-term investment is of individual importance to the investor, however, it must be valued individually. A reduction in the carrying amount is not reversed.

Accounting for investments in associated companies and subsidiaries is discussed in Section 3.8.

3.3 Intangible Assets

Intangibles assets are valued according to the general valuation rules for fixed assets. Exceptions are goodwill acquired when a business is purchased, and costs of research and development, which may be capitalized and amortized according to special valuation rules.

Goodwill on consolidation, calculated as the difference between the cost of acquisition and the value of the net assets acquired, should be capitalized and is the dominating intangible asset in the financial reports. The amortization period should not exceed 5 years unless a longer period, not exceeding 20 years, can be justified. The legal amortization rule was changed in 1992. Some companies seem to apply 20 years as the general rule in the amortization of goodwill.

The costs of research and development may be capitalized under certain restrictions and normally amortized over a maximum of 5 years. However, no specific measurement rule exists in the tax code for research and development costs. Consequently, there is a tax incentive to expense these costs as incurred in the financial statements.

3.4 Property, Plant, and Equipment

Accounting legislation requires depreciation in accordance with a rational depreciation plan. In practice, the straight-line depreciation plan dominates. The oil and gas industry uses the unit-of-production method. The general legal requirement to write down fixed assets also applies to property, plant, and equipment. The legislation permits revaluation of fixed assets under certain restrictions. Although the Oslo Stock Exchange has discouraged listed companies from writing up fixed assets, it occurs occasionally for property and plant. The Accounting Advisory Council in 1989 issued a statement proposing prohibition against writing up fixed assets and the introduction of a reversal rule for income recognition of previous write-downs.

3.5 Income Taxes

The preliminary NAS on income taxes follows the general principles of the SFAS 109 and is widely adopted. The main differences from SFAS 109 are related to the method used for netting temporary differences and tax losses carried forward, and the restrictions laid down for the recognition of a deferred tax asset.

Annual income tax expense is recognized on an accrual basis and consists of taxes payable and the periodic deferred tax. The calculation starts out in the balance sheet, identifying temporary differences between accounting and tax values of assets and liabilities. The approach, referred to as the liability method, implies the tax rules at the balance sheet date to be used in the calculations, and the effect of any changes in the taxation rules to be recognized as tax expense immediately. Calculations are on a full provision basis in nominal terms. However, deferred tax acquired when a business combination is purchased should be measured at present value, although undiscounted values are accepted for practical reasons. Temporary differences comprise timing differences and other temporary differences between accounting values and the tax basis. Apart from some special transactions based on continuity for tax purposes, and revaluations of fixed assets in accordance with the restrictions of accounting legislation, accounting for business combinations by the purchase method is the major source of other temporary differences.

The calculation of deferred tax applies an integral approach. The positive and negative timing differences expected to reverse within the same time horizon and tax losses carried forward are combined, and deferred tax is calculated on a net basis. A net positive difference gives rise to a deferred tax liability, and a negative difference gives rise to a deferred tax asset. According to the legislation, however, a deferred tax asset can be recorded only under certain restrictions. Specifically, the realization of tax benefits must be very likely, and the recognized tax asset must not exceed the deferred tax liability recorded in the same balance sheet.

3.6 Pensions

The accounting legislation makes no preference for incorporating pension liabilities in the financial statements or disclosing such liabilities in the extension of the balance sheet. However, more detailed information on pension plans is, in any case, required in the notes. The legal rules have been interpreted to apply only to pension liabilities funded internally. For pension plans administered by independent pension trusts or insurance companies, no pension liabilities are recognized, and only prepaid premiums made for tax purposes are recorded as long-term receivables in the balance sheet. The expenses comprise the annual premiums less the interest earned on the prepaid premiums.

Accounting for pension costs has been one of the most mixed and confusing areas in financial reporting in Norway. Flexibility within the legal framework, the influence of the tax legislation, the absence of a national standard, and technical issues may explain this historical situation. However, the NAS preliminary standard on pension costs (April 1994) has already been implemented by a few listed companies. The Oslo Stock Exchange expects the listed companies to apply the standard in 1994 financial statements. The standard is coherent with the general lines in the foreign and international standards on pension accounting like SFAS 87/ 88, SSAP 24, and the revised IAS 19, and makes a distinction between defined contribution and defined benefits plans. In Norway most pension plans are defined benefits plans.

3.7 Business Combinations

The recommendation on accounting for business combination covers the consolidation of a parent company and its subsidiaries, as well as legal mergers. It prescribes two accounting methods, the purchase method and the pooling-of-interests method, as acceptable but not as alternatives. The basic principle of the recommendation is that the accounting method shall reflect the economic reality of the combination: a transaction or continuity. Basically, the recommendation is an elaborate interpretation of the transaction concept. A business combination should be accounted for under the purchase method when it is an acquisition transaction. In the rare circumstances of a uniting of interests, the pooling-of-interests method should be used. There is a general understanding, however, that the regulation of mergers in the Joint-Stock Companies Act, based on a principle of continuity, implicitly requires the pooling-of-interest method to be used in the case of a legal merger. The Accounting Advisory Council has proposed a change in the legislation on mergers to remedy this situation.

3.8 Investments in Associated Companies and Subsidiaries

An initiative of the Oslo Stock Exchange in 1985 resulted in a recommendation on equity accounting and later on an amendment in legislation introducing the admittance to use the equity method in the consolidated statements for investments in associated joint-stock companies. A significant influence in another company qualifies the investee to be an associated company. If an investor holds 20% or more of the voting power of the investee, the investor normally does have significant influence. In the individual financial statements, the valuation rules of the legislation prohibit the use of equity accounting for investments in associates and subsidiaries organized as joint-stock companies.

The NASB issued a preliminary standard on equity accounting in 1993. The standard recommends that the equity method be used in the consolidated statements as well as in the individual statements for valuation of investments in associated companies and subsidiaries. However, the standard recognizes the present restriction in legislation on the use of the method.

There has been some tradition by Norwegian companies to use the proportionate method (see Section 3.9) for interests in companies other than joint-stock companies. The preliminary NAS approves this practice, provided a substantial part of the owner's operations takes place in such companies and the companies are set up mainly for finance purposes. At this point, the standard differs from the international standards on equity accounting.

3.9 Interests in Joint Ventures

The NASB issued a preliminary standard on accounting for interests in joint ventures in 1994. The standard recommends the proportionate method, in Norway called the *gross method* and internationally often referred to as *proportional consolidation*, as the appropriate treatment of interests in joint ventures. Joint ventures may be jointly controlled operations, assets, or entities. For interests in jointly controlled entities, application of the gross method is restricted. There is a general understanding that the legal framework does not allow the method to be used for interests in joint-stock companies.

3.10 Foreign Currency

Measurements of foreign currency transactions apply the exchange rate at the date of transaction. The valuation of items denominated in a foreign currency is regulated by the valuation rules in the accounting legislation. A recommendation of good accounting practice interprets the legal framework for monetary items. Unrealized losses are expensed and unrealized gains are deferred. Hedging should be considered in the calculation of unrealized losses. Hedging includes balance sheet items and off-balance-sheet transactions. Anticipative hedges are not included. Some listed companies value unhedged exchange positions on an aggregate portfolio basis. For current monetary items, many listed companies apply the closing rate.

Translation of financial statements of foreign operations is not regulated. In practice, foreign balance sheets are normally translated at the closing rate and income statements at the average rate for the year. The effects of exchange rate changes on net foreign investments and transactions designed as hedges of net foreign investments are adjusted directly to equity. For foreign operations that are integral parts of the operations of the reporting company, the temporal method is used for translation of the financial statements.

4. Future Developments

The introduction of deferred tax liabilities and assets has been mentioned as the most important accounting reform in Norway in recent years. An important side effect of the reform was the Ministry of Finance recognizing that legislation was not a convenient means for the regulation of complex areas like accounting for income taxes and, hence, recognizing the need for accounting standards.

In a second subreport from the Accounting Act Committee in 1992, the committee proposed the establishment of a new Accounting Standards Board with legal authority and appointed by the government. The committee, praising the standard-setting by the NASB, essentially proposed that the work continue by the new Board. The report has been submitted for comment.

In the same report the committee proposed a system for simplification by introducing differentiation in the accounting regulation. The simplification is justified by a cost-benefit consideration. The legal framework will be general and apply to all companies. Accounting standards will differentiate large and medium-sized companies. Complaints about increased complexity in accounting moved the committee to draft a proposal allowing small companies to prepare simplified statements and notes and apply the valuation rules in the tax legislation.

The main report from the Accounting Act Committee will be completed in 1994 and will include proposed changes in the legislation in accordance with the EC Directives. The committee will also take the opportunity to update the legal framework accommodating recent developments in accounting standards. The accounting legislation should further facilitate prospective harmonization of accounting standards. Harmonization of accounting legislation with the EC Directives is a constraint to these latter achievements. Liberal interpretations of the Directives seem necessary to achieve an accounting legislation for the future.

Financial Statements

R E S U L T A T R E G N S K A P
O R K L A - K O N S E R N E T

Beløp i mill. kroner	Note	1993	1992
Driftsinntekter	1	**17.858**	16.807
Forbruk av råvarer, halvfabrikata og handelsvarer		**(7.891)**	(7.538)
Lønn og andre personalkostnader	2	**(3.803)**	(3.540)
Andre tilvirknings-, salgs- og adm. kostnader	3	**(3.959)**	(3.678)
Ordinære avskrivninger	13	**(935)**	(861)
Driftskostnader		**(16.588)**	(15.617)
DRIFTSRESULTAT		**1.270**	1.190
Resultat fra tilknyttede selskaper	10	**219**	112
Finansposter, netto	4	**(523)**	(606)
Porteføljegevinster, netto	5	**350**	(381)
RESULTAT FØR SKATTEKOSTNAD OG MINORITETER		**1.316**	315
Skattekostnad	6, 17	**(317)**	(100)
Minoritetsinteresser	15	**(15)**	(4)
ÅRETS RESULTAT		**984**	211

PROFIT AND LOSS ACCOUNT
ORKLA GROUP

Amounts in NOK million	Note	1993	1992
Operating revenue	1	**17,858**	16,807
Raw materials, goods in process and finished goods		**(7,891)**	(7,538)
Wages and other personnel costs	2	**(3,803)**	(3,540)
Other manufacturing, selling and administrative expenses	3	**(3,959)**	(3,678)
Ordinary depreciation	13	**(935)**	(861)
Operating expenses		**(16,588)**	(15,617)
OPERATING PROFIT		**1,270**	1,190
Share of profits from associated companies	10	**219**	112
Financial items, net	4	**(523)**	(606)
Portfolio gains, net	5	**350**	(381)
PROFIT BEFORE TAXES AND MINORITY INTERESTS		**1,316**	315
Taxes	6, 17	**(317)**	(100)
Minority interests	15	**(15)**	(4)
PROFIT FOR THE YEAR		**984**	211

B A L A N S E
ORKLA · KONSERNET

Beløp i mill. kroner	Note	**1993**	1992
EIENDELER			
Betalingsmidler	7	**635**	787
Porteføljeinvesteringer	9	**4.888**	3.766
Kunde- og andre kortsiktige fordringer	3	**2.717**	2.207
Varebeholdninger	8	**1.794**	1.779
Omløpsmidler		**10.034**	8.539
Andeler i tilknyttede selskaper	10	**1.172**	970
Aksjer og andeler i andre selskaper	12	**137**	177
Andre formuesmidler	11	**1.039**	1.108
Goodwill, immaterielle eiendeler m.v.	13	**951**	675
Varige driftsmidler	13	**6.159**	5.274
Anleggsmidler		**9.458**	8.204
Eiendeler		**19.492**	16.743
GJELD OG EGENKAPITAL			
Kortsiktig rentebærende gjeld	16	**1.739**	1.617
Kortsiktig rentefri gjeld	14	**3.803**	3.497
Kortsiktig gjeld		**5.542**	5.114
Langsiktig rentebærende gjeld	16	**6.003**	4.419
Langsiktig rentefri gjeld	17	**1.177**	1.167
Langsiktig gjeld		**7.180**	5.586
Minoritetsinteresser	15	**197**	206
Aksjekapital		**1.219**	1.219
Annen egenkapital		**5.354**	4.618
Egenkapital	18	**6.573**	5.837
Gjeld og egenkapital		**19.492**	16.743
Pantstillelser	19	**426**	690
Garantiansvar og andre forpliktelser	19, 20	**349**	313

B A L A N C E   S H E E T
ORKLA GROUP

Amounts in NOK million	Note	1993	1992
ASSETS			
Cash and bank deposits	7	635	787
Portfolio investments	9	4,888	3,766
Accounts and other short-term receivables	3	2,717	2,207
Inventories	8	1,794	1,779
Current assets		10,034	8,539
Interests in associated companies	10	1,172	970
Shares and investments in other companies	12	137	177
Other receivables	11	1,039	1,108
Goodwill	13	951	675
Fixed assets	13	6,159	5,274
Long-term assets		9,458	8,204
Total assets		19,492	16,743
LIABILITIES AND EQUITY			
Short-term interest-bearing liabilities	16	1,739	1,617
Short-term interest-free liabilities	14	3,803	3,497
Current liabilities		5,542	5,114
Long-term interest-bearing liabilities	16	6,003	4,419
Long-term interest-free liabilities	17	1,177	1,167
Long-term liabilities		7,180	5,586
Minority interests	15	197	206
Share capital		1,219	1,219
Other equity		5,354	4,618
Equity	18	6,573	5,837
Liabilities and equity		19,492	16,743
Mortgages	19	426	690
Guarantees and other commitments	19, 20	349	313

KONTANTSTRØMANALYSE
ORKLA-KONSERNET

Beløp i mill. kroner	1993	1992
Industriområdet (inkl. HK):		
Driftsresultat	1.241	1.170
Ordinære avskrivninger	923	857
Endring netto driftskapital	(217)	217
Kontantstrøm fra driften	1.947	2.244
Netto fornyelses- og miljøinvesteringer	(1.102)	(794)
Fri kontantstrøm fra driften	845	1.450
Finansposter, netto	(417)	(425)
Fri kontantstrøm fra industriområdet (inkl. HK)	428	1.025
Netto kontantstrøm fra investeringsvirksomheten ¹⁾	(1.120)	516
Ekspansjonsinvesteringer, industriområdet	(924)	(802)
Betalte skatter, utbytte og kontantvederlag	(431)	(499)
Diverse kapitaltransaksjoner	84	126
Kontantstrøm etter kapitaltransaksjoner	(1.963)	366
Endring brutto rentebærende gjeld	1.706	(368)
Endring likvide midler/rentebærende fordringer	257	2
Endring netto rentebærende gjeld	1.963	(366)
¹⁾ Investeringsvirksomheten:		
Fri kontantstrøm fra driften	14	20
Porteføljegevinster	350	275
Nedskrivning aksjer	-	(656)
Netto endring bokført verdi porteføljeaksjer	(1.122)	1.058
Eiendomsinvesteringer	(256)	-
Finansposter, netto for investeringsvirksomheten	(106)	(181)
Netto kontantstrøm fra investeringsvirksomheten	(1.120)	516

Kontantstrøm fra driften gir uttrykk for den brutto kontantstrøm konsernet genererer fra industriområdet (inkl. HK), korrigert for endringer i binding av midler til driftskapital.
Fri kontantstrøm fra driften representerer industriområdets (inkl. HK) gjeldsbetjenings- og ekspansjonsevne når nåværende aktivitetsnivå er opprettholdt gjennom fornyelses- og miljøinvesteringer.
Fri kontantstrøm fra industriområdet (inkl. HK) viser områdets ekspansjonsevne etter at gjelden er betjent.
Kontantstrøm etter kapitaltransaksjoner viser konsernets nedbetalingsevne/lånebehov etter gjennomførte ekspansjonsinvesteringer, utbytte til aksjonærene, skatter og øvrige kapitaltransaksjoner.

CASHFLOW STATEMENT
ORKLA GROUP

Amounts in NOK million	1993	1992
Industrial activities (including Head Office):		
Operating profit	**1,241**	1,170
Ordinary depreciation	**923**	857
Changes in net working capital	**(217)**	217
Cashflow from operations	**1,947**	2,244
Net maintenance and environmental investments	**(1,102)**	(794)
Free cashflow from operations	**845**	1,450
Financial items, net	**(417)**	(425)
Free cashflow from industrial activities (incl. H.O.)	**428**	1,025
Net cashflow from investment activities [1]	**(1,120)**	516
Investments for expansion, industrial activities	**(924)**	(802)
Tax, dividends and cash considerations paid	**(431)**	(499)
Miscellaneous capital transactions	**84**	126
Cashflow after capital transactions	**(1,963)**	366
Change in gross interest-bearing debt	**1,706**	(368)
Change in liquid assets/interest-bearing receivables	**257**	2
Change in net interest-bearing debt	**1,963**	(366)
Investment activities:		
Free cashflow from operations	**14**	20
Portfolio gains	**350**	275
Write-down of shares	**-**	(656)
Net change in book value of portfolio shares	**(1,122)**	1,058
Real estate investments	**(256)**	-
Financial items, net for investment activities	**(106)**	(181)
Net cashflow from investment activities	**(1,120)**	516

Cashflow from operations expresses the gross cashflow generated by the Industry area (incl. H.O.), adjusted for changes in funds employed in providing working capital.

Free cashflow from operations represents the Industry area's (incl. H.O.) debt service capacity and the ability to expand when the current level of activity has been maintained through net maintenance and environmental investments.

Free cashflow from industrial activities (incl. H.O.) shows the Industry area's ability to expand after net financial items.

Cashflow after capital transactions shows the Group's ability to repay debt (borrowing requirement) after expansion investments, dividend payments, taxes and miscellaneous capital transactions.

ACCOUNTING PRINCIPLES

1993 GROUP ACCOUNTS

The 1993 Group accounts have been prepared using the same principles as previous years except for the following three areas:

Due to the expectation that long-term interest rates will remain low, the discount rate for non-insured pension obligations has been reduced from 8% to 5%. The resulting increase in the obligation will be expensed over the next 15 years (see note 2).

The Group also changed the principles regarding the conversion of foreign subsidiaries which are regarded as an integrated part of the parent company. The foreign exchange differences arising from translation for these companies are booked to the profit and loss account, while non-monetary items are translated and recorded using historic rates.

The treatment of foreign exchange differences arising on balances denominated in foreign currencies has changed. All items not directly hedged, both on and off balance sheet, are included in an aggregated portfolio valuation.

The latter two changes in accounting policy have marginal effect on the 1993 profit and loss account.

GENERAL

The Group accounts show the consolidated result and financial position of the parent company, Orkla A.S, and its interest in other companies. Interests in companies where the Group holds more than 50% of the voting share capital and exerts a dominant influence are fully consolidated in accordance with the purchase method. Interests in joint ventures, with the exception of limited companies, where Orkla together with others, has a decisive but not controlling influence, are pro rata consolidated in accordance with the gross method. Interests in associated companies where the Group has a strategic interest and significant influence (20-50%), are accounted for in accordance with the equity method. The purchase price of assets and liabilities in subsidiaries, joint ventures and associated companies are used as a basis for recording results in the Group accounts. The Group's equity capital comprises the parent company's equity and amounts earned subsequent to the above mentioned companies becoming subsidiaries, less amortisation of amounts paid for tangible assets in excess of book values, goodwill and minority interests.

ACCOUNTING AND CON-SOLIDATION PRINCIPLES

Accounts consolidated in the Group have been consistently prepared using common accounting and valuation principles, and the presentation of captions in the profit and loss account and balance sheet has been produced using uniform definitions.

Shares in subsidiaries are eliminated and the purchase price to the Group is replaced by the company's assets and liabilities. At the date of acquisition the difference between the purchase price for the shares and the company's aggregate equity capital is allocated to those assets (or liabilities) where market value differs from book value, with any residual being treated as goodwill in the Group accounts.

Foreign subsidiaries, which are not regarded as an integrated part of the parent company, are translated using the closing exchange rate at 31.12. for the balance sheet and the average exchange rate for the year for the profit and loss account. Translation differences are charged directly against equity.

Foreign subsidiaries, which are regarded as an integrated part of the parent company, are converted in two stages. Monetary items are translated at the closing exchange rate and non-monetary items are translated at the historic rate. With regard to the profit and loss account, depreciation and the cost of materials are translated using the historic exchange rate while other items are translated using the average exchange rate for the year. Translation differences are recorded within the caption "other financial items".

In countries where the accumulated inflation over the preceding three years exceeds 100%, the accounts are inflation adjusted. Depreciation and the book value of operating assets are converted using the exchange rate in effect on the date of acquisition. The profit and loss account is translated using the average exchange rate for the year. Other balance sheet items are translated using the year-end closing exchange rate. Translation differences are recorded within the caption "other financial items".

Interests in joint ventures, with the exception of limited companies, are eliminated using the same principles as for subsidiaries. Orkla's share of each account caption is included in the Group accounts, in accordance with the gross method.

Interests in associated companies are consolidated separately and the Group's share of the results after amortization of goodwill is added to the cost of the investment. The treatment of goodwill in associated companies is similar to that adopted for subsidiaries.

The Group's interests in the limited companies Jotun, Göteborgs Kex and Hjemmet Mortensen are treated as associated companies, with the exception that the share of results to be consolidated is before taxes and that the share of the tax charge is separately included within the caption "other taxes" in the Group accounts. These interests would have been treated in accordance with the joint venture rules set out in the draft Norwegian Accounting Standard had the necessary amendments to the Companies Act been made.

CLASSIFICATION, VALUATION AND ACCRUAL PRINCIPLES

The accounts are based on the fundamental principles of historic cost, accruals, going concern, consistency and prudence.

Classification of current assets in the accounts comprises all assets related to the stock cycle, receivables due within one year and "assets not intended to be permanently retained or used in the business". Other assets are classified as fixed assets. The distinction between short and long-term liabilities is determined at one year prior to the maturity date.

Current assets are valued at the lower of cost and market value. Fixed assets are valued at cost less accumulated ordinary depreciation. If the market value of a fixed asset, or group of fixed assets, is less than book value and the fall is considered permanent, then it is written down.

Accounts receivable are valued at expected realisable value at 31.12. The Group's aggregate provision for bad debts on accounts receivable is disclosed in Note 3.

Inventories of materials are valued at the lower of cost and market value based on the FIFO principle. Finished goods and goods in process are valued at the cost of processing. A provision has been made for obsolescence.

Shares and other investments classified as current assets are financial investments and valued using the portfolio principle. The portfolio is managed as a whole and an adjustment is made if the aggregate holdings has a lower market value than the original cost. Individual items in the portfolio which have incurred a permanent diminution in value are written down. Long-term shareholdings and other interests which are not treated as associated companies are recorded using the cost method. The cost method means that shares/interests are recorded at cost and cash payments received are treated as dividends.

Fixed assets are capitalised only if they have an economic useful life in excess of 3 years and a cost price exceeding NOK 15,000. Maintenance of fixed assets is recorded as an operating expense, whereas additions or improvements are capitalised and depreciated in line with the corresponding asset. Asset renewals are capital-

ised. Excess values arising on mergers are allocated in the Group accounts to the relevant fixed assets and depreciated accordingly. Fixed assets are depreciated on a straight line basis using the following annual rates: buildings 2-4%, machinery and fixtures 10-15%, transport equipment and reusable crates 20%, computer equipment and reusable bottles 25%.

Goodwill. On acquiring another company for a consideration exceeding the value of the individual assets, the difference, to the extent it represents an economic value, is recorded in the balance sheet as goodwill. Goodwill is amortised over its useful expected life, based on calculations made at the time of acquisition, but never exceeds 20 years. The value of goodwill is written down if the market value is considered to be less than the book value and the reduction is considered to be permanent.

Pension expenses related to schemes covered by insurance policies are charged to operating expenses. The expenses comprise the annual premiums less the interest earned on the pension premium funds and the return on the insurance scheme. The pension premium funds are recorded in the balance sheet under "other receivables". Pension obligations including employment tax not covered by the insurance scheme are capitalised and disclosed as a liability in the balance sheet. The aggregate of pensions paid and changes in the obligation represent the year's expense for non-insured schemes (see Note 2).

Foreign exchange. The treatment of foreign exchange differs between hedged and unhedged items. "Hedged" means that the economic effect of fluctuations in the relevant currency has been eliminated. Balance sheet items which hedge each other are presented using the closing rate, while balance sheet items which are hedged by off-balance sheet financial transactions are presented using the hedge rate. Hedging transactions undertaken to hedge contractual cashflows are valued together with their related cashflows. Unhedged foreign exchange positions are treated in aggregate on a portfolio basis. If there is an overall net loss on the portfolio it is expensed, but net gains are not recorded as income.

Taxes. The tax charge is based on the financial result and consists of the aggregate of taxes payable and the movement in deferred tax. Deferred tax is calculated in the balance sheet using the nominal tax rate for the timing differences arising between the accounting and tax values.

N O T E S
ORKLA GROUP

NOTE 1

Operating revenue

Amounts in NOK million	1993	1992[1]
Net sales in Norway	12,126	11,909
Net sales in rest of Scandinavia	2,041	1,720
Net sales outside Scandinavia	3,344	2,912
Total net sales	17,511	16,541
Miscellaneous operating revenues	347	266
Operating revenue	17,858	16,807

[1] Revenue of Orkla Finans has been reclassified from "Sales" to "Miscellaneous operating revenues".

NOTE 2

Wages and other personnel costs

Wages and other personnel costs consist of costs directly related to remuneration of employees and representatives, costs related to pension arrangements for both present and former employees and government employment taxes. The costs consist of:

Amounts in NOK million	1993	1992
Wages and holiday pay	(3,213)	(2,978)
Other remuneration	(27)	(43)
Employment tax	(467)	(467)
Pension costs	(96)	(52)
Wages and other personnel costs	(3,803)	(3,540)

Employee bonus

The Board will propose to make a distribution to employees in the Norwegian operations of 0.75 of one month's wages in the form of options exercisable no earlier than 3 years after and no later than 5 years after the issue date. Estimated employment taxes have been charged in the 1993 accounts on the remuneration benefit (NOK 19 million at the date of issue). With the exception of the employment tax this event will be treated as an equity transaction at the date the options are exercised. See Note 18.

Pension arrangements

Insured pension obligations

The Orkla Group companies have, with certain exceptions, established collective pension schemes. The majority of the schemes are supplementary to the State social security (net arrangement) and include age, disablement, spouse and child pensions.

Non-insured pension obligations

At 31.12.1993 the capitalised value of the Group's non-insured pension obligations was calculated at NOK 471 million. In addition, there was NOK 75 million representing an unamortised increase in the estimated amount following the change on 1.1.1993 from a 8% to a 5% discount rate. The amount includes employment tax. A deferred tax allowance is calculated for the pension obligation. No future salary or pension adjustments are assumed in these calculations, except where these are covered by agreements.

Pension expenses and obligations are shown in the Group accounts:

Profit and loss account

Insured schemes		
Gross pension premiums	(124)	(105)
Interest and surplus	77	94
Net pension premiums	(47)	(11)
Non-insured schemes		
Directly paid pensions	(64)	(60)
Change in non-insured obligations and amortisation of estimated change	15	19
Cost of non-insured schemes	(49)	(41)
Total pension costs for the year	**(96)**	**(52)**

Balance sheet

Pensions funds (premium fund, surplus fund and regulation fund)	706	732[1]
Non-insured pension obligations	471	486[1]

Non-insured pension obligations include a total of 3,807 persons at 31.12.1993.

[1] The items have been adjusted for acquisitions etc.

NOTE 3

Other manufacturing, selling and administrative expenses

Other manufacturing, selling and administrative expenses represent a grouping of cost items not specified on other lines in the profit and loss account. Major individual items include transport costs of NOK 664 million, energy costs of NOK 334 million, repair and maintenance costs of NOK 412 million and advertising and research and development costs of NOK 757 million. In addition, losses on receivables of NOK 27 million are included.

Accounts receivable at 31.12. are shown less a provision for bad debts. The provision has developed as follows:

Amounts in NOK million	1993	1992
Bad debt reserve at 01.01.	82	88
Realised losses for the year	(27)	(41)
Provision for bad debts for the year	27	35
Bad debt reserve at 31.12.	82	82

NOTE 4

Financial items, net

Amounts in NOK million	1993	1992
Dividends	99	75
Interest income	98	169
Interest expenses	(699)	(810)
Net foreign exchange gains/losses	4	(15)
Other financial items, net	(25)	(25)
Financial items, net	(523)	(606)

NOTE 5

Portfolio gains, net

Amounts in NOK million	1993	1992
Portfolio shares[1]	350	(355)
Net write-down/losses, ships	-	(26)
Total	350	(381)

[1] Includes a write-down on shares in UNI Storebrand and Elkem of NOK 203 million and NOK 453 million respectively in 1992.

NOTE 6

Taxes

Amounts in NOK million	1993	1992
Tax payable in Norway	(245)	(232)
Tax payable abroad	(33)	(43)
Tax payable gross associated companies	(38)	(29)
Total tax payable	(316)	(304)
Change in deferred tax Norway	10	211
Change in deferred tax abroad	(1)	8
Change in deferred tax gross associated companies	(10)	(15)
Total change in deferred tax	(1)	204
Total tax charge	(317)	(100)

NOTE 7

Cash and bank deposits
This item includes restricted deposits of NOK 158 (204) million for the Group.

NOTE 8

Inventories

Amounts in NOK million	1993	1992
Raw materials	652	608
Goods in process	100	100
Finished goods	1,042	1,071
Total	1,794	1,779

NOTE 9

Portfolio investments

Amounts in NOK million **Owned by Orkla A.S**	Number of shares	Book value	Market value	Share owned %
Norwegian listed shares				
Bank/Insurance				
Bolig & Næringsbanken	228,000	28	35	2.3
UNI Storebrand Pref. Ord.	12,554,639	125	147	
UNI Storebrand Pref. Free	156,570	2	2	
UNI Storebrand Ord.	30,783,159	328	585	12.4
UNI Storebrand Free	170,000	4	3	
Industry				
Alcatel STK	207,400	17	49	2.5
Adresseavisen	267,134	69	69	14.2
Avantor	400,000	15	15	7.2
C. Tybring Gjedde	101,300	14	17	3.8
Dyno	4,900,262	538	603	19.7
Elkem Ord.	8,540,886	408	735	
Elkem Free	1,873,436	60	169	21.1
Gyldendal	127,295	5	32	5.4
Hafslund Nycomed Ord.	4,312,637	295	528	
Hafslund Nycomed Free	600,432	83	77	6.5
Hafslund Nycomed B	1,412,547	136	180	
Helikopterservice	766,000	54	79	3.5
Kverneland	385,888	15	20	5.2
Kværner Ord.	2,002,028	275	676	4.6
Maritime Group	206,400	17	14	3.0
Norsk Forsvarsteknologi	105,200	12	14	0.5
Norsk Hydro	507,000	85	109	0.3
Nora Eiendom	1,562,587	55	266	23.9
Raufoss	756,372	66	65	10.1
Saga Petroleum Ord.	3,163,264	267	226	
Saga Petroleum Free	595,900	43	44	2.9
Skrivervik Data	212,500	14	17	8.5
Simrad Ord.	130,177	11	16	
Simrad B	59,600	6	7	2.8
Miscellaneous		39	55	
Shipping				
Actinor Shipping	315,035	32	42	7.8
Arcade Drilling	3,543,000	21	20	3.3
Bergesen d.y. Ord.	3,018,517	309	439	
Bergesen d.y. B	1,008,000	111	146	7.1
Benor Tankers	632,800	24	23	3.4
Color Line	2,186,546	47	55	5.7
Nordic American Shipping	378,064	17	18	8.9
Smedvig	733,250	73	106	7.0
Skaugen Petrotrans	5,854,786	17	21	5.3
Storli Ord.	174,000	25	31	
Storli B	205,500	21	35	3.5
Miscellaneous		8	12	
Investment Funds				
Omega AMS	9,950	1	2	
Omega Investment Fund	1,951	39	62	
Total Norwegian listed shares		3,831	5,866	

Amounts in NOK million **Owned by Orkla A.S**	Number of shares	Book value	Market value	Share owned %
Foreign listed shares				
Nordic				
BCP B	650,000	41	47	
Chips Pref. [1]	239,784	38	60	11.1
Kymmene	100,000	14	15	
Lassila	34,400	7	8	
Nokia Pref.	80,000	20	30	
Ejendomss. Norden	40,000	11	11	
Ø.K. Holding	50,000	7	10	
Silcon B	20,000	9	9	
Skandia Free	100,000	10	15	
Tampella	840,000	26	27	
Miscellanous		27	30	
Other countries				
Norex	1,415,200	74	112	
Granada Group	200,000	11	12	
Grand Metropolitan	175,000	8	9	
Jardine Matheson Hold.	100,400	6	8	
Ruberoid	533,487	9	11	
Sita Units	9,000	5	10	
Tomkins ord.	300,000	8	8	
Miscellanous		86	90	
Total foreign listed shares		417	522	
Total listed shares		4,248	6,388	
Owned by Orkla A.S				
Unlisted shares				
Benefon	20,000	18	30	4.3
Carl Aller	4,600	27	27	2.6
Dagbladet Ord.	96,466	33	57	14.0
Dagbladet Pref.	71,677	23	42	
Eeg-Henriksen	168,000	10	10	3.1
Eiendomsspar	222,222	36	29	2.3
Holberg Industries	333,250	14	14	18.0
India Lib. Fund		8	8	
Lindex	275,000	25	25	10.0
NetCom	5,251	25	110	22.4
Steen & Strøm Invest	864,800	26	56	8.0
Miscellanous		55	51	
Total unlisted shares		300	459	
Limited partnerships				
Deepsea Drillships		15	0	32.4
European Acquisition		14	14	
Glenwood Venture Ic		2	0	22.9
Glenwood Venture IIb		3	2	4.5
Industrikapital Ltd. I, II, III		54	54	29.8
Stadrill 4/5		1	1	2.5
Total limited partnerships, current assets		89	71	
Shares owned by subsidiaries				
Elkem Ord.	2,180,245	44	188	4.4
Kværner Ord.	180,000	32	61	0.4
Norgeskreditt	241,692	25	33	2.1
Adresseavisen	60,234	3	16	3.2
NetCom [2]	2,550	9		10.9
Miscellanous		6	12	
Miscellanous securities				
Convertible bonds owned by Orkla A.S		74	74	
Options owned by Orkla A.S		3	5	
Miscellanous bonds owned by Orkla Finans A.S		55	54	
Total		4,888	7,361	

[1] In addition Orkla owns 125.000 voting shares in Chips OY. See Note 12.
[2] Total market value is reported among unlisted shares.

NOTE 10

Interests in associated companies

Amounts in NOK million	Share owned %	Orig-inal cost-price	Book value at 01.01.	Additions/retirements during the year	Gains on sale	Share of profit	Share of taxes	Dividend received/price adjustment	Book value 31.12.93	Deprecia-tion of goodwill in 1993	Book value of goodwill at 31.12.
Jotun A.S	41.5	144	383	-	-	71	(32)	(9)	413	(3)	42
Göteborgs Kex AB[1]	49.0	261	254	-	-	21	(9)	(6)	260	(9)	168
Frionor A/S	38.8	83	82	35	-	6	-	-	123	(2)	34
Hjemmet Mortensen A.S	50.0	21	28	-	-	21	(7)	(11)	31	-	-
Drammens Tidende og Buskerud Blad A.S[1]	34.5	-	-	89	-	-	-	-	89	-	64
Asker og Bærum Budstikke A.S	28.7	70	73	-	-	3	-	(3)	73	(2)	28
Bergens Tidende A.S	28.4	-	-	67	9	5	-	-	72	-	14
A/S Østlandets Blad	39.7	17	19	-	-	1	-	-	20	-	6
TVNorge A.S	-	35	46	(35)	97	(11)	-	-	-	-	-
K/S Swan Sea	35.0	18	18	-	-	2	-	-	20	-	-
K/S Knutsen Bøyelaster III	28.0	13	18	7	-	(10)	-	-	15	-	-
Hemne Orkladal Billag A/S[1]	40.1	7	8	1	-	2	-	-	11	(1)	3
Orkla Exolon A.S K/S	42.3	4	19	-	-	-	-	-	19	-	-
Oskar Sylte A.S	44.0	8	9	-	-	1	-	-	10	(1)	5
ANS Rica Nordkapp	35.8	5	5	-	-	-	-	-	5	-	-
Miscellaneous [2]	-	10	8	6	-	1	-	(4)	11	-	1
Total		696	970	170	106	113	(48)	(33)	1,172	(18)	365

[1] With effect from 1.1.1994 Orkla's ownership will satisfy the requirements for accounting these companies as subsidiaries.
[2] Miscellaneous holdings include, amongst others, investments in ANS Karasjokk Hotell, Ekonor A/S, ANS Bodø Engrossenter and LignoTech VerkaufsgmbH.

NOTE 11

Other receivables

The amount includes loans to individuals and companies covered by Section 12-10 and 11-8.16 of the Norwegian Companies Act totalling NOK 45 million, as well as the pension premium fund of NOK 706 million for the Group. The fund may only be used for the payment of future pension premiums. Also included is the Group's deferred tax allowance of NOK 132 million which mainly relates to the treatment of non-insured pension obligations on a gross basis (see Note 17).

NOTE 12

Shares and investments in other companies [1]

Shares

Amounts in NOK million	Number of shares	Book value	Share owned %
Owned by Orkla A.S			
AB Chips OY [2]	125,000	60	10.0
Norsk Vekst	25,000	25	4.2
Total shares		85	
Owned by Group companies			
Viking Askim SB	2,400,000	6	30.0
Norsk Telegrambyrå	4,750	2	22.3
Solo	665	1	46.6
Miscellaneous Media companies in Poland		14	
Vågsøy Bladforlag	4,833	4	35.0
Norsk Avfallshåndtering	3,330	3	2.5
Coca-Cola Dzieren Ltd.	1,508	2	33.0
Miscellaneous		8	-
Total shares		40	
Interests			
K/S Seatern		0.8	10.0
ANS Vagsøy		0.3	2.8
ANS Rik. Kaarbysgt. 18		0.5	9.1
ANS Bygginvestor II		1.0	16.0
Bankbygg Førde ANS		1.3	2.3
ANS Høgset [3]		4.8	16.0
ANS Nordkapp [3]		3.9	13.9
Miscellaneous		0.1	-
Total interests		12	
Total, Group		137	

[1] In companies where the interest is greater than 20%, an evaluation of the Group's influence has concluded that it would not be correct to present the interests as "associated companies".
[2] Relates to voting share capital. In addition to this item, the company owns shares in Chips OY recorded within current assets. In total the company owns 11.7% of the voting share capital and 17.3% of the total share capital of Chips OY.
[3] Of which owned by Orkla A.S: ANS Høgset (7.1%) and ANS Nordkapp (4.2%).

NOTE 13

Fixed assets and goodwill, intangible assets, etc.

Fixed assets

Amounts in NOK million	Accumulated cost at 01.01.	Revaluations at 01.01.	Written down at 01.01.	Depreciated at 01.01.	Book value at 01.01.	Additions in 1993	Disposals in 1993	Ordinary depreciation and write-downs in 1993	Book value 31.12. 1993
Machinery, vehicles	6,985	5	(4)	(4,434)	2,552	1,000	(41)	(729)	2,782
Buildings and plant	2,955	71	(10)	(1,215)	1,801	633	(11)	(131)	2,292
Rental property	192			(37)	155	1	(1)	(4)	151
Other real estate	383	73		(6)	450	71	(3)	(6)	512
Total	10,515	149	(14)	(5,692)	4,958	1,705	(56)	(870)	5,737
Construction in progress	312				312	98			410
Prepaid costs relating to new con.	4				4	8			12
Total	10,831	149	(14)	(5,692)	5,274	1,811	(56)	(870)	6,159

Goodwill, intangible assets etc.

Amounts in NOK million	Accumulated cost at 01.01.	Written down at 01.01.	Depreciated at 01.01.	Book value at 01.01.	Additions in 1993	Ordinary depreciation and write-downs in 1993	Book value 31.12. 1993
Odense Marcipanfabrik	227		(31)	196		(12)	184
Dragsbæk group	70		(13)	57		(4)	53
BOB Industrier	-				271	(7)	264
Kims	227	(115)	(24)	88		(5)	83
Nidar Europe BV	37		(6)	31		(2)	29
Bakers group	87		(30)	57	36	(5)	88
Household products	43		(11)	32	5	(2)	35
Media group	211		(79)	132	2	(11)	123
Chemicals area	45		(22)	23	1	(8)	16
Miscellaneous	126		(67)	59	26	(9)	76
Total	1,073	(115)	(283)	675	341	(65)	951

Investments in and disposals of fixed assets and goodwill

Amounts in NOK million	Investments in:					Disposals at sales price:				
	1989	1990	1991	1992	1993	1989	1990	1991	1992	1993
Goodwill, etc.	72	572	161	45	341					
Machinery, vehicles	545	640	840	952	1,000	43	123	110	72	82
Ships	107	-	-	-	-	1	-	-	73	-
Buildings and plant	150	252	200	153	633	45	834	155	14	27
Rental property	3	183	32	12	1		43	615	2	-
Other real estate	34	70	88	71	71	7	77	136	20	7
Construction in progress	123	136	15	170	98		37			-
Prepaid costs relating to new con.	2	(7)	12	-	8					
Total	1,036	1,846	1,348	1,403	2,152	96	1,114	1,016	181	116

NOTE 14

Short-term interest-free liabilities

Amounts in NOK million	1993	1992
Accounts payable	1,311	1,128
State duties, taxes, holiday pay, etc.	1,096	961
Accrued unassessed taxes	295	241
Allocated to dividend	202	182
Other short-term liabilities	899	985
Total	3,803	3,497

NOTE 15

The minority interests share of:

Amounts in NOK million	1993
Ordinary depreciations	32
Operating profit	30
Profit before taxes and minority	24
Taxes	9

Minority interests
developed as follows in 1993 (NOK million):

Minority interests at 01.01.	206
Minority interests' share of the year's result	15
Increase in connection with establishment of new subsidiaries	5
Reduction on further acquisition of shares in subsidiaries	(7)
Write-down of own shares in Oktav Invest (see Note 18)	(13)
Dividends to minority interests	(9)
Minority interests at 31.12.	197
Minority interests are divided between:	
Ringnes Poland	92
Nora Denmark	42
Bakers	37
Orkla Media group	11
Borregaard group	5
Miscellaneous minorities	10
Total	197

NOTE 16

Foreign currency and loans

Foreign currency loans 1993 (Amounts in thousands)

	Currency	NOK
USD	431,044	3,106,896
SEK	119,271	107,618
DEM	39,341	170,468
NLG	5,000	19,368
FRF	4,000	5,101
GBP	7,800	86,650
CHF	3,150	15,990
Total		3,512,091

In addition to the above loans two of the Group's Norwegian companies have loans totalling DKK 48.5 million from two of the Group's Danish companies.

Interest rate structure of the loan portfolio

The Group's loan portfolio of NOK 7,742 million has the following break-down of interest adjustment dates (including interest hedging instruments and current installments):

1994	1995	1996	1997	1998	After 1998
5,960	763	467	10	10	532

Special loan agreements

Orkla has loan agreements which state that Orkla may not, without approval from the lenders, sell shares in the following companies: Borregaard Industries, Denofa-Lilleborg, Nora and Ringnes.

Foreign currency positions (Amounts in million)

Foreign exchange transactions (forwards, swaps and options)

Purchase currency	Amount	Sale currency	Amount	Type
USD	310.0	NOK	2,247.0	Forward
USD	15.0	NOK	87.3	Swap
USD	15.0	DKK	101.8	Swap
USD	3.3	DKK	22.3	Forward
USD	60.3	SEK	473.9	Forward
DEM	8.2	NOK	36.1	Forward
DEM	9.0	FIM	30.2	Forward
GBP	1.3	USD	2.0	Forward
DKK	4.5	NOK	6.9	Forward
ITL	4,950.0	NOK	2.0	Forward
NOK	14.5	USD	2.2	Option
NOK	111.7	SEK	125.8	Forward
NOK	2.3	NLG	0.6	Forward
NOK	1.1	FRF	0.9	Forward
NOK	24.0	GBP	2.2	Forward
NOK	127.9	FIM	100.8	Forward
NOK	0.6	ATS	1.0	Forward
NOK	1.6	ESP	30.0	Forward

For foreign exchange transactions carried out to hedge loans the principal amount only is given even though the interest amount will normally be hedged. For this type of transaction the loan is booked at the spot rate and the forward premium accrued as interest.

The Group's interest-bearing debt by loan type and maturity

	Balance at		Repayment schedule				After
Amounts in NOK million	31.12.93	1994[1]	1995	1996	1997	1998	1998
Bank loans	4,344	834	807	521	859	1,296	27
Bearer bonds	2,217	203	503	503	3	2	1,003
Convertible bonds [2]	31	31	-	-	-	-	-
Mortgage companies	163	21	18	18	13	11	82
Insurance companies	286	9	8	7	7	7	248
Miscellaneous	74	14	10	2	1	7	40
Of which due within one year	(1,112)	(1,112)	-	-	-	-	-
Total long-term interest-bearing debt	6,003	-	1,346	1,051	883	1,323	1,400
Long-term debt due within one year	1,112						
Bank loans	348						
Commercial paper	200						
Miscellaneous	79						
Total short-term interest-bearing debt	1,739						
Total interest-bearing debt	7,742						

[1] The amounts are entered as short-term debt.
[2] Bondholders may convert the loan into shares during the period up to 1.12.1994 at a rate of NOK 14.00 per share. See Note 18 (Equity capital).

In December 1993, a NOK 500 million bond was issued with a fixed interest rate and with a 8.5 year term. Simultaneously an interest rate swap agreement was entered into under which Orkla will pay a floating interest rate for a corresponding amount and term. The payment date of the loan was 25 February 1994.

Orkla A.S has a group bank account system with Den norske Bank and Christiania Bank og Kreditkasse. The accounts of Orkla A.S are the only accounts directly settled with the banks and all subsidiaries' accounts are treated as internal. At 31.12.1993 the aggregate deposits were NOK 53 million, while the total drawing rights amounted to NOK 450 million.

NOTE 17

Long-term interest-free liabilities, etc.

Long-term interest-free liabilities include deposits on returnable containers (NOK 134 million), non-insured pension obligations [1] (NOK 471 million), deferred tax (NOK 537 million), and certain other minor items (NOK 35 million).

Deferred tax

Deferred tax is determined as follows:

Net positive time differences after possible set-offs relate to:

Amounts in NOK million	31.12.93	31.12.92
Short-term receivables	(56)	6
Shares	(363)	(510)
Inventories	43	46
Other short-term items	(16)	(74)
Total short-term items	(392)	(532)
Fixed assets	1,493	1,342
Pension premium fund	706	668
Other long-term items	155	440
Total long-term items	2,354	2,450
Losses carried forward	(58)	(1)
Basis for calculation of deferred tax	1,904	1,917
Deferred tax	**537**	**566**

Deferred tax allowances

Negative timing differences which cannot be set off:

Non-insured pension obligations	454	426
Other negative differences not set off	28	78
Basis for calculation of deferred tax allowances	482	504
Deferred tax allowances	**132**	**138**
Net deferred tax	**405**	**428**
Change in deferred tax	23	205
Purchase of new companies, conversion differences etc.	(14)	14
Gross associated companies (shown as change in deferred tax, but deducted from the investment)	(10)	(15)
Change in deferred tax profit and loss acc.	**(1)**	**204**

Calculation of the profit before taxes and the year's tax base for Norwegian taxes payable

Profit before taxes (Amounts in NOK million)	1,316
Addition for:	
Changes in timing differences	111
Group items and eliminations	48
Total	159
Deduction for:	
Permanent differences, dividends, etc.	(147)
Cost price regulated shares	(146)
Losses carried forward	(198)
Total	(491)
Deduction for:	
Foreign companies	(6)
Associated companies	(219)
Of which taxable	118
Total	(107)
Taxable income for Norwegian companies	877
Tax calculated on Norwegian activities (28%)	(245)

[1] Unsecured pension obligations are, due to the discounting effect, in principle interest-bearing. The interest element is not, however, shown as interest but included under wage costs. (In the same manner, the pension premium fund does not reduce net interest-bearing liabilities.)

NOTE 18

Changes in equity during 1993

Amounts in NOK million	Share capital	Legal reserve	Temporary restricted reserve	Free reserves	Orkla A.S	Group reserve	Group
Equity at 01.01.	1,219	565	132	1,410	3,326	2,511	5,837
Adjustment of reserves at 01.01.	-	2	7	(9)	-	-	-
Cash consideration Peter Möller	-	(9)	-	(6)	(15)	-	(15)
Result for the year Orkla A.S	-	-	-	8	8	-	-
Group transfer received	-	-	-	818	818	(8)	-
Allocation to dividend	-	-	-	(192)	(192)	(818)	-
Allocation to legal reserve	-	15	-	(15)	-	-	(192)
Transferred to free reserves	-	-	(36)	36	-	-	-
Group profit	-	-	-	-	-	984	984
Write-down of treasury shares in Oktav Invest	-	-	-	-	-	(28)	(28)
Translation differences, foreign subsidiaries etc.	-	-	-	-	-	(13)	(13)
Total	1,219	573	103	2,050	3,945	2,628	6,573

Share capital history

Amounts in NOK million Date/year	Number of shares	Par value	Type of issue	Amount	Ratio	Correction factor [1]	Issue price	Share capital
31.12.1987	7,216,997	100				5.32		721.7
1988	14,433,994	50	split		2:1	2.42		721.7
1988	15,558,110	50	bonus issue	56.2	1:10	2.42		777.9
1988	12,365,274	50	amortization	159.6		2.42		618.3
31.12.1988	12,365,349	50	conversion			2.42		618.3
1989	13,275,874	50	internat. offering	45.5		2.42	365.00	663.8
31.12.1989	13,339,097	50	conversion	3.2		2.42		667.0
1990	26,678,194	25	split		2:1	1.10		667.0
1990	29,346,582	25	bonus issue	66.7	1:10	1.10		733.7
1990	31,646,582	25	internat. offering	57.5		1.10	230.00	791.2
1990	31,886,582	25	merger	6.0		1.10		797.2
31.12.1990	31,894,938	25	conversion	0.1		1.10		797.4
1991	44,314,828	25	merger	310.5		1.10		1,107.9
31.12.1991	44,314,895	25	conversion			1.10		1,107.9
1992	48,746,384	25	bonus issue	110.8	1:10			1,218.7
31.12.1992	48,746,384	25						1,218.7
31.12.1993	48,747,241	25	conversion					1,218.7

[1] The correction factor is multiplied by the number of old shares to make these figures comparable to the number of shares in 1993.

At the 1993 Annual General Meeting the Board was authorised to issue up to 3.3 million new shares without preferential rights for existing shareholders. The authorisation remains in effect until the Annual General Meeting in 1995.

Treasury shares and convertible bonds

Amount in NOK 1,000	Par value	Number of shares	Book value	Interest (%)
Shares				
A/S Drammen Kjexfabrik	4,018	160,708	-	0.3
Rederi-A/S Orkla	4,183	167,319	-	0.3
A/S Meldalsskogen	-	14	-	-
Sætre AS	2	62	-	-
Oktav Invest A.S [3]	25,128	1,005,139	-	2.1
Total shares held in treasury	33,331	1,333,242	-	2.7
Convertible bonds				
A/S Drammen Kjexfabrik	30,097	2,149,785	132,423	
Orkla A.S	413	29,500	4,463	
Total convertible bonds held in treasury	30,510	2,179,285 [1]	136,886	99.7
Total	63,841	3,512,527 [3]	136,886	6.9

[1] Convertible bonds with a nominal value of NOK 30.5 million may be converted into shares at a rate of NOK 14.00 per share. The loan expires on 31.12.1994. An extension will be proposed at the Annual General Meeting.
[2] Members of management within the Group have been allotted options for convertible bonds and shares equivalent to 379,093 of the treasury shares.
[3] Shares of Orkla A.S recorded in Oktav Invest are in accordance with the Companies Act rules and are recorded at zero value. Oktav Invest owns 1,256,424 shares of Orkla A.S and Orkla owns 80% of Oktav Invest.

Share bonus to Group employees
The Board of Orkla Borregaard A.S approved a trial share bonus scheme for employees in May 1990. Due to extensive changes made by the authorities in the regulations for this type of scheme, the Board has decided not to continue the trial scheme. Instead it is proposed to allocate options with a value equivalent to 0.75 of one month's salary which will amount to approximately 600,000 B-shares (see note 2).

NOTE 19

Mortgages and guarantees

Amounts in NOK million	1993	1992
Liabilities secured by mortgages	426	690
Mortgaged assets:		
Machinery, vehicles, etc.	1,099	1,068
Buildings and plant	1,072	1,202
Other real estate	98	97
Construction in progress	189	119
Inventories, etc.	28	78
Total book value	2,486	2,564
Guarantees, etc.:		
Joint and several guarantees	57	58
Subscribed, uncalled limited partnership capital	130	130
Other guarantee liabilities [1]	162	125
Total guarantee liabilities	349	313

[1] Includes guarantee limits for activities within Financial Services of NOK 125 (90) million.

NOTE 20

Other commitments
Orkla A.S has sold options on an obligation to sell 39,000 shares in Nora Eiendom A.S in 1995 at NOK 115 per share.

Orkla A.S has an obligation, but not a right, to purchase further shares in Bakers AS. The option can be exercised between 31.12. 1994 and 30.01.1995. The option relates to 6,765 shares, equivalent to 28.6% of the company and the price amounts to NOK 96 million.

Scan TV A.S has issued options on an obligation to sell 2,167 shares in NetCom A.S at NOK 4,196 per share.

Nora A.S has an obligation to purchase further shares in Dragsbæk Margarinefabrik A.S (50%) and Dacapo A.S (49%) after 1 January 1994. The existing holdings were acquired in 1989 for approximately NOK 60 million. The price for additional shares will be based on indexation of this amount, adjusted for the development in earnings during the 3 years prior to the obligation/right being exercised.

REVISORS BERETNING TIL GENERALFORSAMLINGEN I ORKLA A.S

Vi har revidert årsoppgjøret for Orkla A.S for 1993 som viser et årsoverskudd på 8 mill. kroner for morselskapet og et årsoverskudd på 984 mill. kroner for konsernet. Årsoppgjøret, som består av årsberetning, resultatregnskap, balanse, kontantstrømanalyse, noter og konsernoppgjør, er avgitt av selskapets styre og konsernsjef.

Vår oppgave er å granske selskapets årsoppgjør, regnskaper og behandlingen av dets anliggender for øvrig.

Vi har utført revisjonen i henhold til gjeldende lover, forskrifter og god revisjonsskikk. Vi har gjennomført de revisjonshandlinger som vi har ansett nødvendige for å bekrefte at årsoppgjøret ikke inneholder vesentlige feil eller mangler. Vi har kontrollert utvalgte deler av grunnlagsmaterialet som underbygger regnskapspostene og vurdert de benyttede regnskapsprinsipper, de skjønnsmessige vurderinger som er foretatt av ledelsen, samt innhold og presentasjon av årsoppgjøret. I den grad det følger av god revisjonsskikk har vi gjennomgått selskapets formuesforvaltning og interne kontroll.

Styrets forslag til disponering av årets resultat og egenkapitaloverføringer tilfredsstiller de krav aksjeloven stiller.

Etter vår mening er årsoppgjøret gjort opp i samsvar med aksjelovens bestemmelser og gir et forsvarlig uttrykk for selskapets og konsernets økonomiske stilling pr. 31.12.1993 og for resultatet av virksomheten i regnskapsåret i overensstemmelse med god regnskapsskikk.

Oslo, 3. mars 1994
Arthur Andersen & Co.

Finn Berg Jacobsen
Statsautorisert revisor

AUDIT REPORT TO THE ANNUAL GENERAL MEETING OF ORKLA A.S

We have audited the annual accounts of Orkla A.S for 1993, showing profit of the year of NOK 8 million for Orkla A.S and profit for the year of NOK 984 million for the Orkla Group. The annual accounts, which consist of the Directors' report, profit and loss account, balance sheet, statement of cashflows, notes and the corresponding consolidated accounts, are the responsibility of the Board of Directors and the Group Chief Executive.

Our responsibility is to examine the company's annual accounts, its accounting records and the conduct of its affairs.

We have conducted our audit in accordance with applicable laws, regulations and generally accepted auditing standards. We have performed the auditing procedures we considered necessary to determine that the annual accounts are free of material errors or omissions. We have examined, on a test basis, the accounting mate-

rial supporting the financial statements, assessed the appropriateness of the accounting principles applied, the accounting estimates made by management and evaluated the overall presentation of the annual accounts. We have also evaluated the company's asset management and internal controls to the extent required by generally accepted auditing standards.

The allocation of profit for the year, as proposed by the Board of Directors, complies with the requirements of the Joint Stock Companies Act.

In our opinion. the annual accounts have been prepared in conformity with the Joint Stock Companies Act and present fairly the company's and the Group's financial positions as at 31 December 1993 and the result of the operations for the fiscal year in accordance with generally accepted accounting principles.

Oslo, 3 March 1994
Arthur Andersen & Co.

Finn Berg Jacobsen (sig.)
State Authorised Public Accountant (Norway)

STATEMENT FROM THE CORPORATE ASSEMBLY TO THE ANNUAL GENERAL MEETING OF ORKLA A.S

The Corporate Assembly of Orkla A.S has received the Board of Directors' proposed Profit and Loss account and Balance Sheet for 1993 for Orkla A.S and the Group and recommends that the Annual

General Meeting adopts the accounts and the proposal of the Board of Directors for the allocation of profit for 1993.

Lysaker, 16 March 1994
The Corporate Assembly of Orkla A.S

Øystein Eskeland (sig.)
Chairman of the Corporate Assembly

Sigvard Heurlin
Coopers & Lybrand AB, Stockholm, Sweden
Erling Peterssohn
Upsala University and Coopers & Lybrand AB, Stockholm, Sweden

1. Background

1.1 The Development of Company and Accounting Law

1.1.1 Company Law

The Royal Ordinance on limited companies of October 6, 1848, was the first law on limited companies in Sweden and the Nordic countries. Long before that law came into effect, however, Sweden had enterprises with a structure similar to that of limited companies. The actual predecessors of our present-day limited companies were the trading companies that came into existence during the seventeenth century. The most famous trading company was probably Tjaruhandelskompaniet, chartered in 1648. In an "audit report" from 1652, the "auditors" of this company expressed an opinion on both the accounts of the directors and the matter of discharge from liability. A Swedish law of 1734 contained stipulations concerning companies with joint and several liability of the shareholders. After its inception, limited companies were nevertheless incorporated both with and without royal charter.

The 1848 ordinance was clearly and strongly influenced by the French *code de commerce*. The ordinance was quite brief, containing only fifteen clauses. It prescribed royal sanction of articles of association, if the shareholders were to enjoy freedom from liability for the company's liabilities. The law did not, however, contain any direct prohibition against forming a limited company without the royal sanction.

The ordinance of 1848 was replaced by the Companies Act of June 28, 1895. The act included a number of rules concerning the payment, increase, and reduction of the share capital, legal reserves, distribution of profits, annual returns, audit, discharge from liability, liquidation, and damages payable by directors. According to the wording of the law, the income for the year had to be reported in the management report. It seems, however, that the concept of income was not quite clear, since the law did not include any rules on valuation. Studies of accounting practice toward the end of the nineteenth century indicate that Swedish companies at this time had started to apply the principle of lower of cost and market value in respect of current assets and had started to depreciate fixed assets. Regarding its content and system, this act seems to have been influenced by German rather than French legislation.

The act of 1895 was not long-lived. It was criticized for the insufficient protection it afforded against unsound corporate activities. Consequently, the act of 1910 contained several new features, for example, comprehensive rules regarding the publication of articles of incorporation, the contents of balance sheets, greater civil and criminal liability for the founders, the directors, and the auditors, the right of minority shareholders to appoint their own auditor to participate in the auditors' examination of a company's accounts, and the administration by its board of directors. In many respects the act was clearly influenced by German law. The impact of German legislation is evidenced by the preparatory work, where an account of the German law was given by far the most space.

When the fall of the Kreuger Group was investigated in the 1930s, the accounts of the group were found to be fraudulent. An undermined financial position had been concealed through the complex, international system of group companies. Shortcomings in the Companies Act were revealed, and the experience drawn from the Kreuger case thus played an important role in the preparatory work for a new Companies Act. The preparatory legislative work was initially carried out in consultation with the other Nordic countries. Because of the Second World War, however, this cooperation was interrupted. Thus, only Sweden issued a new Companies Act in 1944. In the act of 1944, the rules regarding the forms of incorporation and publicity on incorporation were made more stringent. In addition, rules on the limitation of distribution of dividends were introduced to protect creditors. The obligation of the board of directors and the managing director to submit annual reports was significantly enhanced. The rules requiring a parent company to prepare consolidated accounts were quite new. The position of the auditors in relation to the board and the majority shareholders was strengthened. The act also stipulated that large companies should be audited by an authorized public accountant. In other companies as well, a minority of the shareholders could demand that at least one auditor should be an authorized public accountant or a registered accountant. The voting rights of shares were restricted so that no share could have more than ten times the voting power of another share. The board's duty of disclosure at general meetings was also enlarged.

The act is characterized by its scope and detail. The Companies Act of 1944 was amended several times during the 30 years it was in force. The so-called law on public control signified considerable extension of public accountability. The new rules were introduced through an amendment to the law in 1950, in response to demands by the trade unions.

The Companies Act of 1944 was replaced by the present Companies Act of 1975. The preparatory work for this act was carried out in close cooperation with the other Nordic countries, which resulted in largely uniform companies acts in these countries during the 1970s.

In 1990 the government appointed a committee to review the Companies Act and propose necessary amendments with regard to the ongoing process of European integration. So far, a few amendments have been integrated into the law. The obstacles to foreign acquisitions of shares in Swedish companies have been removed. The requirement of a minimum share capital has been changed to 100,000 Swedish krona (Skr), that is, approximately ECU 14,000. There will also be two types of limited companies in Sweden in the future, with different requirements regarding, for example, disclosure of financial information. They will be called *private limited companies* and *public limited companies*. The committee is still working with, among other things, amendments to the rules on the responsibilities of the board of directors, the managing director, and the auditors, as well as the rules on merges between limited companies.

1.1.2 Accounting Law

The first Accounting Act became effective in 1855. It introduced the requirement for a book of first entry and an annual accounts book. The annual accounts book was to contain a balance sheet. The act did not, however, contain any rules on valuation. By contrast, the Accounting Act of 1929 did contain valuation rules. It is quite clear from the preparatory work (work documented in a written report supporting a bill to be tabled in parliament) that the purpose of these rules was to measure the profit of the business and not to establish the value of the company. However, rules for the valuation of assets and liabilities had been introduced in the Companies Act of 1910. There is a significant difference between the rules on valuation contained in these two acts regarding the valuation of current assets, where the Accounting Act permits deviation from the principle of lower of cost and market value. Behind the act of 1929 there was also the wish to enable creditors to assess the manner in which insolvent business people had carried on their business. At that time, however, there was no discussion of the accounts as a basis on which to determine a company's tax liability. The situation was quite different during the preparatory work preceding the Accounting Act of 1976.

An essential new feature in this act, as in the Companies Act of 1975, is the demand for increased disclosure in the case of understatement of assets in relation to the rules of the law, which are designed as rules of maximum valuation. As may be seen in Section 2.1, special models for income statements and balance sheets were developed to satisfy this demand for increased disclosure.

In summary, the Accounting Act contains general rules on the preparation of annual accounts, whereas the Companies Act contains special rules, thereby fulfilling a supplementary function in respect of accounting legislation.

1.2 The Development of the Accounting and Auditing Professions

For many years, the bylaws of limited companies in Sweden have made provisions for audits of the companies' accounts. The Companies Act of 1895 prescribed that the administration of the board of directors should be reviewed and that the company's accounts should be examined by one or more auditors. In those days, auditors were often people with business experience, but seldom did they have skill in accounting matters. During the early twentieth century, however, an accounting profession began to develop. An important event in the development of the profession was the action by the Stockholm Chamber of Commerce in 1912, when it adopted its first statutes for authorization of public accountants. One of the prerequisites for authorization of auditors was satisfied by the foundation of the Stockholm School of Economics in 1909, which offered a university education in business administration. In Sweden, chambers of commerce are private and regional organizations. Beginning in 1973 the government took over the task of authorizing public accountants. This is today handled by the Board of Commerce (*Kommerskollegium*), which also acts as a sanctioning body. The educational and experience qualifications for a person to become an authorized public accountant are briefly described below.

No special professional examinations are required, but all authorized public accountants must have a university degree in business administration, of which accounting, information technology, company law, and taxation are compulsory elements. To be granted a license, the authorized accountant must also have 5 years' practical experience, mainly with an authorized accounting firm. The license is valid for a 5-year period, after which a new application must be made.

An authorized public accountant is not allowed to carry out any activities that are incompatible with his or her professional duties as an independent auditor. Most authorized public accountants are members of the Swedish Institute of Authorized Public Accountants (*Foreningen Auktoriserade Revisorer*, FAR). All members of the Institute must comply with the Rules of Professional Ethics agreed to by the members of the Institute.

The Swedish Institute of Authorized Public Accountants was founded in 1923, its objects being to promote a high standard within the profession and to promote rational methods in auditing, accounting, and business organization within Swedish companies. The founder of the Institute, Oskar Sillén, acted as chairman for 18 years and, in this capacity, was also an innovator in the fields of auditing and accounting.

One of the FAR's most important tasks since the mid-1960s has been to prepare recommendations in accounting and auditing matters and professional ethics. During the past 20 years, the institute has also carried out an extensive training program, mainly in the form of basic audit training leading to authorization. Auditing is not offered as a subject at Swedish universities or schools of economics.

When the Accounting Act of 1976 came into being, a body of experts known as the Swedish Accounting Board (*Bokforingsnamuden*, BFN) was founded for the purpose of developing generally accepted accounting principles. The board, which is a state body, has been working alongside the FAR, focusing on accounting issues. In addition, the Federation of Swedish Industries (*Sveriges Industriforbund*, SI) and the Stockholm Chamber of Commerce have issued accounting recommendations relating to listed companies through the Industry and Commerce Stock Exchange Committee (*Naringslivets borskommitte*, NBK). In order to coordinate these activities, the Swedish Accounting Board, the Swedish Institute of Authorized Public Accountants, and the Federation of Swedish Industries together formed in 1989 a foundation and a body of experts, the Swedish Financial Accounting Standards Council (*Redovisningsradet*, RR) to develop and issue recommendations on financial reporting of public companies, replacing the FAR as a standard-setting body.

1.3 International Influence on Accounting and Auditing in Sweden

During the first half of the twentieth century, German accounting theorists such as Eugen Schmalenbach, Fritz Schmidt, and Ernst Walb exercised considerable influence over the subject of accounting at the two Swedish Schools of Economics, in Stockholm and Gothenburg.

Ernst Walb was the first professor of the subject at the Stockholm School of Economics. He was succeeded by Oskar Sillén, who was in an excellent position to carry on the German tradition, because of his earlier studies at the Cologne School of Economics, where Schmalenbach was teaching.

When the Gothenburg School of Economics appointed its first professor of business management and accounting a few decades later, Professor Mahlberg from Germany was chosen. After only a short time he was succeeded by Professor ter Vehn, who had studied in Frankfurt under Professor Schmidt. It may be added that well into the 1960s, the Schools of Economics in Stockholm and Gothenburg were the only ones to offer higher education and research in accounting.

To a limited extent, the American influence manifested itself during the 1940s, becoming increasingly evident during the 1960s. During that period, teaching and research at the Stockholm School of Economics were molded by Professor Sven-Erik Johansson. The influence of leading American accounting theorists, such as William A. Paton, Maurice Moonitz, Arthur L. Sprouse, Edgar O. Edwards, and Philip W. Bell became stronger, partly through literature, partly through research exchange. In Gothenburg, and later at the new seats of learning, teaching and research in the subject of accounting was to come under even stronger influence from the United States. Today the German influence on education is nearly nonexistent, if we disregard the heritage in Swedish legislation and doctrine.

International influence also reaches Swedish accounting practice through the standards that are set by Swedish bodies, especially the Swedish Financial Accounting Standards Council and, previously, the FAR. Other channels of influence are the Swedish multinationals and the international accounting firms. Another source of international influence on accounting practice in Sweden is the international financial market. Of relatively recent origin, this influence is growing in importance. Large Swedish companies that turn to U.S. stock markets for funds must adopt, in certain respects, U.S. GAAP in their reporting.

The main source of international influence on auditing practices in Sweden is the international accounting firms. Most large Swedish accounting firms cooperate with or are members of an international firm. Such cooperation involves exchange of staff, handbooks, manuals, and education programs.

As a member of the International Federation of Accountants (IFAC), the Swedish Institute (FAR) has committed itself to supporting IFAC's endeavors toward high and uniform professional ethical conduct among public accountants and also to work for the observance of the IFAC statements of guidance on ethics in Sweden, as far as this complies with Swedish law. IFAC's International Auditing Guidelines are incorporated (although not completely) into the auditing standards issued by the FAR, thereby influencing auditing practice.

1.4 Sources of Accounting Standards in Sweden

Generally accepted accounting principles in Sweden are derived from the following sources:

- The Swedish Accounting Act (*Bokforingslagen* 1976:125), which established general accounting requirements for private-sector entities

- The Swedish Companies Act (*Aktiebolagslagen* 1975:1385), which sets forth, among other things, accounting regulations for corporate annual reports, consolidated accounts, interim reports, appropriations and dividend distribution, and audit requirements

- Recommendations on Accounting Matters issued by the Swedish Institute of Authorized Public Accountants (FAR), which describe generally accepted accounting principles and interpret certain regulations in the Swedish Companies Act and the Swedish Accounting Act

- Recommendations on accounting matters issued by the Swedish Accounting Board (BFN). The BFN also prepares and issues general advice on accounting matters and the preparation of financial statements.

- Recommendations issued by the Business Community's Stock Exchange Committee (NBK) for Swedish quoted companies. The NBK was formed by the Stockholm Chamber of Commerce and the Swedish Federation of Industries (SI) to issue recommendations concerning information provided to the stock exchange by listed companies.

- During 1988, the BFN, FAR, and SI started negotiations to form an organization for issuing accounting standards. These negotiations resulted in a foundation for the development of generally accepted accounting principles and a council of experts, the Swedish Financial Accounting Standards Council (*Redovisningsrådet*), with the task of preparing and adopting accounting standards for public companies. The BFN, FAR, and SI shall no longer issue recommendations in the domain of the *Redovisningsrådet* (RR).

Generally accepted accounting principles in Sweden could also be described by reference to the accounting and reporting standards actually adopted by high quality public companies. Thus, not only formal sources of accounting standards, but also other current developments and trends give substance to the concept of Swedish GAAP.

2. The Form and Content of Published Financial Statements

2.1 The Form of Financial Statements

The income statement and balance sheet should be set out in the format required by law, as specified in the Swedish Accounting Act, Sections 18 and 19, respectively. Departures from the required format called for by the nature and extent of the business are permitted. Assets and liabilities are segregated between current and noncurrent items in the balance sheet. A noncurrent asset is defined as an asset intended for continuous use or possession by the entity. All other assets are current assets.

According to Swedish tax law, all extra deductions or provisions for tax purposes (tax appropriations or year-end provisions) should be reflected in the income statement in order to be allowed in computing taxable income. When this requirement was first implemented, accounting income and asset values became distorted. Therefore, an accounting model was developed in the 1960s, supported by the Stock Exchange Committee (NBK), which was unique for Sweden for many years but today is also used in other Scandinavian countries. The model, described in the following paragraph, is now prescribed in the Accounting Act.

All tax appropriations, many of which imply asset undervaluation, are reported in a certain segment of the income statement under the heading "appropriations" (sometimes called "allocations" or "year-end provisions"). The "true" before tax accounting income in a Swedish income statement is "income before appropriations and taxes" (sometimes called "income before allocations and tax(es)" or "income before year-end provisions and tax(es)"). To maintain the integrity of asset values in the balance sheet, assets are not reduced by the extra write-offs appearing under the tax appropriations heading in the income statement. Instead, the appropriations and the extra write-offs are reflected in the balance sheet as increases in untaxed reserves, similarly reported in a certain segment of the balance sheet. These reserves should be considered a mixture of equity and deferred tax. Beginning in 1991, and as an effect of a tax reform, the taxable proportion of these untaxed reserves have been around 30%. The reserves may not be used for dividend distribution until they have been carried back to income and included in taxable income.

2.2 The Content of Published Financial Statements

Under the Swedish Companies Act, limited companies are required to lay before their shareholders an annual report containing an administration report, a balance sheet, an income statement, and a statement of changes in financial position. Notes to financial statements are considered an integral part of the statements. A parent company shall also prepare, on a consolidated basis, an income statement, a balance sheet, and a statement of changes in financial position.

2.3 The Scope of Consolidated Financial Statements

The Swedish Company Act stipulates that where a company—directly or indirectly—holds more than half the votes attached to the shares of a Swedish or a foreign legal entity, the company is a parent company and the legal entity is a subsidiary. Furthermore, where a company exercises decisive influence over a legal entity, and a considerable share in its results, the company is a parent company and the legal entity a subsidiary.

Chapter 11 of the Companies Act deals with reporting requirements, and Section 3.1 of this chapter in particular deals with consolidated financial statements. As indicated above, a parent company shall for each financial year prepare, in addition to its annual report, consolidated financial statements consisting of an income statement and a balance sheet. The consolidated financial statements should be prepared to the same date as the balance sheet of the parent company, and group members should have the same financial year, except in extraordinary circumstances.

The consolidated income statement and the consolidated balance sheet shall be a combination of the parent company's financial statements and those of its subsidiaries, prepared in conformity with generally accepted accounting principles in Sweden. Uniform accounting policies should be used for the transactions and other events in similar circumstances. Intercompany balances, dividends, and profits should be eliminated. The consolidated balance sheet should show the group's nonrestricted equity capital or accumulated loss after deduction of intercompany profits, a requirement that is unique to Sweden.

Minority interests should be presented separately in the consolidated balance sheet and the consolidated income statement.

A subsidiary should be excluded from consolidation when control is intended to be temporary. In this case and in such other rare cases when consolidated financial statements are not prepared because difficulties are encountered, the reasons should be stated in the administration report of the parent company.

The methods and valuation principles used in the preparation of the consolidated financial statements should be described in the annual report. In addition, the amount that, according to the annual reports of the group enterprises, should be transferred from the nonrestricted equity capital of the group to the restricted equity capital, should be stated.

As described in Section 3.1 below, the purchase method, the pooling of interest method, and equity accounting are used for the preparation of consolidated financial statements.

2.4 Segmental Disclosure

There are no explicit requirements by law to disclose segmental information. However, BFN has issued a recommendation in this area, effective from January 1991. According to this recommendation, a company and a group of companies should disclose income before depreciation for each independent industry segment. If depreciation could be fairly allocated between industry segments, income after depreciation should be disclosed. Public companies should also disclose the value of their assets employed in each industry segment. Disclosure of information on revenue, income, and assets for geographic areas in agreement with IAS 14 is also recommended for public companies.

2.5 Status of Form and Content

From a regulatory point of view the Swedish standard-setting system is a combination of a system with certain requirements prescribed by law (basic form and content of financial statements, as well as certain valuation principles and certain disclosures) and a self-regulation system (accounting principles and disclosures).

There is no precise legal status of the recommendations and the pronouncements developed under the self-regulation system.

3. Accounting Principles and Practices in Valuation and Income Measurement

3.1 Group Accounts—Methods of Consolidation

3.1.1 Purchase Method

Normally a corporate combination is regarded as a true purchase, and the purchase method for consolidation should be applied.

Under the purchase method, the buyer accounts for the cost of an acquisition as an indirect acquisition of the net assets of the subsidiary. Assets and liabilities thus acquired are restated to their fair value at the date of acquisition. Fair value adjustments are allowed up to 12 months after the date of acquisition.

A positive difference between the purchase price of the shares and the fair value of the net assets is classified as goodwill arising on acquisition. According to the RR Standard on Consolidated Financial Statements, goodwill is an asset to be depreciated over its useful life, which should not exceed 10 years unless a longer period is justified. The amortization period must not, however, exceed 20 years in any case.

When the cost of acquisition is less than the acquirer's interest in the fair values of the assets and liabilities acquired, the fair values of the nonmonetary assets acquired should be reduced proportionally. Alternatively, the negative difference is classified as a long-term liability to be recognized as income on a systematic basis, reflecting the estimated performance of the subsidiary at the date of acquisition.

Although not generally applicable in Swedish accounting, deferred taxes should, when applicable, be provided for in the consolidated financial statements, reflecting temporary differences under the liability method. Discounting is generally not allowed.

3.1.2 Pooling of Interest Method

The pooling of interest method should be applied when the shareholders of previously independent companies decide to unite their interests. One prerequisite is that none of the companies could be defined as an acquirer, or as a dominating party in the transaction.

A number of criteria should be met to justify the pooling of interests method, relating to independence, continuation of ownership, and continuation of the uniting companies' businesses.

Under the pooling of interests method, the values of the assets and liabilities of the acquired company are not adjusted but are retained at the amounts as recorded in the company's balance sheet. The difference between the cost of the shares acquired and the subsidiary's underlying equity does not need to be determined; the cost of the shares acquired will be eliminated against the corresponding amount of the subsidiary's equity. Through the RR Standard on Consolidated Financial Statements, the earlier practice of frequently using the pooling of interest method has been discontinued.

3.1.3 Proportional Consolidation Method

FAR recommends the proportional consolidation method of accounting for an investment in a jointly controlled entity as the benchmark treatment, with the equity method as an allowed alternative.

3.1.4 Equity Accounting

An entity is defined as an associated company to another company (the investor) if the investor holds shares in the entity to the extent that it controls 20% or more, but less than 50%, of the voting power.

Equity financial information is not to be included in the individual balance sheet and income statement of the investor. Such a treatment does not comply with the Swedish Accounting Act. In 1986, however, the FAR issued an exposure draft dealing with investments in associated companies, according to which equity accounting may be used in consolidated financial statements only. The draft has been increasingly applied in practice. An important requirement of the exposure draft deals with the equity in an associated company's undistributed earnings, which must be classified as restricted (nondistributable) consolidated equity. The exposure draft represents, in fact, a departure from a fundamental principle, that is, that the same approach should be applied in the preparation of consolidated financial statements as in the preparation of a single entity's financial statements.

Goodwill arising on equity participations is amortized in the same manner as under the purchase method.

3.2 Foreign Currency Translation

3.2.1 *Translation of the Financial Statements of Foreign Subsidiaries*

The Swedish Companies Act does not specifically regulate how to translate foreign subsidiaries' financial statements for the purpose of consolidation. As a consequence, accounting practice in this area may not have been uniform. In an exposure draft issued by the FAR in the mid-1980s, however, a basis for a uniform accounting treatment has been established. This draft has today reached the status of a proposed but not yet definitive recommendation. It introduced into accounting in Sweden the same view as FAS-52 did in the United States at the beginning of the 1980s, a view that is consistent with IAS 21. The proposed recommendation, accordingly, differentiates between "independent" and "integrated" foreign operations. Where a foreign subsidiary is independent, assets and liabilities of the subsidiary should be translated by using the current rate method (sometimes called the closing rate method). Income statement items should be translated at the exchange rates at the dates of the transactions. If the effects are not material, income statement items may be translated at the current rate. Translation differences should be taken directly to equity, separately disclosed in a note describing changes in consolidated equity.

When a foreign operation is integrated with the reporting company, its financial statements should be translated by using the temporal method and resulting exchange differences arising from translation of monetary items should be included as other exchange gains and losses in the consolidated income statement.

Subsidiaries in countries with particularly high inflation rates (e.g., greater than 25%) raise special problems. Translation of their financial statements by the current rate method usually results in an incorrect description of their financial position and their result of operations. In such cases, even financial statements of independent subsidiaries should be translated by use of the temporal method (or the monetary-nonmonetary method, which, according to a footnote to the applicable FAR recommendation, is another expression of the same method). Alternatively, inflation-adjusted financial statements may be translated by the current rate method.

Exchange differences arising on noncurrent intercompany monetary items that are in effect an extension to or a deduction from a parent's net investment in a foreign subsidiary should be taken to equity. Similarly, if foreign currency loans are designated as, and provide, an effective hedge against a net investment in a foreign subsidiary, exchange differences on the loans may be taken to equity, to the extent that they are covered by exchange differences arising on the net investment.

The Swedish Companies Act requires that the consolidated balance sheet disclose the amount of unrestricted equity or the accumulated deficit of the group after deduction of internal profits. Therefore, it is necessary to split accumulated translation differences between restricted and unrestricted equity or accumulated deficit.

3.2.2 Translation of Foreign Currency Denominated Assets and Liabilities

There are no explicit rules in the Swedish Accounting Act for valuation of receivables and payables denominated in foreign currencies. General rules for the valuation of assets and liabilities have been applied but without uniformity. At the beginning of the 1980s FAR issued an exposure draft on the valuation of receivables and payables denominated in foreign currencies. The exposure draft became a temporary standard and formed a basis for accounting practice development up to and including 1989. In 1989 BFN issued a recommendation on valuation of receivables and payables denominated in foreign currencies, effective from January 1990.

According to the BFN recommendation, receivables and payables denominated in foreign currency should be reported in the balance sheet at the closing rates. The difference between the historical rates (or the closing rates at the previous balance sheet date) and the closing rates should be recorded as a gain or loss in the period in which the exchange rates change. However, unrealized exchange gains arising from long-term receivables and payables should be taken to an untaxed currency reserve in the balance sheet.

If a receivable or a payable denominated in foreign currency is effectively hedged, a change in the currency rate should have no effect on the value of the item in the balance sheet. A transaction should be classified as a hedge only when the intention to hedge was present at the time of entering into the hedging transaction. If the hedge is a foreign currency forward contract, the spot rate at the date of inception of the forward contract should be used for valuation of the underlying receivable or payable.

The discount or premium on a forward contract should be recognized in income over the life of the contract. Other forms of hedging, which are effective hedges as forward contracts, should be treated in the same manner as a forward contract.

3.3 Capital and Reserves

3.3.1 General

Equity is accounted for in somewhat different ways in private firms, partnerships, and limited companies. This review concentrates on limited companies. Shareholders' equity is generally divided between two sub-headings: restricted equity and nonrestricted equity or accumulated deficit. Restricted equity includes share capital, legal reserve, and revaluation reserve. Nonrestricted equity includes nonrestricted reserves (each disclosed separately), retained earnings brought forward, and net income for the year.

3.3.2 Share Capital

Where a company's share capital is divided into several classes of shares, the amount of each class should be disclosed. The number of shares and the face value of each share should also be reported.

Holdings of the company's own shares are generally not permitted, except for interim periods. Any such holdings should be entered as assets having no value, but their aggregated face value should be disclosed, preferably on the balance sheet.

All changes since the preceding balance sheet in the amounts specified under various equity headings should be specified in a note to the balance sheet.

In accordance with the Swedish Companies Act, the regulations of the disclosure of a single entity's equity shall also apply to consolidated accounts, where appropriate.

3.3.3 Restricted Reserves

Two kinds of restricted reserves may appear in a limited company's balance sheet: the statutory reserve and the revaluation reserve.

The Statutory Reserve The following allocations should be made to the statutory reserve:

1. At least 10% of the net income for the year after deduction of any deficit brought forward. Such allocation must continue until the reserve equals 20% of the share capital.
2. Any amount received in excess of the nominal amount at issue of shares
3. Any amount paid by a person whose shares have been declared forfeited
4. Any amount according to the articles of association or approved by the general meeting

The reduction of the statutory reserve requires a decision at the general meeting and may be made for only the following purposes:

1. To cover losses that cannot be covered by nonrestricted equity
2. To increase the share capital through a bonus issue
3. For any other purpose, provided that the court has given consent

The Revaluation Reserve The revaluation reserve arises as a result of the revaluation of noncurrent assets. It may be used only for a necessary write-down of the value of noncurrent assets or for a bonus issue or to cover a deficit—appearing in a balance sheet adopted by the general meeting—provided that the loss cannot be covered by available unrestricted equity.

A decision to use the revaluation reserve to cover a deficit requires consultation with the auditors. Such a decision prevents the company from declaring a dividend for a period of 3 years, in case the share capital is not increased by an amount at least equal to the deficit covered by the revaluation reserve or if the court has not given consent.

3.3.4 Nonrestricted Reserves

Each nonrestricted reserve should be disclosed separately. Such reserves include retained earnings brought forward (losses to be shown as deductions) and net income for the current financial year (a loss to be shown as a deduction).

3.3.5 Distribution Restrictions

Dividends to the shareholders may not exceed the amount that is distributable according to the adopted balance sheet and, regarding a parent company, according to the consolidated balance sheet. The distributable amount includes the net income for the year, retained earnings brought forward, and nonrestricted reserves less reported losses, less the amount that according to the Companies Act or articles of association shall be allocated to restricted equity, and finally, less the amount that according to the articles of association shall otherwise be used for a purpose other than dividends to the shareholders.

Dividends may not be distributed to such an extent that—in the light of the company's or the group's consolidation needs, cash needs, or financial position in other respects—the distribution would be contrary to good business practice.

The general meeting may not declare a dividend that is higher than the dividend proposed or approved by the board of directors, unless otherwise provided in the articles of association.

A company may not grant cash loans to a person who owns shares in the company or who is a member of the board or managing director of the company or of another entity in the same group. The same rule shall apply to persons who are relatives to or are otherwise closely related to a shareholder, to a member of the board, or to the managing director of the company.

3.3.6 *Untaxed Reserves*

Untaxed reserves are the result of tax appropriations. All tax appropriations, some of which imply asset undervaluation, are reported in a certain segment of the income statement. These appropriations are taken directly to the credit of the balance sheet as increases in untaxed reserves. These reserves should be considered a mixture of equity and deferred tax. Since 1991 the tax proportion has been around 30%. Untaxed reserves may not be used directly for dividend distribution. In that case, they will have to be carried back to the income statement and included in the taxable income. Examples of untaxed reserves are inventory reserve, investment reserves, accumulated excess depreciation, and, since 1991, the tax equalization reserve. Most of these untaxed reserves will gradually disappear as a result of recent changes in the tax laws. However, accumulated excess depreciation, together with a new tax appropriation, will appear in the accounts for the future.

The practice described above is not used any longer in group accounts as a result of the RR Standard on Consolidated Financial Statements, effective from January 1992.

3.4 Liabilities and Provisions

3.4.1 *Current Liabilities*

Current liabilities should include amounts payable within one year from the date of the balance sheet. The concept of "normal operating cycle" is not used in Sweden for segregation between current and noncurrent receivables and liabilities. Instead, the one-year rule is the valid criterion for classification purposes. Current liabilities should be segregated among bills payable, trade credits, taxes payable, accrued liabilities and deferred revenues, advances from customers, and other current liabilities. Payables to subsidiary and parent entities should also be disclosed in the balance sheet.

Commitments such as purchase orders or other kinds of contractual obligations do not qualify as liabilities until the corresponding services have been performed. Contingencies are accounted for as liabilities only when they become probable.

3.4.2 Long-Term Debt

The most common forms of long-term debt in Sweden are debentures, bonds, mortgages, and other long-term bank credit. The general accounting treatment applied to these items is basically the same as for current liabilities, that is, they are carried in the balance sheet at their face value.

As with current liabilities, long-term debt must be segregated on the face of the balance sheet between debentures, bonds, bank overdrafts, construction credits, other long-term liabilities, and pension provisions. Long-term payables to subsidiary and parent companies should also be disclosed in the balance sheet.

If a company has raised loans by issuing convertible bonds or bonds containing an option to subscribe to new shares, the amount not yet converted and the time and conditions for conversion or subscription should be disclosed for each loan. Regarding participating debentures, the amount still outstanding and the interest provisions should be disclosed.

3.4.3 Contingencies

A contingent liability is defined as an obligation that may arise dependent upon one or more future events that have some probability of occurrence. The accounting treatment of contingencies depends on the probability of occurrence of the future event that will determine the contingency. If the probability is high, the contingencies should be included among liabilities.

Except for the Accounting Act, there is no accounting standard dealing with contingencies in Sweden. The Accounting Act requires that contingent liabilities be disclosed under the headings (*a*) discounted bills, (*b*) guarantees and other contingent liabilities, and (*c*) pension obligations that are not reported as a liability or covered by the assets of a pension fund. Contingencies are disclosed as memorandum items at the bottom of the balance sheet.

3.4.4 Provisions

General provisions are not permitted, as a provision must relate to a specific existing obligation. Provisions for future expenses or losses are not permitted unless the circumstances giving rise to such an expense have occurred.

Provisions for future expenses relating to warranties may be recognized at the point of sale of the item under warranty.

3.4.5 Untaxed Reserves—Deferred Tax

As mentioned in Section 3.3, untaxed reserves should be considered a mixture of equity and deferred tax. The deferred tax portion is not disclosed in the single-entity balance sheet. According to the RR Standard on Consolidated Financial Statements, however, untaxed reserves should be allocated between tax liability and an equity portion in the balance sheet of the group.

3.5 Property, Plant, and Equipment

Expenditures on capital assets, which result in an enduring improvement of the asset and thereby in an increase in its value, may be capitalized as a part of the cost of the asset. Expenditures to maintain normal operating efficiency should be expensed.

3.5.1 Basis of Valuation

Fixed assets should not be carried at a value higher than cost. For exceptions, see Section 3.5.4.

Fixed assets, which continuously decline in value with age, use, or other comparable causes, shall be subject to annual depreciation at least by an amount corresponding to an appropriate depreciation plan, unless it is obvious that sufficient depreciation has already been made in previous years.

Where the value of a fixed asset has permanently declined, a write-down shall be made as required by generally accepted accounting principles.

3.5.2 Depreciation

As Cost Allocation The Swedish Accounting Act requires fixed assets to be depreciated according to "an appropriate depreciation plan." According to the FAR's recommendations on accounting for tangibles, such a plan should be based on the historical cost concept, an estimation of the useful life of the asset, and an allocation method. The most commonly used method is the straight-line method. However, any method consistently applied that produces a reasonable and systematic allocation over the asset's useful life is acceptable.

As Tax Allowances According to Swedish tax law, companies are allowed to apply a depreciation schedule that implies that machinery and equipment are depreciated in total during a period of 5 years. Companies may choose between an accelerated and a straight-line profile. For many kinds of machinery and equipment, this means an accelerated rate of depreciation compared with "an appropriate depreciation plan." The difference—"the excess depreciation over and above depreciation according to plan"—is disclosed as an appropriation in the single-entity income statement. This tax appropriation will not, however, appear in the income statement of the group.

3.5.3 Disclosure

The accounting policies adopted in relation to valuation and depreciation of fixed assets must be disclosed. Details of cost, accumulated depreciation, and book value of each class of assets must be disclosed in notes to the balance sheet. If any fixed asset is carried at an appraised value, it must be shown. The income statement should disclose the amount of depreciation charged for the accounting period. Details for each class of assets should be presented in notes to the income statement in a way that is consistent with the notes to the balance sheet.

3.5.4 Revaluation

A fixed asset that has an enduring value substantially in excess of the amount at which it was carried in the preceding balance sheet may be revalued at an amount not in excess of that enduring value, provided that the amount of revaluation is used for a necessary write-down of the value of other fixed assets and provided that there are particular reasons for such a compensating adjustment. Real estate assessed for taxation purposes may, however, not be revalued above the tax assessment value.

In limited companies the amount of revaluation of fixed assets may also be used for issuing bonus shares or for appropriation to a revaluation reserve (part of restricted equity).

If an entity chooses to revalue its fixed assets upward, the depreciation should then be applied to the basis of the revalued amount.

3.5.5 Tax Appropriation in the Single-Entity Income Statement

Most tax appropriations, many of which imply asset undervaluation, are reported in a certain segment of the income statement. When one is looking for the "true" before-tax accounting income in a Swedish single-entity income statement, one should look for "income before tax appropriations." In order to maintain the information content of the asset values in the balance sheet, these are not reduced by such extra write-offs, classified as tax appropriations in the income statement. Instead, the appropriations and the extra write-offs are taken directly to the credit of the balance sheet as increases in untaxed reserves. This practice is applied to the single-entity accounts only. No tax appropriations are shown in the group accounts (see Section 3.4.5).

3.5.6 Accounting for Government Grants

BFN has issued a recommendation on accounting for government grants and assistance, effective beginning in 1989. The BFN recommendation is in accordance with the principles of IAS No. 20, "Accounting for Government Grants and Disclosure of Government Assistance." Government assistance should be reported in the income statement under the same heading as the expenses that it is supposed to cover and in a consistent manner from period to period.

The cost of the fixed asset should be reduced by the amount of the government grant. The net cost is the basis for depreciation. Consistent with IAS 20, the gross value of the asset and the amount of the grant should be disclosed in a note to the financial statements.

The accounting policy in relation to government grants and assistance shall be disclosed, if material. Benefits or commitments that will remain for several periods in the future should be continually disclosed. The effect on the company's result and financial position from government assistance should be recognized in multiperiod highlights.

3.5.7 Capitalized Interest Costs

According to FAR's Recommendation No. 3 on accounting for tangible assets, it is acceptable to capitalize interest as a part of the cost of construction of assets and machinery during the construction and installation period. It is only the paid-out interest that can be capitalized. Computed interest on the entity's equity should not be capitalized at all. According to RR's Standard on Inventories, interest cost should be capitalized if the storage period constitutes a significant part of the production process (e.g., when producing wine or cheese).

3.6 Leases

Neither the Swedish Accounting Act nor the Swedish Companies Act regulates accounting for leasing agreements. The only Swedish standard-setter that, so far, has dealt with leasing is FAR Recommendation No. 7. However, this recommendation departs considerably from international accounting standards, that is, IAS No. 17 and FAS-13.

3.6.1 Capital Leases

When the lease contract includes an obligation for the lessee to acquire the ownership rights to the leased object after a specific period and at terms agreed on, the lease contract should be recognized as a fixed asset in the lessee's balance sheet. The remaining lease payments should be recognized as liabilities and the leased object should be reported among pledged assets at net book value. The lessor should report a financial asset.

3.6.2 Operating Leases

When the lease contract does not include an obligation—but possibly a right—to acquire the object after a specific period, it is not necessary for the lessee to recognize the contract in the balance sheet. If a significant proportion of the fixed assets used, other than such buildings, which it is normal for the user not to own, are available as a result of leasing agreements, these circumstances should be disclosed in the administration report or in a note to the balance sheet, together with details about their cost price and the remaining lease expenditures. In this connection, details should be given of an approximate cost value as well as the remaining leasing costs for such assets, analyzed by year of payment.

If a leasing agreement implies a lower depreciation rate than is acceptable, the shortfall shall be disclosed as a liability for release toward the end of the term of the lease.

Where the amount is material, the management report or the notes to the financial statement shall include disclosure of the approximate effect on net income and on the balance sheet resulting from the leasing agreement, implying a faster rate of depreciation than the lessee company applies to assets of a similar type, which it owns.

3.6.3 *Lessor's Accounts*

Regarding the lessor, in the case of operating leases the leased asset should be separately reported in the balance sheet if the leasing activities are significant in relation to the total operation of the lessor company.

3.6.4 *Sale and Leaseback*

Sale and leaseback involves the owner of an asset selling it to a buyer, who then leases the asset back to the original owner.

Certain sale and leaseback transactions cannot be reported as normal sales of fixed assets by the selling company without presenting an incorrect picture of the true nature of the transaction. In such cases the FAR has issued a proposed recommendation that the following should apply:

1. When the sale price is considered to exceed the open market price, and future lease expenses are consequently considered to exceed market rates, the excess of the sale price over market value shall be deferred and released to income over the contracted lease period.

2. If the lease agreement is considered to have no value for future operations, the entire cost thereof shall be provided for in the balance sheet.

3. If the agreement is so constructed that the asset automatically reverts to the seller at the termination of the agreement, or that the seller is obliged to repurchase the asset on predetermined conditions, no transfer of the asset can be considered to have occurred. In such cases, there is no reason to exclude the asset from the original owner's balance sheet. The amount received should then be reported as a loan payable and the book value of the asset in question as a pledged asset.

Disclosure of the asset's value and of the remaining lease payments in sale and leaseback transactions shall be made in the same way as in ordinary lease agreements.

In sale and leaseback situations, it is essential that the selling company disclose the accounting principles applied. When the book gain on a sale and leaseback transaction is taken to income, it is appropriate that there be disclosure in the notes of the fact that it is a question of a gain on the sale of an asset that has been leased back.

3.6.5 Recent Developments

The RR has indicated that a draft Standard on Leases is in progress, which will follow IAS 17 in all material respects.

3.7 Extractive Operations

In order to unify accounting practices in mining, BFN has recently issued a recommendation according to which the expenditure for the acquisition of the actual deposit and expenditure for underground work on plant/facilities (such as roads, galleries, shafts, and inclined drifts) to be used for a period exceeding one year should be capitalized. Expenditure for plant/facilities to be used for a maximum of one year should be treated as current expenses. The expenses that are capitalized should be included in a depreciation plan and should be the subject of annual depreciation. The amount of depreciation should be based on the value of the extraction made (depletion). It should be kept in mind, however, that there is no alternative use for a mine in the event of a planned or ongoing extraction becoming unprofitable. Because of this circumstance, special attention must be paid to the need for a lump-sum write-down pursuant to Section 15 of the Accounting Act.

3.8 Intangible Assets

Where the entity has acquired a business for a consideration that exceeds the value of the acquired assets, the difference may be recognized as a fixed asset to the extent that it represents goodwill. This asset shall be amortized annually by an appropriate amount, at least one-tenth.

Expenditures for technical assistance, research and development, trial runs, market research, and similar activities may be recognized as fixed assets, provided that the expenditures are of material value for the entity during future years. Such assets shall be amortized annually by an appropriate amount, at least one-fifth, unless on account of special circumstances amortization at a lower rate may be considered to be in accordance with generally accepted accounting principles.

Until 1989 there was a lack of uniformity in Sweden regarding reporting practice in the research and development field. Therefore, BFN issued a recommendation on Accounting for Research and Development, with the aim of harmonizing with international accounting practice. This recommendation is in conformity with IAS 9. The general rule is that research and development expenditures should be expensed as incurred unless the criteria set out below are satisfied:

1. The R&D project and expenditures attributed to it should be clearly defined.
2. The R&D project should have a certain application as its goal.
3. The product or process resulting from the R&D project should be intended for sale or internal use.
4. The expected revenue or cost savings as a result of the R&D project should be known with a reasonable probability.
5. There should be adequate resources to complete the R&D project.

Once capitalized, research and development cost must be amortized annually according to the rules stated in the Accounting Act, that is, at least one-fifth annually.

3.8.1 Disclosure

The financial statements—on the face or in notes—should disclose:

- The accounting policy concerning accounting for R&D
- The R&D expenditures expensed in the year and the amortization of R&D expenditures capitalized in previous years
- The R&D expenditures capitalized in total and the accumulated amortization applying to this asset

3.9 Investments in Associated Companies

An entity is defined as an associated company to another company (the investor) if the investor holds shares in the entity to the extent that it controls at least 20% but less than 50% of the voting power .

Equity financial information is not to be included in the balance sheet and income statement of the investor—such a treatment would not comply with the Swedish Accounting Act. However, in 1986 FAR issued an exposure draft dealing with investments in associated companies, according to which equity accounting may be applied in consolidated financial statements only.

In the parent or single company's account, the cost method of accounting is compulsory. However, equity accounting information should be disclosed on the face of the financial statements or in notes. The disclosure should include the investor's share of the associated entity's result after financial items and its share of untaxed reserves and equity.

3.10 Inventories and Work in Progress

3.10.1 Basis of Valuation for Inventories

Inventories should be carried at the lower of cost or fair value. Fair value is defined as net realizable value, but replacement cost, less allowance for obsolescence where appropriate, is permissible for raw materials and semifinished products. Net realizable value is the estimated proceeds from the sale of the inventory, less all further costs necessary for marketing, selling, and distribution to customers and an appropriate share of the entity's administration and storage costs, including interest expenses.

The FIFO method for determining cost should be applied according to the RR and is also prescribed by the tax law.

To determine the carrying amount of inventory, each item should be analyzed separately; where this is impracticable, similar items may be dealt with in aggregate.

3.10.2 Overhead and Interest Cost for Manufactured Inventories

When inventories are manufactured, cost should be determined by using absorption costing based on the entity's normal operating capacity. Cost relating to abnormal circumstances, such as idle facilities, should be excluded. Interest expenses during the production period may not be included, except when the storage period is a considerable part of the production process.

3.10.3 Long-term Contracts

Long-term construction and installation contracts are usually accounted for on the completed contract basis, but the percentage of completion method appears to be slowly gaining acceptance in practice. In the preparatory work of the Accounting Act, long-term contracts are used as an example of a situation in which a departure from the lower of cost or market concept is permissible. However, this deviation should be limited to companies that carry out a few large projects that take a long time to complete. The FAR's Recommendation No. 2 on work in progress permits the percentage of completion method to be used, provided the preparatory work requirements mentioned above are met and the revenue and the costs to complete the contract are determinable.

3.11 Extraordinary or Unusual Items

The RR has issued a Standard on Extraordinary Items, which includes disclosure requirements for comparative purposes, thereby replacing a previous FAR Recommendation on extraordinary items.

The new standard, which is effective January 1, 1994 has been modeled from IAS 8 and classifies virtually all items of income and expense as part of the ordinary activities of the enterprise. The standard has confirmed the profile of the previous FAR Recommendation, which, however, was not always adhered to in practice.

The disclosure requirements of the new standard relate to events and transactions that it is important to observe when the results of operations of an accounting period are compared with other accounting periods or with other entities.

3.12 Taxation

The Swedish corporate tax system was reformed effective from 1991. Additional changes have been made since. The main goal of reform was to reduce the tax rate and at the same time broaden the tax base, with the intention of diminishing the locking-in effects on capital. The new tax system does not contain tax appropriations in the income statement to inventory reserve and the investment reserves.

The basic tax depreciation rules for equipment, allowing depreciation of up to 30% of the remaining balance, continued in the reformed tax system. If this depreciation in a certain year is larger or smaller than the "depreciation according to plan," the difference should appear in the appropriation segment of the single-entity income statement.

Previously allowed untaxed reserves for inventory, work-in-progress, and the profit equalization reserve should be reversed and taxed on a gradual basis. The appropriation segment of the single-entity income statement will then be used for the reversal of untaxed reserves.

As reflected in Section 3.4.5, however, deferred tax accounting has been introduced in the consolidated accounts only, thereby creating income and equity concepts that are in line with dominating international practice.

3.13 Pensions

Pension plans in respect of white-collar employees are governed by nationwide union employer organization agreements. Mainly, two systems are used: one in which actuarially computed premiums are currently paid to an independent pension insurance company and another in which an independent organization computes the actual liability that must be provided for. Under this latter system, the liability must be reported in companies' balance sheets as a long-term liability.

The defined benefits provided for are a function of the employee's salary at each date of computation (balance sheet date). Overfunding is unlikely to occur, and in principle, neither should underfunding. Companies' obligations to pay pensions may be secured and represented by a separate but company-related pension foundation.

Pension expenses in respect of blue-collar employees, under state schemes, are financed by direct charges.

The Swedish Accounting Act requires that pension provisions be separately disclosed on the face of the balance sheet as a long-term liability. However, it is not compulsory to report all pension commitments in that way. It is an acceptable alternative to disclose the actuarially computed amount of such commitments as a contingent liability. This alternative treatment is used mainly in connection with older commitments, often made to the benefit of former owners. The amounts involved for such alternative treatments are usually relatively insignificant.

FAR's recommendation on accounting for pension liabilities and pension expenses requires companies to charge the actual pension expenses for the year to operating income. The effect of any extraordinary circumstances on the pension expenses should be reported as an extraordinary item.

3.14 Earnings per Share

The Companies Act does not require companies to disclose earnings per share. There are requirements regarding disclosure of the number of shares and their nominal value, which makes it possible for analysts to make their own computations. In 1983, however, the NBK issued a recommendation on the format of income statement and financial ratios containing a definition of earnings per share (EPS). The NBK recommended that EPS be disclosed, both including and excluding extraordinary items. The income base used in the computation is calculated by using a comprehensive tax expense for the year, that is, the current tax charge plus or minus changes in the deferred tax (EPS "after full tax"). As the deferred tax is sometimes regarded as irrelevant because of the almost permanent nature of the underlying untaxed reserves, EPS is often calculated by using only the current tax charge (EPS "after tax paid").

4. Expected Future Developments

Until the beginning of the 1980s, financial reporting in Sweden had developed with little influence from the ongoing internationalization and globalization of business in general. Financial accounting standards were based on the requirements of the Accounting Act and Companies Act and were further detailed in accounting recommendations mainly issued by FAR and by certain business associations, for example, the building and construction industry association. Gradually, BFN also took an interest in financial reporting. The system so designed was one of self-regulation that worked fairly well; recommendations issued were principally adhered to by the business community.

With the increasing globalization of capital markets, international influence became more significant. Certain differences between Swedish generally accepted accounting principles and standards generally applied on an international scene became more evident, for example, in the field of accounting for business combinations, in particular regarding the treatment of goodwill.

Mainly because of practice in the field of consolidated financial statements and of accounting for goodwill, it gradually became evident that the Swedish standard-setting system did not work satisfactorily and that there was a need for a change.

Against the above background, FAR, BFN, and the Swedish Federation of Industries decided to form a foundation for the development of good financial reporting standards in Sweden with a board and a council. The council, the Swedish Financial Accounting Standards Council (*Redovisngsrådet*, RR), is responsible for the standard-setting procedure and the preparation of new accounting standards. The council began its activities at the beginning of 1990, and its main objective is to issue accounting standards and to deal with accounting issues relating to listed companies. It is assumed that the standards also will be applied by other companies.

It is also assumed that the standards to be issued, although not enforce-able, will be accepted by the business community. So far this has proved to be true. The RR issued standards on the following topics in 1991–1993:

- Consolidated financial statements (1991)
- Inventories (1992)
- Receivables and payables with regard to special interest agreements and hidden interest compensations (1992)
- Extraordinary items including disclosure requirements for compara-tive purposes (1993)
- Change of accounting principle (1993)

In particular the standard on consolidated financial statements consti-tutes a change in certain respects of some of the practices established during the 1980s; the new Standard does not allow write-off of goodwill against equity. Generally, the standards issued by the RR are in line with IAS.

This ambition might conflict, in certain respects, with the effect of an agreement entered into with the EU and its member states about a Euro-pean Economic Area (EEA). The agreement includes a commitment to adapt parts of the Swedish accounting legislation to the Fourth, Seventh, and Eleventh EC directives and the EC accounting directives for banks and insurance companies.

Some of the suggested changes in legislation are discussed below.

4.1 True and Fair View

The concept of true and fair view will be introduced into Swedish account-ing legislation through the adaptation to the EC directives. The Swedish Accounting Law Committee has pointed out that the concept of true and fair view has become part of the EU legislation and that it cannot be interpreted from the point of view of only British legislation or accounting practices, where it originated.

The committee has also noted that it has not been possible to define the precise meaning of the concept in terms of EU law. According to the committee, annual accounts prepared in accordance with existing law and taking into account applicable recommendations and standards from national and international authoritative bodies should, in most cases, give a true and fair view of a company's financial position and results of operations.

4.2 Group Companies

The Accounting Act, as proposed by the Committee, contains a slightly new definition of a group. Compared with existing law, the suggested definition includes the new criterion that a consortium agreement can form the basis of a group relationship. Also, it has been proposed that the current requirement that a parent company have a considerable share in the results of a subsidiary's business be abolished.

4.3 Associated Companies

The committee suggests that a definition of associated companies be included in the act. Companies are regarded as associated companies if one company holds at least 20% of the votes of another company, which is not a subsidiary, and has a significant influence over that company. This definition complies with current Swedish and international accounting practice. When accounting for associated companies, the committee proposes that the equity method may be used in the annual accounts for each legal entity, but the method *must* be used in the consolidated accounts.

4.4 Display

The directive opens the possibility of introducing two different displays for the balance sheet and four for the income statement. In order to increase the comparability between the annual accounts of different companies, the committee has decided to propose only one display for the balance sheet and the income statement, respectively.

The display for balance sheets chosen from the fourth directive by the Committee differs from the current one as shown in the Swedish Accounting Act inasmuch as the order of liquidity has been reversed, that is, the most easily realizable assets and the liabilities with the earliest maturity date have been placed at the bottom of the balance sheet. Furthermore, the proposal implies that the liabilities that today are disclosed as creditors shall be shown as creditors and provisions. A provision is characterized by the fact that there is some degree of uncertainty regarding the amount and/ or the maturity date.

Two reserves, namely the share premium account and equity method reserve, have been added under equity. The former reserve consists of amounts received as premium on issuing new shares, now included in the legal reserve according to the Swedish Companies Act. When shares or participations in companies accounted for in accordance with the equity method are revalued, these amounts must be transferred to the equity method reserve.

With regard to the income statement, the committee proposes a split of costs by type of function and not by type of expense. As a consequence, depreciation will no longer be disclosed separately in the income statement.

4.5 Change in Accounting Principles

The committee proposes that in those cases in which a company changes its accounting principles, the prior-year figures must be adjusted to make them consistent with the figures for the current year, which is well in line with international practice in this area. It previously has been seen as doubtful if such adjustment—when it results in assets being valued at a higher value than in the previous year's balance sheet—is in accordance with the general ban on upward revaluation of current assets according to the current Swedish Accounting Act. The proposal is considered to be within the scope of the Fourth EU Directive.

4.6 Deferred Tax

According to the committee, it would be most consistent with the requirement for a true and fair view and also with the structure of the EC directives if the accounts were unaffected by tax considerations. Depreciation charged and provisions made purely for tax purposes should therefore not be accounted for in the income statement and the balance sheet but only in the company's tax returns. It would, from a general accounting point of view, be an advantage if the system with untaxed reserves and appropriations to such reserves would be abolished and replaced by accounting for deferred tax. The committee, however, consistent with its own arguments, has refrained from giving a proposal.

4.7 Valuation Rules

The valuation rules in the fourth directive are not materially different from the corresponding current Swedish rules. Some of the accounting practices discussed by the RR, however, such as mark-to-market for marketable securities and percentage of completion for construction contracts, contemplated to be introduced in forthcoming standards in line with IAS do not seem to be in agreement with the committee's proposal.

Assets should not be understated and write-downs of fixed assets must be reversed if the reasons for the write-downs no longer apply. Furthermore, it has been proposed that §14, Section 4 of the Swedish Accounting Act, allowing, under certain circumstances, an upward revaluation of current assets, be abolished.

As for the possibility of upward revaluation of certain types of fixed assets, the committee proposes that this possibility be retained for limited liability companies (but not for partnerships).

In the same way as with write-downs, revaluations must be reversed if the reasons for the revaluation no longer exist. It has been proposed that the present rule in the Swedish Accounting Act that a revaluation of a property may be made only up to its tax assessment value be abolished.

4.8 Consolidated Financial Statements

According to Swedish law, all limited liability companies, which are parent companies, must prepare consolidated financial statements. As a consequence of the adaptation of the Seventh EC Directive, parent companies that are also subsidiaries shall be exempted from the obligation to prepare consolidated financial statements, unless a minority of the shareholders require that such financial statements be prepared. This exemption does not apply if the parent company is a listed company.

Furthermore, the committee proposes that the proportional method be permitted when accounting for joint ventures.

Consolidated financial statements shall, as a main rule, be prepared by using the same accounting principles as are used in the parent company accounts. Other principles may be used if there are special reasons for doing so. In this way, consolidated accounts will be less influenced by tax considerations than is normally the case with single-entity accounts. The committee does not, however, favor a solution in which different accounting principles are used on the single-entity level and group level, respectively, but this is, according to the committee, the only practical option available in view of the strong link that still exists between accounting and taxation under Swedish law.

The adaptation to the EC directives is sometimes viewed among the accounting profession as a step in the wrong direction, from a financial reporting point of view, hindering the development of generally accepted accounting principles in Sweden from being in line with dominant international accounting standards as formulated by IASC.

Financial Statements

ATLAS COPCO-GRUPPEN
RESULTATRÄKNING
Belopp i MSEK

		1993	1992
Rörelseintäkter	Fakturering (NOT 1)	18 906	16 007
Rörelsekostnader (NOT 2)	Kostnader för sålda varor	−12 133	−10 229
	Kostnader för teknisk utveckling, marknadsföring, administration mm	−4 944	−4 127
Rörelseresultat före avskrivningar		1 829	1 651
Avskrivningar	Enligt plan (NOT 3)	−653	−527
Rörelseresultat efter avskrivningar		1 176	1 124
Finansiella intäkter och kostnader (NOT 4)		122	−138
Andel i intressebolag (NOT 11)		22	31
Resultat efter finansiella intäkter och kostnader		1 320	1 017
Skatter (NOT 6)		−432	−408
Minoritetsandelar i årets resultat (NOT 7)		−21	−11
ÅRETS VINST		867	598
Vinst per aktie, SEK (NOT 27)		23:70	16:75

ATLAS COPCO GROUP

CONSOLIDATED INCOME STATEMENT

Amounts in SEK m.

		1993	1992
Operating income	Invoiced sales (NOTE 1)	18,906	16,007
Operating expense (NOTE 2)	Cost of goods sold	−12,133	−10,229
	Technical development, marketing and administrative costs, etc	−4,944	−4,127
Operating profit before depreciation		1,829	1,651
Cost depreciation	In accordance with plan (NOTE 3)	−653	−527
Operating profit after depreciation		1,176	1,124
Financial income and expense (NOTE 4)		122	−138
Share in associated companies (NOTE 11)		22	31
Profit after financial income and expense		1,320	1,017
Taxes (NOTE 6)		−432	−408
Minority interest (NOTE 7)		−21	−11
NET PROFIT		867	598
Earnings per share, SEK (NOTE 27)		23.70	16.75

/ .

ATLAS COPCO-GRUPPEN

BALANSRÄKNING
Belopp i MSEK

TILLGÅNGAR		1993.12.31		1992.12.31	
Omsättningstillgångar	Kassa, bank och kortfristiga placeringar (NOT 8)	2 123		1 938	
	Fordringar (NOT 9)	5 043		4 216	
	Varulager (NOT 10)	4 491	11 657	4 425	10 579
Anläggningstillgångar	Aktier och andelar (NOT 11)	227		224	
	Goodwill (NOT 12)	1 237		989	
	Övriga anläggningstillgångar (NOT 13)	4 701	6 165	4 427	5 640
SUMMA TILLGÅNGAR			**17 822**		**16 219**

SKULDER OCH EGET KAPITAL					
Kortfristiga skulder	*Icke räntebärande skulder*				
	Växelskulder	99		55	
	Leverantörsskulder	1 135		1 003	
	Skatteskulder	303		222	
	Upplupna kostnader och förutbetalda intäkter	2 084		1 533	
	Övriga kortfristiga skulder	1 160		1 059	
	Räntebärande skulder				
	Bank- och reversskulder (NOT 18)	1 678		1 617	
	Kortfristig del av långfristiga skulder	28		488	
	Övriga kortfristiga skulder	27	6 514	24	6 001
Långfristiga skulder	*Icke räntebärande skulder*				
	Övriga långfristiga skulder	80		80	
	Latenta skatteskulder (NOT 20)	546		576	
	Räntebärande skulder				
	Intecknings- och reverslån (NOT 19)	264		267	
	Avsatt till pensioner (NOT 21)	1 905	2 795	1 756	2 679
SUMMA SKULDER			9 309		8 680
Konvertibelt förlagslån (NOT 22)			–		137
Minoritetsintressen (NOT 7)			119		90
Eget kapital	Aktiekapital (NOT 24)	918		885	
	Bundna reserver (NOT 25)	4 417		3 429	
	Disponibla vinstmedel (NOT 26)	2 192		2 400	
	Årets vinst	867	8 394	598	7 312
SUMMA SKULDER OCH EGET KAPITAL			**17 822**		**16 219**
Ställda panter (NOT 28)			237		251
Ansvarsförbindelser (NOT 28)			749		578

ATLAS COPCO GROUP

CONSOLIDATED BALANCE SHEET
Amounts in SEK m.

ASSETS

		1993.12.31		1992.12.31	
Current assets	Cash, bank and short-term				
	investments (NOTE 8)	2,123		1,938	
	Receivables (NOTE 9)	5,043		4,216	
	Inventories (NOTE 10)	4,491	11,657	4,425	10,579
Fixed assets	Shares and participations (NOTE 11)	227		224	
	Goodwill (NOTE 12)	1,237		989	
	Other fixed assets (NOTE 13)	4,701	6,165	4,427	5,640
TOTAL ASSETS			**17,822**		16,219

LIABILITIES AND SHAREHOLDERS' EQUITY

		1993.12.31		1992.12.31	
Current liabilities	*Non-interest-bearing liabilities*				
	Notes payable	99		55	
	Suppliers	1,135		1,003	
	Provision for taxes	303		222	
	Accrued expenses and prepaid income	2,084		1,533	
	Other current liabilities	1,160		1,059	
	Interest-bearing liabilities				
	Bank loans (NOTE 18)	1,678		1,617	
	Current portion of long-term liabilities	28		488	
	Other current liabilities	27	6,514	24	6,001
Long-term liabilities	*Non-interest-bearing liabilities*				
	Other long-term liabilities	80		80	
	Deferred tax liabilities (NOTE 20)	546		576	
	Interest-bearing liabilities				
	Mortgage and other long-term loans (NOTE 19)	264		267	
	Provision for pensions (NOTE 21)	1,905	2,795	1,756	2,679
TOTAL LIABILITIES			**9,309**		8,680
Convertible debenture loan (NOTE 22)			–		137
Minority interest (NOTE 7)			**119**		90
Shareholders' equity	Share capital (NOTE 24)	918		885	
	Restricted reserves (NOTE 25)	4,417		3,429	
	Retained earnings (NOTE 26)	2,192		2,400	
	Net profit	867	8,394	598	7,312
TOTAL LIABILITIES AND SHAREHOLDERS' EQUITY			**17,822**		16,219
Assets pledged (NOTE 28)			237		251
Contingent liabilities (NOTE 28)			749		578

13

ATLAS COPCO AB
RESULTAT- OCH BALANSRÄKNING
Belopp i MSEK

RESULTATRÄKNING

	1993	1992
Rörelseintäkter	238	173
Rörelsekostnader	−85	−116
Rörelseresultat före avskrivningar	153	57
Avskrivningar enligt plan (NOT 3)	−7	−8
Rörelseresultat efter avskrivningar	146	49
Finansiella intäkter och kostnader (NOT 4)	461	282
Resultat efter finansiella intäkter och kostnader	607	331
Bokslutsdispositioner (NOT 5)	−177	−12
Resultat före skatter	430	319
Skatter (NOT 6)	−	0
ÅRETS VINST	430	319

BALANSRÄKNING

TILLGÅNGAR		1993.12.31		1992.12.31	
Omsättningstillgångar	Kassa, bank och kortfristiga				
	placeringar (NOT 8)	1 038		1 174	
	Fordringar (NOT 9)	1 673	2 711	1 676	2 850
Anläggningstillgångar	Aktier och andelar (SID 27)	3 816		3 541	
	Övriga anläggningstillgångar (NOT 13)	415	4 231	790	4 331
SUMMA TILLGÅNGAR			6 942		7 181

SKULDER OCH EGET KAPITAL					
Kortfristiga skulder	Icke räntebärande skulder (NOT 17)	326		198	
	Räntebärande skulder (NOT 17)	1 692	2 018	2 318	2 516
Långfristiga skulder	Räntebärande skulder (NOT 19, 21)		446		436
SUMMA SKULDER			2 464		2 952
Konvertibelt förlagslån (NOT 22)			−		137
Obeskattade reserver (NOT 23)			450		458
Eget kapital	Aktiekapital (36 703 184 aktier				
	à nom 25 SEK) (NOT 24)	918		885	
	Reservfond (NOT 25)	1 737		1 522	
	Disponibla vinstmedel (NOT 26)	943		908	
	Årets vinst	430	4 028	319	3 634
SUMMA SKULDER OCH EGET KAPITAL			6 942		7 181
Ställda panter (NOT 28)			44		5
Ansvarsförbindelser (NOT 28)			636		548

ATLAS COPCO AB

INCOME STATEMENT AND BALANCE SHEET
Amounts in SEK m.

INCOME STATEMENT

	1993	1992
Operating income	**238**	173
Operating expense	**−85**	−116
Operating profit before depreciation	**153**	57
Cost depreciation (NOTE 3)	**−7**	−8
Operating profit after depreciation	**146**	49
Financial income and expense (NOTE 4)	**461**	282
Profit after financial income and expense	**607**	331
Appropriations (NOTE 5)	**−177**	−12
Profit before taxes	**430**	319
Taxes (NOTE 6)	**−**	0
NET PROFIT	**430**	319

BALANCE SHEET

ASSETS

		1993.12.31		1992.12.31	
Current assets	Cash, bank and short-term investments (NOTE 8)	1 038		1,174	
	Receivables (NOTE 9)	1 673	2 711	1,676	2,850
Fixed assets	Shares and participations (PAGE 27)	3 816		3,541	
	Other fixed assets (NOTE 13)	415	4 231	790	4,331
TOTAL ASSETS			6 942		7,181

LIABILITIES AND SHAREHOLDERS' EQUITY

Current liabilities	Non-interest-bearing liabilities (NOTE 17)	326		198	
	Interest-bearing liabilities (NOTE 17)	1 692	2 018	2,318	2,516
Long-term liabilities	Interest-bearing liabilities (NOTE 19, 21)		446		436
TOTAL LIABILITIES			2 464		2,952
Convertible debenture loan (NOTE 22)			−		137
Untaxed reserves (NOTE 23)			450		458
Shareholders' equity	Share capital (36,703,184 shares, par value SEK 25) (NOTE 24)	918		885	
	Legal reserve (NOTE 25)	1 737		1,522	
	Retained earnings (NOTE 26)	943		908	
	Net profit	430	4 028	319	3,634
TOTAL LIABILITIES AND SHAREHOLDERS' EQUITY			6 942		7,181
Assets pledged (NOTE 28)			44		5
Contingent liabilities (NOTE 28)			636		548

16

ATLAS COPCO
FINANSIERINGSANALYSER
Belopp i MSEK

	GRUPPEN		ATLAS COPCO AB	
	1993	1992	**1993**	1992
INTERNT GENERERADE MEDEL				
Resultat efter finansiella				
intäkter och kostnader	1 320	1 017	607	331
Återläggning av icke utdelade				
resultatandelar i intressebolag	−12	−24		
Avskrivningar	653	527	7	8
Realisationsvinst på sålda				
anläggningstillgångar	−15	−9	3	0
Koncernbidrag			−185	190
Betalda skatter	−383	−284	0	−
INTERNT GENERERADE MEDEL FRÅN RÖRELSEN	1 563	1 227	**432**	529
RÖRELSEKAPITAL				
Förändring av kortfristiga fordringar	−827	−559	3	−206
Förändring av varulager	−66	−960	−	−
Förändring av kortfristiga rörelseskulder	909	717	128	92
FÖRÄNDRING AV RÖRELSEKAPITAL	16	−802	**131**	−114
OPERATIVT NETTO FRÅN RÖRELSEN	1 579	425	**563**	415
INVESTERINGAR				
Investeringar i fastigheter, maskiner				
och inventarier*	−488	−858	0	0
Investeringar i aktier och andelar	15	−7	−162	−38
Förvärvade bolag och goodwill	−110	−21		
Avyttrade bolag	17	89		
Investeringar i långfristiga fordringar	13	−13	365	−20
Försäljning av anläggningstillgångar	128	155	0	1
INVESTERINGAR I ANLÄGGNINGSTILLGÅNGAR, NETTO	−425	−655	**203**	−57
ÖVRIGA POSTER				
Utdelning från moderbolaget	−284	−283	−284	−283
Utdelning till minoritetsintressen				
i dotterbolag	−3	−5		
Preskriberade fondaktier	−	1	−	1
Minoritetsandelar i eget kapital	−2	−15		
Förändring av övriga skulder	−36	18	−2	−
Omräkningsdifferenser**	−394	111		
FÖRÄNDRING AV ÖVRIGA POSTER	−719	−173	**−286**	−282
NETTO FRÅN ÅRETS VERKSAMHET	435	−403	**480**	76
FÖRÄNDRING AV RÄNTEBÄRANDE SKULDER	−250	235	**−616**	−138
FÖRÄNDRING AV LIKVIDA MEDEL	185	−168	**−136**	−62

* Investeringar i befintliga fastigheter och maskiner i nyförvärvade företag ingår med 94 (305).

** Av omräkningsdifferenser är 96 (610) hänförliga till eget kapital, latent skatteskuld och minoritetsintressen samt −490 (−499) till anläggningstillgångar.

ATLAS COPCO

STATEMENTS OF CHANGES IN FINANCIAL POSITION

Amounts in SEK m.

	GROUP		ATLAS COPCO AB	
	1993	1992	**1993**	1992
INTERNAL FUNDS GENERATED				
Profit after financial income and expense	**1,320**	1,017	**607**	331
Reversal of undistributed shares in the profit of associated companies	**−12**	−24		
Depreciation	**653**	527	**7**	8
Capital gain from sales of fixed assets	**−15**	−9	**3**	0
Intra-Group transfers			**−185**	190
Taxes paid	**−383**	−284	**0**	−
INTERNAL FUNDS GENERATED FROM OPERATIONS	**1,563**	1,227	**432**	529
WORKING CAPITAL				
Change in short-term receivables	**−827**	−559	**3**	−206
Change in inventories	**−66**	−960	**−**	−
Change in short-term operating liabilities	**909**	717	**128**	92
CHANGE IN WORKING CAPITAL	**16**	−802	**131**	−114
NET FUNDS FROM OPERATIONS	**1,579**	425	**563**	415
INVESTMENTS				
Investments in property, plant and equipment*	**−488**	−858	**0**	0
Investments in shares and participations	**15**	−7	**−162**	−38
Companies and goodwill acquired	**−110**	−21		
Divested companies	**17**	89		
Investments in long-term receivables	**13**	−13	**365**	−20
Sales of fixed assets	**128**	155	**0**	1
NET INVESTMENTS IN FIXED ASSETS	**−425**	−655	**203**	−57
OTHER ITEMS				
Dividend from Parent Company	**−284**	−283	**−284**	−283
Dividend to minority interests in subsidiaries	**−3**	−5		
Lapsed bonus shares	**−**	1	**−**	1
Minority interest in shareholders' equity	**−2**	−15		
Change in other liabilities	**−36**	18	**−2**	−
Translation differences**	**−394**	111		
CHANGE IN OTHER ITEMS	**−719**	−173	**−286**	−282
NET INTERNAL FUNDS GENERATED	**435**	−403	**480**	76
CHANGE IN INTEREST-BEARING LIABILITIES	**−250**	235	**−616**	−138
CHANGE IN LIQUID ASSETS	**185**	−168	**−136**	−62

* The amounts include investments of sᴇᴋ 94 m. (305) in existing properties and machinery at newly-acquired companies.

** Of the total translation differences, sᴇᴋ 96 m. (610) is attributable to shareholders' equity, deferred tax liabilities and minority interests, and sᴇᴋ −490 m. (−499) to fixed assets.

Note to the Atlas Copco Group statements of changes in financial position

Changes in foreign exchange rates in recent years have caused an extremely high increase in total Group assets. This affects the traditional Statement of Changes in Financial Position which, as a result, does not provide an accurate picture of actual financial flows.

Net result from operations

The Statement of Changes in Financial Position shows cash flow from operations (net funds from operations) of SEK 1,579 m. (425). The actual payment flows, however, provided a cash flow of SEK 2,169 m. (1,448). This calculation takes into account items that do not affect cash flows, such as differences arising in translation of the working capital in subsidiaries, a negative effect of SEK 504 m. (485) – as well as a negative effect of SEK 102 m. (528) on the initial working capital of acquired companies. The positive cash effect of the working capital released is attributable primarily to reductions in inventory.

Investments

Group investments in buildings, machinery and equipment amounted to SEK 488 m. (858), including SEK 94 m. (305) for fixed assets in newly acquired companies.

Following the large investments during 1990 and 1991, mainly in the Compressor Technique business area, the rate of investing has decreased to a level slightly below that which is expected to apply during the next few years.

The self-financing ratio, defined as internally generated funds as a percentage of investments in machinery and buildings, was 397 percent (222).

Net from year's operations

Actual cash flow from the year's operations amounted to SEK 687 m. (42). The difference between this figure and the figure of SEK 435 m. (−403) given in the Statement of Changes in Financial Position, relates to translation differences that do not affect cash flow.

Net indebtedness

Net indebtedness pertains to the Group's interest-bearing liabilities less cash, bank deposits and short-term investments. Net indebtedness also includes SEK 1,905 m. in the item Provision for pensions, which is classified as an interest-bearing liability.

Five-year condensed Statement of Changes in Financial Position 1989−1993

Internal funds generated	6,234
Change in working capital	−877
Net funds from operations	5,357
Net investments in fixed assets	−4,468
Dividends paid	−1,299
Other items, net	−529
Net internal funds generated	−939
New issue of shares	1,203
Change in interest-bearing liabilities	8
Change in liquid assets	272

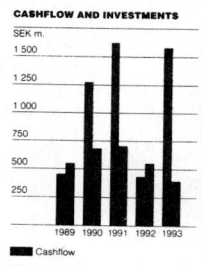

CASHFLOW AND INVESTMENTS

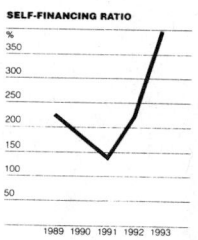

SELF-FINANCING RATIO

NET INDEBTEDNESS	1989	1990	1991	1992	1993
Net indebtedness, January 1	−1,933	−2,605	−1,852	−1,811	−2,214
Company acquisitions	−600	−924	−465	−759	−332
Effect of changes in exchange rates	0	0	0	−403	−252
New issue of shares	−	1,203	−	−	−
Cash effect, excluding above items	−72	474	506[1)	759	1,019
Net from year's operations	−672	753	41	−403	435
Net indebtedness, December 31	−2,605	−1,852	−1,811	−2,214	−1,779
Provision for pensions	924	1,058	1,257	1,756	1,905
Net indebtedness, excluding Provision for pensions, December 31	−1,681	−794	−554	−458	126

1) Includes adjustment of SEK 110 m. for change in accounting principles.

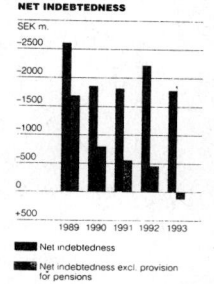

NET INDEBTEDNESS

NOTES TO FINANCIAL STATEMENTS

SEK m. unless otherwise noted

Accounting principles

International guidelines

Atlas Copco follows in all essential respects the guidelines prepared by the OECD for companies that operate internationally.

These guidelines have been observed in the preparation of this Annual Report, except for certain information which, for competitive reasons, cannot be currently disclosed.

Accordingly, the Annual Report contains the following information:

	Page number
Company structure	
– name and address	Page 2
of the Parent Company	and inside cover
– shares and participations in	
subsidiaries, percentage	Shares and
holdings and shareholdings	participations,
among companies	page 27
	Page 6
	Business areas,
	pages 36–53
Geographic areas of oper-	Sales and service
ations and the primary	organization,
activities conducted there	page 59
Invoicing by geographical	
area and for important	Pages 2, 6–7
product groups	Note 1, page 20
Capital expenditures by	Page 8
geographical area and	Business areas,
by business area	pages 36–53
Statements of Changes in	
Financial Position for the	
Atlas Copco Group	Page 14
Average number of	
employees by	
geographical area and	Page 10
by business area	Note 30, page 26
Research and development	Page 10
costs for the company	Page 19
as a whole	Note 2, page 20
Principles applied for internal	
pricing	Page 19
Accounting principles for	
consolidated accounts	Page 17

The Company also views positively the guidelines with respect to multinational companies and the labor market which have been prepared by the United Nations Organization for labor matters (ILO).

In conformity with international standards, the following designations have been used in this Annual Report:

Currency: SEK = Swedish kronor.
Other currencies: See Exchange rates, page 29.
Suffix m. = millions.

Change in accounting principles

Effective in 1993, Atlas Copco applies the American accounting rules in respect of the cost of health care and drugs for retired employees (FAS 106) and new procedures for tax accounting (FAS 109). The new principles are applied retroactively in accordance with the recommendations of Sweden's Financial Accounting Standards Council regarding changes in accounting principles and this means that the accumulative effect is shown as an adjustment entry against consolidated shareholders' equity.

Values for the year under comparison have been recalculated in accordance with the change in principles. Corresponding adjustments have also been made to the affected key figures. See further NOTE 29.

Consolidation

The consolidated accounts have been prepared in accordance with the recommendations of the Swedish Financial Accounting Standards Council.

The Consolidated Balance Sheet and Income Statement of the Atlas Copco Group cover all companies in which the Parent Company, directly or indirectly, holds more than 50 percent of the voting rights, as well as those companies in which the Group in some other manner has a decisive influence and a substantial participation in operating income from their operations.

The consolidated accounts have been prepared in accordance with the purchase method, which means that assets and liabilities are reported at market value according to the acquisition plan. If the acquisition cost exceeds the market value of the company's net assets, calculated as above, the difference is reported as goodwill, see below.

Companies acquired during the year have been reported in the Consolidated Income Statement, with the amounts relating to the period following the date of acquisition.

Earnings of companies divested during the year have been deducted from consolidated earnings on the basis of the Group's reported net assets in these companies at the time of the divestment.

The Consolidated Balance Sheet and Income Statement are shown without untaxed reserves and appropriations. Under Swedish law, this may only be done in consolidated statements.

Untaxed reserves reported in individual Group companies have been apportioned in such a manner that deferred taxes are reported as a long-term liability, while the remaining amount is included in restricted reserves in the Consolidated Balance Sheet.

Deferred taxes are thus calculated individually for each company on the basis of current local income tax rates at the estimated date of the reversal for taxation, i.e. generally the next accounting year. The tax calculated in this manner relating to the appropriations for the year in the individual companies is included in the Group's tax expense as deferred taxes while the remaining amount is included in the consolidated net profit. If the tax rate is changed, the change in tax liabilities is reported among tax expenses for the year.

NOTES TO FINANCIAL STATEMENTS

Goodwill

The acquisition of well-established companies active in an international environment normally means that the acquisition price substantially exceeds tangible net worth. The market price is determined primarily by future expectations, which are based on the company's market position and know-how.

A company acquisition, in which the acquisition price exceeds the company's net assets, valued at market prices, results in intangible assets, which are capitalized and amortized over a certain period.

Goodwill is normally amortized over ten years, while goodwill arising from strategic acquisition is amortized over a period of 20 years.

The economic life of assets is appraised annually to determine whether the selected amortization plan is sufficient.

Associated companies

Companies in which the Atlas Copco Group has between 20 and 50 percent of the voting rights, and in which it has a substantial ownership involvement, are reported as associated companies.

Holdings in associated companies are reported in the Consolidated Income Statement and Balance Sheet in accordance with the equity method.

Atlas Copco's share of income before appropriations in associated companies is reported in the Income Statement under the heading Financial income and expense.

Shares of taxes in associated companies are reported in consolidated tax expense.

The acquisition cost of shares is reported among Shares and participations in the Balance Sheet, increased or reduced by the shares in income and less dividend received. Undistributed income in these companies is reported among restricted reserves in consolidated shareholders' equity.

Internal profits have been eliminated in appropriate cases.

Translation of accounts of foreign subsidiaries

Atlas Copco applies the current-rate method in translating the accounts of foreign subsidiaries, in accordance with the suggested recommendations of the Swedish Institute of Authorized Public Accountants FAR. In applying this method, the subsidiaries are primarily reported as independent units with operations conducted in foreign currencies and in which the Parent Company has a net investment. The exceptions to this approach are those subsidiaries which are located in high-inflation countries. The accounts of such subsidiaries are translated according to the monetary/non-monetary method. In accordance with FAR's suggested recommendations, such a procedure is regarded as providing a more accurate picture of the earnings and financial positions of these companies.

In accordance with the current-rate method, all assets and liabilities in the balance sheets of subsidiaries are translated at year-end rates, and all items in the income statements are translated at the average exchange rate for the year. Translation differences that arise are a result of the fact that net investment is translated at year-end at a rate different from that used at the beginning of the year. This translation difference does not affect earnings, but is instead transferred directly to shareholders' equity.

For those subsidiaries treated according to the monetary/non-monetary method, all non-monetary items, real estate (land and buildings), machinery and equipment, inventories, shareholders' equity and deferred tax, are translated at the acquisition date rates. Other items, monetary items, are translated at year-end rates. The income statement items have been translated at the average rate for the year, except for the cost of goods sold, depreciation and deferred taxes, which have been translated at the investment rate. Exchange differences arising in connection with the translation of the accounts, and which accordingly relate to companies in countries with high inflation have been included in the Income Statement.

The principle applied by Atlas Copco in the translation of the accounts of foreign subsidiaries essentially corresponds with the recommendations of the International Accounting Standards Committee (IAS 21), and with the corresponding American recommendations (FAS 52).

Choice of Methods

In a particular respect, FAR's suggested recommendations require that the user chooses translation procedures according to the specific situation. This applies to the classification of the foreign subsidiaries as either independent or integrated companies. How the company is defined leads directly to the choice of translation method. The accounts of independent companies are translated according to the current-rate method, and integrated companies according to the monetary/non-monetary method.

Based on the criteria defined for classification of companies, the great majority of Atlas Copco's subsidiaries should be regarded as independent companies.

As a consequence, the accounts of all subsidiaries of the Atlas Copco Group are translated according to the current-rate method except for the companies in high-inflation countries, primarily Latin America. The operational currency of these companies is regarded as being the USD, and is therefore translated in two stages.

In the first stage, translation is made to USD in accordance with the monetary/non-monetary method, whereby translation differences arising are charged to consolidated income. In the second stage, the company's balance sheet items are translated to SEK according to the year-end rate and the income statement items according to the average rate for the year. The resulting translation differences are transferred directly to shareholders' equity.

For Group companies in Brazil, an inflation-adjusted year-end report is prepared in the local currency. This is subsequently translated to USD in accordance with the year-end rate and then to SEK, whereby translation differences arising are transferred directly to shareholders' equity.

Receivables and liabilities in foreign currencies

Receivables and liabilities in foreign currencies are translated at the year-end rate.

For individual Swedish companies, these receivables and liabilities are reported in accordance with Directive R7 of the Swedish Accounting Standards Board. Unrealized exchange-rate gains on long-term receivables and liabilities are allocated to a currency exchange reserve and are reported as appropriations.

In the case of currency exchange through a swap agreement, the loan is valued at the year-end rate for the swapped currency. In cases where the swapped loan, translated at the year-end rate for the original currency, exceeds the booked liability, the difference is included under contingent liabilities.

Hedging of net investments

Forward contracts and loans in foreign currency have been arranged in some Group companies to hedge the Group's net assets in foreign subsidiaries. Foreign exchange gains and losses on such contracts, less current and deferred tax, are not included in income for the year but are offset against translation differences arising in connection with the translation of the foreign subsidiaries' net assets.

Interest-rate differences arising between currencies are distributed evenly over the term of each contract.

Inventories

Inventories are valued at the lower of cost or market, in accordance with the "first in/first out" principle and the net sales value.

Group inventories are shown after deductions for obsolescence and for internal profits arising in connection with deliveries from the product companies to the sales companies.

Transfer pricing between companies is based on comparable market prices.

Depreciation

The Atlas Copco Group uses three depreciation concepts; cost depreciation, book depreciation and current cost depreciation.

Cost depreciation is based on original cost and is applied according to the straight-line method over the economic life of the asset. Goodwill is amortized in accordance with a plan established for each specific case.

Book depreciation is used in each individual company in accordance with the maximum amount permitted by tax legislation in each country. The difference between book depreciation and cost depreciation is reported under "Appropriations" in the Income Statement. The total value is reported in the Balance Sheet among untaxed reserves under the heading "Accumulated additional depreciation". In the case of the Group, untaxed reserves and appropriations are eliminated.

Current cost depreciation is used as the basis for price and profitability calculations and is based on the replacement value of the asset. Depreciation is applied on a straight-line basis over the economic life of the asset. The following economic lives are used for cost depreciation and current cost depreciation:

Machinery and equipment	3 to 10 years
Vehicles	4 to 5 years
Buildings	25 to 50 years

Research and development costs

Research and development costs are expensed as incurred.

Product development costs and warranty costs

Product development costs are charged against operations when they are incurred.

Estimated costs of product warranties are charged against cost of sales at the time the products are sold.

Definitions

Profit margin
Profit after financial income and expense as a percentage of invoiced sales.

Return on capital employed
Profit after financial income and expense plus interest paid and foreign exchange differences as a percentage of average total assets less non-interest-bearing liabilities.

In calculating capital employed in the business areas, in contrast to the calculation for the Group, deferred tax liabilities are not deducted.

Return on equity capital
Profit after financial income and expense less full tax and minority interest as a percentage of average shareholders' equity.

Rate of equity capital
Shareholders' equity and minority interest, as a percentage of total capital.

Degree of self-financing
Internal funds generated as a percentage of investments in machinery and buildings.

Capital turnover ratio
Invoiced sales divided by average total assets.

Cash flow
The total of internally generated funds from operations and changes in working capital.

Interest coverage ratio
Profit after financial income and expense plus interest paid and foreign exchange differences divided by interest paid and foreign exchange differences.

Earnings per share
Profit after financial income and expense less full tax and minority interest plus interest expense after tax on the convertible debenture loan, divided by the average number of shares outstanding after full conversion.

Notes

1. Invoiced sales by market

	Group	
	1993	1992
Europe incl CIS	9,830	9,200
of which Sweden	894	783
of which EU	7,197	6,992
North America	3,344	2,356
South America	890	689
North Africa/Middle East	767	641
Southern Africa	633	559
India/East Asia	2,708	2,046
Oceania	734	516
	18,906	16,007

Group revenues and operating income by business area are shown in the Board of Directors' Report and in the individual sections for each business area.

2. Operating expense

Operating expenses include costs for major restructuring projects amounting to SEK 100 m. (100). The amounts reported relate to identified and approved costs for projects that are not estimated to provide any future earnings. Of the appropriations remaining from the two most recent years, SEK 79 m. (76) had not been utilized at year-end 1993.

Appropriations for future restructuring charges have been made in the balance sheets of companies acquired during the year. At year-end 1993 SEK 14 m. (9) remained, which will be utilized during 1994.

Deferred taxes have been taken into account in the above calculations.

Capital gains/losses arising from continual scrapping and/or divestment of fixed assets are included in reported operating expenses in an amount of SEK +15 m. (+9).

	Group	
	1993	1992
Technical development costs	582	479
Marketing and administrative costs	4,362	3,648
	4,944	4,127

The above costs include taxes of SEK 15 m. (16) in Sweden based on pension liabilities and pension payments, profit tax and payroll tax respectively.

3. Depreciation

	Group		Parent Company	
	1993	1992	1993	1992
Goodwill (NOTE 12)	82	66	–	–
Machinery and equipment	479	381	5	7
Buildings	92	80	2	1
	653	527	7	8

Current cost depreciation for the Group amounted to SEK 762 m. (648) and thus exceeded cost depreciation by SEK 109 m. (121). See further Current cost accounting page 31.

4. Financial income and expense

	Group		Parent Company	
	1993	1992	1993	1992
Dividends received				
from subsidiaries			378	285
from others	1	1	0	0
Interest				
from subsidiaries			104	117
from others	391	324	219	187
to subsidiaries			−161	−88
to others	−303	−442	−137	−226
Foreign exchange differences	33	27	58	7
Write-down of financial receivable	–	−48		
	122	−138	461	282

The interest portion of the year's provision for pensions in Swedish companies is not charged against operating income but shown as interest expense. The amount has been calculated on the basis of provisions for pensions at January 1 and December 31 and at an interest rate of 6.1 percent (8.1) for index pensions. The interest portion for 1993 amounted to SEK 52 m. (71). The corresponding sum for the Parent Company amounts to SEK 25 m. (30). No such division has occurred in the Group's foreign companies. The average pension liability for these companies amounts to SEK 1,000 m.

During 1992, net financial items were charged with a write-down of SEK 48 m. in connection with the bankruptcy of Gota AB.

5. Appropriations

Tax legislation in Sweden and in other countries allows companies to retain untaxed profits through tax-deductible allocations to untaxed reserves. By utilizing these regulations, companies can dispose and retain earnings within the business without being taxed. The untaxed reserves created through this means may not be used for dividends.

The untaxed reserves first become subject to tax when they are withdrawn. Should the company report a loss, certain untaxed reserves can be used to cover the loss without being taxed.

	Parent Company	
	1993	1992
Difference between book depreciation and cost depreciation (NOTE 23)	8	4
Allocation to tax equalization reserve	–	−206
Group contributions, net	−185	190
	−177	−12

Under certain circumstances, the transfer of earnings, in the form of Group contributions can be made between Swedish companies within the same Group. The contribution is a tax deductible expense for the donor and taxable income for the receiver. During 1993, the Parent Company received contributions from Atlas Copco Tools AB and made contributions to Atlas Copco Construction and Mining Technique AB and Uniroc AB.

6. Taxes

	Group	
	1993	1992
Taxes paid		
Swedish taxes	1	−1
Foreign taxes	382	285
Deferred taxes	43	110
Taxes in associated companies	6	14
	432	408

Total tax expenses for the year, amounting to SEK 432 m. (408) corresponded to 32.7 percent (40.1) of income after financial items.

When eliminating untaxed reserves, deferred tax has been calculated separately for each company in accordance with the applicable local income tax rate at the date of expected reversal to taxation.

Changes in tax rates in Sweden, among other countries, had a favorable impact, amounting to SEK 74 m. (13), on tax expense. Applying unchanged rates, tax expense in 1993 was equal to 38.3 percent (41.4) of profit after financial items.

The federal tax rate in Sweden was 30 percent in 1993, calculated on nominal book income plus non-deductible items and less tax-exempt revenue and other deductions. Other deductions in the Parent Company include mainly so-called Annell deductions (for capital stock issues) and tax-exempt dividends received from holdings of shares in subsidiaries.

Changes in tax legislation in Sweden have resulted in a reduction of the federal tax rate to 28 percent, effective in 1994. As specified in the new regulations, Annell deductions cannot be utilized after 1993. Instead, effective in 1994, the possibility of making allocations to a profit-equalization reserve has been introduced.

Capital-based tax equalization reserves (K-Surv) in the Group's Swedish companies amount to SEK 484 m. (487). Up to and inlucing 1993, allocations were based on a company's equity capital. Under the new tax regulations, beginning in 1994 existing reserves are to be recovered at a rate of 20 percent annually over five years. Half of the amount, with certain limitations, may be recovered tax-free. The full amount, SEK 47 m. (140) of the transitional reserve for inventory reserves was withdrawn.

7. Minority interest in subsidiaries' equity and earnings

Minority interest in income after financial income and expense amount to SEK 36 m. (22).

The Income Statement reports the minority shares in the Group's profit after tax as totaling SEK 21 m. (11). These minority interests primarily relate to Atlas Copco India, Atlas Copco Malaysia and subsidiaries of Chicago Pneumatic.

	Group
Minority interest Dec. 31, 1992	90
Minority acquired	−2
Dividends	−3
Translation differences	13
Net profit	21
Minority interest Dec. 31, 1993	119

8. Cash, bank and short-term investments

	Group		Parent Company	
	1993	1992	1993	1992
Cash, bank	1,283	1,082	198	318
Financial investments				
Government Treasury bills	696	149	696	149
Treasury notes	–	207	–	207
Other short-term investments	44	400	44	400
Other investments	100	100	100	100
	2,123	1,938	1,038	1,174

Financial investments and other investments that are to be held to maturity are valued at acquisition cost.

Investments related to trade are valued at market rates.

The Parent Company's guaranteed credit at predetermined interest-rate levels amounted to SEK 2,910 m.

The subsidiaries' granted but unutilized overdraft facilities amounted to SEK 1,675 m.

9. Receivables

	Group		Parent Company	
	1993	1992	1993	1992
Notes receivable	445	405	–	–
Receivables from subsidiaries			1,584	1,561
Trade receivables	3,728	3,108	16	4
Prepaid expenses and accrued income	333	222	57	89
Other receivables	537	481	16	22
	5,043	4,216	1,673	1,676

10. Inventories

	Group	
	1993	1992
Raw materials	201	218
Work in progress	691	709
Semi-finished goods	1,183	1,097
Finished goods	2,416	2,401
	4,491	4,425

NOTES TO FINANCIAL STATEMENTS

11. Shares and participations

	Number of shares	Per- cent held	Par value loc cur[1]	Book value SEK m.
Associated companies				
VOAC Hydraulics AB	250,000	50	100	72
Atlas Copco- Diethelm Ltd, Thailand	49,000	49	100	1
Nanjing Huarui Construction Machinery Ltd, China	1	25	[2]	8
Nanjing Atlas Copco Construction Machinery Ltd, China	1	51	[2]	9
NEAC Compressor Service GmbH & Co KG, Germany	1	50	[2]	0
NEAC Compressor Service Verwaltungs GmbH, Germany	1	50	[2]	0
Pneumatic Equipment Corp., Philippines	2,398	30	100	0
Toku-Hanbai KK, Japan	200,000	50	500	48
Adjustment for consolidation of associated companies				54
				192
Other companies				
Shares and participations reported by Atlas Copco AB (as specified on page 27)				17
Shares and participations reported by subsidiaries Bhagwati Foundries Ltd, India	84,480	50	100	2
Atlas Copco Yugoslavia Inc., Serbia	100,000	60[3]	[2]	0
Honda Power Equipment Sweden AB	1,250	25	1,000	2
Rasa Corporation, Japan	400,000	5	50	0
Misc. shares and participations				14
				35
Total for the Group				227

[1] Value per share [2] Without par value
[3] This company was not included in the consolidated accounts, since the relevant data had not been secured due to the conditions prevailing in Serbia.

The Parent Company's holdings of shares in listed companies (SILA) had a book value at year-end 1993 of SEK 10 m. (17) and a market value of SEK 18 m. (22). The figures for the preceding year include the divested shares in Bilspedition.

Associated companies
The Atlas Copco Group's share in the income after financial items of associated companies amounted to SEK 22 m. (31). Dividends from these companies amounted to SEK 8 m. (7). The

Group's share in the shareholders' equity and the untaxed reserves of associated companies, with deduction for deferred tax at the end of the fiscal year was SEK 192 m. (176).

12. Goodwill

Change in goodwill value as shown in the Balance Sheet:

	1993	1992
Acquired goodwill, Jan. 1	1,298	1,198
Accumulated depreciation	−309	−215
Acquired goodwill	206	21
Depreciation for the year	−82	−66
Translation differences	124	51
Planned residual value, Dec 31	1,237	989

Acquired goodwill pertains to the Robbins Company, Kango and Worthington-Creyssensac.

13. Other fixed assets

	Group		Parent Company	
	1993	1992	1993	1992
Long-term receivables from subsidiaries			331	694
Long term receivables	80	93	7	9
Deferred tax receivable	361	225	–	–
Construction work in progress	61	70	–	–
Machinery and equipment (NOTE 14)	1,804	1,763	14	23
Buildings (NOTE 15)	1,693	1,613	42	43
Land (NOTE 16)	702	663	21	21
	4,701	4,427	415	790

14. Machinery and equipment

	Group		Parent Company	
	1993	1992	1993	1992
Cost	5,130	4,513	71	88
Accumulated cost depreciation	−3,326	−2,750	−57	−65
Planned residual value	1,804	1,763	14	23
Accumulated depreciation in excess of cost depreciation (NOTE 23)			−12	−20
Book value, net	1,804	1,763	2	3

The estimated acquisition value of premises, machines, vehicles, major computer and office equipment leased by the Group is SEK 228 m. (179). The leasing costs for this property and equipment, SEK 53 m. (39), are reported under operating expenses. Future costs for non-cancellable leasing contracts amount to SEK 130 m. (112).

15. Buildings

	Group		Parent Company	
	1993	1992	1993	1992
Cost	2,551	2,320	63	63
Undepreciated amount of revaluations	7	8	0	0
Accumulated cost depreciation	−865	−715	−21	−20
Planned residual value	1,693	1,613	42	43
Accumulated depreciation in excess of cost depreciation (NOTE 23)			−10	−10
Book value, net	1,693	1,613	32	33
Tax assessment value	229	228	29	29

The amount shown for Group "Tax assessment value" relates exclusively to buildings in Sweden, the book value of which amounts to SEK 404 m. (416).

16. Land

	Group		Parent Company	
	1993	1992	1993	1992
Cost	678	639	17	17
Revaluations	24	24	4	4
Book value, net	702	663	21	21
Tax assessment value	129	132	23	26

The amount shown for Group "Tax assessment value" relates exclusively to land and land improvements in Sweden, the book value of which amounts to SEK 279 m. (280).

17. Current liabilities

Short-term non-interest-bearing and interest-bearing liabilities are reported in the Parent Company's balance sheet as follows:

	Parent Company	
	1993	1992
Suppliers	5	14
Provision for taxes	3	11
Accrued expenses and prepaid income	316	97
Other current liabilities	2	76
Total non-interest-bearing liabilities	326	198
Bank loans (NOTE 18)	727	781
Liabilities to subsidiaries	965	1,091
Current portion of long-term liabilities	0	446
Total interest-bearing liabilities	1,692	2,318

18. Bank loans

Short-term bank loans are shown in the Balance Sheet of the Group as follows:

	1993	1992
PARENT COMPANY		
Available under "USD 200 m. Eurocommercial Paper Program" Outstanding USD 24.3 m.	202	204
Available under "USD 100 m. US Commercial Paper Program" Outstanding USD 25.5 m.	212	−
Other short-term loans and promissory notes	313	577
The Parent Company's bank loans and promissory notes	727	781
SUBSIDIARIES	951	836
Group bank loans	1,678	1,617

19. Long-term loans

Long-term liabilities in the Balance Sheet of the Parent Company pertain to long-term loans and provision for pensions.

Bond loans	1993	1992
PARENT COMPANY		
1978 11⅝% loan SEK 100 m.	−	6
1988 loan LUF 300 m.	−	53
1988 loan CHF 100 m.	−	351
Less: next year's maturities	−	−410
Bond loans	−	−

Mortgage loans and promissory notes	1993	1992
PARENT COMPANY		
Available under "USD 100 m. Medium Term Note Program" Outstanding USD 5 m.	42	70
Other mortgage loans and promissory notes	0	2
Less: next year's maturities	0	−36
Parent Company's mortgage loans and promissory notes	42	36
SUBSIDIARIES	250	273
Less: next year's maturities	−28	−42
Group mortgage loans and promissory notes	264	267

The Group's short- and long-term loans can be divided into the following currencies:

			1993	1992
Currency	Amount m.	SEK m.	%	%
USD	98	816	41	24
FRF	114	161	8	11
ITL	27,595	134	7	7
DEM	25	121	6	17
JPY	1,634	122	6	4
CAD	21	128	6	3
AUD	17	96	5	1
NLG	12	52	3	4
Others		367	18	29
		1,997	100	100

NOTES TO FINANCIAL STATEMENTS

Based on the currency exchange rates prevailing on Dec. 31, 1993, mortgage loans and promissory notes are amortized as follows:

	Group	Parent Company
1994	28	0
1995	149	42
1996	58	—
1997 – and thereafter	57	—
	292	42

20. Deferred tax liabilities

Deferred tax liabilities have been calculated individually for each company on the basis of local tax rates, see accounting principles, page 17.

21. Provision for pensions

This item pertains mainly to the Swedish companies and corresponds to the actuarially calculated amount of pension obligations under the negotiated supplementary pension plan in excess of the National Supplementary Pension Plan. In accordance with a recommendation of FAR, a certain portion of the year's pension cost is shown as interest expense (NOTE 4). "Provision for pensions" is accordingly included among interest-bearing liabilities.

	Group		Parent Company	
	1993	1992	1993	1992
Swedish companies				
FPG/PRI-pensions	792	820	362	357
Other pensions	57	49	42	43
Companies outside Sweden	1,056	887		
Total provision for pensions	1,905	1,756	404	400

Pensionsregistreringsinstitutet (FPG/PRI) is an organization which administers employee pension plans.

22. Convertible debenture loan

Pertains to 1987/1993 convertible debenture loan issued to employees in the Atlas Copco Group. The loan carried interest at a fixed rate of 10 percent. The conversion period was August 14, 1989 through March 1, 1993. After adjustment for the issue of bonus shares in 1989, the conversion price was SEK 150 per share. See also page 58.

23. Untaxed reserves

Untaxed reserves are reported in the Parent Company balance sheet as a compounded item. The distribution is shown below. These are totally eliminated in the consolidated accounts. See Accounting principles, page 17.

	Parent Company	
	1993	1992
Accumulated additional depreciation		
Machinery and equipment	12	20
Buildings	10	10
Tax equalization reserve	428	428
	450	458

Accumulated additional depreciation	Machinery and equipment	Buildings
Opening value, Jan. 1, 1993	20	10
Dissolutions	−8	—
Closing value, Dec. 31, 1993	12	10

24. Share capital

	Group	Parent Company
Share capital, Dec. 31, 1992	885	885
Conversion of debenture loan	23	23
Non-cash issue	10	10
Share capital, Dec. 31, 1993	918	918

25. Restricted reserves

	Group	Parent Company
Restricted reserves, Dec. 31, 1992	3,429	1,522
Premium on conversion and non-cash issue	226	226
Less taxes	−11	−11
Transfers between restricted and unrestricted capital	773	
Restricted reserves, Dec. 31, 1993	4,417	1,737

The increase in restricted reserves for the Atlas Copco Group relates primarily to translation differences and the portion of shareholders' equity in allocations made to untaxed reserves in individual companies.

26. Retained earnings

	Group	Parent Company
Retained earnings, Dec. 31, 1992	2,377	908
1992 net profit	604	319
Effect of changes in accounting principles (NOTE 29)	17	
Unrestricted reserves, Dec. 31, 1992	2,998	1,227
Dividend to shareholders	−284	−284
Transfers between restricted and unrestricted capital	−773	
Translation differences	251	
Retained earnings, Dec. 31, 1993	2,192	943

Group shareholders' equity has been affected by the translation differences arising from the application of the current method of accounting in an amount of SEK 647 m. By hedging the net assets of the foreign subsidiaries, translation differences have been reduced by SEK 396 m.

Unrestricted shareholders' equity for the Atlas Copco Group has been defined as follows:

The Parent Company's unrestricted shareholders' equity, increased by the Group's share of each subsidiary's unrestricted equity, to the extent that it can be distributed without the Parent Company having to write-down the shares in the subsidiary.

From this amount, the Group's share in accumulated losses and other reductions of capital in subsidiaries have been deducted to the extent that these amounts have not affected share values in the Parent Company's accounts. In the Consolidated Balance Sheet eliminated internal profit has also been charged against the Group's unrestricted shareholders' equity.

Of the Group's retained earnings, SEK 11 m. will be transferred to statutory reserves in accordance with the proposals of the Board of Directors of the respective companies.

In evaluating the Atlas Copco Group's retained earnings and profit for the year, it should be noted that a substantial portion was earned in companies outside Sweden, from which in certain cases the transfer of profit to the Parent Company is subject to taxation or restrictions.

27. Earnings per share

	Group	
	1993	1992
Net profit	867	598
Interest on convertible loan after deduction for 30-percent tax	1	10
Adjusted profit after full tax and full conversion	868	608
Average number of shares after full conversion	36,591,330	36,319,969
Earnings per share, SEK	23.70	16.90

28. Assets pledged and Contingent liabilities

	Group		Parent Company	
	1993	1992	1993	1992
Real estate mortgages	80	91	1	1
Chattel mortgages	47	89	–	–
Short-term investments	39	–	39	–
Receivables	71	71	4	4
Assets pledged	237	251	44	5
Notes discounted	77	122	–	–
Sureties and other contingent liabilities	672	456	636	548
Contingent liabilities	749	578	636	548

Of the contingent liabilities reported in the Parent Company SEK 549 m. (401) relates to contingent liabilities on behalf of subsidiaries.

Loans in accordance with Chap. 12, Paragraph 7 of the Swedish Companies Act were granted during the period 1987 to 1990 to employees in conjunction with the offer related to savings invested in Atlas Copco shares through the Atlas Copco General Savings Fund. A dispension was granted by the County Board in the particular counties.

	Parent	
	Group	Company
Number of borrowers	147	147
Loans reported in the balance sheets as receivables	0	0

Borrowers in the Parent Company also include employees in other Swedish companies.

29. Change in accounting principles

Effective 1993, Atlas Copco applies the American accounting rules in accordance with FAS 106 (Employer's accounting for post-retirement benefits other than pensions) pertaining to costs of health care and drugs for retired employees and new procedures for tax accounting (FAS 109).

The new principles have been applied retroactively and the cumulative effect of the change is reported as an adjustment item in consolidated shareholders' equity.

The effect on shareholders' equity at January 1, 1993 for "post-retirement benefits" amounted to SEK −91 m. and for change in tax accounting to SEK +108 m.

A pro forma consolidated income statement and pro forma balance sheet are presented below.

	1992	
	Established	According to new principles
Operating profit after depreciation	1,134	1,124
Net financial items	−138	−138
Share in associated companies	31	31
Profit after financial income and expense	1,027	1,017
Taxes	−412	−408
Minority interest	−11	−11
Net profit	604	598
Earnings per share, SEK	16.90	16.75
Cash, bank and short-term investments	1,938	1,938
Receivables	4,216	4,216
Inventories	4,425	4,425
Fixed assets	5,421	5,640
Total assets	16,000	16,219
Non-interest-bearing liabilities	4,478	4,528
Interest-bearing liabilities	4,000	4,152
Convertible debenture loan	137	137
Minority interest	90	90
Shareholders' equity	7,295	7,312
Total liabilities and shareholders' equity	16,000	16,219

NOTES TO FINANCIAL STATEMENTS

30. Other information regarding personnel

Remunerations etc paid to certain members of the Board, the President and CEO, and to other members of Group management

The Chairman of the Board received SEK 150,000 in fees, SEK 2,088,447 in the form of a bonus, fees from a Group company amounting to FRF 50,000 and a certain ten-year pension effective from the age of 65. A fee of SEK 60,000 and a bonus of SEK 125,000 was paid to each other non-employed Board member and to each deputy for such a member a fee of SEK 30,000 and a bonus of SEK 62,500. Vice Chairman, Tom Wachtmeister, received SEK 68,000 in special compensation plus FRF 50,000 and USD 50,000 in fees from Group companies, plus a pension based on 70 percent of his former salary. A special ten-year pension commitment exists that becomes effective during ten years at the age of 65. Board member Jacques van der Schueren received BEF 1,300,000 in fees from a Group company and Board member Otto Grieg Tidemand received BEF 525,000 in fees from a Group company plus an old-age pension. The President and Chief Executive Officer received a salary of SEK 2,291,849, a bonus payment of SEK 1,027,000 and fees from Group companies in the amount of USD 66,000, FRF 50,000 and CAD 14,000. In addition, a pension commitment exists that is estimated to provide approximately 55 percent of pensionable salary upon retirement after the age of 60.

Notice of termination served by the Company on a member of management with 20 years of service extends over a period not exceeding 30 months. This applies to the President and other members of Group management, with certain individual exceptions within a given framework. Deductions will be made from salaries during notice-of-termination periods in the event of income being received from an another employer or other business operations. From the age of 60 a pension commitment which is estimated to provide approximately 70 percent of the salary at that age currently exists in the category designated "other members of Group management."

Value added and interested parties

The value added corresponds to the Group's total invoicing, SEK 18,906 m., reduced by costs for the purchase of raw materials, wholly and partially finished goods as well as services, SEK 11,513 m. The figure obtained is a measure of the company's productive contribution, i.e. the value added through processing etc.

In 1993, the value added amounted to SEK 7,393 m. (6,442), an increase of approximately 15 percent, while value added per employee increased by approximately 21 percent.

The value added is distributed among interested parties, i.e. employees, creditors, government, municipalities and shareholders. Remaining funds are retained in the company to cover costs for wear on plants and equipment (depreciation) and to provide for continued expansion of operations (retained in the business).

Distribution of value added:

	1993		1992	
	SEK m.	%	SEK m.	%
Wages and salaries	4,142	56	3,554	55
Social costs	1,422	19	1,237	19
Depreciation	653	9	527	8
Capital costs, net	−144	−2	107	2
Corporate and municipal taxes	432	6	408	6
Dividends paid	287	4	288	5
Retained in business	601	8	321	5
Value added, total	7,393	100	6,442	100
Value added per employee, SEK thousands	405		336	

Geographic distribution of personnel and distribution of women and men:

	Total number	Distribution as %	
		Women	Men
Europe	10,842	19	81
of which Sweden	2,748	18	82
of which EU	7,523	19	81
North America	2,572	14	86
South America	1,234	13	87
North Africa/Middle East	234	26	74
Southern Africa	445	20	80
India/East Asia	2,412	7	93
Oceania	508	19	81
	18,247	16	84

A detailed presentation showing the average number of employees, and wages, salaries and other remuneration paid, prepared in conformity with the Swedish Companies Act, is included in the Annual Report filed with the National Patent & Registration Office in Sweden and may be obtained free of charge from Atlas Copco's headquarters in Nacka, Sweden.

NOTES TO FINANCIAL STATEMENTS

Financial operations

The market in 1993

The turmoil that characterized the currency market in 1992 continued in 1993. The peak was reached on August 2, when the allowed rate fluctuations within the European Rate Mechanism (ERM) were changed from plus/minus 2.25 percent to plus/minus 15 percent for most currencies. This was a temporary setback for plans for a common European currency.

The German mark maintained its strong position in Europe during 1993, although the British pound increased about 4 percent in value relative to the mark. This can be attributed to the economic recovery that was discernible in England. The currencies that declined most in value relative to the German mark were the Italian lira, the Spanish peseta, the Portuguese escudo, the Finnish markka and, in particular, the Swedish krona, which fell 10 percent. (See table on page 29.)

Interest rates dropped sharply in most markets throughout the world. The short-term rate for the U.S. dollar was stable, at a very low level, while corresponding rates for the German mark and Swedish krona — two other important borrowing currencies for Atlas Copco — each declined by about three percentage units.

Political upheaval and unrest in Eastern Europe and the failed coup d'état in Russia in October had limited repercussions in the world's financial markets.

Financial risks

Atlas Copco's daily operations give rise to financial risks, primarily in the foreign exchange and interest-rate areas. Changes in exchange rates and interest rates therefore have a direct impact on Group earnings.

Coordination of financial operations
The Group Treasurer has basic responsibility for the Atlas Copco Group's financing operations and currency management.

Financial management's task is to define the financial risks and to limit their negative impact on Group earnings through the selection of financial strategies.

The daily transactions are carried out by the Group's internal bank, which also provides services in the areas of export financing and cash management.

In addition, the internal bank is responsible for coordinating the financial operations in countries in which there are more than one Atlas Copco company by i e establishing local cash pools. These cash pools, which serve as an extension of the internal bank's operations, have been established in 19 countries.

Borrowing risk
Borrowing risk pertains to the risk that it may be difficult to obtain sources of financing at a given time.

Atlas Copco companies finance their capital employed through local borrowing in local currencies. A substantial portion of this borrowing is handled by Atlas Copco's internal bank which borrows funds in the open market and lends them to Group companies on market terms. To limit borrowing risk, the Parent Company has guaranteed but unutilized credit facilities of USD 350 m., equal to SEK 2,910 m., with Swedish and international banks. In December 1993, the Atlas Copco Group's net borrowing amounted to SEK 1,997 m. (2,396). During the year the Group's net indebtedness, less liquid funds, which had amounted to SEK 458 m. at year-end 1992, was converted to a surplus of SEK 126 m. These figures do not include the item Provision for pensions.

Currency risk
Currency risk is the risk that changes in foreign exchange rates will have a negative impact on the value of the Group's commercial transactions and net assets outside Sweden.

The Group Treasurer is responsible for managing Atlas Copco's total currency exposure. Accordingly, risks arising in the divisions are covered in the Group's internal bank through centralized netting and currency hedges. Loans, forward contracts and options are employed as part of the program to reduce sensitivity to movements in foreign exchange rates.

Atlas Copco's currency policy is to minimize currency risks in commercial flows of currencies, so-called transaction risks. Each division manages its own risks and determines the period and the manner in which hedging is effected. In principle, flows of currencies are hedged only for the

The chart shows Atlas Copco's sensitivity to changes in the USD/BEF exchange rate, expressed in Swedish kronor. A change of one percent in the rate increases/decreases Group profit by SEK 11 m.

SENSITIVITY TO CURRENCY MOVEMENTS

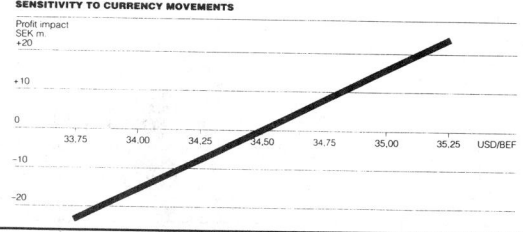

Profit impact
SEK m.

period estimated to be required to adapt to changes in foreign exchange rates. These periods vary from division to division and amount, on average, to approximately four months for the Group as a whole. Changes in exchange rates thus impact relatively quickly on Group earnings.

The Group's net commercial flows, which can give rise to a transaction risk, amounts to SEK 3,000 m. per year. Its "surplus" currencies — currencies in which revenues exceed disbursements — are well distributed geographically, while the "deficit" currencies are concentrated in Europe. As the accompanying chart shows, the USD/BEF exchange rate is the single most important one for the Atlas Copco Group. This is due to the growing importance of the United States as a market and to the high percentage of production in Belgium within the Compressor Technique business area. The most important currency exposure in the Construction and Mining Technique business area and the Industrial Technique business area is related to the USD/SEK exchange rate. The annual impact on the Group of a change of one percentage unit in the USD/BEF exchange rate amounts to approximately SEK 11 m., when the value of the U.S. dollar rises by one percent relative to the Belgian franc, Group income increases by SEK 11 m.

The currency risk in net assets outside Sweden — shareholders' equity in non-Swedish Group companies — is minimized through forward contracts and currency swaps, among other measures.

At year-end 1993, the value of the Group's net assets outside Sweden was approximately SEK 6,000 m. Exchange differences arising as a result of the hedging of foreign exchange rates are offset in shareholders' equity against translation differences arising when net assets of subsidiaries are translated at year-end exchange rates. (See Note 26 on page 24.) Interest-rate differences — the difference between foreign and Swedish interest rates in the forward contracts and swap contracts employed in hedging operations — are reported in the consolidated net interest item. The net interest-rate difference in 1993 amounted to SEK 141 m. (20).

An additional effect of changes in exchange rates occurs when translating earnings to Swedish kronor since the Group's consolidated accounts are reported in kronor. Due to the weakening of the krona, this effect was positive in the amount of approximately SEK 130 m.

Interest-rate risk
Interest-rate risk is the risk that changes in interest-rate levels will affect Group income negatively. Group loans have largely had short fixed-interest-rate periods. As a result of declining interest rates, this has had a positive effect on the Group's net interest expense. At year-end 1993,

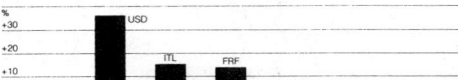

TRANSACTIONS EXPOSURE IN KEY GROUP CURRENCIES

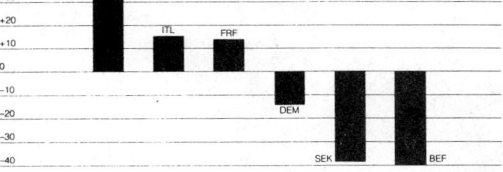

The chart shows the Group's most important surplus and deficit currencies. These are shown as a percentage of the Group's total net exposure of SEK 3,000 m.

the average fixed-rate period was four months. During the year, to further improve the Group's borrowing potential, Atlas Copco's European commercial paper program was increased to USD 200 m.

Credit risk
Credit risk is the risk of loss on short-term investments of liquid funds. The internal bank is responsible for managing the Parent Company's liquid funds which amounted to SEK 1,038 m. in December 1993.

Investments in money markets and bond markets are concentrated in Sweden, via the internal bank. These operations are governed by a highly restrictive policy with regard to credit risk; only a limited group of creditworthy borrowers are accepted. There were no credit losses in 1993.

Exchange rates

Country	Value	Currency code	Year-end rate 1993	Year-end rate 1992	Average rate 1993	Average rate 1992
Australia	1	AUD	5.64	4.85	5.31	4.31
Austria	100	ATS	68.50	62.50	67.00	53.50
Belgium	100	BEF	23.00	21.50	22.50	18.30
Canada	1	CAD	6.22	5.54	6.01	4.84
France	100	FRF	142.00	128.50	137.50	110.50
Germany	100	DEM	481.00	437.50	471.00	375.50
Great Britain	1	GBP	12.33	10.67	11.68	10.25
India	100	INR	27.00	24.50	25.00	21.50
Italy	100	ITL	0.485	0.478	0.492	0.472
Japan	100	JPY	7.44	5.66	7.01	4.63
Luxemburg	100	LUF	23.00	21.50	22.50	18.30
The Netherlands	100	NLG	430.00	389.00	419.00	333.50
Norway	100	NOK	111.00	102.00	109.50	94.00
Singapore	1	SGD	5.21	4.30	4.86	3.60
South Korea	100	KRW	1.023	0.907	0.976	0.776
Spain	100	ESP	5.84	6.15	6.10	5.70
Switzerland	100	CHF	567.00	482.50	528.00	418.00
U.S.A.	1	USD	8.32	7.03	7.77	5.84

NOTES TO FINANCIAL STATEMENTS

International accounting principles

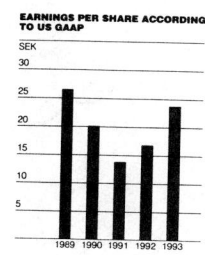

EARNINGS PER SHARE ACCORDING TO US GAAP

SEK

1989 1990 1991 1992 1993

The consolidated accounts for the Atlas Copco Group follow Swedish accounting practices. Swedish accounting practices, however, diverge from international practices on certain points. A calculation of the income for the year and financial position, taking into account the major differences between Swedish accounting practice and the U.S. GAAP and IAS standards is provided below.

U.S. accounting principles, U.S. GAAP

Revaluation of assets
Certain properties have been written up to amounts which exceed the acquisition cost. In specific situations, such revaluations are permitted by Swedish accounting practice. According to U.S. GAAP, revaluations of assets are not reported in the Balance Sheet.

Capitalization of interest expenses
In accordance with Swedish accounting practice, the Group has expensed interest payments arising from the external financing of newly constructed fixed assets. According to U.S. GAAP, such interest expenses are capitalized.

Forward contracts
Hedging transactions via forward contracts are reported in the Swedish accounts on the basis of budgeted volume. For a contract to be treated as a hedge in accordance with U.S. GAAP, there must be a firm commitment. The effect of the difference in accounting principles is not substantial and is not included in the accompanying reconciliation.

Pension provisions
In the U.S. other rules govern accounting of pension provisions. In general, these rules are applied by Atlas Copco's U.S. subsidiaries. Compared with Swedish accounting practice for FPG/PRI pension provisions, there are differences, primarily in the selection of the discount rate and in that the calculation of equity value is based on the salary or wage at the date of retirement. Possible differences have not been quantified and are not included in the following U.S. GAAP account presentation.

Accounting for Post-Retirement Benefits
Effective in 1993 Atlas Copco applies FAS 106 in reporting costs of health care and drugs for retired employees. In accordance with Swedish accounting principles, shareholders' equity at January 1, 1993 is adjusted for the effects of the change in principles, as well as the values for the preceding year. FAS 106 provides two alternatives for reporting the transition. A company can either account for the entire estimated costs in income for the year, or the costs can be distributed over a maximum of 20 years. The Group's reporting in accordance with U.S. GAAP reflects the first alternative. The effect of the change in principle is reported as "Prior year adjustments" and amount to a reduction of SEK 91 m.

Company acquisitions
In accordance with Swedish accounting practices, the Secoroc Group has been included in the consolidated accounts for 1988 according to the pooling of interests method. The U.S. GAAP

Application of U.S. GAAP would have the following approximate effect on consolidated net income and shareholders' equity for the Group:		
U.S. GAAP	1993	1992
Income as reported in the Consolidated Income Statement	867	598
Items increasing/decreasing reported net income:		
Depreciation of revaluations	1	1
Capitalization of interest expenses	−6	0
Depreciation of goodwill	−12	−10
Deferred taxes	2	0
Prior year adjustments	17	6
Calculated net profit	869	595
Calculated earnings per share, SEK	23.75	16.65
After full conversion, SEK	23.75	16.80
Total assets	18,337	16,533
Total liabilities	9,486	8,765
Shareholders' equity as reported in the Consolidated Balance Sheet	8,394	7,312
Net adjustments in reported shareholders' equity	457	456
Approximate shareholders' equity	8,851	7,768

Application of IAS would have the following approximate effect on consolidated net income and shareholders' equity for the Group:		
IAS	1993	1992
Income as reported in the Consolidated Income Statement	867	598
Items increasing/decreasing reported net income:		
Depreciation of revaluations	1	1
Calculated net profit	868	599
Calculated earnings per share, SEK	23.75	17.20
After full conversion, SEK	23.75	16.75
Total assets	17,800	16,197
Total liabilities	9,767	9,199
Shareholders' equity as reported in the Consolidated Balance Sheet	8,394	7,312
Net adjustments in reported shareholders' equity		
Proposed dividend	−330	−283
Other adjustments	−31	−31
Approximate shareholders' equity	8,033	6,998

criteria for the application of the pooling of interests method differs in certain respects from the criteria then applicable, according to Swedish practises. One of the criteria in U.S. GAAP is that none of the merging companies may be a subsidiary of another company during the two years preceding the merger. On the date of acquisition, Secoroc was a subsidiary of Kinnevik, as a result of which it is impossible to apply the pooling of interests method according to U.S. GAAP.

Deferred taxes
Effective in 1993, Atlas Copco applies FAS 109, which requires that operations in each year be charged with the tax for that year. Consequently, deferred tax is calculated on all the differences between book valuation and valuations for tax purposes (temporary differences). Accrued loss carryforwards are anticipated in those cases in which it is more likely than not that these will be utilized. In accordance with Swedish accounting principles shareholders' equity at January 1, 1993 is adjusted for the effect of the change in principles, as well as the values for the preceding year. In accordance with U.S. GAAP, the effect of the change in principles is reported as "Prior year adjustments" and amounts to SEK 108 m.

No adjustment has been made for deferred taxes on the translation differences arising from the use of the monetary/non-monetary method, since such differences are regarded as marginal.

Translation differences in shareholders' equity
According to Swedish accounting practice, all account items included in shareholders' equity must be classified in the Balance Sheet as restricted equity (share capital and restricted reserves) or as unrestricted equity. The accumulated exchange differences arising from the translation of the financial statements of foreign companies are distributed among restricted and unrestricted equity in the Consolidated Balance Sheet.

According to U.S. GAAP, this currency component is shown as a separate item in the Balance Sheet. In the sale/discontinuation of foreign subsidiaries, the result from the discontinuation shall also include accumulated translation differences.

International Accounting Standards, IAS
With the exception of only a few points, Atlas Copco's accounting principles are in accordance with IAS.

Revaluation of assets
As in the case of U.S. GAAP, it is not permitted to report revaluations of assets.

Proposed dividend
According to Swedish accounting principles, the proposed dividend is not normally debited until it has been approved by the Annual General Meeting of shareholders. According to IAS, the dividend proposed by the Board of Directors is entered as a liability.

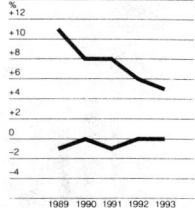

DIFFERENCE US GAAP/SWEDISH ACCOUNTING

■ Equity
■ Earnings per share
(the plus symbol denotes that the US GAAP is greater)

Current cost accounting

One result of the highly variable rate of inflation is that traditional accounting based on historical cost can give an inaccurate picture of a company's income and financial position.

Current cost accounting aims at taking price changes into consideration on the resources used and consumed by the company in its production operations, both in the valuation of assets and in calculating income. Since current cost accounting to a relatively large extent is based on estimations, it cannot meet the same demand for precision as conventional accounting.

In the valuation of assets, accounting based on current cost is characterized by the fact that historical cost is abandoned in favor of other principles, such as replacement cost.

Atlas Copco has chosen to use a model that focuses on three concepts of income to report this effect:
☐ current cost-based operating income
☐ current cost-based income before financial items
☐ real income after financial items

Current cost-based operating income
Current cost-based operating income is an "operative" income figure which should show the degree to which sales revenues covered the replacement value of goods sold. Current cost-based operating income of the Atlas Copco Group in 1993 amounted to SEK 1,075 m. (968).

This income figure is SEK 101 m. (156) lower than the traditional operating income. This is due to two factors. Price changes occurred during the year on goods that are included in the Company's products. These goods are estimated to cost SEK 8 m. less (1992: SEK 35 m. more) to purchase than they did on the purchase date. Income has also been charged with current cost depreciation that is SEK 109 m. (121) higher than depreciation based on historical cost. This means that the wear on the Company's facilities has been assigned a cost based on the amount that would be required to replace these facilities with new ones today.

PROFIT MARGIN

■ Traditional accounting
■ Current cost accounting

NOTES TO FINANCIAL STATEMENTS

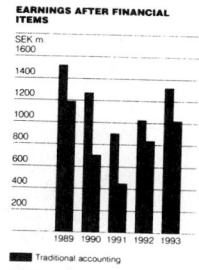

EARNINGS AFTER FINANCIAL ITEMS
SEK m

■ Traditional accounting
■ Current cost accounting

RETURN ON EQUITY
%

	1989	1990	1991	1992	1993
Inflation	7%	10%	7%	2%	4%

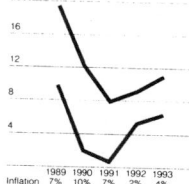

■ Traditional accounting
■ Current cost accounting

Current cost-based income before financial items

Price increases result in an increase in the value of the company's assets. Inventories and fixed assets are subject to price gains. In accordance with traditional accounting, unrealized price gains should not be credited to income. In contrast, both unrealized and realized price gains should affect income in current cost-based accounting.

Atlas Copco's current cost-based income before financial items was SEK 1,237 m. (1,095). Price losses of SEK 16 m. (1992: price gains SEK 42 m.) occurred on inventories and the Company's fixed assets increased in value by SEK 178 m. (85).

Real income after financial items

If a real profit is to be regarded as having arisen, the purchasing power of the equity capital should have increased during the year. Therefore, a so-called purchasing-power adjustment must be made on the equity capital. To enable the purchasing power of equity capital to be maintained it should have increased by the average annual price increase, or by SEK 360 m. (159) during the year. The annual average price increase in 1993 has been estimated at 4 percent (2). Atlas Copco's real income after financial items is thus SEK 1,021 m. (829). This income figure is SEK 299 m. (188) lower than the traditional income and corresponds to a real profit margin of 5.4 percent (5.2).

The real net profit for the year is SEK 299 m. lower than the traditional income and amounted to SEK 568 m. (410).

Adjustment of the Balance Sheet

The adjustment of the Balance Sheet involves stating inventories and fixed assets at current values instead of at cost. Total assets thereby increase by SEK 1,078 m. (1,018) since hidden reserves in inventories and assets are shown openly. The main effects are shown below:
□ Machinery, buildings and land are stated at a value that is SEK 1,047 m. (982) higher.
□ Inventory is shown at a value SEK 23 m. (31) higher.
□ Shareholdings are shown at a value SEK 8 m. (5) higher.

Equity capital and unrealized price changes are reported at a value of SEK 1,078 m. higher, which means that the rate of equity capital including minority interest thereby amounts to 51 percent, as against 48 percent in accordance with traditional accounting.

Return on shareholders' equity amounts to 6.4 percent (5.2), compared with 11.0 percent (9.0) according to the traditional method. The reduction in return is attributable to lower actual earnings and to the fact that equity is SEK 1,078 m. higher as a result of current cost accounting.

Current cost income statement

	1993	1992
Invoiced sales	18,906	16,007
Current cost of goods sold	−17,069	−14,391
Current cost depreciation	−762	−648
Operating income	1,075	968
Price changes, inventory	−16	42
Price changes, fixed assets	178	85
Operating income before financial items	1,237	1,095
Financial items	144	−107
Purchasing power adjustment, equity capital	−360	−159
Real income after financial items	1,021	829
Taxes	−432	−408
Minority interest	−21	−11
Net profit	568	410

Current cost balance sheet

ASSETS	1993	1992
Cash, bank and short-term investments	2,123	1,938
Receivables	5,043	4,216
Inventories	4,514	4,456
Fixed assets	7,220	6,627
Total assets	18,900	17,237

LIABILITIES AND SHAREHOLDERS' EQUITY		
Current liabilities	6,514	6,001
Long-term liabilities	2,914	2,906
Unrealized price changes	1,078	1,018
Shareholders' equity	8,394	7,312
Total liabilities and shareholders' equity	18,900	17,237

Reconciliation between traditional and current cost accounting

Income according to traditional accounting		1,320
Change, unrealized price changes:		
Price change, goods sold	8	
Price change, depreciation	−109	−101
Price change for the year:		
Inventory	−16	
Equipment	178	162	61
Adjustment for inflation		−360
Real income after financial items		1,021

VINSTDISPOSITION

Förslag till vinstdisposition

Enligt Atlas Copco ABs balansräkning står följande belopp till bolagsstämmans förfogande:		Styrelsen och verkställande direktören föreslår att dessa vinstmedel disponeras på följande sätt:		
Balanserade vinstmedel		Till Aktieägarna utdelas		
från föregående år	SEK 943 294 148	9:00 SEK per aktie	SEK	330 328 656
Årets vinst	SEK 430 020 202	I ny räkning balanseras	SEK	1 042 985 694
	SEK 1 373 314 350		SEK	1 373 314 350

Nacka den 10 mars 1994

PETER WALLENBERG
Ordförande

TOM WACHTMEISTER		ANDERS SCHARP
CURT G OLSSON	OTTO GRIEG TIDEMAND	GEORG KARNSUND
GÖSTA BYSTEDT	JACOB WALLENBERG	JACQUES VAN DER SCHUEREN
BERT-OLOF SVANHOLM		MICHAEL TRESCHOW Verkställande direktör
BO HENNING	BENGT LINDGREN	LARS-ERIK SOTING

REVISIONSBERÄTTELSE

Vi har granskat årsredovisningen, koncernredovisningen, räkenskaperna samt styrelsens och verkställande direktörens förvaltning för år 1993. Granskningen har utförts enligt god revisionssed.

Vid vår granskning har vi biträtts av KPMG Bohlins Revisionsbyrå AB.

att vinsten disponeras enligt förslaget i förvaltningsberättelsen samt

att styrelsens ledamöter och verkställande direktören beviljas ansvarsfrihet för räkenskapsåret.

Moderbolaget

Årsredovisningen har upprättats enligt aktiebolagslagen.

Vi tillstyrker
att resultaträkningen och balansräkningen fastställs,

Koncernen

Koncernredovisningen har upprättats enligt aktiebolagslagen.

Vi tillstyrker
att koncernresultaträkningen och koncernbalansräkningen fastställs.

Nacka den 17 mars 1994

STEFAN HOLMSTRÖM Auktoriserad revisor	OLOF HEROLF Auktoriserad revisor

33

APPROPRIATION OF PROFIT

Proposed distribution of profit

As shown in the balance sheet of Atlas Copco AB, the following funds are available for appropriation by the Annual General Meeting:

The Board of Directors and the President propose that these earnings be appropriated as follows:

Unappropriated earnings from preceding year	SEK	943,294,148
Net profit for the year	SEK	430,020,202
	SEK	1,373,314,350

To the shareholders, a dividend of SEK 9.00 per share	SEK	330,328,656
To be retained in the business	SEK	1,042,985,694
	SEK	1,373,314,350

Nacka, March 10, 1994

PETER WALLENBERG
Chairman

TOM WACHTMEISTER   ANDERS SCHARP

CURT G OLSSON   OTTO GRIEG TIDEMAND   GEORG KARNSUND

GÖSTA BYSTEDT   JACOB WALLENBERG   JACQUES VAN DER SCHUEREN

BERT-OLOF SVANHOLM   MICHAEL TRESCHOW
President

BO HENNING   BENGT LINDGREN   LARS-ERIK SOTING

AUDITORS' REPORT

We have examined the Annual Report, the Group accounts, the financial statements and the administration of the Company by the Board of Directors and the President for the year 1993. Our examination was carried out in accordance with generally accepted auditing standards.

We have been assisted in our examination by KPMG Bohlins AB.

Parent Company

The Annual Report has been prepared in accordance with the Swedish Companies Act.

We recommend:
that the Income Statement and Balance Sheet be adopted,

that the net profit for the year be disposed of in accordance with the proposal in the Board of Directors' Report, and

that members of the Board of Directors and the President be granted discharge from liability for the fiscal year.

Group

The Group accounts have been prepared in accordance with the Swedish Companies Act.

We recommend:
that the Consolidated Income Statement and the Consolidated Balance Sheet be adopted.

Nacka, March 17, 1994

STEFAN HOLMSTRÖM   OLOF HEROLF
Authorized Public   Authorized Public
Accountant   Accountant

SWITZERLAND

Bernard Raffournier
University of Geneva, Switzerland

1. Background

1.1 The Legal, Institutional, and Economic Environment of Accounting

Switzerland is a confederation of 26 cantons, all of which have considerable political, economic, and fiscal autonomy. The power to legislate is shared among the federal state, the cantons, and more than 3,000 communes. Switzerland has three official languages: German, French, and Italian. The currency is the Swiss franc (SFr).

Federal laws constitute a common basis, assuring a basic level of homogeneity within the country. To a large extent, they are comprised in the Civil Code *(Zivilgesetzbuch —Code Civil —Codice Civile)*, the Code of Obligations (*Obligationenrecht—Code des Obligations—Codice delle Obligazioni*), and the Penal Code (*Strafgesetzbuch—Code Pénal —Codice Penale*). Every canton and commune may, within the limits of its own powers, promulgate additional laws.

The main political characteristic of Switzerland is its system of direct democracy, which enables citizens to have a say on any administrative or legislative project. This system gave rise to the initiative and referendum rights.

The initiative right makes it possible for a sufficient group of electors to propose a change in the Constitution and, in some cantons, a new law. The referendum right enables the people to oppose the implementation of a new federal or cantonal law by submitting the project to a referendum.

These popular rights theoretically preclude the implementation of any governmental project that does not have people's agreement. A recent example was the negative result of the referendum on the participation of Switzerland in the European Economic Area. However, an increase in the number of initiatives in recent years has led to a high level of abstention, which often makes it possible for well-organized lobbying groups to block decisions detrimental to their personal interests.

The public sector is limited to specific industries (e.g., public transport, telecommunications). Nevertheless, the economy is far from perfectly liberal because there are severe restrictions on competition. Some activities (agriculture in particular) are protected from international competition by guaranteed high prices. The main obstacle to competition, however, is the existence of many cartels of producers, importers, and distributors that contribute to keeping prices higher than in comparable countries. These cartels are perfectly legal, although a law project is being drawn up in order to prevent abuses. In addition, many cantonal regulations often preclude suppliers outside the canton from bidding for public-sector orders.

In recent years, Swiss economic and political life has been dominated by discussions on the place of Switzerland in Europe and on its relationship with the EU. The government finally decided that Switzerland should participate in the European Economic Area in order to prepare for future membership in the EU. Swiss legislation has been revised with this perspective in order to make it compatible with European directives. This movement stopped after a referendum rejected Swiss participation in the European Economic Area. Nevertheless, Switzerland remains largely dependent on the EU because 72% of its imports and 58% of its exports are with EU member states. In the field of accounting, a consequence of this influence is that more and more companies draw up their financial statements in accordance with the Fourth and Seventh EC directives.

1.2 The Sources of Accounting Regulation

In the sphere of accounting, Switzerland has been, for a long time, a poorly regulated country. Until 1984, the only source of accounting regulation was the Code of Obligations (CO), part of Swiss company law, which contains some general accounting principles that apply to all enterprises (articles 957–964) and more detailed rules for companies limited by shares (articles 662–670).

The preceding version of company law dated back to 1936 and included only a few provisions concerning accounting. Its main features were the prohibition of valuation bases other than historical cost and the authorization of hidden reserves practically without limitation. For the rest, the law stated that accounting had to comply with usual business practices.

As far back as the early 1970s, a revision was undertaken, which ended in 1991 with the adoption of articles 620–763 of the Code of Obligations. The aim of the revision was:

- To increase transparency
- To strengthen the protection of shareholders
- To improve the structure and functioning of companies
- To facilitate the raising of capital
- To prevent abuses

The new company law includes several provisions concerning accounting and goes much further than the initial regulation. More detailed accounting rules have been adopted, and disclosure requirements have been largely expanded.

The law was implemented on July 1, 1992, except for articles governing consolidated financial statements, which became effective one year later.

A second source of accounting regulation was introduced in 1984 with the creation of the Foundation for Accounting and Reporting Recommendations (*Fachkommission für Empfehlungen zur Rechnungslegung* [FER]— *Fondation pour les recommandations relatives à la présentation des comptes*—*Fondazione per le racommandazioni concernenti la presentazione dei conti*). The objective of this standard-setting body, created on the initiative of the Swiss Institute of Certified Accountants and Tax Consultants, is to establish Accounting and Reporting Recommendations (ARR) in order to harmonize accounting practices, improve comparisons, and increase the quality of financial statements in Switzerland. Members represent various interests such as auditing firms, industry, banks and insurance companies, employer and employee organizations, financial analysts and stock exchanges, universities, public administration, and other parties interested in accounting.

At present, nine recommendations have been issued. They are much less detailed and prescriptive than International Accounting Standards, probably because their achievement needs a more complete consensus among conflicting interests.

The *Swiss Handbook of Auditing*, published by the Swiss Institute of Certified Accountants and Tax Consultants, is the third source of accounting harmonization. It provides, for all the headings of financial statements, more precise guidelines than the FER recommendations.

Until now, the stock exchange authorities have played a minor role in the evolution of accounting and disclosure practices. Swiss stock exchanges require only limited information from listed companies. The most frequently advanced explanation is that the Swiss market is dominated by large banks that can easily obtain inside information.

1.3 Taxation

Consistent with the structure of the political system, the Confederation, the cantons, and municipalities have their own taxing jurisdictions. All have the power to levy taxes within certain limits. Taxation may thus vary considerably from canton to canton and even from commune to commune. The system has become so complex that a harmonization of direct cantonal and communal taxes has been undertaken. This process is expected to be completed by the end of the year 2000.

The main federal taxes are the direct federal tax and the indirect sales tax. The direct federal tax is assessed on the income of individuals and the revenues of enterprises. The sales tax applies to any transaction or import of goods. Its rate is 6.2%. In 1995, this tax will be replaced by a 6.5% value added tax (VAT), whose creation was finally approved by a referendum at the end of 1993. Direct taxes on revenues and income provide the main part of the resources of cantons.

A breakdown of federal, cantonal, and communal taxes is as follows:

Direct taxes on revenues and capital	56%
Sales taxes	21%
Other taxes	23%
	100%

Total taxes as percentage of gross domestic product amount to 21%

1.4 Auditing

1.4.1 The Role of Auditors

The auditing requirements for companies are stated by the Code of Obligations (articles 727–731a).

Auditors are elected by the general meeting of shareholders for a maximum period of 3 years. Renewals are permitted without limitation. The general meeting of shareholders may remove them at any time.

Auditors must be independent from the board of directors or from any majority shareholder. They must also be independent from any company within the same group, if a shareholder or creditor so requests.

Auditors must have the necessary qualifications with regard to the company to be audited. In fact, small firms may be audited by nonqualified persons, but higher professional standards are required if the company has bonds outstanding, is listed on a stock exchange, or exceeds a certain size (total assets greater than 20 million Swiss francs, revenues greater than 40 million SFr, more than 200 employees).

The role of auditors is to ascertain whether accounting records, financial statements, and proposals for profit appropriation comply with the law and the company's articles of incorporation. In their report to the meeting of shareholders, the auditors recommend the approval, with or without qualification, or the rejection of the financial statements.

Auditors of companies that are required to be audited by specially qualified professionals must provide the board of directors with a report explaining the conduct and the results of the audit.

Consolidated financial statements of companies that are required to prepare such statements must be audited by specially qualified professionals who must ascertain whether these statements comply with the law and principles governing consolidation.

1.4.2 The Auditing Profession

Because the auditing profession is not protected by law, anybody may practice as an independent accountant. Nevertheless, most qualified auditors are members of the Swiss Institute of Certified Accountants and Tax Consultants (*Schweizerische Kammer der Bücher-, Steuer- und Treuhandexperten—Chambre suisse des experts comptables, fiduciaires et fiscaux—Camera svizzera dei periti contabili, fiduciari e fiscali*; in abbreviated form, *Treuhand Kammer—Chambre Fiduciaire—Camera Fiduciaria*), which is the only organization authorized to deliver the legally protected title of Certified Accountant (*Dipl. Bücherexperte—Expert-comptable diplômé—Perito contabile diplomato*).

Applicants must have several years of professional experience in an audit firm and pass an examination for which they generally prepare in a school managed by the institute. Although no academic degree is required, more and more young certified accountants hold a university degree.

2. The Form and Content of Published Financial Statements

2.1 Disclosure Requirements

2.1.1 Contents of the Annual Report

Before the Swiss company law was revised, legal disclosure requirements were quite limited. The only constraint was to prepare once a year a balance sheet and a profit and loss account. The notes to the accounts were not mandatory, and the law did not even mention consolidated financial statements.

Things have changed considerably since the implementation of the revised company law (July 1, 1992). The Code of Obligations (article 662) now requires the board of directors to prepare individual financial statements, a management report, and in some cases, consolidated financial statements. Financial statements consist of the profit and loss account, the balance sheet, and the notes to the accounts.

The management report must discuss the business operations and the financial and business condition of the company. It also indicates any increase in capital during the period and quotes the auditors' opinion on the financial statements (CO, article 663d).

Some large companies voluntarily disclose additional information, in particular a value-added statement and information concerning employees.

2.1.2 The Consolidated Financial Statements

If a company controls, by a majority of votes or any other means, one or more other companies, consolidated financial statements must be prepared

(CO, article 663e). It is noteworthy that the term "any other means" theoretically extends the obligation of consolidated financial statements to horizontal groups, that is, groups in which control does not result from internal financial linkages but from the existence of a common management.

To be exempted from the duty to prepare consolidated financial statements, a corporation, together with its subsidiaries and during two consecutive years, must not exceed two of the following thresholds :

- Total assets of 10 million SFr
- Sales of 20 million SFr
- Average of 200 employees per annum (CO, article 663e)

A corporation already included in the consolidated financial statements of a parent company is also exempted from preparing its own consolidated financial statements, providing the statements of the parent corporation have been prepared and audited according to Swiss or equivalent foreign requirements (CO, article 663f). The provisions of the Seventh EU Directive are generally considered as equivalent foreign requirements.

In any event, consolidated financial statements are mandatory if the following conditions apply:

- The company has bonds outstanding.
- The shares of the corporation are listed on a stock exchange.
- Shareholders whose combined holdings represent at least 10% of the capital-stock so request.
- The statements are necessary to provide as reliable a determination as possible of the company's financial condition and income (CO, article 663e).

2.1.3 Publication of Financial Statements

Companies that have bonds outstanding or whose shares are listed on a stock exchange must either publish their individual and consolidated financial statements in the Swiss Gazette of Commerce or send a copy of them to any interested person (CO, article 697h).

All other corporations must make these statements available for inspection only by creditors who have a legitimate interest. Disputes are settled in court.

2.2 The Balance Sheet

There is no legal format for the balance sheet. It may be presented horizontally (in columns) or vertically (in a list). The order of classification does not matter; current assets and short-term liabilities may be presented first or after fixed assets and owners' equity.

Before the company law was revised, the balance sheet of some firms conveyed little information, many items being grouped under the same heading. A minimum structure is now required by law. According to the Code of Obligations (article 663a), the balance sheet must distinguish among current assets, fixed assets, liabilities, and equity. These headings must also be broken down as follows:

- Current assets:
  —Cash and cash equivalents
  —Accounts receivable from sales of goods and rendering of services
  —Other accounts receivable
  —Inventories
- Fixed assets:
  —Investments
  —Property, plant, and equipment
  —Intangibles
- Liabilities:
  —Accounts payable for deliveries of supplies and services rendered
  —Other short-term liabilities
  —Long-term liabilities
  —Provisions for risks and expenses
- Equity:
  —Capital
  —Legal and other reserves
  —Net income

In addition, the following items must be shown separately:

- Capital not paid-in
- Aggregate amount of participations
- Accounts receivable from and liabilities to other companies of the same group or shareholders who hold a participation in the company
- Accrued assets and liabilities
- Net loss

The balance sheet must also include the accounting numbers for the preceding year.

2.3 The Profit and Loss Account (Income Statement)

In past years, the income statement was sometimes quite limited. Some firms did not even mention sales, making their profit and loss account begin with gross margin.

Since the implementation of the "new" Code of Obligations (article 663), the profit and loss account includes operating and nonoperating revenues and expenses, as well as extraordinary gains and expenses. Its minimum structure is as follows:

- Revenues:
    —Sales of goods and rendering of services
    —Financing revenues
    —Gains from the sale of fixed assets
- Expenses:
    —Purchases of materials and goods
    —Labor expenses
    —Financing expenses
    —Depreciation

No particular format is required. The income statement may still be presented in columns or in a list; revenues and expenses may be classified by nature or by function, but it must mention the corresponding accounting numbers for the preceding year.

2.4 The Notes to the Accounts

Before the company law was revised, the only information to be disclosed in addition to the balance sheet was the fire insurance value of tangible assets. The primary aim of this information was to enable readers of financial statements to appreciate the extent of hidden reserves in fixed assets.

Article 663b of the Code of Obligations greatly extended the list of items that must be disclosed in the notes to the accounts. These items are:

- The aggregate amount of sureties, guarantees, and security interests in favor of third parties
- The aggregate amount of assets pledged, mortgaged, or assigned to secure commitments of the company and assets subject to a reservation of title
- The aggregate amount of debts resulting from leasing agreements not recorded on the balance sheet
- The fire insurance value of tangible assets
- Liabilities to pension funds
- The amounts, interest rates, and maturity dates of bonds issued by the company
- Any participation that is material for the determination of the company's financial condition and earnings
- The aggregate amount of reductions of reserves for replacement costs and additional hidden reserves if such amount exceeds the aggregate amount of newly established reserves of this kind and if the consequence is a significantly more favorable income
- Information about items that have been revalued and the amount of this revaluation
- Information about the acquisition, sale, and number of its own shares held by the company, including those held by another corporation in which the company holds a majority interest, and the conditions governing the acquisition or sale of the company's own shares
- The amount of an authorized or conditional increase of capital

In addition, companies whose shares are listed on a stock exchange must disclose the identity and participation of major known shareholders. Groups of shareholders bound by a voting agreement and individual shareholders are deemed to be major shareholders if they hold more than 5% of all voting rights (CO, article 663c).

Nevertheless, article 663h of the Code of Obligations states that information that may be detrimental to the company or the group in a material respect may be omitted, provided the auditors are informed about the reasons for noninclusion.

The law does not require companies to disclose their valuation policies or changes in valuation policies. The reason is probably to be found in the existence of hidden reserves.

Nevertheless, the obligation to disclose the net variation of hidden reserves makes manipulations of income figures more apparent.

Companies that prepare consolidated financial statements must also disclose notes to these statements. They must specify the consolidation and valuation principles used (CO, article 663g).

If a company deviates from these principles, it must disclose such deviations and include the information necessary for an analysis of the group's financial condition and earnings.

The FER has issued a recommendation on the notes to the consolidated financial statements. This standard (ARR 8) requires information exceeding legal requirements, in particular:

- A description of consolidation principles (consolidation method, currency translation, treatment of internal profits, etc.)
- A description of valuation principles and changes of these principles
- Information on the scope of consolidation
- The evolution of tangible fixed assets and their accumulated depreciation
- A breakdown of sales by regions and by activities
- Information on research and development activities and subsequent (post balance sheet) events

In practice, the extent of the notes to the financial statements varies considerably among firms. Some companies disclose notes quite similar to those of competitors within the EU, while others comply only with legal requirements.

In 1990, that is, before the implementation of the new company law, the author conducted research into the extent of information in the annual reports of a sample of Swiss publicly traded firms. He computed a disclosure index on the basis of requirements of the Fourth EEC Directive, whose value could theoretically range from 0 (no disclosure) to 100 (full conformity with the Fourth Directive). This study has been replicated with 1992 data. The results are as follows:

	1990 Data (53 companies)	1992 Data (161 companies)
Disclosure index		
Maximum	82.8	96.3
Minimum	8.7	8.3
Mean value	43.3	41.8

2.5 The Statement of Changes in Financial Position

A statement of changes in financial position, or a cash flow statement, is not legally required. The Code of Obligations does not even mention it. Nevertheless, ARR 1 of the FER makes this statement an integral part of the financial statements. It argues that information concerning funds flows must be shown in a specific statement if not clearly evident from other parts of the annual report.

The FER has issued a recommendation on the statement of changes in financial position. According to this standard (ARR 6), the purpose of this statement is to describe funds flows arising from operating, investing, and financing activities. Flows from operating activities must be separately disclosed.

ARR 6 does not require this statement to be centered on changes in cash and cash equivalents. Other funds concepts may be chosen, in particular:

- Cash and cash equivalents less short-term financial liabilities
- Net monetary current assets (cash and cash equivalents plus accounts receivable less short-term liabilities)
- Net financial position (cash and cash equivalents plus financial accounts receivable less financial liabilities)

Working capital is, however, considered less appropriate.

In practice, more and more companies disclose a statement of changes in financial position. For example, in 1993, among a sample of 57 listed companies, only seven did not present such a statement. The most commonly used format is a cash-flow statement, as shown below:

Fund whose changes are described:

Cash and cash equivalents	40	(80%)
Net financial position	5	(10%)
Working capital	5	(10%)
	50	

2.6 The Auditors' Report

The auditors must present to the annual general meeting of shareholders a written report in which they recommend the approval, with or without qualification, or the rejection of the financial statements (CO, article 729). This report must name all persons who have conducted the audit and confirm that the qualification and independence requirements are met.

If the company is required by law to prepare consolidated financial statements, the auditors must also ascertain whether these statements comply with the law and the rules of consolidation (CO, article 731a).

The financial statements of Sandoz, a large pharmaceutical company, reproduced in the appendix to this chapter, are representative of the recent effort of many Swiss firms to comply with International Accounting Standards and provide high-quality information.

3. Accounting Policies and Practices in Valuation and Income Measurement: Implications for the Analyst

3.1 Hidden Reserves

In Switzerland, as in other countries, some enterprises may be tempted to smooth their income by means of hidden reserves. Several motives have been advanced to explain the creation of hidden reserves, such as:

- Tax reduction
- Protection against competitors
- Prevention of excessive dividend claims prejudicial to the internal financing of the firm's growth
- Prevention of excessive claims of employees
- Prevention of prejudicial stock price movements after a decrease in earnings

The main difference is that, in Switzerland, the creation of hidden reserves is expressly allowed by the law. The Code of Obligations (article 669) states that hidden reserves may be created in order to ensure prosperity to the enterprise or to distribute dividends as constantly as possible. The only constraint is that these reserves must be reported to the auditors. As a result, Swiss companies make large use of hidden reserves by recognizing excessive depreciation of assets or creating unjustified provisions.

By definition, the extent of hidden reserves in financial statements is difficult to assess. An economic journal, however, in collaboration with a Swiss securities rating company, published from 1989 to 1992 a ranking of the most profitable Swiss companies, based on an estimation of their "true" (undistorted) income. In some cases, reported income represents less than 25% of estimated real earnings.

When confronted with the financial statements of Swiss companies, analysts must be conscious of the widespread use of hidden reserves.

3.2 Group Accounts

Group accounts are not subject to special provisions. The Code of Obligations states that consolidated financial statements must conform to the same principles as individual accounts (CO, article 663g).

The only specific requirement concerns the notes to the group statements, which must include a description of the consolidation and valuation principles used and, in case of changes, the information necessary for an analysis of the group's financial position and earnings.

Recommendations on consolidation and consolidation principles can be found in the FER standards and, to some extent, in the *Swiss Handbook of Auditing*.

3.2.1 The Scope of Consolidation

The scope of consolidation is defined neither by law nor by professional standards. ARR 2 of the FER does not specify conditions for inclusion in the scope of consolidation. It only mentions, as possible criteria, majority of voting rights, control, and uniform management. Companies can use either an extended conception of control, as in the EU, or a more limited one, as in the United States.

In fact, most Swiss companies limit the scope of consolidation to subsidiaries in which they have a majority interest. Among exceptions are Nestlé, whose main criterion is effective management, and Holderbank, which extends the scope of consolidation to enterprises control of which results from an agreement.

Cases of exclusions are not better specified. ARR 2 cites, as examples of possible exclusions, companies that are not material to the consolidated financial statements or whose activities are too different from those of the group as a whole. In practice, the main reason put forward for the exclusion of certain subsidiaries is small size or immateriality. Other reasons are dissimilar activities from the rest of the group or severe restrictions imparing the ability to transfer funds to the parent.

ARR 2 stipulates that nonconsolidated investments must be recorded at cost, at proportional intrinsic value, or according to the equity method.

3.2.2 The Methods of Consolidation

According to ARR 2, the only method of consolidation is full consolidation. Swiss companies conform to generally accepted principles of consolidation, as follows:

- Subsidiaries under control are consolidated under the full consolidation method.
- Associates in which the parent holds directly or indirectly voting rights of 20% or more are accounted for by using the equity method.
- Companies held at less than 20% are recorded at cost.

Joint ventures are generally accounted for under proportional consolidation. Examples are Bobst, Electrowatt, Holderbank, Motor Columbus,

Nestlé, Rieter, and Sika. Other firms prefer to use the equity method or even maintain their interests in joint ventures at cost.

3.2.3 Intercompany Transactions

ARR 2 states that intercompany assets and liabilities, as well as expenses and income from intercompany transactions, must be eliminated. Dividends from consolidated subsidiaries are specifically mentioned.

In practice, intercompany assets and liabilities are always eliminated. Some companies omit eliminating intercompany profits included in inventories, generally on the grounds that they are immaterial.

3.2.4 The Consolidation of Capital

Until recently, many Swiss companies used the former German method for the consolidation of capital. Under this method, the carrying value of investments in subsidiaries is eliminated against the corresponding part of the reported capital and reserves of the subsidiary at each balance sheet date, with any difference being reported as "consolidation difference." There is no restatement of the subsidiary's assets and liabilities to fair values at the acquisition date.

Although this method is rejected by international standards and ARR 2, it is still legal in Switzerland. In practice, most listed companies have, in recent years, renounced the former German method. Although the description is often unclear, we found, in a sample of 57 companies, only one firm still using the former German method in 1992.

There are two other methods of consolidation:

- The "purchase" method, whereby the cost of an acquisition is accounted for by restating the identifiable assets and liabilities of the subsidiary to their fair value at the date of acquisition
- The pooling of interests method, under which the combined assets, liabilities, and reserves of the parent and its subsidiary are recorded at their existing carrying amounts

There is no legal or professional requirement concerning this issue, and most companies do not even indicate which method they use. On the basis of information disclosed in annual reports, it seems, however, that companies generally use the "purchase" method.

3.2.5 The Treatment of Goodwill

Goodwill represents the excess of the cost of acquisition over the fair value of the net identifiable assets of the subsidiary at the date of acquisition. It either can be recognized as an asset in the consolidated financial statements or immediately adjusted against shareholders' interests. In the absence of any provision concerning goodwill in the law and in FER recommendations, both treatments are allowed in Switzerland.

As could be expected, most companies choose to deduct goodwill from retained earnings, probably to avoid a decrease of income in subsequent years because of goodwill amortization.

Nevertheless, some companies prefer recording goodwill as an asset. A significant number of firms concurrently apply either treatment, depending on the characteristics of the subsidiary.

The following treatments of positive goodwill were obtained from a sample of 43 groups disclosing the necessary information:

Deducted from retained earnings	30	(70 %)
Recognized as an asset	7	(16 %)
Both treatments	6	(14 %)
	43	

When recorded as an asset, goodwill is amortized over its "useful life," which varies from 5 to 40 years.

3.3 Foreign Currency Translation

3.3.1 Translation of Financial Statements in Foreign Currencies

ARR 4 indicates that translation of financial statements of foreign subsidiaries can be achieved by one of the following methods:

- Closing/current rate method
- Temporal method
- Monetary/nonmonetary method

The first two methods are similar to those described in IAS 21.

Under the closing rate method, all balance sheet items other than shareholders' equity are translated at the closing rate, whereas revenues and expenses are converted at the closing rate or at a periodic average rate.

Translation differences arising on the translation of the balance sheet are taken into the shareholders' equity; those resulting from the translation of revenues and expenses at an average rate may be either recognized in income or taken to shareholders' equity.

The temporal method introduces a distinction between monetary items, which are translated at the closing rate, and nonmonetary items, converted at the historical rate or, in the case of valuation adjustments, at the rate existing on the date of the revaluation. Revenues and expenses are translated at the rate that existed when the transaction occurred, except depreciations, which are converted at the same rate as the corresponding balance sheet items.

All translation differences are normally recognized in income.

The monetary/nonmonetary method differs from the temporal method by the fact that all nonmonetary items are translated at historical cost whether or not their value has been adjusted. The other difference is that translation differences can be either recorded in the profit and loss account or taken to shareholders' interests.

ARR 4 describes a variant whereby inventories are classified as monetary items and thus translated at the closing rate.

ARR 4 does not provide rules for the choice of translation methods. It just indicates that a combination of methods should be avoided, except when the net investment approach is used.

According to this approach defined in IAS 21, the translation method depends on the nature of the operating and financing activities of the subsidiary:

- For companies with a high degree of autonomy, the closing/current rate method should be used.
- Financial statements of companies whose activities form an integral part of the parent should be translated by using the temporal method.

These rules can be applied but they are not mandatory.

In practice, a small number of groups refer to well-defined translation methods. Most of them use exclusively the closing/current rate method, translating assets and liabilities at the closing rate and revenues and expenses at an average annual rate. Translation differences are generally taken to shareholders' interests.

3.3.2 Translation of Foreign Currency Transactions

The only available reference for translation of foreign currency transactions is the *Swiss Handbook of Auditing*. According to this book (§ 2.2931), transactions in foreign currencies should be recorded at the exchange rate existing at the date of the transaction (benchmark treatment), but many alternative rates can be used, as the rate at the settlement date, the closing rate, and an average or fixed rate.

In the balance sheet, receivables and liabilities in foreign currencies must be converted at the closing rate. Translation differences on the same currency and whose maturity is similar must be compensated. The resulting net difference should be recognized in income in case of loss and deferred if favorable.

In practice, most companies translate foreign currency items at the closing rate and recognize differences, favorable or not, in income.

Some corporations mention that exchange differences on long-term intercompany investments are taken to retained earnings.

There is no provision concerning forward contracts, but several firms indicate that foreign currency receivables and payables covered by forward contracts are translated at contracted future rates.

3.4 Capital and Reserves

3.4.1 Share Capital

In the new company law, the minimum share capital has been increased to 100,000 SFr. Simultaneously, the minimum per value of shares has been reduced from 100 to 10 SFr because the market value of the individual shares of many publicly traded companies had become too high compared with international standards.

There are two types of shares: bearer shares and registered shares. The main difference between them concerns the means of transfer. Bearer shares may be transferred by simple physical delivery, whereas transferring registered shares requires registration of the acquirer in the company's share ledger and, possibly, the company's consent.

Companies may also issue shares with preferential rights consisting, in particular, of supplementary or cumulative dividends, participation in the distribution of assets remaining upon liquidation, and preemptive rights for newly issued shares.

Companies may hold their own shares, up to an aggregate par value of 10% of total capital (i.e., share capital + participation capital). The corresponding voting rights are suspended as long as the company holds these shares.

A necessary condition for the acquisition of its own shares is that the company have available reserves at least equal to the amount of funds necessary for the acquisition. At the time of the acquisition, this amount is transferred to a special reserve (reserve for own shares), which will be released only when these shares are sold or cancelled.

3.4.2 Participation Capital

In addition to share capital, many companies issue participation capital represented by participation certificates. In past decades, these certificates, essentially nonvoting shares, have became a popular tool for financing publicly held companies.

Holders of participation certificates are not entitled to vote, but their pecuniary rights are at least the same as those of common shareholders. There is no minimum amount, but participation capital must not exceed twice the amount of share capital.

3.4.3 Reserves

There are three types of reserves:

- General reserve
- Special reserves
- Statutory and additional reserves

The general reserve is required by law. The Code of Obligations states that 5% of the annual profit must be allocated to the general reserve until it equals 20% of paid-in capital. After this level has been attained, additional allocations must be made, notably an amount of 10% of all dividends paid in excess of a primary dividend corresponding to 5% of the annual profit. The use of the general reserve is mainly restricted to the covering of losses.

Two special reserves are also prescribed by law. They are the reserve for own shares (see above) and the revaluation reserve (see below). The articles of incorporation my provide that additional reserves be set up and specify their purpose and use.

3.5 Liabilities and Provisions

The main issue under liabilities and provisions concerns hidden reserves. According to the *Swiss Handbook of Auditing* (§ 2.2624), hidden reserves cannot be created by recording fictitious liabilities in the balance sheet, but excessive and even unjustified provisions may be constituted practically without limitation.

3.6 Property, Plant, and Equipment

3.6.1 Valuation

In individual financial statements, fixed assets must be valued at historic acquisition or manufacturing costs net of the necessary depreciation (CO, article 665). Any deviation from historical costs is prohibited.

The only exception is for companies whose accumulated losses exceed half of capital and statutory reserves. In that case, the Code of Obligations (article 670) allows a revaluation of real property and participations up to the current acquisition or manufacturing costs. The revaluation difference must be taken to a special reserve (revaluation reserve), which may be reduced only by a conversion into share capital, a write-down, or the sale of the corresponding assets (CO, article 671b).

Although they are not subject to special legal provisions, a generally accepted opinion is that consolidated financial statements may be prepared with alternative valuation bases. ARR 5 states that possible valuation bases for consolidated accounts are historical cost and current cost. It adds that current cost can be based on actual current cost, replacement cost, or a similar cost basis.

The only condition is that uniformity and consistency are ensured. The valuation basis is considered uniform if it is used for all companies being consolidated and for all items in the consolidated financial statements. Deviations from uniformity and consistency are allowed only when objectively motivated and disclosed.

In their consolidated financial statements, several companies depart from historical costs for the valuation of fixed assets.

The extent of revaluation greatly differs among firms, revalued assets being:

- Land only
- Real estate (land and buildings)
- All tangible assets
- Tangible assets less real estate

Revaluation methods also are quite diverse. Some companies apply price indexes, while others use market values or both methods.

3.6.2 Depreciation

The basis for depreciation is generally the acquisition or manufacturing cost. A residual value is rarely deducted. Depreciation may also be based on replacement cost. All depreciation methods may be used (straight-line, declining balance, etc.). Depreciation may also be based on the quantity of goods produced by the asset (units of production method).

Useful lives of assets should normally be chosen in accordance with the general objective of financial statements, which is to provide an "as reliable as possible" measure of the company's position and earnings. In practice, the choice is largely influenced by other considerations, in particular, taxation and hidden reserves.

In Switzerland, tax rules are closely aligned with accounting principles. An expense may be deducted for taxation purpose only if recognized in income. Tax considerations may thus have a considerable influence on the choice of useful lives of fixed assets, firms tending to increase depreciation in order to minimize taxes.

Hidden reserves generally have a large impact on depreciation. Firms willing to create hidden reserves often choose to overestimate the depreciation of fixed assets. Alternatively, those willing to cancel hidden reserves in order to increase their profits tend to reduce the annual depreciation charge. If necessary, they may even reverse depreciation charged in previous years, provided the resulting carrying amount does not exceed the value of the asset, estimated on a going concern basis.

As a result of hidden reserves, it is not exceptional in individual statements to find land with a nil carrying value, buildings depreciated at obviously excessive rates, or equipment entirely depreciated in the year of acquisition.

By comparison with the fire insurance value of fixed tangible assets, which must be disclosed in the notes to the accounts, it is possible to have a rough view of the amount of hidden reserves contained in property, plant, and equipment.

Because consolidated financial statements are not subject to special valuation rules, hidden reserves should have an impact on them too. However, this impact is probably less than on individual statements for several reasons. First, because group accounts are not considered for tax purpose, companies are less motivated to maintain hidden reserves in these statements. Second, because the consolidated financial statements are the result of an aggregation of several individual companies' accounts, they can hardly be used to evaluate the performance of a particular subsidiary. Hidden reserves are thus less necessary to protect a company from competitors.

Finally, whereas individual accounts are mainly used on a national basis, consolidated statements of large companies are more directed to international users. They thus must comply with international standards prohibiting hidden reserves. In addition, reporting abnormally low earnings would place Swiss companies at a competitive disadvantage for obtaining financing on international markets.

Unfortunately, it is impossible to validate these assumptions empirically because, with a few exceptions, firms do not reveal whether hidden reserves have been excluded from their consolidated financial statements. However, depreciation rates disclosed in the notes to the group accounts seem generally close to real useful lives.

3.6.3 Special Issues

The composition of acquisition or manufacturing costs is not defined either by law or by the FER.

Concerning borrowing costs, the *Swiss Handbook of Auditing* notes that interest related to the construction of buildings and equipment may be incorporated in the cost of these assets (§ 2.28 M). It also considers that fixed government grants should be deducted from the cost of corresponding assets.

3.7 Assets Whose Services Are Acquired by Means of Leases

According to the *Swiss Handbook of Auditing*, leases must be accounted for as follows:

- Operating leases should always be charged to income.
- Finance leases may be either charged to income or reflected in the balance sheet of the lessee.

The distinction is based on criteria used by international standards (transfer of ownership by the end of the lease term, lease containing a bargain purchase option, lease term for major part of the useful life of the asset, etc.).

When a finance lease is recorded as an asset, IAS 17 applies:

- At the inception of the lease, an asset and a liability are recorded at an amount equal to the fair value of the lease property.
- Subsequent rentals are apportioned between the finance charge and the reduction in the outstanding liability.
- The asset is depreciated on a systematic basis consistent with the depreciation policy adopted for assets owned by the lessee.

The notes to the accounts must mention the aggregate amounts of obligations arising from leasing agreements not recorded in the balance sheet (CO, article 663b).

In consolidated financial statements, finance leases are generally recorded in the balance sheet.

3.8 Oil, Gas, and Other Mineral Resources

Oil, gas, and other mineral resources are of little importance in Switzerland, so there is no specific standard that applies to them.

3.9 Intangible Assets

3.9.1 Intellectual Property Rights

Intangible assets are not subject to specific valuation rules. Intellectual property rights (e.g., licences, patents, copyrights) may be recorded as assets, provided the general principles of asset valuation are respected. In practice, firms generally recognize as assets only acquired property rights. Recognition of commercial brands in the balance sheet is exceptional.

In individual financial statements, acquired goodwill may be recorded as an asset. The *Swiss Handbook of Auditing* (§ 2.28 Mbis) states that it must be amortized over a period normally not exceeding 8 years.

Goodwill created by the firm itself cannot be recorded in the balance sheet.

3.9.2 Research and Development Costs

Research costs, as usually defined, cannot be recorded as assets. According to the *Swiss Handbook of Auditing*, development costs may be deferred to future periods if two conditions are met:

- They can be attributable to a separately identified product.
- A profit may be expected from these costs.

In practice, development costs are generally charged to income when incurred.

3.9.3 Other Deferred Costs

The Code of Obligations (article 664) enables companies to defer to future periods foundation costs, capital increase costs, and organization costs, provided they are recorded as separate items and written off within 5 years.

We did not find any company using this opportunity in its consolidated financial statements.

3.10 Participating Interests

In individual financial statements, participations are subject to the general valuation rules of assets. They must be valued at acquisition cost less necessary write-downs (CO, article 665). The use of the equity method is prohibited.

Participations exceptionally may be revalued in conformity with CO article 670 when the holding company has cumulative losses exceeding half its share capital and statutory reserves (see Section 3.5.1, above).

In group accounts, nonconsolidated participations are valued at cost or by the equity method. The choice depends on the percentage of voting rights held. Most companies use the following rules:

- Participations from 20% to 50% of voting rights: equity method
- Participations less than 20% of voting rights: acquisition cost

3.11 Inventories

The Code of Obligations (article 666) states that inventories must be valued at the lower of historical cost (acquisition or manufacturing costs) and net realizable value. Hidden reserves may be constituted for inventories as well as for other assets.

According to the *Swiss Handbook of Auditing*, manufacturing costs include overhead expenses other than those related to administrative and selling activities. The allocation of fixed production overhead should be based on the capacity of the facilities. Borrowing interests may be considered as part of production overhead.

Most companies include at least a part of indirect costs in the valuation of inventories. Nevertheless, some firms value finished goods at the direct cost of production.

Work-in-progress whose production period exceeds one year may be accounted for under the percentage of completion method, whereby revenue is recognized in income as the contract activity progresses. This method is widely used by firms engaged in long-term contracts. Some companies simultaneously apply this method and the completed contract method, under which revenue is recognized only when the contract is completed or substantially completed.

All costs formulas may be used for the purpose of assigning costs to inventories (average cost; FIFO; LIFO; highest-in, first out; fixed costs; etc.). In practice, only the first two methods are widely used. Some companies use them simultaneously for different sets of goods.

A write-down of one-third of historical cost may be deducted for tax purposes. Unfortunately, it is generally impossible to know to what extent this opportunity has been used.

In consolidated financial statements, alternatives to historical cost may be used. According to ARR 5, inventories may be valued at actual current cost, replacement cost, or on a similar cost basis. In practice, however, this opportunity is rarely used. The main exception was Ciba-Geigy, which, until 1992, valued its inventories at indexed prices.

3.12 Taxation

Swiss companies are taxed on income and on equity. In a group, every company is taxed separately; there is no group taxation system based on consolidated earnings. Pure holdings are generally exempted from income taxation and taxed on equity at reduced rates.

The basis for income taxation is net income adjusted for expenses exceeding common business practices. Tax adjustments consist mainly of reversing hidden reserves to income. Other adjustments are generally not significant because firms often align their accounting choices to tax standards.

Taxation methods differ among cantons and are relatively complex. Only a few cantons base taxes on current year's income. In most cases, taxes are assessed on last year's profit or on the average taxable income of the preceding 2 years. In this latter case, taxes remain the same during 2 consecutive years. It means, for example, that taxes due in 1994 and 1995 are assessed on the average taxable profit of 1992 and 1993.

When the harmonization of cantonal and communal legislations is completed (normally by the end of the year 2000), a one-year period will be used for both federal and cantonal taxes.

Depending on cantons, tax losses may be deducted in arriving at taxes to be paid in a future period ranging from 2 to 7 years.

Taxes are not based on income only. They also depend on return on equity. For example, an income of 100,000 SFr will be more heavily taxed in a company whose equity is 500,000 SFr than in another with capital and reserves of 1,000,000 SFr.

The federal income tax is currently computed at rates between 3.63% and 9.8% of taxable income. Most cantonal rates are higher. Table 1 shows the impact of income taxes and canton differences.

Companies are also taxed on equity. Taxable equity includes capital and reported and hidden reserves. The federal tax rate is 0.0825% of taxable capital. Cantonal rates vary from 0.26% to 0.9%.

As a result of some distinctive features of the Swiss fiscal system (taxes based on an average profit of 2 years and on return on equity), the annual tax expense can hardly be linked to the income of a particular year. That is the reason why firms generally charge to income the amount of taxes to be paid in the next year.

Nevertheless, in consolidated financial statements, some companies try to apply the international standards on accounting for income taxes (IAS 12).

With a few exceptions, they use the "liability method," whereby the expected effects of current timing differences are reported as liabilities or as assets and adjusted for changes in tax rate or for new taxes.

Taxes payable on undistributed profits of subsidiaries are not accrued unless these profits are expected to be distributed.

Information disclosed is not sufficiently detailed to draw a full description of how deferred taxes are calculated. Only a small number of companies mention the treatment applied to tax losses and whether all timing differences have been provided for (i.e., whether the full or the partial provision approach has been used).

3.13 Pensions

In Switzerland, pensions are funded by a two-level system. At the age of 65 (men) or 62 (women), individuals are entitled to a basic pension corresponding to what is considered the minimum living wage. Funds necessary for the payment of pensions of people already retired are provided by the contributions of enterprises and employees to a fund managed by the federal state.

Additional retirement benefits result from plans supplied by contributions of enterprises and employees to separate funds. In the private sector, these plans are defined contribution schemes. It means that amounts to be paid as retirement benefits are determined by reference to contributions to these funds together with investment earnings thereon.

Because of the characteristics of the Swiss pension scheme, most firms do not have to create a provision for pension costs.

Contributions to the state-managed fund are based on the wages of people currently employed. The rates are the result of an equilibrium between retired and working people in the entire country. Since there is no direct link between them and the position of a particular firm, contributions must be charged to income along with corresponding wages.

Contributions to the other funds are also recognized as expenses at the time of payment. As long as there is no increase in the firm's obligations, no provision is necessary.

4. Expected Future Developments

In recent years, there has been a large movement toward better transparency and more disclosure by Swiss companies. This change is the result of both an increase in legal requirements (new company law) and a voluntary effort on the part of some companies willing to comply with international standards. This movement will likely continue and even intensify in the future.

At the professional level, several new recommendations are being prepared by the FER, in particular on deferred taxes and intangible assets. Until now, the FER recommendations have been rather permissive, generally allowing several different treatments. More stringent texts may be expected in the future as a consequence of the IASC effort to reduce options in accounting standards.

At the request of the Swiss stock exchange association, professors Zünd and Behr presented in 1991 a report on desirable accounting and disclosure regulation for listed companies. Favorable reactions have been recorded from a large number of companies, some of them even asking for a straightforward implementation of International Accounting Standards. Consequently, publicly traded companies should probably shortly comply with additional accounting and disclosure requirements. However, this will have no effect on most large firms whose financial statements are already in accordance with IAS or European directives.

No additional requirement is expected for nonlisted enterprises. Since the FER recommendations are not compulsory, most small firms will probably continue to depart occasionally from generally accepted principles. The end of hidden reserves, in particular, is not expected in the foreseeable future.

The only event that could cause a thorough change in accounting practices would be the adhesion of Switzerland to the European Union, with the resultant implementation of the Fourth and Seventh Directives. Despite the people's recent rejection of the European Economic Area, many observers anticipate this event to take place by the end of the century.

Useful Address

Treuhand Kammer
Schweizerische Kammer der Bücher-, Steuer- und Treuhandexperten
Postfach 892
CH - 8025 Zürich
Tel.: (41) 01 252 32 12
Fax: (41) 01 252 39 11

Financial Statements

s SANDOZ

KONZERN-BILANZEN PER 31. DEZEMBER 1993 UND 1992

AKTIVEN	*	1993 in Mio Fr.	%	1992 in Mio Fr.	%
Anlagevermögen					
Sachanlagen	1	6 610		6 358	
Immaterielle Anlagen	2	120		74	
Finanzielle Anlagen	3	358		235	
Total Anlagevermögen		**7 088**	35,1	6 667	37,0
Umlaufvermögen					
Vorräte	4	2 972		3 027	
Forderungen aus Lieferungen und Leistungen	5	2 737		2 563	
Übriges Umlaufvermögen	6	1 224		1 129	
Wertschriften	7	1 481		1 598	
Flüssige Mittel	8	4 699		3 026	
Total Umlaufvermögen		**13 113**	64,9	11 343	63,0
TOTAL AKTIVEN		**20 201**	100,0	18 010	100,0

*   *Die Erläuterungen im Anhang auf den Seiten 44 bis 57 sind Bestandteil der Konzern-Rechnungslegung.*

s SANDOZ

CONSOLIDATED BALANCE SHEETS AT 31 DECEMBER 1993 AND 1992

ASSETS	*	1993 Sfr. millions	%	1992 Sfr. millions	%
Long-term assets					
Tangible fixed assets	1	6 610		6 358	
Intangible assets	2	120		74	
Financial fixed assets	3	358		235	
Total long-term assets		7 088	35.1	6 667	37.0
Current assets					
Inventories	4	2 972		3 027	
Trade accounts receivable	5	2 737		2 563	
Other current assets	6	1 224		1 129	
Marketable securities	7	1 481		1 598	
Cash and short-term deposits	8	4 699		3 026	
Total current assets		13 113	64.9	11 343	63.0
TOTAL ASSETS		20 201	100.0	18 010	100.0

* *The notes on pages 44 to 57 form an integral part of the consolidated financial statements.*

⌒ **SANDOZ**

PASSIVEN	*	1993 in Mio Fr.	%	1992 in Mio Fr.	%
Eigenkapital					
Aktienkapital	9	629		629	
– Inhaberaktien im Eigenbesitz		36 –		39 –	
Partizipationskapital	10	187		187	
– im Eigenbesitz		50 –		50 –	
Reserven	11	8 121		7 106	
Konzerngewinn des Geschäftsjahres		1 706		1 495	
Total Eigenkapital		**10 557**	**52,2**	**9 328**	**51,8**
Anteile Minderheitsaktionäre		**195**	**1,0**	**175**	**1,0**
Fremdkapital					
Langfristige Verbindlichkeiten					
Finanzielle Verbindlichkeiten	12	1 762		1 301	
Latente Steuern	13	512		562	
Übrige	14	872		698	
Total langfristige Verbindlichkeiten		3 146		2 561	
Kurzfristige Verbindlichkeiten					
Lieferanten		1 031		1 178	
Finanzielle Verbindlichkeiten	15	2 943		2 339	
Übrige	16	2 329		2 429	
Total kurzfristige Verbindlichkeiten		6 303		5 946	
Total Fremdkapital		**9 449**	**46,8**	**8 507**	**47,2**
TOTAL PASSIVEN		**20 201**	**100,0**	**18 010**	**100,0**

* *Die Erläuterungen im Anhang auf den Seiten 44 bis 57 sind Bestandteil der Konzern-Rechnungslegung.*

s **SANDOZ**

EQUITY AND LIABILITIES	*	1993 Sfr. millions	%	1992 Sfr. millions	%
Equity					
Share capital	9	629		629	
– bearer shares held by the Group		36 –		39 –	
Participation capital	10	187		187	
– held by the Group		50 –		50 –	
Reserves	11	8 121		7 106	
Net income for the year		1 706		1 495	
Total equity		**10 557**	52.2	9 328	51.8
Minority interests		**195**	1.0	175	1.0
Liabilities					
Long-term liabilities					
Financial debts	12	1 762		1 301	
Deferred taxes	13	512		562	
Others	14	872		698	
Total long-term liabilities		**3 146**		2 561	
Short-term liabilities					
Trade accounts payable		1 031		1 178	
Financial debts	15	2 943		2 339	
Others	16	2 329		2 429	
Total short-term liabilities		**6 303**		5 946	
Total liabilities		**9 449**	46.8	8 507	47.2
TOTAL EQUITY AND LIABILITIES		**20 201**	100.0	18 010	100.0

*   *The notes on pages 44 to 57 form an integral part of the consolidated financial statements.*

⑀ **SANDOZ**

KONZERN-ERFOLGSRECHNUNGEN 1993 UND 1992

		1993 in Mio Fr.	%	1992 in Mio Fr.	%
	*				
Umsatz	23/24	15 100	100,0	14 416	100,0
Herstellkosten der verkauften Waren		5 773 –		5 519 –	
Bruttomarge		**9 327**	**61,8**	8 897	61,7
Marketing und Vertrieb		4 416 –		4 298 –	
Forschung und Entwicklung	18	1 744 –		1 496 –	
Administration und allgemeine Unkosten		978 –		1 095 –	
Operatives Ergebnis	25	**2 189**	**14,5**	2 008	13,9
Finanzertrag netto	19	104		27	
Übriger Aufwand und Ertrag	20	99 –		55 –	
Gewinn vor Steuern und Minderheitsanteilen		**2 194**		1 980	
Steuern	21	481 –		470 –	
Gewinn vor Minderheitsanteilen		1 713		1 510	
Minderheitsanteile		7 –		15 –	
KONZERNGEWINN		**1 706**	**11,3**	1 495	10,4

* *Die Erläuterungen im Anhang auf den Seiten 44 bis 57 sind Bestandteil der Konzern-Rechnungslegung.*

$ **SANDOZ**

**CONSOLIDATED INCOME STATEMENTS FOR THE YEARS ENDED
31 DECEMBER 1993 AND 1992**

		1993 Sfr. millions	%	1992 Sfr. millions	%
	*				
Sales	23/24	15 100	100.0	14 416	100.0
Cost of goods sold		5 773 –		5 519 –	
Gross margin		**9 327**	61.8	8 897	61.7
Marketing and distribution		4 416 –		4 298 –	
Research and development	18	1 744 –		1 496 –	
Administration and general overheads		978 –		1 095 –	
Operating income	25	**2 189**	14.5	2 008	13.9
Financial income, net	19	104		27	
Other income and expense	20	99 –		55 –	
Income before taxes and minority interests		**2 194**		1 980	
Taxes	21	481 –		470 –	
Income before minority interests		1 713		1 510	
Minority interests		7 –		15 –	
NET INCOME OF THE GROUP		**1 706**	11.3	1 495	10.4

* *The notes on pages 44 to 57 form an integral part of the consolidated financial statements.*

⌣ SANDOZ

KONZERN-MITTELFLUSSRECHNUNGEN 1993 UND 1992

	1993 in Mio Fr.	1992 in Mio Fr.
26		
Konzerngewinn	1 706	1 495
Abschreibungen auf		
– Sachanlagen	731	646
– Immateriellen und finanziellen Anlagen	59	40
Minderheitsanteile am Ergebnis	7	15
Veränderung latente Steuern und		
übrige langfristige Verbindlichkeiten	142	70
Cash Flow vor Veränderung des Netto-Umlaufvermögens	**2 645**	**2 266**
Veränderung Vorräte	6	157 –
Veränderung Forderungen aus Lieferungen und		
Leistungen und übriges Umlaufvermögen	281 –	235 –
Veränderung Lieferanten	176 –	101
Übrige	75 –	122
Geldfluss aus betrieblichen Aktivitäten	**2 119**	**2 097**
Investitionen in Sachanlagen	1 010 –	1 192 –
Investitionen immaterielles und		
finanzielles Anlagevermögen	205 –	106 –
Veränderung Wertschriften	138	301 –
Verkaufserlöse aus Sach- und immateriellen Anlagen	34	76
Akquisitionen (ohne erworbene flüssige Mittel)	146 –	503 –
Geldfluss aus Investitions-Aktivitäten	**1 189 –**	**2 026 –**
Kapital und Agio aus ausgeübten Optionen	83	—
Veränderung langfristige finanzielle Verbindlichkeiten	419	9 –
Veränderung kurzfristige finanzielle Verbindlichkeiten	592	157
Dividendenausschüttung an Dritte	347 –	259 –
Geldfluss aus Finanzierungs-Aktivitäten	**747**	**111 –**
Umrechnungsdifferenz auf flüssigen Mitteln	4 –	13 –
Netto-Veränderung der flüssigen Mittel	**1 673**	**53 –**

* *Die Erläuterungen im Anhang auf den Seiten 44 bis 57 sind Bestandteil der Konzern-Rechnungslegung.*

43

⅀ **SANDOZ**

CONSOLIDATED STATEMENTS OF FUNDS FLOW FOR THE YEARS ENDED 31 DECEMBER 1993 AND 1992

	1993 Sfr. millions	1992 Sfr. millions
	* 26	
Net income	1 706	1 495
Depreciation on:		
– Tangible fixed assets	731	646
– Intangible and financial fixed assets	59	40
Minority interests	7	15
Change in deferred taxes and other long-term liabilities	142	70
Cash flow before working capital changes	**2 645**	**2 266**
Change in inventories	6	157 –
Change in trade accounts receivable and other current assets	281 –	235 –
Change in trade accounts payable	176 –	101
Others	75 –	122
Net cash provided from operating activities	**2 119**	**2 097**
Investment in tangible fixed assets	1 010 –	1 192 –
Investment in intangible and financial fixed assets	205 –	106 –
Change in marketable securities	138	301 –
Sale of tangible and intangible fixed assets	34	76
Acquisitions (net of cash acquired)	146 –	503 –
Net cash used in investing activities	**1 189 –**	**2 026 –**
Capital and premium from exercise of debenture warrants	83	—
Change in long-term financial debts	419	9 –
Change in short-term financial debts	592	157
Dividends paid to third parties	347 –	259 –
Net cash used in financing activities	**747**	**111 –**
Net effect of currency translation on cash and short-term deposits	4 –	13 –
Net change in cash and short term deposits	**1 673**	**53 –**

*   *The notes on pages 44 to 57 form an integral part of the consolidated financial statements.*

•

s **SANDOZ**

NOTES TO THE CONSOLIDATED FINANCIAL STATEMENTS
(Notes include pages 44 to 57)

Accounting Policies

Introduction

The financial reporting of the Sandoz Group is prepared in accordance with the standards formulated by the International Accounting Standards Committee (IASC). The Group financial statements have been audited by the Société Fiduciaire Suisse-Coopers & Lybrand SA, Basle, and the individual financial statements of the significant subsidiaries have also been audited.

Scope of consolidation

All companies in which Sandoz Ltd., Basle, holds either a direct or indirect equity investment and possesses the majority of the voting rights or exercises direct or indirect control through other means are fully consolidated.

The most significant companies included in the consolidation for the first time in 1993 are:

- FEB Ltd., Manchester (UK), consolidated as from January 1993 (Construction & Environment Division)
- Spectrum Ltd., Minneapolis (Minn., USA), consolidated as from May 1993 (Chemicals Division)
- Reforma-Dianata B.V., Veenendaal (NL), consolidated as from August 1993 (Nutrition Division)

- Veneziani SpA, Triest (I), consolidated as from August 1993 (Construction & Environment Division)

The participation agreement with Gazzoni 1907 SpA of Bologna (I) became legally binding on 15 December 1993. The company will be consolidated as from 1 January 1994 and is included in other investments under financial fixed assets in the 1993 consolidated balance sheet.

The most significant company divested in 1993 (February) was NK Lawn & Garden Co., Minneapolis (Minn., USA) of the Seeds Division.

Associated companies (investments of between 20% and 50% in a company's equity) are consolidated using the equity method, so long as a significant influence is exercised by the Group. All other minority investments are valued at their acquisition cost less impairments in value.

Principles of consolidation

The financial statements of the companies included in the consolidation have been prepared as of the date of the consolidated financial statements using the historical cost convention and applying uniform presentation and valuation principles.

The purchase method of accounting is used for acquired subsidiaries.

Intercompany income and expenses, receivables and payables have been offset. Unrealized profits at the year end resulting from group internal transactions have been eliminated.

Sales are recognized when deliveries and services to third parties are invoiced and are reported net of sales taxes and rebates. Sales and profits of long-term service contracts in progress are recognized based on their percentage of completion.

The minority interests in the equity and the results of consolidated companies are separately disclosed in the balance sheet and income statement.

Tangible fixed assets

Tangible fixed assets have been valued at historical acquisition or production costs and depreciated on a straight-line basis to the income statement, in accordance with the related Group guidelines over the following maximum estimated useful lives:
- Buildings   40 years
- Machinery and equipment   16 years
- Furniture, vehicles,   5 to computer hardware   10 years

Land is valued at acquisition cost. In high-inflation countries tangible fixed assets and related depreciation are indexed in accordance with inflation. Tangible fixed assets which are financed by leases giving rights to use the assets as if owned are capitalized with their estimated

s SANDOZ

present value and depreciated in the same manner as other fixed assets.

Intangible assets

Purchased intangible assets – such as patents, trademarks and other rights – are capitalized at historical cost and depreciated on a straight-line basis to the income statement over their estimated useful lives, with a maximum of ten years.

Goodwill

Goodwill, arising when the acquisition cost of an investment in a company is in excess of the fair value of net assets acquired, is fully written off against reserves in the year of acquisition.

Financial fixed assets

Associated companies are accounted for by the equity method. All other minority investments are reported at their acquisition cost and loans at their nominal value. Adjustments are made for any permanent impairment in value. The net result is included in other income and expense.

Inventories

Purchased products are valued at acquisition cost while self-manufactured products are valued at manufacturing costs including related production overheads.

Inventory is substantially valued at average cost in the balance sheet and this value is used for the cost of goods sold in the income statement.

Adjustments have been deducted for inventories with a lower market value or which are slow-moving. Unsaleable inventory has been fully written-off.

Trade accounts receivable

The reported values represent the invoiced amounts, less adjustments for doubtful receivables.

Marketable securities

Marketable security portfolios are valued at the lower of acquisition cost or market value. The net result is included in financial income.

Foreign currency conversion

Income, expense and funds flow of the consolidated companies have been translated into Swiss francs using the respective yearly average sales-weighted exchange rates. The balance sheets are translated using the year-end exchange rates. Exchange rate differences relating to the translation of shareholders' equity and long-term Group internal financings of consolidated companies, arising from exchange rate movements compared to the prior year and differences resulting from the translation of the net income are allocated to

reserves. The exception to this is for Group companies in high-inflation countries, where translation and transaction differences are charged to the income statement.

All other transaction differences on current business operations are recorded in the income statement.

Financial instruments

Financial instruments (contracts or options for foreign currencies, interest rates and similar instruments) which relate to financial assets or interest-bearing liabilities are valued in the same manner as the related balance sheet positions at the lower of historical cost or market value. Adjustments are recorded in financial income and expense.

Gains and losses arising from the use of financial instruments for the purpose of hedging other risks are recorded in the income statement when the gains and losses arising from the underlying hedged position are recognized.

All other financial instruments are valued at fair market value with the resulting gains of losses recorded in financial income and expense.

Deferred taxes

Deferred taxes have been calculated using the Comprehensive Liability Method. These are cal-

SANDOZ

culated on the timing differences
that arise between the recognition of items in the balance
sheets of Group companies used
for tax purposes and those prepared for consolidation purposes. The withholding tax on possible distributions of retained
earnings of Group companies
has not been taken into account
since, generally, the retained
earnings are reinvested. The
total deferred tax, calculated
using applicable tax rates, is
included in long-term liabilities.
The amount relating to the
reporting period is recorded in
the income statement.

**Pension fund, post-retirement and
termination benefits**

**a) Defined benefit
pension plans**

The liability in respect of de-
fined-benefit pension plans is
the Projected Benefit Obligation
periodically calculated by independent actuaries. The charge
for such pension plans representing the net periodic pension
cost is included in personnel
expenses.

**b) Post-retirement benefits
other than pensions**

The US subsidiaries of the Sandoz
Group provide healthcare and
life insurance benefits for the
majority of their retired employees and their eligible dependents. The cost of these benefits
are actuarially determined and
accrued over employees' wor-

king lives. Personnel costs and
long-term liabilities include the
expense and related liability,
respectively.

c) Termination benefits

These are provided in accordance with the legal requirements
of certain countries.

Research and development

Research and development
expenses are fully charged to the
income statement except for
fixed assets, which are depreciated over their estimated useful
lives.

s. **SANDOZ**

DETAILS OF CHANGES IN THE GROUP'S TANGIBLE FIXED ASSETS DURING THE YEARS ENDED 31 DECEMBER 1993 AND 1992

in Sfr. millions	Land	Buildings	Machinery and equipment	Furniture, vehicles, computer hardware	Plant under construction	Total 1993 Sfr. millions	Total 1992 Sfr. millions
Cost							
at 1 January	374	3 640	4 186	1 742	1 225	11 167	10 320
Consolidation changes	2	16	40	11	0	69	14
Additions and reclassifications	5	707	683	259	644 –	1 010	1 192
Disposals	4 –	84 –	74 –	143 –	2 –	307 –	300 –
Currency translation effects	1	17 –	69 –	5 –	27 –	117 –	59 –
at 31 December	**378**	**4 262**	**4 766**	**1 864**	**552**	**11 822**	**11 167**
Accumulated depreciation							
at 1 January		1 531 –	2 248 –	1 030 –		4 809 –	4 413 –
Consolidation changes		0	12 –	8 –		20 –	3 –
Additions		163 –	310 –	258 –		731 –	646 –
Disposals		66	89	134		289	229
Currency translation effects		7	48	4		59	24
at 31 December		**1 621 –**	**2 433 –**	**1 158 –**		**5 212 –**	**4 809 –**
Book values at 31 December	**378**	**2 641**	**2 333**	**706**	**552**	**6 610**	**6 358**
Insured values at 31 December						**15 083**	**15 107**

* *The capitalized cost of tangible fixed assets under lease contracts at 31 December 1993 amounts to Sfr. 52 million with a book value of Sfr. 35 million (1992: Sfr. 43 million and Sfr. 28 million, respectively)*

---

s **SANDOZ**

DETAILS TO THE CONSOLIDATED FINANCIAL STATEMENTS

		1993 Sfr. millions	1992 Sfr. millions

1 **Tangible fixed assets**

Detailed information regarding the breakdown of tangible fixed assets by categories and their changes is shown on page 47.

2 **Intangible assets**
in Sfr. millions

	Cost		Accumulated depreciation		Book values	
	1993	1992	1993	1992	1993	1992
at 1 January	121	109	47 –	52 –	74	57
Additions	86	50	24 –	29 –	62	21
Disposals	21 –	39 –	5	34	16 –	5 –
Currency translation effects	1 –	1	1			1
at 31 December	**185**	**121**	**65 –**	**47 –**	**120**	**74**

	1993	1992
	120	**74**

3 **Financial fixed assets**

	1993	1992
Investments in associated companies	123	144
Other investments	202	68
Long-term loans	33	23
Total	**358**	**235**

4 **Inventories**

	1993	1992
Raw material, consumables	1223	1165
Finished products, work in progress	1749	1862
Total	**2972**	**3027**

5 **Trade accounts receivable**

	1993	1992
Total	2844	2649
Provision for doubtful receivables	107 –	86 –
Total net	**2737**	**2563**

ﾐ **SANDOZ**

		1993 Sfr. millions	1992 Sfr. milions
6 **Other current assets**			
Other receivables		726	795
Prepaid expenses/accrued income		498	334
Total		**1224**	**1129**

7 **Marketable securities**

Market value including related financial instruments		**1709**	**1684**

8 **Cash and short-term deposits**

These comprise time deposits with prime-name banks, cash on hand and bank current account balances.

9 **Share capital**

Shares of Sfr. 100 par value each	No. of shares 31.12.1993		
Registered shares	**5 477 404**	**548**	**548**
Bearer shares	815 404	81	81
Less:			
– Reserved for Sandoz Overseas Finance Ltd., B.V.I. (SOFI) debentures with equity warrants	110 629 –	11 –	14 –
– Deposited with banks, at the disposal of the Board of Directors	249 340 –	25 –	25 –
Total bearer shares net	**455 435**	**45**	**42**
Total share capital net		**593**	**590**

⅍ **SANDOZ**

10 Participation capital	No. of BPCs 31.12.1993	1993 Sfr. millions	1992 Sfr. millions
Bearer Participation Certificates (BPCs) of Sfr. 100 par value each	1 870 448	187	187
Less:			
– Reserved for SOFI debentures with equity warrants	154 489 –	16 –	16 –
– Deposited with banks, at the disposal of the Board of Directors (issued 1992)	340 000 –	34 –	34 –
Total participation capital net	**1 375 959**	**137**	**137**

11 Reserves		
Balance at 1 January	7 106	6 512
– Retained earnings of previous year	1 148*	855*
– Goodwill amortization	115 –	176 –
– Translation differences	98 –	85 –
– Premium from exercise of debenture warrants	80	—
Total reserves at 31 December	**8 121**	**7 106**
Net income for the year	**1 706**	**1 495**
Total equity at 31 December (items 9, 10 and 11 plus net income)	**10 557**	**9 328**
* After dividends paid to third parties	347	259

֍ **SANDOZ**

	1993 Sfr. millions	1992 Sfr. millions
12 Long-term financial debts		
2¹/₄% debentures with equity warrants 1987/97 of Sfr. 150 million issued in April 1987 by Sandoz Overseas Finance Ltd., British Virgin Islands, and guaranteed by Sandoz Ltd., Basle (all warrants exercised by end of August 1991) Maturity (at 100%) on 18 May 1997, with early repayment options on 18 May 1995 and 18 May 1996 (at 100%).	150	150
4% debentures with equity warrants 1991/98 of US$ 500 millions issued in September 1991 by Sandoz Overseas Finance Ltd., British Virgin Islands, and guaranteed by Sandoz Ltd., Basle	735	710
Each debenture of US$ 10000 carries 70 Sandoz Ltd. bearer share and 80 Sandoz Ltd. BPC subscription rights, 25 of which entitle the holder, from 11 November 1991 until 11 January 1995, to purchase a bearer share or a BPC at a price of Sfr. 2410 or Sfr. 2240, respectively.		
To cover the exercise of these rights Sandoz Overseas Finance Ltd. acquired a total of 140000 bearer shares and 160000 BPCs (par value Sfr. 100 in both cases) and placed them on deposit with a leading bank. This stock acquired in this way is dividend-bearing.		
A total of 29371 bearer shares and 5511 BPCs had been sold under option rights by 31 December 1993. Maturity on 30 September 1998, earlier redemption possible only for tax reasons.		
6³/₈% debenture 1993/2000 of US$ 300 million issued in March 1993 by Sandoz Overseas Finance Ltd., British Virgin Islands, and guaranteed by Sandoz Ltd., Basle Maturity on 3 March 2000. Early repayment possible only for tax reasons.	441	—
Liabilities to banks and other financial institutions	474	479
Obligations under capital leases	39	28
Subtotal	1839	1367
Less current portion	77 –	66 –
Total	**1762**	**1301**

s **SANDOZ**

Long-term financial debts (continued)		1993 Sfr. millions	1992 Sfr. millions
Breakdown by maturity	1994		87
	1995	114	98
	1996	97	81
	1997	250	234
	1998	773	
	Thereafter	528	801
Total		**1762**	**1301**
– Portion secured (normally against fixed assets)		380	
Breakdown by currency	US$	1181	718
	SFr.	156	157
	ATS	94	105
	Yen	252	225
	Others	79	96
Total		**1762**	**1301**

13 Deferred taxes

	1993	1992
Liabilities due to fixed assets	586	578
Assets principally due to personnel benefit provisions	251 –	222 –
Others	177	206
Total	**512**	**562**

14 Other long-term liabilities

	1993	1992
Pension funds, incl. termination benefits	436	453
Post-retirement benefits in respect of US Group companies	281	245
Others	155	—
Total	**872**	**698**

15 Short-term financial debts

	1993	1992
Current portion of long-term financial debts	77	66
Bank and other financial institutions (incl. employees' accounts)	2079	1738
Commercial paper	787	535
Total	**2943**	**2339**

s **SANDOZ**

16 Other short-term liabilities	1993 Sfr. millions	1992 Sfr. millions
Other payables	545	522
Accrued expenses	775	813
Provisions for:		
– Current income and other taxes	258	192
– Social security/pension funds	195	91
– Others	556	811
Total	**2329**	**2429**

17 Pension funds

The Group has, apart from the legally required social security schemes, numerous independent pension plans. The assets are principally kept externally. For certain Group companies, however, no independent assets for the pension benefit obligations exist. In these cases, a related provision (including termination benefits) has been created, which is included in the balance sheet under long-term liabilities. The cost to the employer is included in the income statement.

During 1993, the calculation of the anticipated liability for active and retired employees for all important defined benefit pension plans produces the following:

– Present value of the anticipated benefits of active and retired employees	4887	4335
– Assets of the pension plans*	5482	4668
– **Surplus**	**595**	**333**
* portion included in the balance sheet as long-term liabilities	436	453

18 Research and development

Pharmaceuticals	1331 –	1116 –
Other	413 –	380 –
Total	**1744 –**	**1496 –**

⌔ **SANDOZ**

	1993 Sfr. millions	1992 Sfr. millions
19 **Financial income, net**		
Income from cash, short-term deposits and marketable securities	487	359
Financial expense	283 –	286 –
Exchange rate differences	100 –	46 –
Total	**104**	**27**
20 **Other income and expense**		
Results from financial fixed assets	27	15 –
Other income	96	65
Other expense	130 –	105 –
Restructuring costs	92 –	—
Total	**99 –**	**55 –**
21 **Taxes**		
Current income taxes	340 –	284 –
Deferred income taxes	34	27 –
Capital and other taxes	175 –	159 –
Total	**481 –**	**470 –**

Income taxes have been calculated on the basis of profit for the financial year, taking account taxes deferred due to timing differences.

	1993 Sfr. millions	1992 Sfr. millions
22 **Personnel expenses**		
Wages and salaries	3027 –	2925 –
Social security and pension plans	865 –	823 –
Others	107 –	59 –
Total	**3999 –**	**3807 –**

S. **SANDOZ**

---

23 **Divisional breakdown of key figures 1993 and 1992** (in Sfr. millions)

Division	Sales		Investments in tangible fixed assets		Net operating assets[1] at 31.12.		Employees at 31.12.	
	1993	1992	1993	1992	1993	1992	1993	1992
Pharmaceuticals	7 348	6 870	590	726	4 913	4 529	24 092	24 305
Nutrition	1 722	1 746	99	78	574	561	5 911	5 878
Seeds	981	1 021	58	63	750	773	4 292	5 237
Total **Life Sciences**	**10 051**	**9 637**	**747**	**867**	**6 237**	**5 863**	**34 295**	**35 420**
Chemicals	2 500	2 452	133	172	2 199	2 186	8 464	8 362
Agro	1 315	1 228	48	70	973	990	3 249	3 498
Const.&Environ.	1 234	1 099	63	62	654	559	4 782	4 357
Total **Chemicals & Environment**	**5 049**	**4 779**	**244**	**304**	**3 826**	**3 735**	**16 495**	**16 217**
Others			19	21	786[2]–	1 079[2]–	1 760[3]	1 723[3]
Total Group	**15 100**	**14 416**	**1 010**	**1 192**	**9 277**	**8 519**	**52 550**	**53 360**

24 **Regional breakdown of key figures 1993 and 1992** (in Sfr. millions)

Region	Sales		Investments in tangible fixed assets		Net operating assets[1] at 31.12.		Employees at 31.12.	
	1993	1992	1993	1992	1993	1992	1993	1992
Europe	6 401	6 559	577	723	4 948	4 592	29 034	29 344
USA / Canada	4 643	4 281	273	280	2 103	2 140	11 491	12 072
Asia	2 760	2 382	128	156	1 604	1 298	7 455	7 390
Latin America	876	788	27	21	499	375	3 840	3 835
Africa / Australia	420	406	5	12	123	114	730	719
Total Group	**15 100**	**14 416**	**1 010**	**1 192**	**9 277**	**8 519**	**52 550**	**53 360**

1 *Long-term and current assets (excluding marketable securities, cash and short-term deposits) less non-interest-bearing liabilities*
2 *Deferred taxes and non-allocated provisions*
3 *Group management, Finance and other non-allocated functions*

ઽ **SANDOZ**

	1993 Sfr. millions	1992 Sfr. millions
25 **Operating income**		

Total operating income breaks down as follows:

	1993 Sfr. millions	1992 Sfr. millions
1 **Life Sciences** Pharmaceuticals, Nutrition, Seeds	1681	1601
2 **Chemicals & Environment** Chemicals, Agro, Construction & Environment	508	407
Total	**2189**	**2008**

26 **Consolidated statements of funds flow**

The consolidated statements of funds flow are based on the statements of the individual Group companies translated using average sales-weighted exchange rates and are therefore not directly comparable with the consolidated balance sheets.

However, this does not apply to cash and short-term deposits, which are translated at year-end rates and the resultant exchange gain or loss shown.

27 **Commitments and contingencies**

Commitments
Commitments arising from fixed-term leases in effect at
31 December are as follows:

	1993	1992
1993	–	81
1994	89	60
1995	65	41
1996	42	30
1997	30	23
1998	25	–
Thereafter	122	131
Total	**373**	**366**
Expense	113 –	171 –

Long-term research (primarily pharmaceutical) and other
agreements concluded with various institutes and specialized
companies entailed costs over the next five years, respectively
as follows:

	1993	1992
	510	400

s **SANDOZ**

Contingencies	1993 Sfr.	1992 Sfr.

The Group companies have to observe the laws, government orders and regulations of the country in which they operate. A number of them are currently involved in administrative proceedings arising out of the normal conduct of their business.

A number of Group companies are also the object of litigation arising out of the normal conduct of their business, as a result of which claims could be made against them which, in whole or in part, might not be covered by insurance.

In the opinion of management, however, the outcome of the actions referred to will not materially affect the Group's financial position.

28 **Group and other associated companies**

These are listed on pages 76 to 79.

29 **Currency translation rates**

Year-end rates used to translate the consolidated balance sheets (equivalent to average rate for December):

	1993	1992
1 US$	1.47	1.42
100 DM	85.75	89.90
100 FF	25.05	26.40
1 £	2.18	2.21
100 Lit	-.0869	-.1012
100 Yen	1.34	1.15

Averages sales-weighted rates used for the consolidated income statements and consolidated statements of funds flow:

	1993	1992
1 US$	1.48	1.41
100 DM	89.55	89.94
100 FF	26.28	26.51
1 £	2.21	2.46
100 Lit	-.0944	-.1146
100 Yen	1.33	1.11

.S. **SANDOZ**

BERICHT DER KONZERN-RECHNUNGSPRÜFER

**An die Generalversammlung der
SANDOZ AG
Basel**

Wir haben die vom Verwaltungsrat vorgelegte konsolidierte Jahresrechnung des Sandoz-Konzerns, bestehend aus der auf den Seiten 40
bis 57 wiedergegebenen Konzern-Bilanz, Konzern-Erfolgsrechnung,
Konzern-Mittelflussrechnung und dem Anhang zur Konzern-Rech-
nung, für das am 31. Dezember 1993 abgeschlossene Geschäftsjahr
im Sinne der gesetzlichen Vorschriften geprüft. Unsere Prüfung
erfolgte nach den «International Standards on Auditing» der «International Federation of Accountants». Wir bestätigen, dass wir die
gesetzlichen Anforderungen an Befähigung und Unabhängigkeit
erfüllen.

Nach unserer Auffassung vermittelt die konsolidierte Jahresrechnung
ein den tatsächlichen Verhältnissen entsprechendes Bild der Vermö-
gens-, Finanz- und Ertragslage, in Übereinstimmung mit den «International Accounting Standards» (IAS) des «International Accounting
Standards Committee», den im Anhang wiedergegebenen Konsoli-
dierungs- und Bewertungsgrundsätzen sowie den gesetzlichen Vorschriften.

Wir empfehlen, die vorliegende konsolidierte Jahresrechnung zu
genehmigen.

Basel, 25. März 1994

Schweizerische Treuhandgesellschaft –
Coopers & Lybrand AG

Prof. C. Helbling
Dipl. Bücherexperte

M. B. Cheetham
Chartered Accountant
Leitender Revisor

,Ŝ. **SANDOZ**

REPORT OF THE GROUP AUDITORS

To the General Meeting of
SANDOZ LTD
Basle

We have audited the consolidated financial statements of the Sandoz
Group presented by the Board of Directors, consisting of the consolidated balance sheet, consolidated income statement, consolidated
statement of funds flow and the notes ot the consolidated financial
statements on pages 40 to 57, for the year ended December 31, 1993
in accordance with the provisions of the law. Our audit was conducted in accordance with the International Standards on Auditing
issued by the International Federation of Accountants. We confirm
that we meet the legal requirements concerning professional qualification and independence.

In our opinion, the consolidated financial statements give a true and
fair view of the financial position, results of operations and changes
in financial position, in accordance with the International Accounting
Standards (IAS) issued by the International Accounting Standards
Committee, the principles of consolidation and valuation described in
the notes to the consolidated financial statements and also with provisions of the law.

We recommend that the financial statements submitted to you be
approved.

Basle, March 25, 1994

Société Fiduciaire Suisse –
Coopers & Lybrand SA

Prof. C. Helbling   M. B. Cheetham
Swiss certified public accountant   Chartered Accountant
                                     Lead auditor

58

֍ **SANDOZ**

BILANZ DER SANDOZ AG VOR DER GEWINNVERTEILUNG

	31. Dezember 1993 Franken	%	31. Dezember 1992 Franken	%
AKTIVEN				
Beteiligungen	2 691 646 967		2 740 215 966	
Total Anlagevermögen	2 691 646 967	67,4	2 740 215 966	63,6
Forderungen:				
Konzerngesellschaften	700 644 026		887 450 254	
Dritte	89 621 561		76 602 355	
Wertschriften	256 116 094		278 369 264	
Flüssige Mittel	234 615 568		306 903 009	
Aktive Rechnungsabgrenzungen	18 841 232		17 389 677	
Total Umlaufvermögen	1 299 838 481	32,6	1 566 714 559	36,4
TOTAL AKTIVEN	3 991 485 448	100,0	4 306 930 525	100,0

◎ **SANDOZ**

SANDOZ LTD BALANCE SHEET PRIOR TO PROFIT APPROPRIATION

	31 December 1993 Sfr.	%	31 December 1992 Sfr.	%
ASSETS				
Participations	2 691 646 967		2 740 215 966	
Total long-term assets	2 691 646 967	67.4	2 740 215 966	63.6
Receivables from:				
Group Companies	700 644 026		887 450 254	
Others	89 621 561		76 602 355	
Securities	256 116 094		278 369 264	
Liquid assets	234 615 568		306 903 009	
Accrued income	18 841 232		17 389 677	
Total current assets	1 299 838 481	32.6	1 566 714 559	36.4
TOTAL ASSETS	3 991 485 448	100.0	4 306 930 525	100.0

⒮ **SANDOZ**

	31. Dezember 1993 Franken	%	31. Dezember 1992 Franken	%
PASSIVEN				
Aktienkapital	629 280 800		629 280 800	
Partizipationskapital	187 044 800		187 044 800	
Allgemeine Reserve	1 576 096 199		1 544 096 199	
Reserve für eigene Aktien	86 000 000		89 000 000	
Freie Reserven	651 913 757		648 913 757	
Total	**3 130 335 556**		**3 098 335 556**	
Verfügbarer Gewinn:				
Gewinnvortrag	10 808 422		8 159 596	
Jahresgewinn	461 063 057		391 822 878	
Bilanzgewinn	471 871 479		399 982 474	
Total Eigenkapital	**3 602 207 035**	90,2	**3 498 318 030**	81,2
Verbindlichkeiten:				
Konzerngesellschaften	5 333 740		456 858 697	
Dritte	6 069 241		1 282 428	
Rückstellungen	304 025 000		285 430 000	
Passive Rechnungsabgrenzungen	73 850 432		65 041 370	
Total Fremdkapital	**389 278 413**	**9,8**	**808 612 495**	**18,8**
TOTAL PASSIVEN	**3 991 485 448**	**100,0**	**4 306 930 525**	**100,0**

▵ **SANDOZ**

	31 December 1993 Sfr.	%	31 December 1992 Sfr.	%
EQUITY AND LIABILITIES				
Share capital	629 280 800		629 280 800	
BPC capital	187 044 800		187 044 800	
General reserve	1 576 096 199		1 544 096 199	
Reserve for shares held by Group	86 000 000		89 000 000	
Free reserves	651 913 757		648 913 757	
Total	**3 130 335 556**		**3 098 335 556**	
Available profit				
Balance from previous year	10 808 422		8 159 596	
Net profit for the year	461 063 057		391 822 878	
Total available profit	471 871 479		399 982 474	
Total equity	**3 602 207 035**	90.2	**3 498 318 030**	81.2
Liabilities to				
Group Companies	5 333 740		456 858 697	
Others	6 069 241		1 282 428	
Provisions	304 025 000		285 430 000	
Accrued expenses	73 850 432		65 041 370	
Total liabilities	**389 278 413**	9.8	**808 612 495**	18.8
TOTAL EQUITY AND LIABILITIES	**3 991 485 448**	100.0	**4 306 930 525**	100.0

ERFOLGSRECHNUNG DER SANDOZ AG

	1993 Franken	1992 Franken
ERTRAG		
Beteiligungserträge	321 201 144	349 189 082
Zins- und Wertschriftenerträge	121 000 057	92 942 792
Übrige Erträge	93 798 224	83 090 551
Total Ertrag	**535 999 425**	**525 222 425**
AUFWAND		
Finanzaufwand	36 839 558	28 003 409
Verwaltungsaufwand	4 975 629	3 586 421
Abschreibungen und Wertberichtigungen	16 215 839	91 959 393
Übriger Aufwand inkl. Steuern	16 905 342	9 850 324
Total Aufwand	**74 936 368**	**133 399 547**
JAHRESGEWINN	461 063 057	391 822 878

S **SANDOZ**

SANDOZ LTD STATEMENT OF INCOME

	1993 Sfr.	1992 Sfr.
REVENUE		
Income from participations	321 201 144	349 189 082
Income from investments and securities	121 000 057	92 942 792
Other income	93 798 224	83 090 551
Total revenue	**535 999 425**	**525 222 425**
EXPENDITURE		
Financial expenses	36 839 558	28 003 409
Administrative expenses	4 975 629	3 586 421
Depreciation and value adjustments	16 215 839	91 959 393
Other expenditure (incl. taxes)	16 905 342	9 850 324
Total expenditure	**74 936 368**	**133 399 547**
NET PROFIT FOR THE YEAR	**461 063 057**	**391 822 878**

ꜱ **SANDOZ**

GEWINNVERWENDUNG

Antrag an die Generalversammlung	1993 Franken	1992 Franken
Verfügbarer Gewinn		
Jahresgewinn	461 063 057	391 822 878
Vortrag vom Vorjahr	10 808 422	8 159 596
Total verfügbarer Gewinn	**471 871 479**	**399 982 474**
Gewinnverwendung		
Ausschüttung einer Dividende von brutto Fr. 58.– auf 6 043 468 Aktien (Vorjahr Fr. 47.–) und	350 521 144	284 042 996
von brutto Fr. 58.– auf 1 530 448 Partizipationsscheine (Vorjahr Fr. 47.–)	88 765 984	71 931 056
Total Dividende brutto	439 287 128	355 974 052
Tantième	–	1 200 000
Zuweisung an die allgemeine Reserve	–	32 000 000
Total Gewinnverwendung	**439 287 128**	**389 174 052**
Vortrag auf neue Rechnung	32 584 351	10 808 422

ᔑ **SANDOZ**

PROPOSALS FOR PROFIT APPROPRIATION

	1993 Sfr.	1992 Sfr.
Available profit		
Net profit for the year	461 063 057	391 822 878
Balance brought forward from previous year	10 808 422	8 159 596
Total available profit	471 871 479	399 982 474
Appropriation		
Payment of a dividend of Sfr. 58 gross on 6 043 468 registered and bearer shares (1992: Sfr. 47) and	350 521 144	284 042 996
of Sfr. 58 gross on 1 530 448 BPCs (1992: Sfr. 47)	88 765 984	71 931 056
Total gross dividend payments	439 287 128	355 974 052
Directors' fees	–	1 200 000
Transfer to general reserve	–	32 000 000
Total appropriation	439 287 128	389 174 052
Balance to be carried forward	32 584 351	10 808 422

s SANDOZ

NOTES TO THE FINANCIAL STATEMENTS 1993 OF SANDOZ LTD
(as at 31 December 1993)

1. Contingent liabilities

At 31 December 1993 total guarantees stood at Sfr. 2865.2 million (31.12.92: Sfr. 1347.5 million). They were made up as follows:

	Sfr. millions
Guarantees in favour of Group Companies, associated companies and agents (in use at balance-sheet date Sfr. 195.5 million)	299.9
Guarantee to cover the capital and interest of the outstanding debentures with equity warrants of the 2¼% Sandoz Overseas Finance Ltd., B.V.I., issue 1987/97 of Sfr. 150 million	163.5
Guarantee to cover the capital and interest of the oustanding debentures with equity warrants of the 4% Sandoz Overseas Finance Ltd., B.V.I., issue 1991/98 of US$ 500 million	882.0
Guarantee to cover the capital and interest of the Sandoz Overseas Finance Ltd., B.V.I., 6⅜% debenture 1993/2000 of US$ 300 million	637.8
Repurchase agreement for the Sandoz Corporation, New York, commercial paper program of US$ 600 million (US$ 417 million = Sfr. 613 million issued at balance-sheet date)	882.0
Total	**2865.2**

2. Participations

The principal participations of Sandoz Ltd. are shown on pages 76 to 79 of this report.

3. Shares and BPCs held by the Company itself or by its affiliates

Bearer shares

Of the 140000 shares of par value Sfr. 100 originally transferred to Sandoz Overseas Finance Ltd., British Virgin Islands, to be held in reserve for exercise of the warrants on the US$ 500 million 4% debenture 1991/98, 29371 had been put into circulation as a result of such exercise by 31 December 1993. This leaves a remainder of 110629 shares, while a further 249340 bearer shares of par value Sfr. 100 each are held by a consortium of banks for issue at the discretion of the Board. These latter shares are not eligible for dividend.

Bearer Participation Certificates

Of the 160000 bearer participation certificates of par value Sfr. 100 originally transferred to Sandoz Overseas Finance Ltd., British Virgin Island, to be held in reserve for exercise of the warrants on the US$ 500 million 4% debenture 1991/98, 5511 had been put into circulation as a result of such exercise by 31 December 1993. This leaves a remainder of 154489 BPCs, while a further 340000 BPCs of par value Sfr. 100 each are held by a consortium of banks for issue at the discretion of the Board. These latter BPCs are not eligible for dividend.

A special reserve of Sfr. 86 million (1992: Sfr. 89 million) has been created out of free reserves for these shares and BPCs.

⅃ **SANDOZ**

4. Major shareholders

As far as can be ascertained
from the information available,
shareholders owning 2% or
more of the Company's registered capital are as follows:

	% holding of total share capital
Emasan AG, Basle	10.0
Sandoz Foundation for Employee Participation, Basle	7.4
Sandoz Foundation for Employee Welfare, Basle	5.8
Swiss Life Insurance and Pension Company, Zurich	5.5
Morgan Guaranty Trust Company of New York, New York	1.8

ॐ **SANDOZ**

COMMENTS ON THE FINANCIAL STATEMENTS 1993 OF SANDOZ LTD

General

The Sandoz Ltd. financial statements comply with the requirements of the new Swiss Company Law, which came into force on 1 July 1992. The figures for 1992 have also been adjusted to the new requirements.

BALANCE SHEET

Foreign currency translation/ Exchange rates

Balance sheet items are translated at year-end rates.

Assets

Participations

These are valued at acquisition cost less impairment of value.

Receivables from Group Companies

These comprise short-term interest-bearing current account receivables and loans, together with royalties and interest.

Other receivables

This item includes outstanding withholding tax repayments and claims under double taxation agreements.

Marketable securities

The securities portfolio comprises certificates of deposit of leading Swiss banks and notes issued by other prime-name institutions. Valuation is at the lower of cost or market, the amount shown being the value after the application of the necessary adjustments.

Liquid assets

These comprise mainly time deposits and current account balances held with banks and the post office.

Accrued income

A substantial component of this item is accrued income from fixed-interest investments.

Equity and liabilities

Share capital

The Company's share capital continues to comprise 5 477 404 registered and 815 404 bearer shares, each with a par value of Sfr. 100.

BPC capital

The Company's BPC capital continues to comprise 1 870 448 BPCs, each with a par value of Sfr. 100.

Reserves

General reserve

Sfr. 32 million from the previous year's profits have been allocated to this reserve, which now stands at Sfr. 1576 million. Sfr. 1319 million of this sum derive from premiums paid by Shareholders and BPC holders in connection with capital increases or the exercise of equity option rights attached to debentures.

Reserve for shares held by Group

This reserve has been reduced by Sfr. 3 million in keeping with the number of rights exercised in connection with the Sandoz Overseas Finance Ltd., British Virgin Islands, debenture.

Free reserves

These have increased by Sfr. 3 million to Sfr. 652 million as a result of a transfer from the reserve for shares held by Group.

Liabilities to Group Companies

In addition to short-term liabilities, all liabilities with a maturity of more than 12 months were repaid in full during 1993.

.S. **SANDOZ**

Provisions

This item includes provisions for general and transfer risks.

Accrued expenses

These comprise provisions for taxes and other expenses pertaining to business trans-actions.

INCOME STATEMENT

Revenue

Income from participations

The total of Sfr. 321.2 million represents dividends derived from participations net of non-recoverable withholding tax.

Income from investments and marketable securities

This item comprises income from liquid funds and securities, interest on intra-Group loans, and exchange gains.

Other income

This item is made up principally of royalties and other fees accruing from the sale and licens-ing of trademarks and patents, of fees received for guarantees and directorships and of the net proceeds from the sale of a participation.

Expenditure

Financial expenses

This item consists almost entirely of interest paid to Group Companies.

Administrative expenses

Fees for auditing, consultancy and other services account for most of this item.

Depreciation and value adjustments

This item comprises write-offs on participations and provisions made as cover against the risks involved in the Group's world-wide activities.

Other expenditure (including taxes)

The principal components of this item are capital and income taxes.

S **SANDOZ**

BERICHT DER REVISIONSSTELLE

**An die Generalversammlung
der SANDOZ AG
Basel**

Als Revisionsstelle Ihrer Gesellschaft haben wir die Buchführung
und die vom Verwaltungsrat vorgelegte Jahresrechnung für das am
31. Dezember 1993 abgeschlossene Geschäftsjahr im Sinne der
gesetzlichen Vorschriften geprüft. Unsere Prüfung erfolgte nach aner-
kannten Grundsätzen des Berufsstandes. Wir bestätigen, dass wir die
gesetzlichen Anforderungen an Befähigung und Unabhängigkeit
erfüllen.

Aufgrund unserer Prüfung stellen wir fest, dass die Buchführung
und die Jahresrechnung sowie der Antrag über die Verwendung des
Bilanzgewinnes Gesetz und Statuten entsprechen.

Wir empfehlen, die vorliegende Jahresrechnung zu genehmigen

Basel, 25. März 1994

Schweizerische Treuhandgesellschaft –
Coopers & Lybrand AG

Prof. C. Helbling
Dipl. Bücherexperte
Leitender Revisor

G. Stoll
Dipl. Bücherexperte
Leitender Revisor

ṡ **SANDOZ**

REPORT OF THE AUDITORS

**To the General Meeting of
SANDOZ LTD
Basle**

As auditors of your company we have examined the books of account and the financial statements presented by the Board of Directors for the year ended 31 December 1993 in accordance with the provisions of law. Our audit was conducted in accordance with the auditing standards promulgated by the profession. We confirm that we meet the legal requirements concerning professional qualification and independence.

Based on our examination we conclude that the books of account and the financial statements and the proposed appropriation of the available profit are in accordance with the law and the articles of incorporation.

We recommend that the financial statements submitted to you be approved.

Basle, 25 March 1994

Société Fiduciaire Suisse –
Coopers & Lybrand SA

Prof. C. Helbling
Swiss certified public accountant
Lead auditor

G. Stoll
Swiss certified public accountant
Lead auditor

TURKEY

Unal Tekinalp
Center for Research and Practice in European Law
University of Istanbul

1. Background

1.1 Historical Overview

The development and enactment of legislation concerning independent accounting, financial reporting, and the accounting and auditing profession in Turkey have taken place only comparatively recently. Consequently, the contribution of such legislation to accounting regulation or self-regulation has not been considerable.

Accounting law in Turkey has not experienced a development parallel to company law and has remained under the influence of taxation law, without any character independent of that law. In 1982, however, the Capital Market Law (CML) was enacted, and the Capital Market Board (CMB) was established. Consequently, accounting law entered a new phase of development.

Although the first draft law for regulation of the accounting and auditing professions had been prepared as early as 1932, it was only put into force in 1989, by Law No. 3568 concerning Independent Accounting, Financial Consulting and Sworn Financial Consulting (the "Independent Accounting Law"). Under the terms of the Independent Accounting Law, the Union of Chambers of Independent Accountants, Financial Consultants and Sworn Financial Consultants was established. The delay was caused by the long fight between the accounting and auditing specialists on one side and lawyers on the other. Specific rules concerning auditing were enacted in 1987.

The communiqués issued by the CMB and the Central Bank of Turkey should be regarded as partial efforts at regulation. However, there has been a certain degree of overlap between the above-mentioned regulations and the Independent Accounting Law.

1.2 Development of Company Law

Modern legislation concerning companies was enacted in Turkey for the first time in 1850, with the Law on Commerce. This law, however, merely set out certain provisions about the structures of the various types of partnerships and companies and, to a somewhat inadequate extent, about the rights of their shareholders. The law also specified the accounting books that business firms were to keep and laid down the obligations for them to that effect. Nevertheless, these provisions were not related to the principles of accounting.

The present Turkish Code of Commerce (TCC), dated 1957, which superseded the Turkish Code of Commerce of 1926, is not based on the philosophy of disclosure, and therefore it also does not regulate financial reporting.

With the 1938 passage of the "Law on Organization, Administration and Auditing of State Economic Enterprises that are Fully Owned by the State" (Law No. 3460), state enterprises were regarded as a whole rather than being considered one by one. Even so, the preparation of consolidated financial statements was not adopted.

Law No. 3460 (1938) began a process of development for public enterprises from the standpoint of the introduction and improvement of generally acceptable principles of accounting and also of financial reporting and auditing.

At present, state enterprises are governed by Decree Law No. 233 (1983), which provides that the accounts of state enterprises, companies, and their subsidiaries be kept in such a manner as to present well-ordered information on financial conditions, operations, costs, and investments (Article 33.1); they should be drawn up in accordance with a certain model (Article 34.1); and the balance sheet and other statements should be published in the official Gazette after they have been audited and approved by the Grand National Assembly (Article 34.3). With the enactment of the Tax Laws in 1949 and 1950, an accounting jurisprudence was created in Turkey, aimed at determining the tax base in the most accurate manner. Through the numerous amendments that were subsequently made, such an accounting law became firmly established in Turkey, as a result of the fact that the Tax Procedure Law is a "code" that fully discloses the principles of accounting and balance sheet preparation as well as valuation principles.

Regarding the banking industry, neither the Law for Protection of Bank Deposits No. 2243 (1933), nor Banking Law No. 2999 (1936), which superseded the former, covered the subjects of financial reporting and disclosure to a great extent, but the disclosure principle was introduced to a limited extent with Banking Law No. 7129, which came into force in 1958. Under Banking Law No. 3182 (1985), which is currently in force, and other related legislation, the scope of the disclosure principle has since been enlarged and the trends are in that direction.

Banks are obliged to prepare their accounts, annual balance sheets, and profit and loss accounts in accordance with the uniform accounts plan, standard-type balance sheet and profit and loss account models, and their notes. These models had been prepared by the Turkish Banks Association and came into force with the approval of the Under Secretariat for the Treasury and Foreign Trade of the Prime Ministry. This rule applies also to the branch offices of foreign banks in Turkey.

Similar regulations govern insurance companies. The accounts plan that banks should apply, its explanations, as well as generally accepted accounting principles and their applications and the accounts plan related to overdue claims were published in 1985.

The CML, which covers companies that offer their securities to the public, companies whose ownership is available to the public at large, that is, joint-stock and public limited companies (Article 11), brokers operating in the capital market (Articles 31–34), and unit trusts (Article 35) founded according to the open-end principle, constituted another milestone in the jurisprudence of accounting in Turkey.

The CML adopted as its model the Securities and Exchange Act of the United States and created an agency called the Capital Market Board, or CMB, resembling the U.S. Securities and Exchange Commission and which was equipped with vast powers that included indicating the accounting standards to be applied by corporations covered by the CML.

The main objective of the CML was to establish the control of the CMB over new issues of securities to the public and the requirement for corporations to obtain permission from the said authority for such a purpose, and to enlarge the scope of application of the disclosure principle and to enhance its effectiveness.

Thus, a rapid development of a wide scope was achieved in the law governing corporations—or at least some of them—from the points of view of both disclosure and financial reporting. Under the CML, companies that offer to the public such securities as commercial paper, debentures, share certificates, or bonds, or the number of whose shareholders is established to be more than one hundred and thus are considered to be public companies, will be obliged to draw up their balance sheets and profit and loss accounts according to the forms and principles to be established by the CMB (Article 16).

This authority of the CMB is not confined to determining the layouts of the financial statements; it also covers the laying down of accounting principles to be observed. The CMB discharged that duty in 1983 with the publication of the "Communiqué on Principles Governing Standard Financial Statements and Reports" and, in 1984, the "Unified Chart of Accounts."

The "Communiqué on Principles and Rules Appertaining to Financial Statements and Reports in the Capital Market" (January 1989), which was generally well received, was complemented by the "Communiqué on Principles and Rules Appertaining to Intermediate Financial Statements" (July 1989). The latter was amended by publication of the "Standard Unified Chart of Accounts Plan and the Principles for Application of the Plan" (1989). Detailed regulation was introduced in 1992 by the "General Communiqué Concerning Implementation of Accounting System" by the Ministry of Finance.

1.3 The Evolution of Current Accounting Thought

The provisions of the Turkish Code of Commerce (TCC) that have been subject to justified criticism are those concerning auditing (Articles 347–359). The principal points of criticism have been the following: the internal auditor (or committee of auditors), which is a statutory requirement, was not required to be expert in the field; the auditor or the committee of auditors were not, in practice, able to perform their auditing duties continually; it is impossible with a few auditors to fulfill the principle of having the auditing function carried out by a team that should consist of members complementing one another.

However, because the provisions relating to auditors were contained not only in the part of the TCC dedicated to auditors but also in other parts of the TCC, and in addition to their auditing duties, the auditors have been assigned such other duties as calling the general meeting of shareholders, inserting items in the agenda, hearing complaints, and, when required, representing the company in courts of law, it has been difficult to change the system.

In spite of all these difficulties, the view that a corporation should be audited by an expert institution that is independent of the company has become ever more widespread.

When the CMB published its "Regulations on Auditing by Independent Auditor in the Capital Market" in 1987, the first step was taken toward the application of auditing practice in its full sense, notwithstanding the legal and practical difficulties that may arise with two sources of auditing. True, the Banking Law had already introduced the employment of expert auditors to the Turkish legal system, but that slight improvement was not sufficient to eliminate all the drawbacks of the system. In fact, immediately after the publication of the Regulations, the Central Bank issued its Communiqué Serial No. 1 on Bank Audits (1987).

With a view to firmly establishing independent auditing institutions, the CMB issued Communiqué Serial X, No. 3, on "General Principles Appertaining to Independent Auditing Establishments and Auditors" (June 1987), "Communiqué on Principles and Rules Appertaining to Independent Auditing Work and Reporting" (1987), and their attachments, which were prepared in considerable detail.

1.4 The Present Accounting Environment

The role of law in the determination of accounting requirements had been quite limited before the 1980s. Until that time, the influence of fiscal auditors and of the Ministry of Finance inspectors had been considerable. In their audits of tax returns and accounting records, they made their examinations and drew up their reports for the Ministry of Finance, often from the standpoint of generally accepted accounting principles, and created the establishment of some accounting standards, albeit from a taxation standpoint.

At present, the influence of these inspectors and auditors continues on statutory and self-regulatory bodies. One reason is that the said bodies have recruited their own specialized personnel from among the inspectors and auditors, who also became partners with many of the international auditing companies that established operations in Turkey in the 1970s.

Today also, the great majority of those who are allowed to operate under Law No. 3568 as chartered financial advisors and who are empowered to perform auditing functions consist of the above-mentioned inspectors and auditors. The question remains whether those who in the past always performed audits with the fiscal interests of the government in mind will be able to give a new character, not dominated by tax considerations, to generally acceptable accounting principles in Turkey.

Since 1982, the CMB has been functioning as a law-making body in this respect under the authority granted to it by law. The characteristic feature of the communiqués published by the CMB has been the determining role of the philosophy of disclosure found in them. The rules they have laid down are aimed at realizing disclosure both through the substance (i.e., the contents) of the financial statements and their form (i.e., the layout of the statements), as well as the procedure for their being made public.

There is no doubt that the CMB took into account the EC Fourth Directive and that its principles and provisions have had a significant influence on the drafting of the CMB's communiqués. Communiqué Series XI, No. 1, contains accounting principles parallel to the Fourth Directive, among them the principle of the "true and fair view." However, this was not laid down as an explicit superior rule (the true and fair override), and an explicit indication of that principle in Turkish legislation would not necessarily entail its full application in practice, because that principle can enjoy full application only at such times as the Fourth Directive is fully implemented and the concept of a "true and fair view" becomes established.

2. The Form and Content of Published Financial Statements

The disclosure philosophy, as explained above, is a recent phenomenon in Turkey and has been applied to only a limited number of corporations.

State economic enterprises that are closed to the outside world and make their financial reporting to a closed circle are not included.

As for corporations that are not covered by the CML and are subject only to the TCC, the possibility of applying the disclosure principle to them is almost negligible. The reason that the TCC is inadequate in this respect is that the relevant provisions of the TCC were borrowed from the Code of Obligations of Switzerland, which at that time failed to incorporate the disclosure principle and has only recently been amended in this direction.

2.1 Turkish Code of Commerce

The TCC does not put forward specimens of financial statements that companies must conform to and has not included any provisions about financial reporting, even at a minimum level. The principles governing the drawing-up of balance sheets were limited to the provisions in its Article 75 such that "the balance sheets and income statements should be drawn up in the Turkish currency and in a clear, complete and easily understandable manner."

Since Turkish balance sheet jurisprudence has remained under the influence not of traditional auditing practice but of taxation law, however, even this inadequate provision could not be fully observed in practice. That inadequate provision also applies to partnerships with limited liability and partnerships limited by shares, the latter being quite rare. It must be pointed out, however, that no legal provisions existed, in particular for partnerships with limited liability, regarding accounting and the balance sheet, which are entirely dominated by taxation law.

Needless to say, the TCC, which has not included the disclosure principle even at the minimum scale, does not recognize the "true and fair view" doctrine. On the other hand, in academic texts, the necessity of adopting the disclosure principle as well as the true and fair view doctrine has been pointed out since the 1960s.

From 1987 onward, changes have started to take place with the communiqués. Both the CMB and the Ministry of Finance have issued regulations concerning financial reporting and accounting standards that are in compliance with directives of the EU. These are Communiqué XI/1 and Communiqué No. 1 concerning implementation of the Unified Chart of Accounts.

2.2 Communiqué XI/1

Communiqué XI/1, which is in force at present, has, on the one hand, introduced detailed rules on the subject of financial statements, such as balance sheet principles, financial reporting, and disclosure and, on the other hand, provides specimens that should be used as a guide for such financial statements as balance sheet, profit and loss account, and cash flow table. Furthermore, the minimum data that should be included in the reports of the board of directors and of auditors have been indicated by the CMB.

Finally, a specimen "cost of sales table," to be drawn up by intermediary companies, and "profit distribution table" have been provided in the attachment to this Communiqué.

Although Communiqué XI/1 and Communiqué No.1 have reduced the differences between Turkish Legislation and International Accounting Standards, the differences arising from Turkish tax legislation persist.

2.2.1 Basic Concepts of Accounting

Section 1 of Communiqué No. XI/1 lays down certain basic concepts of accounting. Thirteen basic concepts are stated, some of which are valuation rules concerning:

- Going concern
- Consistency from year to year
- Prudence
- Accruals
- Separate valuation of the components of asset and liability items
- Correspondence of the opening balance sheet for one year with the closing balance sheet for the preceding year

In addition, Section 1 stipulated certain concepts such as the concepts of full disclosure, materiality principle, social responsibility, impartiality, substance over form, entity, and the kind of currency and measurement of cost.

Full Disclosure (Presentation and Disclosure) In the definition of the concept of full disclosure, it was stated that "the full disclosure concept means that the financial statements should be clear and comprehensible enough to enable the persons or institutions that will use such tables to reach decisions." Developments that may take place in the future, however, have been required to be included (Article 10), and the accuracy of financial statements has been laid down as a requirement (Article 47). Communiqué XI/1 embodies the true and fair view principle of the EC Fourth Directive in its Articles 4.4, 5, 10–14, and 47. It is certain, however, that Communiqué XI/1 does not regard that principle as an overriding rule, as expressed in Articles 2.4 and 2.5 of the Fourth Directive.

Materiality Concepts have been defined in Communiqué XI/1 in such a form as to be considered within the scope of the full disclosure principle. According to the definition, the relative significance of an accounting item or financial phenomenon must be at a level in which its value can influence the analysis to be made on the basis of the financial statements and the decisions to be reached. It is a condition that significant items and financial phenomena and other points of importance should be included in the financial statements (Article 11).

Taking Article 47 into consideration on the accuracy of financial statements, we can say that the true and fair view principle has been expressed in this provision.

The accuracy of financial statements requires that:

1. While they are in accordance with the generally accepted accounting principles and the accounting standards published by the CMB, they also reflect some exceptional facts.
2. They have been prepared in accordance with the accounting policies chosen by the undertakings with the purpose of conforming to generally accepted accounting principles and to the standards published by the CMB.
3. Together with their footnotes and attachments, they are satisfactory, clear, understandable, and suitable for interpretation.

4. The significant developments are stated in sufficient detail and reflect important points and developments.

Social Responsibility   The principle of *social responsibility* relates to conforming to generally accepted accounting principles and standards of bookkeeping and acting within the framework of the aim of enlightening individuals and various institutions and of the objectives of disclosure in a consciousness of social responsibility. The basic responsibility of the managers of undertakings and of accounting departments is to prepare the relevant data in an accurate and correct form and to present them for the use of interested parties (Article 12).

The Principle of Impartiality   *Impartiality* means that the presentation of financial and accounting information and the financial statements should be of such content and in such a form that they may be of use to everyone. Such information and financial statements may not be prepared or offered in such a way as to allow only some people to use them to meet their requirements (Article 13.1). This principle means that in case changes in the assets or liabilities of an undertaking and their effects on equity cannot be measured on a cost basis, valuation made through estimation and appraisal should be made in such a way as to reach the same conclusions that an impartial specialist would reach in this respect (Article 13.2).

The Principle of Substance over Form   *Substance over form* means that substance, rather than the legal form, should be taken as the basis for reflecting operations on the accounting records and in their analyses. In case a difference arises between the form and the substance in the application of a principle or a rule, precedence should be given to the substance in principle (Article 14).

Communiqué XI/1 of the CMB has provided a legal basis that ensures widespread application of generally accepted accounting principles. Although it is assumed in some academic texts that the requirement laid down in Article 75 of the TCC that the balance sheets of undertakings should be drawn according to "commercial principles" denotes that the generally accepted principles have been adopted in Turkish jurisprudence under a legal provision, Communiqué XI/1 is much more explicit in this respect and assumes that the general accounting principles are the accounting standards contained in the directives issued by the CMB; or in connection with points that have not been regulated by CMB, the principles that conform to accounting concepts generally used in the same business sector for undertakings of comparable size and that are generally approved in academic circles; or those adopted in international standards (Article 4.4).

At the end of this chapter are English and Turkish versions of specimen balance sheet, profit and loss account, funds flow, and cash flow tables to be prepared by companies covered by the regulations of the CMB, including intermediary firms. Communiqué XI/1 states that disclosure will be required not only in financial statements, but also in their footnotes and annexes (Article 46a).

2.2.2 *Reporting of Material Events*

The CMB issued the communiqué "Serial: Vlll, No: 20, Disclosure of material events" in 1993. This communiqué requires that events that may affect the value of capital market instruments or investment decisions be disclosed.

The communiqué has specially determined some material events to be disclosed:

1. Changes in control of the company
2. Acquisition or disposition or leasing of fixed assets
3. Changes in operations (starting a new operation or cessation of an existing one, disputes in court, etc.)
4. Changes in investments
5. Changes in the company's financial situation such as new issues or losing half of the net capital
6. Acquisition or disposition of subsidiaries, undertakings, joint ventures
7. Changes in management, such as the appointment or registration of managers, managerial disputes in court

The communiqué also requires the company's managers and shareholders who control more than 10% of the company's shares to disclose their trading those shares within the first week of the following month. Extraordinary changes in value or volume of the stock and any rumor or publication about the company and its securities are recognized as material events to be disclosed.

The company and related parties should also disclose the material events that are not specifically mentioned in the communiqué but materially affect the value of the stock. Written disclosure should be sent to the CMB and if its shares are traded on a stock exchange, to the related stock exchange, to be disclosed by the CMB and stock exchange. Disclosure should be clear and understandable and not misleading. After it is sent the CMB and the stock exchange, the information can be sent to the press.

3. Accounting Policies and Practices in Valuation and Income Management: Implications for the Analyst

3.1 Group Accounts

Turkish jurisprudence does not contain provisions concerning group accounts either in the TCC, which includes company law, or in the legislation concerning taxation. Some groups of companies prepare consolidated balance sheets; such balance sheets, however, are not filed with any authority but are used for the self-evaluation of such groups. They are often used in connection with joint ventures and other collaborative efforts involving foreign companies, for the purpose of giving the prospective partner an idea of the financial situation of the group.

There is no uniform method for the consolidation of balance sheets that some groups draw up for their own purpose. The analysis of Price Waterhouse in this respect is as follows:

> The acquisition or purchase method is the only method we have seen used in Turkey with goodwill in consolidation being capitalized and amortized over three to five years. Goodwill is generally only recognized in consolidation. While theoretically possible we have not seen either the merger or pooling method or the "Former German" method. However, in the acquisition or purchase method, if it is deemed that assets are overvalued, in

consolidation they are revalued downward thus reducing or eliminating goodwill.

Proportional consolidation whereby there is a line-by-line consolidation based on the actual ownership control percentage, thus eliminating the need to separately set up minority interest, rather than using 100 percent and then setting up minority interest is not normally used. However, it can be used in a joint venture condition.

Equity accounting is used when ownership is between 20 percent and 50 percent. Goodwill is not normally recognized by the investor. Of course if the investor group has goodwill which is being amortized this will lower the annual change in equity to be equitized.

Güven Coopers and Lybrand's analysis of major differences between Turkish law and IAS and generally recognized accounting principles is as follows: Consolidation or the equity method is not required or envisaged by either company law or the tax legislation. Thus, in accounting for business combinations, neither the acquisition (or purchase method) nor the merger (or pooling of interests method) is legally recognized. On the legal amalgamation or fusion of companies, the assets and liabilities of the liquidated company are transferred at balance sheet values, and shares are issued to the shareholders of the liquidated company. Otherwise the rules for liquidation apply.

These comments should, however, be understood in light of the CMB's Communiqué XI/10 related to the "Communiqué Concerning Principles and Rules Related to Preparation of Consolidated Financial Statements in the Capital Markets" issued in 1992. The main points of the Communiqué can be summarized as follows:

1. Communiqué XI/10 does not oblige groups to prepare consolidated financial statements. However, the groups that include any enterprise subject to the CML should prepare their consolidated financial statements according to the procedures detailed in the communiqué if they disclose any consolidated information to the public.

2. The reason for this regulation is the impossibility of obliging the parent companies that are not subject to CML. Thus, it satisfies the need for a true and fair view in any public disclosure by such a group of companies. In fact, the crux is related to the Commercial Law in general.

3. Parent company, subsidiary, and group concepts are defined basically by considering the facts of Turkish enterprises and groups, and the EEC's Seventh Directive [83/349, O.J. 1983, L 193/1], which deals with consolidated accounts so that the relationship between a parent company and a subsidiary is not obtained only by a majority of voting shares but also by the controlling management.

4. According to Communiqué XI/10, a group is: a community of parent company and its subsidiaries that, despite being legally independent of one another, are related in terms of capital, management, and control and that, regardless of their field of activity, are centrally coordinated under the control of the parent company in the areas of planning, organization, management, and finance.

5. To provide complete and comprehensive information about the group as a whole, the parent company will prepare consolidated accounts and financial statements that consolidate the other group companies into the parent company's financial statements.

6. There is no exception for the group companies to be included in the scope of consolidation, regardless of their location or activities.

7. Because in Turkish enterprises, the parent company–subsidiary relationship forms during the establishment stage, and the acquisition of subsidiaries through takeovers in the secondary market is rarely seen, and because of the difficulties in calculating goodwill by going back to the acquisition date, in the Communiqué, goodwill has been calculated as in item No. 8.

8. If there is any share belonging to any group company within any group company's capital and share premiums (paid-in surplus), these shares and the related paid-in surplus and their cost value in the investor company's book should be netted off. In this procedure if the cost value is more, the difference is recognized as positive goodwill and shown as a deduction from reserves in the consolidated statements, but if the cost value is less, the difference is recognized as negative goodwill and shown as an addition to reserves in the consolidated statements.

9. In the consolidated balance sheet, the paid-in capital account is the parent company's paid-in capital. None of the subsidiary's paid-in capital is included in the consolidated balance sheet. Only if the

subsidiaries have shares of the parent company, would the paid-in capital of the consolidated balance sheet be less than the paid-in capital of the parent company.

10. If the group companies have capital liabilities (capital subscriptions due), the related capital receivables should be netted off.

11. The financial statements of the group companies that are not subject to the CML should be revised according to the accounting standards of the CMB (banks and insurance companies may be excepted from such a requirement).

12. Consolidated financial statements are the combination of all the financial statements of the enterprises in the group in which capital participations, receivables, payables, income, and expense accounts belonging to group companies are netted-off.

13. Shares of paid-in capital and profit and loss accounts that belong to minority shareholders should be shown separately.

14. When the companies forming the group (and thus subject to consolidation) have such varied activities that a consolidation would cause unreasonable results, group companies can be categorized in terms of their activities, such as production companies, service companies, financial companies, and trading companies.

15. To allow a true and fair view to the public, all additional and necessary information should be provided in the footnotes.

16. Disclosure of the consolidated financial statements and related information is not obligatory. Only when the groups disclose their consolidated financial statements should they prepare their financial statements, according to Communiqué XI/10. Companies subject to the CML law should submit these statements to CMB within 6 working days.

3.2 Foreign Currency Translation

There is no common practice in connection with the translation of financial statements of foreign subsidiaries and equity participations (associated companies) for consolidation or equity accounting. This is because the preparation of consolidated financial statements is not widespread, and so far, Turkish companies have not had a significant number of subsidiaries or equity participations in foreign countries. The practice in this respect has been limited to a small number of foreign branch offices of banks and subsidiaries of some construction companies and a few large holding companies. The fact that the draft of the communiqué of the CMB concerning consolidation has left the subsidiaries situated abroad outside the scope of consolidation has been a point of criticism.

The analysis of Price Waterhouse in this respect is as follows:

> Equity participations are normally translated using a variation of the closing rate-net investment method or the monetary-nonmonetary method.

Foreign subsidiaries in consolidation normally use either a variation of the temporal method, primarily fixed assets at historical rates and other items at closing rates, or translate all assets and liabilities at the closing rate.

In all cases that we have seen both for equity participations and subsidiaries the translation difference is taken to the income statement.

Foreign currency denominated assets or liabilities are almost always translated at the closing rate. This would be different if an appropriate forward contract existed, but in Turkey they do not normally exist.

Again the translation gain or loss is taken to the income statement.

3.3 Capital and Reserves

3.3.1 Capital

Turkish legislation regulating companies limited by shares (corporations) assumes two kinds of capital: capital fixed in advance and authorized capital.

Capital Fixed in Advance (Predetermined Capital or Basic Capital) Regulated by the TCC, capital fixed in advance is a kind of arrangement whereby the whole of the amount of capital is subscribed by the shareholders before the registration of the company's foundation or before its increase of capital, 25% of the capital being paid in by the shareholders. Thus, the remaining 75% becomes the liability of the subscribers. The significance of this arrangement from the standpoint of accounting jurisprudence is that it gives rise to three concepts: capital, called-up capital, and uncalled capital.

The TCC and the CML are in conflict with regard to the treatment of the uncalled portion of capital fixed in advance. The TCC requires that the capital fixed in advance should be entered in the liabilities side of the balance sheet at its nominal value, and the uncalled portion thereof should be shown on the assets side as a separate item (Article 463.1 and 2).

On the other hand, it is stated in Communiqué Series XI/1 of the CMB and in the balance sheet format attached to it that the total of the capital mentioned in a company's statutes should be included among the liabilities at its nominal value, with the uncalled portion shown as a deduction under the heading "capital subscriptions" and not in the assets as stated in the TCC.

Authorized Capital Authorized capital is regulated under the CML. Such a system of capital formation may be applied only by public companies. Such companies, however, also have the option to choose the system of capital fixed in advance. In the authorized capital system, issued capital is included among the liabilities section of the balance sheet, and the authorized capital is indicated as a footnote.

3.3.2 Reserves

Reserves in Turkish jurisprudence are regulated in detail by the provisions relating to companies limited by shares. These provisions are also applied to partnerships with limited liability (TTC 534) and partnerships limited by shares (TCC 476.2). There are no provisions in the legislation governing person-based companies or ordinary partnerships. Reserves are not regulated under any provisions of taxation law, however.

Reserves are defined in the Turkish law on companies limited by shares as the net worth of the possessions (net assets) exceeding capital. This definition also covers hidden reserves, because Turkish law, following the Swiss law on which it is modeled, has allowed the keeping of hidden reserves. Article 458 of the TCC explicitly allows companies to set aside hidden reserves, and Articles 460, 461, and 462.2 have allowed evaluation of fixed assets at any figure up to their historical price; that is, fixed assets

---

---

must be carried in the balance sheet at no higher than their purchase price, less depreciation (TCC 460, 461, 462.2—the so-called *Hochstwertprinzip* in Swiss Law). Although an attempt was made with Communiqué Series XI/1 of the CMB to prevent companies limited by shares that come under the CML from setting aside hidden reserves, by requiring them to adopt the system of using a fixed historical price, owing to the provisions of Article 458 of the TCC, that attempt did not bear fruit. Because of both Article 458 of the TCC and the possibility of valuing assets at a level up to the extent of their historical value, the doctrine of true and fair view, which is present in Communiqué XI/1 of the CMB, has become a source of equivocation.

It needs to be pointed out that under the Fourth Directive, hidden reserves are not considered compatible with giving a true and fair view. The 1986 directive (No. 86/635/ECC) on the financial reporting of financial and credit institutions allows the use of hidden reserves only as a member state option pending further harmonization. This should not be interpreted as signifying that the use of hidden reserves is generally considered compatible with the financial statements giving a true and fair view in the European Union.

Under Turkish legislation, reserves may be examined variously from the standpoints of (a) whether it is mandatory to set them aside, (b) the purpose for which they are allocated, and (c) disclosure criteria.

Mandatory Reserves   According to the criterion of mandatory reserves, reserves are divided into two categories: legal and optional.

Legal reserves are those that are required by law to be set aside, and their use is regulated by law. Acting contrary to the rules laid down by law for this purpose would constitute a legal offense and might entail a liability on the part of the Board of Directors (TCC 336) or an annulment of the resolution concerned of the shareholders' meeting (TCC 381). The prequisite for declaring a dividend for shareholders, or adopting a resolution for payment of remuneration to Directors out of the annual profit, is that the statutory reserve should have been set aside first (TCC 472).

Statutory reserves consist of two groups: retained earnings (earned surplus) and capital surplus. It is obligatory to set aside one-twentieth of the net profit each year until these retained earnings add up to one-fifth of the capital (TCC 466.1). In Turkish practice, this is designated the "first allocation." The TCC calls this item in the balance sheet "general reserves" (TCC 466.1). Moreover, the TCC requires another allocation of reserves, called in practice the "second allocation." The second allocation is mandatory in the case of companies declaring a dividend for shareholders in excess of 5% of the annual profit, or even if a smaller dividend has been declared, in the event of remuneration being allocated to "other persons sharing the profit," such as directors, owners of founders' shares, company employees, or foundations. Otherwise, a second allocation would not be made (TCC 466.1.N.3). Unlike the first allocation, the second allocation of reserves has no limit. As long as conditions permit, the second allocation may be made no matter what amount has been reached.

Under Turkish law, capital surplus will come into being in either of two circumstances:

1. Shares may be issued at a price exceeding their par value, that is, with a premium. When there is such an issue, the part of the premium that is not allocated to capital redemption or to charity will be set aside as a statutory reserve (TCC 466.2.N.1).
2. The Board of Directors will apply a special procedure to the shareholder who fails to pay in the part of the capital he has subscribed to. According to Article 407.2 the Board may forfeit the title to shares and part payment of a defaulting shareholder and issue new shares in place of those that are forfeited. The part payments will be kept by the company. The amount kept by the company and the proceeds of the subsequent sales will constitute reserves and, after losses that may have been realized on the replacement shares are deducted, must be placed in the general reserve fund.

Optional reserves will be set aside according to the provisions in the Statute or under a resolution adopted at a shareholders' meeting (TCC 467, 469.2). Reserves set aside under the resolution of shareholders are called "extraordinary reserves" in practice. The TCC has not set a limit to the reserves to be set aside under the company statute. The limit set down on the reserves to be set aside under shareholders' resolution is highly vague and their scope is wide. The company in general meeting may, before declaring a dividend, create reserve funds other than or exceeding those prescribed by law or articles if such a course seems to be desirable in order to ensure the continued prosperity of the company or the equalization of dividends (TCC Article 469.2).

The Purpose of Reserves   Reserves may be divided into two categories: (a) reserves whose purpose has not been specified and (b) those whose purpose has been specified. Reserves whose purpose has not been specified may be used for any legitimate purpose. If a purpose has not been specified, however, companies are bound by the purposes indicated in Article 469.2 of the TCC, mentioned above in connection with optional reserves. It is a widespread practice in Turkey to distribute optional reserves as dividends from time to time. It is doubtful, however, that such a practice is motivated by any social considerations other than the aim of declaring stable dividends. The TCC does not contain an explanation of the objective for setting dividends. The TCC does not contain an explanation of the objective for setting aside statutory reserves, but the objective for a part of the "general reserves" has been explained.

The law states that the funds in the general reserves may be used exclusively for making up for losses or for carrying on the company's operations in difficult times, taking measures for preventing unemployment or alleviating its consequences, as long as the general reserves do not exceed one-half of the company's capital (TCC 469.2).

There is freedom of choice in spending the general reserves exceeding the limit set down in the law and in spending the other statutory reserves. Many academics are of the opinion that it is permissible to distribute statutory reserves as dividend, benefiting from the above-mentioned freedom.

As far as a premium is concerned, however, there is no doubt that the law has indicated that it should be used for redemption of capital (TCC 466.2.N.1).

For reserves whose purpose has been specified, the purpose to which reserves are to be allocated may be shown either in the statute or by the General Assembly. In such a case, the reserves can be spent only for the specified purpose. If they are to be spent for another purpose, the statute or the resolution of the shareholders in the general meeting must be amended. However, the resolution of the shareholders in this respect must not be contrary to the principle of good faith; otherwise it would be annulled (TCC 381).

The law has allowed the creation of mutual assistance funds and other similar organizations with the use of the reserves under statute or shareholders' decision and, thus, has emphasized its social character once more.

Disclosure Criterion   According to the third criterion, reserves may be classified as (*a*) apparent (or disclosed) reserves and (*b*) hidden reserves. The statutory and optional reserves make up the apparent reserves. Those reserves set aside by revaluing the assets at a value lower than their actual value at the balance sheet date, or by other means, make up the hidden reserves. According to the TCC, an undervaluation in the balance sheet of the assets of the company at the date of the balance sheet and the creation of other hidden reserves by the directors are permissible if this seems desirable for assuring the continued prosperity of the company or the equalization of dividends.

Other means of creating hidden reserves include high rates of depreciation allowance and provisions. It is not permissible to set aside hidden reserves by showing fictitious debts or by failing to show some assets in the balance sheet.

The administration must inform the auditor about the creation or an application of hidden reserves (TCC Article 458). The Board of Directors is responsible to the internal auditor regarding where the hidden reserves are spent (TCC 458.2).

3.4 Liabilities and Provisions

According to the definition in the TCC, provisions are "Probable losses whether from the execution of contracts involving delivery or acceptance on the part of the company or from similar current transactions, [which] shall be provided for in the balance sheet by reserves" (TCC 465).

It can be seen that provisions may not cover a general purpose. The TCC has indicated a narrow scope for the purpose of provisions, although it has not been restrictive. In other words, provisions may be set aside not in connection with all kinds of loss risks but only "for losses that may arise in future from obligations to deliver or take delivery or similar commitments."

In order to be allowed to set aside a valid provision, the relation between its purpose and any "loss" should not be overlooked. Provisions may not be set aside for probable expenses.

Even though it is not explicitly indicated in Article 465.2 of the TCC, the provisions against losses in value of certain asset items of the balance sheet are of the same character. Likewise, provisions set aside for legal disputes, losses arising from transactions at exchanges for future deliveries, any guarantees supplied to customers, insurance risks, losses arising from foreign exchange and various penalties, as well as amounts set aside for renewal of fixed assets in franchised companies, for expenses that would be distributed among several years and for pensions or severance payments, are of the same character.

Provisions are of two categories: (a) those that are set aside from the annual profit, and (b) those that are set aside in a manner to decrease the profit during the year. Those mentioned in Article 465.2 of the TCC pertain, as a rule, to those set aside from the annual profit, because the term *reserve* has been used for them. That article can be regarded as covering the first category mentioned above only through a broad interpretation.

Provisions are the conventional means used for setting aside hidden reserves. When provisions are released, that is, when the foreseen risk does not materialize, they are converted into reserves. It would be more appropriate to use the term *reverting to their original character* in describing this process, because the law clearly indicates that provisions are "reserves" (TCC 465).

On the other hand, the Tax Procedure Law N.213 defines provisions very narrowly. According to this law, provisions are amounts set aside to cover losses or expenses that have occurred or that may occur in the future and that constitute a liability for the company whose exact amount is not definitely established (Article 288). A matter of controversy among academics and specialists interested in tax jurisprudence is whether an undertaking may set aside provisions at will and deduct them from income for tax purposes. The opinion of the majority is that the provisions set aside may be deducted from taxable income only in cases in which the tax laws clearly allow them to do so. Those cases, on the other hand, are highly limited in number. The fiscal offices and the State Council have permitted the deduction of provisions for severance pay of employees, in spite of arguments against this in academic texts. The CMB, on the other hand, regards it as a provision.

3.5 Property, Plant, and Equipment

3.5.1 Historical Cost Basis

According to tax law, property, plant, and equipment are stated at historical cost (Tax Procedure Law, Article 269). As explained earlier, the TCC allows evaluation of property, plant, and equipment at any figure up to their historical price. Following the TCC,

Fixed assets used in conduct of the business, such as land, building, power installations and machines, means of transport, implements and furniture must not be valued in the balance sheet at a higher figure than their purchase or cost price and appropriate depreciation must be written off.

The same rule applies to rights, concessions, letters patent, process of manufacture, licenses, trademarks and similar actual assets (TCC 460).

Historical cost is defined in a manner similar to GAAP, except that companies are free to either capitalize or expense financing costs related to capital expenditures, even after the related assets are placed in use.

In accordance with a change in the tax legislation dated and enacted in 1983 (Law No. 2791), revaluation of fixed assets, particularly of property, plant, and equipment, is permitted. Revaluation of land is not permitted. Property, plant, and equipment held throughout the year and the related accumulated depreciation are devalued in accordance with the regulations of the Ministry of Finance and Customs at a rate specified each year that is in line with the official inflation rate. The rates used for revaluation purposes have generally been lower than the rates of inflation.

The increase in the net book value of the said assets is permitted to be added to shareholders' equity, giving companies the option of issuing capital shares, which are called "gratis shares," for the amount of the revaluation (Tax Procedure Law Article 298).

3.5.2 Depreciation of Fixed Assets

Depreciation of fixed assets is controlled by the Ministry of Finance and Customs. Both normal and accelerated depreciation methods are accepted and used. Some of the depreciation methods are not in conformity with the IAS, for instance, a full year's depreciation must be allowed in the year of acquisition to avoid any loss of depreciation for tax purposes in future periods; and a 4-year depreciation period is allowed for plant and equipment.

Buildings are depreciated at rates between 2% and 6% per year. Other tangible and intangible assets, except land, are depreciated principally over 4 years by using either the straight-line or the double declining-balance method. A change from straight-line depreciation to the declining-balance method is not permitted, but the opposite change is possible. In periods of losses, companies are not required to make depreciation. However, they then forego their rights to allow for depreciation, and the book value of some assets is never reduced to nil.

3.5.3 Government Grants

Cash grants can be deducted from the asset base, thereby reducing the depreciable base, or distributed to shareholders. This is not in conformity with the IAS rules.

Such distributions take place in fact simply because during the investment years it is likely that new investments face operating losses, in which case such government grants can be passed on to individual shareholders with absolutely no tax effect, and such funds can be reinvested by means of capital increase, thereby keeping the asset base of depreciable assets the same, although the cash grant has been granted, thereby not reducing the depreciable base.

3.5.4 Interest Charges

Interest charges are capitalized during the years of investment. However, whenever the investment period is completed and operations start, even though the loan is long term, the interest charges associated with the operating years must be expensed. Interest capitalized during the investment period finds its way to the income statement by means of depreciation of the assets concerned. According to the tax legislation, care must be taken that interest on those loans associated with specific assets is included or capitalized with those assets.

3.5.5 Real Estate Development

Turkish law does not contain any provisions concerning real estate development in the TCC, in the legislation concerning taxation, or in the capital market regulations.

3.6 Leases

Turkey has a special body of regulation on leases (Law on Financial Rentals of June 1985). Almost without exception, financial leases are considered off-balance-sheet borrowing, and that is the way they are reported. However, audited statements may recognize such leases as financial obligations within the balance sheet. Finance lease contracts provide a purchase option, and there is a fixed minimum lease term. Operating lease contracts are treated as normal rent and do not fall under the body of legislation governing leases. No distinctions exist as to legal and economic ownership for leasing operations, and the lessor remains the owner of the leased assets for legal and tax purposes.

Therefore, there is no distinction of lease contracts between finance and operating lease for tax purposes, and the accounting treatment follows the tax treatment; the lessor must capitalize the asset and bears the depreciation; the installments paid by the lessee are expenses to the profit and loss account.

3.7 Oil, Gas, and Other Mineral Resources

There is no specific reference to the full cost and successful efforts, methods, or their acceptability, which are unique to oil and gas activities. Instead, accounting practices permitted for tax purposes apply (i.e., income tax method).

3.8 Intangible Assets

The Turkish Commercial Code has allowed valuation of legally protected intellectual property rights, such as patents, copyrights, trade names, brand names, and know-how at any figure up to the historical cost (TCC Article 460.2) (see Section 3.5).

According to tax legislation, legally protected intangible assets are stated at cost, to be amortized over their useful lives. If their useful lives cannot be identified clearly, such assets are amortized over 4 years.

Capitalization of establishment or formation costs is optional; nonpatented patents, know-how reflected in the development costs of products or computer software, and brand names are not recognized as assets.

3.9 Participating Interests

Long-term investments are stated at cost plus reserves distributed by way of bonus shares. No consolidation or equity accounting is performed for equity participations.

In practice, provisions of most sorts, and in particular provisions to reduce securities to net realizable value, are not usually made since Turkey is an inflationary country. Securities are almost always valued at cost. For both fixed assets and securities, interest charges and losses on foreign exchange liabilities are often included in the determination of cost. This can occur even after assets come into use.

3.10 Inventories

The most frequently used pricing methods for inventories are average cost and FIFO. The LIFO method can be used only if and when the company's records prove that last purchases have been used or sold first.

Write-downs for tax purposes only should be ignored. Of course, proper accounting valuation write-downs should be made, including provisions for obsolescence and damaged goods.

Normally there are no departures from historical cost, except as above. Sometimes the latest invoice method is used, but this should not be accepted.

Appropriate production and related administrative overheads are added to inventory cost. However, interest or financial charges and marketing expenses should not be included.

Because of the inflationary environment and frequent renegotiations that take place in Turkey, most companies we have seen use the completed contract method; the percentage of completion method would be desirable.

3.11 Taxation

The most important taxes are as follows:

1. Taxes on income
   —Corporation (income) tax
   —Personal income tax (includes withholding on payments abroad)
2. Taxes on wealth
   —Inheritance and gift taxes
   —Motor vehicle tax
   —Property tax
3. Taxes on expenditure
   —Value added tax (VAT)
   —Banking and insurance transactions taxes
   —Stamp duty taxes
   —Municipality taxes

The principal taxes are corporation tax, income tax, VAT, and customs duties; the other taxes are all minor, both from the point of view of the revenue raised and from that of their effect on business transactions. No income taxes are imposed by provincial municipal authorities.

Corporation Tax Rate The taxation of corporations has been changed with a new law effective January 1, 1994. This new law foresees taxing corporations in two stages.

The first tax to be paid is a corporate tax, the rate of which is 25%. There exists an additional fund levy (see below) to be paid on the calculated corporate tax at the rate of 7%. Exemptions, including investment allowance, tourism revenue, and dividend from Mutual Funds and Investment Companies, are permitted for social and economic purposes. The corporate tax (except for the fund amount) cannot be less than 20% of the corporate income before the deduction of exceptions, which is called the minimum corporate tax. However, when the minimum corporate tax is calculated, some of the exempted income is not considered.

The second stage of the taxation of corporations is the application of a withholding tax to the balance, the amount of which is calculated by deducting the corporate tax from corporate income. The rate of the withholding tax is 10% for joint stock companies open to the public (publicly held corporations) and 20% for others (closely held corporations). The fund application at the rate of 7% is also applicable to the minimum corporate tax and the withholding tax application. Payments on account of corporate tax due must be made at the rate of 70% of the previous year's calculated corporate tax. The advance tax payments are deducted from the corporation's ultimate tax liability as shown on the return for the current (or previous) tax year, and any balance is due by the end of the filing period. Any excess is carried forward against payment of advance tax due for the following year.

There is no additional tax on dividends paid by companies, and losses may be carried forward for 5 years but may not be carried back.

Fund Levy   Pursuant to Law No. 3824 dated June 25, 1992, and decrees made thereunder, some fund liabilities exist for the taxpayer. Fund levy contributions are calculated at 7% (see No. 617) of the corporate and withholding taxes.

Income Determination   For corporate tax purposes, a corporation's income is calculated in accordance with the provisions of personal income tax.

Both limited and fully taxpayer corporations are entitled to revalue their fixed assets, excluding land sites and other intangible assets (e.g., royalties and founding expenditures) in accordance with the index published yearly by the Ministry of Finance and Customs (Law No. 2791).

According to tax laws, inventories must be valued at their actual cost. If cost cannot be determined on an individual basis, then a moving-average determination is acceptable. LIFO and FIFO can be used only when it is clearly demonstrated in specific circumstances that they are in accord with the facts.

Certain expenses, including formation expenses, expenses of issuing shares, and the start-up costs of business operations, are deductible. Hidden distributions of profits are not deductible.

Investment Incentive Allowance Investment incentive allowance is defined in the income tax law. The purpose of this incentive is to encourage investment generally; thus, it can be deducted from taxable income. Investment incentive allowances are granted to companies and individuals at rates between 20% and 70% of the cost of specified assets, which are listed in a "General Encouragement Table" published annually in the official Gazette.

Special Provisions There is no special provision for capital gains. Gains resulting from sales of fixed assets subject to depreciation are taxed at the normal rate, and gains are not taxable when proceeds are reinvested in new fixed assets.

Value Added Tax A Value Added Tax (VAT) was introduced in Turkey on October 25, 1984, effective from 1985. VAT Law No. 3065 adopted an EC-type VAT. All commercial, industrial, agricultural, and professional activities are included in the scope of this tax.

The VAT is levied at rates varying from 1% to 23%, with a basic rate of 15%. The rates are as follows:

- Leasing, 1%
- Basic food, 8%
- Natural gas, 8%
- Luxury goods, 23% (Mainly fur, jewelry, perfumes, cosmetics, household equipment, appliance, cars, and pleasure boats)

Banking and the activities of insurance companies are exempt from VAT.

3.11.3 The Taxation of Individuals

All individuals resident in Turkey are liable for personal income tax on their worldwide income, according to the personal Income Tax Law dated December 31, 1960, No.193.

3.12 Pensions

Employee pension schemes involving defined contribution or benefit plans are uncommon in Turkey. Under the Turkish Social Security Law, all employees (except agricultural workers, the self-employed, civil servants, and employees of some large banks) are covered by the social security system, which, as well as other benefits, includes a retirement pension. In accordance with existing labor law, companies are required to make lump sum payments to employees whose employment is terminated because of retirement or for reasons other than resignation or misconduct. However, the lump sum payments cannot be expensed until paid.

4. Expected Future Developments

We can predict that the adaptation of accounting to international standards and the development of financial reporting in Turkey will be multifaceted and comprehensive and will accelerate in the coming years. These developments will underline the importance of the "true and fair view" and the disclosure principles, leading to standards of higher quality from both a scientific and a result-oriented approach. Moreover, they will extend to all companies limited by shares and not only those under the ambit of the CML. It is unlikely that new arrangements in this respect will cover partnerships limited by shares, and partnerships with limited liability, which are not common in Turkey (unlike Germany and France). The existence of government bills for amendment of both CML and TTC, and the fact that the bill for amending CML is now in the last phase before enactment, are all indications verifying the above expectations. Another significant indication is the ever widening incidence of auditing.

Another important development is that an authority (agency) will be created to impose accounting standards when CML is amended.

Turkey has great hopes invested in the implementation of Act 3568. In order for these hopes to come true, however, the construction and practice of this act must be free of the "all is for taxes" mentality.

Financial Statements

C- Finansal Yapıya İlişkin Bilgiler

1-Brisa Bridgestone Sabancı Lastik Sanayi ve Ticaret A.Ş.
31 Aralık 1993 Tarihindeki Ayrıntılı Bilanço (1000.-TL)

Aktif (Varlıklar)

		Cari dönem 31 . 12 . 1993		Önceki dönem 31 . 12 . 1992
I. Dönen varlıklar		1,103,708,206		702,829,272
A. Hazır değerler		9,389,707		5,794,698
1. Kasa	21,109		7,649	
2. Bankalar	9,368,598		5,787,049	
B. Kısa vadeli ticari alacaklar		562,677,349		352,396,239
1. Alıcılar	188,632,586		222,985,763	
2. Alacak senetleri	393,125,178		134,425,405	
3. Alacak senetleri reeskontu (-)	(19,287,776)		(5,313,387)	
4. Verilen depozito ve teminatlar	252,567		50,827	
5. Diğer kısa vadeli alacaklar	512,270		485,423	
6. Şüpheli alacaklar karşılığı (-)	(557,476)		(237,792)	
C. Diğer kısa vadeli alacaklar		56,514,122		47,645,461
1. Kısa vadeli diğer alacaklar	56,514,122		47,645,461	
1.1 İhracat katma değer vergisi	32,790,516		34,883,540	
1.2 İadesi talep edilen KDV	9,936,172		2,430,597	
1.3 Diğer	13,787,434		10,331,324	
D. Stoklar		472,596,714		296,234,189
1. İlk madde ve malzeme	172,082,596		123,798,931	
2. Yarı mamuller	36,261,690		23,620,307	
3. Mamuller	226,064,259		125,228,065	
4. Emtia	21,516,125		9,387,344	
5. Diğer stoklar	125,085		292,581	
6. Verilen sipariş avansları	16,546,959		13,906,961	
E. Diğer dönen varlıklar		2,530,314		758,685
II. Duran varlıklar		1,172,188,813		722,244,388
A. Uzun vadeli ticari alacaklar		1,052,547		2,754,011
1. Alıcılar	477,743		488,176	
2. Alacak senetleri	878,984		563,381	
3. Alacak senetleri reeskontu (-)	(447,263)		(277,432)	
4. Verilen depozito ve teminatlar	43,083		1,879,610	
5. Uzun vadeli diğer alacaklar	100,000		100,276	
B. Finansal duran varlıklar		0		0
1. Diğer finansal duran varlıklar	0		0	
C. Maddi duran varlıklar		1,160,239,531		718,162,808
1. Arazi ve arsalar	291,479		163,478	
2. Yerüstü ve yeraltı düzenleri	33,804,262		23,497,686	
3. Binalar	389,220,544		243,336,728	
4. Makine, tesis ve cihazlar	1,691,804,511		1,176,828,124	
5. Taşıt araç ve gereçleri	26,998,873		16,127,189	
6. Döşeme ve demirbaşlar	16,629,723		12,107,610	
7. Birikmiş amortismanlar (-)	(1,081,811,410)		(790,675,959)	
8. Yapılmakta olan yatırımlar	81,937,413		36,752,535	
9. Verilen sipariş avansları	1,364,136		25,417	
D. Maddi olmayan duran varlıklar		8,216,370		161,161
1. Haklar	8,216,370		161,161	
E. Diğer duran varlıklar		2,680,365		1,166,408
Aktif (varlıklar) Toplamı		2,275,897,019		1,425,073,660

C- Financial Review

1-Brisa Bridgestone Sabancı Lastik Sanayi ve Ticaret A.Ş.
Detailed Balance Sheet as of December 31, 1993 (TL 1,000)

Assets

		Current Period 31.12.1993		Previous Period 31.12.1992
I. Current Assets			1,103,708,206	702,829,272
A. Liquid assets		9,389,707		5,794,698
1. Cash	21,109			7,649
2. Banks	9,368,598			5,787,049
B. Short-term trade receivables		562,677,349		352,396,239
1. Trade	188,632,586			222,985,763
2. Notes receivable	393,125,178			134,425,405
3. Discount of receivable (-)	(19,287,776)			(5,313,387)
4. Deposits and guarantees	252,567			50,827
5. Other short-term receivables	512,270			485,423
6. Provision for doubtful receivable (-)	(557,476)			(237,792)
C. Other short-term receivables		56,514,122		47,645,461
1. Other short-term receivables	56,514,122			47,645,461
1.1 Deferred export V.A.T.	32,790,516			34,883,540
1.2 V.A.T. Claimed back	9,936,172			2,430,597
1.3 Other	13,787,434			10,331,324
D. Inventories		472,596,714		296,234,189
1. Raw materials	172,082,596			123,798,931
2. Semi-finished goods	36,261,690			23,620,307
3. Finished goods	226,064,259			125,228,065
4. Goods for resale	21,516,125			9,387,344
5. Other inventories	125,085			292,581
6. Advances on purchase orders	16,546,959			13,906,961
E. Other current assets		2,530,314		758,685
II. Long term assets			1,172,188,813	722,244,388
A. Long term trade receivables		1,052,547		2,754,011
1. Trade receivables	477,743			488,176
2. Notes receivable	878,984			563,381
3. Discount of notes receivable (-)	(447,263)			(277,432)
4. Deposits and guarantees	43,083			1,879,610
5. Other long term trade receivables	100,000			100,276
B. Investments		0		0
1. Other investments	0			0
C. Tangible fixed assets		1,160,239,531		718,162,808
1. Lands	291,479			163,478
2. Superstructures and infrastructures	33,804,262			23,497,686
3. Buildings	389,220,544			243,336,728
4. Plant, machinery, and equipment	1,691,804,511			1,176,828,124
5. Motor vehicles	26,998,873			16,127,189
6. Furniture and fixtures	16,629,723			12,107,610
7. Accumulated depreciation (-)	(1,081,811,410)			(790,675,959)
8. Construction in progress	81,937,413			36,752,535
9. Advances on purchase orders	1,364,136			25,417
D. Intangible fixed assets		8,216,370		161,161
1. Rights	8,216,370			161,161
E. Other long-term assets		2,680,365		1,166,408
Total assets		2,275,897,019		1,425,073,660

Pasif (Kaynaklar)	Cari dönem 31.12.1993			Önceki dönem 31.12.1992		
I. Kısa vadeli borçlar			800,718,803			520,046,832
A. Finansal Borçlar		317,968,124			196,721,515	
1. Banka kredileri	285,205,906			166,832,807		
2. Uzun vadeli kredilerin anapara taksit ve faizleri	32,759,570			29,886,043		
3. Tahvil anapara taksitleri ve faizleri	2,648			2,648		
4. Diğer finansal borçlar	0			17		
B. Ticari borçlar		320,725,861			189,944,630	
1. Satıcılar	180,035,674			138,783,694		
2. Borç senetleri	158,475,740			55,165,958		
3. Borç senetleri reeskontu (-)	(17,821,553)			(4,006,022)		
4. Alınan depozito ve teminatlar	36,000			1,000		
C. Diğer kısa vadeli borçlar		95,957,857			78,870,952	
1. Ortaklara borçlar	352,131			220,339		
2. Ödenecek giderler	5,050,108			3,278,483		
3. Ödenecek vergi, harç ve diğer kesintiler	37,483,172			28,235,374		
4. Kısa vadeli diğer borçlar	53,072,446			47,136,756		
4.1 Terkin edilecek ihracat KDV	32,790,516			34,883,540		
4.2 Royalty	17,570,520			11,514,742		
4.3 Diğer	2,711,410			738,474		
D. Alınan sipariş avansları		7,232,952			11,356,084	
E. Borç ve gider karşılıkları		58,834,009			43,153,651	
1. Vergi karşılıkları	33,330,646			18,089,247		
2. Diğer borç ve gider karşılıkları	25,503,363			25,064,404		
2.1 Hatalı mamul tazminatı karşılığı	7,800,000			5,400,000		
2.2 Kısa vadeli kredi faiz karşılığı	5,039,534			4,122,683		
2.3 Orta vadeli kredi faiz karşılığı	12,654,781			15,541,721		
2.4 Diğer	9,048					
II. Uzun vadeli borçlar			220,091,952			186,590,716
A. Finansal borçlar		74,777,421			105,338,379	
1. Banka kredileri	74,777,421			105,338,379		
B. Diğer uzun vadeli borçlar		19,993			17,793	
1. Uzun vadeli diğer borçlar	19,993			17,793		
C. Borç ve gider karşılıkları		145,294,538			81,234,544	
1. Kıdem tazminatı karşılıkları	145,294,538			81,234,544		
III. Öz sermaye			1,255,086,264			718,436,112
A. Sermaye		151,875,000			151,875,000	
B. Emisyon primi		2,602,153			2,602,153	
C. Yeniden değerleme değer artışı		810,612,853			414,002,957	
1. Duran varlıklardaki değer artışı	810,612,853			414,002,957		
2. İştiraklerdeki değer artışı						
D. Yedekler		92,745,584			45,465,772	
1. Yasal yedekler	28,293,251			16,651,314		
2. Olağanüstü yedekler	64,452,333			28,814,458		
E. Dönem kârı (Net)		197,250,674			104,490,230	
Pasif (kaynaklar) Toplamı			2,275,897,019			1,425,073,660

Liabilities and shareholders' equity

	Current Period 31 . 12 . 1993		Previous Period 31 . 12 . 1992	
I. Current liabilities		**800,718,803**		**520,046,832**
A. Financial liabilities		317,968,124		196,721,515
1. Bank overdrafts	285,205,906		166,832,807	
2. Current year portion of long term loans	32,759,570		29,886,043	
3. Principal installment and interest of bond	2,648		2,648	
4. Other financial liabilities	0		17	
B. Trade payables		320,725,861		189,944,630
1. Suppliers	180,035,674		138,783,694	
2. Notes payable	158,475,740		55,165,958	
3. Discount of notes payable (-)	(17,821,553)		(4,006,022)	
4. Deposits and guarantees received	36,000		1,000	
C. Other short term liabilities		95,957,857		78,870,952
1. Amounts due to shareholders	352,131		220,339	
2. Accrued liabilities	5,050,108		3,278,483	
3. Taxes, charges and other deductions payable	37,483,172		28,235,374	
4. Short-term other liabilities	53,072,446		47,136,756	
4.1 Deferred export V.A.T.	32,790,516		34,883,540	
4.2 Royalty	17,570,520		11,514,742	
4.3 Other	2,711,410		738,474	
D. Purchase orders received		7,232,952		11,356,084
E. Provisions		58,834,009		43,153,651
1. Provision for taxation	33,330,646		18,089,247	
2. Other Provisions	25,503,363		25,064,404	
2.1 Provision for warranties	7,800,000		5,400,000	
2.2 Provision for short-term loan interest	5,039,534		4,122,683	
2.3 Provision for medium-term loan interest	12,654,781		15,541,721	
2.4 Other	9,048			
II. Long term liabilities		**220,091,952**		**186,590,716**
A. Financial liabilities		74,777,421		105,338,379
1. Bank loans	74,777,421		105,338,379	
B. Other long-term liabilities		19,993		17,793
1. Other long-term liabilities	19,993		17,793	
C. Provision		145,294,538		81,234,544
1. Provision for termination indemnities	145,294,538		81,234,544	
III. Shareholders' equity		**1,255,086,264**		**718,436,112**
A. Capital		151,875,000		151,875,000
B. Share premium		2,602,153		2,602,153
C. Revaluation reserve		810,612,853		414,002,957
1. Revaluation of tangible fixed assets	810,612,853		414,002,957	
2. Revaluation of investments				
D. Reserves		92,745,584		45,465,772
1. Legal reserves	28,293,251		16,651,314	
2. Extraordinary reserves	64,452,333		28,814,458	
E. Net income for the period		197,250,674		104,490,230
Total liabilities and shareholders' equity		**2,275,897,019**		**1,425,073,660**

Brisa Bridgestone Sabancı Lastik Sanayi ve Ticaret A.Ş.
31 Aralık 1993 Tarihindeki Ayrıntılı Gelir Tablosu (1000.-TL)

	Cari dönem 31 . 12 . 1993		Önceki dönem 31 . 12 . 1992	
A. Brüt satışlar		2,708,075,562		1,680,950,973
1. Yurt içi satışlar	1,796,905,893		1,090,728,171	
2. Yurt dışı satışlar	911,169,669		590,222,802	
B. Satışlardan indirimler (-)		(31,073,336)		(17,933,198)
1. Satıştan iadeler (-)	(6,637,081)		(5,544,244)	
2. Satış iskontoları (-)	(24,436,255)		(12,388,954)	
C. Net satışlar		2,677,002,226		1,663,017,775
D. Satışların maliyeti (-)		(1,729,352,447)		(1,103,977,292)
Brüt satış kârı		947,649,779		559,040,483
E. Faaliyet giderleri (-)		(415,091,206)		(230,106,952)
1. Pazarlama, satış ve dağıtım giderleri (-)	(235,139,949)		(124,988,673)	
2. Genel yönetim giderleri (-)	(179,951,257)		(108,118,279)	
Esas faaliyet kârı		532,558,573		328,933,531
F. Diğer faaliyetlerden gelirler ve kârlar		32,540,868		10,807,199
1. Faiz ve diğer temettü gelirleri	182,338		127,296	
2. Faaliyetle ilgili diğer gelirler ve kârlar	32,358,530		10,679,903	
2.1 Acentalık gelirleri	1,955,227		1,046,392	
2.2 Yatırım teşvik gelirleri	1,253,806		0	
2.3 Reeskont gelirleri	23,412,373		4,365,876	
2.4 Hammadde satışları	169,643		111,842	
2.5 Esas faaliyet dışı satışlar	1,413,361		4,107,662	
2.6 Diğer	4,154,120		1,048,131	
G. Diğer faaliyetlerden giderler ve zararlar (-)		(48,455,279)		(15,018,946)
1. Kıdem tazminatı (-)	(6,837,125)		(5,864,092)	
2. Emlak vergisi (-)	(392,166)		(254,261)	
3. Reeskont giderleri (-)	(23,741,060)		(5,849,093)	
4. Hammadde satış maliyeti (-)	(1,467,363)		(132,314)	
5. Esas faaliyet dışı satışlar maliyeti (-)	(644,229)		(576,795)	
6. Diğer (-)	(15,373,336)		(2,342,391)	
H. Finansman giderleri (-)		(281,330,902)		(232,716,828)
1. Kısa vadeli borçlanma giderleri (-)	(218,627,816)		(173,526,043)	
2. Uzun vadeli borçlanma giderleri (-)	(62,703,086)		(59,190,785)	
Faaliyet kârı		235,313,260		92,004,956
I. Olağanüstü gelirler ve kârlar		13,414,820		43,952,414
1. Önceki dönem gelir ve kârları	7,393,642		41,054,717	
2. Diğer olağanüstü gelirler ve kârlar	6,021,178		2,897,697	
J. Olağanüstü giderler ve zararlar (-)		(18,146,760)		(13,377,893)
1. Çalışılmayan dönem giderleri ve zararları (-)	(8,847,801)		(6,766,085)	
2. Önceki dönem gider ve zararları (-)	(6,154,325)		(3,373,005)	
3. Diğer olağanüstü giderler ve zararlar (-)	(3,144,634)		(3,238,803)	
Dönem kârı		230,581,320		122,579,477
K. Ödenecek vergi ve diğer yasal yükümlülükler (-)		(33,330,646)		(18,089,247)
Net dönem kârı		197,250,674		104,490,230

16

Brisa Bridgestone Sabancı Lastik Sanayi ve Ticaret A.Ş.
Detailed Income Statement for the Year Ended December 31, 1993 (TL 1,000)

	Current Period 31 . 12 . 1993		Previous Period 31 . 12 . 1992	
A. Gross sales		2,708,075,562		1,680,950,973
1. Domestic sales	1,796,905,893		1,090,728,171	
2. Export sales	911,169,669		590,222,802	
B. Sales deductions (-)		(31,073,336)		(17,933,198)
1. Sales returns (-)	(6,637,081)		(5,544,244)	
2. Sales discounts (-)	(24,436,255)		(12,388,954)	
C. Net sales		2,677,002,226		1,663,017,775
D. Cost of sales (-)		(1,729,352,447)		(1,103,977,292)
Gross profit		947,649,779		559,040,483
E. Operating expenses (-)		(415,091,206)		(230,106,952)
1. Marketing, selling and distribution expenses (-)	(235,139,949)		(121,988,673)	
2. Administration expenses (-)	(179,951,257)		(108,118,279)	
Trading profit		532,558,573		328,933,531
F. Income and profit from other operations		32,540,868		10,807,199
1. Interest income and other dividends	182,338		127,296	
2. Other income and profits relating to operations	32,358,530		10,679,903	
2.1 Agency income	1,955,227		1,046,392	
2.2 Investment incentive income	1,253,806		0	
2.3 Rediscount income	23,412,373		4,365,876	
2.4 Raw material sales	169,643		111,842	
2.5 Other sales	1,413,361		4,107,662	
2.6 Other	4,154,120		1,048,131	
G. Expenses and losses from other operations (-)		(48,455,279)		(15,018,946)
1. Termination indemnity (-)	(6,837,125)		(5,864,092)	
2. Taxes on real estate (-)	(392,166)		(254,261)	
3. Rediscount expense (-)	(23,741,060)		(5,849,093)	
4. Cost of sales of raw material (-)	(1,467,363)		(132,314)	
5. Cost of other sales (-)	(644,229)		(576,795)	
6. Other (-)	(15,373,336)		(2,342,391)	
H. Financial expenses (-)		(281,330,902)		(232,716,828)
1. Short-term borrowing expenses (-)	(218,627,816)		(173,526,043)	
2. Long-term borrowing expenses (-)	(62,703,086)		(59,190,785)	
Operating profit		235,313,260		92,004,956
I. Extraordinary income and profits		13,414,820		43,952,414
1. Prior period income and profits	7,393,642		41,054,717	
2. Other extraordinary income and profits	6,021,178		2,897,697	
J. Extraordinary expenses and losses (-)		(18,146,760)		(13,377,893)
1. Expenses and losses relating to non-operating activity (-)	(8,847,801)		(6,766,085)	
2. Prior period expenses and losses (-)	(6,154,325)		(3,373,005)	
3. Other extraordinary expenses and losses (-)	(3,144,634)		(3,238,803)	
Income for the period		230,581,320		122,579,477
K. Taxes payable and other statutory obligations (-)		(33,330,646)		(18,089,247)
Net income for the period		197,250,674		104,490,230

16

Brisa Bridgestone Sabancı Lastik Sanayi ve Ticaret A.Ş.
31 Aralık 1993 Tarihinde Sona Eren Yıla Ait Nakit Akım Tablosu (1000.-TL)

	Cari dönem 31 . 12 . 1993		Önceki dönem 31 . 12 . 1992	
A. Dönem başı nakit mevcudu		5,794,698		13,929,996
B. Dönem içi nakit girişleri		2,568,560,019		1,578,768,201
1. Satışlardan elde edilen nakit	2,466,814,363		1,494,498,647	
a. Net satış hasılatı	2,677,002,226		1,663,017,775	
b. Alacaklardaki (satışlardan kaynaklanan)				
artışlar (-)	(210,187,863)		(168,519,128)	
2. Diğer faaliyetlerden gelirler ve kârlardan dolayı				
sağlanan nakit	18,725,337		7,059,841	
3. Olağanüstü gelir ve kârlardan sağlanan nakit	12,161,410		42,486,841	
4. Kısa vadeli borçlardaki artış (alımlarla ilgili olmayan)	98,546,339		31,534,613	
a. Diğer artışlar	98,546,339		31,534,613	
5. Uzun vadeli borçlardaki artış (alımlarla ilgili olmayan)	(27,687,430)		283,178	
a. Diğer artışlar	(27,687,430)		283,178	
6. Diğer nakit girişleri			2,905,081	
C. Dönem içi nakit çıkışları		2,564,965,010		1,586,903,499
1. Maliyetlerden kaynaklanan nakit çıkışı	1,641,975,482		1,044,602,321	
a. Satışların maliyeti	1,729,352,447		1,103,977,292	
b. Stoklardaki artış	176,362,525		108,278,394	
c. Borçlardaki (alımlardan kaynaklanan)				
artış (-)	(144,561,762)		(87,127,854)	
d. Amortisman ve karşılıklar gibi nakit				
çıkışı gerektirmeyen giderler (-)	(119,177,728)		(80,525,511)	
2. Faaliyet giderlerinden dolayı nakit çıkışı		342,000,877		186,179,594
a. Pazarlama satış ve dağıtım giderleri	235,139,949		121,988,673	
b. Genel yönetim giderleri	179,951,257		108,118,279	
c. Nakit çıkışı gerektirmeyen giderler (-)	(73,090,329)		(43,927,358)	
3. Diğer faaliyetlerden giderler ve zararlardan				
dolayı nakit çıkışı		34,311,059		9,787,982
a. Diğer faaliyetlerle ilgili giderler				
ve zararlar	48,455,279		15,018,946	
b. Nakit çıkışı gerektirmeyen giderler				
ve zararlar(-)	(14,144,220)		(5,230,964)	
4. Finansman giderlerinden dolayı nakit çıkışı		283,300,991		239,403,975
5. Olağanüstü gider ve zararlardan dolayı				
nakit çıkışı		(14,394,108)		5,483,422
a. Olağanüstü giderler ve zararlar	18,146,760		13,377,893	
b. Nakit çıkışı gerektirmeyen giderler				
ve zararlar (-)	(32,540,868)		(7,894,471)	
6. Duran varlık yatırımları nedeniyle nakit çıkışı		188,160,225		87,303,429
7. Uzun vadeli borçların anapara ödemeleri				
(alımlarla ilgili olmayan)				
a. Diğer ödemeler				
8. Ödenen vergi ve benzerleri		18,089,247		4,140,167
9. Ödenen temettüler		57,210,418		10,002,609
10. Diğer nakit çıkışları		14,310,819		
D. Dönem sonu nakit mevcudu		9,389,707		5,794,698
E. Nakit artışı/azalışı		3,595,009		(8,135,298)

Brisa Bridgestone Sabancı Lastik Sanayi ve Ticaret A.Ş.
Statement of Cash Flow for the Year Ended December 31, 1993 (TL 1,000)

	Current Period 31 . 12 . 1993		Previous Period 31 . 12 . 1992	
A. Cash balances at beginning of period		5,794,698		13,929,996
B. Cash receipts during the period		2,568,560,019		1,578,768,201
1. Cash received from sales		2,466,814,363		1,494,498,647
a. Net sales	2,677,002,226		1,663,017,775	
b. Increase in receivables (from sales) (-)	(210,187,863)		(168,519,128)	
2. Cash received from other income and profits		18,725,337		7,059,841
3. Cash received from other income and profits		12,161,410		42,486,841
4. Increase in current liabilities (not relating to purchases)		98,546,339		31,534,613
a. Other increases	98,546,339		31,534,613	
5. Increase in long term liabilities (not relating to purchases)		(27,687,430)		283,178
a. Other increases	(27,687,430)		283,178	
6. Other cash receipts				2,905,081
C. Cash payments during period		2,564,965,010		1,586,903,499
1. Cash payments relating to costs		1,641,975,482		1,044,602,321
a. Cost of sales	1,729,352,447		1,103,977,292	
b. Increase in inventories	176,362,525		108,278,394	
c. Increase in liabilities (relating to purchases) (-)	(144,561,762)		(87,127,854)	
d. Expenses not requiring cash payment, such as depreciation and provisions (-)	(119,177,728)		(80,525,511)	
2. Cash payments relating to operating expenses		342,000,877		186,179,594
a. Marketing, selling and distribution expenses	235,139,949		121,988,673	
b. Administration expenses	179,951,257		108,118,279	
c. Expenses not requiring cash payments (-)	(73,090,329)		(43,927,358)	
3. Cash payments relating to other expenses and other losses		34,311,059		9,787,982
a. Other expenses and losses	48,455,279		15,018,946	
b. Expenses and losses not requiring cash payments (-)	(14,144,220)		(5,230,964)	
4. Cash payments relating to financial expenses		283,300,991		239,403,975
5. Cash payments relating to extraordinary expenses and losses		(14,394,108)		5,483,422
a. Extraordinary expenses and losses	18,146,760		13,377,893	
b. Expenses and losses not requiring cash payments (-)	(32,540,868)		(7,894,471)	
6. Cash payments relating to purchases of fixed assets		188,160,225		87,303,429
7. Principal payments of long term loans (not related to purchases)				
a. Other Payments				
8. Taxes and charges paid		18,089,247		4,140,167
9. Dividends paid		57,210,418		10,002,609
10. Other cash payments		14,310,819		
D. Cash balances end of period		9,389,707		5,794,698
E. Cash increase decrease		3,595,009		(8,135,298)

Brisa Bridgestone Sabancı Lastik Sanayi ve Ticaret A.Ş.
31 Aralık 1993 Tarihinde Sona Eren Yıla Ait Fon Akım Tablosu (1000.-TL)

		Cari dönem 31 . 12 . 1993		Önceki dönem 31 . 12 . 1992
A. Kaynaklar		**698,750,269**		**429,980,330**
1. Faaliyet kârından sağlanan kaynak		435,107,402		218,051,537
a- Faaliyet kârı	235,313,260		92,004,955	
b- Amortismanlar	134,655,864		90,424,270	
c- Fon çıkışı gerektirmeyen giderler (+)	80,923,898		46,057,208	
d- Fon girişi sağlamayan gelirler (-)	(15,785,620)		(10,434,896)	
2. Olağanüstü kârdan sağlanan kaynak		13,414,820		43,952,415
a- Olağanüstü kâr	13,414,820		43,952,415	
3. Kısa vadeli borçlardaki artış		250,228,047		167,976,378
B. Kaynak kullanımları		**698,750,269**		**429,980,330**
1. Olağanüstü zarardan dolayı kaynak kullanımı		18,146,760		13,377,893
a- Olağanüstü zarar	18,146,760		13,377,893	
2. Ödenen vergi ve benzerleri		18,089,247		4,140,167
3. Ödenen temettüler		57,210,418		10,002,609
4. Dönen varlıklar tutarındaki artış		386,584,861		301,009,039
5. Duran varlıklar tutarındaki artış (Yeniden değerleme hariç)		188,160,225		87,303,429
6. Uzun vadeli borçlardaki azalış		30,558,758		14,147,193
Net işletme sermayesindeki değişim				
1. Net işletme sermayesinde artış		**120,206,963**		**133,032,661**
2. Net işletme sermayesinde azalış				

Brisa Bridgestone Sabancı Lastik Sanayi ve Ticaret A.Ş.
Statement of Fund Flow for the Year Ended December 31, 1993 and 1992 (TL 1,000)

		Current Period 31 . 12 . 1993		Previous Period 31 . 12 . 1992
A. Sources			698,750,269		429,980,330
1. Sources from operations		435,107,402		218,051,537
a- Operating profit	235,313,260		92,004,955	
b- Depreciation	134,655,864		90,424,270	
c- Expenses not involving outlay of funds (+)	80,923,898		46,057,208	
d- Income not involving receipt of funds (-)	(15,785,620)		(10,434,896)	
2. Fund received from extraordinary profit		13,414,820		43,952,415
a- Extraordinary profit	13,414,820		43,952,415	
3. Increase in long term liabilities		250,228,047		167,976,378
B. Use of funds			698,750,269		429,980,330
1. Fund used in extraordinary loss		18,146,760		13,377,893
a- Extraordinary loss	18,146,760		13,377,893	
2. Taxes and charges paid		18,089,247		4,140,167
3. Dividends paid		57,210,418		10,002,609
4. Increase in current assets		386,584,861		301,009,039
5. Increase in long term assets (excluding revaluation)		188,160,225		87,303,429
6. Decrease in long term liabilities		30,558,758		14,147,193
Change in net working capital				
1. Increase in net working capital			120,206,963		133,032,661
2. Decrease in net working capital				

4-Brisa Bridgestone Sabancı Lastik Sanayi ve Ticaret A.Ş.
1993 Dönemi Mali Oranlar Tablosu

	Cari dönem 31 . 12 . 1993	Önceki dönem 31 . 12 . 1992
I- Likidite Oranları		
1- Cari Oran: (Dönen varlıklar/kısa vadeli borçlar)	1.38	1.35
2- Asit Test Oranı: (Dönen varlıklar-stoklar/kısa vadeli borçlar)	0.79	0.78
II- Mali Bünye Oranları:		
1- Toplam Borçların/Toplam Aktiflere: (Borçlar toplamı/aktif toplamı)	0.45	0.50
2- Öz Sermayenin Toplam Borçlara: (Öz sermaye/borçlar toplamı)	1.23	1.02
III-Faaliyet ve Kârlılık Oranları		
1- Satışların Kârlılık Oranı: (Net dönem kârı/net satışlar)	0.07	0.06
2- Aktiflerin Kârlılık Oranı: (Net dönem kârı/toplam aktifler)	0.09	0.07
3- Özkaynakların Kârlılık Oranı: (Net dönem kârı/özkaynaklar)	0.19	0.17

5. Mali Yapı İle İlgili Önlemler:
Şirketimiz sağlıklı ve güçlü mali bünyesi ile 1993 yılının zor şartlarına rağmen bu dönemi de başarılı bir şekilde tamamlamıştır.

4-Brisa Bridgestone Sabancı Lastik Sanayi ve Ticaret A.Ş.
Financial Ratios

	Current Period 31 . 12 . 1993	Previous Period 31 . 12 . 1992
I- Liquidity ratios		
1- Current ratio (current assets/short term debts)	1.38	1.35
2- Acid test ratio (current assets, inventories/short term debts)	0.79	0.78
II- Financial structure ratios		
1- Total debts/Total assets	0.45	0.50
2- Net worth/Total debts	1.23	1.02
III-Ratios of operation and profitability		
1- Ratio of profitability of sales (net term profit/net sales)	0.07	0.06
2- Ratio of profitability of assets (net term profit/total assets)	0.09	0.07
3- Ratio of profitability of net worth (net term profit/net worth)	0.19	0.17

5. Measures Relevant to Financial Structure :
With its healthy and powerful structure, our company completed the term in question successfully despite the severe conditions prevailing in 1993.

Brisa Bridgestone Sabancı Lastik Sanayi ve Ticaret A.Ş.
Notes to the Detailed Financial Statements for the
Years Ended December 31, 1993 and 1992 (TL 1,000)

1. Accounting Techniques and Valuation Procedures Applied
a) The company prepared its accounting records and its financial statements for the years ended December 31, 1993 and 1992, in accordance with current legislation and Declarations of the Capital Market Board.

b) Inventories :
Inventories are physically counted as of December 31, 1993. Inventories are stated at the lower of cost or net realizable value. Cost is determined by the continuous mobile average method for raw materials, goods for resale and others, and by the monthly average method for semi-finished goods and finished goods.

c) Fixed Assets :
Company values its buildings (excluding land), its plant machinery and equipment, motor vehicles, furniture and fixtures by applying coefficients that are fixed by the Ministry of Finance. The revaluation surplus is included in the shareholders' equity.
Revalued fixed assets except buildings are depreciated by the declining-balance and straight-line methods using the following rates which are in accordance with tax law :

Superstructures and Infrastructures	25 %
Buildings	2-4 %
Plant, machinery and equipment	10-25 %
Motor vehicles	25 %
Furniture and fixtures	10-25 %

d) Intangible fixed assets :
Intangible fixed assets are stated after amortization.

e) Assets and Liabilities in Foreign Currency :
Assets and liabilities in foreign currency are translated into Turkish Lira at exchange rates issued by the Turkish Central Bank at balance sheet dates. Transactions in foreign currencies during the year are translated into Turkish Lira at the rates in effect on transaction dates. Exchange gains and losses resulting from such transactions are included in the statement of income.

f) Revenues and Expenses :
The accruals basis of accounting is applied for the recognition of revenues and expenses. Income is recognized at the time of delivery of goods or termination of service.

g) Termination Indemnities :
In accordance with the requirements of the Capital Market Board, provision is made for potential future payments to employees with rights to termination indemnities under Turkish Employment Legislation.

2. Subsequent Events
With effect January 1, 1994 the upper limit for termination indemnities has been increased to TL 11,806 in respect of each year of service. (1992 - 7.701 TL)

3. Conditional Events
The legal claims pursued against the company in the Employment Court are still outstanding as of December 31, 1993. Potential liabilities are estimated to be TL 1,561,000 (1992 TL 685,533). The amount of claims pursued by the company is TL 10,017 (1992 TL 38,317).

4. Changes in Accounting Estimates
There are no changes affecting the Company's gross margin estimates.

5. Mortgages or Guarantees on Assets
As of December 31, 1993 and 1992 the total amount of mortgages outstanding on tangible fixed assets and relating to long-term loans amounted to TL 224,350,000.

6. Insurance Coverage
As of December 31, 1993 total insurance coverage on assets amounted to TL 2,831,649,505 (1992 TL 1,940,641,772).

7. Mortgages and Guarantees Received
As of December 31, 1993 the total amount of letter of guarantees and mortgages obtained against short-term trade receivables amounted to TL 205,750,381 (1992 TL 157,695,333).

8. Commitments and Contingent Liabilities
Commitments and contingent liabilities are as follows :
a) Commitments :
The Company's export commitment between 1990 and 1998 in accordance with Investment Incentive Certificates amounts to USD 200 million, all of which were exported by December 31, 1993 (1992-USD 169 million). The Company has outstanding commitments until 1995 in respect of further investment amounting to USD 23 million.

b) Contingent Liabilities :
As of December 31, 1993 outstanding contingent liabilities in the form of letters of guarantees given to banks and customs authorities amounted to TL 167,430,571 (1992 TL 106,393,097).

9. Blocked Deposit Amounts at Banks
As of December 31, 1993 blocked deposits at banks amounted to TL 126,530 (1992 TL 71,744).

10. Provision for Marketable Securities
The company has no marketable securities.

11. Marketable Securities Issued By Related Parties

The Company has no marketable securities issued by related parties, classified under marketable security and tangible fixed asset accounts.

12. Related Party Transactions

Balances with related parties are as follows:

	Receivables		Payables	
	31.12.1993	31.12.1992	31.12.1993	31.12.1992
Lisa Lastik İhracat ve Satış A.Ş.	10.113			
Eksa Export San. Mamulleri Sat. ve Araş. A.Ş.	20.208.733	12.276.316		
Olmuksa Mukavva San. ve Tic. A.Ş.	26.416			
Kordsa Kordbezi San. ve Tic. A.Ş.			68.165.219	39.497.455
Temsa Termomekanik San. ve Tic. A.Ş.	3.789.681	2.716.596		
Ak Sigorta A.Ş.			1.848.666	673.596
I-Bımsa Bilgi İşlem Merkezi Tic. ve San. A.Ş.			4.362.519	2.751.561
Insa A.Ş.		3.527		
Pilsa Plastik San. ve Tic. A.Ş.			122.568	137.686
Bridgestone Corporation			5.034.663	1.198.964
Beksa Çelik Kord. San. ve Tic. A.Ş.			13.550.211	3.102.530
Universal Trading (Jersey) Ltd.			19.881.058	25.667.841
Bridgestone Bekaert Steel Corp Ltd.			4.783.957	8.130.234
Yünsa Yünlü San. ve Tic. A.Ş.	4.540			
Teksa Tekstil Tic. ve San. A.Ş.				
Toyotasa A.Ş.			5.704	
Bossa A.Ş.			138.000	
Exsa Handels Gmbh			33.415	
Exsa U.K. Ltd.			111.360	
Hacı Ömer Sabancı Holding A.Ş.			22.646	39.866
Firestone Hispania S.A.			10.616	
BNP AK.			2.979	
Bridgestone Firestone Singapore PTE Ltd.			7.501.260	5.384.123
Total	20.039.483	15.032.682	125.578.466	86.563.990

Furthermore, the Company has deposit and credit balances with one of its shareholders, Akbank T.A.Ş., due to banking transactions.

13. Other

The total amounts receivable from and payable to personnel by the company do not exceed the 1 percent of the balance sheet total.

14. Doubtful Receivables Related to Related Parties

The Company has no doubtful debts receivable from related parties, shareholders and partners.

15. Doubtful Debts Relating to Receivables Due and not yet due

Doubtful debts relating to the Company's receivables as of December 31, 1993 amount to TL 557,476 (1992- TL 237,792).

16. Investment and Affiliated Companies

The Company has no investment and affiliated companies.

17. Bonus Shares Received from Investments and Related Parties

No shares are currently held by the Company in related entities or as investments.

18. The Property Rights on Fixed Assets

There are no property rights given to third parties on the Company's assets.

19. Revaluation of Tangible Fixed Assets

Revaluations of tangible fixed assets and accumulated depreciation are as follows:

	31.12.1991	31.12.1992	31.12.1993
Increase in cost	270,189,345	510,341,230	562,972,551
Increase in accumulated depreciation	(132,764,153)	(264,492,840)	(165,767,504)
Revaluation surplus	137,425,192	245,848,390	397,205.04

20. Assets and Liabilities in Foreign Currency

Assets denominated in foreign currencies without currency rate guarantees as of 1993 are as follows:

	Foreign Currency	1993 Foreign Currency Amount	Foreign Currency Rate	1992 Foreign Currency Amount	Foreign Currency Rate
Foreign currency cash and bank balances					
	STG	1,287.61	21,349.03	1,287.61	12,944.88
	JY	88,411.69	127.23	88,411.69	67.66
	DM	5,295.78	8,389.41	5,295.78	5,297.36
	USD	42,299.07	14,443.57	28,105.75	8,547.29
Export receivables					
	USD			1,080,427.78	8,555.85
Other overseas receivables					
	USD	193,262.94	14,458.03	318,257.54	8,555.85

Liabilities denominated in foreign currencies without currency rate guarantees as of 31.12.1993 are as follows:

	Foreign Currency	1993 Foreign Currency Amount	Foreign Currency Rate	1992 Foreign Currency Amount	Foreign Currency Rate
Drafts with acceptance credit					
	USD	9,098,654.27	14,458.03	6,308,859.00	8,555.85
	STG	35,679.81	21,370.40		
	BF			2,470,871.00	258.33
	JY	202,559,662.00	129.17		
Foreign currency liabilities					
	USD	2,479,806.01	14,458.03	4,235,502.64	8,555.85
	JY	66,244,286.00	129.17	159,780,914.00	68.69
	DM	223,927.00	8,347.59	82,300.00	5,302.66
	BF			1,213,591.20	258.33
	LIT	4,847,850.00	8.47		
	STG	53,310.34	21,370.40	40,529.97	12,957.84
	FFR	115,165.00	2,458.64		
Advance received					
	USD	369,198.12	14,458.03	1,280,657.08	8,555.85
Short-term bank loans					
	USD	8,750,000.00	14,458.03	7,750,000.00	8,555.85
	DM	10,625,000.00	8,347.59	4,500,000.00	5,302.66

21. Bonds Issued

No bonds issued by the Company.

22. Unaccrued Interest Payable

Unaccrued interest payable of long-term and short-term loans as of 31.12.1993 and 1992 are as follows:

	31.12.1993	31.12.1992
A- Short-term loans	13,109,034	8,216,630
1. Export credits	6,750,914	6,467,807
2. Foreign currency loans	6,358,120	1,748,823
B- Long-terms loans	91,465,439	154,167,866
1. Investment credit with currency guarantees	91,117,540	153,012,239
2. Other long-terms loans	347,899	1,155,537
Total	104,574,473	162,384,496

23. Authorized Capital

As of December 31, 1993 and 1992 the authorized capital is TL 607,500,000.

24. Preferred Shares

At December 31, 1993 and 1992, the company had 100 incorporator shares entitled to participate only in the profit, and 5% of the period profit is distributed to the holders of such shares as stipulated in the Articles of Association.

25. Guarantees Given

As of December 31, 1993, the company has given guarantees to AKBANK T.A.Ş. amounting to TL 11.000.000.

26. Personnel

The average number of personnel during the year is as follows:

	1993	1992
Waged	1073	1088
Salaried	379	411
Total	1452	1499

27. Other Events Affecting the Financial Statements

There are no other events affecting the financial statements which should be disclosed.

Brisa Bridgestone Sabancı Lastik Sanayi ve Ticaret A.Ş.
Notes to the Detailed Income Statements for the Years Ended December 31, 1993 and 1992 (TL 1,000)

1. Inventory Cost

Inventories are valued by using the process cost method. Cost is determined by the continuous mobile average method for raw materials, goods for resale and others, and by the monthly average method for semi-finished goods and finished goods.

2. Stocktake

Inventories are physically counted as of December 31, 1993.

3. Financial Expenses Paid to Related Parties and Recorded as an Expense or Capitalized

During the year, interest amounting to TL 40,985,579 (1992 - TL 62,373,852) was charged to the Company by Akbank T.A.Ş. TL 114,191,119 foreign currency loss resulted from long-term and short-term loans was paid to Akbank (1992 - TL 82,673,409)

Furthermore, interest amounting to TL 5,023,936 (1992 - TL 3,225,823) was charged to the Company in respect of a Türk Eximbank credit utilized by the Company through Exsa Export Sanayi Mamulleri Satış ve Araştırma A.Ş., a Sabancı Group Company.

No foreign currency loss was paid to Exsa Export Sanayi Mamulleri Satış ve Araştırma A.Ş. (1992 - TL 1,698,705).

4. Sales/Purchase Transactions with Related Parties

Sales to related parties exceeding 20% of gross sales were as follows :

To Exsa Export Sanayi Mamulleri Satış ve Araştırma A.Ş. :

	1993	1992
Invoice value	274,752,614	279,298,370
Relevant exchange gain	20,047,123	15,210,067
Relevant export incentives and tax rebate	332,631	464,902

To Bridgestone Corporation

	1993	1992
Invoice value	556,432,944	286,837,533
Relevant exchange gain	12,684,867	8,080,611
Relevant export incentives	35,991	331,318

Purchases from related parties exceeding 20% of cost of sales were as follows :

From Kordsa Kord Bezi Sanayi ve Ticaret A.Ş.

1993	1992
332,112,559	218,163,533

5. Goods and Service Sold

Sales of by product and scrap included in domestic and export sales do not exceed 20% of the gross sales.

6. Prior Period Incomes and Expenses

(a) Incomes related to previous years are as follows :

	1993	1992
Energy incentive	1,644,758	
Price support stabilisation fund	15,129	32,429,010
Previous year's return	2,176,877	3,447,095
Foreign currency gain	2,259,068	3,460,893
Export price difference income	237,604	1,131,169
Other	106,206	585,741
Total	7,393,642	41,054,718

(b) Expenses related to previous years are as follows :

	1993	1992
Tire test expense	1,311,350	
Previous year's return	367,073	1,424,085
Export expense	2,151,246	850,977
Foreign currency loss on licence payment	705,858	716,208
Claim adjustment	990,897	
Other	627,901	381,735
	6,154,325	3,373,005

7. Incorporator Shares

Profit per share and dividends per share for ordinary and incorporator shares are as follows :

	1993	1992
a) Profit per share		
151,875,000 shares receiving 12 months' share from profit	1,223 TL/122.3%	648 TL/64.8%
b) Dividends per share		
151,875,000 shares receiving 12 months' share from profits	620 TL/62%	325 TL/32.5%
To 100 incorporator shareholders	115,290 TL/11.529%	61,289 TL/6,128%

III. Kâr Dağıtım Önerisi

Yönetim Kurulu olarak 1.1.1993 - 31.12.1993 döneminde yaratılmış bulunan 230,581,319,959 TL kârın Esas Mukavelenamemizin 28. maddesi mucibi Kurumlar Vergisi, Gelir Vergisi Stopajı, Fon Payı ve Birinci Tertip Yasal Akçe tenzil edildikten sonra kalan 185,721,608,333 TL kârın aşağıda tabloda görüldüğü şekilde;

Brisa Bridgestone Sabancı Lastik Sanayi ve Ticaret A.Ş.
31 Aralık 1993 Tarihinde Sona Eren Yıla Ait Öngörülen Kâr Dağıtım Tablosu (1000 TL.)

	Cari dönem 31.12.1993		Önceki dönem 31.12.1992	
A. Dönem karının dağıtımı				
1. Dönem kârı		230,581,320		122,579,477
2. Geçmiş yıllar zararları				
3. Ödenecek vergiler		(33,330,646)		(18,089,247)
- Gelir vergisi	(31,150,136)		(16,905,838)	
- Diğer vergi ve benzerleri	(2,180,510)		(1,183,409)	
4. Birinci tertip yasal yedek		(11,529,066)		(6,128,974)
Net dağıtılabilir dönem kârı		185,721,608		98,361,256
5. Ortaklara birinci temettü		(104,389,870)		(55,309,602)
-Adi hisse senedi sahiplerine	(92,860,804)		(49,180,628)	
-İmtiyazlı hisse senedi sahiplerine	(11,529,066)		(6,128,974)	
6. Memur ve işçilere temettü				
7.Yönetim kuruluna temettü		(3,253,275)		(1,722,069)
8. Ortaklara ikinci temettü		(1,301,696)		(178,747)
-Adi hisse senedi sahiplerine	(1,301,696)		(178,747)	
-İmtiyazlı hisse senedi sahiplerine				
9. İkinci tertip yasal yedek		(11,261,232)		(5,512,963)
10.Olağanüstü yedek		65,515,535		35,637,875
B. Hisse başına kâr (TL/%)				
1. Adi hisse senedi sahiplerine (TL/%)		1223 / 122.3		648 / 64.8
C. Hisse başına kâr payı				
1. Adi hisse senedi sahiplerine (TL/%)		620 / 62		325 / 32.5
2. 100 adet kurucu hisse senedi sahiplerine (TL/%)		115290 / 11529		61289/6128

tefrikine ve 151,875,000,000.-TL sermayeyi temsil eden hisse senetleri için %62 oranında temettü payı ile imtiyazlı hisse senetleri ve Yönetim Kurulu kâr paylarının 18/4/94 tarihinden itibaren dağıtılmasına karar vermenizi teklif eder saygılarımızı sunarız.

Yönetim Kurulu adına
Başkan

Sakıp SABANCI

III. Proposal for Profit Distribution

The Board of Directors hereby submits and kindly requests resolution for distribution beginning from April 4, 1994 of the profit worth TL 185,721,608,333 after Corporate Tax, Withholding, Defense Industry Support Fund and 1st Legal Reserves Deductions from the profit worth TL 230,581,310,959 generated in the period of 1.1.1993 - 31.12.1993 according to Article 28 of Articles of Association as given below;

Brisa Bridgestone Sabancı Lastik Sanayi ve Ticaret A.Ş.
Statement of Proposed Profit Distribution for the Year Ended December 31, 1993 (TL 1,000)

		Current Period 31 . 12 . 1993		Previous Period 31 . 12 . 1992
A. Distribution of profit for the period				
1. Income for the period		230,581,320		122,579,477
2. Debts from previous years				
3. Taxes payable		(33,330,646)		(18,089,247)
- Income tax	(31,150,136)		(16,905,838)	
- Other taxes and charges	(2,180,510)		(1,183,409)	
4. First legal reserve		(11,529,066)		(6,128,974)
Distributable net profit for the period		185,721,608		98,361,256
5. First dividend to shareholders		(104,389,870)		(55,309,602)
-To ordinary shareholders	(92,860,804)		(49,180,628)	
-To privileged shareholders	(11,529,066)		(6,128,974)	
6. Dividends to staff and workers				
7. Dividends to the board of directors		(3,253,275)		(1,722,069)
8. Second dividend to shareholders		(1,301,696)		(178,747)
-To ordinary shareholders	(1,301,696)		(178,747)	
-To privileged shareholders				
9. Second legal reserve		(11,261,232)		(5,512,963)
10.Extraordinary reserves		65,515,535		35,637,875
B. Profit per share (TL/%)				
1. To ordinary shareholders (TL/%)		1223 / 122.3		648 / 64.8
C. Dividends per share				
1. To ordinary shareholders (TL/%)		620 / 62		325 / 32.5
2. To holders of 100 incorporator shares (TL/%)		115290 / 11529		61289/6128

where 62% of dividend on shares representing TL 151,875,000,000 of capital and their usufruct and shares of Board of Directors.

Respectfully yours,
For the Board of Directors
Chairman

Sakıp Sabancı

Brisa Bridgestone Sabancı Lastik Sanayi ve Ticaret A.Ş.
1993 Hesap Dönemine Ait Bağımsız Denetçi Raporu

Brisa Bridgestone Sabancı Lastik Sanayi ve Ticaret Anonim Şirketi'nin 31 Aralık 1993 ve 1992 tarihli bilançolarını ve aynı tarihlerde sona eren yıllara ait gelir, fon akım, nakit akım, satışların maliyeti ve öngörülen kâr dağıtım tablolarını incelemiş bulunuyoruz. İncelemelerimiz, genel kabul görmüş denetim ilke, esas ve standartlarına uygun olarak yapılmış ve dolayısıyle hesap ve işlemlerle ilgili olarak muhasebe kayıtlarının kontrolü ile gerekli gördüğümüz diğer denetleme yöntem ve tekniklerini içermiştir.

Görüşümüze göre, söz konusu mali tablolar Brisa Bridgestone Sabancı Lastik Sanayi ve Ticaret Anonim Şirketi'nin 31 Aralık 1993 ve 1992 tarihlerindeki gerçek mali durumunu ve bu tarihlerde sona eren hesap dönemlerine ait gerçek faaliyet sonuçlarını Sermaye Piyasası Kurulu'nun tebliğlerinde belirlenmiş ve bir önceki hesap dönemi ile tutarlı bir şekilde uygulanan genel kabul görmüş muhasebe ilkelerine uygun olarak doğru bir biçimde yansıtmaktadır.

İstanbul,
2 Şubat 1994

Denet Yeminli Mali Müşavirlik A.Ş.

Ömür Günel

Independent Auditors' Report for the 1993 Accounting Period

We have examined the balance sheet of Brisa Bridgestone Sabancı Lastik Sanayi ve Ticaret A.Ş. as of December 31, 1993 and 1992 and the related statements of income, funds flow, cash flow cost of sales and proposed profit distribution for the years then ended. Our examinations were made in accordance with generally accepted auditing standards and, accordingly, included such tests of the accounting records and such other auditing procedures as we considered necessary in the circumstances. In our opinion, the financial statements referred to above present fairly the financial position of Brisa Bridgestone Sabancı Lastik Sanayi ve Ticaret A.Ş. as of December 31, 1993 and 1992, and the results of its operations for the year then ended, in conformity with generally accepted accounting principles issued by the Capital Market board, applied on a consistent basis.

İstanbul,

February 2, 1994

Denet Yeminli Mali Müşavirlik A.Ş.

Ömür Günel

Auditor's Report Summary

To The General Assembly of Brisa Bridgestone Sabancı Lastik Sanayi ve Ticaret A.Ş.
(Brisa Bridgestone Sabancı Tire Manufacturing and Trading Company)

Company's	- Title	:	Brisa Bridgestone Sabancı Lastik Sanayi ve Ticaret A.Ş.
	- Center	:	İstanbul
	- Capital	:	151.875.000.000.-TL
	- Field of activity	:	Manufacturing and sales of vehicle tires

- Name and duty period of Auditors and : Yalçın Küçükertunç - Yukio Saruwatari -
relation with company; or personnel   Mehmet Sıddıkoğlu - Duty Period is one year,
                                         we are not shareholders and personnel of the company.

- Number of Auditors' Committee, : Number of participated Board
and participated Board Meeting   Meetings was 4, number of Auditors'
                                   Committee meeting was 6.

- Scope of studies on partnership : From the side of tax regulations and
accounts, records and document,   commercial code, in the first week of the
date of studies and conclusion   the 3rd, 6th 9th and 12th months,
                                   controls and investigations were made and
                                   nothing to be criticized was found.

- Number and conclusion of cash : 4 times cash counts were made and were
counts which is made according   found in line with existing records
to subparagraph 3 of paragraph
1 of article 353 of the Turkish
Commercial Code.

- The date and conclusion of : In the investigation made in the first
investigation which is made   working day of every month, it was
according to subparagraph   determined that existing securities
4 of paragraph 1 of article 353 of are in accordance with records.
the Turkish Commercial Code.

- Complaints and irregularities : There were no complaints and irregularities.
received, and actions to be taken

We have examined Brisa Bridgestone Sabancı Lastik Sanayi ve Ticaret A.Ş. accounts and procedures for the 1.1.1993 -
31.12.1993 period as required by the Turkish Commercial Code, the Articles of Association of the Company, other
regulations and generally accepted accounting principals and standards.

In our opinion, the enclosed balance sheet prepared as of 31.12.1993 shows the financial position of the company at
the date mentioned above; income statement for 1.1.1993 - 31.12.1993 period, reflects the actual and accurate results
of the company's activities; profit distribution proposal is appropriate to partnership of Articles of Association and
Legislation.

We herewith submit the balance sheet and income statement for your approval and release of the Board of Directors.
18.2.1994

AUDITORS' COMMITTEE

Yalçın KÜÇÜKERTUNÇ
Yukio SARUWATARI
Mehmet SIDDIKOĞLU

EASTERN EUROPE: OVERVIEW

Two facts rapidly became obvious as we began to assemble the material on Eastern Europe. The first fact is that this is a time of extraordinarily rapid and fascinating change in accounting in Eastern Europe. The second fact, related to the first, is that the task of presenting a concise but clear picture of what is going on is an extremely difficult one.

The background, of course, is that the countries of Eastern Europe are moving politically and economically away from central control, away from the "command" type of economy, toward a market-based economy in which prices and profits have economic meaning. The various countries are moving along this path at quite different speeds. Some have much greater political uncertainties and obstacles to overcome than others. Some have helpful vestiges of cultural and institutional history dating from before the Second World War. No one can be sure, however, that progress in any of the countries will be smooth and uninterrupted.

The essential role of accounting in a command economy is to assist in the monitoring of economic plans. The focus is on reporting what has happened to the local planners and, thus, to the central planners. Quantitive (i.e., physical) measures of output acquired a dominant position in planning, despite attempts (e.g., the 1965 economic reform in the USSR) to introduce financial indicators. Consequently, there was a bias against economy and efficiency in the use of materials—when planning was done in tons, sheet glass became heavier and paper became thicker. There was also a bias against product innovation because the necessary disruptive changes to production schedules jeopardized the short-term fulfillment of quantitative performance indicators, that is, crude units of output, such as the number of pairs of shoes manufactured.

The scale of changes involved in creating, from such beginnings, an accounting framework and profession capable of meeting the informational needs of diversified market-based economic decision-making should need no further emphasis.

Simultaneously with the transformation of their economic systems, the countries of Central and Eastern Europe are aspiring to an increasingly close relationship with the European Union in order to incorporate the principal features of competitive market economies.

Therefore, for a consideration of the development of accounting (and especially with respect to corporate reporting and external auditing) in the former socialist countries of Central and Eastern Europe, it may be sensible to keep in mind the words contained in the preamble to the EU Company Law Fourth Directive: that the publication of annual accounts and reports of companies with limited liability "is of special importance for the protection of members and third parties."

The Fourth Directive also affirms the necessity to establish minimum legal requirements "as regards the extent of the financial information that should be made available to the public by companies that are in competition with one another."

Publication means that the annual accounts and reports are made accessible to the general public (e.g., by a copy, available for inspection by members of the general public, being lodged with a registrar of companies, or in some other way, such as a copy being made available upon application to the company's registered office). The public disclosure of certain financial information relating to the performance of a business enterprise is a wider requirement than disclosure to the providers of its capital or to state agencies. Indeed, there is no *a priori* reason for the provision of financial information to state agencies and its public disclosure to be the subject of common legislation.

It is considered that the public disclosure of financial information promotes confidence in the conduct of business transactions. By providing a measure of protection to creditors and by acting as a curb on fraud, the public disclosure of financial information is conducive to increased business activity. A public interest in the disclosure of financial information is recognized as equally valid, irrespective of how the company's capital has been provided (i.e., whether by private investors, financial institutions, or the state). The public disclosure of financial information on the performance of companies is a feature of a well-functioning market economy.

It might be supposed that the period required for the transition to the norms of corporate reporting and external auditing observed in the advanced market economies will be less lengthy for the Visegrad states (i.e., the Czech Republic, Hungary, Poland, and Slovakia) than for some other countries (e.g., Bulgaria and Rumania). Most of the Visegrad states, having entered into agreements of association with the European Union, hope to be in a position by the year 2000 to apply for full membership.

The capacity for the realization of accounting reform and the manner of its realization depend on the nature of the accounting experience accumulated within each country and the quality of the external expert assistance provided.

The German standardized accountancy system was extended to Bohemia and Moravia (1938–1945) and to the parts of Poland annexed by Germany (1939–1944). Jaruga, in the chapter on Poland, emphasizes the significance of the German experience for early post-1945 accounting development in Poland. Elsewhere in Central and Eastern Europe, excluding the USSR, standardized accountancy systems had not been introduced before 1945.

After the end of the Second World War, the task of postwar reconstruction was the principal concern of the newly installed governments throughout Central and Eastern Europe. It was, perhaps, not surprising that the state should take a direct interest in accounting (compare with France during the same period) and assume a responsibility for accounting, especially financial accounting, to be implemented in enterprises.

Both Dolezal, in the chapter on the Czech Republic, and Jaruga, however, stress that beginning in 1950 Soviet influence was paramount in the development of accounting. State-directed accounting development became a well-established practice in the Central and East European countries.

Nevertheless, with the collapse of the communist regimes, the state continues to exercise a critical role in the creation of the institutional structures and regulatory arrangements for a relatively smooth transition to an effectively functioning market economy. The acknowledgment of a continuation of the interest of the state in accounting (e.g., for the assessment and collection of taxes from business enterprises, the collection of data for the generation of macroeconomic statistics) is evidenced by the approach taken to accounting reform:

- State determination and direction of accounting change

- Legal provisions applicable to all manner of micro entities (and not specifically to companies favored with limitation of liability for the debts incurred)

- Preference for uniformity in financial accounting

- Responsibility for cost and management accounting (i.e., internal accounting) devolved to enterprises
- Emphasis placed upon reporting to state agencies

Paradoxically, the gradual adoption of the norms of corporate reporting in advanced market economies is being used in the first instance for the reform of reporting to agencies of the state authorities. Public disclosure of financial information on the performance of enterprises is treated as a subsidiary consideration. There does seem to be a presumption that disclosure to shareholders and to others (e.g., bankers, suppliers) with a financial interest in the activities of a business enterprise is principally a matter of private arrangement.

However, the governing councils of the stock exchanges established in Budapest, Prague, Warsaw, and elsewhere may be expected to give steadily increasing attention to the quality of corporate reporting. In the meantime, recognition of the desirability of the public disclosure of financial information on company performance for the effective functioning of a market economy proceeds slowly.

What is the status of the newly introduced accounting legislation? Is the legislation intended to be binding upon the preparers of financial statements or is it merely exhortatory of preferred accounting practice? The greater the scope of continuing state control over accounting, the greater the probability of new accounting requirements being observed. But how will adherence to the new accounting legislation be ensured? Are accounting and other personnel in the enterprises both willing and able to observe the spirit of new legislation?

An interesting escape clause in Poland, mentioned by Jaruga, is that certain economic entities, such as joint ventures, may be relieved of the requirement to observe the accounting provisions contained in Polish law, provided the needs of the fiscal and statistical authorities are satisfied.

In the countries of Central and Eastern Europe, associations for persons with a professional interest in accounting were established rapidly during 1990–1992, although somewhat similar associations had been established earlier in Hungary, Poland, and Yugoslavia. Some of these associations of interested persons may evolve into professional associations exercising functions similar to those exercised by the professional accounting associations in Western Europe. However, the influence of such associations on the state's policymakers seems to be negligible at the present time and may continue to be so.

Institutional arrangements for the regulation of the activities of auditors (e.g., Chamber of Auditors) are in the process of being developed under state direction in some countries. Transitional arrangements for the designation of suitable persons as auditors are likely to be superseded eventually by educational and training requirements intended to approximate to the provisions of the EU Company Law Eighth Directive. Both Dolezal and Jaruga mention that national auditing standards are being adopted.

Given the many and diverse difficulties encountered in ensuring a successful transition to a market economy, it is reasonable to suppose that some time may well elapse before the quality of audits becomes generally comparable to that achieved in Western European countries.

Apart from the countries assigned a separate chapter, new accounting legislation has been adopted elsewhere in Central and Eastern Europe. For example, a new accounting law has been adopted in Rumania. As in other countries, the law is intended to apply to all economic entities (i.e., sole proprietors, partnerships, and companies) and also to other entities (e.g., municipalities and public institutions). Financial accounting and cost accounting are distinguished. Regulation by law is restricted to the former, the latter now being regarded as the perogative of the enterprise.

Accounting law in Rumania is concerned primarily with the clerical aspects of keeping accounting records. A modified chart of accounts incorporating the additional accounts required in a market economy has been prepared.

A professional organization is being formed with a two-tier membership: accounting experts and authorized accountants (compare with *expert comptable* and *comptable agréé* in France), with the task of audit reserved to the former. Thus, the need for a public accountancy profession has been recognized. For both state enterprises and enterprises in which there is a state shareholding, however, the Ministry of Finance retains the right to nominate or appoint auditors. For privatized businesses, the annual balance sheet is to be published in the official bulletin.

In 1991, an accounting law was adopted in Bulgaria. As in Rumania, Bulgarian Accounting Law deals with the clerical aspects of account keeping: requisites of primary documents and compilation and retention of accounting records.

The development of the national chart of accounts, primary documentation, accounting techniques, and accounting standards is the responsibility of the Ministry of Finance. However, both the national chart of accounts and the national accounting standards are subject to approval by the Council of Ministers.

The chief accountant, in determining the form of accounting, is required to ensure its consistency with:

1. Subsequent financial and tax control over the activities of the enterprise
2. Interconnection with statistics on the basis of statistical indicators
3. A unified classification of accounting entries on the basis of an authorized national classification

There are requirements to observe the principles of going concern, prudence, completeness, consistency, and comparability. Prudence is defined as encompassing the recognition of depreciation and all reasonable risks and possible losses over future reporting periods.

With respect to revenue recognition, "should any reasonable doubt exist over the receipt of an outstanding payment its recognition as income should be deferred." The profession of certified public accountant is being established as independent although subject to supervision by the Ministry of Finance. A certified public accountant is responsible for approving the annual financial reports of enterprises. There is a provision in accounting law that any disagreement concerning the approval of an annual financial report shall be resolved by reference to the Ministry of Finance (and not, for example, by reference to a civil court). This is an interesting and not untypical example of the mixture of "state control" and "professional independence" thinking that permeates many developments in Eastern Europe.

One more brief technical point may be helpful, concerning the concept of *funds*. In command economy accounts, *funds* is a capital/liability/reserve concept, representing the money put in by the state, and has nothing whatever to do with the modern concept of funds as a liquidity concept. Furthermore, a number of such "funds" were often kept separately for particular purposes. This system operated in a fairly pure form in China until recently. A number of designated funds existed within an enterprise—for example, state fixed fund, state current fund, enterprise fixed fund, enterprise current fund, even accumulated depreciation fund. Each fund could be used only for the appropriate purpose, thus creating in effect a number of separate self-balancing parts of the balance sheet. Even in China, however, this system is now breaking down.

The chapters presented here are diverse in their individual coverage and style. They reflect the personality, background, and cultural context of their individual authors. Each chapter gives a clear sketch of the state of financial reporting in the relevant country and how it got there. Each chapter points forward, though with no great certainty or precision. Taking this relatively brief part of the guide as a coherent entity, however, gives a whole rather greater than the sum of its parts. It is not too late to have here on record clear vestiges of the recent past; yet the hopes (and uncertainties) of the future shine through.

Most significantly of all, perhaps, the trials and tribulations of change and the fundamentally subservient nature of accounting to its economic, political, and cultural environment are here caught on the wing and illustrated as perhaps never before.

Note: The editors are particularly grateful to Derek Bailey for his invaluable help in the preparation of this section of the Guide.

Jan Dolezal

BDO CS s.r.o., Prague

Editors' note: Until January 1, 1993 Czechoslovakia had a federal structure. There were, for example, three Ministries of Finance, a Czech Ministry, a Slovak Ministry and a Federal Ministry. As of January 1, 1993 the Federation was dissolved, and the Czech and Slovak Republics are now entirely independent of each other. The separation, while unexpected, was peaceful, and practical cooperation is often close. The long-term effect is difficult to predict, although the Czech Republic may well have greater resources. In the short term both republics are, in an accounting sense, proceeding in a similar direction. What follows, however, is written from a Czech perspective.

1. Background

1.1 Accounting Background

The development of accounting systems in the Czech Republic has undergone several substantial changes of direction during the twentieth century. During the first 45 years of the century, there was a strong influence from the accounting practice and accounting principles used in the German-speaking countries of Europe. Law No. 116/1946, "On Uniform organization of Accounting in Enterprises," laid down accounting practice in the period 1946–1952, emphasizing the utilization of accounting information for purposes of enterprise direction. This was the period in which the construction of a centrally directed and centrally planned economy began, and there was a corresponding influence on the accounting system. The first steps toward uniformity of accounting in the economy were made. Financial accounting, operational (internal) accounting, and auxiliary accounting (including payroll, inventories, etc.) were separate parts of this system.

In 1953 a system of registration in the national economy was introduced by Law No. 41/1952, "On Principles of Accounting Registration." This system, used in the period 1953–1965, was based on practice in the Soviet Union. It was predetermined primarily to meet the demands of centralized direction of the economy, and thus weakened the economic functions of accounting and the independence of enterprises. Historical costs were used for the valuation of assets, and the demands of costing were emphasized over external reporting considerations.

Further development of centrally organized and widely understood information systems came about with three new pieces of legislation in 1971: Law No. 21/1971, "On Uniform Social-Economic Information System," Government Decree No. 153/1971, "On Information System of Enterprises," and the Federal Ministry of Finance Decree No. 154/1971, "On Accounting."

From 1971, accounting in Czechoslovakia was organized by the Federal Ministry of Finance. The ministry stipulated the basic accounting principles and bookkeeping regulations, including formats of financial statements, as well as regulations for checking and approving the annual financial statements of organizations. Financial accounting and cost accounting formed a system that used the same pricing and other principles.

In keeping their accounts (drawing up their schedule of accounts and keeping records of their economic operations), enterprises proceed according to the chart of accounts and the directive to the chart of accounts. This chart of accounts, containing general accounts, is obligatory for enterprises. Enterprises must choose from it and include in their charts of accounts all accounts relating to their activity. In selected sections of the chart of accounts (classes of accounts and groups of accounts), organizations may form accounts and analytical accounts according to their own needs, especially with regard to intra-enterprise management.

Since 1989, and consistent with broader political and economic changes, accounting legislation has been updated. Government Decree No. 136/1989, "On Information Systems of Enterprises," and the Federal Ministry of Finance Decree No. 23/1990, "On Accounting," introduce greater independence for enterprises in cost accounting and stimulate the wide application of computers. This law is now valid in both separated states—in the Czech Republic and the Slovak Republic.

Basic principles of the Fourth and Seventh EC Directives were embodied in this law, thereby substantially changing the previous regulations and accounting practice. These changes concern especially valuation principles, preparation, publication, and auditing of financial statements and other parts of the accounting system.

1.2 The Auditing Profession

For a long time, the balance sheet and income statements of Czech and Slovak enterprises were approved by senior administrators or by central authority (ministry). Laws approved during 1989 and 1990 introduced independent auditing of the annual statements and economic activity of certain legal forms of enterprises, by one or two (in the case of enterprises with foreign capital participation) independent auditors. The law on accounting requires the audit of financial statements for all stock companies and large limited liability companies or cooperatives (with turnover exceeding 40 million Czech crowns or equity exceeding 20 million Czech crowns). The distinction between stock companies and limited liability companies is precisely as in German law. A similar distinction is incorporated into the Polish Commercial Code and may be compared with the distinction between public companies and private companies in the United Kingdom.

The audit includes checking whether

1. The annual financial statements (consolidated financial statements) give a true and fair view of the assets, liabilities, equity, financial position, and income of the company
2. The accounting records are kept fully and properly

After checking the annual statements and the economic activity of the enterprise, the auditors prepare a written report. Until 1993, the scope of the report and other more detailed provisions concerning auditors and their activity were detailed in Federal Ministry of Finance Decree No. 63/1989.

Law No. 526/1992, "On the Auditors and the Chamber of Auditors in Czech Republic," prepares a basis for auditing to the level that is used in the developed countries. This law includes the qualification requirements for auditors (in the case of foreign persons, if they meet the requirements of their own particular country, an examination in Czech accounting and tax law is required), the scope of auditors' duties, the appointment and revocation of auditors, and the assessment of their qualifications and work.

Today the Czech auditing profession is headed by the Chamber of Auditors, which was founded in February 1993. Members of the Chamber are both certified auditors (there were about 600 of them in 1993) and assistant auditors. The Chamber of Auditors organizes the examinations and education of its members and prepares Czech national auditing standards on the basis of international ones. The first four national auditing standards concerning audit objective, audit evidence, audit report, and documentation were prepared and published and came into effect on January 1, 1994.

2. The Form and Content of Published Financial Statements

For many years the content of financial reporting was influenced by the command economy with its centralized direction. Therefore, the contents, formats, and system of approval of financial statements were not compatible with those used in Western Europe and other countries with a market economy.

Enterprises (including joint ventures within the Czech Republic) must file financial statements in the structure, extent, and terms stated by the Federal Ministry of Finance (since 1993, the Czech Ministry of Finance) in Decree Nr. V/l–31 388/1992. As of 1993, enterprises must present the following financial reports:

- Profit and loss account
- Balance sheet
- Notes to the accounts

The financial statements are filed with the tax collection office (together with two copies of the tax return) and the statistical authority. Copies of the financial statements are not filed with a registrar for stock corporations nor with the Prague Stock Exchange.

In the Czech Republic, uniform financial statements for profit-making organizations are used. Different financial statements are required from nonprofit organizations, banks, insurance companies, and small businesses. In the conditions of the newly developing market economy and for East-West joint ventures, the problem of the publication of data on their operations is of fundamental importance to enterprises. The law on accounting requires publication of financial statements for all stock companies and large limited liability companies or cooperatives (with turnover exceeding 40 million Czech crowns or equity exceeding 20 million Czech crowns). The Ministry of Finance gives the precise layout of financial statements for different types of businesses and also the minimal structure of published statements. These represent a simplification of the obligatory state formats of the balance sheet and income statement.

To give a better view on the development of company operations, items in the financial statements show figures not only for the last period (year), but also for the preceding year.

The content of the notes to the accounts is established by the Ministry of Finance Decree of September 8, 1993. Full notes are obligatory for enterprises that must be audited. Abbreviated notes can be presented by other (small) companies.

Full notes include:

1. General information—detailed information on participations in the group companies, the number and structure of employees, including personnel cost, salaries, and benefits of the members of the management and supervisory boards

2. A description of accounting policies and principles—valuation of assets and contents of inventory prices, changes in valuation, depreciation and accounting methods, including reasons for these changes and the effect on individual items of the balance sheet and profit and loss account, transfer of foreign currency items into Czech crowns

3. Additional information for the financial statements:
   - Investments (number and par value of shares shown by type and with gains from these shares, market value of these shares)
   - Changes in stockholders' equity
   - Distribution of profits
   - Overdue receivables and liabilities
   - Contingencies
   - Revenues by segments

- Provisions
- Rented (leased) property not shown in the balance sheet
4. Cash flow statement

A presentation of consolidated financial statements is required by the accounting law for companies with a participation greater than 20% in other companies. Consolidation rules are in the process of being prepared. The Ministry of Finance is preparing a simplified version of consolidation rules and procedures. These rules are expected to be issued in 1994.

Since 1993 the publication of financial statements has been obligatory, being realized through a special business journal (*Obchodni vestnik*). In addition, enterprises prepare an annual report, and some of them publish the information in newspapers.

The requirements for the disclosure of financial information are not affected by stock companies being listed or quoted on the Prague Stock Exchange. As a precondition for a listing, however, stock companies are required to prepare much more detailed information. Since 1993 listed stock companies have been required to present audited half-yearly financial statements.

In accordance with Czech business law, the financial statements are approved by an annual meeting of shareholders, as is the decision on the appropriation of profits.

3. Accounting Policies and Practices in Valuation and Income Measurement: Implications for the Analyst

Foreign accountants and accounting firms studying the financial reports of Czech enterprises should bear in mind the following accounting policies and practices in valuation and income measurement.

3.1 Capital and Reserves

Until 1992 state enterprises were the most common legal form of enterprise. Until 1990 state enterprises presented the following compulsory items of capital:

1. Fund of fixed assets: reflecting the original value of property, plant, and equipment diminished by accumulated depreciation and loans used for the purchase of property, plant, and equipment. This item did not include the value of land.

2. Fund of current assets: the part of capital received from the state that was devoted to current assets. Its amount could be increased when necessary by transfer from the development fund, and vice versa.

3. Securities and investments fund: the par value of purchased securities and investments in other companies. Its amount equaled the amount of securities and investments included in assets.

4. Development fund: a reserve for the future development of the enterprise. It contained accumulated depreciation not yet used, the amount of income devoted to future development of the enterprise, and the estimated future cost of research.

In 1991, all the above funds of state enterprises merged into one single item, known as equity.

By 1994, in the process of privatization, most state enterprises were converted to share companies or limited liability companies.

The minimum subscribed capital is 1,000,000 Czech crowns for a share corporation and 100,000 Czech crowns for a limited liability company. Sole proprietorships and partnerships have no given limits of capital.

Two types of reserves exist—capital and revenue reserves. Capital reserves consist of:

1. The premium paid in connection with the issuance of new shares or received by conversion of convertible debentures

2. Other capital input that does not form a part of share capital

3. Received gifts or state subsidies (these items remain in the balance sheet and are not written off)

The reserve fund is an obligatory general reserve for all forms of enterprise (except for sole proprietorships). In a stock corporation, this fund is created from the profit after tax at the rate of at least 20% of the profit in the first year (but not more than 10% of the stockholders' equity) and 5% in following years until the amount of this fund reaches the level of 20% of total shareholder equity. In a limited liability company, this fund is created from the profit after tax at the rate of at least 10% of the profit in the first year (but not more than 5% of the stockholders' equity) and 5% in following years until the amount of this fund reaches the level of 10% of total shareholder equity.

There are other possible statutory reserves—social reserve and bonus reserve, which are optional for joint ventures and privatized companies (formerly mandatory for state enterprises). Bonus reserve can be used to allow the participation of the staff in the company profit.

3.2 Liabilities and Provisions

Since 1993 a distinction has been made between long-term and short-term liabilities and provisions. Current portions of long-term liabilities are not measured and disclosed separately.

Provisions include legal and other provisions. Legal provisions are deductible for tax purposes and are precisely stipulated by law No. 593/1992, "On Provisions for Measurement of the Income Tax Basis." Legal provisions include:

- Provisions for bad debt (up to 100%), when the debtor is declared bankrupt
- Provisions for repairs of plant and equipment
- Special bank provisions
- For overdue loans (10% of the average amount of these loans)
- For long-term loans (2%)
- For guarantees given (2%)
- Special insurance provisions

Other provisions depend on decisions of the enterprise, and they are not tax deductible.

The structure of liabilities includes:

- Long-term liabilities (including accounts and notes payable, bonds, and prepayments received)

- Short-term liabilities (including accounts and notes payable, prepayments received, wages payable, tax payable, deferred taxes)
- Bank loans (subdivided into short-term and long-term loans)
- Other liabilities (deferred expenses, prepaid revenues, differences in exchange rates)

Provisions are based on appropriate calculations. Liabilities and issued bonds are measured at par value.

3.3 Property, Plant, and Equipment

Until 1991, in the Czech Republic, property, plant, and equipment accounts did not include land. For a long time land was considered to be property of the state and thus not measured and registered in accounts. Today the land is already included in the assets and accounts of companies at prices given by a decree. These prices may differ from the market value of a particular piece of land.

Equipment and machines must be included only when their cost is higher than 10,000 Czech crowns. Equipment under this limit can be shown in the balance sheet or transferred directly into expense. This choice depends on management. Property, plant, and equipment (except for land) are measured at original cost; only when purchased from another enterprise that used the asset before must it be revalued at the second purchase cost. The replacement value is used only for property, plant, and equipment received as a gift, received free after the termination of a financial leasing contract, or newly found during stock-taking. Machines and equipment under 10,000 Czech crowns can be written off in the expense immediately after being purchased.

In the balance sheet fixed assets are disclosed subdivided into tangible, intangible, and financial assets. The depreciation charge in property, plant, and equipment is normally calculated on a straight-line basis. The percentage of depreciation depends on the class of asset and its useful life, given by an internal instruction of the enterprise. For tax purposes, depreciation rates are given for individual classes of property, plant, and equipment by Law No. 586/1992, "On the Income Tax." In this law separate rates for straight-line and accelerated depreciation are shown.

3.4 Assets Acquired by Means of Leases

Assets acquired by means of leases are not included as assets on the balance sheet of the lessee. They are registered separately and treated as off-balance-sheet items. In the cases of both operating and financial leasing, the assets are shown and depreciated in the accounts of the lessor.

The leasing rules are dominated by tax regulations. Financial leasing exists when:

- The lease period exceeds 40% of the depreciation period given in the tax law and exceeds the minimal period of 3 years (for immovables, the minimal period is 8 years).
- The purchase price at the end of the leasing period is not higher than book value if the straight-line depreciation method was used.

3.5 Oil, Gas, and Other Mineral Resources

Until 1992 oil, gas, and other mineral resources were not included in the assets of the enterprises. They were considered to be state property. Since 1993 they are included in the land account and land price (when purchased). This amount is decreased as the resource is extracted, and the depletion is booked in expenses.

3.6 Participations

Investments in other companies are measured at purchase price (purchase cost without expenses related to the purchase, such as commissions). Investments in subsidiaries, in associated companies, and in other companies are disclosed separately.

3.7 Inventories

Materials are measured from the moment of purchase up to the time of their consumption at cost. When bought from various enterprises for different prices, the materials are measured and disclosed at actual cost. Since January 1, 1993 only the average cost and FIFO methods of valuation of inventories have been allowed. Work in progress and finished goods are measured at planned or actual cost (full or direct).

3.8 Taxation

Companies and enterprises must pay taxes to the state budget, as laid down by the law. Since 1993 substantial taxation changes have been approved in the Czech Republic. The principal method of direct taxation is income tax at the rate 45% of taxable profit (a decrease to 42% is expected during 1994). The taxable income can be different from commercial income (shown in the profit and loss account). Two major reasons exist:

1. Temporal differences—different accounting and tax depreciation methods and rates, provisions that are not recognized for tax purposes
2. Definite differences—expenses that are not recognized for tax purposes and income taxed by the paying company (e.g., dividends, bond interest)

Deferred tax has been introduced in the Czech Republic. However, this includes only differences between the accounting and tax depreciation of fixed assets.

In addition, enterprises pay a payroll tax for every employee. The amount of this tax depends on the earnings of the employee, the number of children and other persons dependent on the employee, and so on.

In 1993 a value added tax (VAT) was introduced, and this tax is paid by enterprises. Two rates of VAT are used—23% for goods and 5% for services, with some exceptions shown in the law.

The taxation system includes also:

- A consumption tax, levied on petrol, spirits, wine, beer, and tobacco products
- An immovables tax, levied on land and buildings
- A road tax, levied on cars and trucks used for business purposes
- An inheritance tax, gift tax, and tax on transfer of immovables

3.9 Pension Costs

In the Czech Republic, social security for the illness and old age of workers and other staff has been provided by special insurance companies. In 1993, enterprises paid a special insurance transfer to the insurance companies. Its level amounts to 36% of payroll paid by the company (27% social insurance and 9% health insurance), and 13.5% paid by the employee (9% social and 4.5% health insurance).

3.10 Intangibles

Until 1990 Czechoslovak financial or accounting legal regulations did not recognize intangible assets as a special form of property. Therefore, in balance sheets there were no such items as patents, licenses, trademarks, or goodwill. Some intangible assets (e.g., patents) could be treated as a special category of deferred charges.

Since 1991 partially, and fully since 1993, the idea has been accepted to show intangible assets in the accounts of enterprises. Since 1993 a more detailed structure of intangible assets greater than 20,000 Czech crowns has been presented: organization cost, intangible results of research activities, software, rights, and other intangible assets. Amortization of these intangibles is included during the useful life of the latter, up to a maximum of 5 years. Purchased intangible assets less than 20,000 Czech crowns can be treated as an expense.

Purchased intangibles are measured at cost (inclusive expenses related to the purchase, such as transportation expense, commission). Lower of cost or replacement value is used for the valuation of self-produced intangible assets.

In the process of privatization, goodwill may occur on the balance sheet. It arises if a privatized business is purchased at a price different from book value in the accounts of the privatized business. This item is amortized over a period of 15 years.

4. Expected Future Developments

Since the revolution in November 1989, the economy, accounting practice, financial reporting, and accounting systems in the Czech Republic have been in a phase of rapid evolution toward the European level common for a market economy. A fundamentally new legislation on accounting and taxation is valid from January 1993. The taxation burden has gradually been diminished, and further decrease can be expected. For 1994 a decrease in the income tax rate to 42% is planned.

The accounting methodology and financial reporting reflect the influence of International Accounting Standards and the EC Directives. A first simplified version of consolidation rules occurred early in 1994. Further refinement after several years of experience is planned.

The auditors' opinion on financial reports has become obligatory for most larger enterprises. A further growth in the number of auditors and the organization of their activity will be ensured. These measures will raise the prestige of the accountancy profession to the level common in developed countries.

Useful Address

Komora auditoru Ceske republiky
(Chamber of the Auditors in the Czech Republic)
Opletalova 55/57
111 21 Praha 1
post box 772
Czech Republic
Tel. +42-2-2421 2670
Fax. +42-2-2421 1905

Financial Statements (from a Czech company, 1993)

ROZVAHA

	v tis. Kč	
	1992	1993
Aktiva celkem	209,102	246,002
Stálá aktiva	79,481	86,944
- nehmotný investiční majetek	504	1,508
- hmotný investiční majetek	78,977	85,436
- finanční investice		
- podílové cenné papíry a vklady v podnicích ve skupině		
- ostatní finanční investice		
Oběžná aktiva	128,458	154,314
- zásoby	64,670	76,230
- dlouhodobé pohledávky		
- krátkodobé pohledávky	51,956	79,159
- finanční majetek	11,832	− 1,075
Ostatní aktiva	1,163	4,744
Pasíva celkem	209,102	246,002
Vlastní jmění	124,007	138,130
- základní jmění	104,589	104,589
- kapitálové fondy	-	1,058
- fondy tvořené ze zisku	11,532	10,208
- hospodářský výsledek minulých let	7,886	7,886
- hospodářský výsledek účetního období		14,389
Cizí zdroje	83,791	107,200
- zákonné rezervy		
- jiné rezervy		
- dlouhodobé závazky		
- krátkodobé závaky	47,589	60,600
- bankovní úvěry a výpomoci	36,202	46,600
- dlouhobé bankovní úvěry		
- krátkodobé bankovní úvěry a výpomoci	36,202	46,600
Ostatní pasíva	1,304	672

BALANCE SHEET (IN THOUSAND CZECH CROWNS)

	1992	*1993*
Total assets	209,102	246 002
Fixed assets	79,481	86,944
- intangible fixed assets	504	1,508
- tangible fixed assets	78,977	86,436
- financial investments		
- participating interests		
in affiliated undertakings		
- other investments		
Current assets	128,458	154,314
- inventories	64,670	76,230
- long-term accounts receivable		
- short-term account receivable	51,956	79,159
- financial assets, cash	11,832	- 1,075
Other assets	1,163	4,744
Total liabilities	209,102	246,002
Equity	124,007	138,130
- capital stock	104,589	104,589
- capital reserves	—	1,058
- revenue reserves	11,532	10,208
- undistributed profit of previous years	7,886	7,886
- profit for current year		14,389
Liabilities	83,791	107,200
- legal provisions		
- other provisions		
- long-term accounts and notes payable		
- short term accounts and notes payable	47,589	60,600
- bank loans	36,202	46,600
- long-term bank loans		
- short-term bank loans	36,202	46,600
Other liabilities	1,304	672

VÝKAZ ZISKŮ A ZTRÁT

	1993
Tržby za prodej zboží	7,973
Náklady vynaložené na prodané zboží	7,788
+ Obchodní marže	185
Výroba	209,194
Tržby za prodej vlastních výrobků a služeb	206,265
Změna stavu vnitropodnikových zásob vlastní výroby	763
Aktivace	2,165
Výrobní spotřeba	140,982
+ Přidaná hodnota	68,396
Osobní náklady	21,596
Daně a poplatky	295
Jiné provozní výnosy	4,289
Jiné provozní náklady	6,007
Odpisy nehmotného a hmotného investičního majetku	8,728
Zúčtování rezerv, opravných položek a časového rozlišení provozních výnosů	
Tvorba rezerv, opravných položek a časového rozlišení provozních nákladů	
* Provozní hospodářský výsledek	36,060
Finanční výnosy	328
Finanční náklady	6,521
Zúčtování rezerv a opravných položek do finančních výnosů	
Tvorba rezerv a opravných položek na finanční náklady	
* Hospodářský výsledek z finančních operací	– 6,193
Splatná daň z příjmů za běžnou činnost	14,620
Odložená daň z příjmů za běžnou činnost	
** Hospodářský výsledek za běžnou činnost	15,247
Mimořádné výnosy	2,388
Mimořádné náklady	3,246
Splatná daň z příjmů z mimořádné činnosti	
Odložená daň z příjmů z mimořádné činnosti	
* Mimořádný hospodářský výsledek	– 858
*** Hospodářsky výsledek za účetní období	14,389

PROFIT AND LOSS ACCOUNT

	1993
Sales of goods	7,973
Cost of sales	7,788
+ Gross Margin	185
Production	209,194
Sales of own products and services	206,265
Changes in work in progress and in finished goods	764
Production for own consumption	2,165
Cost of production	140,982
+ Value added	68,397
Staff expenses	21,596
Taxes	295
Other production income	4,289
Other production expenses	6,007
Depreciation and amortization	8,728
Use of provisions and deferred expenses	
Creation of provisions and accrued expenses	
* Operating profit or loss	36,060
Financial revenues	328
Financial expenses	6,521
Use of provisions and deferred financial expenses	
Creation of provisions and accrued financial expenses	
* Financial profit or loss	-6,193
Tax payable from operations	14,620
Deferred tax from operations	
*Net profit or loss on ordinary activities	15,247
Extraordinary revenues	2,388
Extraordinary expenses	3,246
Tax payable on extraordinary operations	
Deferred tax on extraordinary operations	
* Profit or loss on extraordinary operations	-858
*** Profit or loss for accounting period	14,389

Auditors' Report

Auditors' report to the members of...

We have audited the financial statements and the annual report (pages 25 to 28) in accordance with Auditing Standards issued by the Chamber of the Auditors in Czech Republic.

In our examination we have found that the financial statements are consistent with the accounting records organized in conformity with valid legislation.

The financial statements and annual report give in our opinion a fair view of the assets, liabilities, equity, financial situation and results of the activity of the company for accounting period 1993.

Prague, March 24th 1994

BDO CS s.r.o.
Certified Accountants and Consultants
Kvestorska 2
Praha 4

HUNGARY

Maria Borda
EU PHARE
Financial Sector Development Program
Ministry of Finance, KPMG Hungary

1. The History of Accounting Development

The development of Hungarian accounting can be divided into three periods:

1. During the nineteenth and the first half of the twentieth centuries Hungarian accounting was strongly influenced by Western European countries.
2. Between 1948 and 1988, accounting developments were geared to the requirements of a centrally planned economic system.
3. Since 1988 the transition to a market economy has had to be facilitated by new accounting functions. In January of 1992 a new accounting law, basically in line with EC Directives and International Accounting Systems, was introduced.

Before discussing the three periods, this chapter gives an overview of the legal infrastructure of Hungarian accounting.

1.1 Development of the Legal Framework of Accounting

The Budapest Commodity and Security Exchange was established in 1864. The first company law in Hungary, the so-called Commercial Law No. XXXVII/1875, came into force in 1875. This law incorporated an act relating to shares as well.

The first law on notes was enacted in 1890, the issuance of bonds first being regulated by an act of 1897, and the first law on mortgages having been passed in 1876. At the beginning of the twentieth century, together with most other developed capitalist countries, Hungary became a signatory to the Hague Treaty on Notes. A special law (No. V/1930) on private limited companies was enacted in 1930. By enactment of these laws, the legal standards of business life in Hungary corresponded to European norms generally.

Today, after a 40-year break, Hungary has the most developed legal framework in Eastern Europe for privatization and joint ventures. To create a real market economy, the overwhelming proportion of state property rights must be transferred to the private sector. The announced goal of the government is that the proportion of state property be reduced from 90% in 1989 to about 30%–40% in the next few years. In 1993, 50% of the GDP came from the private sector.

In 1989, Hungary was the first Eastern bloc country to establish Western European legal standards of business, by enacting Law No. VI/1988 on business associations, and Law No. XXIV/1988 on investment by foreigners in Hungary. The latter permitted special tax benefits in favor of foreign participants. Unified Entrepreneurs' Profit Taxes Law No. XI/1988 could result in tax holidays of up to 5 years and 60% tax benefit for another 5 years for companies to which foreigners have contributed more than 30% of the capital, if the company operated specific manufacturing enterprises or in the hotel industry. The last year in which foreigners could enjoy the special tax benefit was 1993. The last year of tax benefits allowable under this program is 2003. Since 1994 a tax break has been granted for any investors in companies in which exports are increased or new jobs are created. Law No XIII/1989 on the transformation of business organizations and companies also has great significance for privatization. The main purpose of the law is to provide rules for the transformation of state-owned companies into business associations, declaring simultaneously the principle of general (legal) succession. Furthermore, it provides rules for the transformation of a company into another type of company, including mergers and split-ups.

The Hungarian Stock Exchange—facilitated by Law No. VI/1990 on Securities and the Stock Exchange—was the first to reopen in Central and Eastern Europe. On the basis of Law No. VII/1990, the National Property Agency—a policy advisory and review body—was established to ensure that state assets are sold at "fair" prices.

In 1992 a state holding company was established by Law No. LIII/1992 for the management and sale of state assets. Backing the transformation law, valuation decree No. 30/1989 established the principles of initial share pricing and net asset valuation. In 1992 after the rapid change of legal environment, this decree was replaced by Law No. LIV/1992 on the privatization of state property.

A two-tier banking system could have been introduced as a result of Law No. LX/1991 on the National Bank of Hungary and Law No. LXIX/1991 on commercial banks and banking activities, both of which came into force on December 1, 1991. They were based on the EC Banking Directives. A set of amendments to the banking law came into force on December 31, 1993. A very strict law, Law No. IL/1991 on bankruptcy, liquidation, and final accounts, was introduced in 1992.

As Hungary's economy is restructured, its national economy will be brought into the world market. In addition to greater exports to developed capitalist countries, Hungary must attract foreign capital and, along with it, modern technology.

Joint ventures are considered to be among the most important vehicles of privatization and foreign investment in Hungary. In 1989 the number of joint ventures grew from about 300 to more than 1000. By 1991 the number of joint ventures with more than 50 employees had increased to 11,000. In 1991–1993 the amount of capital invested in Hungary was as great as the total for all the other former eastern bloc countries.

In Hungary, the law on accountancy has occupied a central place in accounting regulations. The first law on accountancy was incorporated within the Commercial Law of 1875. After the Second World War, responsibility for accounting regulation lay with the Ministry of Finance. In 1968, during the period of central economic planning, Law No. 33/1968 on accountancy came into force. It was followed by Law No. II/1979 on public finances, which included the regulation of accounting and auditing.

When the new conditions of economic development came into existence, the old accounting model did not work. A need arose to introduce accounting standards consistent with the generally accepted accounting principles used in the developed market economies. The new law, Law No. XVIII/1991 on accounting, was introduced on January 1, 1992. Law No. CVIII/1993, which amended Law No. XVIII/1991 on accounting, came into force in January 1994.

The provisions of the new laws were worked out by the accounting department of the Ministry of Finance, taking into consideration the opinions of future users of accounting information, such as the World Bank, academics, experts from international accounting firms, foreign and domestic accounting and auditing associations, and the worldwide accounting profession.

Today the function of accounting in Hungary is to facilitate the creation of a market economy through privatization and joint ventures. To meet this requirement, radical accounting changes are needed. The new law brings into accounting practice the essential technical and conceptual changes.

1.2 The Development of Accounting Theory to the End of the Second World War and Influences from Other Countries

During the nineteenth century and the first half of the twentieth century, the development of Hungarian accounting was deeply influenced by practice in other European countries, especially Germany. At that time in Europe, different accounting theories, different allocation techniques of the costs to products, unit cost calculation methods, and theories on balance sheets were developed. The most notable theorists were Hügli, Schär, Schmalenbach, Niklisch, Mellerovich, Schmidt, and Kosiol.

Various account theories were used for the development of the chart of accounts. According to the two account line theory, which was worked out by Hügli (1887), Schär (1888), and Niklisch (1911), asset and liability accounts are differentiated. The balance sheet is based on the two account line theory. The third account line is the group of cost accounts for detailed recording of the operating costs. The fourth account line is the group of net income accounts. The profit and loss statement is based on the four account line theory (Schmalenbach, 1927). The current chart of accounts in Hungary is based on Schmalenbach's related theory.

The different balance sheet theories—dynamic, static, and organic—concern the relationships between the goal of setting a balance sheet and the asset valuation methods. The goal of setting a balance sheet can be to show the realized result—profit or loss—of a given period, the current value of invested assets, or both of these. Generally, according to these theories, the term *realized result* represents the difference between the selling price of an item and its acquisition cost. This is the conventionally reported "gross margin" according to generally accepted accounting principles.

The difference between the current replacement cost of an item and its acquisition cost, termed "holding gain or loss," is considered "nonrealized profit or loss." When the goal is to show the realized profit or loss of a given period in the balance sheet, the actual acquisition cost of assets—their historical cost—should be used in the valuation process. This "dynamic" balance theory can be classified as either classical (Schmalenbach) or "cash-oriented" (Kosiol).

If the goal of setting a balance sheet is to show the current market value of invested assets, their replacement cost should be used in the valuation process. The related balance sheet theory is called static (Niklisch). Whenever the goal of setting a balance sheet is to show both the realized result of a period and the current value of the invested asset, the double valuation method should be used. This means parallel use for acquisition and replacement costs in the valuation process. This is the "organic" theory (Schmidt). This method is used to separate "realized profit" from the profit that comes from price changes, a concern during periods of high inflation. The theoretical basis of the balance sheet and income statement in Hungary is the classical dynamic balance sheet theory.

Although the aforementioned directions in accounting theory in Continental Europe were necessary and useful, to some extent they neglected the managerial approach and failed to assist the planning function of management. Whereas managerial accounting developed quickly in Western Europe in the late 1940s and 1950s, in Hungary the accounting field was influenced primarily by Soviet experience, where accounting was subordinated to central planning.

1.3 Accounting and Auditing under the Central Planning System (1948–1988)

During the period when the national economy was under direct central control, the main tasks of accounting were to provide factual data on the economic activity of enterprises, to measure and control fulfillment of the planned targets at both enterprise and national levels, to provide information for sectoral and national aggregations, and for the derivation of national indices.

Accounting became a tool for macro-level monitoring of the firm. In providing data for reliable planning and control decisions at the national level, however, accounting was successful only to certain degree. The main limitations were:

1. The accounting data structuring process was designed to report production and national income statistics instead of well-integrated financial results.

2. In the absence of market mechanisms, money and prices could not fulfill their function in nationwide structural decision making, and accounting valuations lost their driving and incentive nature.

3. The external valuation of the enterprise's performance could not be manifested in the form of security prices.

Under the central planning system, accounting failed the function of providing information for managerial decision-making and could not serve as an efficient micro-managerial tool.

Financial statements supplied data that could be summarized to provide a general view of the aggregate activities by region, industry, and the entire economy. In order to achieve this, uniformly applicable normative rules of bookkeeping were laid down by detailed regulations.

The scheme of accounts determined the rules for the general ledger and the basic requirements of physical accounts. According to the pre-1992 Accounting Law, the Minister of Finance regulated by decrees the bookkeeping system of all Hungarian firms and public organizations through a General Compulsory Scheme of Accounts. The basic documentation systems, a product cost-tracing system, and the principles of financial statements, valuation methods, and disclosure of financial statements were also regulated. Accounting rules were strongly influenced by tax regulation and other elements of economic regulation.

The contents of the closing financial statements were strictly regulated and the preprinted formats obligatory. The ordinary annual financial report consisted of a balance sheet, an income statement (in summary and in detail), a profit distribution statement (for taxation), a statement of costs detailed by type, and other statements of supplementary information.

The financial report had to be presented to the Board of Directors or to the General Meeting. The Board of Directors or the General Meeting was authorized to accept the balance sheet and the stated profit or loss and the profit distribution.

The acceptance and approval of the balance sheet were documented by the signature of the head of the authorizing body (i.e., the chair of the Board of Directors or the General Meeting). The approved balance sheet, together with the income statement, had to be lodged with the Court of Registration by May 31 of the year after the accounting period. Copies of the deposited documents also had to be filed with the local tax authority.

Under this old accounting legislation, the approved balance sheet, the ledger statements supporting the balance sheet, and the inventory and analytical records were audited by the tax authority within financial and economic audits but could be revised by the company itself under a system of self-audit. Financial audits and self-audits were carried out to verify the validity and completeness of the approved balance sheet, the profit distribution, and the settlements due within the central budget and to ensure compliance with inventory-taking and valuation rules.

State financial auditing extended to economic activity as a whole and the analysis of the success of financial and economic decisions, as well as the impact of economic regulations. It helped the central and the enterprise-level leadership in the assessment of management activity and in the evaluation of decisions taken or missed.

Under financial audits, the Taxes and State Financial Audit Board examined:

1. The business organization's balance sheet and income statement to verify that the assets and the profit or loss of business activities were included to reflect a true picture of the business and that accounting, bookkeeping, and the system of documentation comply with legislative provisions
2. Compliance with the rules pertaining to the payment of taxes and other fiscal liabilities toward the state and the use of budgetary subsidies (for example, consumer and producer price subsidies) (Since January 1991 these subsidies have been significantly reduced.)

The Board carried out financial audits of each business organization, usually every second year. The state auditors included their findings that required action on the part of the authorities in protocols. The protocol played a similar role to that of the audit report in the case of companies that were audited by an independent auditor. The content and form of the protocol was defined by Law No. II/1979 on public finance. An audited company might comment on the contents of the protocol orally at the closing meeting or in writing within days of receiving the protocol.

Auditing started from the requirements of both rational flexibility and strict formal discipline, as required by economic activity. Auditing had to help maintain economic and auditing order, as well as detect abuses that might occur.

Under the "New Economic Mechanism" of the 1970s and 1980s, attempts were made to introduce innovative changes. For example, some domestic prices were allowed to approximate to world prices, the administrative regulation of wages and salaries was abolished, and value-added taxation and personal income taxes were adapted. Under the centralized economic system, however, none of them achieved the desired results. Now the goal is to move from the centralized economic system to a true market economy.

1.4 The Auditing Profession Today

The traditions of the Hungarian auditing profession date from 1932, when the Association of Hungarian Auditors (AHA) was founded. During the period of central planning, the independent audit function did not find its place within the existing economic structure, and the AHA was not active. The recent significant economic changes in Hungary created the need for control over the professional, educational, and ethical standards of accountants. In 1987 the AHA was reestablished and soon became internationally accepted.

A national professional organization of accountants, the AHA has taken part since 1988 in the annual congress of the European Accounting Association. In 1992 the AHA became a member of the International Federation of Accountants (IFAC). Meetings are in process with the *Federation des Experts Comptables Européens* (FEE). AHA, with 2500 members, could be considered a basis for the development of an independent auditing profession in Central and Eastern Europe.

In 1991 the AHA changed its name to Hungarian Chamber of Auditors (HCA). The provision of the law on HCA is in preparation.

Decree No. 46/1992 on Independent Audit defined the required qualification process for a Hungarian Chartered Accountant. The requirements are in line with the requirements of the Eighth EU Directive.

The preconditions for starting the study for earning the chartered accountant "degree" are as follows:

- University degree
- "Degree" of certified accountant
- 4 years of practical experience in the field of accounting or auditing

If the candidate can so certify, 3 years of auditing practice working with a registered chartered account would be acceptable instead of 4 years of practical experience.

After the necessary examinations are passed, the "degree" of Registered Hungarian Chartered Accountant is given by the Ministry of Finance. The registered chartered accountants could be chosen and employed as statutory auditors of the business associations in line with the Eighth EU Directive.

1.5 The Accounting System Today

1.5.1 Goal of the New Law on Accountancy

The purpose of the law on accountancy is to introduce accounting regulations in line with international accounting principles, ensuring the production of information that is sufficiently comprehensive and accurate to enable a true and fair view of the income-generating capabilities, development of the net assets and financial position of an economic entity to be shown. The law defines the reporting and bookkeeping requirements of those subject to its legislation and the basic principles to be followed in the course of the preparation of the financial reports and of bookkeeping (based on internationally accepted principles). It establishes rules for independent auditing and disclosure and the publication data of financial statements.

1.5.2 Scope and Effective Date of the New Legislation

The requirements of the act extend to

1. Entrepreneurs
2. Budgetary organizations
3. Other organizations
4. The National Bank of Hungary

The act defines *entrepreneurs* as every such natural person, legal entity, or economic organization not being a legal entity pursuing in its own name and upon its own risks manufacturing activities or providing services for compensation for the purposes of making a profit and accumulating wealth in a businesslike manner, including financial and insurance institutions. *Budgetary organizations* shall include the central budgetary organization, local government, institutions, and associations founded thereby, the trustee of the social security fund, and the separated state financial fund. *Other organizations* include housing cooperatives, social organizations, special interest groups, the Church, foundations, partnerships that are legal entities performing legal representations, investments funds, and the waterworks association.

The scope of the law does not extend to foreign entrepreneurs who have a majority holding or a 100% stake in a business operating but not registered in Hungary.

Law No. XVIII/1991 on accounting came into effect on January 1, 1992; Section 8 on the consolidated annual report is supposed to come into effect in January 1995. Law No. CVIII/1993, which amends Law No. XVIII/1991 on accounting came into force in January 1994. It brought forward the effective date of the introduction of the consolidated annual reporting requirements.

These two laws will be referred as accounting law. On December 31, 1991, companies should have closed their records in the usual manner in accordance with the previous regulations. In 1992 companies needed to prepare an "arranging balance sheet, income statement and other year-end-reports," which acted as a transition between the old system and the new legislation.

1.5.3 *The New Approach*

Generally Accepted Accounting Principles (GAAP) form the underlying basis of financial reporting by most reporting entities in countries that have an established system of financial reporting. These principles are not regulations, and neither do they cater to all accounting possibilities. They have generally been used by countries to develop their own system of financial reporting and/or regulation. They have evolved over a considerable period of time to enable a greater degree of comparability among financial reports of different years, of different companies, and of different countries.

These principles usually establish what would be reasonable accounting practice and what would generally lead to accounts presenting a true and fair view of their financial position at a point in time and results over a period of time. They have a certain breadth, and where there is a choice between two or more reasonable policies, companies may select their own accounting policies from those detailed in the general principles. The use of different accounting principles affects a set of financial statements, and companies are therefore required to disclose the accounting principles used in preparing their financial statements.

The 1992 accounting law enacted in Hungary has the following characteristics:

1. It is based on internationally accepted accounting principles, although it does not seek to introduce all these principles.
2. There is now an element of choice. The new regulations enable companies to select the appropriate principles on which to establish their accounting information system. The degree of choice permitted by law is, however, restricted.
3. A new relationship will arise between accounting and tax regulations. The regulations are now independent of each other. The taxable income and the tax amount to be paid are defined by the profit tax law. Accounting income is defined by the accounting law.

1.5.4 European Community Standards as a Basis for the Accounting Law

Accounting law is based on the Fourth, Seventh, and Eighth Directives of the Council of European Communities. It also takes into consideration International Accounting Standards issued by the International Accounting Standards Board and International Auditing Guidelines. The Fourth

Directive includes the regulation of financial statements of limited liability corporations. The Seventh Directive lays down the basic rules pertaining to the preparation of consolidated financial statements. The Eighth Directive covers the appointment and qualification of persons responsible for carrying out the statutory audits of accounting documents.

The Fourth Directive contains the central requirement for the role of financial statements. It prescribes two different balance sheet formats and four different formats for the income statement. Member states may prescribe one of the formats or permit companies to choose one of the formats for themselves. The layout of the balance sheet presentation, called horizontal format, is prescribed by Article 9 of the Fourth Directive, which is used most commonly in the majority of continental European countries. It is shown in Figure 1 at the end of the chapter. The other layout, prescribed by Article 10, is called the vertical format and is most common in the United Kingdom. The new Hungarian law stipulates that all companies must adopt the balance sheet format of Article 9.

The income statement formats prescribed by the directive present the total cost model and the cost of sales models either vertically or horizontally. The new law permits companies to adopt the model that is considered to be the most appropriate to the nature of the business. The model must, however, be presented vertically. The two models are presented in Figures 2 and 3. The total cost model is based on the principle of the gross income statement, which derives from Continental European practice. The cost of sales model follows the functional approach of classification of expenses. In Anglo-Saxon practice usually the cost of sales model is used; in Western Europe either of the models is applied.

The horizontal format of the income statement means that in showing the profit of the period against all revenues, all costs and expenses are compared.

2. The Form and Content of Published Financial Statements

2.1 The Objective of Financial Reporting

The predominant objective of financial statements is to provide information on the financial performance of the company upon which management, present and future investors, creditors, and other interested parties may base their decisions. Companies shall prepare a report on their economic resources and the claims on them (net assets, financial position and operating performance, general income) during a period, supported by their accounting records.

2.2 Differentiation of Financial Reports According to the Size and Method of Bookkeeping

The type of report required by a company is determined by its size and method of bookkeeping. There are three different types of report:

1. Annual Report
2. Simplified Annual Report
3. Simplified Balance Sheet

The reports prepared are the responsibility of the entity and its authorized representatives. The accounting period is based on the calendar year.

Financial reporting should include explanations and interpretations to help users understand the financial information provided. Supporting notes and the business report satisfy this objective. In 1992 and 1993 the content of the financial statements was determined by Figures 1–4 and further breakdown was not permitted. Since 1994 further breakdown and analysis have been permitted if they are considered helpful to the reader.

2.2.1 Annual Report

A company that operates a double-entry bookkeeping system and that meets two of the three criteria detailed below in two consecutive years is required to prepare an annual report. The criteria are as follows:

1. Total assets of at least 150 million forints (Ft)
2. Annual net sales of at least Ft 300 million
3. Average number of employees exceeds 100 in any given year

The annual report consists of a balance sheet, an income statement, notes to the accounts, and a business report. The structure, format, and contents of the annual report must be consistent from one year to the next to ensure true comparability. Comparative figures are to be shown for both the balance sheet and the income statement.

Assets and liabilities in the balance sheet and revenues and expenditures in the income statement are to be shown gross and are not to be netted off. The annual report shall be prepared in a clear and transparent form, in the structure and form prescribed by law. It shall be prepared in the Hungarian language and in thousand forints.

2.2.2 Simplified Annual Report

Companies that operate a double-entry bookkeeping system but do not meet the size criteria referred to above are required only to produce a simplified annual report. This consists of a balance sheet and an income statement, as shown in Figures 2 and 4 or 5 and notes to the accounts.

2.2.3 Simplified Balance Sheet

An entrepreneur—whose net sales do not exceed Ft 50 million in two consecutive years—keeping single-entry books must prepare a simplified balance sheet with an accounting reference date of December 31. The simplified balance sheet must be prepared in the form prescribed by the new legislation, on the basis of properly maintained account books. The format of the simplified balance sheet is shown in Figure 6.

In the simplified balance sheet, depreciation and any loss of value of intangible goods and tangible assets shall be accounted for, irrespective of whether the result is a profit or a loss. Equity consists of subscribed capital, capital reserve, and reserves. The reserve represents the amount of accumulated retained earnings accounted for from the commencement of business. This amount could be negative in the case of a loss. The categories of accumulated retained earnings and balance sheet profit or loss for the financial year are not to be used.

When a specific reserve is provided to cover overdue receivables and losses due to bad debts, the amount of the general turnover tax charged and included in the amount of the receivable shall not be taken into account, if the payment of the general turnover tax is linked to financial performance.

Specific reserves are to be created to cover contingent liabilities that are not presented in the balance sheet. These should be disclosed but not booked. The specific reserves generally should be presented only in the simplified balance sheet but not booked. This is because the profit and loss statement is prepared by using a cash basis of accounting for those who maintain records under the single-entry method of bookkeeping.

Specific reserves to cover guarantee obligations are not required. Accordingly, in the simplified balance sheet, foundation and reorganization expenses should not be capitalized. Because of the cash basis of accounting, prepaid and accrued expenses and deferred income are not applicable and may not be presented in the balance sheet.

The general rules of valuation of assets and liabilities explained below are to be applied with the exception of the following items. The entrepreneur who must pay the charged general turnover tax to the state budget linked to financial performance shall present the accounts receivable in the amount net of the general turnover tax, until the receivables are settled in cash or by draft, or until it is ascertained that the receivables cannot be collected.

Self-manufactured inventories may be included at their sales price less realization costs less the anticipated profit margin. Fixed asset renovation costs are not required to be capitalized. Companies reclaiming from the state budget the general turnover tax charged in advance only after payment has been made should include short-term receivables arising from the supply of goods or the performance of services at the amount billed, net of the deductible general turnover tax. The simplified balance sheet must be supported by an inventory taking.

Double-Entry Bookkeeping All companies except those in which net sales do not exceed Ft 50 million in two consecutive years, the budgetary organizations, and the National Bank of Hungary must maintain double-entry account books. Ledger accounts are classified, and the double-entry bookkeeping standards are summarized in the uniform chart of accounts. Under the new law, however, the application of the uniform chart of accounts is no longer mandatory. The main goal of the chart is to facilitate the organization of bookkeeping and financial reporting.

The chart lays down nine classes of accounts and, within them, the groups of accounts and their types. Classes 1–4 include the balance sheet accounts, Classes 1–3 the assets accounts, and Class 4 the accounts of equities, specific reserves, and liabilities. Classes 5, 8, and 9 include data needed for the presentation of income statements.

Class 5 is used for recording operating costs by types. It contains all the material costs, labor, labor-related costs, depreciation allowance, and other costs. Labor-related costs include social insurance and contributions to the unemployment fund. This accounting of costs by types provides the basic data for the national economic information system in accordance with the new law.

In Class 6, overhead (indirect) costs used to be collected by departments. Class 7 has been used for accounting for direct costs by products. Under the new system, Classes 6 and 7 are no longer required but may be used as previously or as management determines. For example, these classes may be used to establish responsibility/cost centers within the organization.

Class 8 includes accounts for expenses. It specifies the accounts for recording direct costs and various other cost of sales that are not represented in the direct cost of products or services, financial and extraordinary expenses, and profit tax levied. Class 9 accounts for sales, other revenue, and revenue from financial transactions and extraordinary revenue.

The Chart of Accounts at Company Level   A company shall establish a chart of accounts, which must be based on the uniform chart of accounts determined by the act. The use of account classes as determined by the act is compulsory, although a company may choose to increase account categories within the standard classes. The goal of the company chart of accounts is to facilitate preparation of the financial statements required by the accounting law, taking into consideration the specific goals of company management and the specific conditions of the company.

Single-Entry Bookkeeping   Entrepreneurs who are required to produce only a simplified balance sheet and whose annual net sales revenue does not exceed Ft 50 million in two consecutive years may keep single-entry account books. Single-entry bookkeeping is basically a record of cash receipts and payments. The increase or decrease in cash results in changes in revenue or expenses, or in accounts receivable or in accounts payable or in owner's capital.

The journal ledger and analyzed cash book are considered to be the most usual methods of single-entry bookkeeping. In the journal ledger, the input and output general sales tax items are always recorded separately. Because only cash-in and cash-out transactions are recorded in the journal ledger, it must supplemented by the physical (analytical) records, which provide information for preparing the simplified balance sheet.

2.3 The Content of Financial Statements in the Annual Report

2.3.1 Balance Sheet

In 1988, important changes were made in the required content and structure of the balance sheet. The distinction between funds for current assets, fixed assets, and other special funds, which characterized the period 1946–1987, was dominated in favor of a homogeneous "funds for assets" account. In the long run, this treatment facilitates the establishment of an interest in asset values. Instead of a segmented view of asset categories, corporate leadership could now focus on the effective management of the entire asset base.

Since 1989 customers' advance payments have been registered on the liabilities side as an accrual, the opposite of the previous practice, when they had been netted out against accounts receivable. Another change has been made by taking the intangible assets (this category was introduced in 1988) out of the gross value of fixed assets and putting them under a separate balance sheet account title.

As a result of these changes, the Hungarian balance sheet of the early 1990s resembles more closely than previously that of the Anglo-Saxon and World Bank model.

The balance sheet lists the assets according to mobility (liquidity) and the liabilities according to solvency due date, in descending order.

The prescribed format of balance sheet under the new accounting law is shown in Figure 1.

Assets Assets should be classified as long-term assets, current assets, or prepaid expenses and accrued income. The classification of assets between long-term assets and current assets is based on the business purpose and expected use of the assets. Assets that are expected to be realized in cash, sold, or consumed within one year are to be considered current assets.

Long-term assets. Long-term assets comprise (*a*) intangible assets, (*b*) tangible assets, and (*c*) financial assets. *Intangible assets* include rights, concessions, intellectual goods, and goodwill. Research and development costs and foundation and reorganization expenses may be capitalized and presented as intangible assets if they have the potential for providing the company with a future benefit. In the case of capitalization of foundation expenses, dividends shall not be paid unless the after-tax profits and the accumulated retained earnings, adjusted by the amount of loss carried forward, exceed the amount of the capitalized foundation and reorganization expenses not yet written off.

Tangible assets. Tangible assets include land, forests, plant buildings, technical equipment, machines, vehicles, plant and shop furnishings, and other equipment.

Financial assets. Financial assets are long-term investments in equity shares of other companies acquired to obtain control over a company or to obtain a long-term interest in the earnings of a subsidiary. Such assets also include other long-term investments and long-term loans granted.

Current assets. Assets that are expected to be realized in cash, sold, or consumed within one year are current assets. Current assets include inventories, receivables, marketable securities, and monetary assets.

Prepaid expenses and accrued income. Prepaid expenses and accrued income include expenditures incurred in the accounting period but that relate to the following accounting period and income earned in the accounting period but not received until the following accounting period.

Owners' Equity and Liabilities   The liability side of the balance sheet must be presented under the following classifications: owners' equity, specific reserves, liabilities, and accrued expenses and deferred income.

Owner's equity. Owners equity includes:

1. Subscribed (registered) capital
2. Capital reserve (share premium account)
3. Accumulated retained earnings (profits)
4. Loss carried forward from the previous years
5. Balance sheet profit or loss for the financial year

Subscribed capital is that part of equity that is registered as such by the Court of Registration.

Capital reserve may include the following items:

- The difference between the par and issued value of the shares
- The amount of capital permanently transferred by the founders to the company
- The difference between the value of the convertible currency cash contribution of the foreign partner of a company that operates with foreign participation upon issue and its value calculated at the exchange rate at the time of its use
- The amount of capital permanently transferred by other companies to the company
- The value of share-vouchers subscribed by cooperative members and asset-notes acquired by employees

Accumulated retained earnings comprise the opening accumulated retained earnings plus the balance sheet profit for the previous period, less brought-forward losses amortized through retained earnings, plus or minus accumulated retained earnings transferred to or from other companies, less the amount transferred to subscribed capital, less the amount used for dividend or profit sharing of the period. The losses to be amortized through accumulated retained earnings come from two sources:

1. Certain losses, as laid down by profit tax legislation, which may be carried forward and amortized over a number of years through the accumulated retained earnings reserve
2. Losses that may not be carried forward. These must be written off through the accumulated retained earnings reserve in the following year.

Loss carried forward from the previous years includes the amount of loss that can be amortized over the following years to the accumulated retained earnings.

Balance sheet profit or loss for the financial year is the after-tax profit or loss, increased by the amount of accumulated retained earnings used for dividend or profit sharing of the given period and reduced by the whole amount of the declared dividend or profit sharing. This should equal the profit figure in the income statement.

The old equity section of the balance sheet did not show the profit after taxation and dividends but rather the total of annual earnings before tax. The amount of the accumulated assets fund was adjusted by net earnings only after the year-end accounts had been finalized. At the year end, the profit tax account had a debit balance with the amount of tax paid in advance that appeared in the equity section of the balance sheet. The amount of tax payable for the year under review was worked out in a separate profit reconciliation. Now, under the new system, the profit distribution is included in the preparation of the year-end balance sheet and income statement.

Specific reserves. Under the new system, a category of specific reserve has been created. The concept of a specific reserve allows for the provision for certain anticipated losses and expenses and can allow for the deferral of the recognition of gains or profits until they are certain to be realized.

Specific reserves may be deducted from the amount of profit before tax. They should cover potential losses from receivables overdue, bad debts, and advance payments made, and to cover obligations of early retirement pension and redundancy payments. Specific reserves may be created to cover guarantee obligations. If the entity does not create such reserves, all guarantee obligations should be classified and disclosed in a note to the accounts. The amount of such reserves shall be detailed in a note.

Insurance companies may form specific reserves to cover long-term obligations and to balance out damage fluctuations between years. The risk reserve requirements pertaining to financial institutions have been regulated by a separate law, Law No. LXIX/1991 on banks and banking activities.

Liabilities. Liabilities are classified as short or long term. Short-term liabilities are loans and credits received with a maturity of less than a year and include the portion of long-term liabilities to be repaid within one year of the accounting date. The amount of the latter shall be disclosed in a note. Short-term liabilities include advance payments received from customers, shown as noncash liabilities.

Long-term liabilities are due more than one year after the accounting date.

Accrued expenses and deferred income. Accruals and deferred income should be used to account for cash receipts received before the balance sheet date but which relate to revenues arising in the next accounting period, costs relating to the current accounting period that will be invoiced in the next period, claims arising from damages, penalties for defaults relating to the current period that have been enforced or submitted against the firm between the accounting date and the preparation of accounts (payments for damages and legal costs that become known during this period), and proposed bonus payments and related social security contributions for both employee and executive staff relating to the current period.

Under the new system, the executive bonus payment will not be separated from the nonexecutive one. The amount of bonuses announced but not paid will be shown in the balance sheet as accruals.

2.3.2 Income Statement (Profit and Loss Account)

The income statement shows the balance sheet profit or loss as the after tax profit or loss of regular and extraordinary activities of the firm, increased by the amount of accumulated retained earnings used for the dividend or (profit-sharing) of the year and reduced by the announced dividend amount. The statement contains the total revenue of the enterprise (i.e., receipt from sales and other income), as well as the total expenses (costs of sales, overhead costs not distributed to products, so-called period costs, and other expenses).

Two models are used in developing the income statement permitted by the law. These are the total cost model and the cost of sales model. The prescribed format for the total cost model is shown in Figure 4.

The main categories of this format and their relationship can be described as follows:

1. Net sales and other revenues
2. Changes in self-produced inventory and work in progress plus capitalized self-manufactured fixed assets
3. Gross production value (1 + 2)
4. Material and material-type expenditures
5. Value added production (3 – 4)

6. Labor and labor-related costs plus depreciation allowance plus other costs plus other expenditures

7. Profit or loss of business activity (5 − 6)

8. Profit or loss of financial transactions

9. Profit or loss from regular business activities (7 + 8)

10. Extraordinary profit or loss

11. Profit before tax (9 + 10)

12. Tax payment liability

13. After-tax profit

14. Amount of accumulated retained earnings used for dividend or profit sharing of the period

15. Dividend or profit sharing of the period announced

16. Balance sheet profit or loss for the financial year (13 + 14 − 15)

The gross income statement presents the opportunity for calculation of value added production, which is widely used in western European countries.

The other format of income statement is the cost of sales model. It is shown in Figure 5.

If the cost of sales model is used, the structure of the income statement is usually based on a functional approach. This means that in showing the profit of the period against net sales, the manufacturing costs of the products and services sold, the marketing costs of the period, and finally, the general administration expenses of the period are all detailed.

In the old practice, the cost of sales model was used, but the functional approach was not followed. Hungarian companies, following the principle of direct costing, tried to separate fixed and variable costs within the income statement, or at least to separate them directly and indirectly by tracing the costs of products and services. Unlike Western practice, the direct costs of goods sold included direct marketing costs of products and services as well manufacturing costs.

Under the new system, if the cost of sales model is used, marketing costs are now separated from the direct costs of sale and are disclosed within indirect costs of sale as sales costs. Financial revenues and expenses should be disclosed separately from the other components of the old category of other revenue and expenses. Specific provisions may now be made for anticipated losses from doubtful debts and receivables overdue and to cover obligations under early retirement pension and redundancy payment guarantee. These provisions are to be charged in the income statement as other expenses. The distinction of profits and losses from ordinary and extraordinary activities has also been introduced. The profit tax charged on the period is also recorded as other expenses.

2.3.3 Notes to the Accounts

The notes to the accounts contain the additional information necessary for providing a reliable, true and fair view of the net assets, financial position, and net income disclosed in the balance sheet and income statement. They contain both numerical data and explanatory text.

The notes disclose the accounting policies adopted by the company from the alternatives offered by law and the effect of the applied methods on net assets, the financial position, and net income. For example, the notes provide detailed information on depreciation rates of tangible and intangible assets. They also contain details of the major shareholders of the company, the number of the company's employees, research and development costs, and the profit tax liability.

The notes should also give information on the portion of any liabilities in the balance sheet that are due in more than 5 years and details of any mortgages or guarantees entered into by the company. Any contingent liabilities that require disclosure in order to give a full picture of the company's position but that are not included in the balance sheet should also be included.

The notes should also include details of the gross opening value of intangible assets and tangible assets, the increase or decrease in these assets, the accumulated depreciation, and depreciation charged for the year, by balance sheet items.

2.3.4 Business Report

The business report must include a fair review of the position of the company's business and its development. It should cover significant events, particularly those that take place after the balance sheet date. Details relating to the purchase of a company's own shares and of the company's research and development policy should be given. The business report should be compatible with the view presented by the rest of the accounts.

2.3.5 *Filing under the New Legislation*

All companies incorporated in the Trade Register keeping double- or single-entry books must file their annual reports, containing the auditor's report as well as the proposal or resolution pertaining to the use of the after-tax profit, with the Court of Registration by May 31 of the year following the accounting period.

All companies limited by shares, limited companies with prime capital in excess of Ft 50 million, single-person limited liability companies, and firms issuing bonds, as well as any other company that so desires, must publish their financial reports containing the auditor's report and the notes to the accounts but not the business report.

The requirement to publish financial statements will gradually become more stringent. Since January 1, 1994, all companies with net sales revenues in excess of Ft 1 billion have been required to publish their statements. After January 1, 1996, all companies with net sales revenues in excess of Ft 300 million, and after January 1, 1998 all companies keeping double-entry books, will be required to publish their statements, containing the auditor's report.

2.4 Review of the Financial Report

Under the new legislation, the balance sheet must be signed by a person authorized to represent the entity. The financial report must be presented to the board of directors and/or the general meeting. The financial report with the profit distribution, the dividend proposal, and profit tax amount are presented to the ultimate decision-making body of the business organization—the general meeting—with comments by the supervisory committee and the auditor, where mandatory audit is required. The board of directors, or the general meeting, is authorized to accept the balance sheet and the profit or loss statement, and the profit distribution (the size of dividend payment, the amount of profit tax, settlement of losses). The deadline for filing the financial report, audited where a mandatory audit is required, is May 31 following the end of the accounting period. The deadline for reporting to the tax authority is February 28 following the end of the accounting period.

Under the new legislation, the name and content of the former state financial and economic auditing shall be changed. It is known as tax auditing and shall have a limited scope. It does not cover management's economic decision making but checks that the accounting income calculation conforms to accounting legislation and that the taxable income is in accordance with tax requirements. The self-audit system used by companies will be basically unchanged.

Under the tax legislation concerning the approved balance sheet, the ledger statements supporting the balance sheet, the inventory, and analytical records may be audited by the tax authority under tax audits and revised by the company itself under self-audit.

Tax audits and self-audits are carried out to verify the validity and completeness of the approved balance sheet, the profit distribution, and the due settlements with the central budget, and compliance with inventory-taking and tax valuation rules. If it is found during the tax audit or self-audit that the balance sheet is wrong, the necessary adjustments must be made on the basis of the relevant provisions in force during the period when the error was made.

2.5 The Function of Independent Auditors

The overall goal of independent auditing is to assess the performance of management in its strategic decision making and to provide audited information upon which external users of the accounts, for example, shareholders, lenders, and potential investors, may base their decisions. The charter of a business association may stipulate that the conduct of management be audited by an independent auditor instead of, or in addition to, the supervisory committee.

It is mandatory to appoint independent auditors for companies limited by shares and for one-person limited liability companies, and for limited liability companies with a stock capital of more than Ft 50 million. Independent auditors must be qualified as chartered accountants and registered with the Ministry of Finance. There should be no family connections or business ties between the auditor and the client company. The auditors must be independent in order to be impartial in undertaking their duties. In the case of the transformation of a state-owned enterprise into a business association, the transforming balance sheet also should be audited by an independent auditor in accordance with the Law on Transformation and Law No. LIV/1992 on the privatization of state properties. If a company limited by shares decides to publicly trade its securities, the main financial statements should be audited by an independent auditor as well. In accordance with the Law on Securities and Stock Exchange, the company prospectus should include these audited financial statements.

The auditor's function is to examine the report presented to each general meeting or board meeting—especially the balance sheet and the whole financial report—and make sure they contain valid figures and comply with legislative provisions.

The auditor has access to the company's books, may seek information from executives and employees, and may examine the company's pay office, portfolio and inventories, agreements, and bank accounts. The auditor must attend the board meeting or general meeting and give an opinion on the audited balance sheet and reports. If the auditor finds that the company's capital may be expected to decrease significantly, or if there is any other such fact for which executives may be held liable, the auditor must let the supervisory committee know and may, at the same time, request that the ultimate decision-making body of the company be convened.

A primary function of the auditor is to review and certify the balance sheet and the balance sheet report and give an opinion. For this purpose, the auditor must examine the balance sheet and the financial report impartially and thoroughly and in turn countersign the reviewed balance sheet. The auditor may refuse to countersign if the balance sheet and financial report contain false figures, if the form in which they have been prepared violates legislative provisions, or if deliberate fraud has occurred. The auditor may also sign the report with a proviso, providing the auditor identifies on the report the problems that have been identified. The auditor should draw attention to any unfavorable change in capital, financial position, or profitability. The auditor has a duty of confidentiality to the client with respect to the facts, data, and business information that come to the auditor's attention in the course of the audit.

The auditor must prepare an audit report, in writing, on the financial report review, the income statement, and the statement of profit distribution in compliance with respective legislative provisions that the capital, assets, and liabilities in the balance sheet and the company's revenues, costs, expenses, and profit or loss in the income statement reflect a true and fair picture and comply with the relevant legislative provisions. To illustrate the standard form audit report used in Hungary, an actual example of an audit report is shown below.

Auditor's Report for the Stockholders—XYZ Hungaria Kft.

We have audited the accompanying balance sheet of XYZ Hungaria Kft. "the Company" as of 31 December 1993 and the related profit and loss account and supplement (collectively "the financial statement") for the period then ended included in the Company's 1993 Annual Report. The Annual Report is the responsibility of management.

Our responsibility is to express an opinion on the financial statements on the basis of our audit and to assess whether the related accounting information contained in the Business Report included in the Annual Report is consistent with that contained in the financial statements.

We conducted our audit in accordance with the applicable laws and regulations in force in Hungary and with International Standards on Auditing. Those standards require that we plan and perform the audit to obtain reasonable assurance about whether the financial statements are free of material misstatement. An audit includes examining, on a test basis, evidence supporting the amounts and disclosures in the financial statements. An audit also includes assessing the accounting principles used and significant estimates made by management, as well as evaluating the overall financial statement presentation. Our work with respect to the Business Report was limited to the aforementioned scope, and did not include a review of any information other than that drawn from the audited accounting records of the Company. We believe that our work provides a reasonable basis for our opinion. In our opinion:

The Annual Report has been compiled in accordance with Law XVIII of 1991 on Accounting and with general accounting principles in Hungary. The Annual Report provides a true and fair view of the financial position of the Company as of 31 December 1993 and the results of its operations for the year ended.

Budapest, 7 May 1994.
(Translation of the original statutory version which has been signed.)
HCA Name
Hungarian Chartered Accountant

3. Accounting Policies and Practices in Valuation and Income Measurement

3.1 Principles and Theories behind Accounting Policies and Practices

The old accounting system broadly conformed to the principles of the accrual basis of accounting. The effects of business transactions were generally recognized when they occurred, regardless of when the cash was actually received or paid. An example, however, of the failure to apply the accrual accounting principle consistently was in the area of bad debts. By using historical cost valuations without applying the principle of prudence, the conventional financial statements failed to reflect the result of management's decisions in the company's current economic environment.

Under the new legislation the financial report is prepared by using generally accepted accounting principles. These includes the principles of:

- Going concern
- Completeness
- Truth
- Lucidity
- Consistency
- Continuity
- Accrual/matching
- Prudence
- Gross settlement
- Individual valuation
- Time deferral

The considerations of materiality and substance over form have not yet been introduced by the new accounting legislation. In Western accounting the concept of prudence exerts a significant influence on profit measurement and the accounting methods used in the preparation of financial statements. It renders accounting "entrepreneur friendly." However, the concept of prudence should not be used for the creation of hidden reserves.

The new Hungarian accounting legislation has, with some few exceptions, been drawn up in accordance with the principle of prudence (see exceptions later). Even the application of direct costing valuation of manufactured stock is considered to be more prudent than the full absorption costing methods, more commonly used in Anglo-Saxon countries.

3.2 Participations, Consolidation Policy, Group Accounts

3.2.1 Accounting Methods for Participations

In developed market economies there are three basic methods used in accounting for long-term investments.

1. Cost method or lower of cost or market value method
2. Equity method
3. Consolidation

The determination of the method of accounting for long-term investments depends on the purpose of the investment and on the percentage of voting stock that the investing company owns.

Hungarian Law No. VI/1988 on business association identifies types of long-term investments:

1. When the company has a majority holding or exercises decisive control over a second company, the holding company is known as the parent company. The majority owned company is defined as a holding that exceeds 50% of the subscribed capital carrying voting rights in the subsidiary, called the subsidiary.

2. A significant holding is held by the parent company that has significant influence over the control of another company and where the value of its investment exceeds 25% of the subscribed capital of the other company but does not exceed 50%.

3. Mutual participation exists between two limited companies if each of them has acquired the shares amounting to more than one quarter part of the registered capital of the other one or if more than one quarter part of the votes are due to it in the general assembly of the other limited company.

Cost Method or Lower of Cost or Market Value Method   Under the new legislation, companies having a minority participation (the percentage of voting stock less than 25%) in another company will account for the investment using the cost method. Under the cost method an investor records its investments at acquisition cost. The investor recognizes as income only dividends received. In the balance sheet such investments are valued at the lower of cost or market value. Any write-down in the value of the investment is shown under financial expenses in the income statement.

Securities Shown among Current Assets   If the security is listed on the Stock Exchange and the market value is permanently (for at least one year preceding the balance sheet preparation date) below cost as of the preparation date of balance sheet, the price listed on the Stock Exchange as of the balance sheet date should be used. If the security is not listed on the Stock Exchange and the market value is below cost as of the preparation date of the balance sheet, this lower market value as of the preparation date is to be used.

Companies having a majority holding or exercising decisive control over subsidiaries, with the exceptions defined above, should prepare a consolidated annual report. This involves the production of consolidated accounts designed to present a true picture of the group of companies' transactions with third parties. To this end, all intercompany balances are eliminated, together with any intragroup sales and the effect of intercompany transfers of fixed assets.

When significant holding is held, the equity method is used. For consolidation of mutual participations, proportional consolidation is applied.

3.2.2 Overview: The Scope of Group Accounts

Under international business practice, the main advantages of consolidation include the following:

1. A reduction in the financial risk of operating a single business unit of legally separated companies
2. To meet more effectively the requirement of tax legislation, especially in the case of foreign subsidiaries
3. To expand or diversify with the minimum of capital investment

In pre-1992 Hungarian accounting practice, different, methods of consolidation, such as acquisition or purchase, merger or pooling, or the "former German method" had not yet been introduced. Increasing national and international economic integration resulted in the growing importance of the introduction of consolidation.

In Hungary under Law No. XVIII/1991 on accounting and Law No. CVIII/1993, which amended the law on accounting, the requirement of consolidation came into effect on January 1, 1994.

A parent company need not prepare a consolidated financial report if:

1. The parent company is itself a subsidiary of a company that is seated in Hungary
2. On the balance sheet date in 2 consecutive years preceding the subject year, two of the following three indices do not exceed the following limits:
   a. The balance-sheet grand total does not exceed Ft 500 million.
   b. The annual net revenue does not exceed Ft 1,000 million.
   c. The average number of employees in the subject year does not exceed 250 persons.

When defining the above indices, the added figures of the parent company and subsidiaries before consolidation shall be taken into consideration.

It is not mandatory to involve a subsidiary in the preparation of the consolidated annual report if:

- It would cost an unreasonable amount of money
- The investment has been acquired for the sole purpose of resale and classified as a current asset in the parent company balance sheet
- Substitutional legal restrictions prevent the parent company from exercising its right
- Without consolidation the financial report will provide a true and fair view on the financial position and result of the company

The exemption defined above shall not apply to parent companies that are financial institutions or insurance companies or if on the balance sheet date the shares of the parent companies or their subsidiaries are publicly traded.

Consolidated financial statements, however, are not the basis either for taxation or for profit distribution.

The consolidated annual report consists of a consolidated balance sheet, a consolidated profit and loss account (income statement), and consolidated summary notes.

The balance sheet and profit and loss account of a consolidated annual report differ from the balance sheet (Figure 2) and profit and loss account (Figures 4 and 5) of an annual report in accordance with Figures 7 and 8.

3.2.3 Steps for Preparation of the Consolidated Annual Report

In the course of the preparation of the consolidated annual report, the following shall be performed:

- Any adjustments arising from the use of different evaluation methods, for assessing the items of the consolidated balance sheet and profit and loss account (that is, a standard evaluation method shall be used)
- Conversion into forints of the items of the balance sheets and profit and loss accounts drawn up in foreign currencies
- Capital consolidation
- Debt consolidation (canceling any receivables and liabilities existing between the companies involved in consolidation)
- Omission of interim results (canceling any profit and loss items arising from transactions between the companies involved in consolidation that are included in the value of assets)
- Consolidation of revenues and expenditures (canceling any revenues and expenditures arising from transactions between the companies involved in consolidation)
- Consolidation of jointly managed enterprises
- Capital consolidation of associated enterprises
- Definition of tax difference due to consolidation

3.2.4 Foreign Currency Translation for Consolidation

For translating items of financial statements drawn up in a foreign currency of a subsidiary, the following exchange rate can be applied:

1. The exchange rate prevailing at the date selected in accordance with the accounting law for items in the balance sheet (with the exception of the balance sheet profit amount). This value, however, cannot be higher than the value calculated at the official foreign exchange medium rate published by National Bank of Hungary as of the balance sheet date.

2. The official foreign exchange medium rate published by the National Bank of Hungary as of the balance sheet date for all items of the balance sheet. The balance sheet profit also shall be valued at this rate.

3. For items of the profit and loss account:
   - Depreciation, loss in value, material-type expenses at the exchange rate applying to the corresponding balance sheet items
   - The balance sheet profit valuation shown above
   - The monthly rate—at the end of month for the rest of the items of the profit and loss account

Translation differences are recorded:

- Partly in the preliminary balance sheet of the given company as a change (adjustment) in equity
- Partly in the preliminary profit and loss account of the given company as other revenues and/or other expenses

The adjustments, arising from different evaluation methods, are recorded in the same way as translation differences.

3.2.5 Capital Consolidation

The primary method of capital consolidation is the Anglo-Saxon purchase or acquisition method. The value of the share due to the parent company from the subsidiary shall be taken at the amount of the parent's ownership ratio. There are two methods: the book value method and the current value method.

According to the book value method, the book values in the individual balance sheets (as adjusted as a result of the application of identical valuation principles) are compared with the cost of the investment. If a debit balance arises, this must be allocated to the relevant balance sheet headings—attachable to the assets and liabilities—in the proportion of shares held. Any amount remaining is to be recorded as goodwill on the asset side of the balance sheet. In the case of a credit balance, the hidden reserves are attachable to the assets and the hidden debts are attachable to the liabilities. The remaining credit balance arising must be recorded as a consolidation difference on the liability side of the balance sheet (negative goodwill, or "badwill").

According to the current value method, the subsidiaries' book values are replaced by updated value at the date of acquisition of the share, or the first time the subsidiary is involved in consolidation. In that case, hidden reserves are fully reflected. After the revaluation, however, the proportional net equity of the subsidiary is not allowed to exceed the cost of the investment. Thus, no "badwill" can arise from applying method 2.

Any debit or credit balances between proportional net equity and the acquisition cost of the shares are classified as goodwill or "badwill." Disclosed hidden reserves relating to other shareholders are dealt with by inclusion in the minority interest.

Goodwill arising at the time of the first consolidation is written off—amortized systematically over the years that are likely to benefit (maximum years: 15).

The capital consolidation difference entered among liabilities may be accounted to the credit of the profit if it is certain that at the consolidated balance sheet date this difference amount is a realized profit.

The difference between the shares from the affiliate shareholders' equity due to the parent company and the calculated shares at the time of the first consolidation should be shown in the consolidated balance sheet as a correction of the shareholders' equity.

When the consolidated annual report is prepared, the number of shares from the shareholders' equity of the affiliate not due to the parent company must be shown among the liabilities—separately within the shareholders' equity—in the consolidated balance sheet as minority interest (shares of external members, other owners).

The law offers several options to companies with regard to capital consolidation. The preferred capital consolidation method will probably be the book value method because of its simplicity.

3.2.6 *Proportional and Equity Consolidation*

For consolidation of jointly managed enterprises—companies have the ownership right on an equal basis—the proportional consolidation method can be used. When a significant holding is held by the parent company, the equity method of long-term investment can be applied for the consolidation of associated enterprises.

If proportional consolidation is applied, the same principles as for capital consolidations are to be followed. The consolidation differences are handled as described above.

When the equity method is used, the given share in the subsidiary shall be entered in a separate line of the parent company balance sheet.

3.2.7 *Debt and Income (Revenues and Expenses) Consolidation*

The elimination of intercompany debt, of intercompany revenues and expenses, as well as of intercompany profits and losses in principle follows the requirements of the Seventh EU Directive.

3.2.8 *Record of Corporate Tax Difference due to Consolidation*

Timing differences incurred in connection with consolidation measures (e.g., intercompany profit elimination) must be addressed by recording deferred tax. If the tax payable based on the individual profit and loss accounts is more than the tax payable according to the consolidated profit and loss account, then the difference shall be entered separately in the consolidated balance sheet as a deferred profit tax liability and in the consolidated profit and loss account as tax difference.

3.2.9 *Summary of the Consolidation Procedure*

The consolidated balance sheet is prepared in the following way:

1. The investment account in the parent company's balance sheet is eliminated and replaced with the individual assets and liabilities of the subsidiary.
2. Intercompany receivables and payables are eliminated.
3. The minority interest in the subsidiary's net assets is shown among equities.

The consolidated income statement is prepared in the following way:

1. Sales and purchases of goods and services between the parent and its subsidiaries (purchases for the buying company and sales for the selling company) are eliminated.
2. Income and expenses on loans receivable or bond indebtedness between the parent and its subsidiaries are eliminated.
3. Items related to the transfer of participation and dividends between the parent and its subsidiaries are eliminated. The amount of the minority interest in the subsidiary's income is the result of multiplying the subsidiary's net income by the minority's percentage of ownership. Typically, the minority's interest in the subsidiary's income appears as a deduction in calculating consolidated net income.

Consolidated income, therefore, comprises the parent's net income and that of its subsidiaries, less the minority interest and adjusted for the effect of any intercompany transactions.

When consolidated accounts are analyzed, particular attention should be given to notes regarding foreign currency translation and tax differences.

3.3 Foreign Currency Translation

Foreign currency transactions are restricted because the domestic currency—the Hungarian forint—is not fully convertible. The currency, however, is actually convertible for commercial purposes. The import is fully liberalized.

The accounting law established the exchange rate mechanism until full convertibility is achieved. In accordance with the law, foreign cash contributions should be valued at the middle rate of the National Bank of Hungary (NBH) in force when the cash contribution or the actual payment was made (historical rate). As the foreign currency is used, the difference between the historical and the ongoing rate—the selling rate at the date of use—is accounted for against the capital reserve.

Foreign currency cash balances are valued in the balance sheet at their book value. If their forint value, calculated at the buying rate advertised by the financial institution authorized to perform foreign exchange transactions and performing the given transaction, on the last day of the accounting period is less than their book value, they will be valued at the closing rate. If the forint value of currencies that are not transferable or listed by the financial institution authorized to perform foreign exchange transactions is calculated at the free market rate valid on the last day of the accounting period at less than their book value, the calculated value shall be used.

Accounts receivable in foreign currencies are valued at the buying rate advertised by the financial institution authorized to perform foreign exchange transactions and performing the given transaction on the contractual date of payment, if the given currency rate has not decreased and the cash has not been collected as of the date the balance sheet is prepared. If the currency rate described above has decreased, the closing buying rate will be used. If cash has been collected as of the date the balance sheet is prepared, the buying rate advertised by the given financial institution on the settlement of payment will be used for valuation of the receivables.

Accounts payable in foreign currencies are valued at the selling rate advertised by the financial institution authorized to perform foreign exchange transactions and performing the given transaction on the contractual day of payment if the given currency rate is decreasing or has not changed and the debt has not been repaid as of the date of the balance sheet preparation. If the given currency rate is increasing, the closing selling rate described above shall be used.

If payment has been made by the date the balance sheet is prepared, accounts payable are valued at the selling rate advertised by the given financial institution valid on the day of the financial performance.

3.4 Capital and Reserves

In 1988 the homogeneous "funds for property" account was introduced. The general fund and changes in the general fund were differentiated within the homogenous property fund. The general fund balance sheet account title referred to registered property value. The other account covered the changes in the general fund, including, for example, the net profit for the period and other changes in the property value that had not yet been registered. In 1989 additional changes were introduced. The existing general fund became the founder's property, the so-called registered capital, and the increases in the general fund were renamed the accumulated property fund, similar to accumulated retained earnings in Anglo-Saxon practice.

Since 1992 accounting law has required the following structure of the owner's equity account:

- Registered (subscribed) capital
- Capital reserve (share premium account)
- Accumulated retained earnings (result reserve)
- Loss carried forward from previous years
- Balance sheet profit or loss for the financial year

Law No. VI/1988 defines the minimum amount of foundation capital (as registered capital) for limited companies and companies limited by shares. Registered capital and capital reserve are defined as a nondistributable element of the owner's equity. Capital reserve does not include the revaluation reserves as unrealized revaluation surpluses. Under the new law, the revaluation reserve has not been introduced yet. Assets, as well as fixed assets, are not to be valued at a value higher than their historical cost.

Result reserve can be available for supplementing the balance sheet profit if it is not tied up in accordance with the accounting or another law and the amount of equity following this transaction exceeds the amount of the registered capital.

3.5 Liabilities and Provisions

Liabilities and provisions are valued in the balance sheet at their book value. If the repayable amount of a liability is higher than the amount received, the repayable amount shall be entered in the balance sheet among other liabilities. The difference between the repayable and received amount shall be shown among prepaid expenses.

Outstanding commitments and contingencies should be disclosed in the notes to accounts.

The category of provisions was introduced by the new accounting legislation. Provisions shall be reported among the liabilities, such as specific reserves created from pretax profit in line with the Fourth EU Directive. Planning for provision for bad debt usually is based on the grouping of accounts receivable on the basis of their maturity.

3.6 Property, Plant, and Equipment

Property, plant, and equipment are valued at historical cost. Under the old legislation, no departure from the historical cost basis was permitted. The straight-line, time, and production depreciation methods were used. The norms for depreciation used to be compulsory. The new law brought the depreciation of tangible assets within the scope of managerial decision making.

For financial reporting any kind of depreciation rate can be used that reflects the useful life of the asset. The amount of depreciation above the planned depreciation amount shall be accounted for the period if the market value at balance sheet preparation date is less than the book value of the asset. There is a difference between depreciation requirements for financial reporting and tax reporting, because the depreciation norms are obligatory when prescribed by the tax law.

If the depreciation rates used for financial reporting differ from the tax rate, the difference should be shown within the notes to accounts.

Interest charges on loans for ongoing investments are capitalized as part of the cost of property and plant. That type of interest charge does not affect the net income of the account year. After the plant is brought into operation, the interest charge is recorded as a period expense against the revenues of the periods concerned.

In the pre-1992 accounting procedure, low-value, short-lived items were distinguished from fixed assets. Furniture, manufacturing tools, and fixtures with acquisition costs less than Ft 50,000 ($500) and useful lives of less than 3 years were defined as low-value, short-lived items. These items were depreciated by 50% on first utilization and by 50% in the years of consumption. The new law eliminated this category of current assets.

3.7 Land

The valuation of land depends on when it was purchased. During the past 40 years at one time it used to be recorded without value. The law on land ownership was enacted in 1994. The accounting techniques should be used in accordance with the new land law (for example, under Accounting for Mortgages).

3.8 Leased Assets

In Hungarian practice, the capital or finance lease accounting method has not been introduced by the new accounting legislation. All leases are considered operating leases. This helps managers in the use of off-balance sheet financing. However, the law does require disclosure in the notes of off-balance sheet financing.

3.9 Oil, Gas, and Other Mineral Resources

In the case of oil, gas, and other mineral resources, depletion is based on the value of the natural resource.

3.10 Intangible Assets

Intangible assets, purchased or self-generated, are valued at cost. Before 1992 there was no amortization of intangible assets, which hindered their wider use. This was legislated for by the new law.

Amortization rates defined by the law are as follows:

- Rights and concessions are written off over 6 years or longer.

- Research and development costs, as well as foundation and reorganization costs, are written off over a period of 5 years or less.
- Patents, license, and other intellectual product costs are written off over the useful life of the assets.
- Goodwill shall be written off over a period of 5 years or more up to a period of 15 years. Disclosure is required if the amortization period is more than 5 years.

The purchase cost of rights and concessions can be capitalized and written off over a period of 6 years or longer.

Under international standards research and development costs are usually expended unless certain conditions are satisfied (IAS 9).

3.11 Inventories

The valuation of inventories is based on historical costs. Before 1989, for the valuation of purchased inventory, the so-called standard cost adjusted by the actual price difference was widely used. FIFO was also allowed as a cost flow assumption for merchandise inventory. Self-produced inventories were valued at factory unit cost, later at direct unit cost.

Under the new law, the actual acquisition cost, LIFO and FIFO cost flow assumptions, or the weighted average method are to be used for the valuation of purchased inventory. The purchase cost includes the purchase price reduced by any discount, increased by any extra charge related to the purchase or delivery cost, taxes, and customs charges with the exception of VAT, and any fees and duties charged by the authorities.

Under the new law, the direct unit cost continues to be used for the valuation of self-produced goods, but it cannot include any selling costs. The direct unit cost includes material costs, wage expenditures, and costs that have been verifiably closely related to manufacture or product. No provision is allowed for slow-moving or obsolete items of inventory, own and purchased.

If the market value of inventories has declined below cost as of the date of the balance sheet, the lower of cost and net realizable value should be shown in the balance sheet. The losses in value, defined above, should be recorded as other costs (Figure 4, line VII and Figure 5, line 07).

Under long-term contracts the direct cost of unfinished construction and installation may be defined by proportioning on the basis of the degree of performance and the customer's certificate.

The difference of the year-end closing and opening stock shall be taken into consideration as change in self-manufactured assets (Figure 4, line 04).

3.12 Taxation

In Hungary, the reported income and taxation income of companies used to be the same. The distinction between taxable income and accounting income was introduced by the new accounting legislation. Tax liability is the annual amount of tax liability payable for profits on the basis of the tax return. The state uses all possible means for increasing the state budget receipt. The profit tax law strictly defines the components of taxable income and the adjustments necessary to the accounting incomes to get the taxable income. The most relevant components are as follows:

- Depreciation rates of fixed assets
- The level of creation of and the titles of specific reserves
- Representation costs rated to be accounted for taxable income

Accelerated depreciation rates are usually not allowed for taxation. The system of investment incentives is rarely exercised. A certain negative deferred profit tax effect exists that is not recorded. In 1994 the general corporate tax rate dropped to 36% from 40%. Advance tax payment should be made by companies on the basis of the actual profit generation of the previous year. In 1994 a minimum tax rate was introduced. The minimum tax is computed as 2% of a corporation's adjusted revenues.

In 1994 the maximum personal income tax rate increased to 44% from 40% on gross incomes over Ft 550,000 per annum.

In 1994 the general VAT rate is 25%, with the exception of previously zero rated items, including most foodstuffs, which became taxable at 10% effective in 1993.

3.13 Social Security, Pension, and Health Care Contribution

In Hungary the social contribution and pension system developed under the centralized planning system. The amount of contribution is defined centrally. The 1994 rate of social security contribution is 44% and the contribution to the unemployment fund is 5.3%. Both are paid by business organizations and are considered cost elements. Employees pay a pension contribution of 6%, a health care contribution of 4%, and a contribution to the unemployment fund of 1.5%, calculated on gross wages and salaries. There is no specific reserve created for pensions. However, since 1994 specific provision may have been made for scheduled early retirement and redundancy payment.

4. Expected Future Developments

To bring the Hungarian economy into the world market, to enlarge foreign capital invested, and to facilitate the privatization process, it is essential that financial statements be prepared according to internationally accepted standards. In order to comply with international and European Union standards, Hungary has been facing up to the problem of an aggressive accounting transition.

The goal of the new accounting legislation is to define the requirements concerning firms' accounting procedures and financial reporting systems in the new conditions of the economy. The new law approaches the internationally accepted principles of accountancy, and it is based on the Fourth, Seventh, and Eighth Directives of the Council of the European Union. However, the EU directives are being taken as the basic model, but the adaptation of the accounting system in different countries is specific because history, traditions, and concepts are different.

The adaptation of the European Union Council's directives will require a lot of experience, and it takes time, as will the transformation of Hungary from a centrally planned economy to a market economy. Some of the main problems to be expected in adopting the EU Council Directives are discussed in the following sections.

4.1 Training Programs for Practitioners

The process of implementing the new law is difficult. It is obvious, however, that without the systematic training of accountants, success cannot be achieved. The whole accounting profession faces an enormous task. The Ministry of Finance has elaborated a training plan and conducted a training program for accounting practitioners who practice under the new law. The World Bank, the EU, the OECD, EU PHARE, German Nordrhein Westfallen Regierung, and the United Nations Working Group on Accounting Standards have offered their help in training Hungarian accountants. International accounting firms and accounting associations that have opened offices in Hungary have an important role in this training process, too. EU PHARE Financial Sector Development Program also offered its assistance in training.

To deepen the understanding of Hungarian professionals with respect to the international accounting and auditing environment, and to provide guidance in specific technical fields, different accountancy projects will be designed and funded by the PHARE Program. The projects are as follows:

- The translation and publication of up-to-date International Accounting and Auditing Standards
- The preparation of recommendations for the improvement of university curricula in accounting, auditing, and taxation
- A training program in consolidated financial reporting
- The preparation of recommendations for the Ministry of Finance on the legislative treatment of inflation accounting
- Design of a one-year pilot specialist accounting and finance training program in English, which is available for use by universities and colleges. It is aimed at providing trainees with a sound grasp of the essential technical language in the field of accountancy and finance tailored to Hungarian circumstances.
- The training of trainers in which university lecturers will be trained to deliver the specialized accounting and finance training program in English, thus ensuring the essential continuity and self-sustainment of the training program

4.2 Current Influence of the Former Overregulated Accounting System on the Profession; Changing Approach

The former overregulated accounting system has a strong influence on the current accounting profession. During the past 40 years accountants in

Hungary had to follow strict rules, prescribed in detail. They had no time to consider things, and there was no room for consideration. Accountants did not have the opportunity to build an accounting and reporting system that fit the goals and strategies of their companies. Under such circumstances, the accountants within management usually have been regarded as low skilled technicians, or "bookkeepers." The entire profession lost its reputation, so it was not able to attract the most talented young people.

The new accounting regulation has absolutely different characteristics. The law forms the underlying basis of financial reporting. The principles of the law are not obligatory rules, and neither do they cater to all accounting possibilities. The new law requires accountants to apply a new approach in their everyday work. They must make decisions to meet the principles of the new laws. To use the acquisition cost of the assets is no longer the only possibility for accounting valuation. In certain cases, accountants must make their best estimation for stating the market value of assets.

Accountants also must consider the time value of money when making accounting decisions. When setting the accounting policy of a company, they have to be not only bookkeepers but economists and marketing experts and to cope with the strategic requirements of the company at the same time. A 2-week course on the new accounting law is not enough to equip accountants with what they need to cope with and manage the change to the new approach. Accounting reform needs to be accomplished in the minds of accountants, which takes longer.

The principle of substance over form and materiality meets the principles of the new accounting law, but they are not clearly defined in the law. Concepts of materiality and substance over form are not widely accepted by practitioners. They do not affect the overall presentation of the financial accounts. There are many criticisms of the idea that the calendar year should always be equal to the financial year. In the creation of provisions, for example, sometimes economic realities are missing because the wording of the law is preferred over the substance of the law. One is allowed to create provision for bad debt, for example, only if the receivable is overdue on the last day of the year. If the accountant knows that on January 2 the debtor's business will be closed, but on December 31 the receivable is not overdue, the accountant is not allowed to create provision for it.

4.3 Problems Connected with the Introduction of Differentiation between Tax and Financial Reporting

The tax law strictly defines the component of taxable income. Usually taxable income is higher than accounting income, given the accounting law. To avoid double recording of the components, companies sometimes use the taxable income rates for the financial reporting goal. In that case, their financial accounts would not present a true and fair view of their financial position at a point in time and results over a period of time. The auditor's task is to persuade them to meet both requirements.

4.4 Underdevelopment of the Social Institutional Framework

Hungary inherited its social security system from the centrally planned economy. Although there are some new elements of social security based on private ownership, basically it is outdated. A new institutional framework for social security and health care in line with a market economy needs further development. The principles for the creation of a specific reserve should be differentiated. Currently there is no disclosure of pension contributions or directors' remuneration.

4.5 The Lack of Inflation Accounting Techniques

On the basis of accounting legislation in force, assets are not allowed a value higher than their acquisition costs. In 1991 the inflation rate reached 35%. During recent years it decreased, but currently it is still about 20%. During the past 5–6 years the foreign exchange rate increased annually 15%–16% on average, because of devaluation of the forint.

The foreign exchange liability shall be valued in the balance sheet at the forint value converted at the foreign exchange selling rate advertised by the authorized commercial bank on the last day of the year. The exchange loss is recorded as other expenses in the profit and loss account. In many cases the loss exceeds the amount of subscribed capital. A provision on the legislative treatment of inflation accounting has been prepared by the Ministry of Finance. This provision would introduce the revaluation of long-term assets and establish the corresponding revaluation reserve in line with the Fourth EU Directive.

The goal of the planned amendments to the accounting law is to provide some solutions for handling inflation in accounting to reflect a true and fair view of the income generation process and financial position of the economic unit. The revaluation of fixed assets is one of the most debated and criticized topics in the accounting field. Hungary must face this difficult task in the near future.

4.6 The Lack of a Cash Flow Approach in Financial Accounting

The Hungarian legislation, like the Fourth EU Directive, does not meet the requirement of international accounting standards to produce a statement of cash flows as part of the accounts package. This statement reports the major sources and uses of cash. It explains how the financing, investing, and operating activities of a firm affect the cash balance for a period, and it is considered to be of great importance to both creditors and investors and the company management itself.

In international practice according to the latest developments, less emphasis is placed on profitability in the form of a single earnings figure (earnings per share) and more upon viability in the form of cash flow information. A business may be profitable in the sense that it is selling its products or service at prices greater than the cost of providing them or making gains by holding assets whose value is appreciating, but unless it is able to convert its "profits" into cash, it will not survive. The Hungarian accounting practice misses the cash flow approach, and an economy in transition to a market economy cannot fail to be aware of cash flows.

4.7 The Introduction of Consolidated Annual Accounts

The accounting law introduced the consolidation requirement effective January 1, 1994. The theory and practice of consolidation are totally new for the majority of practitioners. Course materials and hand-outs must be prepared, and courses are to be organized to impart new knowledge to accountants. The University of Economics and Hungarian Chamber of

Auditors have launched a course on consolidation. EU PHARE also will launch a Train the Trainer course on consolidation.

4.8 From the Backward-Looking Emphasis to a Forward-Looking Orientation

In developed market economies the announced goal of the future development of financial reporting is to turn away from its essentially backward-looking orientation. The report should give more assistance to management in its strategic planning and should also include information on future prospects.

4.9 The Lack of Effective Support Infrastructure for the Accountancy Profession

The EU PHARE Financial Sector Development Program, represented by the Ministry of Finance PHARE Program Management Unit (MoF PHARE PMU) wishes to encourage and assist the accountancy profession to establish appropriate professional bodies that correspond with current EU practices.

The structure of the accountancy profession should be designed to maximize its contribution to the wealth creation process in the economy.

In 1993 Arthur Andersen & Co. reviewed the operations of accounting, auditing, and tax advisory associations in six EU member states to determine the different systems established for ensuring the best development of bookkeeping, accounting, auditing, and tax advisory practice at all levels nationally. Upon findings of the review, the consultant was asked to recommend a system appropriate to the development of the Hungarian bookkeeping, accounting, auditing, and tax advisory professions at all levels, existing structure and financial realities, made in close cooperation with relevant representatives of the Hungarian professions.

On the basis of the above study and intensive consultations with the representatives of the profession, the key elements of the recommended structure are as follows:

- The operation of three self-standing professional bodies

- The possible creation of a common service unit as a technical means to provide differentiated services to and for the professional bodies to cover their common functions.

PHARE now seeks to encourage and assist the Hungarian accounting, auditing, and tax advisory professions with ECU 500,000 for the establishment of professional bodies that are appropriate to their current and future needs. The parallel future operation of the following autonomous but cooperating professional bodies seems the most feasible concept, taking into account current circumstances:

1. Professional body for auditors
2. Professional body for accountants
3. Professional body for tax advisers

It is envisaged that the national professional bodies, by supporting and integrating existing and future initiatives in this field, will develop a comprehensive regional network of support services.

One of the professional bodies, the Hungarian Chamber of Auditors (HCA), is already operational. Elements of the establishment phase of the professional bodies are therefore clearly not valid for the HCA.

There are different possible ways of establishing the professional bodies, such as

1. Establish the national body first, which will build up the regional network on the basis of the proven needs of the profession (top-down model)
2. Encourage local bodies to establish in a process of self-formation. This will result in the need to establish an association and achieve the aim of a national body (bottom-up model)

The second scenario has the risk that the most efficient utilization will not be made of PHARE funds and makes monitoring possibilities uncertain.

The recommended professional bodies should:

- Be appropriate to the traditions and present level of development of the Hungarian bookkeeping, accounting, and auditing profession at all levels

- Take account of existing structures and financial realities

In order to establish and maintain efficiently and effectively operating professional bodies (to EU standards), the professional bodies will have to cover the following tasks. The most important functions that will be provided by the professional bodies are:

- To combine the forces of the membership in order to provide protection of the common interest
- To help and assist its membership to cope with problems arising in their everyday work and to solve these problems in accordance with the principals of the accounting law, and to improve their approach to reflect the requirements of the accounting law on the basis of the demands of a market economy
- To provide training for the profession and to ensure that the members keep up with the developments of the profession
- To elaborate codes of ethics
- To create a system for self-regulation of the professions
- To elaborate and maintain professional standards
- To provide a constant review of accounting, auditing, and taxation legislation and to make recommendations for amendment or updating

There are two different clearly distinct phases of development of the professional bodies—the establishment phase and the operational phase.

To facilitate the establishment of professional bodies, public meetings were held in January 1994 of all those interested in establishing two of the three professional bodies (accountants and tax advisers). Each meeting was well attended, and the attendees at each elected a representative consultative and steering committee to negotiate with PHARE on the establishment of the future professional bodies.

The two new committees (and a committee representing the Hungarian Chamber of Auditors) are developing terms of reference for consultancy assistance with the preparation of business plans for their future professional bodies.

The consultant will prepare an integrated business plan for the three professional bodies for a 3-year period, which sets out their goals to meet their members' needs and the strategy for achieving them. The business plan will be detailed, timetabled, and budgeted and will be split into the following separate sections:

Section I. Business Plan for Auditors' Professional Body

Section II. Business Plan for Accountants' Professional Body

Section III. Business Plan for Tax Advisers' Professional Body

Section IV. Business Plan for Common Service Unit

Section V. Summary reflecting the three professions' development as a whole—auditing, accounting, and tax advising are considered in their entirety in a consistent and integrated manner.

Sections I to IV inclusive of the overall budgeted business plan will cover, among other things, the following:

1. The articles of association of the professional bodies and common service unit

2. A statement of proposed measurable objectives to be achieved in the first year

3. A list of activities to be undertaken

4. A quarterly breakdown of income and expenditure. Such estimations should be based on assumptions clearly stated and justified.

The first year of the plan will include detailed budgets, activities, and targets, while the second and third years will be covered in broader outline but will nevertheless describe major activities and budgetary implications. For the implementation of business plans ECU 1 million will be available, financed by PHARE.

During the past few years, as Hungary moved from the centrally planned economy into a market economy, rapid economic changes have taken place. It is now clear that a market economy cannot operate successfully without a modern accounting framework supported by an efficient, effective, and progressive accountancy profession. The reformed accounting and financial reporting system will ensure appropriate accounting valuations for a market economy, to provide the desired drive and incentive.

If Hungary is to take its place in the international business world, the financial and managerial accounting systems must develop congruently with internationally accepted standards and requirements. Accounting developments will lead to a strong accountancy profession built on a strong theoretical base and in which the emphasis is on looking forward to the demands of the future.

Acknowledgments

The author acknowledges with thanks Prem Prakash, Ph.D, University of Pittsburgh, U.S.A., for his help given by their common working paper, written in 1989, on the role of accounting in facilitating economic development, and Eva Tihanyi, Ph.D., for her helpful questions and comments when this chapter was written.

Financial Statements

Figure 1

HUNGARIA   KFT

MÉRLEG/ESZKÖZÖK	1992.12.31. eFt	1993.12.31. eFt
01. **A. BEFEKTETETT ESZKÖZÖK**	132,225	139,047
02. **I. IMMATERIÁLIS JAVAK**		
03. VAGYONI ÉRTÉKŰ JOGOK		
04. ÜZLETI VAGY CÉGÉRTÉK		
05. SZELLEMI TERMÉKEK		
06. KISÉRLETI FEJLESZTÉS AKTIVÁLT ÉRTÉKE		
07. ALAPÍTÁS-ÁTSZERVEZÉS AKTIVÁLT ÉRTÉKE		
08. **II. TÁRGYI ESZKÖZÖK**	132,225	139,047
09. INGATLANOK	50,755	49,704
10. MŰSZAKI BERENDEZÉSEK, FELSZERELÉSEK, JÁRMŰVEK	74,423	88,848
11. EGYÉB BERENDEZÉSEK, FELSZERELÉSEK, JÁRMŰVEK	7,047	495
12. BERUHÁZÁSOK		
13. BERUHÁZÁSOKRA ADOTT ELŐLEG		
14. **III. BEFEKTETETT PÉNZÜGYI ESZKÖZÖK**		
15. RÉSZESEDÉSEK		
16. ÉRTÉKPAPÍROK		
17. ADOTT KÖLCSÖNÖK		
18. HOSSZÚ LEJÁRATÚ BANKBETÉTEK		
19. **B FORGÓESZKÖZÖK**	68,337	107,840
20. **I. KÉSZLETEK**	11,827	12,943
21. ANYAGOK	11,822	12,834
22. ÁRUK		
23. KÉSZLETEKRE ADOTT ELŐLEGEK	5	99
24. ÁLLATOK		
25. BEFEJEZETLEN TERMELÉS ÉS FÉLKÉSZ TERMÉKEK		
26. KÉSZTERMÉKEK		10
27. **II. KÖVETELÉSEK**	29,247	63,918
28. KÖVETELÉSEK ÁRUSZÁLLÍTÁSBÓL ÉS SZOLGÁLTATÁSBÓL	7,729	37,730
29. VÁLTÓKÖVETELÉSEK		
30. JEGYZETT, DE MÉG BE NEM FIZETETT TŐKE		
31. ALAPÍTÓKKAL SZEMBENI KÖVETELÉSEK		
32. EGYÉB KÖVETELÉSEK	21,518	26,188
33. **III. ÉRTÉKPAPÍROK**		
34. ELADÁSRA VÁSÁROLT KÖTVÉNYEK		
35. SAJÁT RÉSZVÉNYEK, ÜZLETRÉSZEK, ELADÁSRA VÁS. RÉSZV.		
36. EGYÉB ÉRTÉKPAPÍROK		
37. **IV. PÉNZESZKÖZÖK**	27,263	30,979
38. PÉNZTÁR, CSEKK	10	885
39. BANKBETÉTEK	27,253	30,094
40. **C. AKTÍV IDŐBELI ELHATÁROLÁSOK**	1,667	678
41. ESZKÖZÖK ÖSSZESEN:	202,229	247,565

Figure 1 (continued)

MÉRLEG/FORRÁSOK		1992.12.31. eFt	1993.12.31. eFt
42.	D. SAJÁT TŐKE	152,410	152,410
43.	I. JEGYZETT TŐKE	152,410	152,410
44.	II. TŐKETARTALÉK		
45.	III. EREDMÉNYTARTALÉK		
46.	IV. ELŐZŐ ÉVEK ÁTHOZOTT VESZTESÉGE		
47.	V. MÉRLEG SZERINTI EREDMÉNY		
48.	E. CÉLTARTALÉKOK		4,663
49.	1. CÉLTARTALÉK A VÁRHATÓ VESZTESÉGEKRE		4,363
50.	2. CÉLTARTALÉK A VÁRHATÓ KÖTELEZETTSÉGEKRE		300
51.	3. EGYÉB CÉLTARTALÉKOK		
52.	F. KÖTELEZETTSÉGEK	49,819	61,076
53.	I. HOSSZÚ LEJÁRATÚ KÖTELEZETTSÉGEK	27,092	
54.	BERUHÁZÁSI ÉS FEJLESZTÉSI HITELEK		
55.	EGYÉB HOSSZÚ LEJÁRATÚ HITELEK		
56.	HOSSZÚ LEJÁRATRA KAPOTT KÖLCSÖNÖK		
57.	TARTOZÁSOK KÖTVÉNYKIBOCSÁTÁSBÓL		
58.	ALAPÍTÓKKAL SZEMBENI KÖTELEZETTSÉGEK	27,092	
59.	EGYÉB HOSSZÚ LEJÁRATÚ KÖTELEZETTSÉGEK		
60.	II. RÖVID LEJÁRATÚ KÖTELEZETTSÉGEK	22,727	61,076
61.	VEVŐTŐL KAPOTT ELŐLEGEK		
62.	KÖTELEZETTSÉGEK ÁRUSZÁLLÍTÁSBÓL ÉS SZOLGÁLTATÁSBÓL	8,239	33,419
63.	VÁLTÓTARTOZÁSOK		
64.	RÖVID LEJÁRATÚ HITELEK		
65.	RÖVID LEJÁRATÚ KÖLCSÖNÖK		
66.	EGYÉB RÖVID LEJÁRATÚ KÖTELEZETTSÉGEK	14,488	27,657
67.	G. PASSZÍV IDŐBELI ELHATÁROLÁSOK		29,416
68.	FORRÁSOK ÖSSZESEN:	202,229	247,565

Figure 2

Hungaria KFT Balance Sheet
at 31 December 1993

	Assets	31 December, 1992 (THUF)	31 December, 1993 (THUF)
01	A. Invested Assets		
02	I. Intangible Assets		
03	Rights/Concessions		
04	Goodwill		
05	Intellectual Goods		
06	Capitalized Research and Development		
07	Capitalized Formation and Reorganization Expenses		
08	II. Tangible Assets	132,225	139,047
09	Land and Buildings	50,755	49,704
10	Plant and Machinery	74,423	88,848
11	Other fixtures, fittings tools and equipment	7,047	495
12	Tangible Assets under construction		
13	Advance Payments Towards Investments		
14	III. Financial Assets		
15	Participating Interest		
16	Long term investments in shares and securities		
17	Loans Granted		
18	Long term bank deposits		
19	B. Current Assets	68,337	107,840
20	I. Stocks (Inventories)	11,827	12,943
21	Raw materials	11,822	12,8322
22	Commodities		
23	Advance payments on stocks	5	99
24	Animals		
25	Work in progress		
26	Finished goods	0	10
27	II. Receivables	29,247	63,918
28	Accounts receivable	7,729	37,730
29	Bills of exchange		
30	Capital subscribed not yet paid		
31	Claims against founders		
32	Other receivables	21,518	26,188
33	III. Securities		
34	Bonds bought for resale		
35	Shares bought for resale		
36	Other securities		
37	IV. Monetary Assets	27,263	30,979
38	Cash, Cheques	10	885
39	Bank Deposits	27,253	30,094
40	C. Prepaid Expenses and Accrued Income	1,667	678
41	**TOTAL ASSETS**	**202,229**	**247,565**

Liabilities		31 December, 1992 (THUF)	31 December, 1993 (THUF)
42 D.	Owner's Equity	152,410	152,410
43 I.	Subscribed Capital	152,410	152,410
44 II.	Capital Reserves		
45 III.	Accumulated Retained Earnings		
46 IV.	Loss carried forward from previous years		
47 V.	Balance Sheet profit or Loss for the financial year		
48 E.	Specific Reserves	0	4,663
49	Reserves for expected losses	0	4,363
50	Reserves for expected obligations	0	300
51	Other Specific Reserves		
52 F.	Liabilities	49,819	61,076
53 I.	Long Term Liabilities	27,092	0
54	Investments and Developments credits		
55	Other long term credits		
56	Long Term loans		
57	Bonds Payable		
58	Obligations to founders	27,092	0
59	Other long term liabilities		
60 II.	Short Term Liabilities	22,727	61,076
61	Advance payments form customers		
62	Accounts payable	8,239	33,419
63	Bills of exchange		
64	Short Term Credits		
65	Short Term Liabilities		
66	Other Short Term Liabilities	14,488	27,657
67 G.	Accruals and Deffered income	0	29,416
68	**TOTAL LIABILITIES**	**202,229**	**247,565**

Figure 3

EREDMÉNYKIMUTATÁS	1992 eFt	1993 eFt
01. BELFÖLDI ÉRTÉKESÍTÉS NETTÓ ÁRBEVÉTELE	208,123	456,495
02. EXPORT ÉRTÉKESÍTÉS NETTÓ ÁRBEVÉTELE		1,508
I. ÉRTÉKESÍTÉS NETTÓ ÁRBEVÉTELE	208,123	458,003
II. EGYÉB BEVÉTELEK	157	5,438
03. SAJÁT ELŐÁLLÍTÁSÚ ESZKÖZÖK AKTIVÁLT ÉRTÉKE		
04. SAJÁT TERMELÉSŰ KÉSZLETEK ÁLLOMÁNYVÁLTOZÁSA		
III. AKTÍVÁLT SAJÁT TELJESÍTMÉNYEK ÉRTÉKE		
05. ANYAGKÖLTSÉG	141,332	354,770
06. IGÉNYBE VETT ANYAGJELLEGŰ SZOLGÁLTATÁSOK ÉRTÉKE	630	3,616
07. ELADOTT ÁRUK BESZERZÉSI ÉRTÉKE		
08. ALVÁLLALKOZÓI TELJESÍTMÉNYEK ÉRTÉKE		
IV. ANYAGJELLEGŰ RÁFORDÍTÁSOK	141,962	358,386
09. BÉRKÖLTSÉG	3,316	7,474
10. SZEMÉLYI JELLEGŰ EGYÉB KIFIZETÉSEK	1,203	2,209
11. TÁRSADALOMBIZTOSÍTÁSI JÁRULÉK	1,402	3,147
V. SZEMÉLYI JELLEGŰ RÁFORDÍTÁSOK	5,921	12,830
VI. ÉRTÉKCSÖKKENÉSI LEÍRÁS	8,046	15,833
VII. EGYÉB KÖLTSÉGEK	4,963	18,004
VIII. EGYÉB RÁFORDÍTÁSOK	257	8,029
A. ÜZEMI (ÜZLETI) TEVÉKENYSÉG EREDMÉNYE	47,131	50,359
12. KAPOTT KAMATOK ÉS KAMATJELLEGŰ BEVÉTELEK	3,315	6,179
13. KAPOTT OSZTALÉK ÉS RÉSZESEDÉS		
14. PÉNZÜGYI MŰVELETEK EGYÉB BEVÉTELEI		
IX. PÉNZÜGYI MŰVELETEK BEVÉTELEI	3,315	6,179
15. FIZETETT KAMATOK ÉS KAMATJELLEGŰ BEVÉTELEK	8	1,660
16. PÉNZÜGYI BEFEKTETÉSEK LEÍRÁSA		
17. PÉNZÜGYI MŰVELETEK EGYÉB RÁFORDÍTÁSAI		
X. PÉNZÜGYI MŰVELETEK RÁFORDÍTÁSAI	8	1,660
B. PÉNZÜGYI MŰVELETEK EREDMÉNYE	3,307	4,519
C. SZOKÁSOS VÁLLALKOZÓI EREDMÉNY	50,438	54,878
XI. RENDKÍVÜLI BEVÉTELEK	86	285
XII. RENDKÍVÜLI RÁFORDÍTÁSOK		106
D. RENDKÍVÜLI EREDMÉNY	86	179
E. ADÓZÁS ELŐTTI EREDMÉNY	50,524	55,057
XIII. ADÓFIZETÉSI KÖTELEZETTSÉG		
F. ADÓZOTT EREDMÉNY	50,524	55,057
18. EREDMÉNYTART. IGÉNYBEVÉTELE OSZT-RA, RÉSZES-RE		
19. FIZETETT (JÓVÁHAGYOTT) OSZTALÉK ÉS RÉSZESEDÉS	50,524	55,057
G. MÉRLEG SZERINTI EREDMÉNY	0	0

Figure 4

Hungaria Kft.
Profit and Loss Account, Version "A"
For the year ended 31 December 1993

Profit and Loss Account	1992	1993
01 Net domestic sales revenues	208,123	456,495
02 Net export sales revenues	0	1,508
I Net sales revenues (01 + 02)	208,123	458,003
II Other revenue	157	5,438
03 Capitalized value of self-manufactured assets		
04 Changes in stock of self-manufactured assets		
III Capitalized value of own performance (03 + 04)		
05 Materials costs	141,332	354,770
06 Value of material-type services used	630	3,616
07 Purchase value cost of goods sold		
08 Value of subcontractors' performance		
IV Material-type expenditures (05 + 06 + 07 + 08)	141,962	358,386
09 Labor costs	3,316	7,474
10 Other payments to personnel	1,203	2,209
11 Social security contributions	1,402	3,147
V Labor related costs (09 + 10 + 11)	5,921	12,830
VI Depreciation allowance	8,046	15,833
VII Other costs	4,963	18,004
VIII Other expenses	257	8,029
A Profit or loss from business activity (I+II+III+IV+V+VI+VII+VIII)		
12 Interest received and	3,315	6,179
13 Dividend and participation received		
14 Other revenue from financial transactions		
IX Revenue from financial transactions (12+13+14)	3,315	6,179
15 Paid interest and interest-	8	1,660
16 Write-off of financial transactions		
17 Other expenditure on financial transactions		
X Expenditure on financial transactions (15+16+17)	8	1,660
B Profit or loss from financial transactions (IX-X)	3,307	4,519
C Regular business profit or loss (+-A+-B)	50,438	54,878
XI Extraordinary revenue	86	285
XII Extraordinary expenditure	0	106
D Extraordinary profit or loss (XI-XII)	86	179
E Profit or loss before tax (+-C+-D)	50,524	55,057
XIII Tax payment liability		
F After tax profit or loss (+-E-XIII)		
18 Use of accumulated retained earnings for dividends or participation		
19 Dividend and participation announced	50,524	55,057
G Balance sheet profit or loss for the financial year (+-F+18-19)	0	0

NOTES TO THE BALANCE SHEET

Tangible fixed assets

Buildings and equipment are recorded at cost less accumulated depreciation. Depreciation is calculated on a monthly basis using the straight line method at rates based on the expected useful lives of the respective assets, an in accordance with the rates laid down in the Act LXXXVI of 1991 on Company Tax, appendix 2. These rates are shown below:

Category of asset	Depreciation rates of assets purchased prior to 1992	Depreciation rates purchased in 1992
Machinery and equipment	12%	14,5%
Real estate	3%	3%

The assets used in conjunction with the blowing machine are depreciated over 3 years, which is the estimated useful life of the machine as prescribed in the law.

Tangible assets purchased for under 20 THUF are expensed to the profit and loss in full and registered in Class 0 in the Chart of Accounts.

The general ledger is supported by a manual fixed asset register showing cost, accumulated depreciation, net book value, and depreciation charged in the period for each asset. The register is generated from the same source documentation as the general ledger.

The company performs a physical count of tangible assets and ensures that the value is accurate every two years. In the intervening time the value and quantity of the assets are based on the amounts recorded in the manual fixed asset register.

The cost of "contributions in kind" are detailed in the listings and the joint venture agreement.

The additions to fixed assets for the year ended 1993 are detailed below:

Asset category	THUF
Real estate	556
Machinery and equipment	21,746
Vehicles	353
	22,655

Included within the machinery and equipment category are capitalized costs of 15,123 THUF relating to the lease of the B-40 bottle blowing machine.

Tangible fixed assets in 1993

Cost	Real estate equipment, machinery and fittings (THUF)	Technical equipment and vehicles (THUF)	Other (THUF)	Total Cost (THUF)
1 January 93	51,821	81,976	200	133,997
Additions	556	21,746	353	22,655
Small value assets	0	10,000	0	10,000
31 December, 93	52,377	113,722	553	166,652
Accumulated Depreciation				
1 January 93	1,066	10,706	0	11,772
Charge for the year	1,607	14,168	58	15,833
31 December	2,673	24,874	58	27,605
Net book value				
31 December 93	49,704	88,848	495	139,047

The small value assets were transferred from inventory at 1 January 1993 in accordance with the law XVIII on accounting.

Inventories

Inventories are valued at the lower of cost, determined on a "first in first out" basis, and net realisable value.

Raw material purchases were made from foreign companies. Inventory at the 31 December 1993 was valued using the exchange rate in effect on the invoice date.

In compliance with Hungarian legislation, custom duties of 2,395 THUF have been included within the valuation of closing stock.

The detailed stock listing reconciles to the stock accounts in the general ledger.

The company holds copies of:

— the purchase invoice;

— delivery notes which details the number of bottles delivered; and

— minutes indicating unusual stock movements

All stock items were expensed on the date of purchase. The company maintained minimum stock levels to meet production requirements.

Movements in stock are vouched to delivery notes and sales invoices.

A physical stock count is done on a monthly basis because of the high turnover of stock.

The stocktake was completed as at 31 December 1993. The finished goods stock levels maintained are low as Hungaria manufactures bottles to sales orders.

The 1992 stock value has been adjusted as shown in the table below to reflect the new Hungarian accounting law effective from 1 January 1992.

Stock	1 January 1993	31 December 1993
Stock after rearrangement	11,827	12,943

The adjustment reflects small value assets which were classified in stock in 1992 being transferred to tangible fixed assets. The cost of assets transferred was 10,000 THUF.

Receivables, liquid assets, and prepaid expenses

The receivables from sales can be found in the debtors ledger account. Receivables due from the joint venture owners have been classified under other debtors in accordance with the Hungarian accounting law.

Included in the Balance Sheet line for trade debtors are outstanding balances from joint venture owners, holding a combined shareholding of 4.4%. This amounted to 37,730 THUF.

Hungarian Accounting law requires intercompany balances to be shown in other short term receivables. The year end balance of company B, which has a shareholding of 56% in company Hungaria Kft., has been classified here.

As well as debtors ledger a separate ledger is kept for all sales, for VAT recording purposes.

Included in other receivables are amounts owed from employees.

Hungaria Kft. has two bank accounts with OKHB Rt, a settlement account and a foreign exchange transaction account.

Equity and liabilities

Equity

The issued share capital of Hungaria Kft. is 152,410 of which 39.6% is held by a foreign investor.

Liabilities

Separate general ledger accounts are maintained for foreign and domestic creditors.

The company accounted for customs duty payables, local government taxes, and payroll creditors on a timely basis. Payments were made on their due dates.

No corporate income taxes have been provided for in the financial statements of Hungaria Kft. as the result of a legislated tax holiday applicable to companies which operate in certain "Activities of Special Importance" and which meet minimum capital and foreign ownership thresholds. As a result the company is free from the obligation to pay corporation tax and technical development fund tax ("Profit Tax Law" 12 paragraph (4), and Law from the Technical Development Fund 8 paragraph (3)b).

At 31 October 1993 the company circularized its creditors and reconciled the replies to the company's accounting records.

Included in other short-term liabilities is a liability due to company B of 945 THUF. Intercompany balances should be disclosed in this category under Hungarian Accounting Law.

A provision of 4,363 THUF for doubtful debtors was made in the financial statements of Hungaria. This is in compliance with Hungarian Accounting Law XVIII.

Liquidity position analysis

1. Current assets in proportion of short term liabilities:

31 Dec.1992	31 Dec.1993
3:1	1.76:1

2. Short-term liabilities in proportion of equity:

31 Dec,1992	31 Dec,1993
11.24%	24.67%

Information regarding the Profit and Loss Account

Version "A" of the profit and loss account was used by Hungaria Kft.

Subsequent event

At the shareholders' General Meeting on 9 March 1994 board members fees of 150 THUF and management bonuses of 123 THUF were approved. An additional social security and unemployment insurance liability resulted from the bonus approval of 60 THUF. The resulting profit after tax figure of 55,057 THUF was distributed as a dividend.

Types of cost

Costs were accounted for and grouped in accordance with version "A." Costs were matched to revenues earned in the correct accounting period in accordance with the accruals concept.

Direct costs include the customs and transportation fees.

Costs that have been separately identified include:

— cost of energy
— consumables for materials
— other materials
— depreciation of assets with a value under 20 THUF

Other and extraordinary expenses

Extraordinary revenues and expenses have been recorded in Class 8 and 9. This is in compliance with the Hungarian accounting law. The extraordinary income and costs relate to claims and penalties received from and paid to insurance companies.

Sales and other revenues

The majority of net sales for the year ended 31 December are domestic sales. Sales to foreign companies have not been significant in 1993.

Monthly reconciliations are performed between the total sales value and the number of unit sold. The VAT payable on these sales is also reconciled on a monthly basis.

Other revenues:	(THUF)
Exchange rate gain	5,171
Other	267
Total	5,438

Other costs:	(HUF)
Stationary	86,629
Newspapers and publications	56,558
Postage	159,770
Other supplies	5,685,900
Costs of public utilities	1,283,318
Statistical dues	10,275,350
Insurance fees	456,475
Total	18,004,000

Other expenses:	(THUF)
Education fund tax	110
Local tax	1,394
Unemployment contributions	320
Provisions	4,663
Loss from exchange rate differences	1,507
Interest on late payments	35
Total	8,029

Analysis of profit

	1992 (THUF)	1993 (THUF)	Difference (THUF)
Trading profit	47,131	50,359	3,228
Profit on financial transactions	3,307 .	4,519	1,212
Profit on ordinary activities	50,438	54,878	4,440
Extraordinary profit	86	179	93
Profit after taxation	50,524	55,057	4,533
Retained profit of the year	0	0	0

Analysis of revenues

	1992 (THUF)	1993 (THUF)	1993/1992 (%) (THUF)
Net domestic sales	208,123	456,495	219
Net external sales	0	1,508	100
Other revenues	157	5,438	3,464
Total	208,280	463,441	

Analysis of costs and expenses

Costs and expenses	1992 (THUF)	1993 (THUF)	1993/1992 (%) (THUF)
Cost of raw materials	141,332	354,770	251
Material-type cost	630	3,616	574
Wages and salaries	3,316	7,474	225
Other staff emoluments	1,203	2,209	184
Social insurance contribution	1,402	3,147	224
Depreciation	8,046	15,833	197
Other costs	4,963	18,004	363
Other expenses	257	8,029	3,124

Wages and salaries

The average number of people employed by Hungaropet Kft. for the year ended 1993 was 11. These employees were grouped as follows:

	(THUF)
1 staff managing director	
1 staff commercial manager	
1 staff administrator	
1 staff part-time worker chief account	
7 staff manual workers	
Distribution of wages and salaries	
Manual workers	5,759
Intellectual workers	1,715
Total	7,474

Figure 5
Income Statement Format
(Cost of Sales Model)

Version B

01   Net domestic sales revenue
02   Net export sales revenue
   I   Net sales revenues (01 + 02)
   II   Other revenues
03   Direct prime costs of sale
04   Purchase value of goods sold, value of subcontractor's performance
   III Direct costs of sale (03 + 04)
05   Sales costs
06   Administration costs
07   Other general overheads
   IV   Indirect costs of sale (05 + 06 + 07)
   V   Other expenses and expenditures
   A/ Profit or loss from business activities
   (I + II – III – IV – V)

The remainder of the format corresponds to lines 12–19, IX–XIII and B–G of Version A.

Figure 6
Simplified Balance Sheet

Assets

A. Investments
   I.   Intangible goods
   II.   Tangible assets
   III. Financial investments
B. Current assets
   I.   Inventories
   II.   Receivables
        Less: general turnover tax charged on receivables
   III. Securities
   IV. Cash

Liabilities

C. Equity
   I.   Subscribed capital
   II.   Capital reserves
   III. Reserve
D. Specific reserves
E. Liabilities
   I.   Long-term liabilities
   II.   Short-term liabilities
        Less: deductible general turnover tax on liabilities

Figure 7
*Additional Information Required for
the Consolidated Balance Sheet*

Reference is made to classifications shown in Figure 2.
The following additional details shall be given:

A/III/1. Participation
A/III/2. Shares in other companies as long term investment
A/III/3. The lines of loans given to

— company with majority holding
— company with a significant holding
— other companies

A/III/4. Long term bank deposits
B/II/5. Other receivables due from

— company having a majority holding
— company having a significant holding
— other companies

B/III/1. Bonds bought for resale
B/III/2. Own shares, participations
B/III/3. Other securities held in

— company having a majority holding
— company having a significant holding
— other companies

B/III/2. Own shares and other shares, purchased for resale, from

— company having a majority holding
— company having a significant holding
— other companies

D/I/1. Issued capital

— issued by companies involved in consolidation
— issued by jointly managed enterprises
— issued by associated enterprises
— repurchased own shares, business shares

F/I/6. Other long-term liabilities

— companies involved in consolidation
— jointly managed enterprises
— associated enterprises
— other entrepreneurs

F/II/6. Other short-term liabilities

— companies involved in consolidation
— jointly managed enterprises
— associated enterprises
— other entrepreneurs

Figure 8

*Additional Information for
the Consolidated Income Statement*

Reference is made to the classifications shown in Figure 4.
The following details shall be given:

01 Net domestic sales revenue

02 Net export sales revenue

II. Other revenue from

12 Interest received and interest-related revenues

13 Dividend and profit-sharing received

15 Paid interest and interest-related payments

19 Dividend and profit-sharing paid (approved)

The above-listed items shall be detailed in a breakdown by

— companies involved in consolidation
— jointly managed enterprises
— associated enterprises
— other entrepreneurs

POLAND

Alicja Jaruga
Lodz University, Lodz, Poland

1. Background

Accounting in Poland dates back to the fifteenth century. The earliest merchant books preserved cover the period 1421–1454 and belonged to Jan Pis of Gdansk. The first bookkeeping manuals were published in 1530. To this period also belong the oldest preserved inventories and books of large landed estates; the first manuals of economy and accountancy date from 1558.

Elements of state accounting appeared as a result of the separation of the Royal Treasury from the Court Treasury in the fifteenth century. Parliament approved this separation and constituted the Treasury Tribunal in 1591. In the middle of the seventeenth century, the Army Treasury was established, with special consideration given to the so-called hibernation, that is, winter quarters. The first Polish budget was passed by Parliament in 1768, and the Constitution of 1792 established a right for Parliament to approve public revenue and expenditures. The Constitution of Poland (the first to be written after the American Constitution) and Polish budgeting principles served as a model for many European countries.

Similarly to other countries of both Central and Western Europe, Poland was influenced by the accounting principles of northern Italy. In the Royal Salt Mine in Wieliczka, the economic records were kept by two generations of an Italian family.

In the nineteenth century Poland was partitioned by three powers: Russia, Prussia, and Austria; thus, legislation of those countries naturally had some effect on accounting codification in Poland. The greatest effect, though, was the Napoleonic Code proclaimed in 1807 and in force from 1808, which applied in the Duchy of Warsaw and later in the Kingdom of Poland. The code was still in operation in the independent Second Republic of Poland, until 1934, when the Polish Commercial Code was proclaimed. A considerable role was also played by an institutionalized market of securities established in the Kingdom of Poland in 1817 (Decree of the

1465

King's Governor-General on Establishment of Commercial Exchange and Exchange Brokers in Warsaw). Books were initially verified by the magistrate of the Commercial Tribunal.

In the remaining areas of Poland, the market and trade laws of the Russian Empire (volumes X and XI of the collection of laws) were in force, and also the Commercial Code, or *Reichsgesetz*, of the German Empire, which was also effective in the Austro-Hungarian Empire. In 1899 the Shares Regulation was issued, which among other things authorized industrial and commercial chambers to prepare lists of auditors who could audit statutes and reports of joint-stock companies.

Apart from commercial codes, the source of accounting regulation was of a fiscal character, and taxation increasingly influenced the shape of accountancy. This was clearly apparent by the twentieth century, when income tax rates were increased considerably. Thus appeared the "natural conflict of interests" of enterprises and fiscal authorities.

In public accountancy, attention should be paid to the impact of commercialization and, after the enfranchisement of peasants, the commercialization of agriculture, and also the demands made by credit companies, which contributed to the regulation of accounting principles.

In the period of the Second Republic, accounting for companies was regulated by the Commercial Code (1934) and by fiscal legislation, as well as by the jurisdiction of professional accountants. Tax requirements took priority. In practice, this meant there was an obligation to prepare so-called trade or commercial accounts and tax accounts. (The tax accounts were a restatement of the trade or commercial accounts). The influence of the stock exchange was marginal, because the capital market was only beginning to develop in a country that had been reintegrated from the three partitioned parts. Registered companies had to publish their financial reports, however, which were subject to auditing. A well-paid accounting and auditing profession developed. In 1907 the Association of Accountants was established, but the influence of the professional body upon accounting regulations was slight.

In the interwar period, legal norms concerning accounting were the consequence not only of the commercial code and fiscal law, but also of the penal, civil, and bankruptcy laws. A registered merchant was obliged to present a financial statement in court at the end of the financial year. Establishment reports of companies were inspected by auditors.

Reports of joint stock companies were also verified by auditors and presented to a registered court and the Ministry of Industry and Trade. Annual financial statements were published in journals. Annual statements could be revised at the request of a partner by auditors appointed by a commercial court (court of experts).

In the period of German occupation during the Second World War, also called the Fourth Partitioning of Poland, a uniform German chart of accounts was introduced. This was to have a significant influence on accountancy in Poland in the immediate postwar period, before the period of the command, centrally planned economy, with the dominance of state ownership.

On the basis of the German model, the first uniform accounting plan was introduced in 1946. Because of the adoption of Soviet financing and economic planning systems in 1951–1953, however, the Soviet accounting plan was introduced. Successive reforms of this plan were carried out in 1959, 1974, and 1985. The accounting plan reform of 1974 was partly influenced by the French experience, adapted to the circumstances of a centrally planned economy. During the same period, by order of the Minister of Finance, principles of accountancy were promulgated (in 1945, 1954, 1967, 1972, and 1983).

The main characteristic of the changes in legal sources of accounting in this period was the introduction of the uniform measures of the financial law, with a wide range of influence, in place of general principles derived from the commercial code or from tax legislation. The financial law implicitly covered the scope of financial accounting to a considerable extent, reducing accountancy to the role of economic record keeping. Generally speaking, we can distinguish the accountancy of enterprises (state and cooperative), from that of state budgetary entities. The former is based on the financial law, whereas the latter is based on the budgetary law.

The Central Statistical office exerted considerable influence on financial reporting. The professional body of State Authorized Accountants (SAA) had been in existence since 1956, its main objective being to determine whether public enterprises had fully and in due time accounted for their activities with the fiscal authorities. Financial reports were not published: the emphasis was on the legal form.

At the end of the 1980s, the rapid transition to a market economy, commercialization, corporatization and privatization of state enterprises, as well as the establishment of joint ventures with foreign capital, created a need for the restructuring of accountancy and financial reporting. Free market pricing has been reintroduced, state subsidies for enterprises have been eliminated or severely restricted, and domestic convertible currency and varying rates of exchange have been introduced. Inflation has been substantially reduced. The share of the private sector in the economy is increasing. Commercial banks have been being set up.

Poland now faces a return to legal, democratic, and institutional forms after some 50 years. This must be achieved in the context of the globalization and internationalization of financial markets, the development of financial instruments, and the formation of transnational economic communities. Also relevant are the EC legal provisions embracing accountancy (the Fourth, Seventh, and Eighth Directives), as well as the harmonization processes incorporated in International Accounting Standards.

This was the background to the first phase of accountancy restructuring carried out by the Accounting Department of the Ministry of Finance. An order of the Minister of Finance on accounting principles came into force on January 1, 1991. Apart from this order, the Commercial Code of 1934 is still operating, with slight amendments. The whole system is based on laws relating to:

- Financial regulation of state-owned enterprises
- Economic activity with the participation of foreign entities
- Cooperatives
- Fiscal obligations
- Budgetary law
- Security and exchange

There are separate regulations for accounting in banking and insurance institutions, as well as for such enterprises as charities.

Existing accounting requirements are determined mainly by statutory bodies, but the draft of the order was opened for discussion and evaluation by the Accountants Association in Poland, as well as by academics.

As of 1991, neither a National Council of Accounting, on the French model, nor any self-regulatory bodies after the U.K. fashion, have been appointed. The auditing profession is now in the process of being thoroughly remodeled in compliance with the Eighth EC Directive. On October 19, 1991 the Act on Auditing and Publication of Financial Statements and on Chartered Auditors and their Self-government was promulgated. The act regulates legal questions and constitutes a National Chamber of Chartered Auditors. The bodies of the Chamber are as follows:

- National Congress
- National Council of Chartered Auditors
- National Auditing Committee
- National Disciplinary Attorney

The act introduces compulsory annual auditing of the financial reports of the majority of business and governmental entities, conforming with EC Directives. The purpose of auditing is to prepare a written statement confirming the true (*praiwdnowe*) and fair (*rzetelne*) preparation of financial statements (reports). Chartered auditors (*biegli rewidenci*) can operate as sole practitioners and/or chartered auditing firms. The National Council has already registered more than 8,000 chartered auditors and more than 241 accounting firms, including the Big Six. The former State Authorized Accountants have been given an opportunity to be registered as chartered auditors if they prove practical experience and appropriate training. New qualification requirements are expected before the end of 1994 from the State Examination Committee, appointed by the Minister of Finance and nominated by the National Council of Chartered Auditors.

Newly established auditing rules were implemented for the first time in 1993. The first three tentative auditing standards were published by the National Council, alongside the IFAC ones, as a basic source for this undertaking.

The financial reports of listed companies must be published within two weeks after approval by the annual meeting of shareholders. Financial statements of state-owned enterprises, cooperatives, and companies are presented after auditing to the Treasury Chamber (Internal Revenue Office) and central statistical office.

There are two formats of the income statement, the first, containing cost by nature (items), intended mainly for small enterprises. Small firms are also allowed to present summarized balance sheets.

As far as government grants are concerned, there are three kinds, which take the following accounting treatments:

1. Subsidies for certain articles with prices fixed centrally at a low level, which are treated as revenues

2. Subsidies for economic entities to equalize the so-called planned deficit of specific state or communal enterprises, which are treated as revenues

3. Subsidies for financing certain investments (construction), treated as business capital (registered capital)

2. The Form and Content of Published Financial Statements

The new form of published financial statements in Poland is quite similar to that presented in the Fourth EC Directive. The main statements are summarized on pages 1478–1483.

The historical cost principle is common practice in Poland, with the exception of instances of controlled revaluation.

2.1 Balance Sheet

2.1.1 Capital and Reserves

Capital is usually divided into share capital and reserve capital. The company statute determines the proportions of the two. Share premium account (over nominal values) revaluation reserves, and long-term reserves are all disclosed separately. Unpaid shares are disclosed as receivables (an asset). The last section is profit or loss brought forward.

2.1.2 Liabilities and Provisions

Long-term bank loans and amounts owed to credit institutions are distinguished from short-term and overdue ones. Creditors payable consist of trade creditors, tax and other budgetary creditors, wages payable, amounts owed to affiliated undertakings, and other creditors. Special funds are created according to national law provisions. Deferred income is permitted to increase, respectively, revenues or extraordinary profits in the accounting period concerned. Expenses can be accrued for up to 3 years.

Provisions, reserves, and other liabilities consist of provisions for bad debts, mainly arising from insolvency. These provisions should be written off after one year. Reserves for contingent losses are written off similarly.

Profit or loss for the financial year must be equal to the net financial result shown in the income statement.

2.2 Fixed Assets

Fixed assets are measured at historical cost. Depreciation rates are determined by law. Accelerated depreciation has been allowed since 1992; however, the straight line method is the norm. Equipment is depreciated over up to 5 years.

Goodwill is recognized as an asset and amortized over up to 5 years. Only positive goodwill is recognized under the Ministry of Finance order. Development costs are recognized as expenses and can be deferred for up to 5 years, if they meet specified criteria.

The costs of property rights, for example, are recognized as intangible assets valued at historical cost.

2.2.1 Financial Assets

Shares in affiliated undertakings and participating interests are valued at their acquisition price or at an actual realizable value if lower at the end of a financial year. Revaluation differences should be transferred to financial expenses.

When the nominal value of bonds is lower than the issue price, a premium is recognized immediately as financial revenue. Discount is recognized as an immediate expense.

2.3 Current Assets

Materials are valued at their acquisition prices, unless at the end of the year the net selling price is lower. The resulting difference is transferred to the profit and loss account.

Finished goods are valued at manufacturing cost or at net market value if lower. FIFO, LIFO, or weighted average cost methods can be used to assign costs to inventories. Inventories of work in progress are measured on the basis of the percentage of completion method. The definition of overheads regarded as included in manufacturing costs is traditionally stricter than in general international practice.

Monetary assets in foreign currency are valued at nominal value and rates of exchange given by the National Bank of Poland and, at the end of the financial year, at the average rate given by the same bank. Exchange differences on foreign monetary operations are recognized in financial results.

Deferred taxes are not recognized. Income tax and VAT are the two main types of taxation. Personal income tax was reintroduced in 1992.

Pensions and social security arrangements differ greatly from those in Western Europe. The combined rate based on payroll is 35% in 1993 and is totally transferred to the State Social Security Institution.

3. Accounting Reforms: 1991, 1992

Fundamental transformations in the Polish economic structure, occurring in Poland as a consequence of political and social changes, have created the need for a far-reaching restructuring of the Polish accounting system. On the one hand, the process of transition to a market economy is taking place. The main elements of this are the creation of a capital market, decentralization, privatization, the introduction of competition, tax reform, and the reduction of subsidies. On the other hand, Poland has opened up to the world, particularly to the European Community. Contacts are being established with many international organizations, especially the World Bank and the International Monetary Fund. More and more foreign partners are entering into joint ventures, and an increasing number of enterprises are taking advantage of foreign bank loans.

In this situation, the previous accounting regulations in Poland, appropriate for a centrally planned economy, have had to be changed. The main stress is shifting to the final product of the accounting system, that is, financial statements: their legibility, clarity, and comparability for all users—not only the government or fiscal authorities, but also capital providers, potential and actual creditors, borrowers and suppliers, employees, and company management that is responsible for the effective utilization of resources. Changes in business management can be efficient only if based on current economic information, which is supplied chiefly by the accounting system. There is thus a need for restructuring the financial accounting system to form the basis for preparing information necessary for decision making and its evaluation, and second, producing the information essential for decision making, which means focusing on the role and place of the managerial accounting system at the level of the economic entity. This means that accounting should have been defined much more comprehensively than was the case in the centrally planned economy and that the objectives of accountancy, as well as the main users of financial statements, are different.

These changes in Polish accountancy, and the new approach to the accounting system, are reflected in the new accounting law embodied in the Order of the Minister of Finance, in force since January 1, 1991 (with further amendments) for all economic entities, irrespective of their legal form and size.

The complex system of accounting in Poland used to be complicated by the fact that accountancy chiefly served the needs of tax laws, which resulted in financial statements being adjusted solely to suit fiscal requirements and not prepared to facilitate the evaluation of the capital, economic, and financial position of a firm or to serve the needs of business. The new accounting law is an attempt to approximate international practice and to eliminate differences. There are three different patterns of financial statements. One pattern is for companies and state-owned businesses, a second one for organizations financed directly from the state budget, and a third for banks.

Market economies have adopted basic accounting concepts as a framework and a reference point for preparing accounting regulations and for an intellectual appraisal of accounting language. Accounting reflects economic realities through these concepts, basing upon them principles, standards, and rules that have a supranational dimension, for they are the achievement of the accounting science throughout the world, as shown in international accounting regulations and in the form of EC Directives. Sometimes it is considered optimal to secure the comparability of financial statements within the EC, so an accounting harmonization has been carried out to the level allowing mutual understanding of economic principles and leaving enough freedom for specific solutions in the ever-changing economic and social context. Having taken this fact into consideration, the authors of the new accounting regulation in Poland decided to base their solutions on the EC Directives (particularly the Fourth Directive of July 25, 1978 about accounting in companies), while considering also the IASC's treatment.

In the order of the Minister of Finance on Accounting Principles (further called the Order), a majority of the resolutions included in the Fourth Directive have been taken into account. The degree of compliance with specific articles varies, but it comes within the range of possible solutions allowed by the directive to be incorporated into the national law of member countries. At the time of writing, the Seventh Directive had not been taken account of.

All principal accounting rules included in the Fourth Directive (Article 31) have been incorporated in Order 4 (paragraph 3). That does not mean that they were not present in former arrangements, only that they were not articulated. Fundamental accounting concepts in the form of the accruals basis, consistency, going concern, prudence concepts, and others, being the basis for creating accounting systems in enterprises, are becoming compatible with generally accepted accounting principles applied throughout the world, where the "true and fair view" is a basic principle of the credibility and reliability of accounting information.

The discussion of the new accounting law that follows will be limited to pointing out new elements that were not present in earlier solutions or that appeared in a different form. The order does not regulate all issues related to economic entity accounting. It comprises the above-mentioned general accounting principles, bookkeeping (both traditional and computerized, ledgers, books), stocktaking procedures, asset and liability valuation methods, and principles disclosing financial statements, including the pattern of a balance sheet measuring the financial result, as well as methods of preparing an income statement. A number of other issues such as depreciation of fixed, intangible, and legal assets are embraced by separate rules, whereas others, for example, assets valuation under conditions of inflation, accounting for leases, and accounting for capital investments, have been regulated separately.

The basis of bookkeeping in economic entities is to be their own plan of accounts, approved by their own directors. This leaves a considerable degree of freedom to enterprises in creating their own system of accounting. A proper plan of account should include the definition of principles that depend only on the firm's management. Bookkeeping may be entrusted to specialized units rendering such services. Certain economic units, by permission of the Minister of Finance, may carry on accounting according to principles different from those provided under Polish law. This means, for instance, that joint ventures may base their accountancy treatment on Western solutions. The accepted accounting should in consequence give a numerical basis for preparing the required financial statements, that is, the balance sheet and the income statement, in such a way as to give a "true and fair view" of a firm's activities, financial position, and changes to all parties concerned, that is, to the fiscal authorities and preparers of national statistics, as well as other financial statement users. The models of balance sheet and income statement (two formats) included here conform in their contents with the formats prescribed by the Fourth EC Directive. The form of balance sheet is similar to that prescribed by paragraph 10 of the Fourth Directive, and the income statement to the one included in paragraphs 24 and 26 of the Fourth Directive. Small firms may prepare simplified statements, which obviously affords the opportunity of simplified bookkeeping.

In 1991 the Securities Commission was established under the Security and Mutual Funds Act. The responsibilities of the commission are as follows:

1. Inspecting the observance of rules of fair trade and competition in the field of public trading in securities
2. Inspiring, organizing, and undertaking measures to ensure the smooth operation of the securities market
3. Cooperating with state administrative bodies, the National Bank of Poland, securities-market institutions, and participants in public trading in securities in designing economic policy of the state that will promote the development of the securities market
4. Disseminating knowledge of the principles governing the operation of the securities market
5. Undertaking other measures provided for by the law

The Securities Commission is likely to have a significant effect on the quality and content of financial statements of publicly quoted companies.

The approach of the Commission has been heavily influenced by the Fourth EC Directive and the U.S. Securities and Exchange Commission requirements. An independent audit in the generally accepted international manner is essential for all quoted companies.

Taking into account continuing changes in the Polish economy, such as the transformation of public enterprises into commercial partnerships and the development of a securities market, present accounting regulations in Poland are appropriate only for the first period of adapting the economy to market mechanisms and institutions. Gradual transition is also necessary for changing the accounting philosophy and the concepts underlying accounting standards and their harmonization at the international level. Great efforts are required to change the mentality of accountants, to adapt to thinking in free-market terms and increase their knowledge of world solutions.

New accounting programs have been adopted in universities, vocational schools, and professional training institutions.

Democratization, commercialization, and privatization during the transition to a free market economy impose enormous pressures on accounting development and training. The centuries of national tradition and experience provide a strong basis for successfully meeting the challenge of European harmonization.

4. Expected Future Developments

As has already been mentioned, the 1991 Order on Accounting was promulgated by the Minister of Finance. Every change in the Budgetary Act, Acts on Taxes, and others have had an immediate impact on this order. Besides, the Commercial Code (of 1934, with further amendments) is still binding for companies (listed, with limited liability, and others) in cases not regulated by the order. All this, along with acquired experience and knowledge, combined to create a need for developing the Accounting Law. Its first draft is currently being discussed widely, and it is scheduled to take effect on January 1, 1995.

The proposed changes refer to:

1. Definition of the entity: it will be limited to economic subjects only. The same holds in the case of state-owned enterprises, which still generate about half of GNP and account for around 40% of total employment.

2. The scope of matters to be regulated by the new law. It should cover the following issues:

   —Accounting and bookkeeping system, its principles and methodology, because there is not as yet a body authorized to set professional standards

   —Consolidation in accordance with the Seventh EC Directive

   —Extensive description of current accounting policy

   —Special issues, such as accounting for restructuring, improvement, or liquidation of an enterprise. It is a vital question because of the frequent occurrence of such processes in the period of transition.

3. Observance of the rule that financial reports should reflect "economic substance," which results in assets and liabilities valuation, adoption of principles for depreciation, and making provisions in conformity with EC Directives and the IASC, even if tax requirements provide otherwise.

4. Laying down the rules for the audit and publication of financial statements and reports.

It is important to be aware of the great weight of the new law, which is to replace corresponding parts of the Commercial Code. GAAP are being elaborated simultaneously. There are no plans to introduce a uniform chart of accounts. Only a basic, standard chart of accounts has been published (revised version, 1993).

The accounting profession and academics have been heavily involved in commenting on the draft of the Act on Accounting. Representatives of the legal profession participate in monitoring the consistency of the new law. The continuing development of accounting legislation in Poland will undoubtedly lead to the successful entry of the Polish economy into the European market.

Format of Polish Financial Statements (from 1991)

Balance Sheet

Aktywa
A. Adtywa zmniejszające kapitaly własne
  I. Należne wplaty na poczet kapitalu
B. Majątek trwaly
  I. Rzeczowe i zrównane z nimi składniki majątku trwalego
    1. Grunty
    2. Budynki i budowle
    3. Urządzenia techniczne, maszyny, wyposażenie produkcyjne i handlowe
    4. Środki transportu
    5. Inne srodki trwale
    6. Wyposażenie
    7. Inwestycje rozpoczęte
    8. Neleżnosci z tytulu zaliczek na inwestycje
  II. Wartości niemateialne i prawne
    1. Nabyte koncesje, patenty, licencje, znaki towarowe i podobne wartosci
    2. Wartość firmy
    3. Należności z tytulu zaliczek na wartości niematerialne i prawne
  III. Finansowe skladniki majątku trwalego
    1. Udzialy w obcych jednostkach
    2. Dlugoterminowe papiery wartościowe
    3. Udzielone pożyczki dlugoterminowe
    4. Inne finansowe skladniki majątku trwalego

Assets
A. Assets decreasing equity
  1. Subscribed capital unpaid
B. Fixed assets
  1. Tangible assets
    1. Land
    2. Buildings
    3. Plant and machinery
    4. Transport means
    5. Other fixed assets
    6. Equipment
    7. Tangible assets in course of construction
    8. Payments on account
  II. Intangible assets
    1. Concessions, patents, licences, trademarks and similar rights and assets
    2. Goodwill
    3. Payments on account
  III. Financial assets
    1. Shares in undertakings
    2. Long term securities
    3. Long term loans
    4. Other financial assets

C. Majątek obrotowy
  I. Zapasy
    1. Materialy
    2. Produkcja nie zakończona
    3. Produkty gotowe
    4. Towary
    5. Zaliczki na poczet dostaw zapasów
  II. Należności i roszczenia
    1. Należności z tytulu dostaw, robót i uslug
    2. Należności od budżetów
    3. Należności wewnątrzzakladowe
    4. Pozostale należności
    5. Roszczenia sporne
  III. Środki pieniężne
    1. Środki pieniężne w kasie
    2. Środki pieniężne w banku
    3. Inne środki pieniężne
  IV. Krótkoterminowe papiery wartościowe
  V. Rozliczenia międzyokresowe
D. Inne aktywa

C. Current Assets
  I. Stocks
    1. Raw materials
    2. Work in progress
    3. Finished goods
    4. Merchandises
    5. Payments on account
  II. Debtors
    1. Trade debtors

    2. Receivables from budget
    3. Intercompany receivables

    4. Other debtors
    5. Debatable claims
  III. Cash
    1. Cash in hand
    2. Cash at bank
    3. Other cash
  IV. Short term securities

  V. Prepayments and accrued income
D. Other Assets

Pasywa

A. Kapitaly (fundusże) wlasne
   I. Kapitaly
   II. Kapital ze sprzedaży akcji wlasnych powyżej ich wartości nominalnej
   III. Fundusze
   IV. Zmiany kapitalów (funduszy) na skutek przeszacowania aktywów lub pasywów (przyrost - wielkość dodatnia, zmniejszenie - wielkość ujemna)
   V. Nierozliczony wynik finansowy z lat ubieglych
      1. zysk (wielkość dodatnia)
      2. strata (wielkość ujemna)
   VI. Wieloletnie rezerwy celowe
B. Kredyty i pożyczki
   I. Dlugoterminowe kredyty bankowe i pożyczki
      1. Kredyty bankowe
      2. Pożyczki
   II. Pozostale kredyty i pożyczki
      1. Kredyty bankowe
      2. Pożyczki
   III. Kredyty bankowe i pożyczki przeterminowane
C. Zobowiązania, fundusze specjalne i rozliczenia międzyokresowe
   I. Zobowiązania
      1. Zobowiązania z tytulu dostaw, robót i uslag
      2. Zobowiązania wekslowe
      3. Zobowiązania wobec budżetów
      4. Zobowiązania z tytulu wynagrodzeń
      5. Zobowiązania wewnatrzzakladowe
      6. Pozostale zobowiązania
   II. Fundusze specjalne
      1. Zakladowy fundusz socjalny
      2. Zakladowy fundusz micszkaniowy
      3. Inne fundusze specjalne

Liabilities and Equity

A. Equity
   I. Capital
   II. Share premium capital

   III. Funds (for state-owned enterprises)
   IV. Revaluation reserve

   V. Profit or loss brought forward

      1. Profit
      2. Loss
   VI. Long term special purpose reserves
B. Bank and other loans
   I. Long term bank and other loans

      1. Bank loans
      2. Other loans
   II. Other than long term loans
      1. Bank loans
      2. Other loans
   III. Overdue bank and other loans

C. Payables, special funds and accruals
   I. Payables
      1. Trade creditors

      2. Bills of exchange payables
      3. Amounts owed to budget

      4. Amounts owed to workers

      5. Intercompany payables

      6. Other creditors
   II. Special funds
      1. Social fund
      2. Lodging fund

      3. Other special funds

III. Rozliczenia międzyokresowe
  1. Przychody przyszłych
     okresów
  2. Rozliczenia międzyokresowe
D. Rezerwy i inne pasywa
  I. Rezerwy
  II. Inne pasywa
E. Wynik finansowy
  I. Wynik netto
    1. zysk (wielkość dodatnia)
    2. strata (wielkość ujemna)

III. Accruals and deferred income
  1. Deferred income

  2. Accruals
D. Reserves and other liabilities
  I. Reserves
  II. Other liabilities
E. Financial Result for the year
  I. Net Result
    1. Profit (positive value)
    2. Loss (negative value)

Income Statement

Koszty i śtraty	Charges

Koszty i śtraty

A. Koszt uzyskania przychodów
  I. Koszty wg rodzauów
    1. amortyzacja majątku trwalego
    2. zużycie materialów i energii
    3. uslugi obce
    4. wynagrodzenia
    5. narzuty na wynagrodzenia
    6. ...
    7. ...
    8. ...
    9. pozostale
  II. Zmiana stanu producktów
    1. zmniejszenie (wielkość dodatnia)
    2. zwiększenie (wielkość ujemna)
A. Koszt uzyskania prychodów
  I. Koszt wytworzenia (techniczny) sprzedanych produktów
    1. ...
    2. ...
  II. Koszty ogólnego zarządu (ogólnozakladowe) oraz koszty sprzedaży
  III. Koszty handlowe
  IV. Wartość sprzedanych towarów w cenie zakupu
  V. Koszty operacji finansowych
    1. odsetki od kredytów i pozyczek
    2. pozostale
  VI. Podatek obrotowy i inne obsiążenia prychodów ze sprzedąży
    1. Podatek obrotowy
    2. Inne obciażenia prżychhodów
B. Zysk na dzialalności gospodarczej
C. Straty nadzwyczajine
  I. Straty losowe
  II. Pozostale straty
D. Zysk brutto
E. Obowiązkowe amniejszenia zysku
  I. Podatek dochowy
  II. Inne obowiązkowe odpisy z zycku roku bieżącego
F. Zysk netto

Charges

A. Expense
  I. Costs by nature
    1. depreciation
    2. raw materials
    3. external services
    4. payroll
    5. payroll deductions
    6. ...
    7. ...
    8. ...
    9. others
  II. Changes in stocks of finished goods and Work-in-Progress
    1. increasing
    2. decreasing
A. Expenses
  I. Cost of Finished Goods Sold
    1. ...
    2. ...
  II. Administrative and selling expenses
  III. Commercial expenses
  IV. Cost of Goods Sold
  V. Financial Expenses
    1. Credit and Loans Interests Payable
    2. Others
  VI. Turnover Tax and other charges on sales
    1. Turnover Tax
    2. Other charges on sales
B. Profit on ordinary activities
C. Extraordinary Losses
  I. Emergency losses
  II. Others
D. Gross Profit
E. Obligatory charges on the profit
  I. Income Tax
  II. Other charges
F. Net Profit

Przychody i zyski

A. Przychody ze sprzedazy
- I. Produktów
  1. ...
  2. ...
- II. Przychody ze sprzedaży towarów
- III. Przychody z operacji finansowych
  1. z tytulu udzialów w innych jednostkach
  2. odsetki od kredytów i pożyczek
  3. pozostale
- IV. Wynik na pozostalej sprzedaży
  1. zysk (wielkość dodatnia)
  2. strata (wielkość ujemna)
- V. Dotacje przedmiotowe i inne zwiçkszenia przychodów ze sprzedaży

B. Strata na dzialalności gospodarczej
C. Zyski nadzwyczajne
- I. Zyski losowe
- II. Pozostale zyski

D. Strata brutto
E. Obowiązkowe zwiększenia straty
F. Strata netto

Income

A. Turnover
- I. Turnover from sale of finished goods
  1. ...
  2. ...
- II. Turnover from sale of merchandises
- III. Financial revenues
  1. revenues from participating undertakings
  2. credit and loans interests received
  3. others
- IV. Results of other activities
  1. profit (positive value)
  2. loss (negative value)
- V. Subventions and Subsidies

B. Loss on ordinary activities
C. Extraordinary profits
- I. Unexpected profits
- II. Other profits

D. Gross Loss
E. Obligatory charges of loss
F. Net Loss

Notes to the balance sheet

In separate items should be disclosed:

1. Adjustment amounts of assets which are preceded by Roman numerals in part B and presented in net value. It should be made for each item separately.

2. Amounts of receivables, claims (item C, II, Assets) and liabilities (item C, I, Liabilities) divided into short term (amounts payable within one year) and long term (amounts payable after more than one year)

3. Amount of uncertain liabilities which are coming from off-balance sheet register, e.g., notes discounting

4. Value of R&D equipment which is a charge in the profit and loss account

5. Long-term liabilities owed to the state treasury or local government for land renewal

6. Amounts owed to the state or local treasury for building acquisition

Notes to the profit and loss account

I. Expenses and extraordinary losses which are not recognized by tax regulations as cost of sales
   1) . . .
   2) . . .

II. Revenues which are not recognized by tax regulations
   1) . . .
   2) . . .

III. Other allowed changes in taxable income
   1) . . .
   2) . . .

IV. Total amount of taxable income

V. Consequences of changes in accounting policy (valuation of assets, liabilities) in amount of financial result for the year (increasing, positive value; decreasing, negative value)
   1) change category . . .   amount . . .
   2) change category . . .   amount . . .

FORMER SOVIET UNION

Valerii V. Kovalev
Yaroslav V. Sokolov
St. Petersburg Institute of Commerce and Economics
Alexander D. Larionov
St. Petersburg University of Finance and Economics
Leonid I. Kravchenko
Victor I. Strazhev
Belorussian State Economics University, Minsk, Belarus
Vanlovas Lakis
Jonas Mackevicius
Vilnius University, Lithuania
J. and T. Alver
University of Tartu, Estonia
Derek Bailey
Thames Valley University, England

1. The Political and Economic Situation of the Former Soviet Union

1.1 Political Situation

The Union of Soviet Socialist Republics (USSR), as it was known, was the largest country in the world, lying 75% in Asia and 25% in Europe. The population was about 300 million people, of whom slightly fewer than 50% were Russians. Its population consisted of about 150 ethnic groups, the largest of which were Russians (148 million) and Ukrainians (45 million).

The Soviet administrative and territorial structure consisted of several levels. The USSR was the union of 15 republics: Russia, Ukraine, Byelorussia, Kazakhstan, Uzbekistan, Kirgizia, Moldavia, Azerbaijan, Georgia, Armenia, Tadjikstan, Turkmenistan, Lithuania, Latvia, and Estonia. Some of the multinational republics such as Russia, Azerbaijan, Georgia, and Uzbekistan, were further divided into autonomous districts.

Parallel to this, ethnically more homogeneous parts of the country were divided into administrative regions (*oblast*) or larger regions (*Krai*).

At a meeting in Minsk in December 1991, the political leaders of the Slavic republics, Yeltsin (Russia), Kravchuk (Ukraine), and Shuskevich (Byelorussia) agreed on the establishment of the Commonwealth of Independent States (CIS). Other former Soviet republics joined the CIS. The statute of the CIS was signed by the heads of ten states (excluding Azerbaijan, Georgia, Estonia, Lithuania, and Latvia) on January 22, 1993 and later was ratified by the Parliaments. Later, Azerbaijan and Georgia joined the CIS. Some of the states joined the CIS because of economic problems, hoping to solve these problems with the help of Russia. By the beginning of 1994, all of them (excluding Turkmenistan) were debtors of Russia. At present the CIS comprises 12 independent states (excluding the Baltic republics).

According to the statute, the CIS was established for cooperation in political, economic, cultural, humanitarian, and other spheres of life. The CIS is not a state and has no supra-national power. Any independent state can join or leave the CIS. The supreme organ of authority of the CIS is the Council of Heads of the States. The council has meetings twice a year. Some other councils and committees have been founded, as follows:

- The Council of Heads of Governments (which has four meetings per year)
- The Council of Ministers of Foreign Affairs
- The Committee for Coordination and Consultancy (which is located in Minsk, works permanently, and was created as an executive organ of the CIS for solving current problems and tasks). Each state delegates two representatives to the committee.
- The Council of the Ministers of Defense–General Headquarters of Joined Armed Forces
- The Economic Court
- The Commission on Human Rights

The Interparliamentary Assembly of Member States of the CIS was established to coordinate policy. It is located in St. Petersburg. Other organs for industrial cooperation (councils and committees) will be established if necessary.

Because of the many differences in economic and political life in the member states, the CIS is an artificial creation. Each republic intends to find its own way to development. Many republics prefer to solve their problems in any other than the way approved by Russia, even if the way suggested by Russia is the best.

For example, because it is ahead economically, Russia has made many significant changes in accounting during the past 5 years. During these years there were many positive and negative results of the transformation of the accounting system. Such changes were made jointly with foreign experts. Nevertheless, the Ukrainian specialists in accountancy refused to use any of the current achievements of Russian scientists and practitioners and declared their intention "to create an accounting system in accordance with the international accounting standards," thinking that the current accounting system in Russia does not operate in accordance with IAS and, simultaneously, asking the international accounting institutions to help them.

Without doubt, Russia is ahead of other members of the CIS in radical political and socioeconomic change. The final abolition of the so-called Soviet system of management can be considered the main political result of 1993. The national referendum on the new Constitution of Russia and the election of the Parliament were held on December 12, 1993.

According to the new Constitution, the Russian Federation consists of 89 equal-in-rights subjects:

- 21 republics
- 6 territories (*krai*)
- 49 provinces (*oblasty*)
- 2 federal cities (Moscow and St. Petersburg)
- 1 autonomous province
- 10 autonomous areas (*okrug*)

The Constitution:

- Abolished the old Soviet system
- Transformed Russia into a federation with powerful presidential authority

- Stopped the disintegration of Russia
- Declared the equal rights of private, federal, municipal, and other forms of property
- Declared that land and other mineral resources could have private, federal, municipal, and other forms of ownership

According to the Constitution, *Russia* is a shortened version of the full title, *Russian Federation*. As indicated earlier, however, within the Russian Federation there are a number of areas (e.g., Bashkiria, Tatarstan) in which live significant numbers of minority nationalities. In these areas many people have aspirations for an increasing degree of autonomy from control by Moscow.

1.2 Economic Situation

1.2.1 The Global Recession

The recession has become one of the main features of the economy in Russia. In 1993, the Gross Domestic Product was 162.3 trillion rubles, which was 12% lower than it was in 1992.

Industrial production is currently concentrated on large enterprises—about 2% of large industrial enterprises produce more than 40% of the total volume of production. At the end of 1993, the index of industrial production, calculated by the Center of the Economical Conjuncture of the Russian Federation as the geometric average of indices of the 42 most important types of products, was approximately 68% of the level of December 1991.

One of the most serious problems in Russia is the problem of monopolization. Currently, some products are produced by a single enterprise, for example, trolley busses, scooters, potato harvesters, tunnellers' combines, and films. Oligopoly is peculiar to many industries as well. For example, some types of steel are produced by only three enterprises, magnetic tape is produced by two enterprises, and 96% of polystirol is produced by four enterprises. Thus, the Russian economy is still in a depressive corkscrew. One of the main reasons for the disturbance of the production process is the low level of investment activity.

1.2.2 Inflation

According to official data, consumer goods prices have increased as follows:

- From January 1991 to January 1992 by 8.5 times (850%)
- From January 1992 to January 1993 by 9.5 times (950%);
- From January 1993 to January 1994 by 10 times (1000%) (estimate)

Thus, the rate of inflation has been increasing for the past 3 years. The average weekly rate of inflation in 1993 was 4.48% (the minimum level, 3%, was in April, and the maximum level, 7.5%, was in August).

Toward the end of 1993, the volume of production of all consumer goods stabilized at 60% of the volume of production of January 1990. It is possible to say that the 1993 level of consumption was equal to the standard of the mid-1960s to the beginning of 1970s.

1.2.3 The Social Sphere and Unemployment

By the beginning of 1994, the population of Russia was 148.4 million people, which was 300,000 fewer people than a year before. The total number of fully or partly unemployed people was from 5 to 7.8 million, that is, 10.4% of the labor force (the forecast for 1994 is about 10%–15%). In 1993, employees of 265 enterprises were on strike for a day or longer, four times fewer than a year before.

1.2.4 Privatization

By early 1994, 86,000 enterprises had been privatized, 35% of them were trade enterprises, 29% industrial enterprises, 18% enterprises of consumer service, 9% enterprises of the construction industry, 7% enterprises of public catering, 7% enterprises of motor transport, and 2% agricultural enterprises.

1.2.5 Banking

By the end of 1993, nearly 2,000 commercial and co-operative banks licensed by the Central Bank of Russia and about 4,000 of their branches had been registered; 38% of them are located in Moscow. About 80% of the total financial investment in the national economy was made by commercial banks.

1.2.6 Export-Import Operations

Although the conjuncture of the world market was not favorable, the value of exports from Russia in 1993 reached approximately the same level as the year before, that is, $43 billion. The amount of energy resources exported (oil, gas, etc.) was about 50% of this figure (oil, 19.1%; gas, 17.0%; oil products, 8.0%). The share of machines and equipment exported was 6.7% of the total export.

Imports into Russia amounted to about $27 billion, which was 52% less than in 1992. The structure of import was as follows: machines and equipment, 26.5%; grain, 5.8%; garments, 4.5%; sugar, 3.0%. Russia's import of many strategically important goods decreased from 1992 to 1993: fresh-frozen meat by 75%; grain by 62%; and sugar by 30%. Import of machinery and equipment was approximately $6.6 billion.

Economic relations between Russia and the other former Soviet republics have been deteriorating. By the beginning of 1994, the total amount of their debts to Russia was about 3.5 trillion rubles, including 1.5 trillion rubles for energy resources. All republics have been forced to bring into use their own currency or the temporal substitute of currency. Many of them would like to join the "ruble zone."

1.3 The Baltic States

The Baltic states (Estonia, Latvia, and Lithuania) were the only successor states of the USSR not to accede to the CIS. The three states have attempted to reestablish their national sovereignty.

The armed forces of the former Soviet Union have withdrawn from Lithuania, and an agreement on their withdrawal from Latvia has been concluded. There have been negotiations on their withdrawal from Estonia and for the recognition of transit rights across Lithuania to the Russian enclave of Kaliningrad.

By the end of 1993, in all three republics there had been a considerable privatization of state property, including land, and a substantial development of private enterprise (primarily in the trade and services sectors of the economy).

Convertible national currencies have been introduced in Estonia, Latvia, and Lithuania (kroon, lats, and litas, respectively). Commercial banks have been established in all three republics. In September 1993 a stock exchange was opened in Vilnius, the capital of Lithuania. At the end of 1994 a stock exchange is expected to be opened in Riga, the capital of Latvia.

Each of the Baltic states has introduced new accounting legislation, in repudiation of Soviet accounting practice.

All three republics are confronted with unresolved problems of unbalanced national budgets and severe inflationary pressures (i.e., 200% per annum in Estonia and Latvia and even higher in Lithuania).

Previously, the economies of the Baltic republics were integrated into the Soviet economic system. Since the reestablishment of independence, the three republics have attempted to diversify their external trade by developing new marketing, especially in the Scandinavian and European Union countries. In 1993 the CIS countries accounted for 30% and 75% of the foreign trade of Estonia and Lithuania, respectively (compared with 90% for all the Baltic states in 1990–1991).

The Baltic states have entered into negotiations with the European Union with the objective of achieving agreements on free trade (excluding agricultural produce). Such agreements, which would not be fully operative until the end of the century, are expected to lead to association agreements with the European Union. All three Baltic states aspire to become members of the European Union. It seems likely that these states, small, proud, and independent minded, will become increasingly distinct from the 12 CIS states as time goes on.

2. Accounting and Auditing Practices in Russia

2.1 A Brief History of Accounting in Russia

Over the course of eleven centuries, Russia was transformed from a number of city states and principalities in Eastern Europe into a European power encompassing a huge land area and culturally diverse peoples. An enduring problem has been the creation of administrative structures for the effective governance of such a diverse state while simultaneously promoting economic progress sufficient for supporting its upkeep. Consequently, accounting has been perceived as an administrative control device rather than a business tool.

The history of accounting in the Russian lands may be divided into four periods:

1. 862–1700: The emergence and development of accounting systems based on single entry
2. 1700–1917: The adoption of double-entry bookkeeping from Western Europe
3. 1917–1985: The adaptation of double-entry bookkeeping to the requirements of a centrally planned socialist economy
4. 1985–present: The attempt to modify Soviet accounting in order to accord with international accounting practice

The first period, extending from the foundation of the city state of Novgorod to the introduction of the Westernizing reforms of Peter I, was shaped by the adoption of Christianity (988), the introduction of the Cyrillic alphabet, the promulgation of the first code of law *Russkaya Pravda* (1016), and the influence of the Russian Orthodox Church. The monasteries acquired substantial holdings of land and serfs. Monastic accounting, a form of single-entry record keeping originating in the Eastern Roman Empire, was progressively developed.

The second period commenced with the attempt by Peter I to end the isolation of Russia by modernizing the country through a process of Westernization. His successors continued the development of his innovations through the adoption of mercantile regulations (1727), the establishment of the first Russian bank (1733), the formation of the first joint-stock company (1757), and the publication in Russian, under the title *Key to Commerce* and from an English translation, of the first book on double-entry bookkeeping (1783). The first original Russian books on the subject were published in 1809, and by 1917 a total of 1356 books on accounting had been published. Bookkeeping was adapted to Russian conditions. Later in the nineteenth century, a convertible gold ruble was introduced, as well as taxes on profits and the obligatory publication of the balance sheets of quoted joint-stock companies. These developments provided increasing opportunities for accounting specialists, although no professional associations were established.

The third period was characterized by fundamental changes in all socioeconomic relationships in an attempt to accelerate development after the overthrow of the Tsarist autocracy. The system of accounting was repeatedly transformed as follows:

- 1917–1918: An attempt at national economic stabilization through extensive nationalization of business undertakings and the spread of budgetary accounting
- 1918–1921: Establishment of the regime of "war communism" and centralized control of industry and distribution of all resources and products through allocation and rationing. There was an attempt to combine total accountability with the abolition of money. Monetary accounting ceased.
- 1921–1929: The introduction of the "new economic policy," signaling the establishment of a mixed economy and the restoration of traditional double-entry accounting
- 1929–1953: The construction of the framework of a socialist economic system and the deformation of basic accounting principles
- 1953–1985: The adaptation of accounting to the requirements of a centrally planned economy

The consequence of these changes was the implementation of a system of unified socialist accounting throughout the USSR, the main features of which were:

- A rigid hierarchical structure of the national economic system
- A unified chart of accounts
- The centralized regulation of accounting practice and authoritative prescription of accounting entries for typical transactions
- The unification of primary documentation and uniform treatment of accounting data
- Formats for authorized financial statements prescribed by the Ministry of Finance

- The absence of independent audit and its substitution by strict intradepartmental control

The fourth period was marked by the failure of an attempt to radically reform the Soviet economic system and its subsequent disintegration. As a result, the question of restructuring the national economy arose and, with it, the question of the reorganization of the accounting system. By 1985, it had become evident that the established accounting system was inadequate for the reflection of actual economic processes and even distorted economic reality. It became apparent that all the better accounting practices hitherto developed elsewhere would have to be introduced. The recent period may be regarded as characterized by the gradual adaptation of Soviet accounting to the accounting principles and practices generally accepted in the Western economies.

Apart from the Baltic states, and especially during the period of independence in 1918–1939, the accounting experience was common to all the constituent republics of the USSR. As a result of the disintegration of the USSR at the end of 1991, the pace of accounting change began to vary among the successor republics.

2.2 Contemporary Methodological Aspects of Accounting

Many foreign specialists, especially from the economically developed countries, have a confused notion of the overall difference between the accounting systems inherited by the successor states to the USSR and those in the Western world. First, it is reflected in a confusion between the Soviet experience of accounting and an indigenous accounting tradition existing either before incorporation into the USSR (e.g., the Baltic states) or before 1917. It is expressed in such statements as "Populations that have grown up under communism have never seen a balance sheet or profit and loss account."

Second, it is reflected in the traditional disparagement of Russian developments in accounting. The nadir of national denigration is encapsulated in the words printed on the cover of a popular British accounting text recently published in Russia: "There are hardly 300 persons . . . knowing how to read a profit and loss account."

Before the October Revolution (1917) the works of such leading specialists as N.A. Blatov, A.P. Rudanovsky, and E. Sivers were well known both inside and outside Russia. Their influence continued to be felt within the USSR until about 1930, when, along with the creation of the centrally planned economy, the period now characterized as the deformation of accounting commenced.

Whether or not accounting is a key element of the economic system in any country is determined to a significant extent by the level and direction of economic development. The political and economic circumstances that led to the formation of the centrally planned economy were not able to change the essence of accounting, but there was a change in the priorities, goals, procedures, and functions, as was described in Soviet accounting theory and realized in practice. Thus, the main theoretical concept used by the Anglo-American accounting school could be formulated as follows: the subject of accounting is the calculation of the financial results of business activity for an accounting entity. Although the methods for such a calculation may differ across different economic systems, there is a common obligatory condition: the calculation of the financial results should be in accordance with current legislation and generally accepted accounting principles.

Although accounting in the USSR, as in Western countries, fulfilled the role of stewardship, the difference in the nature of the economic system led to a difference in the determination of accounting priorities and accounting techniques. In the Soviet Union, the purpose of accounting had been declared to be the provision of control for the safeguarding of socialist property and, also, control over the fulfillment of state plans. It was achieved through the organization of strict control and by monitoring business activity and financial results on behalf of the appropriate higher management bodies. Thereby was encompassed a monitoring for the protection and custody of assets, the utilization of the factors of production, and compliance with the established norms for the amount and structure of current assets and the realization (i.e., sale) of products, and finally, the ascertainment of the cost price of production, the financial profit, and the manner of its utilization.

The predominance of the administrative method for the management of the Soviet economy had adversely affected over many years the development of accounting. Planning was undertaken without the necessary economic justification for the tasks stipulated for achievement. The fulfillment of plans was pursued in the absence of a price mechanism grounded in costs, so that production was stimulated by the goal of intervention rather than motivated by the economic result. In these circumstances, management of production proceeded without regard for its outcome, so that accounting became an isolated self-perpetuating activity. It led to a devaluation in the role of accounting for expenditures, the controlling of production costs, and the determination of prices and also in the reporting and analyzing of the results of the realization of products. Because of these negative factors, the more progressive methods of accounting, whether developed by Soviet accountants or transmitted by those with foreign connections, did not receive wide application in Soviet enterprises.

Nevertheless, the financial result of the business activities of Soviet enterprises was carefully calculated. The management and employees of an enterprise, however, were not interested in the financial result, partly because it was unreal and partly because the financial result had no practical effect on the economic and financial position of the enterprise. For these reasons, the falsification of profit was unusual in the centrally planned economy: personal incomes remained unaffected by the size of the profit. The appropriation of profit was made specifically in accordance with special norms (e.g., to a stimulation fund, research and development fund, the industrial ministry), although the overwhelming part of profit was withdrawn to the state budget. The first change in the system of profit appropriation was made in 1965 as a result of the economic reform introduced by Alexei Kosygin, and the proportion of profit withdrawn to the state budget was reduced.

The year 1991 can be called a decisive year in Russian accounting development because of three events:

- The publication of a substantially new chart of accounts
- The issue of a new set of financial statements similar to Western accounting practice
- The beginning of preparatory work for the radical change of accounting and auditing regulation

The main regulative document on Russian accounting, "Regulation on Accounting and Reporting in the Russian Federation," was issued by decree of the Government of Russia on February 16, 1992. The new regulation removed the predominance of the control function by specifying three accounting objectives to be of equal importance:

- Maintenance of control over the presence, movement, and use of material, manpower, and monetary resources in accordance with approved norms and estimates
- Prompt prevention of negative events in the course of business activity, and the identification and mobilization of internal potential for raising efficiency
- Provision of full and reliable information on the performance and financial results of an enterprise considered useful and necessary for operational management and for investors, suppliers, customers, and creditors, tax, financial, and banking authorities, and other users interested in the business activity and financial result of an enterprise

Although these objectives may be open to criticism, their consistency with the objectives of Western accounting is evident.

On the other hand, the conceptual framework of accounting in Russia, as in other former republics of the USSR, has more features in common with the Continental European accounting model than with the Anglo-American accounting model. The overall accounting system is permeated by the notion of taxable income calculation.

Nevertheless, in the contemporary Russian accounting system, all the well-known and generally accepted accounting postulates and principles (such as dual aspect; entity, going concern, monetary unit, and periodicity postulates; cost, revenue, matching, conservatism, full disclosure, uniformity, and comparability principles) to some extent are realized.

In Russia, as in all developed countries, double-entry bookkeeping traditionally provides the foundation for accounting. Primary documents provide the legal foundation for recording transactions in accordance with approved bookkeeping rules. No entry should be made into the accounting records unless the bookkeeper has received a primary document.

Inventory taking is the sole method for assurance of the physical presence of assets and for their valuation. It is the main method of supervision over persons held responsible for assets. Under the terms of the labor contract, assets are always entrusted to persons held financially responsible for their safe custody.

The unified chart of accounts provides the nomenclature of accounts and specifies the accounts affected by, or in correspondence with, representative transactions. Their use is obligatory for all types of enterprises. The accounts contained in the chart are called "synthetic" (first order). These accounts, and their subaccounts, may be expanded into detailed "analytical" (supporting or second order) accounts in conformity with the needs of the enterprise.

The structure of internal accounting consists of primary documents, analytical account schedules, summary account schedules, general ledger, inventory taking schedules, and interim responsibility statements.

External reporting (principally to higher management bodies) consists of the balance sheet, statement of financial results and their utilization, and other supplementary forms. These are unified and obligatory for all types of enterprises. Nonprofit organizations and banks have their own unified chart of accounts and system of financial reporting. Such reporting is carried out according to the statutory regulations and presented within strictly determined time periods.

The information generated by the accounting system is required to be timely, reliable, complete, accurate and objective. Historical cost accounting is the only method permitted for the preparation of internal and external reports.

All these developments in accounting are consistent with the mainstream of Continental European accounting practice, although adapted to Russian conditions.

2.3 The Regulation of Accounting in Russia

The centralization of accounting methodology derives to some extent from former Soviet political and economic legislation. The necessity of organization of a single accounting and statistical system, as well as the leading role of the Council of Ministers of the USSR for this process, was declared in the Soviet constitution. According to this declaration, the Council of Ministers was obliged "to carry out measures" intended to organize accounting and statistics in the country. To that end, four regulations on accounting, "Regulation on Documents and Records for Accounting in Enterprises and Economic Organizations" (1961), "Regulation on Chief Accountants" (1980), "Regulation on Accounting Statements and Balance

Sheets" (1979), and "Chart of Accounts" (the last version under the conditions of the centrally planned economy was issued in 1985 and used until 1992), have been approved by decrees. Thus, there were no special accounting laws in the country, and accounting practice was totally regulated by these four documents. They were supplemented by special obligatory instructions issued periodically by the Ministry of Finance.

All these regulations and instructions were applied throughout the constituent republics of the USSR. Since 1991, with the dissolution of the USSR, the legal requirements for accounting have began to change with the changes in political and economic conditions. In neither Russia nor the other former republics of the USSR, however, is there a corpus of accounting legislation, as in Western countries, although progress has been made in its creation. In Russia, several drafts of the Accounting Law and the Auditing Law, worked out by different bodies, were published for discussion but none has been adopted. These drafts restated the leading role of the Ministry of Finance in the licensing of accountants and auditors, the preparation of methodological regulations, and instructions and in other matters. Unresolved issues concerning the division of responsibilities between the Ministry of Finance and other bodies (e.g., the associations of accountants and auditors) have hindered the creation of a true accountancy and independent audit profession in Russia. A similar situation exists in the other successor republics of the USSR. However, new laws governing some aspects of accounting, and marking both a reorientation toward the market economy and a break with Soviet accounting practice, have been introduced in Estonia (1990), Latvia (1992), and Lithuania (1991),

Nevertheless, the first steps in creating the background for new accounting legislation have been made recently in Russia. Three major fundamentally new normative accounting documents have been issued:

- Regulation on Accounting and Reporting in the Russian Federation, approved by the Government of the Russian Federation on February 16, 1992
- Regulation on Cost Allocation and Conditions of Taxable Income Calculation, approved by the Government of the Russian Federation on August 5, 1992
- Chart of Accounts, approved by the Ministry of Finance of Russia on December 19, 1991

On behalf of the government of Russia, the Regulation on Accounting and Reporting was worked out by the Ministry of Finance of Russia. Some changes and supplements to this regulation were approved by the ministry of Finance on June 4, 1993. The Regulation replaces the 1961, 1979, and 1980 regulations previously mentioned. The regulation determines the methodological and organizational aspects of accounting in Russia and is obligatory for all types of enterprises having business in the country. It comprises: (*a*) general provisions, (*b*) the main principles of accounting practice, (*c*) the organizational structure of accounting, and (*d*) reporting.

The first chapter of the regulation specifies the subject matter of accounting and the three main accounting objectives (as mentioned in the previous section). Each enterprise has the right to construct its own organizational chart for the allocation of accounting tasks among accounting personnel and to select accounting procedures and technology for data processing, within the limits prescribed in the regulation. An enterprise may segregate its structural segments (such as affiliates, branches, housing and public utility facilities, and transport services) into separate balance sheets. Thus, the use of a separate balance sheet for each department of a factory, including each of its production departments, is permitted although not required.

The second chapter states that the only method of accounting that can be used in enterprises is double-entry.

The following conditions must be provided by the chosen system of accounting:

- Observance of the accounting policy declared at the enterprise
- Completeness of accounting data
- Correctness of classification of expenses in a given period
- Demarcation of current expenses and investments
- Agreement of the aggregated balances of the analytical accounts with the balances of the corresponding synthetic accounts

One of the most important features of the regulation is the introduction of a new category for Russian accounting—accounting policy. This term appeared in accounting theory and practice for the first time. All transactions must be supported by the corresponding basic documents, each of which, at a minimum, must contain the name, date, transaction explanation, measures, and the position and printed names of the persons who have signed the documents. Persons issuing and signing the documents are responsible for the correctness of the information as well as for the timeliness of their transfer to the accounting system. The structure of accounting ledgers is recommended by the Ministry of Finance. Corrections in cash payment and cash receipt vouchers, as well as in bank documents, are not tolerated in any form. Basic documents, accounting ledgers, and financial statements must be stored in accordance with established procedure and deposited in archives in due time. The safekeeping of the documents and their transfer to the archives is the duty of an accountant general.

All assets must be valued in accordance with the historical cost principle unless another method is authorized by the Ministry of Finance. All entries are required to be made in the Russian currency.

A physical check of inventories is obligatory for ensuring the reliability of accounting data. The number of inventory checks in each year, the lists of items to be examined on each occasion, and the inventory-taking deadlines shall be decided by the enterprise except where an inventory taking is obligatory.

An inspection of the inventories must be undertaken when:

- Renting or purchasing an enterprise
- Transforming enterprises to partnerships or joint-stock companies
- Preparing annual reports and balance sheets, with the exception of items whose inventory taking was done not earlier than October 1 of the reporting year. (The inventory taking of buildings, structures, and other stationary fixed assets can be carried out once every 2–3 years, and of library stock once every 5 years)
- A materially responsible person is being replaced by another (on the day of acceptance of affairs)
- Cases of established embezzlement and malpractice, as well as of damage done to valuables have been uncovered (immediately upon establishment of such facts)
- A fire or natural calamity has occurred

If during an inventory taking or other inspection, valuables are found to be in excess of the recorded amounts, the discrepancy must be entered into the books and included in the financial results, with subsequent investigation of the reasons for the surplus and the guilty persons.

Losses of valuables, within the limits of norms approved in the established manner, are written off by order of the head of an enterprise either as production (general) costs or against special-purpose funds. The norm of losses can be applied only to cases of actually revealed shortages. Any writing off of material values within the accepted norms of losses before the establishment of the fact of a shortage is forbidden. If there are no established norms, losses are looked upon as abnormal shortages. Shortages of value over and above the norms of losses, as well as losses arising from damage in cases when no individual responsibility has been established, are written off at the discretion of the heads of enterprises either as production costs or against special-purpose funds. Shortages of value over and above the norms established for shortages and losses arising from damage can be written off only after a thorough public investigation into the causes and after taking any necessary measures for the prevention of similar losses and waste in the future.

The third chapter of the regulation explains the principles of organization of accounting in an enterprise. The responsibility for correct organization and regulation of bookkeeping is imposed on the heads of enterprises. If an enterprise does not have its own accounting department, the bookkeeping can be done by a specialist or a firm specializing in such services. A chief accountant is appointed or dismissed by the head of the enterprise and is directly responsible to that person. In all questions related to accountancy and the order and method of control, the chief accountant is guided by the regulation and the normative documents approved in the manner established by the regulation.

A chief accountant ensures the rational organization of bookkeeping at an enterprise, timely entry into the books of production assets and processes, correct execution of documents and accounts, reliable and timely accounting for the expenses of production and operations, supplying of operational accounting data to whom they concern, and preparation of financial statements and their timely submission, as well as organization of performance analyses.

All the documents serving as justification for acceptance and delivery of pecuniary assets, goods, and material valuables, as well as credit and account obligations, are signed by the head of an enterprise and the chief accountant or by persons authorized by the same to do so. Granting the right for signing such documents to such persons should be stated in written form by the head of the enterprise. The above-mentioned documents, unless signed by a chief accountant or by persons authorized to do so, are considered to be invalid and should not be accepted for execution by responsible persons or employees of the accounting service of the given enterprise, nor by the banking institutions.

Chief accountants are forbidden to accept for execution and registration documents on operations that contradict the laws and established order of acceptance, keeping and spending of pecuniary assets, goods, materials, and other valuables. A chief accountant is obliged to draw to the attention of the director (in writing) the unlawful character of such documents. Upon receipt of the director's repeated written instruction about the execution of the actions, the chief accountant must comply with it. In such a case, all responsibility for the operation is borne by the head of the enterprise.

The appointment, dismissal, and transfer of materially responsible persons (cashiers, managers of warehouses, and others) is with the agreement of the chief accountant.

A chief accountant who is dismissed is responsible for transferring all necessary materials to a newly appointed person. The total inventory of the condition of the accounting system must be organized for this purpose.

The fourth chapter of the regulation stipulates the procedures for financial statement preparation and includes general requirements, rules for valuation of the main items included in financial statements, and the procedure for the presentation and approval of accounting statements.

Financial statements must be prepared periodically (monthly, quarterly, and annually). The financial statements must include cumulative (i.e., from the beginning of the year to the current date) accounting data on the possession and financial position of the enterprise. The accounting reports and balance sheets make up a set of authorized forms containing a system of indicators reflecting the possessions and financial situation of the enterprise as well as the results of the financial and economic activity for the period under review. The list of forms to be used in monthly, quarterly, and annual reporting, their standard formats, and the instructions for their compilation are prepared and approved annually by the Ministry of Finance.

The demand for, or the submission of, accounting reports and balance sheets in other than the approved format and the approved manner is prohibited, as is their submission to unapproved addressees. Nevertheless, the ministries and state departments may propose additional reporting formats for subordinate entities although there must be coordination with the Ministry of Finance.

Every enterprise undertakes its own reporting in reflection of its property and the sources of their formation in all areas of activity. Corporations controlling autonomous enterprises and organizations are required to compile consolidated financial statements in addition to their own financial statements.

The fiscal year for all enterprises is the period from January 1 to December 31, inclusive. The fiscal year for newly founded enterprises is a period from the date of their formation to December 31, inclusive. If an enterprise is founded during the last quarter of the year, financial statements for that year are not required. In these circumstances, the first fiscal year will be a period from the date of formation to December 31 of the following year.

When drawing up accounts, reports, and balance sheets, it is necessary to ensure the reliability of the information about the assets and commitments of an enterprise, its financial situation, and the results of its activity in the period under review. The indicators of the accounting reportings and balance sheets must correspond with data processed through the accounting records. Similarly, the indication of the opening balance sheet for the period under review must correspond with the indicators of the balance sheet for the end of the immediately preceding period. Any differences must be explained in the annual report.

Any corrections to the data of the reports and balance sheets, whether of the current year or earlier years (arising after the annual accounting reports and balance sheets have been approved), resulting in alterations to the entries in the accounting records, are reflected in the reports and balance sheets prepared for the period in which the inaccuracies were discovered.

Any corrections required to be made to the data used in the annual reports and balance sheets for the immediately preceding year (and arising before their approval) are made in the reports and balance sheets for the current year but in the accounting records for the preceding December. Any corrections made to the financial statements must be specifically signed and dated, the financial statements also being signed in the normal manner.

2.4 Rules for Valuation

2.4.1 Capital and Financial Investments

The following are examples of capital investments:

- Construction works
- The acquisition of fixed assets, equipment, and tools
- Expenses of geological exploration and drilling
- Expenses of working the land and the resettlement of people in connection with the construction of new enterprises

Investments are reflected in a balance sheet according to the actual expenses of the builder (supplier).

Investments in other enterprises within Russia, capital participations in enterprises abroad, investment in the securities of other enterprises, as well as other financial investments, are reflected in the balance sheet according to the actual costs of an investor enterprise.

2.4.2 Fixed Assets and Intangible Assets

Fixed assets include buildings; structures; transmitting devices; machines and equipment; vehicles; tools, production implements, accessories, and equipment (apart from those items that in accordance with the current rules belong to the current assets); draft and breeding livestock irrespective of their value; perennial plants; and other assets such as library stocks, museum valuables, and zoo animals.

Fixed assets also include expenditures incurred for the improvement of soils (amelioration, reclamation, irrigation, and other works) and for rented buildings, structures, equipment, and other such long-lived items.

Before their being commissioned into permanent operation, capital construction projects, being in temporary operation, are not included as fixed assets. In accounts and balance sheets, expenses on such projects are entered as uncompleted capital construction (account #08).

Plots of land, deposits of mineral resources, and forests and reservoirs given to enterprises are not reflected in balance sheets unless legislation specifically requires that they should be.

Buildings and structures for which construction has been completed, installed equipment, and finished capital construction projects are included as fixed assets after approval of all expenses relating to delivery, assembly, and installation of equipment. Capital investment in perennial plants, as well as in the improvement of soils, is incurred on the areas accepted for exploitation, irrespective of whether or not the whole complex of works is completed.

Completed capital expenditure on rented buildings, structures, equipment, and other objects is included by the lessee in his own fixed assets as a sum of actual expenses. Upon the expiration of the lease term, these expenses, if so envisaged by the lease agreement, are transferred to the lessor, who includes them as increased initial value of the corresponding objects.

Fixed assets are reflected in the balance sheet by a sum equal to their actual initial costs. The initial value can be changed only if the item was reconstructed, additionally equipped, or partly liquidated.

The following items are not classed as fixed assets and are included as current items (low-value and short-life items):

- Items whose service life is less than one year irrespective of their value
- Items whose original cost is less than a certain limit declared in the present regulation (currently, this limit is 100,000 rubles, and it is supposed that in the future it can be corrected annually on January 1 according to the annual rate of inflation; directors of enterprises are permitted to reduce this limit); this condition does not affect agricultural machines, tools, mature draft and breeding livestock
- Special items for fishing (trawls, seines, fishing nets, drag nets, etc.), irrespective of their value and useful life
- Special instruments and special devices, irrespective of their value
- Perennial plants, grown in nurseries as planting out material
- Young animals and feeding animals, poultry, rabbits, beasts of burden, bee swarms, as well as experimental animals

- Items designated for hire, irrespective of their value
- Special clothes, footwear, and bedding, irrespective of their value and useful life

Intangible assets include the rights to use land, water resources, and other natural resources, industrial property as well as intellectual property, and other similar rights. Intangible assets are reflected in the balance sheet in the sum of expenses incurred for their acquisition, including expenses on preparation for use.

Fixed assets are depreciated according to the centrally established norms into costs of production or operation. Intangibles must be amortized into expenses over the period benefited, not to exceed 10 years or the business life of an enterprise according to norms established at the enterprise. Low-value and short-life items are amortized into expenses in one of two ways: (*a*) 50% of their cost is depreciated immediately when the items are transferred for use and the remaining 50% (excluding scrap value) when said objects are written off, or (*b*) 100% of the cost is depreciated immediately when they are transferred for use. Items whose cost is less than one-twentieth of the above-mentioned limit are depreciated immediately when they are transferred for use.

2.4.3 *Raw Materials, Materials, Finished Products, and Commodities*

Raw materials, materials, fuel, purchased semi-products and completed parts, spare parts, and other material valuables are reflected in balance sheets at their actual cost, including all expenses incurred in their acquisition and delivery for storage. Computing the unit costs can be made by one of the following methods:

- Weighted averaged cost
- First-in, first-out (FIFO)
- Last-in, first-out (LIFO)

Finished products are reflected in the balance sheet by a sum equal to their actual production costs.

At retail trade establishments, goods are entered in the balance sheet at their retail (sale) prices, while at wholesale warehouses, trading depots, and wholesale supplying organizations, it is done on the basis of retail prices or purchasing values. The difference between purchasing values and retail prices is entered in the balance sheet as a separate item.

Valuables whose market prices have decreased during the reporting year as well as items that have become partially obsolete are reflected in the balance sheet by a sum equal to the prices of their estimated realization. The difference is charged against the results of economic activity.

2.4.4 Unfinished Production and Expenses of Future Periods

In industries with large-scale or mass production it is admissible to assess incomplete production by normative (planned) net cost. In enterprises making one-of-a-kind or special-order products, unfinished production is reflected in the balance sheet by actual net cost.

Expenses incurred in the period under review but subject to liquidation in subsequent periods are reflected in the balance sheet as a separate item, as prepaid expenses. Such expenses are to be written off in due time.

2.4.5 Funds and Reserves

The statutory capital, representing the resources required at the foundation of the enterprise for the conduct of its economic activities, is shown as a separate item on the balance sheet. Also shown separately is the amount owing by participants (founders) in respect of contributions to capital.

Enterprises may create a reserve fund to meet unforeseen losses and expenses. A provision for doubtful debts may be created on the basis of a survey of debtors made at the end of the year. At the end of the following year, any unused portion of the provision is added to that year's profit.

In order to achieve an even spread of future expenses in the costs of production or operating expenses, enterprises are allowed to create reserves to meet:

- Future payments to workers going on holiday
- Payments of annual bonuses for length of service
- Expenses incurred on repairs of fixed assets

- Production expenses incurred on preparatory work in seasonal branches of industry
- Future expenses incurred on repair of objects for hire

2.4.6 Settlements with Debtors and Creditors; Other Items of a Balance Sheet

Debtors and creditors are shown on the balance sheet in the amounts shown in the accounting records and accepted as correct. Within the prescribed period, discrepancies concerning the amounts due and owing must be referred to the other party for agreement.

The amounts shown in the balance sheet as the amounts due to, or owing by, financial organizations, banks, and higher administrative organizations should be mutually reconciled and agreed. It is forbidden to show unreconciled amounts on the balance sheet.

Assets held through the foreign currency accounts of enterprises, and also the balances for debtors and creditors and other financial assets expressed in foreign currencies are translated into Russian currency for inclusion in a balance sheet. For foreign currency translation purposes, the rate of exchange quoted by the Central Bank of the Russian Federation on the first day after the end of the reporting period is used.

Fines, penalties and sanctions, either admitted by the debtor or imposed by a decision of a court, arbitrator, or some other authority, are written off to expenses immediately unless otherwise decided. Before their payment, or receipt, these amounts are shown in the balance sheets of the payer, or payee, as creditors or debtors, respectively.

Bad debts and other debts recognized as irrecoverable by the enterprise are written off at the discretion of the head of the enterprise and charged against the provision for doubtful debts; or, if no provision for doubtful debts has been created, they are charged to expenses or against reserves. The writing off of a bad debt as a result of a debtor's insolvency does not imply a cancellation of the obligation. From the time of the write-off the bad debt should be recorded in a memorandum (off-balance sheet) account for a period of 5 years to provide for the possibility of subsequent recovery.

The amounts unsettled on creditor accounts for which the debt recovery period has expired are transferred either to profit or to the special purpose funds of the enterprise.

2.4.7 *Profit (Loss) of an Enterprise*

The final financial result of the economic activities of the enterprise is measured as the difference between total revenues (from the sale of products, work, and services; from the sale of fixed assets and other property of the enterprise, and from other sales) and the matching expenses. For revenue recognition, enterprises may use either the cash basis or the accrual basis. The recognition of revenue for the year ahead in the current year may be disclosed, at the discretion of the enterprise, in the section on accounting policy in the annual report.

2.5 National Chart of Accounts

In some Western countries, each company may design its own set of accounts in the way that will reflect the nature of its business and the needs of its management in directing that business. In Russia this process is regulated centrally in that there is a tradition of using a unified chart of accounts worked out by the Ministry of Finance. As already stated, all accounts included in this unified chart are called synthetic accounts. On the basis of this chart, each enterprise may work out additionally a set of analytical accounts as a supplement to some synthetic accounts as needed. The national chart of accounts is used for working out centrally some typical accounting entries and for the preparation of the financial statements (thus, all lines of the balance sheet contain the numbers of corresponding synthetic accounts aggregated in a certain line).

The first unified chart of accounts in Russia was worked out during the 1920s. It was intended only for industrial enterprises. From time to time the chart underwent modification:

In 1961 the first national unified chart of accounts had been prepared and was put into operation. The chart became obligatory for all types of enterprises with the exception of nonprofit organizations and banks. With only insignificant alterations the chart remained in use until 1992.

The latest version of the national chart of accounts was issued by the Ministry of Finance USSR as the second annex to Decree No. 56, dated November 1, 1991. It was decreed that as of January 1, 1992, the revised chart of accounts should be adopted throughout the USSR. With the dissolution of the USSR, the decree ceased to be legally enforceable throughout its former constituent republics. In the Russian Federation, however, the transition to the new from the old chart of accounts ought to have been made during the course of 1992. In Belorussia an enabling regulation, adopted on July 1, 1992, required the revised chart of accounts to be introduced into all enterprises not later than January 1, 1993, A number of the successor republics of the dissolved USSR continued to use the old chart of accounts.

The revised chart of accounts consists of about 100 synthetic accounts and 60 subaccounts grouped into 10 main sections. The structure of the system of accounts is shown in Figure 1.

Each account has its own number used in accounting ledgers and transactions. Some of the account numbers are vacant and will be used for changes to the chart. Because the chart is complicated, most of the accounts are divided into subaccounts. Each account (or subaccount) can be further divided into analytical accounts. For example, account 60, "Settlements with suppliers and contractors," can be divided into analytical accounts according to the number of suppliers.

Accounts included in the first nine sections are called balance-sheet accounts. They are used in double-entry accounting. Section 10 includes special off-balance-sheet accounts reflecting some kinds of transactions. These accounts disclose either values not owned by the enterprise (leased property, goods on consignment, goods delivered to the enterprise by mistake, etc.) or symbolic values.

The nature and economic meaning of all accounts and some typical transactions concerning them are described and explained in the document "Chart of Accounts." It should be mentioned that experts from the United Nations Center on Transnational Corporations took part in working out the Chart of Accounts. Thus, the main aspects of the chart comply with the generally accepted accounting principles used in developed countries.

The Chart of Accounts can be considered the most important element of the accounting system in Russia because it determines accounting practice. The essence of the accounting system used in Russia can be easily understood from analyzing it. The Chart of Accounts provides:

- An interrelated classification, grouping, and generalization of information on the business activities of enterprises

Figure 1. The Structure of National Chart of Accounts.

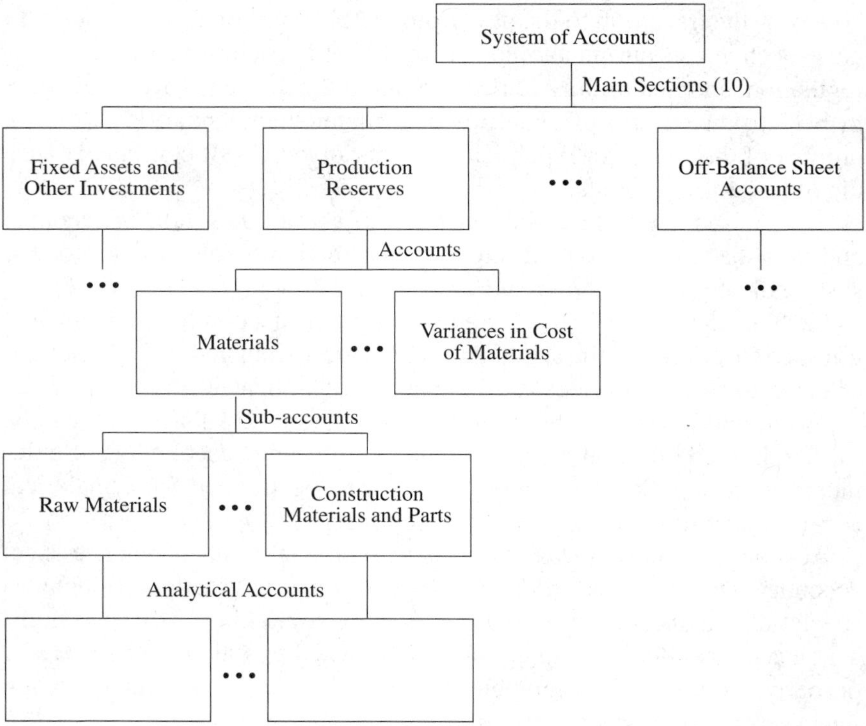

- A unified methodological basis for the organization of accounting in the whole national economy
- An effective system of control of indicators for business activities
- Comparability of accounting procedures used and information generated in the accounting systems of different enterprises
- Common understanding when accountants transfer from one industry to another

2.6 The Form and Content of Published Financial Statements

Since the introduction of the first of the 5-year plans for economic development, in 1929, the recording of data on an enterprise's performance has been realized through three interconnected systems for providing statistical data, accounting data, and operational and technical data.

The recording systems generating statistical data and accounting data provide the data required for the compilation of the periodic statistical and accounting statements presented to organizations external to the enterprise. Therefore, the statements are prepared in accordance with the rules prescribed by superior authorities (e.g., the Ministry of Finance) and are systematized to avoid duplication in the processing (frequently manual) of statistical and accounting data. The recording of operational and technical data is intended to meet the needs of senior personnel within the enterprise. Therefore, this information is often presented in an approximate form at short intervals (e.g., weekly), whereas accounting data are produced according to a monthly cycle. Although statistical data may be produced at monthly intervals, they are used to evaluate enterprise performance over a period extending beyond one year. Traditionally, in the evaluation of an enterprise's performance (i.e., in fulfilling the planned tasks), more weight has been assigned to statistical data than to accounting data.

With the changes in the Russian political and economic environment (the dismantling of the institutional structures of the centrally planned economy and the embarking upon the transformation of the economic system), the accounting, or financial, statements are becoming the prime means for the communication of information on performance both between enterprises and with other organizations. The procedure for the preparation, presentation, and approval of the financial statements is the responsibility of the Ministry of Finance. There is an approved format for all the financial statements, and blank forms for all the financial statements are printed centrally by the state enterprise *Rosblankizdat*. These forms are distributed to the state enterprises by the relevant industrial enterprises and sold to private companies. Periodically the Ministry of Finance issues instructions concerning the content of the quarterly and annual financial statements and the procedure for their compilation.

At the present time (early 1994) the annual financial statements for all enterprises consist of:

- Form no. 1, the balance sheet
- Form no. 2, statement of financial results and their utilization
- Form no. 5, supplement to the balance sheet

Also required is an explanatory text of some 15–20 pages reviewing the activities of the enterprise and, where required, an audit report. The explanatory text is required to clarify and explain the basic factors influencing the financial results and also the main aspects of the financial position of the enterprise.

The industrial ministries have the power to require some additional accounting statements for the provision of a reflection of the particular features of their subordinate enterprises. The format of these additional accounting statements must be approved by the Ministry of Finance.

For all enterprises, the quarterly accounting statements comprise form no. 1 and form no. 2. Both the quarterly and annual accounting reports are presented to:

- The "owners" of the enterprise as stated in its founding document. (Generally the owners are specified as the next higher administrative level within the relevant industrial ministry.)
- The state taxation inspectorate
- The state authorities controlling some aspect of the business activities of the enterprise, as authorized by Russian legislation (e.g., financial agencies acting as intermediaries for financial support made available from the state budget)

With the exception of joint ventures, the quarterly accounting statements are required to be presented within 30 days of the end of the quarter, and annual accounting statements by April 1 of the following year.

The Regulation on Accounting and Reporting in the Russian Federation is concerned exclusively with the provision of accounting statements to state authorities. There is no requirement for the lodging of the accounting statements with an authority (e.g., a registrar) to which there is public access. There is no requirement for public disclosure of information on the financial performance of enterprises (i.e., reflecting the influence of the practice established during the period of the centrally planned economy). The disclosure of financial information to investors is primarily a matter of private arrangement.

Joint ventures are required to present their annual reports by March 15 of the following year to the joint owners and to the state taxation inspectorate. The annual reports are required to meet the provisions of the

Regulation on Accounting and Reporting, although the owners of a joint venture have the right to include additional information. Moreover, joint ventures are empowered independently to produce blank forms in the authorized format for the financial statements.

Compared with the centrally planned economy, the conception of the external reporting function has not changed. That is, the primary consideration is the provision of accounting information to a superior state authority. The industrial ministries and other state departments responsible for subordinate enterprises are required to present aggregated reports within 45 days of the end of each quarter, and aggregated annual reports by April 25 of the following year, to the Ministry of Economics and the State Committee for Statistics.

For an industrial ministry, the aggregated annual reports are required to be prepared separately for the following groups of enterprises:

- Agricultural enterprises
- Material and technical supply enterprises
- Civil engineering and construction enterprises
- Industrial enterprises
- Information and computing services enterprises
- Transport enterprises
- Road repair and maintenance enterprises
- Wholesale, retail, and public catering enterprises
- Geological organizations
- Research organizations
- Public utilities

The financial statements are required to be signed by both the enterprise director and the chief accountant. At the discretion of the owners of an enterprise, the financial statements may be published and thereby made available for all interested in the activities of the enterprise. The form and extent of publication are within the discretion of the enterprise. Before publication, the financial statements are required to be audited by an external auditing firm.

Traditionally, the explanatory text to the annual report has included an analysis of the enterprise's performance (hitherto from the standpoint of plan fulfillment) and an outline of measures for increasing efficiency and improving the financial position. With the transformation of the economic system now being attempted, a modified structure for the annual report has been proposed as follows:

- General information (i.e., general description of business activities, organization chart, key indicators, personnel information)
- Financial statements
- Explanatory notes and comments to the financial statements
- Analytical review (e.g., liquidity, profitability)
- Market perspectives and investment policy
- Other information (e.g., accounting policy, auditor's report, most important contracts and clients)

2.6.1 The Balance Sheet (Form No. 1)

The balance sheet is intended, as before, to reveal the composition of the assets and sources of their formation at the beginning of the first day of the accounting period (i.e., quarter or year). Both assets and liabilities are grouped into three divisions:

Active	*Passive*
Fixed assets and other noncirculating assets	Sources of owned assets
Inventories and expenditures	Long-term liabilities
Monetary assets, debtors and other assets	Creditors and other liabilities

Each line of the balance sheet has been assigned a reference number, which is used in the instructions on the preparation of the financial statements issued annually by the Ministry of Finance. The authorized reporting format for a representative balance sheet (i.e., to be used by all types of enterprises, including joint ventures) for 1993 is shown on pages 1531–1535.

In comparison with the earlier format for the balance sheet, some changes have been introduced:

- A closer approximation to international accounting practice is required.
- Fixed assets are shown net of accumulated depreciation.
- Some new items are introduced, such as intangible assets, reserve fund, provision for doubtful debts, cash held in foreign currencies, bills receivable, and bills payable

2.6.2 Statement of Financial Results and Their Utilization (Form No. 2)

The Statement of Financial Results and their Utilization comprises four sections:

1. Financial results
2. Utilization of profit
3. Payments to state budget
4. Expenses allowed for tax calculation purposes

The first section might be described as an abbreviated profit and loss account. It includes:

- Profit/loss from realization of sales
- Profit/loss from other realization
- Other revenues and expenses (e.g., fines both received and paid, interest received, financial results of earlier years revealed in the current year, losses caused by natural disasters) shown as global amounts. The net total of the three items provides the total profit or loss for the year.

The second section, utilization of profit, provides an expansion of the item of profit utilized shown on the balance sheet (line 471).

The third section, payments to state budgets, provides a summary of all the taxes paid into the state budget.

The fourth section shows the expenses that, although excluded from production costs (and, therefore, not taken into consideration in the determination of profit), nevertheless are allowed for the determination of taxable profit. For example, 30% of the amount spent on environmental protection from net profit is treated as a deductible expense for tax purposes. All these allowable expenses are listed in the instructions of the state taxation inspectorate: "On the Procedure for the Calculation of Tax on Profit and its Payment to the State Budget."

2.7 Taxation

To some extent accounting in Russia is closer to the continental accounting model, the main concept of which was the submission of accounting methodology to the principles of tax legislation. This fact explains why accounting and taxation are so interrelated in Russia, and tax regulations determine the composition of costs.

The Regulation on Cost Allocation and Conditions of Taxable Income Calculation classifies all expenditures that can be included in the cost of production and services. These expenditures, within the norms (limits) set up by additional regulations and other normative documents, are debited to Account 20, "Basic Production," or other similar accounts 23, 25, and 26. Expenses exceeding such norms as well as other expenses not identified in the regulation can't be charged to costs and must be debited to Account 81, "Profit Utilization." For example, interest on commercial credit can be included in costs only within the rate of the Central Bank of Russia.

At present there are three types of taxes in Russia: federal taxes, taxes of republics and provinces, and local taxes. Taxation may be levied on:

- Profit
- The value of certain goods
- Certain types of business activity
- Operations with securities
- The use of raw materials
- The property of individuals and companies
- Value added

- Others items as declared by law

Taxpayers are individuals and companies obliged to pay taxes in accordance with the law. All taxpayers are required to be registered in local offices of the State Tax Service of Russia. A special document confirming this registration must be presented to the bank serving the company.

There are some tax privileges, such as untaxable minimum, exemption for some categories of taxpayers, reduction of tax rates, and deferred taxes. For example, taxable income can be reduced on:

- Net profit used for investments
- 30% of investments for environmental protection
- Input to charity funds within 3% of taxable income
- Dividends paid to owners if they reinvest them

The total amount of reduction must be less than 50% of initial taxable income.

The categories of federal taxes are as follows:

- Taxes being transferred to the federal budget: value added tax, excises, tax on insurance business activity, tax on the income of banks, commodity exchanges tax, tax on security operations, custom tax
- Taxes being transferred proportionally to the federal budget, to the budgets of republics and provinces, and to the local budget: tax for the use of natural resources, tax for the construction and repair of highways and roads
- Taxes being transferred to the local budget: stamp tax, inherited property tax

The categories of taxes of republics and provincial areas are tax for the needs of educational institutions, forestry tax, tax for water used by enterprises, and enterprise property tax. There are more than 20 types of local taxes, such as individuals' property tax, tax for the registration of companies, parking tax, tax on the resale of cars, and tax on enterprises intending to construct in resort zones.

The most significant taxes are the profits tax and VAT tax. The rates of profits tax differ, depending on the type of business activity, as follows:

gambling business, 90% of the pretax profits; video saloons, 70%; banking, 30%; insurance, 25%; brokers' activities, 45%; other business activity, 32%. Thus, most enterprises are required to pay profits tax at the rate of 32%. The rates of value added tax are as follows: 10% for food goods except spirit goods and 20% for other consumer goods.

At present, the tax load is quite significant—the total amount of taxes equals 80%–85% of company income. Such unilateral orientation to stabilization of the state budget at any price does not stimulate the development of production.

2.8 Auditing

Auditing, as the term is understood in Western countries, was never accepted as either a desirable or necessary function in Tsarist Russia or the USSR. The history of Russia has been marked by the pervasive power of the state and either the absence or strict constraints on the exercise of private ownership. Such experience made impossible the emergence of an auditing profession. The very notion of an independent auditor was completely alien to the consciousness of administrators, managers, and professionals. While accepting that their performance needed to be monitored, they believed nevertheless that any report by an evaluator to a superior authority ought to be circumscribed, that is, restricted to what that person had been told and not based on an independent assessment or discovery.

Moreover, government officials did not conceive of a role for independent auditors. All subordinate enterprises were regarded as under their full control, and an external audit, or examination, of the activities of enterprises would not have been welcomed. Russia was, and remains, a country in which administrative law dominates over civil law. Vertical ties (i.e., between superiors and subordinates) always have been more important than horizontal ties (e.g., among enterprises). As a consequence, the terms *control* and *controller* were used in preference to *audit* and *auditor*. The term *inspection* (*reviziya*) was used widely.

A gradual change began in 1987, however, when the initial basic regulations on accounting and auditing for joint venture operations were issued. These regulations required auditing for joint ventures to conform to Western auditing practice. Audits were required to be performed by independent auditors, that is, to be conducted "by a commercial Soviet auditing organization in exchange for a fee." For this purpose, a special-ized organization, *Inaudit*, was created. In practice, the new organization has not been independent but is controlled by the Ministry of Finance.

In recent years many firms providing auditing and consultancy services have been established in Russia. For example, there are more than 150 auditing firms in the city of St. Petersburg. However, the leading role in the development of auditing and consultancy services in Russia and other former Soviet republics has been taken by the Big Six international accounting firms, Arthur Andersen, Coopers & Lybrand, Deloitte & Tou-che, Ernst & Young, KPMG Peat Marwick, and Price Waterhouse. These firms are engaged mainly in privatization and consultancy activities. Many potential foreign investors, as well as participants in joint ventures, prefer to use the services of the international accounting firms. Consequently, no strong competition exists between the Western and indigenous firms in providing auditing and consultancy activities although, because of the lack of detailed legislation, misunderstandings arise concerning the audit re-quirement.

The Temporary Rules for Auditing in the Russian Federation, intro-duced on December 1, 1993, provided for an obligatory audit only for banks and joint ventures. In addition, an enterprise is required to be subjected to audit when it is:

- Nominated for privatization
- Nominated for liquidation
- Intending to issue securities
- Intending to publish financial statements

There is no precise guidance on the manner of conduct of these obliga-tory audits or examinations. Nevertheless, many administrative authorities and commercial banks have already been demanding audit reports in connection with privatization, the issue of securities, the issue of credits and loans, and liquidations. Moreover, local officials of the state taxation inspectorate frequently require the annual financial statements to be sup-ported by an audit report.

During the past 2 years considerable hopes were placed on the adoption and implementation of a law on auditing. A team of specialists (drawn from the international accounting firms, the United Nations Center on

Transnational Corporations, and the largest Russian auditing firms) participated in drafting an auditing law. In May 1993 a revised draft of a law on auditing, incorporating significant amendments, was presented by the President of Russia to the Supreme Soviet. Although approved by the Supreme Soviet after amendment, the president did not sign it.

The differences centered on the following matters. The president conceived that auditors would be assistants to the tax inspectors. Therefore, he proposed to subordinate audit to the state taxation service. The Supreme Soviet, in the pursuit of an expansion of its own power and a curtailment of the power of the president, intended to supervise the exercise of the audit function. Therefore, the Supreme Soviet proposed to establish a United Auditing Chamber endowed with substantial control functions, comparable to the former Soviet Committee of National Control. There was also an opinion that the audit function ought to be subordinated to the Procurator-General. Because these differences could not be resolved, the president issued the aforementioned decree on Temporary Rules for auditing in the Russian Federation.

The deliberations on the role of audit in Russia, as well as in other successor republics of the USSR, reveal a different conception of its function compared with the advanced market economies. Audit was conceived primarily as an inspection function, undertaken as a public duty for the state authorities, rather than a task undertaken by, and on behalf of, the business community. With impetus for the introduction of audit being provided by the politicians, the emphasis has been upon detection rather than verification.

These discussions indicate the uncertainties concerning the design of a regulatory framework for business activity. A confusion was revealed between the role of enterprise-appointed auditors serving the needs of investors and the role of state-appointed inspectors serving a wider public interest. There is confusion between the tasks of audit and investigation. The interests of actual and potential investors in requiring credible information on an enterprise's performance are not adequately appreciated. There has been no discussion of a requirement for the public disclosure of accounting information; instead it is regarded as being protected by commercial secrecy.

Comparable discussions concerning the role of audit have been occurring in other successor republics of the USSR. Generally, audit has been considered from the viewpoint of the state authorities. In Lithuania, however, the view has arisen that audit is wholly a matter of private negotiation in the market economy without the need for any kind of state involvement.

3.9 Expected Future Developments

Since the disintegration of the USSR, the characteristic feature of accounting development in its constituent European republics (Armenia, Azerbaijan, Belarus, Estonia, Georgia, Latvia, Lithuania, Moldova, Russia, and Ukraine) has been disharmonization. The system of unified accounting implemented throughout the former USSR is in the process of being dismantled, not only because of the dismantling of the control structures of the centrally planned economy but also because of the release from Moscow's suzerainty in accounting matters and as an expression of national independence in the successor republics.

In the Caucasian republics (Armenia, Azerbaijan, and Georgia), the recurrent armed conflicts have removed accounting reform from the agenda of matters of current concern. In Moldova, where a *de facto* division of territory exists among different nationalities, an amalgam of Soviet, Ukrainian, Rumanian, and reformed Russian accounting practices has emerged.

In both Belarus and Ukraine, the Soviet accounting system as it existed at the end of 1991 continues to be implemented. To some extent, the adherence to past accounting practice may be regarded as a reflection of sluggish progress in economic reform. It also reflects, however, the deficient resources of accounting expertise for the challenging task of accounting reform. Previously, improvements in accounting were determined in Moscow and transmitted throughout the USSR for implementation. Although it is so no longer, Belarus does tend to be influenced by Russian accounting reforms in devising new accounting regulations.

The smaller the country the more deficient the resources of accounting expertise for the tasks of accounting reform and the more uncertain the process of its realization. Nevertheless, after the declarations of national independence made in 1990, independent initiatives in accounting reform have been attempted in the Baltic republics (Estonia, Latvia, and Lithuania). The proposal, made in that year by leading accounting specialists in the Baltic states, for a common approach to accounting reform in their countries lacked support. Instead, accounting reform has been undertaken separately in each of the Baltic states.

The determination to establish democratic institutions and market economies, and the repudiation of control by Moscow, did imply a need for an early policy decision concerning the manner of realization of the functions of accounting and auditing in the newly evolving society. In 1990 a new accounting law was adopted, perhaps prematurely, by Estonia. It was published in Russian in a number of journals in the former USSR. Somewhat similar accounting laws were adopted in 1992 by Latvia and Lithuania.

These new accounting laws were concerned primarily with administrative and clerical matters affecting the accounting function. This peculiarity may explain why the new laws were extended to a wide range of entities (e.g., municipalities) and not restricted to business undertakings. Thus, henceforth accounting is to be conducted in the relevant national language (whereas the majority of accounting specialists throughout the Baltic states are more conversant with the Russian language).

Paradoxically, the new accounting laws diminished the position of the chief bookkeeper (accountant) (e.g., being no longer required to countersign the balance sheet, a Soviet practice retained in Belarus and Russia) by the responsibility for accounting being transferred to the head of the enterprise. The clause for the protection of commercial secrets has reinforced a predisposition against public disclosure of financial information (e.g., no rules on accounting disclosure have been adopted by the Vilnius stock exchange, which opened in 1993). There is no requirement for copies of the annual financial statements of companies to be lodged with a registrar.

The format and content of financial statements has been authorized separately, usually by an order issued by the Ministry of Finance.

For an Estonian enterprise, the annual balance sheet, in summarized form, is as follows:

	Line No.	*Start of Year*	*End of Year*

Active
1. Liquid assets
2. Production and commercial
   inventories

3. Fixed assets and capital
   work-in-progress
4. Long-term investments
5. Intangible assets
6. Other assets

Passive
7. Short-term liabilities
9. Reserves
10. Interperiod adjustments
11. Owned capital
12. Other liabilities

The ordering of the items within the balance sheet is reminiscent of a format common during the interwar decades (1919–1939) in the Baltic states.

The official form containing the balance sheet, spread over five pages, issued by the Ministry of Finance in 1991 (as also the system of enumeration adopted) is more characteristic of a statistical return than a financial statement. A similar observation may be made with respect to current practice in other successor states of the former Soviet Union.

For an Estonian enterprise, the income statement, in summarized form, is as follows:

	Line No.	Previous Year	Current Year
1. Gross sales			
2. Taxes against sales			
3. Net sales (1 – 2)			
4. Production costs			
5. Operating profit/loss (3 – 4)			
6. Other operating revenues			
7. Other operating expenses			
8. Financial revenue			
9. Financial expenses			
10. Net profit (5 + 6 + 8 – 7 – 9)			
11. Additional tax allowances			

12. Amounts disallowed
13. Taxable profit (10 – 11 + 12)
14. Income tax
15. Miscellaneous payments
16. Net profit (13 – 14 – 15)

The official form segments the income statement into sixteen separate boxes for the insertion of data.

Within 4 months of the end of the accounting year, copies of the financial statements must be presented to the Department of Statistics, the Tax Collection Office, and the owners (e.g., the general meeting of shareholders for a privatized enterprise, the supervising ministry for a state enterprise). Similar requirements exist for the presentation of financial statements in Latvia and Lithuania.

Initially the Soviet chart of accounts, with some modifications, continued to be used in all three Baltic states, although the intention was to develop and introduce new national charts of accounts. In Estonia in 1990 an accounting council and an audit council were established under the Ministry of Finance. The accounting council is charged with issuing instructions or recommendations on accounting practice. The chairperson, appointed for a 3-year term by the government, is an accounting specialist, and at least one other member must be a lawyer. The audit council is charged with the determination of professional qualifications, licensing, supervision of auditing activities, and the resolution of disputes between auditors and clients. In 1991 an audit council, with similar powers and a membership nominated by the Ministry of Finance, was established in Latvia.

For the larger enterprises, auditing became obligatory in 1993 in Estonia and Latvia. In Estonia the auditor is required to verify both the condition and the legality of the enterprise's accounting and the reliability of its external reporting. In Latvia the scope of audit is widened to incorporate an efficiency audit

In 1992 in Lithuania an audit commission was established for the purpose of determining the persons qualified to undertake audits. In the Baltic states the normal qualification for designation as an auditor is the possession of a higher education in economics (accounting was treated as a branch of economics and not as an independent discipline in the Soviet

Union) or law and at least 5 years of practical experience in either accounting or law. There is no recognized system for the education and training of auditors.

In Lithuania audit is obligatory only for commercial banks. The balance sheet, income statement, and auditor's opinion are required to be published (e.g., in a newspaper) within 4 months of the end of the accounting year.

Stock companies in Lithuania are required to appoint an accountant and the general meeting of shareholders to elect an auditor, but there is no requirement for an annual audit. The prevailing view in Lithuania seems to be that any need for an audit can be met voluntarily through privately negotiated contracts without the need for legislation.

Latvia and Lithuania introduced new national charts of accounts at the beginning of 1994. For both countries the new charts of accounts were distinguished from the old Soviet chart of accounts by the separate classification of balance sheet accounts (i.e., for assets and liabilities) and operational accounts (i.e., for income and expenditures). Since 1993 no national chart of accounts has been obligatory in Estonia.

Piecemeal and frequent changes to laws and regulations are increasing the inconsistencies (e.g., among basic accounting legislation, tax rules, charts of accounts, and financial statement formats) and destabilizing accounting practice (causing, for example, a lack of comparability between successive financial statements). These difficulties are augmented by the absence of an established procedure for the development of technical standards of accounting. Its establishment is hindered, however, by the lack, in these minority European languages, of a standardized and accepted accounting terminology relevant to the application of business accounting in the context of a market economy.

The resolution of these problems, the existence of which aggravates not only the task of accounting reform but also of economic renewal, is likely to be protracted.

Regarding Russia itself, at the present time foreign assistance in the development of accounting is being concentrated on the major Russian cities, especially Moscow and St. Petersburg. The main work of transforming accounting to suit the emerging requirements of the newly evolving economic system is being undertaken by the Russian Ministry of Finance, with the assistance of specialists provided by the United Nations

Center for Transnational Corporations, the European Union, the World
Bank, and the leading international accounting firms. The main effort is
being directed to the development of a regulatory framework for accounting. Of the several proposals under consideration, the one that seems to be
gaining most support is a proposal for a multi-level approach to accounting regulation. The first level would comprise a basic law on accounting
and auditing. The second level would comprise the obligatory regulations
defining the conceptual framework of accounting (categories, objectives,
postulates, principles, etc.). The third level would comprise the accounting
standards. The fourth level would comprise the explanatory materials and
instructions for helping the practical accounting workers to observe the
revised requirements.

It is presumed that the draft of the initial accounting standards will
eventually appear, including accounting standards concerning:

- Disclosure of accounting policies
- Financial reporting of enterprises and organizations
- Consolidated financial statements
- Accounting for tangible assets and their depreciation
- Accounting for intangibles
- Valuation and accounting for materials, products, and goods
- Accounting for equity and settlements with owners
- Accounting for financial results and their utilization
- Accounting for cash, financial investments, and foreign currency
  translations

The drawing of a distinction among accounting law, accounting regulations, and practical guidance would enable a corresponding allocation of
responsibilities to be made among different authorities. However, little
consideration seems to have been given to the institutional structures
needed for ensuring the observance of the reformed accounting. Even less
consideration has been given to the public disclosure of accounting information, being regarded in general as a matter of private negotiation (e.g.,
between the directors of an enterprise and its major providers of capital).

In 1989 the USSR Ministry of Finance authorized the establishment of
an Association of Accountants, open to all with an interest in accounting.

A number of the Soviet republics established their own accounting association as an expression of national identity and the movement toward independence. Within the Russian Federation additional associations have been established in some regions and cities. All these associations lack the power and authority to influence the formation of accounting policy. There are no professional accounting associations in the countries of the former USSR. Some progress is being made in the issue of licenses as evidence of competence to act as an auditor, although formal arrangements for the education and training of entrants to an audit profession have not been achieved.

Accounting education and training in the countries of the former Soviet Union are being reexamined and restructured, partly as a consequence of the general overhaul of the provision of higher education. Accounting education is carried out at institutions of higher education and, at a lower educational level, in technical colleges and vocational schools. The scope for training has diminished as enterprises have sought to reduce their commitments.

There has been progress in the reform of the accounting curricula to reflect the requirements of the evolving market economy. Training programs on Western accounting techniques have been developed through the cooperation of the United Nations Center for Transnational Corporations and Russian and Western academics. A special contribution to the development of these programs has been made by the Center for International Accounting at the University of Texas at Dallas. These training programs have been mounted at Russian and Ukrainian institutions of higher education for students, academics, and accounting specialists in commerce and industry. Some well-known Western accounting textbooks have been published in Russian language editions. Other forms of cooperation between Russian and Western accounting specialists are under consideration. Much remains to be achieved.

Useful Addresses

St. Petersburg Institute of Commerce & Economics
Novorossiiskaya str., 50
St. Petersburg, 194018
Russia
Tel: (812) 247-81-00
Fax: (812) 247-43-42

St. Petersburg Chamber of Auditors
Italianskaya str., 23
St. Petersburg
Russia
Tel: (812) 311-61-29

Lithuanian Accountants and Auditors Association
Pomenkalio 31-9
232669 Vilnius
Lithuania
Tel: 62-05-98

Sample Financial Statements, Former Soviet Union

Balance Sheet of Enterprise

Form No. I per CKUD

	Codes
	0710001

on I _____ 19___ _____ Date (year, month, day)

Enterprise, organization _____ per OKPO

Branch (type of activity)_____ per OKONKh

Authority for management of state property _____ per OKPO

Unit of measurement: 000s roubles _____ Control total

Address _____

Date of dispatch

Date of receipt

Submission period

Active 1	*Line code* 2	*At start of year* 3	*At end of year* 4
I BASIC MEANS AND OTHER NON-CIRCULATING ASSETS			
Intangible assets:			
initial value (04)	010		
amortization (05)	011		
written down value	012		
Basic means			
initial (renovated) value (01, 03)	020		
depreciation (02)	021		
written down value	022		
Equipment for installation (07)	030		
Capital construction in progress (08)	040		
Long-term investments (06)	050		
Proprietors (75)	060		
Other non-circulating assets	070		
Total of Section 1	080		
II INVENTORIES AND EXPENDITURES			
Production inventories (10, 15)	100		
Livestock for rearing and fattening (11)	110		
Low-valued and short-lived appliances:			
initial value (12)	120		
depreciation (13)	121		
written down value	122		

Work-in-progress (20, 21, 23, 29, 30)
| | |
Deferred expenses (31) — 140
Finished output (40) — 150
Commodities:

Work-in-progress (20, 21, 23, 29, 30)	
Deferred expenses (31)	140
Finished output (40)	150
Commodities:	
selling price (41)	160
trade mark-up (42)	161
purchase price	162
Materials handling expenses attributable	
to commodities inventory (44)	170
Value added tax on purchases (19)	175
Other inventories and expenditures	178
Total of Section II	180

III   MONETARY RESOURCES, DEBTORS AND OTHER ASSETS
Debtors:	
goods, work and services (45, 62, 76)	200
bills receivable (82)	210
subsidiary enterprises (78)	220
state budget (68)	230
personnel for other operations (73)	240
other debtors	250
Advanced payments to suppliers (61)	260
Short-term investments (58)	270
Monetary resources:	
cash (50)	280
bank (51)	290
foreign currency (52)	300
other monetary resources (55, 56, 57)	310
Other circulating assets	320
Total of Section III	330
Losses:	
earlier years (87)	340
current year	350
GRAND TOTAL	
(lines 080, 180, 330, 340, and 350)	360

Passive	*Line code*	*At start of year*	*At end of year*
1	*2*	*3*	*4*
I SOURCES OF OWNED ASSETS			
Authorized capital	(85)	400	
Reserve fund (860)	410		
Special purpose funds (88)	420		
Designated financing and receipts (96)	430		
Leasing liabilities (97)	440		
Proprietors (75)	450		
Unappropriated profit of earlier years (87)	460		
Profit:			

current year (80)	470	X
utilized (81)	471	X
unappropriated profit of current year	472	X
Total of Section I	480	

II LONG-TERM LIABILITIES

Long-term bank credits (92)	500
Long-term loans (95)	510
Total of Section II	520

III CREDITORS AND OTHER LIABILITIES

Short-term bank credits (90)	600
Bank credits for employees (93)	610
Short-term loans (94)	620
Creditors:	
goods, work and services (66)	630
bills payable (66)	640
wages (70)	650
social insurance and social security (69)	660
property and personal insurance (65)	670
subsidiary enterprises (78)	680
extra-budgetary payments (67)	690
state budget (68)	700
other creditors	710
Advances received form customers (64)	720
Deferred income (83)	730
Provisions for anticipated expenses and	
payments (89)	740
Provisions for doubtful debts (82)	750
Other short-term liabilities	760
Total of Section III	770
GRAND TOTAL (lines 480, 520 and 770	780
Chief Executive _____	
Chief Accountant _____	

Statement of Financial Results and Their Utilization

Form No. 2 per OKUD

From 1 January to 1_____19____

Date (year, month, day)

Enterprise, organization _____ per OKPO

Branch (type of activity) _____ per OKONKh

Authority for management of state property_____ per OKPO

Unit of measurement: 000s roubles _____

Codes 0710002

I FINANCIAL RESULTS

Item	Line code	Profit	Losses (expenses)
1	*2*	*3*	*4*
Receipts (gross income) from realization of output (work, services)	010	X	
Value added tax	015	X	
Excise duty	020	X	
	030	X	
Cost of realized output (work, services)	040	X	
Realization result	050		
Other realization result	060		
Non-operating revenues and expenses of which:	070		
for securities and participation in joint ventures	071		X
for foreign currency dealings	072		
Total profits and losses	080		
Overall profit or loss	090		
NOTE			
Excess remuneration of enterprise personnel	100		X

II UTILIZATION OF PROFIT

Item	Line code	At end of period
1	*2*	*3*
Payments to state budget	200	
Allocations to reserve (insurance) fund	210	
Applied to:		
accumulation fund	220	
consumption fund	220	
charitable purposes	250	
other purposes	260	
NOTE		
Lease payments, excluding amortization	270	

III PAYMENTS TO STATE BUDGET

Item	Line code	Payable	Paid
1	*2*	*3*	*4*
Property tax	300		
Profit (income) tax	310		
Payment for utilzation of mineral resources and for discarded spoilage	340		
Land tax	350		
Value added tax	355		
Excise duty	356		
Export customs duty	360		
Import customs duty	365		

Personal income tax	380
Other taxes	386
Econmic sanctions	390

IV EXPENDITURES ALLOWED AGAINST PROFIT TAX

Item	*Line code*	*At end of period*
1	*2*	*3*
For financiang capital investment	500	
For implementation of environmental protection mesures	520	
For upkeep of institutions for public health, national education, culture and sport; homes for elderly and invalids; pre-school institutions and children's holday camps; housing fund (within expenditure norms approved by local societs) (521)	530	
For charitable pruposes to ecological and sanitation funds, publica organizations, invalids, religious organizations and other similar purposes	540	
	550	
	560	
	570	
	580	
	590	

Chief Executive _____   Chief Accountant _____

INDEX

Anglo-Saxon countries, *cont.*
disclosure practice, 240
Angola, 668, 698
Annex (notes). *See also* Notes
Austria, 1039–1040, 1045
Portugal, 677, 679–680
Annexe, 51, 54, 55
Annual accounts. *See also* Notes
Belgium, 47–48
Iceland, 1116–1117, 1119, 1121–1122
Italy, 432–435
Luxembourg, 543–544
Norway, 1146–1149
Spain, 826–842
Annual report
Hungary, 1409–1410, 1428
Italy, 415, 432–433
Netherlands, 565–566, 575–578
Spain, 840–842
Switzerland, 1254
Anonymos eteria (AE) (Greece), 325
APB. *See* Auditing Practices Board
Appendix (notes), Greece, 328–330
Appropriations, Sweden, 1193, 1207
ARBED (Luxembourg), 535
Arden (Hon. Mrs. Justice), 922
Armenia, 1523
ARR. *See* Accounting and Reporting Recommendations, Switzerland
Articles of Association, United Kingdom, 913–914
ASB. *See* Accounting Standards Board
ASC. *See* Accounting Standards Committee
Assets. *See also* Current assets; Financial assets; Fixed asset movement analysis; Fixed assets; Intangible assets; Leases; Participations; Property, plant, and equipment; assets by type
acquired by leases (Greece), 335–336
Austria, 1034–1035
Belgium, 62–74
current (Luxembourg), 546
current (Netherlands), 570
current (Norway), 1159–1160
deferred taxation and (Netherlands), 608–609
financial (Finland), 1078
fixed. *See* Fixed assets
foreign currency consolidation in consolidated accounts and, 56–57
foreign currency denominated (Sweden), 1199–1200
foreign exchange differences and (Spain), 853
Hungary, 1413–1414
intangible. *See* Intangible assets

Italian theory and, 385
Italy, 447–452, 476–477, 479–480
leased. *See* Leases
loss of value (Portugal), 696–697
Poland, 1471–1472
Portugal, 685
Republic of Ireland, 757
revaluation of, 63–64
Russia, 1501, 1505–1507
tangible. *See* Tangible assets
translation of foreign-currency denominated (Greece), 333
valuation of. *See* Valuation
Asset Valuation Decree, Netherlands, 597
ASSIREVI (Associazione Italiana Revisori Contabili), 423
Associated companies
Finland, 1082, 1084–1085
Italy, 468
Norway, 1163–1164
Portugal, 683, 692
Sweden, 1212, 1218
United Kingdom, 935, 968
Associated enterprises, Austria, 1043
Association of Accountants, Russia, 1528–1529
Association of Accounting and Business Administration (AECA), Spain, 840–841
Association of Auditors, Finland, 1070
Association of Hungarian Auditors, 1404
Association of State Authorized Accountants (FLE), Iceland, 1129, 1132
Associations, audit (Italy), 423
Athens Stock Exchange (Greece), 325, 339
Atomistic-reductionist perspective, of Besta, 386
Audit
Belgium, 43–46, 50
compliance by firms (Italy), 422
fees (Italy), 423
fees (Greece), 330
Hungary, 1421
Italy, 417–424, 429–432
Luxembourg, 537, 538–543
Audit firms, Italy, 417–424
Auditing
Austria, 1045–1045
Hungary, 1401–1404
Denmark, 115
France, 170–171
Germany, 225–226
Iceland, 1117–1118
Italy, 394, 401–402, 412–424
Norway, 1153–1154